Schroeder's Collectible TOYS
Antique to Modern
Price Guide

OUR #1 BESTSELLING TOY BOOK

2006 TENTH EDITION

Identification & Values
of Over
20,000
Collectible Toys

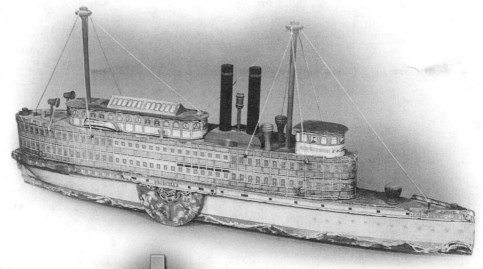

COLLECTOR BOOKS
A Division of Schroeder Publishing Co., Inc.

Editorial Staff:
Editors: **Sharon and Bob Huxford**
Research and Editorial Assistants: **Michael Drollinger, Donna Newnum, Loretta Suiters**
Cover Design: **Beth Summers**
Layout: **Terri Hunter, Heather Warren, Lisa Henderson, Christen Byrd**

COLLECTOR BOOKS
P.O. Box 3009
Paducah, Kentucky 42002-3009
www.collectorbooks.com

Copyright © 2006 Schroeder Publishing Co., Inc.

Searching For A Publisher?

We are always looking for people knowledgeable within their fields. If you feel that there is a real need for a book on your collectible subject and have a large comprehensive collection, contact Collector Books.

The current values in this book should be used only as a guide. They are not intended to set prices, which vary from one section of the country to another. Auction prices as well as dealer prices vary greatly and are affected by condition as well as demand. Neither the editors nor the publisher assumes responsibility for any losses that might be incurred as a result of consulting this guide.

Introduction

Moving into the twenty-first century, it has become obvious that the frenzied activity that characterized the toy market of the 1990s has slowed. But there still is and will no doubt always be a market for good vintage toys.

The Internet is alive and well, and how we collect toys, their availability, and their values have changed dramatically since its inception. Not only are thousands of toys offered daily through eBay sales, many dealers who hate to be tied solely to eBay for an online sales outlet have set up their own ecommerce storefronts. Since we published the first edition of our toy book, besides the drop in the number of toy shows and their poor attendance, we've seen many of the dealers who used to publish catalogs and send out lists completely abandon that approach, finding that even their long-time customer base had virtually evaporated in favor of online dealings.

We can't argue the fact; obviously the Internet is where sales are made, and it's great, to a point. Merchandise moves quickly, dealers make a good living without the hassle of setting up at shows, and buyers can select from thousands of toys on any given day. But most collectors will tell you that it's the impersonal aspect of these kinds of transactions that keeps the tried and true methods of finding treasures — toy shows, traditional auctions, malls, flea markets, and estate and garage sales — alive. They all agree Internet buying will never replace the thrill of discovering and then actually holding that long-sought old toy in their hands as they negotiate the price.

There can be no mistake about it, Internet buying, eBay in particular, has affected values. As more and more people become aware of the online market, whether they have ever been involved in the toy market or not, they suddenly became a 'dealer.' As a result, what was once considered a 'rare' toy may appear multiple times during the same month or even the same day. Supply has outpaced demand, and it has become a buyer's market. Many of these part-time sellers are willing to take a wide range of prices for their items, as they have no use for them past a one-time offering. So buyers can wait for one to sell at the price they're willing to pay, which makes for interesting dynamics. Items produced in large quantities have been targeted in particular; since so many of them have survived and are now making their way to the resale market, their values have plummeted. On the other hand, the truly rare toys are exposed to more buyers, thereby driving values up. Items that are in demand and have a cachet of being rare consistently hit record prices realized via eBay. It is quite obvious that the most desirable toys will always be valuable, while those that are plentiful are worth less in today's market.

But to actually rely on eBay results as a standard by which pricing can be determined is difficult to say the least. Sellers tell us that identical items can sell for as little as $5.00 today and as much as $40.00 in a later sale. If you check on completed auctions as we do every day, you'll find this is very true: eBay is a hit and miss proposition — on any given day, the same piece graded in like condition will sell for vastly different money, depending on who and how many saw the auction and when.

With the volume of merchandise that passes through Internet auctions on any given day, condition has become an even weightier worth-assessing factor than ever before. Dealers report that dolls and toys in played-with condition are another group of collectibles that has fallen in value. Collectors can wait and easily locate better examples of the same items in a short period of time. Unless priced reasonably, 'played-with' toys are passed by more often than not. Mint examples, mint-in-box, or never-removed-from box dolls and toys are still commanding top dollar. An old toy in great condition will bring top dollar at shows, in malls and shops, and most of all on eBay or live toy auctions. Everyone wants to own the best, and many are willing to pay well for the privilege.

When a toy is offered on eBay impacts the results as well, often making the difference between getting top dollar, selling at cost, or selling for less than purchase price. The toy market is much like the stock market with highs and lows changing regularly, based on such things as the economy, the season of the year, and even the weather. During the summer when there are flea markets to attend and other outdoor activities to complete with, selling prices seem to come down.

In its favor, eBay offers a unique opportunity for sellers to develop a customer base through invaluable exposure and contacts with toy collectors and enthusiasts. They often tie their website in with their listings and by doing so increase the traffic to their online stores, often resulting in additional sales.

Dealers tell us that in particular these toys always sell well for them: in the tin market, toys related to characters such as Felix, Popeye, Superman, and Dick Tracey; robots and space-related toys; pressed steel toy trucks by Marx, Structo, and Smith Miller; Transformers; Hot Wheels redlines; slot cars; vintage Disneyana; Barbie accessories; anything monster; Western cowboys; super heroes; or any item in a collecting category that is scarce or in limited supply. Good windups and battery-ops in top condition are always good. Marx, Lehmann, Chein, Wolverine, and Unique Art are some of the more sought-after tin toy manufacturers. The doll market is still reported to be very active, and trolls from the '60s bring amazing prices on eBay right now. TV-related toys from the '60s continue to be strong sellers as well as many toys from the '70s and '80s. Noticeably stagnate are lunch boxes, Pez, Star Wars, G.I. Joe, and Mego figures.

Watch for reproductions! Special editions, limited editions, packaging vartiations, etc., used by various toy companies to target collectors of vintage toys have angered and frustrated collectors, and few are buying into them.

Though it's obvious the venue has shifted and the speculators have switched to some other commodity, there's good news — the true collector is still buying for all the right reasons, the most important of which is personal enjoyment, as it should be. However, the rarest and highest quality unique older toys with intrinsic beauty by nature of their design or manufacture will always be a good investment. The soft end of the market will firm up when the abundance of the more contemporary toys eventually diminishes. As new collectors seek the toys of their youth, many will gravitate to older or newer toys, expanding their collections in both directions outside the parameters of their memories. This foilble of human nature will assure the future value of collectible toys. Our advice: continue to add high quality toys to your collection. There are some real bargains out there right now. Future values are impossible to predict, but if you buy what you like in the best condition you can afford, your collections will continue to appreciate over the long term. As a dealer once told us, a good old toy on the shelf is worth far more than money sitting in a bank. We agree!

In this edition we've tried to bring accurate, up-to-date information concerning market values, but so many of our advisors, experienced though they are, found it impossible to determine fixed prices. We had some advisors who were still reluctant to factor in eBay prices, especially on low-end merchandise, while others gave in to the weight of it and actually lowered values. We left this up to the individual; we have the utmost confidence in their opinions.

Our concept is unique. Though we designed the book first and foremost to be a price guide, we wanted to make it a buying/selling guide as well. So we took many of our descriptions and values from the websites and 'toys for sale' lists of dealers and collectors around the country. In each of those listings we included a dealer's code, so that if you were looking for the particular toy that S5 (for example) had to offer, you'd be able to match his code with his name and address in the Categories of Special Interest section and simply send him an e-mail or call him to see if it were still available. Some of our categories contain listings from live auctions. If we had no active advisor for a particular category, we used an 'A' in the line to indicate auction; pre-sale estimates follow the 'A' in parenthesis. Listings that have neither the 'A' code or the dealer code we mentioned above were either sent to us by collectors who specialize in those specific types of toys or were originally coded but altered at the suggestion of an advisor who felt that the stated price might be far enough outside the market's range to be misleading. In that case, the code was removed from the line.

Each edition contains about 24,000 listings, but even at that we realize that when it comes to the toy market, that only begins to scratch the surface. Our intent is to provide our readers with fresh information, issue after issue. The few categories that are repeated in their entirety in consecutive editions generally are those that were already complete or as nearly complete as we or our advisors could make them. But even those are checked to make sure that values are still current and our information up to date.

The bottom line is that there are two factors determining selling price: the attitude of the individual collector (how strongly he desires to own) and the motivation of the dealer (does he need to turn over his merchandise quickly to replenish and freshen his stock, or can he wait for the most opportune time to turn it over for maximum profit). Where you buy affects prices as well. One of our advisors used this simple analogy: while a soda might cost you $2.50 at the ball park, you can buy the same thing for 39¢ at the corner 7-11. So all we (or anyone) can offer is whatever facts and information we can compile, and ask simply that you arrive at your own evaluations based on the data we've provided, adapted to your personal buying/selling arena.

We hope you enjoy our book and that you'll be able to learn by using it. We don't presume to present it as the last word on toys or their values — there are many specialized books by authors who are able to devote an entire publication to one subject, covering it from 'A' to 'Z,' and when we're aware that such a text book exists, we'll recommend it in our narratives. If you have suggestions that you think will improve our format, let us hear from you — we value your input. Until next time — happy hunting!

— The Editors

Advisory Board

The editors and staff take this opportunity to express our sincere gratitude and appreciation to each person who has contributed their time and knowledge to help us. We've found toys to be *by far* the largest, most involved field of collecting we've ever tried to analyze, but we will have to admit, it's great fun! We've been editing general price guides for twenty years now, and before ever attempting the first one, we realized there was only one way we would presume to publish such a guide — and that would be to first enlist the help of knowledgeable collectors around the country who specialized in specific areas. We now have over fifty toy advisors, and we're still looking for help in several areas. Generally, the advisors are listed following each category's narrative, so if we have mentioned no one and you feel that you are qualified to advise us, have the time, and would be willing to help us out with that subject, please contact us. We'd love to have you on our advisory board. (We want to stress that even if an advisor is credited in a category narrative, that person is in no way responsible for errors — those are our responsibility.) Even if we currently list an advisor for your subject, contact us so that we'll have your name on file should that person need to be replaced. This of course happens from time to time due to changing interests or because they find they no longer have the time.

While some advisors sent us listings and prices, others provided background information and photographs, checked printouts or simply answered our questions. All are listed below. Each name is followed by their code, see the section called Categories of Special Interest for an explanation of how these are used in the listings.

Matt and Lisa Adams (A7)

Sally and Stan Alekna (A1)

Pamela E. Apkarian-Russell (H9)

Bob Armstrong (A4)

Richard Belyski (B1)

Jim Buskirk (B6)

Bill Campbell (C10)

Brad Cassity (C13)

Mark Chase (C2)

Ken Clee (C3)

Joel Cohen (C12)

Donna and Ron Donnelly (D7)

Lee Garmon

Bill Hamburg (H1)

George Hardy (H3)

Dan Iannotti (I3)

Terri Ivers (I2)

Dana Johnson (J3)

Keith and Donna Kaonis (K6)

David Kolodny-Nagy (K2)

Tom Lastrapes (L4)

Michael and Polly McQuillen (M11)

Steven Meltzer (M9)

Gary Mosholder (G1)

Judith Mosholder (M7)

Peter Muldavin (M21)

Dawn Diaz (P2)

Gary Pollastro (P5)

Judy Posner (P6)

John Rammacher (S5)

Charlie Reynolds (R5)

Cindy Sabulis (S14)

Scott Smiles (S10)

Steve Stephenson (S25)

Nate Stoller (S7)

Mark and Lynda Suozzi (S24)

Richard Trautwein (T3)

Judy and Art Turner (H8)

Marci Van Ausdall (V2)

James Watson (W8)

Randy Welch (W4)

Mary Young (Y2)

How to Use This Book

Concept. Our design for this book is two-fold. Primarily it is a market report compiled from many sources, meant to be studied and digested by our readers, who can then better arrive at their own conclusion regarding prices. Were you to ask ten active toy dealers for their opinion as to the value of a specific toy, you would no doubt get ten different answers, and who's to say which is correct? Quite simply, there are too many variables to consider. Where you buy is critical. Condition is certainly subjective, prices vary from one area of the country to another, and probably the most important factor is how badly you want to add the item in question to your collection or at what price you're willing to sell. So use this as a guide along with your own observations.

The second function of this book is to put buyers in touch with sellers who deal in the type of toys they want to purchase. Some of our listings contain a dealer's code, linking that item to a merchant that may have that particular toy in stock. (See the section titled Categories of Special Interest in the Directory.) Even though it may have already sold by the time our book is published, many of them tell us that they often get similar or even the same items in over and over, so if you see something listed you're interested in buying, don't hesitate to call any of them. Remember, though, they're not tied down to the price quoted in the book, since their asking price is many times influenced by what they've had to pay to restock their shelves.

Toys are listed by name. Every effort has been made to list a toy by the name as it appears on the original box. There have been very few exceptions made, and then only if the collector-given name is more recognizable. For instance, if we listed 'To-Night Amos 'n' Andy in Person' (as the name appears on the box lid), very few would recognize the toy as the Amos 'n' Andy Walkers. But these exceptions are few.

Descriptions and sizes may vary. When we were entering data, we often found the same toy had sold through more than one auction gallery or was listed in several dealer lists. So the same toy will often be described in various ways, but we left descriptions just as we found them, since there is usually something to be gleaned from each variation. We chose to leave duplicate lines in when various conditions were represented so that you could better understand the impact of condition on value. Depending on the source and who was doing the measuring, we found that the size of a given toy might vary by an inch or more. Not having the toy to measure ourselves, we had to leave dimensions just as they were given in auction catalogs or dealer lists. *Lines are sometimes coded as to source.* Each listing that represents an auction-realized price will be coded 'A' at the end of the line; often pre-auction estimates will follow in parenthesis. Other letters/number codes identify the dealer who sent us that information or who at that time had the item for sale. See the section called Categories of Special Interest for further explanation. Additional sources of like merchandise will sometimes be noted under the narrative for each category.

As we said before, collectors have various viewpoints regarding auction results. You will have to decide for yourself. Some feel they're too high to be used to establish prices while others prefer them to 'asking' prices that can sometimes be speculative. Because the average auction-consigned toy is in especially good condition and many times even retains its original box, it will naturally bring higher prices than the norm. And auctions often offer the harder-to-find, more unusual items. Unless you take these factors into consideration, prices may seem high, when in reality, they may not be at all. Prices may be driven up by high reserves, but not all galleries have reserves. Whatever your view, you'll be able to recognize and consider the source of the values we quote and factor that into your personal evaluation. For the most part, we found auction prices to be well in line with previously accepted market values.

Categories that have priority. Obviously there are thousands of toys that would work as well in one category as they would in another, depending on the preference of the collector. For instance, a Mary Poppins game would appeal to a games collector just as readily as it would to someone who bought character-related toys of all kinds. The same would be true of many other types of toys. We tried to make our decisions sensibly and keep our sorts simple. We'll guide you to those specialized categories with cross-references and 'See Alsos.' If all else fails, refer to the index. It's as detailed as we know how to make it.

Price ranges. Once in awhile, you'll find a listing that gives a price range. These result from our having found varying prices for the same item. We've taken a mid-range — less than the highest, a little over the lowest — if the original range was too wide to really be helpful. If the range is still coded 'A' for auction, all that were averaged were auction-realized prices.

Condition — how it affects value, how to judge it. The importance of condition can't be stressed enough. Unless a toy is exceptionally rare, it must be very good or better to really have much collector value. But here's where the problem comes in: though each step downward on the grading scale drastically decreases a toy's value, as the old saying goes, 'beauty is in the eye of the beholder.' What is acceptable wear and damage to one individual may be regarded by another as entirely too degrading. Criteria used to judge condition even varies from one auction company to the next, so we had to attempt to sort them all out and arrive at some sort of standardization. Please be sure to read and comprehend what the description is telling you about condition; otherwise you can easily be mislead. Auction galleries often describe missing parts, repairs, and paint touch-ups, summing up overall appearance in the condition code. When losses and repairs were noted in the catalog, we noted them as well. Remember that a toy even in mint restored condition is never worth as much as one in mint original condition. And even though a toy may be rated 'otherwise EX' after losses and repairs are noted, it won't be worth as much as one with original paint and parts in excellent condition. Keep this in mind when you use our listings to evaluate your holdings.

These are the conditions codes we have used throughout the book and their definitions as we have applied them:

M — mint. Unplayed with, brand new, flawless.

NM — near mint. Appears brand new except on very close inspection.

EX — excellent. Has minimal wear, very minor chips and rubs, a few light scratches.

VG — very good. Played with, loss of gloss, noticeable problems, several scratches.

G — good. Some rust, considerable wear and paint loss, well used.

P — poor. Generally unacceptable except for a filler.

Because we do not use a three-level pricing structure as many of you are used to and may prefer, we offer this table to help you arrive at values for toys in conditions other than those that we give you. If you know the value of a toy in excellent condition and would like to find an approximate value for it in near mint condition, for instance, just run your finger down the column under 'EX' until you find the approximate price we've listed (or one that easily factors into it), then over to the column headed 'NM.' We'll just go to $100.00, but other values will be easy to figure by addition or multiplication.

G	VG	EX	NM	M
40/50%	55/65%	70/80%	85/90%	100%
5.00	6.00	7.50	9.00	10.00
7.50	9.00	11.00	12.50	15.00
10.00	12.00	15.00	18.00	20.00
12.00	15.00	18.00	22.00	25.00
14.00	18.00	22.50	26.00	30.00
18.00	25.00	30.00	35.00	40.00
22.50	30.00	37.50	45.00	50.00
27.00	35.00	45.00	52.00	60.00
32.00	42.00	52.00	62.00	70.00
34.00	45.00	55.00	65.00	75.00
35.00	48.00	60.00	70.00	80.00
40.00	55.00	68.00	80.00	90.00
45.00	60.00	75.00	90.00	100.00

Condition and value of original boxes and packaging. When no box or packaging is referred to in the line or in the narrative, assume that the quoted price is for the toy only. Please read the narratives! In some categories (Corgi, for instance), all values are given for items mint and in original boxes. Conditions for boxes (etc.) are in parenthesis immediately following the condition code for the toy itself. In fact, any information within parenthesis at that point in the line will refer to packaging. Collector interest in boxes began several years ago, and today many people will pay very high prices for them, depending on scarcity, desirability, and condition. The more colorful, graphically pleasing boxes are favored, and those with images of well-known characters are especially sought-after. Just how valuable is a box? Again, this is very subjective to the individual. We asked this question to several top collectors around the country, and the answers they gave us ranged from 20% to 100% above mint-no-box prices.

Listing of Standard Abbreviations

These abbreviations have been used throughout this book in order to provide you with the most detailed descriptions possible in the limited space available. No periods are used after initials or abbreviations. When two dimensions are given, height is noted first. When only one measurement is given, it will be the greater — height if the toy is vertical, length if it is horizontal. (Remember that in the case of duplicate listings representing various conditions, we found that sizes often varied as much as an inch or more.)

att	attributed to
bl	blue
blk	black
b/o	battery-operated
brn	brown
bsk	bisque
BRT	black rubber tires
cb	cardboard
CI	cast iron
compo	composition
dbl	double
dk	dark
emb	embosse
EX	excellent
EXIB	excellent in box
EXIC	excellent in container
EXIP	excellant in package
ft, ftd	feet, foot, footed
G	good
GIB	good in box
gr	green
hdl	handle, handled
illus	illustrated, illustration
inscr	inscribed
jtd	jointed
L	long, length
litho	lithographed
lt	light, lightly
M	mint
MBP	mint in bubble pack
mc	multicolored
MDW	metal disk wheels
MIB	mint in box
MIP	mint in package
mk	marked
MOC	mint on card
MOT	mint on tree

MSW	metal spoke wheels
NM	near mint
NOS	new old stock
NP	nickel plated
NPDW	nickel plated disk wheels
NPSW	nickel plated spoke wheels
NRFB	never removed from box
NRFP	never removed from package
orig	original
o/w	otherwise
P	poor
pk	pink
pkg	package
PMDW	painted metal disk wheels
pnt	paint, painted
pr	pair
prof	professional
PS	pressed steel
r/c	remote control
rnd	round
rpl	replaced
rpr	repaired
rpt	repainted
rstr	restored
sz	size
turq	turquoise
unmk	unmarked
unpt	unpainted
VG	very good
VGIB	very good in box
W	width, wingspan
wht	white
WRT	white rubber tires
WWT	white-wall tires
w/	with
w/up	windup
yel	yellow

Action Figures

You will find a wide range of asking prices from dealer to dealer, and under the influence of Internet buying, prices fluctuate greatly. Be critical of condition! Original packaging is extremely important. In fact, when it comes to recent issues, loose, played-with examples are seldom worth more than a few dollars. When no size is given, assume figures are 3¾" or standard size for that line. Unless noted, values are for complete accessories or figures.

See also Character, TV, and Movie Collectibles; Dolls, Celebrity; GI Joe; Star Trek; Star Wars.

A-Team, accessory, Combat Headquarters (w/4 figures), Galloob, MIB, from $45 to $55.00
A-Team, accessory, Command Chopper & Enforcer Van, MIP...$25.00
A-Team, accessory, Corvette (w/Face figure), Galoob, M...$35.00
A-Team, accessory, Interceptor Jet Bomber (w/Murdock figure), Galoob, MIP, from $50 to...$55.00
A-Team, accessory, Off Road Attack Cycle, Galoob, MIP .$20.00
A-Team, accessory, Patrol Boat (w/Hannibal figure), Galoob, MIB $30.00
A-Team, accessory, van w/removable roof, Galoob, M, from $35 to $45.00
A-Team, figure, 3¾", Bad Guys, set of 4 (Cobra, Python, Rattler & Viper), Galoob, MOC (all on 1 card), from $50 to.......$60.00
A-Team, figure, 3¾", Soldiers of Fortune, set of 4 (BA, Face, Hannibal & Murdock), Galoob, MOC (all on 1 card), from $30 to...$50.00
A-Team, figure, 6½", Amy Allen, Galoob, MOC, from $28 to $32.00
A-Team, figure, 6½", BA Baracus, Galoob, MOC, from $32 to $36.00
A-Team, figure, 6½", Cobra, Python, Rattler, or Viper, Galoob, MOC, ea from $12 to $16.00

A-Team, figure, 6½", Face, Hannibal, or Murdock, Galoob, MOC, ea from $20 to $22.00
A-Team, figure, 12", Mr T, talking, Galoob, MIB, from $70 to $80.00
Action Jackson, accessory, Campmobile, Mego, MIB.......$75.00
Action Jackson, accessory, Fire Rescue Pack or Parachute Plunge, Mego, MIB, ea from $12 to $18.00
Action Jackson, accessory, Jungle House, Mego, MIB $75.00
Action Jackson, accessory, Scramble Cycle, Mego, MIB ..$45.00
Action Jackson, accessory, Strap-On Helicopter or Water Scooter, Mego, MIB, ea from $12 to $18.00

Action Jackson, figure, any except Black figure, Mego, MIB, each from $25.00 to $30.00; Action Jackson, figure, Black, Mego, MIB, from $50.00 to $60.00.

Action Jackson, outfit, any, Mego, MIP, ea from $8 to $12.00
Adventures of Indiana Jones, see Indiana Jones (Adventures of)

A-Team, figure, 12", Mr. T, nontalker, Galoob, MIB, from $50.00 to $60.00.

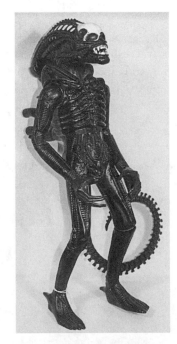

Alien, figure, Alien, 18", Kenner, 1980, M, from $175.00 to $185.00.

Alien, figure, Alien, 18", Kenner, MIB, from $400 to **$475.00**

Aliens, accessory, Evac Fighter or Hovertread, Kenner, MIP, from $15 to...**$18.00**

Aliens, accessory, Power Loader or Stinger XT-37, MIP, ea from $15 to...**$18.00**

Aliens, figure, Series 1, Apone, Bishop, Bull Alien, Drake, Gorilla Alien, or Hicks, Kenner, MOC, ea from $8 to............**$10.00**

Aliens, figure, Series 1, Queen Alien, Ripley, or Scorpion Alien, Kenner, MOC, ea from $15 to..................................**$20.00**

Aliens, figure, Series 2, Flying Queen Alien, Queen Face Hugger, or Snake Alien, Kenner, MOC, ea from $12 to ..**$16.00**

Aliens, figure, Series 3, Arachnid Alien, Clan Leader Predator, King Alien, or Swarm Alien, Kenner, MOC, ea from $18 to..**$22.00**

Aliens, figure, Series 3, Atax, Kenner, 1994, Mattel, MOC, from $10.00 to $15.00.

Aliens, figure, Series 3, Cracked Tusk Predator, Kill Krab, or Lava Predator, Kenner, MOC, ea from $10 to **$15.00**

Aliens, figure, Series 3, Mantis Alien, Night Cougar Alien or Night Storm Predator, Kenner, MOC, ea from $10 to **$15.00**

Aliens, figure, Series 3, Panther, Rhino, Spiked Tail, Stalker, or Wild Boar, Kenner, MOC, ea from $10 to **$15.00**

Aliens, figure set, Series 2, Alien vs Predator, Kenner, MOC, from $28 to..**$32.00**

American West, figure, Buffalo Bill Cody or Cochise, Mego, MIB, ea from $65 to.......................................**$75.00**

American West, figure, Buffalo Bill Cody or Cochise, Mego, MOC, from $80 to...**$90.00**

American West, figure, Davy Crockett, Mego, MIB, from $90 to **$100.00**

American West, figure, Davy Crockett, Mego, MOC, from $125 to...**$135.00**

American West, figure, Sitting Bull, Mego, MIB, from $75 to **$85.00**

American West, figure, Sitting Bull, Wild Bill Hickok, or Wyatt Earp, Mego, MOC, ea from $100 to.........................**$115.00**

American West, figure, Wild Bill Hickok or Wyatt Earp, Mego, MIB, ea from $65 to...**$75.00**

American West, horse, Shadow, Mego, MIB, from $125 to **$135.00**

American West, playset, Dodge City, Mego, MIB, from $150 to **$175.00**

Archies, figure, any, Marx, MIP, ea from $70 to...............**$80.00**

Archies, figure, any, Marx, NM, ea from $12 to...............**$18.00**

Avengers, figure, any figure from any series, Toy Biz, MIP, from $6 to...**$10.00**

Avengers, figure gift sets, Ant-Man/Giant Man, Hulk, Iron Man, The Wasp, Toy Biz, MIP, ea from $18 to..................**$22.00**

Banana Splits, any figure, Sutton, 1970s, MIP, ea from $115 to **$130.00**

Batman, see also Captain Action, Pocket Super Heroes, Super Heroes & Super Powers

Batman (Animated), accessory, Aero Boat, BATV Vehicle, Batcycle, or Bat-Signal Jet, Kenner, 1992-95, MIP, ea from $18 to **$32.00**

Batman (Animated), accessory, Batcave, Kenner, MIP, from $100 to...**$130.00**

Batman (Animated), accessory, Batmobile, Kenner, MIP, from $50 to...**$60.00**

Batman (Animated), accessory, Crime Stalker, Hoverboat, Ice Hammer, or Joker Mobile, Kenner, MIP, ea from $12 to **$18.00**

Batman (Animated), accessory, Robin's Dragster, Kenner, MOC, from $275 to..**$300.00**

Batman (Animated), accessory, Street Jet or Turbo Batplane, Kenner, MIP, ea from $18 to.......................................**$26.00**

Batman (Animated), figure, Anti-Freeze, Bane, Bruce Wayne, Ground Assault, or Infrared Batman, Kenner, MOC, ea from $8 to..**$12.00**

Batman (Animated), figure, Battle Helmet Batman, High-Wire Batman, or Poison Ivy, Kenner, MOC, ea from $28 to **$38.00**

Batman (Animated), figure, Man-Bat, Kenner, MOC, from $24.00 to $28.00.

Batman (Animated), figure, Bola Trap Robin or Sky Dive Batman, Kenner, MOC, ea from $8 to..................$12.00

Batman (Animated), figure, Catwoman, Radar Scope Batman, or Rapid Attack Batman, Kenner, MOC, ea from $22 to ..$26.00

Batman (Animated), figure, Combat Belt Batman, Kenner, MOC, from $35 to.................................$38.00

Batman (Animated), figure, Knight Star Batman, Lightning Strike Batman, or Mech-Wing Batman, Kenner, MOC, ea from $8 to.................................$12.00

Batman (Animated), figure, Man-Bat, Kenner, M, from $6 to $8.00

Batman (Animated), figure, Penguin, Kenner, MOC, from $60 to $65.00

Batman (Animated), figure, Riddler, Tornado Batman, or Two Face, Kenner, MOC, ea from $22 to $26.00

Batman (Animated), figure set, Ninja Batman & Robin, Kenner, MOC, from $18 to..................................$22.00

Batman (Dark Knight), accessory, Batcycle, Batwing, or Bola Bullet, MIP, ea from $35 to..........................$45.00

Batman (Dark Knight), accessory, Batjet, Kenner, MIP, from $65 to $70.00

Batman (Dark Knight), accessory, Batmobile, Kenner, MIP, from $70 to $80.00

Batman (Dark Knight), accessory, Joker Cycle, Kenner, MIP, from $20 to..$25.00

Batman (Dark Knight), figure, Blast Shield, Claw Climber, Power Wing, Thunder Whip, Kenner, MOC, ea from $20 to $30.00

Batman (Dark Knight), figure, Bruce Wayne, Kenner, MOC, from $18 to..$22.00

Batman (Dark Knight), figure, Crime Attack, Iron Winch, Shadow Wing, or Wall Scaler, Kenner, MOC, ea from $18 to $22.00

Batman (Dark Knight), figure, Knockout Joker, Kenner, MOC, from $45 to..$55.00

Batman (Dark Knight), figure, Night Glider, Kenner, MOC, from $30 to..$40.00

Batman (Dark Knight), figure, Sky Escape Joker, Kenner, MOC, from $22 to..$28.00

Batman (Movie), accessory, Batcave Master Playset, Toy Biz, MIB, from $65 to $75.00

Batman (Movie), accessory, Batmobile (Turbine Sound), Toy Biz, MIB, from $25 to $30.00

Batman (Movie), accessory, Joker Cycle (Detachable Launching Sidecar), Toy Biz, MIB, from $20 to..................$25.00

Batman (Movie), figure, Batman (any except sq jaw), Toy Biz, MOC, ea from $10 to $15.00

Batman (Movie), figure, Batman (sq jaw), Toy Biz, MOC, from $18 to $22.00

Batman (Movie), figure, Bob (Joker's Goon), Toy Biz, MOC, from $20 to..$25.00

Batman (Movie), figure, Joker (hair curl), Toy Biz, MOC, from $20 to $25.00

Batman (Movie), figure, Joker (Squirting Orchid), Toy Biz, MOC, from $18 to..$22.00

Batman & Robin, accessory, Batmobile, Batmobile (Sonic), or Ice Hammer, Kenner, MIP, ea from $18 to..................$22.00

Batman & Robin, accessory, Ice Fortress, Kenner, MIP, from $8 to $12.00

Batman & Robin, accessory, Iceglow Bathammer, Kenner, MIP, from $45 to $55.00

Batman & Robin, accessory, Jet Blade, Kenner, MIP, from $18 to $22.00

Batman & Robin, accessory, NightSphere, Kenner, MIP, from $20 to $30.00

Batman & Robin, figure, Aerial Combat Batman or Mr Freeze (Jet Wing w/Ring), Kenner, MIP, ea from $18 to.......$22.00

Batman & Robin, figure, 5", Bane, Batman (Ambush Attack) or Batman (Battle Board w/Ring), Kenner, 1997-98, ea from $6 to $10.00

Batman & Robin, figure, 5", Batgirl, MIP, from $4 to.........$6.00

Batman & Robin, figure, 5", Batman (Heat Scan), Batman (Hover Attack), Batman (Ice Blade), Kenner, MIP, ea from $6 to $10.00

Batman & Robin, figure, 5", Batman (Ice Blade & Ring), Kenner, MIB, from $12 to $15.00

Batman & Robin, figure, 5", Batman (Laser Cape & Ring), Kenner, MIP, from $6 to..$10.00

Batman & Robin, figure, 5", Batman (Neon Armor & Ring), Batman (Rotoblade & Ring), Kenner, MIP, ea from $12 to..$15.00

Batman & Robin, figure, 5", Batman (Neon Armor), Batman (Snow Tracker), Kenner, MIP, ea from $6 to.............$10.00

Batman & Robin, figure, 5", Batman (Sky Assault & Ring), Batman (Thermal Shield & Ring), Kenner, MIP, ea from $12 to..$15.00

Batman & Robin, figure, 5", Batman (Snow Tracker), Batman (Wing Blast), Kenner, MIP, ea from $6 to..................$10.00

Batman & Robin, figure, 5", Bruce Wayne (Battle Gear) or Frostbite, Kenner, MIP, ea from $6 to $10.00

Batman & Robin, figure, 5", Jungle Venom Poison Ivy, Robin (Iceboard), Robin (Razor Skate), Kenner, MIP, ea from $4 to $6.00

Batman & Robin, figure, 5", Mr Freeze (Ultimate Armor w/Ring), Kenner, MIP, ea from $12 to.......................$15.00

Batman & Robin, figure, 5", Robin (Talon Strike) or Robin (Triple Strike), Kenner, MIP, ea from $12 to.............$15.00

Batman & Robin, figure, 12", Batgirl, Kenner, 1997-98, MIB, from $30 to..$36.00

Batman & Robin, figure, 12", Batman, Kenner, 1997-98, MIB, from $20..$28.00

Batman & Robin, figure, 12", Ice Battle Batman, Mister Freeze, or Robin, Kenner, 1997-98, MIB, ea from $20 to $25.00

Batman & Robin, figure, 12", Ultimate Batman or Ultimate Robin, Kenner, 1997-98, MIB, ea from $18 to..........$22.00

Batman & Robin, figure set, Batman & Poison Ivy, 12", Kenner, 1997-98, MIB, from $35 to..........................$45.00

Batman & Robin, figure set, Batman vs Poison Ivy, Kenner, 1998, MIP, from $35 to..$45.00

Batman & Robin, figure set, Challengers of the Night, Kenner, 1998, MIP, from $12 to..$18.00

Batman & Robin, figure set, Cold Night at Gotham, Brain vs Brawn, or Guardians of Gotham, Kenner, 1998, MIP, ea from $8 ....$12.00

Batman & Robin, figure set, Wayne Manor Batcave, Kenner, MIP, from $45 to $55.00

Batman & Robin (Deluxe), figure, Batgirl w/Icestrike Cycle, Kenner, MIP, from $18 to $22.00

Batman & Robin (Deluxe), figure, Batman, Kenner, MIP, from $8 to $12.00

Batman & Robin (Deluxe), figure, Robin, Kenner, MIP, from $8 to $12.00

Batman & Robin (Deluxe), figure, Robin (Glacier Battle), Kenner, MIP, from $12 to $15.00

Batman Crime Squad, accessory, Attack Jet, Kenner, MOC, from $12 to $16.00

Batman Crime Squad, figure, Air Assault Batman, Fast Pursuit Batman, or Landstrike Batman, Kenner, MOC, ea from $12 to $16.00

Batman Crime Squad, figure, Bomb Control Batman or Disaster Control Batman, Kenner, MOC, ea from $22 to $28.00

Batman Crime Squad, figure, Piranha Blade Batman, Sea Claw Batman, or Ski Blast Robin, Kenner, MOC, ea from $12 to $16.00

Batman Crime Squad, figure, Skycopter Batman or Triwing Batman, Kenner, MOC, ea from $22 to...........................$28.00

Batman Crime Squad, figure, Stealthwing Batman, Supersonic Batman, or Torpedo Batman, Kenner, MOC, ea from $12 to $16.00

Batman Forever, accessory, Batboat or Batwing, Kenner, MIB, ea from $22 to $28.00

Batman Forever, accessory, Batcave, Batmobile, or Triple Action Vehicle Set, Kenner, MIB, ea from $35 to $45.00

Batman Forever, accessory, Robin Cycle, Kenner, MIB, from $10 to $15.00

Batman Forever, accessory, Sky Blade or Sky Drop, Kenner, MIP, ea from $25 to $45.00

Batman Forever, accessory, Wayne Manor, Kenner, MIB, from $45 to $55.00

Batman Forever, figure, Attack Wing Batman, Laser Disc Batman, or Lightwing Batman, Kenner, MOC, ea from $20 to $28.00

Batman Forever, figure, Batarang Batman or Ice Blade Batman, Kenner, MOC, ea from $10 to...................................$15.00

Batman Forever, figure, Blast Cape Batman, Fireguard Batman, Hydro Claw Robin, Kenner, MOC, ea from $12 to...$16.00

Batman Forever, figure, Bruce Wayne or The Riddler, Kenner, MOC, ea from $30 to $35.00

Batman Forever, figure, Catwoman, Penguin Commandos, or Robin, Kenner, MOC, ea from $18 to.......................$24.00

Batman Forever, figure, Firebolt Batman, Night Climber Batman, or Rocket Blast Batman, MOC, ea from $25 to $30.00

Batman Forever, figure, Manta Ray Batman, Martial Arts Robin, or Neon Armor Batman, Kenner, MOC, ea from $12 to..$16.00

Batman Forever, figure, Night Hunter Batman, Power Beacon Batman, or Recon Hunter Batman, Kenner, MOC, ea from $12 to..$16.00

Batman Forever, figure, Polar Blast Batman, Powerwing Batman, or Shadow Wing Batman, Kenner, MOC, ea from $12 to..$16.00

Batman Forever, figure, Riddle (w/Bazooka) or Tripel Strike Robin, Kenner, MOC, ea from $10 to......................$15.00

Batman Forever, figure, Skyboard Robin, Solar Shield Batman, or Sonar Sensor Batman, Kenner, MOC, ea from $12 to...$16.00

Batman Forever, figure, Street Biker Robin, Street Racer Batman, or Transforming Bruce Wayne, Kenner, MOC, ea from $12 to..$16.00

Batman Forever, figure, Talking Riddler, Tide Racer Robin, Kenner, MOC, ea from $18 to $22.00

Batman Forever, figure, Transforming Dick Grayson, Two-Face, or Wing Blast Batman, Kenner, MOC, ea from $12 to....$16.00

Batman Forever, figure set, Guardians of Gotham City, Kenner, MOC, from $30 to $35.00

Batman Returns, accessory, All-Terrain Batskiboat, Kenner, MIP, from $40 to $45.00

Batman Returns, accessory, Bat Cave Command Center, Kenner, MIB, from $65 to $75.00

Batman Returns, accessory, Batmissile Batmobile, Kenner, MIB, from $130 to $150.00

Batman Returns, accessory, Batmobile, Kenner, MIP, from $135 to $145.00

Batman Returns, accessory, Bruce Wayne Custom Coupe (w/figure), Kenner, MIB, from $45 to $55.00

Batman Returns, accessory, Camo Attack Batmobile, Kenner, MIP, from $75 to $85.00

Batman Returns, accessory, Robin Jetfoil, Kenner, MIP, from $20 to $25.00

Batman Returns, Bat Cycle, Kenner, MIP, from $20 to $25.00

Batman Returns, figure, Aerostrike Batman, Air Attack Batman, or Arctic Batman, Kenner, MOC, ea from $12 to $16.00

Batman Returns, figure, Batman, 16", Kenner, MIB, from $60 to $65.00

Batman Returns, figure, Bola Strike Batman, Bruce Wayne, or Catwoman, MOC, ea from $12 to............................$18.00

Batman Returns, figure, Claw Climber Batman, Crime Attack Batman, or Deep Dive Batman, Kenner, MOC, ea from $12 to $16.00

Batman Returns, figure, Glider Batman, High Wire Batman, or Hydrocharge Batman, Kenner, MOC, ea from $12 to ...$16.00

Batman Returns, figure, Jungle Tracker Batman, Laser Batman, or Night Climber Batman, Kenner, MOC, ea from $12 to $16.00

Battlestar Galactica, accessory, Colonial Scarab, Mattel, MIB, from $65 to..$70.00

Battlestar Galactica, accessory, Colonial Steller Probe, Colonial Viper, or Cylon Raider, Mattel, MIB, ea from $65 to...$75.00

Battlestar Galactica, figure, 3¾", 1st series, any character, Mattel, MOC, ea from $30 to $35.00

Battlestar Galactica, figure, 3¾", 2nd series, Baltar, Noray, Cylon Commander, Lucifer, Mattel, MOC, ea from $80 to $115.00

Battlestar Galactica, figure, 12", Colonial Warrior or Cylon Centurian, Mattel, MIB, ea from $75 to $80.00

Best of the West, accessory, Buckboard w/Horse & Harness, Marx, MIB, from $175 to $200.00

Best of the West, accessory, Circle X Ranch, Marx, MIB, from $150 to $175.00

Best of the West, accessory, Covered Wagon, Marx, MIB, from $175 to $200.00

Best of the West, accessory, Fort Apache Playset, Marx, MIB, from $150 to $175.00

Best of the West, accessory, Jeep & Horse Trailer, Marx, later issue, M, from $50.00 to $75.00.

Best of the West, accessory, Jeep & Horse Trailer, Marx, MIB, from $125 to $150.00

Best of the West, accessory, Travel Case, Marx, NM $30.00

Best of the West figure, Bill Buck, Marx, M, from $275 to .$325.00

Best of the West, Best of the West, figure, Bill Buck, Marx, MIB, from $400 to $450.00

Best of the West, figure, Captain Maddox, Marx, M, from $75 to $100.00

Best of the West, figure, Captain Maddox, Marx, MIB, from $150 to $200.00

Best of the West, figure, Chief Cherokee, Marx, M, from $125 to $150.00

Best of the West, figure, Chief Cherokee, Marx, MIB, from $175.00 to $215.00.

Best of the West, figure, Daniel Boone, Marx, M, from $75 to $110.00

Best of the West, figure, Daniel Boone, Marx, MIB, from $175 to $215.00

Best of the West, figure, Davy Crockett, Marx, MIB, from $225 to $260.00

Best of the West, figure, Fighting Eagle, Marx, M, from $150 to $175.00

Best of the West, figure, Fighting Eagle, Marx, MIB.......$230.00

Best of the West, figure, General Custer, Marx, M, from $90 to $115.00

Best of the West, figure, General Custer, Marx, MIB, from $175 to $225.00

Best of the West, figure, Geronimo, Marx, MIB, from $125 to $165.00

Best of the West, figure, Geronimo with Storm Cloud, Marx, M, from $75.00 to $100.00.

Best of the West, figure, Geronimo w/Storm Cloud, Marx, MIB, from $150 to $200.00

Best of the West, figure, Jamie West, Marx, M, from $50 to $75.00

Best of the West, figure, Jamie West, Marx, MIB, from $75 to $110.00

Best of the West, figure, Jane West, Marx, M, from $50 to $75.00

Best of the West, figure, Jane West, Marx, MIB, from $100.00 to $125.00.

Best of the West, figure, Jane West w/Flame, Marx, M, from $75 to $100.00

Best of the West, figure, Jane West w/Flame, MIB, from $150 to $200.00

Best of the West, figure, Janice West, Marx, M, from $50 to ..$75.00

Best of the West, figure, Janice West, Marx, MIB, from $85 to ..$100.00

Best of the West, figure, Jay West, Marx, M, from $50 to ..$75.00

Best of the West, figure, Jay West, Marx, MIB, from $75 to $100.00

Best of the West, figure, Jed Gibson, Marx, M, from $400 to $450.00

Best of the West, figure, Johnny West, Marx, M, from $75 to $85.00

Best of the West, figure, Johnny West, Marx, MIB, from $100 to $150.00

Best of the West, figure, Johnny West (later version w/quick-draw arm), Marx, NMIB $60.00

Best of the West, figure, Johnny West w/Comanche, Marx, M, from $75 to $100.00

Best of the West, figure, Johnny West with Thunderbolt, Marx, MIB, from $165.00 to $185.00.

Best of the West, figure, Josie West, Marx, M, from $50 to ..$75.00

Best of the West, figure, Josie West, Marx, MIB, from $80 to $110.00

Best of the West, figure, Princess Wildflower, Marx, complete, M, from $75 to $125.00

Best of the West, figure, Princess Wildflower, Marx, MIB, from $150 to $175.00

Best of the West, figure, Sam Cobra, Marx, M, from $75 to ..$125.00

Best of the West, figure, Sam Cobra, Marx, MIB, from $175 to $225.00

Best of the West, figure, Sam Cobra (later version w/quick-draw grip), Marx, MIB $50.00

Best of the West, figure, Sam Cobra w/Thunderbolt, Marx, M, from $75 to $100.00

Best of the West, figure, Sam Cobra w/Thunderbolt, Marx, MIB, from $175 to $225.00

Best of the West, figure, Sheriff Garrett, Marx, M, from $150 to $165.00

Best of the West, figure, Sheriff Garrett, Marx, MIB, from $175 to $200.00

Best of the West, figure, Zeb Zachary, Marx, M, from $175 to ..$225.00

Best of the West, figure, Zeb Zachary, Marx, MIB, from $275 to $325.00

Best of the West, horse, Comanche, Marx, M, from $50 to ..$75.00

Best of the West, horse, Comanche, Marx, MIB, from $100 to $130.00

Best of the West, horse, Flame (palomino), Marx, MIB, from $125 to $150.00

Best of the West, horse, Pancho, Marx, MIB, from $65 to ..$85.00

Best of the West, horse, Pancho, Marx, M, from $35 to ...$45.00

Best of the West, horse, Thunderbolt, Marx, M, from $50 to $75.00

Best of the West, horse, Thunderbolt, Marx, MIB, from $100 to $130.00

Big Jim, accessory, Baja Beast, Mattel, MIB, from $60 to ...$70.00

Big Jim, accessory, Boat & Buggy Set, Mattel, MIB, from $45 to $55.00

Big Jim, accessory, Devil River Trip (w/figure & alligator), Mattel, MIB, from $45 to $55.00

Big Jim, accessory, Jungle Truck, Mattel, MIB, from $45 to $55.00

Big Jim, accessory, Motorcross Honda, Mattel, MIB, from $45 to $55.00

Big Jim, accessory, Rescue Rig, Mattel, MIB, from $45 to ...$55.00

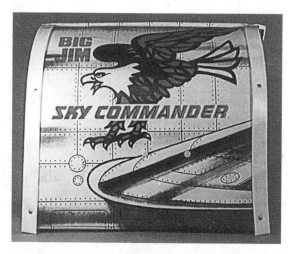

Big Jim, accessory, Sky Commander, Mattel, M, from $40.00 to $50.00.

Big Jim, accessory, Sky Commander, Mattel, MIB, from $60 to ..$70.00

Big Jim, accessory, Sport Camper w/Boat, Mattel, MIB, from $35 to $45.00

Big Jim, figure, Big Jack, Big Jeff, Big Josh, or Dr Steel, Mattel, M, ea from $18 to $22.00

Big Jim, figure, Big Jack, Big Jeff, Big Josh, or Dr Steel, Mattel, MIB, ea from $45 to $55.00

Big Jim, figure, Big Jack (Gold Medal), Mattel, M, from $22 to $25.00

Big Jim, figure, Big Jack (Gold Medal), Mattel, MIB, from $70 to $80.00

Big Jim, figure, Big Jim, Mattel, M, from $20 to $25.00

Big Jim, figure, Big Jim, Mattel, MIB, from $65 to $85.00

Big Jim, figure, Big Jim (Gold Medal Olympic Boxing Match), Mattel, M, from $42 to $45.00

Big Jim, figure, Big Jim (Gold Medal Olympic Boxing Match), Mattel, MIB, from $75 to $85.00

Big Jim, figure, Big Jim (Gold Medal), Mattel, M, from $22 to $25.00

Big Jim, figure, Big Jim (Gold Medal), Mattel, MIB, from $70 to...$80.00

Big Jim, outfit, any, Mattel, MIP, ea from $12 to..............$15.00

Big Jim's PACK, accessory, Beast, Mattel, MIP, from $85 to..$110.00

Big Jim's PACK, accessory, Frogman, Mattel, MIP, from $38 to $42.00

Big Jim's PACK, accessory, Howler, Mattel, MIP, from $55 to...$65.00

Big Jim's PACK, accessory, LazerVette, Mattel, MIP, from $90 to...$110.00

Big Jim's PACK, accessory, LazerVette Blitz-Rig, Mattel, MIP, from $150 to $175.00

Big Jim's PACK, accessory, Martial Arts, Mattel, MIP, from $10 to $15.00

Big Jim's PACK, accessory, Secret Spy, Mattel, MIP, from $35 to...$45.00

Big Jim's PACK, figure, Big Jim (Commander), gold pants, Mattel, M, from $40 to...$60.00

Big Jim's PACK, figure, Big Jim (Commander), gold pants, Mattel, MIP, from $150 to.....................................$175.00

Big Jim's PACK, figure, Big Jim (Commander), wht pants, Mattel, M, from $35 to...$45.00

Big Jim's PACK, figure, Big Jim (Commander), wht pants, Mattel, MIP, from $75 to.....................................$110.00

Big Jim's PACK, figure, Big Jim (Double Trouble), Mattel, M, from $75 to..$80.00

Big Jim's PACK, figure, Big Jim (Double Trouble), Mattel, MIB, from $150 to $175.00

Big Jim's PACK, figure, Dr Steel, Mattel, MIB, from $75 to..$100.00

Big Jim's PACK, figure, Torpedo Fist, Mattel, M, from $35 to $45.00

Big Jim's PACK, figure, Torpedo Fist, Mattel, MIB, from $100 to $150.00

Big Jim's PACK, figure, Warpath or The Whip, Mattel, M, ea from $30 to..$40.00

Big Jim's PACK, figure, Warpath or The Whip, Mattel, MIB, ea from $100 to...$150.00

Big Jim's PACK, figure, Zorack the Enemy, Mattel, M, from $40 to $60.00

Big Jim's PACK, figure, Zorack the Enemy, Mattel, MIB, from $100 to..$150.00

Bionic Woman, accessory, Beauty Salon, Kenner, MIB, from $65 to...$75.00

Bionic Woman, accessory, Bubblin' Bath 'n Shower, Kenner, MIB, from $50 to $75.00

Bionic Woman, accessory, House Playset, Kenner, MIP, from $25 to...$50.00

Bionic Woman, accessory, Spots Car, Kenner, MIB, from $90 to...$110.00

Bionic Woman, figure, Jaime Sommers, Kenner, MIB, from $125 to...$150.00

Bionic Woman, figure, Fembot, Kenner, MIB, from $175.00 to $200.00.

Bionic Woman, figure, Jaime Sommers (w/Mission Purse), Kenner, MIB, from $160 to..$180.00

Bionic Woman, outfits, any, Kenner, MOC, ea from $10 to .$20.00

Black Hole, figure, 3¾", Captain Holland, Dr Alex Durant, or Dr Hans Reinhardt, Mego, MOC, from $22 to..........$28.00

Black Hole, figure, 3¾", Harry Booth or Kate McCrae, Mego, MOC, from $22 to..$28.00

Black Hole, figure, 3¾", Humanoid, Mego, MOC, from $650 to $675.00

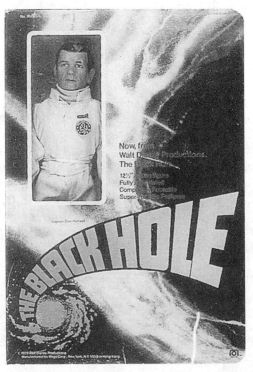

Black Hole, figure, 12", Captain Holland, Mego, MIB, from $70.00 to $80.00. (Photo courtesy Joseph Bourgeois)

Black Hole, figure, 3¾", Maximillian, Mego, MOC, from $70 to $80.00

Black Hole, figure, 3¾", Old Bob, Mego, MOC, from $150 to $175.00

Black Hole, figure, 3¾", Pizer, Mego, MOC, from $45 to $55.00

Black Hole, figure, 3¾", Sentry Robot, Mego, MOC, from $70 to $80.00

Black Hole, figure, 3¾", STAR, Mego, MOC, from $275 to $325.00

Black Hole, figure, 3¾", VINcent, Mego, MOC, from $65 to $75.00

Black Hole, figure, 12", Dr Alex Durant, Mego, MIB, from $70 to $80.00

Black Hole, figure, 12", Dr Hans Reinhardt, Mego, MIB, from $70 to $80.00

Black Hole, figure, 12", Harry Booth, Mego, MIB, from $85 to $90.00

Black Hole, figure, 12", Kate McCrae, Mego, MIB, from $95 to $100.00

Black Hole, figure, 12", Pizer, Mego, MIB, from $70 to $80.00

Blackstar, accessory, Battle Wagon, Galoob, MIB, from $70 to $80.00

Blackstar, accessory, Ice Castle, Galoob, MIB, from $70 to $80.00

Blackstar, accessory, Triton, Galoob, MIB, from $45 to $55.00

Blackstar, accessory, Warlock, Galoob, MIB, from $45 to ...$55.00

Blackstar, accessory, Wind Machine w/2 Trobbits, Galoob, MIB, from $55 to.......................................$65.00

Blackstar, figure, Blackstar, Galoob, M, from $8 to...........$12.00

Blackstar, figure, Blackstar, Galoob, MIB, from $20 to $30.00

Blackstar, figure, Blackstar (w/Laser Light), Galoob, M, from $8 to $12.00

Blackstar, figure, Blackstar (w/Laser Light), Galoob, MIB, from $30 to $40.00

Blackstar, figure, Devil Knight (w/Laser Light), Galoob, M, from $20 to $30.00

Blackstar, figure, Devil Knight (w/Laser Light), Galoob, MIB, from $40 to $50.00

Blackstar, figure, Gargo, Galoob, M, from $8 to $12.00

Blackstar, figure, Gargo, Galoob, MIB, from $30 to.........$40.00

Blackstar, figure, Gargo (w/Laser Light), Galoob, M, from $8 to.......................................$12.00

Blackstar, figure, Gargo (w/Laser Light), Galoob, MIB, from $30 to $40.00

Blackstar, figure, Kadray, Galoob, M, from $8 to $12.00

Blackstar, figure, Kadray, Galoob, MOC, from $30 to $40.00

Blackstar, figure, Kadray (w/Laser Light), Galoob, M, from $8 to $12.00

Blackstar, figure, Kadray (w/Laser Light), Galoob, MOC, from $30 to $40.00

Blackstar, figure, Klone (w/Laser Light), Galoob, M, from $12 to $18.00

Blackstar, figure, Klone (w/Laser Light), MOC, from $40 to..$50.00

Blackstar, figure, Lave Loc (w/Laser Light), Galoob, M, from $12 to $18.00

Blackstar, figure, Lava Loc (w/Laser Light), Galoob, MOC, from $40 to $50.00

Blackstar, figure, Mara, Galoob, M, from $25 to $35.00

Blackstar, figure, Mara, Galoob, MOC, from $55 to.........$65.00

Blackstar, figure, Meuton, Galoob, M, from $8 to............$12.00

Blackstar, figure, Meuton, Galoob, MOC, from $30 to.....$40.00

Blackstar, figure, Neptul, Galoob, M, from $12 to............$18.00

Blackstar, figure, Neptul, Galoob, MOC, from $45 to......$55.00

Bonanza, accessory, wagon (4-in-1), American Character, M, from $35 to.......................................$45.00

Bonanza, accessory, wagon (4-in-1), American Character, MIB, from $75 to $110.00

Bonanza, figure, Ben, Little Joe, Hoss, or Outlaw, American Character, M, ea from $50 to $75.00

Bonanza, figures, Ben, Little Joe, Hoss, and Outlaw, American Character, MIB, each from $125.00 to $175.00.

Bonanza, figure w/horse, any, American Character, M, ea from $65 to $85.00

Bonanza, figure w/horse, any, American Character, MIB, ea from $175 to.......................................$225.00

Bonanza, horse, any, American Character, Mego, M, ea from $25 to $35.00

Bonanza, horse, any, American Character, MIB, ea from $65 to.......................................$80.00

Buck Rogers, accessory, Draconian Marauder, Mego, MIP, from $35 to $45.00

Buck Rogers, accessory, Land Rover, Mego, NMIB, from $30 to.......................................$50.00

Buck Rogers, accessory, Laserscope Fighter, Mego, MIB, from $35 to $45.00

Buck Rogers, accessory, Star Fighter, Mego, MIB, from $45 to $55.00

Buck Rogers, accessory, Star Fighter Command Center, Mego, MIB, from $75 to $125.00

Buck Rogers, accessory, Star Seeker, Mego, MIP, from $55 to .$75.00

Buck Rogers, figure, 3¾", Adrella or Killer Kane, Mego, MOC, from $14 to.......................................$18.00

Buck Rogers, figure, 3¾", Buck Rogers, Mego, MOC, from $55 to.......................................$65.00

Buck Rogers, figure, 3¾", Dr Huer or Draco, Mego, MOC, ea from $18 to.......................................$22.00

Buck Rogers, figure, 3¾", Draconian Guard, Mego, MOC, from $18 to $22.00

Buck Rogers, figure, 3¾", Tiger Man or Wilma Deering, Mego, MOC, ea from $24 to $28.00

Buck Rogers, figure, 3¾", Twiki, Mego, MOC, from $40 to ..$50.00

Buck Rogers, figure, 12", any accept Tiger Man, Mego, MIB, ea from $65 to...$75.00

Buck Rogers, figure, 12", Killer Kane, Mego, MIB, from $65.00 to $75. 00. (Photo courtesy Joseph Bourgeois)

Buck Rogers, figure, 12", Tiger Man, Mego, MIB, from $120 to...$130.00

Captain Action, accessory, Action Cave, Ideal, MIP, from $600 to...$675.00

Captain Action, accessory, Anti-Gravitational Power Pack, Ideal, MIB, from $200 to.......................................$275.00

Captain Action, accessory, Directional Communicator, Ideal, MIB, from $275 to..$325.00

Captain Action, accessory, Headquarters, Ideal, MIB, from $450 to..$550.00

Captain Action, accessory, Inter-Galactic Jet Mortar, Ideal, MIB, from $275 to...$325.00

Captain Action, accessory, Parachute Pack, Ideal, MIB, from $200 to...$230.00

Captain Action, accessory, Silver Streak Amphibian Car, Ideal, MIB, from $1,000 to..$1,500.00

Captain Action, accessory, Silver Streak Garage, Ideal/Sears, MIB, from $1,500 to..$1,800.00

Captain Action, accessory, Survival Kit, Ideal, MIB, from $225 to...$250.00

Captain Action, accessory, Weapons Arsenal, Ideal, MIB, from $175 to...$200.00

Captain Action, figure, Action Boy, Ideal, M, from $225 to ..$250.00

Captain Action, figure, Action Boy, Ideal, MIB, from $850 to..$875.00

Captain Action, figure, Action Boy (space suit), Ideal, MIB, from $900 to...$1,000.00

Captain Action, figure, Captain Action, Ideal, M (Lone Ranger box), from $200 to......................................$230.00

Captain Action, figure, Captain Action, Ideal, MIB (Lone Ranger box), from $475 to $525.00

Captain Action, figure, Captain Action, Ideal, M (parachute offer), from $275 to..$300.00

Captain Action, figure, Captain Action, Ideal, MIB (parachute offer), from $650 to.......................................$675.00

Captain Action, figure, Captain Action, Ideal, M (photo box), from $280 to..$325.00

Captain Action, figure, Captain Action, Ideal, MIB (photo box), from $850 to...$875.00

Captain Action, figure, Dr Evil, Ideal, M (from photo box), from $225 to...$275.00

Captain Action, figure, Dr Evil, Ideal, MIB (from photo box), from $425 to...$475.00

Captain Action, outfit, Aquaman, Ideal, MIB, from $550 to..$625.00

Captain Action, outfit, Aquaman (w/ring), Ideal, MIB, from $875 to...$975.00

Captain Action, outfit, Batman, Ideal, M, from $175 to ..$200.00

Captain Action, outfit, Batman, Ideal, MIB, from $650 to ..$675.00

Captain Action, outfit, Batman (w/ring), Ideal, MIB, from $1,000 to...$1,200.00

Captain Action, outfit, Buck Rogers (w/ring), Ideal, M, from $425 to...$500.00

Captain Action, outfit, Buck Rogers (w/ring), Ideal, MIB, from $2,000 to..$2,500.00

Captain Action, outfit, Captain America, Ideal, MIB, from $825 to..$875.00

Captain Action, outfit, Captain America (w/ring), Ideal, MIB, from $950 to.......................................$1,100.00

Captain Action, outfit, Flash Gordon, Ideal, M, from $175 to $225.00

Captain Action, outfit, Flash Gordon (w/ring), Ideal, M, from $200 to...$250.00

Captain Action, outfit, Flash Gordon (w/ring), Ideal, MIB, from $750 to..$775.00

Captain Action, outfit, Green Hornet (w/ring), Ideal, M, from $1,500 to...$1,800.00

Captain Action, outfit, Green Hornet (w/ring), Ideal, MIB, from $6,000 to..$6,500.00

Captain Action, outfit, Lone Ranger, Ideal, M, from $150 to..$175.00

Captain Action, outfit, Lone Ranger (w/ring), Ideal, MIB, from $900 to..$1,100.00

Captain Action, outfit, Phantom (w/ring), Ideal, MIB, from $850 to...$875.00

Captain Action, outfit, Robin, Ideal, M, from $700 to ..$750.00

Captain Action, outfit, Robin, Ideal, MIB, from $900 to...$1,100.00

Captain Action, outfit, Steve Canyon, Ideal, M, from $200 to..$225.00

Captain Action, outfit, Steve Canyon, Ideal, MIB, from $600 to..$650.00

Captain Action, outfit, Steve Canyon (w/ring), Ideal, M, from $175 to...$200.00

Captain Action, outfit, Steve Canyon (w/ring), Ideal, MIB, from $775 to..$800.00

Captain Action, outfit, Super Boy, Ideal, MIB, from $750 to $850.00

Captain Action, outfit, Superman, Ideal, M, from $150 to $175.00

Captain Action, outfit, Super-man (with ring), Ideal, MIB, from $900.00 to $1,000.00.

Captain Action, outfit, Tonto (w/ring), Ideal, MIB, from $900 to $1,000.00

Captain America, see also Marvel Super Heroes

Charlie's Angels (Movie), figure, any, Jakks Pacific, MIB, ea...$40.00

Charlies Angels (TV Series), figure, any, Hasbro, MOC, ea...$80.00

Charon, figure, Charon, Mattel, M, from $25 to $28.00

CHiPs, accessory, motorcycle (for 3¾" figures), Mego, MOC, from $25 to...$35.00

CHiPs, accessory, motorcycle (for 8" figures), Mego, MIP, from $70 to $80.00

CHiPs, accessory, motorcycle w/ramp (for 3¾" figures), Mego, MIP, from $45 to...$55.00

CHiPs, figure, 3¾", Jimmy Squeaks, Mego, MOC, from $12 to $16.00

CHiPs, figure, 3¾", Jon, Mego, MOC, from $18 to..........$22.00

CHiPs, figure, 3¾", Ponch, Mego, MOC, from $15 to.....$18.00

CHiPs, figure, 3¾", Sarge, Mego, MOC, from $22 to.......$28.00

CHiPs, figure, 3¾", Wheels Willie, Mego, MOC, from $12 to $16.00

CHiPs, figure, 8", Jon, Mego, MOC $52.00

CHiPs, figure, 8", Ponch, Mego, MOC $42.00

CHiPs, figure, 8", Sarge, Mego, MOC...............................$52.00

CHiPs, figure w/motorcycle, 3¾", Ponch or Jon, MOC, from $25 to $30.00

Clash of the Titans, Calibos, Mattel, M, from $15 to $18.00

Clash of the Titans, figure, Calibos, Mattel, MOC, from $40 to...$45.00

Clash of the Titans, figure, Charon, Mattel, MOC, from $60 to...$65.00

Clash of the Titans, figure, Kraken, Mattel, M, from $60 to...$65.00

Clash of the Titans, figure, Kraken, Mattel, rare, MOC, from $240 to...$260.00

Clash of the Titans, figure, Pegasus, Mattel, M, from $20 to...$22.00

Clash of the Titans, figure, Pegasus, Mattel, MOC, from $60 to...$65.00

Clash of the Titans, figure, Perseus, Mattel, M, from $15 to...$18.00

Clash of the Titans, figure, Perseus, Mattel, MOC, from $40 to...$45.00

Clash of the Titans, figure, Thallo, Mattel, M, from $15 to .$18.00

Clash of the Titans, figure, Thallo, Mattel, MOC, from $40 to.$45.00

Clash of the Titans, figure set, Pegasus & Perseus, Mattel, M, from $40 to...$45.00

Clash of the Titans, figure set, Pegasus & Perseus, Mattel, MIP, from $75 to...$100.00

Comic Action Heroes, accessory, Batcopter, w/Batman figure, Mego, MIP, from $90 to.................................$110.00

Comic Action Heroes, accessory, Batmobile, w/Batman figure, Mego, MIP, from $150 to.................................$160.00

Comic Action Heroes, accessory, Collapsing Tower w/Wonder Woman figure & Invisible Plane, Mego, MIP, from $200 to...$225.00

Comic Action Heroes, accessory, Exploding Tower w/Spider-Man figure, Mego, MIP, from $225 to.................$275.00

Comic Action Heroes, accessory, Fortress of Solitude w/Super-man figure, Mego, MIP, from $175 to.................$225.00

Comic Action Heroes, accessory, Spider-Car w/Spider-Man & Green Goblin figures, MIP, from $75 to...................$125.00

Comic Action Heroes, accessory, The Mangler, Mego, MIP, from $250 to...$275.00

Comic Action Heroes, figure, Aquaman, Batman, Captain America, or Joker, Mego, M, ea from $18 to..............$22.00

Comic Action Heroes, figure, Aquaman, Batman, Captain America, or Joker, Mego, MOC, ea from $70 to........$80.00

Comic Action Heroes, figure, Green Goblin, Mego, M, from $20 to...$25.00

Comic Action Heroes, figure, Green Goblin, Mego, MOC, from $120 to...$130.00

Comic Action Heroes, figure, Hulk, Mego, MOC, from $50 to...$60.00

Comic Action Heroes, figure, Penguin, Shazam, or Spider-Man, M, ea from $70 to $80.00

Comic Action Heroes, figure, Robin, Superman, or Wonder Woman, Mego, M, ea from $55 to $60.00

Comic Action Heroes, figure, Robin, Superman, or Wonder Woman, Mego, MIP, ea from $60 to $70.00

Commando (Schwarzenegger), figure, 3¾", any except Matrix, Diamond Toymakers, M, ea from $8 to.....................$12.00

Commando (Schwarzenegger), figure, 3¾", Matrix, Diamond Toymakers, M, from $35 to.................................$45.00

Commando (Schwarzenegger), figure, 8", any except Matrix, Diamond Toymakers, M, ea from $12 to...................$18.00

Commando (Schwarzenegger), figure, 8", any except Matrix, Diamond Toymakers, MIP, ea from $35 to $45.00

Commando (Schwarzenegger), figure, 8", Matrix, Diamond Toymakers, M, from $30 to..$40.00

Commando (Schwarzenegger), figure, 18", Matrix, Diamond Toymakers, M, from $50 to...$75.00

Commando (Schwarzenegger), figure, 18", Matrix, Diamond Toymakers, MIP, from $100 to $150.00

Dukes of Hazzard, accessory, 3¾", Cadillac w/Boss Hogg or Police Car w/Sheriff Roscoe, M, ea from $35 to $45.00

Dukes of Hazzard, accessory, 3¾", Cadillac w/Boss Hogg or Police Car w/Sheriff Rosco figure, MIP, ea from $75 to $85.00

Dukes of Hazzard, accessory, 3¾", Jeep w/Daisy figure or General Lee w/Bo & Luke figures, Mego, MIP, ea from $45 to..$55.00

Dukes of Hazzard, accessory, 3¾", Jeep w/Daisy or General Lee w/Bo & Luke figures, Mego, M, ea from $20 to $30.00

Dukes of Hazzard, figure, 3¾", Uncle Jesse, MOC, from $14.00 to $18.00.

Dukes of Hazzard, figure, 8", Bo (pictured) or Luke, MOC, each from $28.00 to $32.00.

Dukes of Hazzard, figure, 3¾", Bo, Luke, or Boss Hogg, Mego, M, ea from $8 to..$10.00

Dukes of Hazzard, figure, 3¾", Bo, Mego, MOC, from $12 ..$16.00

Dukes of Hazzard, figure, 3¾", Boss Hogg, Mego, MOC, from $18 to...$22.00

Dukes of Hazzard, figure, 3¾", Cletus, Cooter, Coy, Rosco, Jesse, or Vance, MOC, ea from $28 to..............................$32.00

Dukes of Hazzard, figure, 3¾", Cletus, Cooter, Coy, or Vance, M, ea from $14 to..$18.00

Dukes of Hazzard, figure, 3¾", Daisy, Mego, M, from $10 to..$12.00

Dukes of Hazzard, figure, 3¾", Daisy, Mego, MOC, from $25 to...$28.00

Dukes of Hazzard, figure, 3¾", Luke, Mego, MOC, from $18...$22.00

Dukes of Hazzard, figure, 8", Bo or Luke, Mego, M, ea from $12 to...$16.00

Dukes of Hazzard, figure, 8", Boss Hogg, Mego, M, from $18 to...$22.00

Dukes of Hazzard, figure, 8", Boss Hogg, Mego, MOC, from $38 to...$42.00

Dukes of Hazzard, figure, 8", Coy (Bo), Daisy, or Vance (Luke), Mego, M, ea from $25 to $28.00

Dukes of Hazzard, figure, 8", Coy (Bo) or Vance (Luke), Mego, MOC, ea from $48 to $52.00

Dukes of Hazzard, figure, 8", Daisy, Mego, MOC, from $48 to...$52.00

Emergency, accessory, Fire House, LJN, MIP, from $175 to $200.00

Emergency, accessory, Rescue Truck, LJN, MIP, from $225 to...$250.00

Emergency, figure, John or Roy, LJN, MOC, ea from $65 to.$75.00

Evel Knievel, figure, Evel Knievel, Ideal, 1973-74, MIP, from $40.00 to...$60.00

Evel Knievel, figure Robby Knievel, Ideal, 1973-74, MIP, from $50 to...$70.00

Flash Gordon, figure, Dale Arden, Mego, MOC, from $80 to $90.00

Flash Gordon, figure, Dr Zarkov, Mego, MOC, from $90 to...$110.00

Flash Gordon, figure, Flash Gordon, Mego, MOC, from $90.00 to $100.00. (Photo courtesy Joseph Bourgeois)

Flash Gordon, figure, Ming the Merciless, Mego, MOC, from $80 to $90.00

Happy Days, accessory, Fonzie's Garage, Mego, MIB, from $140.00 to $160.00.

Happy Days, accessory, Fonz's Jalopy or Motorcycle, Mego, MIB, ea from $75 to $85.00

Happy Days, figure, any, Mego, MOC, ea from $75 to $85.00

Hulk Hogan, figure, Hasbro, M, from $12 to $15.00

Indiana Jones & the Temple of Doom, figure, Giant Thugee or Mola Ram, LJN, M, ea from $45 to..........................$55.00

Indiana Jones & the Temple of Doom, figure, Giant Thugee or Mola Ram, LJN, MOC, ea from $65 to......................$75.00

Indiana Jones & the Temple of Doom, figure, Indiana, LJN, M, from $60 to...$70.00

Indiana Jones & the Temple of Doom, figure, Indiana, LJN, MOC, from $145 to..$165.00

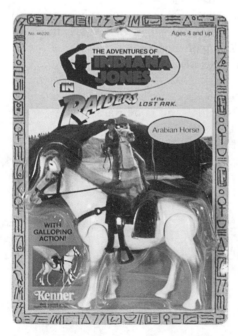

Indiana Jones in Raiders of the Lost Ark, accessory, 4", Arabian Horse, Kenner, MOC, from $65.00 to $75.00.

Indiana Jones in Raiders of the Lost Ark, accessory, 4", Convoy Truck, Kenner, MIB, from $145 to..........................$165.00

Indiana Jones in Raiders of the Lost Ark, accessory, 4", Map Room, Kenner, M, from $35 to $40.00

Indiana Jones in Raiders of the Lost Ark, accessory, 4", Map Room, Kenner, MIB, from $90.00 to $100.00.

Indiana Jones in Raiders of the Lost Ark, accessory, 4", Streets of Cairo, Kenner, M, from $45 to $50.00

Indiana Jones in Raiders of the Lost Ark, accessory, 4", Streets of Cairo, Kenner, MIB, from $90 to $100.00

Indiana Jones in Raiders of the Lost Ark, accessory, 4", Well of Souls, Kenner, M, from $60 to..................................$65.00

Indiana Jones in Raiders of the Lost Ark, figure, 4", Belloq, Kenner, M, from $20 to..$25.00

Indiana Jones in Raiders of the Lost Ark, figure, 4", Belloq, Kenner, MOC, from $60 to...$70.00

Indiana Jones in Raiders of the Lost Ark, figure, 4", Belloq (Ceremonial Robe), Kenner, M, from $16 to $20.00

Indiana Jones in Raiders of the Lost Ark, figure, 4", Belloq (Ceremonial Robe), Kenner, MOC or M (mailing bag), ea from $45 to $50.00

Indiana Jones in Raiders of the Lost Ark, figure, 4", Cairo Swordsman, Kenner, M, from $14 to........................$18.00

Indiana Jones in Raiders of the Lost Ark, figure, 4", Cairo Swordsman, Kenner, MOC, from $35 to....................$45.00

Indiana Jones in Raiders of the Lost Ark, figure, 4", German Mechanic, Kenner, M, from $24 to $26.00

Indiana Jones in Raiders of the Lost Ark, figure, 4", German Mechanic, Kenner, MOC, from $70 to.................$80.00

Indiana Jones in Raiders of the Lost Ark, figure, 4", Indiana w/whip, Kenner, M, from $75 to $85.00

Indiana Jones in Raiders of the Lost Ark, figure, 4", Indiana w/whip, Kenner, MOC, from $200 to $250.00

Indiana Jones in Raiders of the Lost Ark, figure, 4", Indiana Jones (German uniform), Kenner, M, from $24 to $26.00

Indiana Jones in Raiders of the Lost Ark, figure, 4", Indiana (German Uniform), Kenner, MOC, from $90 to.....$100.00

Indiana Jones in Raiders of the Lost Ark, figure, 4", Marion Ravenwood, Kenner, M, from $90 to......................$110.00

Indiana Jones in Raiders of the Lost Ark, figure, 4", Marion Ravenwood, Kenner, MOC, from $300.00 to $375.00.

Indiana Jones in Raiders of the Lost Ark, figure, 4", Sallah, Kenner, M, from $25 to......................................$35.00

Indiana Jones in Raiders of the Lost Ark, figure, 4", Sallah, Kenner, MOC, from $95 to...$100.00

Indiana Jones in Raiders of the Lost Ark, figure, 4", Toht, Kenner, M, from $15 to..$18.00

Indiana Jones in Raiders of the Lost Ark, figure, 4", Toht, Kenner, MOC, from $38 to...$42.00

Indiana Jones in Raiders of the Lost Ark, figure, 12", Indiana, Kenner, M, from $140 to.......................................$160.00

Indiana Jones in Raiders of the Lost Ark, figure, 12", Indiana Jones, Kenner, MIB, from $200.00 to $275.00.

James Bond, figure, Bond (Pierce Brosnan), Medicom, MIB...$85.00

James Bond, figure, 12", Bond, Gilbert, MIB, from $300 to ..$350.00

James Bond, figure, 12", Odd Job, Gilbert, MIB, from $200 to...$225.00

James Bond (Moonraker), figure, Bond, Mego, MIB, from $140 to...$160.00

James Bond (Moonraker), figure, Bond (w/suit & accessories), Mego, MIB, from $475 to.......................................$525.00

James Bond (Moonraker), figure, Drax or Holly, Mego, MIB, ea from $200...$225.00

James Bond (Moonraker), figure, Jaws, Mego, MIB, from $475 to...$525.00

Johnny Apollo (Astronaut), figure, Jane Apollo, Marx, MIB, $100 to...$130.00

Johnny Apollo (Astronaut), figure, Johnny Apollo, Marx, MIB, $150 to...$175.00

Johnny Apollo (Astronaut), figure, Kennedy Space Center Astronaut, Marx, MIB, from $130 to......................$150.00

Knight Rider, accessory, Knight 2000 Voice Car with Michael figure, Kenner, M, from $25.00 to $30.00. (Photo courtesy June Moon Collectibles)

Knight Rider, accessory, Knight 2000 Voice Car w/Michael figure, Kenner, MIB, from $45 to $55.00

Knight Rider, figure, Michael Knight, Kenner, M, from $8 to...$10.00

Knight Rider, figure, Michael Knight, Kenner, MOC, from $18 to...$20.00

Legend of the Lone Ranger, accessory, Western Town, Gabriel, MIB, $75 to...$100.00

Legend of the Lone Ranger, figure, Buffalo Bill Cody, Butch Cavendish, or Gen Geo Custer, Kenner, M, ea from $10 to...$15.00

Legend of the Lone Ranger, figure, Buffalo Bill Cody, Gabriel, MOC, from $24 to.......................................$28.00

Legend of the Lone Ranger, figure, Butch Cavendish, Gabriel, MOC, from $24 to.......................................$28.00

Legend of the Lone Ranger, figure, Lone Ranger, Gabriel, M, from $15 to...$20.00

Legend of the Lone Ranger, figure, Lone Ranger, Gabriel, MOC, from $24 to...$28.00

Legend of the Lone Ranger, figure, Tonto, Gabriel, M, from $8 to...$10.00

Legend of the Lone Ranger, figure, Tonto, Gabriel, MOC, from $14 to $18.00

Legend of the Lone Ranger, figure w/horse, any, Gabriel, M, ea from $25 to $30.00

Legend of the Lone Ranger, figure w/horse, any, Gabriel, MOC, ea from $45 to $55.00

Legend of the Lone Ranger, horse, Scout, Gabriel, MOC, from $18 to $22.00

Legend of the Lone Ranger, horse, Silver, Gabriel, MOC, from $28 to $32.00

Legend of the Lone Ranger, horse, Smoke, Gabriel, MOC, from $24 to $26.00

Lone Ranger, see also Captain Action

Lone Ranger Rides Again, accessory, Blizzard Adventure, Gabriel, M, from $15 to.................................$20.00

Lone Ranger Rides Again, accessory, Blizzard Adventure, Gabriel, MIB, from $25 to...............................$30.00

Lone Ranger Rides Again, accessory, Carson City Bank Robbery, Gabriel, M, from $25 to........................$30.00

Lone Ranger Rides Again, accessory, Carson City Bank Robbery, Gabriel, MIB, from $45 to....................$50.00

Lone Ranger Rides Again, accessory, Hidden Rattler Adventure, Gabriel, M, from $15 to.........................$20.00

Lone Ranger Rides Again, accessory, Hidden Rattler Adventure, Gabriel, MIB, from $25 to......................$30.00

Lone Ranger Rides Again, accessory, Landslide Adventure, Gabriel, MIB, from $25 to..............................$30.00

Lone Ranger Rides Again, accessory, Mysterious Prospector, Gabriel, M, from $45 to..............................$50.00

Lone Ranger Rides Again, accessory, Mysterious Prospector, Gabriel, MIB, from $70 to............................$75.00

Lone Ranger Rides Again, accessory, Red River Flood Waters, M, from $15 to..$20.00

Lone Ranger Rides Again, accessory, Red River Flood Waters, MIB, from $25 to.....................................$30.00

Lone Ranger Rides Again, accessory, Tribal Teepee and Prairie Wagon, MIB, ea from $25.00 to $30.00.

Lone Ranger Rides Again, accessory, Tribal Teepee, Gabriel, M, from $15 to...$20.00

Lone Ranger Rides Again, figure, any, Gabriel, M, each from $30.00 to $35.00, MIB, ea from $65.00 to $75.00; figure and horse sets, any, Gabriel, M, each from $45.00 to $50.00, MIB, each from $65.00 to $75.00.

Lord of the Rings, figure, any, Toy Vault, 1998-99, M, ea from $8 to $10.00

Lord of the Rings, figure, any, Toy Vault, 1998-99, MOC, ea from $12 to $18.00

Lost in Space, accessory, Bubble Fighter, Trendmasters, M, from $25 to $30.00

Lost in Space, accessory, Bubble Fighter, Trendmasters, MIB, from $75 to $85.00

Lost in Space, accessory, Jupiter 2, Trendmasters, M, from $25 to $30.00

Lost in Space, accessory, Jupiter 2, Trendmasters, MIB, from $65 to $85.00

Lost in Space, accessory, Jupiter 2 (Classic), Trendmasters, M, from $45 to $55.00

Lost in Space, accessory, Jupiter 2 (Classic), Trendmasters, MIB, from $90 to $115.00

Lost in Space, figure, Cyclops, Trendmasters, M, from $25 to $30.00

Lost in Space, figure, Cyclops, Trendmasters, MOC, from $55 to $65.00

Lost in Space, figure, Don West (Battle Armor), Trendmasters, M, from $4 to $6.00

Lost in Space, figure, Dr Judy Robinson (Cryo Suit), Trendmasters, M $5.00

Lost in Space, figure, Dr Judy Robinson (Cryo Suit), Trendmasters, MOC, from $8 to $10.00

Lost in Space, figure, Dr Smith (Proteus Armor), Trendmasters, M $5.00

Lost in Space, figure, Dr Smith (Proteus Armor), Trendmasters, MOC, from $8 to $10.00

Lost in Space, figure, Dr Smith (Sabotage-Action), Trendmasters, M, from $8 to $10.00

Lost in Space, figure, Dr Smith (Sabatoge-Action), Trendmasters, MOC, from $14 to $18.00

Lost in Space, figure, Future Smith, Trendmasters, M, from $6 to $8.00

Lost in Space, figure, Future Smith, Trendmasters, MOC, from $10 to..$12.00

Lost in Space, figure, John Robinson (Proteus Armor), Trendmasters, M, from $4 to..............................$6.00

Lost in Space, figure, John Robinson (Proteus Armor), Trendmasters, MOC, from $8 to.........................$10.00

Lost in Space, figure, Judy Robinson, Trendmasters, M, from $8 to..$10.00

Lost in Space, figure, Judy Robinson, Trendmasters, MOC, from $14 to..$16.00

Lost in Space, figure, Judy Robinson (Cryo Chamber), Trendmasters, M...$5.00

Lost in Space, figure, Judy Robinson (Cryo Chamber), Trendmasters, MOC, from $8 to.........................$10.00

Lost in Space, figure, Major Don West (Battle Armor), Trendmasters, MOC, from $8 to.........................$10.00

Lost in Space, figure, Will Robinson, Trendmasters, M, from $8 to..$10.00

Lost in Space, figure, Will Robinson, Trendmasters, MOC, from $14 to..$18.00

Lost in Space, figure, Will Robinson (Cryo Chamber), Trendmasters, M...$5.00

Lost in Space, figure, Will Robinson (Cryo Chamber), Trendmasters, MOC, from $8 to.........................$10.00

Lost in Space, figure, 9" (Classic), Cyclops, Trendmasters, M, from $25 to..$30.00

Lost in Space, figure, 9" (Classic), Cyclops, Trendmasters, MIP, from $45 to..$55.00

Lost in Space, figure, 9" (Classic), Don West, Trendmasters, M, from $10 to..$12.00

Lost in Space, figure, 9" (Classic), Don West, Trendmasters, MIP, from $18 to..$22.00

Lost in Space, figure, 9" (Classic), Dr Smith, Trendmasters, M, from $20 to..$25.00

Lost in Space, figure, 9" (Classic), Dr Smith, Trendmasters, MIP, from $38 to..$42.00

Lost in Space, figure, 9" (Classic), Judy Robinson, Trendmasters, M, from $10 to.....................................$12.00

Lost in Space, figure, 9" (Classic), Robot B9, Trendmasters, M, from $25 to..$30.00

Lost in Space, figure, 9" (Classic), Robot B9, Trendmasters, MIP, from $45 to..$55.00

Lost in Space, figure, 9" (Classic), Tybo the Carrot Man, Trendmasters, M, from $18 to.........................$22.00

Lost in Space, figure, 9" (Classic), Tybo the Carrot Man, Trendmasters, MIP, from $38 to.....................$42.00

Lost in Space, figure, 9" (Classic), Will Robinson, Trendmasters, M, from $15 to.....................................$18.00

Lost in Space, figure, 9" (Classic), Will Robinson, Trendmasters, MIP, from $28 to.................................$32.00

M*A*S*H, accessory, 3¾", Ambulance (w/Hawkeye figure), Tri-Star, MIP, from $25 to.........................$30.00

M*A*S*H, accessory, 3¾", Helicopter (w/Hawkeye figure), Tri-Star, MIP, from $25 to.........................$30.00

M*A*S*H, accessory, 3¾", Jeep (w/Hawkeye figure), Tri-Star, MIB, from $25 to $30.00

M*A*S*H, accessory, 3¾", Military Base, Tri-Star, MIB, from $50 to..$65.00

M*A*S*H, figure, 3¾", BJ, Col Potter, Father Mulcahy, Hawkeye, Klinger, or Winchester, Tri-Star, MOC, ea from $15 to..$20.00

M*A*S*H, figure, 3¾", Hot Lips, Tri-Star, MOC, from $20 to..$25.00

M*A*S*H, figure, 3¾", Klinger (in dress), Tri-Star, MOC, from $25 to..$35.00

M*A*S*H, figure, 8", BJ, Hawkeye, or Hot Lips, Tri-Star, MOC ea from $55 to..$65.00

Major Matt Mason, accessory, Astro Trac, Mattel, MIB, from $100 to..$125.00

Major Matt Mason, accessory, Fireball Space Cannon, Mattel, MIB, from $75 to....................................$100.00

Major Matt Mason, accessory, Gamma Ray Guard, Mattel, MIB, from $100 to..$120.00

Major Matt Mason, accessory, Moon Suit Pak, MIB, from $100 to..$115.00

Major Matt Mason, accessory, Rocket Launch, Mattel, MIB, from $70 to..$80.00

Major Matt Mason, accessory, Satellite Locker, Mattel, MIB, from $65 to..$75.00

Major Matt Mason, accessory, Space Crawler Action Set (w/figure), Mattel, MIB, from $75 to $100.00

Major Matt Mason, accessory, Space Probe, Mattel, MIB, from $70 to..$80.00

Major Matt Mason, accessory, Space Station, Mattel, MIB, from $250 to..$300.00

Major Matt Mason, accessory, Uni-Tred & Space Bubble, M, from $90 to..$100.00

Major Matt Mason, accessory, Uni-Tred & Space Bubble, MIB, from $175 to..$200.00

Major Matt Mason, figure, Callistro, Mattel, M, from $90 to..$110.00

Major Matt Mason, figure, Callistro, Mattel, MOC, from $200 to..$225.00

Major Matt Mason, figure, Captain Lazer, Mattel, M, from $125 to..$135.00

Major Matt Mason, figure, Captain Lazer, Mattel, MIP, from $275 to..$325.00

Major Matt Mason, figure, Doug Davis (w/helmet), Mattel, M, from $100 to..$125.00

Major Matt Mason, figure, Doug Davis (w/helmet), Mattel, MOC, from $250 to....................................$275.00

Major Matt Mason, figure, Jeff Long, Mattel, M, from $150 to..$175.00

Major Matt Mason, figure, Jeff Long (w/helmet), Mattel, MOC, from $450 to $500.00

Major Matt Mason, figure, Major Matt Mason, Mattel, M, from $75 to..$85.00

Major Matt Mason, figure, Major Matt Mason, Mattel, MOC, from $175 to..$200.00

Major Matt Mason, figure, Scorpio, Mattel, M, from $350 to $375.00

Major Matt Mason, figure, Scorpio, Mattel, MOC, from $775 to $800.00

Major Matt Mason, figure, Sgt Storm, Mattel, M, from $100 to $125.00

Major Matt Mason, figure, Sgt Storm, Mattel, MOC, from $350 to...$375.00

Man From UNCLE, accessory, Arsenal Set #1 or #2, Gilbert, MIP, from $35 to...$45.00

Man From UNCLE, accessory, Jumpsuit Set, Gilbert, M, from $20 to...$30.00

Man From UNCLE, accessory, Jumpsuit Set, Gilbert, MIP, from $40 to...$50.00

Man From UNCLE, accessory, Scuba Set, Gilbert, M, from $25 to...$35.00

Man From UNCLE, accessroy, Scuba Set, Gilbert, MIP, from $50 to...$75.00

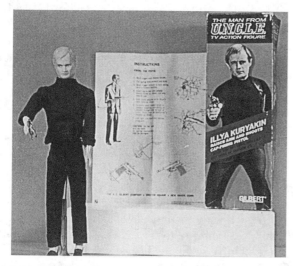

Man From UNCLE, figure, Illya Kuryakin, Gilbert, M, from $175.00 to $200.00, MIB, from $325.00 to $375.00.

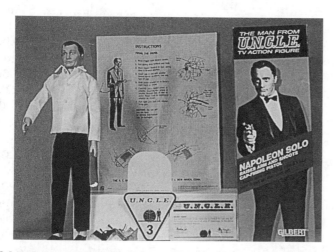

Man From UNCLE, figure, Napoleon Solo, Gilbert, M, from $175.00 to $200.00, MIB, from $325.00 to $375.00.

Marvel Super Heroes, accessory, Training Center, Toy Biz, MIB, from $25 to...$35.00

Marvel Super Heroes, figure, Annihilus, Deathlok, Hulk, Human Torch, Mr Fantastic, or Thing, Toy Biz, MOC, ea from $15 to...$18.00

Marvel Super Heroes, figure, Captain America, Toy Biz, MOC, from $18 to...$22.00

Marvel Super Heroes, figure, Daredevil, Toy Biz, M, from $18 to...$20.00

Marvel Super Heroes, figure, Daredevil, Toy Biz, MOC, from $34 to...$38.00

Marvel Super Heroes, figure, Dr Doom or Dr Octopus, Toy Biz, MOC, ea from $24 to...$28.00

Marvel Super Heroes, figure, Green Goblin (back lever) or Thor (back lever), Toy Biz, MOC, ea from $38 to.............$42.00

Marvel Super Heroes, figure, Green Goblin (no lever) or Thor (no lever), Toy Boz, MOC, ea from $24 to $28.00

Marvel Super Heroes, figure, Human Torch (fireball flinging action), Toy Biz, MOC, from $15 to $18.00

Marvel Super Heroes, figure, Invisible Woman (catapult), Toy Biz, MOC, from $15 to...$18.00

Marvel Super Heroes, figure, Invisible Woman (vanishing), Toy Biz, MOC, from $140 to...$160.00

Marvel Super Heroes, figure, Mr Fantastic (5-way stretch), Toy Biz, MOC, from $18 to...$20.00

Marvel Super Heroes, figure, Punisher (cap-firing or machine gun sound), Silver Surfer (chrome), Toy Biz, MOC, ea $15 to...$18.00

Marvel Super Heroes, figure, Spider-Man (ball joints or web tracer), Toy Biz, MOC, ea from $15 to.......................$18.00

Marvel Super Heroes, figure, Spider-Man (web climbing or web-shooting), Toy Biz, MOC, ea from $30 to.................$35.00

Marvel Super Heroes, figure, Venom or Tongue-Flicking Venom, Toy Biz, MOC, ea from $18 to...$22.00

Marvel Super Heroes (Secret Wars), accessory, Doom Copter, Mattel, MIP, from $30 to...$35.00

Marvel Super Heroes (Secret Wars), accessory, Doom Copter (w/Dr Doom figure), Mattel, MIP, from $45 to..........$50.00

Marvel Super Heroes (Secret Wars), accessory, Doom Cycle, Mattel, MIP, from $18 to...$22.00

Marvel Super Heroes (Secret Wars), figure, Baron Zemo, Mattel, MOC, from $34.00 to $38.00.

Marvel Super Heroes (Secret Wars), accessory, Doom Cycle (w/Dr Doom figure), Mattel, MIP, from $30 to $35.00

Marvel Super Heroes (Secret Wars), accessory, Doom Roller, Mattel, MIP, from $18 to $22.00

Marvel Super Heroes (Secret Wars), accessory, Freedom Fighter, Mattel, MIP, from $25 to $30.00

Marvel Super Heroes (Secret Wars), accessory, Tower of Doom, Mattel, MIP, from $30 to $40.00

Marvel Super Heroes (Secret Wars), accessory, Training Center, Mattel, MIP, from $20 to $25.00

Marvel Super Heroes (Secret Wars), figure, Captain America, Mattel, MOC, from $24 to $28.00

Marvel Super Heroes (Secret Wars), figure, Daredevil, Mattel, MOC, from $34.00 to $38.00.

Marvel Super Heroes (Secret Wars), figure, Dr Doom, Dr Octopus, Kang, or Magento, Mattel, MOC, ea from $18 to $22.00

Marvel Super Heroes (Secret Wars), figure, Falcon, Mattel, MOC, from $38 to $42.00

Marvel Super Heroes (Secret Wars), figure, Hobgoblin, Mattel, MOC, from $55 to $60.00

Marvel Super Heroes (Secret Wars), figure, Iron Man, Mattel, MOC, from $34 to $38.00

Marvel Super Heroes (Secret Wars), figure, Spider-Man (blk outfit), Mattel, MOC, from $48 to $52.00

Marvel Super Heroes (Secret Wars), figure, Spider-Man (red & bl outfit), Mattel, MOC, from $38 to $42.00

Marvel Super Heroes (Secret Wars), figure, Wolverine (blk claws), Mattel, MOC, from $70 to $80.00

Marvel Super Heroes (Secret Wars), figure, Wolverine (silver claws), Mattel, MOC, from $38 to $42.00

Marvel Super Heroes (Talking), figure, any, Toy Biz, MIP, ea from $20 to...$25.00

Masters of the Universe, accessory, Battle Cat, Mattel, MIP, from $45 to $55.00

Masters of the Universe, accessory, He-Man & Wind Raider, Mattel, MIP, from $22 to $28.00

Masters of the Universe, accessory, Jet Sled, Mattel, MIP, from $12 to $18.00

Masters of the Universe, accessory, Mantisaur, Mattel, MIP, from $20 to $30.00

Masters of the Universe, accessory, Monstroid, Mattel, MIP, from $70 to..$80.00

Masters of the Universe, accessory, Night Stalker, Mattel, MIP, from $28 to $32.00

Masters of the Universe, accessory, Panthor, MIP, from $45 to $55.00

Masters of the Universe, accessory, Screech, Mattel, MIP, from $35 to $45.00

Masters of the Universe, accessory, Stilt Stalkers, Mattel, MIP, from $18 to $22.00

Masters of the Universe, accessory, Weapons Pak, Mattel, MIP, from $12 to..$18.00

Masters of the Universe, accessory, Zoar, Mattel, MIP, from $28 to $32.00

Masters of the Universe, figure, Battle Armor He-Man or Battle Armor Skeletor, Mattel, MOC, ea from $38 to $42.00

Masters of the Universe, figure, Beast Man or Blade, Mattel, MOC, ea from $65 to $75.00

Masters of the Universe, figure, Blast Attack, Buzz-Off, or Buzz-Saw Hordak, Mattel, MOC, ea from $38 to...............$42.00

Masters of the Universe, figure, Clamp Champ or Clawful, Mattel, MOC, ea from $42 to $48.00

Masters of the Universe, figure, Dragstor the Evil Horde, Mattel, MOC, from $38 to......................................$42.00

Masters of the Universe, figure, Evil-Lyn, Mattel, MOC, from $48 to $52.00

Masters of the Universe, figure, Extender, Mattel, MOC, from $30 to $35.00

Masters of the Universe, figure, Faker, Mattel, MOC, from $115 to..$125.00

Masters of the Universe, figure, Faker II, Mattel, MOC, from $70 to...$75.00

Masters of the Universe, figure, Fisto, Mattel, MOC, from $38 to.$42.00

Masters of the Universe, figure, Grizzlor (blk), Mattel, MOC, from $145 to $155.00

Masters of the Universe, figure, Grizzlor the Evil Horde, Mattel, MOC, from $38 to..................................$42.00

Masters of the Universe, figure, Gwilder, Mattel, MOC, from $70 to $75.00

Masters of the Universe, figure, He-Man, Mattel, MOC, from $120 to...$135.00

Masters of the Universe, figure, He-Man (Thunder Punch), Mattel, MOC, from $65 to $70.00

Masters of the Universe, figure, Hordak or Horde Trooper, Mattel, MOC, ea from $38 to $42.00

Masters of the Universe, figure, Jitsu or King Hiss, Mattel, MOC, ea from $40 to $50.00

Masters of the Universe, figure, King Randor, Mattel, MOC, from $70 to......................................$75.00

Masters of the Universe, figure, Leech, Mattel, MOC, from $30 to $35.00

Masters of the Universe, figure, Man-At-Arms, Mattel, MOC, from $38 to...$42.00

Masters of the Universe, figure, Man-E-Faces, Mattel, MOC, from $45 to...$55.00

Masters of the Universe, figure, Mantenna or Mekaneck, Mattel, MOC, ea from $38 to $42.00

Masters of the Universe, figure, Mer-Man, Mattel, MOC, from $45 to $55.00

Masters of the Universe, figure, Modulok, Mattel, MOC, from $30 to $35.00

Masters of the Universe, figure, Moss Man or Multi-Bot, Mattel, MOC, ea from $38 to $42.00

Masters of the Universe, figure, Ninjor, Mattel, MOC, from $75 to $85.00

Masters of the Universe, figure, Orko, Mattel, MOC, from $45 to $55.00

Masters of the Universe, figure, Prince Adam, Mattel, MOC, from $55 to...$65.00

Masters of the Universe, figure, Ram-Man, Mattel, MIB, from $55.00 to $65.00.

Masters of the Universe, figure, Rattlor, Mattel, MOC, from $30 to $35.00

Masters of the Universe, figure, Rattlor (red neck), Mattel, MOC, from $28 to...$32.00

Masters of the Universe, figure, Rio Blast, Mattel, MOC, from $38 to $42.00

Masters of the Universe, figure, Roboto, Mattel, MOC, from $30 to $35.00

Masters of the Universe, figure, Rokkon, Mattel, MOC, from $30 to $35.00

Masters of the Universe, figure, Rotar, Mattel, MOC, from $65 to $75.00

Masters of the Universe, figure, Saurod, Mattel, MOC, from $65 to $75.00

Masters of the Universe, figure, Scare Glow Spector, Mattel, MOC, from $70 to...$80.00

Masters of the Universe, figure, Skeletor, Mattel, MOC, from $110 to...$120.00

Masters of the Universe, figure, Skeletor (Terror Claws), MOC, from $65 to...$70.00

Masters of the Universe, figure, Snake Face, Mattel, MOC, from $40 to $50.00

Masters of the Universe, figure, Snout Spout, Mattel, MOC, from $38 to $42.00

Masters of the Universe, figure, Sorceress, Mattel, MOC, from $65 to $75.00

Masters of the Universe, figure, Spikor, Mattel, MOC, from $38 to $42.00

Masters of the Universe, figure, Stratos, Mattel, MOC, from $70 to $80.00

Masters of the Universe, figure, Sy-Klone, Mattel, MOC, from $38 to $42.00

Masters of the Universe, figure, Teela, Mattel, MOC, from $60 to $70.00

Masters of the Universe, figure, Trap Jaw, Mattel, MOC, from $80 to $90.00

Masters of the Universe, figure, Tri Klops, Mattel, MOC, from $38 to $42.00

Masters of the Universe, figure, Tung Lasher, Mattel, MOC, from $45 to...$50.00

Masters of the Universe, figure, Twistoid, Mattel, MOC, from $70 to $80.00

Masters of the Universe, figure, Two-Bad, Mattel, MOC, from $28 to $32.00

Masters of the Universe, figure, Webstor, Mattel, MOC, from $28 to $32.00

Masters of the Universe, figure, Whiplash, Mattel, MOC, from $25 to $30.00

Masters of the Universe, figure, Zodac, Mattel, MOC, from $45 to $55.00

Micronauts, accessory, Astro Station, Mego, MIB, from $20 to $25.00

Micronauts, accessory, Battle Cruiser, Mego, MIB, from $55 to $65.00

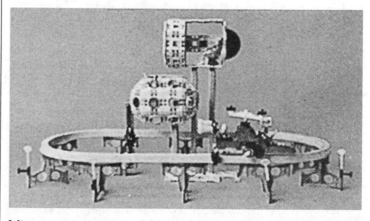

Micronauts, accessory, Microrail City, Mego, M, from $18.00 to $22.00, MIB, from $40.00 to $45.00.

Micronauts, accessory, Hornetroid, Mego, MIB, from $45 to **$50.00**

Micronauts, accessory, Mega City, Mego, MIB, from $35 to **$35.00**

Micronauts, accessory, Mobile Exploration Lab, Mego, MIB, from $30 to....................................**$40.00**

Micronauts, accessory, Neon Orbiter, Mego, MIB, from $20 to **$25.00**

Micronauts, accessory, Rocket Tubes, Mego, MIB, from $45 to **$55.00**

Micronauts, accessory, Star Searcher, Mego, MIB, from $35 to **$45.00**

Micronauts, figure, Andromeda, Mego, MIB, from $25 to..**$30.00**

Micronauts, figure, Antron, Mego, MOC, from $75 to ..**$100.00**

Micronauts, figure, Baron Karza, Mego, MIB, from $30 to...**$35.00**

Micronauts, figure, Biotron, Mego, MIB, from $25 to **$30.00**

Micronauts, figure, Centaurus, Mego, MOC, from $150 to...**$175.00**

Micronauts, figure, Force Commander, Mego, MIB, from $25 to...**$30.00**

Micronauts, figure, Giant Acroyeat, Mego, MIB, from $25 to...**$30.00**

Micronauts, figure, Kronos, Mego, MOC, from $150 to...**$175.00**

Micronauts, figure, Lobros, Mego, MOC, from $150 to....**$175.00**

Micronauts, figure, Membros, Mego, MOC, from $75 to .**$100.00**

Micronauts, figure, Microtron, Mego, MIB, from $15 to **$20.00**

Micronauts, figure, Nemesis Robot, Mego, MIB, from $12 to **$18.00**

Micronauts, figure, Oberon, Mego, MIB, from $25 to **$30.00**

Micronauts, figure, Phobos Robot, Mego, MIB, from $25 to..**$30.00**

Micronauts, figure, Repto, MOC, from $50 to **$75.00**

Micronauts, figure, Time Traveler (solid yel or orange), Mego, MOC, from $20 to **$25.00**

Micronauts, figure, Time Traveler (translucent yel or orange), Mego, MOC, from $12 to **$18.00**

Official World's Greatest Super Heroes, see Super Heroes

One Million BC, accessory, Tribal Lair, Mego, MIB, from $150 to..**$175.00**

One Million BC, accessory, Tribal Lair Gift Set (w/5 figures), MIB, from $350 to **$375.00**

One Million BC, figure, Dimetrodon creature, Mego, MIB, from $200 to...**$225.00**

One Million BC, figure, Grok, Mada, Orm, Trag, or Zon, Mego, MOC, ea from $45 to **$55.00**

One Million BC, figure, Hairy Rhino creature, Mego, MIB, from $250 to...**$275.00**

One Million BC, figure, Tyrannosaur creature, Mego, MIB, from $250 to...**$275.00**

Planet of the Apes, accessory, Action Stallion, r/c, Mego, 1970s, MIB, from $75 to **$110.00**

Planet of the Apes, accessory, Battering Ram, Jail, or Dr Zaius Throne, Mego, 1970s, MIB, ea from $35 to **$45.00**

Planet of the Apes, accessory, Catapult & Wagon, Mego, 1970s, MIB, from $125 to....................................**$165.00**

Planet of the Apes, accessory, Forbidden Zone Trap, Fortressor Treehouse (w/5 figures), Mego, 1970s, MIB, ea $175 to **$225.00**

Planet of the Apes, accessory, Action Stallion, with remote control, Mego, 1970s, M, from $45.00 to $55.00.

Planet of the Apes, accessory, Village, Mego, 1970s, MIB, from $175 to..**$225.00**

Planet of the Apes, figure, 7", any, Hasbro, 1999, MIP, ea from $5 to **$8.00**

Planet of the Apes, figure, 8", Astronaut, any, Mego, 1970s, ea from $90 to **$130.00**

Planet of the Apes, figure, 8", Astronaut, any, Mego, 1970s, MIB, from $240 to...**$260.00**

Planet of the Apes, figure, 8", Cornelius, Dr Zaius, Galen, or Zira, Mego, 1970s, MIB, ea from $175 to................**$225.00**

Planet of the Apes, figure, 8", Cornelius, Dr Zaius, Galen, or Zira, Mego, 1970s, MOC, ea from $75 to **$125.00**

Planet of the Apes, figure, 8", General Urko or Soldier Ape, Mego, 1970s, MIB, ea from $240 to.........................**$260.00**

Planet of the Apes, figure, General Ursus, Mego, 1970s, MOC, from $240.00 to $260.00.

Planet of the Apes, figure, 8", General Urko, General Ursus or Soldier Ape, Mego, 1970s, MOC, ea from $175 to ...**$225.00**

Planet of the Apes, figure, 12", any, Hasbro, 1999, MIP, from $18 to **$22.00**

Pocket Super Heroes, accessory, Batcave, Mego, MIB, from $275 to..............$325.00

Pocket Super Heroes, accessory, Batmachine, Mego, MIB, from $75 to..............$125.00

Pocket Super Heroes, accessory, Batmobile (w/Batman & Robin), Mego, MIB, from $175 to..............$225.00

Pocket Super Heroes, accessory, Spider-Car (w/Spider-Man & the Hulk), Mego, MIB, from $75 to..............$100.00

Pocket Super Heroes, accessory, Spider-Machine, Mego, MIB, from $75 to..............$125.00

Pocket Super Heroes, figure, Aquaman, Captain America, or Green Goblin, Mego, MOC (wht card), ea from $90 to..........$110.00

Pocket Super Heroes, figure, Batman, Mego, MOC (red card), ea from $65 to..............$75.00

Pocket Super Heroes, figure, Batman, Mego, MOC (wht card), from $120 to..............$130.00

Pocket Super Heroes, figure, Gen Zod, Mego, MOC (red card), from $20 to..............$30.00

Pocket Super Heroes, figure, Incredible Hulk, Mego, MOC (red card), from $28 to..............$32.00

Pocket Super Heroes, figure, Incredible Hulk, Mego, MOC (wht card), from $38 to..............$42.00

Pocket Super Heroes, figure, Jor-El or Lex Luthor, MOC (red card), from $18 to..............$22.00

Pocket Super Heroes, figure, Robin, Mego, MOC (red card), from $55 to..............$65.00

Pocket Super Heroes, figure, Robin, Mego, MOC (wht card), from $90 to..............$110.00

Pocket Super Heroes, figure, Spider-Man, Mego, MOC (red card), from $45 to..............$55.00

Pocket Super Heroes, figure, Spider-Man, Mego, MOC (wht card), from $90 to..............$110.00

Pocket Super Heroes, figure, Superman, Mego, MOC (red card), from $35 to..............$45.00

Pocket Super Heroes, figure, Superman, Mego, MOC (wht card), from $70 to..............$80.00

Pocket Super Heroes, figure, Wonder Woman, Mego, MOC (wht card), from $70 to..............$80.00

Power Lords, figure, any, MOC, ea from $20 to..............$30.00

Rambo, accessory, .50 Caliber Anti-Aircraft Gun or .50 Caliber Machine Gun, Coleco, MIP, ea from $10 to..............$15.00

Rambo, accessory, Defender 6x6 Assault Vehicle, Coleco, MIB, from $28 to..............$32.00

Rambo, accessory, SAVAGE Strike Cycle, Coleco, MIB, from $18 to..............$22.00

Rambo, accessory, SAVAGE Strike Headquarters, Coleco, MIB, from $50 to..............$60.00

Rambo, accessory, Skywolf Assault Jet, Coleco, MIB, from $25 to..............$30.00

Rambo, accessory, Swamp Dog, Coleco, MIB, from $18 to..............$22.00

Rambo, accessory, 106 Recoilless Anti-Tank Gun or 81mm Motar, Coleco, MIP, ea from $10 to..............$15.00

Rambo, figure, Black Dragon, Colonel Troutman, General Warhawk, or Gripper, Coleco, MOC, ea from $8 to..$12.00

Rambo, figure, Dr Hyde, Snakebite, TD Jackson, or X-ray, Coleco, MOC, ea from $18 to..............$22.00

Rambo, figure, KAT, Mad Dog, Nomad, Rambo, or Rambo w/Fire Power, Coleco, MOC, ea from $8 to..............$15.00

Rambo, figure, Sgt Havoc, Turbo, or White Dragon, Coleco, MOC, ea from $8 to..............$15.00

Rambo, Skyfire Assault Copter, Coleco, MIB, from $28 to...$32.00

Robocop (Ultra Police), accessory, Robo-Command vehicle w/figure, Kenner, MIB, from $28 to..............$32.00

Robocop (Ultra Police), accessory, Robo-Jailer vehicle, Kenner, MIB, from $38 to..............$42.00

Robocop (Ultra Police), figure, any, Kenner, 1988-90, MOC, ea from $15 to..............$25.00

Robotech, accessory, Armoured Cyclone, Matchbox, MIB, from $18 to..............$22.00

Robotech, accessory, Bioroid Hover Craft, Matchbox, MIB, from $22 to..............$28.00

Robotech, accessory, Bioroid Invid Fighter, Dana's Hover Cycle, or Excaliber MkVI, Matchbox, MIB, ea from $30 to...$50.00

Robotech, accessory, Gladiator, Invid Scout Ship, Invid Shock Trooper, or Raider X, Matchbox, MIB, ea from $30 to .$45.00

Robotech, accessory, SDF-1 Playset, Matchbox, MIB, from $350 to..............$375.00

Robotech, accessory, Spartan, Tactical Battle Pod, or Veritech Fighter, Matchbox, MIB, ea from $30 to..............$45.00

Robotech, accessory, Veritech Hover Tank or Zentraedi Officer's Battle Pod, Matchbox, MIB, ea from $30 to..............$45.00

Robotech, accessory, Zentraedi Powered Armor, Matchbox, MIB, from $45 to..............$50.00

Robotech, figure, 3¾", Bioroid Terminator, Lisa Hayes, or Micronized Zentraedi, Matchbox, MOC, ea from $10 to..............$18.00

Robotech, figure, 3¾", Corg, Lunk, Max Sterling, Miriya (red), or Rick Hunter, Matchbox, MOC, ea from $18 to $28.00

Robotech, figure, 3¾", Dana Sterling, Roy Fokker, or Scott Bernard, MOC, ea from $28 to..............$38.00

Robotech, figure, Miriya (blk), 3¾", Matchbox, MOC, from $60 to..............$70.00

Robotech, figure, 3¾", Rand, Robotech Maste, or Zor Prime, Matchbox, MOC, ea from $10 to..............$18.00

Robotech, figure, 8", any, Matchbox, MOC, ea from $12 to..$22.00

Robotech, figure, 12", Dana Sterling, Lisa Hayes, Lynn Minmei, or Rick Hunter, Matchbox, MIB, ea from $45 to.......$55.00

Rookies, figure, Chris, Mike, Terry, or Willie, LJN, MOC, from $25 to..............$30.00

Rookies, figure, Lt Riker, LJN, MOC, from $30 to..........$35.00

Schwarzenegger Commando, see Commando (Schwarzenegger)

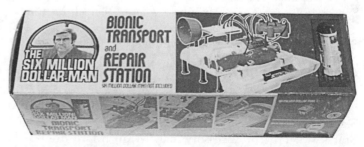

Six Million Dollar Man, accessory, Bionic Transport and Repair Station, Kenner, MIB, from $40.00 to $50.00.

Six Million Dollar Man, accessory, Mission Control Center, Kenner, MIB, from $65 to $75.00

Six Million Dollar Man, accessory, OSI Headquarters, Kenner, MIB, from $65 to $75.00

Six Million Dollar Man, accessory, Venus Space Probe, Kenner, MIB, from $250 to..$300.00

Six Million Dollar Man, figure, Bionic Bigfoot, Kenner, MIB, from $175 to $200.00

Six Million Dollar Man, figure, Maskatron, Kenner, MIB, from $145 to...$155.00

Six Million Dollar Man, figure, Oscar Goldman, Kenner, MIB, from $90 to $110.00

Starsky & Hutch, figure, Huggy Bear (or any other figure), Mego, MOC, each from $45.00 to $55.00.

Six Million Dollar Man, figure, Steve Austin, Kenner, MIB, from $100.00 to $125.00.

Super Heroes, figure, 5", Batgirl (Bend 'n Flex), Mego, MOC, from $100 to $125.00

Super Heroes, figure, 5", Captain America (Bend 'n Flex), Mego, MOC, from $90 to..$100.00

Super Heroes, figure, 5", Catwoman (Bend 'n Flex), Mego, MOC, from $160 to..$180.00

Super Heroes, figure, 5", Joker, (Bend 'n Flex), Mego, MOC, from $125 to $150.00

Super Heroes, figure, 5", Mr Mxyzptlk (Bend 'n Flex), Mego, MOC, from $120 to..$130.00

Super Heroes, figure, 5", Penguin (Bend 'n Flex), Mego, M, from $30 to..$35.00

Super Heroes, figure, 5", Penguin (Bend 'n Flex), Mego, MOC, from $125 to $150.00

Super Heroes, figure, 5", Riddler (Bend 'n Flex), Mego, MOC, from $125 to $150.00

Super Heroes, figure, 5", Shazam (Bend 'n Flex), Mego, MOC, $120 ....$130.00

Super Heroes, figure, 5", Spider-Man (Bend 'n Flex), Kenner, MOC, from $90 to..$100.00

Super Heroes, figure, 5", Supergirl (Bend 'n Flex), Mego, MOC, from $160 to $180.00

Six Million Dollar Man, figure, Steve Austin (w/bionic arm), Kenner, MIB, from $275 to $325.00

Six Million Dollar Man, figure, Steve Austin (w/engine block), Kenner, MIB, from $145 to $155.00

Six Million Dollar Man, figure, Steve Austin (w/girder), Kenner, MIB, from $175 to..$225.00

Space: 1999, accessory, Moonbase Alpha, Mattel, MIB, from $150 to..$175.00

Space: 1999, figure, any except Zython Alien, Mattel, MOC, ea from $55 to...$65.00

Space: 1999, figure, Zython Alien, Mattel, MOC, from $250 to..$275.00

Spider-Man, figure, 5", any, Toy Biz, MOC, ea from $5 to $8.00

Star Gate, figure, any, Hasbro, MOC, ea from $4 to $6.00

Starsky & Hutch, accessory, car, Mego, MIB, from $150 to $175.00

Super Heroes, see also Pocket Super Heroes

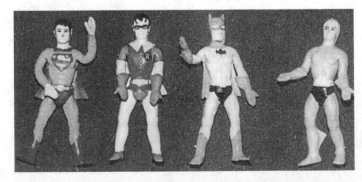

Super Heroes, figure, 5", Superman (Bend 'n Flex), Mego, MOC, from $60.00 to $80.00; Robin, MOC, from $60.00 to $80.00; Batman, MOC, from $100.00 to $125.00; Aquaman, MOC, from $100.00 to $125.00.

Super Heroes, figure, 5", Tarzan (Bend 'n Flex), Mego, MOC, from $55 to...$65.00

Super Heroes, figure, 5", Wonder Woman (Bend 'n Flex), Mego, MOC, from $75 to..$100.00

Super Heroes, figure, 8", Aquaman, Mego, M, from $55 to....$60.00

Super Heroes, figure, 8", Aquaman, Mego, MIB (window box) or MOC, ea from $140 to $160.00

Super Heroes, figure, 8", Batgirl, Mego, M, from $125 to....$130.00

Super Heroes, figure, 8", Batgirl, Mego, MIB or MOC, ea from $250 to...$275.00

Super Heroes, figure, 8", Batman (Fist-Fighting), Mego, M, from $145 to...$155.00

Super Heroes, figure, 8", Batman (Fist-Fighting), Mego, MIB, from $400 to...$425.00

Super Heroes, figure, 8", Batman (pnt mask), Mego, M, from $65 to...$70.00

Super Heroes, figure, 8", Batman (pnt mask), Mego, MIB, from $155 to...$165.00

Super Heroes, figure, 8", Batman (removable mask), Mego, M, from $150 to...$175.00

Super Heroes, figure, 8", Batman (removable mask), Mego, MOC, from $650 to..$700.00

Super Heroes, figure, 8", Batman (removable mask), MIB, from $500 to...$550.00

Super Heroes, figure, 8", Captain America, Mego, MIB $175.00

Super Heroes, figure, 8", Captain America, Mego, MOC, from $100 to..$125.00

Super Heroes, figure, 8", Catwoman, Mego, M, from $140 to...$160.00

Super Heroes, figure, 8", Catwoman, Mego, MIB, from $300 to...$325.00

Super Heroes, figure, 8", Catwoman, Mego, MOC.........$425.00

Super Heroes, figure, 8", Conan, Mego, MIB, from $350 to.$375.00

Super Heroes, figure, 8", Conan, Mego, MOC, from $450 to...$475.00

Super Heroes, figure, 8", Green Goblin, Mego, MIB, from $225.00 to $250.00.

Super Heroes, figure, 8", Falcon, Mego, MIB, from $125 to...$150.00

Super Heroes, figure, 8", Falcon, Mego, MOC, from $400 to...$425.00

Super Heroes, figure, 8", Green Arrow, Mego, M, from $100 to...$125.00

Super Heroes, figure, 8", Green Arrow, Mego, MIB, from $400 to...$425.00

Super Heroes, figure, 8", Green Arrow, Mego, MOC, from $500 to...$525.00

Super Heroes, figure, 8", Green Goblin, Mego, M...........$85.00

Super Heroes, figure, 8", Green Goblin, Mego, MOC, from $850 to...$900.00

Super Heroes, figure, 8", Human Torch, Mego, MIB, from $75 to...$85.00

Super Heroes, figure, 8", Human Torch, Mego, MOC, from $45 to...$55.00

Super Heroes, figure, 8", Incredible Hulk, Mego, M, from $20 to $25.00

Super Heroes, figure, 8", Incredible Hulk, Mego, MIB, from $90 to...$110.00

Super Heroes, figure, 8", Incredible Hulk, Mego, MOC, from $45 to...$55.00

Super Heroes, figure, 8", Iron Man, Mego, MIB, from $120 to $130.00

Super Heroes, figure, 8", Iron Man, Mego, MOC, from $400 to...$425.00

Super Heroes, figure, 8", Isis, Mego, MIB, from $200 to $225.00

Super Heroes, figure, 8", Iris, Mego, M, from $70 to $80.00

Super Heroes, figure, 8", Isis, Mego, MOC, from $75.00 to $100.00.

Super Heroes, figure, 8", Joker, Mego, M, from $55 to......$65.00

Super Heroes, figure, 8", Joker, Mego, MIB, from $185 to ..$210.00

Super Heroes, figure, 8", Joker, Mego, MOC, from $140 to....$160.00

Super Heroes, figure, 8", Joker (Fist-Fighting), Mego, MIB, from $525 to $550.00

Super Heroes, figure, 8", Lizard, Mego, MIB, from $150 to........$175.00

Super Heroes, figure, 8", Lizard, Mego, MOC, from $675 to $700.00

Super Heroes, figure, 8", Mr Fantastic, Mego, MIB, from $125 to $150.00

Super Heroes, figure, 8", Mr Fantastic, Mego, MOC, from $55 to $65.00

Super Heroes, figure, 8", Mr Mxyptlk (open mouth), MOC, from $145 to $165.00

Super Heroes, figure, 8", Mr Mxyzptlk (smirk), Mego, MIB, from $140 to $160.00

Super Heroes, figure, 8", Penguin, Mego, MIB, from $145 to $165.00

Super Heroes, figure, 8", Penguin, Mego, MOC, from $125 to $130.00

Super Heroes, figure, 8", Riddler, Mego, MIB, from $200 to..$225.00

Super Heroes, figure, 8", Riddler, Mego, MOC, from $525 to $550.00

Super Heroes, figure, 8", Riddler (Fist-Fighting), Mego, MIB, from $500..$550.00

Super Heroes, figure, 8", Robin (Fist-Fighting), Mego, MIB, from $440.00 to $460.00.

Super Heroes, figure, 8", Robin (pnt mask), Mego, M, from $65 to $75.00

Super Heroes, figure, 8", Robin (pnt mask), Mego, MIB, from $125 to..$150.00

Super Heroes, figure, 8", Robin (pnt mask), Mego, MOC, from $75 to $100.00

Super Heroes, figure, 8", Robin (removable mask), M, from $200 to $225.00

Super Heroes, figure, 8", Robin (removable mask), Mego, MIB, from $650 to $700.00

Super Heroes, figure, 8", Robin (removable mask), Mego, MIB (solid box), from $1,425......................................$1,450.00

Super Heroes, figure, 8", Shazam, Mego, M, from $55 to....$65.00

Super Heroes, figure, 8", Shazam, Mego, MIB, from $150 to $175.00

Super Heroes, figure, 8", Shazam, Mego, MOC, from $130 to $140.00

Super Heroes, figure, 8", Spider-Man, Mego, MIB, from $75 to $100.00

Super Heroes, figure, 8", Spider-Man, Mego, MOC, from $40 to $50.00

Super Heroes, figure, 8", Spider-Man, Mego, M, from, $20 to.$25.00

Super Heroes, figure, 8", Supergirl, Mego, M, from $300 to $325.00

Super Heroes, figure, 8", Supergirl, Mego, MIB or MOC, ea from $400 to..$425.00

Super Heroes, figure, 8", Superman, Mego, M, from $50 to $60.00

Super Heroes, figure, 8", Superman, Mego, MIB (solid box), from $700 to $750.00

Super Heroes, figure, 8", Superman, Mego, MIB (window box), from $150 to $175.00

Super Heroes, figure, 8", Superman, Mego, MOC, from $75 to $100.00

Super Heroes, figure, 8", Tarzan, Mego, MIB, from $100 to $125.00

Super Heroes, figure, 8", Tarzan, Mego, MOC, from $200 to $215.00

Super Heroes, figure, 8", Thing, Mego, M, from $40.00 to $45.00.

Super Heroes, figure, 8", Thing, Mego, MIB, from $155 to $165.00

Super Heroes, figure, 8", Thing, Mego, MOC, from $55 to....$65.00

Super Heroes, figure, 8", Thor, Mego, M, from $145 to....$165.00

Super Heroes, figure, 8", Thor, Mego, MIB, from $350 to....$375.00

Super Heroes, figure, 8", Thor, Mego, MOC, from $400 to....$425.00

Super Heroes, figure, 8", Wonder Woman, Mego, M, from $100 to $115.00

Super Heroes, figure, 8", Wonder Woman, Mego, MIB, from $300 to..$325.00

Super Heroes, figure, 8", Wonder Woman, Mego, MOC, from $400 to..$425.00

Super Heroes, figure, 8", Wonder Woman (Fly-Away Action), Mego, M, from $128 to..............................$132.00

Super Heroes, figure, 8", Wonder Woman (Fly-Away Action), Mego, MIB, from $245 to..........................$165.00

Super Heroes, figure, 8", Wondergirl, Mego, M, from $100 to..$115.00

Super Heroes, figure, 8", Wondergirl, Mego, MOC, from $350 to..$375.00

Super Heroes, figure, 12½", Batman (Fly-Away Action), Mego, MIB, from $225 to..............................$250.00

Super Heroes, figure, 12½", Batman, Mego, MIB, from $120 to..$130.00

Super Heroes, figure, 12½", Batman (Magnetic), Mego, MIB, from $200 to..$225.00

Super Heroes, figure, 12½", Captain America, Mego, MIB, from $150 to..$175.00

Super Heroes, figure, 12½", Captain America (Fly-Away Action), Mego, MIB, from $150 to....................$175.00

Super Heroes, figure, 12½", General Jod, Mego, MIB, from $75 to..$100.00

Super Heroes, figure, 12½", Incredible Hulk (Fly-Away Action), Mego, MIB, from $90 to........................$110.00

Super Heroes, figure, 12½", Lex Luthor, Mego, MIB, from $90 to..$110.00

Super Heroes, figure, 12½", Robin (Fly-Away Action), Mego, MIB, from $225 to..............................$250.00

Super Heroes, figure, 12½", Robin (Magnetic), Mego, MIB, from $225 to..$250.00

Super Heroes, figure, 12½", Spider-Man (Fly-Away Action), Mego, MIB, from $75 to............................$100.00

Super Heroes, figure, 12½", Spider-Man, Mego, MIB, from $100 to..$125.00

Super Heroes, figure, 12½", Superman (Fly-Away Action), Mego, MIB, from $75 to............................$100.00

Super Heroes, figure, 12½", Superman, Mego, MIB, from $120 to..$130.00

Super Naturals, accessory, Ghost Finder, Tonka, 1986, MIB, from $25 to..$30.00

Super Naturals, accessory, Lionwings Battle Creature, Tonka, 1986, MIB, from $15 to............................$20.00

Super Naturals, figure, any Ghostlings, Tonka, M, ea from $2 to..$4.00

Super Naturals, figure, any Ghostlings, Tonka, MOC, ea from $5 to...$8.00

Super Naturals, figure, any Warrior, Tonka, M, ea from $3 to....$5.00

Super Naturals, figure, any Warrior, Tonka, MOC, from $8 to..$10.00

Super Powers, accessory, Batcopter, Kenner, MIB, from $75 to..$100.00

Super Powers, accessory, carrying case, Kenner, M, from $20 to..$25.00

Super Powers, accessory, Darkseid Destroyer, Kenner, MIB, from $45 to..$55.00

Super Powers, accessory, Delta Probe One, Kenner, 1984, MIB, from $30 to..$35.00

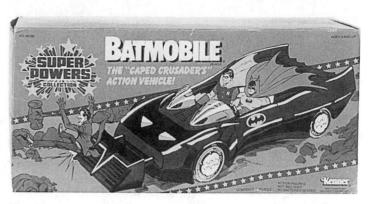

Super Powers, accessory, Batmobile, Kenner, MIB, from $100.00 to $125.00.

Super Powers, accessory, Hall of Justice, Kenner, MIB, from $100 to..$150.00

Super Powers, accessory, Kalibak Boulder Bomber, Kenner, MIB, from $20 to..$30.00

Super Powers, accessory, Lex-Sor 7, Kenner, MIB, from $20 to..$30.00

Super Powers, accessory, Supermobile, Kenner, MIB, from $25 to..$35.00

Super Powers, figure, Aquaman, Kenner, M, from $15 to..$20.00

Super Powers, figure, Aquaman, Kenner, MOC, from $45 to..$50.00

Super Powers, figure, Batman, Kenner, M, from $38 to....$42.00

Super Powers, figure, Batman, Kenner, MOC, from $70 to..$80.00

Super Powers, figure, Brainiac, Kenner, M, from $18 to...$20.00

Super Powers, figure, Brainiac, Kenner, MOC, from $28 to..$32.00

Super Powers, figure, Clark Kent, Kenner, M (mail-in), from $60 to..$65.00

Super Powers, figure, Clark Kent, Kenner, MOC (mail-in), from $70 to..$80.00

Super Powers, figure, Cyborg, Kenner, M, from $155 to..$160.00

Super Powers, figure, Cyborg, Kenner, MOC, from $250.00 to $275.00. (Photo courtesy June Moon)

Super Powers, figure, Cyclotron, Kenner, M, from $38 to...**$40.00**

Super Powers, figure, Cyclotron, Kenner, MOC, from $70 to **$80.00**

Super Powers, figure, Darkseid, Kenner, M, from $6 to.......**$8.00**

Super Powers, figure, Darkseid, Kenner, MOC, from $18 to ..**$20.00**

Super Powers, figure, Desaad, Kenner, M, from $12 to **$15.00**

Super Powers, figure, Desaad, Kenner, MOC, from $25 to...**$35.00**

Super Powers, figure, Dr Fate, Kenner, M, from $40 to.....**$45.00**

Super Powers, figure, Dr Fate, Kenner, MOC, from $70 to ..**$75.00**

Super Powers, figure, Firestorm, Kenner, M, from $18 to...**$20.00**

Super Powers, figure, Firestorm, Kenner, MOC, from $38 to ..**$40.00**

Super Powers, figure, Flash, Kenner, M, from $12 to **$15.00**

Super Powers, figure, Flash, Kenner, MOC, from $25 to ..**$28.00**

Super Powers, figure, Golden Pharaoh, Kenner, M, from $55 to **$60.00**

Super Powers, figure, Golden Pharaoh, Kenner, MOC, from $75 to...**$100.00**

Super Powers, figure, Green Arrow, Kenner, M, from $28 to .**$30.00**

Super Powers, figure, Green Arrow, Kenner, MOC, from $45 to...**$50.00**

Super Powers, figure, Green Lantern, Kenner, M, from $32 to...**$35.00**

Super Powers, figure, Green Lantern, Kenner, MOC, from $45 to **$50.00**

Super Powers, figure, Hawkman, Kenner, M, from $28 to ..**$30.00**

Super Powers, figure, Hawkman, Kenner, MOC, from $50 to...**$60.00**

Super Powers, figure, Joker, Kenner, MOC, from $25 to ..**$35.00**

Super Powers, figure, Kalibak, Kenner, M, from $6 to **$8.00**

Super Powers, figure, Kalibak, Kenner, MOC, from $18 to...**$20.00**

Super Powers, figure, Lex Luthor, Kenner, M, from $6 to ...**$8.00**

Super Powers, figure, Lex Luthor, Kenner, MOC, from $16 to **$18.00**

Super Powers, figure, Mantis, Kenner, M, from $12 to **$15.00**

Super Powers, figure, Mantis, Kenner, MOC, from $28 to..**$32.00**

Super Powers, figure, Martian Manhunter, Kenner, M, from $18 to...**$20.00**

Super Powers, figure, Martian Manhunter, Kenner, MOC, from $40 to **$50.00**

Super Powers, figure, Mister Freeze, Kenner, M, from $28 to **$30.00**

Super Powers, figure, Mister Freeze, Kenner, MOC, from $60 to **$70.00**

Super Powers, figure, Mister Miracle, Kenner, M, from $65 to **$70.00**

Super Powers, figure, Orion, Kenner, M, from $28 to.......**$30.00**

Super Powers, figure, Orion, Kenner, MOC, from $50 to ..**$60.00**

Super Powers, figure, Parademon, Kenner, M, from $18 to..**$20.00**

Super Powers, figure, Parademon, Kenner, MOC, from $30 to **$35.00**

Super Powers, figure, Penguin, Kenner, M, from $18 to ...**$22.00**

Super Powers, figure, Penguin, Kenner, MOC, from $40 to..**$45.00**

Super Powers, figure, Plastic Man, Kenner, M, from $60 to ..**$70.00**

Super Powers, figure, Plastic Man, Kenner, MOC, from $130 to...**$140.00**

Super Powers, figure, Red Tornado, Kenner, MOC, from $75 to...**$80.00**

Super Powers, figure, Red Tornado, M, from $35 to **$40.00**

Super Powers, figure, Robin, Kenner, M, from $28 to.......**$30.00**

Super Powers, figure, Samurai, Kenner, M, from $48 to ...**$50.00**

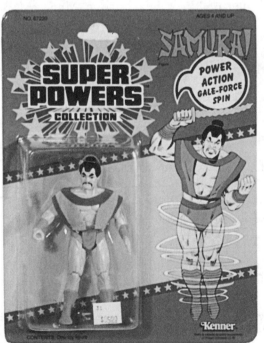

Super Powers, figure, Samurai, Kenner, MOC, from $90.00 to $100.00.

Super Powers, figure, Mister Miracle, Kenner, MOC, from $100.00 to $135.00. (Photo courtesy June Moon)

Super Powers, figure, Shazam, Kenner, M, from, $28 to ...**$30.00**

Super Powers, figure, Shazam, Kenner, MOC, from $50 to...**$60.00**

Super Powers, figure, Steppenwolf, complete w/ID card & comic book, Kenner, M, from $32 to **$38.00**

Super Powers, figure, Steppenwolf, Kenner, MIP (mail-in), from $18 to **$22.00**

Super Powers, figure, Steppenwolf, Kenner, MOC, from $75 to...**$80.00**

Super Powers, figure, Superman, Kenner, MOC, from $32 to $38.00

Super Powers, figure, Tyr, Kenner, M, from $45 to............$48.00

Super Powers, figure, Tyr, Kenner, MOC, from $70 to $80.00

Super Powers, figure, Wonder Woman, Kenner, M, from $16 to...$18.00

Super Powers, figure, Wonder Woman, Kenner, 1986, MOC, from $38 to...$42.00

Super Powers, Parademon, Kenner, MOC, from $30 to ...$35.00

Supernaturals, accessory, Tomb of Domb, Tonka, 1986, MIB, from $25 to...$30.00

Teen Titans, figure, Aqualad, Mego, M, from $175 to....$200.00

Teen Titans, figure, Aqualad, Mego, MOC, from $300 to...$325.00

Teen Titans, figure, Kid Flash, Mego, M, from $175 to ..$200.00

Teen Titans, figure, Kid Flash, Mego, MOC, from $400 to ..$425.00

Teen Titans, figure, Speedy, Mego, M, from $250 to $275.00

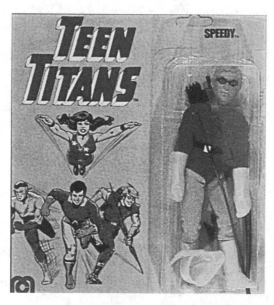

Teen Titans, figure, Speedy, Mego, MOC, from $450.00 to $475.00. (Photo courtesy Wallace M. Chrouch)

Teen Titans, figure, Wondergirl, Mego, M, from $150 to..$175.00

Teen Titans, figure, Wondergirl, Mego, MOC, from $400 to...$425.00

Waltons, accessory, barn or country store, Mego, MIB, ea from $75 to...$100.00

Waltons, accessory, farmhouse (w/6 figures), Mego, MIB, from $250 to..$275.00

Waltons, accessory, farmhouse (only), Mego, M, from $125 to...$175.00

Waltons, accessory, truck, Mego, MIB, from $65 to..........$75.00

Wizard of Oz, accessory, Emerald City (for 8" figures), Mego, MIB, from $300 to...$325.00

Wizard of Oz, accessory, Wizard of Oz & His Emerald City (for 4" figures), Mego, MIB, from $100 to $125.00

Wizard of Oz, figure, 4", Munchkin, any, Mego, MIB, ea from $160 to...$160.00

Wizard of Oz, figure, 8", any except the Wicked Witch or the Wizard, MIB, ea from $45 to $55.00

Wizard of Oz, figure, 8", Wicked Witch, Mego, MIB, from $90 to...$115.00

Wizard of Oz, figure, 8", Wizard, Mego, MIB, from $245 to ..$265.00

Waltons, figure sets, John Boy and Mary Ellen, Mom and Pop, or Grandpa and Grandma, Mego, MIB, each set from $45.00 to $55.00. (Photo courtesy David Morgan)

Wonder Woman, figure, Nubia, Queen Hippolyte, or Steve Trever, Mego, M, ea from $45 to $48.00

Wonder Woman (TV Series), figure, Nubia, Queen Hippolyte, or Steve Trever, Mego, MIB, ea from $90 to............$115.00

Wonder Woman (TV Series), figure, Wonder Woman (w/Diana Prince outfit), Mego, M, from $110 to.....................$120.00

Wonder Woman (TV Series), figure, Wonder Woman (w/Diana Prince outfit), Mego, MIB, from $190 to $215.00

World's Greatest Super Heroes, or Official World's Greatest Super Heroes, see Super Heroes or Pocket Super Heroes

World's Greatest Super Knights, figure, Black Knight, Mego, MIB, from $275 to...$325.00

World's Greatest Super Knights, figure, Ivanhoe, Mego, MIB, from $200 to $250.00

World's Greatest Super Knights, figure, King Arthur, Mego, MIB, from $175 to...$225.00

World's Greatest Super Knights, figure, Sir Galahad, Mego, MIB, from $250 to...$275.00

World's Greatest Super Knights, figure, Sir Lancelot, Mego, MIB, from $275 to...$300.00

WWF, figure, Akeem, Hasbro, M, from $16 to $18.00

WWF, figure, Akeem, Hasbro, MOC, from $35 to $40.00

WWF, figure, Animal (Shotgun Sat Night #1), Jakks, MOC, from $8 to...$10.00

WWF, figure, Bret Hart (Superstars #1), Jakks, MOC, from $18 to...$22.00

WWF, figure, Bret Hart (Superstars #2), Jakks, MOC, from $15 to...$18.00

WWF, figure, Diesel (Superstars #3 reissue), Jakks, MOC, from $15 to...$18.00

WWF, figure, Dusty Rhodes, Hasbro, M, from $65 to.......$70.00

WWF, figure, Dusty Rhodes, Hasbro, MOC, from $140 to ..$160.00

WWF, figure, Greg The Hammer Valentine, Hasbro, MOC, from $12 to...$15.00

WWF, figure, Honky Tonk Man, Hasbro, M, from $12 to ..$15.00

WWF, figure, Honky Tonk Man, Hasbro, MOC, from $12 to ..$15.00

WWF, figure, Hulk Hogan, Hasbro, MOC, from $12 to...**$15.00**

WWF, figure, Hulk Hogan (mail-in), Hasbro, M, from $35 to .**$40.00**

WWF, figure, Hulk Hogan (mail-in), Hasbro, MIP, from $45 to...**$55.00**

WWF, figure, Hulk Hogan (no shirt), Hasbro, MOC, from $8 to..**$12.00**

WWF, figure, Jake 'The Snake' Roberts, Hasbro, M, from $6 to..**$8.00**

WWF, figure, Jake 'The Snake' Roberts, Hasbro, MOC, from $8 to...**$12.00**

WWF, figure, Jim 'The Anvil' Neidhart, Hasbro, M, from $4 to..**$5.00**

WWF, figure, Jim 'The Anvil' Neidhart, Hasbro, MOC, from $8 to **$10.00**

WWF, figure, Jimmy Snuka, Hasbro, MOC, from $12 to...**$15.00**

WWF, figure, Lex Lugar, Hasbro, MOC, from $15 to.......**$18.00**

WWF, figure, Macho Man, Hasbro, MOC, $18 to............**$22.00**

WWF, figure, Mr Perfect (w/Perfect Plex), Hasbro, MOC, $18 to **$22.00**

WWF, figure, Nasty Boys, Hasbro, MOC (2-pak), from $70 to...**$75.00**

WWF, figure, New Age Outlaws (2-Tuff #2), Jakks, MOC, from $12 to...**$15.00**

WWF, figure, Razor Ramon, Hasbro, M, from $16 to............**$18.00**

WWF, figure, Razor Ramon, Hasbro, MOC, from $28 to ..**$32.00**

WWF, figure, Rick Rude, Hasbro, MOC, from $28 to......**$32.00**

WWF, figure, Rowdy Roddy Piper, Hasbro, MOC, from $28 to **$32.00**

WWF, figure, Sid Justice, Hasbro, MOC, from $16 to......**$18.00**

WWF, figure, The Warlord, Hasbro, MOC, from $16 to ..**$18.00**

WWF, figure, Typhoon w/Tidal Wave, Hasbro, M, from $16 to.**$18.00**

WWF, figure, Typhoon w/Tidal Wave, Hasbro, MOC, from $28 to..**$32.00**

WWF, figure, Undertaker, Hasbro, MOC, from $24 to.....**$26.00**

WWF, figure, Undertaker (mail-in), Hasbro, MOC, from $45 to...**$55.00**

WWF, figure, Undertaker & Kane (2-Tuff #4), Jakks, MOC, from $12 to...**$15.00**

WWF, figure, 1-2-3 Kid, Hasbro, MOC, from $35 to........**$40.00**

X-Men/X-Force, figure, Arctic Armor Cable, Avalanche, or Cable Cyborg, Toy Biz, MOC, ea from $8 to.............**$10.00**

X-Men/X-Force, figure, Black Tom, Blob, or Bonebraker, Toy Biz, MOC, from $12 to...**$16.00**

X-Men/X-Force, figure, Bridge or Brood, Toy Biz, MOC, ea from $12 to...**$16.00**

X-Men/X-Force, figure, Cable I, Cable II, or Cable III, Toy Biz, MOC, ea from $12 to **$16.00**

X-Men/X-Force, figure, Cable V, Toy Biz, MOC, from $12 to..**$16.00**

X-Men/X-Force, figure, Cannonball (pk), Toy Biz, MOC, from $30 to...**$33.00**

X-Men/X-Force, figure, Cannonball (purple), Toy Biz, MOC, from $18 to...**$22.00**

X-Men/X-Force, figure, Commando, Toy Biz, MOC, from $8 to..**$10.00**

X-Men/X-Force, figure, Deadpool, Toy Biz, MOC, from $34 to **$36.00**

X-Men/X-Force, figure, Deadpool (1995) or Domino, Toy Biz, MOC, ea from $10 to **$12.00**

X-Men/X-Force, figure, Forearm, Toy Biz, MOC, from $18 to...**$22.00**

X-Men/X-Force, figure, Genesis, Toy Biz, MOC, from $6 to...**$8.00**

X-Men/X-Force, figure, Gideon or Grizzly, Toy Biz, MOC, ea from $16 to...**$18.00**

X-Men/X-Force, figure, Kane I or Kane II, Toy Biz, MOC, ea from $16 to...**$18.00**

X-Men/X-Force, figure, Killspree, Toy Biz, MOC, from $12 to.**$14.00**

X-Men/X-Force, figure, Killspree II, Toy Biz, MOC, from $8 to...**$10.00**

X-Men/X-Force, figure, Krule or Kylun, Toy Biz, MOC, from $12 to...**$14.00**

X-Men/X-Force, figure, Longshot, Toy Biz, MOC, from $16 to...**$18.00**

X-Men/X-Force, figure, Mojo, Toy Biz, MOC, from $8 to ..**$10.00**

X-Men/X-Force, figure, Nimrod, Toy Biz, MOC, from $8 to...**$10.00**

X-Men/X-Force, figure, Pyro, Toy Biz, MOC, from $16 to..**$18.00**

X-Men/X-Force, figure, Quark, Toy Biz, MOC, from $12 to ..**$14.00**

X-Men/X-Force, figure, Random or Rictor, Toy Biz, MOC, ea from $16 to...**$18.00**

X-Men/X-Force, figure, Rogue, Toy Biz, MOC, from $24 to ..**$28.00**

X-Men/X-Force, figure, Sabretooth I or Sabretooth II, Toy Biz, MOC, ea from $16 to **$18.00**

X-Men/X-Force, figure, Shatterstar I or Shatterstar II, Toy Biz, MOC, ea from $10 to **$15.00**

X-Men/X-Force, figure, Shatterstar III, Toy Biz, MOC, from $8 to...**$10.00**

X-Men/X-Force, figure, Silver Samurai, Toy Biz, MOC, from $15 to...**$18.00**

X-Men/X-Force, figure, Slayback, Toy Biz, MOC, from $14 to **$16.00**

X-Men/X-Force, figure, Stryfe, Toy Biz, MOC, from $24 to...**$28.00**

X-Men/X-Force, figure, Sunspot, Toy Biz, MOC, from $14.00 to $18.00.

X-Men/X-Force, figure, Urban Assault, Toy Biz, MOC, from $8 to $10.00

X-Men/X-Force, figure, Warpath I or Warpath II, Toy Biz, MOC, from $16 to $18.00

X-Men/X-Force, figure, X-Treme, Toy Biz, MOC, from $16 to $18.00

Zorro (Cartoon Series), figure, Captain Ramon or Sgt Gonzales, M, ea from $5 to $8.00

Zorro (Cartoon Series), figure, Captain Ramon or Sgt Gonzales, Gabriel, MOC, ea from $15 to $18.00

Zorro (Cartoon Series), figure, Tempest or Picaro, Gabriel, M, ea from $8 to $10.00

Zorro (Cartoon Series), figure, Tempest or Picaro, Gabriel, MOC, ea from $20 to $25.00

Zorro (Cartoon Series), figure, Zorro or Amigo, Gabriel, M, ea from $6 to $8.00

Zorro (Cartoon Series), figure, Zorro or Amigo, Gabriel, MOC, ea from $18 to $20.00

Activity Sets

Activity sets that were once enjoyed by so many children are finding their way back to some of those same kids, now grown up, more or less. The earlier editions, especially, are carrying pretty respectible price tags when they can be found complete or near complete.

The following listings are complete unless noted otherwise.

See also Character, TV, and Movie Collectibles; Coloring, Activity, and Paint Books; Disney; Playsets; and other specific categories.

Big Burger Grill, Kenner, 1967, EXIB $35.00

Cartoon-O-Graph Sketch Board, features Warner Bros cartoon characters, Moss Mfg Co, 1940s-50s, EXIB.............$75.00

Colorforms My House Printer Kit, 1962, EXIB.................$25.00

Colorforms Totem Pole Kit, 1958, NMIB $50.00

Creepy Crawlers, see Thingmaker

Fulton Sign Writer, Fulton Specialty Company, EXIB, from $40.00 to $50.00. (Photo courtesy Linda Baker)

Crime Lab, Amsco, 1976, unused, MIB $50.00

David Berglas Conjouring Tricks Magic Set, Kay Ltd/London, EXIB..$100.00

Design-O-Marx Set, 1960s, scarce, unused, MIB.............$50.00

Drawing Teacher, Milton Bradley, EXIB $100.00

Hanna-Barbera, rubber stamp set, with 20 H-B characters, 1960s, NMIB...$150.00

Hocus-Pocus Magic Set, Adams, 1962, unused, MIB $85.00

Hocus Pocus Magic Set, Adams, 1976, NMIB.................$50.00

Jerry the Magicians's Complete Magic Act, 1940s-50s, unused, EX (in photo envelope)...$50.00

Johnny Toymaker Car Molding Set, EXIB $55.00

Magic Kit of Tricks & Puzzles, Transogram, 1960s, MIB...$75.00

Magic Set, w/10 tricks, Redhill, 1930s-40s, MIB $50.00

Magician Magic Set, features Bill Bixby, 1974, NMIB......$70.00

Mandrake the Magician Kit, briefcase-style box w/clasp, 1950s, complete, NMIB...$75.00

Mandrake the Magician Magic Tricks, KFS, 1949, w/6 complete tricks, VG+IB $35.00

Martian Magic Tricks, Gilbert, 1963, scarce, NMIB, from $250 to..$300.00

Master Magic, Sherms S set, 1930s-40s, EXIB...............$100.00

Mighty Men & Monster Maker Set, 1978, EXIB.............$30.00

Mister Funny Face Clay & Plastic, 1953, EXIB $100.00

Modelcast N' Color Kit, features Huckleberry Hound & the Flintstones, Standard Toycraft, 1960, unused, MIB..$100.00

Moled Master Combat Set, Kenner, 1963, EXIB $50.00

Monster Machine, Gabriel, MIB....................................$25.00

Mr Magic Set, Adams, 1960s, NMIB $50.00

Mr Potato Head & Pete the Pepper Set, Hasbro, 1960s, MIB $30.00

Mr Potato Head In The Parade Set, Hasbro, 1968, MIB ..$35.00

Mysto Magic (Exhibition Set), AC Gilbert, #2.5, Gilbert, 1938, VGIB, $150.00.

Picture Maker Hot Birds Skyway Scene, Mattel, 1970s, MIB $75.00

Play-Doh Fun Factory, 1960s, rare, MIB.........................$50.00

Power Mite Workshop, Ideal, 1969, EXIB $130.00

Power Shop, Mattel, 1960s, NMIB..................................$50.00

Pre-Flight Training Cockpit, Einson, 1942, NMIB...........$50.00

Pretzel Jetzel Factory, Transogram, 1965, EXIB.................$50.00

Shaker Maker Bugglies Set, Ideal, 1962, MIB $30.00

Shrink Machine, Wham-O, unused, MIB.........................$85.00

Shrinky Dinks, My Little Pony, 1980s, MIB (sealed)........$25.00

Shrunken Head Apple Sculpture, Milton Bradley, 1975, MIB...$75.00

Simple Sewing Cards For Nimble Fingers, Milton Bradley,
EXIB...$150.00

Simple Stitch Quilting, Fisher-Price Arts and Crafts #737, MIB, from $6.00 to $10.00. (Photo courtesy Brad Cassity)

Sneaky Pete's Magic Show, Remco #702, 1950s-60s,
VG+IB..$85.00

Soft Drink Stand, Amsco, complete with original Kool-Aid packages, EXIB, A, $100.00. (Photo courtesy Bertoia Auctions)

Space Faces, Pressman, 1950s, unused, NMIB................$175.00
Space Scientist Drafting Set, 1950s, EXIB.......................$65.00
Specks & Things Molding Set, MIB $50.00
Starmaster Astronomy Set, Reed, 1950s, EXIB................$50.00
Suzy Homemaker Sweet Shoppe Soda Fountain, Topper, 1960s,
MIB $50.00
Tasket Basket Shape Sorter, Holgate, 1953, NM $35.00
Thingmaker (Triple), Mattel, EXIB $125.00
Thingmaker Creepy Crawlers, 1st issue, Mattel, 1964,
EXIB...$75.00
Thingmaker Creepy Crawlers Collection Case, Mattel, 1964,
NM...$50.00
Thingmaker Creepy Crawlers II, Mattel, 1978, NMIB.....$50.00

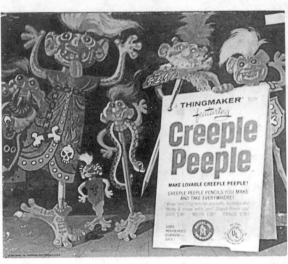

Thingmaker Creeple Peeple, Mattel, 1965, MIB, $100.00.

Thingmaker Fright Factory, Mattel, MIB (sealed)..........$150.00
Thingmaker Fun Flowers Maker Pak, Mattel, 1966, EXIB...$30.00
Thingmaker Giant Creepy Crawlers Maker Pack #2, Mattel,
1965, EXIB..$75.00
Thingmaker Men Set, Mattel, 1965, EXIB $75.00
Thingmaker Mini Dragon Maker Pack, Mattel, 1967, MIB
(sealed) $150.00
Tinker Fish, Toy Tinkers, 1927, EXIB..............................$50.00
Tinker Spot, Toy Tinkers, 1930s, EXIB $60.00
Tinkerbeads No 4, Toy Tinkers, 1928, EX (in tin container)...$80.00
Trix Stix, Harry Dearly, 1952, MIP..................................$50.00
Vac-U-Form Playset, Mattel, 1962, NMIB $100.00
Voodini Magic Set, Transogram, 1960, NMIB $50.00
Winky Dink Paint Set, Pressman, 1950s, EX $75.00
Wire Puzzle Set, Gilbert, 1930s, MIB (sealed) $75.00
Young Magicians Box of Tricks, Saalfield, 1958, NMIB ...$50.00

Advertising

The assortment of advertising memorabilia geared toward children is vast — plush and cloth dolls, banks, games, puzzles, trucks, radios, watches, and much, much more. And considering the popularity of advertising memorabilia in general, when you add to it the crossover interest from the realm of toys, you have a real winning combination! Just remember to check for condition very carefully; signs of play wear are common. Think twice about investing much money in soiled items, especially cloth or plush dolls. (Stains are often impossible to remove.)

For more information we recommend B.J. Summers' Guide to Coca-Cola, Collectible Soda Pop Memorabilia, and Antique & Contemporary Advertising Memorabilia, all by B.J. Summers; Cracker Jack Toys and Cracker Jack, the Unauthorized Guide to Advertising, both by Larry White; Pepsi-Cola Collectibles, Vols I, II, and III, by Bill Vehling and Michael Hunt.

Advisor: Larry White (W7), Cracker Jack

See also Bubble Bath Containers; Buddy L (and other vehicle categories); Character, TV, and Movie Collectibles; Disney; Pin-Back Buttons; Premiums; other specific categories.

A&W Root Beer, bears, bean-stuffed plush, 2 different, 1997-98, ea from $15 to...$20.00

AC Spark Plugs, figure, AC man w/1 arm extended & other on hip, wht & gr w/AC on chest, gr hat, 6", EXIB.......$160.00

AC Spark Plugs, figure, Sparky the Horse, inflatable vinyl w/logo, Ideal, 1960s, 24x15" L, EX..........................$100.00

Alka-Seltzer, charm, glass-covered lenticular form w/metal frame & mirrored back, flickers, 1960s, 1¼", EX+.............$50.00

Alka-Seltzer, figure, Speedy, vinyl, 1960s, 5½", EX, from $275.00 to...$300.00

Allied Van Lines, doll, gr uniform & hat, Lion Uniform Inc, 14", MIB...$1,200.00

Allied Van Lines, semi truck, Grimland, litho tin, orange w/blk trim, silver roof on trailer, 7½", EXIB, A.................$165.00

Alpo, w/up figure, Dan the Dog, walks on his front paws, 1970s, 3", EX+...$12.00

Arden Milk, bank, plastic truck, NM.............................$60.00

Aunt Jemima, Breakfast Bear, plush, 13", M.................$175.00

Aunt Jemima, doll, Aunt Jemima, stuffed oilcloth, Aunt Jemima 'cross-stiched' on wht apron, 1950s, 12", NM, from $40 to...$50.00

Aunt Jemima, doll, Diana, stuffed oilcloth, hands behind back, heart-shaped mouth, 1950s, 9", NM, from $40 to......$50.00

Aunt Jemima, doll, Uncle Mose, stuffed oilcloth, holding top hat, glancing up, 1950s, 12", from $40 to...................$50.00

Aunt Jemima, Wade doll holding lollipop, stuffed printed oilcloth, 1950s, 9", NM, from $40.00 to $50.00. (Photo courtesy Joleen Ashman Robinson and Kay Sellers)

Aunt Jemima, Jr Chef Pancake Set, Argo Industries, 1949, EX...$150.00

Baskin-Robbins, figure, Pinky the Spoon, bendable vinyl, 1990s, 5", NM+...$6.00

Bazooka Bubble Gum, doll, Bazooka Joe, stuffed print cloth, 1970s, 19", EX+...$10.00

Betty Crocker, Doll & Bake Set, stuffed print cloth doll w/baking kit, Kenner, 1970s, unused, MIB..........................$25.00

Big Boy, bank, ceramic figure holding hamburger, M.....$500.00

Big Boy, bank, plastic figure wearing red & wht checked overalls, 1970s, 9", NM...$20.00

Big Boy, bank, pnt vinyl figure, chubby version, 1960s-70s, 9", NM...$50.00

Big Boy, comic book, Adventures of Big Boy #1.............$250.00

Big Boy, comic book, Adventures of Big Boy #2-#5, NM, ea...$50.00

Big Boy, comic book, Adventures of Big Boy #6-#10, NM, ea...$35.00

Big Boy, comic book, Adventures of Big Boy #11-#100, NM, ea...$25.00

Big Boy, comic book, Adventures of Big Boy #101-#250, NM, ea...$10.00

Big Boy, comic book, Adventures of the Big Boy #300/Happy 25th Birthday, dated April 1982, unused, EX, P6......$12.00

Big Boy, doll, stuffed cloth w/Big Boy on wht T-shirt, red & wht overalls, 15", MIP (Yes, I'm Your Pal on cb header) ..$25.00

Big Boy, figure on surfboard w/wave, PVC, 1990, 3", EX....$5.00

Big Boy, kite, paper w/Big Boy logo, 1960s, M.............$100.00

Big Boy, kite, paper w/Big Boy logo, 1960s, unused, MIP...$250.00

Big Boy, yo-yo, wood w/die-stamp seal, 1960s, M.............$10.00

Blue Bonnet Margarine, doll, Blue Bonnet Sue, stuffed cloth w/yel yarn hair, 1980s, NM.................................$5.00

Borden, bank, Beauregard, red plastic figure, Irwin, 1950s, 5", EX...$65.00

Borden, Elsie's Funbook Cut-Out Toys & Games, 1940s, EX...$65.00

Borden, Elsie's Good Food Line punch-out train, cb, 1940s, 25x37", unpunched, M (EX envelope)...................$150.00

Borden, figure, Elsie, vinyl, aqua dress w/striped skirt, wht apron, gold felt shoes & bib, 22", EX+.................................$100.00

Borden, figure, Elsie the Cow, plush w/vinyl head, has moo sound, 1950s, 12", VG+...$50.00

Borden, figure, Elsie the Cow, PVC, 3½", M, from $10 to..$20.00

Borden, game, Elsie the Cow, Jr Edition, EXIB.............$125.00

Borden, milk truck, Keystone #D402, white-painted pressed steel with red Borden's decal, 9", EXIB, A, $385.00. (Photo courtesy Bertoia Auctions)

Borden, milk truck, Divco, 1950s, diecast metal, cream w/red lettering, 4", NM, A $120.00

Borden, night light, Elsie the Cow head figure, rubber-type compo, 9", NM $180.00

Borden, pull toy, Elsie the Cow (The Cow That Jumped Over the Moon), wood, 1940s, EX+ $35.00

Borden, push-button puppet, Elsie, wood, EX................$125.00

Bosco Chocolate, doll, Bosco the Clown, vinyl, EX+.......$50.00

Bosco Chocolate, jar pouring top, Bosco the Clown head, plastic, fluted collar, fits on Bosco jar, 1950s premium, EXIB $50.00

Bradford House Restaurants, figure, Bucky Bradford standing on base reading It's Yum Yum Time, vinyl, 1976, 9", EX, P6 ....$35.00

Burger Chef, hand puppet, Burger Chef, cloth body & hat w/vinyl head, 1970s, EX $10.00

Burger Chef, pillow figure, Burger Chef, stuffed printed cloth, 1970s, EX $12.00

Burger King, bear, Crayola Christmas, plush, 4 different, 1986, EX, ea...$10.00

Burger King, doll, Burger King, stuffed print cloth, 1972, M, $10.00.

Burger King, doll, Burger King, stuffed cloth, 1973, or 1977, 16", NM, ea $10.00

Burger King, doll, Burger King, stuffed cloth, 1980, 18", EX ..$10.00

Burger King, doll, Magic King, Knickerbocker, 1980, 20", MIB...$20.00

Buster Brown, see also Character, TV, and Movie Collectibles

Buster Brown, hobby horse, wood w/pnt advertising as saddle, 28x36", very rare, VG..$300.00

Buster Brown Shoes, bank, molded plastic ball shape w/busts of Buster & Tige on top, 1960s, 3½" dia $25.00

Buster Brown Shoes, booklet, Playing Movies w/Buster Brown, 1910s-20s, 20 pgs, EX+ $75.00

Buster Brown Shoes, clicker, tin shoe-sole form, bl (Blue Ribbon) lettering on yel, VG $20.00

Buster Brown Shoes, clicker, tin w/head image of Buster & Tige, VG $20.00

Buster Brown Shoes, doll, Buster, 1974, stuffed cloth, 14", NM...$40.00

Buster Brown Shoes, kite, 1940s, NM.............................$40.00

Buster Brown Shoes, paddle ball toy, Froggy the Gremlin graphics on die-cut cb, Ed McConnell, 1940s, EX+ $75.00

Buster Brown Shoes, shoe box w/Treasure Hunt Game on side, 1930s, unused, from $50 to...$75.00

Butterfinger Candy Bar, doll, Butterfinger Bear, plush, 1987, 15", M...$25.00

Campbell's Soup, Campbell Kids Shopping Game, Parker Bros, 1955, scarce, NMIB..$65.00

Campbell's Soup, coloring book, A Story of Soup, 1977, EX .$25.00

Campbell's Soup, comic book, Captain America & Campbell Kids, 1980s promotional item, EX+ $25.00

Campbell's Soup, doll, boy & girl, beanbag type in Alphabet Soup outfits, 2001, 8", MIP, ea.............................$12.00

Campbell's Soup, doll, boy & girl, pnt vinyl w/movable heads, Product People, 1970s, 7", NM, pr...........................$50.00

Campbell's Soup, doll, boy & girl, rag type, 1970s, MIB, pr..$75.00

Campbell's Soup, doll, cheerleader, vinyl, 1967, 8", EX...$75.00

Campbell's Soup, chef doll, composition with molded hair, cloth outfit and hat, painted shoes and socks, Horsman, 12", MIB, $250.00; boy doll in cap and shorts, composition with molded hair, painted shoes and socks, 12", MIB, $250.00. (Photo courtesy McMasters Doll Auctions)

Campbell's Soup, doll, farm kids, cloth, she in denim dress & straw hat & he in red shirt & jeans, 2000, 7", MIP, ea...$12.00

Campbell's Soup, doll, girl, rubber & vinyl w/cloth outfit, Ideal, 1955, 8", EX, minimum value $125.00

Campbell's Soup, doll, Paul Revere & Betsy Ross replicas, 1976, 10", M, ea from $45 to...$65.00

Campbell's Soup, doll, pirate, Home Shopper, 1995, 10", EX
(soup can box) $80.00
Campbell's Soup, doll, Scottish outfit, vinyl w/molded hair, from
$85 to..$100.00
Campbell's Soup, kaleidoscope, replica of soup can, 1981,
EX..$40.00
Campbell's Soup, semi truck, diecast metal, M'm M'm Good!
and Kids perched on crescent moon on trailer, 12½",
MIB..$50.00
Campbell's Soup, wristwatch, 4 different, 1980s, MIB, ea ..$50.00
Cheer, doll, Cheer Girl, plastic w/cloth clothes, Proctor & Gam-
ble, 1960, 10", NM $20.00
Cheetos, doll, Chester Cheeta, 18", NM (w/orig tag).......$40.00
Chevrolet, mask, winking mascot w/hat labeled 'See the New
1940 Chevrolet,' die-cut cb, 12", EX+ $600.00

**Chiclet Company, Chicklet Zoo, complete set of 12, collected
with gum wrappers, EX, A, $15,000.00. (Photo courtesy
Gary Metz)**

Chiquita Bananas, doll, stuffed print cloth, 16", M $30.00
Chiquita Bananas, doll, uncut print cloth, framed, NM...$50.00
Chuck-E Cheese Pizza, bank, vinyl figure, 7", EX............$10.00
Chuck-E Cheese Pizza, doll, plush, Show Biz Pizza Time, 1996,
10", M $10.00
Chuck-E Cheese Pizza, hand puppet, plush, 1992, 9", EX...$12.00
Cities Service, Fix-All wrecker, plastic, gr & wht, Marx, 11",
EXIB..$100.00
Clark Bar, figure, boy in striped shirt holding Clark bar, vinyl,
1960s, 8½", EX $175.00
Coca-Cola, ball & cup, wooden ball on string attached to cup
on hdl w/Coke advertising, 1960s, NM....................$45.00
Coca-Cola, bang gun, G Man/It's the Real Thing, M.......$20.00
Coca-Cola, bank, can shape w/repeated red & wht diamond
design, NM..$85.00
Coca-Cola, bank, pig wearing hat, red plastic w/wht Drink
Coca-Cola/Sold Everywhere on sides, EX.................$35.00
Coca-Cola, book, Freckles & His Friends, Whitman Better Lit-
tle Book, premium, 1927, VG+ $35.00
Coca-Cola, bus, VW van, Taiyo, 1950s, litho tin, 7½", VG...$235.00
Coca-Cola, car, Ford Taxi, Taiyo, litho tin, friction, 9", MIB...$400.00
Coca-Cola, carousel, metal w/mc Coca-Cola graphics, EX ..$50.00
Coca-Cola, doll, Buddy Lee dressed as Coca-Cola route driver,
2nd limited ed, 1997-98, 13", M $350.00
Coca-Cola, figure, bear holding Coke bottle, wht plush, 1990s,
MIB..$15.00

**Coca-Cola, dispenser,
red, with two of four
glasses, 1950s, EXIB,
$60.00.**

Coca-Cola, figure, Frozen Coca-Cola mascot, stuffed cloth,
1960s, NM $150.00
Coca-Cola, game, Broadsides, Milton Bradley, 1940s-50s,
VG+ $150.00
Coca-Cola, game, checkers, metal pegs fit in holes on board
w/wave logo, 1970s, NM+ $75.00
Coca-Cola, game, Double-Six Dominos, brn vinyl case w/Sprite
Boy logo, 1970s, EX......................................$40.00
Coca-Cola, game set, 12 games (ping-pong, checkers, domi-
noes, etc), Milton Bradley, 1942, M (w/orig shipping
box) $1,900.00
Coca-Cola, jigsaw puzzle, Teenage Party, NMIB.............$100.00

**Coca-Cola, truck, Buddy L, 1960s, pressed steel, yellow with
white plastic grille cover, white-wall tires, plastic cases, bottles, and two metal handcarts, 16", NMIB, A, $825.00.
(Photo courtesy Randy Inman Auctions)**

Coca-Cola, truck, Buddy L, 1960s, #5426, PS, yel w/chrome
grille, WWT, w/plastic cases & bottles, 15", G, A.....$75.00
Coca-Cola, truck, Buddy L, 1960s, #5426, PS, yel w/chrome grille,
WWT, w/plastic cases & bottles, 15", EX, A $300.00

Coca-Cola, truck, Les-Paul, PS, Mack cab w/ad header on 2-tier bed, yel w/red, 22½", NM $400.00

Coca-Cola, truck, Marx, plastic, 2-tiered, w/cases, yel w/red detail, 11" L, NMIB, A..$275.00

Coca-Cola, truck, Marx #991, PS, stake bed w/Sprite Boy signs, covered wheel wells, yel, 20", G..............................$135.00

Coca-Cola, truck, Marx #1088, litho tin, stake bed w/Sprite Boy signs, red, yel & bl, NMIB $1,300.00

Coca-Cola, truck, Metalcraft, 1930s, PS, A-frame, electric lights, BRT, glass bottles, red & yel, 11", EX $1,400.00

Coca-Cola, truck, Sanyo, 1950s, litho tin, BRT, wht, yel & red, 13", NMIB $375.00

Coca-Cola, truck, Smith-Miller, contemporary, PS GMC cab, wooden open box bay & cases, metal divider, BRT, red, 14", EX $400.00

Coca-Cola, truck, Smith-Miller, 1940s, PS Ford cabover (Hollywood Calif), wood A-frame bed, wood cases, red, 14", VG+, A..$2,400.00

Coca-Cola, truck, Smith-Miller, 1950s, PS GMC cab w/2-tiered bed, BRT, cases w/glass bottles, red, 14", NOS $1,500.00

Coca-Cola, truck, Solido, Ford pickup (1936), die-cast, 1.18 scale, NM $35.00

Cracker Crack, palm puzzle, A-Maze Puzzle, plastic & paper, various designs & colors, W7, ea $3.40

Cracker Jack, airplane on stand (put-together), plastic, W7 ..$6.75

Cracker Jack, Animals Collect a Set, litho tin, W7..........$92.00

Cracker Jack, B-Series 35, Transfer Fun, paper, any of 32, W7, ea..$3.00

Cracker Jack, B-Series 77, Slate Fun, paper/plastic, any of 32, W7, ea $2.50

Cracker Jack, bank, litho tin book, W7, ea.....................$325.00

Cracker Jack, book, Animated Jungle Book, paper, W7 ...$90.00

Cracker Jack, book, Hello 1980, paper, any of 20, W7, ea..$7.50

Cracker Jack, booklet, Bess & Bill of Cracker Jack Hill, paper, any of 12, W7, ea..$90.00

Cracker Jack, booklet, Cracker Jack Riddles, paper, W7, ea .$16.50

Cracker Jack, booklet, Words of Wisdom, paper, W7.....$145.00

Cracker Jack, bookmark, dog, rocket, etc, plastic, various colors, W7, ea..$4.75

Cracker Jack, bookmarks, metal, Cracker Jack, dog, etc, any of 4, W7, ea $9.50

Cracker Jack, Breakfast Set, agateware in matchbox, W7 ..$25.00

Cracker Jack, candleholder, single, metal, gold color, W7 ...$3.75

Cracker Jack, charm, anchor, wht metal, W7 ....$2.75

Cracker Jack, charm, dirigible, wht metal w/celluloid insert, W7...$62.50

Cracker Jack, charm, hammer, wht metal, W7 ....$1.50

Cracker Jack, charm, man eating watermelon, wht metal, W7...$8.75

Cracker Jack, chicken figure, chenile, W7 ....$7.50

Cracker Jack, dollhouse miniature, sugar bowl w/floral design, wht metal, W7 ....$2.75

Cracker Jack, eyeglasses, Cracker Jack Wherever You Look, paper w/celluloid inert, W7 ....$72.50

Cracker Jack, figure, man made of wooden beads & wire, W7 ....$27.50

Cracker Jack, Flip-Action Movie, various subjects, paper, W7 ....$11.50

Cracker Jack, flip book, Hand Cinema, paper, W7...........$16.50

Cracker Jack, fob, alphabet letter, plastic, various colors, W7, ea...$4.50

Cracker Jack, fortune teller, Cracker Jack, paper, W7.......$95.00

Cracker Jack, game, Cracker Jack Magink Question Box, paper, W7 ....$33.50

Cracker Jack, game, Drawing Made Easy, paper, W7 ....$35.00

Cracker Jack, globe, metal, W7 ....$60.00

Cracker Jack, Handy Andy, paper, any of 12, W7, ea $67.50

Cracker Jack, hat, Me for Cracker Jack, paper, W7 ....$425.00

Cracker Jack, horse & wagon, Cracker Jack, wht metal, W7 ....$450.00

Cracker Jack, jigsaw puzzle, Akron blimp, paper, W7.....$135.00

Cracker Jack, license plate card, paper, any of 50, W7, ea ..$17.50

Cracker Jack, lenticular, various scenes & colors, plastic, W7, ea...$6.25

Cracker Jack, locomotive, Cracker Jack Line #512, metal, 1920s, 2", EX, $125.00.

Cracker Jack, mirror back, Cracker Jack the Great Connection, metal & glass, W7 ....$115.00

Cracker Jack, Mysticolor Paint Set, W7, ea $4.50

Cracker Jack, NIT, plastic, various figures & colors, W7 ....$5.50

Cracker Jack, palm puzzle, boy riding duck, paper w/metal rim, Germany, W7, ea $27.50

Cracker Jack, palm puzzle, moon over city, Cracker Jack box on back, paper & plastic, W7 ....$85.00

Cracker Jack, pencil sharpener, clock face, wht metal, W7...$39.00

Cracker Jack, Picture Panorama, any of 14, W7, ea..........$15.50

Cracker Jack, pin-back button, pretty lady, w/paper insert, any of 12, W7, ea $98.50

Cracker Jack, pinball game, w/graphics, Gordy, 1995, 5x10", MIP..$6.00

Cracker Jack, pipe, lion head, Germany, W7 ....$20.00

Cracker Jack, postcard, The Cracker Jack Bears, paper, any of 16, W7, ea..$19.50

Cracker Jack, puzzle, image of early toys, 500 pcs, complete, unused, MIB...$10.00

Cracker Jack, Series #48, Tag Along, plasticized paper, any of 15 ....$5.00

Cracker Jack, slide card, Animal, any of 26, W7, ea...........$9.50

Cracker Jack, slide card, Cracker Jack Movies, paper, W7 ..$137.50

Cracker Jack, spinner, Cracker Jack Golf, paper & wood, W7 ....$125.00

Cracker Jack, spinner, Keep 'Em Flying, metal, W7..........$55.00

Cracker Jack, spinner, Golf, metal, W7, $125.00. (Photo courtesy Larry White)

Cracker Jack, spinner, You're It, finger pointing, metal, W7 ..$13.00

Cracker Jack, squeaker w/American flag, Me for Cracker Jack on back, paper, W7 ....$110.00

Cracker Jack, Squeeze Faces, paper, any of 9, W7, ea $15.00

Cracker Jack, stand-up, Cracker Jack 1389, plastic, various colors, W7, ea $7.25

Cracker Jack, stand-up, Herby, metal, W7, $29.50. (Photo courtesy Larry White)

Cracker Jack, stand-up, Indian, cowboy, etc, plastic, NOSCO, W7, ea $2.75

Cracker Jack, stand-up, motorcyclist, metal, various japanned colors, W7, ea $27.50

Cracker Jack, stickers, glow-in-the-dark, paper, any of 56, W7, ea $1.75

Cracker Jack, streamliner, Cracker Jack, train cars, plastic, various colors, W7, ea $4.50

Cracker Jack, streamliner, metal, red & yel, W7 ....$9.50

Cracker Jack, streamliner, Tootsietoy Zephyr, metal, W7..$27.50

Cracker Jack, stud, Cracker Jack Air Corps, metal, W7 ...$29.50

Cracker Jack, Tele-Viz, paper, any of 10, W7 ....$65.00

Cracker Jack, tennis racquet, metal, Dowst, W7 ....$6.50

Cracker Jack, Tiny Tatoos, paper, various colors, any of 16, W7 .$1.50

Cracker Jack, train, Kerchoo, plastic, various colors, W7, ea ..$5.25

Cracker Jack, train, litho tin, engine & 2 passenger cars, 2¼" ea, EX, A $140.00

Cracker Jack, train track, Cracker Jack, plastic, Canadian prize, W7 ....$20.00

Cracker Jack, Trick Mustache, paper punch-out card, W7...$13.50

Cracker Jack, trophy, World Famous Musician, etc, plastic, W7, ea $5.50

Cracker Jack, truck, Express, litho tin, W7 ....$74.50

Cracker Jack, visor, Cracker Jack, paper, W7.................$325.00

Cracker Jack, Water Flowers in 8-sided paper box, W7....$43.50

Cracker Jack, whistle, airplane w/flag design, metal, W7...$49.50

Cracker Jack, whistle, bear on spherical chamber, Made in Japan, metal, W7 ....$49.50

Cracker Jack, whistle, Close End w/Fingers, metal, W7 ...$15.00

Cracker Jack, whistle, dirigible, litho tin, W7.................$42.50

Cracker Jack, whistle, playing card on front, metal, any of 6, W7, ea $37.50

Cracker Jack, zodiac coin, plastic, various colors, any of 12, W7 ....$5.50

Crayola, figure, Crayola Ballerina, plush, Gund, 14", M...$10.00

Crayola, figure, Crayola Bear, plush, 7½", EX...................$15.00

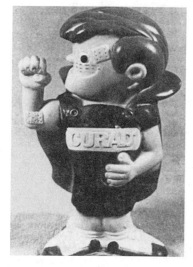

Curad, The Taped Crusader bank, plastic figure, 8", $6.00.

Curel Lotion, doll, Curel Baby, plastic w/jtd arms & legs, 1980, 6", EX $20.00

Curity, doll, Miss Curity, compo, wht nurse's dress & Miss Curity on wht hat, American, 1940s, 21", VG+ $275.00

Dairy Queen, figure, Dairy Queen Kid, stuffed cloth, 1974, EX $20.00

Dairy Queen, figure, Marsh Mallo, plush moose, 1980s, 7", scarce, EX...$12.00

Dairy Queen, figure, Sweet Nell, plush, 1974, 12", EX.....$20.00

Dairy Queen, whistle, plastic ice-cream cone shape, 2", NM ..$5.00

Del Monte, figures, Fluffy Lamb, Lushie Peach, or Reddie Tomato, plush, 1980s, EX, ea.............................$20.00

Dominos Pizza, figure, Noid, plush, 1988, 19", MIP..........$20.00

Dominos Pizza, figure, Noid as sorcerer, PVC, 1980s, 2½", MIP $6.00

Dominos Pizza, yo-yo, Nobody Delivers Faster, plastic, Humphery, NM+..$5.00

Dots Candy, doll, Dots Candy Baby, beanbag type w/vinyl face & hands, Hasbro, 1970s, MIB $15.00

Dubble Bubble Bubble Gum, beanie, mc suede w/metal top button, rnd Fleers... logo on front, 1930s, rare, EX+.....$100.00

Dunkin Donuts, figures, koala bears, plush, 2 different, 4½", EX+, ea $6.00

Eli's Cheescake, doll, cloth, holding lg wht cloth fork, 6", EX $8.00

Energizer Batteries, Christmas ornament, Energizer Bunny, clear plastic, 1992, 3", M $5.00

Energizer Batteries, Christmas Stocking, plush Energizer Bunny, mail-in item, 1980s, 28", MIP $20.00

Energizer Batteries, figure, Energizer Bunny, beanbag type, Creata, 1999, 7", MIP...$15.00

Energizer Batteries, figure, Energizer Bunny, plush, flip-flop shoes, 25", MIP...$85.00

Energizer Batteries, flashlight, Energizer Bunny w/movable arms & head, 4", MIP..$8.00

Eskimo Pie, doll, Eskimo Pie Doll, stuffed cloth, 1964-74, 15", EX, from $15 to..$20.00

Fanny Farmer Candies, delivery truck, Japan, 1950s, tin, friction, red & wht, 8", Fair, A $40.00

Fig Newtons, doll, balancing cookie on her head & holding lg cookie in her hand, plastic, Nabisco, 1980s, 4½", NM $15.00

Flintstones Vitamins, figure, Fred Flintstone, inflatable vinyl w/removable plastic clothes, 1970s, M $12.00

Fruit Stripe Gum, figure, Yipes, plush, 15", EX $50.00

Fruit Stripe Gum, figure shaped like pack of gum riding motorcycle, bendable vinyl, 1967, 7½", EX+.........................$175.00

Funny-Face Drink, book, How Freckle Face Got His Freckles, Pillsbury, 1965, EX...$28.00

Funny-Face Drink, masks, die-cut paper images of 6 different characters, Pillsbury, 1960s, unused, M, ea from $250 to $275.00

Funny-Face Drink, mugs, various character faces pnt on plastic, Pillsbury, 3", NM, ea from $10 to $12.00

Funny-Face Drink, pitcher, Goofy Grape, molded plastic, Pillsbury, 10", EX, from $65 to $85.00

General Electric, Radio Man, painted wood and composition bead-like majorette figure, red and white with yellow trim, black shoes, 1930s, 18½", EX+, A, $920.00. (Photo courtesy James Julia Auctions)

General Mills, bank, Twinkles the Elephant, molded plastic, store item, 1960, 9½" L, EX $350.00

General Mills, mask, Count Chocula, 1970s, plastic, NM ..$35.00

General Mills, ring, secret compartment; Frankenberry, NM $275.00

General Mills, tent, Cocoa Puffs Train Station, lithoed material, 1961, EX $100.00

Generl Mills, Cocoa Puffs Train, litho tin, 4 attached cars, 12", 1959-61, EX $75.00

Gilmore/Red Lion, tanker truck, Dorman Prod, w/gas pump & cans, PS, 26", NM $1,950.00

Gilmore/Red Lion, tanker truck, Smith-Miller, metal, 1949 GMC, red & wht, BRT, 22", EX..............................$450.00

Green Giant, bank, Little Sprout figure, compo, plays Valley of the Green Giant, 8½", EX...................................$50.00

Green Giant, doll, girl, vinyl w/rooted hair, yel & gr dress & hat, corn motif on purse, 1950s, 17", M $40.00

Green Giant, figure, Jolly Green Giant, vinyl, 1970s, 10", EX+ $90.00

Green Giant, figure, Little Sprout, talker, MIP.................$55.00

Green Giant, figure, Little Sprout, vinyl, 1970s, 6½", EX ..$8.00

Green Giant, jump rope, Little Sprout hdls, MIP.............$20.00

Green Giant, tractor-trailer, Green Giant Brands, 22", G+ ..$200.00

Hamburger Helper, figure, Helping Hand, plush, 14", M...$10.00

Hardee's, Gilbert Giddyup doll, stuffed print cloth, 1971, EX, $25.00. (Photo courtesy Joleen Ashman Robinson and Kay Sellers)

Harley-Davidson, doll, Harley Hog, 9", M $25.00

Hawaiian Punch, doll, Punchy, beanbag type, 1997, 10", MIP...$15.00

Hawaiian Punch, doll, Punchy, stuffed cloth, 20", NM $65.00

Hawaiian Punch, game, Mattel, 1978, NMIB..................$50.00

Heinz, H-57 Rocket Blaster, w/instructions, MIB.............$15.00

Heinz, talking alarm clock, Aristocrat Tomato figure & Heinz label-shaped clock on rnd base, plastic, 1980s, 10x6", NM $125.00

Hershey's, plush bear wearing Hershey's sweater, 7", NM+ ...$8.00

Holiday Inn, gorilla beanbag figure, give-away item, 1990s, 3½", EX $5.00

Hush Puppies, plush dog, Presents, 1980s, 10", EX+.........$14.00

Hush Puppies, plush dog, tan & maroon bean-bag type, Applause, 5x6", EX+..$8.00

Icee, bank, Icee Bear, vinyl figure, 1970s, 8", VG $20.00
Jell-O, puppet, Mr Wiggle, red vinyl, 1966, M $125.00

Jewel Tea, delivery truck, 1940s, pressed steel, brown with gold advertising, 10", EX, A, $350.00. (Photo courtesy Randy Inman)

Keebler, bank, Ernie the Keebler elf, ceramic, 10", M $50.00
Keebler, doll, Ernie, cloth beanbag type, 5", EX+ $6.00
Keebler, figure, Ernie, vinyl, 1970s, 7", NM $25.00
Kellogg's, Bath-Tub Toy, Pop! in boat, vinyl, store item, Talbot
    Toys, 1984, 6x4", NMIB.....................................$10.00
Kellogg's, doll, Bean Bag Bunch, w/tag, MIP...................$10.00
Kellogg's, figure, Snap!, Crackle! & Pop!, pnt squeeze vinyl,
    1975, 7½", EX, set of 3 ....$50.00
Kellogg's, figure, Snap!, Crackle! & Pop!, vinyl, store items,
    1984, 5", MIB, ea $10.00
Kellogg's, figure, Tony the Tiger, inflatable vinyl, 1950s, 45",
    EX..$300.00
Kellogg's, figure, Toucan Sam, vinyl, store item sold w/Rice
    Krispies Dolls, 1984, 5", NMIB..............................$5.00
Kellogg's, Friction Powered Mover, Crackle!, plastic, store item,
    1984, 2½", NMOC $10.00
Kellogg's, hand puppets, Snap!, Crackle! & Pop!, 1950, cloth &
    vinyl, 8", EX, ea $75.00
Kellogg's, jigsaw puzzle, Keep Going w/Kellogg's, child throwing
    baseball, 1930s, 8x6", EX+ $65.00
Kellogg's, Magic Color Cards, Rice Krispies, 1930s, complete,
    unused, EX+ (EX+ envelope)..................................$65.00
Kellogg's, Paul Jung & Lou Jacobs Shuttle Action Toy, 1953,
    10", NM $45.00
Kellogg's, push puppet, Pop!, plastic, store item, 1984, 4½",
    MOC $6.00
Kellogg's, sleeping bag, shows Tony the Tiger & other Kellogg's
    characters, 1970s, EX..$50.00
Kellogg's, Smaxey the Seal Action Cutout, 1959, 5", EX ..$10.00
Kentucky Fried Chicken, bank, Colonel Sanders figure w/cane
    on sm rnd base, Starling Plastics, 1965, 12½", EX+ ..$30.00
Kentucky Fried Chicken, coloring book, Favorite Chicken
    Stores, 1960s, EX $25.00
Kentucky Fried Chicken, hand puppet, Colonel Sanders, plastic,
    1960s, EX $20.00
Kentucky Fried Chicken, mask, Colonel Sanders face, molded
    plastic, 1960s, NM $55.00
Kentucky Fried Chicken, nodder, Colonel Sanders, pnt compo,
    Kentucky Fried Chicken on base, 1980s, 7½", EX.....$65.00
Kentucky Fried Chicken, Wacky Wobbler, PVC Colonel
    Sanders figure, MIB $25.00

Kentucky Fried Chicken, nodder, The Colonel, holding a bucket of chicken, plastic, 7", NM, $ 12.00.

Kiwi Fruit, figures, plush, 1985-90, set of 3, 10½", 11" & 17", M,
    ea...$30.00
Knoor Soup, doll set, hard plastic, dressed in costumes from vari-
    ous countries, Best Foods, 1963-64, M, pr.................$15.00
Kool-Aid, bank, mascot pitcher standing on base, hard plastic,
    mechanical actions, 1970s, 7", NM..........................$50.00

Kool-Aid, dancing guitar player, plastic multicolored pitcher figure on round base, battery-operated, 8½", $50.00.

Kool-Aide, dispenser, MIB..$50.00
Kool-Aid, figure, Kool-Aid Man w/barbells, PVC, 2", EX ..$4.00
Kraft, figures, Cheesasaurus Rex in various sporting poses, PVC,
    1990s premiums, M, ea $10.00
Kraft Foods, pull toy, Kraft TV Theatre cameraman seated on rolling
    camera base, plastic, 1950s Velveeta premium, EX........$100.00
Kraft Macaroni & Cheese, wristwatch, 1980s, M $10.00
Lee Jeans, doll, Buddy Lee as train engineer in Lee overalls, bl
    shirt & bl & wht striped hat, 13", EX $150.00
Lifesavers, bank, cb & metal cylinder w/Lifesavers graphics,
    1960s, 12", EX..$20.00
Little Ceasar's Pizza, doll, Pizza Pizza Man holding slice of pizza,
    plush, 1990, EX $5.00
Log Cabin Syrup, pull toy, Log Cabin Express, NMIB....$900.00
M&M Candy, figure, peanut shape, beanbag, golfer or witch, 6",
    M, ea $10.00

Little Debbie, doll, vinyl with cloth dress and straw hat, 1980s, 11", NM, $85.00.

M&M Candy, figure, peanut shape, bendable arms or legs, 7", M, ea $15.00

M&M Candy, figure, plain shape, beanbag, various colors, 6", M, ea $5.00

M&M Candy, figure, plain shape, plush, dressed as bride, 36", EX $40.00

M&M Candy, figure, plain shape, plush, 4½", M................$5.00

M&M Candy, figure, plain shape, plush, 8", M...................$8.00

M&M Candy, figure, plain shape, plush, 12", M..............$10.00

M&M Candy, figure, plain shape, plush, 48" from fingertip to fingertip, NM $75.00

Maypo Oat Cereal, bank, Marky Maypo figure, plastic, 1960s, EX $100.00

McDonald's, action figures, several different, Remco, 1976, NM, ea $25.00

McDonald's, bank, Grimace, compo, 1985, NM...............$15.00

McDonald's, bank, Ronald McDonald bust, plastic, Taiwan, 1993, EX...$40.00

McDonald's, bop bag, Grimace, 1978, 8", MIP $10.00

McDonald's, doll, Fry Girl, stuffed cloth, 1987, 4", M $5.00

McDonald's, doll, Fry Girl, stuffed cloth, 1987, 12", NM ..$10.00

McDonald's, doll, Fry Guy, stuffed cloth, 1987, 12", NM ..$12.00

McDonald's, doll, Hamburgler, cloth, purple stripes, early 1970s, 15", NM $200.00

McDonald's, doll, Hamburgler, cloth w/vinyl head & hat, cloth cape, blk stripes, 1980s, 11", NM+ $20.00

McDonald's, figure, Grimace, plush, plastic eyes, 8", M ..$10.00

McDonald's, figure, Ronald McDonald, cloth, raised arms, 1987, 13", NM $20.00

McDonald's, figure, Ronald McDonald, cloth w/plastic head, yarn hair, real shoe laces, Dakin, 15", 1991, M..........$15.00

McDonald's, figure, Ronald McDonald, vinyl w/cloth costume, Remco, 1976, 7", MIB $30.00

McDonald's, game, McDonald's, Milton Bradley, 1975, MIB ..$25.00

McDonald's, game, Playland Funburst, Parker Bros, 1984, MIB $20.00

McDonald's, playset, McDonaldland, Remco, 1976, MIB...$125.00

Michelin Tires, figure, Mr Bib, cloth, Chase Bag Co, 1967, 21", EX $40.00

Michelin Tires, figure, Mr Bib holding baby, rubber, 7", NM...$125.00

Michelin Tires, puzzle, put together to form a figure of Mr Bib on motorcycle, MIP $55.00

Michelin Tires, ramp walker, w/up Mr Bib figure, MIB ..$125.00

Michelin Tires, yo-yo, Mr Bib in blk outline on wht, EX...$10.00

Moxie, toy car with horse and rider, lithographed tin, VG+, A, $700.00. (Photo courtesy Wm Morford)

McDonald's, doll, Ronald McDonald, stuffed printed cloth, Chase Bag Co., 1970s, two different versions, 17", EX, $20.00 each. (Photo courtesy Gary Henriques and Audre DuVall)

Mr Clean, figure, wht-pnt vinyl standing w/arms crossed, Proctor & Gamble, 1960s, 8", EX...$75.00

Mr Softee, truck, Japan, 1960s, wht & bl litho tin w/rubber tires, friction, 4", NM $65.00

Nabisco, doll, Mr Salty, stuffed cloth, 1983, NM, minimum value $25.00

Nalplex Paint, hand puppet, Dutch Boy mascot, cloth body w/vinyl head, 1960s premium, 16", unopened, NMIP ..$60.00

Nestlé, book, Magic Tricks, 1970s, NM............................$8.00

Nestlé, cup, plastic w/bunny ears forming hdl, 4", EX.........$8.00

Nestlé, doll, P Nutty as Morsel Family Clown, Trudy Co, 1984, 10", EX+...$18.00

Nestlé, figure, Quik Bunny, bendable, 6", EX....................$6.00

Nestlé, figure, Quik Bunny, plush, w/'Q' necklace, 1980s, 21", EX..$25.00

Old Dutch Cleanser, mechanical toy, cast iron, Old Dutch girl with can and broom on articulated base, EX, A, $11,500.00. (Photo courtesy Bertoia Auctions)

Oreo Cookies, figure, Oreo Cookie w/bendable arms & legs, 4½", M $6.00

Oscar Mayer, puppet, Little Oscar, plastic w/printed image, EX+ $6.00

Oscar Mayer, whistle, plastic wienermobile, 2x1¼", NM ..$15.00

Oscar Mayer, Wienermobile, plastic, Little Oscar pops up when wheels move, earliest version, 1950s, 10" L, EX $100.00

Oscar Mayer, Wienermobile pedal car, EX.....................$125.00

Ovaltine/Bovril, dbl-decker bus, w/up, Tri-Ang, 1950s, 4x7", EX+ $100.00

Pepsi-Cola, dispenser/bank, b/o, Linemar, 1950s, 10", unused, EXIB..$350.00

Pepsi-Cola, pull toy, puppy w/hot dog wagon, wood, 10", EX $250.00

Pepsi-Cola, truck, Buddy L, wood, gr Railway Express truck w/wht Pepsi=Cola advertising, w/accessories, 16", NMIB $1,000.00

Pepsi-Cola, truck, Buddy L, 1970s, metal, 2-tier open bay w/Enjoy Pepsi ad panel, bl & wht, w/cases, 16", EXIB..............$100.00

Pepsi-Cola, truck, Marx, tin, wht w/plastic cases on open bay, P=C cap logos on doors & back, 1940s-50s, 7", NM, A.......$100.00

Pepsi-Cola, truck, Ny-Lint, metal, 3-part open-sided bays w/Pepsi ads on inside walls, 16", no accessories o/w VG.........$100.00

Pepsi-Cola, truck, Ny-Lint, metal, 3-part open-sided bays w/Pepsi ads on inside walls, 16", w/accessories, VGIB $175.00

Pepsi-Cola, truck, Smith-Miller, contemporary, metal GMC Cabover w/wood open box bay & cases, metal divider, 13", NM, A $165.00

Pepsi-Cola, truck, Solido, Chevy pickup (1946), die-cast, 9½", M, from $15 to $25.00

Pillsbury, bank, ceramic Poppin' Fresh figure, 1980s premium, M $35.00

Pillsbury, figure, Poppin' Fresh, talker, Mattel, 16", NM...$100.00

Pillsbury, figure, Poppin' Fresh, vinyl, standing w/arms open on sq plastic base w/emb name, 1971, 7½", EX, P6 ....$28.00

Pillsbury, finger puppet, cat (Biscuit) or dog (Flapjack), vinyl, 1974, ea...$35.00

Pillsbury, finger puppet, Poppin' Fresh, Poppie Fresh, Bun Bun (girl), or Popper (boy), vinyl, 1974, ea....................$25.00

Pillsbury, puppet, Poppin' Fresh, plastic w/vinyl head, 1971, EX $25.00

Pizza Hut, bank, Pizza Hut Pete, plastic, 1969, 8", EX+ $25.00

Pizza Hut, kite, Garfield, MIP...$5.00

Planters, badge, die-cut tin full image of Mr Peanut w/bendable pocket tab, 1930s, 1½", NM......................................$25.00

Planters, bank, clear plastic Mr Peanut figure, 1950s-70s, EX, from $90 to $150.00

Planters, beachball, yel w/image of Mr Peanut in bl, 1970s, 13½" dia, EX...$10.00

Planters, coloring book, America, an Ecology Coloring Book, 1970s, unused, M, P6..$15.00

Planters, coloring book, 12 Months, 1970s, unused, M, P6...$12.00

Planters, coloring book, 50 States, 1970s, unused, M, P6 ..$15.00

Planters, figure, Mr Peanut, cloth, Chase Bag Co, 1967, 21", EX...$40.00

Planters, figure, Mr Peanut, cloth, Chase Bag Co, 1970, 18", NM $25.00

Planters, figure, Mr. Peanut, painted wood with bead-type arms and legs, 8½", VG, A, $125.00. (Photo courtesy James Julia Auctions)

Planters, frisbee, wht plastic w/Heritage logo, M $15.00

Planters, game, Planters Peanut Party, lg premium version, 1930s, unused, NM..$100.00

Planters, hand puppet, Mr Peanut, rubber, 1942, 6", EX, from $750 to..$1,000.00

Planters, nodder, Mr Peanut figure, pnt compo, 1960s, 7", VG $80.00

Planters, top, pnt wood w/ad label on top, 1940s, 2½", EX.$150.00

Planters, whistle, plastic Mr Peanut figure, 1970s, NM, P6...$6.00

Planters, yo-yo, Mr Peanut image, Humphery, 1976, NM ..$12.00

Popsicle, Music Maker Truck, Mattel, plastic, 11", VG, $150.00.

Post Cereals, doll, Sugar Bear, cloth, Sugar Crisps, 5", EX+..$8.00

Post Cereals, doll, Sugar Bear, cloth, 2 different (1 in sweater & 1 in shorts), Sugar Crisp, 5", EX+, ea $8.00

Post Cereals, Puppet Theater w/3 Crispy Critters Puppets, cb, mail-in offer, 1966, uncut & unused, NMIP $250.00

Purina, squeak toy, chuck wagon, vinyl, 1975, 8", NM.....$30.00

Quaker Oats, Co, Quisp Space Beanie, pk plastic w/propeller on top, 1967, EX+...$300.00

Quaker Oats Co, bank, Cap'n Crunch figure, pnt plastic, 1970s, EX..$35.00

Quaker Oats Co, bank, Quisp figure, cermaic, 1960s, NM...$100.00

Quaker Oats Co, Cavern Helmet, plastic w/headlight, 1967, EX...$225.00

Quaker Oats Co, coloring book, Cap'n Crunch, Whitman, 1968, unused, EX $25.00

Quaker Oats Co, doll, Cap'n Crunch, plush, 1990, 18", M...$20.00

Quaker Oats Co, Guppy Sailing Ship, plastic, assembled, Cap'n Crunch Cereal, 1967, 10" L, EX..............................$200.00

Quaker Oats Co, kaleidoscope, Cap'n Crunch, 1964-65, cb, 7", EX...$35.00

Quaker Oats Co, Quake Cavern Helmet, plastic, 1967, 10", EX...$225.00

Raid, figure, Raid Bug, plush, 1980, EX+ $25.00

Raid, figure, Raid Bug, w/up, mean expression, 4", NM....$50.00

RCA, figure, Radiotron Man in parade outfit w/RCA Radiotrons chest banner, pnt beaded wood, 16", EX+, A $880.00

RCA, TV Service Truck, Marx, plastic, opening rear door, extension ladder on top, 8½", NMIB, A..................$200.00

Richfield Gasoline, tank truck, American National, 1920s, PS, blk w/wht trim, gold lettering, 27", rstr, A............$1,500.00

Sambo's Restaurant, figure, tiger mascot, stuffed plush, 7", NMIB $100.00

Sealtest, rider truck, Roberts Co, PS, gray w/red Sealtest Milk decals, red frame & steering wheel, 22", EX+IB, A .$880.00

Sears, delivery truck, Marx, tin, 2-tone gr, Shop at Sears & Save on sides of van w/opening rear doors, 25", VG, A ...$225.00

Seven-Up, figure, Fresh-Up Freddie, stuffed cloth w/rubber head, Canada, 15", EX...$75.00

Seven-Up, figure, Spot, bendable, 3", NM $5.00

Seven-Up, figure, Spot, folds away into cloth bag shaped like 7-Up can, premium item, 12", EX+ $15.00

Seven-Up, figure, Spot w/suction-cup hands, Commonwealth, 1980s, 6", NM+...$8.00

Shoney's, bank, Shoney's Bear, vinyl, 1990s, 8", NM $15.00

Smokey Bear, see US Forest Service

Snickers Candy Bar, doll, fits into bag resembling Snickers bar, Mars, 1990s, 12", EX...$12.00

Snow Crop Frozen Foods, bear, Teddy Snow Crop, wht plush w/molded vinyl face, rnd red cloth label, 1950s, 9", EX ..$50.00

Snow Crop Frozen Foods, hand puppet, Teddy Snow Crop, wht plush w/molded vinyl face, red cloth label, 1950s, EX ..$25.00

Snow Crop Frozen Foods, toy van, H/Japan, 1960s, litho tin, BRT, friction, 8½" L, EX+.......................................$100.00

Snuggle Fabric Softener, figure, Snuggles the bear, plush, Lever Bros, 1983, 6", EX+..$15.00

Snuggle Fabric Softener, figure, Snuggles the bear, plush, Lever Bros, 1986, 14", EX+..$30.00

Snuggle Fabric Softener, figure, Snuggles the bear, plush beanbag type, Lever Bros, 1999, 8", NM $15.00

Snuggles Fabris Softener, hand puppet, Snuggles the bear (full body), Lever Bros, 1990s, 15", EX+.............................$15.00

Squirt, doll, Squirt Boy, 1960s, 17", VG, $200.00. (Photo courtesy Randy Inman Auctions)

Star-Kist, bank, ceramic Charlie the Tuna figure standing on tuna can, 1988, 9½", NM..$20.00

Star-Kist, figure, Charlie the Tuna, 'Talkin' Patter Pillow,' stuffed print cloth, Mattel, 1970s, 15", NM+ $25.00

Star-Kist, figure, Charlie the Tuna, stuffed pillow figure, 1970s, 36", EX $15.00

Star-Kist, figure, Charlie the Tuna, vinyl w/removable hat, Product People, 1970s, 7", EX+ $12.00

Star-Kist, lamp base, Charlie the Tuna figure, pnt plaster, 1970s, 12½", EX+ $65.00

Star-Kist, truck, Tonka, 1950s, PS, red cab w/bl box van, opening rear doors, ads on cab & van, 14½", VG $500.00

Star-Kist, Wack Wobbler, Charlie the Tuna figure, PVC, M..$15.00

Sunbeam Bread, doll, Little Miss Sunbeam, stuffed cloth, 17", NM..$35.00

Swiss Miss Chocolate, doll, Swiss Miss, stuffed cloth w/vinyl face & yel yarn hair, EX, minimum value........................$25.00

Taco Bell, dog, beanbag type, w/tags, 1999, M.................$12.00

Texaco Service Station Playset, steel with plastic accessories, unopened, NOS, $250.00.

Tastee Freeze, figure, Miss Tastee Freeze, hard plastic, 1950s, 7", NM...$20.00

Teddy Grahams, doll, plush bear w/purple velvet jacket & purple shoes, Nabisco, 10", M.................................$15.00

Texaco, bank, red plastic gas pump w/star logo on rnd wht globe, Ideal, 9", EXIB...$300.00

Texaco, doll, Cheerleader, 1971, 11", NRFB....................$20.00

Texaco, helmet w/speaker on top, plastic, Wen-Mac/USA, EX ..$75.00

Texaco, pencil case, red plastic pump form w/blk rubber gas hose & hinges, Hasbro, 8", NM....................................$175.00

Tootsie Roll, Train Game, Hasbro, 1969, EXIB $55.00

Tupperware, plush figures, seal (Tupper Seal) & bear (I Love Tupperware), Interpur, 1980s, 10" & 8", rare, EX, ea........$20.00

Tyson Chicken, figure, Chicken Quick, stuffed cloth, 13", VG..$15.00

US Forest Service, bank, Smokey Bear, Let Smokey Bank on You Too, red plastic, 1950s, 5", EX.....................$50.00

US Forest Service, bank, Smokey Bear seated on stump w/shovel & hand on hat, ceramic, 6", NM+ $50.00

US Forest Service, bank, Woodsy Owl standing on rnd base maked Give a Hoot..., ceramic, 1970s, 8½", EX........$50.00

US Forest Service, book, Smokey Bear's Story of the Forest, 1968, softcover, 16 pgs, VG, P6............................$22.00

US Forest Service, book & stamp kit, The Story of Smokey Bear, Ladybird, 1990s, MIP......................................$10.00

US Forest Service, figure, Smokey Bear, plush, Knickerbocker, 22", complete, VG, P6......................................$75.00

US Forest Service, figure, Smokey Bear, plush body w/plastic hands & feet, Smokey belt, Ideal, 1950s, 15½", EX+ ..$50.00

US Forest Service, figure, Woodsy Owl & frowning flower on sq base mk Give a Hoot..., ceramic, 1960s-70s, 3¾", EX $35.00

US Forest Service, tatoos, Smokey Bear Temporary Tatoos, 6 different, Gordy Toys, 1990s, MIP.........................$8.00

US Postal Service, pull toy, 3-wheeled US Mail car w/Mr Zip driver, plastic, Kusan/US Postal Service, 6x8x12", VG+..$85.00

Vlasic Pickles, figure, Vlasic Stork, fluffy wht fur w/glasses & bow tie, Trudy Toys, 1989, 22", NM..........................$40.00

Ward's Tip Top Cakes, devil face mask promoting 'Devil's Food Sandwich,' red, blk & wht litho on die-cut cb, unused, NM $65.00

Wilkins Coffee, hand puppet, pnt rubber ad character, 1950s, 7½", EX..$115.00

Wilrick's Grape Drink, shaker cup, features Major Space character, yel & purple plastic, 7½", EX...........................$35.00

Woodsy Owl, see US Forest Service

Wrigley's Chewing Gum, Mother Goose booklet, Introducing the Sprightly Spearman (illus throughout), 1915, 28 pgs, EX $60.00

Advertising Signs, Ads, and Displays

Nowadays, with the intense passion toy buffs pour into their collections, searching for advertising items to complement those collections is a natural extension of their enthusiasm, adding even more diversity to an already multifaceted collecting field.

Barbie, display doll #3 in Evening Splendor outfit, upswept do, stand/book, M doll in EX pk box, A.....................$3,025.00

Barbie (World of) Fashions, Barbie, Ken, Brad, and Christie in 3-D plastic display case, 1969 – 70, dolls are M in case, $1,430.00. (Photo courtesy Bertoia Auctions)

Batman Wallets, die-cut cb sign w/lettering over logo, Standard Plastic/Mattel/NPP, 1960s, fits on rack, 6x16", EX....$75.00

Bozo the Capitol Clown Squeeze Me All Rubber Toy, die-cut cb sign, Capitol Records, 1940s-50s, 5½x14", EX $50.00

Custer's Last Stand, display for cereal box premium, 5 pre-cut cb litho items depicting Custer's last battle, 1950s, EX ..$35.00

Disney Classics, advertising plaque, ceramic, pk flowers crown top of wht scrolled banner w/name, Schmid/WD, 4x6", EX $32.00

Donald Duck Products, promo card w/name & image of Donald promoting his products, 1940s-50s, 14x10", unused, EX+ $75.00

Dr Seuss, die-cut bin topper, The Newest Book...Collection of Songs For Beginning Singers! 1960s, 12x9", EX......$200.00

Duncan Yo-yo, die-cut paper yo-yo-shaped sign reading ....Sold Here, red, blk & wht, 1960s-70s, 13", dia, EX $65.00

Duncan's Beginners' Yo-yo, red & wht cb display box w/24 wooden yo-yos in assorted colors, 1950s, 9x9½", EX+, A $375.00

Family Affair Electric Cord Organ, lithoed store poster showing Buffy at organ w/family, 1971, 44x22", M $50.00

Gabby Hayes Western Gun Collection, cb folder display w/complete set of 6 guns, premiums for Quaker, 1951, 7x12", EX $125.00

Guns by Hubley, blk metal hook rack w/litho tin header sign, no guns, 1950s-60s, 17x23x7", EX.............................$100.00

Halloween Masks, sign, Free Halloween Mask (While They Last) With 2 lbs Brazil Nuts (Kernel Nut), 1950s, 8x19", EX $75.00

Krazy Kat Balloons, cb tri-fold display w/assortment of balloons featuring Krazy Kat, Ashland Rubber, 1950s, 14" T, EX.......$50.00

McDonald's New Food Changables, translucent plastic sign w/flicker image, 1988, 21x21", EX+ $75.00

Micro-Lite Flash-Gun, cb sign featuring Mountie using Flash-Gun, Goes Bang When It Flashes, yel, 1950s, 15x10", VG+ $50.00

Mr Magoo for G-E Bulbs, die-cut cb floor display featuring Mr Magoo, UPA, 1960, 69x21x18", rare, EX $200.00

Master Caster, promotional car models punchboard display with chance to win one of four cars, unused, EX+, $1,750.00. (Photo courtesy Noel Barrett Auctions)

Tonka, oval porcelain dealer sign, 1968, 11x23", MIB, $325.00. (Photo courtesy Randy Inman Auctions)

Walt Disney Slotties, die-cut cb Donald Duck figure holding ...50¢ sign, 6-pc construction, 14", rare, EX............$125.00
Walt Disney's Pinocchio, paper poster, The 48 Page Book Free/Cocomalt...¢, WDP, 1939, 16x10", rare, VG...$175.00

Mr Magoo's G-E Bulb Fair, 2-sided cb display for G-E 3-Way Soft-White Bulbs, 1960s, 17x7", EX+........................$80.00
New Haven Animated Character Watches, die-cut cb standup, images of Gene Autry, Dick Tracy, Annie Oaklie, 1950s, 12", VG..$125.00
Parachute Men, display box w/24 plastic toy figures, RL Albert & Son #509, 1960s, M (EX box)...............................$75.00
PEZ, display, molded plastic head image of Peter PEZ the clown holding Pilot PEZ, 2-sided, fits on rack, 1960s, 18", EX+.........$150.00
Popeye Flashlite, die-cut cb standup w/fold-out 3-D effect, shows Popeye in crow's nest, Bantamlite, 1950s, EX $65.00
Popeye Official Pipe It Lites It Toots, display card w/5" plastic pipe w/glowing top (b/o), Micro-Lite, 1958, VG+.....$60.00
Popsicle 5 Star Comedy Party, paper poster w/images of comedy stars including Winchell & Mahoney, 1950s, 15x8", NM $125.00
Rin-Tin-Tin Dog Supply Center, display rack for choke chains, 2 Rinty images & 10 hooks, Screen Gems, 1956, 8x4x20", VG+...$100.00
Roadmaster Tricycles, saleman's sample scale model, red & wht w/BRT, NP handlebars w/red grips, 13", EX+, A $165.00
Robin Hood Shields, cb display w/3 of 12 shields, Official Films, 1950s, 11x10½", VG $50.00
Rolling Stones 'Official Vari-Vue Badge,' cb standup display, orange, blk & wht litho w/head shots, 1970s, 11x14", NM+...$75.00
Roy Rogers Wagon Train of Bargains, brn & yel litho cb dispay, folds for standup, 1950s, 8x13", unused, NM...........$150.00
Schwinn 'Quality Features,' red & wht litho tin display featuring real bike parts, 23x25", EX, A $935.00
Space Man Watch, cb display of 12 watches in 4 different colors, Ichimura/Japan, NM+, A $135.00
Squirt, paper litho sign, 18" Squirt Doll for $2.95...$5.95 Value!, 1962, 10x21", M $50.00
Star Kist, cb litho sign, Charlie's Official Little League Baseball Free..., 1960s premium promotion, 25x17", EX+ $75.00
Thundercaps, cb display box w/die-cut header, Magic Marxie/Super Sound Caps, Marx, 1950s, 12x4x25" L, VG $50.00
Trick or Treat Headquarters For Candy Hand Outs, 2-sided hanging sign, orange & blk die-cut cb, 1950s-60s, 21x14", EX+ $75.00

Aeronautical

Toy manufacturers seemed to take the cautious approach toward testing the waters with aeronautical toys, and it was well into the second decade of the twentieth century before some of the European toy makers took the initiative. The earlier models were bulky and basically inert, but by the 1950s, Japanese manufacturers were turning out battery-operated replicas with wonderful details that advanced with whirling motors and flashing lights.

For more information see *Big Book of Toy Airplanes* by W. Tom Miller, Ph.D.

See also Battery-Operated Toys; Cast Iron, Airplanes; Gasoline-Powered Toys; Model Kits; Pull Toys; Robots and Space Toys; Windups, Friction, and Other Mechanicals.

Air France ALBA Airliner, Joustra, w/up, litho tin, 6 plastic props, red, wht, yel, 22x24" W, EX (Est: $300-$400) $385.00
Air France F-PA-N-AM Airliner, w/up, b/o lights, litho tin, 4-prop, red, 21x24" W, VG+, A (Est: $200-$300)......$260.00
Air Mail Helicopter, KO, 1960s, b/o, litho tin w/plastic dome, w/pilot, 10" L, EXIB, A (Est: $25-$50) $90.00
Airplane, Wyandotte, 1940s, PS, 4-prop, cut-out windows, WRT (rpl), 14" W, VG+, A (Est: $75-$125).....................$130.00
American Airlines N305AA (Flagship Caroline), Linemar, b/o, litho tin, 4 props, 19" W, VG, A (Est: $150-$200)..$190.00
American Airways Twin Engine, Wyandotte, 1950s, litho tin, yel w/red, bl & wht trim, 12½" W, A (Est: $75-$125) $440.00
Army Plane, Marx, w/up, litho tin w/camoflauge detail, 4-prop, w/sparkling guns, 18" W, VG, A (Est: $150-$200)..$220.00
Army Tank Transport Plane, Buddy L, 1940s, PS, 2-prop, orange & brn, 27" W, missing tanks, G, A (Est: $75-$125)..$165.00

Army Scout Plane NX-107, Steelcraft, pressed steel, 22" wingspan, VG, A (Est: $400.00 to $600.00), $550.00. (Photo courtesy Bertoia Auctions)

Biplane, Tipp & Co, w/up, b/o lights, yel w/bl & wht bands on wings, 1 prop, 16" W, VG, A (Est: $500-$700) **$465.00**

Boeing B-50, Y, friction, tin, 4-prop, 19" W, NM+IB, A (Est: minimum $400)................**$1,025.00**

Capital Airlines, Linemar, r/c, litho tin, 4-prop, wht & gray w/red detail, 14" W, EX, A (Est: $75-$125).............**$200.00**

Cargo Plane, Orobr, w/up, b/o lights, wood, yel w/red trim, 1 prop, 14" W, VG, A (Est: $500-$700) **$165.00**

Cargo Plane #1416, Tippco/Germany, w/up, litho tin, yel w/bl stripes, red prop, 12½" W, VG, A (Est: $250-$350) ..**$330.00**

China Clipper, Wyandotte, PS w/wooden wheels, 13" W, NM, A (Est: minimum $125) **$365.00**

Cragstan Flying Plane (w/Pylon Tower), b/o, litho tin, 9" W, EXIB, A (Est: $100-$200) **$135.00**

Cragstan Smoking Jet Plane, TN, 1950s, b/o, litho tin, EXIB, A (Est: minimum $175) **$250.00**

D-A LBA, Marklin, wind-up, operating flaps, 22" wingspan, VG+, A (Est: $1,200.00 – $1,500.00), $1,200.00.

DNSA R-93 Bomber, Japan, w/up, litho tin, gr w/red trim, 1-prop, 2 pilots, 6½", EX, A (Est: $350-$450)............**$220.00**

Douglas CK Tri-Motor Top-Wing, prewar, litho tin, orange w/red, wht & bl trim, 9½", VG, A (Est: $350)........**$660.00**

E-695 Tri-Motor Passenger Plane, Gunthermann, w/up, tin, cream w/blk stripes on wings, 23" W, VG, A (Est: $1,000-$1,200)..**$935.00**

Early Airship, Ernst Plank, hand-painted tin, 15" long, EXIB, A (Est: $12,000.00 – $15,000.00), $16,500.00. (Photo courtesy Bertoia Auctions)

F-POV Single Engine Passenger Plane, Joustra/France, w/up, litho tin, red & yel, 12½" W, EX, A (Est: $300-$400) **$330.00**

F-252 Top Wing, JEP, w/up, tin, silver w/orange, bl & wht trim, red prop, 16" W, G, A (Est: $800-$1,200) **$350.00**

Flying Boat D9-340, German, w/up, litho tin, orange w/silver-tone wings, tail & props, 16" W, A (Est: $2,500-$3,500)...**$575.00**

Flying Plane w/Air Traffic Control Tower, Cragstan, b/o, litho tin, 9", incomplete o/w EXIB, A (Est: $150-$250) ..**$140.00**

Ford Tri-Motor, Steelcraft, PS, gr w/red top wing, red hubs, 23" W, VG+, A (Est: $200-$300)................................**$600.00**

Green Shell (TWA), Japan, w/up, litho tin, 2-prop, 11½" W, G, A (Est: $50-$75)..**$110.00**

Jet Plane Base, Y, 1950s, b/o, litho tin, w/9" L plane, NMIB, A (Est: minimum $350) **$650.00**

Jet Plane Base, Y, 1950s, b/o, litho tin, w/9" L plane, VG+, A (Est: $150-$200)..**$330.00**

Lighted Jet Plane, see US Air Force FW-996 Fighter Jet

Lockheed Air Lines Monoplane, Modern Toys, w/up, tin, silver w/red & bl trim, 3-prop, 14" W, VG, A (Est: $600-$800) **$1,430.00**

Lockheed F104A Starfighter, Momoya, friction, litho tin, 10" L, NMIB, A (Est: minimum $125) **$245.00**

Lockheed Sirus, Steelcraft, 22" W, VG, A (Est: $1,250-$1,500)..**$1,320.00**

Navy Emergency Helicopter (Cragstan), NGS/Japan, friction, tin, red, wht & bl, 2 pilots, 11", NMIB, A (Est: minimum $65)..**$100.00**

Navy F9F-5 207 Panther Jet, Y, friction, litho tin, fold-up wings, 8½" L, NM, A (Est: minimum $125) **$225.00**

NX-130 Top Wing, Steelcraft, 1930s, 1-prop, 23" W, G, A (Est: $600-$800) **$520.00**

Pan Am Airliner, Y, friction, 4-prop, 11½" W, EXIB, A (Est: minimum $125) **$250.00**

Pan Am Clipper Jet, Japan, b/o, litho tin, 4 engines, wht & silver w/bl detail, 16½" W, G, A (Est: $75-$125) **$165.00**

Pan Am DC-7, Japan, b/o, litho tin, wht & bl w/silver wings, 24" W, G+IB, A (Est: $100-$200) **$385.00**

Pan American Airways NI023V Clipper, Gama, friction, lithographed tin, 15x20" wingspan, G, A (Est: $100.00 – $200.00), $190.00. (Photo courtesy Randy Inman Auctions)

Pan Am World Airways N7015Y Airliner, Y, 1950s, 4-prop, 9½", NMIB, A (Est: minimum $75) **$280.00**

Passenger Plane, w/up, litho tin, early top-wing w/1 prop, silver bl & red trim, 17" W, G, A (Est: $250-400) **$150.00**

Piston Action Plane (USAF), TN, b/o, litho tin, 1-prop, silver, pilot in domed cockpit, 12" W, EXIB, A (Est: $75-$125)..**$220.00**

Pure Oil NC-16113 Monoplane, Metalcraft, 1930s, PS, wht, 17" W, missing single prop, Fair+, A (Est: $300-$500) $715.00

Red Arrow Jet, Y, friction, litho tin, 10" L, EX, A (Est: minimum $85) $135.00

Seven Seas Douglas DC 7C, Daiya, litho tin, friction, 11½" W, EXIB, A (Est: minimum $150) $200.00

Sky Circus-SPAD III, b/o, litho tin & plastic biplane, 10½" W, EXIB, A $100.00

Sky Cruiser Two-Motored Transport Plane 50234, Marx, friction, litho tin w/2 plastic props, NMIB, A (Est: minimum $200) $350.00

Space Shuttle Columbia, Japan, b/o, tin & plastic, 10", NMIB, A (Est: $50-$100) $275.00

Spirit of Linemar Biplane, Linemar, 1950s, b/o, litho tin, 11" L, EX+ $150.00

Stunt Plane SPAD X-III, TPS, 1960s, b/o, litho tin & plastic, 10½" W, EXIB, A (Est: $75-$125) $85.00

Super Skyliner C-A/MTY, w/up, litho tin, yel w/red trim, 17" W, missing single prop o/w VG+, A (Est: $300-$500) ..$200.00

The Red Arrow, Henry Katz, 1930, litho tin, red fuselage w/yel top wing, tail & prop, 18" W, VG, A (Est: $100-$200) $245.00

Tiger X-15 Top Wing, Usagiya, friction, 1-prop, 7½" L, NMIB, A (Est: minimum $100) $140.00

Top Wing, Shieble, 1930s, pressed steel, 27" wingspan, G, A (Est: $300.00 – $500.00), $660.00. (Photo courtesy Randy Inman Auctions)

Top Wing, Wyandotte, 1940s, PS, 1-prop, blk & orange, 10" W, G, A (Est: $50-$75) $50.00

Top Wing, Wyandotte, 1940s, PS, 4-prop, wht body w/red wing, 9" W, EX, A (Est: $50-$75) $150.00

TV News Airplane, Taiyo, litho tin, friction, camerman turns, prop spins, 14" W, EXIB, A (Est: minimum $175) ..$350.00

TWA DC-7, Cragstan, b/o, litho tin, wht w/red & gray trim & gray wings, 24" W, Fair+, A (Est: $75-$125) $120.00

United Airlines DC-7, 1950s, friction, litho tin w/rubber tires, 4-prop, 11" W, NMIB, A (Est: minimum $150) $350.00

United Mainliner N 37530 (Air Plane Ways), Japan, friction, 4 props, 10" L, NM+IB, A $350.00

US Air Force FE-996 Fighter Jet (Lighted Jet Plane), b/o, litho tin, bump-&-go action, 12½" E, NMIB, A (Est: $225) $275.00

US Air Force Jet Plane, TN/Cragstan, 1950s, b/o, red/wht/bl tin, smoking taillight, w/39 punchout figures, 13" L, EXIB $250.00

US Army Bomber (Military Aeroplane), Marx, litho tin, w/up, gr w/wht lettering, 18" W, NM+IB, A (Est: minimum $175) $350.00

US Army 712, Marx, litho tin, w/up, red, wht & bl, dual wing machine guns, 8" W, VG+, A (Est: minimum $125) ..$150.00

USAF F-86 Jet Fighter, Nikko, 1950s, w/up, litho tin, red, wht & bl w/yel accent, 7½" L, EX, A (Est: minimum $95) $225.00

USAF FA 985 Starfire Jet, Y, 1950s, friction, litho tin, EXIB, A (Est: minimum $85) $125.00

USAF F60 Jet Fighter, 1950s, litho tin, friction, red, yel & gr, lithoed pilots, 5½" W, VG, A (Est: minimum $50) ...$50.00

USAF Night Fighter, Japan, friction, litho tin, 9" W, NM+IB, A (Est: minimum $150) $285.00

USAF Tornado North American B-45, Japan, 1960s, friction, litho tin, red, wht & silver, 16" W, EX+ $175.00

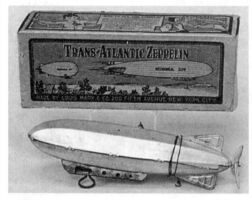

Zeppelin (Trans-Atlantic), Marx, wind-up, tin, 9½" long, VGIB, A (Est: $200.00 – $300.00). $465.00. (Photo courtesy Bertoia Auctions)

Banks

The impact of condition on the value of a bank cannot be overrated. Cast-iron banks in near-mint condition with very little paint wear and all original parts are seldom found and might bring twice as much (if the bank is especially rare, up to five times as much) as one in average, very good original condition with no restoration and no repairs. Overpainting and replacement parts (even screws) have a very negative effect on value. Mechanicals dominate the market, and some of the hard-to-find banks in outstanding, near-mint condition may exceed $20,000.00! (Here's a few examples: Girl Skipping Rope, Calamity, and Mikado.) Modern mechanical banks are also emerging on the collectibles market, including Book of Knowledge and James D. Capron, which are reproductions with full inscriptions stating that the piece is a replica of the original. Still banks are widely collected as well, with more than 3,000 varieties having been documented. Beware of unmarked modern reproductions. All of the banks listed are cast iron unless noted otherwise.

The following listings were compiled from various auctions with the estimates given in parenthesis.

For more information we recommend *The Dictionary of Still Banks* by Long and Pitman; *The Penny Bank Book* by Moore; *The Bank Book* by Norman; and *Penny Lane* by Davidson. For information on glass banks we recommend *Collector's Guide to Glass Banks* by Charles V. Reynolds.

Advisor: Dan Iannotti (I3), modern mechanicals

See also Advertising; Battery-Operated; Character, TV, and Movie Collectibles; Disney; Political; Reynolds Banks; Robots, Miscellaneous; Rock 'n Roll; other specific categories.

Key:
B of K — Book of Knowledge
J&ES — J&E Stevens
JH — John Harper
K&R — Kyser & Rex
SH — Shepard Hardware

MECHANICAL BANKS

Administration Building Columbian Exposition (Columbia Magic Savings Bank), Introduction Co, rpt, A (Est: $100-$200)..$100.00
Always Did 'Spise a Mule, B of K, NM, I3......................$175.00
Always Did 'Spise a Mule (Boy on Bench), J&ES, G, A (Est: $300-$400) $550.00
Always Did 'Spise a Mule (Jockey), J&ES, VG, A (Est: $500-$700)..$630.00
Artillery Bank, B of K, NM, I3......................................$225.00
Artillery Bank, J&ES, VG, A (Est: $600-$800) $660.00
Automatic Coin Savings Bank Building, Drop a Coin & I Will Tell Your Fortune emb on roof, VG, A (Est: $1,200-$1,500)..$1,100.00
Bad Accident, J&ES, VG, A (Est: $1,200-$1,500) $1,050.00
Bill E Grin, J&ES, old recast, A (Est: $300-$500)..........$825.00
Billy Goat, J&ES, rpt, A (Est: $600-$800) $500.00
Bird on Roof, J&ES, VG, A (Est: $500-$700).............$1,100.00
Bismark Bank, J&ES, blk, VG, A (Est: $1,200-$1,400) ..$935.00
Bismark Bank, J&ES, gray, VG, A (Est: $1,800-$2,200)...$1,430.00
Bobby Riggs & Billy Jean King, John Wright, limited edition of 250, scarce, M, I3..$800.00
Bowler's Strike, Richards/Wilton, scarce, NM, I3..........$600.00
Bowling Saving's Bank, b/o, 11" L, EXIB, A (Est: $50-$100) ..$135.00
Boy on Trapeze, B of K, M, I3......................................$300.00
Boy Robbing Bird's Nest, J&ES, EX, A (Est: $5,000-$6,000)...$6,600.00
Boy Scout Camp, J&ES, G+, A (Est: $4,000-$5,000)...$4,025.00
Boy Stealing Watermelon, K&R, VG, A (Est: $2,000-$2,600) $2,200.00
Buddy Bank, tin Buddy L leaning on glass jar, shake Buddy's left hand & right arm dumps coin, 4", EX, A (Est: $100-$200) $165.00

Boy on Trapeze, Barton & Smith, EX+, A (Est: $8,000.00 – $10,000.00), $24,000.00. (Photo courtesy Bertoia Auctions)

Bull Dog Bank, J&ES, bl collar & blanket, VG, A (Est: $500-$500)..$715.00
Bull Dog Standing, Judd, VG, A (Est: $500-$700).........$300.00
Butting Buffalo, B of K, M, I3......................................$200.00
Butting Buffalo, K&R, VG, A (Est: $2,000-$3,000) ..$2,200.00
Cabin Bank, J&ES, VG, A (Est: $300-$400) $450.00
Calumet Baking Powder Can, tin or cb, EX, A (Est: $100-$150) .$220.00
Cat & Mouse, B of K, NM, I3......................................$200.00
Cat & Mouse (Cat Balancing), J&ES, EX, A ($1,500-$2,000) $1,320.00
Cat & Mouse (Cat Standing), J&ES, VG, A (Est: $1,500-$1,800) $1,320.00
Cat Boat, Richards/Wilton, NM, I3.............................$700.00
Chief Big Moon, J&ES, EX, A (Est: $2,000-$2,500) ..$2,475.00
Cigar Smoker (Monica Lewinsky Bust), Sandman Designs, 1 of 50, unused, M, I3..$400.00
Clown (Arched Top), England, litho tin, EX, A (Est: $300-$400) $220.00
Clown Head, Chein, litho tin, VG, A (Est: $25-$50) $85.00
Clown on Globe, J&ES, EX, A (Est: $3,500-$4,500)..$4,025.00
Clown on Globe, J&ES, VG, A (Est: $2,000-$3,000)...$2,090.00
Cow (Kicking), B of K, NM, I3......................................$315.00
Creedmoor, B of K, M, I3......................................$250.00
Creedmore, J&ES, VG, A (Est: $300-$400) $385.00
Cresent Cash Register, J&ES (?), VG, A (Est: $300-$400) $330.00

Confectionary, Kyser & Rex, VG, A (Est: $3,000.00 – $4,000.00), $5,225.00. (Photo courtesy Bertoia Auctions)

Cross-Legged Minstrel (Automatic Negro), J Levy Co, VG, A $715.00
Cupola, J&ES, 1870s, rpt, A (Est: $2,000-$3,000)......$1,870.00
Dapper Dan, Marx, litho tin, VG, A (Est: $400-$600) ..$500.00
Darktown Battery, J&ES, VG, A (Est: $1,800-$2,200) ..$2,750.00
Dentist, B of K, EX, I3 ....$175.00
Dentist, J&ES, some rstr, A (Est: $5,000-$7,000) $4,655.00
Dinah, JH, G, A (Est: $250-$350) $360.00
Dog on Turntable, Judd, EX, A (Est: $300-$400) $400.00
Eagle & Eaglets, B of K, M, I3 ....$225.00
Eagle & Eaglets, J&ES, EX, A (Est: $700-$900)............$825.00
Elephant (Three Stars), VG, A (Est: $200-$300) $250.00
Elephant Howdah (Man Pops Out), Enterprise, VG, A (Est: $200-$300) $330.00
Elephant Howdah (Pull Tail), Enterprise Mfg, VG, A (Est: $300-$400) $500.00
Elephant Howdah (Pull Tail), Hubley, VG, A (Est: $200-$300)..$220.00
Elephant on Wheels (w/Tusks), K&R, VG, A (Est: $1,500-$2,000) $1,760.00

Ferris Wheel Bank, Hubley, VG, A (Est: $4,000.00 – $5,000.00), $7,150.00. (Photo courtesy Bertoia Auctions)

Football Bank, JH, VG, A (Est: $1,500-$1,800) $1,100.00
Fortune Teller Savings Bank, Baumgarten & Co, rpt, A (Est: $500-$600) $275.00
Fowler, J&ES, rstr, A (Est: $4,000-$6,000)..................$3,850.00
Frog Bank (Two Frogs), J&ES, G, A (Est: $300-$400) ...$500.00
Frog Bank (Two Frogs), J&ES, VG, A (Est: $500-$700) ..$825.00
Frog on Rock, Kilgore, G, A (Est: $200-$400) $420.00
Frog on Round Base (Lattice), J&ES, EX, A (Est: $500-$700) $700.00
Frog on Round Base (Lattice), J&ES, G, A (Est: $200-$400) $350.00
Frog on Stump, G, A (Est: $300-$600)..........................$485.00
Girl in Victorian Chair, recast, rpt, A (Est: $300-$500) ..$360.00
Girl Skipping Rope, J&ES, VG, A (Est: $12,000-$15,000) $15,400.00
Hall's Excelsior, J&ES, VG, A (Est: $300-$400) $300.00
Hall's Liliput, J&ES, VG, A (Est: $300-$400) $690.00
Hold the Fort (Five Holes), EX, A (Est: $2,500-$3,000) ..$3,850.00
Hole In One Bank, b/o, VGIB, A (Est: $50-$100) $115.00

Harold Lloyd, lithographed tin, EX, A (Est: $800.00 – $1,000.00), $2,750.00. (Photo courtesy Bertoia Auctions)

Home Bank (no dormer windows), J&ES, EX, A (Est: $3,500-$4,000) $5,775.00
Horse Race (Straight Base), J&E, VG, A (Est: $1,800-$2,200) $3,025.00
Humpty Dumpty, B of K, M, I3 ....$175.00
Humpty Dumpty, SH, G, A (Est: $400-$600) $440.00
Independence Hall Tower, Enterprise, VG, A (Est: $500-$700) $825.00
Indian Shooting Bear, J&E Stevens, VG, A (Est: $600-$800) $935.00

Initiating Bank (Second Degree), Mechanical Novelty Works, VG, A (Est: $5,000.00 – $7,000.00), $4,125.00. (Photo courtesy Bertoia Auctions)

Joe Socko, Straits Corp, VG, A (Est: $100-$150) $100.00
Jolly 'N,' JH, movable eyes, fixed ears, VG, A (Est: $100-$200)..$220.00
Jolly 'N,' JH, top hat, movable eyes, fixed ears, G, A (Est: $200-$300)..$330.00
Jolly 'N,' Starkie, aluminum, movable eyes & ears, VG, A (Est: $100-$200)..$165.00
Jolly 'N,' Starkie, aluminum, straw hat, movable eyes & ears, VG, A (Est: $200-$300)................................$300.00
Jolly 'N,' Sydenham & McOustra, movable eyes, fixed ears, pk lips, VG, A (Est: $200-$300) $275.00
Jonah & the Whale, B of K, M, I3 ....$175.00
Jumbo on Wheels, J&ES (?), G, A (Est: $500-$700) $360.00

Jonah and the Whale, Shepard Hardware, VG+, A (Est: $3,000.00 – $4,000.00), $3,565.00. (Photo courtesy Bertoia Auctions)

Kiltie Bank, JH, VG, A (Est: $800-$1,000) $715.00
Leap Frog, B of K, NM, I3 ....$335.00
Leap Frog, SH, EX, A (Est: $1,800-$2,200)...............$3,300.00
Leap Frog, SH, VG, A (Est: $1,200-$1,600) $1,980.00
Lion & Monkey (Double Peanut), K&R, G, A (Est: $400-$600)...$660.00
Lion & Monkey (Single Peanut), K&R, EX, A (Est: $1,000-$1,200)..$935.00
Lion & Two Monkeys, K&R, VG, A (Est: $800-$1,200) ..$990.00
Lucky Wheel Money Box, W&R Jacob & Co, litho tin, VG, A...$250.00
Magic Bank, J&ES, VG, A (Est: $400-$600) $660.00
Magician, B of K, MIB, I3 ....$325.00
Magician, J&ES, VG, A (Est: $3,000-$4,000) $4,320.00
Magie, Germany, litho tin, VG, A (Est: $1,500-$2,000) ..$2,475.00
Mama Katzenjammer, Kenton, 2nd casting, VG, A (Est: $300-$500)..$825.00
Memorial Money Box, Enterprise, rstr, A (Est: $250-$350)..$220.00
Mikado, K&R, rare, VG, A (Est: $15,000-$20,000) ..$16,500.00
Milking Cow, B of K, NM, I3 ....$175.00
Minstrel, Saalheimer & Strauss, litho tin, VG, A (Est: $300-$400)..$440.00
Monkey, James Capron, MIB..............................$200.00
Monkey & Coconut, J&ES, VG, A (Est: $1,200-$1,400)..$1,870.00
Monkey & Parrot, Saalheimer & Strauss (?), litho tin, VG, A (Est: $200-$300) $220.00
Monkey Bank, Hubley, VG, A (Est: $200-$300)............$220.00
Monkey Tips Hat (Bank/Thank You), Chein, litho tin, EX, A (Est: $40-50)..$100.00
Monkey w/Tray, Germany, litho tin, G (Est: $100-$200) ..$85.00
Mule Entering Barn, J&ES, VG, A (Est: $500-$700).....$770.00
New Bank, J&ES, VG, A (Est: $400-$600).................$1,320.00
Novelty Bank, J&ES, VG, A (Est: $600-$800) $715.00
Octagonal Fort Bank, G, A (Est: $1,800-$2,200)........$2,090.00
Organ Bank (Boy & Girl), B of K, NM, I3 ....$200.00
Organ Bank (Boy & Girl), K&R, VG, A (Est: $800-$1,200) $1,540.00
Organ Bank (Cat & Dog), K&R, EX, A (Est: $1,200-$1,500)..$1,760.00
Organ Bank (Medium w/Monkey), K&R, VG, A (Est: $300-$400)..$330.00
Organ Bank (Miniature w/Monkey), K&R, VG, A (Est: $500-$700)..$440.00

Owl (Slot in Book), B of K, NM, I3 ....$175.00
Owl (Slot in Book), Kilgore, VG, A (Est: $175-$250)...$385.00
Owl (Turns Head), J&ES, EX, A (Est: $600-$800) $660.00
Paddy & the Pig, B of K, NM, I3.........................$200.00
Paddy & the Pig, J&ES, VG, A (Est: $1,300-$1,500) ..$1,320.00
Pay Phone Bank, J&ES, VG, A (Est: $800-$1,000) $1,200.00
Penny Pineapple (Hawaii 50th State), EX+, A (Est: $100-$200) $275.00
Pig (Slot in Back), Fair, A (Est: $100-$200)...................$360.00
Pig in Highchair, J&ES, VG, A (EST: $250-$500) $430.00
Popeye Knockout Bank, Straits Mfg, litho tin, EX+, A (Est: $600-$800)...$715.00
Professor Pug Frog, J&ES, rpt, A (Est: $1,500-$2,500)..$1,870.00
Professor Pug Frog, J&ES, VG, A (Est: $4,000-$5,000)...$4,485.00
Punch & Judy, B of K, NM, I3............................$175.00
Punch & Judy, SH, VG, A (Est: $1,000-$1,500).........$1,150.00
Punch & Judy/One Penny, Harry James Banks & Sons, CI & tin, EX, A (Est: $3,000-$4,000)..................................$4,125.00
Rabbit in Cabbage, Kilgore, VG, A (Est: $300-$400) $330.00

Red Riding Hood, J&E Stevens, VG+, A (Est: $20,000.00 – $25,000.00), $38,500.00. (Photo courtesy Bertoia Auctions)

Robot (The), Starkie, 9", VG, A (Est: $4,000-$5,000) $4,600.00
Rooster, K&R, VG, A (Est: $300-$600) $450.00
Safety Locomotive, VG, A (Est: $250-$350)..................$330.00
Santa Claus (Standing at Chimney), SH, VG, A (Est: $800-$1,000)...$935.00
Scotchman, Saalheimer & Strauss, 1930s, litho tin, EX, A (Est: $500-$700) $600.00
Sentry, Saalheimer & Strauss, litho tin, VG, A (Est: $600-$800)..$935.00
Shoot the Chute, J&ES, second casting, A (Est: $4,000-$6,000)..$5,500.00
Snap It Building (8-sided), Judd, EX, A (Est: $300-$400) ..$250.00
Speaking Dog, J&ES, rnd trap, EX, A (Est: $2,500-$3,000)...$3,025.00
Speaking Dog, JH (English), rectangular trap, VG, A (Est: $800-$1,000)...$1,035.00
Speaking Dog, SH, VG, A (Est: $400-$600) $660.00
Squirrel & Tree Stump, Mechanical Novelty Works, VG, A (Est: $250-$350) $600.00
Stollworck's Victoria Vending Bank (A Penny Saved..), Stollworck, litho tin/glass, 1-penny, 7", EX, A (Est: $800-$1,000) ..$500.00

Stollworck's Victoria Vending Bank (Cherub in Window), Stollwork, litho tin/glass, 2-penny, 7", VG, A (Est: $100-$150) $275.00

Stump Speaker, SH, G, A (Est: $700-$900) $1,200.00

Tabby, Fair, A (Est: $200-$300) $250.00

Tammany Bank, B of K, NMIB, I3 ....$200.00

Tammany Bank, J&ES, EX, A (Est: $1,000-$1,200) ...$1,320.00

Tammany Bank, J&ES, G, A (Est: $250-$450) $375.00

Tank & Cannon, Starkie, EX, A (Est: $1,000-$1,200)...$935.00

Teddy & the Bear, B of K, NM, I3..............................$300.00

Teddy and the Bear, J&E Stevens, VG, A (Est: $800.00 – $1,000.00), $715.00. (Photo courtesy Bertoia Auctions)

Thrifty Animal Bank, Buddy L, litho tin, Fair, A (Est: $250-$350)..$440.00

Toad on Stump, J&ES, Fair, A (Est: $200-$300) $440.00

Treasure Chest Music Bank, Faith Mfg, 1930s, EX, A (Est: $600-$800)..$880.00

Trick Dog, Hubley, solid base, VG, A (Est: $200-$300)....$385.00

Trick Dog, Hubley, 6-part base, EX, A (Est: $1,000-$1,200)....$715.00

Trick Pony, B of K, NM, I3 ....$350.00

Trick Pony, SH, VG, A (Est: $800-$1,200) $800.00

Trick Savings Bank, Chas Toliner, wood, EX, A (Est: $100-$200)..$135.00

Try Your Weight Scale, Germany, litho tin, Fair, A (Est: $200-$300)..$110.00

Two Ducks, rpt, A (Est: $1,200-$1,500) $1,050.00

Uncle Remus, B of K, M, I3 ....$200.00

Uncle Sam, Richards/Wilton, rear trap, scarce, NM, I3 ..$450.00

Uncle Sam, SH, VG, A (Est: $1,500-$2,000) $1,665.00

Uncle Tom (Star/No Lapels), K&R, VG, A (Est: $400-$600)...$880.00

United States Bank, J&ES, EX+, A (Est: $2,500-$3,000) ..$7,150.00

US & Spain, B of K, M, I3 ....$175.00

Vending Bank, see Stollworck's Victoria Vending Bank

Watch Dog Safe, J&ES, EX, A (Est: $300-$500).............$500.00

William Tell, B of K, M, I3..$200.00

William Tell, J&ES, VG, A (Est: $400-$600) $465.00

Wireless Bank, John Hugo Mfg, VG, A (Est: $100-$200) ..$250.00

World's Banker (The), Germany, Fair, A (Est: $1,000-$1,500) $1,050.00

World's Fair Bank, J&ES, VG, A (Est: $500-$700) $715.00

REGISTERING BANKS

Bean Pot, CI, 3", EX..$250.00

Beehive Registering Savings Bank, NP CI, 5½", EX......$275.00

Ben Franklin Trift Bank, litho tin, 4", VG, A (Est: $50-$100) ..$45.00

Dandy Self-Registering Savings Bank, tin, 5", NM $350.00

Dime Register (Barrel), Kyser & Rex, 4", EX+, A (Est: $200.00 – $300.00), $245.00. (Photo courtesy Bertoia Auctions)

Donald Duck Bank, Marx, litho tin, 4", EX....................$350.00

Dopey Dime Register, litho tin, Disney, 1938, VG+.........$75.00

Liberty Penny Bank, litho tin, rnd w/image of Abe Lincoln on yel background, 5½" dia, VG, A (Est: $50-$100)......$45.00

Mickey Mouse Dime Register, WDE 1939, EX $300.00

Penny Saver, CI, 5", VG...$80.00

Popeye Daily Dime Bank, KFS, litho metal, VG $80.00

Snow White & the Seven Dwarfs Dime Register, litho tin, 2½" sq, VG, A (Est: $100)..$225.00

Superman, litho tin, 1940s, 2½" sq, EX+.......................$200.00

Watch Your Savings Grow, Golliwog & friends, litho tin, EX+..$275.00

STILL BANKS

Andy Gump Seated Reading Newspaper, mc pnt, 4½", EX, A (Est: $1,200-$1,400)..$935.00

Andy Gump Standing on Either Side of Money Box w/Money Bag on Top, General Thrift, lead, 6", EX, A (Est: $500-$600)..$220.00

Arcade Steamboat, silver pnt, 2 coin slots on top, 2 working spoke wheels, 7½" L, VG, A (Est: $100-$150)........$110.00

Baby in Egg (aka Doll's Head Bank), flesh-toned baby in blk-pnt egg, EX (Est: $200-$300)..$330.00

Bank Building (Copula), BANK emb above door w/steps flanked by windows, wht, red & bl, 3", EX, A (Est: $75-$125) $600.00

Barrel of Fun Bank, wht metal, children emb on front, children emb on front of barrel, 3½", EX, A (Est: $50-$75)..$110.00

Battleship Maine, J&ES, 10½", EX+ (Est: $2,500-$3,000) ..$7,150.00

Battleship Oregon, J&ES, japanned w/gold detail, 5", VG, A (Est: $100-$200)..$300.00

Bear Standing w/Right Foot Forward, Hubley, brn, 6¼", EX, A (Est: $150-$250)..$220.00

Bear Stealing Pig, gold w/red detail, 5½", VG, A (Est: $800-$1,000)..$825.00

Black Boy Bust (Two-Faced), AC Williams, blk face w/gold hat & shoulders, lg, EX, A (Est: $150-$200)..................$165.00

Black Boy Bust (Two-Faced), AC Williams, blk face w/gold hat & shoulders, silver collar, sm, EX, A (Est: $75-$125) $100.00

Building & Dog on 4-Footed Platform, japanned, 5½", EX, A (Est: $150-$250) $795.00

Bulldog w/Collar Sitting Upright, AC Williams, 4½", EX, A (Est: $75 to $125)......................................$110.00

Buster Brown & Tige Good Luck Bank, Arcade, Buster & Tige w/horse encircled by horseshoe, 5", EX, A (Est: $175-$225) $300.00

Buster Brown Standing Next to Seated Tige, AC Williams, gold w/red detail, 6", VG, A (Est: $75-$125) $165.00

Calumet Baking Powder, tin can w/paper label, 5½", EX, A (Est: $75-$125)..$88.00

Camel, AC Williams, gold w/red & brn detail, emb moon & stars on blanket, 7¼", EX, A (Est: $300-$400)........$300.00

Campbell's Soup Kids, AC Williams, figures joined & walking in wide stride, gold pnt, 3x4", EX, A (Est: $200-$300)..$165.00

Captain Kidd Stanging by Tree Truck w/Shovel, US, mc pnt, 5x4", VG, A (Est: $250-$350) $250.00

Castle With Two Towers, John Harper, japanned, 7", VG, A (Est: $400.00 – $600.00), $825.00. (Photo couresy Bertoia Auctions)

Cat Crouching w/Ball, AC Williams, 1905, 5½", Fair, A (Est: $50-$75) $140.00

Cat Crouching w/Ball, AC Williams, 5½", VG, A (Est: $200-$300)...$275.00

City Bank Building, England, emb name above arched door & 2 windows, steps lead to door, 4", VG, A (Est: $200-$250)..$135.00

Clown w/Pointed Hat Standing, AC Williams, gold or silver w/red trim, 6", VG, A (Est: $100-$150)..................$190.00

Coffee Money Coffee Mill, pnt ceramic mill w/2 CI wheels, wht, 6", VG, A (Est: $50-$100)......................................$55.00

Columbia Tower, Grey Iron, japanned, 7", rpt, A (Est: $200-$300)...$275.00

Counting House (Federal Trust Vaults), footed sq building w/clock, gold-pnt highlights, 6", EX, A (Est: $500-$800) $1,150.00

Cow, Arcade, wht w/blk spots, 2½x4½" L, EX, A (Est: $250-$350)...$355.00

Deposit (Large Print) Bank Building, Grey Iron, japanned, 4¼", VG, A (Est: $75-$125).......................................$135.00

Dog w/Neck Bow & Bee (Puppo Bank), Hubley, 1920s, 5", VG, A (Est: $75-$125) $60.00

Dogpatch USA, Capp Ent, set of 4 w/Li'l Abner, Pappy, Mammy & Daisy Mae, pnt ceramic, 7¼", EX+, A (Est: $400-$600)...$220.00

Donkey w/Hinged Saddle, pnt wht metal w/advertising, 4", VG, A (Est: $50-$75) $55.00

Doughboy Standing, Grey Iron, ca 1919, brn uniform, brimmed hat, 7", EX, A (Est: $400-$500) $275.00

Duck, AC Williams, 1920s, gold or silver, 5", G, A (Est: $50-$75)...$88.00

Duck, yel w/red top of head & bill, eyes looking up, 4", VG, A (Est: $175-$225) $275.00

Elephant (Circus) Sitting Upright w/Bobbing Head, sm yel hat, ruffled collar, red dots, 5" L, G, A (Est: $75-$125) $55.00

Elephant w/Howdah (Swinging Trunk), AC Williams, bronze tone, 5x7", VG, A (Est: $50-$100) $65.00

Ford Model T Touring Car w/Driver, Arcade, 6½", rpt, A (Est: $100-$200) $385.00

Foxy Grandpa Standing w/Hands in Pockets, Hubley, brn, 5", EX, A (Est: $300-$400) $165.00

Gas Pump, US, red w/gold globe, 5¾", VG, A (Est: $200-$300) $220.00

General Sheridan on Rearing Horse, Arcade, gold, 6", VG, A (Est: $200-$300)...$330.00

Give Me a Penny (Sharecropper), Wing/Hubley, blk pants w/red shirt, toes show on 1 foot, 5½", VG, A (Est: $250-$350) $330.00

Globe, Grey Iron, globe spins on base, red, 5¼", A (Est: $100-$200)...$165.00

Golliwog Standing w/Hands on Tummy, JH, mc pnt, 6", VG, A (Est: $200-$300)...$355.00

Grand Father's Clock, England, very rare, 5½", EX, A (Est: $500-$700)...$1,045.00

House With Bay Windows, rare version painted yellow with green dormers and tan roof, 5", EX, A (Est: $2,500.00 – $3,000.00), $3,850.00. (Photo courtesy Bertoia Auctions)

Home Savings Bank Building w/Dog Finial, J&ES, japanned w/gold trim, 6¼", VG, A (Est: $150-$200) $165.00

Horse (Circus) w/Front Feet on Tub, AC Williams, blk w/orange blanket, 5½", EX (Est: $100-$150) $165.00

House (Two-Story), AC Williams, silver & gold w/red or gr roof, 4", VG, A (Est: $100-$175)..............................$88.00

House w/Porch, Grey Iron, cast porch w/2 figures at front door, 2 chimneys, 4", EX, A (Est: $250-$350) $500.00

Indian Scout w/Tomahawk, mc pnt, 6", EX, A (Est: $200-$300) $355.00

Jitney Bank, litho tin, 5", Fair, A (Est: $150-$250) $220.00

Junior Cash (Register), J&ES, NP, 5", EX+, A (Est: $300-$400) $250.00

Kitten w/Neck Bow Sitting Upright, pnt CI, wht w/bl bow, 5", Fair, A (Est: $50-$75) $45.00

Liberty Bell (1905), JH, electoplated copper, 3¾", EX, A (Est: $100-$200) $165.00

Liberty Bell w/George Washington, emb image, red w/gold trim, 3", VG, A (Est: $50-$100)..............................$65.00

Lion on Circus Tub w/Rope in Mouth, AC Williams, 1934, pnt CI, gold w/red rope, blue tub, 5½", G, A (Est: $75-$125)..$88.00

Log Cabin (Lincoln), Kyser & Rex, 4" T, VG, A (Est: $800.00 – $1,000.00), $1,200.00. (Photo courtesy Bertoia Auctions)

Mail Box (US Mail), AC Williams, pnt CI w/steel back, red, gr or blk w/gold trim, 5", VG, A (Est: $75-$125)...........$88.00

Mail Box (US Mail/Letters), Hubley, gr w/gold trim, movable coin drop, 4", EX+, A (Est: $75-$125).....................$130.00

Mammy w/Spoon (Aunt Jemima), AC Williams, bl dress w/silver apron, red bandanna, 5", EX, A (Est: $200-$300) $330.00

Mickey Mouse, France, aluminum figure standing w/hands on hips, blk w/red shorts, Fair, A (Est: $300-$400) $500.00

Money Bag (100,000), silver pnt w/gold trim, 3½", VG, A (Est: $250-$350) $190.00

Money Bag (200,000), rare version, 3½", VG, A (Est: $400-$500)..$520.00

Mutt & Jeff (One Standing & One Seated), AC Williams, gold pnt, 5¼x3¼", VG, A (Est: $75-$125) $75.00

Padlock, Wyandotte, plastic, w/combination dial, 9", EX, A (Est: $50-$100)..$25.00

Pass 'Round the Hat (Derby Hat), brn w/gold trim, EX+, A (Est: $250-$300)..$440.00

Pay-Phone Bank, J&ES, NP, early wall-type, insert coin & turn crank & bell rings, no sz given, VG, A (Est: $350-$450) $525.00

Penny Basket, ca 1902, 3" T, G, A (Est: $50-$100)........$190.00

Pig W/Neck Bow Seated, Shimmer Toy Co, NP, 5" L, G, A (Est: $150-$250) $165.00

Policeman Standing w/Arms at Sides, Arcade, 1920s, bl dbl-breasted coat w/gold trim, 5½", VG, A (Est: $200-$300) $520.00

Possum, Arcade, gold, 2⅜x4⅜", G, A (Est: $150-$200) ..$300.00

Puppo Bank, see Dog w/Neck Bow & Bee

Rhinoceros, Arcade, blk w/gold horn & pnt features, 2⅝x5", VG, A (Est: $200-$300)................................$355.00

Riverboat (Side-Wheeler), pnt CI, 7½", P, A (Est: $75-$175) $700.00

Roper Stove, Arcade, wht-pnt CI & sheet metal, burner covers lift up, 3¾x3¾", EX, A (Est: $175-$250) $190.00

Safe (Security Bank), japanned w/gold trim, lettering on lock, 5", EX, A (Est: $75-$125) $140.00

Safe (Security Safe Deposit), 6", EX, A (Est: $125.00 – $175.00), $220.00. (Photo courtesy Randy Inman Auctions)

Safe (The Globe), silver-tone globe on legs w/emb lettering on door, 5", VG, A (Est: $125-$175) $715.00

Safe (White City Puzzle Safe No 10), CI, japanned, 4", VG, A (Est: $50-$100)..$110.00

Santa, figure in hooded robe w/hands together in front, P, A (Est: $50-$75) $130.00

Save & Smile Money Box, England, man's head in hat w/feet, but no body, mc pnt, 4", EX, A (Est: $200-$300) $245.00

Save for a Rainy Day (Duck on Tub), wht w/blk top hat & umbrella tucked under wing, red tub, 6", EX, A (Est: $200-$250)..$220.00

Sharecropper, AC Williams, blk pants, gold shirt w/red trim, toes show on 1 foot, 5½", EX+, A (Est: $200-$300) $275.00

Sharecropper, see also Give Me a Penny

Skyscraper (6 Posts), AC Williams, silver w/gold roof & posts, 6½", EX, A (Est: $500-$700) $300.00

Soldier (Early) Standing w/Rifle, Hubley, brn w/gold trim, 6", EX, A (Est: $300-$400)................................$330.00

State Bank Building, Kenton, japanned, VG, A (Est: $100-$200)..$190.00

Statue of Liberty, Kenton, silver w/gold accents, 10", VG, A
(Est: $400-$500) $700.00
Stollwerk's Chocolade Sparbuchse, Germany, ca 1908, litho tin
building, 3¼" W, EX, A (Est: $50-$100) $165.00
Stove (Parlor), blk w/nickel finish, 7", EX, A (Est: $150-$250).$385.00
Teddy (Roosevelt) Bust, AC Williams, gold w/silver glasses, 5",
EX, A (Est: $150-$250) $355.00

Tower Bank 1891, Kyser & Rex, 7", EX, A (Est: $2,000.00 – $2,500.00), $3,025.00. (Photo courtesy Bertoia Auctions)

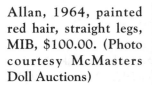

Turkey, AC Williams, japanned w/red detail on head, 4" EX, A
(Est: $250-$350) $300.00
US Bank Mailbox on Pedestal w/Eagle Finial, late 1800s, maroon
w/gold eagle, 9¼", EX, A (Est: $1,400-$1,800) $1,540.00
Wise Monkeys (See/Hear/Speak No Evil), gold pnt, 3x3½", VG,
A (Est: $150-$200) $165.00

Barbie and Friends

Barbie was first introduced in 1959, and since then her face has changed three times. She's been blond and brunette; her hair has been restyled over and over, and it has varied in length from above her shoulders to the tips of her toes. She's worn high-fashion designer clothing and pedal pushers. She's been everything from an astronaut to a veterinarian, and no matter what her changing lifestyle required, Mattel (her 'maker') has provided it for her.

Though Barbie items from recent years are bought and sold with fervor, those made before 1970 are the most sought after. You'll need to do a lot of studying and comparisons to learn to distinguish one Barbie from another, but it will pay off in terms of making wise investments. There are several books available; we recommend them all: *The Story of Barbie, Second Edition*, by Kiturah B. Westenhouser; *Barbie Doll Fashion, Vol. 1, 1959 – 1967, Vol. II, 1968 – 1974, Vol. II, 1975 – 1979*, by Sarah Sink Eames; *Barbie, The First 30 Years, 1959 Through 1989, 2nd Edition*, by Stefanie Deutsch; *Collector's Encyclopedia of Barbie Doll Exclusives* and *Collector's Encyclopedia of Barbie Doll Collector's Editions*, by J. Michael Augustyniak; and *The Barbie Years*, by

Patrick C. and Joyce L. Olds (all published by Collector Books).

As a general rule, a mint-in-box doll is worth about twice as much as a mint doll with no box. The same doll, played with and in only good condition, is worh half as much (or even less). Never-removed-from box examples sell at a premium.

See also Advertising Signs, Ads, and Displays.

DOLLS

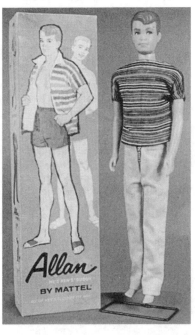

Allan, 1964, painted red hair, straight legs, MIB, $100.00. (Photo courtesy McMasters Doll Auctions)

Allan, 1965, bendable legs, MIB $300.00
Barbie, #1, 1958-59, blond or brunette hair, MIB, ea from $5,250
to...$5,775.00
Barbie, #2, 1959, blond or brunette hair, MIB, ea from $5,250
to $6,800.00
Barbie, #3, 1960, blond or brunette hair, MIB, ea from $925
to $1,025.00
Barbie, #4, 1960, blond or brunette hair, MIB, ea from $425
to...$450.00
Barbie, #5, 1961, blond hair, MIB, from $375 to $425.00
Barbie, #5, 1961, red hair, orig swimsuit, NM................$375.00
Barbie, #6, blond, brunette or titian, MIB, ea................$425.00
Barbie, American Airline Stewardess, 1963, NRFB.......$700.00
Barbie, American Girl, 1964, blond, brn, or brunette hair,
NRFB, ea $1,500.00
Barbie, American Girl, 1964, platinum cheek-length hair, orig
swimsuit, NM...$650.00
Barbie, American Girl, 1964, red hair, replica swimsuit,
NM...$600.00
Barbie, Angel Lights, 1993, NRFB................................$100.00
Barbie, Angel of Peace (White or Black), 1999, Timeless Senti-
ments, NRFB $50.00
Barbie, Arctic, 1996, Dolls of the World, NRFB $25.00
Barbie, Army Desert Storm (Black or White), 1993, Stars &
Stripes, NRFB, ea..$30.00
Barbie, Autumn in London, 1999, City Season Collection,
NRFB $45.00

Barbie, Avon Representative (White or Hispanic), 1999, NRFB, ea $50.00

Barbie, Ballerina Barbie on Tour, 1976, NRFB $125.00

Barbie, Barbie Celebration, 1987, NRFB $30.00

Barbie, Barbie Sign Language (Black or White), 1999, NRFB, ea $20.00

Barbie, Bay Watch (Black or White), 1995, NRFB, ea.....$20.00

Barbie, Brazilian, 1989, Dolls of the World, NRFB...........$75.00

Barbie, Bubble-Cut, 1962, blond or brunette hair, MIB, ea..$250.00

Barbie, Bubble-Cut, 1962-64, side part, any hair color, MIB, ea $950.00

Barbie, Busy Talking Barbie, 1972, MIB, $200.00. (Photo courtesy McMasters Doll Auctions)

Barbie, Calvin Klein, 1996, Bloomingdale's, NRFB..........$40.00

Barbie, Celebration Cake Barbie (any), 1999, NRFB, ea...$20.00

Barbie, Children's Doctor, 2000, NRFB $20.00

Barbie, Chinese, 1993, Dolls of the World, NRFB............$30.00

Barbie, Color-Magic, 1966, blond hair, MIB $1,200.00

Barbie, Color-Magic, 1966, brunette, MIB $2,500.00

Barbie, Cool Times, 1989, NRFB $25.00

Barbie, Cut & Style (any), 1995, NRFB, ea.....................$20.00

Barbie, Dorothy (Wizard of Oz), 1994, Hollywood Legends Series, NRFB $350.00

Barbie, Dramatic New Living, 1970, MIB........................$225.00

Barbie, Dream Glow (Black), 1986, MIB..........................$30.00

Barbie, Dream Glow (Hispanic), 1986, MIB....................$40.00

Barbie, Dream Glow (White), 1986, MIB.........................$35.00

Barbie, Dutch, 1994, Dolls of the World, MIB..................$35.00

Barbie, Easter Party, 1995, NRFB $20.00

Barbie, Elizabethan, 1994, Great Eras, MIB $50.00

Barbie, Enchanted Evening, 1991, JC Penney, NRFB $50.00

Barbie, Enchanted Princess, 1993, Sears, NRFB..............$75.00

Barbie, Eskimo, 1982, Dolls of the World, NRFB.............$65.00

Barbie, Evening Sparkle, 1990, Hill's, NRFB...................$35.00

Barbie, Fabulous Fur, 1986, NRFB..................................$65.00

Barbie, Fantastica, 1992, MIB $55.00

Barbie, Fantasy Goddess of Asia, 1998, Bob Mackie, NRFB...$150.00

Barbie, Feelin' Groovy, 1987, NRFB...............................$175.00

Barbie, Fire Fighter, 1995, Toys R Us, NRFB...................$50.00

Barbie, Flower Seller (My Fair Lady), 1995, Hollywood Legend Series, NRFB..$70.00

Barbie, Fountain Mermaid (Black or White), 1993, NRFB, ea $20.00

Barbie, French Lady, 1997, Great Eras Collection, NRFB ..$50.00

Barbie, Gap Barbie (Black or White), 1996, Gap Stores, NRFB, ea $65.00

Barbie, Glinda (Wizard of Oz), 2000, NRFB....................$25.00

Barbie, Goddess of the Sun, 1995, Bob Mackie, NRFB..$175.00

Barbie, Gold Medal Skater or Skier, 1975, NRFB, ea $75.00

Barbie, Grand Premier, 1997, Barbie Collectors Club, NRFB...$225.00

Barbie, Great Shapes (w/Walkman), 1984, NRFB............$30.00

Barbie, Great Shapes (White or Black), 1984, NRFB $25.00

Barbie, Growin' Pretty Hair, 1971, NRFB........................$475.00

Barbie, Hawaiian Superstar, 1977, MIB $75.00

Barbie, Holiday, 1988, NRFB, minimum value...............$500.00

Barbie, Holiday, 1989, NRFB $250.00

Barbie, Holiday, 1990, NRFB $200.00

Barbie, Holiday, 1991, NRFB $200.00

Barbie, Holiday, 1992, NRFB $150.00

Barbie, Holiday, 1993, NRFB $175.00

Barbie, Holiday, 1994, NRFB $150.00

Barbie, Holiday, 1995, NRFB $75.00

Barbie, Holiday, 1996, NRFB $50.00

Barbie, Holiday, 1997, NRFB $35.00

Barbie, Holiday, 1998, NRFB $25.00

Barbie, Indiana, 1998, University Barbie, NRFB..............$15.00

Barbie, Island Fun, 1988, NRFB......................................$20.00

Barbie, Jamaican, 1992, Dolls of the World, NRFB..........$50.00

Barbie, Jewel Essence, 1996, Bob Mackie, NRFB $125.00

Barbie, Kellogg Quick Curl, 1974, Kellogg Co, NRFB $60.00

Barbie, Kenyan, 1994, Dolls of the World, NRFB $40.00

Barbie, Knitting Pretty (pk), 1964, NRFB...................$1,265.00

Barbie, Knitting Pretty (royal bl), 1965, NRFB.............$635.00

Barbie, Lights 'N Lace, 1991, NRFB $25.00

Barbie, Lily, 1997, FAO Schwarz, NRFB $150.00

Barbie, Live Action on Stage, 1970, MIB, $225.00. (Photo courtesy McMaster's Auctions)

Barbie, Malibu (Sunset), 1971, NRFB $65.00

Barbie, Malt Shop, 1993, Toys R Us, NRFB $30.00

Barbie, Medieval Lady, 1995, Great Eras Collection, NRFB.$60.00

Barbie, Miss America, 1972, Kellogg Co, NRFB $175.00

Barbie, Moon Goddess, 1996, Bob Mackie, NRFB.........$175.00

Barbie, Moonlight Magic, 1993, Toys R Us, NRFB $75.00

Barbie, My First Barbie, 1981, NRFB $25.00

Barbie, NASCAR 50th Anniversary, 1998, NRFB...........$25.00

Barbie, Native American #2, 1994, Dolls of the World, NRFB $40.00

Barbie, Nifty Fifties, 2000, Great Fashions of the 20th Century, NRFB $50.00

Barbie, Nutcracker, 1992, Musical Ballet Series, NRFB ..$150.00

Barbie, Opening Night, 1993, Classique Collection, NRFB...$75.00

Barbie, Oreo Fun, 1997, NRFB.............................$35.00

Barbie, Paleontologist, 1997, Toys R Us, NRFB $25.00

Barbie, Party in Pink, 1991, Ames, NRFB $25.00

Barbie, Party Sensation, 1990, NRFB.........................$55.00

Barbie, Peach Blossom, 1992, NRFB.........................$40.00

Barbie, Peach Pretty, 1989, K-Mart, MIB.....................$35.00

Barbie, Peaches 'N Cream, 1985, MIB $35.00

Barbie, Pepsi Spirit, 1989, Toys R Us, NRFB $75.00

Barbie, Perfume Party, 1988, NRFB.........................$30.00

Barbie, Phantom of the Opera, 1998, FAO Schwarz, NRFB ..$125.00

Barbie, Picnic Party, 1992, Osco, NRFB $30.00

Barbie, Pilgrim, 1995, American Stories Collection, NRFB...$20.00

Barbie, Pink & Pretty, 1982, MIB.............................$60.00

Barbie, Pink Sensation, 1990, Winn Dixie, NRFB $25.00

Barbie, Pioneer, 1995 or 1996, American Stories Collection, NRFB, ea...$20.00

Barbie, Police Officer (White or Black), 1993, Toys R Us, NRFB...$75.00

Barbie, Polly Pockets, 1994, Hill's, NRFB.....................$30.00

Barbie, Portrait in Blue (White or Black), 1998, Wal-Mart, NRFB $25.00

Barbie, Pretty Hearts, 1991, MIB $25.00

Barbie, Queen of Hearts, 1994, Bob Mackie, NRFB.......$250.00

Barbie, Queen of Sapphires, 2000, Royal Jewels, NRFB..$125.00

Barbie, Quick Curl (DeLuxe), 1976, Jergens, NRFB $100.00

Barbie, Quick Curl Miss America, 1974, MIB $80.00

Barbie, Rising Star Barbie, 1998, Grand Old Opry, NRFB .$75.00

Barbie, Rockettes, 1993, FAO Schwarz, NRFB $120.00

Barbie, Romantic Wedding 2001, 2000, Bridal Collection, NRFB $50.00

Barbie, Russian, 1988, Dolls of the World, NRFB $35.00

Barbie, Safari, 1983, Disney, MIB.............................$25.00

Barbie, Sapphire Sophisticate, 1997, Toys R Us, NRFB ...$30.00

Barbie, Savvy Shopper, 1994, Bloomingdale's, NRFB $50.00

Barbie, School Spirit Barbie, 1993, Toys R Us, NRFB......$30.00

Barbie, Scottish, 1981, Dolls of the World, NRFB............$80.00

Barbie, Sea Princess, 1996, Service Merchandise, NRFB ..$45.00

Barbie, Sentimental Valentine, 1997, Hallmark, NRFB...$30.00

Barbie, Serenade in Satin, 1997, Barbie Couture Collection, MIB...$100.00

Barbie, Sheer Illusion #1 or #2, 1998, Designer Collection, NRFB, ea...$80.00

Barbie, Snap 'N Play, 1992, NRFB $20.00

Barbie, Snow Princess, 1994, Enchanted Seasons, blond hair, NRFB $130.00

Barbie, Snow Princess, 1994, Mattel Festival, brunette hair, NRFB $1,100.00

Barbie, Snow White, 1999, Children's Collector Series, NRFB $40.00

Barbie, Something Extra, 1992, Meijer, NRFB $25.00

Barbie, Songbird, 1996, NRFB $25.00

Barbie, Southern Beauty, 1991, Winn Dixie, NRFB.........$30.00

Barbie, Southern Belle, 1994, Great Eras Collection, NRFB...$75.00

Barbie, Sports Star, 1979, NRFB.............................$25.00

Barbie, Standard, 1967, any hair color, MIB, ea $475.00

Barbie, Starlight Dance, 1996, Classique Collection, NRFB...$45.00

Barbie, Steppin' Out Barbie 1930s, 1999, Great Fashions of the 20th Century, NRFB...$55.00

Barbie, Strawberry Sorbet, 1999, Avon, NRFB, $25.00. (Photo courtesy J. Michael Augustyniak)

Barbie, Sugar Plum Fairy, 1997, Classic Ballet Series, NRFB...$30.00

Barbie, Swan Lake Ballerina, 1991, NRFB $200.00

Barbie, Swirl Ponytail, 1964, blond or brunette hair, NRFB, ea $650.00

Barbie, Swirl Ponytail, 1964, brunette, NRFB $650.00

Barbie, Swirl Ponytail, 1964, platinum hair, NRFB.....$1,300.00

Barbie, Talking, 1968, blond, brunette or red hair, NRFB, ea...$400.00

Barbie, Talking, 1970, blond, brunette or red hair, NRFB...$300.00

Barbie, Ten Speeder, 1973, NRFB.............................$30.00

Barbie, Thailand, 1998, Dolls of the World, NRFB.........$25.00

Barbie, Theatre Date, 1964, NRFB $660.00

Barbie, Twirly Curls, 1983, MIB.............................$45.00

Barbie, Twist 'N Turn, 1966, blond hair, MIB.................$600.00

Barbie, Twist 'N Turn, 1967, long straight red hair w/bangs, MIB $600.00

Barbie, Twist 'N Turn, 1969, flipped hairdo, blond or brunette, NRFB, ea $475.00

Barbie, Twist 'N Turn, 1971, any color hair, eyes centered, MIB, ea...$250.00

Barbie, Twist 'N Turn, 1971, brunette hair, NRFB $500.00

Barbie, Unicef, 1989, NRFB.............................$20.00

Barbie, Winter Fantasy, 1990, FAO Schwarz, NRFB......$200.00

Barbie, Wonder Woman, 2000, Pop Culture Collection, NRFB $40.00

Barbie, Working Woman (White or Black), 1999, NRFB, ea ..$25.00

Barbie, Xavier, 1999, University Barbie, NRFB $16.00

Barbie, Yuletide Romance, 1996, Hallmark, NRFB $30.00

Brad, Talking, 1970, NRFB $225.00

Brad, 1970, darker skin, bendable legs, NRFB $200.00

Casey, Twist 'N Turn, 1968, blond or brunette hair, NRFB ..$300.00

Chris, 1967, any hair color, MIB $200.00

Christie, Beauty Secrets, 1980, MIB...............................$60.00

Christie, Fashion Photo, 1978, MIB................................$95.00

Christie, Golden Dream, 1980, MIB................................$50.00

Christie, Kissing, 1979, MIB...$45.00

Christie, Pink & Pretty, 1982, NRFB.............................$45.00

Christie, Pretty Reflections, 1979, NRFB $85.00

Christie, Sunsational Malibu, 1982, NRFB....................$55.00

Christie, Superstar, 1977, MIB $80.00

Christie, Talking, 1969, brunette or red hair, NRFB $350.00

Christie, Twist 'N Turn, 1968, red hair, MIB $300.00

Francie, Busy, 1972, NRFB...$425.00

Francie, Growin' Pretty Hair, 1971, MIB........................$180.00

Francie, Malibu, 1971, NRFB...$75.00

Francie, Twist 'N Turn, blond or brunette, long hair, no bangs, MIB..$1,200.00

Francie, Twist 'N Turn, 1966, Black, 1st issue, red hair, MIB $1,200.00

Francie, Twist 'N Turn, 1966, Black, 2nd issue, blk hair, MIB $1,500.00

Francie, Twist 'N Turn, 1969, blond or brunette, long hair w/bangs, MIB...$425.00

Francie, Twist 'N Turn, 1969, blond or brunette, short hair, MIB $465.00

Francie, 1966, brunette hair, bendable legs, MIB, $375.00. (Photo courtesy McMasters Doll Auctions)

Francie, 30th Anniversary, 1996, NRFB $65.00

Ginger, Growing Up, 1977, MIB.......................$100.00

Jamie, New & Wonderful Walking, 1970, blond hair, MIB, $225.00. (Photo courtesy McMasters Auctions)

Kelley, Quick Curl, 1972, NRFB $175.00

Kelly, Yellowstone, 1974, brunette hair, NRFB.............$575.00

Ken, 1961, flocked hair, straight legs, MIB, ea $125.00

Ken, 1962, pnt blond or brunette hair, MIB $125.00

Ken, Air Force, 1994, Stars 'N Stripes, NRFB $30.00

Ken, Arabian Nights, 1964, NRFB $425.00

Ken, Army, 1993, Stars 'N Stripes, NRFB......................$25.00

Ken, Beach Blast, 1989, NRFB.......................................$15.00

Ken, Busy, 1972, NRFB $150.00

Ken, California Dream, 1988, NRFB $25.00

Ken, Crystal, 1984, NRFB...$40.00

Ken, Dream Date, 1983, NRFB.......................................$30.00

Ken, Earring Magic, 1993, NRFB...................................$40.00

Ken, Fashion Jeans, 1982, NRFB....................................$35.00

Ken, Gold Medal Skier, 1975, NRFB $75.00

Ken, Hawaiian, 1979, MIB $55.00

Ken, Henry Higgins, 1996, Hollywood Legends Series, NRFB $65.00

Ken, In-Line Skating, 1996, FAO Schwarz, NRFB...........$25.00

Ken, Jewel Secrets, 1987, NRFB......................................$30.00

Ken, King Arthur, 1964, NRFB.......................................$500.00

Ken, Live Action on Stage, 1971, NRFB.........................$150.00

Ken, Marine Corps, 1992, Stars 'N Stripes, NRFB $30.00

Ken, Mod Hair, 1972, MIB...$70.00

Ken, New Look, 1976, longer or shorter hair, NRFB, ea ..$75.00

Ken, Ocean Friends, 1996, NRFB $20.00

Ken, Rhett Butler, 1994, Hollywood Legend Series, NRFB ..$55.00

Ken, Rocker, 1986, MIB $40.00

Ken, Sea Holiday, 1993, FAO Schwarz, NRFB................$40.00

Ken, Sport & Shave, 1980, MIB $40.00

Ken, Sun Charm, 1989, MIB...$25.00

Ken, Sun Lovin' Malibu, 1979, NRFB $30.00

Ken, Superstar, 1977, MIB..$100.00

Ken, Talking, 1960s, NRFB $150.00

Ken, Walk Lively, 1972, MIB $150.00

Ken, Western, 1982, MIB $45.00

Midge, 1963, brunette hair, straight legs, MIB................$150.00

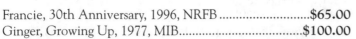

Midge, 1965, any hair color, bendable legs, MIB $450.00
Midge, Cool Times, 1989, NRFB.................................$30.00
Midge, Earring Magic, 1993, NRFB $30.00
Midge, Ski Fun, 1991, MIB..$30.00
Midge, Winter Sports, 1995, Toys R Us, MIB..................$40.00
Midge, 30th Anniversary, 1992, porcelain, MIB, D2......$175.00
Nikki, Animal Lovin', 1989, NRFB..............................$30.00
PJ, Deluxe Quick Curl, 1976, MIB..............................$65.00
PJ, Fashion Photo, 1978, MIB $95.00
PJ, Free Moving, 1976, MIB $85.00
PJ, Gold Medal Gymnast, 1975, NRFB.........................$120.00
PJ, Live Action, 1971, orig outfit, M.........................$150.00
PJ, Malibu, 1978, MIB $55.00

Skooter, 1966, any hair color, bendable legs, MIB, $275.00. (Photo courtesy McMasters Doll Auctions)

PJ, Malibu (The Sun Set), 1971, blond hair, NRFP, $100.00. (Photo courtesy McMasters Doll Auctions)

Stacey, Talking, any hair color, MIB $400.00
Stacey, Twist 'N Turn, 1969, any hair color, NRFB $500.00
Teresa, All American, 1991, MIB.................................$25.00
Teresa, California Dream, 1988, MIB...........................$30.00
Teresa, Country Western Star, 1994, NRFB....................$30.00
Teresa, Rappin' Rockin,' 1992, NRFB............................$45.00
Tutti, 1967, any hair color, MIB.................................$165.00
Tutti, Night Night Sleep Tight, 1966, NRFB $275.00
Whitney, Style Magic, 1989, NRFB $35.00

CASES

Barbie, Francie, Casey & Tutti, hard plastic, EX, from $50
    to...$75.00
Barbie, Stacey, Francie & Skipper, pk hard plastic, rare, NM,
    from $75 to $100.00
Barbie, vinyl w/head image of Bubble-Cut Barbie on diamond
    pattern, plastic window, w/Swirl Ponytail Barbie doll, VG,
    A $650.00
Barbie, 1961, red vinyl, Barbie pictured in 4 different outfits, EX,
    from $30 to...$40.00
Barbie, 1963, pk vinyl, Bubble-Cut Barbie wearing Solo in the
    Spotlight, rare, NM, from $75 to..................$85.00
Barbie, 1967, vinyl, Barbie wearing All That Jazz surrounded by
    flowers, from $30 to $40.00
Barbie & Ken, 1963, blk vinyl, Barbie wearing Party Date &
    Ken wearing Saturday Night Date, EX.....................$65.00
Barbie & Midge, pk vinyl, Barbie wearing Rain Coat & Midge
    wearing Sorority Meeting, NM, from $45 to.............$55.00
Barbie & Stacey, 1967, vinyl, NM, from $65 to...............$75.00
Barbie & Stacey Sleep 'n Keep, 1960s, vinyl, several color varia-
    tions, NM...$75.00
Barbie Goes Travelin', vinyl, rare, NM $100.00
Barbie on Madison Avenue, FAO Schwarz, 1992, blk back-
    ground, pk hdl, M $40.00
Circus Star Barbie, FAO Schwarz, 1995, M $25.00
Fashion Queen Barbie, 1963, red vinyl, w/mirror & wig stand,
    EX $100.00
Francie & Casey, vinyl, Francie wearing Groovy Get-Up &
    Casey wearing Iced Blue, rare, from $65 to...............$75.00

PJ, New & Groovy Talking, 1969, orig swimsuit, beads & glasses,
    NM...$150.00
PJ, Sun Lovin' Malibu, 1979, MIB $50.00
PJ, Sunsational Malibu, 1982, MIB $40.00
PJ, Talking, 1970, MIB $250.00
Ricky, 1965, MIB...$150.00
Scott, 1980, MIB...$55.00
Skipper, 1964, any hair color, straight legs, MIB $130.00
Skipper, 1965, any hair color, MIB..............................$175.00
Skipper, Deluxe Quick Curl, 1975, NRFB $65.00
Skipper, Dramatic New Living, 1970, MIB....................$130.00
Skipper, Dream Date, 1990, NRFB..............................$25.00
Skipper, Growing Up, 1976, MIB................................$100.00
Skipper, Hollywood Hair, 1993, NRFB $30.00
Skipper, Homecoming Queen, 1989, NRFB $20.00
Skipper, Music Lovin,' 1985, NRFB.............................$30.00
Skipper, Sunsational Malibu, 1982, MIB $40.00
Skipper, Super Teen, 1980, NRFB................................$30.00
Skipper, Totally Hair, 1991, NRFB.............................$30.00
Skipper, Twist 'N Turn, 1969, any hair style or color, MIB...$250.00
Skipper, Western, 1982, NRFB...................................$40.00
Skipper, Workout Teen Fun, 1988, NRFB.......................$25.00

Ken, 1962, gold vinyl w/black plastic handle, metal clasp, with hang tag, NM, $35.00. (Photo courtesy McMasters Doll Auctions)

Ken, gr vinyl w/plastic hdl, lg image of Ken w/3 smaller images of Barbie in casual wear, 1961, NM, from $30 to.......$40.00

Midge, 1963, bl vinyl, Midge wearing Movie Date, rare, NM, from $100 to $125.00

Miss Barbie, 1963, wht vinyl, w/orig wig, wig stand & mirror, rare, EX $150.00

Skooter, 1965, bl vinyl, Skooter wearing Country Picnic & chasing butterflies, rare, from $125 to.............................$175.00

Tutti Play Case, bl or pk vinyl w/various scenes, EX, ea from $30 to $40.00

CLOTHING AND ACCESSORIES

Barbie, After Five, #934, 1962, NRFP $300.00
Barbie, All Decked Out, #17568, 1997, NRFP $20.00
Barbie, All Turned Out, #4822, 1984, NRFP $20.00
Barbie, Barbie in Hawaii, #1605, 1964, NRFP................$300.00
Barbie, Beach Dazzler, #1939, 1981, NRFP $10.00
Barbie, Beautiful Bride, #1698, 1967, NRFP $2,500.00
Barbie, Brunch Time, #1628, 1965, NRFP.....................$400.00
Barbie, Busy Morning, #981, 1960, NRFP $325.00
Barbie, Cinderella, #872, 1964, NRFP............................$475.00
Barbie, City Fun, #5717, 1983, NRFP $10.00
Barbie, Club Meeting, #1672, 1966, NRFP $400.00
Barbie, Cotton Casual, #912, 1959, NRFP $125.00
Barbie, Cruise Stripes, #918, 1959, NRFP $175.00
Barbie, Day 'N Night, #1723, 1965, NRFP $75.00
Barbie, Disco Dazzle, #1011, 1979, NRFP $15.00
Barbie, Dog 'n Duds, #1613, 1964, NRFP $350.00
Barbie, Drum Majorette, #875, 1964, NRFP..................$225.00
Barbie, Enchanted Evening, #983, NRFP $350.00
Barbie, Evening Outfit, #2221, 1978, NRFP....................$30.00
Barbie, Evening Splendour (reissue), #961, 1964, NRFP...$15.00
Barbie, Fashion Bouquet, #1511, 1970, NRFP...............$350.00
Barbie, Fashion Shiner, #1691, 1967, NRFP..................$300.00
Barbie, Floral Petticoat, #921, 1959, NRFP...................$125.00
Barbie, Fraternity Dance, #1638, NRFP.........................$600.00
Barbie, Friday Night Date, #979, 1960, NRFP...............$225.00
Barbie, Galaxy A Go-Go, #2742, 1986, NRFP.................$30.00
Barbie, Glamour Group, #1510, 1970, NRFP.................$350.00

Barbie, Gold 'N Glamour, #1647, NRFP........................$475.00
Barbie, Gold Spun, #1957, 1981, NRFP..........................$15.00
Barbie, Golden Glory, #1645, complete, M, D2 ....$250.00
Barbie, Graduation, #945, 1963, NRFP...........................$60.00
Barbie, Great Coat, #1459, 1970, NRFP.........................$90.00
Barbie, Groovin' Gauchos, #1057, 1971, NRFP.............$300.00

Barbie, Hair Fair, #4044, 1974, NRFP, $55.00. (Photo courtesy McMasters Doll Auctions)

Barbie, Holiday Dance, #1639, 1965, NRFP..................$625.00
Barbie, In the Limelight, #2790, 1979, NRFP..................$15.00
Barbie, Indian Print Separates, #7241, 1975, NRFP.........$35.00
Barbie, Invitation to Tea, #1632, 1965, NRFP $575.00
Barbie, Jumpin' Jeans, Pak, 1964, NRFP $85.00
Barbie, Knit Separates, #1602, 1964, NRFP $175.00
Barbie, Lady in Blue, #2303, 1978, NRFP.......................$15.00
Barbie, Light 'N Lazy, #3339, 1972, NRFP......................$75.00
Barbie, Little Red Riding Hood & the Wolf, #880, 1964, NRFP...$500.00
Barbie, Lunch on the Terrace, #1649, 1966, NRFP........$350.00
Barbie, Madras Plaid, #3485, 1972, NRFP....................$120.00
Barbie, Make Mine Midi, #1861, 1969, NRFP...............$300.00
Barbie, Masquerade, #944, 1963, NRFP.........................$200.00
Barbie, Maxi 'N Mini, #1799, NRFP..............................$400.00
Barbie, Midi-Marvelous, #1870, 1969, NRFP................$160.00
Barbie, Midnight Blue, #1617, NRFP $850.00
Barbie, Movie Groovie, #1866, 1969, NRFP $125.00
Barbie, My First Picnic, #5611, 1983, NRFP..................$10.00
Barbie, Now Knit, #1452, 1970, NRFP..........................$100.00
Barbie, Olympic Warm-Ups, #7243, 1975, NRFP...........$40.00
Barbie, Overall Denim, #3488, 1972, NRFP..................$110.00
Barbie, Pajama Party, #1601, 1964, NRFP $75.00
Barbie, Patio Party, #1708, 1965, NRFP.........................$50.00
Barbie, Peachy Fleecy, #915, 1959, NRFB.....................$150.00
Barbie, Perfectly Pink, #4805, 1984, NRFP $10.00
Barbie, Picnic in the Park, #16077, 1996, NRFP $30.00
Barbie, Plush Pony, #1873, 1969, NRFP........................$175.00
Barbie, Princess Aurora, #9329, 1976, NRFP..................$40.00
Barbie, Rare Pair, #1462, 1970, NRFP $125.00
Barbie, Reception Line, #1654, 1966, NRFP..................$600.00
Barbie, Red Flair, #939, 1962, NRFP $175.00
Barbie, Royal Ball, #2668, 1979, NRFP...........................$15.00
Barbie, Scuba Do's, #1788, 1970, NRFP.........................$65.00

Barbie, Sea-Worthy, #1872, 1969, NRFP.......................$225.00
Barbie, Shape-Ups, #1782, 1970-71, NRFP..................$200.00
Barbie, Sharp Shift, #20, 1970, NRFP........................$110.00
Barbie, Sheath Sensation, #986, 1961, NRFP $150.00
Barbie, Silken Flame, #977, 1960, NRFP.....................$175.00
Barbie, Silver Serenade, #3419, 1971-72, NRFP $350.00
Barbie, Silver Sparkle, #1885, 1969, MIP....................$200.00
Barbie, Skate Mates, #1793, 1970, NRFP....................$130.00

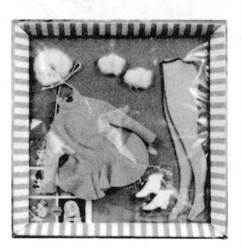

Barbie, Skater's Waltz, 1965, NRFP, $450.00. (Photo courtesy McMasters Doll Auctions)

Barbie, Ski Party Pink, #5608, 1983, NRFP.....................$10.00
Barbie, Skin Diver, #1608, 1964, NRFP...........................$125.00
Barbie, Slip On Wrap 'n Tie, #1910, 1981, NRFP $10.00
Barbie, Snap Dash, #1824, 1968, NRFP...........................$140.00
Barbie, Snug Fuzz, #1813, 1968, NRFP $250.00
Barbie, Star of the Snow in Golden Glow, #9741, 1977,
     NRFP $15.00
Barbie, Stormy Weather, #949, 1964, NRFP $100.00
Barbie, Sugar Plum Fairy, #9326, 1976, NRFP $40.00
Barbie, Sunny Sleep Ins, #3348, 1973, NRFP..................$50.00
Barbie, Swinging Easy, #955, 1963, NRFP......................$200.00
Barbie, Togetherness, #1842, 1968, NRFP.....................$175.00
Barbie, Topsy Twosider, #4826, 1984, NRFP...................$10.00
Barbie, Tour-Ins, #1515, 1969, NRFP............................$50.00
Barbie, Trail Blazer, #1846, 1968, NRFP........................$250.00
Barbie, Tropicana, #1460, 1967, NRFP.........................$170.00
Barbie, Two-Way Tiger, #3402, 1971, NRFP $110.00
Barbie, United Airlines Stewardess, #7703, 1973, NRFP ..$75.00
Barbie, Velvet Touch, #2789, 1979, NRFP $15.00
Barbie, Victorian Velvet, #3431, 1971, NRFP $175.00
Barbie, Walking Pretty, Pak, 1971, NRFP......................$130.00
Barbie, White Delight, #3799, 1982, NRFP.....................$15.00
Barbie, Wild 'N Wonderful, #1856, 1968-69, NRFB $200.00
Barbie, Wild Things, #3439, 1971, NRFP.......................$250.00
Barbie, Yellow Go, #1816, 1967, NRFP.........................$800.00
Barbie, Zokko!, #1820, 1968, NRFP $200.00
Barbie & Stacey, All the Trimmings Fashion Pak, #0050, 1970,
     MOC..$75.00
Francie, Beach Outfit, #7710, 1973, NRFP $200.00
Francie, Cheerleading Outfit, #7711, 1973, NRFP...........$80.00
Francie, Clam Diggers, #1258, 1966, NRFP....................$275.00
Francie, Dancing Party, #1257, NRFP..............................$275.00

Francie, First Things First, #1252, 1966, NRFP.............$115.00
Francie, Furry-Go-Round, #1294, Sears Exclusive, 1967,
     NRFP..$500.00
Francie, Hill Riders, #1210, 1968, NRFP.......................$75.00
Francie, Hip Knits, #1265, 1966, NRFB $225.00
Francie, In-Print, #1288, 1967, NRFP $150.00
Francie, Little Knits, #3275, 1972, NRFP.....................$125.00
Francie, Long on Leather, #1769, 1970, NRFP.............$155.00
Francie, Merry-Go-Rounders, #1230, NRFB $375.00
Francie, Midi Bouquet, #3446, 1971, NRFP.................$125.00
Francie, Peach Plush, #3461, 1971, NRFP....................$250.00
Francie, Pretty Frilly, #3366, 1972, MIB $200.00
Francie, Quick Shift, #1266, 1966, NRFP $200.00
Francie, Satin Happenin,' #1237, 1970, NRFP............$75.00
Francie, Slightly Summery Fashion Pak, 1968, NRFP......$95.00
Francie, Striped Types, #1243, 1970, NRFP.................$75.00
Francie, Summer Number, #3454, 1971-72 & 1974, MIP...$175.00
Francie, Totally Terrific, #3280, 1972, MIP $225.00
Francie, Two for the Ball, #1232, MIB $225.00
Francie, Wedding Whirl, #1244, 1970-71 & 1974, complete,
     M..$275.00

Francie, Wild Flowers, #3456, 1971, NRFP, $65.00. (Photo courtesy McMasters Doll Auctions)

Francie, Zig-Zag Zoom, #3445, 1971, NRFP.................$125.00
Francie & Casey, Cool It! Fashion Pak, 1968, MIP $50.00
Francie & Casey, Corduroy Cape, #1764, 1970-71, MIB..$150.00
Francie & Casey, Culotte-Wot?, #1214, 1968-69, MIB..$300.00
Francie & Casey, Floating In, #1207, 1968-69, MIB $200.00
Francie & Casey, Tennis Time, #1221, 1969-70, MIP $150.00
Francie & Casey, Victorian Wedding, #1233, 1969-70, MIB...$300.00
Jazzie, Mini Dress, #3781 or #3783, 1989, NRFP, ea.........$10.00
Julia, Brrr-Furrr, #1752, 1969, NRFP.............................$175.00
Kelly, #24310, 1999, NRFP...$5.00
Ken, Army & Air Force, #797, 1963, NRFP...................$250.00
Ken, Baseball, #9168, 1976, NRFP................................$70.00
Ken, Casual Suit, #9167, 1976, NRFB $70.00
Ken, City Sophisticate, #2801, 1979, NRFP..................$15.00
Ken, Date With Barbie, #5824, 1983, NRFP..................$10.00
Ken, Evening Elegance, #1415, 1980, NRFP..................$15.00
Ken, Fountain Boy, #1407, 1964, NRFP.......................$150.00

Ken, Fun at McDonalds, #4276, 1983, NRFP $15.00
Ken, Fun on Ice, #791, 1963, NRFP $125.00
Ken, Get-Ups 'N Go Doctor, #7705, 1973, MIP.............$75.00
Ken, Going Bowling, #1403, 1964, NRFP $85.00
Ken, Groom, #9596, 1976, NRFP $15.00
Ken, Gym Shorts (bl) & Hooded Jacket, #2795, 1979,
    NRFP $60.00
Ken, Hiking Holiday, #1412, 1965, NRFP $250.00
Ken, Jazz Concert, #1420, 1966, NRFP........................$300.00
Ken, King Arthur, #773, NRFP $400.00
Ken, Midnight Blues, #1719, 1972, NRFP....................$115.00
Ken, Mr Astronaut, #1415, 1965, NRFP $725.00
Ken, Night Scene, #1496, 1971, NRFP $100.00
Ken, Outdoor Man, #1406, 1980, NRFP........................$15.00
Ken, Pepsi Outfit, #7761, 1974, NRFP...........................$40.00
Ken, Rain or Shine, #4999, 1984, NRFP $10.00
Ken, Running Start, #1404, 1981, NRFP $10.00
Ken, Safari, #7706, 1973, NRFP.....................................$70.00
Ken, Sea Scene, #1449, 1971, NRFP $60.00

Ken, Ski Champion, #798, 1963, NRFP, $150.00. (Photo courtesy McMasters Doll Auctions)

Ken, Special Date, #1401, NRFP $150.00
Ken, Summer Job, #1422, 1966, NRFP $450.00
Ken, Town Turtle, #1430, 1969-70, complete, M $200.00
Ken, United Airlines Pilot Uniform, #7707, 1973, NRFP ..$100.00
Ken, Western Winner, #3378, 1972, NRFP $60.00
Ken, White Is Right Fashion Pak, 1964, NRFP $40.00
Ken, Wide Awake Stripes, #3378, 1972, NRFP $60.00
Ken & Brad, Sun Fun Fashion Pak, 1971, MIP................$75.00
Ken & Brad, Way Out West, #1720, 1972, MIP.............$175.00
Midge, Orange Blossom, #987, 1962, NRFP $75.00
Ricky, Saturday Show, #1502, 1965, NRFB $90.00
Skipper, All Over Felt, #3476, NRFP $150.00
Skipper, Bandana Print, #9023, 1975, NRFP $40.00
Skipper, Budding Beauty, #1731, 1970, NRFP $75.00
Skipper, Confetti Cutie, #1952, 1968, NRFP $250.00
Skipper, Dressed in Velvet, #3477, 1971, NRFP.............$125.00
Skipper, Fun Time, #1920, 1965, NRFP..........................$225.00
Skipper, Get-Ups 'N Go Flower Girl, #7847, 1974-76, MIP...$100.00
Skipper, Goin' Sleddin,' #3475, 1971, NRFP....................$75.00
Skipper, Hearts 'N Flowers, #1945, 1967, NRFB $300.00

Skipper, Ice Cream 'N Cake, #1970, 1969-70, MIP........$200.00
Skipper, Ice Skatin', #3470, 1971-72, MIP $150.00
Skipper, Jazzy Jammys, #1967, MOC, A........................$25.00
Skipper, Jeepers Creepers, #1966, 1969, NRFP.............$125.00

Skipper, Land & Sea, #1917, 1965, NRFP, $125.00. (Photo courtesy McMasters Doll Auctions)

Skipper, Little Miss Midi, #3468, 1971, NRFP $70.00
Skipper, Nifty Knickers, #3291, 1972, NRFP...................$85.00
Skipper, Party Pair, #3297, 1972, NRFP..........................$75.00
Skipper, Popover, #1943, 1967, NRFP $175.00
Skipper, Quick Change, #1962, 1968, NRFP $200.00
Skipper, Real Sporty, #1961, 1968, NRFP......................$200.00
Skipper, Rolla-Scoot, #1940, 1967, NRFP......................$180.00
Skipper, School's Cool, #1976, 1969-70, MIP $200.00
Skipper, Shoe Parade Fashion Pak, 1965, NRFP...............$45.00
Skipper, Skating Fun, #1908, NRFB $175.00
Skipper, Skimmy Stripes, #1956, 1968, MIP..................$200.00
Skipper, Summer Slacks Fashion Pak, 1970, MIP.............$75.00
Skipper, Tea Party, #1924, 1966, NRFP $325.00
Skipper, Velvet Blush, #1737, 1970, NRFP......................$85.00
Skipper & Fluff, Fun Runners, #3372, 1972, MIP.............$50.00
Skipper & Fluff, Slumber Party Fashion Pak, 1971, MIP..$65.00
Skipper & Fluff, Some Shoes Fashion Pak, 1971, MIP $65.00
Skipper & Fluff, Sporty Shorty Fashion Pak, 1971, MIP ..$65.00
Skipper & Fluff, Super Snoozers, #3371, 1972, NRFB......$55.00
Stacey, Stripes Are Happening, #1544, 1968, NRFP........$75.00
Tutti, Birthday Beauties, #3617, 1968, NRFP................$160.00
Tutti, Clowning Around, #3606, 1967, NRFP...............$195.00
Tutti, Pink PJs, #3616, 1968-69, MIP...........................$150.00
Tutti & Chris, Sea-Shore Shorties, #3614, 1968-69, MIP ..$150.00
Twiggy, Twiggy Turnouts, #1726, 1968, NRFP.............$250.00

Furniture, Rooms, Houses, and Shops

Action Sewing Center, 1972, MIB....................................$50.00
Barbie & Ken Little Theatre, 1964, complete, NMIB....$600.00
Barbie & Skipper Deluxe Dream House, Sears Exclusive, 1965,
    MIB, minimum value $175.00
Barbie & Skipper School, 1965, rare, MIB $500.00
Barbie & the Beat Dance Cafe, 1990, MIB......................$35.00
Barbie & the Rockers Dance Cafe, 1987, MIB $50.00
Barbie & the Rockers Hot Rockin' Stage, 1987, MIB $40.00

Barbie Baby-Sitting Room, Canada, MIB $100.00
Barbie Beauty Boutique, 1976, MIB $40.00
Barbie Cafe, JC Penney Exclusive, 1993, MIB.................$45.00
Barbie Cafe Today, 1971, MIB.......................................$400.00

Barbie Cookin' Fun Kitchen, MIB, $100.00. (Photo courtesy Paris and Susan Manos)

Barbie Deluxe Family House, 1966, complete, VG $135.00
Barbie Dream Armoire, 1980, NRFB $35.00
Barbie Dream Bath Chest & Commode, 1980, lt pk, MIB ..$25.00
Barbie Dream Bed & Nightstand, 1984, pk, MIB $25.00
Barbie Dream Dining Center, 1984, MIB.........................$25.00
Barbie Dream Glow Vanity, 1986, MIB............................$20.00
Barbie Dream House, 1961, 1st edition, complete, NM .$150.00
Barbie Dream House Bedroom, 1981, MIB $6.00
Barbie Dream House Kitchen Set, 1981, MIB....................$6.00
Barbie Dream Kitchen-Dinette, #4095, 1964, MIB........$600.00
Barbie Dream Luxury Bathtub, 1984, pk, MIB.................$20.00
Barbie Dream Store Makeup Department, 1983, MIB......$40.00
Barbie Fashion Salon, Sears Exclusive, 1964, MIB.........$225.00
Barbie Fashion Wraps Boutique, 1989, MIB $35.00
Barbie Glamour Home, 1985, MIB $125.00
Barbie Lively Livin' Room, MIB......................................$50.00
Barbie Mountain Ski Cabin, Sears Exclusive, MIB...........$50.00
Barbie Playhouse Pavilion, Europe, MIB..........................$75.00
Barbie Teen Dream Bedroom, MIB $50.00
Barbie Unique Boutique, Sears Exclusive, 1971, MIB $185.00
Barbie Vanity & Shower, Sears Exclusive, 1975, MIB......$50.00
Barbie's Apartment, 1975, MIB.....................................$140.00
Barbie's Room-Fulls Country Kitchen, #7404, 1974, NRFB .$100.00
Barbie's Room-Fulls Firelight Living Room, 1974, MIB ..$100.00
California Dream Barbie Hot Dog Stand, 1988, NRFB $50.00
Cool Tops Skipper T-Shirt Shop, 1989, complete, MIB ...$25.00
Francie & Casey Housemates, 1966, complete, NM.........$200.00
Francie House, 1966, complete, M $150.00
Go-Together Chair, Ottoman and End Table, MIB........$100.00
Go-Together Chaise Lounge, MIB $75.00
Go-Together Couch, 1964, MIB.......................................$30.00
Go-Together Dining Room, Barbie & Skipper, 1965, MIB..$50.00
Go-Together Lawn Swing & Planter, 1964, complete, MIB..$150.00
Go-Together Living Room, Barbie & Skipper, 1965, MIB...$60.00
Ice Capades Skating Rink, 1989, MIB $70.00
Jamie's Penthouse, Sears Exclusive, 1971, MIB $475.00

Living Pretty Cooking Center, 1988, MIB........................$25.00
Living Pretty Refrigerator/Freezer, 1988, MIB.................$30.00
Magical Mansion, 1989, MIB...$125.00
Movietime Prop Shop, 1989, MIB....................................$50.00
Party Garden Playhouse, 1994, MIB $275.00
Pink Sparkles Armoire, 1990, NRFB................................$25.00
Pink Sparkles Refrigerator/Freezer, #4776, 1988, NRFB...$30.00
Pink Sparkles Starlight Bed, 1990, MIB...........................$30.00
Skipper & Skooter Double Bunk Beds and Ladder, MIB ..$100.00
Skipper Dream Room, 1964, MIB..................................$300.00
Skipper's Deluxe Dream House, Sears Exclusive, 1966, MIB...$500.00

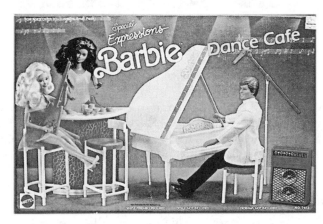

Special Expressions Barbie Dance Cafe, Woolworth, 1991, EXIB, $50.00.

Superstar Barbie Beauty Salon, 1977, MIB $55.00
Superstar Barbie Photo Studio, Sears Exclusive, 1977, MIB...$45.00
Surprise House, 1972, MIB...$100.00
Susy Goose Barbie & Midge Queen Size Chifferobe, NM ..$100.00
Susy Goose Barbie & Midge Vanity, 1963, MIB, A $100.00
Susy Goose Canopy Bed, 1962, MIB................................$150.00
Susy Goose Chifferobe, 1964, MIB................................$275.00
Susy Goose Four Poster Bed Outfit, M $35.00
Susy Goose Ken Wardrobe, M $50.00
Susy Goose Mod-A-Go-Go Bedroom, 1966, NRFB.....$2,300.00
Susy Goose Queen Size Bed, Sears Exclusive, 1963, NRFB ..$200.00
Susy Goose Skipper's Jeweled Bed, 1965, MIB $150.00
Susy Goose Skipper's Jeweled Vanity, Sears Exclusive, 1965, NRFP $100.00
Susy Goose Vanity, Bench & Throw Rug, M...................$35.00
Susy Goose Wardrobe, 1962, EX $35.00
Town & Country Market, 1971, MIB $135.00
Tutti Playhouse, 1966, M..$100.00
Workout Center, 1985, MIB..$30.00
World of Barbie House, 1966, MIB $175.00

GIFT SETS

Army Barbie & Ken, 1993, Stars 'N Stripes, MIB $60.00
Ballerina Barbie on Tour, 1976, MIB $175.00
Barbie & Her Horse Dancer, Canada, MIB.......................$75.00
Barbie & Ken Campin' Out, 1983, MIB $75.00

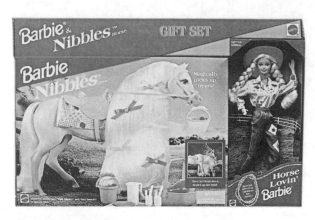

Barbie & Nibbles Horse Gift Set, BJ's Wholesale Clubs, 1996, NRFP, $40.00. (Photo courtesy J. Michael Augustyniak)

Barbie Beautiful Blues, Sears Exclusive, 1967, MIB $3,000.00
Barbie Dance Club & Tape Player Set, #4217, 1989, MIB...$75.00
Barbie Loves Elvis, 1996, NRFB..$75.00
Barbie Snap 'N Play Deluxe Gift Set, JC Penney Exclusive, 1992, MIB $40.00
Barbie Travel in Style, Sears Exclusive, 1968, MIB.....$1,500.00
Barbie 35th Anniversary Gift Set, 1994, NRFP $150.00
Barbie's 'Round the Clock Gift Set, 1964, MIB..............$700.00
Barbie's Olympic Ski Village, MIB $75.00
Barbie's Sparkling Pink Gift Set, 1963, MIB..................$600.00
Barbie's Wedding Party, 1964, MIB.............................$700.00
Beauty Secrets Barbie Pretty Reflections, 1980, NRFB ..$100.00
Birthday Fun at McDonald's, 1994, NRFB......................$75.00
Bright & Breezy Skipper, Sears Exclusive, 1969, NRFB ..$975.00
Cinderella, 1992, NRFB $125.00
Dance Magic Barbie & Ken, 1990, NRFB.......................$50.00
Dance Sensation Barbie, 1985, MIB $35.00
Dolls of the World II, 1995, NRFB $100.00
Dramatic New Living Skipper Very Best Velvet, Sears Exclusive, 1970-71, NRFB $1,500.00
Francie & Her Swingin' Separates, Sears Exclusive, 1966, MIB.$600.00
Golden Dreams Glamorous Nights, 1980, NRFB $100.00
Golden Groove Barbie, Sears Exclusive, 1969, NRFB...$2,000.00
Halloween Party Barbie & Ken, Target, 1998, NRFB.......$65.00
Happy Birthday Barbie, 1985, NRFB $50.00
Happy Meal Stacie & Whitney, JC Penney Exclusive, 1994, MIB $30.00
Hollywood Hair Barbie, #10928, 1993, MIB....................$35.00
Ken Red, White & Wild, Sears Exclusive, 1970, NRFB..$525.00
Live Action PJ Fashion 'N Motion, Sears Exclusive, 1971-72, NRFB..$1,500.00
Living Barbie Action Accents, Sears Exclusive, 1970, MIB..$450.00
Loving You Barbie, 1984, MIB $75.00
Malibu Barbie Beach Party, M (M case)............................$75.00
Malibu Barbie Fashion Combo, 1978, NRFB....................$80.00
Malibu Ken Surf's Up, Sears Exclusive, 1971, MIB........$350.00
New & Wonderful Walking Jamie & Furry Friends, NMIB, A..$600.00
New 'N Groovy PJ Swingin' in Silver, MIB, A................$770.00

New Talking Barbie Dinner Dazzle Set, Sears Exclusive, 1968, MIB..$1,500.00
Night Night Sleep Tight Tutti, NRFB $300.00
On Parade With Barbie, Ken & Midge, #1014, 1964, MIB...$650.00
Pretty Pairs Nan 'N Fran, 1970, NRFB $250.00
Skipper Bright 'N Breezy, Sears Exclusive, 1969, MIB...$2,000.00
Skipper Party Time, 1964, NRFB..................................$500.00
Stacey & Butterfly Pony, 1993, NRFB $30.00
Stacey Nite Lighting, Sears Exclusive, 1969, NRFB ...$2,000.00
Stacey Stripes Are Happening, Sears Exclusive, 1968, MIB..$1,500.00
Sun Sensation Barbie Spray & Play Fun, Wholesale Clubs, 1992, MIB $60.00
Superstar Barbie & Ken, 1978, MIB...............................$175.00
Superstar Barbie Fashion Change-Abouts, 1978, NRFB..$100.00
Superstar Barbie in the Spotlight, 1977, MIB................$125.00
Talking Barbie Golden Groove Set, Sears Exclusive, 1969, MIB .$1,500.00
Talking Barbie Mad About Plaid, Sears Exclusive, 1970, NRFB...$1,200.00
Talking Barbie Perfectly Plaid, Sears Exclusive, 1971, MIB...$500.00
Travelin' Sisters, 1995, NRFB...$70.00
Tutti & Todd Sundae Treat, 1966, NRFB $500.00
Walking Jamie Strollin' in Style, NRFB $450.00
Wedding Party Midge, 1990, NRFB...............................$150.00
Workin' Out Barbie Fashions, BJ's Wholesale Clubs, 1997, NRFB $25.00

VEHICLES

Allan's Roadster, 1964, aqua, MIB $500.00
ATC Cycle, Sears Exclusive, 1972, MIB $65.00
Austin Healy, Irwin, 1962, red & wht, very rare, NRFB..........$3,500.00
Barbie & Ken Dune Buggy, Irwin, 1970, pk, MIB...........$250.00
Barbie & the Rockers Hot Rockin' Van, 1987, MIB.........$60.00
Barbie Silver 'Vette, MIB...$30.00
Barbie Travelin' Trailer, MIB...$40.00

Barbie's Mercedes, Irwin, EX, $150.00.

Barbie's Own Sports Car, NMIB.....................................$150.00
Beach Buggy for Skipper, Irwin, 1964, rare, MIB, minimum value..$500.00
Beach Bus, 1974, MIB..$45.00
California Dream Beach Taxi, 1988, MIB........................$35.00
Ken's Classy Corvette, 1976, yel, MIB $75.00
Ken's Dream 'Vette, 1981, dk bl, MIB............................$100.00

Ken's Hot Rod, Sears Exclusive, 1964, red, MIB $900.00
Snowmobile, Montgomery Ward, 1972, MIB $65.00
Sports Plane, Sears Exclusive, 1964, MIB....................$3,600.00
Star 'Vette, 1977, red, MIB.......................................$100.00
Starlight Motorhome, 1994, MIB................................$45.00
Sunsailer, 1975, NRFB..$55.00
Western Star Traveler Motorhome, 1982, MIB $50.00
1957 Belair Chevy, 1989, 1st edition, aqua, MIB $150.00
1957 Belair Chevy, 1990, 2nd edition, pk, MIB $125.00

MISCELLANEOUS

Ballerina Dress-Ups, Colorforms, 1977, complete, EXIB..$15.00
Barbie & Ken Sew Magic Add-Ons, 1973-74, complete, MIB ..$55.00
Barbie & the Rockers, purse, vinyl, w/comb & cologne, M ..$15.00

Barbie Autographs Book, 1961, black vinyl with colored graphics, unused, NMIB, $30.00. (Photo courtesy McMasters Doll Auctions)

Barbie Beauty Kit, 1961, complete, M $125.00
Barbie Cutlery Set, Sears Exclusive, 1962, MIP................$50.00
Barbie Dictionary, bl vinyl w/head image of Bubble-Cut Barbie
    encircled by lettering & stars graphics, 1963, G, A ...$20.00
Barbie Electric Drawing Set, 1970, complete, MIB $75.00
Barbie Electronic Drawing Set, Sears Exclusive, 1963, MIB...$200.00
Barbie Ge-Tar, 1965, M $325.00
Barbie Make-Up Case, 1963, NM $25.00
Barbie Nurse Kit, 1962, MIB.......................................$300.00
Barbie Pretty-Up Time Perfume Pretty Bath, 1964, complete,
    M $150.00
Barbie Queen of the Prom Game, Mattel, 1960, complete,
    NMIB...$50.00
Barbie Sew Magic Fashion Set, 1973-75, complete, MIB ..$100.00
Barbie Shrinky Dinks, 1979, MIB $30.00
Barbie Snaps 'N Scraps Scrapbook, several color variations, rare,
    ea from $200 to...$250.00
Barbie Young Travelers Play Kit, Sears Exclusive, 1964, MIB..$75.00
Book, Barbie's Fashion Success, Random House, 1962, hard-
    cover, w/dust jacket, NM, D2 ....$50.00
Book, Target's 30th Anniversary Barbie Keep Sake, 1989, hard-
    cover, EX $20.00
Booklet, World of Barbie Fashion, 1968, M $10.00
Carrying Case, cloth w/vinyl trim, Barbie's name & allover
    flower design, grip hdl, zipper, VG, A $75.00
Christie Quick Curl Beauty Center, Sears Exclusive, 1982,
    MIB...$35.00

Collector's Club Lit, 1999, M......................................$40.00
Coloring Book, Barbie & Ken, 1963, unused, NM $50.00

Comic Book, Barbie and Ken, Dell #3, 1963, VG, $30.00. (Photo courtesy McMasters Doll Auctions)

Diary, blk vinyl w/metal clasp & key, image of Barbie in long
    gown & fur stole, EX $100.00
Dictionary, 1963, bl vinyl w/Bubblecut Barbie graphics,
    VG...$35.00
Embroidery Set, Barbie & Ken, 1962, complete, rare, NMIB,
    D2 ....$150.00
Fashion Designer Set, Mattel, 1969, NM (EX+ box) $50.00
Game, Barbie Queen of the Prom, Mattel, 1962, MIB $80.00
Game, Barbie 35th Anniversary, Golden, 1994, MIB.......$60.00
Game, Barbie's Keys to Fame, Mattel, 1963, NMIB.........$40.00
Jumbo Trading Cards, Barbie & Ken, #176-210, Dynamic Toy
    Inc, 1962, VGIB, A $100.00
Knitting for Barbie, cb canister w/metal ends, complete con-
    tents, VG, A $30.00
Luncheon Embroidery Set, 1962, unused, MIB................$30.00
Nurse Kit, #1694, 1962, complete, NMIB $400.00
Ornament, Holiday Barbie, Hallmark, 1993, 1st edition,
    MIB...$75.00
Paper Dolls, Angel Face Barbie, Golden #1982-45, 1983, uncut,
    M $20.00
Paper Dolls, Ballerina Barbie, Whitman #1993-1, 1977, uncut,
    M $30.00
Paper Dolls, Barbie, Whitman #4601, 1963, uncut, M $85.00
Paper Dolls, Barbie & Skipper Campsite at Lucky Lake, Whit-
    man #1836-31, 1980, M, uncut $25.00
Paper Dolls, Barbie Country Camper, Whitman #1990, 1973,
    uncut, M...$30.00
Paper Dolls, Midge Cut-Outs, Whitman #1962, 1963, uncut,
    NM...$150.00
Picture Maker Designer Fashion Set, Mattel, 1969, NMIB..$40.00
Pillow, 1961, lavender vinyl w/Barbie & Ken graphics, 11½" dia,
    VG $25.00
Puzzle, jigsaw; Barbie & Ken, Whitman, 1963, 100 pcs,
    MIB $40.00
Puzzle, jigsaw; Nostalgic Barbie, Am Publishing, 1989, 550 pcs,
    MIB...$25.00

Puzzle, jigsaw; Skipper & Skooter, 1965, 100 pcs, MIB $30.00

Quick Curl Miss America Beauty Center, Sears Exclusive, 1975, MIB $75.00

Record Tote, 1961, blk vinyl w/blk plastic hdls, VG, A ...$55.00

Slippers, quilted cloth bottoms w/stiched vinyl trim, cloth strap w/Barbie logo, NM, A, pr $115.00

Sweet Sixteen Promotional Set, 1974, M $70.00

Tea Party Dinette, 16-piece set, NRFP, $50.00. (Photo courtesy McMasters Doll Auctions)

Tea Set, Barbie, Chilton Globe, 1989, china, 16 pcs, NRFB..$30.00

Tea Set, Barbie, Sears Exclusive, 1962, 42 pcs, MIB.......$200.00

Tea Set, Barbie 25th Anniversary, 1984, complete, M ...$150.00

Tea Set, Tea Party Dinette, Reliable Toy Co, Barbie's name encircled by filigree border on wht plastic, 16 pcs, VGIB, A...$30.00

Umbrella, Barbie, 1962, several variations, EX, ea $65.00

Wagon, Camp Barbie, 1995, 34", EX.................................$50.00

Wallet, blk vinyl w/Bubble-Cut Barbie in evening gown & fur stole w/Barbie Ponytail lettering, dated 1962, VG, A..$20.00

Wallet, pk vinyl w/bust image of Barbie encircled by her name in various lettering, dated 1976, G, A $20.00

Wallet, 1962, blk vinyl w/graphics, VG $25.00

Wristwatch, Barbie & Ken, Bradley, 1963, MIB.............$200.00

Wristwatch, Swirl Ponytail Barbie, 1964, bl or yel band, MIB, ea $400.00

Wristwatch, 30th Anniversary, 1989, MIB $80.00

Yo-yo, Spectra Star, plastic w/paper sticker, MIP $5.00

Battery-Operated Toys

From the standpoint of being visually entertaining, nothing can compare with the battery-operated toy. Most (probably as much as 95%) were made in Japan from the 1940s through the 1960s, though some were distributed by American companies, such as Marx, Ideal, and Daisy, for instance, who often sold them under their own names. So even if they're marked, sometimes it's just about impossible to identify the actual manufacturer. Though batteries had been used to power trains and provide simple illumination in earlier toys, the Japanese toys could smoke, walk, talk, drink, play instruments, blow soap bubbles,

and do just about anything else humanly possible to dream up and engineer. Generally, the more antics the toy performs, the more collectible it is. Rarity is important as well, but first and foremost to consider is condition. Because of their complex mechanisms, many will no longer work. Children often stopped them in mid-cycle, rubber hoses and bellows aged and cracked, and leaking batteries caused them to corrode, so very few have survived to the present intact and in good enough condition to interest a collector. Although it is sometimes possible to have them repaired, it is probably better to wait on a better example. Original boxes are a definite plus in assessing the value of a battery-op and can sometimes be counted on to add from 30% to 50% (and up), depending on the box's condition, of course, as well as the toy's age and rarity.

If the name of the toy is on the toy, that name will be listed first with the box name (if different) listed in parenthesis. If there is no name on the toy, then the name on the box will be listed first. Some cross-referencing has been used to help identify toys without boxes. For more information we recommend *Collecting Toys* by Richard O'Brien (Books Americana).

Advisor: Tom Lastrapes (L4)

See also Aeronautical; Boats; Japanese and Other Tin Replica Vehicles; Games; Marx; Robots and Space Toys.

ABC Toyland Express, MT, 1950s, litho tin, 14½", NM ..$125.00

Accordion Bear, Alps, 1950s, r/c microphone, 10½", NMIB, A..$725.00

Accordion Player Hobo (w/Monkey), Alps, 1950s, seated hobo plays accordion while monkey plays cymbals, NMIB, A.........$350.00

Acro-Chimp Porter, YM, 1960s, 9", NMIB....................$100.00

Acrobatic Umbrella, lady in cloth outfit holding litho tin umbrella, 10", GIB, A...$110.00

Air Control Tower (w/Airplane & Helicopter), Bandai, 1960s, 10½", EXIB, A...$250.00

All Stars Mr Baseball Jr, K, 1950s, 8", EXIB, A $825.00

Animated Squirrel, S&E, 1950s, 9", MIB $225.00

Annie Tugboat, Y, 1950s, litho tin, 12½", NM $140.00

Answer Game Machine (Robot), Ichida, 1960s, 15", NMIB, A...$450.00

Anti-Aircraft Jeep, see Super Control Anti-Aircraft Jeep

Antique Fire Car, TN, 1950s, 10", EXIB.........................$350.00

Antique Gooney Car, Alps, 1960s, litho tin w/vinyl-headed figure, 9", EX $75.00

Army Shearchlight Truck, Daisy, plastic & tin, 11½", MIB..$75.00

Arthur A-Go-Go Drummer, Alps, 1960s, 10", G, A $245.00

Arthur A-Go-Go, Alps, 1960s, 10", NM+IB, A, $575.00. (Photo courtesy Don Hultzman)

Aston Martin Secret Ejector Car, #M101, r/c, 11", EX ..$250.00
Astro Dog, Y, 1960s, r/c, 11", EXIB, A............................$175.00
Astro Racer, Daiya, 1960s, 12", NMIB....................$975.00
Auto-Matic (Rock 'N Roll Monkey), see Rock 'N Roll Monkey
B-Z Porter (Baggage Truck), MT, 1950s, litho tin, 8" L, EXIB, A $130.00
B-Z Rabbit, MT, 1950s, litho tin, 7" L, EX $100.00
Baby & Carriage Pony Tail Girl, Rosko/S&E, 1950s, girl in cloth dress & pony tail pushing carriage, 8" T, EXIB, A ...$175.00
Baby Bertha the Watering Elephant, Mego, 1960s, plush w/cloth headdress & back blanket, r/c, 9" L, MIB, A.............$475.00
Baby Carriage, TN, 1950s, litho tin carriage w/plastic baby, 13", EXIB, A $120.00
Baggage Porter, Cragstan, plush dog pulling tin 2-wheeled stake cart, 12", EXIB, A..$125.00
Ball Blowing Clown (w/Mystery Action), TN, 1950s, cloth costume, 11", EXIB, A..$175.00
Ball Playing Bear, 1940s, bear, goose, umbrella & celluloid balls in wire spiral on litho tin base, 11", EXIB, A............$920.00
Balloon Blowing Monkey w/Lighted Eyes, Alps, 1950s, plush w/cloth overalls, 12", EXIB, A $130.00
Balloon Vendor, Y, 1960s, litho tin w/cloth outfit, 11", GIB, A..$165.00
Barber Bear, TN, 1950s, plush, tin base, 10", EXIB $450.00
Barber Bear, TN, 1950s, plush, tin base, 10", nonworking, G, A..$150.00
Barky Puppy, Alps, plush dog, walks, stops & barks, r/c, 9" T, EXIB..$50.00
Barney Bear the Drumming Boy, Alps, 1950s, r/c, 11", NM+IB, A..$200.00
Barney Bear the Drumming Boy, Alps, 1950s, r/c, 11", VGIB, A..$100.00
Bartender, TN, 1960s, wht-haired gent in red jacket standing behind litho tin bar, 12", EXIB, A...........................$30.00
Bartender w/Revolving Eyes, TN, 1950s, 11½", NMIB, A ..$250.00
Batman, Fairylite, litho tin, walks and arms swing, 11½", NMIB, A...$3,100.00
Batman Flying Batplane, Remco, 1966, performs aerial stunts, plastic, r/c, 12", EXIB $125.00
Batmobile (Mystery Action/Blinking Warning Light & Engine Noise), Ahi, 1970s, blk w/red trim, w/Batman figure, 12", EX $225.00

Batmobile (Mystery Action/Blinking Warning Light & Engine Noise), Ahi, 1970s, bl w/red trim, w/Batman & Robin, 12", NMIB..$550.00
Bear Target Game, MT, 1950s, litho tin, 9", NMIB, A...$300.00
Bear the Cashier, MT, 1950s, plush bear seated at desk w/telephone & cash register, 8" T, EXIB, A....................$330.00
Bear the Shoe Maker, TN, 1950s, 8½", EX+, A $200.00
Bear the Xylophone Player, Y, 1950s, plush & tin, r/c, 10", EX, A..$275.00

Beauty Parlor, S&E, 1950s, 9½x6½" long, EX, A, $525.00. (Photo courtesy Bertoia Auctions)

Beethoven the Piano Playing Dog, see Pianist (Jolly Pianist)
Big Dipper, Technofix, 1960s, 3 cars travel track, litho tin, 21" L, EX $150.00
Big John the Chimpee Chief, Alps, 1960s, chimp in Indian headdress seated at drum, 13", EXIB, A....................$80.00
Big Ring Circus (Circus Parade), MT, 1950s, litho tin circus truck, 13", EXIB..$200.00
Big Top Champ Circus Clown, Alps, 1960s, 14", NMIB ..$150.00
Big Wheel Ice Cream Truck, Taiyo, 1970s, 10", EX........$100.00
Bimbo the Drumming Clown, Cragstan, 1950s, r/c, 11", EXIB, A..$220.00
Birdwatcher Bear, MT, plush, seated w/bird on paw, 10", VG $440.00
Black Smithy Bear, TN, 1950s, plush bear seated at anvil, 10", EXIB, A..$330.00
Blacksmith Bear, A-1, 1950s, plush bear standing at anvil & 'brick' fire pit, 9", EXIB, A $375.00
Blinky the Clown (w/the Light in His Eyes), Amico, 1950s, playing drum or xylophone, cloth costume, r/c, 11", EXIB, ea..$200.00
Blushing Gunfighter, Y, 1960s, litho tin w/cloth shirt, 11", NMIB..$250.00
Blushing Willie, Y, 1960s, wht-haired gent pouring himself a drink, 10", EXIB..$75.00
Bobby Drinking Bear, Y, 1950s, plush, r/c, 10", VGIB....$600.00
Boil Over Car (Automoball), MT, 1950s, 10", EXIB......$150.00
Bongo Monkey (With Bongo Drums & Lited Eyes), Alps, 1960s, plastic hat, 10", EXIB, A $175.00

Brave Eagle (Beating Drum & Raising War Hoop), TN, 1950s, cloth outfit, 13", VG+IB, A $55.00

Bruin the Bear & His Ball Playing Act, Cragstan, tin & celluloid, 10", NMIB..$500.00

Bruno Accordion Bear, Y, 1950s, r/c, 10", EXIB, A $350.00

Bubble Bear, MT, 1950s, litho tin bear seated on base blowing bubbles, 9½", EXIB, A $330.00

Bubble Blowing Boy, Y, 1950s, litho tin, boy seated on base blowing bubbles, 8", EXIB, A $230.00

Bubble Blowing Bunny, Y, 1950s, plush elephant standing at bucket on litho tin base, 7" T, GIB, A $130.00

Bubble Blowing Monkey, Alps, 1950s, 11", EXIB, A......$115.00

Bubble Blowing Musician, Y, 1950s, 10", EXIB $250.00

Bubble Blowing Popeye, Linemar, litho tin, 12", EXIB, A, $1,430.00. (Photo courtesy Don Hultzman)

Bubble Blowing Popeye, Linemar, 1950s, litho tin, 12", VG, A $825.00

Bubble Blowing Washing Bear, Y, 1950s, plush bear in cloth dress standing at wash tub on litho tin base, 8", EXIB, A ..$375.00

Bubble Kangaroo, MT, 1950s, 9", NM+IB, A $300.00

Bubble Lion, MT, 1950s, litho tin, 7", EXIB...................$125.00

Bubbling Bull, see Wild West Rodeo ....$.09

Bumper Automatic Control Bus, Bandai, 15", EXIB, A ..$225.00

Bunny the Busy Secretary, MT, plush & tin, 7½", NMIB, A..$600.00

Bunny the Magician, Alps, 1950s, plush, 14", VG+IB, A...$330.00

Burger Chef, Y, 1950s, plush & litho tin, 9", EXIB.........$175.00

Busy Housekeeper (Bear), Alps, 1950s, pushing sweeper, plush w/cloth dress, 9", EXIB, A $200.00

Busy Housekeeper (Rabbit), Alps, 1950s, pushing sweeper, plush w/cloth dress, 10", EXIB, A $220.00

Busy Secretary, Linemar, 1950s, 7½" T, EXIB................$250.00

Calypso Joe, Linemar, 1950s, r/c, 10", EX $350.00

Cappy the Happy Baggage Porter, Alps, 1960s, 12", MIB..$275.00

Captain Blushwell, Y, 1960s, gent pouring himself a drink, 11", VG+IB, A $55.00

Captain Hook, Marusan, 1950s, 11", rare, EX, minimum value.$750.00

Captain Kidd Pirate Ship, Yonezawa, 1960s, 13", rare, MIB..$275.00

Cement Mixer #25, Masaduya, 1950s, 10", NMIB, A $200.00

Cement Mixer/Tools Truck, Japan, 1950s, litho tin, orange & yel w/silver-tone cement drum, 10½", EX, A $100.00

Central Cable Streamliner, TN, litho tin train engine & car, 13½", EXIB, A...$85.00

Champion Weight Lifter, YM, 1960s, plush dressed monkey w/lg barbell, 10", EXIB, A $115.00

Chap the Obedient Dog, Rosko, 1960s, MIB..................$150.00

Charlie the Funny Clown, Alps, 1960s, clown in cloth outfit on circus car, 10" L, EXIB, A..$220.00

Charlie Weaver Bartender, TN, 1960s, NM+IB, $125.00. (Photo courtesy Don Hultzman)

Chee Chee Chihuahua, Mego, 1960s, 8", EX $50.00

Cheerful Dachshund, Y, 1960s, plush, r/c, 9", EXIB $50.00

Chef Cook, Y, 1960s, 9", EXIB, A.................................$130.00

Chimpy the Jolly Drummer, Alps, plush monkey seated at drum w/cymbals, 9", EXIB...$50.00

Chippy the Chipmunk, Alps, 1950s, 12", MIB...............$125.00

Cindy the Meowing Cat, Tomiyama, 1950s, 12", EX........$75.00

Cine Bear (Camera Shooting Bear), Linemar, 1950s, litho tin & plush, w/5 plastic worms, 11", EXIB, A....................$935.00

Circus Fire Engine, MT, 1960s, litho tin & plastic, 11", EX ..$200.00

Circus Lion, Rock Valley, 1950s, plush, seated atop drum roaring, w/whip & flannel carpet, 10", VG+IB, A.........$430.00

Circus Parade, see Big Ring Circus ....$.09

Circus Queen (Seal), Kosuge, 1950s, 11", rare, MIB......$375.00

Clancy the Great, Ideal, 1960s, MIB.............................$275.00

Climbing Linesman (Clown), TPS, 1950s, clown in cloth costume climbing metal rod atop vehicle, 24" (assembled), EXIB...$675.00

Clown & Lion, MT, 1960s, clown spins up & down pole as lion roars, litho tin base, 13", NMIB, A $325.00

Clown the Magician, Cragstan, #40244, 1950s, cloth costume, 11", VGIB, A...$200.00

Clown Violinist, Alps, clown w/plastic head, cloth costume seated on litho tin barrel lying on its side, 10½", EX..$85.00

Clucking Clara, CK, 1950s, NM $130.00

Coffeetime Bear, TN, 1960s, plush & tin, 10", EX $150.00

Coffeetime Bear, TN, 1960s, plush & tin, 10", EXIB $250.00

College Jalopy, Linemar, 10", NMIB.............................$375.00

Collie, Alps, 1950s, barks and begs, eyes light up, plush, r/c, 7", EXIB..$75.00

Comic Choo Choo, Cragstan, 1960s, 10", EX $65.00

Communication Truck, MT, 1950s, friction, b/o lights, 12", NMIB..$250.00

Coney Island Rocket Ride, Remco, 1950s, 14", EXIB..$1,100.00

Cragstan Crapshooter Y, 1950s, 10", EXIB, A $165.00

Cragstan Melody Band (Daisy the Jolly Drummer Duck), Alps, 1950s, plush & litho tin, eyes light up, 9", EXIB, A ..$275.00

Cragstan Melody Band (Mambo the Jolly Drumming Elephant), Alps, 1950s, plush & litho tin, eyes light up, 9", EXIB, A..$150.00

Cragstan Playboy, 1960s, 13", EXIB $125.00

Cragstan Telly Bear, S&E, 1950s, plush, litho tin desk, 9", EXIB, A $275.00

Cragstan Tootin'-Chuggin' Locomotive w/Mystery Action (Santa Fe), litho tin, 24", EXIB, A $100.00

Crowing Rooster, Y, 1950s, plush, wht, yel & orange, 9", EXIB, A $75.00

Cycling Daddy, Bandai, 1960s, man w/pipe in mouth & cloth outfit riding tricycle, 10", EXIB, A.........................$120.00

Cymbal Playin' Monkey, lt brn plush w/pointed hat, metal cymbals, r/c, 12", VGIB, A......................................$40.00

Cymbal Playin' Turn-Over Monkey, TN, 1960s, brn plush w/metal cymbals, r/c, 8", EXIB, A $35.00

Daisy the Jolly Drumming Duck, see Cragstan Melody Band

Dalmatian (The Jolly Drumming Dog), Cragstan, plush, 9", EXIB, A $150.00

Dancing Dan (w/His Mystery Mike), Bell Prod, 1950s, 16", EXIB, A $170.00

Dancing Merry Chimp, Kuramochi, 1960s, 11", NM $150.00

Dandy the Happy Drumming Pup, Cragstan, 1950s, plush dog seated at litho tin drum set, 9", EXIB, A..................$165.00

Dandy Turtle, DSK, 1950s, 8", M $150.00

Dashee the Derby Hat Dachshund, Mego, 1970s, plush w/plastic hat, r/c, MIB..$80.00

Dennis the Menace (Playing Xylophone), TN, 1950s, 8", EXIB, A $315.00

Dentist Bear, S&E, 1950s, plush & tin, 10", MIB..........$500.00

Dilly Dalmatian, Cragstan, 1950s, plush, r/c, 8", VGIB, A ..$100.00

Dip-ie the Whale, SH, 1960s, 13", M $275.00

Distant Ealry Warning Radar Station, see Radar N Scope

Dixie the Dog (Dachshund), Linemar, r/c, 10" T (at head), EXIB $75.00

Dog Shuttling Train Set, Y, 1950s, 38" (extended), EXIB...$300.00

Donald Duck Locomotive, MT, 1970, tin & plastic, 9", M ...$175.00

Dozo the Steaming Clown, Rosko, 1960s, standing w/broom, cloth costume, 14", VGIB, A $275.00

Dragster Racer (Bump & Go Action), Sears, 13", EXIB, A ..$220.00

Dream Boat (Rock 'N Roll Hot Rod), TN, tin, 7", EX..$225.00

Dream Boat (Rock 'N Roll Hot Rod), TN, tin, 7", NMIB....$400.00

Drinker's Saving Bank, Illfelder, 1960s, 10" L, EXIB, A ...$90.00

Drinking Bear, Alps, 1970s, plush, seated w/milk bottle, 10", G, A $55.00

Drinking Captain, S&E, cloth outfit, 12", MIB..............$125.00

Drinking Dog, Y, plush & tin, NM+IB, A $110.00

Drinking Licking Cat, TN, plush & tin, 10½", EX $125.00

Drinking Licking Cat, TN, 1950s, plush & tin, NM+IB ..$250.00

Drumming Bunny, wht plush w/red nose, standing beating drum, 12", EXIB, A $65.00

Drumming Mickey Mouse (Lighted Eyes), Linemar, r/c, 11", EXIB, A $935.00

Dune Buggy (w/Surf Board), TPS, tin & plastic, w/driver, 10" L, EX+IB $100.00

El Toro, TN, 1950s, litho tin, NMIB, A $225.00

Electro #21 Midget Racer, Y, 1950s, litho tin, red version, w/driver, 10", VG+, A $1,375.00

Electro #21 Midget Racer, Y, 1950s, litho tin, scarce bl version, w/driver, 10", NMIB, A $4,400.00

Electro Lastomat Truck, Schuco #6084, r/c steering, 14", NMIB, A $700.00

Electro Matic Filling Station & Car, Distler, litho tin station (battery box) w/plastic car, 6½" L station, EXIB, A.........$200.00

Electro Matic 7500 Porsche, Distler, 10", EXIB, A.........$550.00

Electro Mercedes 280-SL Convertible, Schuco, 10½", EXIB, A $520.00

Electronic Periscope-Firing Range, Cragstan, 1950s, VGIB..$100.00

Emergency Service Searchlight Truck, Lumar, litho tin, wht w/yel trim, 19", VG, A $165.00

Excalibur Car, Bandai, 1960s, litho tin, 10", EX............$125.00

Expert Motor Cyclist, MT, 1950s, litho tin, 12", EX $375.00

Expert Motor Cyclist, MT, 1950s, litho tin, 12", NMIB, A ..$1,050.00

Farm Truck, Alps, 1960s, 11", MIB $325.00

Farm Truck (John's Truck), TN, 1950s, 9", MIB.............$350.00

Father Bear, MT, 1950s, plush, seated in rocking chair reading & drinking, EXIB, A $170.00

FBI Godfather Car, Bandai, 1970s, 10", MIB..................$125.00

Feeding Bird Watcher, Linemar, 1950s, plush mama bird & babies in nest perched on litho tin tree trunk, 7" L, EXIB, A $440.00

Ferrari Gear Shift Car, Bandai, 11", EXIB......................$250.00

Fido the Xylophone Player, Alps, 1950s, plush, 9", EXIB, A $130.00

Fighter F-50 Jet Plane, KO, 'chunky' plastic plane w/pilot under clear dome, 9", VGIB, A $140.00

Fighting Bull, Alps, 1960s, 10", MIB..............................$175.00

Fire Boat, MT, 1950s, 15", MIB.....................................$350.00

Fire Chief Car, litho tin, open car w/2 figures, siren by windshield, simulated spoke wheels, 10" L, EXIB, A.......$135.00

Fire Chief Car (FD), Japan, litho tin w/red light on top, antenna on trunk, emblem on door, 11" L, nonworking, G, A..$45.00

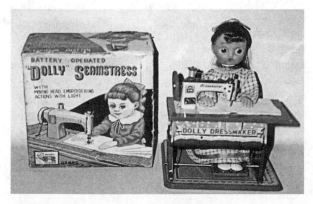

Dolly Dressmaker (Seamstress), TN, 1950s, 6", EXIB, A, $430.00. (Photo courtesy Don Hultzman)

Fire Chief Car (Ford), Japan, litho tin, red w/red light & 2 sirens on top, 12½", EX, A $80.00

Fire Engine (Mystery Action), S&H, 1960s, litho tin w/wht plastic extension ladder, 13½", EXIB, A $50.00

Fire Patrol, MT, litho tin, rider on motorcycle, 12", rare, EXIB $1,750.00

Fire Tricycle, TN, litho tin, w/driver, 10" L, EXIB, A.....$650.00

Fishing Bear (Lighted Eyes), Alps, 1950s, plush & tin, 11", EXIB, A $220.00

Fishing Panda Bear (Lighted Eyes), Alps, 1950s, plush & tin, 11", EXIB, A $275.00

Flexi the Pocket Monkey, Alps, 1960s, 12", MIB $200.00

Flintstone Yacht, Remco, 1960s, 17", NM $225.00

Flying Circus, Tomiyco, 1960s, 14" T, EXIB, A $465.00

Ford GT, Bandai, 11", NMIB...$110.00

Ford Mustang Fastback 2x2, plastic, lt bl, 16", EXIB (box mk 2x2 Cool & 'Pow!'), A $165.00

Ford Mustang Fastback 2x2, plastic, lt bl, 16", VGIB (box mk 2x2 Cool & 'Pow!') $100.00

Frankenstein, Poynter, 1970s, mostly plastic, standing on 'rock' base, red & wht striped shirt, belly showing, 13", VGIB.........$110.00

Frankenstein (Mod Monster — Blushing Frankenstein), TN, 1960s, standing on litho tin base w/name, 13", EXIB, A...........$175.00

Frankenstein (Monster), TN, 1960s, 13", VG+..............$100.00

Frankie the Roller Skating Monkey, Alps, 1950s, plush w/cloth outfit, r/c, 12", VGIB, A..$115.00

Fred Flint-stone's Bedrock Band, Alps, 1960s, 10", MIB, $750.00. (Photo courtesy Don Hultzman)

Fred Flintstone's Bedrock Band, Alps, 1960s, 10", VGIB...$365.00

French Cat, Alps, 1950s, 10" L, MIB $125.00

Friendly Joco My Favorite Pet, Alps, 1950s, dressed monkey, r/c, 10", EXIB $125.00

Friendly Puppy Barking & Begging, Alps, 1950s, plush, r/c, 8", EXIB, A $35.00

Funland Cup Ride, Sansco, 1960s, tin & plastic, 6½", VGIB..$150.00

Funland Cup Ride, Sansco, 1960s, 7", NM+IB................$350.00

Future Fire Car, TN, 1950s, 9", VG $225.00

Galloping Cowboy Savings Bank, Y (Cragstan), 1950s, 8x7", MIB..$1,275.00

Galloping Horse & Rider, Cragstan, 12", EXIB, A $230.00

Genie Bottle, Hobby Craft/Hong Knog, plastic, 12", NM+IB, A...$65.00

Gino Neapolitan Balloon Blower, Rosko/Tomiyama, 1960s, 11", MIB...$175.00

GM Coach Bus, Y, 1950s, litho tin, bump-&-go action, doors open to passengers debarking, 16", EXIB, A $300.00

Go Stop 'Benz Racer #7, Marusan, 10", EXIB, A............$250.00

Godzilla, Japan, r/c, 10", EXIB (Japanese box), A $935.00

Godzilla Monster, Marusan, 1970s, 12", M $450.00

Gomora Monster, Bullmark, 1960s, 8", M......................$350.00

Good Time Charlie, MT, 1960s, figure by lamppost w/cigar & whiskey bottle, 13", EX+IB, A $150.00

Gorilla, see also Roaring Gorilla Shooting Gallery, Shooting Gorilla, or Walking Gorilla

Gorilla, TN, 1950s, wht or brn plush, r/c, 10", EXIB, ea ..$350.00

Grand-Pa Panda Bear, MT, 1950s, plush, cloth vest, seated in rocking chair, 9", EXIB, A..$200.00

Grandpa Bear (Smoking & Rocking w/Lighted Pipe), Alps, plush, 9", EXIB $225.00

Grasshopper, MT, 1950s, 6", M.....................................$350.00

Green Caterpillar, Daiya, tin & fabric, 10" L, NMIB, A...$200.00

Green Hornet Secret Service Car, ASC, 1960s, 11", EX+..$700.00

Greyhound Bus w/Headlights, Linemar, 1950s, 10", MIB..$250.00

Gypsy Fortune Teller, Ichida, 1950s, 10", VG+IB, A, $1,265.00. (Photo courtesy Don Hultzman)

Hamburger Chef, K, 1960s, 8", MIB $250.00

Handy-Hank Mystery Tractor w/Light, TN, 1950s, 11", EXIB, A...$88.00

Happy 'N Sad Magic Face Clown, Y, 1960s, cloth costeene, r/c, 10", VGIB, A $130.00

Happy 'N Sad Magic Face Clown, Y, 1960s, cloth costume, r/c, 11", EXIB, A $385.00

Happy Band Trio, MT, 1970s, 11x11", NMIB, A............$500.00

Happy Fiddler Clown, Alps, 10", NM+IB, A.................$325.00

Happy Naughty Chimp, Daishin, 1960s, 10", M..............$50.00

Happy Santa, Alps, 1950s, plush outfit, walking w/drum, r/c, 11", VGIB, A $160.00

Happy Santa (w/Lighted Eyes), Alps, 1950s, Santa in cloth suit seated at drum set, 9", EXIB, A $150.00

Happy Singing Bird, MT, 1950s, 3" L, M $75.00

Happy the Clown Puppet Show, Y, 1960s, 10", EXIB.....$275.00

Happy the Clown Puppet Show, Y, 1960s, 10", NM+IB, A ..$400.00

Hasty Chimp, Y, 1960s, 9", MIB, from $100 to..............$125.00

High Jinks at the Circus, TN, 1960s, clown & monkey, plush & tin, 10", VGIB, A $175.00

Highway Patrol (Patrolman on Motorcyle), MT, 1950s, litho tin, 12", EXIB $825.00

Highway Patrol (TV Patrol) Car, Taiyo, 12½", EX+IB, A..$150.00

Highway Patrol Car, Okuma, blk & wht Oldsmobile, r/c, 11½", EXIB, A $150.00

Highway Patrol Motorcycle, MT, 1950s, 12", VGIB $465.00

Hiller Hornet Helicopter, Alps, 1950s, 12" L, MIB........$300.00

Home Washing Machine, Y, 1950s, 6", MIB $100.00

Honda Big Rider Motorbike #34, TPS, 1960s-70s, 10", NMIB $125.00

Hong Kong Rickshaw, PMC, 1960s, 9", EXIB, A $90.00

Hoop Zing Girl, Linemar, 1950s, 12", MIB..................$375.00

Hoopy the Fishing Duck, Alps, 1950s, 10", NMIB.........$375.00

Hooty the Happy Owl, Alps, 1960s, 9", MIB.................$200.00

Hot Rod #158 (Dream Boat), TN, 1950s, teen driver, 10", EX+, A $275.00

Hovercraft (Brace), TPS, 1950s, hovers by stream of air, r/c, 8", NMIB, A...$225.00

Hungry Baby Bear, Y, 1950s, plush momma bear in cloth dress feeding baby bear, 9", EXIB $150.00

Hungry Cat, Linemar, 1960s, cat swipes at fishbowl, 9", EXIB, A $520.00

Hungry Hound Dog, Y, 1950s, 10", M........................$400.00

Hungry Sheep, MT, 1950s, plush, r/c, 8" T, EXIB, A......$220.00

Hy-Que the Amazing Monkey, TN, 1960s, plush, 17", EXIB, A...$230.00

I May Look Busy/I'm the Boss (Telephone Bear), see Telephone Bear (I May Look Busy/I'm the Boss)

Ice Cream Baby Bear, MT, 1950s, 10", rare, NM $475.00

Indianapolis 500 Racer, Sears/TN, 1950s, 15", NMIB....$450.00

Indian Joe, Alps, 1960s, beating drum between legs, cloth outfit, 12", VG...$100.00

Indian Signal Choo-Choo, Kanto Toys, 1960s, 10", EXIB, A $55.00

ITV (International TV Broadcasting Van), Gakken/Japan, r/c, nonworking o/w NMIB, A $225.00

Jaguar Champ O' Raver, ASC, r/c, tin, w/driver, 8", NM+IB, A $100.00

James Bond 007 Aston Martin, Gilbert, 11½", NM, A..$175.00

Jeep (Tipping Action), Linemar, duck driver, litho tin, 8" L, EXIB, A $180.00

Jig-Saw Magic, Z Co, 1950s, 7x5x9", MIB....................$100.00

Joco the Drinking Monkey, Linemar, 1950s, plush w/plastic face, dressed in tux w/top hat, 10", EXIB, A $115.00

Johnny Speed Mobile, Remco, 1960s, 15", MIB.............$350.00

Jolly Bambino, Alps, 1950s, plush monkey seated in highchair, 9", MIB $750.00

Jolly Bambino, Alps, 1950s, plush monkey seated in highchair, 9", VGIB, A $300.00

Jolly Daddy the Smoking Elephant, Marusan, 1950s, plush in cloth outfit, r/c, 9", VGIB $150.00

Jolly Peanut Vendor, Cragstan, plush bear pushing peanut cart, 9", EXIB, A $330.00

Jolly Pianist, see Pianist (Jolly Pianist)

Journey Pup, S&E, 1950s, 8" L, M.............................$50.00

Jumbo (the Elephant), Alps, 1960s, plush w/circus blanket & headdress, picks up pole w/truck, r/c, 9½" T, G+IB..$175.00

Jumbo (the Roaring Elephant), Alps, 1960s, plush, w/circus blanket & headdress, 11" T, EXIB, A $85.00

Jumbo the Bubble-Blowing Elephant, Y, 1950s, 7", GIB ..$125.00

Jungle Jumbo, BN-C Toy, 1950s, hunter on plush elephant, 10", VGIB $325.00

Jungle Trio, Linemar, 1950s, litho tin, 7x6½" dia, EXIB ..$775.00

King Size Fire Engine, Bandai, 1960s, 13", M $150.00

King Zor, Ideal, 1961, 26" L, very rare, M...................$1,000.00

Kissing Couple, Ichido, 1950s, 11", MIB.....................$350.00

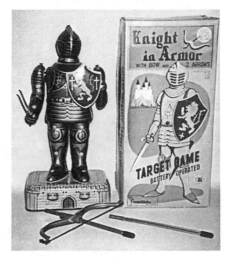

Knight in Armor Target Game, MT, 1950s, 12", NMIB, A, $500.00. (Photo courtesy Don Hultzman)

Knitting Grandma (Lighted Eyes), TN, 1950s, plush bear, 9", VGIB, A $170.00

Lady Carrying Jug (On Head), China, cloth outfit, 9", VGIB, A $130.00

Lady Pup Tending Her Garden, Cragstan, 1950s, cloth outfit, 8½", EXIB...$250.00

Last Chance (Western Style Music Box), Linemar, tin & plastic, cowboy dances to music, 5", NMIB......................$375.00

Laughing Clown (Robot), Waco, mc plastic, 14", NM+IB, A..$200.00

Leo the Growling Pet Lion (w/Magic Face-Change Action), Tomiyama, 1970s, 9", MIB.............................$275.00

Light House, Alps, 1950s, litho tin, 6½x8½", EX, A $600.00

Light-A-Wheel Lincoln, Rosko, 1950s, bump-&-go action, 10½", NM, A...$150.00

Linemar Hauler, Linemar, 1950s, 14", MIB..................$250.00

Linemar Music Hall, 6", EXIB..................................$325.00

Lite-O-Wheel Go-Kart, Rosko, 1950s, 11", EXIB, A $175.00

Little Indian, TN, 1960s, 9", rare, NM $175.00

Little Poochie in Coffee Cup, Alps, 1960s, 9", M............$80.00

Loop the Loop Clown, TN, 1960s, cloth costume, litho tin base, 12", EXIB, A $85.00

Lucky Cement Mixer Truck, MT, 1960s, 12", M $150.00

Lucky Crane, MT, 1950s, tin, w/toys, 8½", rare, EXIB...$675.00

Mac the Turtle w/The (Whiskey) Barrel, Y, 1960s, 9", EXIB, A..$275.00

Magic Action Bulldozer, TN, 1950s, 10", MIB..............$250.00

Magic Beetle, Linemar, 7", EXIB, A............................$55.00

Magic Man (Clown), Marusan, 1950s, puffs smoke, r/c, 12", EXIB...$250.00

Magic Snow Man, MT, 1950s, holding broom, 11", EXIB, A $140.00

Main Street, Linemar, 1950s, 20", very rare, M, minimum value...$1,200.00

Major Tooty (Drum Major), Alps, tin, 11", NM+IB, A...$125.00

Make-Up Bear, MT, 1960s, 9", rare, NM $700.00

Mambo the Jolly Drumming Elephant, see Cragstan Melody Band

Man From UNCLE, Headquarters Transmitter, NMIB ..$375.00

Man From UNCLE Talking Patrol Car, Rico, 1960s, 19", EXIB $575.00

Marching Bear, Alps, 1960s, plush bear w/drum & cymbals, 10", EXIB, A...$50.00

Marshal Wild Bill, Y, 1950s, cloth outfit, r/c, 10½", VGIB, A...$185.00

Marvelous Locomotive, 1950s, TN, 10", M $100.00

Maxwell Coffee-Loving Bear, TN, 1960s, plush & tin, 10", EXIB $250.00

McGregor, TN, 1960s, 12", EXIB, A............................$115.00

Melody Camping Car, Y, 1970s, 10", NM $150.00

Mercedes, see also Electro Mercedes

Mercedes Benz 250SL Convertible, Bandai, w/vinyl driver, 10", NM+, A..$150.00

Merry-Go-Round Truck #1700, TN, 1950s, 8½" L, EXIB, A ..$300.00

Mew-Mew the Walking Cat, MT, 1950s, plush, r/c, 7", VGIB, A..$85.00

Mexicali Pete the Drum Player, Alps, 1960S, cloth-dressed figure seated playing drum, 10", EXIB, A......................$175.00

Mickey Mouse & Donald Duck Fire Truck, MT, 1960s, litho tin, 16", EX+IB, A..$330.00

Mickey Mouse Locomotive, MT, 1960s, 9", NM $175.00

Monorail Set, Haji, 1950s, complete, EXIB...................$175.00

Mother Bear (Sitting & Knitting In Her Old Rocking Chair), MT, 1950s, plush, 10", EXIB, A............................$150.00

Mother Duck & Baby, see Worried Mother Duck & Baby

Mother Goose, Cragstan, plush, 10", VGIB, A................$75.00

MP Jeep, TN, 1950s, 10", NM.....................................$100.00

Mr Al-E-Gator (The Amazing), Alps, 1950s, r/c, 13" L, NMIB, A $200.00

Mr Baseball Jr, see All Stars Mr Baseball Jr.

Mr Fox the Magician (w/The Magical Disappearing Rabbit), Y, 1960s, 9", EX, A...$220.00

Mr Fox the Magician (w/The Magical Disappearing Rabbit), Y, 1960s, 9½", EXIB, A.......................................$550.00

Mr Magoo Car, Hubley, 1960s, 9", EXIB, A..................$285.00

Mr McPooch Taking a Walk & Smoking His Pipe, SAN, 1950s, plush dog in cloth outfit, r/c, 8", EXIB....................$150.00

Mr Traffic Policeman, litho tin, traffic cop standing next to stoplight on base, 14", VGIB $350.00

Mumbo Jumbo (w/Drum), Alps, 1960s, boy in native outfit seated playing bongo-type drums w/drum sticks, 11", EXIB, A $185.00

Mumbo Jumbo Hawaiian Dancer, Alps, 1960s, 10", MIB..$300.00

Mumbo Jumbo Hawaiian Drummer, Alps, 1960s, 10", VG..$150.00

Musical Bulldog, Marusan, 1950s, 8½", NMIB, A..........$975.00

Musical Comic Jumping Jeep, Alps, 12", M...................$175.00

Musical Dancing Sweethearts, KO, 1950s, 10", rare, NM..$500.00

Musical Ice Cream Truck, Bandai, 1960s, 11", NM........$150.00

Musical Jackal, Linemar, 1950s, 10", very rare, MIB...$1,100.00

Musical Jolly Chimp, C-K, 1960s, 10", EXIB, A.............$80.00

Mickey the Magician, Linemar, 1960s, 10", NM+IB, A, $1,750.00. (Photo courtesy Don Hultzman)

Musical Marching Bear, Alps, 1950s, remote control, 10", EXIB, A, $400.00. (Photo courtesy Don Hultzman)

Mickey the Magician (The Great Mickey), Linemar, 1960s, 10½", VGIB $1,200.00

Mickey the Magician/Great Mickey, Linemar, 10", VG, A..$650.00

Mighty Mike (The Barbell Lifter Bear), K, 1950s, plush, cloth shorts, 11", EXIB, A...$400.00

Mischief (Mischievous Monkey), MT, 1950s, 13", EX+IB, A $250.00

Miss Friday the Typist, TN, 1950s, 8" T, EXIB...............$175.00

Mobile Loudspeaker (Truck), Remco, 1950s, 22", NMIB, A..$125.00

Monkee-Mobile, ASC, 1960s, 12", EX $325.00

Monkee-Mobile, ASC, 1960s, 12", EXIB.......................$465.00

Monkey on a Picnic, Cragstan, plush, 9½", EXIB, A $300.00

Monkey the Shoe Maker, TN, 1950s, 9", rare, NMIB $650.00

Musical Melody Mixer, Taiyo, 1970s, 11", M.................$100.00

Mystery Action Tractor, Japan, 1950s, 7", MIB $150.00

Mystery Plane, TN, 1950s, pilot in open cockpit, litho tin, 10" L, EXIB, A..$300.00

Mystery Police Car, TN, 1960s, 10", NM......................$275.00

NAR Television Truck, Linemar, 1950s, litho tin, 11" L, EXIB..$775.00

Naughty Dog & Busy Bee, MT, plush pup & bee, 10", EXIB, A $65.00

NBC Television/RCA Victor Truck, Japan, 8", G+, A..$275.00

Nutty Nibbs, Linemar, 12", EXIB, A.............................$950.00

Ol' Rip Sleepy Head, Y, 1950s, 9½", EXIB, A $315.00
Old Fashioned Bus, MT, 13", NMIB.................................$85.00
Old Fashioned Car, SH, 1950s, jalopy w/driver, 9", EXIB, A $65.00

Open Sleigh, MT, 1950s, 15" long, EXIB, A, $500.00. (Photo courtesy Don Hultzman)

Over Land Express Locomotive #3140, MT, 1950s, 15", NMIB, A $30.00
Overland Stage Coach, MT, 1950s, litho tin, 15" L, EXIB...$175.00
Pa Pa Bear, Marusan, plush w/cloth outfit, tin shoes, standing smoking pipe, r/c, 9", NMIB, A $90.00
Passenger Bus, Y, 1950s, working headlights, opening & closing door, 16", EXIB, A $250.00
Pat O'Neill, TN/Rosko, 1960s, tin, cloth outfit, 11", EXIB...$275.00
Patrol Auto-Tricycle, see Police Patrol Auto-Tricycle
PD 26 Patrol (Police Patrol w/Lited Shooting Gun), Alps, 1950s, litho tin & palstic, w/driver, 10", EXIB $250.00
Peppermint Twist Doll, Haji, 1950s, 12", EXIB, A $245.00
Peppy Puppy w/Bone, Y, 1950s, 7", M $75.00
Pesky Pup the Shoe Steeler, Y, 1950s, 8", M..................$110.00
Pet Turtle, Alps, 1960s, tin & vinyl, 8", NM+IB, A.......$150.00
Pete the Talking Parrot, TN, 1950s, 18", M....................$250.00
Peter the Drumming Rabbit (Lighting Eyes), Alps, 1950s, plush w/cloth pants, r/c, 12", EXIB, A $150.00
Pianist (Jolly Pianist), Marusan, 1950s, plush dog seated at litho tin piano, 8½", EXIB, A $300.00
Picnic Bear (It Drinks), Alps, 1950s, plush, 12", EXIB...$100.00
Picnic Bunny (It Drinks) Alps, 1950s, plush, 10", NM+IB, A..$125.00
Pierrot Monkey Cycle, MT, 1950s, 9" T, EXIB, A $330.00
Piggy Cook, Y, 1950s, 10", EXIB $175.00
Pinky the Juggling Clown, Rock Valley, 1950s, cloth costume, 10", EXIB, A $200.00
Pinocchio (Xylophonist), TN/Rosko, 1962, 10", EXIB, A..$150.00
Pioneer Covered Wagon, Ichida, 1960s, litho tin w/vinyl wagon cover, 15" L, EXIB, A $120.00
Pipie the Whale, Alps, 1950s, 12", NM $325.00
Pistol Pete, Marusan, 1950s, litho tin figure w/cloth outfit, 10", EXIB, A $350.00
Plane w/Tow Car, Bandai, litho tin, 26" L, EX+IB, A $575.00
Playboy Cadillac, AHI, 1950s, 8" L, VGIB, A...............$200.00

Playful Puppy w/Caterpillar, MT, plush, litho tin base, 7½" T, EXIB, A $130.00
Playing Monkey, S&E, 9½", NM+IB, A.........................$150.00
Pleasant Kappa, ATD, 1950s, 10", NM $950.00
Pluto, Linemar, 1960s, plush, r/c, 10" L, EXIB, A $65.00
Police Auto-Tricycle, TN, litho tin, 10", EXIB $400.00
Police Cadillac, MIB...$250.00
Police Car (w/Siren & Flashing Dome Light), Linemar, 1950s, r/c, 7", EXIB $85.00
Police Car (1954 Chevy), Marusan, 10", EX $550.00
Police Car w/Stick Shift, TM, 1960s, 12", NMIB..........$175.00
Police Command Car ('63 Chevy Convertible), TN, tin, 13½", VGIB $175.00
Police Dept Jeep, Japan, wht litho tin, w/2 officers, 11", VG+, A $125.00
Police DP 35 (Flashing Light Police Squad Car), Japan, litho tin, 8", EXIB, A $175.00
Police Patrol Car (1950s Ford), Marusan, tin, blk & wht, 10", EX, A $350.00
Polzia Stardale, Taiyo, mk Fiat (not Ford), 12½", unused, NMIB, A $125.00
Popcorn Eating Bear, MT, 1950s, EX $175.00
Popcorn Vender (sic) Truck, TN, 1950s, litho tin, 9", EXIB, A .$330.00
Popcorn Vendor (Bear), S&E, 1960s, 8", MIB..............$575.00
Popcorn Vendor (Duck), TN, 1950s, 8", EX...................$300.00
Popeye & Olive Oyl Tumbling Buggy, Hong Kong, 1981, 7", NMIB $60.00
Popeye in Rowboat, Linemar, 1950s, 10", EX.............$2,420.00
Popeye in Rowboat, Linemar, 1950s, 10", EXIB..........$7,700.00
Porsche 911R, Schuco, plastic, 10", NM+IB $150.00
Power Construction Truck, Alps, 12" L, NMIB, A.........$235.00
Pretty Peggy Parrot, Rosko, plush, 11", EXIB.................$275.00

Professor Owl, Y, 1950s, 8", NMIB, $425.00. (Photo courtesy Don Hultzman)

Puffy Morris (Cigarette Smoker), Rosko, Y, 1960s, uses real cigarette, 11", EXIB..$275.00
Quick Draw McGraw Target Car w/Baba Looie, EXIB...$200.00
Rabbits & the Carriage, S&E, 1950s, plush rabbit pushing tin carriage w/plush rabbit, 9", EXIB, A $330.00
Racer #7, Marusan, litho tin, silver w/red number & trim, driver w/wht helmet, 10", nonworking, G+, A $85.00

Radar 'N Scope (Distant Early Warning Radar Station), MT, 1950s, 7x10", EX+IB $375.00

Railroad Hand Car, KDP, 1950s, litho tin, 6" L, EXIB, A ..$75.00

Rambling Ladybug, MT, 1960s, 8", EX..................................$100.00

Red Gulch Bar (Western Bad Man), MT, 1960s, 10", MIB, A, $925.00. (Photo courtesy Don Hultzman)

Red Gulch Bar (Western Bad Man), MT, 1960s, 10" T, VGIB $465.00

Rembrandt the Monkey Artist, Alps, 1950s, 8", rare, M ..$500.00

Return Tram, MT, 1950s, 30", rare, NM $350.00

Rex Doghouse, Tel-E-Toy, 1950s, 5", M $130.00

Ricky the Begging Poodle, Rosko, 1950s, plush, r/c, 8", VGIB, A...$45.00

River Steam Boat (With Whistle & Smoke), MT, litho tin, 14", VG+IB, A $75.00

Road Roller, MT, 1950s, NM+ $150.00

Roaring Gorilla Shooting Gallery, MT, 1950s, 9", NMIB, A $225.00

Roaring Gorilla Shooting Gallery, MT, 1950s, 9", VG+IB, A $125.00

Robo Tank TR2, TN, 1960s, 6", NM+............................$180.00

Rock 'N Roll Monkey (Auto-Matic), Alps, 1950s, tin & plush, 12", EXIB..$275.00

Roof-O-Matic Charger (Car), TN, litho tin, 15", NM+IB, A $150.00

Rooster, litho tin, blk & wht horizontal stripes, 7", EXIB, A $115.00

Roulette Man, dressed man standing at roulette table, complete w/chips & plastic cloth, 9", EXIB, A......................$220.00

Sam the Shaving Man, Plaything Toy Co, 1960s, 12", EXIB, A...$275.00

Sammy Wong the Tea Totaler, Rosko/TN, 1950s, 10", EXIB, A...$385.00

Santa Bank, Trim-A-Tree/Noel Decorations, plush figure seated on top of house, 11", EXIB $150.00

Santa Claus, Alps, 1950s, standing in plush suit ringing bell & carrying toy sack, wht fur boots, 9½", EXIB, A $65.00

Santa Claus (Merry Christmas), Santa in cloth suit ringing bell behind Merry Christmas stand, 9", EXIB, A............$100.00

Santa Claus #M-750 (Eyes Light Up/Sitting on House), HTC, 1950s, plush, EXIB..$65.00

Santa Claus in Reindeer Sleigh (Mystery Action), MT, 1950s, 17", EXIB, A $300.00

Santa Claus on Scooter, MT, 1950s, litho tin w/fur beard, 9", EXIB, A $125.00

Santa Fe Diesel Battery Cable Train w/Headlight, TN, 1950s, 2-car set, litho tin, 7", EXIB, A $90.00

Santa Fe Train Set, TN, 1950s, litho tin, 22", EXIB, A....$55.00

School Bus System (Stop-Go School Bus), yel, 13" L, EXIB, A $200.00

Scotch Watch (Lighted Eyes), Flare, plush Scottie dog w/plaid neck bow, r/c, 8", VGIB, A..................................$65.00

Shoe Shine Bear (Lighted Pipe), TN, 1950s, seated, plush w/vinyl snout, glasses on forehead, cloth apron, 9", EXIB, A..$120.00

Shoe Shine Joe (Lighted Pipe), TN, 1950s, plush monkey, 9½", EXIB, A $175.00

Shooting Bear, Marusan, 1950s, remote control, 10", EXIB, A, $400.00. (Photo courtesy Don Hultzman)

Shooting Gorilla, MT, 1950s, litho tin gorilla w/articulated arms standing on base, w/gun & darts, 10", EXIB, A $490.00

Showdown Sam Robot Target Game, figure w/pistol in ea hand, 10", complete, EXIB, A $115.00

Showroom Electric Sedan (1957 Dodge), 9½", nonworking o/w EXIB, A $250.00

Shutter Bug (Eyes Open), TN, 1950s, 9", NM+IB $800.00

Shutter-Bug (Eyes Open), TN, 1950s, 9", VGIB, A $400.00

Shuttling Dog Train, Japan, 15" L, complete, nonworking o/w VG+IB, A $85.00

Shuttling Train & Freight Yard, Alps, 1950s, litho tin, 16", EXIB, A $100.00

Sight Seeing Bus, Bandai, tin w/figure under clear roof dome, passengers lithoed on side windows, 15", NM+IB, A $200.00

Sightseeing Bus No 6026, red, wht & bl w/clear see-through top, 14", EXIB, A $100.00

Singing Circus Truck, Tomy, 1960s, 10½", G+, A............$75.00

Skating Circus Clown, TPS, 1950s, cloth outfit, r/c, 6", VG+IB $1,540.00

Skipping Monkey, TN, 1960s, plush dressed monkey w/rope, 10", EXIB, A $65.00

Sleeping Baby Bear, Linemar, litho tin w/cloth outfit & bedding, 9½", VGIB...$220.00

Sleeping Baby Bear, Linemar, 1950s, plush bear in bed, 9" T, EXIB...$350.00

Sloppy Pup, V, 1950s, plush, wht w/blk spots, r/c, 10", VGIB, A...$30.00

Smokey Bill on Old-Fashioned Car, TN, 1960s, 9", MIB ..$250.00

Smoking & Shoe Shining Panda Bear, Alps, 1950s, plush, 10", EXIB...$250.00

Smoking Bunny, Cragstan, plush, r/c, 10", VG+IB, A....$275.00

Smoking Grandpa (in Rocking Chair), SAN, 1950s, 8½", NM+IB $300.00

Smoking Pa Pa Bear, SAN, standing, plush in cloth outfit, r/c, 8", VGIB $90.00

Smoking Popeye, Linemar, 1950s, 9", NM $1,500.00

Smoking Popeye, Linemar/ KFS, 1950s, 9", NMIB, very rare, minimum value $3,000.00. (Photo courtesy Bertoia Auctions)

Smoky Bear, SAN, 1950s, plush, cloth outfit, r/c, 9", EXIB, A...$350.00

Snake Charmer, Linemar, 1950s, 8", NMIB....................$575.00

Snappy Puppy, Alps, 1960s, plush, 9", VGIB $50.00

Snappy the Happy Bubble Blowing Dragon, TN, 1960s, tin, plush & plastic, 30" L, NM+IB, A.......................$3,950.00

Sneezing Bear (Lighted Eyes), Linemar, 1950s, plush, w/box of tissues, 9", EXIB...$275.00

Space Patrol (Snoopy), MT, 1960s, litho tin, Snoopy in rocket ship, 11½" L, EXIB, A..$200.00

Space Traveling Monkey, Yanoman, 1960s, monkey in wht spacesuit & plastic helmet carrying 2 suitcases, 9", EXIB, A........$125.00

Spanking Bear, Linemar, 1950s, plush momma bear in cloth dress spanking plush baby bear, 10", EXIB, A..........$285.00

Squirmy Hermy the Snake, HTC, r/c, tin, 12", NMIB, A ..$225.00

Stop-Go Bus, see School Bus System

Strange Explorer, DSK, 1960s, 8", EXIB $275.00

Strutting My Fair Dancer, Haji, 1950s, figure on rnd base, 9", EXIB, A $285.00

Super Boy, TN, tin, 12½", NMIB, A $1,800.00

Super Coach (Transcontinental Bus), TN, w/horn noise, 16", NMIB, A...$100.00

Super Control Anti-Aircraft Jeep, S&E, tin, 9", NMIB, A..$100.00

Super Racer #42, 1950s, rare bl flame version, w/driver, 19", nonworking o/w+, A.......................................$2,640.00

Super Susie, Linemar, 1950s, 8x6", EX+IB, A $525.00

Superman Tank, Linemar, 1950s, 11", NMIB.............$3,500.00

Surry Jeep, TN, 1960s, 11", M......................................$200.00

Suzette the Eating Monkey, Linemar, 1950s, plush & tin, 9", G, A...$150.00

Suzette the Eating Monkey, Linemar, 1950s, 9", EXIB...$350.00

Swimming Duck, Bandai, 1950s, 8", rare, NM $150.00

Swimming Fish, Koshibe, 1950s, 11", NM.....................$125.00

Switchboard Operator, Linemar, 1950s, 7½x7", EXIB, A, $825.00. (Photo courtesy Bertoia Auctions)

Tarzan, Marusan, 1966, 13", VGIB (Japanese box) $1,600.00

Taxi, Linemar, working light-up sign on top, r/c, 7½", NMIB, A...$85.00

Teddy Balloon Blowing Bear, Alps, 1950s, plush w/cloth outfit, 11", EXIB, A...$120.00

Teddy Bear Swing, TN, 1950s, plush bear on trapeze, 14", EXIB, A $550.00

Teddy the Artist, Electro Toy/Y, 1950s, plush bear in cloth outfit seated at desk, 10", EXIB..$450.00

Teddy the Boxing Bear (Teddy the Champ Boxer), Y, 1950s, plush w/vinyl face, cloth shorts, 10", EXIB, A.........$400.00

Teddy-Go-Kart, Alps, 1960s, plush bear pulling cart, 10", EXIB $175.00

Telephone Bear, Linemar, 1950s, plush bear in cloth overalls seated in straight chair w/phone, 9", EXIB, A.........$160.00

Telephone Bear (I May Look Busy/I'm the Boss), Linemar, 1950s, plush bear at litho tin desk, 8", EXIB............$200.00

Telephone Bear (Ringing & Talking in His Old Rocking Chair), MT, 1950s, wht plush w/red candlestick phone, 10", EXIB, A $185.00

Telephone Rabbit (Ringing & Talking in Her Old Rocking Chair), MT, 1950s, wht plush, pk overalls, 10", EXIB, A.........$175.00

Telephone Talking Bear, MT, 1950s, plush in cloth overalls, tin base & telephone, 9", NM+IB, A.............................$200.00

Tin Man Robot (The Wizard of Oz), Remco, 1969, b/o, plastic, 21", MIB $200.00

Tom & Jerry Comic Car, Rico Co/Spain, tin auto w/Tom driving, 13" L, EX+IB...$350.00

Tom Tom Indian, Y, 1960s, 11", M................................$75.00

Topo Gigio Xylophone Player, TN, 1960s, 11", very rare, MIB, minimum value $1,200.00

Tractor (Robot Driver/Visible Lighted Piston Movement), Linemar, 1950s, tin w/rubber treads, 9½", MIB, A $425.00

Tractor on Platform, TN, 1950s, tin w/rubber treads, 9" L, NM+IB, A $130.00

Tractor T-27, Amico, 1950s, 12", rare, M $125.00

Transport Express (Overland), MT, litho tin cabover semi, 17", EXIB, A $150.00

Traveler Bear, K, 1950s, plush bear carrying tin suitcase, r/c, 8", nonworking o/w VG, A...$120.00

Traveler Bear, K, 1950s, plush bear carrying tin suitcase, r/c, 8", NMIB...$375.00

Tric-Cycling Clown, MT, 1960s, cloth costume, 12", VGIB, A $300.00

Trolly Bus, roof extends over open cab w/driver, passengers lithoed on windows, 13", EX, A $45.00

Trumpet Monkey, Alps, 1950s, plush & tin, 10", EXIB, A...$160.00

Tugboat (Annie), Japan, litho tin, b/o, 13", EXIB (Est: $100-$200)..$100.00

Tugboat (w/Realistic Noises & Puffs of Real Smoke...), SAN/Cragstan, 1950s, litho tin, 13", EXIB $175.00

Tuggy the Tugboat, Japan, litho tin, 13", EXIB, A..........$125.00

Tumbles the Bear, YM, 1960s, 9", NMIB.......................$150.00

Tumbling Bozo the Clown, Sonsco, 1970s, 8", M $160.00

Tumbling Monkey, brn plush w/vinyl fave, ears, hands & feet, red & wht striped outfit, 7", VGIB, A......................$80.00

TV Broadcasting (VW) Van, Gakken Toy/Japan, 1960s, 8", EXIB..$325.00

Twirly Whirly Rocket Ride, Alps, 1950s, 13", EXIB, A, $800.00. (Photo courtesy Bertoia Auctions)

Twirly Whirly Rocket Ride, Alps, 1950s, litho tin, 13", VGIB...$550.00

Two-Gun Sheriff, Cragstan, cloth outfit, plastic hat, r/c, 10", EXIB, A $200.00

Union Mountain Monorail, TN, 1950s, MIB................$225.00

Unmarked Secret Agents Car, Spesco, bump-&-go action, 14½", NM+IB, A $225.00

Vertol AirPort Service Helicopter, Alps, 1950s, 13", NMIB...$250.00

VIP the Busy Boss, S&E, 1950s, 8", EXIB.....................$200.00

Waddles Family Car, Y, 1960s, MIB $150.00

Wagon Master, MT, 1960s, 18" L, NM..........................$150.00

Wal-Boot Hobo, Tomy, 1960s, 20", NM $100.00

Walking Bear, brn plush, realistic, walking on all fours, r/c, 6" L, VGIB, A..$65.00

Walking Bear w/Xylophone, Linemar, 1950s, plush w/tin shoes & xylophone, 10", EXIB, A....................................$350.00

Walking Donkey, Linemar, 1950s, plush, r/c, 9", VGIB, A ..$140.00

Walking Elephant, Linemar, 1950s, plush w/red back blanket, r/c, 9" T, VGIB, A $85.00

Walking Elephant (Carrying Free Flying Ball), MT, 1950s, plush, r/c, 9" T, EXIB, A $110.00

Walking Gorilla, Linemar, plush, eyes light, has voice, r/c, 6½", NMIB...$275.00

Walking Horse (Cowboy Rider), Linemar, 1950s, litho tin, r/c, 7", EXIB $350.00

Wee Little Baby Bear (Reading Bear/Lighted Eyes), Alps, plush, 10", EXIB...$375.00

Western Bad Man, see Red Gulch Bar

Whirlybird Helicopter, Remco, 1960s, 25", NMIB........$250.00

Whistling Hobo, Waco, 1960s, 13", EXIB, A $100.00

Windy the Juggling Elephant, TN, 1950s, plush elephant on tin drum balancing umbrella on nose, 10", G+IB, A ...$200.00

Worried Mother Duck & Baby, TN, 1950s, 7", MIB $250.00

Worried Mother Duck & Baby, TN, 1950s, 7", VGIB, A ..$100.00

X-1018 Tank, MT, 9", NMIB, A $125.00

Xylophone, Ace, 1950s, 6" L, NM.................................$60.00

Yellow Cab (Coin Operated Battery Cab), Ichiko, yel tin w/red top, driver and passengers lithoed on windows, 9", NMIB, A $1,100.00

Yo-yo Clown, S&E, 1960s, 10", rare, MIB $425.00

Bicycles, Motorbikes, and Tricycles

The most interesting of the vintage bicycles are those made from the 1920s into the 1960s, though a few later models are collectible as well. Some of the '50s models were very futuristic and styled with sweeping Art Deco lines; others had wonderful features such as built-in radios and brake lights, and some were decked out with saddlebags and holsters to appeal to fans of Hoppy, Gene, and other western heroes. Watch for reproductions.

Condition is everything when evaluating bicycles, and one worth $2,500.00 in excellent or better condition might be worth as little as $50.00 in unrestored, poor condition. But here are a few values to suggest a range.

Note: A girl's bicycle does not command the price as a boy's bicycle in the same model. The value could be from ⅓ to ½ less than a boy's.

Advisor: Richard Trautwein (T3)

AMF Spiderman Jr Roadmaster, boy's, 1978, EX $100.00

Barnes White Flyer Tandem, rstr, from $1,200 to........$1,500.00

Bowden Space Lander, boy's, limited reissue of the 1950 model, EX, from $700 to $900.00

Cleveland Deluxe Roadmaster, boy's, prewar, light on front fender, horn tank, rear carrier, 24", EX, A $225.00

Cleveland Racing Bicycle, boy's, 1896, wooden wheels, cork handgrips, leather seat, 38", VG, from $250 to........$300.00

Colson Bullnose, boy's, 1939, light on front fender, EX rstr, A $1,800.00

Colson Firestone Cruiser, girl's, 1930s, 3-ribbed snap-in tank, Delta front fender light, Fair, from $110 to.............$200.00
Columbia Airrider, boy's, 1940-42, EX.........................$800.00
Columbia Chainless 2-Speed Safety, boy's, 1903, EX, from $1,200 to...$2,700.00
Columbia Model 40, boy's, 1890s, rstr........................$650.00
Columbia Superb, boy's, 1941, VG, from $300 to..........$525.00
Columbia 3-Speed Playbike, boy's, 1970s-80s, VG..........$75.00
Crescent #12 Pneumatic Safety, girl's, 1890s, G.............$225.00
Elgin Blackhawk, boy's, 1934, rstr.............................$2,000.00
Elgin Bluebird, boy's, 1936, VG, from $8,000 to.......$12,100.00
Elgin Deluxe, girl's, 1940, G, from $350 to...................$550.00
Elgin Robin, boy's, 1937, G, from $1,900 to..............$2,750.00

Elgin Sport Model, girl's, 1940s, G, from $350.00 to $550.00. (Photo courtesy Copake Auction, Inc.)

Evans, boy's, 1960s, middleweight truss frame, G, A $75.00
Evinrude Imperial Steam Flow, boy's, 1937, EX, from $9,500 to $1,400.00
Evinrude Streamflow, boy's, 1937, all aluminum, extremely rare (recalled due to engineering flaws), old rstr, G.....$6,600.00
Greyhound, girl's, 1920s, VG $150.00
Hawthorn Comet, boy's, Montgomery Ward, 1938, EX, from $600 to...$800.00
Hawthorn Zep, boy's, 1938, rstr, EX, from $2,900 to...$3,630.00
Hawthorn 2-Speed, boy's, Montgomery Ward, 1937, EX, from $100 to...$200.00
Hendee Indian Electric, boy's, 1918, G older rstr, from $2,600 to $3,200.00
Huffman Dayton Super Streamline, boy's, 1937, older rstr, from $1,900 to..$2,420.00
Huffy American Thunderbird, boy's, 1960s, G, from $75 to .$100.00
Huffy BMX, boy's, 1970s, VG, from $100 to...................$150.00
Huffy Radio, boy's, 1955, orig pnt & graphics, EX $4,400.00
Humber Sports Classic English 3-Speed, boy's, 1960s, Strumy Archer gears and handbrakes, rear book rack, EX ...$100.00
Indian, 1937, boy's, complete w/leather saddlebags, orig condition, VG $1,300.00
Iver Johnson, boy's, red body w/chrome fenders, wooden rims, rear kickstand, w/saddle bag, 36", EX $10,000.00
JC Higgins, boy's, Winderide Spring Fork, EX, from $800 to..$900.00
JC Higgins Flow Motion, girl's, 1948, G, from $100 to ..$150.00
JC Higgins Murray, boy's, 1948, rstr, from $150 to.........$200.00

Mercury, boy's, 1937, w/dbl lamp speedo/lamp combination, rstr, EX, from $2,200 to $3,850.00

Monarch Firestone Pilot, 1941, G, A, $175.00. (Photo courtesy Copake Auction, Inc)

Monarch Firestone Pilot, boy's, 1941, chrome headlight & rear rack, VG $400.00
Monarch Silver King Flo Cycle, boy's, 1938, rstr, EX, A...$2,090.00
Monarch Silver King Model M1, boy's, 1938, EX...........$900.00
Monarch Silver King Racer, boy's, 1935, rstr, from $1,000 to...$1,500.00
Monarch Silver King Wingbar, girl's, 1939, EX $600.00
Monarch Silver King 26-X, boy's, 1939, rare, EX, from $2,000 to...$3,000.00
Moulton Mark III, boy's, 1970, G, A..............................$330.00
Murray Fire Cat, boy's, 1977, VG..................................$250.00
Raleigh Chopper, boy's, 1970s, EX, from $150 to $250.00
Raleigh Space Rider 3-Speed, boy's, 1968, EX $75.00
Raleigh Superb, girl's, 3-speed, Brooks saddle, G, from $75 to...$100.00
Roadmaster Luxury Liner, girl's, 26", EX, from $500 to ..$700.00
Ross Polo Bike Jr Convertible, boy's, VG, from $100 to..$150.00
Schwinn Aero-Cycle, boy's, 1936, rstr, EX $3,150.00
Schwinn American w/Bendix 2-Speed, boy's, 1960, w/Cadet speedometer, G, from $75 to $100.00
Schwinn Apple Krate Sting Ray, boy's, 1971, NM (NOS), from $1,500 to...$2,300.00
Schwinn Auto Cycle Super Deluxe, boy's, 1941, rstr, EX ..$3,100.00
Schwinn Bantam, girl's, 1960, G $75.00
Schwinn Black Phantom, boy's, 1950s, balloon tires, rstr, from $1,000 to...$1,500.00
Schwinn Black Phantom, girl's, 1950s, balloon tires, rstr...$800.00
Schwinn Collegiate 5-Speed Sport, boy's, 1970, EX, from $150 to...$250.00
Schwinn Fair Lady, 1960s, VG, from $150 to $250.00
Schwinn Green Phantom, boy's, 1951, 26", EX.............$700.00
Schwinn Grey Ghost Sting Ray, boy's, 1971, 5-speed, 54", rstr..$650.00
Schwinn Grey Ghost Sting Ray 5-Speed, boy's, 1971, w/suspended banana seat, 54", rstr.................................$650.00
Schwinn Lady's Standard Model BC308, VG, from $100 to ..$200.00
Schwinn Mark IV Jaguar, boy's, 1960s, w/West Wind tires, VG .$1,200.00
Schwinn Model B, girl's, w/spring fork and fender headlight, VG...$250.00

Schwinn Predator, boy's, 1970s, fenderless chrome frame, Tuff wheels, G+ $50.00
Schwinn Red Phantom, boy's, 1950s, rstr....................$1,000.00

Schwinn Sting Ray, girl's, 1970s, with add-on Stewart-Warner three-speed transmission. G, A, $55.00. (Photo courtesy Copake Auction. Inc)

Schwinn Sting Ray Tornado, boy's, 1970s, NM, from $150 to $250.00
Sears Free Spirit, boy's, 1960s, EX, from $100 to $150.00
Sears Spaceliner, boy's, 1960s, G, from $100 to $150.00
Shelby Airflo, boy's, 1938, rstr, EX, from $3,290 to.....$4,620.00
Shelby Airflo, girl's, 1938, rstr, EX, from $1,300 to $1,980.00
Shelby Traveler, boy's, 1938, G $175.00
Silver King Hex Tube, boy's, 1948, aluminum frame w/spring fork, EX rstr, A $1,800.00
Swiss Army, boy's, 1941, VG, from $700 to.................$1,000.00
Vista Banana 3-Speed, boy's, 1970s, 20", M, from $200 to..$550.00
Waverly Scorcher, boy's, Indiana Cycle Co, 1894, EX...$1,600.00
Western Flyer Buzz Bike 2+1, boy's, 1960-70, G............$475.00

MOTOR VEHICLES

Honda Passport Scooter, 1981, EX.................................$500.00
Monarch Super-Twin, 1949, EX....................................$3,200.00
Schwinn B-10E, boy's, 1934, rstr, from $1,800 to........$2,420.00
Spaceliner, girl's, Sears, 67", EX $200.00
Whizzer, Cleveland Welding Co, late 1940s, Roadmaster frame, 26", VG, A $1,500.00

TRICYCLES

AMF Junior Tow-Trike, w/Delta front light, cleated tires, rear boom w/crank & chain pulley, NM..........................$350.00
Bell Car, name stenciled on paddle-formed seat, 27" L, VG, A $230.00
Colson Fairy, 1920s, chain drive, EX rstr, A $375.00
Early American, CI w/wooden seat & handlebars, VG ..$575.00
Gendron Pioneer, no fenders, 19½", G.......................$375.00
Jaxon, 1950s, w/unusual rear 3 wheels, hard tires, G, A ..$355.00
Murray Airflow Jr, 17½", G..$200.00

Monark Silver King, 1939, extremely rare, VG, A $5,250.00. (Photo courtesy Copake Auction. Inc.)

Pony Tricycle, hide-covered pony w/leather trappings, sulky seat w/metal trim 3 spoke wheels, 39" L, G, A................$180.00
Telephone Repairman Trike, Garton, wood tool box on rear, gr & wht, 32", VG (Est: $95) $110.00
V-Room! Trike, Mattel, w/plastic engine, 35", EX, A (Est: $25) $60.00

Black Americana

Black subjects were commonly depicted in children's toys as long ago as the late 1870s. Among the most widely collected today are the fine windup toys made both here and in Germany. Early cloth and later composition and vinyl dolls are favorites of many; others enjoy ceramic figurines. Many factors enter into evaluating Black Americana, especially in regard to the hand-made dolls and toys, since quality is subjective to individual standards. Because of this, you may find wide ranges in dealers' asking prices.

Advisor: Judy Posner (P6)

See also Banks; Battery-Operated Toys; Schoenhut; Windups, Friction, and Other Mechanicals.

Amos 'N' Andy Fresh Air Taxi, 1930s, NM, A $740.00
Banjo, plastic w/image of various figures around steamboat spewing musical notes from 2 stacks, 22", EX, from $200 to......$300.00
Bank, boy seated on tree stump on box base, compo w/wood box, pnt detail, side drawer, Germany, 1920s, 8½", EX, A ..$420.00
Bank, litho tin cylinder w/blk, yel & red image of a minstrel playing a banjo, red lid, England, prewar, 4", NM, A.......$185.00
Book, Andy's Exciting Day, England, 1930s, heavy paper, 24 pgs, EX, A $130.00
Book, die-cut Christmas stocking w/Golly & other toys, tag reads A Merry Christmas/To..& From.., England, prewar, EX+, A $125.00
Book, Frawg, 1930s, hardback, 5 stories, 127 pgs, NM+, A..$200.00
Book, Kellogg's Story Book of Games #1, features Little Black Sambo, Cinderella, etc, premium, 1931, VG, P6.......$60.00

Book, Kids of Many Colors, 1901, hardback, 156 pgs, EX+, A..$220.00

Book, Little Black Sambo, Bannerman, 1949, hardback, w/5 mechanical multi-action pgs, 9x18", NM, A...........$140.00

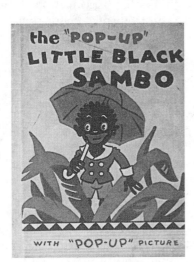

Book, *Little Black Sambo* (the Pop-Up), Blue Ribbon, 1934, NM, $275.00. (Photo courtesy Larry Jacobs)

Book, Little Colored Boy & Other Stories, Abingdon Press, undated but from late 1800s, hardback, 64 pgs, EX, P6................$125.00

Book, Sambo's Family Funbook, 'Fun, Games & Puzzles,' Featuring JT & the Tiger Kids, restaurant premium, 1978, EX, P6...$30.00

Book, Ten Little Colored Boys, USA, 1942, hardback w/ea pg having a die-cut head, EX, A $120.00

Book, Treasury of Steven Foster, Random House, 1st ed, 1946, hardback, 224 pgs, EX, P6 ....$55.00

Book, Well Done Noddy!, by Enid Blayton, hardback, EX, P6...$30.00

Coloring Book, Little Brown Koko, illus by Dorothy Wadstaff, 1941, 22 pgs, unused, EX $125.00

Doll, baby, 1930s-40s, 10", med brn-pnt compo body w/3 pigtails, cloth diaper, NM $75.00

Doll, Beloved Belindy, Georgene Dolls, 15", stuffed cloth w/button eyes, head scarf, NMIB, A $3,275.00

Doll, girl, Beecher (?), 20", shoe-button eyes, applied red felt mouth & short blk hair, dressed, G, A.....................$920.00

Doll, girl, Simon & Halbig #0739, 17", wood & compo body w/brn bsk socket head, set eyes, blk wig, cloth dress, EX........$650.00

Doll, girl, Simon & Halbig #1009 (Le Petit Parisian label), 22", antique wht silk dress & bonnet w/wht leather shoes, VG..........$1,680.00

Doll, girl, Simon & Halbig #1079, 11", compo & wood body w/bsk head, dk brn w/glass eyes, long wig, dress/pinafore, VG+...$450.00

Doll, girl, Simon & Halbig #1358, 17", brn bsk w/socket head sleep eyes, blk wig, red dress w/wht pinafore, straw hat, EX...$4,500.00

Doll, Golliwog, England prewar, 19", blk stuffed body w/wool hair, goggle eyes, bl pants, red tails, ruffled shirt, EX...........$60.00

Doll, Golliwog, 16", stuffed blk body w/wool hair, goggle eyes, red & wht checked pants, gr jacket, red bow tie, NM, A $130.00

Doll, Golliwog, 1950s-60s, 13", bl pants w/red vest & tails, yel bow tie, EX, P6 ....$40.00

Doll, Golliwog, 23", stuffed knitted-wool body w/wool hair, goggle eyes, knitted red & wht striped top & bl pants, EX, A...$60.00

Doll, Mammy, Chase Stockinet Doll, 26", pnt features, caracul hair, cloth dress, apron & head scarf, EX.............$8,800.00

Doll, Mammy, folk art, 10", straw-stuffed blk cloth w/mc cloth outfit, red neckerchief & head bandana, EX, A $240.00

Doll, Mammy, Norah Wellings, 13", brn velvet w/brn glass eyes, pnt features, blk mohair wig w/print scarf, VG, A...$150.00

Doll, Pappy, folk art, 1890s, 10", straw-stuffed blk cloth body w/stitched features, shirt & pants, hat & tie, EX, A ..$220.00

Doll, Picanniny, 14", stuffed blk cloth body w/dress, pinafore & pantaloons, plain face w/stitched eyes only, EX, A..$120.00

Doll, Pretty Pairs (Nan 'N Fran), bendable arms and legs, in flannel print pajamas with lace trim, NRFB, $200.00. (Photo courtesy McMasters Doll Auctions)

Doll, primitive man, 23", blk cloth w/embroidered features, wht cloth eyes, yarn hair, 19th c outfit, leather shoes, G, A...........$500.00

Doll, Topsy Turvy, 12", stuffed cloth w/life-like pnt features, red & wht clothing, VG, A $520.00

Game, Bean-Em, All Fair, 1930s, EX+IB, A $285.00

Game, Chuckler's Game, USA, 1930s, 9" sq, EXIB, A ..$100.00

Game, Jolly Darkie Target Game, McLoughlin Bros, early, complete, EX+IB $500.00

Game, Jolly Darkie Ten Pins, McLoughlin Brothers, EX+IB, A, $1,000.00. (Photo courtesy Wm Morford)

Game, Little Black Sambo, Cadaco-Ellis, 1940s, complete, EXIB...$100.00

Game, Pickaninny Bowling Game, Bavaria/England, 1920s, mini version (scarce), EX+IB (rare box), A....................$285.00

Game, Poosh-M-Up Jr 4-IN-1 Pinball Game, Northwestern Prod, 1920s, 17", EX+, A...$90.00

Game, Sambo Target, Wyandotte, 1930s, 23", EX, A.......$75.00

Game, Snake Eyes, Selchow & Richter, 1940s, EXIB, A..$85.00

Game, target head, 1880s, chromo litho die-cut blk head w/red open mouth ready to receive beanbags or balls, 13", VG, A...$230.00

Game, Watch On De Rind, All Fair, 1931, complete, rare, NMIB, A...$675.00

Game, White Eyed Coon Ring Toss, Spear Bavaria/England, 1900s, NMIB, A $730.00

Game, Zoo Hoo, USA, 1920s, complete, very rare, NMIB, A..$125.00

Kobe Toy, half-figure on wooden box opens mouth & brings watermelon slice to mouth, 3½" T, VG+, A $255.00

Kobe Toy, minstrels (2) seated at table w/hand crank, heads & hands move, 4½", EX, A $275.00

Marionette, Jambo the Jiver, Talent Products, 1948, 14", jtd wood w/cloth outfit, VG $225.00

Mariontte, minstrel strumming banjo, Pelham, 13", wood w/cloth outfit, MIB...$200.00

Mechanical Toy, Best Maid Pickanniny Seesaw, Japan, prewar, w/up, celluloid boy & girl on seesaw under umbrella, 8", NMIB $700.00

Mechanical Toy, Bojangle Dancer, Clown Toy Co, push the button on tin base & articulated wood dancer performs, NMIB $175.00

Mechanical Toy, Boy or Girl Walker, Fisher-Price, w/up, wood w/cloth clothing, pnt features, 6", rare, VG, A, ea ..$575.00

Mechanical Toy, Dancing Bellhop, articulated flat-sided pnt wood figure, push on stick to work, USA, 1930s, 16", NM, A $125.00

Mechanical Toy, Dancing Man, England, 1930s, flat articulated litho tin figure on rnd base, push tab for action, 8", VG+ $550.00

Mechanical Toy, Double Dancers, w/up, jtd wood couple in cloth outfits dance atop wood box, 10½" T, EX, A..........$1,430.00

Mechanical Toy, Gentleman's Head in Top Hat on Block Base, w/up, jaw moves as to talk, 7" T, EX (partial box), A ..$880.00

Mechanical Toy, Harlum Strutter, Sonsco/Occupied Japan, figure dances under street sign, tin/celluloid, 8½", EXIB, A..$275.00

Mechanical Toy, Jigger on Cotton Bale, Japan, Pat 1910, w/up, litho tin, nonworking a/missing suitcase o/w VG, A $1,100.00

Mechanical Toy, Minstrel Man, lever activated, litho tin, legs & arms move wildly, bl jacket, checked pants, hat, 8", VG..........$330.00

Mechanical Toy, Our New Clergyman, Ives, w/up, cloth-dressed figure w/pulpit on wooden box w/front label, 10", EX+, A...$4,400.00

Mechanical Toy, Preacher at Pulpit, American Toy, w/up, cloth-dressed figure on 3-tiered wooden box pulpit, 11", VG, A...$3,575.00

Mechanical Toy, Preacher at the Pulpit (Our New Clergyman), Ives, w/up, 9", EXIB (wood box), A......................$4,400.00

Mechanical Toy, Tap Dancer, w/up, celluloid figure in cloth outfit dances under street sign, Alps/Occupied Japan, 9", NMIB, A $250.00

Mechanical Toy, The Dixie Dancer, Ellsworth Haas Co, tap the end of wood paddle & articulated dancer performs, 8", G..$125.00

Mechanical Toy, Trumpet Player, w/up, plastic figure in cloth outfit on tin base sways & plays, etc, TN, 10", NM+IB, A $350.00

Musical Pack O' Fun, Oh Susannah!, Star Bright, 1950s, 5-in-1 activity set w/record, complete & unused, EX, P6 .....$55.00

Musical Toy, Dixieland Banjo-Uke, plastic, Spec Toy, 12", NM, A $50.00

Pin, golliwog tennis player, enameled brass figure holding tennis/banminton racket, bl, red & yel, 1½", 1960s, EX+ $25.00

Pull Toy, cloth-dressed boy bell ringer on metal four-wheeled platform, articulated axle allows figure to move, 6" L, VG, A, $715.00. (Photo courtesy Bertoia Auctions)

Puppet Set, grandparents, parents & 3 children, pnt rubber, Child Craft, 1965, 8½", EX+, A $60.00

Puzzle, Darktown Fire Brigade, jigsaw, heavy cb, shows stereotypical fire dept scene, Parker Bros, 1890s, complete, EXIB $425.00

Puzzle, Little Black Sambo, fr-tray, Sambo giving jacket to tiger, 1930s, 7½x8½", VG..$35.00

Squeeze Toy, Golliwog figure, pnt rubber, goggle-eyed, Robertson's Marmalade premium, 1950s, 4", EX+, A.........$100.00

Tea Set, matt porcelain w/golliwog graphics by Florence Upton, 1904, 5 pcs, M..$250.00

Wrapped Crayons, cb box w/image of blk minstrel w/cut-out mouth showing crayons inside, England, 1950s, 4" sq, NM, A $45.00

Boats

Though some comercially made boats date as far back as the late 1800s, they were produced on a much larger scale during WWI and the decade that followed and again during the years that spanned WWII. Some were scaled-down models of battleships measuring nearly three feet in length. While a few were actually seaworthy, many were designed with small wheels to be pulled along the carpet or out of doors on dry land. Others were motor-driven windups, and later a few were even battery operated. Some of the larger manufacturers were Bing (Germany), Dent (Pennsylvania), Orkin Craft (California), Liberty Playthings (New York), and Arnold (West Germany).

Advisor: Richard Trautwein (T3)

See also Battery-Operated Toys; Cast Iron, Boats; Paper-Lithographed Toys, Tootsietoys, Windups, Friction, and Other Mechanicals; other specific manufacturers.

Aircraft Carrier, Japan, 1950s, pnt wood, lt gray w/2 wht stripes on deck, red bottom, w/planes, EX, A (Est: $150-$250)...$200.00

Aircraft Carrier, Linemar, litho tin, b/o, 14", EXIB, A (Est: $200-$300) $200.00

Aircraft Carrier (Ventura), plastic, b/o, w/accessory planes, 22", VG+, A (Est: $150-$150) $100.00

Aircraft Carrier #59, Japan, litho tin, friction, w/accessory planes & helicopter, 14½", G, A (Est: $50-$100) $120.00

Armada, Hess, litho tin, w/up, lg flagship w/5 smaller boats, 34½" overall, G, A (Est: $200-$300)......................$600.00

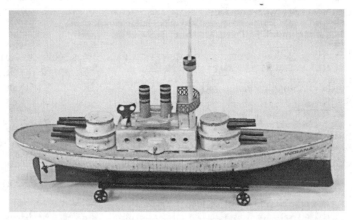

Battleship, Carette, painted tin, windup, red and white with two black stacks, 20½", VG, A (Est: $1,500.00-$2,000.00), $3,300.00. (Photo courtesy Bertoia Auctions)

Battleship, Fleischmann (?), pre-WWII, pnt tin, w/up, movable gun turrets, 2 stacks, 14", VG, A (Est: $500-$700)....$600.00

Battleship, France, pnt tin, w/up, 2 stacks & 2 masts, 2 turrets, deck hatch opens, overpnt, 19", A (Est: $800-$1,200)..$465.00

Battleship, Orbor, litho tin, w/up, 2 stacks & 2 crow's nests, guns on deck, wht w/red trim, 11", EX, A (Est: $500-$700) $825.00

Battleship, Remco, plastic, b/o, wht w/gray & orange detail, mk USA, 33", incomplete, GIB, A (Est: $50-$100)......$110.00

Battleship (B3), Orkin, PS, w/up, w/fire control towers, deck guns, 24", Fair...$2,000.00

Battleship (HMS Edinburgh), Marx, litho tin, friction, 14½", NM, A (Est: minimum $75)...................................$100.00

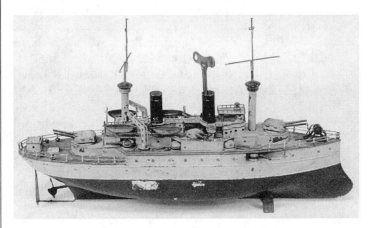

Battleship (Indiana), pressed steel, windup, white with red trim, 25", $3,600.00. (Photo courtesy Bertoia Auctions)

Battleship (Los Angles), Ventura, plastic, b/o, 35", EX, A (Est: $250-$400) $520.00

Battleship (USN on Hull), Dent, pnt CI & tin, articulated front axel, 19", no guns o/w VG, A (Est: $1,500-$2,000) .$2,750.00

Boat, Carette, pnt tin, w/up, sailor figure standing on deck w/single stack, wht & red, 7", rstr, A (Est: $200-$300)....$355.00

Cabin Cruiser, ITO/Japan, pnt wood, b/o, maroon & wht w/gray, wht & orange cabin, railed, 29", EX, A (Est: $300-$450)...$330.00

Cabin Cruiser, Japan, pnt wood, b/o, tapered & rounded tail, hinged cabin cover, 17½", EX.................................$950.00

Cabin Cruiser (Dragon), Japan, pnt wood, b/o, dragon design on sides, 18", EX, A (Est: $450-$550) $465.00

Cabin Cruiser (Typhon), JEP, pnt tin, w/up, lt bl & wht, 12", EXIB..$160.00

Cabin Cruiser (Vacationer #22), Linemar, 1950s, litho tin, b/o, w/outboard motor, 12", NMIB, A (Est: minimum $125)...........$175.00

Destroyer #3012, Ives, pnt tin, w/up, gray w/2 blk stacks, 2 masts & guns on deck, rpt, 13", A (Est: $400-$500) $250.00

Ferry Boat, Bing, pnt tin, w/up, wht over red, enclosed upper deck w/windows, 19", overpt.................................$800.00

Ferry Boat (Hendrick Hudson), Kuramochi (CK), litho tin, w/up, 10½", G+, A (Est: minimum $225) $420.00

Fishing Boat (American Scout), pnt balsa wood, blk & red hull w/wht deck, 51", G+, A ($600-$800) $525.00

Gunboat, Carette, tin, flywheel friction, metallic w/red & wht trim, brass-plated guns, 10", VG, A (Est: $300-$400)..........$115.00

Gunboat, Carette, tin, w/up, 3 stacks, red w/blk & wht trim, 8½", nonworking, overpt, A (Est: $200-$300) $110.00

Gunboat, Ernst Planck, store display, pnt tin, electric motors & lighting, 4 stacks, 36", EX, A (Est: $6,000-$8,000) $5,500.00

Gunboat, Germany, pnt tin, w/up, 2 stacks & gun stations, 2-tone brn w/wht line trim, 8", EXIB, A (Est: $300-$400) $350.00

Motor Boat, wood, gas-powered, dk brn w/wht bottom, 33", P+, A (Est: $200-$400) $220.00

Ocean Liner, Arnold, litho tin, w/up, red & blk w/wht upper deck, 2 yel & blk stacks, 12", VG, A (Est: $400-$600) $385.00

Ocean Liner, Arnold, tin, wht w/red center trim, 2 red & blk stacks, 10 lifeboats, 17½", VG $350.00

Ocean Liner, Bing, pnt tin, w/up, 3 stacks, 2 masts, 2 lifeboats, red, wht & bl, 16", Fair, A (Est: $400-$600)...........$660.00

Ocean Liner, Carette, pnt tin, w/up, 4 stacks, 2 crow's nest, red & wht w/blk trim, 13", rstr, A (Est: $1,000-$1,200) $1,265.00

Ocean Liner, Fleischmann, pnt tin, w/up, red deck, wht hull w/bl band, 1 stack, railed deck, 20", VG, A (Est: $400-$500) $600.00

Ocean Liner, Fleischmann, painted tin, windup, white deck with black and red hull, two crow's nests with flags, 21", restored, A (Est: $1,000.00 – $1,500.00), $1,980.00. (Photo courtesy Bertoia Auctions)

Ocean Liner, German, pnt tin, w/up, blk & red w/2 blk & red stacks, wht engine house, 8", EX, A ($100-$200) ...$150.00

Ocean Liner, German, pnt tin, w/up, wht, blk & red w/2 tan stacks, nonworking, 16", some rstr, A (Est: $800-$1,200) $3,520.00

Ocean Liner, w/up, pnt tin, dk bl w/yel deck, 2 red stacks, railed deck, 10½", G, A (Est: $175-$350) $120.00

Ocean Liner, Wolverine, litho tin, w/up, 15", EXIB, A (Est: $75-$125)....................................$165.00

Ocean Liner (America), Wyandotte, PS hull w/litho tin deck, wht & bl, 12", VG, A (Est: $50-$75).......................$130.00

Ocean Liner (Queen of the Sea), Masudaya, tin, b/o, bump-&-go, rotating antenna, fog horn, 22", NM+IB, A (Est: minimum $200) $300.00

Oceanliner, Carette, tin, w/up, 3 stacks, 2 crow's nests, wht/bl/red hull, brn deck, 21", overpt..................$1,200.00

Oceanliner, Germany, pnt tin, w/up, wht & bl, 1 bl stack, 2 flag poles, w/life boats, 20", VG+.....................................$900.00

Oceanliner (Leviathan), Bing, pnt tin, w/up, 3 stacks, observation deck, red, wht & bl, 39", VG, from $3,000 to $4,400.00

Oceanliner (SS United States), pnt wood, b/o, 2 stacks, 12 tin lifeboats, wht/blk/red, 23½", VG, A (Est: $250-$350)...$190.00

Patrol Boat (Sally), Ives, pnt tin, w/up, single stack, mast & lifeboat, 9½", some rpt, A (Est: $350-$450)........$1,870.00

PT Boat, Japan, pnt wood, b/o, bl w/red bottom, w/accessory planes, 16", VG+, A (Est: $75-$125)......................$195.00

Racing Boat, TMY, pnt wood, b/o, wht w/natural wood decking, NP trim, EX, A (Est: $400-$500)..........................$500.00

Racing Boat (B-24), Japan, pnt wood, b/o, maroon w/B-24 on gr tail fin, NP trim, 15", VG, A (Est: $500-$600) $935.00

Racing Boat (G-4), Japan, pnt wood, b/o, maroon & wht, w/outboard motor, 14½", VG, A (Est: $275-$350) $465.00

Racing Boat (Hydroplane U-27), pnt wood, b/o, 23½", EX $800.00

Racing Boat (Shark), Japan, pnt wood, b/o, dbl fins, shark design pnt on nose, 16½, EX+..............................$900.00

Racing Boat (Swallow), Japan, pnt wood, b/o, wht, maroon & gr, 15", EX+IB...$900.00

River Boat, Carette, painted tin, steam-powered, 15", repainted, A (Est: $600.00 – $800.00), $500.00. (Photo courtesy Bertoia Auctions)

Riverboat (Klaus Peter), France, pnt tin & brass, gear-driven anchor & pronounced keel, rpt, 11" $800.00

Sailboat, Star Prod/England, pnt wood, 20", EXIB........$150.00

Sailboat (Ocean Star), Star Prod/England, pnt wood & steel, complete, 24", EX (P box)....................................$135.00

Sailboat (Peggy Jane), litho tin, 36" T, VG+, A (Est: $75-$125) $130.00

Showboat, litho tin w/die-cut smoke coming from whistle, 13", EXIB, A (Est: $50-$100) $65.00

Side-Wheeler, Kellerman, tin, w/up, lithoed pilot house & deck, 10", VG...$400.00

Sightseeing Boat (USS Statue of Liberty), Japan, pnt wood, b/o, celluloid windows, NP rails, 18", VG, A (Est: $300-$400) $440.00

Sightseeing Boat (USS Statue of Liberty), Japan, pnt wood, b/o, celluloid windows, NP rails, 18", EX, A (Est: $550-$650) $770.00

Speed Ship, Masudaya, 1950s, litho tin, w/up, red & bl w/yel trim, guns fore/aft, railed deck, 7", NMIB, A (Est: mimimum $85)....**$150.00**

Speedboat, Japan, pnt wood, b/o, bl w/red & wht, bl seats, NP rail & cleats, 19½", EX, A (Est: $350-$450) **$550.00**

Speedboat, Japan, pnt wood, b/o, blk over wht w/gr striping, bl decking, NP trim, 17½", EX, A (Est: $200-$250) ...**$440.00**

Speedboat, Japan, pnt wood, b/o, maroon & gr w/wht striping, natural decking, NP detail, 17", EX, A (Est: $175-$225)..**$355.00**

Speedboat, Japan, pnt wood, b/o, rounded fan tail, NP detail, railed motor cover, 23", EX+, A (Est: $1,000-$1,200)........**$1,540.00**

Speedboat, Japan, pnt wood, wht & bl w/maroon fin on rnd tail, 15½", EX, A (Est: $850-$950).....................**$1,760.00**

Speedboat, Rico, pnt wood, b/o, wht & red w/natural deck, 13", Fair (VG box), A (Est: $75-$175)..............................**$65.00**

Speedboat (Chris Craft), Japan, pnt wood, b/o, yel & red, bl seats, NP detail, EX+, A (Est: $175-$225) **$1,045.00**

Speedboat (Columbia), tin, 2 US flags, rpt, 13", A (Est: $200-$300)...**$135.00**

Speedboat (Dragon), Japan, pnt wood, b/o, wht & red w/dragon design on sides, NP trim, 16½", EX, A (Est: $250-$350)...**$220.00**

Speedboat (Fairy Craft), Dewitt Speed Craft, w/up, blk celluloid body, 16", EX (w/case), A...............................**$300.00**

Speedboat (G-7), Japan, pnt wood, b/o, celluloid windshield, NP horns & cleats, 16½", EX, A (Est: $200-$275)........**$385.00**

Speedboat (Hornby), Meccano, tin & plastic, w/up, red & wht, 13", EXIB, A (Est: $75-$125)...................................**$140.00**

Speedboat (Little Wonder), Union Toy Co, brass, steam-powered, open hull w/sm boiler, 9", EX, A (Est: $300-$500)....**$715.00**

Speedboat (Lucky Boat), Japan, pnt wood, b/o, lion w/anchor decals on sides, 16½", EX, A (Est: $300-$350)........**$385.00**

Speedboat (Miss America), Lindstrom, litho tin, w/up, 7½", EX, A (Est: $50-$75)...**$100.00**

Speedboat (Miss America), Mengel Playthings, wood hull w/brass prop & deck cover, w/up, 14", EX, A (Est: $400-$500)...**$220.00**

Speedboat (Rocket), Japan, pnt wood, b/o, nose w/metal finial twin screw, 34", EX+, A (Est: $1,500-$1,750)......**$2,750.00**

Speedboat (Sea Eagle), Japan, pnt wood, b/o, gr & bl w/lg eagle design, applied eyes, 16½", EX, A (Est: $350-$450)..**$355.00**

Speedboat (Tiger), Japan, pnt wood, b/o, maroon & wht w/tiger's head on sides, NP trim, 16", EX, A (Est: $300-$350)..**$440.00**

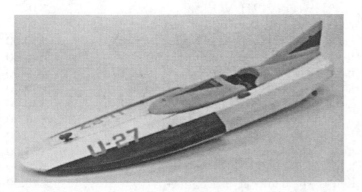

Speedboat (U-27 Hydroplane), painted wood, 23½", EX, $600.00. (Photo courtesy Bertoia Auctions)

Steam Launch, Weeden, modeled after 'The Glouster' w/open hull showing brass boiler, 13", VG, A (Est: $400-$500) **$275.00**

Steamboat, Arnold, pnt tin, w/up, 2-tone gr w/wht line trim, single stack, 12", G, A (Est: $125-$250)................**$170.00**

Submarine, Ives, pnt tin, w/up, able to submerge, gr w/red band, 9", rpt..**$180.00**

Submarine, Japan, pnt tin, w/up, wht, gray & blk, 9½", EXIB..**$150.00**

Submarine, Japan, painted wood with tin deck, battery-operated, 27", EX, A (Est: $800.00 – $900.00), $600.00. (Photo courtesy Bertoia Auctions)

Submarine (Diving), Wolverine, tin, w/up, unused, 13", MIB, A (Est: minimum $135) **$270.00**

Torpedo Boat, Bing, pnt tin, w/up, 2-tone gray, 4 stacks, observation deck, 23", overpt, A (Est: $1,200-$1,700) **$3,300.00**

US Merchant Marine Ship, Germany, pnt tin, w/up, 2-tone gray & wht, 1 stack, 10½", G, A (Est: $125-$250).........**$270.00**

Books

Books have always captured and fired the imagination of children, and today books from every era are being collected. No longer is it just the beautifully illustrated Victorian examples or first editions of books written by well-known children's authors, but more modern books as well.

One of the first classics to achieve unprecedented success was *The Wizard of Oz* by author L. Frank of Baum — such success, in fact, that far from his original intentions, it became a series. Even after Baum's death, other authors wrote Oz books until the decade of the 1960s, for a total of more than forty different titles. Other early authors were Beatrix Potter, Kate Greenaway, Palmer Cox (who invented the Brownies), and Johnny Gruelle (creator of Raggedy Ann and Andy). All were accomplished illustrators as well.

Everyone remembers a special series of books they grew up with, the Hardy Boys, Nancy Drew Mysteries, Tarzan — there were countless others. And though these are becoming very collectible today, there were many editions of each, and most are very easy to find. Generally the last few in any series will be most difficult to locate, since fewer were printed than the earlier stories which were likely to have been reprinted many times. As is true of any type of book, first editions or the earliest printing will have more collector value.

Big Little Books came along in 1933 and until edged out by the comic-book format in the mid-1950s sold in huge volumes, first for a dime and never more than 20¢ a copy. They were printed by Whitman, Saalfield, Goldsmith, Van Wiseman, Lynn, and World Syndicate, and all stuck to Whitman's original layout — thick hand-sized sagas of adventure, the right-hand page with an exciting cartoon, well illustrated and contrived so as to bring the text on the left alive. The first hero to be immortalized in this arena was Dick Tracy, but many more were to follow. Some of the more collectible today feature well-known characters like G-Men, Tarzan, Flash Gordon, Little Orphan Annie, Mickey Mouse, and Western heroes by the dozens. (Note: At the present time, the market for these books is fairly stable — values for common titles are actually dropping. Only the rare, character-related titles are increasing.)

Little Golden Books were first published in 1942 by Western Publishing Co. Inc. The earliest had spines of blue paper that were later replaced with gold foil. Until the 1970s the books were numbered from 1 to 600, while later books had no numerical order. The most valuable are those with dust jackets from the early '40s or books with paper dolls and activities. The three primary series of books are Regular (1 – 600), Disney (1 – 140), and Activity (1 – 52). Books with the blue or gold paper spine (not foil) often sell at $8.00 to $15.00. Dust jackets alone are worth $20.00 and up in good condition. Paper doll books are generally valued at about $30.00 to $35.00, and stories about TV Western heroes at $12.00 to $18.00. First editions of the 25¢ and 29¢ cover-price books can be identified by a code (either on the title page or the last page); '1/A' indicates a first edition while a 'number/Z' will refer to the twenty-sixth printing. Condition is important but subjective to personal standards. For more information we recommend *Collecting Little Golden Books, Vols I and II*, by Steve Santi. The second edition also includes information on Wonder and Elf books.

Advisors: Ron and Donna Donnelly (D7), Big Little Books

See also Black Americana; Coloring, Activity, and Paint Books; Rock 'n Roll; and other specific categories.

BIG LITTLE BOOKS

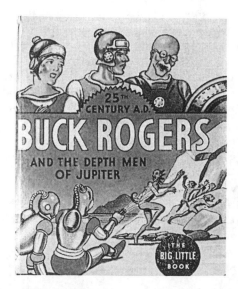

Buck Rogers and the Depth Men of Jupiter, #1169, EX, $140.00. (Photo courtesy Larry Jacobs)

Adventures of Jim Bowie (TV Series), 1958, EX+............$25.00
Adventures of Krazy Kat & Ignatz Mouse in Koko Land, 1934, VG $100.00
Alice in Wonderland, 1933, EX+................................$100.00
Alley Oop and Dinny in the Jungles of Moo, 1938, EX+ ..$45.00
Bambi, #1469, 1942, EX+ $40.00
Blondie & Baby Dumpling, 1937, EX+ $40.00
Buck Rogers & The Planetoid Plot, 1936, VG $85.00
Convoy Patrol, 1942, EX $25.00
Cowboy Malloy, 1940, VG+..$20.00
Dan Dunn on the Trail of Wu Fang, 1938, EX+ $65.00
Death by Shortwave, 1938, VG....................................$20.00
Dick Tracy & the Stolen Bonds, 1934, EX....................$65.00

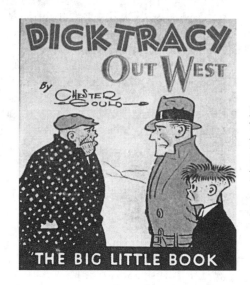

Dick Tracy Out West, #723, EX, $65.00. (Photo courtesy Larry Jacobs)

Don Winslow Navy Intelligence Ace, 1942, EX..............$50.00
Donald Duck & Ghost Morgan's Treasure, 1946, VG $55.00
Eddie Cantor in an Hour With You, 1934, EX+ $65.00
Eddie Cantor in Laughland, 1934, VG...........................$25.00
Ella Cinders Plays Duchess, 1938, EX $50.00
Fighting Heroes Battle for Freedom, 1943, VG................$18.00
Flash Gordon & the Ape Men of Mor, 1942, VG............$75.00
G-Man vs the Fifth Column, 1941, EX $30.00
Gang Busters Smash Through, 1942, EX+ $50.00
Gene Autry & the Mystery of Paint Rock Canyon, 1947, EX+ $50.00
Ghost Avenger, 1943, VG $18.00
Hal Hardy in the Lost Land of the Giants, 1938, EX+ $50.00
Houdini's Big Little Book of Magic, 1927, EX $50.00
Inspector Wade of Scotland Yard, 1940, VG $18.00
It Happened One Night, 1935, EX+ $80.00
Jack London's Call of the Wild, 1935, EX+ $50.00
Jackie Cooper in Peck's Bad Boy, 1934, VG+ $30.00
Jungle Jim & the Vampire Woman, #1139, EX...............$45.00
Junior G-Men, 1937, EX...$30.00
Just Kids & Deep-Sea Dan, 1940, VG+ $25.00
Kayo in the Land of Sunshine, 1937, EX $35.00
Ken Maynard in Gun Justice, 1934, VG $40.00
Kit Carson and the Mystery Riders, 1935, VG................$35.00
Last of the Mohicans, 1936, VG...................................$30.00

Li'l Abner & Sadie Hawkins Day, 1940, VG $25.00
Little Jimmy's Gold Hunt, 1935, VG $35.00
Little Orphan Annie & the Gooneyville Mystery, 1947, EX...$50.00
Little Women, 1934, VG...$35.00
Lone Ranger on the Barbary Coast, 1944, EX+ $50.00
Mickey Mouse & the Magic Carpet, 1935, VG $150.00
Mickey Mouse & the Magic Lamp, 1942, VG $50.00
Mickey Mouse & the Sacred Jewel, 1936, EX $80.00
Mickey Mouse Sails for Treasure Island, 1935, VG...........$75.00
Moon Mullins & Kayo, 1933, EX+...............................$50.00
Nancy & Sluggo, 1946, EX+ $45.00
Nevada Rides the Danger Trail, 1938, EX+ $35.00
Once Upon a Time, 1933, EX+ $60.00
Our Gang on the March, 1942, EX $40.00
Phantom & the Sky Pirates, 1945, EX+ $75.00
Popeye & the Deep-Sea Mystery, 1939, EX+ $75.00
Popeye & the Jeep, 1937, EX+ $85.00
Popeye in Quest of His Poopdeck Pappy, 1937, VG $40.00
Porky Pig & Petunia, 1942, EX+ $60.00
Prairie Bill & the Covered Wagon, 1934, EX $50.00
Radio Patrol Outwitting the Gang Chief, 1939, EX $25.00
Rangers of the Rio Grande, 1938, VG $18.00
Red Ryder & Circus Luck, 1947, EX+.........................$45.00
Red Ryder & the Squaw-Tooth Rustlers, 1946, VG.........$25.00
Roy Rogers & the Deadly Treasure, 1947, EX+..............$65.00
Roy Rogers & the Dwarf-Cattle Ranch, 1947, VG...........$25.00
Roy Rogers & the Snowbound Outlaws, 1949, VG $20.00
Shadow & the Ghost Makers, 1942, VG $100.00
Smilin' Jack & the Jungle Pipe Line, 1947, EX................$35.00
Smokey Stover the Foolish Foo Fighter, 1942, EX+ $45.00
Story of Charlie McCarthy & Edger Bergen, 1938, VG ...$25.00
Story of Skippy, 1934, Big Big Book, EX $95.00
Story of Skippy, 1934, premium, EX...........................$100.00
Story of Will Rogers, 1935, EX+...............................$45.00
Tarzan & the Lost Empire, 1948, VG $35.00
Tarzan in the Land of the Giant Apes, 1949, EX $50.00
Terry & the Pirates Meet Again, 1936, VG $75.00
Texas Rangers in Rustler Strategy, 1936, VG..................$50.00
Three Musketeers, 1935, EX+ $65.00
Tim McCoy & the Sandy Gulch Stampede, 1939, EX+ ...$50.00
Tim McCoy in the Prescot Kid, 1935, EX+....................$75.00

Tom Mix and Tony Jr. in Terror Trail, #762, EX, $50.00. (Photo courtesy Larry Jacobs)

Tom Mix in the Texas Bad Man, 1934, EX $50.00
Tom Swift & His Giant Telescope, 1939, VG.................$25.00
Uncle Don's Strange Adventure, 1935, VG....................$20.00
Union Pacific, 1939, EX+.......................................$50.00
Walt Disney's Mickey & the Beanstalk, EX $35.00
Walt Disney's Pluto the Pup, 1938, EX $50.00
Walter Lantz Presents Andy Panda's Rescue, 1949, EX+..$30.00
Wells Fargo, 1938, EX+ $50.00
World of Monsters, 1935, EX+ $60.00
Zane Grey's King of the Royal Mounted Gets His Man, 1938, EX+ $50.00
Zip Saunders King of the Speedway, 1939, VG............$18.00

LITTLE GOLDEN BOOKS

Airplanes, #180, A ed, 1953, 28 pgs, VG $8.00
All Aboard!, #152, A ed, 1952, 28 pgs, VG+ $15.00

Annie Oakley and the Rustlers, #221-25, A edition, NM, $22.00.

Baby's Book, #10, 1st ed, 1942, 42 pgs, VG+ $35.00
Barbie, #125, 1st ed, 1954, 24 pgs, EX+ $10.00
Bedtime Stories, #2, 1st ed, 1942, 42 pgs, VG $30.00
Buffalo Bill Jr, #254, A ed, 1956, 24 pgs, VG...................$18.00
Bugs Bunny, Pioneer, #161, 1st ed, 1977, 24 pgs, NM.........$8.00
Christopher & the Columbus, #103, A ed, 1951, 28 pgs, NM..$15.00
Daisy Dog's Wake-Up Book, #102, 1st ed, 1974, 24 pgs, EX+ $12.00
Dale Evans & The Lost Gold Mine, #213, A ed, 1954, 28 pgs, NM...$25.00
Danny Beaver's Secret, #160, A ed, 1953, 28 pgs, VG+ ...$12.00
Emerald City of Oz, #151, A ed, 1952, 28 pgs, EX...........$40.00
Fairy Princess Superstar Barbie, #162, 1st ed, 1977, 24 pgs, EX+ $8.00
Friendly Book, #199, A ed, 1954, 28 pgs, VG...................$12.00
Gene Autry, #230, A ed, 1955, 28 pgs, EX+ $25.00
Gingerbread Man, #165, A ed, 1953, 28 pgs, EX+...........$12.00
Golden Book of Fairy Tales, #9, 1st ed, 1942, 42 pgs, EX+...$42.00
Golden Book of Flowers, #16, 1st ed, 1943, 43 pgs, VG $25.00
Hansel & Gretel, #17, 1st ed, 1943, 42 pgs, EX $25.00
Here Comes the Parade, #143, A ed, 1950, 28 pgs, VG+ ..$15.00
House that Jack Built, #218, A ed, 1954, 28 pgs, EX+......$12.00

How Big, #83, A ed, 1948, 28 pgs, VG...................................$15.00

Howdy Doody & the Princess, #135, A ed, 1952, 28 pgs, VG+ $20.00

Indian Indian, #149, A ed, 1952, 28 pgs, VG+ $15.00

Laddie & the Little Rabbit, #116, A ed, 1952, 28 pgs, EX+ ..$15.00

Land of the Lost The Surprise Guest, #136, 1st ed, 1975, 24 pgs, EX+ $12.00

Little Yip-Yip, #73, A ed, 1950, 42 pgs, EX+ $18.00

Lively Little Bunny, #15, 1st ed, 42 pgs, 1943, VG...........$25.00

Lone Ranger & Tonto, #297, A ed, 1957, 24 pgs, VG......$18.00

Maverick, #354, A ed, 1959, 24 pgs, EX+ $20.00

Mr Rogers' Neighborhood (Henrietta Meets Someone New), #133, 1st ed, 1974, 24 pgs, NM $8.00

Night Before Christmas, #20, 1st ed, 1946, 42 pgs, EX.....$20.00

Open Up My Suitcase, #207, A ed, 1954, 28 pgs, VG......$18.00

Party Pig, #191, A ed, 1954, 28 pgs, VG $20.00

Poky Little Puppy, #8, 1st ed, 1942, 42 pgs, EX.................$35.00

Puss in Boots, #137, A ed, 1952, 28 pgs, EX+ $12.00

Road to Oz, #144, A ed, 1951, 28 pgs, VG $22.00

Rootie Kazootie Detective, #150, A ed, 1953, 28 pgs, VG $25.00

Rootie Kazootie Joins the Circus, **A edition, EX, $25.00;** *Tenggren's Snow White and Rose Red,* **A edition, EX, $12.00.**

Roy Rogers & the New Cowboy, #177, A ed, 1953, 28 pgs, VG $20.00

Sailor Dog, #156, A ed, 1953, 28 pgs, VG $20.00

Scuffy the Tugboat, #30, 1st ed, 1946, 42 pgs, EX+ $25.00

Steve Canyon, #356, A ed, 1959, 24 pgs, EX+ $20.00

Three Little Kittens, #1, 1st ed, 1942, 42 pgs, VG............$30.00

Tom & Jerry Meet Little Quack, #181, A ed, 1953, 28 pgs, VG $8.00

Uncle Wiggily, #148, A ed, 1953, 28 pgs, VG+ $18.00

Waltons & the Birthday Present, #134, 1st ed, 1975, 24 pgs, EX+ $8.00

Where Jesus Lived, #147, 1st ed, 1977, 24 pgs, NM+ $8.00

Whistling Rainy Day Play Book, #133, A ed, 1951, 28 pgs, VG $15.00

Wild Kingdom, #151, 1st ed, 1976, 24 pgs, NM+ $8.00

Wizard of Oz, #119, 1st ed, 1975, 24 pgs, NM.................$10.00

Woody Woodpecker at the Circus, #149, 1st ed, 1976, 24 pgs, NM $8.00

TELL-A-TALE BY WHITMAN

Animal Jingles, 1951, EX..$18.00

Aristocats, 1970, EX...$9.00

Barbie & Skipper Go Camping, 1974, EX+ $9.00

Captian Kangaroo & the Too-Small House, 1958, EX+ ...$14.00

Cinderella, 1954, image of Cinderella w/mice at her feet among the flowers, EX..$6.00

Donald Duck on Tom Sawyer's Island, 1978, EX $6.00

Eloise & the Old Blue Truck, 1971, EX+ $8.00

Fanny Forgot, 1946, EX $15.00

Fury, 1958, VG...$10.00

Gene Autry & the Lost Dogie, 1953, EX $20.00

Hey There It's Yogi Bear, 1964, NM...............................$15.00

Hop, Skippy & Jump, 1947, VG.....................................$10.00

Huckleberry Hound the Rainmaker, 1963, EX...................$15.00

I Love My Grandma, 1960, VG.......................................$10.00

Jim Jump, 1954, EX+ $10.00

Johnny Appleseed, 1967, EX+ $5.00

Land of the Lost The Dinosaur Adventure, 1975, EX+ $6.00

Lassie & The Kittens, by E Grant, 1956, VG.....................$5.00

Lassie Finds a Friend, 1960, EX $10.00

Let's Visit the Farm, 1948, VG.......................................$10.00

Little Lulu Has an Art Show, 1964, NM+ $10.00

Little Lulu Uses Her Head, 1955, EX $20.00

Me Too!, 1962, VG...$5.00

My Little Book About Flying, 1978, NM+ $5.00

Nancy & Sluggo in The Big Surprise, 1974, VG.................$6.00

Once Upon a Windy Day, 1947, VG+ $12.00

Pebbles Flintstone's ABC's, 1966, EX.............................$15.00

Peter's Pencil, 1953, VG..$10.00

Pinocchio, 1961, EX...$6.00

Poor Kitty, 1945, EX+ $15.00

Rackety Boom, 1953, shows truck on the farm, VG $15.00

Rainbow Brite & the Magic Belt, 1985, NM $5.00

Rescuers, 1977, EX+...$5.00

Ruff & Reddy Go to a Party, 1958, EX+...........................$25.00

Runaway Ginger, 1949, VG $8.00

Sherlock Hemlock & the Great Twiddlebug Mystery, EX+ ..$8.00

Snooty, 1944, VG $12.00

Snow White & the Seven Dwarfs, 1957, head images of Snow White & dwarfs, EX...$6.00

Sylvester & Tweety Bird in A Visit to the Vet, by J Lewis, EX .$5.00

That Donkey, 1954, VG..$6.00

Tom & Jerry in Model Mice, 1951, VG..............................$8.00

Uncle Wiggily & the Alligator, 1953, VG+ $6.00

Under Dog, 1966, VG+ $8.00

Wally Gator in Guess What's Hiding at the Zoo, 1963, VG ..$6.00

Yogi Bear's Secret, 1963, VG+.......................................$15.00

WHITMAN MISCELLANEOUS

Adventures of Sherlock Holmes, 1965, EX+ $10.00

Andy Panda's Rescue, by Walter Lantz, Tiny Tot Tale #2942, 1949, EX...$10.00

Bugs Bunny & the Secret Storm Island, Dell Fast Action, NM $75.00

Bugs Bunny's Big Invention, 1953, EX $10.00

Crusader Rabbit in Bubble Trouble, 1960, Tip Top Tales, EX+ $25.00

Donald Duck, linen, WDE, 1935, EX, A $125.00

Gene Autry & the Golden Ladder Gang, W Hutchinson, 1950, EX $18.00

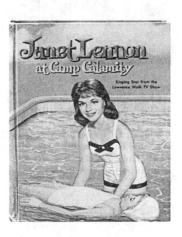

Janet Lennon at Camp Calamity, Barlow Meyer, illustrated authorized edition, Whitman #1539, 1962, EX, $18.00.

Little Orphan Annie & the Gooneyville Mystery Book, 1947, EX+ $50.00

Mickey Mouse & His Friends, #904, 1936, EX, A $150.00

Mickey Mouse 6 Wee Little Books Set, WDE, 1934, unused, NMIB, A $400.00

Munsters & the Great Camera Caper, #1510, 1965, EX...$15.00

Roy Rogers & the Gopher Creek Gunman, EX (w/dust jacket) $40.00

Roy Rogers & the Raiders of Sawtooth Ridge, #2329, EX ..$25.00

Roy Rogers' Trigger to the Rescue, Cozy Corner #2038, 1950, EX $30.00

Thimble Theatre Starring Popeye, Big Big Book, 1935, EX..$50.00

Tom & Jerry Meet Mr Fingers, #2006, 1967, EX $15.00

Tony & His Pals (Tom Mix), 1934, EX (w/dust jacket) $65.00

Tortoise & the Hare, 1935, hardback, EX $60.00

Twinkles and Sanford's Boat, General Mills premium, 1962, EX..$20.00

WONDER BOOKS

A Surprise For Felix, 1959, NM, $15.00. (Photo courtesy June Moon)

Astronaut & the Flying Bus, #853, 1965, VG+ $15.00

Babar the King, #602, 1953, VG+ $16.00

Baby Animal Friends, #604, 1954, EX+ $8.00

Baby Elephant, #541, 1950, VG $8.00

Bunny Sitter, #774, 1963, EX+ $8.00

Casper & Wendy Adventures, #855, 1969, VG $10.00

Casper the Friendly Ghost in Ghostland, #850, 1983, NM $8.00

Count the Baby Animals, #702, 1958, EX $6.00

Five Little Finger Playmates, #522, 1949, VG $8.00

Fred Flintstone: Fix-It Man, #917, 1976, EX+ $8.00

Hoppy the Curious Kangaroo, #579, 1952, image of Hoppy looking up & hopping over the city, EX+ $10.00

How the Clown Got His Smile, #566, 1951, VG+ $8.00

Huckleberry Hound in The Big Blooming Bush, #944, 1976, EX+ $10.00

Kitten's Secret, #527, 1950, VG+ $10.00

Littlest Angel, #755, 1960, image of angel diving downward from the heavens, EX+ $12.00

Littlest Christmas Tree, #625, 1954, VG $12.00

Magilla Gorilla & the Super Kite, #707, 1976, EX+ $12.00

Ollie Bakes a Cake (Kukla, Fran & Ollie), #829, 1964, VG+ $6.00

Pecos Bill, #767, 1961, EX $10.00

Three Mice & a Kitten, #533, 1950, VG $20.00

Wonder Book of Bible Stories, #577, 1951, EX+ $10.00

Wonder Book of Trains, #569, 1952, VG $8.00

MISCELLANEOUS

Adventues of Sonny Bear, by Frances Margaret Fox, illus by Warner Carr, Rand McNally, 1916, 1st ed, hardback, EX $48.00

Adventures of Andy Panda, Dell Fast Action, NM $75.00

Adventures of Charlie McCarthy & Edger Bergen, Dell Fast Action, NM $85.00

Adventures of Isabel, by Ogden Nash, Trumpet Club Special Edition, 1992, softcover, VG $18.00

Adventures of Mickey Mouse/Book 1, by David McKay, 1931, softcover, VG+ $75.00

Adventures of Superman, by George Lowther, Random House, 1942, hardback, EX+ $150.00

Alice in Wonderland (Movie Edition), Grosset & Dunlap, 1934, 297 pgs, hardback w/Charlotte Henry illus, EX $75.00

Alphabet Book, illus by Connie Ringel Bailey, Saalfield, 1934, linen-like, EX, P6...$30.00

American Indian Tales & Legends, by Vladimir Hulpach, Paul Hamlyn Co, 1966, hardback, VG..............................$18.00

At the Zoo Picture Book, illus by George Trimmer, Merrill, 1946, hardback, 14 pgs, EX, P6 ....$30.00

Baby's Animal Real Cloth Picture Book, Merrill, 1955, 8 pgs, NM, P6...$20.00

Bambi, Grosset & Dunlap, 1942, EX+ $35.00

Batman — Three Villains of Doom, Signet, 1966, 160 pgs, EX+ $20.00

Billy Whisker's Treasure Hunt, illus by Francis Brundage, Saalfield, 1st ed (?), 1928, 156 pgs, EX, P6 ....$45.00

Black Beauty, by Anna Sewell, Winston publisher, 1927, cloth cover, EX, $60.00. (Photo courtesy Marvelous Books)

Flash Gordon and the Ape Men of Mor, NM, $125.00. (Photo courtesy Larry Jacobs)

Black Stallion Returns, by Walter Farley, Random House, 1983, hardback, EX............$15.00

Blondie's Family, Treasure Book #887, King Features Syndicate, 1954, hardback, EX............$20.00

Bobbsey Twins & Their Schoolmates, by Laura Lee Hope, Grosset & Dunlap, 1928, hardback, G+ $10.00

Bonzo's Annual, by Dean, British, 1930s, 124 pgs, VG $75.00

Buck Rogers & the Children of Hopetown, by R Dwight, Golden Press, 1979, hardback, EX $12.00

Captain Marvel in The Return of the Scorpion, Dell Fast Action, NM............$225.00

Cat & the Fiddler, by Jacky Jeter, Parents' Magazine Press, 1968, 1st ed, hardback, EX+............$15.00

Cave of the Lost Fraggle, by M Teitelbaum, Weekly Reader Books, 1984, EX............$8.00

Charge of the Light Brigade, by Alfred Lord Tennyson, Golden Press, 1964, hardback, EX+............$25.00

Chuck Squirrel, Goldsmith Publishing, 1922, die-cut cover of lg squirrel, EX, P6............$30.00

Cowboys, by Douglas & Marie Gorsline, Random House, 1978, softcover, EX+............$15.00

Crocks of Gold, by Carol Ryie Brink, Saalfield #4110, 1940, VG+............$15.00

Dale Evans Prayer Book for Children, Big Golden Book, 1956, hardback, VG+............$10.00

Dilly the Dinosaur, by Tony Bradman, Weekly Reader Books, 1987, hardback, VG+............$10.00

Fairy Tales, retold by Katherine Gibson, illus by Erika, Whitman Publishing, 1945, hardback, 68 pgs, EX, P6............$25.00

Fantasia (Stories From Walt Disney's), Random House/WDP, 1940, hardback, EX+............$100.00

Fire House, by Leo Manso, World Publishing, 1949, Rainbow Playbook, spiralbound hardback, EX............$25.00

First Book of the Antarctic, by JB Icenhower, F Watts Co, 1956, 7th printing, hardback, EX+............$18.00

Flash Gordon in The Sand World of Mongo, by H Elias, 1976, paperback, EX............$10.00

Flintstone's Bedrock Rockmobile Race, by H Elias, 1980, EX............$8.00

Fonzie Drops In, by Johnston, #2, 1974, paperback, EX ...$10.00

Fraggle Countdown, by M Muntean, Holt-Rinehart & Princeton, 1985, EX $6.00

Ghost Busters Training Manual, by C Brown, Antioch Publishing, 1984, w/stickers, NM+............$8.00

Gingerbread Boy, Platt & Munk, 1932, paperback, 12 pgs, EX, P6............$18.00

God's Plan for Growing Things, by Mary Alice Jones, Rand McNally Junior Elf Book #8112, hardcover, 1964, EX+...$8.00

Happy-Go-Hoppy, by Myna Lockwood, Golden Press, 1972, hardback, VG+............$18.00

Helen Keller The Story of My Life, by Helen Keller, Pendulum Press, 1969, softcover, VG............$10.00

Here's to You Charlie Brown, by C Schulz, 1970, hardback, EX+............$8.00

Hoppity, by Marjorie Barrows, Rand McNally Junioe Elf #8144, 1967, hardback, VG+............$12.00

Horse Who Had His Picture in the Paper, by Phyllis McGinley, illus by Helen Stone, 1951, 1st ed, hardback, EX, P6 ..$28.00

How Fletcher Was Hatched, by Harry & Wende Devlin, Parents' Magazine Press, 1969, 1st ed, hardback, EX $12.00

Huckleberry Hound & the Dream Pirates, by H Elias, Modern Promotions, 1972, booklet, EX............$6.00

It's the Great Pumpkin Charlie Brown, by C Schulz, 1967, 1st ed, hardback, VG............$12.00

Jasper & the Watermelons, Diamond Publishing, 1945, 36 pgs, hardback, scarce, VG............$75.00

Junk Day on Juniper Street..., by Lilian Moore, Parent's Magazine Press, 1969, 1st ed, hardcover, EX+ $15.00

Knight Rider, by G Larson & R Hill, Pinnacle Books, 1983, paperback, EX+............$10.00

Land of the Giants — The Hot Spot, #2, by M Leinster, 1969, Pyramid, 1st ed, paperback, VG $5.00

Lassie Come Home, by Eric Knight, Holt, Rinehart & Winston Co, 1978, 1st ed of reissue, hardback, EX+ $18.00

Little Auto, by Lois Lenski, Oxford University Press, 1944, hardback, VG, P6............$25.00

Little Brown Bear, by Alice E Radford, illus by Clayton Rawson, Rand McNally, 1934, hardback, 68 pgs, EX, P6............$35.00

Little Deer, by Naoma Zimmerman, Rand McNally & Co, 1956, hardback, VG............$10.00

Little Dorothy & Toto of Oz, Rand McNalley, 1939, hardback, EX+ $75.00

Little Indian of the Prairies, Platt & Munk Co #3300B, 1935, paperback, VG $12.00

Little Red Riding Hood and the Big Bad Wolf, McKay, 1934, hardback, NM, $65.00. (Photo courtesy Larry Jacobs)

Little Tiger, by Mabel Watts, Rand McNally Jr Elf #8097, 1962, hardback, EX+ $10.00

Masters of the Universe — The Trap, Golden Storybook, 1983, VG $5.00

Masters of the Universe — Time Trouble, by R McKenzie, Golden Super Adventure Book, 1984, paperback, EX ..$6.00

McBroom & the Big Wind, by Sid Fleischman, WW Norton & Co, 1967, 1st ed, hardback, EX+ $10.00

Meet the Care Bears, Random House, 1983, mini, EX $8.00

My Daddy's Office, by Robert Jay Misch, Alfred A Knoph, 1946, hardback, VG $12.00

My First Zoo Book, by Andy Cobb, Rand McNally Jr Elf #820, 1952, hardback, EX $10.00

Night Before Christmas, by Clement C Moore, Random House, 1975, EX $10.00

Night Before Christmas, Merrill, 1961, linen-like, 12 pgs, cover shows Santa standing among the toys, EX, P6 ....$24.00

Nursery Songs & Rhymes, compliled & arranged by Catherine Allison w/pictures by Marion Smith, Lowe, 1944, hardback, EX $25.00

Nutcracker Suite From Fantasia, D Davis & Co Ltd, Australia, 1940, hardback, 32 pgs, EX+ (w/dust jacket)...........$100.00

Once Upon a Time — Story of the Frog Prince, Rand McNally Jr Elf #8068:15, 1960, hardback, VG $10.00

Osmond Brothers, by J Hudson, Scholastic Books, 1972, 1st ed, paperback, EX $10.00

Partridge Family in the Haunted Hall, by M Avalone, Curtis Books, 1970, paperback, EX.............................$8.00

Pastoral From Walt Disney's Fantasia, Harper & Bros/WDP, 1940, 1st ed, 36 pgs, hardback, EX $75.00

Peanuts, figure, Snoopy (Valentine), cloth, pk shirt w/red bow tie, blk suspenders w/hearts, Whitman Candy, 6", EX ..$6.00

Peter Rabbit in The Tale of the Flopsy Bunnies, by B Potter, McDonald's ed, 1988, paperback, EX $10.00

Peter Rabbit the Magician, by Mel Richards, Strathmore, 1942, spiral-bound hardback, VG, P6 ....$45.00

Pilgrims Progress, by Mary Godolphin, McLoughlin Bros, 1884, hardback, EX...$65.00

Pinocchio, Grosset & Dunlap, 1939, EX+ $50.00

Pinocchio (Walt Disney's), Random House, 1939, hardback, EX+ $40.00

Pirate's Apprentice, by Peter Wells, John C Winston Co, 1st ed, 1943, hardback, VG...$38.00

Pony Express, by Gaylord Dubois, Artist & Writers Guild/Grosset & Dunlap, 1944, hardback, EX, P6 ....$28.00

Popeye Puppet Show, Pleasure Books, 1936, EX+............$75.00

The Pop-Up Goldilocks and the Three Bears, Blue Ribbon, 1934, with three pop-up pictures, NM, $200.00; *The Pop-Up Little Orphan Annie and Jumbo the Circus Elephant,* with three pop-up pictures, Blue Ribbon Books, EX, $250.00. (Photos courtesy Larry Jacobs and David Longest)

Pups & Pussies, Linenette, Samuel Gabriel & Sons, 1930s, 12 pgs, EX, P6 ....$20.00

Puss in Boots/Pop-Up Book With Moving Figures, illus By V Kubasta, 1972, hardback, 6 pop-ups, EX, P6 ....$22.00

Pussy Cat Talks to Her Kittens, by Fannie E Mead, Rand McNally Jr Elf Book #8060, 1942, hardback, EX+.....$15.00

Raggedy Ann & Andy & the Magic Wishing Pebble, by C Dubowski, Random House, 1987, NM+......................$8.00

Raggedy Ann's Book of Go-Togethers, Random House, 1988, hardback, EX..$8.00

Rainbow Brite in Twink's Magic Carpet Ride, by J Lewis, Golden Book, 1985, hardback, EX $8.00

Real Ghostbusters — The Great Ghost Show, Wanderer Book, 1987, paperback, NM+ $5.00

Road Runner in A Very Scary Lesson, by Schroeder, Merrigold Press, hardback, NM+...$8.00

Rocket Away! by Francis Frost, 1953, 1st ed, hardback, EX, P6 ....$35.00

Santa's Circus, White Plains Greeting Card Corp, 1952, spiral-bound, 3 pop-ups, EX...$40.00

Sgt Preston & Yukon King, by MH Comfort, Rand McNally, 1955, NM+ $10.00

Shaun Cassidy Scrapbook, by C Berman, Tempo Books, 1978, NM...$10.00

Shirley Temple's Favorite Poems, Saalfield #1720, 1936, EX+..**$30.00**

Simpsons Christmas Book, by M Groening, Harper Collins, 1990, hardback, EX..**$8.00**

Skip Sees the Signs, by Virginia Novinger, Whitman, 1st ed, 1953, hardback, 36 pgs, EX, P6.........................**$28.00**

Snow White's Party/A Mini Pop-Up Book, Windmill Books/Dutton & Co, 1976, 1st ed, hardback, 6 pop-ups, EX, P6..**$25.00**

Speak Up Charlie Brown Talking Storybook, Mattel #4812, 1971, cb w/vinyl pgs, NM+ **$125.00**

Steadfast Tin Soldier, by Hans Christian Andersen, Little Brown & Co, 1983 ed, hardback, EX+ **$30.00**

Stories From Uncle Remus, by Joel Chandler Harris, Saalfield, 1934, with AB Frost illustrations, NM in dust jacket, $125.00. (Photo courtesy Marvelous Books)

Strawberry Shortcake & the Birthday Surprise, by E Doyle, Parker Bros, 1983, hardback, NM+ **$10.00**

Strawberry Shortcake & the Fake Cake Surprise, Little Pop-Up Book, 1982, NM+..**$10.00**

Strike-Out King, by Julian De Vries, World Publishing, 1948, hardcover, EX..**$10.00**

Tale From the Care Bears — Sweet Dreams for Sally, Parker Bros, 1983, hardback, EX..**$8.00**

Tales From Shakespeare, by Charles & Mary Lamb, John C Winston Co, 1924, hardback, EX...............................**$25.00**

Talking Typewriter, by Margaret Pratt, Lothrop, Lee & Shepard, 1940, hardback, 40 pgs, EX, P6 ....**$45.00**

Talks About Animals, Donohue & Co, 1920s (or earlier), hardback, EX, P6..**$38.00**

Teeny Tiny Witches, by Jan Wahl, GP Putman's Sons, Weekly Reader Book Club, 1979, hardcover, VG..................**$10.00**

Television Book of Choo-Choo, Bonnie Book, illus by Oscar Fabres, Lowe, 1949, EX, P6 ....**$25.00**

Thunder Cats in Quest for the Magic Crystal, Random House, 1985, booklet, EX...**$6.00**

Treasure Island, by Robert Louis Stevenson, John C Winston Co, 1924, hardback, EX+ **$30.00**

Valentine Bears, by Eve Bunting, Weekly Reader Books, 1983, hardback, VG...**$10.00**

Weather-Smurfing Machine, Random House/Mini-Storybook, 1982, EX+ **$6.00**

Who Cried for Pie?, by Veronica Buffington, Troll Associated, 1970, hardback, VG...**$18.00**

Wizard of Oz (Movie Edition), Bobbs-Merrill, 1939, blk-on-gr hardback, w/dust jacket (scarce), EX **$125.00**

Yogi Bear & The Bubble Gum Lions, Ottenheimer Publishing, 1974, booklet, NM+ **$10.00**

Yonie Wondernose, by Marguerite De Angeli, 1944, EX, P6...**$25.00**

Breyer

Breyer collecting seems to be growing in popularity, and though the horses dominate the market, the company also made dogs, cats, farm animals, wildlife figures, dolls, and tack and accessories such as barns for their models. They've been in continuous production since the 1950s, all strikingly beautiful and lifelike in both modeling and color. Earlier models were glossy, but since 1968 a matt finish has been used, though glossy and semiglossy colors are now being reintroduced, especially in special runs. (A special run of Family Arabians was done in the glossy finish in 1988.)

One of the hardest things for any model collector is to determine the value of his or her collection. The values listed below are for models in excellent to near mint condition. This means no rubs, no scratches, no chipped paint, and no breaks — nothing that cannot be cleaned off with a rag and little effort. A model which has been altered in any way, including having the paint touched up, is considered a customized model and has an altogether different set of values than one in the original finish. The models listed herein are completely original. For more information we recommend *Breyer Animal Collector's Guide* by Felicia Browell.

CLASSIC SCALE

Andalusian Foal (#3060FO), Cloud's Legacy, smutty palomino w/wht mane & tail, star, 2003 ....**$28.00**

Andalusian Foal (#3060FO), Precious Beauty & Foal Gift Set, bay blanket appaloosa w/blk points, socks, 1996-97.....**$6.00**

Andalusian Mare (#3060MA), Bay Andalusian, dk bay w/blk points, stripe, 3 socks, 2003 ....**$12.00**

Andalusian Mare (#3060MA), Classic Andalusian Family, dapple gray w/darker points, socks, 1979-93 ....**$11.00**

Andalusian Stallion (#3060ST), Classic Andalusian Family, alabaster w/gray-shaded points, gray or pk hooves, 1979-93..**$11.00**

Andalusian Stallion (#3060ST), Spirit Kiger Mustang Family, Action, buckskin w/blk points, Wal-Mart, 2002-current ..**$19.00**

Arabian Foal (#3055FO), alabaster w/lt gray mane, tail & hooves, 1973-82..**$12.00**

Arabian Foal (#3055FO), Drinkers of the Winds, rose gray w/darker gray points, right hind sock, Toys R Us, 1993................**$10.00**

Arabian Mare (#3055MA), Arabian Mare & Foal Set, lt bay w/blk points, dappling, front socks/hind stockings, 1997-98..**$11.00**

Arabian Mare (#3055MA), Collector's Arabian Family Set, blk w/broad blaze, front socks, JC Penney, 1988-90........**$16.00**

Arabian Stallion (#3055ST), Classic Arabian Family, lt brn bay w/blk points, diamond star, socks, Sears Book, 1984-85 ..**$18.00**

Arabian Stallion (#3055ST), liver chestnut with lighter mane and tail, striped left stockings, right hind socks, 2001 – 2002, $13.00. (Photo courtesy Felicia Browell)

Black Beauty (#3040BB), Black Beauty Family, blk w/star, right front stocking, 1980-93 ....$11.00

Black Beauty (#3040BB), Quarter Horse, sorrel w/lighter mane & tail, gray hooves, 2002 ....$13.00

Black Stallion (#3030), King of the Wind Set, red bay w/blk points, wht spot on right hind ankle, 1990-93 ....$12.00

Black Stallion (#3030BS), Arabian, seal bay w/blk points, star, socks, 2002-02 ....$12.00

Bucking Bronco (#190), Dakota Bucking Bronco, palomino w/wht mane & tail, dappling, shaded muzzle, hind socks, 1995-96 ....$16.00

Bucking Bronco (#190), gray w/darker mane & tail, bald face, stockings, 1961-67 ....$43.00

Charging Mesteño (#4812ME), Grulla Charging Mustang & Dun Foal Set, grulla w/brn points, Wal-Mart, 1995 ...$12.00

Cutting Horse (#491), Cutting Horse & Calf Set, chestnut w/darker mane & tail, hind socks, 2004 ....$31.00

Duchess (#3040DU), Lady Roxanna, King of the Wind Set, alabaster w/gray mane & tail, darker hooves, 1990-93 ....$11.00

Fighting Mesteño (#4811ME), Rufo & Diablo, bay roan w/blk points, shading, blaze, front stockings, Wal-Mart, 2001 ..$13.00

Fighting Sombra (#4811ME), Runaway, Mustang Kiger, cocoa dun w/brn points, left hind sock, BLM Adopt-a-Horse, 1997 ....$17.00

Ginger (#3040GI), Black Beauty Family, chestnut w/darker mane, tail & hooves, stripe & snip, 1980-93 ....$12.00

Ginger (#3040GI), Pinto Family, grulla pinto with black points and bald face, $20.00. (Photo courtesy Felicia Browell)

Ginger (#3040GI), Classics Bareback Riding Set, buckskin blanket appaloosa w/blk points, blaze, front sock, 2002-current $20.00

Hobo (#625), Hobo the Mustang of Lazy Heart Ranch, buckskin w/blk mane & tail, shading, 1975-80 ....$32.00

Hollywood Dun It (#478), buckskin with black points, dorsel stripe, leg barring, small star, 1998 – current, $21.00. (Photo courtesy Felicia Browell)

Jet Run (#3035JR), Pinto Sporthorse, blk pinto w/blk & wht mane, wht tail & legs, blk head w/star, 2001-current...$12.00

Jet Run (#3035JR), US Olympic Team, lt chestnut w/darker mane & tail, front socks, Sears Wish Book, 1987 ......$16.00

Johar (#3030JO), Dapple Gray Mare & Bay Foal, lt dapple gray w/wht mane & tail, shaded leg jts, Wal-Mart, 2002-current $15.00

Johar (#3030JO), The Black Stallion Returns Set, alabaster w/gray mane, tail & hooves, 1983-93 ....$12.00

Keen (#3035KE), Liver Chestnut Appaloosa Sporthorse, liver chestnut blanket appaloosa w/darker points, socks, 1998 ....$11.00

Keen (#3035KE), Olympic Team Set, gray w/lighter lower legs, gray hooves, Sears Wish Book, 1987 ....$16.00

Kelso (#601), Black Jack, blk pinto w/wht mane, tail & left foreleg, pk muzzle, right hind stocking, 3 socks, 1995-96...$12.00

Kelso (#601), dk bay/brn w/blk points, w/ or w/o right hind sock, 1975-90 ....$17.00

Kelso (#601), Ladies of the Bluegrass, red chestnut w/blaze, left front sock, QVC, 2002 ....$20.00

Lipizzan Stallion (#620), alabaster w/lightly shaded mane & tail, pk/natural hooves, 1975-80 ....$21.00

Lipizzan Stallion (#620), Pegasus, alabaster w/pk hooves, wings fit in slots on back, 1984-87 ....$29.00

Man O' War (#602), red chestnut w/darker mane & tail, w/stripe or star, 1975-90 ....$17.00

Man O' War (#602), War Admiral, blk bay, Wal-Mart, 2003-current $24.00

Merrylegs (#3040ML), Black Beauty Family, dapple gray w/wht mane & tail, lighter face & lower legs, 1980-83 ....$12.00

Merrylegs (#3040ML), Martin's Dominique Champion Miniature Horse, semigloss blk, 3 socks, 1994-95 ....$14.00

Mesteño (#480), Pirro (Pirro & Eldorado), chestnut pinto w/wht face, stockings, Wal-Mart, 2001 ....$13.00

Mesteño (#480), Spirit (Spirit Kiger Mustang Family), buckskin w/blk points, Wal-Mart, 2002...................................$13.00

Mesteño — Reflections, see Reflections Mesteño

Mesteño Foal (#4810FO), Rojo (Nekana & Rojo), red dun w/chestnut points, shaded, leg bars, Wal-Mart, 2001...**$7.00**

Mesteño's Mother (#4810MO), Alona (Alona & Damita Set), buttermilk dun w/blk points, leg bars, Wal-Mart, 2001.......**$12.00**

Mesteño's Mother (#4810MO), Cloud's Legacy, bl roan w/blk points & head, narrow star/strip/snip, 2003-current ..**$28.00**

Might Tango (#3035MT), Pinto Sport Horse, bay pinto w/blk mane & tail, wht head, stockings, gray hooves, 2004-current...**$12.00**

Might Tango (#3035MT), US Olympic Team Set, bay w/blk points, hind socks, Sears Wish Book, 1987 ....**$15.00**

Mustang Foal (#3065FO), Cloud's Legacy, grulla w/blk mane & tail, star, shaded leg joints w/bars, 2004-current **$28.00**

Mustang Foal (#3065FO), Mustang Family, grulla w/chestnut mane & tail, knee & hock stripes, hind socks, JC Penney, 1992...**$9.00**

Mustang Mare (#3065MA), Mustang Family, chestnut pinto w/chestnut mane & tail, gray hooves, Sears Wish Book, 1976-90 ....**$12.00**

Mustang Stallion (#3065ST), Mustang Family, buckskin w/blk points, knee stripes, no dorsel stripe, Sears Wish Book, 1985...**$15.00**

Mustang Stallion (#3065ST), Three-Piece Gift Set, grulla pinto with darker points and head, hind socks, high white on front legs, 1998 – 1999, $13.00. (Photo courtesy Felicia Browell)

Polo Pony (#626), bay w/blk points, early ones w/socks, molded woodgrain base, 1976-82 ....**$29.00**

Quarter Horse Foal (#3045FO), Dapple Gray Mare & Bay Foal Set, red bay w/blk points, Wal-Mart, 2002...................**$7.00**

Quarter Horse Foal (#3045FO), palomino w/wht mane & tail, socks, gray hooves, 1975-82.....................................**$11.00**

Quarter Horse Mare (#3045MA), bay w/blk points, socks, gray hooves, 1974-93..**$12.00**

Quarter Horse Mare (#3045MA), Quarter Horse Family, dk chestnut w/darker or blk points, hind socks, JC Penney, 1991 ....**$15.00**

Quarter Horse Stallion (#3045ST), Quarter Horse Family, dk chestnut/bay w/darker points, hind sock, JC Penney, 1991 ....**$16.00**

Rearing Stallion (#180), bay w/blk mane & tail, bald face, stockings, hooves, 1965-80 ....**$17.00**

Rearing Stallion (#180), Promises, dk bay pinto w/bay & blk mane & tail, wht hind legs, front socks, 1994-95 ......**$15.00**

Reflections Mesteño (#481), buckskin w/blk points, leg bars, 1996 ....**$16.00**

Rojo (#4812RO), Roano (Adriano & Roano Set), chestnut blanket appaloosa, shaded, front socks, Wal-Mart, 2001 ....**$10.00**

Ruffian (#606), dark bay w/blk points, star, left hind sock, 1977-90 ....**$16.00**

Ruffian (#606), Whispers, gray appaloosa w/extensive blanket, gray mane & lower tail & hooves, blaze, 1997...........**$13.00**

Sagr (#3030SA), Arabian Stallion, blk w/high stockings, 2003-current..**$12.00**

Sagr (#3030SA), Bay Arabian w/blk points, left front sock, 1998...**$12.00**

Shire A (#627A), dapple gray with shaded knees, hocks, and muzzle, half blaze, high stockings, blue and white ribbons, 2002 – current, $14.00. (Photo courtesy Felicia Browell)

Silky Sullivan (#00387), Ladies of the Bluegrass, dk gray w/blk points, blaze, 3 socks, QVC, 2002 ....**$20.00**

Silky Sullivan (#603), T Bone, blk roan w/blk points, gray speckles, 1991-92 ....**$13.00**

Swaps (#604), Black Mist (Misty II, Black Mist & Twister Set), blk pinto w/wht legs, blaze, natural hooves, 1996-99...**$15.00**

Swaps (#604), chestnut w/darker mane & tail, star, hind sock & lt hoof w/3 dk hooves, 1975-90 ....**$17.00**

Terrang (#605), Ambrosia, palomino w/wht mane & tail, shaded, front socks & hind stockings, 1997 ....**$13.00**

Terrang (#605), dk brn w/darker mane & tail, lighter hind leg, 1975-90 ....**$17.00**

Wahoo King (#466), Roping Horse & Calf Set, bay w/blk points, hind socks, 2000 ....**$16.00**

PADDOCK PALS SCALE

American Saddlebred (#9030), bay w/blk points, wht 5-point star, 1985-88..**$7.00**

American Saddlebred (#9030), English Show Horse & Rider Set, blk w/3 stockings, star & stripe, w/rider figure, 2003......**$9.00**

Arabian Stallion (#9001), bay w/blk points, 1984-88.........**$8.00**

Arabian Stallion (#9001), Half-Arabian, bay pinto w/bicolor mane & gray striped tail & hooves, narrow blaze, 1999-2000....**$6.00**

Clydesdale (#9025), chestnut w/blk mane & tail, bald or solid face, stockings, gray hooves, 1984-88 ....**$9.00**

Clydesdale (#9025), red bay w/blk points, broad wht blaze, stockings, 1999-2003 ....**$6.00**

Morgan Stallion (#9005), buckskin w/blk points, socks, pk/natural hooves, 1999-2000...**$6.00**

American Saddlebred (#9030), black with right hind sock, gray hooves, 1900 – 2000, $5.00; American Saddlebred (#9030), dapple rose gray with black points, hind socks, resist dapples, star-shaped star, 2001 – current, $6.00. (Photo courtesy Felicia Browell)

Morgan Stallion (#9005), seal brn w/blk points, 1984-88 ..$8.00

Quarter Horse Stallion (#9015), Breyer Prade of Breeds, smoke gray w/blk points, socks, JC Penney, 1988.....................$8.00

Quarter Horse Stallion (#9015), liver chestnut blanket appaloosa w/lighter tail, darker lower legs, shaded face, 2001-03 ....$6.00

Thoroughbred Stallion (#9010), dk gray w/blk points, hind socks, 1989-94...$7.00

Throughbred Stallion (#9010), Breyer Parade of breeds, dk bay w/blk points, bald face, hind sock, JC Penney, 1988....$100.00

Unicorn (#9020), wht w/gray shading on mane, tail beard & hooves, wht & gold horn, 1999-2003.........................$6.00

Unicorn (#9020), wht w/powder bl mane, tail, beard & feathers, gold horn, Montgomery Ward, 1985 ....$31.00

STABLEMATE SCALE

American Saddlebred (#5608), Just About Horses Special Edition Stablemates Gift Set, blk w/star & snip, hind socks, 1998...$9.00

Andalusian (#5606), Horse Foal Gift Set, buckskin w/blk points, 2003...$6.00

Andalusian (#5606), Just About Horses Special Edition Stablemates Set, dk dapple gray w/blk points, snip, socks, 1998 ....$9.00

Appaloosa (#5601), Little Red Stable Set, chestnut pinto w/darker mane & tail, bl eyes, bald face, 3 socks, 1999-01 ....$9.00

Appaloosa (#5601), Silver Cup Series/First Collection 2002, glossy bay pinto w/blk points, hind sock, QVC $12.00

Arabian Mare (#5011), dapple gray w/darker mane & tail, stockings, gray hooves, 1975-76..$22.00

Arabian Mare (#5011), Hidalgo Arabian Adventure Set, fleabit gray w/shaded points, chestnut speckles, 2004-current ..$13.00

Arabian Mare (#5011), palomino w/wht mane, tail & face, socks, gray hooves, 1995-97 ....$5.00

Arabian Rearing (#5603), Just About Horses Special Edition Gift Set, chestnut w/lighter mane & tail, blaze, socks, 1998...$9.00

Arabian Stallion (#5010), dapple gray w/darker mane & tail, stockings, 1975-76..$32.00

Arabian Stallion (#5010), Stablemate Set, gray w/blk mane & tail, socks, gray hoves, Sears Wish Book, 1989.............$8.00

Arbian Rearing (#5603), Silver Cup Series/First Collection 2002, glossy chestnut w/shaded mane & tail, socks/stockings $13.00

Cantering Foal (#5614), Flocky Set II, flocked buckskin appaloosa w/blk mane & tail, hind stockings, BreyerFest, 2001 ....$12.00

Citation (#5020), from J.C. Penney's Twelve-Piece Stablemate Set, palomino with white mane and tail, gray hooves and shaded muzzle, blaze, 1997, $5.00; Citation (#5020), from Sears' Wish Book Twelve-Piece Stablemate Gift Set, peppercorn appaloosa with darker points, spots over back, faint hind socks, 1998, $5.00. (Photo courtesy Felicia Browell)

Citation (#5020), bay w/dk points, left hind sock, 1975-90..$8.00

Citation (#5020), Stablemates Assortment III, med gray w/blk points, Sears Wish Book, 1991 ....$7.00

Clydesdale (#5604), Just About Horses Special Edition Gift Set, bl roan w/blk points, bald face, stockings, 1998 ....$9.00

Clydesdale (#5604), Red Stable Set, dun w/blk & chocolate points, blaze, 3 stockings, 2003-current......................$23.00

Draft Horse (#5055), dk chestnut w/darker mane & tail, socks, gray hooves, Riegseckers, 1985.................................$33.00

Draft Horse (#5055), 12-Piece Stablemate Set, blk pinto w/wht blaze, belly, chest & legs, JC Penney, 1996...................$6.00

Morgan Mare (#5038), chestnut w/darker mane & tail, hind stockings, lighter lower fore legs, gray hooves, 1976..$24.00

Morgan Mare (#5038), Hidalgo Arabian Adventure Set, alabaster w/gray-shaded face, natural hooves, 2004-current $13.00

Morgan Prancing (#5612), liver chestnut w/lighter flaxen mane & tail, blaze, socks, natural hooves, 1999-2002 ....$3.00

Morgan Prancing (#5612), Silver Cup Series/Second Collection 2002, glossy seal bay w/blk mane & tail, shading, QVC...$13.00

Morgan Stallion (#5035), bay w/blk mane, tail, knees & hocks, left hind sock, 1976-88 ....$13.00

Morgan Stallion (#5035), Stablemate Assortment II, red chestnut w/socks, Sears Wish Book, 1990..........................$8.00

Morgan Stallion (#5035), 12-Piece Stablemate Set, brn-shaded chestnut w/darker mane & tail, JC Penney, 1997 ....$5.00

Mule (#5609), blk leopard appaloosa w/blk tail & face, gray shading, blk spash spots, 1998-2002 ....$4.00

Native Dancer (#5023), blood bay w/blk points, Sears Wish Book, 1989 ....$8.00

Native Dancer (#5023), Set of 12 Miniatures, bay w/vague right socks, JC Penney, 1995 ....$5.00

Paso Fino (#5610), Hildago Stablemate Mustang Playset, dapple rose gray w/darker points, Blockbuster, 2004..............$11.00

Paso Fino (#5610), Just About Horses Special Edition Gift Set, smutty buckskin w/blk points, shaded back, 1998........$9.00

Quarter Horse Mare (#5048), buckskin w/blk points, no dorsal stripe, socks, gray hooves, 1976-88............................$11.00

Quarter Horse Mare (#5048), chestnut with darker mane and tail, stockings, black hooves, 1976, $27.00. (Photo courtesy Felicia Browell)

Quarter Horse Stallion (#5045), matt/semigloss chestnut w/darker mane & tail, socks/stockings, gray hooves, 1976..........$25.00

Quarter Horse Stallion (#5045), Paint, grulla pinto w/gray body, darker points, 1998 ....$5.00

Saddlebred (#5002), dapple gray w/darker points, bald face, gray hooves, 1975-76...$33.00

Saddlebred (#5002), 12-Piece Stablemate Set, dk red chestnut w/darker points, right hind sock, JC Penney, 1997 ....$19.00

Scrambling Foal (#5613), Fun Foals Gift Pack, mostly wht bay pinto w/blk mane on upper neck, shaded muzzle, 2002..$9.00

Scratching Foal (#5616), Fun Foals Gift Set, palomino w/wht mane & tail, blaze, wht chin, socks, 2002-current $9.00

Seabiscuit (#5024), Assortment III, matt/semigloss dapple gray w/blk points, Sears Wish Book, 1991 ....$8.00

Shetland Pony (#5605), Just About Horses Special Edition Gift Set, brn/chestnut w/silver dapple, wht mane & tail, 1998.........$9.00

Silky Sullivan (#5022), chestnut w/darker mane & tail, right hind stocking, 1976-94 ....$7.00

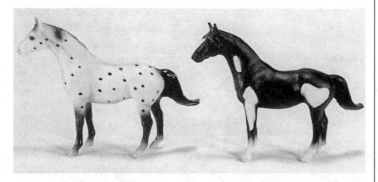

Silky Sullivan (#5022), from J.C. Penney's Twelve-Piece Stablemates Set, left: black leopard appaloosa with black points and spots, 1996, $5.00; right: black pinto with fairly symetrical markings, pink muzzle, socks, $5.00. (Photo courtesy Felicia Browell)

Standard Bred (#5611), Just About Horses Special Edition Gift Set, med chestnut, right front & left rear socks, 1998....$9.00

Swaps (#5021), bay w/blk points, 12-Piece Stablemate Set, JC Penney, 1996 ....$6.00

Swaps (#5021), blk leopard appaloosa w/blk points, sm spots, Sears Wish Book, 1989 ....$8.00

Thoroughbred, Just About Horses Special Edition Gift Set, lt gray shading w/darker, mane, tail, face & hooves, 1998 ....$9.00

Thoroughbred (#5602), dappled gray w/blk mane & tail, star/stripe/snip, hind sock, from Reflections Set, Toys R Us, 2002 ....$10.00

Thoroughbred Lying Foal (#5700LF), Lying & Standing Foals, bay w/darker mane & tail, w/ or w/o hind stockings, 1975-76 ....$12.00

Thoroughbred Lying Foal (#5700LF), Morgan Mare & Foal, buckskin w/blk points, 1997-99 ....$3.00

Thoroughbred Mare (#5026), matt/semigloss blk, front socks & hind stockings, gray hooves, 1975-88.........................$8.00

Thoroughbred Mare (#5026), Saddle Club Collection, solid blk, 1994-95 ....$5.00

Thoroughbred Standing Foal (#5700SF), Fun Foals Gift Pack, dusty dun w/chocolate points, 3 socks, 2002-current..$10.00

Thoroughbred Standing Foal (#5700SF), Stable Set, dk bay w/darker mane, tail, legs & stockings, 1976-80.........$11.00

Trotting Foal (#5615), Horse & Foal Gift Set, leopard appaloosa w/shaded mane, tail & forelegs, chestnut spots, 2003 ..$5.00

Warmblood (#5607), Double Exposure, glossy grulla w/darker points, star/stripe, right socks, Just About Horses, 2003 ....$13.00

Warmblood (#5607), Just About Horse Special Edition Gift Set, blk pinto w/star, natural hooves, 1998.........................$9.00

TRADITIONAL SCALE

Action Stock Horse Foal (#235), Alo (Great Spirit III), lt bay pinto w/wht spots, blk mane/tale, socks, JC Penney, 2003.........$17.00

Action Stock Horse Foal (#235), appaloosa w/blk points & hooves, blanket over hind quarters, 1984-88.............$13.00

Action Stock Horse Foal (#235), chestnut w/flaxen mane & tail, 1984-86 ....$13.00

Action Stock Horse Foal (#235), Frisky Foals Set, yel dun w/gray shading, JC Penney, 1992 ....$15.00

Adios (#50), Clayton Quarter Horse, dapple palomino w/wht mane & tale, resist dappling, stockings, 1995-96.......$24.00

Adios (#50), Quarter Horse Stallion, blk roan w/blk points, gray speckles, no shaded muzzle, 1990 ....$27.00

Adios (#50), Vales of Phoenix, buckskin w/blk points, 1978..$232.00

Amber (#488), Twin Appaloosa Foals, bay blanket appaloosa w/ blk mane & tail, wht blaze, 2 socks, Sears, 1998........$17.00

Amber (#488), Twin Palomino Foals, palomino w/wht mane, tail & blaze, lighter lower legs, 2004 ....$30.00

American Saddlebred Stallion (#571), Blue Note, glossy bay w/shading, blk mane, tail & above socks, QVC, 2002..$66.00

Appaloosa Performance Horse (#99), Appaloosa Stallion, gray w/blk points, hind blanket pattern, JC Penney, 1984 ..$44.00

Appaloosa Performance Horse (#99), lt bay blanket w/blk mane & tail, blk knees, socks, Mid-States Distributing, 2000......$32.00

Aristocrat Champion Hackney (#496), bay w/blk points, socks, 1995-96 ....$22.00

Ashley (#489), Great Spirit Mare & Foal, bay pinto w/blk tail & top of mane, wht legs & rear, bay head, JC Penney, 2001 ....$19.00

Ashley (#489), Twin Morgan Foals, chestnut w/wht star, right socks, 1997-99...$15.00

Balking Mule (#207), bay/chestnut w/darker mane & tail, gray hooves, brn or dk red bridle, 1968-73 ....$74.00

Balking Mule (#207), Black Horse Ranch (400), blk appaloosa w/blanket pattern, blk spots, socks, dk brn bridle, 1993 ..$64.00

Belgian (#92), Buddy, glossy liver chestnut w/reddish mane & tail, bald face, socks, 1998 ....$48.00

Belgian (#92), semigloss blk, wht-on-lt bl ribbon, Disney World, 1984-85 ....$62.00

Belgian (#92), smoke w/wht mane & tail, bald face, stockings, gray hooves, red-on-yel ribbon, 1965-71 ....$66.00

Big Ben (#483), chestnut w/star & stripe, hind socks, 1997-current..$31.00

Big Ben (#483), Hickstead, glossy red bay w/shading, blk points, broad blaze, hind striped hooves & socks, QVC, 2002 ..$57.00

Black Beauty (#89), Black Beauty, black with various stockings, diamond-shaped star, 1979 – 1988, $32.00; Faded Grey, dark dappled gray with black points, bald face or narrow blaze, socks/stockings, dark gray hooves, 1989 – 1990, $26.00; Dream Weaver (Limited Edition), sorrel with flaxen mane and tail, right stockings, broad blaze and white muzzle, 1991, $20.00 – $35.00. (Photo courtesy Felicia Browell)

Black Beauty (#89), Donovan Running Appaloosa Stallion, gray w/blanket pattern & chestnut spots, 3 socks, 1995-97 ....$24.00

Black Stallion (#401), Majestic Arabian Stallion, leopard appaloosa w/blk points, brn & blk splash spots, 1989-90.................$26.00

Black Stallion (#401), Sapphire (Medallion Series), buckskins w/blk points, 3 socks, Toys R Us, 1996......................$31.00

Brown Sunshine (#484), Maynard's Miss Sheba, buckskin w/chocolate points, dorsal/shoulder strip, leg bars, 2003-current..$29.00

Brown Sunshine (#484), sorrel w/wht mane & tail, lighter lower legs, gray hooves, 1996-97 ....$23.00

Buckshot (#1121), Mustang, dun roan with black and dark brown points, shaded body, lighter over haunches, three socks, 2000 – 2001, $27.00. (Photo courtesy Felicia Browell)

Buckshot (#415), Spanish Barb, chestnut pinto w/darker mane, tail & lower front legs, wht hind legs, 1988-89..........$26.00

Cantering Welsh Pony (#104), bay w/blk points, yel or bl ribbons, 1971-1973...$74.00

Cantering Welsh Pony (#104), Plain Pixie, red roan w/chestnut shading & red speckles, 1992-1993 ....$25.00

Cedarfarm Wixom (#573), Belle Fleur, glossy lt gray w/shading, dk gray mane & tail, red & wht tail ribbon, 2003 ...$205.00

Cedarfarm Wixom (#573), Belle Fleur, lt gray w/shading, dk gray mane & tail, fine speckles, red & wht tail ribbon, 2003..$79.00

Cedarfarm Wixom (#573), matt blk w/slight dappling, gray chestnuts, bl tail bow, 2001-03 ....$34.00

Chestnut Stock Horse Foal (#236), flaxen mane & tale, gray hooves, left hind stocking..$13.00

Clydesdale Foal (#84), dapple gray (sm dapples), darker gray mane & tail, socks, Horses Int'l, 1988......................$46.00

Clydesdale Foal (#84), Satin Star, chestnut w/wht, yel or cream mane, tail, & blaze, stockings, gray hooves, 1994-95..$15.00

Clydesdale Mare (#83), Clydesdale Family Set, red bay w/blk mane & tail, wht legs & belly, bald face, JC Penney, 1982-84 ....$46.00

Clydesdale Mare (#83), Shire Mare, dk chestnut & bay w/darker points, broad blaze, pk muzzle, stockings, 1992-93.....$27.00

Clydesdale Stallion (#80), muscle version, bay w/blk mane & tail, bald face, stockings, red bobs, JC Penney, 1982-84.......$46.00

Clydesdale Stallion (#80), muscle version, semigloss mahogany bay w/blk points, wht stockings/blaze, gold bobs, 1998-02 ...$28.00

Clydesdale Stallion (#80), muscle version, woodgrain, no markings, 1961 (?)-1965 ....$177.00

Clydesdale Stallion (#80), no muscle version, bay w/dk mane & tail, stockings, 1958 (?)-1961 (?)...........................$117.00

Cody (#471), Buster, buckskin pinto w/blk & wht mane & tail w/blk points, blk spot on muzzle, 1999-2001..............$27.00

Cody (#471), Easy Jet, chestnut w/darker mane & tail, shaded muzzle, star-stripe, Quarter Horse Outfitters, 2001 ....$40.00

Donkey (#81), gray w/stockings, dk mane & tail, pale muzzle, or bay variation, 1958-74, ea $22.00

El Pastor (#61), bay w/blk points, solid face, left socks, 1987 ....$124.00

El Pastor (#61), Jamoca Jazz, liver chestnut pinto, State Line Tack, 2003..$43.00

El Pastor (#61), Tersoro, palomino w/wht mane, tail, narrow blaze, gray-shaded muzzle & hooves, stockings, 1992-95 ....$26.00

Family Arabian Foal (#9), lt chestnut w/flaxen mane & tail, narrow blaze, JC Penney, 1983..........................$17.00

Family Arabian Foal (#9), Shah, glossy bay w/blk mane & tail, narrow blaze, stockings, blk hooves, 1961-66 ....$12.00

Family Arabian Foal (#9), Spirit of the Wind Set, dapple gray w/blk points, bald face, JC Penney, 1991 ....$15.00

Family Arabian Mare (#8), chestnut/sorrel w/flaxen mane & tail, socks, JC Penney, 1983.......................................$34.00

Family Arabian Mare (#8), Dickory, charcoal w/wht mane & tail, bald face, socks, gray hooves, 1967-73 ....$21.00

Family Arabian Stallion (#7), Fleck, glossy gray appaloosa w/blk points, splash spots on rear, wht barrel, 1963-67........$24.00

Family Arabian Stallion (#7), matt or semigloss blk, no markings, Model Congress, Bently Sales Co, 1978 ....$63.00

Family Arabian Stallion (#7), No Doubt, red roan w/chestnut points, speckled roaning, left socks, Toys R Us, 1997 ..$24.00

Fighting Stallion (#31), Chaparral, buckskin pinto w/blk & wht mane & tail, front socks/blk knees, wht back legs, 1992 ..$34.00

Fighting Stallion (#31), King, glossy alabaster, gray mane, tail & hooves, pk & gray shaded muzzle, 1961-64 ....$98.00

Fighting Stallion (#31), King, woodgrain, narrow blaze, socks, blk hooves, 1963-73 ....$109.00

Five Gaiter (#52), American Saddlebred, dapple gray w/wht mane & tail, bald face, socks, pk hooves, ribbons, 1987-88 ....$39.00

Five Gaiter (#52), Commander, glossy alabaster w/pk shaded muzzle, gray hooves, turq-on-yel ribbons, red eyes, 1962-66...$138.00

Five Gaiter (#52), Commander, glossy alabaster w/pk-shaded muzzle, gray hooves, turq-on-yel ribbons, blk eyes, 1962-66...$133.00

Five Gaiter (#52), Kentucky Saddlebred, chestnut w/darker mane & tail, narrow blaze, 3 socks, 1992-93 ....$27.00

Five Gaiter (#52), Storm, glossy dapple gray w/blk points, resist dapples, gold braids, Sears Wish Book, 2000..............$60.00

Foundation Stallion (#64), American Indian Pony, fleabit gray w/reddish gray points, fine speckles, 1988-91 ....$26.00

Foundation Stallion (#64), bay appaloosa w/blk points, blanket, hind socks, Wild Horses of America, JC Penney, 1993 ....$31.00

Foundation Stallion (#64), blk, no markings, 1977-87.....$26.00

Friesian (#485), Action Drafters Set, dk bay w/blk points, sparse resist dappling, left hind sock, 1994-95......................$30.00

Friesian (#485), Jack Frost, speckled gray w/darker points, 1999..$60.00

Fury Prancer (#(P45), woodgrain, may or may not have hat reins, 1960 ....$211.00

Fury Prancer (#P45), TV's Fury, glossy blk w/elongated diamond star, low socks, gray hooves, 1957 (?)-65 ....$54.00

Galiceno (#100), Crillo Pony, yel dun w/darker points, dorsal stripe, blaze, shaded muzzle, right hind sock, 1998-99...$23.00

Gem Twist (#495), Champion Show Jumper, alabaster w/gray-shaded tail, knees & socks, natural hooves, 1993-95 ...$28.00

Grazing Foal (#151), Adorable Horse Foal Set, bay appaloosa w/blk points, blanket pattern w/spash spots, JC Penney, 1991 ....$16.00

Grazing Foal (#151), blk w/bald face, stockings, 1964-70..$32.00

Grazing Foal (#151), from Grazing Mare and Foal Gift Set, liver chestnut with lighter mane and tail, stockings, pink/natural hooves, stripe, and snip, 2000 – current, $17.00. (Photo courtesy Felicia Browell)

Grazing Mare (#141), Grazing Mare & Foal, matte or semigloss mahogany bay w/blk points, 2 socks, 1998-99............$24.00

Haflinger (#156), Mountain Pony, sorrel w/gray knees & socks, 1991-92 ....$22.00

Haflinger (#156), sorrel w/flaxen mane & tail, faint socks, gray hooves, Horses Int'l, 1984-85 ....$27.00

Halla (#63), Famous Jumper, bay w/blk points, sm star, 1977-85...$28.00

Halla (#63), Nobel Jumper, dapple gray w/blk points, hind socks, 1990-91 ....$29.00

Hanoverian (#58), dapple gray w/wht base coat, dk gray mane, tail & knees, wht spatters, socks, Horses Int'l, 1986..$203.00

Hanoverian (#58), dk bay w/blk points, 1980-84 ....$29.00

Hanoverian (#58), Pan 'N Go, bay leopard appaloosa w/blk points, shaded, spatter spots, 2000-03 ....$32.00

Henry (#482), Norwegian Fjord, dun w/dk gray wht mane & tail, blk dorsal stripe, dk gray striped knees & hooves, 1996 ....$23.00

Huckelberry Bey (#472), Gold Rush, palomino w/wht mane & tail, shaded muzzle, star, right socks, BreyerFest, 2002 ......$1,059.00

Huckleberry Bey (#472), Paradigm, glossy dapple gray w/blk points, dk shading w/some peach on head & mane, QVC, 2001 ....$71.00

Ideal American Quarter Horse (#497), Offspring of Go Man Go, red roan w/solid points, coon tail, 'J bar' brand, 1998..$31.00

Ideal American Quarter Horse (#497), Pretty Buck, buckskin/dun w/blk points, Best Remunda Ranch Series, 2003 ....$32.00

In-Between Mare (# unknown), Family Mare, glossy gray appaloosa, 1961 ....$1,482.00

Indian Pony (#175), alabaster w/lt gray mane & tail, red hand print on left haunch, bl sq on left neck, 1970-71 ....$211.00

Indian Pony (#175), Black Horse Ranch, blk leopard appaloosa w/gray points, blk spots, stockings, 1987 ....$89.00

Indian Pony (#175), Cheyenne American Mustang, blk points, chestnut-shaded head, stripe & snip, left fore sock, 1995-96..$31.00

Indian Pony (#175), Ichilay, lt gray w/darker gray points, red speckle roaning, Indian symbols, 1993.....................$36.00

Iron Metal Chief (#486), Fanfare, glossy Gold Charm w/wht mane & tail, bald face, stockings, Breyer 50 Years, 2000 ....**$119.00**

Iron Metal Chief (#486), Missouri Fox Trotter, bay w/blk points, shaded body, star & stripe, gr & yel ribbons, 1999-2001 ..**$31.00**

John Henry (#445), Joe Patchen Sire of Dan Patch, blk w/star & stripe, pk shaded muzzle, stockings, 1991-93..............**$26.00**

John Henry (#445), Western Horse, dk chestnut w/darker mane & tail, star & stripe, socks, JC Penney, 1994 ....**$28.00**

Jumping Horse (#300), bay w/blk mane & tail, bald face, front socks, 1965-88..**$27.00**

Jumping Horse (#300), Jumping Gem Twist, alabaster w/shaded tail, gray hocks, knees, shaded hooves, QVC, 1995...**$70.00**

Justin Morgan (#1142), Montana Harvest, dapple buckskin w/blk points, shaded body w/resist dapples, socks, 2001-03 ....**$32.00**

Justin Morgan (#65), lt chestnut w/darker mane & tail, shaded knees & hocks, left hind sock, JC Penney, 1988........**$28.00**

Khemosabi (#460), Arabian Stallion, rose gray w/darker points, restist dapples in rosy chestnut, socks, 1999-2000 .....**$23.00**

Lady Phase (#40), Breyer Traditional Horse Set, dapple gray w/blk points, bald face, dorsal stripe, JC Penney, 1990..........**$59.00**

Lady Phase (#40), Family Appaloosa Mare, blk leopard appaloosa, gray points, stenciled spots, 1992-94 ....**$33.00**

Lady Roxanna (#425), Cinnamon, bay appaloosa w/blk points, wht spots, blanket w/dk spots, star, socks, limited ed, 1996..**$20.00**

Lady Roxanna (#425), Prancing Arabian Mare, chestnut w/flaxen mane & tail, 3 socks, gray hooves, 1988-89 ....**$22.00**

Le Fire (#581), chestnut with right front sock and three stockings, natural hooves, star and odd-shaped blaze with snip, gray-shaded muzzle, 2002 – current, $35.00. (Photo courtesy Felicia Browell)

Le Fire (#581), palomino w/wht mane & tail, stripe snip, front socks/rear stockings, QVC's Baby's First Steps..., 2002..**$25.00**

Legionario (#68), Spanish Pride, bay w/blk points, left fore stocking, 1991-92...**$29.00**

Legionario (#68), Stardust, dapple gray w/wht mane & tail, lg wht dapples, socks, Toys R Us, 1997 ....**$26.00**

Llanarth True Briton (#494), Sunny Boy, Welsh Cob, shaded palomino w/wht mane & tail, shaded knees, socks, 1997..**$28.00**

Lonesome Glory (#572), Mosaic, bay pinto w/blk points, wht left hind leg, half apron face, Connoisseur Series, 2001....**$575.00**

Lonesome Glory (#572), Mosaic, bay pinto w/blk points, wht left hind leg, half apron face, glossy version, 2001...**$700.00**

Lying Down Foal (#245), blk appaloosa w/bald face, rear blanket, 1969-84 ....**$19.00**

Lying Down Foal (#245), Serenity Set, buckskin w/dk points, bald face, rear blanket, JC Penney, 1995....................**$15.00**

Man O' War, War Admiral, bay w/blk points, dk shading, gray hooves, blk halter, gold hardware, 2003-current........**$31.00**

Man O' War (#47), Traveller (Gen Lee's Horse), lt shaded gray w/blk mane & tail, Horses in American History, 1998-99 ....**$41.00**

Marabella (#487), Fortuna, soft dappled gold w/wht mane & tail, shaded knees & hocks, socks & stockings, QVC, 2002...**$51.00**

Marabella (#487), 1999-2000, Morgan Mare, liver chestnut w/flaxen mane & tail, strip/snip, lighter lower legs, 1999-2000 .....**$27.00**

Midnight Sun (#60), High Flyer Tennessee Walker, chestnut pinto, blaze, stockings, bl & wht braids, 1995-96 ......**$27.00**

Midnight Sun (#60), Tennessee Walking Horse, red bay w/blk points, red & wht braids, gray hooves, 1988-89.........**$30.00**

Midnight Sun (#60), Three Pintos Collector Set, blk pinto w/blaze, natural hooves, gold & blk ribbons, JC Penney, 1999 ....**$30.00**

Misty (#20), Marguerite Henry's Misty, glossy palomino pinto, old Misty pinto pattern, 1973 (?) **$110.00**

Misty (#20), Marguerite Henry's Misty, palomino pinto w/dbl eye circles, old Misty pinto pattern, 1972 ....**$80.00**

Misty's Twilight (#470), chestnut pinto w/darker lower half of wht tail, blaze, wht legs, 1991-95 ....**$26.00**

Misty's Twilight (#470), Romanesque, lt dapple gray w/shaded muzzle, hocks, knees & hooves, 1999-2000 ....**$26.00**

Morgan (#48), blk w/bald face, front socks, back stockings, 1965-1987 ....**$38.00**

Morgan (#48), Lippitt Pegasus, red bay w/blk points, star, left hind sock, 1994-95 ....**$26.00**

Morganglanz (#59), chestnut w/flaxen mane & tail, stripe, stockings, gray hooves, 1980-87 ....**$21.00**

Morganglanz (#59), Swedish Warmblood, palomino w/wht mane & tail, gray shading, stocking, JC Penney, 1996 ....**$25.00**

Mustang (#87), Black Horse Ranch, alabaster w/gray mane & tail, very lt gray hooves, 1988..................................**$89.00**

Mustang (#87), Diablo, glossy alabaster w/lt gray mane, tail & hooves, blk eyes, 1961-66................................**$129.00**

Mustang (#87), Diablo, glossy alabaster w/lt gray mane, tail & hooves, red eyes, earlier version **$140.00**

Mustang (#87), Gray Hawk, bl roan pinto, w/Indian markings, QVC, 2002..**$50.00**

Mustang (#87), Renegade, semigloss blk pinto w/frame overo pattern, wht face, left front hock, Toys R Us, 1998 ...**$35.00**

Nursing Foal (#3155FO), Special Delivery Mare & Foal Gift Set, bright bay w/blk points, stripe & snip, socks, QVC, 2001 ....**$17.00**

Nursing Foal (#3155FO), Thoroughbred Mare & Foal Gift Set, lt chestnut w/darker mane & tail, 1973-84 ....**$14.00**

Old Timer (#200), alabaster w/lt gray mane & tail, dk brn harness, yel hat, 1966-76 ....**$33.00**

Old Timer (#200), buckskin w/blk points, bald face, socks, blk harness w/gold band, bl hat, 1998-99 ....**$26.00**

Pacer (#46), liver chestnut w/slightly darker mane & tail, socks, halter w/gold trim, 1967-87 ....**$27.00**

Pacer (#46), TRU Horse of a Different Color, iridescent gold w/wht mane & tail, silvery shadings, Toys R Us, 2001.............**$35.00**

Pacer #46, matt/semigloss dapple gray w/darker gray points, stockings, Riegseckers, 1984......................................$162.00

Peruvian Paso (#576), Cobrizo, bay w/metallic undertones, blk points, star/stripe/snip, right front sock, 2004............$57.00

Peruvian Paso (#576), dapple gray w/darker points, shaded, 2002-current $31.00

Phantom Wings (#18), Stock Horse Foal, brn appaloosa w/darker points, sm blanket on rear, 1979-82 ....$14.00

Phantom Wings (#18), Three Generations Appaloosa Set, bay appaloosa w/darker points, 3 socks, JC Penney, 1993...$16.00

Phar Lap (#90), Liver Chestnut Paint, pinto w/blaze, hind socks, 1998-99 ....$24.00

Phar Lap (#90), Phar Lap Famous Race Horse, red chestnut w/reverse C-shaped star, hind legs, 1985-88................$29.00

Pluto (#475), Embajador XI, Andalusian, med dapple gray w/lighter face, flank & tail, darker legs, 1996-97 ....$24.00

Pluto (#475), Royal Lipizzaner Stallion, very lt dapple gray w/darker mane, tail, knees & socks, Spiegel, 1993 ..$166.00

Pony of the Americas (#155), chestnut leopard appaloosa w/stenciled spots, gray hooves, added shoes, 1976-80 ....$28.00

Pony of the Americas (#155), Just Justin Quarter Pony, coffee dun w/blk points, blaze, 1993-95 ....$20.00

Proud Arabian Foal (#218), Amira (Princess), Tour Raffle Model, shaded rose gray with black points, dappling and shading, three socks, 2002, $543.00. (Photo courtesy Felicia Browell)

Proud Arabian Foal (#218), Joy, glossy alabaster w/blk & dk gray mane, tail & hooves, 1956-60 ....$31.00

Proud Arabian Foal (#218), Spot, glossy gray appaloosa w/blk & dk gray points & hooves, 1956-60..............................$84.00

Proud Arabian Mare (#215), matt/semigloss mahogany bay w/black points, socks, 1972-80 ....$30.00

Proud Arabian Mare (#215), Parade of Breeds, lt bay w/blk points, right hind socks, QVC, 1995..........................$27.00

Proud Arabian Mare (#215), Pride, glossy alabaster w/lt gray shaded mane, tail, muzzle & hooves, 1956-60 ....$82.00

Proud Arabian Stallion (#211), Black Horse Ranch, red bay w/blk points, pk nose, 1987 ....$65.00

Proud Arabian Stallion (#211), Cappuccino, liver chestnut w/hind socks, Toys R Us, 1998 ....$30.00

Proud Arabian Stallion (#211), matt or semigloss mahogany bay w/blk points, blaze, socks or stockings, 1971-80........$36.00

Quarter Horse Gelding (#97), Traditional Horse Set, palomino w/wht mane & tail, stockings, brn halter, JC Penney, 1990..$29.00

Quarter Horse Gelding (#97), Two Bits, buckskin w/blk points, blk & dk brn halter, w/o dorsal stripe, 1961-81.........$32.00

Quarter Horse Yearling (#101), Calypso, dun w/darker red mane & tail, red shaded knees, hocks & ankles, stock, 1995-96...$24.00

Quarter Horse Yearling (#101), liver chestnut, crooked blaze, hind socks, gray hooves, 1970-80 ....$29.00

Racehorse (#36), glossy chestnut w/bald face, stockings, blk hooves & halter, 1956-67 ....$71.00

Racehorse (#36), woodgrain w/star, socks, blk hooves, blk halter, Tenite sticker, 1958 (?)-66..............................$134.00

Rejoice (#479), Charisma, palomino pinto w/wht mane & tail, shaded muzzle, front stockings, hind stockings, QVC, 2001...$57.00

Rejoice (#479), National Show Horse, bay pinto w/blk points, star, hind socks, right front stocking, 1999-current....$29.00

Roemer (#465), Quiet Fox Hunters Set, seal bay/brn w/blk points, diamond star, 3 socks, Sears Wish Book, 1992.............$30.00

Roemer (#465), Sandstone, lt bay w/darker points, paler face, Toys R Us, 1998 ....$32.00

Roy the Belgian (#455), Belgian Brabant, gray dun w/darker points, chestnut shading, 1991-93......................$26.00

Roy the Belgian (#455), Legacy Gift Set II, lt gray w/shaded, muzzle, knees, hocks & hooves, Sears Wish Book, 1999 .....$29.00

Rugged Lark (#450), Quiet Foxhunters Set, dappled gray w/darker points & shading, sm dapples, bald face, Sears, 1992 ....$29.00

Running Foal (#130), bay chestnut w/blk mane, tail & hooves, bald face, stockings, 1963-87 ....$13.00

Running Foal (#130), Frisky Foals Set, blk blanket appaloosa w/splash spots, star & snip, stockings, JC Penney, 1992 ..$20.00

Running Mare (#120), chestnut pinto, flaxen mane & tail w/chetnut tip, blaze on lower face, 3 stockings, 1991-93 ....$25.00

Running Mare (#120), woodgrain (lt or dk), no markings, blk hooves, 1963-65..$132.00

Running Stallion, glossy charcoal w/wht points, bald face, 1968-71 ....$164.00

Running Stallion (#210), bay chestnut w/blk mane & tail, bald face, stockings, 1971-76/1978-80 ....$32.00

Running Stallion (#210), Running Thunder, semigloss dk dapple gray w/blk points, 1993-94...................................$30.00

Saddlebed Weanling (#62), Parade of Breeds, alabaster w/lt gray mane & tail, shaded muzzle, darker hooves, QVC, 1995.............$25.00

Saddlebred Weanling (#62), chestnut w/slightly darker mane & tail, 3 socks, 1984 ....$134.00

San Domingo (#67), chestnut pinto (mostly wht), chestnut medicine hat, natural hooves, 1978-87 ....$28.00

San Domingo (#67), Dude Ranch Trail Horse Set, semigloss bay w/blk points, shaded, star/stripe/snip, Sears, 1997......$29.00

Scratching Foal (#168), Adorable Horse Set, alabaster w/lt gray mane, tail, knees & hocks, JC Penney, 1991..............$21.00

Scratching Foal (#168), liver chestnut w/darker mane & tail, stockings, 1970-71 ....$64.00

Sham (#410), Marguerite Henry's Sham, red bay w/blk points, 1984-88 ....$33.00

Sham (#410), Rana, dk grayish brown w/grayish tan mane & tail, stockings, 1992-93 ....$27.00

Sham (#410), Sham the Godolphin Arabian, red bay w/blk points, '95' stamped on inner hind leg, QVC, 1995 ..**$32.00**

Sherman Morgan (#430), chestnut w/darker mane & tail & hooves, stripe, right hind sock, 1987-90 ....**$47.00**

Sherman Morgan (#430), Justin Morgan, glossy shaded bay w/blk points, gray hooves, QVC, 2002.......................**$48.00**

Shetland Pony, (#23), bay pinto w/blk mane & tail, blaze, natural hooves, 1989-1991..**$19.00**

Shetland Pony, (#23), glossy lt chestnut pinto w/wht mane, chestnut tail w/wht tip, bald face, pk shading, 1960-73.........**$21.00**

Shire (#95), dapple gray w/dk gray points, wht stockings, 1972-73/1975-76 ....**$56.00**

Shire (#95), shaded light bay w/blk points, 1998-99 ....**$28.00**

Silver (#574), Black Beauty, blk w/star, right front sock, gray hooves, 2001-current..**$34.00**

Silver (#574), Hidalgo, chestnut pinto w/lighter tail, 2-color mane, intricate pattern, 2004-current.......................**$31.00**

Smoky (#69), Northern Lights, metallic bl & gr, no markings, 2003 ....**$35.00**

Smoky (#69), Remington, Pinto, bay pinto w/blk points, apron face, socks, natural hooves, 1997................................**$24.00**

Spirit (#577), Stallion of the Cimarron Collection, buckskin w/blk mane & tail, shaded muzzle & lower legs, 2002 ....**$31.00**

Stock Horse Foal (#228), American Quarter Horse Foal, bay w/blk points, shading, star/stripe/snip, socks, 1999-2001 ....**$15.00**

Stock Horse Foal (#228), Bay Quarter Horse Stock Foal, bay w/blk points, hind socks, 1983-88 ....**$17.00**

Stock Horse Foal (#228), Paint Foal, brown dun with black points, primitive leg bars above high stockings, dorsal stripe, shoulder stripe, star-stripe-snip, white on barrel, 2002 – current, $15.00. (Photo courtesy Felicia Browell)

Stock Horse Foal (#228), Palomino Horse & Foal Set, palomino w/wht mane & tail, bald face, stockings, M Ward, 1983 ....**$44.00**

Stock Horse Mare (#227), Goin' for Approval, Chestnut snowflake appaloosa w/darker mane & tail, hind socks, 1996-97 ....**$21.00**

Stock Horse Mare (#227), Sorrel Quarter Horse Stock Mare, flaxen mane & tail, stripe, right hind sock, 1982.......**$26.00**

Stock Horse Stallion, Paint Horse Stallion, liver chestnut pinto w/darker mane & tail, sm patches, hind socks, 1989-90..**$24.00**

Stock Horse Stallion (#226), Bay Quarter Horse Stock Stallion, bay w/blk points, 1981-88...**$25.00**

Stock Horse Stallion (#226), Brown & White Pinto Stock Horse, bay pinto w/blk points, stockings, JC Penney, 1984....**$31.00**

Stormy (#19), Buckaroo & Skeeter, bay pinto w/crescent-shaped star, 3 socks, Toys R Us, 1995 ....**$13.00**

Strapless (#583), dk bay w/tiny star, 2003 ....**$35.00**

Strapless (#583), Winsome, blk pinto w/apron face, bl left eye, right socks, left hind stocking, Just About Horses, 2003 ....**$353.00**

Stud Spider (#66), Appaloosa American Classic Set, gray leopard appaloosa w/blk points, hind sock, Sears Wish Book, 1990 ....**$42.00**

Stud Spider (#66), blk appaloosa w/stenciled blanket pattern over back half, thin star, front sock, 1978-89.............**$28.00**

Stud Spider (#66), Smooth Copper Quarter Horse, bay w/blk points, shaded, right hind & fore socks, 1997-98.......**$25.00**

Susecion (#580), Baby's First Steps Mare & Foal Set, palomino w/wht mane & tail, 3 socks, QVC, 2002....................**$42.00**

Thoroughbred Mare (#3155MA), Cupid & Arrow Gift Set, lt bay w/blk points, heart-shaped star, hind socks, 2002-current..**$38.00**

Thoroughbred Mare (#3155MA), from Thoroughbred Mare and Foal Gift Set, dapple gray with resist dappling, left hind and right fore socks, lighter barrel and head, 2000 – current, $27.00; from QVC's Special Delivery Mare and Foal set, bright bay with black points, socks, stripe, and snip, 2001, $32.00. (Photo courtesy Felicia Browell)

Thoroughbred Mare (#3155MA), Pinto Mare & Suckling Foal Set, bay pinto w/blk pints, socks, Sears Wish Book, 1982-83..**$38.00**

Touch of Class (#420), Century Finale, chestnut pinto (mostly wht), SLT brand on right hip, 1999 ....**$29.00**

Touch of Class (#420), Selle Francais, dk chestnut w/darker mane & tail, blaze, stockings, gray hooves, 1991-92..**$25.00**

Trakehner (#54), bay w/blk points, brand on left thigh, 1979-84...**$30.00**

Trakehner (#54), Spotted Trakehner Warmblood, blk pinto w/wht hind legs, wht over rump, stripe, 1998-99.......**$26.00**

Western Pony (#45), Gambler, palomino w/wht mane & tail, bald face, gray-shaded muzzle, socks, complete w/saddle, 1997-98...**$19.00**

Western Horse (#57), glossy blk, gold hooves, complete w/saddle, 1956-60 ....**$73.00**

Western Horse (#57), glossy palomino, stockings, gray hooves, complete w/saddle, 1956-67 ....**$38.00**

Western Horse (#57), palomino, complete w/saddle, QVC, 1995 ....**$26.00**

Western Pony (#45), semigloss plum brn, diamond star, socks (pnt-on), complete w/saddle, 1956 (?) $64.00

Western Prancing Horse (#110), Cheyenne, glossy blk pinto w/bald face, socks, complete w/saddle, 1961-66.........$69.00

Western Prancing Horse (#110), Ranger Cow Pony, dun w/brn points, wht blaze, socks, complete w/saddle, 1994-95 ..$23.00

Zippo Pine Bar (#466), chestnut w/star & stripe, right hind stocking, 1999-current...............................$28.00

Zippo Pine Bar (#466), Zip's Chocolate Chip, bay w/blk points, star/stripe, socks, striped hooves, metallic sheen, 2003 ..$31.00

OTHER ANIMALS

Alpine Goat (#1512), brn, blk & wht w/brn horns, 1999-2002..$7.00

Australian Shepherd (#1515), bl merle w/wht ruff & feet, wht spot in muzzle, 2000-current...........................$6.00

Beagle (#1527), Popular Dog Two-Piece Gift Set, wht w/brn, 2004-current $10.00

Bear (#306), dk brn w/lighter face, dk nose, 1967-71 ....$37.00

Bear Cub (#308), dk brn w/lighter face, dk nose, 1967-71..$22.00

Bighorn Ram (#78), brn & tan w/lighter head, horns & lower legs, darker hooves, 1997-current.......................$25.00

Black Angus Bull, see also Walking Black Angus Bull..........$.09

Black Angus Bull (#365), no markings, 1978-current $25.00

Black Labrador (#1507), Popular Dog Two-Piece Gift Set, blk, 2004-current.................................$9.00

Border Collie (#1518), blk & wht, 2000-current $5.00

Boxer (#1), Pug Boxer, chocolate brown/brindle with darker face and muzzle, white belly and feet, 1995 – 96, $21.00. (Photo courtesy Felicia Browell)

Boxer (#1), semigloss woodgrain w/wht face stripe, blk muzzle, 1959-65..................................$242.00

Brahma Bull (#70), matt/semigloss lt gray w/shaded quarters, darker neck, lt horns w/dk tips, 1958-67 ....$27.00

Buffalo (#76), med brn w/dk brn head & mane, wht horns w/dk tips, 1965-91 ....$30.00

Calf (#347), Brown Swiss, cocoa brn, 1972-73 ....$31.00

Calio Cat (#1517), wht, brn & blk, 2000-current...............$3.00

Cat, see Calico Cat or Silver Tabby

Charolais Bull (#360), alabaster, 1975-95 ....$21.00

Collie (#2), Honey Collie, golden bicolor w/darker shading, blk nose, pk tongue, 1995-96...........................$19.00

Collie (#2), Lassie, semigloss chestnut & wht, gold or blk eyes, 1958-65 ....$45.00

Cougar (#822), Rufo & Diablo, tan & wht w/blk muzzle, from American Wild Mustangs, Wal-Mart, 2001 ....$7.00

Cow (#341), Brown Swiss, cocoa brn w/lighter legs, horns are forward, 1972-73 ....$50.00

Cow (#341), Cow Family, blk & wht pinto pattern, horns point forward & slightly down, 1974-89 ....$27.00

Cow (#341), Holstein, black and white, 2001 – current, $24.00. (Photo courtesy Felicia Browell)

Cutting Calf (#492), Cutting Horse & Calf set, lt tan w/shading, gray ears & hooves, pk nose, 2000-01 ....$10.00

Dalmatian (#1516), Lots of Spots, wht w/matt blk spots, brn-shaded nose, JC Penney, 2000-current $7.00

Deer (#301BU), Buck, tan w/blk nose & hooves, w/bl ribbon, 1965-73 ....$12.00

Deer (#303DO), Doe, tan w/blk nose & hooves, w/bl ribbon, 1965-73 ....$12.00

Deer (#303FA), Fawn, tan w/wht spots, blk nose & hooves, 1965-73 ....$9.00

Elephant Trumpeting (#91), solid battleship gray, 1958-60...$145.00

Elk (#77), brn (lt or dk brn), darker neck, antlers angled back or up, 1968-97 ....$23.00

English Foxhound (#1519), Fox Hunting Gift Set, brn & wht, 2001-2003 ....$7.00

German Shepherd (#327), matt/semigloss charcoal gray w/shaded body, lighter face & legs, 1972-73 ....$46.00

German Shepherd (#327), Rin-Tin-Tin, matt/semigloss brn w/darker back, lighter face & legs, 1958-66 ....$44.00

Golden Retriever (#1519), Popular Dog Two-Piece Gift Set, lt golden color, 2004-current..................................$9.00

Great Dane (#1520), brindle w/blk muzzle, tiger-striped, blk paws, 2001-2002...$8.00

Hereford Bull, see Walking Hereford Bull

Irish Setter, red w/shaded muzzle, 2004-current $6.00

Jack Russell Terrier (#1505), Flock Set I, brn & wht, BreyerFest Special, 2001..$10.00

Jasper the Market Hog (#355), wht & gray w/dk spots, pk nose & hooves, 1974-2004 ....$12.00

Kitten (#335), Leonardo Kitten, gray tabby w/wht paws, golden eyes, 1994-95 ....$21.00

Kitten (#335), Siamese Kitten, gray or seal point, bl or gr eyes, 1966-71 ....$64.00

Lassie, see Collie

Miniature Sicilian Donkey (#1522 ?), gray dun w/dorsal stripe & bar, pale muzzle, 2001-current $8.00

Montana Mountain Goat (#312), alabaster w/shading, blk horns, 1973-76 (1989 reissue w/gray horns is same price).......$37.00

Moose (#79), very dk brn w/shading over shoulders & neck, lt knees & antlers, 1999-current $25.00

Polled Hereford Bull (#74), red-brn & wht, 1968-current ..$26.00

Poodle (#67), silver-gray, 1968-73 ....$43.00

Pronghorn Antelope (#210), chestnut & wht w/striped neck, shaded muzzle, gray antlers, 1997-current $25.00

Red Fox (#820), Fox Hunting Gift Set, glossy red chestnut w/blk points, wht throat tail tip & inner ears, 2001-03 ....$6.00

Rin-Tin-Tin, see German Shepherd

Roping Calf (#474?), Roping Horse & Calf Set, tan w/wht chest, bald face, gray hooves, 2000 ....$9.00

Rottweiler (#1525), blk & red, pk tongue, 2004-current $6.00

Shetland Sheepdog (#1504), Popular Small Dog 3-Piece Gift Set, bl merle, grayer back, 2004-current $11.00

Silver Tabby (#1511), blk, gray & wht, 1999-current $3.00

Spanish Fighting Bull (#73), blk, wht horns w/dk tips, 1970-85 ....$57.00

Saint Bernard (#328), matt/semigloss brown and white, 1972 – 1981, $33.00; Brandy, gold and white with brown shading on head, 1995 – 1996, $20.00. (Photo courtesy Felicia Browell)

Texas Longhorn Bull (#75), lt brn & tan w/bald face, stockings, shaded horns, 1961-89 ....$27.00

Walking Black Angus Bull (#72), glossy & textured, wht of eyes shown, gold halter, 1960-62/1963-78 ....$76.00

Walking Hereford Bull, glossy, semigloss or matt dk brn to red brown & wht, 1958-81, ea $37.00

Welsh Corgi (#1506), golden brn & wht, 1999-current $4.00

Wolf (#821), Tipi Set, gray w/wht on face & throat, 2001-03 ....$10.00

Bubble Bath Containers

Since back in the 1960s when the Colgate-Palmolive Company produced the first Soaky, hundreds of different characters and variations have been marketed, bought on demand of the kids who saw these characters day to day on TV by parents willing to try anything that might make bathtime more appealing. Purex made their Bubble Club characters, and Avon and others followed suit. Most Soaky bottles came with detachable heads made of brittle plastic which cracked easily. Purex bottles were made of a softer plastic but tended to loose their paint.

Rising interest in US bubble bath containers has created a collector market for those made in foreign countries, i.e, UK, Canada, Italy, Germany, and Japan. Licensing in other countries creates completely different designs and many characters that are never issued here. Foreign containers are generally larger and are modeled in great detail, reminiscent of the bottles that were made in the US in the '60s. Prices may seem high, considering that some of these are of fairly recent manufacture, but this is due to their limited availability and the costs associated with obtaining them in the United States. We believe these prices are realistic, though many have been reported much higher. Rule of thumb: pay what you feel comfortable with — after all, it's meant to be fun. And remember, value is affected to a great extent by condition. Unless noted otherwise, our values are for examples in near-mint condition. Bottles in very good condition are worth only about 60% to 65% of these prices. For slip-over styles, add 100% if the bottle is present.

Advisors: Matt and Lisa Adams (A7)

Alvin (Chipmunks), Colgate-Palmolive, red sweater w/wht A, w/puppet, neck tag & contents, M, A7 ....$50.00

Alvin (Chipmunks), Colgate-Palmolive, wht sweater w/blk A, cap head, NM, A7 ....$30.00

Alvin (Chipmunks), Ducair Bioescence, holding microphone, w/contents, M, A7 ....$25.00

Anastasia, Kid Care, 1997, NM $8.00

Astroniks Robot, Ducair Bioescence, gold buck-toothed robot on red base, EX+, A7 ....$15.00

Atom Ant, Purex, 1965, NM, from $50 to $70.00

Augie Doggie, Purex, orange w/gr shirt, orig tag, EX, A7 ..$45.00

Baba Looey, Purex, 1960s, brn w/bl scarf & gr hat, NM, A7 ..$35.00

Baba Looey, Roclar, 1977, NM $15.00

Baloo Bear, Colgate-Palmolive, 1966, NM, A7 ....$20.00

Bambi, Colgate-Palmolive, sitting & smiling, NM, A7 ....$25.00

Bamm-Bamm, Purex, blk or gr suspenders, NM, A7, ea ...$35.00

Barney, Kid Care, 1994, yel hat & puppy slippers, NM $8.00

Barney Rubble, Milvern (Purex), bl outfit w/yel accents, NM, A7 ....$35.00

Barney Rubble, Roclar (Purex), brn outfit w/yel accents, MIB, A7 ....$20.00

Batman, Colgate-Palmolive, 1966, NM, A7, from $75 to ..$90.00

Batman, Kid Care, 1995, bl & gray w/yel belt, M, A7 ......$10.00

Batmobile, Avon, 1978, bl & silver w/decals, EX, A7 ......$20.00

Bear, Tubby Time, 1960s, NM $35.00

Beatles, any character, Colgate-Palmolive, EX, ea from $100 to $150.00

Beauty & the Beast, Cosrich, orig tag, M, A7, ea from $5 to ..$8.00

Betty Bubbles, Lander, 1960s, NM $15.00

Big Bad Wolf, Tubby Time, cap head, EX, A7 ....$35.00

Bobo Bubbles, Lander, 1950s, NM $30.00

Bozo the Clown, Colgate-Palmolive, 1960s, NM, A7 ......$30.00

Bozo the Clown, Step Riley, cap head, EX, A7 ....$30.00

Broom Hilda, Lander, 1977, EX, A7 ....$30.00

Brutus (Popeye), Colgate-Palmolive, 1965, red shorts w/red & wht striped shirt, EX, A7 ....$40.00

Bugs Bunny, Colgate Palmolive, lt bl & wht, NM, A7 .....$25.00

Bugs Bunny, Colgate-Palmolive, gray, wht & orange w/cap ears, EX, A7 ....$30.00

Bugs Bunny, Kid Care, in swim trunks w/surfboard, M, A7..$8.00

Bullwinkle, Colgate-Palmolive, several color variations, NM, A7, ea..$45.00

Bullwinkle, Fuller Brush, 1970s, NM $60.00

Butterfly Princess Barbie, Kid Care, orig tag, M, A7..........$5.00

Care Bear, AGC, 1984, NM..$10.00

Casper the Ghost, Colgate-Palmolive, wht w/lavender & bl accents, EX, A7 ....$30.00

Cecil (Beany & Cecil), Purex, 1962, NM $40.00

Cement Truck, Colgate-Palmolive, bl & gray w/movable wheels, EX+, A7...$35.00

Charlie Brown, Avon, red baseball outfit, NM, A7 ....$20.00

Cinderella, Colgate-Palmolive, 1960s, movable arms, NM, A7 ....$30.00

Creature From the Black Lagoon, Colgate-Palmolive, 1960s, NM, A7, from $100 to...$150.00

Darth Vader, Omni, 1981, NM...$20.00

Deputy Dawg, Colgate-Palmolive, 1960s, gray, yel & bl w/cap hat, VG (VG box), A7 ....$30.00

Dick Tracy, Colgate-Palmolive, 1965, NM, A7 ....$50.00

Dino & Pebbles, Cosrich, 1994, NM................................$15.00

Donald Duck, Colgate-Palmolive, 1960s, wht, bl & yel w/cap head, EX, A7...$20.00

Dopey, Colgate-Palmolive, 1960s, purple, yel & red, NM .$20.00

Dum Dum, Purex, 1964, wht w/pk accents, rare, NM, from $75 to...$100.00

El Cabong, Knickerbocker (Purex), blk, yel & wht, rare, NM, from $100 to $150.00

Elmer Fudd, Colgate-Palmolive, 1960s, hunting outfit, NM ..$25.00

Elmo, Kid Care, 1997, NM...$10.00

Ernie (Sesame Street), Minnetonka, holding rubber duckie, orig tag, M, A7 ....$8.00

ET, Avon, 1984, NM...$15.00

Felix the Cat, Colgate-Palmolive, 1960s, bl, red or blk, EX, A7 ....$30.00

Fozzie Bear, Muppet Treasure Island, Calgon, 1996, NM..$10.00

Fred Flintstone, Milvern (Purex), 1960s, red outfit w/blk accents, EX+, A7..$30.00

Garfield, Kid Care, lying in tub, NM, A7 ....$10.00

Genie (Aladdin), Cosrich, M, A7 ....$5.00

GI Joe (Drill Instructor), DuCair Bioescence, 1980s, NM..$15.00

Goofy, Colgate-Palmolive, 1960s, red, wht & blk w/cap head, NM, A7..$20.00

Gravel Truck, Colgate-Palmolive, 1960s, orange & gray w/movable wheels, EX, A7...$35.00

Gumby, M&L Creative Packaging, 1987, NM.................$30.00

Harriet Hippo, Merle Norman, in party hat, NM, A7......$10.00

Holly Hobbie, Benjamin Ansehl, 1980s, several variations, M, ea from $15 to...$20.00

Huckleberry Hound, Knickerbocker (Purex), bank, red & blk, orig neck tag, 15", M, A7, from $45 to.....................$60.00

Huckleberry Hound & Yogi Bear, Milvern (Purex), 1960s, MIB (sealed), A7 ....$75.00

Hunchback of Notre Dame, Kid Care, in robe w/scepter, M, A7 ....$5.00

Incredible Hulk, Benjamin Ansehl, standing on rock, M, A7...$25.00

Jasmine (Aladdin), Cosrich, w/bird or mirror, orig tag, M, A7, ea $6.00

Jiminy Cricket, Colgate-Palmolive, 1960s, gr, blk & red or gr, blk & yel, EX+, A7, ea $30.00

Magilla Gorilla, Purex, 1960s, NM, $60.00.

Frankenstein, Colgate-Palmolive, 1963, NM, from $100.00 to $125.00.

Kermit the Frog, Calgon, Treasure Island outfit, w/tag, M, A7 ..$8.00

Lamb Chop (Shari Lewis), Kid Care, holding duck, w/tag, M, A7...$8.00

Lippy the Lion, Purex, 1962, purple vest, rare, EX, A7 ....$35.00

Little Mermaid, Kid Care, 1991, tail up, NM...................$10.00

Little Orphan Annie, Lander, 1977, NM.........................$25.00

Lucy (Peanuts), Avon, 1970, red dress w/top hat, MIB, A7 ..$20.00

Mad Hatter, Avon, 1970, bronze w/pk hat & clock, EX, A7 ..$20.00

Mickey Mouse, Avon, 1969, MIB, A7.............................$30.00

Mickey Mouse, Colgate-Palmolive, red whirt & wht pants, cap head, NM, A7...$30.00

Mickey Mouse as Band Leader, Colgate-Palmolive, 1960s, NM...$25.00

Mighty Mouse, Colgate-Palmolive, yel & red, lg head, EX, A7...$25.00

Miss Piggy, Muppet Treasure Island, Calgon, 1996 ....$10.00

Morocco Mole, Purex, 1966, rare, EX, from $75 to........$100.00

Mr Do Bee, Manon Freres, 1960s, w/sticker, rare, NM, from $50 to...$75.00

Mr Jinks w/Pixie & Dixie, Purex, w/contents, MIB..........$30.00

Mr Magoo, Colgate-Palmolive, 1960s, red or bl outfit, EX, A7, ea...$25.00

Mr Robottle, Avon, 1971, MIB, A7.................................$20.00

Mummy, Colgate-Palmolive, 1960s, NM, from $100 to ..$125.00

Oil Truck, Colgate-Palmolive, gr & gray w/movable wheels, VG, A7...$35.00

Pebbles & Dino, Cosrich, Pebbles on Dino's back, M, A7..$6.00

Pebbles Flintstone, Purex, 1960s, several color variations, EX, A7, ea...$35.00

Peter Potamus, Purex, 1960s, purple w/wht or yel shirt, w/contents & orig tag, M, ea...$20.00

Pinocchio, Colgate-Palmolive, 1960s, red & wht or solid brn or red, M, ea...$20.00

Pluto, Colgate-Palmolive, 1960s, orange w/cap head, NM ..$20.00

Popeye, Colgate-Palmolive, 1967, wht w/bl accents, w/contents, NMIB, A7...$50.00

Popeye, Colgate-Palmolive, 1977, bl w/wht accents, NM, A7...$35.00

Porky Pig, Colgate-Palmolive, 1960s, red or bl tuxedo, EX+, A7, ea...$25.00

Power Rangers, Kid Care, 1994, any character, M, A7, ea..$8.00

Punkin' Puss, Purex, 1966, orange w/bl outfit, VG, A7....$30.00

Quick Draw McGraw, Purex, 1960s, several variations, NM, A7, ea...$30.00

Race Car, Tidy Toys, several variations w/movable wheels, NMIB, A7, ea...$40.00

Raggedy Ann, Lander, 1960s, NM $50.00

Rainbow Brite, Hallmark, 1995, NM $10.00

Red Power Ranger, Centura (Canada), 1994....................$20.00

Ricochet Rabbit, Purex, movable arms, VG, A7 ....$35.00

Robin, Colgate-Palmolive, 1966, EX, from $75 to $100.00

Robocop, Cosway, 1990, NM..$15.00

Schoolhouse, Avon, 1968, red, MIB, A7 ....$15.00

Schroeder, Avon, 1970, MIB, A7....................................$25.00

Secret Squirrel, Purex, 1966, rare, VG, A7, from $40 to ..$60.00

Simba, Kid Care, M, A7 ....$6.00

Simon (Chipmunks), Colgate-Palmolive, 1960s, 3 color variations, w/tag & puppet, M, A7, ea $50.00

Skeletor (Masters of the Universe), Ducair Bioescence, NM, A7...$15.00

Smokey Bear, Colgate-Palmolive, 1960s, NM, A7 ....$25.00

Snaggle Puss, Purex, 1960s, pk w/gr hat, NM, A7 ....$50.00

Snoopy & Woodstock, Avon, 1974, on red skis, MIB, A7..$20.00

Snoopy as Flying Ace, Avon, 1969, MIB, A7 ....$20.00

Snoopy as Flying Ace on Doghouse, Minnetonka, M, A7..$10.00

Snoopy as Joe Cool, Minnetonka, 1996, NM $10.00

Snoopy in Tub of Bubbles, Avon, 1971, MIB, A7.............$20.00

Snow White, Colgate-Palmolive, 1960s, bank, bl & yel, VG, A7...$25.00

Snow White, Colgate-Palmolive, 1960s, movable arms, NM...$35.00

Speedy Gonzales, Colgate-Palmolive, 1960s, EX $25.00

Spider-Man, Benjamin Ansehl, orig tag, M, A7 ....$25.00

Splash Down Space Capsule, Avon, 1970, MIB, A7 ....$20.00

Spouty Whale, Roclar (Purex), bl, orig card, M...............$20.00

Squiddly Diddly, Purex, 1960s, purple w/pk shirt, rare, NM, A7, from $60 to...$75.00

Superman, Avon, 1978, complete w/cape, MIB, A7.........$35.00

Superman, Colgate-Palmolive, 1965, EX, A7 ....$50.00

Sylvester the Cat and Tweety Bird (Sylvester holding Tweety), DuCair Bioescence, 1988, M, from $10.00 to $30.00. (Photo courtesy Greg Moore and Joe Pizzo)

Sylvester & Tweety, Minnetonka, Tweety standing on Sylvester's head, M, A7 ....$8.00

Sylvester the Cat w/Microphone, Colgate-Palmolive, 1960s, EX, A7...$30.00

Tasmanian Devil in Inner Tube, Kid Care, 1992, EX, A7...$8.00

Teenage Mutant Ninja Turtles, Kid Care, 1990, any character, M, A7, ea $8.00

Tennessee Tuxedo, Colgate-Palmolive, 1965, w/ice-cream cone, NM, A7...$30.00

Tex Hex (Brave Starr), Ducair Bioescence, w/tag, M, A7 ..$15.00

Theodore (Chipmunks), Colgate-Palmolive, wht w/bl T or gr w/red sweater & gr T, w/tag & puppet, M, A7, ea......$50.00

Three Little Pigs, Tubby Time, 1960s, any character, rare, M, A7, ea...$40.00

Thumper, Colgate-Palmolive, 1960s, EX, A7 ....$25.00

Tic Toc Tiger, Avon, orange w/yel hands & hat, M, A7 ...$15.00

Tic Toc Turtle, Avon, 1968, gr w/yel face & pk hands, MIB, A7 ....$20.00

Tommy (Rugrats), Kid Care, 1997, NM $8.00

Top Cat, Colgate-Palmolive, 1963, EX, $30.00.

Touche Turtle, Purex, lying on stomach, gr w/pk accents, EX, A7 ....$35.00

Touche Turtle, Purex, standing, NM, A7 ....$45.00

Tweety on Cage, Colgate-Palmolive, NM, A7 ....$25.00

Wally Gator, Purex, 1963, rare, NM, from $45 to.............$60.00

Watering Can, Avon, 1962, yel w/flowers, NM, A7 ....$15.00

Wendy the Witch, Colgate-Palmolive, 1960s, NM, A7 ...$30.00

Whitey the Whale, Avon, 1959, EX, A7 ....$15.00

Winkie Blink Clock, Avon, 1975, yel w/bl hands & hat, MIB, A7 ....$15.00

Winnie the Pooh, Johnson & Johnson, 1997, NM $6.00

Winsome Witch, Purex, 1965, rare, NM, A7....................$30.00

Wolfman, Colgate-Palmolive, 1963, red pants, NM, from $100 to $125.00

Woodsy Owl, Lander, early 1970s, EX............................$35.00

Woody Woodpecker, Colgate-Palmolive, 1977, NM........$45.00

Yaaky Doodle Duck, Roclar (Purex), w/contents & neck card, M, A7 ....$20.00

Yoda (Star Wars), Omni, 1981, NM $20.00

Yogi Bear, Milvern (Purex), brn, rare, NM, A7 ....$50.00

Yogi Bear, Purex, powder/bank, gr hat & yel tie, NM, A7 ..$30.00

101 Dalmatians, Kid Care, red & blk doghouse w/2 pups, M, A7 ....$5.00

FOREIGN

Action Man (Dr X), Rosedew Ltd/UK, 1994, topper, NM, A7 ....$15.00

Action Man (Night Creeper), Rosedew Ltd/UK, 1994, topper, silver gun, w/suction cups, M, A7 ....$15.00

Action Man (Space Commando), Rosedew Ltd/UK, 1994, bl & gray combat uniform, M, A7 ....$35.00

Aladdin, Grosvenor/UK, 1994, flying on carpet w/girl & monkey, M, A7...$30.00

Alf, PE/Germany, 1980s, NM, A7......................................$40.00

Alice in Wonderland, Aidee Int'l Ltd/UK, 1993, NM, A7..$30.00

Aliens, Grosvenor/UK, 1993, topper, M, A7 ....$20.00

Ariel (Little Mermaid), Damascar/Italy, 1995, sitting on purple rock, NM, A7...$30.00

Ariel (Little Mermaid), Prelude/UK, 1994, sitting on clear bubbles, NM, A7 ....$20.00

Baloo (Jungle Book), Boots/England, 1965, NM $70.00

Barney Rubble, Damascar/Italy, 1995, wearing Water Buffalo hat, w/bowling ball, M, A7......................................$35.00

Bart Simpson, Grosvenor, 1991, w/wht towel & soap, NM, A7 ....$25.00

Bashful, Grumpy & Happy, Grosvenor/UK, 1994, topper, M, A7 ....$15.00

Batman, Grosvenor/UK, 1992, gray suit & blk cape, NM, A7...$25.00

Batman (Animated), Damascar/Italy, 1995, NM, A7.......$30.00

Batmobile (Batman Forever), Prelude/UK, 1995, blk w/silver wheels, body lifts for bottle, NM, A7 ....$25.00

Beast (Beauty & the Beast), Prelude/UK, 1994, movable arms, comes apart at waist, NM, A7 ....$25.00

Belle (Beauty & the Beast), Prelude/UK, 1994, yel gown, w/hands crossed & head tilted back, NM, A7 ....$25.00

Big Bird, Grosvenor/UK, 1995, topper, sitting in bubbles w/teddy bear, M, A7 ....$10.00

Boo Boo Bear, Damascar/Italy, M, $35.00.

Bubba Saurus, Belvedere/Canada, 1995, bank, pk dinosaur, M, A7 ....$15.00

Bugs Bunny, Centura/Canada, 1994, in purple robe holding carrot, NM, A7...$20.00

Bugs Bunny, Prelude/UK, 1995, cloth hand puppet, slips over bottle, M, A7...$20.00

Casper the Ghost, Damascar/Italy, 1995, sitting on pumpkin, glow-in-the-dark, M, A7 ....$35.00

Casper's Friends, Damascar/Italy, 1995, 3 ghosts sitting on trunk, NM, A7 ....$35.00

Cinderella, Damascar/Italy, 1994, gray & wht gown, NM, A7...$35.00

Cindy Bear, Damascar/Italy, 1995, sitting on purple rock, NM, A7...$35.00

Cookie Monster, Jim Henson/PI/UK, 1995, bl w/wht cloth towel, NM, A7...$20.00

Daffy Duck, Prelude/UK, 1994, wearing shark suit, M, A7 ..$20.00

Daffy Duck, Prelude/UK, 1995, cloth hand puppet, slips over bottle, M, A7 ....$20.00

Darth Vader, Grosvenor/UK, 1995, holding light saber, movable arm, M, A7...$20.00

Dino (Flintstones), Rosedew/UK, 1993, M, A7.............$30.00

Dino (Flintstones), Rosedew/UK, 1993, topper, NM, A7...$15.00

Doc & Dopey, Grosvenor/UK, 1994, topper, NM, A7......$15.00

Donald Duck, Centura/Canada, 1994, standing on red base, NM, A7..$20.00

Donald Duck (Mickey & Pals), Centura/Canada, 1995, Donald driving yel boat, NM, A7.......................................$20.00

Dopey & Sneezy, Grosvenor/ UK, 1994, NM, A7 ....$30.00

Flipper Riding a Wave, Euromark/England, 1996, NM $20.00

Forever Friends, Grosvenor/England, 1995, NM $20.00

Fred Flintstone, Damascar/Italy, 1994, w/golf club, NM, A7...$35.00

Fred Flintstone, Rosedew/UK, 1994, w/bowling ball, NM, A7...$30.00

Garfield, Grosvenor/England, 1981, NM $25.00

Genie (Aladdin), Centura/Canada, 1994, holding microphone, NM, A7..$20.00

Genie (Aladdin), Damascar/Italy, 1994, released from lamp, real hair, NM, A7 ....$35.00

Goofy, Centura/Canada, 1995, coming out of shower/tub, M, A7...$20.00

Huckleberry Hound, Secol/UK, 1960s, bl w/yel bow tie, rare, EX, A7..$100.00

Hulk Hogan, Fulford/Canada, 1986, Hulkmania on shirt, NM...$20.00

Jasmin (Aladdin), Damascar/Italy, 1994, in purple dress, head tilted, M, A7...$30.00

Joker (Batman), Prelude/UK, 1995, topper, NM, A7 ....$15.00

Jungle Land Boat, Top Care/Canada, 1995, NM $15.00

Magic Princess, Boots/England, 1996, NM $20.00

Matchbox Indy Race Car, Grosvenor/UK, 1995, topper, red w/blk & wht checker flag, NM, A7................................$15.00

Mickey Mouse, Centura/Canada, 1994, NM $20.00

Mickey Mouse, Disney/Canada, 1994, pie-eyed, traditional outfit, M, A7...$25.00

Mickey Mouse, Prelude/UK, 1994, topper, pie-eyed, legs crossed, NM, A7..$15.00

Minnie Mouse, Disney World/UK, 1989, red dress, yel shoes, flower & umbrella, NM, A7 ....$30.00

Minnie Mouse, Prelude/UK, 1994, topper, pie-eyed, w/legs crossed, red skirt, NM, A7....................................$15.00

Mr Men, UK, yel & orange hat, M, A7............................$40.00

Nala (Lion King), Centura/Canada, 1994, sitting on pk base, M, A7...$20.00

Noddy, Grosvenor/UK, 1994, topper, sitting w/coffee cup, NM, A7 ....$15.00

Olive Oyl, Damascar/Italy, 1995, sitting w/hands clasped, NM, A7...$35.00

Oscar the Grouch, Grosvenor/UK, 1994, taking a bath in trash can w/I Hate Baths sign, NM, A7 ....$25.00

Paddington Bear, Grosvenor/UK, 1989, topper, EX (EX window box), A7..$20.00

Papa Smurf, IMPS Brussels/Germany, 1991, bl w/red pants & hat, M, A7...$30.00

Pebbles & Bamm-Bamm, Damascar/Italy, 1995, sitting on sabertooth tiger, M, A7...$35.00

Peter Rabbit, Grosvenor/UK/Canada, 1991, bl coat, NM, A7...$20.00

Piglet (Winnie the Pooh), Prelude/UK, topper, waving, M, A7...$15.00

Pocahontas, Grosvenor/UK, 1995, standing on rock in dive position, NM, A7..$20.00

Pocahontas, Grosvenor/UK, 1995, topper, in canoe w/raccoon, NM, A7..$15.00

Popeye, Rosedew Ltd/UK, 1987, on blk base holding spinach can, M, A7...$30.00

Pumba (Lion King), Prelude/UK, 1994, M, A7 ....$20.00

Robin, Damascar/Italy, 1995, squatting on eagle head statue, M, A7...$35.00

Rupert Bear, UK, 1995, topper, in yel airplane, M, A7.....$20.00

Scooby Doo, Damascar/Italy, 1995, brn, M, A7 ....$35.00

Simba (Lion King), Prelude/UK, 1994, sitting on rock w/paw up, NM, A7..$20.00

Sleeping Beauty, Damascar/Italy, 1994, holding roses, NM, A7...$35.00

Sneezy & Sleepy, Grosvenor/UK, 1994, topper, NM, A7 ..$15.00

Snow White, Rosedew/UK, 1994, standing w/arms crossed, M, A7...$25.00

Spider-Man, Euromark/UK, 1995, walking over trash can & tire, NM, A7..$20.00

Superman, Euromark/UK, 1994, NM...............................$25.00

Superman, Euromark/UK, 1994, topper, kneeling, M, A7 ..$15.00

Sylvester, Prelude/UK, 1995, cloth hand puppet, slips over bottle, M, A7...$25.00

Tasmanian Devil, Prelude/UK, 1995, mouth wide open, movable arms, M, A7...$25.00

Tom & Jerry, Damascar/Italy, 1995, sitting in drum, NM, A7...$35.00

Tweety Bird, Prelude/UK, 1995, bl robe & wht towel, NM, A7...$35.00

Two-Face (Batman), Prelude/UK, 1995, topper, NM, A7...$15.00

USS Enterprise (Star Trek), Euromark/UK, 1994, NM $30.00

Wile E Coyote, Prelude/UK, 1995, w/rocket backpack, NM, A7...$35.00

Wilma Flintstone, Damascar/Italy, 1993, standing on turtle shell, M, A7...$35.00

Winnie the Pooh, Boots/UK, blk base, M, A7...................$35.00

Yogi Bear, Damascar/Italy, 1994, standing on gr base w/purple grass, M, A7...$35.00

101 Dalmatians, Grosvenor/UK, 1994, father w/pup on head & 1 between legs, NM, A7 ....$35.00

101 Dalmatians, Grosvenor/UK, 1994, topper, pups on pillow w/red sunglasses, M, A7...$15.00

Buddy L

First produced in 1921, Buddy L toys have escalated in value over the past few years until now early models in good original condition (or restored, for that matter) often bring prices well into the four figures when they hit the auction block. The business was started by Fred Lundahl, founder of Moline Pressed Steel Co., who at first designed toys for his young son, Buddy. They were advertised as being 'Guaranteed Indestructible,' and indeed they were so sturdy and well built that they just about were. Until wartime caused a shortage, they were made of heavy-gauge pressed steel. Many were based on actual truck models; some were ride-ons, capable of supporting a grownup's weight. Fire trucks with hydraulically activated water towers and hoisting towers that actually worked kept little boys entertained for hours. After the war, the quality of Buddy Ls began to decline, and wood was used to some extent. Condition is everything. Remember that unless the work is done by a professional restorer, overpainting and amateur repairs do nothing to enhance the value of a toy in poor condition. Professional restorations may be expensive, but they may be viable alternatives when compared to the extremely high prices we're seeing today.

The following listings are from various auctions, and the estimates have been included. The prices reflect a 10% buyer's premium.

See also Advertising; Aeronautical; Boats; Catalogs.

CARS

Flivver Coupe, 1920s, blk, MSW, 11", EX+, A (Est: $800-$1,200) $1,430.00
Flivver Coupe, 1920s, blk, MSW, 11", G+, A (Est: $500-$700)..$715.00
Flivver Roadster, 1920s, blk, MSW, 11½", G, A (Est: $500-$800)..$770.00
Flivver Roadster, 1920s, blk, MSW, 11½", NM, A (Est: $2,500-$3,500) $2,200.00
Greyhound Bus, automatic door, ringing bell, b/o lights, bl & wht, 16", G+, A (Est: $150-$250)............................$275.00

Motor coach, 1920s, green with nickel-plated disk wheels and trim, 29", VG, A (Est: $4,000.00 – $6,000.00), $5,500.00. (Photo courtesy Randy Inman Auctions)

CONSTRUCTION

Bucket Loader, 1940s, 4-wheeled cart, 22", old rpt, A (Est: $75-$125) $75.00

Concrete Mixer, 1920s, rubber treads, gray, 17", restored, A (Est: $1,000.00 – $1,500.00), $2,200.00. (Photo courtesy Randy Inman Auctions)

Concrete Mixer, 1940s, #832, 10", G+, A (Est: $75-$125)..$165.00
Construction Crane, 1950s, 4-wheeled, orange, yel & gr, 24", Fair, A (est: $50-$75) $65.00
Derrick, #241, 24", G, A (Est: $800-$1,200)..............$1,800.00
Hoisting Tower, 1920s, #350, 38", G, A (Est: $400-$600)..$550.00
Mobile Power Digger, 1950s, 20", G, A (Est: $175-$225)..$175.00
Pile Driver, 1920s, #260, 21", rstr, A (Est: $300-$500)...$825.00
Sand Screener, 1920s, #300, 22", broken gears o/w VG+, A (Est: $1,200-$1,500) $1,540.00
Steam Shovel, 1920s, #220, 21", VG, A (Est: $150-$250)...$200.00
Steam Shovel, 1920s, #220A, heavier version, 22", G, A (Est: $600-$800) $1,430.00
Steam Shovel, 1940s, 20", G, A (Est: $25-$50)................$30.00

FIREFIGHTING

Aerial Ladder Truck, open seat, hydraulic, w/headlights & bumper, , 40", VG, A (Est: $3,000-$5,000)..........$4,620.00
Aerial Ladder Truck, 1920s, open seat, NP extension ladders, NPDW, 40", VG, A (Est: $3,500-$4,500) $2,875.00
Aerial Ladder Truck, 1930s (?), red/yel slant pnt, NP grille & ladders, BRT, 4-wheeled, 29", rstr, A (Est: $400-$600) $1,430.00
Aerial Ladder Truck, 1950s, GMC cab, orange, 6-wheeled, 26", missing accessory ladders, Fair, A (Est: $50-$75).....$100.00
Aerial Ladder Truck, 1960s, mk Buddy L 3/BKFD, 27", missing accessory ladders o/w VG+IB, A (Est: $150-$250)..$165.00
Extention Ladder Truck, 1940s, red w/wht nose pnt diagonally, aluminum ladders, 6-wheeled, 30", G, A (Est: $75-$125)...$440.00
Fire Hose & Water Pumper Truck, 1940s, 12½", EX, A (Est: $25-$50) $100.00
Hook & Ladder Truck, 1920s, NPDW, complete w/accessories, 28", rstr, A (Est: $1,000-$1,500) $1,485.00
Hook & Ladder Truck, 1920s, NPDW, complete w/orig accessories, G, A (Est: $700-$900) $1,100.00

Hook & Ladder Truck (Rear Stear), 1940s, open U-shaped back w/high seat, 20", no accessories, G, A (Est: $100-$150) $60.00

Ladder Truck, b/o lights, red w/yel ladders, 20", VG, A (Est: $300-$400) $400.00

Pumper Truck, 1920s, open seat, red w/NP boiler, MDW, no headlights or bumper, 24", rstr, A, (Est: $1,200-$1,500) $1,200.00

Pumper Truck, 1930s, open seat, red with gold trim, with headlights and bumper, 24", G+, A (Est: $3,000.00 – $5,000.00), $6,820.00. (Photo courtesy Randy Inman)

RIDERS

Baggage Truck, 1953, cream over gr, BRT, 6-wheeled, 25", no seat or hdl o/w VG, A (Est: $275-$350) $165.00

Delivery Truck, 1920s International, 24", old rpt, A (Est: $200-$300) $450.00

Delivery Truck, 1930s International, stake bed, 2-color horizontal pnt, 23", complete, G+, A (Est: $250-$400) $600.00

Delivery Truck, 1930s International with stake bed, two-color slant detail, 25", EX+IB, A (Est: $2,000.00 – $3,000.00), $2,200.00. (Photo courtesy Randy Inman Auctions)

Dump Truck, 1930s International, curved cab, 25", G, A (Est: $800-$1,200) $1,045.00

Dump Truck, 1930s International, sq cab w/visor, 20", rstr, A (Est: $150-$250) $240.00

Dump Truck, 1930s International, working headlights, 24", complete, Fair+, A (Est: $400-$700) $500.00

Dump Truck, 1950s, gray w/blk seat, 20", no hdl, G, A (Est: $75-$125) $70.00

Fire Water Tower Truck, red, BRT, removable seat, w/hdl, 42", VG, A (Est: $2,000-$3,000) $2,475.00

Sand & Gravel Truck, 2-color slant detail, opening lift gate, 21", complete, EX, A (Est: $400-$600) $300.00

Wrecker, 1938 International, 28", no seat or pull rod o/w VG, A (Est: $2,000-$2,500) $1,980.00

TRAINS

Industrial Balliste Car, opening side doors, 8", NM (P box), A (Est: $3,000-$4,000) $1,980.00

Industrial Set, locomotive, 4 cars, roundhouse, track & turntable, ea car about 10", G+, A (Est: $3,000-$4,000) $1,100.00

Industrial Set, locomotive, 5 cars, about 8" ea, Fair+, A (Est: $300-$400) $825.00

Industrial Set, locomotive, 6 cars, roundhouse, track & turntable, ea car approx 10", VG+, A (Est: $4,000-$6,000) $2,300.00

Industrial Set, locomotive, 7 cars & track, about 8" ea, G+, A (Est: $1,000-$1,500) $1,100.00

Mining Train, locomotive, five work cars and twelve pieces of track, 36" overall, EX+ A (Est: $1,000.00 – $1,200.00), $1,725.00. (Photo courtesy James D. Julia Inc.)

Outdoor Caboose, red, 20", VG, A (Est: $1,200-$1,500) ..$825.00

Outdoor Coal Car, blk, 22", EX, A (Est: $800-$1,200) ..$1,045.00

Outdoor Dredger on Flatbed Car, 30", rstr, A (Est: $500-$800) $1,320.00

Outdoor Gondola Car, dual bottom dump doors, EX, A (Est: $800-$1,000) $5,225.00

Outdoor Locomotive & Tender, blk, 43", EX+, A (Est: $2,500-$3,500) $2,860.00

Outdoor Locomotive & Tender, blk, 43", rstr, A (Est: $800-$1,200) $1,155.00

Outdoor Locomotive & Tender w/5 Cars & Caboose, w/4 pcs of track, rstr, A (Est: $1,500-$2,000) $2,200.00

Outdoor Overhead Yard Crane, 5-crank action, pulleys allow crane movement, 33x45x12", VG+, A (Est: $2,500-$3,500) .$2,760.00

Outdoor Pile Driver on Flatbed Car, 27", rstr, A (Est: $500-$800) $1,200.00

Outdoor Steam Shovel on Flatbed Car, 28", partially rstr, A (Est: $1,200-$1,500) $1,430.00

Outdoor Stock Car, red, opening side doors, 22", VG, A (Est: $800-$1,000) $1,200.00

Outdoor Stock Car, 1920s, red, opening side doors, 22", EX+, A (Est: $1,200-$1,500).............................$2,200.00

Outdoor Tank Car, red and black, 19", VG, A (Est: $1,000.00 – $1,500.00), $1,100.00. (Photo courtesy Bertoia Auctions)

Outdoor Tank Car, yel, scarce version, 19", G, A (Est: $1,000-$1,200) $1,650.00

Outdoor Wrecking Crane on Flatbed Car, 30", Fair+, A (Est: $1,500-$2,500) $2,530.00

Zephyer, 2-car, Burlington Route decal, b/o lights, about 46", missing pull rod, G, A (Est: $300-$500)...............$1,200.00

TRUCKS AND VANS

Air Force Searchlight Truck, 1950s, plastic searchlight, BRT, 4-wheeled, 15", incomplete, G, A (Est: $50-$75).........$30.00

Air Force Supply Truck, 1950s, bl, w/cloth topper, BRT, 15", G+, A (Est: $50-$75) $185.00

Airway Delivery Truck, 1950s, GMC cab w/box van, gr, 4-wheeled, VG, A (Est: $150-$200) $245.00

Allied Van Lines Semi, blk & orange, removable van roof, BRT, 6-wheeled, 29", G, A (Est: $300-$400)...............$300.00

Anti-Aircraft Unit w/Electric Searchlight Trailer, 1950s, GMC cab, bl, 24", VG+, A (Est: $150-$250) $400.00

Army Supply Corps, 1950s, GMC cab, canvas cover, 4-wheeled, 14½", EX, A ($150-$250) $330.00

Army Transport w/Howitzer Gun, army gr, w/cloth canopy cover, BRT, 4-wheeled, 17" truck, EX, A (Est: $250-$300)...$275.00

Baggage Stake Truck, 1920s, MDW, 27", no accessories, VG+, A (Est: $3,500-$4,500)..............................$5,500.00

Boat Hauler, 1960s, lt bl w/wht grille, WWT, 2 red & wht plastic boats, 27", VG, A (Est: $350-$450).........................$190.00

Camper Truck, 1960s, WWT, 15", VG, A (Est: $50-$75) ..$65.00

Cement Truck, 1960s, red w/wht revolving cement drum, 8-wheeled, 15", NM+, A (Est: $150-$250) $220.00

City Dray, 1930s International w/stake bed, b/o lights, yel & gr diagonal pnt, red hubs, 19", VG, A (Est: $300-$400)..$465.00

City Ice Co Stake Truck, Steelcraft, early long-nosed cab w/visor, red w/wht bed, NPDW, 22", VG, A (Est: $300-$500)...$465.00

Coal Truck, 1920s, doorless cab, V-shaped bed, blk w/red chassis & hubs, MDW, 25", P, A (Est: $700-$900).............$990.00

Curtiss Baby Ruth Semi, 29", EX, A (Est: $350.00 – $450.00), $465.00. (Photo courtesy Bertoia Auctions)

Dump Truck, see also Hydraulic Dumper

Dump Truck, 1920s, doorless cab, blk, NPDW w/red hubs, 6-wheeled, rstr, A (Est: $300-$400) $600.00

Dump Truck, 1920s, enclosed cab, electric lights, blk & red, BRT, 4-wheeled, 20", Fair, A (Est: $75-$125)..........$300.00

Dump Truck, 1920s, open seat, chain-lift bed, red, MDW w/red hubs, 4-wheeled, 25", P, A (Est: $150-$200) $185.00

Dump Truck, 1920s, open seat, hydraulic, blk, MDW w/red hubs, 4-wheeled, 24", old rpt, A (Est: $200-$300) ..$230.00

Dump Truck, 1920s, open seat, rope lift, blk, MDW w/red hubs, 4-wheeled, 24", VG, A (Est: $700-$900) $1,200.00

Dump Truck, 1930s, enclosed cab, electric lights, yel & red, MDW, 4-wheeled, 20", rstr, A (Est: $50-$75)..........$175.00

Dump Truck, 1930s, enclosed cab, NP lights & grille, curved dump bed, BRT, 4-wheeled, 24", rstr, A (Est: $150-$250) $88.00

Dump Truck, 1940s, enclosed cab w/curved dump bed, blk wooden wheels, 4-wheeled, 17", VG, A (Est: $75-$125) $110.00

Dump Truck, 1960s, enclosed cab w/side-crank dump bed, BRT, 6-wheeled, 14", VG, A (Est: $50-$75).....................$40.00

Electric Emergency Unit, 1950s, yel, 14½", rstr, A (Est: $50-$75) $55.00

Electronic Loud Speaker Unit (Truck), 1950s GMC, 14", incomplete, VG+, A (Est: $50-$100)...............................$55.00

Emergency Auto Wrecker, 1940s, yel w/red boom, NP grille, 15", VG+, A (Est: $100-$150) $230.00

Emergency Auto Wrecker, 1950s, red & wht, BRT, 17", VG, A (Est: $75-$125) $130.00

Express Line Tractor-Trailer, 1930s, box van w/removable roof, 25", G+, A (Est: $250-$400)...............................$300.00

Express Line Truck, red cab mk Fire Chief, gr van trailer, simulated spoke wheels, 6-wheeled, 23", G, A (Est: $350-$550) $345.00

Express Line Van, 1920s, roof extends over open seat, solid sides, blk, NPDW, red hubs, 24", G, A (Est: $700-$900)..$700.00

Express Line Van, 1920s, van roof extends over open seat, solid sides, blk/gr/red, MDW, 25", EX, A (Est: $1,200-$1,400) $1,760.00

Express Truck, 1930s, electric lights, removable roof, opening doors, 6-wheeled, gr w/ads, 23", rpt, A (Est: $150-$250)........$185.00

Farm Supplies Dump Truck, 1940s, diagonal 2-color pnt, 20", VG+IB, A (Est: $400-$600)....................................$460.00

Farm Supplies Dump Truck, 1940s, 2-color diagonal pnt, 20", G, A (Est: $200-$300)..............................$110.00

Fast Freight Semi, 1950s, Open U-shaped trailer w/chain across open back, 6-wheeled, 20", NMIB............................$650.00

Fast Freight Semi, 1950s, open U-shaped trailer w/chain across open back, 6-wheeled, 20", VG, A (Est: $150-$200)...$100.00

Flivver Dump Truck, 1920s, blk, MSW, 11", Fair, A (Est: $300-$500)..$385.00

Flivver Huckster Delivery Truck, 1920s, blk, MSW, 14½", G, A (Est: $2,000-$3,000)...........................$2,860.00

Flivver Pickup Truck, 1920s, blk, MSW, 12", VG+, A (Est: $1,500-$2,000)..................................$1,155.00

Freight Hauler, 1950s, GMC cab, orange, 8-wheeled, 22", G, A (Est: $75-$125)..................................$200.00

Highway Maintenance Dump Truck & Sand Hopper, 1950s, orange, 14", ea, G, A (Est: $75-$125)......................$90.00

Horse Transport, modern cabover, plastic & PS, rust & cream, 8-wheeled, 11", G, A (Est: $10-$20)..........................$20.00

Hydraulic Dumper, 1950s, gr & wht, 10-wheeled, 20", VG, A (Est: $100-$200)....................................$240.00

Hydraulic Dumper, 1961, turq, BRT, 6-wheeled, 20", VG, A (Est: $200-$300).......................................$110.00

Hydraulic Heavy Hauling Dumper Truck, 1950s, red w/wht dump bed, BRT, 4-wheeled, 21", Fair, A (Est: $50-$100)..$65.00

Hydraulically Operated Dump Truck, 1950s, orange, 4-wheeled, 14", P, A (Est: $25-$50).............................$22.00

Ice Truck, 1920s, doorless cab, w/canvas cover, 26", G+, A (Est: $1,500-$1,800)...................................$2,400.00

Jr Air Mail Truck, bk & red, 22", G, A (Est: $2,000-$2,500)...$3,740.00

Jr Dairy Truck, 1920s, 23", overpnt, G, A (Est: $700-$900)..$1,045.00

Jr Dump Truck, 1930s, enclosed cab w/visor, opening doors, BRT, rear duals, 22", G, A (Est: $1,200-$1,500) ..$1,200.00

Junior Dump Truck, 1930s, rear dual wheels, 24", VG, A (Est: $1,500.00 – $2,000.00), $2,530.00. (Photo courtesy Bertoia Auctions)

Jr Tanker Truck, 25", rstr, VG+, A (Est: $1,500-$2,000) ..$1,760.00

Kennel Truck, 1960s, bl, WWT, incomplete o/w G, A (Est: $25-$50)..$28.00

Lumber Truck, 1920s, #203A, doorless cab, blk, MDW, red hubs, 25", no racks, Fair, A (Est: $1,200-$1,500)..............$900.00

Machinery Truck, 1950s, gr w/lt yel bed, BRT, 6-wheeled, 23", VG+, A (Est: $200-$250)...............................$250.00

Merry-Go-Round Truck, 1960s, 13", NM, A (Est: $250-$350)...$330.00

Milk Delivery Stake Truck, 1930s, enclosed cab w/visor, opening doors, BRT, 24", P, A (Est: $600-$800)................$1,100.00

Mobile Artillery Unit Half-Truck, 1940s, 13½", missing 1 rear track o/w VG, A (Est: $50-$75)...........................$110.00

Mobile Repair Unit, 1940s International, 2-color horizontal pnt, BRT, 4-wheeled, 28", EX, A (Est: $250-$400)........$465.00

Motor Market Truck, 20", G, A (Est: $200-$250)...........$600.00

Motor Truck, 1930s, wht w/yel nose, 2-tiered bay w/ad panel, 20", no accessories, rstr, A (Est: $75-$125)..............$130.00

Pickup Truck, 1960s, lt bl, WWT, 12", no tailgate o/w VG, A (Est: $25-$50)...$22.00

Playboy Truck Co Wrecker, Steelcraft, early long-nosed cab w/visor, wht w/blk boom, 21", G, A (Est: $200-$300)...............$200.00

Pure Ice Truck, 1930s International, red over wht, BRT, 22", EX, A (Est: $300-$500)...............................$825.00

Railway Express Agency Truck, 1930s, electric lights, six-wheeled, Wrigley's ad, 23", A (Est: $1,500.00 – $2,500.00), $2,300.00. (Photo courtesy Randy Inman Auctions)

Railway Express Van, 1925, van roof extends over open seat, screened sides, MDW, 24", EX, A (Est: $2,000-$2,500).............$4,125.00

Red Baby Express Truck (International Harvester), doorless cab, NPSW, 25", VG, A (Est: $600-$800)......................$600.00

Repair-It Service Truck, 1950s, red cab w/wht dump bed, w/accessories, 21", EXIB, A...................................$440.00

Repair-It Unit Tow Truck, 1940s, wht over red, gr boom (rpl), 6-wheeled, 24", G, A (Est: $150-$175)......................$245.00

Robotoy Dump Truck, electric lights, 21", no transformer, Fair+, A (Est: $400-$500)...$400.00

Rockin' Giraffes Truck, 1960s, WWT, complete w/2 giraffes, 13½", G+, A (Est: $75-$125) $250.00

Sand & Gravel Dump Truck, 1920s, #202A, blk, red hubs, 24", older rpt, A (Est: $500-$700)....................................$600.00

Sand & Gravel Truck, 1940s, 13½", EX, A (Est: $200-$300)..$110.00

Sand & Stone Dump Truck, 1950s, 6-wheeled, 14½", EX, A (Est: $125-$150)...$200.00

Scoop & Dump Truck, 1950s, 10-wheeled, 22", Fair, A (Est: $75-$125)..$55.00

Scoop & Dump Truck, 1950s, 4-wheeled, 18", G, A (Est: $50-$75)...$75.00

Scoop & Dump Truck, 1950s, 6-wheeled, 18", VG, A (Est: $50-$100) $85.00

Sheffield Farms Select Grade-A Milk Tanker Truck #857, 25", VGIB, A (Est: $1,500.00 – $2,500.00), $2,530.00. (Photo courtesy Randy Inman Auctions)

Shell Fuel Oils Tanker, 1938 International, yel w/diagonal red on nose, 21", VG+, A (Est: $300-$500) $260.00

Shell Truck, 1940s, yel, cut-out detail on curved bed, open chained tailgate, 13", VG, A (Est: $200-$300) $130.00

Son-ny Parcel Post Delivery Truck, screened van w/roof extended over open seat, 26", VG+, A (Est: $700-$900) $550.00

Stake Truck, 1950s, red w/silver stake sides, BRT, 15", rstr, A (Est: $25-$50) $45.00

State Hi-Way Dept Dump Truck, 1950s, 4-wheeled, 14", rstr, A (Est: $50-$100) $55.00

State Hi-Way Dept Dump Truck & Air Compressor, 1950s, 4-wheeled w/2-wheeled compressor, 20", rstr, A (Est: $50-$100) $75.00

Super Market Delivery Truck, 1940s, wht, BRT, no accessories, 13", VGIB, A (Est: $100-$200) $130.00

Super Market Delivery Truck, 1940s, wht, BRT, w/accessories, 13", G, A (Est: $75-$125) $85.00

Tank Line Truck, 1920s, doorless cab, blk w/red frame, NPDW, red hubs, 25", VG+, A (Est: $700-$900) $715.00

Tank Line Truck w/Sprinkler, 1920s, doorless cab, MDW, no cans, 26", rpt, A (Est: $1,500-$1,750) $1,200.00

Tank Line Truck w/Sprinkler, 1920s, doorless cab, MDW, w/cans, 26½", EX, A (Est: $3,000-$3,500) $4,950.00

Tank Truck, 1930s, wht cab w/red tank body, BRT, red hubs, 4-wheeled, 20", rstr, A (Est: $150-$250) $165.00

Telephone & Maintenance Truck, 1940s, #450, 2-tone gr, no accessories, 16", A (Est: $25-$50) $80.00

Tow Truck, see also Wrecking Truck

Tow Truck, 1960s, bl w/red light on top of wht cab, blk boom, spare on side of curved bed, 15", VG, A (Est: $50-$75) $110.00

US Mail Truck #2592, 1940s, Buy Defense Bonds, army gr, BRT, 6-wheeled, 20", VG+, A (Est: $250-$350) $175.00

Utilities Service Truck, 1950s, GMC, orange w/lg blk crane, 15", EX, A (Est: $100-$150) $385.00

Van Freight Carriers Semi, 1940s, trailer w/removable roof, 6-wheeled, 20", VG, A (Est: $150-$250) $90.00

Wrecking Truck, 1920s, #209, open bench seat, NPDW, 32" (w/boom extended), VG+, A (Est: $600-$800).......$990.00

Wrecking Truck, 1940s, red, bk & gray w/blk boom, silver-pnt grille, emb lettering, 17", VG, A (Est: $50-$100).....$65.00

Wrigley's Spearmint Delivery Truck, 1950s, metallic bl-gr w/decal on side of van, 15", some rpt, G, A (Est: $100-$200)..$100.00

Zoo Truck, 1960s, 13", incomplete, P, A (Est: $10-$20) ...$22.00

WOODEN VEHICLES

Greyhound Bus, 1940s, bl & wht w/wht hubs, 18", G, A (Est: $300-$500) $410.00

Long Distance Moving Van, 26", VG+, A (Est: $200.00 – $300.00), $440.00. (Photo courtesy Noel Barrett Auctions)

Milk Farms Delivery Truck, sliding side doors, w/5 orig milk bottles & carrying case, 13", G, A (Est: $150-$300).......$90.00

Woody Station Wagon, 1940s, 19", Fair, A (Est: $100-$200) $80.00

CONTEMPORARY MODELS

Baggage Truck, 1930s version, blk w/yel stake bed, red hubs, 26", complete, MIB, A (Est: $500-$600)........................$935.00

Filvver Touring Car, Cowdry, blk, MSW, 11", M, A (Est: $800-$1,200) $1,155.00

Fivver Tank Line Truck, Cowdry, blk, MSW, w/2 milk cans, 15", M, A (Est: $1,200-$1,500) $2,090.00

Flivver Center Door Fire Chief's Car, Cowdry, red, MSW, 11", MIB, A (Est: $600-$900) $1,430.00

Flivver Center Door Sedan, Cowdry, blk, MSW, 11", MIB, A (Est: $500-$800) $825.00

Flivver Pickup, Cowdry, blk, MSW, 12", M, A (Est: $800-$1,200) $1,320.00

Flivver Pure Ice Truck, Cowdry, blk w/yel bed, MSW, 15½", M, A (Est: $1,200-$1,500) $1,540.00

Flivver Richfield Delivery Van, Cowdry, blk, MSW, 11½", M, A (Est: $1,200-$1,500)................................$1,430.00

Flivver Wrecker, Cowdry, blk, MSW, 16", M, A (Est: $1,200-$1,500) $1,430.00

Outdoor RR Flatcar, 19", M, A (Est: $100-$200) $130.00

Pile Driver, swivel cab, steel 'Caterpillar' treads, steam-powered, 24x19", M, A (Est: $150-$300) $485.00

Red Baby Truck, T-Reproductions, 1930s version, opening doors, red, NPDW, 24", MIB, A (Est: $500-$600) $880.00

Steam Shovel, swivel cab, steel 'Caterpillar' treads, red & blk, 18x22", M, A (Est: $150-$300)................................$230.00

Red Baby Wrecker, Era Toys, 1920s version, 25", VG+, A (Est: $700.00 – $800.00), $1,265.00. (Photo courtesy Noel Barrett Auctions)

Wrecker, Joe Ertl, 1920s version, red & blk w/disk wheels, 26", M, A (Est: $300-$400) $575.00

MISCELLANEOUS

Catapult Hangar, w/monocoupe, 12" W hanger, VG+, A (Est: $1,000-$1,500) $1,200.00
Dandy Digger, 1920s, #33, 28", EX, A (Est: $125-$175)...$140.00

Fire Station, 1940s, painted wood, 16x16", VG+, A (Est: $500.00 – $800.00), $250.00. (Photo courtesy Randy Inman Auctions)

Giant Digger, 44", missing seat, G, A (Est: $100-$200) ...$75.00
Hangar w/3 Planes, 1920s, 20", Fair+, A (Est: $800-$1,200) ..$1,200.00
Tool Box, blk & red wooden box w/metal corners, 11x23", no insert tray or tools o/w VG, A (Est: $25-$50)............$45.00

Building Blocks and Construction Toys

Toy building sets were popular with children well before television worked its mesmerizing influence on young minds; in fact, some were made as early as the end of the eighteenth century. Important manufacturers include Milton Bradley, Joel Ellis, Charles M. Crandall, William S. Tower, W.S. Read, Ives Manufacturing Corporation, S.L. Hill, Frank Hornby (Meccano), A.C. Gilbert Brothers, The Toy Tinkers, Gebruder Bing, R. Bliss, S.F. Fischer, Carl Brandt Jr., and F. Ad. Richter (see

Anchor Stone Building Sets by Richter). Whether made of wood, paper, metal, glass, or 'stone,' these toys are highly prized today for their profusion of historical, educational, artistic, and creative features.

Richter's Anchor (Union) Stone Building Blocks were the most popular building toy at the beginning of the twentieth century. As early as 1880, they were patented in both Germany and the USA. Though the company produced more than six hundred different sets, only their New Series is commonly found today (these are listed below). Their blocks remained popular until WWI, and Anchor sets were one of the first toys to achieve international 'brand name' acceptance. They were produced both as basic sets and supplement sets (identified by letters A, B, C, or D) which increased a basic set to a higher level. There were dozens of stone block competitors, though none were very successful. During WWI the trade name Anchor was lost to A.C. Gilbert (Connecticut) who produced Anchor blocks for a short time. Richter responded by using the new trade name 'Union' or 'Stone Building Blocks,' sets considered today to be Anchor blocks despite the lack of the Richter's Anchor trademark. The A.C. Gilbert Company also produced the famous Erector sets which were made from about 1913 through the late 1950s.

Note: Values for Richter's blocks are for sets in very good condition; (+) at the end of the line indicates these sets are being reproduced today.

Advisor: George Hardy (H3), Anchor Stone Building Sets by Richter

American Model Builder Set #6, EXIB...........................$150.00
American Skyline, Elgo, 1950s, NMIB......................$35.00
Auburn Rubber Building Bricks, 1950s, EXIC.................$40.00
Block City #B-500, 1960, EXIC...$50.00
Built-Rite Army Trench w/6 Soldiers, 1940s, MIB........$100.00
Built-Rite Fort w/Soldiers, 1940s, EXIB..........................$125.00

Dayton Steel Worker Set, VGIB, $200.00. (Photo courtesy Bertoia Auctions)

Falcon Building Lumber Set, EXIB (wood box)..............$150.00
Fisher-Price Construx Action Building System #6331 Mobile Missiles/Military Series, NMIB, from $50 to..............$75.00
Gabriel Tinkertoy No 30040, EXIC $25.00

Gabriel Tinkertoy No 30060, Gabriel, motorized, EXIC ..$35.00
Gilbert Erector Set #1 (Tru Model), EXIB.....................$200.00
Gilbert Erector Set #3, MIB $200.00
Gilbert Erector Set #4, VGIB.......................................$125.00
Gilbert Erector Set #5½, MIB.......................................$175.00
Gilbert Erector Set #6½, MIB.......................................$165.00
Gilbert Erector Set #7, EXIB (wood box) $250.00
Gilbert Erector Set #7, GIB (wood box) $75.00
Gilbert Erector Set #7½, EXIB (wood box) $350.00
Gilbert Erector Set #8, EXIB (wood box) $850.00
Gilbert Erector Set #8½, EXIB (wood box) $950.00
Gilbert Erector Set #10½", VGIB (metal box)...............$100.00
Halsam American Logs, EXIB $50.00
Halsam American Plastic Bricks, 1950s, EXIC $35.00
Hasbro Fire Alarm Set, Hasbro, NMIB...........................$135.00
Ideal Super City Heliport Building Set, 1968, EX (EX vinyl
   case) $50.00
Ideal Super City Skyscraper Building Set, 1960s, EXIB....$75.00
Ideal Super City Town & Country, VGIB........................$50.00
Kenner Girder & Panel Constructioneer Set #8, EXIB..$100.00
Kenner Girder & Panel Hydro-Dynamic Double Set #18,
   VGIB...$200.00
Kenner Girder & Panel Hydro-Dynamic Single Set #17,
   VGIB $175.00
Kenner Girder & Panel International Airport, 1977, EXIB..$40.00
Kenner Mold Master Road Builder, 1964, NMIB $125.00

Lionel Construction Set #222, unused, NMIB, $100.00. (Photo courtesy Stout Auctions)

Marklin #7 Racer, w/up motor, BRT, 14½" (assembled), EX,
   A $715.00
Marklin Auto-Baukasten, contemporary reissue of 1930s race
   car, MIB, A $185.00
Marklin Fire Aerial Ladder Truck, 1990s reissue of early model, w/up,
   electric lights, 2 figures, 18" (assembled), NM, A $330.00
Marklin Reichspost Truck, 1989 reissue of early model, w/up, 15"
   (assembled), M, A $400.00
Marklin Sedan, BRT, opening door, working steering, 14"
   (assembled), G, A $520.00
Marklin Standard Oil Tank Truck, 1990s reissue of early model,
   w/up, 17" (assembled), M $300.00
Meccano Aeroplane Constructor #0, EXIB $375.00

Meccano Aeroplane Constructor #1, VGIB.................$325.00
Meccano Aeroplane Constructor #2, EX+IB.................$450.00

Meccano Motor Car Constructor Set #1, VGIB, each set for $350.00; Meccano Motor Car Constructor Set #2, EX+IB, $450.00. (Photo courtesy Bertoia Auctions)

Meccano Racer, assembled, w/up, w/hand-controlled lever, 13",
   VG, A (Est: $150-$200) $770.00
Meccano Roadster Constructor, EXIB $500.00
Metalcraft Spirit of St Louis Airplanes, builds over 250 air-
   planes, VGIB $450.00
Metalcraft Train Kit, stock car, caboose & tracks, EXIB...$300.00
Questor Big Tinkertoy Construction Set for Little Hands, 1976,
   EXIC $25.00
Questor Tinkertoy Design Blocks, EXIC.........................$30.00
Questor Tinkertoy Giant Engineer, EXIC $25.00
Questor Tinkertoy Junior Architect, EXIC $25.00
Questor Tinkertoy Little Designer, EXIC $25.00
Questor Tinkertoy Locomotive & Driver, EXIC...............$15.00
Questor Tinkertoy Master Builder, EXIC $25.00
Renwal Busy Mechanic Construction Kit #375-198, EXIB...$300.00
Renwal Drawbridge Set #155, rare, EXIB $250.00
Schoenhut Aeroplane Builder, EXIB $250.00
Schoenhut Dirigible Builder, EXIB.............................$1,000.00
Schoenhut Hollywood Home Builder, EXIB....................$165.00
Schuco Elektro Champion Deluxe Set, VGIB................$325.00
Schuco Montage-Mercedes 190SL Kit, #2097, EX+IB...$165.00
Spalding Big Boy Tinkertoy, 1950s-60s, EXIC $45.00
Spalding Curtain Wall Builder No 640, 1959-64, EXIC...$40.00
Spalding Executive Tinkertoy Set, 1966, EXIC $35.00
Spalding Major Tinkertoy, 1964, EXIC $25.00
Spalding Motorized Tinkertoy, EXIC $60.00
Spalding Teck Tinkertoy, 1963, EXIC $25.00
Spalding Tinker Zoo No 717, 1970, EXIC $15.00
Spalding Tinker Zoo No 737, 1962-70, EXIC..................$25.00
Spalding Tinkertoy Panel Builder #600, 1958, EXIC.......$30.00
Spalding Tinkertoy Panel Builder #800, 1958, EXIC.......$40.00
Spalding Tinkertoy Wonder Builder, 1953-54, EXIC $30.00
Spaulding Junior Tinkertoy, 1963, EXIC..........................$25.00
Toy Tinkers Double Tinkertoy, 1927, EXIC $40.00
Toy Tinkers Giant Tinker, 1926, EXIB...........................$225.00
Toy Tinkers Special Tinkertoy w/Windlass Drive, 1943, EXIC..$35.00
Toy Tinkers Tinkerblox, 1917-20, EXIB...........................$60.00
Union Stone Blocks, dbl-layer set w/some metal components,
   appears complete, GIB (15x10") $225.00

ANCHOR STONE BUILDING SETS BY RICHTER

American House & Country Set #206, VG, H3............$600.00
American House & Country Set #208, VG, H3............$600.00
American House & Country Set #210, VG, H3............$700.00
DS Set #E3, w/metal parts & roof stones, VG, H3 ....$80.00
DS Set #5, w/metal parts & roof stones, VG, H3 ....$150.00
DS Set #5A, w/metal parts & roof stones, VG, H3 ....$150.00
DS Set #7, w/metal parts & roof stones, VG, H3 ....$270.00
DS Set #7A, w/metal parts & roof stones, VG, H3 ....$200.00
DS Set #9A, w/metal parts & roof stones, VG, H3 ....$250.00
DS Set #11, w/metal parts & roof stones, VG, H3 ....$675.00
DS Set #11A, w/metal parts & roof stones, VG, H3 ......$300.00
DS Set #13A, w/metal parts & roof stones, VG, H3 ......$325.00
DS Set #15, w/metal parts & roof stones, VG, H3 ......$1,500.00
DS Set #15A, w/metal parts & roof stones, VG, H3 ......$475.00
DS Set #19A, w/metal parts & roof stones, VG, H3 ......$475.00
DS Set #21A, w/metal parts & roof stones, VG, H3 ......$975.00
DS Set #23A, w/metal parts & roof stones, VG, H3 ......$750.00
DS Set #25A, w/metal parts & roof stones, VG, H3 ...$1,500.00
DS Set #27, w/metal parts & roof stones, VG, H3 ......$6,000.00
DS Set #27B, w/metal parts & roof stones, VG, H3....$2,000.00
DS Set #3A, w/metal parts & roof stones, VG, H3..........$80.00
Fortress Set #402, VG, H3............$100.00
Fortress Set #402A, VG, H3 ....$130.00
Fortress Set #404, VG, H3............$250.00
Fortress Set #404A, VG, H3 ....$275.00
Fortress Set #406, VG, H3............$500.00
Fortress Set #406A, VG, H3............$400.00
Fortress Set #408, VG, H3............$1,000.00
Fortress Set #408A, VG, H3............$800.00
Fortress Set #410, VG, H3............$1,800.00
Fortress Set #410A, VG, H3............$1,000.00
Fortress Set #412A, VG, H3............$1,500.00
Fortress Set #414, VG, H3............$5,000.00
German House & Country Set #301, VG, H3............$500.00
German House & Country Set #301A, VG, H3 ....$500.00
German House & Country Set #303, VG, H3............$1,000.00
German House & Country Set #303A, VG, H3 ....$2,000.00
German House & Country Set #305, VG, H3 ....$3,000.00
GK-AF Great-Castle Set, VG, H3............$9,950.00
GK-NF Set #6, VG, H3 (+)............$140.00
GK-NF Set #6A, VG, H3 (+)............$160.00
GK-NF Set #8, VG, H3............$300.00
GK-NF Set #8A, VG, H3 (+)............$180.00
GK-NF Set #10, VG, H3............$480.00
GK-NF Set #10A, VG, H3 (+)............$200.00
GK-NF Set #12, VG, H3............$680.00
GK-NF Set #12A, VG, H3 (+)............$250.00
GK-NF Set #14A, VG, H3............$250.00
GK-NF Set #16, VG, H3............$1,180.00
GK-NF Set #16A, VG, H3............$300.00
GK-NF Set #18A, VG, H3............$400.00
GK-NF Set #20, VG, H3 ....$2,000.00
GK-NF Set #20A, VG, H3............$500.00
GK-NF Set #22A, VG, H3............$500.00
GK-NF Set #24A, VG, H3............$600.00

GK-NF Set #26A, VG, H3............$1,000.00
GK-NF Set #28, VG, H3............$4,000.00
GK-NF Set #28A, VG, H3............$1,200.00
GK-NF Set #30A, VG, H3............$1,200.00
GK-NF Set #30A, VG, H3............$1,200.00
GK-NF Set #32B, VG, H3............$1,600.00
GK-NF Set #34, VG, H3............$7,000.00
KK-NF Set #5, VG, H3............$110.00
KK-NF Set #5A, VG, H3............$100.00
KK-NF Set #7, VG, H3............$200.00
KK-NF Set #7A, VG, H3............$115.00
KK-NF Set #9A, VG, H3............$120.00
KK-NF Set #11, VG, H3............$315.00
KK-NF Set #11A, VG, H3............$275.00
KK-NF Set #13A, VG, H3............$300.00
KK-NF Set #15A, VG, H3............$450.00
KK-NF Set #17A, VG, H3............$750.00
KK-NF Set #19A, VG, H3............$2,500.00
KK-NF Set #21, VG, H3............$4,500.00
Neue Reihe Set #102, VG, H3............$100.00
Neue Reihe Set #104, VG, H3............$150.00
Neue Reihe Set #106, VG, H3............$200.00
Neue Reihe Set #108, VG, H3............$300.00
Neue Reihe Set #110, VG, H3............$600.00
Neue Reihe Set #112, VG, H3............$1,000.00
Neue Reihe Set #114, VG, H3............$1,500.00
Neue Reihe Set #116, VG, H3............$2,000.00

California Raisins

The California Raisins made their first TV commercials in the fall of 1986. The first four PVC figures were introduced in 1987, the same year Hardee's issued similar but smaller figures, and three 5½" Bendees became available on the retail market. In 1988 twenty-one more Raisins were made for retail as well as promotional efforts in grocery stores. Four were graduates identical to the original four characters except standing on yellow pedestals and wearing blue graduation caps with yellow tassels. Hardee's increased their line by six.

In 1989 they starred in two movies: *Meet the Raisins* and *The California Raisins — Sold Out*, and eight additional characters were joined in figurine production by five of their fruit and vegetable friends from the movies. Hardee's latest release was in 1991, when they added still four more. All Raisins issued for retail sales and promotions in 1987 and 1988 (including Hardee's) are dated with the year of production (usually on the bottom of one foot). Of those released for retail sales in 1989, only the Beach Scene characters are dated, and these are actually dated 1988. Hardee's 1991 series is also undated.

Advisor: Ken Clee (C3)

Beach Theme Edition, female w/boom box, purple glasses, gr shoes, CALRAB-Applause, 1988, M $20.00
Beach Theme Edition, female w/tambourine, gr shoes & bracelet, CALRAB-Applause, 1988, M $15.00

Beach Theme Edition, hula girl, gr skirt, yel shoes, bracelet, CALRAB-Applause, 1988, M..........................$15.00

Beach Theme Edition, male in beach chair, orange sunglasses, brn base, CALRAB-Applause, 1988, M.....................$20.00

Beach Theme Edition, male w/surfboard, board not connected to foot, CALRAB-Applause, 1988, M............................$10.00

Christmas Issue, candy cane or red hat, CALRAB, 1988, M, ea..$7.50

Commercial Issue (1st), guitar player, red guitar, CALRAB, 1988, M, $8.00. (Photo courtesy Larry DeAngelo)

Commercial Issue (1st), hitchhiker winking (Winky), CALRAB, 1988, M..$5.00

Commercial Issue (1st), male singer w/microphone in left hand (not touching face), CALRAB, 1988, M $6.00

Commercial Issue (1st), Sunglasses II, aqua glasses & sneakers, eyes not visible, CALRAB, 1988, M...........................$4.00

Commercial Issue (1st), Sunglasses II, aqua glasses & sneakers, eyes visible, CALRAB, 1988, M $35.00

Commercial Issue (2nd), bass player, gray slippers, CALRAB, 1988, M...$8.00

Commercial Issue (2nd), drummer, CALRAB-Applause, 1988, M..$10.00

Commercial Issue (2nd), female singer, reddish purple shoes, bracelet, CALRAB-Applause, 1988, M $12.00

Commercial Issue (2nd), female tambourine player (Ms Delicious), yel shoes, CALRAB-Applause, 1988, M........$15.00

Commercial Issue (3rd), female singer w/microphone, yel shoes & bracelet, CALRAB-Applause, 1988, M.................$12.00

Commercial Issue (3rd), Hip Band Guitarist (Jimi Hendrix), headband, yel guitar, CALRAB-Applause, 1988, M...$30.00

Commercial Issue (3rd), saxophone player, blk beret, bl eyelids, CALRAB-Applause, 1988, M $15.00

Hardee's 1st Promotion, male in sunglasses, index finger touching face, 1987, M...$3.00

Hardee's 1st Promotion, male singer w/microphone, right hand pointing up, CALRAB, 1987, M..............................$3.00

Hardee's 1st Promotion, male w/hands up & thumbs touching forehead, CALRAB, 1987, sm, M $3.00

Hardee's 1st Promotion, saxophone player, gold sax, no hat, CALRAB, 1987, M...$3.00

Hardee's 2nd Promotion, Captain Toonz, bl boom box, yel glasses & sneakers, Applause, 1988, sm, M, from $1 to.............$3.00

Hardee's 2nd Promotion, FF Strings, bl guitar & orange sneakers, Applause, 1988, sm, M, from $1 to................................$3.00

Hardee's 2nd Promotion, Rollin's Rollo, roller skates, yel sneakers & hat mk H, Applause, 1988, sm, M, from $1 to ...$3.00

Hardee's 2nd Promotion, SB Stuntz, yel skateboard & bl sneakers, Applause, 1988, sm, M, from $1 to $3.00

Hardee's 2nd Promotion, Trumpy Trunote w/trumpet, bl sneakers, Applause, 1988, sm, M, from $1 to $3.00

Hardee's 2nd Promotion, Waves Weaver I, yel surfboard, connected to foot, Applause, 1988, sm $5.00

Hardee's 2nd Promotion, Waves Weaver II, yel surfboard, not connected to foot, Applause, 1988, sm, M..................$2.00

Hardee's 4th Promotion, Alotta Style, purple boom box, CALRAB-Applause, 1991, sm, MIP (w/collector's card)..................$15.00

Hardee's 4th Promotion, Anita Break shopping w/Hardee's bags, CALRAB-Applause, 1991, sm, MIP (w/collector's card) $15.00

Hardee's 4th Promotion, Benny w/bowling ball & bag, CALRAB-Applause, 1991, sm, MIP (w/collector's card) $15.00

Key Chains (Graduate), in sunglasses w/index finger touching face, CALRAB-Applause, 1988, M............................$85.00

Key Chains (Graduate), male singer w/microphone, right hand pointing up, CALRAB-Applause, 1988, M $85.00

Key Chains (Graduate), male w/hands up & thumbs touching forehead, CALRAB-Applause, 1988, M $85.00

Key Chains (Graduate), saxophone player, CALRAB-Applause, 1988, M $85.00

Key Chains (1st), male in sunglasses, index finger touching face, CALRAB, 1987, M..$5.00

Key Chains (1st), male singer w/microphone, right hand pointing up, CALRAB, 1987, M..$5.00

Key Chains (1st), male w/hands pointing up & thumbs touching forehead, CALRAB, 1987, M......................................$5.00

Key Chains (1st), saxophone player, gold sax, no hat, CALRAB, 1987, M $5.00

Key Chains (2nd), female singer w/microphone, yel shoes, bracelet, CALRAB-Applause, 1988, sm, M...............$45.00

Key Chains (2nd), Hip Band Guitarist (Hendrix), headband, yel guitar, CALRAB-Applause, 1988, M.........................$65.00

Key Chains (2nd), male singer w/microphone, left hand extended w/open palm, CALRAB-Applause, 1988, sm, M..........$45.00

Key Chains (2nd), saxophone player, CALRAB-Applause, 1988, sm, M $45.00

Meet the Raisins 1st Edition, Banana White, yel dress, Applause-Claymation, 1989, M $20.00

Meet the Raisins 1st Edition, piano player, bl piano, red hair, gr sneakers, Applause-Claymation, 1989, M..................$35.00

Meet the Raisins 1st Edition, Lick Broccoli, gr & blk w/red & orange guitar, Applause-Claymation, 1989, M $20.00

Meet the Raisins 1st Edition, Ruby Bagaman w/cigar, purple shirt & flipflops, Applause-Claymation, 1989, M......$20.00

Meet the Raisins 2nd Edition, AC in 'Gimme-5' pose, CALRAB-Applause, 1989, M..................................$225.00

Meet the Raisins 2nd Edition, Cecil Tyme (carrot), CALRAB-Applause, 1989, M...$250.00

Meet the Raisins 2nd Edition, Lenny Lima Bean, purple shirt, CALRAB-Applause, 1989, M..................................$175.00

Meet the Raisins 2nd Edition, Mom w/yel hair & pk apron, CALRAB-Applause, 1989, M, from $150 to..........$200.00

Post Raisin Bran Issue, Graduate, sunglasses, yel base, CALRAB-Claymation, 1988, from $45 to......................$65.00

Post Raisin Bran Issue, Graduate, yel base, CALRAB-Claymation, 1988, M, from $45 to $65.00

Post Raisin Bran Issue, Graduate saxophone player, yel base, CALRAB-Claymation, 1988, from $45 to.................$65.00

Post Raisin Bran Issue, Graduate singer, yel base, CALRAB-Claymation, 1988, from $45 to $65.00

Post Raisin Bran Issue, male in orange sunglasses with right hand pointing up and left hand pointing down, CALRAB, 1987, M, $2.00; male singer with microphone, right hand in fist, CALRAB, 1987, M, $2.00; saxophone player, inside of sax painted red, CALRAB, 1987, M, $2.00; male (Hands) with left hand pointing up and right hand pointing down, CALRAB, 1987, M, $2.00. (Photo courtesy Larry DeAngelo)

Special Edition, Michael Raisin, Applause, 1989, M........$15.00

Special Lovers Edition, Valentine Girl & Boy holding hearts, CALRAB-Applasue, 1988, M, ea............................$8.00

Unknown Promotion, male w/bl surfboard, board connected to fot, CALRAB, 1988, M...$40.00

Unknown Promotion, male w/bl surfboard in right hand, board not connected to foot, CALRAB, 1987, M $75.00

MISCELLANEOUS

Activity Book, EX, C3 ....$12.00

Auto Sun Shield, roll-away type, suction cup mounting, 16¾x51", MIP (sealed)..$15.00

Autograph book, rainbow-colored pgs, Autumn Rose/CALRAB, 1988, MIP (sealed) $12.00

Bank, figure standing w/Sun-Maid Raisins box, CALRAB, 1987, 7", MIB..$8.00

Bank, molded raisin figure, holds Raisin Bran Cereal, 1988, NM $10.00

Beach Towel, singer w/3 musicians, bl, 58x29", EX $12.00

Bed Sheet, Raisins doing their line dance, cotton, CALRAB, 1988, 64x84", EX $8.00

Belt, yel w/purple characters, Lee, EX $10.00

Book, California Raisins What's Cool, CALRAB, 1988, 5x8", M $12.00

Califronia Raisins Board Game, 1987, MIB (sealed) $8.00

Card Game, CALRAB, 1987, MIP.....................................$6.00

Cassette Tape, Christmas w/the Califronia Raisins, 1988, M ..$15.00

Chalkboard, Rose Art, 1980s, NM+.................................$20.00

Chalkboard, w/eraser, Rose Art/CALRAB, 1988, MIP $20.00

Collector's Club New Member's Kit w/Watch Set, 1988, M, C3...$40.00

Colorforms Play Set, 1980s, complete, EXIB $15.00

Computer Game, Box Office, MIB (sealed)......................$20.00

Costume, w/wht gloves, CALRAB, 1987, 33", EX $10.00

Crayon-By-Number Set, Rose Art, 1980s, EXIB..............$20.00

Figures, plush, Hardee's promotion, from a set of four, each from $3.00 to $4.00.

Fingertronic Puppet, male or female, Bendy Toys/CALRAB, 1988, MIB $25.00

Gift Wrap, bl or purple background, MIP, C3, ea..............$12.00

Inflatable Figure, vinyl, Imperial Toys, 1987, 42", MIB $50.00

Key Chains, various plastic figures, NM, C3, ea................$6.00

Lunch Box, yel plastic w/bl scene, w/vacuum bottle, Thermos, 9x4x8", EX $15.00

Mad Magazine, Calif Raisin on front cover, Sept, 1988, EX...$12.00

Magnets, singers, sax player, orange sunglasses & bl shoes, Applause, 1988, M, ea $45.00

Mug, mc scenes, Applause, 1987, M..................................$8.00

Photo Album, 3-ring binder, 24 pgs, CALRAB, 1988, M...$20.00

Pillow, plush Raisin figure w/12" arms & legs, EX............$10.00

Pinback Buttons, many different, sm, ea, C3.....................$6.00

Poster, Calif Raisins Tour, cities on bottom w/Sold Out, 34x22", NM...$12.00

Puffy Stick-Ons, 1987, MIP..$8.00

Radio, AM only, figure w/poseable arms & legs, MIB.....$200.00

Record, I Heard It Through the Grapevine, 45 rpm, 1987, EX (w/sleeve) $10.00

Record, Rudolph the Red-Nosed Reindeer, 45 rpm, Atlantic, NM (w/sleeve) $10.00

Record, Signed Sealed Delivered/Same, 45 rpm, Atlantic, 1988, EX+ (sleeve) $15.00

Record, When a Man Loves a Woman/Sweet, Delicious & Marvelous, Buddy Miles lead vocals, NM+ (w/sleeve).....$20.00

Sandwich Stage, slice-of-bread shaped stage w/3 figures, Del Monte mail-in, EX $25.00

Sleeping Bag, w/vinyl case, M, C3....................................$45.00

Sunglasses, child's, MOC $5.00

Suspenders, yel w/purple figures & red I Heard It Through the Grapevine, EX $20.00

Valentine Cards, set of 38, Cleo/CALRAB, 1988, MIB $4.00

Video, Meet the Calif Raisins, Atlantic, 1988, NRFB........**$8.00**
Wall Clock, female Raisins w/tambourines, b/o, 8½" dia, M.**$35.00**
Watch figural, Applause, 1988, MIP.................................**$5.00**
Welcome Mat, band members w/sun on bl, 18x30", EX ...**$55.00**
Windsock, character on bl, Windsicals, 44x27", MIP.......**$15.00**

Candy Containers

As early as 1876, candy manufacturers used figural glass containers to package their candy. They found the idea so successful that they continued to use them until the 1960s. The major producers of these glass containers were Westmoreland, West Bros., Victory Glass, J.H. Millstein, J.C. Crosetti, L.E. Smith, and Jack and T.H. Stough. Some of the most collectible and sought after today are the character-related figures such as Amos 'N Andy, Barney Google, Santa Claus, and Jackie Coogan, to name a few.

There are many reproductions; know your dealer. For a listing of these reproductions, refer to *Schroeder's Antiques Price Guide*.

The following listings were found at auction, including some hand-painted composition character candy containers. We have included the estimates to give a better idea of price trends.

For other types of candy containers, see Halloween; Pez Dispensers.

GLASS

Airplane (Passenger), emb w/3 windows, tin prop, 5" L, G, A
    (Est: $150-$300) **$115.00**

Amos 'N Andy in Car, Victory, 1920s, 4¼" long, VG, A (Est: $200.00 – $400.00), $360.00. (Photo courtesy James D. Julia Inc.)

Barney Google on Pedestal, 1920s, 3¾", VG+, A (Est: $150-
    $200)..**$140.00**
Barney Google Standing by Barrel, 1920s, tin lid on barrel, 3x4",
    VG, A (Est: $600-$900) **$1,320.00**
Baseball Player Standing by Barrel, 1920s, mk P on shirt & hat,
    3x4", VG, A (Est: $500-$600) **$860.00**
Baseball Player Standing on Sqaure Base, ca 1916, 5", VG+, A
    (Est: $400-$600)...**$800.00**
Bear on Circus Tub Holding Fan, TG Stough, ca 1916, blow through
    tube to turn fan, 4¼", VG, A (Est: $250-$500) **$175.00**
Black & White Taxi, Westmoreland Specialty Co, blk & wht
    checked tin top, tin spoke wheels, 4" L, VG, A (Est: $400-
    $600)...**$690.00**
Black Cat for Luck, 4¼", VG, A (Est: $800-$1,200) ..**$1,265.00**

Camera on Tripod, 1910s, G, A (Est: $150-$250).........**$115.00**
Cannon, pnt glass w/tin 2-wheeled carriage, pewter screw-on
    cap, 4¾" L, VG, A (Est: $200-$400) **$460.00**
Colorado Boat, mk Serial No 56661, wooden deck & stacks,
    6½" L, G, A (Est: $100-$200)..................................**$100.00**
Felix Standing Next to Barrel, Pat Sullivan, 1920s, 3½", VG+,
    A (Est: $200-$400)..**$430.00**

Flossie Fisher's Funnies Bed, gold and black lithographed tin with a glass panel, 3¾" long, G, A (Est: $1,000.00 – $1,500.00), $690.00; Flossie Fisher's Funnies China Closet, gold and black lithographed tin with a front glass panel, 4", G, A (Est: $600.00 – $800.00), $400.00. (Photos courtesy James D. Julia Inc.)

Flossie Fisher's Funnies Chair, Borgfeldt/c Helene NYCE, gold &
    blk litho tin & glass, 3", G, A (Est: $200-$400) **$230.00**
Happy Fat Standing on Drum, Borgfeldt, ca 1915, 4¾", G, A
    (Est: $75-$150) **$90.00**
Hearse, 1920s, glass balloon spoke wheels, 4" L, VG, A (Est:
    $350-$450) **$345.00**
Irish Hat (It's a Long Way to Tipperary), 1920s, 3", VG, A (Est:
    $1,000-$1,200) **$630.00**
Jackie Coogan Standing on Round Base, 1920s, 5", VG, A (Est:
    $400-$600) **$300.00**
Lamp (Christmas), West Bros, sq glass base pnt brick red
    w/Santa in oval, 4-sided tin shade, G, A (Est: $200-
    $400)..**$175.00**
Lamp (Library), clear glass dome shade w/'fringe' on fluted metal
    base, 4" , VG, A (Est: $250-$400) **$230.00**
Laundry Delivery Truck, mk West Spec Co, tin top mk Laundry,
    tin spoke wheels, 4½" L, G, A (Est: $400-$700) **$420.00**
Liberty Motor Biplane, West Glass Co, ca 1920, glass fuselage
    w/tin wings, 6" W, VG, A (Est: $1,500-$2,500) ...**$1,035.00**
Los Angeles Dirigible, mk VG Co Jenet PA USA, 1920s, silver
    pnt, 6" L, VG, A (Est: $150-$200)..........................**$460.00**
Motorcycle w/Rider & Sidecar, Victory, mk ¼ Oz Avor VG Co
    Jenet PA, VG, A (Est: $200-$400) **$460.00**
Rabbit Family, mk VG Co Jeannette PA Avor Oz, 1920s,
    mama, papa & baby rabbit on base, 5x4", VG, A (Est:
    $600-$800)...**$485.00**
Rabbits (Mama & Daughter) Standing Upright in Dress, mk
    w/VG logo/USA Avor, 5¼", G, A (Est: $450-$650) ..**$175.00**
Santa Claus Standing, legs go down into rnd container, red robe,
    metal screw-lid bottom, 5", VG, A (Est: $100-$150) ..**$330.00**

Santa Claus Standing by Chimney, LE Smith, 1920s, 4", VG, A (Est: $200-$300) $200.00

Santa Claus Stepping Into Chimney, USA, metal screw-lid bottom, 5", EX, (Est: $100-$125) $70.00

Santa Standing, USA, hands clasped together, pnt features, metal screw-lid bottom, 4½", VG, A (Est: $75-$100) $110.00

Sedan, West Bro's #2862, early limo style w/flat top, glass spoke wheels, 2½x4" L, VG, A (Est: $600-$800)..............$715.00

Spark Plug, USA, 1920s, orange pnt blanket, 3x4", G, A (Est: $75-$150) $115.00

Spirit of St Louis Airplane, Westmoreland, 1920s, glass fuselage w/name on tin wing, 6" W, VG, A (Est: $400-$600)..$690.00

Steamship, milk glass, emb detail, 4x6¼" L, G, A (Est: $50-$75) $30.00

Stop & Go Sign, 1920s, tin sign screws onto bulbous glass bottom, 4¼", G, A (Est: $200-$300) $400.00

Toonerville Trolley, mk 1922 by Fontaine Fox/7 Depot Line, VG, A (Est: $300-$500)..................................$375.00

Uncle Sam Standing by Barrel, ca 1918, 4x3¾", VG, A (Est: $450-$600) $660.00

US Express Wagon, ca 1913, glass wagon body on tin base w/tin spoke wheels, wire hdl, 6½" L, VG, A (Est: $300-$500) $150.00

Yellow Taxi, Westmoreland Specialty Company, 4" long, G, A (Est: $400.00 – $600.00), $800.00. (Photo courtesy James D. Julia Inc.)

HAND-PAINTED COMPOSITION

Alphonse Emerging From Eggshell w/Feet Showing, Germany, 5⅛", A (Est: $300-$400) $165.00

Bobby Blake Holding Rabbit in Arm, Germany, red outfit w/lg yel hat, 6", EX, A (Est: $300-$400) $100.00

Brownie (Palmer Cox) Emerging From Egg w/Tall Skinny Legs, Germany, pointed ears, 8½", VG, A (Est: $500-$600) $220.00

Brownie (Palmer Cox) w/Tall Skinny Legs, Germany, rnd ears, yel & blk striped legs, 9½", EX+, A (Est: $700-$900) $1,430.00

Brownie Standing in Eggshell Suit, Germany, wht suit & top hat w/red band, rnd base, 5¼", EX, A (Est: $700-$900) ..$135.00

Brownie Standing w/Hands on Round Tummy, Germany, gr sailor suit, pointed hat, rnd base, 6¼", VG, A (Est: $200-$300)..$135.00

Buster Brown Seated on Tige, Germany, 6¼", EX, A (Est: $600-$800) $1,430.00

Buster Brown Standing, Germany, lg rnd eyes, red pants, bl top hat, 4½", EX, A (Est: $200-$300) $165.00

Campbell Kid, Germany, bl hat, red coat & yel pants, rnd base, 4½", EX, A (Est: $200-$300) $110.00

Campbell Kids, Germany, wht w/bl plaid, blk shoes, wht w/pk stripes, red shoes, 4¼" EX, A (Est: $300-$400), pr..$190.00

Dolly Dimple Holding Chick, Germany, wht w/gr detail on hat & dress, blk shoes, rnd base, 6", EX, A (Est: $300-$400)..$100.00

Foxy Grandpa Seated on Egg, Germany, 5", VG, A (Est: $200-$300)..$135.00

Foxy Grandpa Seated Sideways on Chicken, Germany, 6½", EX, A (Est: $600-$800)..$245.00

Happy Hooligan Seated Sideways on Chick, Germany, 5¼", EX, A (Est: $300-$400)..$135.00

Katzenjammer Kid (Fritz) Emerging From Eggshell w/Feet Showing, Germany, 5", EX, A (Est: $200-$300)..............$110.00

Katzenjammer Kid (Hanz) Riding Rooster, Germany, 6¾", EX, A (Est: $800-$1,000)..$300.00

Mama Katzenjammer Holding 'Nodding' Hanz and Fritz, Germany, 6", EX, A (Est: $1,000.00 – $1,200.00), $1,320.00. (Photo courtesy Bertoia Auctions)

Mamma Katzenjammer Standing Holding Switch, Germany, wearing eye glasses, 6¼", EX, A (Est: $400-$500)...$410.00

Mamma w/Son & Daughter Emerging From Eggshells, Germany, w/scarves wrapped around necks, 5x5", EX, A (Est: $500-$600)..$330.00

Papa Katzenjammer Standing w/Hands on Round Tummy, Germany, rnd base, 4½", EX, A (Est: $300-$400) $100.00

Snookums Playing w/Roller Devil's Toy, Germany, on rectangular wood base, no sz given, EX, A (Est: $400-$600)........$245.00

Yellow Kid Emerging From Eggshell, Germany, 2¾", EX, A (Est: $200-$300) $300.00

Cast Iron

Realistically modeled and carefully detailed cast-iron toys enjoyed their heyday from about the turn of the century (some companies began production a little earlier) until about the 1940s when they were gradually edged out by lighter-weight toys that were less costly to produce and to ship. (Some of the cast irons were more than 20" in length and very heavy.) Many were vehicles faithfully patterned after actual models seen on city streets at the time. Horse-drawn carriages were phased out when motorized vehicles came into use.

Some of the larger manufacturers were Arcade (Illinois), who by the 1920s was recognized as a leader in the industry; Dent (Pennsylvania); Hubley (Pennsylvania); and Kenton (Ohio). In the 1940s Kenton came out with a few horse-drawn toys which are collectible in their own right but naturally much less valuable than the older ones. In addition to those already noted, there were many minor makers; you will see them mentioned in the listings. For more detailed information on these companies, we recommend *Collecting Toys* by Richard O'Brien (Books Americana)

The following listings have been compiled from major toy auctions. The estimates have been added at the end of each listing for comparison. You will see that some toys have sold for way over or way under the estimate, and some have sold within range. This is a new feature that we are sure will facilitate the use of this guide.

See also Banks; Dollhouse Furniture; Guns; Pull and Push Toys.

AIRPLANES

America, Hubley, 17" wingspan, two pilots, rare, EX, A (Est: $3,000.00 – $4,000.00), $3,570.00. (Photo courtesy Bertoia Auctions)

Big Bang Carbide, 13", EX, A (Est: $300-$400) **$550.00**

Bremen, Hubley, 7" W, VG, A (Est: $200-$300) **$385.00**

DO-X Top Wing Seaplane, Hubley, 3½", VG, A (Est: $400-$500)..**$550.00**

DO-X Top-Wing Seaplane, Hubley, 7½" W, WRT, VG, A (Est: $2,500-$3,500) **$4,125.00**

Fokker Monocoupe, Vindex, 8" W, EX, A (Est: $5,000-$6,000) **$5,775.00**

Ford Cabin Aeroplane, Dent, 12½" W, 3 NP motors, overpnt, A (Est: $2,500-$3,500)................................**$1,980.00**

Lindy, Hubley, 6" W, EX+, A (Est: $400-$600) **$600.00**

Lindy, Hubley, 10" W, 2 figures, some overpnt, A (Est: $2,000-$2,500)...**$1,870.00**

Sea Gull, Kilgore, 8" W, G+, A (Est: $400-$600)...........**$700.00**

Sea Gull, Kilgore, 8" W, VG+, A (Est: $600-$800)........**$935.00**

Spirit of St Louis, AC Williams, 4" W, EX, A (Est: $300-$400)...**$330.00**

Travel Air Mystery, Kilgore, 7" W, G, A (Est: $300-$400) **$330.00**

UX 166, AC Williams, 6½" W, NP prop, NPSW, G, A (Est: $100-$150) **$175.00**

BELL TOYS

Alligator & Boy (Darky & the Alligator) on 4-Wheeled Flat-Sided Log Base, Gong Bell, 7½", EX, A (Est: $3,500-$4,500) **$6,035.00**

Alligator & Boy (Gator Baiter) on 4-wheeled grassy platform, att: NN Hill, 9", EX, A (Est: $2,200-$2,600) **$5,175.00**

Alligator w/Bell on Back, 7", EX, A (Est: $300-$500)....**$275.00**

Are You a Buffalo?, Gong Bell, 6", NM, A (Est: $3,000-$4,000)..**$12,650.00**

Baby Quieter, J&E Stevens, 7½", NM, A (Est: $2,500-$3,500) **$4,600.00**

Bear in Sweater Standing on 4-Wheeled Open Platform, Gong Bell, 8", EX, A (Est: $1,750-$2,750).....................**$8,900.00**

Black Boys (2) Sawing Watermelons on 4-Wheeled Grassy Platform, NN Hill, 8½", EX+, A (Est: $3,000-$3,500)...**$9,485.00**

Boy and Racoon In and Out of Log on Four-Wheeled Base, Gong Bell, 9", heart-shaped spokes, EX, A (Est: $2,500.00 – $3,500.00), $11,500.00. (Photo courtesy James D. Julia, Inc.)

Boy Fishing on 4-Wheeled Base, NN Hill, 6", G, A (Est: $1,400-$1,600) **$1,495.00**

Boy Pulling Cat's Tail on 4-Wheeled Grassy Platform, NN Hill, 6", head facing straight, EX, A (Est: $2,500-$3,000) **$5,175.00**

Boy Pulling Cat's Tail on 4-Wheeled Grassy Platform, NN Hill, 6", head turned, G, A (Est: $1,500-$2,000) **$3,565.00**

Boy Scout, Gong Bell, 7", boy w/pouch holding rod w/bell on 4-wheeled open platform, VG, A (Est: $3,000-$4,000) ..**$4,885.00**

Captain & the Kids, Gong Bell, 8", G+, A (Est: $7,000-$9,000) **$13,225.00**

Cossack & the Jap on Ornate 4-Wheeled Platform, Gong Bell, 7", EX+, A (Est: $12,000-$14,000) **$25,300.00**

Couple on Seats Rock Back & Forth to Ring Bell, Gong Bell, MSW (2 lg & 1 sm), 7", G, A (Est: $1,000-$1,200).............**$2,750.00**

Couple on Seesaw on 3-Wheeled Platform, Gong Bell, 7", G+, A (Est: $1,400-$1,800) **$1,550.00**

Daisy on 4-Wheeled Horse Sleigh, Gong Bell, 8½", VG, A (Est: $1,000-$1,200)...**$1,950.00**

Darky & the Alligator, see Boy and Alligator

Ding Dong Bell Pussy's Not in the Well, Gong Bell, 9", 2 figures & well, EX, A (Est: $2,000-$2,500).....................**$6,325.00**

Drummer Boy, J&E Stevens, 10", VG, A (Est: $6,000-$8,000) **$10,350.00**

Duck w/Bell in Mouth on 4-Wheeled Open Platform, Gong Bell, 5", EX, A (Est: $1,000-$1,200) $2,530.00

Ducks & Jester on Two Bell Wheels, 4" L, G, A (Est: $50-$100) $200.00

Eagle w/Bell in Mouth on Open frame, Gong Bell, 5½", patriotic colors, EX+, A (Est: $1,000-$1,200) $2,585.00

Elephant w/Tusks & Trunk Out on 4-Wheeled Grassy Platform, NN Hill, 7", no bell o/w EX, A (Est: $800-$1,000) .. $1,150.00

Fish on 2 Wheels, Gong Bell, 5½", VG, A (Est: $800-$1,000) $920.00

Galloping Horses (2) w/Riders on 4 Wheels, Wilkins, 6½", bell between flat-sided figures, EX, A (Est: $2,500-$2,500) .. $4,885.00

Gator Baiter, see Alligator & Boy

Girl & Doll Under Blanket w/Horse Head on Wheeled Frame, Gong Bell, 9", 2 lg heart wheels & 2 sm, G+, A (Est: $500-$800) $275.00

Goose With Bell in Mouth and Rider on Four-Wheeled Base, Gong Bell, 7", EX, A (Est: $2,500.00 – $3,500.00), $4,300.00. (Photo courtesy James D. Julia, Inc.)

Horse & Rider on 4-Wheeled A-Frame Platform, Wilkins, 6½", VG, A (Est: $800-$1,000) $575.00

Horse Pulling Heart-Shaped Spoke Wheels w/Center Bell, Gong Bell, 1890s, 8", tin horse, VG, A (Est: $300-$400) .. $330.00

Hunter Shooting at Rabbit Coming Out of Hole on 4-Wheeled Platform, NN Hill, 6", VG, A (Est: $2,000-$2,500) .. $2,875.00

Independence 1776-1876 (Eagle Atop Bell on 4-Wheeled Open Platform), Gong Bell, 9½", EX, A (Est: $1,200-1,500) $2,645.00

Jigger w/Bells on Feet Flanked by 2 Bells on 4-Wheeled Bar, 7", Fair, A (Est: $200-$300) $300.00

Jonah Pops In & Out of Whale's Mouth on 4-Wheeled Base, NN Hill, 6", EX, A (Est: $800-$1,200) $2,700.00

Jonah Standing on Whale's Head While Dangling Bell in Front of Whale's Mouth, Gong Bell, 5½", G, A (Est: $800-$1,000) $1,600.00

Kids (4) on 4-Wheeled Double Ripper Sled, NN Hill, 8½", some old rstr, A (Est: $6,000-$8,000) $5,175.00

Mary & Her Little Lamb on 4-Wheeled Open Platform, Gong Bell, 8", G, A (Est: $1,800-$2,200) $2,300.00

Miss Liberty in 4-Wheeled Shell Leaf Chariot, Kyser & Rex, 8", VG, A (Est: $5,000-$7,000) $14,375.00

Monkey in 4-Wheeled Chariot w/'Mushroom'-Type Bell, Kyser & Rex, 6", EX, A (Est: $2,000-$2,500) $2,000.00

Monkey Sulky on 3-Wheeled Platform, Gong Bell, 7", EX, A (Est: $1,000-$1,200) $1,200.00

Monkey w/Coconut on 4-Wheeled Log, 6½", VG, A (Est: $800-$1,200) $525.00

Mule Kicking Bell on 2-Wheeled Platform, 8", G, A (Est: $300-$500) $600.00

Mule Kicking Bell on 4-Wheeled Platform, Gong Bell, 8", VG, A (Est: $800-$1,000) $2,415.00

Paul Revere on Horse Pulling 2-Wheeled Double Bells, 9" L, EX, A (Est: $100-$200) $85.00

Pig Cart w/Clown Driver, Gong Bell, 6", EX, A (Est: $700-$900) $460.00

Pig w/Clown Rider, Gong Bell, 5½", bell attached to nose, front legs rest on 2 lg wheels, EX, A (Est: $600-$800) .. $1,150.00

Rastus & His Mother on 4-Wheeled Open Platform, 7", chain w/bell connects figures, VG, A (Est: $2,400-$2,800) $3,450.00

Saratoga Chimes, J&E Stevens, 11", VG, (Est: $2,500-$3,000) $3,565.00

Surf Boat, Ives, 8", 2 tin figures in boat w/A-frame holding bell in center, VG rstr, A (Est: $4,000-$6,000) $6,900.00

Swing on Sleigh w/4 Wheels, att: Ives, 9½", EX+, A (Est: $7,000-$9,000) $8,625.00

Tramp Bell Ringer on 4-Wheeled Open Frame, Gong Bell, 6", EX+, A (Est: $1,000-$1,500) $1,600.00

Trick Pony on Four-Wheeled Base, Gong Bell, 8", EX+, A (Est: $1,500.00 – $2,000.00), $3,565.00. (Photo courtesy James D. Julia, Inc.)

Turtle (4-Wheeled) w/Clown Atop Bell On Back, Gong Bell, 6½", EX, A (Est: $700-$1,000) $690.00

Turtle w/Frog on Back, unknown mfg, 7", bell on frog's nose, EX, A, (Est: $300-$500) $500.00

Uncle Sam & the Don on 4-Wheeled Platform, Gong Bell, 7", EX, A (Est: $3,000-$4,000) $4,310.00

Waddler, see Duck w/Bell in Mouth

Washer Woman at Tub on 4-Wheeled Platform, Ives, 7½", heart-shaped spoke wheels, EX, A (Est: $6,000-$8,000) $4,600.00

Wild Mule Jack, Gong Bell, 8", G+, A (Est: $500-$700) $345.00

BOATS

Adirondack Side-Wheeler, Dent, 15", NM, A (Est: $2,000-$2,500) $5,175.00

Battleship Maine, 8½", VG, A (Est: $2,000-$2,500) ..$3,850.00

Battleship New York 20, Dent, 20", VG, A (Est: $800-$1,200) $1,200.00

City of Chicago Side-Wheeler, Wilkens, 16", dbl side wheels, NM, A (Est: $800-$1,200).................................$1,100.00

City of New York Side-Wheeler, Wilkins, 15", EX+, A (Est: $1,500-$2,000)..................................$5,865.00

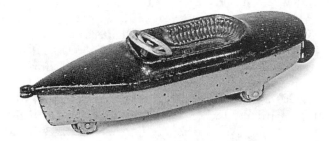

Motorboat, Freidag, 1920s, 10", EX+, A (Est: $1,200.00 – $1,500.00), $5,500.00. (Photo courtesy James D. Julia, Inc)

New Orleans Side-Wheeler, Wilkins/Harris, 10½", EX, A (Est: $1,000-$1,200) $975.00

Priscilla Side-Wheeler, Dent, 10½", EX, A (Est: $700-$900) $800.00

Racing Skull w/Pace Man & 4 Rowers, US Hardware, 9½", VG, A, (Est: $2,000-$2,500) $4,600.00

Racing Skull w/Pace Man & 8 Rowers, Union, 14½", EX, A (Est: $2,500-$3,500).................................$8,280.00

Showboat, Arcade, 11", VG, A (Est: $800-$1,000) $1,725.00

Speedboat, Hubley, 5½", cast driver w/hand on motor, VG, A (Est: $150-$200) $250.00

CHARACTER

Alphonse & Gaston Car, Kenton, 7½", Gloomy Gus driving, EX, A (Est: $8,000-$10,000) $13,800.00

Alphonse 'Rubber Neck' Nodder in Mule-Drawn Two-Wheeled Cart, Kenton, 6½", MSW, EX, A (Est: $250-$350) ..$525.00

Amos 'N' Andy Fresh Air Taxicab Co Touring Car, Dent, 6", MSW, w/2 figures & dog, VG, A (Est: $400-$500)...................................$1,760.00

Andy Gump #348 Car, Arcade, 7", MDW, w/figure, EX, A (Est: $3,000-$4,000) $3,450.00

Andy Gump #348 Car, Arcade, 7", MDW, w/figure, G, A (Est: $1,200-$1,500) $1,320.00

Andy Gump Driver Figure, Arcade, 4½", G+, A (Est: $200-$300)..$440.00

Brownie Riding Galloping Horse, Hubley, 5", w/cast 4-wheeled base, EX, A (Est: $1,200-$1,400)..........................$2,415.00

Comical Cop Standing in Mule Cart, Jones & Bixler, 8", mule is kicking, 2 MSW, EX+, A (Est: $800-$1,200).......$2,070.00

Happy Hooligan Derby Car, NN Hill, 6", MSW, EX, A (Est: $2,500-$3,000)................................$5,750.00

Happy Hooligan Nodder in Mule-Drawn Two-Wheeled Cart, Hubley, 6½", MSW, VG, A (Est: $250-$350) $550.00

Mama Katzenjammer Spanking Child in Donkey Cart, Kenton, 11½", w/Captain & Fritz, EX, (Est: $1,800-$2,200) ..$1,950.00

Mama Katzenjammer Standing in 2-Wheeled Mule Cart, Harris, 8", G, A (Est: $400-$500) $400.00

Nodders Wagon (Foxy Foxy Grandpa and Happy Hooligan), Hubley, 14", G+, A (Est: $10,000.00 – $12,000.00), $8,625.00. (Photo courtesy James D. Julia, Inc.)

Popeye Patrol Motorcycle, Hubley, 8½", EX, A (Est: $2,250-$2,750) $5,225.00

Popeye Patrol Motorcycle, Hubley, 8½", G, A (Est: $1,500-$2,000) $1,980.00

Popeye Spinach Delivery Cycle, Hubley, 6", VG, A (Est: $400-$600) $715.00

Punch (Punch & Judy) in Goat Cart, unknown mfg, 7", VG, A (Est: $800-$1,000) $575.00

Rubber Neck (Foxy Grandpa Riding on 2-Wheeled Mule Cart), Kenton, 6½", EX+, A (Est: $250-$350) $630.00

Toonerville Trolley, Dent, 4½", w/figure, EXIB, A (Est: $1,000-$1,200)..$975.00

Uncle Sam in Eagle Chariot, Kenton, 12", 2 horses, VG, A (Est: $2,500-$3,500)................................$2,875.00

Yellow Kid Standing in 2-Wheeled Goat Cart, Kenton, 7½", VG, A (Est: $250-$350)................................$385.00

CIRCUS ANIMALS AND ACCESSORIES

Bandwagon, Hubley, 22", 4 horses & 6 musicians, no driver, VG+, A (Est: $2,000-$2,500) $3,450.00

Bandwagon, Ives, 31", wagon emb w/horses, eagles & lions, 4 horses, driver & 8 musicians, EX+, A (Est: $7,500-$8,500) $23,000.00

Calliope Wagon, Hubley, 9", 2 horses, w/driver, NM, A (Est: $700-$800) $1,495.00

Calliope Wagon, Hubley, 12", 2 horses, w/driver, EX+, A (Est: $1,500-$2,000) $3,680.00

Calliope Wagon, Hubley, 16", 2 horses, w/driver, EX, A ($1,200-$1,400) $4,400.00

Eagle Wagon, Hubley, eagle emb on sides, gold trim, 2 horses, w/driver, VG+, A (Est: $250-$350) $400.00

Lion Wagon, Hubley, 12", enclosed wagon w/lion emb on sides, gold trim, 2 horses, driver, NM, A (Est: $1,200-$1,500) $1,955.00

Monkey on Trapeze Sits Atop Wagon w/Mirrored Sides, Hubley, 12½", 2 horses, w/driver, VG+, A (Est: $1,200-$1,500) $3,220.00

Overland Circus Band Wagon, Kenton, 16", 2 horses, 6 band members & driver, VG, A (Est: $200-$350)............$520.00

Overland Circus Cage Truck, Kenton, 9", w/lion, PMDW, w/driver, EX, A (Est: $1,750-$2,250) $825.00

Overland Circus Cage Wagon, Kenton, 14", w/bear, 2 horses & driver, EX, A (Est: $300-$400)............................$385.00

Overland Circus Calliope Truck, Kenton, 7", NM, A (Est: $1,200-$1,500) $1,840.00

Royal Circus Band Wagon, Hubley, 23", 4 horses, driver & 6 band members, EX, A (Est: $1,500-$2,000) $1,045.00

Royal Circus Cage Wagon, Hubley, 9½", simple box style w/bear, 2 horses, no driver, Fair+, A (Est: $150-$300) $100.00

Royal Circus Cage Wagon, Hubley, 9½", w/bear, 2 horses & driver, EX+, A (Est: $500-$700) $630.00

Royal Circus Cage Wagon, Hubley, 12", NM, A (Est: $800.00 – $1,000.00), $2,415.00. (Photo courtesy James D. Julia, Inc.)

Royal Circus Cage Wagon, Hubley, 12", w/tiger, 2 horses & driver, VG+, A (Est: $400-$600) $1,495.00

Royal Circus Lion Wagon, Hubley, 9", lion emb on sides, gold trim, 2 horses, w/driver, NM, A (Est: $800-$1,000)............$1,380.00

CONSTRUCTION

Austin Roller-A-Plane, Arcade, 7½", no driver, Fair+, A (Est: $150-$250) $410.00

Avery Tractor, Arcade, 1920s, 4½", roadwork vehicle w/roof over driver's seat, 4 MSW, VG, A (Est: $400-$500) $135.00

Bates 40 Steel Mule Tractor, Vindex, 1929, no sz given, cast treads, NP driver, G, A (Est: $8,000-$10,000) ...$11,000.00

Buckeye Ditcher, Kenton, 12" L, chain treads, EX+, A (Est: $1,200-$1,500) $1,650.00

Caterpillar Tractor, Arcade, 6½", enclosed nose w/emb side vents, chain-link treads, NP driver, G, A (Est: $250-$350)..$650.00

Caterpillar Tractor, Arcade, 8", enclosed nose w/emb side vents, chain-link treads, NP driver, VG, A (Est: $550-$850) $1,650.00

Caterpillar Tractor, Arcade, 8", enclosed nose w/emb side vents, steel treads, NP driver, EX, A (Est: $2,000-$2,500)..$1,760.00

Caterpillar Tractor, Arcade, 8", open-sided nose w/exposed engine, steel treads, NP driver, G, A (Est: $550-$750) $1,200.00

Caterpillar Tractor, Arcade, 8", open-sided nose w/exposed engine, steel treads, NMIB (No 270 Y), A (Est: $1,800-$2,200) $2,760.00

Contractor's Dump Truck, Kenton, 10", w/3 dump buckets, MDW, w/driver, VG, A ($800-$1,000)....................$880.00

Contractors Dump Truck, Kenton, 10", EX+, A (Est: $2,000.00 – $2,500.00), $2,090.00. (Photo courtesy Bertoia Auctions)

Contractor's Dump Wagon (Motorized), Kenton, 9", w/3 dump buckets, PMSW, EX+, A (Est: $800-$1,000)...........$550.00

Contractors Wagon w/3 Dump Buckets, Kenton, 8", NPDW, EX, A (Est: $400-$500)..$990.00

Fordson Industrial Tractor, Arcade, BRT w/Whitehead & Kales emb on disk wheels, w/driver, EX+, A (Est: $500-$700) $715.00

Fordson Tractor w/Front-end Loader, Hubley, 9", MSW, NP driver, VG, A (Est: $1,500-$2,000).........................$1,980.00

Gallion Master Road Roller, Kenton, 7", cast driver, NM, A (Est: $700-$900) $515.00

General Steam Shovel (Mack) Truck, Hubley, 8½", WRT, G, A (Est: $200-$300)..$260.00

General Steam Shovel (Mack) Truck, Hubley, 10", WRT, VG, A (Est: $400-$500) $500.00

Huber Road Roller, Hubley, 8", army gr w/NP rollers & driver, EX, A (Est: $500-$700) $800.00

Huber Road Roller, Hubley, 8", army gr w/NP rollers & driver, G, A (Est: $300-$500)..$400.00

Huber Road Roller, Hubley, 8", orange w/NP rollers, no driver, VG+, A (Est: $150-$200) $300.00

Ingersoll-Rand Air-Compressor Truck, Hubley, 1933, 8", Mack cab w/cast driver, MSW, VG+, A (Est: $6,000-$7,000)..$9,350.00

International Diesel TracTracTor, Arcade, 1940s, 7½", blk rubber treads, NP driver, EX, A (Est: $2,500-$3,000).......$3,300.00

Jaeger Cement Mixer Truck, Kenton, 7", NP drum, WRT, G, A (Est $200-$300) $400.00

Lansing Cement Cart, Vindex, 6½", rnd-bottom bucket w/metal spoke wheels, gr & red, EX, A (Est: $2,000-$2,500) $1,980.00

Machine Hauler, AC Williams, 28½", truck pulling 3 trailers w/construction vehicles, EX, A (Est: $3,000-$4,000)...........$4,950.00

Mack Hoist Truck, Arcade, 1932, 7", NP winch, WRT, cast driver, VG, A (Est: $1,200-$1,500)......................$1,540.00

Monarch Bulldozer, Hubley, 1932, 5½", articulated action when pulled, cast driver, G, A (Est: $600-$800) $355.00

Morgan Crane, Kenton, 9x16x12", EX, A (Est: $2,500-$3,500) $2,200.00

Oh Boy Tractor, Kilgore, 1930s, 6", rubber wheel treads, cast driver, EX, A (Est: $1,200-$1,500)......................$3,025.00

P&H Steam Shovel, Vindex, 12" long, EX+, A (Est: $5,000.00 – $7,000.00), $8,250.00. (Photo courtesy Bertoia Auctions)

Panama Steam Shovel (Mack) Truck, Hubley, 12", WRT, 10-wheeled, cast driver & 2 operators, NM, A (Est: $2,000-$2,500) $2,585.00

Panama Steam Shovel (Mack) Truck, Hubley, 12", MSW, 10-wheeled, cast driver & 2 operators, VG, (Est: $1,200-$1,500) $1,980.00

Panama Steam Shovel (Mack) Truck, Hubley, 14", WRT, 6-wheeled, cast driver & 2 operators, rstr, A (Est: $300-$400) $1,045.00

Road Grader, Dent, 5", 4 MSWs, driver holding 2 spoke wheel contols, G, A (Est: $150-$225) $65.00

Road Roller & Trailer, Wallworks Foundry/England, 14½" overall, EX, A (Est: $1,200-$1,500)......................$465.00

Road Sweeper, Dent, 8", w/stand-up driver, EX, A (Est: $4,000-$5,000) $6,875.00

Sand Loading Shovel, Arcade, 8½" L, side lever lifts shovel, cast driver, VG, A (Est: $1,000-$1,200) $1,320.00

Steam Roller, Dent, 5", upright boiler & wooden rollers, EX, A (Est: $300-$400) $465.00

Steam Shovel, Arcade, 10x9", w/chain treads on spoke wheels, red w/gr, EX+, A (Est: $6,000-$7,000) $9,350.00

Steam Shovel, 3", NP shovel & axles, wht rubber treads, VG+, A (Est: $75-$150)......................................$115.00

Street Sweeper, Dent, 7½", wire brush on front, front sprocket wheels, standing driver, EX, A (Est: $2,500-$3,000) ..$3,300.00

Trac Tractor (1937 Diesel), Arcade, 7½", NP treads & driver, VG, A (Est: $1,500-$1,800) $1,100.00

Trac Tractor, see also International Diesel Trac Tractor

FARM TOYS

See also Horse-Drawn.

Allis-Chalmers Tractor, Arcade, 6", blk rubber front wheels & wooden rear wheels, cast driver, VG, A (Est: $250-$350)..............$165.00

Allis-Chalmers Tractor, Arcade, 6", BRT w/silver-pnt hubs, cast driver, EX, A (Est: $300-$400)......................$300.00

Allis-Chalmers Tractor, Arcade, 6", salesman's sample, blk-pnt wooden wheels, cast driver, NM, A (Est: $800-$1,000) $1,100.00

Allis-Chalmers Tractor, Arcade, 7", 2 lg back BRT & 2 sm front BRT, NP driver, overpt, A (Est: $150-$200)............$190.00

Allis-Chalmers Tractor, Hubley, 6½", BRT, w/driver, EX+, A (Est: $500-$700)....................................$1,100.00

Allis-Chalmers Tractor & Mower, Arcade, 9", BRT, cast driver, VG, A (Est: $200-$300)..............................$220.00

Allis-Chalmers Tractor & Spreader, Arcade, 12" overall, WRT, w/driver, spreader has lever action, G, A (Est: $125-$250) $100.00

Allis Chalmers Tractor and Two-Wheeled Dump Trailer, Arcade, 8", NM, A (Est: $500.00 – $700.00), $410.00. (Photo courtesy Bertoia Auctions)

Allis-Chalmers WC Tractor, Arcade, 7", BRT, NP driver, NM, A (Est: $1,500-$2,000)..............................$3,300.00

Avery Tractor, 4½", resembles early train engine, 4 MSWs, EX, A (Est: $300-$400)......................................$275.00

Case Combine, Vindex, 7½x12", EX, A (Est: $2,500-$3,500)..$5,775.00

Case L Tractor, Vindex, 7", MSW, NP driver, EX+ ($1,200-$1,500) $2,750.00

Case L Tractor, Vindex, 7", MSW w/treads, NP driver, EX+, A (Est: $2,000-$2,500)..............................$7,150.00

Case Manure Spreader, Vindex, 12", EX, A (Est: $1,500-$2,000) $1,320.00

Case 3-Bottom Plow, Vindex, 10", MSW, EX+, A (Est: $1,200-$1,500)..$990.00

Disc Harrow (Tandem), Arcade, 7", EXIB, A (Est: $500-$700)..$2,750.00

Farmall A Cultivision Tractor, Arcade, 7", BRT, NP driver, EX, A (Est: $400-$500)......................................$520.00

Farmall M Tractor, Arcade, 6", BRT, cast driver, G, A (Est: $200-$300) $190.00

Farmall M Tractor, Arcade, 7", BRT, NP driver, EX, A (Est: $400-$600)..$385.00

Farmall Tractor, Arcade, 6", MSW, cast driver, NMIB, A (Est: $1,200-$1,500) $7,700.00

Farmall Tractor, Arcade, 6", WRT, cast driver, NM, A (Est: $700-$900) $2,090.00

Ford 9N Tractor, Arcade, 3½", blk-pnt wooden wheels, cast driver, EX+, A (Est: $250-$350) $245.00

Ford 9N Tractor, Arcade, 6½", saleman's sample, BRT, w/driver, M, A (Est: $2,000-$3,000) $2,475.00

Ford 9N Tractor, Arcade, 9", salesman's sample, BRT, w/driver, NM, A (Est: $1,500-$2,000)..................$2,200.00

Fordson Tractor, AC Williams, 6", MSW, cast driver, VG, A (Est: $600-$800) $220.00

Fordson Tractor, Arcade, 6", MSW (2 lg back w/grids & 2 sm front), NP driver, EX, A (Est: $500-$750)...............$255.00

Fordson Tractor, Dent, 6", MSW (2 lg back wheels w/grids & 2 sm front w/no grids), NP driver, G, A (Est: $1,000-$1,200)..$3,575.00

Fordson Tractor, North & Judd, 4", MSW, NP driver, VG, A (Est: $250-$300) $355.00

Fordson Tractor, Skolund & Olson, 6", 4 MSW, NP driver, EX, A (Est: $3,000-$4,000) $1,430.00

Fordson Tractor & Hay Rake, Arcade, no sz given, MSW, NP driver, tin wire prongs on hay rake, EX, A (Est: $1,000-$1,200) $2,200.00

Fordson Tractor & Thraser, Arcade, 16" overall, MSW (2 lg back & 2 sm front), NP driver, EX+, A (Est: $1,200-$1,500) $1,980.00

Fordson Tractor w/Front Scoop, Hubley, 9½" L, PMSW, w/driver, EX, A (Est: $3,000-$4,000) $1,980.00

Fordson Tractor w/Miami Scraper, Dent, 11" overall, NPSW, w/driver, very rare, EXIB, A (Est: $2,000-$3,000) ..$6,050.00

Hay Rake, Arcade, 7", NPSW, w/seat, NM, A (Est: $600-$800) $1,100.00

Hay Wagon, Vindex, 8", VG, A (Est: $1,700.00 – $2,000.00), $1,430.00. (Photo courtesy Bertoia Auctions)

Industrial Fordson Tractor, Arcade, BRT, Whitehead & Kales emb on disk wheels, NP driver, G, A (Est: $400-$500) $355.00

John Deere (Horse-Drawn) Hand Plow, 10", NP, no horse, EX, A $220.00

John Deere A Tractor, Arcade, 7½", BRT, NP driver, VG, A..$385.00

John Deere Combine, Vindex, 1928, 13½", w/standing figure, EX, A (Est: $4,000-$6,000)...................................$5,500.00

John Deere D Tractor, Vindex, 6", MSW, NP driver, G, A (Est: $1,500-$1,750) $880.00

John Deere D Tractor, Vindex, 6", MSW, NP driver, NM (Est: $1,500-$2,000) $3,300.00

John Deere Farm Spreader Wagon, Vindex, 9", MSW, 2 horses, w/driver, VG, A (Est: $1,500-$2,000) $1,680.00

John Deere Gas Engine, Vindex, 3½" T, EX, A (Est: $500-$700)...$1,150.00

John Deere Harvester, Vindex, 13½" L, w/rpl figure, VG+, A (Est: $4,000-$5,000)...$4,675.00

John Deere Hay Loader, Vindex, 9", very rare, EX, A (Est: $3,000-$4,000)...$4,675.00

John Deere Hay Loader, Vindex, 9", very rare, NM, A (Est: $4,000-$5,000)...$6,325.00

John Deere Manure Spreader, Vindex, 14", MSW, single seat, no horses, VG, A (Est: $1,200-$1,500) $1,430.00

John Deere Thrasher, Vindex, 15", EX, A (Est: $2,000-$3,000) $3,300.00

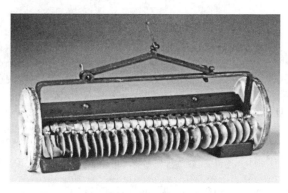

John Deere Van Brunt Drill, Vindex, 10", EX, A (Est: $1,800.00 – $2,200.00), $2,475.00. (Photo courtesy Bertoia Auctions)

John Deere Wagon, Vindex, 12½", adjustable frame w/removable seat, no horse, VG, A (Est: $1,200-$1,500)..$1,760.00

John Deere 3-Bottom Plow, Vindex, 9", NM, A (Est: $1,500-$2,000) $2,475.00

John Deere 3-Bottom Plow, Vindex, 9", VG, A (Est: $750-$1,000) $800.00

McCormick-Deering Spreader, Arcade, 15", BRT, EX, A (Est: $400-$500) $355.00

McCormick-Deering Spreader, Arcade, 15", NPSW, EX+, A (Est: $500-$700) $440.00

McCormick-Deering Thresher, Arcade, 10", EX+, A (Est: $600-$800)...$600.00

McCormick-Deering Tractor & Bailer, Arcade, 17" overall, tractor w/SMW (2 lg & 2 sm), VG, A (Est: $175-$350)........$345.00

McCormick-Deering Tractor & Hay Rake, Arcade, 11", G+, A (Est; $150-$200) $330.00

McCormick-Deering Weber Wagon, Arcade, 12", removable seat, 2 horses, no driver, EX, A (Est: $600-$800) $465.00

McCormick-Deering Weber Wagon, Arcade, 12", removable seat, 2 horses, no driver, G, A (Est: $150-$175) $170.00

McCormick-Deering 10-20 Tractor, Arcade, 1925, 7", BRT, no driver, VG, A (Est: $200-$300) $275.00

McCormick-Deering 10-20 Tractor, Kilgore, 6", NPSW, NP driver, EX+, A (Est: $600-$800) $1,200.00

McCormick-Deering 10-20 Tractor & 2-Bottom Plow, Arcade, 14" overall, MSW, NP driver, EX+, A (Est: $500-$700)..$1,200.00

McCormick-Deering 2-Bottom Plow, Arcade, 7", VG, A (Est: $400-$600) $165.00

Oliver Orchard Tractor, Hubley, 5", M, A (Est: $400.00 – $500.00), $825.00. (Photo courtesy Bertoia Auctions)

Oliver Superior Spreader, Arcade, 10", BRT, VG, A (Est: $500-$700)..$410.00

Oliver Tractor, Arcade, 7", 4 BRT, w/driver, G+, A (Est: $200-$300)..$285.00

Oliver Tractor & Row Corn Picker, Arcade, 10" overall, BRT, cast driver, NM, A (Est: $500-$600).........................$355.00

Oliver 2-Bottom Plow, Arcade, 6" L, NP spoke wheels, G, A (Est: $300-$400)...................................$385.00

Oliver 70-Row Crop Tractor, Arcade, 7", BRT, NP driver, EX, A $500.00

Thrasher, Arcade, 10", rpt, A (Est: $400-$500)..............$250.00

Tractor, Kilgore, 6", back wheel covers over 2 lg MSW w/grids, 2 sm front MSW, NP driver, rpt, A (Est: $200-$250)..$355.00

Tractor & Farm Trailer, Kenton, 1928, 10½" overall, NPSW, NP driver, disk wheels on trailer, EX+, A (Est: $600-$800) ...$1,430.00

Tractor & Wagon, Arcade, 9", MSW (2 lg & 2 sm) on tractor, NPDW on wagon, w/driver, G, A (Est: $100) $125.00

Tractor w/Dump Trailer, Arcade, 8" overall, WRT (2 lg back & 2 sm front), 2 WRT on trailer, VG+, A (Est: $300-$400)......$135.00

Two-Bottom Plow, Arcade, 5½" L, NPSW, EX, A (Est: $300-$500)..$100.00

Wallis Tractor, Freidag, 5", MSW, cast driver, G, A (Est: $2,500-$3,000) $3,025.00

Firefighting

Accessory, Aerial Ladder, Ives, 24" T (extended), NP ladders mounted on base, w/2 firemen, VG, A (Est: $600-$800).............$2,300.00

Accessory, Burning 2-Story Building, Carpenter, 17" T, lady in distress & 2 firemen, EX, A (Est: $28,000-$32,000)...$54,625.00

Accessory, Engine House, Carpenter, 21" L, wood sides w/CI windows & doors, curved tin roof, VG, A (Est: $5,000-$6,000) $7,475.00

Accessory, Extension Ladder, Ives, 33" T (extended), no base, w/4 firemen, VG, A (Est: $400-$600) $1,150.00

Accessory, Fire Engine House & Horse-Drawn (2) Pumper Wagon, Ives, 13" wagon, cast driver, EX, A (Est: $4,000-$6,000) $16,100.00

Aerial Ladder Truck, Kenton, 12", open frame, red, NP ladders & driver, MDW, yel hubs, side levers, G, A (Est: $700-$900 ....$1,650.00

Ahrens-Fox Ladder Truck, Hubley, 7½", open, red w/red ladders & driver, WRT, EX, A (Est: $400-$600).................$410.00

Ahrens-Fox Pumper Truck, Hubley, 9", open, red, NP detail, ladders & driver, WRT, VG, A (Est: $1,200-$1,500) $800.00

Aherns-Fox Pumper Truck, Hubley, 11", EX+, A (Est: $2,250.00 – $2,500.00), $4,675.00. (Photo courtesy James D. Julia, Inc.)

Ahrens-Fox Pumper Truck, Hubley 11", open, red, NP detail, ladders & driver, WRT, rstr, A (Est: $400-$500) $715.00

Chemical Truck, see Mack Chemical Truck

Fire Chief Coupe, Arcade, 5", cast bell on hood, WRT, VG, A (Est: $500-$600) $465.00

Fire Chief Coupe, Arcade, 6½", NPSW, NP driver, EX, A (Est: $800-$1,000) $4,025.00

Fire Chief Coupe, Dent, 5", slanted windshield, bell cast on hood & driver in window, NPDW, VG, A (Est: $400-$500) $600.00

Fire Chief Coupe, Kenton, 5½", bell cast on hood, driver cast in window, NPDW, VG, A (Est: $400-$500)...............$660.00

Fire Pumper Wagon, Hubley, 18", MSW, 2 horses, no figures o/w EX, A (Est: $200-$400) $185.00

Fire Truck, Arcade, 13½", open, red w/silver trim, revolving hose reel, BRT, 6 figures, VG, A (Est: $400-$600) ..$500.00

Fire Truck, Hubley, 13½", open, red w/silver-pnt windshield, grille & bumper, NP ladder & driver, wooden pipe for hose, WRT, NM, A (Est: $800-$1,000) $2,475.00

Hook & Ladder Truck, Arcade, 16", open, red w/yel ladders, 3 cast figures, 6-wheeled, G, A (Est: $300-$400) $440.00

Hook & Ladder Truck, Dent, 19", open, red w/yel ladders, NPDW, yel hubs, 4-wheeled, 2 figures, EX+ (Est: $1,800-$2,200) $3,160.00

Horse-Drawn Aerial Hook & Ladder Wagon, Wilkins, 23", 2 horses, w/front & rear drivers, EX+, A (Est: $2,000-$2,500) $6,325.00

Horse-Drawn Chemical Wagon, Wilkins, 19½", 2 horses (1 wht & 1 palomino), w/driver, VG+, A (Est: $4,500-$5,500)...$12,075.00

Horse-Drawn Chief's Cart, Shimer, 15", 1 horse, w/driver, w/sledgehammer & axe, VG, A (Est: $1,500-$2,000)............$1,950.00

Horse-Drawn Chief's Cart, Wilkins, 11½", 1 horse, w/driver, EX, A (Est: $1,500-$2,000) $2,875.00

Horse-Drawn FD Chief Wagon, Hubley, 15", 1 horse, driver, G, A (Est: $300-$400)...$245.00

Horse-Drawn Fire Patrol #55, Carpenter, 16", MSW, 2 horses, w/driver & 2 seated figures, EX, A (Est: $2,500-$3,500) $4,885.00

Horse-Drawn Fire Patrol Wagon, Hubley, 15½", 2 horses, 3 figures seated in back, EX+, A (Est: $1,000-$1,200).........$2,070.00

Horse-Drawn Fire Patrol Wagon (Phoenix), Ives, 21", 2 horses, driver & 6 riders, VG+, A (Est: $1,200-$1,500) ..$4,025.00

Horse-Drawn Hook & Ladder Wagon, Carpenter, 27", 2 horses, front & rear drivers, VG, A (Est: $2,000-$2,500) ..$3,160.00

Horse-Drawn Hook & Ladder Wagon, Dent, 26", 1 horse, w/driver, VG, A (Est: $500-$700) $385.00

Horse-Drawn Hook & Ladder Wagon, Ideal, 32", 3 horses, w/front & rear drivers, EX, A (Est: $2,000-$4,000) $2,300.00

Horse-Drawn Hook & Ladder Wagon, Wilkins, 21", 3 horses, w/driver, G, A (Est: $400-$600) $440.00

Horse-Drawn Hook & Ladder Wagon 126, Hubley, 32", 3 horses, front & back drivers, EX, A (Est: $700-$900) $1,320.00

Horse-Drawn Hose Reel Cart, Carpenter, 14", 2-wheeled, 1 horse, w/driver & rear figure, VG, A (Est: $1,500-$1,800) .$1,550.00

Horse-Drawn Hose Reel Wagon, Hubley, 13", 2 horses, rpr/rpt, A (Est: $300-$500) $385.00

Horse-Drawn Hose Reel Wagon, Ideal, 21½", 2 horses, w/driver, EX, A (Est: $3,000-$4,000) $17,250.00

Horse-Drawn Hose Reel Wagon, Ives, 17", 1 horse, w/driver, EX+, A (Est: $2,000-$2,500) $4,885.00

Horse-Drawn Hose Reel Wagon, Wilkins, 14", 2 horses, w/driver, VG, A (Est: $600-$800) $1,035.00

Horse-Drawn Hose Reel Wagon, Wilkins, 15½", 2 horses (1 palomino), w/driver, VG+, A (Est: $2,500-$3,500)...$4,600.00

Horse-Drawn Ladder Truck, Hubley, 16½", 3 horses, VG+, A (Est: $200-$400) $115.00

Horse-Drawn Ladder Wagon, Arcade, 16", MSW, 3 horses, w/driver, EX, A (Est: $175-$225) $285.00

Horse-Drawn Pumper Wagon, Arcade, 13", MSW, 3 horses, w/driver, EX, A (Est: $125-$175) $160.00

Horse-Drawn Pumper Wagon, Carpenter, 18", marked #14, MSW, 2 horses, driver & rear figure, VG+, A (Est: $2,000-$2,500) $3,450.00

Horse-Drawn Pumper Wagon, Carpenter, 19", 2 horses, w/driver & rear standing figure, EX, A (Est: $2,500-$3,500) $6,035.00

Horse-Drawn Pumper Wagon, Dent, 22", 3 horses, EX, A (Est: $700-$900) $1,045.00

Horse-Drawn Pumper Wagon, Ideal, 22½", 2 horses, w/driver & rear standing figure, EX, A (Est: $3,000-$4,000)...$18,400.00

Horse-Drawn Pumper Wagon, Kenton, 13", 3 horses, w/driver, EX, A (Est: $175-$250) $175.00

Horse-Drawn Pumper Wagon, Kenton, 15", 2 horses, w/driver, EX, A (Est: $500-$700) $1,495.00

Horse-Drawn Pumper Wagon, Pratt & Letchworth, 18", 2 horses, driver & rear standing figure, VG, A (Est: $2,000-$2,500) $2,760.00

Horse-Drawn Pumper Wagon, Welker & Crosby, 17", blk w/red & gold trim, 2 horses, driver, VG+, A (Est: $2,000-$2,600) $5,175.00

Horse-Drawn Pumper Wagon, Wilkens, 10", 3 horses, w/driver, VG, A (Est: $250-$350) $355.00

Horse-Drawn Pumper Wagon, Wilkins, 14", 2 trotting horses, w/driver, VG, A (Est: $600-$800) $1,035.00

Horse-Drawn Pumper Wagon, Wilkins, 14½", 2 galloping horses, w/driver, VG, A (Est: $600-$800) $1,035.00

Horse-Drawn 40th Water Tower, Wilkins, 40" long, EX, A (Est: $3,000.00 – $4,000.00), $18,975.00. (Photo courtesy James D. Julia, Inc.)

Ladder Truck, see also Mack Ladder Truck or Pontiac Ladder Truck

Ladder Truck, AC Williams, 7", take-apart body, open, red w/NP trim & ladders, WRT, VG, A (Est: $700-$900).......$440.00

Ladder Truck, Arcade, 10", 1930s Pontiac, red w/NP grille & lights, BRT, ladders, 2 cast figures, VG, A (Est: $200-$300) $350.00

Ladder Truck, Arcade, 16", 2-pc w/open cab, BRT (6-wheeled), 3 figures, 2 yel ladders, G+, A (Est: $200-$400) $570.00

Ladder Truck, Arcade, 18", Mack, open, red w/3 yel ladders, NPSW, NP driver, VG+, A (Est: $400-$500) $600.00

Ladder Truck, Arcade, 22½", open w/open frame, red, NP supports & hose reel, yel ladders, gr service box, blk-pnt MSW, pnt driver, VG, A (Est: $800-$1,000).......$4,400.00

Ladder Truck, Hubley, 8", open, red, red ladders, NP trim, NPDW, red-pnt driver w/NP hat, EX, A (Est: $175-$250) $550.00

Ladder Truck, Hubley, 11", open, red w/NP fenders, running boards, grille, trim & 2 figures, WRT, G, A (Est: $200-$300) $285.00

Ladder Truck, Hubley, 11", red w/blk chassis, electric lights, crank action, WRT, EX, A (Est: $3,500-$4,500)..$9,350.00

Ladder Truck, Hubley, 13½", open, red w/silver-pnt windshield, grille & bumper, NP ladders & driver, WRT, NM, A (Est. $800.00-$1,000.00) $2,200.00

Ladder Truck, Hubley, 16", open, red w/silver-pnt grille & windshield, WRT, NP ladders & driver, EX, A (Est: $500-$800) $715.00

Ladder Truck, Kenton, 9", open, red w/2 NP ladders, MDW, cast driver, G, A (Est: $150-$250) $140.00

Ladder Truck, Kenton, 19", open, red w/gold trim, PMDW, yel hubs, 2 figures, no accessories, G, A (Est: $100-$200)...........$250.00

Ladder Truck, Kenton, 7½", open, railed bed, red, yel ladder, NP grille, driver on right, G, A (Est: $500-$700).......$1,650.00

Ladder Truck, Kilgore, 5", cast side ladders, NP bell/grille/lights/bumper, 2 cast riders, WRT, EX+, A (Est: $300-$400) $660.00

Ladder Truck, Skoglund & Olson, 16", open, red, NP hose reel/ladders/supports, WRT, driver, EX, A (Est: $2,000-$3,000) $2,750.00

Mack Chemical Truck, Arcade, 15", open, red, 2 ladders, NP reel & driver, MSW w/rear duals, G, A (Est: $2,000-$2,500) $2,750.00

Mack Ladder Truck, Arcade, 21", open, red, metal ladders, NP driver & steering wheel, WRT, EX, A (Est: $1,200-$1,500) $4,400.00

Patrol Truck, Kenton, 6½", open, red w/gold trim, PMDW w/yel hubs, 3 NP figures in back, Fair+, A (Est: $150-$250)..$200.00

Patrol Truck, Kenton, 9", open, red w/gold trim, PMDW w/yel hubs, w/driver & 3 figures, VG, A (Est: $500-$700)...$600.00

Patrol Truck, Kenton, 9", open, red w/gold trim, WRT w/red hubs, w/driver & 3 figures, G+, A (Est: $300-$500)............$600.00

Patrol Wagon, Dent, 20½", MSW (2 lg/2 sm), 3 horses, driver & 4 firemen, rpt, A (Est: $500-$700).........................$275.00

Pontiac Ladder Truck, Arcade, 9½", red, yel metal ladders, BRT, driver & standing rider, EXIB, A (Est: $1,000-$1,200) ...$2,090.00

Pontiac Pumper Truck (1936), Kenton, 5", red & blk, NP boiler top & grille, cast driver, rare, G, A (Est: $350-$450).........$385.00

Pumper Truck, AC Williams, 1937, 7", take-apart body, EX, A (Est: $1,000.00 – $1,200.00), $1,650.00. (Photo courtesy Bertoia Auctions)

Pumper Truck, Arcade, 6½", open, red, WRT, cast driver, G, A (Est: $75-$125) $60.00

Pumper Truck, Dent, 10½", brn w/gold trim, PMDW, no driver, VG, A (Est: $700-$900) $440.00

Pumper Truck, Hubley, 6½", 2 cast figures in open seat, NP grille, bumper & boiler top, WRT, EX (Est: $400-$500)........$135.00

Pumper Truck, Hubley, 8", open, red w/gold trim, cast driver, MDW, VG, A (Est: $150-$250)............................$130.00

Pumper Truck, Hubley, 8½", open, red w/NP fenders, grille, trim & 2 figures, WRT, G, A (Est: $150-$250) $220.00

Pumper Truck, Hubley, 10", open, red, NP fenders, grille & boiler top, WRT, no figures, G+, A (Est: $200-$300)..........$385.00

Pumper Truck, Hubley, 10", open, red w/gold trim, b/o headlights, WRT, cast driver, G+, A (Est: $300-$400) ...$350.00

Pumper Truck, Hubley, 13½", open, red w/NP boiler & trim, hubs & driver, MDW, VG, A (Est: $1,500-$2,500)........$1,980.00

Pumper Truck, Kenton, 7½", open, red w/separate NP grille & bumper, driver cast on right, WRT, EX, A (Est: $500-$700) $520.00

Pumper Truck, Kenton, 10½", open, red w/gold boiler top, WRT, cast driver, G, A (Est: $150-$250) $175.00

Pumper Truck, Kenton, 10½", open, red w/silver boiler top, WRT, cast driver, EX, A (Est: $400-$500)...............$330.00

Pumper Truck, Kenton, 12½", open, red w/gold trim, NPDW, yel hubs, driver, VG, A (Est: $1,200-$1,500)............$1,600.00

Pumper Truck, Kenton, 14½", open, red w/NP & gold trim, BRT/MSW, pnt driver, rear figure, G+, A (Est: $400-$600) $770.00

Pumper Truck, Kilgore, 5", open, red w/gold hats on 2 cast riders & hood bell, NP grille, WRT, EX, A (Est: $200-$300)....$355.00

Water Tower Truck, Hubley, 15", open, bl w/NP trim, NPDW, eagle on sides, 2 cast drivers, G, A (Est: $400-$500) ..$465.00

Water Tower Truck, Kenton, 11½", open frame & seat, red w/bl tower, MDW, side lever, driver, EX, A (Est: $700-$900).........$2,200.00

HORSE-DRAWN AND OTHER ANIMALS

See also Farm (Horse-Drawn John Deere and Horse-Drawn McCormick Deering), Firefighting.

Bad Accident (Mule Cart), J&E Stevens, 9", w/driver, EX, A (Est: $1,000-$1,200)..$1,500.00

Barouche, Pratt & Letchworth, 18", MSW, 2 horses, w/driver, VG, A (Est: $4,000-$6,000) $8,050.00

Beer Wagon, Kenton, 15", MSW, 2 horses, w/driver, EX (Est: $700-$900) $1,100.00

Beer Wagon, Kenton, 15", MSW, 2 horses, w/driver, VG, A (Est: $400-$600) $715.00

Boy's Express Wagon, Pratt & Letchworth, 17", EX, A (Est: $4,000.00 – $5,000.00) $10,925.00. (Photo courtesy James D. Julia, Inc.)

Brake (Four Seat), Pratt & Letchworth, 1890, 27", MSW, 4 horses, 8 figures, G, A (Est: $12,000-$15,000)...$22,000.00

Buckboard, Harris, 14", 2 goats, lady driver, VG, A (Est: $2,000-$2,500) $3,565.00

Buckboard, Wilkens, 12½", 4 MSW, 1 horse, no driver, VG, A (Est: $500-$700)..$355.00

Cab, Hubley, 10¾", open bench seat w/enclosed passenger compartment, 4 MSW, 1 horse, VG, A (Est: $300-$400) $300.00

Carriage, Kenton, 16", enclosed passenger w/oval cutouts, 1 horse, w/driver & lady passenger, EX, A (Est: $300-$500)....$220.00

Cart, Wilkens, 13", stake sides, 2 MSW, single horse, w/driver, VG, A (Est: $300-$400)..$220.00

Chariot w/Clown, Hubley, 9½", mule-drawn, EX, A (Est: $600-$800) $1,150.00

Chariot w/Roman Driver, Hubley, 10", 3 horses, w/Roman driver, VG+, A (Est: $600-$800) $1,380.00

City Delivery Wagon, Harris, 15½", 2 horses, w/driver, VG, A (Est: $2,500-$3,500)...$4,600.00

Coal Cart, Ives No 0 tag, 1912, 10½", mule-drawn, 2 MSW, Black driver, w/shovel, EX, A (Est: $900-$1,100) $1,495.00

Coal Wagon, Dent, 15", w/orig tin coal chute, 1 horse, w/driver, unused, NM+, A (Est: $2,000-$2,500) $3,160.00

Coal Wagon, Hubley, 16", 1 horse, EX, A (Est: $1,200-$1,400) $2,530.00

Coal Wagon, Kenton, 18½", 2 horses, driver, EX, A (Est: $800-$1,000) $1,540.00

Consolidated Street RR #372 Trolley, Wilkins, 13", 1 horse, w/driver, EX, A (Est: $1,400-$1,800) $2,240.00

Contractor's Dump Wagon, see also Dump Wagon

Contractor's Dump Wagon, Arcade, 13", BRT, 2 horses, w/driver, EX, A (Est: $500-$700) $465.00

Contractor's Dump Wagon, Arcade, 13", MSW, 1 horse, w/driver, EX, A (Est: $500-$700) $465.00

Contractor's Dump Wagon, Kenton, 15½", 3 dump buckets, MSW, 2 horses, w/driver, G, A (Est: $300-$400) $600.00

Doctor's Cart, Wilkens, 10½", 4 lg spoke wheels, w/bulbous doctor in top hat, EX, A (Est: $1,200-$1,500) $1,380.00

Dog Cart, Pratt & Letchworth, ca 1895, 13", 2 MSW, 1 horse, driver, EX, A (Est: $1,500-$2,000) $2,750.00

Dog Cart, 10", EX, A (Est: $1,000.00 – $1,200.00), $2,300.00. (Photo courtesy James D. Julia, Inc.)

DPW Street Sweeper, Wilkens, 12½", open frame w/MSW, bristle roller, 1 horse, driver, VG, A (Est: $1,500-$2,000)...$1,550.00

Dray Cart, Pratt & Letchworth, 10½", 2-wheeled, 1 horse, standing driver, NM, A (Est: $800-$1,000)..........$2,645.00

Dray Wagon, Arcade, 13", open curved sides, MSW, 2 horses, w/driver, EX, A (Est: $1,000-$1,200) $2,475.00

Dray Wagon, Dent, 16", w/4 farm tools, 2 horses, w/driver, EX+, A (Est: $1,200-$1,500) $1,780.00

Dray Wagon, Hubley, 23", open stake & chain sides w/6 wooden barrels, 2 horses, driver, VG, A (Est: $700-$900)..$1,540.00

Dray Wagon, Ives, 14", 1 horse, w/driver on high seat, VG, A (Est: $1,000-$1,200)...$1,440.00

Dray Wagon, Kenton, 15", solid sides, MSW, 2 horses, w/driver, EX, A (Est: $200-$300) $250.00

Dray Wagon, Pratt & Letchworth, 13", 1 horse, driver on high seat, VG+, A (Est: $1,800-$2,200).........................$2,415.00

Dray Wagon, Shimer, 14", NP, MSW, 2 horses, w/driver, 6 wooden barrels, VG, A (Est: $700-$900) $440.00

Dray Wagon, Welker & Crosby, 1890, high seat, stake sides, MSW (2 lg/2 sm), 1 horse, rpt, A (Est: $1,200-$1,500) $3,300.00

Dray Wagon, Wilkins, 13", low sides, MSW (2 lg back & 2 sm front, 1 horse, stand-up driver, EX, A (Est: $600-$800) $1,650.00

Dump Wagon, Arcade, 14½", side-dump action, NPSW, 2 horses, NM, A (Est: $8,000-$12,000)...................$6,600.00

Dump Wagon, Hubley, 14", 2 horses, w/driver, EX, A (Est: $500-$700) $1,265.00

Dump Wagon, see also Contractor's Dump Wagon

Eldorado Wagon, Shimer, 5½", ox-drawn Conestoga wagon, red & wht, VG, A (Est: $250-$350) $190.00

Elephant Cart, Harris, 6½", MSW, elf driver, VG, A (Est: $200-$300)..$77.00

Elephant Cart, Kenton, 7½", 2 MSW, driver, all silver, G, A (Est: $200-$300) $55.00

Express Wagon, Dent, 12", removable bench seat, MSW, 1 horse, driver, VG, A (Est: $400-$500) $165.00

Farm Wagon, Arcade, 11", BRT, 2 horses, w/driver, EX+, A (Est: $500-$700)...$220.00

Flatbed Wagon, Arcade, 13", 4 MSW, 1 horse, NP driver, VG, A (Est: $300-$400) $275.00

Flying Artillery, Ives, 22", 4-wheeled gun wagon, 2 horses, driver & horse rider, VG, A (Est: $1,500-$2,000) $3,220.00

Flying Artillery, Pratt & Letchworth, 33½", EX, A (Est: $18,000.00 – $22,000.00), $60,375.00. (Photo courtesy James D. Julia, Inc.)

Goat Cart, Harris, 6¾", brownie figure seated in shell seat, 2 MSW, G, A (Est: $300-$400) $135.00

Greyhound Cart, Kenton, 7", NP finish, VG, A (Est: $250-$350)..$220.00

Groceries Wagon, Wilkens, no sz given, roof extends over seat, MSW (2 lg & 2 sm), 1 horse, EX, A (Est: $100-$200)...$410.00

Hansom Cab, Arcade, 10½", 1 horse, driver, EX, A (Est: $700-$900)..$825.00

Hansom Cab, Dent, 13½", 1 horse, w/driver & lady passenger, EX, A (Est: $1,200-$1,500).................................$1,950.00

Hansom Cab, Ives, 13", 1 horse, no driver, EX, A (Est: $1,500-$2,000) $1,550.00

Hansom Cab, Pratt & Letchworth, 11½", 1 horse, no driver, VG, A (Est: $1,000-$1,400)......................................$935.00

Hay Wagon, Hubley, 15", vertically slatted sides, 2 oxen, Black driver standing, G, A (Est: $700-$900) $920.00

Hay Wagon, Vindex, 14½", flatbed w/front & back stake sides, MSW, 2 horses, EX, A (Est: $1,500-$1,750) $2,200.00

Horse Cart, Carpenter, Pat 1884, 13", 2-wheeled, VG, A (Est: $150-$250) $190.00

Horses (2), Arcade, 5", blk w/red & gold harness, NP hitch, single wheel on front of ea, NMIB, A (Est: $1,000-$1,200)...$2,200.00

Ice Wagon, Arcade, 11", enclosed w/ICE emb on sides, MSW, 2 horses, w/driver, VG, A (Est: $600-$800)................$465.00

Ice Wagon, Hubley, 15", 2 horses, w/driver, EX+, A (Est: $1,600-$1,800) $3,795.00

Ice Wagon, Shimmer, 13", 2 horses, w/driver, EX+, A (Est: $800-$1,000) $1,780.00

Landau, Hubley, 15", opening doors, MSW, 2 horses, driver, EX+, A (Est: $3,500-$4,500) $8,625.00

Lion Cart w/Hindu, att: Kenton, 7½", EX+, A (Est: $500-$600)..$1,435.00

Log Wagon, Hubley, 15", figure on top of log, 1 ox, Fair, A (Est: $200-$300) $410.00

Log Wagon, Kenton, 15", driver seated on log sideways, 4 MSW, 1 horse, G, A (Est: $300-$400) $500.00

McCormick-Deering Spreader, Arcade, 13½", MSW, 2 horses, EX+, A (Est: $700-$900)..................................$1,045.00

Milk Wagon, Kenton, 13", 1 horse, driver, EX, A (Est: $250-$350)..$275.00

Mower, Wilkens, 10½", MSW, 2-wheeled, w/swing-out blade, 2 horses, driver, EX, A (Est: $2,500-$3,500) $2,475.00

Mule Cart, Ives, 14", japanned articulated mule & 2-wheeled cart, EX, A (Est: $1,500-$2,000) $1,380.00

Mule Cart, Wilkins, 10½", w/driver, G+, A (Est: $800-$1,000) $1,380.00

Ox Cart, Hubley, 12", stake sides, 1 ox, driver seated, EX, A (Est: $800-$1,000)..$1,600.00

Ox Cart, Hubley, 13", box cart, 1 ox, driver standing, EX, A (Est: $1,000-$1,200)..$935.00

Ox Cart, Hubley, 13", box cart, 1 ox, driver standing, G+, A (Est: $400-$600) $400.00

Ox Cart, Ives, Pat 1883, no sz given, 2-wheeled open box cart w/2 oxen, MSW, VG, A (Est: $400-$600)..............$385.00

Ox Cart, Wilkens, 13", 2-wheeled, MSW, 1 ox, w/driver, Fair, A (Est: $200-$300)..$355.00

Ox Stake Cart, Kyser & Rex, 11", 2 MSW, Black driver, EX, A (Est: $1,000-$1,200)..$1,200.00

Ox Wagon, Kyser & Rex, 13", open stake sides, 4 MSW, 2 oxen, driver, VG, A (Est: $600-$800) $465.00

Plantation Cart, see Ox Cart

Pleasure Cart, Kenton, 10", 1 horse, lady passenger in 2-wheeled cart, EX, A (Est: $800-$1,000) $3,100.00

Polar Ice Wagon, Ives, 14", 2 horses, no driver, VG, A (Est: $1,500-$1,800) $1,265.00

Police Ice Wagon, Kenton, 14½", 2 horses, driver, EX, A (Est: $1,000-$1,200) $770.00

Pony Cart, Carpenter, 11½", 1 horse, no figure, EX, A (Est: $500-$600) $800.00

Pony Cart, Shimer, 10", 2 MSW, NP driver, VG, A (Est: $300-$400)..$75.00

Pony Cart, Wilkins, 10½", 1 horse, w/lady driver in fancy 2-wheeled cart, NM, A (Est: $700-$900)...................$920.00

Pure Lake Ice Wagon, Harris, 13½", 2 horses, w/driver, G, A (Est: $2,000-$2,500)................................$2,875.00

Rabbit Cart, Kenton, 5", pulled by rabbit & w/rabbit driver, NP, 2 MSW, VG, A (Est: $300-$400)...................$500.00

Sand & Gravel Wagon, 15½", MSW, 2 horses, w/driver, VG+, A (Est: $250-$350)..$150.00

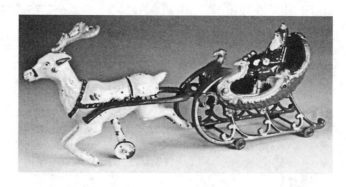

Santa Sleigh, Hubley, 14½", single reindeer, EX+, A (Est: $2,000.00 – $2,500.00), $4,600.00. (Photo courtesy James D. Julia, Inc.)

Santa Sleigh, Hubley, 16", 2 reindeer, Santa figure, EX+, A (Est: $2,000-$2,500)..................................$4,300.00

Second Regiment Ambulance Wagon, 15", MSW, 2 horses, no driver, Fair+, A (Est: $300-$500) $650.00

Sleigh, Hubley, 14½", 1 horse, lady driver, EX, A (Est: $800-$1,000) $1,745.00

Sleigh, Hubley, 14½", 2 horses, lady driver, rstr, A (Est: $400-$600)..$550.00

Sprinkler Wagon, Wilkins, 14½", driver on seat cast atop cylindrical tank, MSW, 2 horses, EX, A (Est: $7,000-$9,000) ...$16,100.00

Sulky, Kenton, 8", MSW, w/driver, EX, A (Est: $75-$125)..$80.00

Surrey, Hubley, 14½", 2-seater, 1 horse, w/driver & lady passenger, EX, A (Est: $2,500-$3,500) $6,900.00

Surrey, Kenton, 12", cloth canopy, 2 horses, w/driver & passenger, EX+, A (Est: $400-$500)..................................$300.00

Tally Ho, Carpenter, 27½", enclosed carriage w/4 horses, driver & 6 passengers, EX+, A (Est: $35,000-$45,000) $92,000.00

Transfer Wagon, Dent, 19", 3 horses, w/driver, EX+, A (Est: $2,000-$2,500)..$3,620.00

Trap, 13", 1 horse, w/couple and child in back, EX, A (Est: $3,000-$4,000)..$8,050.00

Phaeton, Kenton, 17½", EX+, A (Est: $5,000.00 – $6,000.00), $12,650.00. (Photo courtesy James D. Julia, Inc.)

Victor Cart, Ives, 9½", articulated horse, EX, A (Est: $1,000-$1,500) $3,450.00

Wagon, Arcade, 11", buckboard type, BRT (2 lg & 2 sm), 2 horses, driver, EX, A (Est: $700-$900).....................$440.00

Wagon, Wilkens, 22", sheet-metal flatbed w/roped sides & rear fenders, 2 horses, w/driver, VG, A (Est: $1,000-$1,200) $520.00

World's Fair St R Trolley, Wilkins, 15", 1 lg horse, EX, A (Est: $1,600-$2,000) $1,435.00

MOTOR VEHICLES

Note: Description lines for generic vehicles may simply begin with 'Bus,' 'Coupe,' or 'Motorcycle,' for example. But more busses will be listed as 'Coach Bus,' 'Coast-To-Coast,' 'Greyhound,' 'Interurban,' 'Mack,' or 'Public Service' (and there are other instances); coupes may be listed under 'Ford,' 'Packard,' or some other specific car company; and lines describing motorcycles might be also start 'Armored,' 'Excelsior-Henderson,' 'Delivery,' 'Policeman,' 'Harley-Davidson,' and so on. Look under 'Yellow Cab' or 'Checker Cab' and other cab companies for additional 'Taxi Cab' descriptions. We have given any lettering or logo on the vehicle priority when entering descriptions, so with this in mind, you should have a good idea where to look for your particular toy. Body styles (Double-Decker Bus, etc.) have also been given priority.

Air Flow, see Chrysler Air Flow

Ambulance, see also City Ambulance or Chevy Ambulance

Ambulance, Kenton, 7", roof extends over open seat, w/driver, EX, A..$1,200.00

Ambulance, Kenton, 10", NP version, VG, A (Est: $1,500.00 – $2,000.00), $1,725.00. (Photo courtesy James D. Julia, Inc.)

Ambulance, Kenton, 10", roof extends over open seat, pnt version, MSW, w/driver, VG, A (Est: $1,750-$2,250) $1,550.00

American Gasoline Tank Truck, see Mack Tank Truck (American Gasoline Tank Truck)

Anchor Truck Co Stake Truck, North & Judd, 9", Ford Model T, NPSW, NP driver, VG, A (Est: $600-$800) $520.00

Anthony Dump Truck, see Ford Anthony Dump Truck

Arctic Ice Cream Truck, Kilgore, 7", NPDW, Fair, A (Est: $300-$500)..$520.00

Army Motor Truck, Hubley, 9", open seat, stake bed, MSW, G, A (Est: $200-$300)....................................$265.00

Army Motor Truck, Kenton, 14½", NM, A (Est: $1,500.00 – $2,500.00), $2,470.00. (Photo courtesy James D. Julia, Inc.)

Auto (1900s), Kenton, 9", canopy-type curved roof over open sides, MSW, passenger & driver, G, A (Est: $1,500-$2,000) $715.00

Auto Carrier, Arcade, 14", Austin cab, 3 Austins on flatbed trailer, WRT, VG, A (Est: $400-$600).....................$550.00

Auto Carrier, Arcade, 14", curved top cab, 3 Austins on flatbed trailer, WRT, EX, A (Est: $500-$700).....................$660.00

Auto Carrier, Arcade, 14", Ford Model A cab, flatbed trailer, WRT, no autos, VG, A (Est: $400-600) $400.00

Auto Carrier, Arcade, 15", curved-top cab, 3 Pontiac autos w/NP grilles on flatbed trailer, EX, A (Est: $1,750-$2,250) $1,430.00

Auto Carrier, Arcade, 19", Ford Model A cab, 3 Fords in flatbed trailer, MSW, EX, A (Est: $2,000-$2,500) $880.00

Auto Carrier, Arcade, 20", curved-top cab, 3 1933 Plymouth autos on flatbed trailer, WRT, EX, A (Est: $2,000-$2,500).$1,540.00

Auto Carrier, Arcade, 25", Ford Model A cab, 3 Model A autos on flatbed trailer, MSW, EX, A (Est: $2,000-$2,500) $7,700.00

Auto Carrier, Arcade, 25", 1934 Ford cab, 3 Fords on flatbed trailer, WRT, EX, A (Est: $5,000-$7,500) $3,850.00

Auto Carrier, Hubley, 10", cabover, 4 autos on 2-tier trailer, WRT, EX+, A (Est: $500-$750).............................$520.00

Auto Carrier, Hubley, 10", flat-top cab, 3 Buick coupes cast on flatbed trailer, EX+, A (Est: $1,000-$1,200).........$1,320.00

Auto Carrier, Hubley, 12", flat-top cab w/side spare, 2 roadsters on flatbed trailer, WRT, VG, A (Est: $1,000-$1,200)......$715.00

Auto Carrier, Kenton, 13", take-apart cab, 2 autos w/type-I NP grilles on flatbed trailer, EX, A (Est: $5,000-$6,000)..$7,700.00

Auto Express Truck, Hubley, 9", open sides, MSW, w/driver, VG, A (Est: $800-$1,100)....................................$630.00

Auto Pulling House Trailer, see also Coupe Pulling House Trailer

Auto Pulling House Trailer, AC Williams, 12", 1930s long-nosed auto w/low roof, curved back, EX, A (Est: $500-$750) ..$990.00

Auto Pulling House Trailer, Hubley, 6½", WRT, EX, A (Est: $300-$400) $300.00

Auto Pulling Mullins Red Cap Trailer, Arcade, 8½", trailer w/opening top, BRT, VG, A (Est: $500-$700) $715.00

Aviation Gas Truck, Kilgore, 12", NPSW, G+, A (Est: $1,200-$1,500) $3,630.00

Bell Telephone Truck, Hubley, 4", red, WRT, EX, A (Est: $175-$225)..$355.00

Bell Telephone Truck, Hubley, 5", gr, WRT, VG, A (Est: $150-$200)..$275.00

Bell Telephone Truck, Hubley, 8", gr, NPSW, NP ladder & tools, VG, A (Est: $400-$500) $1,150.00

Bell Telephone Truck, Hubley, 9", gr, WRT, w/pole trailer, pully & NP ladders, EX+, A (Est: $1,200-$1,500)............$935.00

Bell Telephone Truck, Hubley, 10", gr, MSW, no accessories, G, A (Est: $200-$300)......................................$320.00

Bell Telephone Truck, Hubley, 10", gr, WRT, w/auger & accessories, VG, A (Est: $200-$300) $350.00

Bell Telephone Truck, Hubley, 10", complete with accessories, NMIB, A (Est: $2,500.00 – $3,500.00), $3,960.00. (Photo courtesy James D. Julia, Inc.)

Bell Telephone Truck, Hubley, 10", red, WRT, w/pole trailer & tools, EX+, A (Est: $1,200-$1,500) $2,200.00

Bell Telephone Truck, Hubley, 10", red, WRT, w/pole trailer & tools, G, A (Est: $300-$400)...........................$300.00

Bell Telephone Truck, Hubley, 11", gr, WRT, w/pole trailer & tools, Fair+, A (Est: $400-$600) $385.00

Blue Streak Roadster, Kilgore, 5½", WRT, EX, A (Est: $800-$1,000)..$465.00

Borden's Milk Bottle Truck, Arcade, 6", WRT, VG, A (Est: $500-$700) $715.00

Borden's Milk Truck, Hubley, 6", wht, WRT, pnt grille, VG, A (Est: $500-$800)..$1,100.00

Borden's Milk Truck, Hubley, 7½", wht, MSW, NP grille, opening rear door, w/driver, EX, A (Est: $1,500-$1,700).......$2,090.00

Bugatti Racer, Skoglund & Olson, 7", boat-tail style w/WRT, rstr, A (Est: $600-$800)................................$1,200.00

Buick Coupe (1927), Arcade, 8½", rear spare, WRT on MSW, NP driver, NM, A (Est: $4,000-$6,000) $6,600.00

Buick Sedan (1927), Arcade, 8½", rear spare, WRT on MSW, NP driver, G, A (Est: $850-$1,050).....................$1,760.00

Buick Sedan (1927), Arcade, 8½", rear spare, WRT on MSW, NP driver, VG+, A (Est: $2,500-$3,000) $3,300.00

Burney Automobile, AC Williams, 1930s, 4½", streamline style w/nose curving downward, NPSW, Fair, A (Est: $500-$700) $275.00

Bus, AC Williams, 4½", take-apart body w/long nose, orange & blk, WRT w/red hubs, EX+, A (Est: $800-$1,200)..$1,100.00

Bus, Arcade, 13", NPDW w/rear duals, 2 spares mounted on ea side on long nose, NP driver, VG, A (Est: $1,500-$2,000) .$1,680.00

Bus, Freidag, 9", long nose, NPDW, VG, A (Est: $300-$400)...$440.00

Bus, Hubley, 7½", resembles stretch limo, bl w/silver-pnt fenders & bumpers, WRT, P, A (Est: $50-$100) $85.00

Bus, Kenton, 1936, 3½", take-apart body, bright yel, WRT, EX, A (Est: $300-$400)..$220.00

Bus, Kenton, 1936, 4½", take-apart body, bright yel, WRT, EX, A (Est: $800-$1,000)..$330.00

Bus, Kenton, 1936, 7", take-apart body, bright yel, WRT w/red hubs, EX, A (Est: $2,500-$3,500) $2,750.00

Bus, see also Double-Decker, Greyhound, Interurban, etc.

Bus, Skoglund & Olson, 11", long nose, NP grille, WRT, VG, A (Est: $300-$400) $550.00

Cement Mixer Wagon, Kenton, 14", MSW, 1 horse, w/driver, EX, A (Est: $600-$800)..................................$1,870.00

Central-Garage Wrecker, Skoglund & Olson, 12" overall, WRT, VG+, A (Est: $600-$800) $1,750.00

Champion Panel Delivery Truck, Champion, 8", WRT, EX, A (Est: $400-$600)..$440.00

Champion Police Motorcycle, Champion, 7½", NPSW, cast driver, G+, A (Est: $200-$300) $275.00

Champion Police Motorcycle, Champion, 7½", WRT, cast driver, NM, A (Est: $250-$350) $920.00

Champion Police Motorcycle, Champion, 7½", WRT, cast driver, VG, A (Est: $300-$500) $385.00

Checker Cab, Arcade, 9", Checker emb above windshield, orange & blk, NP trim, WRT, driver, EX+, A (Est: $60,000-$75,000) $20,350.00

Chevy Ambulance, Arcade, 1930s, 3½", wht w/blk fenders, NP grille & bumper, VG, A (Est: $250-$350) $355.00

Chevy Coupe, Skoglund & Olson, 8", NP grille & headlights, rear spare, VG+, A (Est: $400-$500)....................$650.00

Chevy Coupe (1925), Arcade, 6½", MSW, rear spare, NP driver, EX+, A (Est: $700-$900) $880.00

Chevy Coupe (1928), Arcade, 8", NPDW, rear spare, G, A (Est: $500-$750) $550.00

Chevy Coupe (1928), Arcade, 8", WRT, rear spare, NM, A (Est: $1,200-$1,400)..$2,530.00

Chevy Coupe (1934), Arcade, 4", open rumble seat, WRT, VG, A (Est: $250-$300)..$275.00

Chevy Panel Van (1934), Arcade, 3½", NP grille (extends up hood), bumper & headlights, EX+, A (Est: $250-$350)..$465.00

Chevy Roadster, Arcade, 6½", MSW, rear spare, NP driver, EX, A (Est: $1,000-$1,200) $1,650.00

Chevy Sedan (1920s), Arcade, 6¾", WRT w/spoke wheels, gold side stripe, EX+, A (Est: $800-$1,000) $2,200.00

Chevy Sedan (1920s), Arcade, 8", NPDW, EX, A (Est: $1,600-$1,800) $2,700.00

Chevy Sedan (1920s), Arcade, 8", NPDW, G, A (Est: $850-$1,050)..$900.00

Chevy Stake Truck (1924), Arcade, 9", doorless cab, WRT w/spoke wheels, NP driver, VG, A (Est: $1,200-$1,500)..$1,100.00

Chevy Stake Truck (1934), Arcade, 3½", take-apart body, NP grille, lights & bumper, WRT, EX, A (Est: $200-$300)...........$330.00

Chevy Touring Car (1924), Arcade, 6½", MSW, NP driver, EX, A (Est: $600-$800) $1,540.00

Chevy Wrecker, Arcade, 3½", NP grille, lights & bumper, EX, A (Est: $200-$300)......................$660.00

Chicago Motor Coach (Double-Decker Bus), Arcade, 13", rear steps, WRT, NP driver, EX, A (Est: $2,250-2,500)..$2,520.00

Chrysler Airflow Sedan, Hubley, 4½", WRT, G, A (Est: $50-$100)......................$110.00

Chrysler Airflow Sedan, Hubley, 4½", WRT, VG, A (Est: $75-$125)......................$330.00

Chrysler Airflow Sedan, Hubley, 6", WRT, G, A (Est: $75-$125)......................$170.00

Chrysler Airflow Sedan, Hubley, 6", WRT, VG+, A (Est: $200-$300)......................$350.00

Chrysler Airflow Sedan, Hubley, 8", electric lights, EX+, A (Est: $2,000.00 – $2,400.00), $2,000.00. (Photo courtesy James D. Julia, Inc.)

Chrysler Airflow Sedan, Hubley, 8", WRT, electric lights, G rstr, A (Est: $500-$800)......................$600.00

Chrysler Airflow Sedan, Hubley, 8", WRT, electric lights, VG+, A (Est: $1,200-$1,500)......................$1,540.00

Chrysler Convertible Coupe & Airstream Trailer, Sealoff, no sz given, NP trim, w/driver, EX+IB, A (Est: $400-$600) $990.00

City Ambulance (1920s), Arcade, 6", WRT, EX, A (Est: $400-$500)......................$720.00

Coal Truck, Dent, 6½", open slanted bed w/Coal emb on sides, NPDW, NP driver & shovel, G+, A (Est: $200-$400) ..$260.00

Coal Truck, Hubley, 15", open seat, coal bed w/slanted back, PMSW, w/driver, VG, A (Est: $400-$500) $770.00

Coal Truck, Kenton, 8", Coal emb on bed w/slanted back, NP grille & bumper, WRT, G, A (Est: $600-$800) $600.00

Coal Truck, Kenton, 10½", dump bed w/slanted back, WRT, w.driver, VG, A (Est: $1,200-$1,500)....................$1,100.00

Coal Wagon (Motorized), Kenton, 8", open bench seat w/center-steering, MDW, w/driver, EX, A (Est: $500-$600) $400.00

Coast to Coast Stake Truck, AC Williams, 10", NPSW, 6-wheeled, rpt, A (Est: $250-$300)......................$275.00

Coupe, AC Williams, 5", low top w/'2-pane' windshield, long nose & short back, WRT, Fair, A (Est: $400-$600) ..$220.00

Coupe, AC Williams, 5", take-apart body, extended front bumper, plain rear end, WRT, EX, A (Est: $250-$350) $440.00

Coupe, AC Williams, 7½", NP rumble seat, extended front bumper, cast side spare, WRT, EX+, A (Est: $700-$900) $550.00

Coupe, Freidag, 5½", 1925 model w/slightly slanted windshield frame, MSW, NP driver, VG, A (Est: $300-$400) ...$465.00

Coupe, Hubley, 6", take-apart body, WRT, w/spare, NP grille, VG, A (Est: $250-$350)......................$275.00

Coupe, Hubley, 6½", 1920s model w/straight windshield frame, rear spare, NPDW, cast driver, EX, A (Est: $500-$600) $715.00

Coupe, Hubley, 9", NPDW, rear spare, w/driver, G+, A (Est: $250-$350)......................$650.00

Coupe, Kenton, 6½", slanted windshield frame, rear spare, NPDW, NP driver, EX, A (Est: $400-$600)..............$715.00

Coupe, Kenton, 8", straight windshield frame w/visor, rear spare, MDW, NP driver, EX, A (Est: $2,000-$3,000).......$1,750.00

Coupe, Kenton, 9½", slanted windshield frame, rare spare, MDW, NP driver, VG, A (Est, $1,200-$1,500)....$1,200.00

Coupe, Kenton, 10½", straight windshield frame w/visor, rear spare, w/driver, VG, A (Est: $3,000-$3,500) $3,575.00

Coupe, unknown mfg, 8½", sleek styling w/V-shaped bumper, low top, rear spare, WRT, VG, A ($1,750-$2,250).......$2,090.00

Coupe Pulling House Trailer, Kenton, 9" overall, take-apart body w/type-III NP grille, WRT, VG, A (Est: $1,000-$1,500)......................$660.00

Crash Car, Hubley, 6½", WRT w/spokes, cast police figure, VG, A (Est: $400-$600)......................$355.00

Crash Car, Hubley, 11½", Indian decal, BRT w/spokes, police figure, NM, A (Est: $3,000-$4,000)......................$6,325.00

Crash Car, Hubley, 11½", Indian decal, BRT, VG, A (Est: $2,000-$2,500)......................$3,850.00

Delivery Panel Truck, Freidag, 7½", NPSW, w/driver, older rstr, A (Est: $400-$600) $1,020.00

Delivery Van, Arcade, 8½", side spares, NPDW, NP driver, VG+, A (Est: $3,000-$4,000)......................$3,080.00

Delivery Van, Arcade, 8½", side spares, NPDW, NP driver, Wyman's stenciled on sides, EX, A (Est: $3,000-$4,500) $4,125.00

Dodge Coupe (1922), Arcade, 9", MDW, w/driver, EX+, A (Est: $1,500-$1,750)......................$3,850.00

Dodge Coupe (1922), Arcade, 9", MSW, w/driver, Fair, A (Est: $600-$900) $935.00

Dodge Coupe (1934), Champion, 7", NP grille, rear spare, WRT, EX, A (Est: $2,000-$3,000)......................$935.00

Double-Decker Bus, see also Chicago Motor Coach, Yellow Coach, etc.

Double-Decker Bus, Arcade, 8", long nose, rear curved steps, NM, A (Est: $800-$1,000)......................$1,725.00

Double-Decker Bus, Arcade, 8", long nose, rear curved steps, VG, A (Est: $300-$400)......................$715.00

Double-Decker Bus, Arcade, 8", streamline model, rear curved steps, cast driver, 3 passengers, EX+, A (Est: $400-$600) $660.00

Double-Decker Bus, Arcade, 8", streamline model, rear straight steps, BRT, 2 NP passengers, NM, A (Est: $500-$600)...........$920.00

Double-Decker Bus, Arcade, 10", WRT, red & gr, VG+, A (Est: $700-$900) $770.00

Double-Decker Bus, Freidag, 9", long nose, rear curved steps, EX, A (Est: $1,500-$2,000)......................$1,980.00

Double-Decker Bus, Freidag, 9", long nose, rear curved steps, G, A (Est: $350-$450)......................$440.00

Double-Decker Bus, Kenton, 6½", long nose, rear straight steps, no passengers, VG+, A (Est: $400-$500)................$600.00

Double-Decker Bus, Kenton, 7½", long nose, rear straight steps, w/3 passengers, VG+, A (Est: $400-$500)..............$650.00

Double-Decker Bus, Kenton, 10", long nose, rear curved steps, EX, A (Est: $600-$800)................................$465.00

Double-Decker Bus, Kenton, 12", long nose, rear straight steps, w/3 passengers, G+, A (Est: $500-$600)..................$825.00

Dray Truck, Kenton, 9", open seat, stake bed, PMSW, G, A (Est: $400-$500)..$600.00

Dump Truck, AC Williams, 8", 1920s cab w/visor, bed w/slanted back, shallow sides, WRT, VG+, A (Est: $150-$200)..$250.00

Dump Truck, Freidag, 8", doorless, w/dumping action, MSW, G, A (Est: $450-$650)..$880.00

Dump Truck, Kilgore, 5½", flat-top cab w/bottom of grille curving outward, WRT, VG, A (Est: $300-$400)...........$220.00

Dump Truck, Skoglund & Olson, 10½", early model w/flat rood & visor, low-sided bed, WRT, rpt, A (Est: $200-$300)..$260.00

Elgin Street Sweeper, Hubley, 8½", VG+, A (Est: $3,500.00 – $4,000.00), $5,050.00. (Photo courtesy James D. Julia. Inc.)

Express Stake Truck, Kilgore, 5½", flat-top cab w/bottom of grille curving outward, WRT, NM, A (Est: $400-$600)..$1,100.00

Express Truck, see also Mack Express Truck

Fageol Safety Coach, Arcade, 8", NPDW, VG, A (Est: $250-$350)..$230.00

Fageol Safety Coach, Arcade, 12", MDW, NP driver, G, A (Est: $300-$500)..$165.00

Faegol Safety Coach, Arcade, 12", WRT, NP driver, EX+, A (Est: $700-$900)..$1,870.00

Flowers Delivery Cycle, Hubley, 4½", 3-wheeled, WRT, cast driver, VG, A (Est: $600-$800)................................$2,090.00

Ford Anthony Dump Truck, Arcade, 8½", open seat, NPWS, EX, A (Est: $1,200-$1,500)........................$990.00

Ford Anthony Dump Truck, Arcade, 8½", open seat, NPSW, VG, A (Est: $750-$950)................................$850.00

Ford Brewster Coupe (1934), Hubley, 4", NP grille, rear spare, WRT, EX+, A (Est: $300-$400)..............................$410.00

Ford Brewster Roadster (1934), Hubley, 4", NP grille, bumper & headlights, rear spare, WRT, EX+, A (Est: $300-$400)...$500.00

Ford Brewster Sedan (1934), Hubley, 4", NP grille, bumper & headlights, rear spare, WRT, EX, A (Est: $300-$400).........$245.00

Ford Brewster Town Car (1934), Hubley, 4", NP grille, bumper & headlights, rear spare, WRT, EX+, A (Est: $350-$450).$330.00

Ford Coupe (1935), AC Williams, 4", take-apart body, red & blk w/NP grille & headlights, WRT, EX+, A (Est: $700-$900)..$825.00

Ford Coupe (1935), AC Williams, 6½", take-apart body w/NP grille, WRT, EX, A (Est: $500-$600)......................$935.00

Ford Coupe (1936), AC Williams, 4½", take-apart body, red w/NP trim & running boards, EX, A (Est: $500-$600).........$660.00

Ford Dump Truck, Arcade, 1930s, 5½", dump bed w/slanted back, BRT, NM, A (Est: $300-$400)......................$190.00

Ford Fordor Sedan (1935), Arcade, 4½", NP grille, bumper & headlights, rear spare, WRT, EX, A (Est: $400-$600)..$770.00

Ford Model A Coupe, Arcade, 5", rumble seat, NPSW, G, A (Est: $150-$250)..$275.00

Ford Model A Coupe, Arcade, 5", rumble seat, NPSW, VG, A (Est: $150-$250)..$500.00

Ford Model A Dump Truck, Arcade, 6", NPSW, VG, A (Est: $175-$225)..$220.00

Ford Model A Sedan, Arcade, 6½", NPSW, NP driver, EX, A ($1,000-$1,200)..$2,200.00

Ford Model A Sedan, Kilgore, 3", NPDW, cast driver & passengers at windows, EX+, A (Est: $150-$200).............$165.00

Ford Model A Wrecker, Arcade, 8", w/Weaver boom, NPSW, G, A (Est: $200-$300)..$230.00

Ford Model T Coupe, AC Williams, 5", cast curtains in rear window, MSW, VG, A (Est: $300-$400).................$165.00

Ford Model T Coupe, Arcade, 6½", higher trunk, PMSW, no driver, Fair, A (Est: $50-$150).............................$185.00

Ford Model T Coupe, Arcade, 7", lower trunk, PMSW, w/driver, G, A (Est: $200-$300)......................................$440.00

Ford Model T Coupe, Dent, 6", blk w/gold side stripe, MSW, cast driver, VG, A (Est: $400-$600)........................$410.00

Ford Model T Coupe, Kilgore, 6½", no visor, opening rumble seat, gray color, MSW, driver, G, A (Est: $400-$500).........$355.00

Ford Model T Coupe, Kilgore, 6½", w/visor, cast rear, NPSW, 2 spring-mounted figures, EX+, A (Est: $500-$700)...$990.00

Ford Model T Dump Truck, Dent, 8", open bench seat, slanted dump bed w/lever, MSW, w/driver, G, A (Est: $1,200-$1,500)..$825.00

Ford Model T Pickup Truck, Arcade, 8½", NPSW, NP driver, G, A (Est: $150-$250)..$715.00

Ford Model T Sedan, Arcade, 5", center door, blk w/gold stripe, NPSW, w/driver, EX, A (Est: $250-$350)...............$355.00

Ford Model T Sedan, Arcade, 6½", center door, blk w/gold stripe, PMSW, no driver, G, A (Est: $200-$300).....$440.00

Ford Model T Sedan, Arcade, 6½", center door, blk w/gold stripe, PMSW, NP driver, EX+ (Est: $800-$1,000)..........$1,045.00

Ford Model T Sedan, Arcade, 6½", center door, blk w/gold stripe, PMSW, NP driver, NMIB, A (Est: $1,500-$2,000)..$2,475.00

Ford Model T Sedan, Arcade, 6½", center door, rare orange w/gold stripe, NPSW, NP driver, EX, A (Est: $700-$900)..$1,870.00

Ford Model T Sedan, Dent, 6", blk w/blk-pnt SW, blk-pnt driver, G, A (Est: $600-$900)......................................$250.00

Ford Model T Stake Truck, Arcade, 7½", NPSW, no driver, EX+, A (Est: $250-$350)......................................$440.00

Ford Model T Stake Truck, Arcade, 7½", NPSW, NP driver, VG, A (Est: $100-$200)..$300.00

Ford Model T Stake Truck, Arcade, 9", WRT, rstr, A (Est: $150-$250)..$330.00

Ford Model T Stake Truck, see also Anchor Truck Co Stake Truck

Ford Model T Touring Car, Arcade, 6½", 'cloth' top up, MSW, NP driver, 6½", EX, A (Est: $250-$350) $275.00

Ford Model T 1-Ton Flatbed Truck w/Bell Bank, Arcade, no sz, Ford dealer ad on rooftop, Fair, A (Est: $1,500-$2,000) $1,100.00

Ford Panel Truck (1936), AC Williams, 4", take-apart body w/NP trim, WRT, VG, A (Est: $600-$700) $825.00

Ford Roadster (1936), AC Williams, 4", take-apart body, WRT, EX, A (Est: $600-$700)..........................$880.00

Ford Sedan (Century of Progress 1933), Arcade, 6", orange w/blk top, WRT, G, A (Est: $400-$500)..................$385.00

Ford Sedan (1936), AC Williams, 4½", take-apart body, EX, A (Est: $900.00 – $1,200.00), $1,045.00. (Photo courtesy Bertoia Auctions)

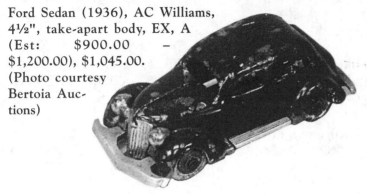

Ford Sedan Pulling The Covered Wagon House Trailer, Arcade, 12", NP grille, WRT, NM, A (Est: $6,000-$7,000) $9,350.00

Ford Stake Truck (1935), Arcade, 4½", NP grille, lights & bumper, WRT, EX, A (Est: $600-$800) $410.00

Ford Weaver Wrecker, Arcade, 7", NPSW, VG (Est: $400-$600) $410.00

Ford Weaver Wrecker, Arcade, 11½", red w/gr boom, MSW w/WRT, NP driver, EX+ (Fair box), A (Est: $1,500-$2,000) $3,850.00

Ford Wrecker (1933), Arcade, 6½", cast boom, NP front, WRT, VG+ ($700-$900) $400.00

Fruehauf Co Semi Tank Truck, AC Williams, 7", emb Gasoline...Motor Oil..., 6-wheeled, NPSW, G, A (Est: $200-$300)....................$275.00

Gasoline Tank Truck, Kenton, 4", take-apart model w/type II NP grille, WRT, EX+, A (Est: $1,000-$1,200) $1,045.00

Golden Arrow Racer, Hubley, 8½", tail-fin, articulated flames on hood, NPDW, w/driver, EX, A (Est: $800-$1,200) $2,090.00

Golden Racer, see Racer

Graham Coupe (1933), Kilgore, 6½", take-apart body w/NP finish, WRT, EX+, A (Est: $2,500-$3,500)...............$1,100.00

Graham Dump Truck (1933), Kilgore, 6½", take-apart body w/NP grille, headlights & bumper, VG, A (Est: $2,000-$2,500) $1,045.00

Graham Roadster (1933), Kilgore, 7", take-apart body, cast open rumble seat, NP trim, EX, A (Est: $2,750-$3,000) ..$1,980.00

Graham Sedan (1933), Kilgore, 7", take-apart body w/NP grille, headlights & bumper, WRT, VG, A (Est: $2,000-$2,500) $1,320.00

Graham Stake Truck (1933), Kilgore, 6½", take-apart body, NP grille, lights & bumper, WRT, EX, A (Est: $2,000-$2,500) $1,100.00

Graham Wrecker (1933), Kilgore, 6½", take-apart body, NP grille, headlights & bumper, WRT, VG, A (Est: $2,000-$2,500) $715.00

Great Lakes Exposition, see Greyhound Lines

Greyhound Lines Bus, Arcade, 9", NP front & back, WRT, G, A (Est: $450-$650)....................$350.00

Greyhound Lines Century of Progress Chicago 1933 GMC Tandem Bus, Arcade, 14", WRT, VG, A (Est: $500-$600)........$220.00

Greyhound Lines Century of Progress Chicago 1934 Tandem Bus, Arcade, 5½", WRT, VG, A (Est: $250-$350)..$300.00

Greyhound Lines Century of Progress Chicago 1935 Bus, Arcade, 14", WRT, VG, A (Est: $400-$600)...........$410.00

Greyhound Lines GMC Bus, Arcade, 7½", red long-nose w/gold striping, WRT, VG, A (Est: $300-$400) $220.00

Greyhound Lines GMC Tandem Bus, Arcade, 10½", G, A (Est: $150-$200) $185.00

Greyhound Lines Great Lakes Exposition 1935 Tandem Bus, Arcade, 11", WRT, G+, A (Est: $400-$500) $410.00

Greyhound Lines Great Lakes Exposition 1937 Tandem Bus, Arcade, 11", WRT, G, A (Est: $350-$450)..............$385.00

Greyhound Lines New York World's Fair Bus, Arcade, 7", BRT, EX, A (Est: $200-$300)....................$220.00

Greyhound Lines New York World's Fair Bus, Arcade, 8", BRT, EX+, A (Est: $300-$400) $330.00

Greyhound Lines New York World's Fair Bus, Arcade, 10½", bl w/wht roof, EX+, A (Est: $400-$500) $520.00

Greyhound Lines San Francisco-1939-New York Bus, Arcade, 9", NP front, bl & wht, BRT, EX, A (Est: $900-$1,250)..$715.00

Greyhound Lines 1937 Great Eastern Bus System, Arcade, 7½", red w/blk stripe, WRT, EX+, A (Est: $800-$1,000) $3,300.00

Harley-Davidson Civilian Hillclimber Motorcycle, Hubley, 8½", BRT (spokes), w/driver, VG, A (Est: $6,500-$7,500).$8,800.00

Harley-Davidson Civilian Motorcycle, Hubley, 6", EX, A (Est: $400-$600) $650.00

Harley-Davidson Civilian Motorcycle, Hubley, 6", VG, A (Est: $200-$300) $375.00

Harley-Davidson Civilian Motorcycle w/Sidecar, Hubley, 6½", EX, A (Est: $600-$800)....................$1,045.00

Harley-Davidson Civilian Motorcycle w/Sidecar, Hubley, 9", BRT (spokes), driver & passenger, VG+, A (Est: $6,500-$7,500) $7,150.00

Harley-Davidson Jr Police Motorcycle, Hubley, 5½", NPSW, cast driver, EX+, A (Est: $300-$400) $600.00

Harley-Davidson Police Motorcycle, Hubley, 5½", WRT (spokes), cast driver, EX, A (Est: $250-$350)..........$330.00

Harley-Davidson Police Motorcycle, Hubley, 9", BRT (spokes), w/driver, G, A (Est: $250-$350)....................$465.00

Harley-Davidson Police Motorcycle w/Sidecar, Hubley, 5", WRT, integral driver, Fair, A (Est: $100-$150) $260.00

Harley-Davison Civilian Motorcycle w/Sidecar, Hubley, 6", BRT (spokes), integral driver, Fair, A (Est: $150-$200) ..$385.00

Hathaway's Bakery Truck, see International Delivery Van

Hillclimber Motorcycle w/#2 Rider, Hubley, 7", WRT, cast driver, VG, A (Est: $800-$1,200) $935.00

Hubley Delivery Van, Hubley, 4½", gr, NPDW, Hubley emb on side panels, EX, A (Est: $225-$275) $715.00

Hupmobile Coupe, Kenton, 7½", take-apart body w/NP grille, WRT, rpt, A (Est: $2,000-$2,500) $3,025.00

Hupmobile Sedan, Kenton, 7½", take-apart body w/NP grille, WRT, VG, A (Est: $2,000-$3,000) $4,125.00

Ice Truck, see also Studebaker Ice Truck

Ice Truck, Arcade, 7", snub nose, Ice emb on sides of railed bed, NP grille, open back, w/ice, VG, A(Est: $250-$350) $300.00

Ice Truck, Kenton, 7 ", long nose, Ice emb on sides of railed bed, NP grille, open back, WRT, EX, A (Est: $400-$600) ..$935.00

Indian Civilian Motorcycle, Hubley, 9", 4-cylinder, BRT w/spokes, w/driver, G, A (Est: $300-$400) $935.00

Indian Civilian Motorcycle, Hubley, 9", EX, A (Est: $3,000.00 – $3,500.00), $8,250.00. (Photo courtesy Bertoia Auctions)

Indian Crash Car, see Crash Car

Indian Police Motorcycle, Hubley, 8½", orig front wheel clicker, BRT (spokes), w/driver, EX, A (Est: $400-$500).....$990.00

Indian Police Motorcycle, Hubley, 9½", 4-cylinder, BRT (spokes), w/driver, Fair+, A (Est: $400-$600)..........$500.00

Indian Police Motorcycle w/Sidecar, Hubley, 9", BRT, w/driver, w/orig pull string, VG, A (Est: $1,000-$1,200) $1,725.00

Indian Tricycle w/Stake Bed, Hubley, 6", PMSW, cast driver, G+, A (Est: $150-$200) $600.00

Ingersoll Rand Truck, see Mack Ingersoll Rand Truck

Interchangable Set, AC Willimas, 1930s, 1 frame w/4 different body styles, G+IB, A (Est: $600-$800) $800.00

International Delivery Van (1932), Arcade, 9½", Hathaway's, rear door opens, WRT, driver, EX+, A (Est: $2,000-$2,500)..$1,980.00

International Delivery Van (1936), Arcade, 9½", WRT, no driver, VG, A (Est: $1,200-$1,500).........................$3,630.00

International Dump Truck, Arcade, 9", cabover, lever-op dump bed w/open back, BRT, Fair, A (Est: $250-$300).....$350.00

International Dump Truck, Arcade, 10", long tapered nose, NP grille & extended bumper, no driver, G+, A (Est: $550-$750) $1,300.00

International Dump Truck, Arcade, 10½", early model w/NP winch bar & driver, BRT, G, A (Est: $300-$400)....$275.00

International Dump Truck, Arcade, 10½", low dump bed, WRT w/rear duals, NP driver, VG, A (Est: $1,500-$1,750) ..$1,200.00

International Pickup Truck, Arcade, 9", BRT, G, A (Est: $500-$600)..$220.00

International Red Baby Dump Truck, 11", nickel-plated disc wheels, EX+, A (Est: $800.00 – $1,000.00), $1,100.00. (Photo courtesy Bertoia Auctions)

International Red Baby Dump Truck, Arcade, 11", WRT, w/driver, G, A (Est: $200-$400).......................................$385.00

International Red Baby Wrecker, Arcade, 11", NPDW, EX+, A (Est: $500-$600)...$1,840.00

International Stake Truck (1920s), Arcade, 11", WRT, Fair, A (Est: $200-$300)...$440.00

International Stake Truck (1930s), Arcade, 11½", NP grille & bumper, WRT, G, A (Est: $450-$650)..................$1,320.00

International Stake Truck (1941), Arcade, 11½", BRT, overpnt, A (Est: $400-$600)..$300.00

International Yellow Baby Dump Truck, Arcade, 11", PMDW, w/driver, EX, A (Est: $1,000-$1,200) $2,475.00

Interurban Bus, Kenton, 11", bl w/blk front fenders, PMDW, VG, A (Est: $700-$900) $1,430.00

LaSalle Coupe (1934), Dent, 4", take-apart body w/NP grille, WRT, VG, A (Est: $400-$600) $465.00

LaSalle Panel Truck (1935), Dent, 4", take-apart body w/NP grille, WRT, EX, A $715.00

LaSalle Pickup (1935), Dent, 4½", take-apart body w/NP grille, WRT, EX, A (Est: $400-$600) $275.00

LaSalle Roadster (1934), Dent, 4", take-apart body w/NP grille, WRT, EX, A (Est: $400-$500) $600.00

LaSalle Sedan (1934), Dent, 4", take-apart body w/NP grille, WRT, NM, A (Est: $700-$900) $715.00

LaSalle Wrecker (1935), Dent, 4½", take-apart body w/NP grille, WRT, VG, A (Est: $600-$700)...................$1,200.00

Lincoln Zephyr, Skoglund & Olson, 9½", NP, skirted rear fenders, WRT, VG+, A (Est: $300-$400) $230.00

Lincoln Zephyr (1939), Hubley, 5", silver trim, WRT, hitchless version, EX+, A (Est: $300-$400)............................$385.00

Lincoln Zephyr Pulling House Trailer, Hubley, 9½" overall, WRT, EX, A (Est: $400-$600) $220.00

Lincoln Zephyr Yellow Cab, see Yellow Cab

Lionelton Transit Co Double-Decker Bus, Arcade, 8", rear spiral steps, NP driver, WRT, EX+, A (Est: $1,500-$1,750)...........$1,200.00

Livestock Stake Truck, Kilgore, 8", NPSW, VG+, A (Est: $250-$350)...$500.00

Lincoln Zephyr Pulling House Trailer, Hubley, 13½" overall, EX+, A (Est: $1,000.00 – $1,200.00), $2,475.00. (Photo courtesy Bertoia Auctions)

Log Truck, Skoglund & Olson, 17", 1920s truck w/open bed holding 3 logs, WRT, 6-wheeled, VG+, A (Est: $400-$500) ..$1,320.00

Lubrite Gasoline Tanker Truck, Arcade, 13", MSW, NP driver, G, A (Est: $750-$950) $1,430.00

Mack Coal Truck, Arcade, 10", dump bed w/removable divider, BRT w/rear duals, NP driver, VG, A (Est: $500-$600)...........$700.00

Mack Coal Truck, Arcade, 10", dump bed w/removable divider, BRT w/rear duals, NP driver, EX+, A (Est: $1,000-$1,200)...................................$1,320.00

Mack Dump Truck, Arcade, 7½", side dump, WRT w/rear dualls, NP driver, NM, A (Est: $2,250-$2,750) $4,675.00

Mack Dump Truck, Arcade, 9", side dump action, VG, A (Est: $2,500.00 – $3,500.00), $5,225.00. (Photo courtesy Bertoia Auctions)

Mack Dump Truck, Arcade, 9", side dump, WRT, rear duals, w/driver, G, A (Est: $1,500-$2,000) $1,760.00

Mack Dump Truck, Arcade, 12", MSW, NP T-bar, WRT w/rear duals, EX, A (Est: $2,000-$2,500) $2,070.00

Mack Dump Truck, Champion, 8", bed w/slanted back, WRT, w/driver, VG+, A (Est: $150-$250) $120.00

Mack Dump Truck, Dent, 12", MSW, Fair+, A (Est: $150-$250) $600.00

Mack Dump Truck, Dent, 15", MSW, no driver, EX, A (Est: $1,000-$1,200) $1,300.00

Mack Dump Truck, Hubley, 7", open windshield, NPSW, cast driver, NM, A (Est: $600-$800) $2,070.00

Mack Dump Truck, Hubley, 7½", w/windshield frame, WRT, cast driver, NM, A (Est: $2,250-$2,750) $4,675.00

Mack Dump Truck, Hubley, 9", NPSW, cast driver, NMIB (No 743 on box label), A (Est: $1,500-$2,000)...........$4,300.00

Mack Dump Truck, Hubley, 11", opening tailgate, G, A (Est: $500-$600) $520.00

Mack Express Truck, Dent, 4½", roof over stake bed, MDW, cast driver, VG, A (Est: $200-$300) $245.00

Mack Gasoline Tank Truck, Arcade, 12", gr w/gr rubber tires, NP driver, G+, A (Est: $800-$1,000).....................$880.00

Mack Hoist Truck, Arcade, 11", WRT, w/driver, VG, A (Est: $2,500-$3,500) $2,530.00

Mack Ice Truck, Arcade, 8½", NPSW, NP driver, w/tongs & block of ice, VG, A (Est: $800-$1,000) $880.00

Mack Ice Truck, Arcade, 10½", NPSW, NP driver, w/tongs & 4 blocks of ice, G+, A (Est: $1,750-$2,250)...........$1,760.00

Mack Ingersoll Rand Truck, Hubley, 8", MSW, cast driver, EX, A (Est: $5,000-$6,000) $10,925.00

Mack Junior Supply Co. Express Truck, Dent, 15", G, A (Est: $4,000.00 – $6,000.00), $4,400.00. (Photo courtesy Bertoia Auctions)

Mack Milk Stake Truck, Arcade, 11", WRT w/rear duals, NP driver, 4 milk cans, EX, A (Est: $3,000-$4,000)...$4,400.00

Mack Open Bed Truck, Champion, 8", WRT (emb Champion), rpr/rpt, A (Est: $200-$300) $110.00

Mack Panama Steam Shovel Truck, see Construction

Mack Stake Truck, AC Williams, 7", MSW, old rpt, A (Est: $50-$150)..$175.00

Mack Stake Truck, Champion, 7", NPSW, VG, A (Est: $200-$250)..$245.00

Mack Stake Truck, Dent, 15½", chain around stakes on flatbed, MSW, w/driver, EX, A (Est: $2,500-$3,500) $6,240.00

Mack Stake Truck, Hubley, 5½", WRT, cast driver, VG, A (Est: $300-$400) $100.00

Mack Tank Truck, Hubley, 4½", MSW, G (Est: $50-$150) $130.00

Mack Tank Truck, Hubley, 6½", BRT, cast driver, Fair, A (Est: $50-$100)...$175.00

Mack Tank Truck, Hubley, 11", MSW, NP driver, orig pull string, EX+, A (Est: $1,500-$2,000) $2,875.00

Mack Tank Truck, 13", PS tank body, WRT w/rear duals, NP driver, VG, A (Est: $2,000-$2,250)..........................$1,100.00

Mack Tank Truck (American Gasoline), Arcade, 13", 'Powerful As It's Name,' WRT, NP driver, VG, A (Est: $2,500-$3,000)..$3,025.00

Mack Tank Truck (American Oil Co), Dent, 11", WRT, cast driver, made in 1960s from orig parts, A (Est: $300-$400) $550.00

Mack Tank Truck (American Oil Co), Dent, 15", MSW, w/driver, made in 1960s from orig parts, EX, A (Est: $600-$800)..$1,100.00

Mack Tank Truck (Gasoline), Arcade, 13", NPSW, NP driver, EX+, A (Est: $1,200-$1,500) $2,750.00

Mack Tank Truck (Gasoline), Arcade, 13", NPSW, NP driver, G, A (Est: $400-$600)..............................$660.00

Mack Tank Truck (Webaco Oil Co), Arcade, 13", NPSW, rear duals, NP driver, VG, A (Est: $2,500-$3,000)......$2,750.00

Mack Wrecker, Arcade, 10½", Weaver boom, MSW, NP driver, EX, A (Est: $2,000-$2,500)...........................$2,200.00

Mack Wrecker, Champion, 9", cast wench, NP barrel & lever, NPDW, VG, A (Est: $250-$350) $250.00

Merchants Delivery Truck, Kenton, 6", MSW, cast driver, VG, A (Est: $600-$800)....................................$800.00

Motor Express Semi, Hubley, 9", NM, A (Est: $1,200.00 – $1,500.00), $880.00. (Photo courtesy Bertoia Auctions)

Moving Van, see also USCO Moving Van

Moving Van (1936), Kenton, 8" overall, take-apart truck cab w/type-I NP grille pulling van, WRT, VG, A (Est: $700-$900) $1,320.00

Nash Coupe (1934), Arcade, 4½", NP grille, bumper & headlights, WRT, VG, A (Est: $300-$400) $330.00

Nash Lafayette Open Roadster (1936), Kenton, 7", NP grille & frame, WRT, VG, A (Est: $500-$700) $825.00

Nash Lafayette Sedan Pulling Farm Trailer, Kenton, 13", NP grille, bumpers & runners, WRT, VG+, A (Est: $1,000-$1,200) $3,300.00

Nash Sedan (1934), Arcade, 4½", NP grille, bumper & headlights, WRT, EX, A (Est: $700-$900) $385.00

Nash Stake Truck, Arcade, 4½", take-apart body, NP grille, lights & bumper, WRT, VG, A (Est: $300-$400) $245.00

National Trailways (Santa Fe Trailways) Bus, Arcade, 9", red & wht w/NP grille, WRT, NM, A (Est: $1,500-$2,000) $2,475.00

National Trailways Bus, Arcade, 9", red & wht w/NP grille & headlights, WRT, EX, A (Est: $700-$1,000)............$990.00

New York World's Fair Bus, see Greyhound Lines

Nash Lafayette Coupe and House Trailer, Kenton, 13½", NM, A (Est: $7,500.00 – $10,000.00), $9,900.00. (Photo courtesy Bertoia Auctions)

New York World's Fair Train, Arcade, 7", motor car w/canopied passenger car, BRT, w/NP driver, VG+IB, A (Est: $300-$400)..$400.00

Nite Coach, Kenton, 6½", NPDW, G, A (Est: $200-$400) ..$465.00

Nu-Car Transport, Hubley, 16", w/4 autos, WRT, VG+, A (Est: $800-$1,000) $1,045.00

Oil/Gas Tank Truck, Kenton, 8", early model w/sq cab, MDW, G+, A (Est: $200-$300) $600.00

Oldsmobile Coupe, Vindex, 1929, 8", NPSW, no driver, VG, A (Est: $4,000-$5,000)............................$3,575.00

Packard Club Sedan, Vindex, #53, 1929, 9½", NPSW, no driver, EX+IB, A (Est: $20,000-$25,000) $19,800.00

Packard Coupe, AC Williams, 4", take-apart body w/NP grille, 'shovel nose' hood, WRT, G, A (Est: $175-$250) ...$245.00

Packard Coupe (1933), AC Williams, 7", take-apart body w/NP grille, 'shovel nose,' hood, WRT, EX, A (Est: $450-$650) $550.00

Packard Roadster, AC Williams, 4½", take-apart body, WRT, EX+, A (Est: $275-$350) $520.00

Packard Sedan, AC Williams, 4", take-apart body w/NP grille, 'shovel nose' hood, WRT, G, A (Est: $175-$250) ...$165.00

Packard Sedan (1933), AC Williams, 7", take-apart body w/NP grille, 'shovel nose' hood, WRT, VG, A (Est: $500-$600)..$600.00

Packard Sedan (1936), AC Williams, 7", WRT, EX, A (Est: $600-$800) $520.00

Packard Stake Truck, AC Williams, 4", take-apart body w/NP grille, 'shovel nose' hood, WRT, VG, A (Est: $300-$400)..$385.00

Packard Straight-8 Sedan, Hubley, 11, EX, A (Est: $15,000.00 – $20,000.00), $20,700.00. (Photo courtesy James D. Julia, Inc.)

Packard Stake Truck (1933), AC Williams, 7", take-apart body w/NP grille, 'shovel-nose,' WRT, VG, A (Est: $400-$600) $550.00

Panama Steam Shovel Truck, see Construction

Parcel Express Panel Truck, Dent, 8", NPDW, side spare, w/driver, EX+, A (Est: $5,000-$6,000) $7,320.00

Parcel Post Delivery Cycle, Hubley, 9½", Harley-Davidson decal on gas tank, w/driver, EX, A (Est: $1,800-$2,000) ..$2,800.00

Patrol Truck, Hubley, 12", open, gr, gold trim, NPSW, Patrol & eagle emb on sides, 4 figures, G, A (Est: $200-$300) ..$400.00

Patrol Truck, Kenton, 9½", bl, Patrol emb on sides of railed bed w/benches, MDW w/red hubs, EX, A (Est: $800-$1,000) $1,760.00

PDQ Delivery Cycle, Vindex, 8½", BRT, w/driver, EX, A (Est: $2,500-$3,000) $5,775.00

Peerless Racer, Kenton, 6", MSW, cast driver, G, A (Est: $400-$500) $275.00

Peerless Racer, Kenton, 8", MSW, cast driver, extremely rare, G, A (Est: $2,500-$3,500) $1,760.00

Phaeton (1936), Kenton, 4", take-apart body w/type-II NP grille, WRT, EX+, A (Est: $600-$800) $990.00

Phaeton (1936), Kenton, 4", take-apart body w/type-III NP grille, WRT, G, A (Est: $400-$600).....................$355.00

Phaeton (1936), Kenton, 4", take-apart model w/type-I NP grille, WRT, EX, A (Est: $600-$800)....................$1,320.00

Pickup Truck, Kenton, 4", take-apart body w/type-I NP grille, WRT, EX, A (Est: $500-$600) $465.00

Pickup Truck, Kenton, 4", take-apart body w/type-II NP grille, WRT, very rare, EX+, A (Est: $600-$800)...............$550.00

Pickup Truck, Kenton, 4", take-apart body w/type-III NP grille, EX+, A (Est: $500-$700) $600.00

Pickwick Nite Coach, Kenton, 11", MDW, scarce, Fair, A (Est: $400-$600) $1,100.00

Pickwick Nite Coach, Kenton, 11", MDW, scarce, VG+, A (Est: $2,000-$3,000) $5,720.00

Pierce Arrow Coupe (1930s), AC Williams, 4", take-apart body, WRT, EX+, A (Est: $250-$350)...............................$410.00

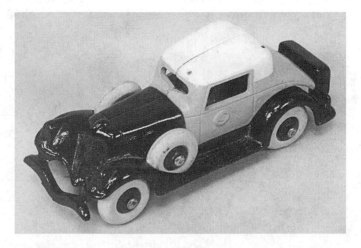

Pierce-Arrow Coupe (1930s), Hubley, 6½", take-apart body, NM, A (Est: $700.00 – $900.00), $2,475.00. (Photo courtesy Bertoia Auctions)

Pierce Arrow Silver Arrow Sedan (1935), Arcade, 7", NP grille & front bumper, WRT, EX, A (Est: $1,200-$1,500) $880.00

Pierce Arrow 'Woody' Wagon, Hubley, 5", take-apart body, WRT, EX, A (Est: $200-$300) $500.00

Plymouth Sedan, AC Williams, 6", WRT (rpl), cast spare on running board, G, A (Est: $200-$300).....................$135.00

Plymouth Sedan (1933), Arcade, 4", NP grille, bumper & headlights, WRT, EX, A (Est: $500-$700) $520.00

Plymouth Wrecker, 4½", long-nosed cab w/short bed, NP grille, lights & bumper, WRT, VG, A (Est: $300-$400)....$330.00

Police 'Patrol' Motorcycle, 6½", BRT, integral driver, G, A (Est: $100-$200) $120.00

Police Armored Motorcycle w/Sidecar, Hubley, 8½", BRT, w/driver & passenger, G, A (Est: $1,000-$1,200).........$1,320.00

Police Motorcycle, see also Champion, Harley-Davidson, Indian, etc.

Police Motorcycle, AC Williams, 7", 2-cylinder engine, WRT, cast driver, VG, A (Est: $200-$300).......................$190.00

Police Motorcycle, Champion, 7", WRT, w/driver, VG, A (Est: $350-$450) $300.00

Police Motorcycle, Hubley, 6", electric headlight, BRT w/spokes, driver, NM, A (Est: $600-$800).............................$935.00

Police Motorcycle, Hubley, 6", electric headlight, WRT w/spokes, driver, G, A (Est: $300-$400) $275.00

Police Motorcycle, Kilgore, 5", handlebars are separately cast, WRT, w/driver, EX, A (Est: $750-$1,000)............$1,045.00

Police Motorcycle w/Sidecar, Hubley, 8½", electric headlight, BRT, EX, A (Est: $1,000-$1,250) $4,125.00

Police Motorcycle w/Sidecar, Hubley, 9", Hubley decal on gas tank, BRT w/spokes, Fair+, A (Est: $250-$350)......$440.00

Pontiac (1930s) & Farm Trailer, Kenton, 8", take-apart body w/type III NP grille, WRT, VG, A (Est: $700-$900) ..$825.00

Pontiac (1930s) & House Trailer, Kenton, 9½", take-apart body w/type-III NP grille, WRT, EX, A (Est: $1,200-$1,750) $1,760.00

Pontiac (1930s) Stake Truck, Arcade, 6", NP grille & headlights, WRT, EX+, A (Est: $600-$800) $520.00

Pontiac Coupe (1930s), Kenton, 4", take-apart model w/type-I grille, WRT, EX+, A (Est: $500-$700) $1,870.00

Pontiac Roadster, Vindex, 1929, 7", opening rumble seat, rear spare, MSW, VG, A (Est: $3,500-$4,500) $1,980.00

Pontiac Sedan (1930s), Arcade, 4", NP grille, bumper & headlights, WRT, EX+, A (Est: $300-$400) $355.00

Pontiac Sedan (1930s), Arcade, 6", NP grille, bumper & headlights, BRT, G, A (Est: $200-$300).........................$200.00

Pontiac Sedan (1930s), Kenton, 4", take-apart body w/type-I NP grille, WRT, VG+, A (Est: $450-$500) $385.00

Pontiac Sedan (1930s), Kenton, 4", take-apart body w/type-II NP grille, WRT, EX, A (Est: $400-$600).................$550.00

Pontiac Stake Truck, Arcade, 6½", NP grille, WRT, VG, A (Est: $300-$400) $330.00

Pontiac Wrecker (1930s), Kenton, 4½", NP grille, WRT, VG, A, (Est: $350-$450)...$165.00

Pontiac Wrecker (1930s), Kenton, 4½", take-apart body w/type-III NP grille, WRT, VG, A (Est: $350-$450)...........$165.00

Pontiac Wrecker (1930s), Kenton, 4½", take-apart body w/type-I NP grille, WRT, EX, A (Est: $350-$450) $355.00

Pontiac Wrecker (1930s), Kenton, 4½", take-apart w/Type-II NP grille, WRT, very rare, EX, A (Est: $500-$600) $715.00

Public Service Bus, Dent, 14", open windows, rear spare, MDW, NP driver, EX, A (Est: $4,500-$5,500) $8,160.00

Racer, see also Golden Arrow Racer

Racer, AC Williams, 8½", tail-fin model w/emb side pipes, BRT, cast driver, VG, A (Est: $400-$600) $385.00

Racer, AC Williams, 8½", tail-fin model w/emb 12-cylinder hood, WRT, NP driver, EX, A (Est: $500-$700) $300.00

Racer, Arcade, 1920s, 7½", gas tank cast behind open seat, NPSW, NP driver, EX, A ($400-$600) $400.00

Racer, Champion, 5", tail-fin model, WRT, w/driver, VG, A (Est: $300-$400) $165.00

Racer, Champion, 8", tail-fin model, WRT, w/driver, EX+, A (Est: $1,000-$1,200)..............................$1,980.00

Racer, Champion, 8½", tail-fin model w/very long hood, NPDW, w/driver, G+, A (Est: $150-$250) $330.00

Racer, Dent, 6½", boat-tail w/8 emb cylinders, radiator & headlights, cast driver, NPSW, G, A (Est: $150-$300) ...$200.00

Racer, Freidag, 6½", boat-tail, NPDW, 2 drivers, Fair+, A (Est: $600-$800) $600.00

Racer, Hubley, 6½", early model w/open bench seat, MSW, w/driver, EX, A (Est: $350-$450) $165.00

Racer, Hubley, 6½", tail-fin model w/vents emb on side of hood, WRT, NP driver, EX, A (Est: $100-$200).................$180.00

Racer, Hubley, 6½", 12 emb pistons, grille-mounted light, NP side lever, WRT, w/driver, EX+, A (Est: $750-$1,000) $1,870.00

Racer, Hubley, 8", early model w/open high-back bench seat, MSW, driver at center wheel, G, A (Est: $400-$500) $385.00

Racer, Hubley, 11", tail-fin model w/articulated flames on hood, BRT w/spokes, w/driver, G, A (Est: $1,200-$1,500) ..$1,045.00

Racer, Kenton, 6½", back curves downward, emb pistons on hood, WRT, driver, G, A (Est: $400-$500) $220.00

Racer, Kenton, 9", long nose w/flat radiator, bullet-shaped back, MSW, NP driver, rstr, A (Est: $500-$800) $600.00

Racer, Kenton, 10½", boat-tail back, emb side vents, MDW, w/driver, VG, A (Est: $1,500-$2,000) $935.00

Racer #1, Hubley, 8", WRT, cast driver, VG+, A (Est: $200-$400)...$175.00

Racer #5, Hubley, 9", hood opens to reveal motor, MDW, w/driver, Fair, A (Est: $300-$400) $600.00

Racer #5, Hubley, 9½", hood opens to reveal motor, WRT, w/driver, EX, A (Est: $1,500-$1,750) $2,090.00

Racer #8, Arcade, 5½", tail-fin model, WRT, driver, EX, A (Est: $200-$300) $165.00

Racer #9, Arcade, 8", bullet-type, MDW, driver, Fair, A (Est: $500-$600) $1,870.00

Railway Express Truck, Hubley, 4", WRT, EX, A (Est: $200-$250)...$330.00

Red Baby, see International Red Baby

Reo Coupe, Arcade, 7½", pnt grille, cast side spare, WRT, EX, A (Est: $2,000-$2,500)...................................$2,750.00

Reo Coupe, Arcade, 9", EX+, A (Est: $3,500.00 – $5,000.00), $4,400.00. (Photo courtesy Bertoia Auctions)

Roadster, Arcade, 6", opening rumble seat, extended cast bumper, MSW, EX+, A (Est: $500-$700) $550.00

Roadster, ca 1934, 8½", sleek styling w/wide V-shaped, bumper, rear spare, WRT, VG, A (Est: $1,750-$2,250) $1,430.00

Roadster, Freidag, 9", boat-tail racer-type body w/wide-set MSW, rear spare, plain flat grille, VG, A (Est: $700-$800)..$935.00

Roadster, Hubley, 6½", take-apart body, cast 'fold-down' windshield, 2 side spares, BRT, VG, A (Est: $300-$400)...$190.00

Racer #2, Vindex, 11", VG, A (Est: $1,500.00 – $2,000.00), $4,125.00. (Photo courtesy Bertoia Auctions)

Racer #5, Arcade, 8", tail-fin model, WRT, 2 cast drivers, EX+, A (Est: $800-$1,000) $2,475.00

Roadster, Kenton, 4½", take-apart body w/type-III grille, NM+, A (Est: $800.00 – $1,000.00), $1,870.00. (Photo courtesy Bertoia Auctions)

Roadster, Hubley, 7", 1920s model, roof w/portholes extends over open seat, MSW, w/driver, EX, A (Est: $700-$900) ..$990.00

Roadster, Kenton, 4½", take-apart body w/type-II NP grille, WRT, EX, A (Est: $600-$800) $990.00

Roadster, Kenton, 6", open seat, slanted back, MDW, w/driver on right side, VG, A (Est: $250-$350)....................$135.00

Roadster, Kenton, 7", open seat, flat back, PMDW, w/driver, G, A (Est: $150-$200)...$685.00

Roadster, Kilgore, 8", opening rumble seat & cast spare, MDW, NP driver, VG, A (Est: $400-$500) $410.00

Roadster, Kilgore, 10½", take-apart body, NP detail & disk wheels, fold-down windshield, EX, A (Est: $2,000-$2,500) $1,100.00

Roadster (Sport), Dent, 5½", extended cast front bumper, NPDW, 2 figures in rumble seat, G, A (Est: $300-$400) $165.00

Runabout, Clark, 8", pnt wood & CI w/iron flywheel mechanism, MSW, lady driver & child, VG, A (Est: $800-$1,000) .$825.00

Runabout, Kenton, 5½", center steering, MDW, w/driver, VG, A (Est: $400-$500)..$350.00

Santa Fe Trailways Bus, see National Santa Fe Trailways Bus

Say It With Flowers Delivery Cycle, Hubley, 7", VG, A (Est: $3,000-$5,000)..$8,250.00

Say It With Flowers Delivery Cycle, Hubley, 11", VG, A (Est: $12,000-$15,000) $33,000.00

Sedan, AC Williams, 5", take-apart body w/extended cast front bumper, WRT, EX, A (Est: $250-$350) $440.00

Sedan, AC Williams, 8", sleek modernistic style, covered wheels, WRT, G, A (Est: $700-$900) $440.00

Sedan, Arcade, 4½", WRT, EX, A (Est: $150-$250)......$110.00

Sedan, Champion, 7½", take-apart Art-Deco body style w/rear spare, WRT, EX+, A (Est: $1,500-$1,750)...............$880.00

Sedan, Dent, 4", 1920s model w/straight windsield frame, U-shaped, NPDW, no driver, EX, A (Est: $200-$300)..$500.00

Sedan, Dent, 5½", 1920s model w/slightly slanted windshield frame, WRT, cast driver, EX, A (Est: $400-$500)....$275.00

Sedan, Hubley, 6", 1920s model w/visor, NPDW, cast driver, G, A (Est: $300-$500) $150.00

Sedan, Hubley, 7½", NP V-shaped grille & bumpers, WRT, G, A (Est: $75-$125) $185.00

Sedan, Kenton, 6½", low roof w/visor, extended cast bumper, MDW, driver on right side, EX, A (Est: $3,000-$3,500) $2,200.00

Sedan, Kenton, 6½", slanted windsield frame, rear spare, NPDW, NP driver, EX, A (Est: $400-$600)............$715.00

Sedan, Kenton, 8", slanted windshield frame, rear spare, MDW, NP driver, EX, A (Est: $1,500-$2,000) $1,540.00

Sedan, Kenton, 8½", low roof w/visor, separate NP bumper, MDW, driver on right side, EX, A (Est: $3,500-$4,500)........$1,200.00

Sedan, Kenton, 10", separate NP bumper, MDW, driver on right side, G, A (Est: $10,000-$12,000) $2,475.00

Sedan, Skoglund & Olsun, 8", 1920s model, WRT, rear spare, G+, A (Est: $400-$500) $935.00

Sedan Pulling Trailer, Kenton, 10" overall, VG, A (Est: $100-$200)...$385.00

Special Delivery Cycle, Kilgore, 4½", hinged rear compartment, NPSW, integral driver, G, A (Est: $100-$150)........$285.00

Stake Truck, AC Williams, 7", WRT (rpl), Fair+, A (Est: $75-$125)...$110.00

Stake Truck, Champion, 4½", take-apart body w/top part of cab & bed cast together, WRT, VG, A (Est: $250-$350) $190.00

Stake Truck, Champion, 7", cab w/flat top & hood, high box stake bed, NP grille & bumper, VG, A (Est: $500-$700) $330.00

Stake Truck, Freidag, 8", MSW, G, A (Est: $450-$650) ..$850.00

Stake Truck, Hubley, 6½", take-apart body, 6-wheeled, BRT, EX, A (Est: $500-$700).......................................$245.00

Stake Truck, Hubley, 7", open seat, WRT, w/driver, EX, A (Est: $300-$400)...$465.00

Stake Truck, Kenton, 7", high box stake bed w/solid back, NP grille & bumper, WRT, VG, A (no estimate) $440.00

Stake Truck, Kenton, 8", semi w/open stake bed w/solid back, curved front end, WRT, 6-wheeled, VG, A (Est: $300-$400) $200.00

Studebaker Convertible, Hubley, 4½", WRT, EX, A (Est: $150-$250)...$220.00

Studebaker Dump Truck, Hubley, 7", slanted dump bed, NP grille & lights, pnt bumper, EX, A (Est: $300-$400) $190.00

Studebaker Ice Truck, Arcade, 7", WRT, cast driver, w/tongs & 3 blocks of ice, EX+, A (Est: $1,750-$2,000) $2,475.00

Studebaker Roadster, Hubley, 7", take-apart body w/NP trim, rear spare, WRT, EX, A (Est: $400-$600) $715.00

Studebaker Sedan, Hubley, 5", NP trim, WRT, EX, A (Est: $175-$225)..$300.00

Studebaker Sedan, Hubley, 7", take-apart body w/NP trim, rear spare, WRT, EX, A (Est: $400-$600) $520.00

Studebaker Town Car, Hubley, 7", take-apart body, EX, A (Est: $400.00 – $600.00), $520.00. (Photo courtesy Bertoia Auctions)

Stutz Bearcat, Kilgore, 10", open seat, NPDW, rstr, A (Est: $300-$400)..$550.00

Stutz Bearcat Racer, Kenton, 7½", gas tank cast behind open seat, MSW, w/driver, A (Est: $350-$400) $600.00

Tank, Arcade, 8", camouflage pnt, rubber treads, turret door opens, NM (Est: $100) $300.00

Tank Truck, Hubley, 7", long nose w/NP grille, WRT, VG, A (Est: $175-$225) $185.00

Tank Truck, Kenton, 7", cab & tank cast together, NP grille, lights & bumper, WRT, EX, A (Est: $750-$1,000)............$1,540.00

Tank Truck, Skoglund & Olson, 10½", early model w/flat roof & visor, WRT, w/driver, VG rpt, A (Est: $300-$400)..**$465.00**

Taxi, Arcade, 8½", blk & orange flat top Buick w/WRT, orange hubs, w/driver, G+, A (Est: $1,500-$1,800) **$1,430.00**

Taxi, Dent, 8", #543, lemon yel w/bl trim, rear spare, MDW, w/driver, VG, A (Est: $500-$700).........................**$465.00**

Taxi, Freidag, 5", #453, orange & blk, MDW, cast driver, VG, A (Est: $400-$500)...**$770.00**

Taxi, Hubley, 8", black and white, EX, A (Est: $1,500.00 – $2,000.00), $2,000.00. (Photo courtesy Bertoia Auctions)

Taxi, Hubley, 8", orange w/blk trim on doors & hood, rear spare, NP driver, VG, A (Est: $750-$950) **$600.00**

Taxi, Kenton, 6", orange & blk, PMDW, NP driver, VG, A (Est: $400-$500) **$355.00**

Taxi, Kenton, 8", roof extends over open bench seat, MSW, w/passenger & driver, EX, A (Est: $900-$1,200) **$660.00**

Taxi, Kenton, 10", orange w/blk running boards & fenders, rear spare, MSW, driver, G, A (Est: $1,200-$1,400)....**$1,100.00**

Terraplane Coupe, Hubley, 6", NP grille & bumper, rear spare, WRT, EX, A (Est: $350-$450) **$465.00**

Terraplane Phaeton, Hubley, 6", NP grille & bumper, rear spare, WRT, VG, A (Est: $400-$500) **$355.00**

Terraplane Phaeton, Hubley, 6", take-apart body, NP bottom part, rear spare, EX, A (Est: $400-$500) **$520.00**

Terraplane Pickup Truck, 6", NP grille & bumper, WRT, EX, A (Est: $300-$500)...**$275.00**

Terraplane Sedan, Hubley, 6", NP grille & V-shaped bumper, rear spare, WRT, VG, A (Est: $350-$450)...............**$550.00**

Terraplane Wrecker, Hubley, 6", take-apart body, NP grille, lights, bumper & boom, WRT, VG, A (Est: $300-$400) **$220.00**

Texaco Tanker, Kenton, 7½", name emb on tank, NP grille, lights & bumper, WRT, 4-wheeled, EX, A (Est: $750-$1,000) **$1,200.00**

Texaco Tanker, Kenton, 10", EX, A (Est: $2,500.00 – $3,500.00), $2,475.00. (Photo courtesy Bertoia Auctions)

Tiller Auto, Hubley, 4", center steering, MSW, w/driver, VG, A (Est: $350-$450) **$245.00**

Tiller Auto, Kenton, 4½", center steering, MSW, w/driver, VG, A (Est: $350-$450)...**$300.00**

Tiller Auto, Kenton, 6", center steering, MSW, w/driver, G, A (Est: $300-$400)...**$100.00**

Touring Car, AC Williams, 9½", open, MSW, no figures, VG+, A (Est: $200-$300)..**$440.00**

Touring Car, AC Williams, 12", open, MSW, w/driver & lady passenger, EX, A (Est: $900-$1,100)....................**$800.00**

Touring Car, Dent, 8", open w/no windshield, tapered hood, MSW, NP driver, NM, A (Est: $700-$900)..........**$2,200.00**

Touring Car, Hubley, 6", take-apart body, top up, WRT, w/spare, NP grille, EX+, A (Est: $400-$600)....................**$1,200.00**

Terraplane Roadster, Hubley, 6", EX, A (Est: $350.00 – $450.00), $550.00. (Photo courtesy Bertoia Auctions)

Touring Car, Hubley, 11½", EX, A (Est: $8,000.00 – $10,000.00), $10,925.00. (Photo courtesy James D. Julia, Inc.)

Touring Car, Hubley, 10", open w/no windshield, right steering, MSW, 2 passengers & driver, VG, A (Est: $1,000-$1,200)..$825.00

Touring Car, Hubley, 10", removable canopy top, MSW, passenger & driver, EX, A (Est: $1,200-$1,500)..............$2,750.00

Touring Car, Jones & Bixler, 9½", 'soft' top over open front seat, MSW, passenger & driver, G, A (Est: $1,500-$1,750)..$1,200.00

Touring Car, Kenton, 6", open front seat w/roof over backseat, rear doors, headlamps, blk, MSW, G, A (Est: $300-$500)...$200.00

Touring Car, Kenton, 9", top up, MSW, w/driver & lady passenger, VG+, A (Est: $1,400-$1,600)........................$1,150.00

Touring Car, Kenton, 9½", open w/no windshield, MDW, w/lady passenger & driver, VG, A (Est: $700-$900)...........$500.00

Tow Truck, Champion, 8", NP grille, WRT, G, A (Est: $150-$250)..$250.00

Tractor-Trailer, Arcade, 11", VG+, A (Est: $400.00 – $600.00), $2,400.00. (Photo courtesy James D. Julia, Inc.)

Traffic Car, Hubley, 9", 3-wheeled motorcycle w/stake cart, WRT w/spokes, w/integral driver, G+, A (Est: $400-$500)..$715.00

Traffic Car, Hubley, 11", 3-wheeled motorcycle w/stake cart, BRT w/spokes, w/driver, scarce, VG, A (Est: $1,500-$2,000)..$3,080.00

USCO Moving Van, Arcade, 13", VG+, A (Est: $7,000.00 – $9,000.00), $6,960.00. (Photo courtesy James D. Julia, Inc.)

Truck & Trailer Set, Kenton, 7" truck w/3 6" trailers marked Ice, Oil/Gas, Speed, Fair, A (Est: $450-650)..............$1,430.00

Twin Coach, AC Williams, 16", cast aluminum, yel over gr w/wht stripe, WRT, yel hubs, EX, A (Est: $800-$1,000) $3,500.00

US Air Mail Cycle, Hubley, 9½", BRT, opening rear door, no driver, VG+, A (Est: $1,500-$2,000)....................$2,420.00

Valley View Dairy Truck, Dent, 8", sliding doors, WRT, made in 1960 from orig parts, EX, A (Est: $200-$300) $770.00

Weaver Wrecker, see Ford Weaver Wrecker

Webcao Oil Co Tank Truck, see Mack Tank Truck (Webaco Oil Co)

White Delivery Van, Arcade, 8", White emb on grille, 2 side spares, WRT, NP driver, G, A (Est: $3,000-$4,000).............$1,760.00

Willy's Knight Sedan, Kenton, 8", rear spare, red & blk (rare), MDW, NP driver, VG, A (Est: $4,000-$4,500)....$2,475.00

Woody Wagon, see Pierce Arrow 'Woody' Wagon

Wrecker, AC Williams, 5½", take-apart body, open cab w/high bed, NP hook, WRT, cast driver, EX, A (Est: $300-$400) $660.00

Wrecker, AC Williams, 6½", NP real & hook, EX+, A (Est: $300-$400) $880.00

Wrecker, Arcade, 5½", NP boom, BRT w/silver hubs, VG, A (Est: $300-$400) $275.00

Wrecker, Champion, 4½", take-apart body, NP grille, lights, bumper & tow hook, WRT, NM, A (Est: $350-$450)...............$880.00

Wrecker, Champion, 7", NP grille, WRT, G+, A (Est: $200-$300)..$300.00

Wrecker, Hubley, 5", low body w/long tapered nose, NP boom & hook, WRT, NM, A (Est: $300-$400) $135.00

Wrecker, Hubley, 6", take-apart body, NP grille & wench, VG, A (Est: $225-$275)......................................$220.00

Wrecker, Kilgore, 6", flat-top cab w/bottom of grille curving out, boom on block-type bed, WRT, EX, A (Est: $400-$500) $715.00

Wrecker, see also Auto Wrecker, Ford, International, Yellow Cab, etc.

Yellow Cab, Arcade, 6½", Pontiac (1935), NP grille, WRT, G, A (Est: $400-$600)......................................$550.00

Yellow Cab, Arcade, 8", bank, lattice work on rear windows, PMDW, w/driver, no grille insert, VG+, A (Est: $800-$1,200)..$935.00

Yellow Cab, Arcade, 8", curved top, no visor, orange & blk, MDW, NP driver, VG, A (Est: $300-$400) $440.00

Yellow Cab, Arcade, 8", GMC (1927), flat top w/visor, MDW, NP driver, EX+, A (Est: $2,500-$3,500) $4,400.00

Yellow Cab, Arcade, 8", GMC (1927), flat top w/visor, WRT, NP driver, G+, A (Est: $1,200-$1,500) $1,045.00

Yellow Cab, Arcade, 8", Parmalee, yel w/blk top, NP grille, headlights & bumper, WRT, VG+, A (Est: $2,500-$3,500) $2,645.00

Yellow Cab, Arcade, 8½", coupe w/rear spare, wht pnt MDW, rear spare, NP driver, VG, A (Est: $1,400-$1,600)........$1,380.00

Yellow Cab, Arcade, 9", curved top, no visor, MDW, NP driver, VG+, A (Est: $600-$800) $700.00

Yellow Cab, Arcade, 9", curved top, no visor, WRT, NP driver, Fair, A (Est: $200-$300)..................................$250.00

Yellow Cab, Dent, 8", #543, MDW, rear spare, cast driver, VG, A (Est: $1,000-$1,400) $1,320.00

Yellow Cab, Friedag, 7½", blk & yel, PMDW, yel hubs, w/driver, EX, A (Est: $200-$300)................................$520.00

Yellow Cab, Hubley, 8", Lincoln Zephyr, NP trim, rear luggage rack, WRT, w/driver, EX, A (Est: $600-$800).........$600.00

Yellow Cab Bus, Fageol, 12", Phone Circle 5000/Yellow Cab Express/Baggage on sides, VG, A (Est: $3,000-$4,000)..$4,885.00

Yellow Cab Delivery Van (Stukenberg & Brochers...), Arcade, 8½", WRT, w/driver, VG, A (Est: $2,000-$3,000).........$12,100.00

Yellow Cab Fageol Safety Coach, 12", VG, A (Est: $3,000.00 – $4,000.00), $4,885.00. (Photo courtesy James D. Julia, Inc.)

Yellow Coach Double-Decker Bus, Arcade, 13", BRT, VG+ (Est: $1,500-$1,800).......................................$2,070.00

Yellow Coach Double-Decker Bus, Arcade, 13", WRT, EX+, A (Est: $1,800-$2,200)................................$2,760.00

Yellow Coach Double-Decker Bus, Arcade, 13", WRT, G, A (Est: $800-$1,000)................................$1,600.00

TRAINS

Blue Line Train Set, Harris, locomotive, tender, passenger car & baggage car, 12", G (Est: $700-$900)................$660.00

Camelback 600 & 999 Locomotive & Tender, Kenton, 14" L, EX, A (Est: $400-$500)..$410.00

Camelback 600 Locomotive With LS&MS Tender and Gondola, Kenton, 1920s, 23" overall, NM, A (Est: $300.00 – $400.00), $2,240.00. (Photo courtesy James D. Julia, Inc.)

Cannonball, Ives, 1893, 4-4-0 loco, 189 tender, Limited Vestibule Express, Union Line boxcar, VG, A (Est: $1,500-$2,000)..$2,875.00

Century (of Progress) Engine, Kenton, rnd nose, sm upper deck, WRT, 1 of 3 in set, 7½", EX, A (Est: $800-$1,200)...$600.00

Locomotive, early, w/cow catcher, 2 lg SW & 2 sm SW, blk w/red trim, 8½", Fair, A (Est: $50-$75)..................$120.00

Locomotive, Ives, Pat 1884, 7", w/up, bl w/red & gold trim, 2 lg back MSW, cow catcher, VG, (Est: $450-$500)......$660.00

Locomotive, Niagara Falls 819 Passenger Car & 2 open cars mk 21619 NYC & HRRR 38, Buffalo, VG, A (Est: $1,000-$1,200)..$600.00

Locomotive, Walker & Crosby, w/wooden domes & boiler, figure on platform, no sz given, VG, A (Est: $1,200-$1,400).....$1,100.00

Locomotive With W&CRR Tender and Two Gondolas, Welker & Crosby, 28" overall, VG, A (Est: $1,500.00 – $2,000.00), $4,025.00. (Photo courtesy James D. Julia, Inc.)

Locomotive #857 w/Pennsylvania RR Tender & Panama Side-Dump Car, Hubley, 23" L overall, VG, A (Est: $1,000-$1,200)..$975.00

Locomotive #999 w/NYC & HRRR Tender w/2 Passenger/Baggage Cars, Pratt & Letchworth, 60" L, VG, A (Est: $700-$900)..$4,300.00

Locomotive w/Tender & Pullman Car, 18", Fair+, A (Est: $50-$75)..$330.00

Locomotive w/Tender & 2 Gondolas, Carpenter, 1880s, 20" overall, MSW, w/gondola driver, G+, A (Est: $300-$400).......$430.00

Locomotive 2-4-0 w/PRR Tender & Caboose, Hubley, 15" overall, VG+, A (Est: $150-$250)..............................$285.00

MCRR Train Set, Dent, locomotive, 2 stock cars w/sliding doors & caboose, 12" L, G, A (Est: $600-$800)................$550.00

NYC & HPRR Train Set, Pratt & Letchworth, loco & tender (23"), buffet (15"), coach (20"), EX, A (Est: $6,000-$8,000)..$1,045.00

PRR Locomotive & Tender, 9½", Fair, A (Est: $25-$50)..$130.00

Railplane, Arcade, 8½", VG, A (Est: $125-$175)..........$130.00

CONTEMPORARY MODELS

Arcade Taxi, 9", gr & blk, WRT w/gr hubs, NP driver, EX, A ($100-$200)..$150.00

Arcade Zegel Moving & Storage White Van, Ironman, 13", bl w/wht trim, NP grille, tires & spares, NM, A (Est: $400-$500)..$935.00

Chrysler Airflow, Selhoff, 10½", signed and dated 10/92, M, A (Est: $500.00 – $600.00), $440.00. (Photo courtesy Bertoia Auctions)

Chrysler Airflow Convertible & Clipper Trailer, Selhoff, 25" overall, WRT, signed & dated 11/92, M, A (Est: $800-$1,000)..$990.00

Meteor Hearse, Motorcade, 10", with 'Gideon' decal on windows, NM, A (Est: $400.00 – $500.00), $600.00. (Photo courtesy Bertoia Auctions)

Milk Tank Truck, Selhoff, 14", wht w/red detail, NP grille, WRT, signed & dated 4/91, NM, A (Est: $400-$500)........$575.00
Sunset Foundry Delivery Van, Sunset Toy Co, 9", blk & yel, WRT, opening rear door, EX, A (Est: $200-$300)...$440.00
Texaco Tank Truck, Selhoff, 14", red w/wht detail, NP grille, WRT, blk hubs, NM, A (Est: $400-$500)................$450.00

MISCELLANEOUS

Arcade Service, wood, wht w/gr stenciling, 13", VG, A (Est: $150-$250) $300.00
Arcade Service Station, wood, wht w/gr stenciling, 13" L, VG, A (Est: $50-$100)..$100.00
Automotive Repair Ramp, pnt CI, 6-footed angled ramp, 14½", EX, A (Est: $150-$250)..$1,540.00
Baby Buggy, Kilgore, NP push hdl & 4 NPSW, 5¼", EX, A (Est: $100-$150) $275.00
Bank, Arcade, gas pump, ball globe on tall sq body w/beveled base, dial on front, w/hose, 5¾", G, A (Est: $250-$350) $300.00

Arcadia Airport With Twin-Engine Plane, painted wood, 8x12½", G, A (Est: $250.00 – $350.00), $440.00. (Photo courtesy Randy Inman Auctions)

Barrett Cravens Hand-Truck, name emb on 2 runners, NPSW, 4", EX, A (Est: $250-$350) $275.00
Bear, Arcade, in stride, NP, 4", G, A (Est: $150-$250)...$990.00
Cannon (Young America), rapid fire action w/crank hdl, 2 spoke wheels, w/cannon balls, 15", G+, A (Est: $150-$300) ..$120.00
Engine (Horizontal), Kenton, w/hand-crank flywheel mechanism, 10½" L, VG, A (Est: $800-$1,000)............$3,025.00
Engine (Vertical), Kenton, mechanisim on 4-footed base, 8½x6½", EX, A (Est: $700-$900) $1,650.00
Gas Pump, AC Williams, ball globe, rope nozzle, 4¾", EX+, A (Est: $300-$400)..$520.00
Gas Pump, Arcade, Arcade Gas emb on rnd globe, 6", G, A (Est: $150-$250) $440.00
Gas Pump, Arcade, Arcade Gas on rnd flat-sided globe, rnd dial below, did not come w/hose, 6", EX+, A (Est: $400-$500)..$770.00
Gas Pump, Arcade, plain gold-pnt rnd globe w/red base, 5½", G, A (Est: $150-$250)..$330.00
Gas Pump, Kilgore, Gas on rnd globe, gallon gauge on front, w/crank & hose, 6½", EX, A (Est: $300-$400)........$355.00
Gas Pumps, Arcade, 3 sq-type on integral oblong base, red w/silver tops, 5", G, A (Est: $100-$200) $190.00

National Wagon, Kenton, 7¼", VG, A (Est: $250.00 – $350.00), $220.00. (Photo courtesy Bertoia Auctions)

Horse & Jockey, Hubley, brn horse w/blk mane & tail, red & wht separate jockey, 4¾", EX, A (Est: $200-$300)..**$250.00**

McCormick-Deering Cream Separator, Arcade, w/bucket, 5", EX+, A (Est: $500-$700) **$600.00**

Monkey, att: Ives, dressed articulated figure wearing fez mounted on wooden base, 4¼", VG, A (Est: $200-$300) **$230.00**

Scraper, Arcade, 2 MSWs, 7", EX, A (Est: $100-$200)..**$440.00**

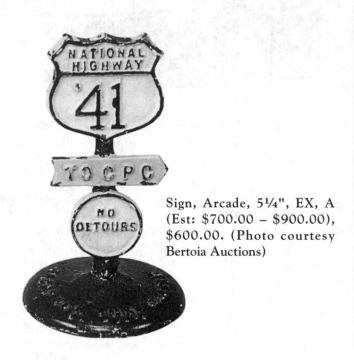

Sign, Arcade, 5¼", EX, A (Est: $700.00 – $900.00), $600.00. (Photo courtesy Bertoia Auctions)

Sign, Do Not Park Here, Freidag, oval on rnd base, orange & blk, 12", G, A (Est: $50-$150) **$685.00**

Sign, Don't Park Here, sidewalk lollipop type, 5", VG, A (Est: $25-$50) **$120.00**

Sign, Go, T shape on rnd base w/May 1925 emb on pole, 5", EX+, A (Est: $250-$400) **$245.00**

Sign, Main St, emb Warner Bros Screen Classic on 2 sides of base, 5½", G, A (Est: $250-$300) **$465.00**

Stop Light, Kilgore, Stop emb under 4-sided light, yel & red, 9", Fair+, A (Est: $300-$500) **$550.00**

Tricycle w/Rider, Ideal, 3¾", G, A (Est: $225-$275)......**$190.00**

Water Pump w/Bucket, Arcade, operating hdl, 7½", VG, A (Est: $100-$150) **$165.00**

Catalogs

In any area of collecting, old catalogs are a wonderful source for information. Toy collectors value buyers' catalogs, those from toy fairs, and Christmas 'wish books.' Montgomery Ward issued their first Christmas catalog in 1932, and Sears followed a year later. When they can be found, these 'first editions' in excellent condition are valued at a minimum of $200.00 each. Even later issues may sell for upwards of $75.00, since it's those from the '50s and '60s that contain the toys that are now so collectible.

American Flyer, 1949, G...$25.00

Aurora, 1973, M $125.00

Black Beauty Bicycles, 1917, G...$50.00

Breyer Animal Creations, 1976, EX......................................$20.00

Fisher-Price Toys, 1950, EX..$135.00

Gimbels, Christmas, 1953, VG+ $40.00

Hartland Plastic, sales brochure, late 1950s, 16 pgs (accordion-type folding), 5½x3", EX $50.00

Hasbro Romper Room, 1972, EX..$50.00

Hot Wheels International Collector's Catalog By Mattel, 1968, M...$25.00

Iver Johnson's Arms & Cycle Works, 1899, EX.............$150.00

Johnson Smith Novelties, 1940, 96 pgs featuring gags, magic tricks, character toys, etc, EX $40.00

Keystone Steam Shovels & Trucks, 1925, 6x4", G $130.00

Lionel Trains, 1942, M $135.00

Marx, 1975, 48 pgs, EX...$50.00

Mattel, 1966, VG+..$45.00

Mattel Toys, 1968, NM...$40.00

Merchandising Supplement, 1960s, 12 pgs, product campaigns (Nabisco, Clorox, etc) featuring PEZ, Marx, Chein, etc, NM...$50.00

Nylint, 1967, EX..$35.00

Ohio Art Fall & Winter 1956, 16-pg catalog w/Roy Rogers Ranch Lantern on cover, w/bl vinyl cover, EX+ $50.00

Ohio Art Spring & Summer Toys, 1956, 8-pg brochure featuring Roy Rogers Horseshoe Sets, w/bl vinyl sleeve, EX+ ..$50.00

Parker Brothers Games & Toys, 1976, EX.........................$80.00

Railroading With American Flyer, 1946, NM $150.00

Roy Rogers & Dale Evans Catalogue & Merchandising Manual, 1953, 82 pgs, laser copy (not original), M................$100.00

Schoenhut's Humpty Dumpty Circus, 1918, VG, $150.00.

Steiff, 1957, features 150 animals, 15 pgs, M $35.00

Thingmaker, Mattel, 1967, EX $15.00

Tinkertoys, 1927, 1931 or 1935, EX, ea.............................$50.00

Ventriloquist Figures By Fred Maher, #1, 1950, 16 pgs, EX+ ..$65.00

Walt Disney Character Merchandise, 1938-39, complete, VG..**$500.00**

Weeden Toy Steam Engines, 1937, 20 pgs, EX $32.00

Wolverine Toys, 1973, EX...$20.00

Tinkertoys for 1924, EX, $50.00. (Photo courtesy Craig Strange)

Character and Promotional Drinking Glasses

Once given away by fast-food chains and gas stations, a few years ago you could find these at garage sales everywhere for a dime or even less. Then, when it became obvious to collectors that these glass giveaways were being replaced by plastic, as is always the case when we realize no more (of anything) will be forthcoming, we all decided we wanted them. Since many were character-related and part of a series, we felt the need to begin to organize these garage-sale castaways, building sets and completing series. Out of the thousands available, the better ones are those with super heroes, sports stars, old movie stars, Star Trek, and Disney and Walter Lantz cartoon characters. Pass up those whose colors are worn and faded. Unless another condition or material is indicated in the description, values are for glass tumblers in mint condition. Cups are plastic unless noted otherwise.

There are some terms used in our listings that may be confusing if you're not familiar with this collecting field. 'Brockway' style tumblers are thick and heavy, and they taper at the bottom. 'Federal' is thinner, and top and diameters are equal. For more information we recommend *McDonald's Drinkware* by Michael J. Kelly and *The Collector's Guide to Cartoon and Promotional Drinking Glasses* by John Hervey. See also Clubs, Newsletters, and Other Publications.

Advisor: Mark E. Chase (C2)

Al Capp, Dogpatch USA, ruby glass, oval portraits of Daisy or Li'l Abner, ea from $15 to $20.00
Al Capp, Shmoos, USF, 1949, Federal, 3 different sizes (3½", 4¾", 5¼"), from $10 to $20.00
Al Capp, 1975, flat bottom, Daisy Mae, Li'l Abner, Mammy, Pappy, Sadie, ea from $35 to.....................................$50.00
Al Capp, 1975, flat bottom, Joe Btsfplk, from $35 to $50.00
Al Capp, 1975, ftd, Daisy Mae, Li'l Abner, Mammy, Pappy, Sadie, ea from $35 to..$50.00
Al Capp, 1975, ftd, Joe Btsfplk, from $40 to.....................$60.00

Animal Crackers, Chicago Tribune/NY News Syndicate, 1978, Eugene, Gnu, Lana, Lyle Dodo, ea from $7 to $10.00
Animal Crackers, Chicago Tribune/NY News Syndicate, 1978, Louis, scarce..$25.00
Arby's, Actor Series, 1979, 6 different, smoked-colored glass w/blk & wht images, silver trim, numbered, ea from $3 to........$5.00
Arby's, Bicentennial Cartoon Characters Series, 1976, 10 different, 5", ea from $8 to $15.00
Arby's, Bicentennial Cartoon Characters Series, 1976, 10 different, 6", ea from $10 to $20.00
Arby's, see also specific name or series
Archies, Welch's, 1971 & 1973, many variations in ea series, ea from $3 to...$5.00
Baby Huey & Related Characters, see Harvey Cartoon Characters
Batman & Related Characters, see also Super Heroes
Batman Forever, McDonald's, 1995, various emb glass mugs, ea from $2 to...$4.00
Battlestar Galactica, Universal Studios, 1979, 4 different, ea from $7 to...$10.00
Beatles, Dairy Queen/Canada, group photos & signatures in wht starburst, gold trim, ea from $95 to $125.00
Beverly Hillbillies, CBS promotion, 1963, rare, NM......$200.00
Bozo the Clown, Capital Records, 1965, Bozo head image around top w/related character at bottom, ea from $10 to $15.00
Bozo the Clown, Capital Records, 1965, Bozo on 3 sides only, from $8 to...$10.00
Buffalo Bill, see Western Heroes or Wild West Series
Bugs Bunny & Related Characters, see Warner Bros
Bullwinkle, Rocky & Related Characters, see Warner Bros or PAT Ward
Burger Chef, Friendly Monster Series, 1977, 6 different, ea from $15 to $25.00
Burger King, Collector Series, 1979, 5 different Burger King characters featuring Burger Thing, etc, ea from $3 to..$5.00

Burger King, pitcher, 'Where Kids Are King,' from $30.00 to $35.00. (Photo courtesy Mark Chase and Michael Kelly)

Burger King, Put a Smile in Your Tummy, features Burger King mascot, from $5 to $6.00

Burger King, see also specific name or series

California Raisins, Applause, 1989, juice, 12-oz, 16-oz, ea from $4 to $6.00

California Raisins, Applause, 1989, 32-oz, from $6 to $8.00

Captain America, see Super Heroes

Casper the Friendly Ghost & Related Characters, see Arby's Bicentennial or Harvey Cartoon Characters

Charlie McCarthy & Edgar Bergen, Libbey, 1930s, set of 8, M (EX illus display box) $600.00

Children's Classics, Libbey Glass Co, Alice in Wonderland, Gulliver's Travels, Tom Sawyer, from $10 to $15.00

Children's Classics, Libbey Glass Co, Moby Dick, Robin Hood, Three Musketeers, Treasure Island, ea from $10 to....$15.00

Children's Classics, Libbey Glass Co, The Wizard of Oz, from $25 to $30.00

Chilly Willy, see Walter Lantz

Chipmunks, Hardee's (no logo on glass), 1985, Alvin, Simon, Theodore, Chipettes, ea from $1 to............................$3.00

Cinderella, Disney/Libbey, 1950s-60s, set of 8 ....$120.00

Cinderella, see also Disney Collector Series or Disney Film Classics

Daffy Duck, see Warner Bros

Dick Tracy, Domino's Pizza, M, from $100.00 to $125.00.

Dick Tracy, 1940s, frosted, 8 different characters, 3" or 5", ea from $50 to..$75.00

Dilly Dally, see Howdy Doody

Disney, see also Wonderful World of Disney or specific characters

Disney Characters, 1936, Clarabelle, Donald, F Bunny, Horace, Mickey, Minnie, Pluto, 4¼" or 4¾", ea from $30 to..$50.00

Disney's All-Star Parade, 1939, 10 different, ea from $25 to ..$50.00

Donald Duck, Donald Duck Cola, 1960s-70s, from $10 to ..$15.00

Donald Duck or Daisy, see also Disney or Mickey Mouse (Happy Birthday)

Dynomutt, see Hanna-Barbera

ET, Pepsi/MCA Home Video, 1988, 6 different, ea from $15 to..$25.00

ET, Pizza Hut, 1982, ftd, 4 different, from $2 to $4.00

Fantasia, see Disney Film Classics or Mickey Mouse (Through the Years)

Flintstones, see also Hanna-Barbera

Flintstones, Welch's, 1962 (6 different), 1963 (2 different), 1964 (6 different), ea from $4 to $6.00

Ghostbusters II, Sunoco/Canada, 1989, 6 different, ea from $3 to..$5.00

Goonies, Godfather's Pizza/Warner Bros, 1985, 4 different, ea from $3 to..$5.00

Green Arrow or Green Lantern, see Super Heroes

Hanna-Barbera, Pepsi, 1977, Dynomutt, Flintstones, Josie & the Pussycats, Mumbly, Scooby, Yogi & Huck, ea from $10 to $20.00

Hanna-Barbera, 1960s, jam glasses featuring Cindy Bear, Flintstones, Huck, Quick Draw, Yogi Bear, rare, ea from $60 to..$90.00

Happy Days, Dr. Pepper or Dr. Pepper/Pizza Hut, 1977, any character from either series, each from $6.00 to $10.00. (Photo courtesy Mark Chase and Michael Kelly)

Harvey Cartoon Characters, Pepsi, 1970s, action pose, Baby Huey, Hot Stuff, Wendy, ea from $8 to $10.00

Harvey Cartoon Characters, Pepsi, 1970s, static pose, Baby Huey, Casper, Hot Stuff, Wendy, ea from $12 to $15.00

Harvey Cartoon Characters, Pepsi, 1970s, static pose, Richie Rich, from $15 to..$20.00

Harvey Cartoon Characters, Pepsi, 1970s, static pose, Sad Sack, scarce, from $25 to..$30.00

Harvey Cartoon Characters, see also Arby's Bicentennial Series

He-Man & Related Characters, see Masters of the Universe

Honey, I Shrunk the Kids, McDonald's, 1989, plastic, 3 different, ea from $1 to $2.00

Hopalong Cassidy, milk glass w/blk graphics, Breakfast Milk, Lunch Milk, Dinner Milk, ea from $15 to $20.00

Hopalong Cassidy, milk glass w/red & blk graphics, 3 different, ea from $20 to...$25.00

Hopalong Cassidy's Western Series, ea from $25 to..........$30.00

Hot Stuff, see Harvey Cartoon Characters or Arby's Bicentennial

Howard the Duck, see Super Heroes

Howdy Doody, Welch's/Kagran, 1950s, 6 different, emb bottom, ea from $10 to...$15.00

Huckleberry Hound, see Hanna-Barbera

Incredible Hulk, see Super Heroes

Indiana Jones & the Temple of Doom, 7-Up (w/4 different sponsers), 1984, set of 4, from $8 to.............................$15.00

James Bond 007, 1985, 4 different, ea from $10 to $15.00

Joker, see Super Heroes

Jungle Book, Disney/Canada, 1966, 6 different, numbered, 5", ea from $30 to...$65.00

Jungle Book, Disney/Canada, 1966, 6 different, numbered, 6½", ea from $20 to..$40.00

Jungle Book, Disney/Pepsi, 1970s, Bagheera or Shere Kahn, unmk, ea from $35 to...$60.00

Jungle Book, Disney/Pepsi, 1970s, Mowgli, unmk, from $15 to...$20.00

Jungle Book, Disney/Pepsi, 1970s, Rama, unmk, from $25 to..$35.00

Laurel & Hardy, see Arby's Actor Series

Leonardo TTV, see also Arby's Bicentennial Series

Leonardo TTV Collector Series, Pepsi, Underdog, Go-Go Gophers, Simon Bar Sinister, Sweet Polly, 6", ea from $10 to $15.00

Leonardo TTV Collector Series, Pepsi, Simon Bar Sinister, Sweet Polly, 5", ea from $6 to.....................................$10.00

Leonardo TTV Collector Series, Pepsi, Underdog, 5", from $6.00 to $10.00.

Little Mermaid, 1991, 3 different sizes, ea from $6 to.......$10.00

Masters of the Universe, Mattel, 1983, He-Man, Man-at-Arms, Skeletor, Teels, ea from $5 to $10.00

Masters of the Universe, Mattel, 1986, Battle Cat/He-Man, Man-at-Arms, Orko, Panthor/Sketetor, ea from $3 to...........$5.00

McDonald's, McDonaldland Action Series or Collector Series, 1970s, 6 different ea series, ea from $2 to....................$3.00

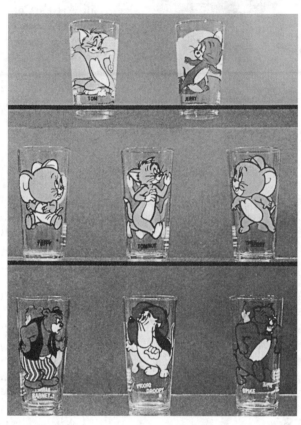

MGM Collector Series, Pepsi, 1975, Top row: Tom or Jerry, 5", each from $6.00 to $10.00; Middle row: Tuff, Tom, Jerry, 6", each from $5.00 to $10.00; Bottom row: Barney, Droopy, Spike, 6", each from $5.00 to $10.00. (Photo courtesy Mark Chase and Michael Kelly)

Mickey Mouse, Happy Birthday, Pepsi, 1978, Clarabelle & Horace or Daisy & Donald, ea from $5 to..................$10.00

Mickey Mouse, Happy Birthday, Pepsi, 1978, Donald, Goofy, Mickey, Minnie, Pluto, Uncle Scrooge, ea from $5 to ..$7.00

Mickey Mouse, Mickey's Christmas Carol, Coca-Cola, 1982, 3 different, ea from $5 to $7.00

Mickey Mouse, Pizza Hut, 1980, milk glass mug, Fantasia, MM Club, Steamboat Willie, Today, ea from $2 to $5.00

Mickey Mouse, see also Disney Characters

Mickey Mouse, Through the Years, K-Mart, glass mugs w/4 different images (1928, 1937, 1940, 1955), ea from $3 to......$5.00

Mickey Mouse Club, 4 different w/filmstrip bands top & bottom, ea from $10 to...$20.00

Mister Magoo, Polomar Jelly, many different variations & styles, ea from $25 to..$35.00

Pac-Man, Bally Midway MFG/AAFES/Libbey, 1980, Shadow (Blinky), Bashful (Inky), Pokey (Clyde), Speedy (Pinky), ea $4 to $6.00

Pac-Man, Bally Midway Mfg/Libbey, 1982, 6" flare top, 5⅜" flare top or mug, from $2 to $4.00

Pac-Man, Arby's Collector Series, 1980, rocks glass, from $2.00 to $4.00.

PAT Ward, Collector Series, Holly Farms Restaurants, 1975, Boirs, Bullwinkle, Natasha, Rocky, ea from $20 to **$40.00**

PAT Ward, Pepsi, late 1970s, action pose, Bullwinkle w/balloons, Dudley in Canoe, Rocky in circus, 5", ea from $5 to ..**$10.00**

PAT Ward, Pepsi, late 1970s, static pose, Boris, Mr Peabody, Natasha, 5", ea from $10 to **$15.00**

PAT Ward, Pepsi, late 1970s, static pose, Boris & Natasha, 6", from $15 to..**$20.00**

PAT Ward, Pepsi, late 1970s, static pose, Bullwinkle, 5", from $15 to **$20.00**

PAT Ward, Pepsi, late 1970s, static pose, Bullwinkle (brn lettering/no Pepsi logo), 6", from $15 to............................**$20.00**

PAT Ward, Pepsi, late 1970s, static pose, Bullwinkle (wht or blk lettering), 6", from $10 to.......................................**$15.00**

PAT Ward, Pepsi, late 1970s, static pose, Dudley Do-Right, 5", from $10 to...**$15.00**

PAT Ward, Pepsi, late 1970s, static pose, Dudley Do-Right (blk lettering), 6", from $10 to..**$15.00**

PAT Ward, Pepsi, late 1970s, static pose, Dudley Do-Right (red lettering/no Pepsi logo), 6", from $10 to **$15.00**

PAT Ward, Pepsi, late 1970s, static pose, Rocky, 5", from $15 to..**$20.00**

PAT Ward, Pepsi, late 1970s, static pose, Rocky (brn lettering/no Pepsi logo), 6", from $10 to **$15.00**

PAT Ward, Pepsi, late 1970s, static pose, Rocky (wht or blk lettering), 6", from $10 to...**$15.00**

PAT Ward, Pepsi, late 1970s, static pose, Snidley Whiplash, 5", from $8 to...**$10.00**

PAT Ward, Pepsi, late 1970s, static pose, Snidley Whiplash (wht or blk lettering), 6", from $10 to **$15.00**

PAT Ward, see also Arby's Bicentennial Series

Peanuts Characters, ftd, Snoopy sitting on lemon or Snoopy sitting on lg red apple, ea from $2 to................................**$3.00**

Peanuts Characters, Kraft, 1988, Charlie Brown flying kite, Lucy on swing, Snoopy in pool, Snoopy on surfboard, ea.....**$2.00**

Peanuts Characters, McDonald's, 1983, Camp Snoopy, wht plastic w/Lucy or Snoopy, ea from $5 to **$8.00**

Peanuts Characters, milk glass mug, At Times Life Is Pure Joy (Snoopy & Woodstock dancing), from $3 to..............**$5.00**

Peanuts Characters, milk glass mug, Snoopy for President, 4 different, numbered & dated, ea from $5 to **$8.00**

Peanuts Characters, Dolly Madison Bakery, Top row: Snoopy for President, four different, each from $3.00 to $5.00; Bottom row: Snoopy Sport Series, four different, each from $3.00 to $5.00. (Photo courtesy Mark Chase and Michael Kelly)

Peanuts Characters, milk glass mug, Snoopy in various poses, from $2 to..**$4.00**

Peanuts Characters, plastic, I Got It! I Got It!, I Have a Strange Team, Let's Break for Lunch!, ea from $3 to **$5.00**

Peanuts Characters, Smuckers, 1994, 3 different, ea from $2 to **$4.00**

Penguin, see Super Heroes

Peter Pan, see Disney Film Classics

Pinocchio, Dairy Promo/Libbey, 1938-40, 12 different, ea from $15 to **$25.00**

Pinocchio, see also Disney Collector's Series or Wonderful World of Disney

Pluto, see Disney Characters

Pocahontas, Burger King, 1995, 4 different, MIB, ea **$3.00**

Popeye, Coca-Cola, 1975, Kollect-A-Set, any character, ea from $3 to **$5.00**

Popeye, Popeye's Famous Fried Chicken, 1978, Sports Scenes, Popeye, from $7 to **$10.00**

Popeye, Popeye's Famous Fried Chicken, 1978, Sports Scenes, Brutus, Olive Oyl, Swee' Pea, ea from $10 to **$15.00**

Popeye, Popeye's Famous Fried Chicken, 1979, Pals, 4 different, ea from $10 to **$15.00**

Popeye, Popeye's Famous Fried Chicken/Pepsi, 1982, 10th Anniversary Series, 4 different, ea from $7 to............**$10.00**

Quick Draw, McGraw, see Hanna-Barbera

Raggedy Ann & Andy, going down slide, skipping rope, stacking blocks, riding in wagon, ea from $5 to **$10.00**

Rescuers, Pepsi, 1977, Brockway tumbler, Bernard, Bianca, Brutus & Nero, Evinrude, Orville, Penny, ea from $5 to........**$10.00**

Rescuers, Pepsi, 1977, Brockway tumbler, Madame Medusa or Rufus, ea from $15 to................................$25.00

Richie Rich, see Harvey Cartoon Characters

Riddler or Robin, see Super Heroes

Road Runner & Related Characters, see Warner Bros

Rocky & Bullwinkle, see Arby's Bicentennial or PAT Ward

Roy Rogers Restaurant, 1883-1983 logo, from $3 to..........$5.00

Sad Sack, see Harvey Cartoon Characters

Scooby Doo, see Hanna-Barbera

Sleeping Beauty, American, late 1950s, 6 different, ea from $8 to..$15.00

Sleeping Beauty, Canadian, late 1950s, 12 different, ea from $10 to..$15.00

Smurf's, Hardee's, 1982 (8 different), 1983 (6 different), ea, from $1 to..$3.00

Snidley Whiplash, see PAT Ward

Snoopy & Related Characters, see Peanuts Characters

Snow White & the Seven Dwarfs, Bosco, 1938, ea from $20 to..$30.00

Snow White & the Seven Dwarfs, Libbey, 1930s, verses on back, various colors, 8 different, ea from $15 to..................$25.00

Snow White & the Seven Dwarfs, see also Disney Collector's Series or Disney Film Classics

Star Trek, Dr Pepper, 1976, 4 different, ea from $15 to $20.00

Star Trek, Dr Pepper, 1978, 4 different, ea from $25 to $30.00

Star Trek II, The Search for Spock, Taco Bell, 1984, 4 different, ea from $3 to..$5.00

Star Trek: The Motion Picture, Coca-Cola, 1980, 3 different, ea from $10 to..$15.00

Star Wars Trilogy: Empire Strikes Back, Burger King/Coca-Cola, 1980, 4 different, ea from $5 to................................$7.00

Star Wars Trilogy: Return of the Jedi, Burger King/Coca-Cola, 1983, 4 different, ea from $3 to................................$5.00

Star Wars Trilogy: Star Wars, Burger King/Coca-Cola, 1977, 4 different, ea from $8 to................................$10.00

Sunday Funnies, 1976, Brenda Star, Gasoline Alley, Moon Mullins, Orphan Annie, Smilin' Jack, Terry & the Pirates, $5 to..$7.00

Sunday Funnies, 1976, Broom Hilda, from $90 to..........$125.00

Super Heroes, DC Comics or NPP/Pepsi Super (Moon) Series, 1976, Batgirl, Batman, Robin, Shazam!, ea from $10 to............$15.00

Super Heroes, DC Comics or N.P.P./ Pepsi Super (Moon) Series, 1976, Super Girl or Wonder Woman, each from $12.00 to $20.00.

Super Heroes, DC Comics or NPP/Pepsi Super (Moon) Series, 1976, Aquaman, Flash, Superman, ea $12 to.............$20.00

Super Heroes, DC Comics/Pepsi, 1978, Brockway, flat bottom, Batman, Robin, Wonder Woman (red boots), ea from $8 to..$15.00

Super Heroes, DC Comics/Pepsi, 1978, Brockway, flat bottom, Aquaman, Shazam!, Superman, The Flash, ea from $8 to........$10.00

Super Heroes, DC Comics/Pepsi, 1978, Brockway, rnd bottom, Batman, Robin, Shazam!, 5½", ea from $15 to..........$25.00

Super Heroes, DC Comics/Pepsi, 1978, Brockway, rnd bottom, Superman, The Flash, Wonder Woman, ea from $15 to..$25.00

Super Heroes, DC Comics/Pepsi Super (Moon) Series, 1976, Green Arrow, from $20 to................................$30.00

Super Heroes, DC Comics/Pepsi Super (Moon) Series, 1976, Green Lantern, Joker, Penguin, Riddler, ea from $25 to..........$30.00

Super Heroes, Marvel, 1978, Federal, flat bottom, Captain America, Hulk, Spider-Man, Thor, ea from $40 to....$75.00

Super Heroes, Marvel, 1978, Federal, flat bottom, Spider-Woman, from $100 to................................$150.00

Super Heroes, Marvel/7 Eleven, 1977, ftd, Amazing Spider-Man, from $25 to................................$30.00

Super Heroes, Marvel/7 Eleven, 1977, ftd, Captain America, Fantastic Four, Howard the Duck, Thor, ea from $10 to....$15.00

Super Heroes, Marvel/7 Eleven, 1977, ftd, Incredible Hulk, from $10 to..$15.00

Super Heroes, NPP/Pepsi Super (Moon) Series, 1976, Green Lantern, Joker, Penguin, Riddler, ea from $20 to.......$30.00

Superman, NPP/M Polanar & Son, 1964, 6 different, various colors, 4¼" or 5¾", ea from $20 to................................$25.00

Sylvester the Cat or Tasmanian Devil, see Warner Bros

Tom & Jerry & Related Characters, see MGM Collector Series

Underdog & Related Characters, see Arby's Bicentennial or Leonardo TTV

Universal Monsters, Universal Studio, 1980, ftd, Creature, Dracula, Frankenstein, Mummy, Mutant, Wolfman, ea $125 to..$150.00

Walter Lantz, Pepsi, 1970s, Chilly Willy or Wally Walrus, ea from $25 to..$45.00

Walter Lantz, Pepsi, 1970s, Cuddles, from $40 to............$60.00

Walter Lantz, Pepsi, 1970s, Space Mouse, from $150 to..$200.00

Walter Lantz, Pepsi, 1970s, Woody Woodpecker, from $7 to ..$15.00

Walter Lantz, Pepsi, 1970s-80s, Anty/Miranda, Chilly/Smelley, Cuddles/Oswald, Wally/Homer, ea from $20 to........$30.00

Super Heroes, DC Comics or N.P.P./Pepsi Super (Moon) Series, 1976, Penguin, DC Comics: from $40.00 to $60.00.

Walter Lantz, Pepsi, 1970s-80s, Buzz Buzzard/Space Mouse, from $15 to $20.00

Walter Lantz, Pepsi, 1970s-80s, Woody Woodpecker/Knothead & Splinter, from $15 to $20.00

Walter Lantz, see also Arby's Bicentennial Series

Warner Bros, Acme Cola, 1993, bell shape, Bugs, Sylvester, Taz, Tweety, ea from $4 to $8.00

Warner Bros, Arby's, 1988, Adventures Series, ftd, Bugs, Daffy, Porky, Sylvester & Tweety, ea from $25 to $30.00

Warner Bros, Marriott's Great America, 1975, 12-oz, 6 different (Bugs & related characters), ea from $20 to..............$30.00

Warner Bros, Marriott's Great America, 1989, Bugs, Porky, Sylvester, Taz, ea from $7 to $10.00

Warner Bros, Pepsi, 1973, Brockway 12-oz tumbler, Bugs, Porky, Road Runner, Sylvester, Tweety, ea, from $5 to.........$10.00

Warner Bros, Pepsi, 1973, Federal 16-oz tumbler, Bugs Bunny, wht lettering, from $5 to..$10.00

Warner Bros, Pepsi, 1973, Federal 16-oz tumbler, Cool Cat, blk lettering, from $5 to..$10.00

Warner Brothers, Pepsi, 1973, Federal 16-ounce tumbler, Elmer Fudd, white lettering, from $5.00 to $8.00.

Warner Bros, Pepsi, 1973, Federal 16-oz tumbler, Henry Hawk or Slow Poke Rodriquez, blk lettering, ea from $25 to ...$40.00

Warner Bros, Pepsi, 1973, Federal 16-oz tumbler, Speedy Gonzales, blk lettering, from $6 to $10.00

Warner Bros, Pepsi, 1973, wht plastic, 6 different, Bugs, Daffy, Porky, Road Runner, Sylvester, Tweety, ea from $3 to ..$5.00

Warner Bros, Pepsi, 1976, Interaction, Beaky Buzzard & Cool Cat w/kite or Taz & Porky w/fishing pole, ea from $8 to......$10.00

Warner Bros, Pepsi, 1976, Interaction, Bugs & Yosemite w/cannon, Yosemite & Speedy Gonzales panning gold, ea $10 to...$15.00

Warner Bros, Pepsi, 1976, Interaction, Foghorn Leghorn & Henry Hawk, from $10 to $15.00

Warner Bros, Pepsi, 1976, Interaction, others, ea from $5 to...$10.00

Warner Bros, Pepsi, 1979, Collector Series, rnd bottom, Bugs, Daffy, Porky, Road Runner, Sylvester, Tweety, ea $7 to..$10.00

Warner Bros, Pepsi, 1980, Collector Series, Bugs, Daffy, Porky, Road Runner heads on star, names on band above, ea $6 to..$10.00

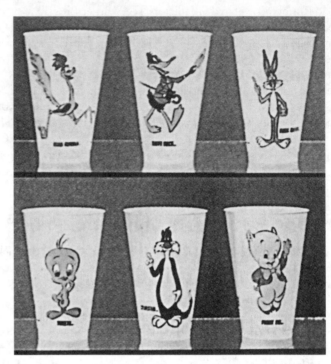

Warner Brothers, plastic, 1970s (with 1966 copyright), any character, rare, each from $3.00 to $5.00. (Photo courtesy Mark Chase and Michael Kelly)

Warner Bros, Six Flags, 1991, clear, Bugs, Daffy, Sylvester, Wile E Coyote, ea from $5 to $10.00

Warner Bros, Six Flags, 1991, clear, Yosemite Sam, from $10 to...$15.00

Warner Bros, Welch's, 1974, action poses, 8 different, phrases around top, ea from $2 to..$4.00

Warner Bros, Welch's, 1976-77, 8 different, names around bottom, ea from $5 to..$7.00

Warner Bros, 1995, Taz's Root Beer/Serious Suds, clear glass mug, from $5 to...$7.00

Warner Bros, 1996, 8 different w/ea character against busy background of repeated characters, names below, ea from $4 to...$6.00

Warner Bros, 1998, 6 different w/characters against vertically striped background, ea from $4 to $6.00

WC Fields, see Arby's Actor Series

Western Heroes, Annie Oakley, Buffalo Bill, Wild Bill Hickok, Wyatt Earp, ea from $8 to...$12.00

Western Heroes, Lone Ranger, from $10 to $15.00

Western Heroes, Wyatt Earp, fight scene or OK Corral gunfight, name at top, from $12 to $22.00

Wild West Series, Coca-Cola, Buffalo Bill, Calamity Jane, ea from $10 to..$15.00

Wile E Coyote, see Warner Bros

Winnie the Pooh, Sears/WDP, 1970s, 4 different, ea from $7 to...$10.00

Wizard of Oz, see also Children's Classics

Wizard of Oz, Coca-Cola/Krystal, 1989, 50th Anniversary Series, 6 different, ea from $7 to $10.00

Wizard of Oz, Swift's, 1950s-60s, fluted bottom, Emerald City or Flying Monkeys, ea from $8 to $15.00

Wizard of Oz, Swift's, 1950s-60s, fluted bottom, Glinda, from $15 to $25.00

Wizard of Oz, Swift's, 1950s-60s, fluted bottom, Wicked Witch, from $35 to...$50.00

Wonder Woman, see Super Heroes

Wonderful World of Disney, Pepsi, 1980s, Alice, Bambi, Lady & the Tramp, Pinocchio, Snow White, 101 Dalmatians, $15 to..$20.00

Woody Woodpecker & Related Characters, see Arby's Bicentennial or Walter Lantz

Yogi Bear or Yosimite Sam, see Hanna-Barbera

Ziggy, Number Series, 1-8, ea from $4 to.............................$8.00

Ziggy, 7-Up Collector Series, 1977, Here's to Good Friends, 4 different, ea from $3 to $5.00

Character Bobbin' Heads

Frequently referred to as nodders, these papier-maché dolls reflect accurate likenesses of the characters they portray and have become popular collectibles. Made in Japan throughout the 1960s, they were sold as souvenirs at Disney, Universal Studios, and Six Flags amusement parks, and they were often available at roadside concessions as well. Papier-maché was used until the mid-'70s when ceramic composition came into use. They were very susceptible to cracking and breaking, and it's difficult to find mint specimens — little wonder, since these nodders were commonly displayed on car dashboards!

Our values are for nodders in near-mint condition. To calculate values for examples in very good condition, reduce our prices by 25% to 40%.

Advisors: Matt and Lisa Adams (A7)

Donald Duck, celluloid with tin base, Japan, 6", EX, A, $300.00. (Photo courtesy Bertoia Auctions)

Andy Griffith, ceramic, 1992, NM $75.00
Barney Fife, ceramic, 1992, NM $75.00
Beetle Bailey, NM, from $150 to $200.00
Charlie Brown, sq blk base, NM, from $75 to.................$125.00
Charlie Brown, 1970s, NM, from $45 to.........................$60.00
Charlie Brown as Baseball Player, ceramic, Japan, NM $50.00
Chinese Boy & Girl, 5½", NM, pr $65.00
Colonel Sanders, 2 different, NM, ea from $125 to........$175.00
Dagwood, compo, Kiss Me on gr base, 1950s, 6", EX, from $150 to...$200.00
Danny Kaye & Girl Kissing, NM, pr, from $150 to $200.00
Dobie Gillis, NM, from $300 to $400.00
Donald Duck, Irwin/WDP, 5", EX $100.00
Donald Duck, rnd gr base, 1970s, NM $75.00
Donald Duck, Walt Disney World, sq wht base, NM........$75.00
Donny Osmond, wht jumpsuit w/microphone, NM, from $100 to...$150.00
Dr Ben Casey, NM, from $125 to $175.00
Dr Kildare, compo, rnd wht base, 1960s, 7", EX, from $100 to...$150.00
Dr Kildare, from $125 to...$175.00
Dumbo, rnd red base, NM, from $75 to $100.00
Goofy, arms at side, sq wht base, Disneyland, NM............$75.00
Goofy, arms folded, sq wht base, Walt Disney World, NM...$75.00

Hobo, composition, Japan, 1960s, NM, $65.00; Chinaman, composition, Japan, 1960s, NM, $65.00. (Photo courtesy June Moon)

Linus, sq blk base, Lego, NM, from $75 to $125.00
Linus as Baseball Catcher, ceramic, Japan, NM $60.00
Little Audrey, NM, from $100 to $150.00
Lt Fuzz (Beetle Bailey), NM, from $150 to $200.00
Lucy, no base, 1970s, sm, NM, from $45 to.....................$60.00
Lucy, sq blk base, Lego, NM, from $75 to $125.00
Lucy as Baseball Player, ceramic, NM, from $45 to $60.00
Mammy (Dogpatch USA), NM $75.00
Mary Poppins, wood, w/umbrella & satchel, Disneyland, 1960s, 5¾", M, from $100 to..$150.00
Maynard Krebs (Dobie Gillis), holding bongos, NM, from $300 to..$400.00
Mickey Mouse, red, wht & bl outfit, Disney World, NM .$75.00

Looney Tunes Characters, Top row: Bugs Bunny, Foghorn Leghorn, Porky Pig, Wile E. Coyote; Bottom row: Speedy Gonzoles, Elmer Fudd, Tweety, Yosemite Sam, NM, each from $175.00 to $250.00. (Photo courtesy Matt and Lisa Adams)

Mickey Mouse, red, wht & bl outfit, sq wht base, Disneyland, NM, from $75 to..$100.00
Mickey Mouse, yel & red outfit, rnd gr base, NM.............$75.00
Mr Peanut, moves at waist, NM, from $150 to $200.00
NY World's Fair Boy & Girl Kissing, NM, from $100 to ..$125.00
Oodles the Duck (Bozo the Clown), NM, from $150 to...$200.00
Peppermint Patti as Baseball Player, ceramic, Japan, NM, from $45 to $60.00
Phantom of the Opera, gr face, Universal, NM, from $150 to ..$200.00
Phantom of the Opera, sq base, rare, NM, from $500 to ..$750.00
Pig Pen, Lego, 1960s, 6", NM, from $75 to $125.00
Pluto, rnd gr base, 1970s, NM $75.00
Raggedy Andy, bank, mk A Penny Earned, NM..............$75.00
Raggedy Ann, bank, mk A Penny Saved, NM...................$75.00
Roy Rogers, compo, sq gr base, Japan, 1960s, M, from $150 to...$200.00
Schroeder, sq blk base, Lego, NM, from $75 to...............$125.00
Sgt Snorkel (Beetle Bailey), NM, from $150 to..............$200.00
Smokey the Bear, rnd base, NM, from $125 to $200.00
Smokey the Bear, sq base, NM, from $125 to $200.00
Snoopey as Joe Cool, no base, 1970s, sm, NM, from $45 to..$60.00
Snoopy, sq blk base, Lego, lg, NM, from $75 to..............$125.00
Snoopy as Baseball Player, ceramic, Japan, NM, from $45 to ..$60.00
Snoopy as Flying Ace, 1970s, NM, from $45 to................$60.00
Snoopy as Santa, 1970s, NM, from $45 to $60.00
Space Boy, blk spacesuit & helmet, NM $75.00
Three Little Pigs, bl overalls & yel cap, rnd red base, NM, ea from $100 to $150.00
Three Stooges, bsk, set of 3, MIB, from $100 to $150.00
Topo Gigio, Rossini/Japan, 1960s, 9", EX........................$55.00
Topo Gigio, w/fruit or w/o fruit, NM, ea $75.00
Winnie the Pooh, 1970s, rnd gr base, NM, from $100 to...$150.00
Wolfman, sq base, rare, NM, from $500 to $750.00
Woodstock, 1970s, NM, from $45 to..................................$60.00
Woodstock as Baseball Player, ceramic, Japan, NM, from $45 to ..$60.00
Zero (Beetle Bailey), NM, from $150 to $200.00

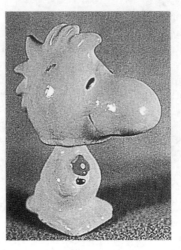

Woodstock, no base, 1970s, sm, NM, $45.00.

Character Clocks and Watches

Clocks and watches whose dials depict favorite sports and TV stars have been manufactured with the kids in mind since the 1930s, when Ingersoll made a clock, a wristwatch, and a pocket watch featuring Mickey Mouse. The #1 Mickey wristwatch came in the now-famous orange box commonly known as the 'critter box,' illustrated with a variety of Disney characters. There is also a blue display box from the same time period. The watch itself featured a second hand with three revolving Mickey figures. It was available with either a metal or leather band. Babe Ruth stared on an Exacta Time watch in 1949, and the original box contained not only the watch but a baseball with a facsimile signature.

Collectors prize the boxes about as highly as they do the watches. Many were well illustrated and colorful, but most were promptly thrown away, so they're hard to find today. Be sure you buy only watches in very good condition. Rust, fading, scratches, or other signs of wear sharply devaluate a clock or a watch. Hundreds have been produced, and if you're going to collect them, you'll need to study *Comic Character Clocks and Watches* by Howard S. Brenner (Books Americana) for more information.

Note: Our values are typical of high retail. A watch in exceptional condition, especially an earlier model, may bring even more. Dealers (who will generally pay about half of book when they buy for resale) many times offer discounts on the more pricey items, and package deals involving more than one watch may sometimes be made for as much as a 15% discount.

Advisor: Bill Campbell (C10)

See also Advertising.

CLOCKS

Bugs Bunny Alarm Clock, Ingraham, 1940s, Bugs resting w/carrot, 4x4" sq, EX, from $150 to $200.00
Bugs Bunny Wall Clock, Seth Thomas, 1970, plastic case, image of Bugs w/carrot, electric, 10" dia, NM $85.00
Cinderella Alarm Clock, Bradley/Japan, image of Cinderella leaving slipper on steps, 3" dia, scarce, MIB $125.00

Batman and Robin Talking Alarm Clock, Janex, 1970s, molded plastic with image of Batman running along side Robin in car, VG+, from $40.00 to $50.00; from $100.00 to $125.00 with box.

Bugs Bunny Talking Alarm Clock, Janex, 1970s, molded plastic with Bugs leaning on clock and sign reading 'Eh, Wake Up, Doc!,' MIB, $75.00.

Davy Crockett Electric Clock, Haddon Prod, 1950s, plastic log cabin form w/rnd dial & Day graphics, 7x11½", NM, A..........$725.00
Felix the Cat, Bright Ideas, 1989, MIB..............................$65.00
Hopalong Cassidy Alarm Clock, US Time, close-up of Hoppy on Topper on rnd face, name on base, EX, C10............$650.00
Howdy Doody Clock-A-Doodle, Bandai/Kagran, EXIB, A..$1,350.00
Howdy Doody Talking Alarm Clock, Janex, It's Howdy Doody Time, plastic, w/Howdy & Clarabelle figures, 7" L, EXIB........$150.00
James Bond 007 Wall Clock, 1981, Roger Moore image, NM+ $50.00
Mickey Mouse Alarm Clock, Bradley, 1960s, lg blk ears atop rnd case w/lg face image on front, footed, 3½" dia, EXIB...$85.00
Mickey Mouse Alarm Clock, Ingersoll, 1930s, electric, sq metal case w/Mickey figure on face, 4" sq, nonworking o/w M, A .$425.00

Mickey Mouse Alarm Clock, Ingersoll, 1930s, w/up, rnd case w/full figure Mickey on face, 4" T, nonworking, VGIB, A..$150.00
Mickey Mouse Alarm Clock, Ingersoll, 1940s, w/up, plastic arched case, full Mickey on face, 4½", NM+IB, A..$400.00
Mickey Mouse Alarm Clock, Ingersoll, 1940s, w/up, plastic arched case, full Mickey on face, 4½", VG, A...........$40.00

Minnie Mouse Alarm Clock, Bradley/WDP, red case with two yellow bells, image and name on face, footed, EXIB, P6, $65.00.

Mickey Mouse Cookie Time Alarm Clock, WDP, EX, $85.00.

Peanuts Alarm Clock, Japan, 1988, silver metal case, character faces as numbers, 3½" dia, MIB.................................$60.00
Pluto Wall Clock, Allied, plastic figure w/clock attached to his chest, hands shaped as dog bones, 8", EXIB............$300.00
Popeye Alarm Clock, Smiths/Great Britain, 1960s, Popeye & Swee Pea, head moves to count seconds on rnd face, 5", VG, A $200.00
Roy Rogers & Trigger Alarm Clock, Ingraham, desert mountain scene on face, 4½" sq, MIB $600.00
Roy Rogers & Trigger Alarm Clock, Ingraham, desert mountain scene, 4½" sq, VG+...$280.00
Shmoo Pendulette Alarm Clock, Lux, 1950, plastic figure, 8", EXIB...$275.00

Sleeping Beauty Alarm Clock, Phinney-Walker, 1950s, Sleeping Beauty petting rabbit & surrounded by 3 birds, 5", EX+..$65.00

Snoopy & Charlie Brown Talking Alarm Clock, Janex, 1974, 2-D image of Snoopy & Charlie beside clock, plastic, MIB.$135.00

Superman Wall Clock, New Haven, 1978, b/o, framed w/image of Superman confronting spaceship, EX+ $40.00

Tweety Bird Talking Alarm Clock, Janex, 1978, b/o, EX..$75.00

POCKET WATCHES

Buck Rogers, Ingraham, 1935, 2½" dia, EX $550.00

Captain Marvel, Fawcett, 1948, rnd chrome case, full figure image, plastic strap, EXIB..$750.00

Dan Dare, Imperial Limited/London, 1950s, 2" dia, EX, $500.00. (Photo courtesy Randy Inman Auctions)

Don Winslow of the Navy, New Haven, 1938-39, EX ..$1,600.00

Donald Duck, Ingersoll, rnd chrome case, Donald w/hands on hips, Mickey emb on back, G...................................$275.00

Lone Ranger, 1970, rnd chrome case, Lone Ranger & Silver, bl strap, silver chain, NM..$100.00

Mary Marvel, Fawcett, 1948, rnd chrome case, full figure, red plastic strap, VG, A..$125.00

Mickey Mouse, Ingersoll, 1930s, box only, 7" L, VG......$175.00

Mickey Mouse, Ingersoll, 1930s, rnd chrome case, full image of Mickey on face, complete w/Mickey fob, GIB, A....$500.00

Mickey Mouse, Ingersoll, 1930s, round chrome case, full image of Mickey on face, EX+, A, $350.00.

Mickey Mouse, Ingersoll, 1930s, rnd chrome case, full image of Mickey on face, nonworking o/w VG, A $190.00

Mickey Mouse, Ingersoll, 1930s, rnd chrome case, full image of Mickey on face, complete w/Mickey fob, NMIB ..$1,750.00

Popeye, New Haven, 1935, 1¾" dia, NM+, from $550.00 to $1,000.00.

Roy Rogers, Bradley, lg image of Roy w/sm image of Roy & Trigger in background, w/stopwatch feature, EX............$600.00

Superman, New Haven, rectangular chrome case, 3-quarter figure, w/stopwatch feature, EX,.............................$600.00

Three Little Pigs, Ingersoll, 1934, image of the Three Little Pigs & the Big Bad Wolf, EX+IB................................$1,200.00

Tom Mix, Ingersoll, 1930s, rnd chrome case, Tom on rearing horse, emb phrase on back, EX $3,500.00

Wizard of Oz, Westclock, 1980s, 4 characters on dial, silver-tone case, unused, MIB...$75.00

Woody (Toy Story), Fossil, 1996, limited ed, M (M box & container) $125.00

WRISTWATCHES

Alice in Wonderland, Ingersoll, image of Alice, fabric strap, EX (EX rnd pk box w/clear plastic teacup), from $250 to..$350.00

Alice in Wonderland, Timex, 1950s, name on rnd face, w/ceramic figure, MIB $300.00

Angelique (Dark Shadows), Abbelare, MIB (coffin box) ..$100.00

Babe Ruth, EX (EX plastic baseball container), $850.00. (Photo courtesy Randy Inman Aucitons)

Bambi, Ingersoll-US Time/WDP, 1949, Birthday Series, rnd chrome case, animated ears for hands, leather band, MIB, A $275.00

Barnabas Collins (Dark Shadows), Abbelare, MIB (coffin box)...$100.00

Batman, Fossil, 1990, limited ed, complete w/pin, M (M litho box), from $150 to...$200.00

Batman, 1966, batwings keep time on rnd face encased in blk plastic wings, NMIB $850.00

Big Bad Wolf/Three Little Pigs, Ingersoll/WD, 1934, rnd case, rare tapered leather band, NMIB, C10, from $2,600 to..$3,000.00

Big Bad Wolf/Three Little Pigs, Ingersoll/WD, 1934, rnd chrome case, metal bracelet band w/wolf & pigs, NM+ $950.00

Big Bad Wolf/Three Little Pigs, Ingersoll/WD, 1935, box only, shows circular image of wolf's head on oblong box, EX $1,000.00

Bionic Woman, MZ Berger, 1970s, image & lettering on face, vinyl band, NM, from $60 to...$80.00

Blondie, Danbros Watch Co/KFS, 1949, rnd chrome case, Blondie, Dagwood & pups on band, NM+IB, A......$950.00

Bongo, Ingersoll/US Time/WDP, Birthday Series, EXIB...$325.00

Bozo the CLown, 1960s, image & name in red, vinyl band, EX $50.00

Buffy & Jody, Sheffield, 1969, image & names on face, visible gears, various bands, M, ea $125.00

Bugs Bunny, Rexall Drug Co/Warner Bors, 1950s, rnd chrome case, animated carrot hands, EX, C10.......................$400.00

Bugs Bunny, Rexall Drug Co/Warner Bros, 1950s, rnd chrome case, animated carrot hands, NM+IB, A $1,600.00

Buzz Lightyear (Toy Story), Fossil, 1996, complete w/Buzz Lightyear plaque, M (M rnd tin box) $75.00

Captain Marvel, Fawcett, 1948, rnd chrome case, vinyl band, VG $160.00

Captain Marvel, Fawcett, 1948, rnd chrome case, vinyl band, unused, NM+IB, A $500.00

Catwoman, Quintel, 1991, digital, NM+ $25.00

Charlie Brown, Determined, 1970s, baseball scene on yel background, black band, EXIB...$175.00

Charlie Brown, Determined, 1970s, baseball scene on yel background, blk band, EX+...$75.00

Charlie Chaplin, Bradley, 1985, Oldies Series, MIB.........$50.00

Cinderella, Ingersoll-US Time, 1950, rnd chrome case, pk band, unused, MIB, A $350.00

Cool Cat, Sheffield, 1960s, full-figure image, VG.............$50.00

Daisy Duck, US Time, 1948, EXIB.................................$300.00

Dale Evans, Bradley, 1950s, oblong chrome case, Dale & Buttermilk on face, leather band, MIB, A $225.00

Dale Evans, Bradley, 1960s, rnd gold-tone case, image of Dale & Buttermilk framed by horseshoe on face, vinyl band, VG......$50.00

Davy Crockett, US Time, 1950s, gr plastic case, tooled leather band, EX+...$100.00

Davy Crockett, US Time, 1950s, gr plastic case, tooled leather band, unused, MIB (w/powder horn display)...........$450.00

Dick Tracy, New Haven/Chester Gould, 1948, rnd chrome case, leather band, EXIB (yel box), A $200.00

Dick Tracy, New Haven/Chester Gould, 1951, rnd chrome case, leather band, NM+IB (wht box), A........................$650.00

Dizzy Dean, Everbrite-Ingersoll, 1933, scarce, M $1,100.00

Donald Duck, Ingersoll, 1936, leather band w/little Donalds, Donald hands, EXIB, C10, from $2,500 to...........$3,000.00

Donald Duck, Ingersoll-US Time/WDP, 1940s, oblong chrome case, animated hands, vinyl band, NM+IB, A.........$725.00

Donald Duck, Ingersoll-US Time/WDP, 1940s, rnd chrome case, complete w/pen & plastic ring, NM+IB (rnd birthday cake box), A..$650.00

Dopey, Ingersoll-US Time/WDP, Birthday Series, EXIB...$250.00

Dr Seuss' Cat in the Hat, 1972, NM $150.00

Dudley DoRight's Little Nell & Horse, Jay Ward, 1972, rnd chrome case, leather band, 17 jewels, EX, C10 ....$145.00

Evel Knievel, Bradley, 1976, vinyl band, EX...................$150.00

Flipper, ITF/MGM, glow-in-the-dark image, M..............$125.00

Frankenstein (Universal Monsters), 1995, glow-in-the-dark, MOC..$25.00

Gene Autry, New Haven, 1951, Six Shooter, brn leather band, unused, MIB..$650.00

Gene Autry, Wilane, 1948, Champion, NMIB...............$400.00

Girl From UNCLE, 1960s, pk face w/blk line drawing & numbers, EX $65.00

Goofy, Helbros/WDP, 1972, runs backwards, rnd chrome case, animated hands, leather band, MIB, A...................$675.00

Goofy, Helbros/WDP, 1972, runs backwards, rnd chrome case, animated hands, leather band, EX+ $400.00

Green Lantern, MIB $85.00

Hopalong Cassidy, Anniversary, w/watch, neckerchief & steer slide, MIB, C10...$150.00

Hopalong Cassidy, US Time/Wm Boyd, 1955, blk plastic case, decorated band, unused, MIB, A.............................$525.00

Howdy Doody, Ideal/Kagran, 1950s, rnd chrome case, plastic band, MIB, A...$650.00

Howdy Doody, Paten Watch Co/Bob Smith, 1954, rnd chrome case, Howdy on face w/movable eyes, MIB, A $1,425.00

Joe Carioca, Ingersoll-US Time/WDP, 1953, chrome case, animated hands, EX+IB (20th birthday box), A $250.00

Joker, Fossil, 1980s, NMIP..$75.00

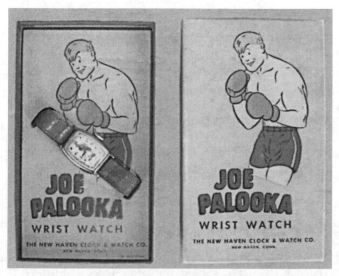

Joe Paloka, New Haven/Ham Fisher, 1948, unused, NMIB, A, $950.00. (Photo courtesy Smith House Toy Company)

Josie & the Pussycats, Bradley, 1971, complete w/3 bands, MIB...$350.00

Kaptain Kool & the Kongs, 1977, Kaptain Kool on face, M...$100.00

Lash LaRue, MIB..$50.00

Li'l Abner Animated, New Haven, 1947, rare, MIB, from $600 to...$800.00

Lone Ranger, New Haven, 1939, MIB, from $500.00 to $800.00. (Photo courtesy Smith House Toy Company)

Lone Ranger, New Haven, 1939, oblong chrome case w/Lone Ranger on face, leather band, MIB, A.................$3,200.00

Lone Ranger Lapel Watch, New Haven, 1939, rnd chrome case w/blk-pnt rim, LR & Silver on front, w/holser & gun fob, EX+IB...$525.00

Man From UNCLE, Bradley, 1960s, very rare w/box, MIB..$200.00

Mary Marvel, Marvel/Fawcett, 1948, rnd chrome case, vinyl band, EX+IB (oblong cb box)..............................$600.00

Mary Marvel, Marvel/Fawcett, 1948, rnd chrome case, vinyl band, unused, MIB (oblong plastic box)..................$660.00

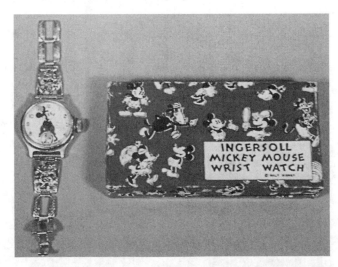

Mickey Mouse, Ingersoll, 1930s, metal link bracelette band, EXIB (red with allover black and white images of Mickey and friends), from $1,000.00 to $1,500.00. (Photo courtesy David Longest and Michael Stern)

Mickey Mouse, Ingersoll, 1930s, rnd gold-tone case, vinyl band, VGIB, A..$150.00

Mickey Mouse, Ingersoll, 1933, rnd chrome case, metal link bracelet band, EXIB (red box w/Mickey & friends images)......$1,200.00

Mickey Mouse, Ingersoll, 1933, rnd chrome case, metal link bracelet band, GIB (red box w/Mickey & friends images)...........$600.00

Mickey Mouse, Ingersoll, 1933, rnd chrome case, metal link bracelet band, NMIB (bl box w/Mickey walking & pointing), C10...$900.00

Mickey Mouse, Ingersoll, 1938, oblong chrome case, metal link bracelet band, VGIB (Mickey in top hat on box), A...$1,500.00

Mickey Mouse, Ingersoll, 1939, oblong gold-tone case, leather band, nonworking o/w EXIB.............................$1,600.00

Mickey Mouse, Ingersoll, 1947, oblong chrome case, leather band, unused, MIB (yel Mickey box), A.................$400.00

Mickey Mouse, Ingersoll, 1947, oblong chrome case, vinyl band, EXIB (yel Mickey box).............................$275.00

Mickey Mouse, Ingersoll, 1947, oblong chrome case, vinyl band, NM+IB (yel Mickey box)..............................$500.00

Mickey Mouse, Ingersoll, 1947, rnd chrome case, vinyl band, NM+IB (yel Mickey box), A.............................$225.00

Mickey Mouse, Ingersoll, 1948, rnd chrome case, luminous face, unused, NMIB (20th birthday box)........................$500.00

Mickey Mouse, Ingersoll, 1950s, rnd chrome case, vinyl band, VGIB (w/Mickey stand-up display in box)..............$350.00

Minnie Mouse, Timex, 1950s, Minnie on rnd face, w/emb celluloid plaque, MIB.......................................$200.00

Orphan Annie, New Haven/Harold Gray, 1935, oblong chrome case, leather band, EXIB (blk & wht oblong box), A..........$1,450.00

Orphan Annie, New Haven/Harold Gray, 1948, oblong chrome case, leather band, NM+IB (gr box w/image of Annie & Tige), A...$450.00

Partridge Family, 1970s, family image on face, NM, from $150 to...$200.00

Pinocchio, Ingersoll-US Time/WDP, 1948, rnd chrome case, luminated face, leather band, MIB (20th birthday box), A .$450.00

Pluto, Ingersoll-US Time/WDP, 1948, rnd chrome case w/luminous face, MIB (20th birthday box), A....................$375.00

Porky Pig, Ingraham/Warner Brothers, 1949, MIB, A, $880.00.

Pocahontas, Time Works/Disney, 1990s, leather strap, unused, MIB $75.00

Pokeman, General Mills premium, 1999, blk plastic band, MIP ..$12.00

Popeye, Bradley, #308, 1964, gr case, EXIB.....................$200.00

Popeye, New Haven/KFS, 1935, different Popeye characters on oblong face, leather band, NMIB, A $4,050.00

Popeye, Unique, 1987, digital, NMIB $50.00

Porky Pig, Sheffield, 1970s, rnd chrome case w/Porky tipping his hat on face, vinyl band, NMIB........................$75.00

Rocky Jones Space Ranger, Ingraham, 1950s, MIB $750.00

Roger Rabbit, Shiraka, 1980s, silhouette, gold case, blk band, unused, MIP..$150.00

Roy Rogers, Ingraham, 1960s, chrome case w/flickering image of Roy on Trigger, leather band, NM+ $150.00

Roy Rogers & Trigger, Bradley, 1960s, rnd chrome case w/close-up image of Roy holding Trigger's bit, vinyl band, VG+ $50.00

Rudolph the Red Nosed Reindeer, Ingersoll, 1947, oblong chrome case, leather band, NM+IB, A $400.00

Smitty, New Haven, 1930s, VGIB, A, $425.00. (Photo courtesy James D. Julia Auctions, Inc.)

Smokey Bear, Hamilton, 1960s, MIB $150.00

Snoopy, Determined, 1969, dancing Snoopy, gold or silver case, various bands, EX $100.00

Snoopy, Timex, 1970s, tennis theme w/articulated hands holding racket on denim background, denim band, NMIB $75.00

Space Patrol, US Time, 1950, chrome case w/expansion band, NM+IB, A $950.00

Superman, Bradley, 1959, chrome case w/Superman flying over cityscape, EXIB..$700.00

Superman, Dabbs, NM $100.00

Superman, Ingraham/NCP, 1948, Supertime #289, oblong chrome case & leather band w/'S,' unused, MIB, A $3,800.00

Superman, New Haven, 1939, Superman from waist up on oval face, leather band, EXIB $1,000.00

Tarzan, Bradley, MIB..$60.00

Three Little Pigs, Ingersoll, 1934, MIB.......................$3,000.00

Tim Holt, MIB $50.00

Tom Corbett Space Cadet, Ingraham, 1950s, rnd chrome case, leather band, NM+IB (w/rocket ship insert), A...$2,600.00

Tom Mix, 1983, 100th Anniversary, M............................$275.00

Wizard of Oz, EKO, 1989, plastic band, unused, MIP.......$50.00

Wonder Woman/Super Hero, Dabs, 1970s, image on rnd face, leather band, NMIB $100.00

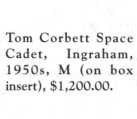

Tom Corbett Space Cadet, Ingraham, 1950s, M (on box insert), $1,200.00.

Woody (Toy Story), Fossil, 1996, complete w/Woody plaque, unused, M (M rnd tin box)................................$75.00

X-Files, Fossil, 2000, M (M see-through cylinder box) $75.00

Zorro, US Time/WDP, 1950s, blk face w/Zorro in red, blk band, EX+ $125.00

Zorro, US Time/WDP, 1950s, blk face w/Zorro in red, blk band, unused, NM+ (EX+ hat box) $350.00

Character, TV, and Movie Collectibles

To the baby boomers who grew up glued to the TV set and addicted to Saturday matinees, the faces they saw on the screen were as familiar to them as family. Just about any character you could name has been promoted through retail merchandising to some extent; depending on the popularity they attain, exposure may continue for weeks, months, even years. It's no wonder, then, that the secondary market abounds with these items or that there is such wide-spread collector interest. For more information, we recommend *Cartoon Toys and Collectibles Identification and Value Guide* by David Longest; and *The World of Raggedy Ann Collectibles* by Kim Avery.

Note: Though most characters are listed by their own names, some will be found under the title of the group, movie, comic strip, or dominate character they're commonly identified with. The Joker, for instance, will be found in the Batman listings.

All items are complete unless noted otherwise.

See also Action Figures; Battery-Operated; Books; Chein; Character Clocks and Watches; Coloring, Activity, and Paint Books; Disney; Dolls, Celebrity; Fisher-Price; Games; Guns; Halloween Costumes; Lunch Boxes; Marx; Model Kits; Paper Dolls; Pin-Back Buttons; Plastic Figures; Playsets; Ramp Walkers; Records; View-Master; Western; Windups, Friction, and Other Mechanicals.

Addams Family, bank, Lurch, ceramic, Koria, 1970s, 8", NM ...$200.00

Addams Family, doll, Morticia, stuffed cloth, 27", NM $50.00

Addams Family, figure, Morticia, hard plastic w/oversized rubber head, 4", 1960s, NM..................................$100.00

Addams Family, figure, Uncle Fester, pnt hard plastic w/movable soft vinyl head, Remco, 1960s, 4½", NM $150.00

Addams Family, hand puppets, Gomez, Morticia, or Uncle Fester, Ideal, 1965, EX, ea..................................$75.00

Addams Family, Uncle Munster's Mystery Light Bulb, Poynnter Prod, 1965, EXIB..................................$125.00

Alf, figure, plush, talker, b/o, Alien Prod, 1980s, 18", EX ..$30.00

Alf, figure, Stick-Around Alf, plush w/suction cups on hands, Coleco, 1988, 8", unused, NRFB..................................$18.00

Alf, finger puppet, plush, Coleco, 1987, MIB $15.00

Alf, hand puppet, Born to Rock, Alien Prod, 1988, 12", M..$18.00

Alf, hand puppet, Cookin' w/Alf, Alien Prod, 1988, MIP (sealed)..................................$22.00

Alf, jacks set, ball & 5 jacks, 1980s, MIP $6.50

Alvin & the Chipmunks, any character, PVC, jtd arms & legs, about 3", NM, ea..................................$4.00

Alvin and the Chipmunks, bank, Alvin, vinyl, M, $25.00. (Photo courtesy David Longest)

Alvin & the Chipmunks, figure, Alvin, stuffed ribbed cloth & felt bodt w/lg applied felt A, Christy, 1959, 5", NM ..$25.00

Alvin & the Chipmunks, figure, any charachter, plush w/vinyl face, Knickerbocker, 1960s, 14", NM, ea $50.00

Alvin & the Chipmunks, figure, any character, plush, Burger King, 1988, 12", NM+, ea..................................$15.00

Alvin & the Chipmunks, soap dispenser, Alvin figure holding bar of soap mk The Chipmunks, Helm Toy, 1984, 10", NRFB $25.00

Alvin & the Chipmunks, Stuff & Lace Set, Hasbro, 1950s-60s, EX+IB $75.00

Alving & the Chipmunks, jack-in-the-box, plastic, shows Alvin singing into microphone on side, Child Guidance, 1983, NM..................................$35.00

American Tail, Christmas stockings, Fievel, 3 different, McDonald's, 1986, 7", EX+, ea $5.00

American Tail, doll, Fievel plush, bl pants, red shirt, bl hat, Caltoy/Sears, 22", NM..................................$15.00

Amos & Andy, figure set, jtd wood, Jaymar, 1930s, 6", NM..$300.00

Andy Panda, see Walter Lantz

Annie (Movie), doll, Annie, Knickerbocker, 1980s, 6", MIB....$45.00

Annie (Movie), doll, any character except Annie, Knickerbocker, 1980s, 7", MIB, ea..................................$35.00

Archies, doll, Archie, stuffed cloth, Presents, 1987, 18", NM+...$28.00

Archies, figure, Reggie, bendable vinyl, standing w/arms out at sides, gray pants, yel jacket, Jesco, 1989, 6½", NM+ ..$60.00

Archies, Jughead Jr Shaver, Ja-Ru, 1986, NRFP $10.00

Archies, Ring Toss, Ja-Ru, 1987, NRFP $10.00

Archies, stencil set, 1980s, MOC $18.00

Aristocats, Colorforms, 1960s, MIB $50.00

Atom Ant, Play Fun Set, Whitman, 1966, NMIB............$50.00

Babar, figure, felt-like beanbag body, Toy Works, 1980s, 10", NM+ $18.00

Babar, figure, stuffed plush, gray w/gr suit & yel crown, button eyes, Gund, 1988, 9", M $12.00

Babar, figure, vinyl, jtd, gr pnt suit w/felt overcoat, c L de Brunhoff, 1988, 7", NM..................................$20.00

Babe, figure, stuffed felt-like material, purple w/chest label reading Babe & Friends, Toy Works, 1990s, 8", NM $10.00

Babe, figure, stuffed plush, pk, talker, sits upright on all fours, Equity Toys, 1990s, 9", NM+..................................$15.00

Baby Huey, figure, stuffed felt-like cloth, Good Stuff, 1999, 9", NM $8.00

Banana Splits, figure, Yellow Dog, plastic w/vinyl head, jtd arms, Dakin, 1970, 7", EX $50.00

Banana Splits, guitar, Snorky Elephant, 1970s, 10", EX ...$25.00

Banana Splits, Kut-Up Kit, Larami, 1970s, MOC (sealed) ..$20.00

Banana Splits, tambourine, plastic & cb, 1970s, MIP.......$35.00

Barney, bank, Baby Bop seated on lg alphabet block, hard vinyl, HEI, 1992, 7", M..................................$12.00

Barney, bank, Barney figure, vinyl, 7½", NM+ $8.00

Barney, figure, Baby Bop, plush, Lyons Group, 1992, 13", M..$10.00

Barney Google & Spark Plug, figure, Spark Plug, ceramic, stylized w/name emb on sides, beige w/blk pnt trim, 3½", NM+..................................$50.00

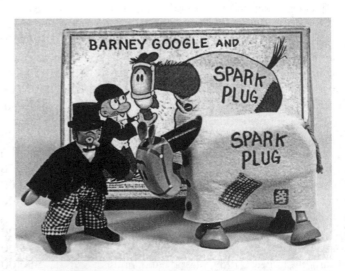

Barney Google and Spark Plug, figure set, Schoenhut, MIB, $2,500.00.

Barney Google & Spark Plug, figure, Spark Plug, stuffed cloth w/blanket mk Sparky, 10", VG+ $225.00

Barney Google & Spark Plug, pull toy, litho tin, figures rock back & forth when pulled, VG, A $825.00

Barney Google & Spark Plug, pull toy, Spark Plug, stenciled wood figure on 4 wheels, mk Spark Plug on blanket, 5", VG..$50.00

Barney Google & Spark Plug, pull toy, Spark Plug Wa-Gee Walker, stuffed cloth w/orig blanket mk Spark Plug, 9", EX+ $550.00

Batman, bank, compo, standing on sq base w/hands on hips, name on base, NPP/Japan, 1966, 7", NM..................$80.00

Batman, Batmobile, Duncan, 1970s, unused, MOC (8x12") ..$75.00

Batman, Batmobile Motorized Kit, Aoshinu/Japan, 1980s, unused, MIP..$80.00

Batman, Cast & Paint Set, 1960s, complete & unused, NMIB $75.00

Batman, coin set, Transogram, 1966, MIP (sealed)..........$35.00

Batman, Color Pin-Ups, litho cb, various images, 1966, 11x14", NMIB, ea $25.00

Batman, Colorforms Cartoon Kit, 1960s, EXIB................$50.00

Batman, doll, Batman, hard vinyl, jtd, bl shorts, gloves & boots w/turq cape, yel belt, Presents, 1988, 15", M $40.00

Batman, doll, Flying Batman, Transogram, 1966, 13", MIP (sealed) $175.00

Batman, doll, vinyl w/movable arms, Japan, 1960s, 14", EX+..$150.00

Batman, figure, Batman w/arms above head, inflatable vinyl, silver body w/bl head, hands & feet, Japan, 1970s, 24", EX+..$25.00

Batman, figure, Robin Jr. (Super Junior) w/1 arm behind back and waving w/the other, squeeze vinyl, 1978, 6½", EX........$30.00

Batman, Give-A-Show Bat-Projector, Chad Valley/NPPI, 1966, NMIB...$500.00

Batman, Gotham City Stunt Set, Tonka, 1989, NMIP $75.00

Batman, hand puppet, Batman, cloth body w/vinyl head, Ideal/NPPI, 1965-66, NM $75.00

Batman, hand puppet, Batman, plastic printed body w/molded vinyl head, Ideal, 1966, EX..$50.00

Batman, hand puppet, Robin, plastic printed body w/molded vinyl head, 1966, NM...$75.00

Batman, Helmet & Cape set, bl hard plastic face helmet w/bl vinyl cape, Ideal, 1966, EXIB..................................$200.00

Batman, kite, Hi-Flyer, 1980s, unused, MIP....................$30.00

Batman, mug, clear plastic w/mc paper wrap, 1966, 5", NM+..$75.00

Batman, night light, pnt vinyl figure standing on sq base, cloth cape, 11", EX..$75.00

Batman, Paint-By-Number Set, Hasbro, 1970s, NMIB $30.00

Batman, pencil box, gun shape, 1966, unused, MOC (sealed) $175.00

Batman, Print Putty, Colorforms, 1966, MIP (sealed)....$150.00

Batman, pull toy, Batboat, Eidai/Japan, EX+.................$75.00

Batman, push-button puppet, Batman, Kohner, 1960s, 3", NM+...$50.00

Batman, push-button puppet, Robin, Kohner, 1960s, 3", rare, NM $75.00

Batman, ring, flashes from Batman to Robin, silver-tone plastic, Vari-Vue, 1960s, EX+ $15.00

Batman, ring, plastic gumball type, 1960s, EX+...............$20.00

Batman, slide-tile puzzle, plastic, ½ image of Batman on wht tiles w/yel moon behind, American Publishing, 1977, MOC $20.00

Batman, Sparkle Paints, Kenner, 1966, EXIB $75.00

Batman, Super Powers Stain & Paint Set, 1980s, complete & unused, NMIP...$40.00

Batman, Trace-a-Graph, Emenee, 1966, EXIB................$35.00

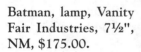

Batman, lamp, Vanity Fair Industries, 7½", NM, $175.00.

Beany and Cecil, doll, Beanie, Bob Clampett, ca 1960, NM, $200.00. (Photo courtesy David Longest)

Batman & Robin, Sip-A-Drink Cup, plastic, w/built-in straw, NPP, 1966, 5", EX+...$30.00

Batman Forever, candy dispenser, head form on rnd base, plastic, DC Comics, 1989, 3", unused, NM $5.00

Batman Returns, bank, vinyl, 1991, 9", EX....................$10.00

Beany & Cecil, bank, Cecil's head, molded plastic, NM ..$35.00

Beany & Cecil, Beany-Copter, Mattel, 1961, NMOC......$75.00

Beany & Cecil, Cecil Disguise Kit, unused, MIB............$115.00

Beany & Cecil, doll, Beany, talker, plush, Mattel, 1961, EXIB $200.00

Beany & Cecil, hand puppet, Cecil, talker, EX.................$50.00

Beany & Cecil, jack-in-the box, Mattel, 1961, M $250.00

Beany & Cecil, record player, Vanity Fair, 1961, EX+....$125.00

Beetle Bailey, nodder, Beetle Bailey, staning w/hands in pockets in gr army fatigues, name on base, Lego, 1960s, 8", NM+ $110.00

Beetle Bailey, nodder, Zero, compo, standing looking sideways in gr army fatigues, name on blk base, Lego, 1960s, 8", NM $110.00

Beetle Baily, doll, stuffed cloth w/vinyl head, brn camo outfit w/yel belt, brn vinyl shoes, Toy Works, 2002, 16", NM+ $15.00

Beetle Baily, stamper set, w/book, crayon & stampers, Ja-Ru, 1980s, complete & unused, MIP $60.00

Ben Casey, doctor kit, Transogram, EX $35.00

Ben Casey, Paint-By-Number Set, Transogram, 1962, MIB (sealed) $125.00

Berenstain Bears, figure, Mamma Bear, plush, gr dress or bl polka-dot dress, both w/hats, Chosum, 1990s, 9", EX+, ea $10.00

Berenstain Bears, figure, Mamma Bear, plush, gr polka-dot dress w/red hat & scarf, Applause, 11", EX $10.00

Berenstain Bears, figure, Sister Bear, plush, gr & purple outfit w/pk flowers, 1990s, 8", EX+ $10.00

Betty Boop, bank, pnt chalkware figure standing on rnd base w/hands on hips, 1950s-60s, 14", VG......................$125.00

Betty Boop, Colorforms Big Dress-Up Set, 1970s, MIB....$45.00

Betty Boop, doll, Betty, compo, gr-pnt dress w/red heart label on hip, gr bloomers & shoes, jtd, 12", rstr.....................$300.00

Betty Boop, doll, Betty, jtd vinyl, M-Toy, 1986, 12", NM+..$45.00

Betty Boop, doll, Betty, stuffed cloth, in Santa outfit & hat w/toy bag standing on top of chimney, KF, 1999, 13", VG+..$10.00

Betty Boop, doll, Ko-Ko the Clown, plush w/rubber head, cloth outfit, Presents, 1987, 12", NM $25.00

Betty Boop, doll quilt, quilted stuffed cloth w/litho Betty Boop design, Fleischer Studios, 1930s, 18x13", EX...........$100.00

Betty Boop, figure, Betty, pnt wood bead type w/jtd limbs, 1930s, 4½", EX..$75.00

Betty Boop, figure, Betty Boop, PVC, 8 different, 1980s, 3", ea..$15.00

Betty Boop, figure, Bimbo, bsk, playing fiddle, Japan, 1930s, 3½", NM...$125.00

Betty Boop, figure, Bimbo, wood & compo, jtd, 7", EX..$325.00

Betty Boop, nodder figure w/hand on hip & in short pk dress w/red heart on rnd base, celluloid, prewar, 7½", EXIB, A..$1,400.00

Betty Boop, tambourine, litho tin, 1930s, 6" dia, EX......$150.00

Beverly Hillbillies, BH Car, plastic w/up w/figures & accessories, Ideal, 1963, 22½", EXIB..$500.00

Beverly Hillbillies, Colorforms w/foyer scene, 1960s, NMIB...$100.00

Beverly Hillbillies, car, Ideal, 1963, EXIB, $550.00.

Beverly Hillbillies, doll, Ellie May, complete w/wardrobe, Unique, Art, 1964, 12", MIB $200.00

Beverly Hillbillies, doll, Jane Hathaway, gr skirt & jacket w/yel blouse, Japan, 1960s, 11½", MIB $400.00

Beverly Hills 90210, dolls, any character, Mattel, 1991, 11½", MIB, ea...$50.00

Bewitched, doll, Samantha, red gown & hat, Ideal, 1965, 11½", M...$300.00

Bimbo, see Betty Boop

Bionic Woman, bank, vinyl figure in jogging suit running on 'rocky' base, Animals Plus, 1976, 10", EX+................$25.00

Bionic Woman, Paint-By-Number Set, Craftmaster, 1970s, MIB..$30.00

Bionic Woman, Pic-A-Show Projector, Kenner, 1970s, MIB..$25.00

Bionic Woman, Play Doh Action Playset, Kenner, 1970s, MIB..$20.00

Bionic Woman, See-A-Show Viewer, Kenner, 1970s, MOC ..$15.00

Bionic Woman, Styling Boutique, Kenner, 1970s, MIB ...$50.00

Blondie, dolls, Dagwood, Knickerbocker, 14", EX+, $700.00; Alexander, Knickerbocker, 9", EX+, $400.00.

Bionic Woman, wallet, bl or pk w/image, Fabergè, 1970s, MIP $200.00

Blondie, doll, Blondie, soft vinyl molded curly blond hair, red cloth dress, red pnt shoes, Presents, 1985, 18", NM+ ..$30.00

Blondie, figure, Daisy the dog, plush, w/orig tag, 1985, EX ..$25.00

Blondie, marionette, Dagwood, 1940s, 14", NM+ $225.00

Blondie, paint set, American Crayon, 1940s, EXIB..........$75.00

Blondie, wallet, EX+...$25.00

Blossom (TV Show), dolls, any character, Tyco, 1993, 9", MIB $35.00

Blues Brothers, dolls, Elwood & Jake, blk cloth suits, hats & sunglasses, Fun 4 All, 1997, 26", MIB, set....................$200.00

Blues Brothers, dolls, Elwood & Jake, shiny blk suits, hats & sunglasses, w/accessories, Fun 4 All, 1997, 12", MIB, ea ...$30.00

Bo-Peep, doll, jtd body w/pnt features, blond mohair wig, pk & wht print dress & hat, w/lamb, Vogue, 8", EX $550.00

Bob Hope, hand puppet, cloth body w/pnt vinyl head, Bob Hope/JVZ Co, 1940s, scarce, EX $75.00

Bonzo, dexterity game, tin & cb, Germany, 4" dia, EX, A ..$100.00

Bonzo, figure, plush, seated, orig Bonzo button on collar, Chad Valley/England, 5" T, VG $250.00

Bonzo, figure set, bsk, 4 different Bonzos playing musical instruments, mk GE Studdy, 1920s, 3", EX, P6 ....$250.00

Boo-Boo, see Hanna-Barbera

Boob McNutt, doll, litho on canvas w/felt pants, jacket & hat, Star Co, 1923, 35", G, A $110.00

Bozo the Clown, bank, Bozo standing on star-shaped base, plastic, Star Merchandise Co, 1960s or 1970s, 5½", EX+IB $30.00

Bozo the Clown, cloth body w/rubber head, yarn hair, Mattel, 1960s, NM $150.00

Bozo the Clown, Decal Decorator Kit, Meyerscord/Capitol Records, 1950s, EX+ $50.00

Bozo the Clown, doll, stuffed cloth, bl w/red-trimmed collar, wht hands, red feet, Ace Novelty, 1989, 10½", NM+ $12.00

Bozo the Clown, doll, stuffed cloth w/vinyl face, red yarn hair, bl & wht polka dots, talker, Mattel, 1962, 21", EX........$40.00

Bozo the Clown, doll, stuffed cloth w/vinyl head, bl & wht polka-dots w/red trim, yel feet, Knickerbocker, 1972, 12", NM...$30.00

Bozo the Clown, doll, stuffed cloth w/vinyl head, hands & shoes, bl outfit w/wht collar, wht trim, Eegee, 1970s, 12", NM $25.00

Bozo the Clown, figure, bendable rubber, Lakeside, 1960s, 6", NM+ $20.00

Bozo the Clown, figure, squeeze vinyl, arms at sides, Dakin, 1974, 5", EX+...$25.00

Bozo the Clown, figure, squeeze vinyl, hands on hips & looking up, turq w/red, wht & bl trim, Holland Hall, 1964, 8", EX.$50.00

Bozo the Clown, figure, vinyl w/cloth collar, jtd arms, Dakin, 1974, 7½", NM $30.00

Bozo the Clown, figure, vinyl w/jtd arms, bl w/yel, red & wht trim, Knixie by Knickerbocker, 1962, 6", EX+...........$40.00

Bozo the Clown, record player, Transogram, EX $65.00

Bozo the Cown, mask, die-cut litho paper, promotes Capitol Records, 1940s-50s, M $65.00

Brady Bunch, banjo, Larami, 1973, 15", MIP.................$65.00

Brady Bunch, Brain Twisters, Larami, 1973, MOC..........$25.00

Brady Bunch, Fishin' Fun Set, Larami, 1973, MOC $30.00

Broomhilda, doll, stuffed cloth, yarn hair, Wallace Berrie, 1983, 14", w/orig hang tag, NM+ $30.00

Buck Rogers, Crayon Ship box, die-cut cb, American Pencil Co #019, 1930s, EX $75.00

Buck Rogers, pencil box, Am. Lead Pencil Co., 1936, 5x8½", EX $75.00

Buck Rogers, ring, flashes from Buck Rogers to Captain Action, chrome band, 1960s, NM $20.00

Buck Rogers, roller skates, PS, streamlined clamp-ons, mk Buck Rogers, Marx, VG+, pr...$2,850.00

Buck Rogers, Strato-Kite, Aero-Kite, 1940s, unused & complete w/instructions, EXIP $50.00

Buffy the Vampire Slayer (TV Show), dolls, any character, Diamond Select, 1999, MIB, ea $30.00

Bugs Bunny, see Looney Tunes

Bullwinkle, see Rocky & Friends

Buster Brown, bandana, mc images of the 'gang' on wht cloth, 1940s Smilin' Ed McConnell radio show premium, 20x23", VG $50.00

Buster Brown, figure, Froggy the Gremlin, soft squeeze rubber, Rempel, 1948, 10", VG+ $65.00

Buster Brown, Magic Hat, blk plastic top hat w/wht Buster figure, Buster pops up, Commonwealth Plastics, 1950s, 3", M..$65.00

Buster Brown, mask, Froggy the Gremlin, die-cut litho cb, radio series premium, Ed McConnell, 1940s, 10x8", EX.....$75.00

Buster Brown, see also Advertising or Premium categories

Buttercup and Spareribs, pull toy, lithograhed tin, Nifty, 7½", VG +, A, $1,025.00. (Photo courtesy Smith House Toys)

Cabbage Patch Kids, bank, baby in diaper, hard vinyl, Appalachian Artworks, 1983, 5½x7" L, NM.............$10.00

Cabbage Patch Kids, bank, kid in yel dress w/piggy bank in hands, 1980s, 7", NM $10.00

Cabbage Patch Kids, figures, set of 4 different athletic poses, PVC, 2½", Arcotoys, 1995, MIB..............................$12.00

Captain America, Flashmite, Jane X, 1970s, MOC..........$75.00

Captain America, hand puppet, Ideal, 1960s, NM $50.00

Captain Kangaroo, doll, Captain Kangaroo, Mattel, 1960s, MIB $150.00

Captain Kangaroo, doll, Mr Green Jeans, stuffed cloth w/yel yarn hair, gr outfit w/red & wht plaid shirt, 1960s, 13", M $30.00

Captain Kangaroo, squeeze toy, Captain Kangaroo standing w/hands in pockets, pnt vinyl, 1950s, 8", MIB...........$65.00

Captain Kangaroo, TV Eras-O-Board Set, Hasbro, 1950s, EXIB $60.00

Captain Marvel, Buzz Bomb (airplane), paper, Fawcett, 1950s, complete & unused, MIP...$125.00

Captain Marvel, Flying Captain Marvel figure, 'No Cutting! No Pasting! Easy to Assemble!..., Fawcett, 1944, MIP, P6 ..$30.00

Captain Marvel, Illustrated Soap, 3 bars w/different images of Mary Marvel, Fawcett, 1940s, complete & unused, MIB $650.00

Captain Marvel, key chain, Fawcett, 1940s, EX+ $50.00

Captain Marvel, Magic Flute, cb w/plastic mouthpiece, w/logo & illus on sides, Fawcett, 1940s, 4½" L, EX+ $50.00

Captain Marvel, Magic Lightning Box, Fawcett, 1940s, EX+ $75.00

Captain Video, Space Ship Set, Dumpont/USA, 1950s, plastic, rare, MIB, A...$225.00

Casey Jones, doll, 12", EXIB, A, $385.00. (Photo courtesy Bertoia Auctions)

Casper the Friendly Ghost, doll, Casper, cloth, 1960s, 15", EX+..$50.00

Casper the Friendly Ghost, doll, Casper, talker, terrycloth w/plastic head, Mattel, 1960s, 15", EX+ $100.00

Casper the Friendly Ghost, doll, Fatso, cloth w/glow-in-the-dark eyes, 1994, 12", EX $10.00

Casper the Friendly Ghost, hand puppet, Casper, cloth w/plastic head, 1960s, 8", NM+...$50.00

Casper the Friendly Ghost, jack-in-the-box, EX+, $50.00. (Photo courtesy David Longest)

Casper the Friendly Ghost, hand puppets, Casper, Fatso & Stretch, glow-in-the-dark, movie promo, Pizza Hut, 1995, EX, ea $6.00

Casper the Friendly Ghost, pull toy, Casper playing xylophone, 1950s, EX+..$75.00

Casper the Friendly Ghost, push-button puppet, Casper, Kohner, EX+ $25.00

Charlie Chaplin, mechanical figure, pnt compo w/cloth outfit, w/cane, squeeze box activates arm & foot motions, 7", EX $220.00

Charlie Chaplin, string rider figure, flat litho tin figure on bicycle rides across string, 8" L, G..................................$200.00

Charlie McCarthy, hand puppet, cloth body w/pnt compo head, 1930s, 11", VG+ $75.00

Charlie McCarthy, pencil sharpener, Bakelite 2-D bust image w/portrait decal, 1930s, 1¾", EX $65.00

CHiPs, wallet, Imperial, 1981, MOC (sealed), $25.00. (Photo courtesy Greg Davis and Bill Morgan)

Charlie McCarthy, scrapbook, spiral bound w/graphic covers, Western Tablet, 1930s, some use, VG $35.00

Charlie McCarthy, soap figure, Kerk Guild, 1930s, unused, VG+IB $75.00

Charlie McCarthy, ventriloquist doll, compo head, hands & feet, blk suit, string-activated, 16", nonworking o/w EX, A $135.00

Charlie's Angels, scrapbook, TV's Superwomen, Tempo Books, 1978, some use, VG $5.00

Charlie's Angels, wallet, vinyl w/circular image of stars, 1977, MOC $35.00

CHiPs, bicycle siren, 1970s, EX...$25.00

CHiPs, Colorforms Playset, 1980s, unused, MIB $50.00

Chitty-Chitty Bang-Bang, Automobile, plastic w/opening wings & inflatable raft, 4 figures, Mattel, 1960s, 5", NMIB $135.00

Christopher Robin, doll, stuffed felt w/pnt features, brn wig, complete rain gear, RJ Wright, 18", EX+IB, A.....$1,200.00

Christopher Robin, doll, stuffed felt w/pnt features, brn wig, complete rain gear, RJ Wright, 18", EX $775.00

Clueless, dolls, any character, Mattel, 1996, 11½", MIB, ea...$40.00

Curious George, doll, plush, beanbag type, Gund, 7", EX...$8.00

Curious George, doll, plush, wht sweater & red hat, Eden Toys, 1980s, 15", EX+ $15.00

Dennis the Menace, doll, Margaret, stuffed cloth w/vinyl head, red hair, pk shirt, blk skirt, Presents, 1987, 10", NM ..$30.00

Dennis the Menace, lamp, pnt plaster figures of Dennis & his dog Ruff, name on base, Hall, 1960s, 17", scarce, EX $100.00

Dennis the Menace, paint set, Pressman, 1954, complete & unused, MIB..$125.00

Dennis the Menace, pinball machine, 5x8", NM+ $10.00

Dick Tracy, coloring set, w/pencils & pictures to color, 1960s, Hasbro, 1967, complete & unused, MIP $100.00

Dick Tracy, Comiccooky Baking Set, Pillsbury, 1930s, complete & unused, MIB $200.00

Dick Tracy, Detective Set, Pressman, 1930s, NMIB.......$200.00

Dick Tracy, Famous Funnies Deluxe Printing Set, unused, 1930s, NMIB...$150.00

Dick Tracy, fingerprint set, w/microscope, magnifying glass, badge & ink pad, Pressman, 1930s, EXIB $200.00

Dick Tracy, hand puppet, cloth w/vinyl head, Ideal, 1960s, NM $75.00

Dick Tracy, handcuffs, metal, John Henry, 1940s, EX+ $30.00

Dick Tracy, Islander Ukette, features Sparkle Plenty, Styron, 1950s, EX+...$75.00

Dick Tracy, Official Hat, Dick Tracy Detective Club tag, brownish gray wool w/cloth hat band, scarce, EX $75.00

Dick Tracy, soap figure, Sparkle Plenty, Castile, display box simulates bed, 4½" figure, EXIB.....................................$50.00

Dick Tracy, Sunny Dell Acres playset, DeLuxe Game Corp., EX, A, $440.00. (Photo courtesy Bertoia Auctions)

Dennis the Menace, Stuff n' Lace Doll, Standard Toycraft, MIP, $40.00.

Dick Tracy, Wrist Radios, Remco, 1950s, EXIB, $100.00. (Photo courtesy Larry Doucet)

Deputy Dawg, figure, cloth w/vinyl head, Ideal/Terrytoons, 1960s, 14", EX+ $75.00

Dick Tracy, Candid Camera, complete w/film & plastic carrying case, Seymour Sales, 1950s, EXIB $75.00

Dick Tracy, Sparkle Paints, Kenner, 1963, complete & unused, NMIB $75.00

Dick Tracy, Talking Phone, b/o, 10 different phrases, Marx, 1960s, EX+ $50.00

Dick Tracy, Wrist Radio, rnd receiver on leather band, Da-Myco Products, 1940s, EXIB $300.00

Dick Tracy, Wrist Radio (2-Way), Chicago Tribune, 1961, VGIB $50.00

Dick Tracy, Wrist Radios (2-Way), plastic, b/o, American Doll & Toy Co, 1960s, EXIB $75.00

Doctor Dolittle, Animal Fist Faces, EXIB $40.00

Doctor Dolittle, bank, NM, $50.00. (Photo courtesy Matt and Lisa Adams)

Doctor Dolittle, Colorforms Cartoon Kit, 1967, NMIB ...$30.00

Doctor Dolittle, doll, Doctor Dolittle, talker, Mattel, 1960s, 24", MIB...$150.00

Doctor Dolittle, doll, Pushmi-Pullyu, talker, Mattel, 1960s, NM $125.00

Doctor Dolittle, hand puppet, Doctor Dolittle, talker, rubber head, Mattel, 1967, 12", NM....................................$50.00

Doctor Dolittle, Stitch-a-Story, Hasbro, NMIP $25.00

Donkey Kong, figure, plush beanbag type w/rubber face, hands & feet, Etone, 5", EX...$7.00

Dr Kildare, doll, plastic, 1960s, 11½", rare, MIB $450.00

Dr Seuss, doll, Cat in the Hat, plush, Coleco, 1980s, EX+...$20.00

Dr Seuss, doll, Cat in the Hat, plush, talker, Mattel, 1970s, EX+...$75.00

Dr Seuss, doll, Horton the Elephant, plush, Coleco, 1980s, NM+..$75.00

Dr Seuss, doll, Horton the Elephant, plush, talker, Mattel, 1970s, EX+ $75.00

Dr Seuss, doll, Thidwick the Moose, cloth, Arcotoys Inc, 1990s, NM+ $10.00

Dr Seuss, doll, Thidwick the Moose, plush, Coleco, 1980s, EX+...$25.00

Dr Seuss, doll, Yertle the Turtle, plush, Coleco, 1980s, EX+ ..$25.00

Dr Seuss, puppet, Cat in the Hat, talker, Mattel, 1970, EX+..$75.00

Dragnet, Crime Lab, Transogram, 1955, incomplete, G+IB...$50.00

Dukes of Hazzard, bank, General Lee (car), plastic, 1981, 17", G...$10.00

Dukes of Hazzard, car, General Lee, plastic, 1980, 10", VG+ ..$25.00

Dukes of Hazzard, car case, vinyl w/photo of cast, holds 24 cars, 1981, EX+ $35.00

Dukes of Hazzard, Etch-A-Sketch Action Pak, 6 different reusable screens, Ohio Art, 1980s, NMIP $10.00

Dynasty (TV Series), dolls, Alexis Colby or Krystal Carrington, World Doll, 1985, 19", MIB, ea...............................$175.00

Elmer Fudd, see Looney Tunes

Emmett Kelly Jr, ventriloquist doll, Horsman, 1978, MIB ..$50.00

Emergency, fire hat and oxygen mask set, $65.00. (Photo courtesy June Moon Collectibles)

ET, Authentic Bendable Extra Terrestrial Figure, Imperial Toy Corp, 1977, MOC (sealed), $18.00.

ET, figure, cloth, Showtime, 1980s, 8", EX+ $15.00

ET, figure, ET holding flowerpot, lights up when hand is moved, Hershey Foods, 2002, 3½", NM+ $5.00

ET, ring, Eviva, 1980s, MOC...$5.00

Family Affair, Buffy and Mrs. Beasley doll set, Mattel, 1960s, 10½", NRFB, $150.00. (Photo courtesy McMasters Doll Auctions)

Family Affair, doll, Buffy w/Mrs Beasley, talker, pk dress, shoes & socks, 1960s, 36", rare, MIB $800.00

Family Affair, make-up & hairstyling set, Buffy, Amsco, 1970s, EX...$50.00

Famous Cartoon Characters From the Funnies, figure set, bsk, Smitty, Herby, Annie, Kayo, etc, 12-pc, restrung o/w EXIB $2,100.00

Fat Albert, doll, Fat Albert, vinyl w/cloth outfit, Remco, 1985, lg, NRFB $50.00

Fat Albert, figure, Bill balancing on a snowboard, PVC, WNK Enterprises, 1990, from a set, 4", NM+ $10.00

Fat Albert, figure, Fat Albert, vinyl, 1973, 3", VG $10.00

Felix the Cat, bop bag, infatable vinyl, 1960s, 11", EX+ ..$35.00

Felix the Cat, crayons, 8 crayons in cb box w/cut-out window, American Lead Pencil Co, 1930s, used, NM $50.00

Felix the Cat, figure, cloth, Wendy's premium, 1997, 5", EX ..$3.00

Felix the Cat, figure, compo w/jtd arms, 13", VG, A......$150.00

Felix the Cat, figure, stuffed mohair, button eyes & nose, toothy grin, neck ribbon, Chad Valley, 9½", EX, A............$165.00

Felix the Cat, figure, wood, blk beaded body w/sq feet, 6", VG, A $250.00

Felix the Cat, figure, wood, blk w/wht features & name on chest, leather ears, jtd arms & legs, Schoenhut, 4", NM, A..$115.00

Felix the Cat, flashlight, w/whistle, 1960s, EX+ $75.00

Felix the Cat, pencil box, School Companion, 1939, empty, EX...$75.00

Felix the Cat, Pencil Color-By-Number Set, Hasbro, MIB (sealed)...$75.00

Felix the Cat, pull toy, Felix chases mouse on 4-wheeled platform, litho tin, 7½" L, EX, A $600.00

Felix the Cat, pull toy, Felix in car, pnt wood, w/pull cord, Nifty/Borgfeldt, 12", EX, A $600.00

Felix the Cat, School Crayons, set of 8, American Pencil Co/Pat Sullivan, 1930s, 4¾x2½" box, used, EX $50.00

Felix the Cat, sparkler, smiling head, litho tin, mk Copyrighted by Pat Sullivan, EX, A..$120.00

Felix the Cat, Speedy Felix car, wood, head bobs up & down as car advances, 12", EX, A $500.00

Felix the Cat, Trophy Spinner, purple base, Wendy's premium, 1996, EX...$3.00

Fievel, see American Tail

Flash Gordon, hand puppet, cloth body w/vinyl head, KFS, 1950s, scarce, EX $75.00

Flash Gordon, Road-Stars Spaceship, die-cast metal, 1975, MOC..$30.00

Flash Gordon, Space Outfit, complete w/vest, cumberbund, belt, sleeves cuffs & spatz, Esquire Novelty, 1950s, NMIB, A ..$150.00

Flash Gordon, table cover, paper, 1978, 54x88", unused, MIP..$25.00

Flash Gordon, tattoos, glow-in-the-dark, Ja-Ru, 1996, MIP...$4.50

Flash Gordon, wrist compass, plastic, FG Inc, 1950s, EX...$65.00

Flintstones, bank, Bamm Bamm sitting on turtle, plastic, 1960s, 11", NM+ $50.00

Flintstones, bank, Fred Loves Wilma, ceramic, EX+ $100.00

Flintstones, bank, Fred standing next to safe, plastic, MIB ..$35.00

Flintstones, bank, Fred standing w/1 arm behind back & pointing to himself w/other, Vandor, 1990, 8½", EX, P6............$38.00

Flintstones, bank, Pebbles crawling on Dino's back while resting on bed emb Dino, ceramic, Japan, 1980s, 6x6", EX, P6 ......$30.00

Flintstones, bath mitt, Dino, 1970s, EX $15.00

Flintstones, bubble pipe, Fred, soft vinyl, NM+ $15.00

Flintstones, Colorforms, 1972, NMIB $30.00

Flintstones, doll, Bamm Bamm, Ideal, 1960s, 15", EX $75.00

Flintstones, doll, Bamm Bamm, stuffed felt-like cloth, Knickerbocker, 1974, 11", NRFB $60.00

Flintstones, doll, Bamm Bamm, vinyl, Dakin, 1970, 7", NM...$30.00

Flintstones, doll, Barney, hard rubber, holding beach ball, 3½", EX+ $5.00

Flintstones, doll, Barney, plastic, movable arms, 1980, 6", EX $15.00

Flintstones, doll, Barney, plush w/vinyl head, fur suit, Knickerbocker, 1962, 11", NM...$60.00

Flintstones, doll, Barney, vinyl, 1980, 6", EX $20.00

Flintstones, doll, Barney, vinyl, Knickerbocker, 1960s, 10", EX+...$85.00

Flintstones, doll, Barney, vinyl w/cloth cave suit, jtd, Dakin, 1970, 7", EX $45.00

Flintstones, doll, Barney, vinyl w/velvet cave suit, jtd arms, Dakin, 1970, 8" (larger version), EX+........................$50.00

Flintstones, doll, Barney (Flintstones Movie), Dakin, 1993, MIB $15.00

Flintstones, doll, Betty, vinyl, bl dress w/blond hair, Hanna-Barbera, 1960s, 12", scarce, EX $75.00

Flintstones, doll, Betty, vinyl, Knickerbocker, 1960s, 10", EX..$100.00

Flintstones, doll, Fred, felt, Travel Buddy, Day's Inn premium, 9", EX...$8.00

Flintstones, doll, Fred, plush w/vinyl head, fur suit, Knicker-bocker, 1960s, 11", EX+................................$55.00

Flintstones, doll, Fred, talker, Mattel, 1993, 15", MIB......$30.00

Flintstones, doll, Fred, vinyl, bendable, holding microphone, 1991, 4", EX................................$5.00

Flying Nun, doll, Hasbro, 1967, 12", rare, MIB, $350.00. (Photo courtesy Greg Davis and Bill Morgan)

Flintstones, doll, Fred, vinyl, Knickerbocker, 10", EX+, $75.00.

Flintstones, doll, Fred, vinyl, Knickerbocker, 1960s, 15", EX+................................$100.00

Flintstones, doll, Pebbles, stuffed body w/vinyl head & limbs, Mighty Star, 1982, 12", EX+................................$20.00

Flintstones, doll, Wilma, vinyl, Knickerbocker, 1960s, 10", EX................................$75.00

Flintstones, figure, Bamm Bamm, squeeze vinyl, seated holding club, 1980s, 3", NM................................$10.00

Flintstones, figure, Dino, cloth, Strottman Int, 1988, 5", EX ..$5.00

Flintstones, finger puppets, any character, Knickerbocker, 1970s, 3", NM, ea................................$10.00

Flintstones, Fun Water Squirters, various, Denny's premium, 1991, M, ea................................$3.00

Flintstones, Give-A-Show Projector, Kenner, 1964, NMIB..$100.00

Flintstones, Magic Movies, Embree, 1965, scarce, NMIB..$25.00

Flintstones, paint box, Transogram, 1960s, EX $25.00

Flintstones, pocket puzzle, Barney & Fred, 1993, MOC $5.00

Flintstones, push-button puppet, Dino, Kohner, 1960s, NM+ ...$30.00

Flintstones, push-button puppet, Fred, Kohner, 1960s, EX ..$50.00

Flintstones, push-button puppet, Hoppy, Kohner, 1960s, NM+ $25.00

Flintstones, push-button puppet, Pebbles, Kohner, 1960s, EX................................$25.00

Flintstones, Tricky Trapeze, w/Fred figure, Kohner, 1960s, 5", NM................................$30.00

Flintstones, wallet, vinyl w/image of Dino, Estelle, 1964, unused, NM+................................$50.00

Flipper, magic slate, Lowe, 1960s, EX+ $25.00

Flipper, ukelele, Mattel, 1960s, EX................................$15.00

Flying Nun, doll, Hasbro, 1967, 4½", rare, MIB.............$175.00

Foghorn Leghorn, see Looney Tunes

Foodini, birthday card, for 5-year-old, Foodini Art Prints/RC Cox, 1950, EX................................$50.00

Foodini, dexterity puzzle, plastic w/tin frame, 5 metal balls, shows Foodini doing magic, A&A Metal Toys, 1950s, 5", VG................................$75.00

Froggy the Gremlin, see Buster Brown

Full House (TV Series), doll, Jesse, vinyl w/cloth outfit, red guitar, Tiger Toys, 1993, 12", MIB................................$50.00

Full House (TV Series), doll set, Danny's Family, Tiger Toys, 1993, from 3" to 7", MIB................................$50.00

Full House (TV Series), doll set, Jesse's Family, Tiger Toys, 1993, from 3" to 7", MIB................................$50.00

Garfield, bank, seated w/arms folded, ceramic, Enesco, 6", EX, P6................................$35.00

Garfield, figure, diecast metal, cowboy Garfield on rocking horse, Ertl, 1990, 3", MOC................................$12.00

Garfield, figure, Golfer, plush, Dakin, 1980s, 10", w/orig hang tag, NM+................................$15.00

Garfield, figure, plush, dressed as angel w/wings & halo, McDonald's promo, 1990s, 7", EX................................$10.00

Garfield, figure, plush, dressed as Halloween witch, Dakin, 1980s, 10½", NM+................................$15.00

Garfield, figure, plush, w/bunny ears, Dakin, 1980s, 4½", NM+................................$12.00

Garfield, figure, squeeze vinyl, plump Garfield w/eyes closed & big toothy grin, 3", Paws, 1990s, M................................$8.00

Garfield, gumball machine, plastic, I'll Share, But It Will Cost You!, Superior Toy, 1970s-80s, EX+................................$32.00

Garfield, music box, Swingin' in the Rain, Garfield swinging on lamppost, plastic, Enesco, 1980s or 1990s, 7½", NM+..$40.00

Garfield, snowdome, Garfield as Santa pointing w/index finger, Enesco, 1980s, NM+................................$15.00

Garfield, tote bag, canvas w/image of Garfield working a puzzle w/his name in red, gray w/red trim, Thermos, 1980s, EX $15.00

Get Smart (TV Series), doll, Agent 99, red dress w/gold belt, Japan, 1967, 11½", rare, MIB.................$400.00

Gilligan's Island, doll, Mary Ann in 2-pc swimsuit, Japan, 1965, 11½", rare, MIB.................$400.00

Gilligan's Island, Gilligan's Floating Island, Playskool, 1977, MIB, $150.00. (Photo courtesy Greg Davis and Bill Morgan)

Good Times (TV Series), doll, JJ, stuffed cloth w/molded head, red suit, Shindana, 1975, 15", rare, MIB.................$150.00

Good Times (TV Series), doll, JJ, talker, stuffed cloth w/Dyn-O-Mite label on chest, Shindana, 21", MIB.................$125.00

Green Hornet, figure, bendable, Lakeside Toys, 1966, 6", MOC.................$175.00

Green Hornet, flicker rings, any of 6, 1966, EX+, ea from $18 to.................$25.00

Green Hornet, hand puppet, Greenway Prod, 1960s, EX+ ..$250.00

Green Hornet, Official Green Hornet Mask, Green Hornet & Kato, Arlington Hat/Greenway, 1966, NMOC (both in 1 pkg).................$225.00

Green Hornet, Stardust Touch of Velvet Art By Numbers, Hasbro, unused, MIB (sealed) $100.00

Gremlins, Colorforms Play Set, 1984, unused, MIB $35.00

Gremlins, figure, Gizmo, plush, Hasbro Softies, 1980s, 12", scarce, EX+ $25.00

Gremlins, figure, Spike, PVC, LJN, 1980s, 2½", EX...........$5.00

Grizzly Adams, figures, Grizzly Adams or Nakuma (Nakoma on box), Mattel, 9½", MIB, ea $85.00

Groucho Marx, hand puppet, cloth body w/vinyl head, wearing detectives outfit w/hat, VG $85.00

Groucho Marx, ventriloquist doll, Eegee, first made in 1981, NM.................$50.00

Gulliver's Travels, drum, litho tin w/mesh & paper top & bottom, Chein/Paramount, 1939, EX $75.00

Gulliver's Travels, handkerchief, cloth, Gulliver in center w/characters around, Paramount, 1939, 9x9½", EX+ $50.00

Gulliver's Travels, masks, 3 different: Gabby, King Bombo & Prince David, Hecker's Flour premiums, 1930s, EX, ea.............$55.00

Gulliver's Travels, mug, wht china w/mc images, gold trim, flat bottom, Hammersley, 1939, 4x3", EX+ $75.00

Gulliver's Travels, plate, china, gold rim, character scene in center & around rim, Hammersley, 1939, 7" dia, EX.......$50.00

Gulliver's Travels, soap set, figural King Bombo, King Little, Princess Glory & Regal Horse, 1939, 2½ to 3½", EX ..$75.00

Gulliver's Travels, top, litho tin w/wood hdl, Chein, 1939, 5" dia, rare, NM $175.00

Gumby & Pokey, Astronaut Adventure Costume, plastic, Lakeside, 1965, unused, MOC (sealed) $25.00

Gumby & Pokey, figure, Goo, bl rubber w/yel hair w/wht bow on top, Trendmasters/Prema Toy, 1990s, 2½", NM+.........$6.00

Gumby & Pokey, figure, Gumby, stuffed gr felt-like material, Good Stuff, 1990s, 17", EX+ $12.00

Gumby & Pokey, figure, Gumby as Santa, gr plush w/red Santa hat & scarf, Ace Novelty, 1988, NM $15.00

Gumby & Pokey, figure, Gumby, bendable, Applause, 1980s, 5½", NM+.................$15.00

Gumby & Pokey, figure, Pokey, bendable, Trendmasters, 1980s or 1990s, 5", EX+ $8.00

Gumby & Pokey, figure, Pokey, plush, red w/blk mane & tail, 'bug eyes,' Ace Novelty, 1988, VG.................$10.00

Gumby & Pokey, figure, Pokey, rubber, red w/blk mane & tail, 'bug eyes,' 1985, 2¼", NM+.................$5.00

Gumby & Pokey, figure, Spark Plug, squeeze rubber, 1923, 5", VG+ $65.00

Gumby & Pokey, hand puppet, Gumby, cloth w/vinyl head, Lakeside, 1965, 9", EX+ $25.00

Gumby & Pokey, hand puppet, Pokey, plush body w/vinyl head, tag reads Gumby's Pal Pokey, Lakeside, 1965, VG.....$25.00

Gumby & Pokey, Jeep, litho tin, Lakeside, 1960s, EX+..$150.00

Hanna-Barbera, see also Flintstones, Jetsons, or Scooby Doo

Hanna-Barbera, bank, Baba Looey, vinyl w/plastic head, Knickerbocker, 1960s, 9", NM+ $40.00

Hanna-Barbera, bank, Huckleberry Hound figure, hard plastic, Knickerbocker, 1960, 10", NM+ $60.00

Hanna-Barbera, bank, Quick Draw McGraw, plastic, orange, bl & wht, 1960s, 10", EX+.................$35.00

Hanna-Barbera, bubble pipe, Yogi Bear, plastic figure, 1965, MIP (sealed).................$35.00

Hanna-Barbera, Ed-U-Cards, Huckleberry Hound, 1961, VGIB $15.00

Hanna-Barbera, Cartoonist Stamp Set, 1960s, EXIB, $100.00. (Photo courtesy David Longest)

Hanna-Barbera, chalk-board, Huckleberry Hound, Pressman Toy Co. 1960s, M, $50.00. (Photo courtesy David Longest)

Hanna-Barbera, figure, Augie Doggie, plush w/vinyl face, Knickerbocker, 1959, 10", EX+ $40.00

Hanna-Barbera, figure, Augie Doggie, squeeze rubber, jtd arms, Bucky, 1973, 8", NM.................$85.00

Hanna-Barbera, figure, Babba Looey, plush w/pnt vinyl face, Knickerbocker, 1959, 14", VG $35.00

Hanna-Barbera, figure, Boo Boo, stuffed cloth w/orange felt hair and gr felt bow tie, Knickerbocker, 1973, 6½", MIB...$50.00

Hanna-Barbera, figure, Boo Boo w/hands behind back, vinyl, mk Bu-Bu on back, Moplas, 1967, margarine give-away, 5", NM+ $32.00

Hanna-Barbera, figure, Cindy Bear, plush w/vinyl face, Knicker-bocker, 1959, 16", EXIB.................$75.00

Hanna-Barbera, figure, Dixie, plush w/felt eyes & tie, Knicker-bocker, 1959, 13", EX+ $50.00

Hanna-Barbera, figure, Huckleberry Hound, plastic, 1960s, 7½", VG+ $20.00

Hanna-Barbera, figure, Huckleberry Hound, plush w/vinyl face & hands, Knickerbocker, 1959, 18", EX+ $50.00

Hanna-Barbera, figure, Huckleberry Hound as policeman w/Billy club, squeeze rubber, Dell, 1960s, 9½", EX+ $50.00

Hanna-Barbera, figure, Huckleberry Hound holding cane and Top hat in hands, squeeze rubber, Dell, 1960s, 6", MIP........$50.00

Hanna-Barbera, figure, Huckleberry Hound holding ice cream cone, squeeze vinyl, wht w/accent colors, 1960s-70s, 7", MIP $75.00

Hanna-Barbera, figure, Magilla Gorilla, cloth body & limbs w/hard plastic head, 1960s, 11", EX $75.00

Hanna-Barbera, figure, Magilla Gorilla, felt body w/vinyl head, bendable arms, Ideal, 1960s, 7½", EX+ $60.00

Hanna-Barbera, figure, Magilla Gorilla, plush, Nanco, 1990, 8½", orig hang tag, NM $10.00

Hanna-Barbera, figure, Magilla Gorilla, plush body w/vinyl head, Ideal, 1960s, 19", EX+ $100.00

Hanna-Barbera, figure, Magilla Gorilla, squeeze rubber, Bucky, 1974, 6½", EX+ $75.00

Hanna-Barbera, figure, Mr Jinks, plush w/vinyl face, Knicker-bocker, 1959, 13", NM.................$75.00

Hanna-Barbera, figure, Pixie or Dixie, plush, Knickerbocker, 1960s, 12", NM+, ea $50.00

Hanna-Barbera, figure, Quick Draw McGraw, plush w/pnt vinyl face, Knickerbocker, 1959, 16", VG $35.00

Hanna-Barbera, figure, Quick Draw McGraw, plush w/vinyl face, Knickerbocker, 1960, 16", NM+ $100.00

Hanna-Barbera, figure, Snagglepus, plastic body w/vinyl head, jtd arms, Dakin, 1971, 10", EX.................$100.00

Hanna-Barbera, figure, Yogi Bear, cloth w/gr tie & hat, Play-By-Play, 1995, 8", NM+.................$8.00

Hanna-Barbera, figure, Yogi Bear, plastic, Knickerbocker, 1960s, 9", EX $50.00

Hanna-Barbera, figures, Yogi Bear & Huckleberry Hound, plush w/vinyl heads, Kellogg's, 1960, 18" & 17", EX, ea $30.00

Hanna-Barbera, flashlight, Huckleberry Hound's face lights up, plastic, Laurie Import Ltd, 1976, 7", MIP.................$15.00

Hanna-Barbera, friction toy, Yogi Bear figure, plastic, w/running action, Fairylite/Hong Kong, 7", EX+IB, A $250.00

Hanna-Barbera, guitar, Yogi Bear Ge-Tar, Mattel, 1960s, EX ..$75.00

Hanna-Barbera, hand puppet, Droop-A-Long, cloth body w/vinyl head, Ideal, NM.................$50.00

Hanna-Barbera, hand puppet, Ricochet Rabbit, cloth body w/vinyl head, Ideal, 1960s, 11", VG+ $25.00

Hanna-Barbera, hand puppet, Yogi Bear, gr hat & tie, Mighty Star, 1980, 12", EX.................$15.00

Hanna-Barbera, hand puppet, Yogi Bear, Knickerbocker, NM...$35.00

Hanna-Barbera, Huckleberry Hound Cartoon Kit, Color-forms, 1962, EXIB, $150.00. (Photo courtesy Davis Longest)

Hanna-Barbera, Huckleberry Hound Fan Club Kit, Better Breakfast, 1960s, complete, VG+ $35.00

Hanna-Barbera, magic slate, Pixie & Dixie, 1959, EX+ ...$20.00

Hanna-Barbera, masks, Huckleberry Hound & Mr Jinx, paper cutouts, Kellogg's, 1960s, EX, ea.................$10.00

Hanna-Barbera, Modelcast 'N Color Kit, Huckleberry Hound & The Flintstones, Standard Toycraft, 1960, NMIB......$80.00

Hanna-Barbera, Paint 'em Pals Paint-By-Number Set, Yogi Bear, Craft Master, 1970s, EXIB $30.00

Hanna-Barbera, pencil sharpener, Quick Draw McGraw, pnt ceramic figure w/plastic sharpener, China, 1960s, 2", NM+ $20.00

Hanna-Barbera, Pin-Mates, Huck & Yogi pin figures attached by chain, silver-tone, Kellogg's Sugar Pops, 1962, 2", EX ..$50.00

Hanna-Barbera, puffy sticker, Huckleberry Hound figure, vinyl, bl body w/yel bow tie, 1970s, 7", MIP $10.00

Hanna-Barbera, pull toy, Magilla Gorilla, vinyl figure, 1960s, EX+ $100.00

Hanna-Barbera, push-button puppets, Magilla Gorilla and Secret Squirrel, Kohner, 1960s, $50.00 each. (Photo courtesy David Longest)

Hanna-Barbera, push-button puppet, Yogi Bear & Cindy Bear Set, Kohner, 1960s, NM $100.00

Hanna-Barbera, 3-D glasses, Yogi Bear, paper, Kellogg's premium, MIP $5.00

Hansel & Gretel, doll, Gretel, compo w/molded pnt features, cloth outfit, w/umbrella, pnt socks & shoes, 8½", EX, A $375.00

Happy Days, Colorforms Presents the Fonz..., 1976, MIB...$25.00

Happy Days, doll, Fonz, stuffed printed cloth, Samet & Wells, 1976, 16", M $50.00

Happy Days, Fonz Viewer, Larami, 1981, MOC (sealed), $25.00. (Photo courtesy Greg Davis and Bill Morgan)

Happy Days, Flip-A-Knot, National Marketing, 1977, MIP ..$20.00

Happy Days, Presto Magix Rub-Down Transfer Game, several different, APC, 1981, MIP, ea $20.00

Happy Days, record player, features the Fonz, Vanity Fair, 1976, EX...$40.00

Happy Days, wallet, Larami, 1981, MIP $20.00

Happy Hooligan, figure, compo, mc pnt, spring action makes upper body wobble, EX...$75.00

Hardy Boys Mysteries, dolls, Frank or Joe, Kenner, 1978, 12", MIB, ea $100.00

Hardy Boys, Sing-A-Long Phonograph, Vanity Fair, electric or battery-operated versions, EX, $75.00 each. (Photo courtesy Greg Davis and Bill Morgan)

Harold Lloyd, badge, emb tin star w/head image & name, 1920s, 4", EX $50.00

Harry & the Hendersons, doll, Harry, plush, talker, Galoob, 1990-91, 20", MIB $60.00

Heathcliff, figure, plush, Applause, 1982, 7", NM+ $8.00

Heathcliff, figure, plush w/printed cloth tie, vest & striped pants, bl cloth jacket & hat, Knickerbocker, 1981, 12", M ..$15.00

Heathcliff, friction toy, Heathcliff as football player, Talbot Toys, 1980s, 3", NRFC (card shaped like Heathcliff) $15.00

Heckle & Jeckle, figure looking upward and with arms at sides, plush, Mighty Star, 1981, 12", w/orig hang tag, NM..$25.00

Heckle & Jeckle, figures, soft foam, 7", NM+, pr $75.00

Heckle & Jeckle, pinball game, 7½", EX...........................$15.00

Heckle & Jeckle, 3-D Target Game, litho on formed plastic, needs assembly, Aldon Ind/Terrytoons/CBS, 1950s, unused, EXIB...$50.00

Hector Heathcote, Colorforms, 1964, EXIB $40.00

Henry, doll, rubber w/wht cloth shorts, red shirt w/wht M, wht plastic hat, wht socks & shoes, Perfekta, 1940s, 10", NM..$100.00

Homey the Clown, see In Living Color

Honey West, doll, Gilbert, 1965, 11½", rare, MIB.........$400.00

Honey West, Pet Set, Gilbert, unused, MIB $85.00

Honeymooners, dolls, any character, Exclusive Premiere, 1997, 9", MIB, ea $25.00

Honeymooners, dolls, Ralph or Ed, Effanbee, 1986, 16", MIB, ea $350.00

Howdy Doody, bank, Mr Bluster, plastic w/flocking, Strauss, 1970s, 9", NM+...$65.00

Howdy Doody, barrette, Clarabell figure w/legs crossed, molded plastic, 1950s, 1¾x1½", scarce, EX $75.00

Howdy Doody, bubble pipe, Howdy, bl plastic figural head, 1950s, 4", VG..$35.00

Howdy Doody, Dangle-Dandy, Howdy's face put together w/string, uncut from Kellogg's Rice Krispies box back, 1950s, EX $25.00

Howdy Doody, earmuffs, furry muffs w/molded head images, 1950s, VG $50.00

Howdy Doody, embroidery kit, Summer Fall-Winter Spring, Milton Bradley, 1950s, VGIB..............................$50.00

Howdy Doody, figure, Howdy as sheriff standing in chaps, squeeze vinyl, 1950s, 13", EX, from $50 to..............$75.00

Howdy Doody, Figurine Painting Kit, Hadley, plaster Howdy Doody figure & pnts, complete & unused, MIB, A .$250.00

Howdy Doody, finger puppet set, 4 different characters, rubber, 5", EX, set $100.00

Howdy Doody, hand puppet, Clarabelle, cloth body w/vinyl head, Bob Smith, 1950s, EX+..........................$30.00

Howdy Doody, hand puppet, Howdy Doody, 1950s, EX+ ..$30.00

Howdy Doody, marionette, Clarabell, Peter Puppet Playthings, 1950s, EXIB $225.00

Howdy Doody, marionette, Flub-A-Dub, cloth & vinyl, Kagran, unused, MIB..$375.00

Howdy Doody, marionette, Flub-A-Dub, compo body w/vinyl head, Peter Puppet Playthings, 1950s, 7", EX+........$150.00

Howdy Doody, marionette, Flub-A-Dub, compo body w/vinyl head, Peter Puppet Playthings, 1950s, 7, EXIB........$225.00

Howdy Doody, marionette, Heidi Doody (Howdy's sister), wood & compo w/cloth outfit, Peter Puppet Playthings, 1950s, EX+ $185.00

Howdy Doody, marionette, Howdy, Peter Puppet Playthings, 1950s, NMIB $175.00

Howdy Doody, marionette, Mr Bluster, wood & compo w/cloth outfit, Peter Puppet Playthings, 1950s, EX $200.00

Howdy Doody, marionette, Princess Summerfall-Winterspring, bsk head, cloth outfit, 13", G+IB..........................$100.00

Howdy Doody, marionette, Zippy, wood & compo w/fur-like accents & cloth outfit, EX+ $175.00

Howdy Doody, push-button puppet, Flub-A-Dub, plastic & wood w/felt trim, Kohner, 1950s, 5", VG+..............$75.00

Howdy Doody, push-button puppet, Howdy at microphone, wood & plastic w/felt bandana, Kohner, 1950s, EX+IB $165.00

Howdy Doody, rings, Action (flasher), 8 different characters, Nabisco, 1960, EX, ea.......................................$20.00

Howdy Doody, soap dish bath toy, pnt soft vinyl figure of Howdy seated on life raft, Stahlwood, 1950s, 5x5", VG $50.00

Howdy Doody, stool, wood w/Mr Bluster riding circus elephant pnt on octagonal seat, 1950s, 12" T, VG $125.00

Howdy Doody, swim ring, inflatable plastic w/graphics, Ideal, 1950s, 21", EX...$50.00

HR Pufnstuf, Witchiepoo, My-Toy, 1970, 19", rare, EX ..$450.00

Hulk Hogan, Colorforms Sparkle Art, 1991, MIB............$15.00

Hulk Hogan, doll, stuffed cloth, Ace Novelty, 1991, 42", EX...$50.00

Hulk Hogan, doll, vinyl, talker, Hasbro, 1990s, 13", MIB...$50.00

Hulk Hogan, doll, vinyl in cloth outfit & cape, 1980s, 18", MIB $100.00

Hulk Hogan, pillow, Ace Novelty, 1991, 5x5", EX $5.00

Humpty Dumpty, figure, wooden bead type w/elastic string coming out of top of head, 4", EX $10.00

Humpty Dumpty, squeak toy, Humpty Dumpty seated on brick wall w/ankles crossed looking upward, rubber, 1960s, 7", EX+ $35.00

I Dream of Jeannie, doll, Jeannie, Libby, 1966, 20", rare, MIB..$600.00

I Dream of Jeannie, dolls, good Jeannie & the wicked twin sister Jeannie, Trendmasters, 1996, 11½", MIB, ea.............$55.00

I Dream of Jeannie, Dream Bottle, with 6½" doll, Remco, 1976, MIB, $200.00. (Photo courtesy Greg Davis and Bill Morgan)

I Dream of Jeannie, knitting & embroidery kit, Harmony, 1975, MOC...$30.00

I Dream of Jeannie, magic slate, Rand McNally, 1975, M ..$30.00

I Spy, camera/gun, plastic, 35mm camera shoots 'bullets,' Ray Line, 1966, EX+ $40.00

I Spy, Weapons Set, Ray Line, 1966, NMIB $200.00

In Living Color (TV Series), doll, Homey the Clown, Acme, 1992, 25", M $50.00

Incredible Hulk, bank, Hulk figure breaking through block wall, vinyl, AJ Renzi, 1977, EX................................$25.00

Incredible Hulk, Crazy Foam, 1979, w/contents, EX $25.00

Incredible Hulk, Flip-It, Tillotson, 1977, MOC................$50.00

Incredible Hulk, frozen pop treat maker, 3 plastic containers w/images of the Hulk, w/holder, 1978, VG+.............$10.00

Incredible Hulk, gumball bank, Hulk figure standing on base w/arms at sides, w/orig gumballs, 1980, 11", unused, M $40.00

Incredible Hulk, TV tray, metal, image of Hulk walking street, 1979, rectangular, EX...................................$25.00

J Fred Mugs (Today Show Chimp), Swing Dings, die-cut cb pcs, Modern Toy, 1950s, EXIB...$75.00

Jackie Coogan, stickpin doll, pipe cleaner style w/litho head, 1920s, 4", EX+ $40.00

James Bond 007, attaché case, complete w/acccessories, EX ..$8.00

James Bond 007, doll, Miss Moneypenny, bl dress, Japan, 1963, 11½", rare, MIB..$400.00

James Bond 007, Electric Drawing Set, Lakeside, 1960s, unused, MIB...$200.00

James Bond 007, hand puppet, Odd Job (Goldfinger), vinyl, Ideal, 1960s, 13", EX+ $100.00

Jeffersons, doll, Florence Johnston, Shindana, 1978, 15", MIB .$100.00

Jerry Mahoney, beanie, cloth w/molded plastic head on top, mechanism inside hat operates mouth, Benay-Albee, 1950s, NM $50.00

Jerry Mahoney, key chain, plastic head w/movable eyes & mouth on metal chain, 2x1", EXOC.................................$50.00

Jerry Mahoney, Paul Winchell TV Fun Kit, Transogram, 1950s, VGIB $125.00

Jerry Mahoney, ventriloquist doll, Juro, 1950s, complete, NMIB $250.00

Jetsons, Colorforms, 1960s, EXIB $75.00

Jetsons, doll, Astro, plush, Nanco, 1989, 10", NM $10.00

Jetsons, doll, Elroy, Applause, 1990, 9", MIP $10.00

Jetsons, doll, Rosie the Robot, vinyl w/cloth outfit, Applause, 1990, 9", w/orig hang tag, EX+ $18.00

Jetsons, figure, Astro, plush, Nanco, 1989, 10", M............$10.00

Jetsons, figure, Astro on pk base w/4 blk wheels, plastic, Applause, 1990, NM+ $5.00

Jetsons, nightlight, Astro sleeping at foot of bed w/Orbity & Elroy, bsk, Giftique, 1986, 3½x6" L, M $35.00

Jetsons, Slate & Chalk Set, 1960s, unused, MIB $100.00

Joan Palooka, doll, Ideal, 1952, 14", EX..........................$135.00

Joe Palooka Jr, doll, soft molded vinyl w/pnt hair & features (slide-glance eyes), cloth outfit, 1960s, 15", NM.....$150.00

Josie & the Pussycats, chalkboard, 1970s, M, from $50 to ..$75.00

Josie & the Pussycats, Slicker Ticker Play Watch, Larami, 1973, MOC...$25.00

Josie and the Pussycats, Vanity Set, Larami, 1973, MOC (sealed), $35.00. (Photo courtesy Greg Davis and Bill Morgan)

Julia (TV Series), doll, talker or non-talker, any outfit, Mattel, 1969-71, 11½", MIB, ea $250.00

Jungle Book, doll, Baloo, plush, 12", EX+ $20.00

Jungle Book, figure, Mowgli, vinyl, Holland Hill, 1960s, 8", EX+...$25.00

Jungle Book, tea set, litho tin set w/tray, plates, cups & saucers, Chein, 1960s, NMIB $75.00

Jurassic Park, Colorforms, 1992, EXIB $20.00

Jurassic Park, school kit, complete w/pencil pouch, ruler, pencil sharpener & eraser, 1992, MIP $8.00

Katzenjammer Kids, doll, Mama, straw-stuffed w/compo head & arms, cloth dress, mouth opens when squeezed, 10", EX..........$175.00

Katzenjammer Kids, Hingees Set, w/2 sheets of unpunched pcs to assemble, Reed & Assoc, 1940s, NM (w/envelope) $75.00

Kayo, doll, papier-maché like w/pull-string movable mouth, pnt clothes & hat, mk Kayo, Williard/FAS, 13", EX......$135.00

Kayo, figure, jtd & pnt wood, Jaymar, 1938, M...............$125.00

Kermit the Frog, see Muppets

King Kong, Colorforms Panoramic Play Set, 1976, EXIB ..$25.00

King Kong, doll, talker, Mattel, 1966, 12", NM..............$150.00

King Kong, Jungle Set With Magnetic Action Hand, Multiple, 1967, complete, NMIB..$250.00

King Leonardo, doll, stuffed cloth, dressed in royal attire, Holiday Fair, 1960s, EX+ $75.00

Knight Rider, Colorforms, Adventure Set, 1982, MIB $35.00

Knucklehead Smiff, ventriloquist doll, vinyl head & hands w/cloth outfit, Juro, 1960s, 24", NM $350.00

Ko-Ko the Clow, see Betty Boop

Knight Rider, K.I.T.T. Dashboard, Illco, 1980s, NM (G box), $75.00.

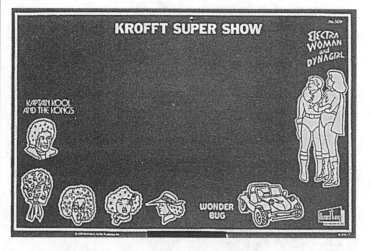

Krofft Super Show, chalkboard, Board King, 1977, 12x18", MIP, $75.00. (Photo courtesy Greg Davis and Bill Morgan)

Kojak, doll, Excel Toy Corp, 1976, 8", MOC $150.00

Koko the Clown, hand puppet, Gund/Out of the Inkwell, 1962, cloth body w/pnt vinyl head, 11", rare, EX $100.00

Krazy Kat, figure, pnt wood bead type, Chein, 1920s, 7", NM.$1,250.00

Krazy Kat, pull toy, litho tin, Krazy Kat chases 2 red mice on base when pulled, Nifty, 7½", VG+ $375.00

Krusher, figure, expandable, Mattel, 1970s, 13½", EX......$65.00

L'il Abner, see Shmoo

Lamp Chop, hand puppet, plush, Shari Lewis Ent, 1991, 12", EX...$12.00

Land Before Time, bank, Littlefoot, plastic, 5", EX............$5.00

Land Before Time, figure, Littlefoot, cloth, 12", NM+ $15.00

Land Before Time, hand puppets, any character, rubber, Pizza Hut, 1988, NM+, ea $10.00

Land of the Giants, Colorforms, 1968, NMIB $60.00

Land of the Lost, Cosmic Signal, Larami, 1975, MOC.....$40.00

Land of the Lost, Explorer's Kit, Larami, 1975, MOC $40.00

Land of the Lost, Give-A-Show Projector, Kenner, 1975, EXIB $35.00

Land of the Lost, magic slate, Whitman, 1975, unused, M .$40.00

Land of the Lost, Secret Look Out, Larami, 1975, MOC ..$40.00

Lassie, figure, plush w/vinyl face, metal collar w/name, Knickerbocker, 1966, 24", NM......................................$50.00

Lassie, Lassie & Timmy Plastic Palette Coloring Set, Standard Toycraft, 1950s, VGIB...$50.00

Lassie, Trick Trainer Set, Mousley, 1950s, EX+IB...........$150.00

Laurel & Hardy, bank, plastic figures, Play Pal, 1970s, NM+, ea $35.00

Laurel & Hardy, doll, Oliver, vinyl, 1950s, 13", VG........$70.00

Laurel & Hardy, marionette, Stan Laurel, stuffed body w/pnt vinyl head, Knickerbocker, 1966, 12", EX...................$50.00

Laurel & Hardy, playset, Laurel & Hardy at the Supermarket, Standard Toykraft/Larry Harmon, 1962, unused, NM ..$30.00

Laurel & Hardy, TV set, w/filmstrips, 1970s, EX+ $30.00

Laurel & Hardy, ventriloquist dolls, Goldberger/Eegee, 1983, 25", MIB, ea...$50.00

Laverne & Shirley, dolls, Laverne & Shirley or Lenny & Squiggy, Mego, 1977, 12", MIB, ea pr $175.00

Laverne and Shirley, Paint by Numbers, Hasbro, 1981, unused, MIB, $50.00. (Photo courtesy Greg Davis & Bill Morgan)

Li'l Abner, dolls, Pappy and Mammy Yokum, NM, $175.00 each.

Linus the Lion-Hearted, doll, talker, Mattel, 1965, NM..$125.00

Little Audrey, Shoulder Bag Leathercraft Kit, Jewel Leathergoods, 1961, EXIB...$75.00

Little House on the Prairie, Colorforms Playset, 1978, MIB...$35.00

Little House on the Prairie, dolls, Laura & Carrie, Knickerbocker, 1978, MIB, ea......................................$35.00

Little King, walking spool figure, pnt wood, moves when top string is pulled & released, Jaymar, 1930s, 3¾", VG+IB $75.00

Little Lulu, charm bracelet, Larami, 1973, MOC $15.00

Little Lulu, doll, rubber, 6", MIP $25.00

Little Lulu, doll, stuffed cloth, red dress w/wht bric-a-brac & collar, red print socks & blk shoes, 14", VG $35.00

Little Lulu, doll, stuffed cloth, western outfit w/brn fringed skirt & red & wht gun holster, 16", EX............................$275.00

Little Lulu, doll, stuffed cloth w/hair, dress & vinyl purse w/her image & name, Margie, 1944, 16", EX....................$275.00

Little Orphan Annie, Colorforms, 1968, NMIB...............$30.00

Little Orphan Annie, doll, cloth, Knickerbocker, 1982, 16", NM+ $15.00

Little Red Riding Hood, doll, cloth w/molded pnt face, blond wig, red cape, M Alexander, 1933-40, 15½", EX, A $400.00

Little Red Riding Hood, tea set, litho tin w/bl background, Ohio Art, 1920s-30s, 9 pcs, EX+ $350.00

Little Red Riding Hood, tea set, litho tin w/wht background & red border, Ohio Art, 1960s, 11 pcs, NM+ $100.00

Looney Tunes, Bake A Craft Stained Glass Kit, features Roadrunner, Road Champs, 1991, complete & unused, MOC...$12.00

Looney Tunes, ball, rubber w/emb images of Porky Pig & friends, 1960s, 6" dia, EX+ $25.00

Looney Tunes, bank, Daffy Duck figure, Applause, 1980s, NM+ $25.00

Looney Tunes, bank, Porky Pig, bsk figure standing w/hands behind back & wearing red jacket, 1930s, EX $150.00

Looney Tunes, bank, Porky Pig head, plastic, Creative Connection, 1990s, 5", NM..$8.00

Looney Tunes, bank, Road Runner running on leafy base w/flowers, compo, Holiday Fair, 1970s, 8", NM....................$50.00

Looney Tunes, bank, Road Runner standing on dirt mound, plastic, Dakin, 1971, 11½", EX+ $45.00

Looney Tunes, bank, Sylvester the Cat, vinyl figure, EX ..$30.00

Looney Tunes, bank, Tasmanian Devil figure, Applause, 1980s, NM+ $25.00

Looney Tunes, bank, Tweety's Bank, Sylvester patting Tweety on the head while Tweety stands on safe, vinyl, 1970s, NM+ $35.00

Looney Tunes, bracelet, brass charm figures of Bugs Bunny, Elmer Fudd, Tweety Bird & Sniffles, etc, 1950s, EX+ $35.00

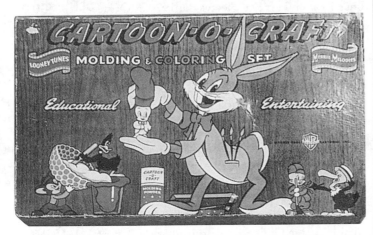

Looney Tunes, Cartoon-O-Craft Molding & Coloring Set, Merrie Melodies/Warner Brothers Cartoons, EXIB, $125.00. (Photo courtesy David Longest)

Looney Tunes, figure, Bugs Bunny as Baseball Player, stuffed cloth with pressed cloth face, Warner Brothers, rare, EX, $300.00. (Photo courtesy David Longest)

Looney Tunes, Cartoon-O-Graph Sketch Board, Metal Moss Mfg/Warner Bros, 1940s, VGIB $75.00

Looney Tunes, Colorforms Cartoon Kit, Bugs Bunny, EXIB...$100.00

Looney Tunes, figure, Auggie Doggie, plush w/vinyl face, Knickerbocker, 1959, 10", EX+ $30.00

Looney Tunes, figure, Baba Looey, plush w/vinyl face, Knickerbocker, 1959, 20", EX+ $75.00

Looney Tunes, figure, Bugs Bunny, bendable vinyl, Applause, 1980s, 4", NM+...$20.00

Looney Tunes, figure, Bugs Bunny, ceramic, squatting w/hands on cheeks & sad expression, Shaw, 1940s, EX+ $75.00

Looney Tunes, figure, Bugs Bunny, cloth, holding basketball, Burger King Space Jam promo, 1996, 8", MIP $9.00

Looney Tunes, figure, Bugs Bunny, plush, Mighty Star, 1970s, 20", NM $18.00

Looney Tunes, figure, Bugs Bunny, plush, 24-K, 1993, 15", EX+...$10.00

Looney Tunes, figure, Bugs Bunny, plush & plastic, talker, Mattel/WB, 1971, NMIB.......................................$110.00

Looney Tunes, figure, Bugs Bunny, soft squeeze rubber, beige or gray, 1930s, EX..$175.00

Looney Tunes, figure, Daffy Duck, bendable, Applause, 1980s, 4", NM+...$25.00

Looney Tunes, figure, Elmer Fudd, rubber, standing w/arms away from body, lg sq chunky legs, Arby's promo, 1988, 3", EX+ $6.00

Looney Tunes, figure, Elmer Fudd, stuffed pillow type, 1970s, EX...$20.00

Looney Tunes, figure, Elmer Fudd, vinyl in cloth hunting outfit, Dakin, 1968, 10", EX..$125.00

Looney Tunes, figure, Foghorn Leghorn, plush, Ace Novelty, 1997, 12", NM $10.00

Looney Tunes, figure, Foghorn Leghorn, plush, Mighty Star, 1987, 12", NM+...$15.00

Looney Tunes, figure, Honey Bunny (Bug's girlfriend) standing w/hand on chin, pk putfit, 1980s, 5", EX $10.00

Looney Tunes, figure, Marvin the Martian, stuffed felt-like material, Starbucks' Coffee promo, 2004, EX+ $5.00

Looney Tunes, figure, Merlin the Mouse, plastic w/vinyl head, cloth jacket, Dakin, 1970, EX+ $30.00

Looney Tunes, figure, Pepe Lepew, plush w/fluffy tail, 16", NM+..$20.00

Looney Tunes, figure, Porkey Pig, plastic, pk vest w/blk jacket, wht bow tie w/bl dots, Dakin, 1970s, 4", NM+..........$22.00

Looney Tunes, figure, Porky Pig, cloth w/vinyl head, Mattel, 1960s, 17", EX+ $25.00

Looney Tunes, figure, Porky Pig, plush, Gund, 1950, 14", EX+ $75.00

Looney Tunes, figure, Porky Pig, squeeze rubber, Sun Rubber, NM...$75.00

Looney Tunes, figure, Road Runner, plush, Mighty Star, 1970s, 13", EX+ $20.00

Looney Tunes, figure, Road Runner running on a cloud of dust, PVC, Tyco, 1994, 1994, MOC $10.00

Looney Tunes, figure, Road Runner Standing tall, plastic w/vinyl head, Dakin, 1968, 9", EX+ $25.00

Looney Tunes, figure, Road Runner standing w/wings at sides, rubber, Arby's promo, 1988, NM+...............................$8.00

Looney Tunes, figure, Sylvester the Cat, plush, Tyco, 1994, 14", NM+ $12.00

Looney Tunes, figure, Sylvester the Cat, rubber, Oak Rubber, 1950s, 6", NM+...$75.00

Looney Tunes, figure, Tasmanian Devil, cloth, knight in armor, Ace Toys, 8", NM+ $8.00

Looney Tunes, figure, Tasmanian Devil, plastic, on base, Superior, 1980s, 7", NM+ $25.00

Looney Tunes, figure, Tasmanian Devil, plush, Mighty Star, 1970s, 13", NM+...$50.00

Looney Tunes, figure, Tweety Bird, beanbag type, Applause, 1997, 6", EX+ **$6.00**

Looney Tunes, figure, Tweety Bird, cloth, Robin Hood outfit, Play-by-Play, 1997, 11", NM $10.00

Looney Tunes, figure, Tweety Bird, soft squeeze rubber, Warner Bros, 1940s, EX...$100.00

Looney Tunes, figure, Wile E Coyote, plush, Mighty Star, 1970s, 18", EX+ $30.00

Looney Tunes, hand puppet, Bugs Bunny, cloth body w/rubber head, Zany, 1940s, EX+ $75.00

Looney Tunes, hand puppet, Elmer Fudd, cloth body w/rubber head, Zany, 1940s, EX+ $75.00

Looney Tunes, hand puppet, Foghorn Leghorn, cloth w/rubber head, Zany, 1940s, EX+ $50.00

Looney Tunes, hand puppet, Foghorn Leghorn, cloth w/vinyl head, 1960s, 9", EX+....................................$30.00

Looney Tunes, hand puppet, Foghorn Leghorn, plush, Warner Brothers, 1970s, EX+, $25.00. (Photo courtesy David Longest)

Looney Tunes, hand puppet, Porky Pig, jiggle eyes, 1950s, NM...$30.00

Looney Tunes, hand puppet, Road Runner, cloth body w/vinyl head, Japan, 1970s, MIB.............................$15.00

Looney Tunes, hand puppet, Sylvester the Cat, Zany, 1940s, EX+ $75.00

Looney Tunes, hand puppet, Tweety Bird, Zany, 1940s, EX+ ..$75.00

Looney Tunes, hand puppet, Wile E Coyote, cloth body w/vinyl head, Japan, 1970s, MIB.............................$15.00

Looney Tunes, jack-in-the-box, Porky Pig, Mattel, 1960s, EX ..$100.00

Looney Tunes, Magic Rub-Off Pictures, Whitman, 1954, EXIB...$40.00

Looney Tunes, pull toy, Bugs Bunny on tricycle w/bell wheels, wood, Brice Toys, 1940s, EX....................................$500.00

Looney Tunes, pull toy, Elmer Fudd in fire chief's car, wood, Brice Toys, 1940s, 9", EX+ $100.00

Looney Tunes, push-button puppet, Marvin the Martian, wood, 1994, NM...$20.00

Looney Tunes, ring, Tweety Bird, plastic, flashes Tweety in 2 different poses, EX, P6 ....$15.00

Looney Tunes, toothbrush holder, Bugs Bunny, pk plastic wall hanger w/decal image of Bugs & phrase, 1950s, 9x5", EX, P6 ....$65.00

Love Boat, Barber Shop, Fleetwood, 1979, MOC (sealed) ..$30.00

Love Boat, Doctor's Kit, Imperial, 1983, MOC (sealed)...$30.00

Love Boat, In Port Set, Fleetwood, 1979, MOC (sealed) ..$30.00

Love Boat, Pacific Princess Playset, Multi-Toys, 1983, MIB..$100.00

Love Boat, Poster Art Kit, Craft Master, 1978, MIP........$50.00

Love Boat, Travel Bag, vinyl, Imperial, 1983, MIP $25.00

Maggie & Jiggs, figure set, wood w/pnt detail, cloth outfits, Schoenhut, 7" & 9", VG+....................................$325.00

Magilla Gorilla, see Hanna-Barbera

Man From UNCLE, flicker ring, silver plastic w/blk & wht photos, 1960s, EX..$20.00

Man From UNCLE, hand puppet, Illya Kuryakin, full figure, vinyl, Gilbert, 1960s, 13", EX................................$110.00

Man From UNCLE, Headquarters Transmitter, b/o, NMIB..$375.00

Man From UNCLE, Pinball Affair Bagatelle Game, graphics on metal w/clear plastic top, Marx, 1966, 25", EX........$100.00

Man From UNCLE, Secret Print Putty, Colorforms, 1965, MOC (sealed)..$50.00

Man From UNCLE, Secret Weapon Set, Ideal, 1965, NMIB...$400.00

Man From UNCLE, THRUSH Buster Car, EXIB $285.00

Marvel Super Heroes, Colorforms Set, 1983, EXIB $15.00

Marvel Super Heroes, Sparkle Paint Set, Kenner, 1967, unused, NMIB...$100.00

Mary Hartline, Super Circus TV Color Show, EC Kropp, 1950s, scarce, EXIB...$75.00

Masters of the Universe, bank, He-Man, HG Toys Ltd., Made in Hong Kong, MIB, $15.00.

Masters of the Universe, Magnetix Playset, American Publishing, 1985, MIP (sealed) $20.00

McGruff the Crime Dog, ventriloquist, Puppet Prod, 28", EX ..$125.00

Mighty Mouse, Basketball Game, 1973, MOC $25.00

Mighty Mouse, figure, plastic w/vinyl head, jtd arms, Dakin, 1978, mk Fun Farm, 10", EX $125.00

Mighty Mouse, figure, squeeze vinyl, Terrytoons, 1950s, 10", EX $50.00

Mighty Mouse, figure, stuffed cloth, Ideal, 1950s, 14", EX+ ..$75.00

Mighty Mouse, flashlight, figural, Dyno, 1970s, 3½", EX+ ...$30.00

Mighty Mouse, Picture Play Lite, Janex, 1980s, EX+........$10.00

Mork & Mindy, Colorforms Sets, several different, MIB, ea from $25 to $30.00

Mork & Mindy, doll, Mindy, jeans & red sweater, Mattel, 1979, 8½", MIB $65.00

Mork & Mindy, doll, Mork, red spacesuit w/silver trim, Mattel, 1979, 9", MIB...$50.00

Mork & Mindy, doll, Mork, talker, stuffed cloth, Mattel, 1979, 16", MIB...$55.00

Mister Magoo, doll, stuffed cloth body with vinyl head, UPA Pictures, 1962, EX, $150.00.

Mork and Mindy, doll, talker, Mattel, 1979, 16", EX, $35.00.

Mr Magoo, hand puppet, cloth body w/vinyl head, 1960s, EX+ $50.00

Mr T, transfer set, 1980s, MIB (sealed) $50.00

Munsters, doll, any character, Presents, 1980s, 10½" to 13", MIB, ea..$65.00

Munsters, doll, any character, stuffed cloth w/cloth outfits, Toy Works, 1990s, 14", w/orig hang tags, M, ea...............$20.00

Munsters, doll, Baby Herman, Ideal, 1965, NM...............$65.00

Munsters, doll, Herman, stuffed cloth w/vinyl head, nontalking version, Mattel, 1964, 20", NM $100.00

Munsters, doll, Herman, talker, Mattel, 1964, 20", rare, MIB..$450.00

Mork & Mindy, Figurine Painting Set, Milton Bradley, 1979, unused, MOC...$20.00

Mork & Mindy, Magic Transfer Set, 1979, MIP...............$15.00

Mork & Mindy, Paint-By-Number Set, Craft Master, 1979, unused, MIB...$35.00

Mortimer Snerd, doll, molded compo w/cable mesh extremities, cloth outfit, Doll of a Thousand Poses on tag, 13", EX, A $300.00

Mortimer Snerd, mask, pnt mesh canvas w/life-like hair , 1930s-40s, EX $40.00

Mortimer Snerd, ventriloquist doll, Juro, 1968, 30½", EX..$50.00

Mr Green Jeans, see Captain Kangaroo

Mr Magoo, doll, cloth body w/vinyl head, Ideal, 1960s, 5", EX+ $75.00

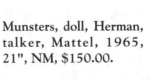

Munsters, doll, Herman, talker, Mattel, 1965, 21", NM, $150.00.

Munsters, doll, Lily, Exclusive Premiere, 1997, 9", MIB ...$30.00

Munsters, doll, Marilyn, Japan, 1964, orange dress, 11½", rare, MIB...$400.00

Munsters, flicker ring, Lily's name/photo, chrome band, 1960s, NM...$20.00

Munsters, hand puppet, Herman, talker, cloth body w/vinyl head, Mattel, 1960s, nonworking o/w VG+..............$75.00

Munsters, Koach Toy w/Motor Noise, plastic, AMT, EX+IB..$1,100.00

Muppets, see also Sesame Street

Muppets, bank, Kermit/pirate w/chest, vinyl, 1989, 10", VG+ ..$20.00

Muppets, bank, Miss Piggy, Sigma, NM $50.00

Muppets, Dress-Up Doll, Great Gonzo, Fisher-Price, 1980s, MIB...$15.00

Muppets, figure, Fozzie Baby Bear, McDonald's, 1988, NM ..$7.00

Muppets, figure, Fozzie Bear or Rowlf, Fisher-Price, 1977-81, NM, ea $10.00

Muppets, figure, Kermit Baby, McDonald's, 1988, EX+ $8.00

Muppets, figure, Kermit Baby, wht outfit w/bl trim, Child Dimension, 1992, 9", EX+ $10.00

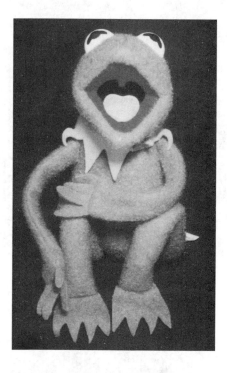

Muppets, figure, Kermit the Frog, Fisher-Price, 1977 – 1983, NM, $12.00. (Photo courtesy Brad Cassity)

Muppets, figure, Miss Piggy, bendable, Just Toys, 5", EX.....$5.00

Muppets, figure, Miss Piggy, plush, blk gown w/long leopard gloves, Applause, 1988, 12", MIP (sealed).................$15.00

Muppets, figure, Red (Fraggle Rock), plush body w/stuffed arms & legs, red shirt, yarn hair, Tommy, 1983, 16", NM ..$25.00

Muppets, figure set, Muppet Babies, set of 4, McDonald's 1996, EX...$10.00

Muppets, hand puppet, Miss Piggy, Fisher-Price, 1978, MIB ..$35.00

Muppets, jack-in-the-box, Big Bird, 1980s, EX+ $15.00

Muppets, stick puppets, any character, Fisher-Price, 1979, MOC, ea from $5 to $10.00

Mutt & Jeff, figure set, celluloid, Stasco, 5¾" & 4½", VG, A..$100.00

Mutt & Jeff, figure set, metal jtd bodies w/pnt compo heads, hands & shoes, felt outfits, 7" & 8", EX+, pr $600.00

Mutt & Jeff, mask, Mutt, die-cut litho cb, Einson-Freeman Co/Shell Oil promotion, 11½x7½", VG+ $35.00

My Favorite Martian, beanie, pink felt, wire antennae w/bells, Benay Albee, 1960s, unused, EX $75.00

My Favorite Martian, Magic Tricks Set, Gilbert, 1964, NMIB $175.00

My Three Sons, doll set, Robbie's Triplets, Remco, 1969, MIB...$350.00

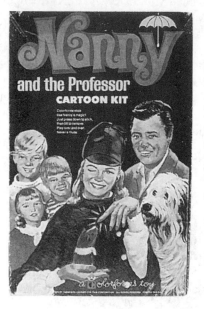

Nanny and the Professor, Cartoon Kit, Colorforms, 1971, MIB, $40.00. (Photo courtesy Greg Davis and Bill Morgan)

New Zoo Revue, doll, Henrietta Hippo, plush, 1977, 17", EX..$60.00

New Zoo Revue, figure, any character, Rushton, 1970s, NM, ea from $25 to..$30.00

New Zoo Revue, figure, Freddie the Frog, Henrietta Hippo, Charlie Owl, bendable, 1973, 3", M, ea $15.00

New Zoo Revue, figure, Freddie the Frog, plush, Kamar, 1977, w/tag, M $40.00

New Zoo Revue, mobile, musical, 1975, MIB.................$25.00

Nick Carter, Finger Print Set, w/16-pg instruction booklet, NY Toy & Game Co, 1930s, EXIB $75.00

Nightmare on Elm Street, figure, Freddie Kruger, complete w/outfits & various body parts, Matchbox, 1989, 8½", MIB...$50.00

Nightmare on Elm Street, figure, Freddy, bendable & twistable, LJN, 1989, 9", MIP..$15.00

Nightmare on Elm Street, figure, Freddy, squishy-squashy type, LJN, 1989, 5", MIP..$12.00

Oswald the Rabbit, bowl, china, tan glaze w/Oswald skating in center & 3 other images, Warwick China, 1930s, 5" dia, NM...$50.00

Oswald the Rabbit, figure, chalkware, flat back, 1930s, 7½", EX+ $50.00

Oswald the Rabbit, figure, stuffed felt body w/wire-framed cloth ears, linen face & rubber hands, Ideal, 1930s, 21", EX $165.00

Partridge Family, bulletin board, 1970s, 18x24", NM.....$100.00

Partridge Family, bus, w/8 figures, Remco/Columbia, 1970s, NMIB (garage box) $1,950.00

Oswald the Rabbit, figure, stuffed cloth, 15", G+, A, $100.00. (Photo courtesy Randy Inman Auctions)

Partridge Family, doll, Laurie, Remco, 1973, 19", MIB...$325.00

Peanuts, bank, Snoopy figure, United Feature, 1960s, 7", EX+..$25.00

Peanuts, bank, Snoopy on Easter egg, Whitman's Candies, 5", EX..$10.00

Peanuts, camera, Snoopy-Matic Instant Load Camera, Helm Toy, 1970s, EXIB..$100.00

Peanuts, Colorforms Batter-Up Snoopy, 1970s, EXIB.......$25.00

Peanuts, Colorforms Happy Birthday Snoopy (Pop-Up), MIB..$35.00

Peanuts, Colorforms Lucy's Winter Carnival, 1970s, NMIB..$50.00

Peanuts, Colorforms Yankee Doodle Snoopy, 1975, EXIB..$40.00

Peanuts, figure, Belle, Dress Me, Knickerbocker #1581, 1980s, EX+..$20.00

Peanuts, figure, Charlie Brown, plastic, Hungerford, 1950s, 8½", EX+...$100.00

Peanuts, figure, Linus, plush, Determind, 1983, 8", MIB..$25.00

Peanuts, figure, Linus, vinyl, jtd, 1966, 7", VG+ $25.00

Peanuts, figure, Lucy, Ideal, 1976, EX+ $35.00

Peanuts, figure, Lucy Pocket Doll, Boucher, 1968, 7", NM+ ..$30.00

Peanuts, figure, Peppermint Patty, foam-stuffed printed terrycloth, Determined, 1970s, 8½", MIP (sealed) $35.00

Peanuts, figure, Peppermint Patty, PVC, arms over hear & wearing #3 tank top, brn shorts & sandals, 1970s, 3", NM....$8.00

Peanuts, figure, Peppermint Patty, stuffed cloth w/printed features, bl overalls & red checked blouse, 6", NM+......$15.00

Peanuts, figure, Peppermint Patty, stuffed printed cloth w/cloth outfit, Ideal, 1970s, MIP $43.00

Peanuts, figure, Pigpen, plastic, Hungerford, 1950s, 8½", EX $75.00

Peanuts, figure, Sally, plastic, Hungerford, 1950s, 6½", EX ...$75.00

Peanuts, figure, Sally, squeeze vinyl, stands w/hands over mouth, pk top, blk pants, wht shoes, Con Agra, 1990s, 6", NM.......$8.00

Peanuts, figure, Snoopy, beanbag type, Red Baron outfit, Whitman Candies, 6", EX $5.00

Peanuts, figure, Snoopy, cloth, Easter, gr outfit w/bunny ears, Whitman Candy, EX...$6.00

Peanuts, figure, Snoopy, cloth pillow type, United F Syndicate, c 1958, 13", EX...$12.00

Peanuts, figure, Snoopy, Dress Me, Knickerbocker, 1983, EX+..$25.00

Peanuts, figure, Snoopy, plush, red neck ribbon w/name, 1970s, 6", EX...$15.00

Peanuts, figure, Snoopy, PVC, Easter, painting egg, 2½", NM...$5.00

Peanuts, figure, Snoopy, rag-type, Ideal, 7", NM+ $25.00

Peanuts, figure, Snoopy as Astronaut, plastic body w/rubber head, Determined, 1969, 9", EX+...............................$65.00

Peanuts, figure, Snoopy as Astronaut, plush, Ideal, 1970s, 14", EX+..$125.00

Peanuts, figure, Snoopy as Astronaut, vinyl, Knickerbocker, 5", EX+ $50.00

Peanuts, figure, Snoopy as Musician, plush, Ideal, 1970s, 14", EX...$125.00

Peanuts, figure, Snoopy as Rock Star, plush w/microphone, wig & shoes, Ideal, 1970s, 14", EX+ $150.00

Peanuts, figure, Snoopy as Viking, PVC, jtd, from McDonald's Snoopy World Tour Series, 1999, M...................$6.00

Peanuts, figure, Woodstock as Santa, plush, Applause, 9", MIP $20.00

Peanuts, finger puppets, set of 6 different characters, Ideal/Determined, MIB...$35.00

Peanuts, guitar, Snoopy, plastic w/crank hdl, Aviva, 1980, EX...$25.00

Peanuts, hairbrush, Charlie Brown, vinyl, 1971, 6", VG+ ..$10.00

Peanuts, jack-in-the-box, Snoopy in doghouse, plastic, Romper Room/Hasbro, 1980s, EX......................................$25.00

Peanuts, kaleidoscope, cb w/metal trim, features the Peanuts gang playing outside, Hallmark, 1970s, 9", EX...........$35.00

Peanuts, marionette, Charlie Brown, Pelham, 1970s, 8", EX+...$50.00

Peanuts, marionette, Snoopy, Pelham, 1970s, 27", EXIB..$200.00

Peanuts, Mattel-O-Phone, 1968, MIB $125.00

Peanuts, megaphone, tin, Head Beagle, shows Snoopy w/megaphone w/Charlie Brown & Lucy on gr, Chein, 1970, 6", NM $35.00

Peanuts, music box, wooden cube showing Peanuts characters, I'd Like to Teach the World to Sing, Schmid, 1972, 4", NM $250.00

Peanuts, nightlight, Snoopy figure, soft vinyl, EX.............$40.00

Peanuts, paint-by-number set, Snoopy, Craft House, 1980s, MIB..$30.00

Peanuts, pencil sharpener, Snoopy, Kenner, 1970s, NM+...$50.00

Peanuts, piano, Schroeder's, Child Guidance, 1970s, EX+ ..$100.00

Peanuts, Picture Maker, plastic stencils of various chracters, Mattel, 1970s, EXIB...$75.00

Peanuts, playset, Camp Kamp, Child Guidance, 1970s, EXIB..$50.00

Peanuts, playset, Charlie Brown's All-Star Dugout, Child Guidance, 1970s, EXIB...$50.00

Peanuts, Pocket Beanbags, Snoopy printed on red cloth beanbag, Butterfly Originals, 1980s, MIP (sealed).............$20.00

Peanuts, pull toy, Push 'N Fly Snoopy, Romper Room/Hasbro, 1980s, EX...$15.00

Peanuts, pull toy, Snoopy Copter, Romper Romm, 1980, NM+ $12.00

Peanuts, punching bag, Charlie Brown, Determined, 1970s, EX $25.00

Peanuts, push-button puppet, Charlie Brown, Ideal, 1977, EX+ $30.00

Peanuts, push-button puppet, Lucy, Ideal, 1970s, EX $25.00

Peanuts, push-button puppet, Snoopy as Joe Cool, Magician, Sheriff or Flying Ace, Ideal, 1977, EX+, ea from $25 to $30.00

Peanuts, roly poly, Snoopy lying atop sphere, gr & yel plastic, makes noise, Danara, 1970s-80s, 4", EX+ $25.00

Peanuts, Snoopy Family Car, plastic, open car w/Snoopy driver & 3 Peanuts passengers, 1970s, NMIB $75.00

Peanuts, Snoopy Snippers Scissors, plastic, Mattel #7410, 1970s, NM+ $50.00

Peanuts, Snoopy Sno-Cones Ice Treat Maker, M, $50.00. (Photo courtesy David Longest)

Peanuts, soap set, yel Charlie Brown, wht Snoopy & pk Lucy figures, Avon, 1970, unused, MIP, ...$25.00

Peanuts, tea set, w/plates, cups, saucers & tray, litho tin, Chein, 1970s, complete, EX $75.00

Peanuts, top, litho tin w/Peanuts characters, Chein, 1960s, EX+ $35.00

Peter Cottontail, soap figures, Peter & cabbage, Daggart & Ramsdell Inc, unused, NM+IB $50.00

Phantom, camera, Larami, 1970s, EX.............................$75.00

Phantom, paint-by-number set, Hasbro, 1960s, some use, EXIB $150.00

Phantom, rub-on transfer set, Hasbro, 1960s, complete & unused, MIP...$175.00

Pink Panther, Cartoonarama, 1970, EXIB $60.00

Pink Panther, figure, plush, Mighty Star, 1984, 12", NM...$25.00

Pink Panther, toothbrush holder, figure seated & brushing his teeth in front of 3-brush holder, ceramic, 1970s, 5", P6 ....$55.00

Pink Panther, w/up figure, plush body w/vinyl jead, plays cymbals w/twists hips, 9", VG $50.00

Pinky Lee, doll, stuffed cloth w/soft vinyl head & hat, compo hands, checked cloth suit, Juro Celebrity, 1950s, 23", EX..........$100.00

Pinky Lee, serving tray, tin w/photo image, 1950s, 10x14", EX+ $30.00

Pinky Lee, squeeze toy, soft vinyl figure, head pops off, Stern, 1950s, 9", EX...$50.00

Pippi Longstockings, figure, PVC, 4", NM $5.00

Pixie & Dixie, see Hanna-Barbera

Planet of the Apes, bank, Dr. Zauis, plastic, 1967, 10", EX, $30.00.

Planet of the Apes, bank, Galen, hard vinyl, Play Pals, 1974, 10½", NM+..$40.00

Pogo, figure, Albert Alligator, vinyl, jtd, detergent promo, 1969, 5½", NM $15.00

Pogo, figure, Churchy La Femme holding fishing pole, pnt vinyl, jtd head & arms, 5", scarce, EX+ $85.00

Pogo, figure, Pogo, vinyl, Walt Kelly, 1969, 4", VG+ $15.00

Pogo, Pogomobile, w/22 different die-cut cb Walt Kelly characters & wire hanger, Simon & Schuster, 1954, EX....$150.00

Popeye, badge, flasher type showing Popeye eating spinach, 1960s, EX+ $10.00

Popeye, bank, Popeye head form w/pipe in mouth, American Bisque, mk USA, scarce, EX $325.00

Popeye, bank, Popeye Knockout Bank, litho tin, Straits MFG/KFS, 1935, EX...$475.00

Popeye, bulletin board, cork, 1980, 16x22", EX..............$25.00

Popeye, Colorforms Birthday Party Set, 1960s, EXIB $30.00

Popeye, Colorforms Puppetforms, 1950s, EXIB.................$30.00

Popeye, figure, Brutus, stuffed cloth w/vinyl head, hands & boots, yel jumpsuit, bl belt, Presents, 1985, 13", NM+ $25.00

Popeye, figure, Brutus, vinyl w/cloth outfit, orig tag, 13", M ..$25.00

Popeye, figure, Olive Oyl, beanbag type, CVS, 2000, 9", NM+ $6.00

Popeye, figure, Olive Oyl, rubber, Ben Cooper, 1970s, EX+..$20.00

Popeye, figure, Olive Oyl, vinyl w/cloth outfit, Dakin #1055, 1960s, 9", w/orig tag, NM $25.00

Popeye, figure, Olive Oyl, wood compo, standing on rnd base w/hands clasped, Syroco/KFS, 1944, 5", EX+, A $150.00

Popeye, figure, Popeye, bendy type, Jesco, 1980s, NM+ ...$12.00

Popeye, figure, Popeye, cloth body w/soft rubber head (w/pipe & winking) & hands, Gund/KFS, 19", VG, A ($150-$250) $125.00

Popeye, figure, Popeye, pnt compo body w/jtd wood arms & legs, KFS, 1935, 13½", G $250.00

Popeye, figure, Popeye, pnt vinyl w/movable head & limbs, Cameo/KFS, 1950s, 13", EX+................................$125.00

Popeye, figure, Popeye, pnt wood bead body w/1933 Century of Progress label on torso, Chein/King Features, 8", EX+..$500.00

Popeye, figure, Popeye, rubber, Ben Cooper, 1970s, EX+...$10.00

Popeye, figure, Popeye, sponge rubber, Lakeside, 1968, 12", EX+...$25.00

Popeye, figure, Popeye, vinyl bead-type w/movable head & limbs, Cameo/KFS, 1950s, 13", EX $125.00

Popeye, figure, Swee' Pea, PVC, presents, 1980s, NM+......$5.00

Popeye, figure, Wimpy, cloth, holding hamburger, Stuffins, 1999, 7", NM+..$10.00

Popeye, figure, Wimpy, rubber, KFS, 1950s, VG $35.00

Popeye, figure, Wimpy, rubber, Schavoir Rubber Co, 1935, NM $275.00

Popeye, figure, Wimpy, squeeze vinyl, Cribmates, 1979, NM+ ..$20.00

Popeye, Funny Face Maker, Jaymar, 1960s, unused, EX+IP...$30.00

Popeye, hand puppet, Popeye, cloth body w/rubber head, 1930s, 11", EX $75.00

Popeye, hand puppet, Popeye, cloth body w/vinyl head, Gund, 1960s, EX+..$25.00

Popeye, hand puppet, Swee' Pea, cloth body w/vinyl head, 1950s, NM $50.00

Popeye, hand puppet, Wimpy, cloth body w/vinyl head, Gund, 1960s, EX+..$25.00

Popeye, iron-on transfer, lg red P in center of bl Popeye name, KFS, 1950s, unused, EX $15.00

Popeye, jack-in-the box, Mattel, 1960s, EX+...................$75.00

Popeye, kaleidoscope, Larami, 1979, EX+.......................$15.00

Popeye, My Popeye Coloring Kit, American Crayon, 1950s, EX $35.00

Popeye, Paddle Wagon, Popeye, Olive Oyl & Wimpy on paddle boat on car body, Corgi Jr, 2x3" L, EX, P6 ....$32.00

Popeye, paint-by-number set, Hasbro, 1960s, unused, EXIB ..$20.00

Popeye, party game, 'Pin the Pipe on Popeye,' lg image at the helm on paper sheet, w/24 cut-out pipes, Whitman, 1937, EX...$75.00

Popeye, pencil box, cb, center image of Popeye flanked by cartoon strip images, Eagle Pencil Co, 1930s, 6x11", EX+........$50.00

Popeye, pin, mc hard plastic figure in profile w/pipe in his mouth, 1960s, 2", EX, P6.....................................$30.00

Popeye, pipe, wood, red, 1940s, EX+.............................$20.00

Popeye, Presto Paints, Kenner, 1961, VG+.....................$100.00

Popeye, push-button puppet, Popeye, Kohner, 1960s, 4", NM+..$50.00

Popeye, push-button puppet, Popeye & Olive Oyle, Kohner, 1949, NM+IB (both in same box), set...................$130.00

Popeye, ring, flashes from Popeye to another character, bl, EX+ $10.00

Popeye, soap figure, Popeye, 1930s, 4", unused, VG, P6...$30.00

Popeye, table cover, bl & red litho on crepe paper, KFS, 1930s, 36" sq, VG...$35.00

Popeye, tambourine, Larami, 1980s, EX+...........................$8.00

Popeye, Thimble Theatre Mystery Playhouse, w/3 compo figures, Harding/KFS, 1939, NM+IB................................$2,000.00

Popeye, toothbrush holder, plastic b/o figure of Popeye standing in boat w/2 toothbrushes, Nasta, 1983, EX $25.00

Popeye, tugboat, inflatable vinyl, Ideal, 1960s, unused, MIP..$50.00

Popeye, wallet, Official, KFS, 1950s, EX+........................$20.00

Popcyc, Wimpy's Musical Hum-Burger, litho tin, Northwest Prod, 3½" dia, EX $100.00

Power Rangers, doll, Pink Power Ranger, cloth, Saban, 1993, 11", NM+ $8.00

Power Rangers, wallet, vinyl, bl & red w/Pnk Power Ranger graphics, 3x5" (closed), EX.....................................$6.00

Prince Valiant, sword, scabbard & shield, EXIB, (C10) ..$450.00

Raggedy Andy, bank, Play Pal, 11", NM+.......................$25.00

Raggedy Andy, bank, vinyl figure dressed in red, wht & bl patriotic attire & wht wig, Royalty, 1974, 9", NM $35.00

Raggedy Andy, doll, pillow type, Bobbs-Merril, 1979, 19", EX+ $15.00

Popeye, pull toy, paper lithograph on wood, metal wheels, KFS, 11x10", VG+, A, $465.00. (Photo courtesy Randy Inman Auctions)

Raggedy Andy, doll, Knickerbocker, 1970s, 14", NM, $32.00. (Photo courtesy June Moon Collectibles)

Raggedy Andy, pencil sharpener, Keep Sharp w/Raggedy Andy, plastic, b/o, Andy figure hugs sharpener, Janex, 1974, 7", NM..$25.00

Raggedy Ann, bank, compo figure standing in yel dress w/bl & pk dots around hem, brn shoes, 1970s, 8½", NM+ $25.00

Raggedy Ann, bank, Play Pal, 1970s, 11", NM+...............$25.00

Raggedy Ann, bank, vinyl figure in brn felt jumper, wht molded blouse & blk molded shoes, red yarn hair, Royalty, 1974, 9", NM..$35.00

Raggedy Ann, Colorforms Play Kitchen, 1975, MIB........$25.00

Raggedy Ann, doll, beanbag type, Applause, 7", EX...........$8.00

Raggedy Ann, doll, Christmas, 1980s, 13", VG $15.00

Raggedy Ann, doll, Christmas, 1980s, 18", EX $25.00

Raggedy Ann, doll, cloth, pk outfit & bonnet, Playskool, 1989, 10", EX $8.00

Raggedy Ann, doll, musical, Knickerbocker, 15", EX+.....$50.00

Raggedy Ann, squeeze toy, vinyl, pk dress w/wht apron, red & wht striped legs, blk shoes, Regent, 1973, 6", MIP (sealed) ..$25.00

Raggedy Ann & Andy, Animal Friends, plastic fencing and animal pcs, Larami, 1977, MOC $12.00

Raggedy Ann & Andy, Colorforms Super Deluxe Playhouse, 1988, MIB $15.00

Raggedy Ann & Andy, crayon box, metal, Chein, 1974, EX+ ..$25.00

Raggedy Ann & Andy, dolls, cloth, Applause, 12", EX, ea..$10.00

Raggedy Ann & Andy, dolls, cloth, Knickerbocker, 1970s, 6½", MIB, ea...$40.00

Raggedy Ann & Andy, dolls, inflatable vinyl, Ideal, 1960s or 1970s, 15", EX+, ea...$15.00

Raggedy Ann & Andy, dolls, Miniature Rag Dolls, Knickerbocker, 1976, 5", MIB, ea $25.00

Raggedy Ann & Andy, figure, Ann & Andy, pnt ceramic, Care Inc, 1970s, 12", EX, ea...$15.00

Raggedy Ann & Andy, mobile, flocked plastic figures hanging from plastic balloons, musical, Dolly Toy Co, 1976, NMIB ...$40.00

Raggedy Ann & Andy, wall plaque, Andy lying on back w/hands under head, yel shirt, Dart, 1977, 14", NM+ $15.00

Rainbow Brite, doll, Lurky, plush, Mattel, 1983, 14", scarce, EX+...$20.00

Rainbow Brite, doll, Sprite, stuffed pillow type, 15", EX ..$10.00

Ren & Stimpy, figure, Ren, plush, Dakin, 1992, 17", NM+ ...$20.00

Ren & Stimpy, dolls, talkers, Mattel, 1992, NRFB, ea......$80.00

Ripcord, Sky Diving Parachute, w/4" plastic figure, Ray Plastics Inc, 1960s, unused, MOC..$40.00

Rocky (Movie), doll, Rocky Balboa, gray sweat outfit w/name on chest & headband, United Artist, 1985, 18", MIB..$100.00

Rocky (Movie), doll, Rocky Balboa, Phoenix Toys, 1980s, 8", NM+ $20.00

Rocky (Movie), hand puppet, w/bobbing head & movable arms w/boxing gloves, Ro-Jus, 12", EX..............................$25.00

Rocky & Friends, bank, Bullwinkle, plastic, Play Pal, 1970s, 12", EX+ $75.00

Rocky & Friends, Colorforms Cartoon Kit, 1960s, EX+IB..$75.00

Rocky & Friends, figure, Boris Badenov, bendable, blk & wht w/ bulging black eyes, Wham-O, 1972, NM+.................$25.00

Rocky & Friends, figure, Boris Badenov, bendable, blk & wht w/bulging lavender eyes, Jesco, 1986, unused, MOC ...$15.00

Rocky & Friends, figure, Bullwinkle, bendable, 1985, 7", M ..$15.00

Rocky and Friends, figure, Snidley Whiplash, bendable, Wham-O, 4½", M, $25.00.

Rocky & Friends, figure, Bullwinkle, plush, Ideal, 1960, 20", NM $75.00

Rocky & Friends, figure, Bullwinkle, plush, red & wht shirt w/gr bow, red Santa hat, Ward Products, 1996, 24", NM+ ..$20.00

Rocky & Friends, figure, Dudley Do-Right, bendable, Wham-O, 1970s, 5", EX+ $25.00

Rocky & Friends, figure, Rocky, bendable, 1985, 5", M....$15.00

Rocky & Friends, figure, Rocky, bendable rubber, Jesco, 1991, MOC (card reads Bullwinkle & Friends) $12.00

Rocky & Friends, figure, Rocky, inflatable vinyl, silver body w/bl cap, Rinco, 1999, 20", M $10.00

Rocky & Friends, figure, Rocky, plastic w/vinyl head, Dakin, 1970s, 6½", NMIB..$100.00

Rocky & Friends, figure, Rocky, plush, Wallace Berrie, 1982, 12", w/orig hang tag, NM+ $25.00

Rocky & Friends, figure, Rocky, plush w/plastic flight helmet & goggles, Nanco, 1991, 24", NM...............................$20.00

Rocky & Friends, playing cards, Bullwinkle, complete, 1962, VGIB..$10.00

Rocky & Friends, Signal Flasher, Bullwinkle, plastic, 1970s, MOC..$25.00

Rocky & Friends, stamp set, Bullwinkle, Larami, 1970, EXIB ..$25.00

Romper Room, lamp base, Do-Bee, pnt plaster figure embracing 'buzz powder' pot, 1960s, 22", EX $50.00

Rootie Kazootie, doll, cloth body w/vinyl head & hands, Effanbee, 1950s, EX+ $50.00

Rootie Kazootie, hand puppet, cloth body w/pnt vinyl head, RK Inc, 1950s, 10", EX $35.00

Rootie Kazootie, magic set, 1950s, NMIB....................$125.00

Rudolph the Red Nosed Reindeer, Kiddy Projector, National Plastic Corp/Fleischer Creation, 1944, EXIB.............$75.00

Ruff & Reddy, finger puppet, vinyl, 1959, 3", EX $150.00

Ruff & Reddy, Karbon Kopee, Wonder Kit, 1960, EXIB ..$75.00

Ruff & Reddy, Magic Rub-Off Picture Set, Transogram, 1950s, unused, NMIB $100.00

Rugrats, doll, Angelica, 2 different, Mattel, 1997, 11" or 12", NM, ea $10.00

Rugrats (Movie), doll, Angelica, vinyl w/yarn hair & safari hat, Mattel, 1998, unused, MIB................................$10.00

Rugrats (Movie), watches, 4 different, plastic, Burger King promo, 1998, MIB, ea $8.00

Santa Claus, bank, nodder figure, pnt compo w/spring-mounted head, 1950s-60s, 6", EX $50.00

Santa Claus, candy container, Santa standing on 4-wheeled platform, red/gr pnt plastic, E Rosen Candy Co, 1950s, 5", NM $50.00

Santa Claus, doll, squeeze vinyl, 1960s, 7", EX $10.00

Santa Claus, doll, stuffed flannel body w/cloth mask face, pnt features, mohair beard/suit trim, musical, 1930s, 28", EX ..$250.00

Santa Claus, puppet, die-cut figure w/moving eyes & mouth, Happi-Times Toy Town promo for Sears, 1948, 13", NM $30.00

Scooby Doo, bank, vinyl figure seated on haunches, gr collar w/yel medallion, 1980s, 6", EX+ $20.00

Scooby Doo, figure, beanbag type, Applause, 1998, 7", EX...$6.00

Scooby Doo, figure, cloth, in night shirt & cap, Play-By-Play, 9", NM+ $8.00

Scooby Doo, figure, plush, seated on haunches, Sutton, 1970, 8", NM $32.00

Scooby Doo, figure, plush, sitting, 1998, 13", EX $8.00

Scooby Doo, figure, Scrappy Doo, vinyl, Dakin, 1982, 6", EX $75.00

Scooby Doo, gumball machine, plastic head, Hasbro, 1968, EX $25.00

Scrappy, bank, metal book form w/emb image of Scrappy & dog on leather-like binding, 3x3½x1", NM+ $75.00

Scrappy, doll, compo w/cloth outfit, Columbia Studios, 1935, 14", VG $200.00

Scrappy, figure, Marge (Scrappy's girlfriend), pnt bsk, Japan, 1930s, 3½", EX+ $30.00

Secret Squirrel, push-button puppet, Kohner, 1960s, EX+...$30.00

Sesame Street, figure, Animal, stuffed felt-type tan cloth w/fuzzy pk head & red hair, Nanco, 1980s-90s, 25", NM $18.00

Sesame Street, figure, Animal as a beachcomber, Just Toys, 1980s-90, 5", NM $6.00

Sesame Street, figure, Big Bird, talker, Playskool, 1970s, 22", VG $25.00

Sesame Street, figure, Elmo, beanbag type, Tyco, 1997, NM $8.00

Sesame Street, figure, Ernie, beanbag type, Applause, 6", EX...$5.00

Sesame Street, figure, Guy Smiley, plush beanbag type w/fuzzy blk hair, lt bl jacket, blk legs, Tyco, 1997, M $10.00

Sesame Street, figure, Honker, beanbag type, Tyco, 1997, EX..$6.00

Sesame Street, figure, Oscar the Grouch, beanbag type, Tyco, 1997, 7", EX $6.00

Sesame Street, figure, Scooter, stuffed felt w/lt gr satin jacket & bl jeans, wht shoes, Fisher-Price, 1978, 17", EX.........$22.00

Sesame Street, hand puppet, Big Bird, plush, Child Guidance, 1980, NM..$18.00

Sesame Street, Lacing Puppets, Big Bird & Ernie, Fisher-Price, 1984, MIP $10.00

Sesame Street, see also Muppets

Shari Lewis, finger puppets, 4 different, Quaker Life Cereal, 1962, 2", M, ea...$25.00

Shari Lewis, puppets, Lamb Chop & Hush Puppy, vinyl heads w/cloth bodies, Quaker Oats, 1962, 7½", EX, ea $30.00

Shirley Temple, ring, photo image on oblong top, narrow band, nonadjustable, EX $80.00

She-Ra, Princess of Power, bank, HG Toys, Hong Kong, MIB, $10.00.

Shmoo, figure, wht plush, oilcloth face w/stenciled features, bl felt hat w/red trim, Gund, 1940s, 11", VG...............$425.00

Shmoo, nesting figures, wht plastic w/blk accents, 1940s, set of 4 from 2½" up to 5½", VG+.......................................$65.00

Simpsons, Activity Pack, Pancake Press, MIP (sealed) $25.00

Simpsons, bank, Bart, plastic figure, Street Kids, 1990, EX+..$8.00

Simpsons, Bath Soap, Bart figure standing w/arms crossed, Cosrich, 1990, 5", NRFB (box reads Wash It, Dude!) $12.00

Simpsons, Crayon-By-Number, Rose Art, MIB $10.00

Simpsons, doll, any character, stuffed cloth, Dan-Dee, 11", NM, ea..$18.00

Simpsons, doll, any character, stuffed felt w/vinyl head, Burger King promo, 1990, Marge is 12", NM+, ea $10.00

Simpsons, doll, any character, stuffed w/vinyl limbs, Presents, 9", M, ea $12.00

Simpsons, doll, Bart, stuffed body w/vinyl head & limbs, pk felt shirt reads Cooties Man!, Dan-Dee, 1990, 11½", NM..$15.00

Simpsons, doll, Bart, stuffed cloth, red & wht striped nightshirt w/toothbrush in hand, Dan-Dee, 1990, 24", M.........$20.00

Simpsons, doll, Maggie, stuffed cloth w/printed face, red felt pacifier, lt bl nightshirt, 1990s, 10½", NM+ $10.00

Simpsons, figure, Bart, Homer, Lisa, Maggie & Marge, PVC, Burger King promo, 1990, 5-pc set, 3" to 4", NM $15.00

Simpsons, figure, bendable rubber, Jesco, 1990, 6", NM+..$10.00

Simpsons, figure, Homer, bendable rubber, Jesco, 1990, 6", NM+..$10.00

Simpsons, figure, Maggie, bendable, Jesco, 1990, 3½", NM+..$6.00

Simpsons, Fun Dough Model Maker, MIB $35.00

Simpsons, key chain, Bart figure, PVC, 3½", 1990, EX $5.00

Simpsons, Paint-By-Number, Rose Art, unused, MIB $10.00

Simpsons, pinball game, Jaru, plastic, MOC $5.00

Simpsons, punch ball set, National Latex Prod, MIP $50.00

Simpsons, Stamper Pak, Rubber Stampede, MIP (sealed) ..$15.00

Simpsons, toy talking watch, plastic, says 'Emm Burger,' w/grill cooking graphics, Burger King promo, NM...............$5.00

Simpsons, Trace 'N Color Drawing Set, Toymax, NMIB..$75.00

Simpsons, Write 'N Wipe, Rose Art, MIB (sealed) $15.00

Simpsons, 3-D Chess Set, MIP (sealed) $35.00

Six Million Dollar Man, Bionic Tatoos & Stickers, Kenner, 1976, unused, MIP..$15.00

Six Million Dollar Man, Play Doh Action Play Set, 1977, MIB (sealed)...$35.00

Six Million Dollar Man, waste can, metal w/lithoed images, 1976, EX..$25.00

Skippy, figure, bsk, movable arms, rnd base, Percy L Crosby/Japan, 1930s, 5½", NM $50.00

Skippy, figure, bsk, standing in bl jacket & red hat, mk Made in Japan, 1930s, 3½", EX, P6 ....$32.00

Smokey the Bear, see Advertising category

Smurfs, bank, molded plastic character, Peyo, 1980s, NM..$35.00

Smurfs, Colorforms, EXIB......................................$25.00

Smurfs, figure, Baby Smurf, plush w/pk jumper, eyelet-trimmed hat, Applause, 1984, 12", NM................................$12.00

Smurfs, figure, Papa Smurf, plush, 7", VG+......................$8.00

Smurfs, figure, Santa w/bag of toys, plush, 10", NM $12.00

Smurfs, figure, Smurfette, cloth, I Smurf You, purple skirt, Applause, 7", NM+.......................................$10.00

Smurfs, figure, Smurfette, plush, in dress, Peyo, 1981, 12", EX+ $15.00

Smurfs, figure, Smurffette, cloth, Have a Happy Day on pk sweater, Applause, 7", NM+ $10.00

Smurfs, figure, Smurfette, vinyl with synthetic hair and cloth outfit, Applause, 1983, M, $8.00.

Smurfs, mug, plastic, Peyo, 1980s, M...............................$15.00

Smurfs, pail, plastic, 1-qt, 1981, VG+ $15.00

Smurfs, phonograph, NMIB.....................................$65.00

Smurfs, pillow, stuffed cloth Smurf house, 14x12", NM ...$15.00

Smurfs, push-button puppet, yel sq base, Peyo, 4", EX........$8.00

Smurfs, record player, Vanity Fair, 1982, EXIB $75.00

Smurfs, sewing cards, MIB (sealed) $25.00

Smurfs, telephone, plastic dial base w/receiver and a Smurf figure standing atop, red, yel, bl & wht, HG Toys, 1982, VG+..$32.00

Smurfs, top, litho tin w/suction cup on bottom, shows Smurfs in outdoor scene, Ohio Art, 1982, 10x9" dia, EX $25.00

Smurfs, w/up walking figure, plastic, Peyo, 1980, 3", NM+..$10.00

Soupy Sales, marionette, stuffed body w/vinyl head, Knicker-bocker, 1966, 13", EX......................................$75.00

Soupy Sales, pen, plastic w/pnt vinyl head topper, lg polka-dot bow tie, 1960s, NM+ $40.00

Space Patrol, drink shaker, spaceship form, United Plastic Corp, 8½", VGIB $50.00

Space Patrol, party cups, paper litho w/Space Patrol graphics, pkg of 6 cups, CA Reed, 1950s, 5", unopened, M......$75.00

Speedy Gonzales, figure, standing w/arms straight out, plastic, lg gray sombrero, felt outfit, 1960s, 12", EX+................$75.00

Speedy Gonzales, figure, vinyl w/cloth outfit, Dakin, 1970, 8", NM+ $30.00

Spider-Man, Action Gumball Machine & Bank, 7" figure, 1984, MIB..$20.00

Spider-Man, American Bricks Set, Playskool, 1977, EXIB...$35.00

Spider-Man, Colorforms Adventure Set, 1974, NMIB.....$25.00

Spider-Man, doll, stuffed talker, Mego, 1974, 28", M.......$50.00

Spider-Man, figure, plastic body w/vinyl head, Imperial, 1976, EX+..$30.00

Spider-Man, finger puppet, 1970, NM $15.00

Spider-Man, hand puppet, plastic body w/vinyl head, Imperial, 1970s, 9", EX+..$25.00

Spider-Man, Presto-Magix Set, rub-ons transfers, 1978, NM ..$8.00

Spider-Man, roller skates, red, blk & bl plastic, EX $20.00

Spider-Man, skydiving parachute, Ahi, 1973, MOC........$35.00

Spider-Man, Spider Van, Buddy L, 1980, EX $20.00

Spider-Man, squirt gun, plastic head figure, 1974, EX $25.00

Spider-Man, walkie-talkies, plastic, battery-op, Nasta, 1984, MIB..$50.00

Sponge Bob Square Pants, doll, beanbag style, Viacom, 2000, 8", NM..$8.00

Sponge Bob Square Pants, doll, cloth, Manco, 2002, 9", EX...$6.00

Starsky & Hutch, AM Wrist Radio, Illco, 1977, MIB....$150.00

Starsky & Hutch, Children's Band Radio, NMIB, $75.00.

Starsky & Hutch, dashboard set, 1976, EX $40.00

Starsky & Hutch, flashlight, Fleetwood, 1976, 7", MOC ..$65.00

Starsky & Hutch, Handcuffs & Wallet Set, Fleetwood, 1976, unused, MOC..$30.00

Starsky & Hutch, Poster Put-Ons, Bi-Rite, 1976, unused, MIP, ea..$10.00

Starsky & Hutch, Shoot-Out Target Set, Berwick (European), 1977, MIB...$75.00

Steve Urkle, doll, talker, Hasbro, 1991, 18", MIB............$50.00

Stuart Little, key-chain figure, talker, 6", EX $8.00

Super Mario, doll, beanbag type, 7", scarce, NM $12.00

Super Mario, doll, cloth body w/rubber head, hands & boots, Applause, 1989, 12", scarce, EX $15.00

Super Mario, doll, plush, Acme, 1988, 11", EX................$10.00

Superman, bank, ceramic, Superman standing on cloud, 1949, 10", EX+ $400.00

Superman, belt buckle, metal, shows red & bl image of Superman breaking chain, 1940s, VG+..............................$75.00

Superman, Crayon-By Numbers Set, Transogram, 1954, EXIB..$100.00

Superman, Crazy Foam Bath Soap, American Aerosol, 1970s, unused, NM+ $60.00

Superman, doll, plush, Knickerbocker, 20", EXIB.............$25.00

Superman, figure, Justice League, plastic, Ideal, 1966, 3", EX+ ..$75.00

Superman, figure, pnt wood & compo bead style w/chest & belt decals, Ideal/Superman Inc, 13", EX $2,600.00

Superman, hand puppet, cloth body w/vinyl head, Ideal/NPPI, 1965-66, EX $150.00

Superman, horseshoe set, Super Swim Inc, 1950s, EXIB..$100.00

Superman, kite, Pressman, 1960s, unused, MIP.............$125.00

Superman, Krypto (Projector) Rag Gun, emb steel, b/o, flashes pictures on wall, w/film, EXIB...................................$475.00

Superman, Krypton Rocket, NCP, 1950s, NM+IB $150.00

Superman, Paint-By-Numbers Watercolor Set, Transogram, 1954, EXIB..$80.00

Superman, pencil box, Mattel, 1966, EX+ $35.00

Superman, pillow, image of flying Superman on felt, 1960s, 12" sq, EX+ $45.00

Superman, push-button puppet, Superman & Supergirl, Kohner, 1968, NMIB, pr (single box) $500.00

Superman, record player, suitcase type w/latch, well illustrated, 1970s, EX+ $75.00

Superman, school bag, vinyl, red & bl w/mc Superman image, blk plastic hdl, Acme, 1950s, EX+ $150.00

Superman, scrapbook, Saalfield/Superman Inc #178, 1940, some use, EX $100.00

Superman, stamp set, 6 character stamps, 1960s, EXIP $30.00

Superman, String Puppet, cloth body w/vinyl head, Madison, 1978, unused, MIB...$125.00

Superman, tile puzzle, blk & wht, Roalex/NPP, 1960s, 2½" sq, VG+OC $65.00

Superman, toothbrush, b/o, Janex, 1970s, EX+................$25.00

Superman, toy watch, plastic, Toy House, 1960s, unused, MIP ..$75.00

Superman, wallet, brn w/emb mc image, Croydon, 1950s, EX+ $75.00

Superman, water pistol, plastic, Multiple Toys, 1960s, unused, MIP $175.00

Superman & Supergirl, push-button puppet set, Kohner, 1960s, EXIB..$175.00

Tarzan, ring, flasher type, Vari-Vue, 1960s, EX+..............$15.00

Teenage Mutant Ninja Turtles, doll, cloth w/string hook, Ace, 1989, 8", NM+ $8.00

Teenage Mutant Ninja Turtles, Power Patch, 2 different iron-ons, Mirage, 1989, MIP, ea.......................................$3.00

Teenage Mutant Ninja Turtles, Tote Pack, Mirage Studios, MIP, from $10.00 to $15.00. (Photo courtesy David Longest)

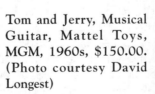

Tom and Jerry, Musical Guitar, Mattel Toys, MGM, 1960s, $150.00. (Photo courtesy David Longest)

The Nanny (TV Series), doll, Nanny, talker, Street Players, 12", MIB $65.00

Three Stooges, Colorforms, 1959, NMIB......................$120.00

Three Stooges, doll, Larry, stuffed cloth body w/rubber head, bl policeman's outfit & hat, 2001, 12", NM+ $10.00

Three Stooges, dolls, any character, Presents, 1988, 14", M, ea...$65.00

Three Stooges, fan club kit, complete, EX $75.00

Three Stooges, Flying Cane, plastic w/spring mechanism, Empire, 1959, 33", EXIP......................................$100.00

Three Stooges, hand puppets, cloth bodies w/vinyl heads, 1950s, NM, ea $50.00

Thunder Cats, puffy stickers, 6 different, Goody, 1985, MIP...$6.00

Tom & Jerry, bank, Gorham, 1980s, NM+ $40.00

Tom & Jerry, figure, Tom holding black top hat, PVC, Turner, 1990, NM+..$5.00

Tom & Jerry, figure set, stuffed cloth w/linen faces, 1940s, 17" & 7½", VG+, pr...$150.00

Tom & Jerry, hand puppet, Tom, cloth w/vinyl head, Mattel/MGM, 1960s, NM $75.00

Tom & Jerry, jack-in-the-box, Mattel, 1965, EX...............$45.00

Tom & Jerry, mug, ceramic, decal shows Jerry tying a string w/a bomb to Tom's tail, MGM, 1970, 3¼" T, EX, P6.......$30.00

Tom Corbett Space Cadet, Cosmic Vision Helmet, Rockhill, 1950, MIB..$285.00

Tom Corbett Space Cadet, flashlight, rocketship w/decals on fin, NM..$250.00

Tom Corbett Space Cadet, Model-Craft Molding & Coloring Set, unused, EXIB..$100.00

Top Cat, bank, Top Cat figure standing on trash can, pnt vinyl, 1960s, 10", NM..$50.00

Topo Gigio, bank, nodder figure w/pineapple, M............$125.00

Topo Gigio, doll, vinyl w/poseable arms, pnt detail w/realistic hair & cloth bow tie, 1963, 12", EX $50.00

Umbriago (Jimmy Durante's Pal), hand puppet, cloth body w/pnt ceramic head, American Merchandise, 1940s, NM (EX box) $75.00

Uncle Wiggily, tea set, wht ceramic w/characters, bl trim, pitcher, 4 cups & saucers,/4 sm plates, Sebring, 1920s, EX $250.00

Underdog, bank, plastic figure, Imco, 1977, 10", NM+ $75.00

Underdog, bank, vinyl figure, Play Pal, 1973, 11", NM+..$85.00

Universal Monsters, figure, Creature From the Black Lagoon, bendable, Ahi, 1974, 5", NM+.................................$100.00

Universal Monsters, figure, Creature From the Black Lagoon, plastic w/jtd arms, 1960s, 13", NM+ $200.00

Universal Monsters, flip movie book, 'Frankenstein in Hiding,' 1960s, 2½", EX+ $18.00

Universal Monsters, night-lights, set of 4 different monsters, EX..$50.00

Universal Monsters, pencil sharpener, Wolfman, gr plastic bust, UP Co, 1960s, 3", NM..$25.00

Universal Monsters, wallet, vinyl w/color images of Creature From the Black Lagoon & Wolfman, 1963, EX+.......$60.00

V (TV Series), Bop Bag, vinyl, 1970s, MIB....................$30.00

V (TV Series), puffy stickers, 6 different, Gordy, 1980s, MIP (sealed) $8.00

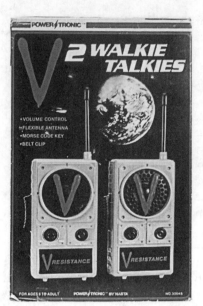

V (TV Series), two Walkie Talkies, Nasta, MOC, $75.00.

Vincent Price, Transparent Watercolors, Sears, 1960s, EXIB..$75.00

Vincent Van Gopher, doll, plush w/pnt vinyl head, blk felt hands, Ideal, 1961, 14", EX.......................................$35.00

Wally Walrus, see Walter Lantz

Walter Lantz, bank, Andy Panda, pnt compo figure, Crown Toy/Walter Lantz Prod, 1939, 5", EX $75.00

Walter Lantz, bank, Andy Panda figure, plastic, 1970s, 7", NM+..$45.00

Walter Lantz, figure, Andy Panda, plush beanbag-style body w/tan plastic shoes, Calif Stuffed Toys, 1982, 10", EX $25.00

Walter Lantz, figure, Chilly Willy, plush, 1980s, NM+.....$30.00

Walter Lantz, figure, Wally Walrus, ceramic, full-length standing pose, 1950s, 5½", NM..$90.00

Walter Lantz, figure, Andy Panda, stuffed felt, with name tag on wrist, NM, $350.00.

Walter Lantz, figure, Woody Woodpecker, squeeze rubber, Vinfloat, 1960, 8", EX+ $50.00

Walter Lantz, hand puppet, Woody Woodpecker, talker, Mattel, 1963, NM...$45.00

Walter Lantz, harmonica, plastic baby grand piano shape featuring Woody Woodpecker, 4x7", EX $15.00

Walter Lantz, Mattel Music Maker, litho tin, featuring Woody Woodpecker, 1960s, VG..$50.00

Walter Lantz, wall plaque, Homer Pigpin figure, Napco, 1958, 6", EX, P6...$75.00

Walter Lantz, wall plaque, Wally Walrus figure w/cane, Napco, 1958, 7", EX, P6...$75.00

Waltons, Farmhouse Playset, w/cb figures & accessories, Amsco, 1975, MIB $75.00

Welcome Back Kotter, chalkboard, gray surface w/circular color image & bordering wht images, Board King, 1970s, EX $50.00

Welcome Back Kotter, Classroom Playset, for 10" dolls, Mattel, 1976, EXIB..$50.00

Welcome Back Kotter, Colorforms Set, 1970s, MIB.........$20.00

Welcome Back Kotter, dolls, any character, Mattel, 10", MOC, ea...$75.00

Welcome Back Kotter, magic slate, 2 different, Whitman, 1977, unused, M, ea...$20.00

Welcome Back Kotter, Paint-By-Number Set, acrylic, 2 different sets, 1970s, unused, MIB, ea $30.00

Wizard of Oz, doll, Scarecrow, Ideal, 1939, 17", NM, $600.00.

Welcome Back Kotter!, Sweat-Hog Calculator, Remco, 1976, MOC, $40.00.

Wizard of Oz, bank, Dorothy, Tin Man, Scarecrow or Cowardly Lion, ceramic, 1960s, NM, ea.....................................$75.00

Wizard of Oz, doll, Cowardly Lion, plastic w/soft rubber head, Toy Time, 1981, 12", complete, scarce, NM+ $15.00

Wizard of Oz, doll, Cowardly Lion, plush, Ideal (Character Doll Series), 1984, 9", NMIB $50.00

Wizard of Oz, doll, Dorothy, Effanbee (Legend Series), 1984, 15", NMIB $125.00

Wizard of Oz, figure, Wicked Witch, squeeze rubber, Burnstein, 1939, 7", EX+ $200.00

Wizard of Oz, figure, Wizard, squeeze rubber, Burnstein, 1939, 7", VG+ $100.00

Wizard of Oz, jack-in-the-box, Scarecrow pops up, litho tin w/Off to See the Wizard cartoon graphics, Mattel, 1960s, EX..$75.00

Wizard of Oz, magic slate, Lowe, 1960s, EX+....................$15.00

Wizard of Oz, mask, Cowardly Lion, die-cut litho cb, Einson-Freeman/Lowe's Inc, 1939, NM...............................$75.00

Wizard of Oz, Paint w/Crayons Set, w/4 pictures, Art Award, 1989, unused, NMIB...$15.00

Wizard of Oz, paint-by-number set, Tin Man, Cowardly Lion & Scarecrow pictures, Craft Master, 1960s, unused, NMIB..$50.00

Wizard of Oz, soap figures, 4 different: Cowardly Lion, Wizard, Tin Man & Scarecrow, Kerk Guild, 1939, unused, EX, set $150.00

Wizard of Oz, Stitch-A-Story Set, Hasbro, 1970s, NM+IB..$25.00

Wonder Woman, Color-A-Deck Card Game, MOC........$50.00

Wonder Woman, Flashmite, Jane X, 1976, MOC $75.00

Wonder Woman, iron-on transfers, several different, 1970s, MIP, ea...$15.00

Wonder Woman, place mat, vinyl face shape w/color image of Wonder Woman & island, 1977, NM.......................$15.00

Woody Woodpecker, see Walter Lantz

Yakky Doodle, see Hanna-Barbera

Yogi Bear, see Hanna-Barbera

Ziggy, doll, cloth, red & wht striped night shirt w/I Love You heart on front, w/hat & moose slippers, 7", EX...........$6.00

Ziggy, doll, in graduation gown & cap, Class of 88, 7", NM...$8.00

Chein

Though the company was founded shortly after the turn of the century, this New Jersey-based manufacturer is probably best known for the toys it made during the 1930s and 1940s. Windup merry-go-rounds and Ferris wheels as well as many other carnival-type rides were made of beautifully lithographed tin even into the '50s, some in several variations. The company also made banks, a few of which were mechanical and some that were character-related. Mechanical, sea-worthy cabin cruisers, space guns, sand toys, and some Disney toys as well were made by this giant company; they continued in production until 1979.

Advisor: Scott Smiles (S10)

See also Banks; Character, TV, and Movie Collectibles; Disney; Sand Toys.

WINDUPS, FRICTION, AND OTHER MECHANICALS

Airplane, top wing with propellers facing the tail, 11" wide, VG+ (P box), $1,320.00. (Photo courtesy Randy Inman Auctions)

Barnacle Bill Walker, 6", VGIB, $250.00. (Photo courtesy Bertoia Aucions)

Aeroswing, 10" L, EXIB	$700.00
Alligator w/Native Rider, 15", EXIB, A	$300.00
Aquaplane, 1939, 8½" L, EXIB, A	$275.00
Aquaplane, 1939, 8½" L, NM	$350.00
Aquaplane (NX4010K), w/pontoons, wings & tail resemble fighter jet, but has single prop, flat-sided pilot's head, VG, A	$65.00
Barnacle Bill Floor Puncher, EX	$400.00
Barnacle Bill in Barrel, 7", EX	$350.00
Bass Drummer, 1930s, 9", NM	$400.00
Big Top Tent, 1961, 10", EXIB	$200.00
Bird Walker, 4½" L, EX+	$175.00
Broadway Trolley, 8", EX+	$150.00
Butterfly Sparkler, 1930, celluloid wings, 5", EXIB	$225.00
Cabin Cruiser, 15", MIB	$350.00
Cabin Cruiser, 15", VG	$150.00
Cathedral Organ, #130, crank-op, 9½", NMIB	$225.00
Clown Balancing Parasol on Nose, 1920s, 8", EX	$200.00
Clown Floor Puncher, celluloid boxing bag, 7½", EX	$750.00

Clown in Barrel, 7½", EX, $400.00. (Photo courtesy Bertoia Auctions)

Clown Walking on Hands, #158, patriotic detail, 5", EX	$150.00
Dan-Dee Oil Truck, 9", EXIB	$900.00
Dan-Dee Oil Truck, 9", G, A	$225.00
Dan-Dee Roadster, 9", EXIB	$1,000.00
Disneyland Ferris Wheel, #172, 17", EXIB	$750.00
Disneyland Rollercoaster, 19" L, NMIB	$850.00
Drummer (Military), 1930s, 7", EX, A	$200.00
Drummer (Parade), #109, 1930s, EXIB	$375.00
Duck Walker, 1930s, 5", EX+	$125.00
Dump Truck (K-18-30), open, blk w/red hubs, 18", rstr	$125.00
Easter Bunny Delivery Cart, #98, 1930s, 9½", EX	$225.00
Edna (Boat), 1910s-20s, EX+	$275.00
Fancy Groceries Truck, 6", EX	$300.00

Disneyland Ferris Wheel, #172, 17", VG, $425.00. (Photo courtesy Bertoia Auctions)

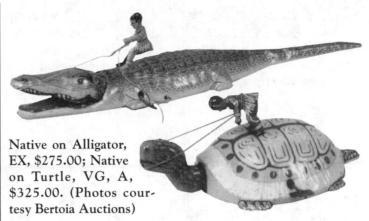

Native on Alligator, EX, $275.00; Native on Turtle, VG, A, $325.00. (Photos courtesy Bertoia Auctions)

Felix the Cat on Scooter, 7", VG $450.00
Ferris Wheel, #172, lithoed base, 17", EX......................$350.00
Ferris Wheel, #172, lithoed base, 17", EXIB $450.00
Fish (Mechanical), #55, 1940s, 11" L, NM.....................$125.00
Greyhound Coast-to-Coast Bus, disk wheels, 9", VG.....$225.00
Happy Hooligan, name on hat, 6", EX............................$450.00
Happy Hooligan, no name on hat, 6", EX.......................$400.00

Penguin, #152, NMIB..$175.00
Playland Merry-Go-Round, #385, bl base, 10", EX.........$375.00
Playland Merry-Go-Round, #385, bl base, 10", EXIB, A ..$550.00
Playland Merry-Go-Round, #387, orange base, 10", EX ..$450.00
Playland Whip, #340, 20" L, MIB (sealed)..................$1,500.00
Playland Whip, #340, 20" L, NMIB...........................$1,000.00
Popeye Floor Puncher, 7", EX, A....................................$825.00
Popeye Floor Puncher, 7", G...$475.00
Popeye Heavy Hitter, 1930s, 12", rare, NM................$4,000.00

Indian Chief Walker, 5", EX, $175.00. (Photo courtesy Bertoia Auctions)

Popeye in Barrel, #258, 1930s, 7", NM, $850.00; Popeye Walker Carrying Two Parrot Cages, 8½", VGIB, $500.00. (Photos courtesy Bertoia Auctions)

Junior Truck, 8", EX...$350.00
Limousine, 1930s, 6", EX+ $275.00
Marine Sergeant, 1960s, 5", EX, A..................................$250.00
Navy Frog Man, plastic flippers, 12", NMOC.................$125.00
Parade Drummer, see Drummer (Parade)
Pelican, #222, 5", NM $125.00

Popeye in Barrel, #258, 1930s, 7", VG+, A $475.00
Popeye Overhead Speed Punching Bag, #255, 1930s, NM ..$300.00
Popeye Shadow Boxer, #254, 1930s, 7", rare, NM.......$1,700.00
Popeye Sparkler, 6", EXIB..$1,000.00
Popeye the Drummer, 7", NM+ $3,000.00
Popeye Walker, 6", EX..$600.00
Popeye Walker, 6", G+ $300.00
Racer #7 (Emmett Racer or Boat-Tail), 20", EX..........$1,500.00

Racer #52, wooden Wheels, EX $200.00
Ride-A-Rocket, EX...$450.00
Roadster, #221, 1920s, 8", EX.......................................$325.00
Roller Coaster, #275, 1930s, red & yel w/amusement pard
     theme, EX+IB $400.00

Roller Coaster, 1950s, park theme with children feeding ducks, 19" long, EX, $200.00. (Photo courtesy Bertoia Auctions)

Ruth (Boat), 1910s-20s, extremely rare, EX+ $425.00
Santa Walker, 5½", EX, A..$475.00
Santa's Gnome, early mk, 6", MIB $325.00
Seaplane, see Aquaplane
Sedan, yel w/red & gr trim, disk wheels, 7", EX, A.........$600.00
Ski Boy, 7½" L, EX $175.00
Ski Boy, 7½" L, EXIB $300.00

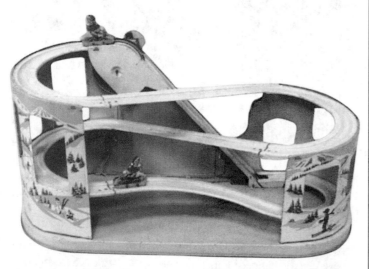

Ski Ride, #320, 18" long, EX, $450.00. (Photo courtesy Bertoia Auctions)

Ski Ride, #320, 18" L, MIB..$600.00
Skin Diver, 11½", NMIB..$200.00

Surf's Up, 10", NMOC...$100.00
Toyville Dump Truck, 9", VG, A $385.00

US Army Sergeant, #153, 5", EX (with original card), A, $250.00. (Photo courtesy Bertoia Auctions)

Yellow Taxi (Main 7570), 1920s, 7", EX $250.00
Yellow Taxi (Main 7570), 1930s, 7", NMIB $425.00

HERCULES SERIES

Army Truck, cloth cover, 29", G $300.00
Clamshell Crane Truck, 28", rare, EX+, A $2,500.00
Coal Truck, 20", G+, A $300.00
Coupe, 1920s, w/rumble seat & luggage rack, 18", EX+ ..$1,200.00

Dairy Products Truck, 19½", EX, A, $1,300.00. (Photo courtesy Smith House Toys)

Ferris Wheel, 17", EX $350.00
Fire Ladder Truck, open seat, 18", no ladders, G, A $185.00
Fire Pumper Truck, open seat, 18", G, A........................$200.00
Ice Truck, #600, 20", VG..$600.00
Mack Dump Truck, 19½", G $400.00
Motor Express Truck, 1928, 19", G $450.00

Motor Express Truck, 19", VG, A, $1,100.00. (Photo courtesy Smith House Toys)

Railway Express Agency Truck, 20", G+ $425.00
Roadster, 1920s, w/rumble seat & luggage rack, 18", EXIB..$2,300.00
Roadster, 1920s, w/rumble seat & luggage rack, 18½", G+ ..$900.00
Royal Blue Line Bus, mid-1920s, 18", G $700.00

Royal Blue Line Bus, 18", VG, $1,000.00. (Photo courtesy Smith House Toys)

Sailboat (Peggy Jane), 36", VG, A $130.00
Tow Truck, 18", VG..$600.00

Tanker Truck, 19", G, $800.00. (Photo courtesy Noel Barrett Antiques and Auctions Ltd.)

MISCELLANEOUS

Bank, church, #29, NM...$125.00
Bank, clown bust, 5", EX $100.00

Bank, elephant on drum, 5", EX....................................$125.00
Bank, monkey, #11, EX..$100.00
Bank, Save for War Bonds & Stamps, dome shape, 4½", NM ..$550.00
Bank, Save for War Bonds & Stamps, shell shape, 6", NM ...$225.00
Bank, Uncle Wiggily, #22, 5", M....................................$225.00
Bank, 1939 World's Fair, 12", NM..................................$275.00
Brake Service/Welding Garage, litho tin, opening door, 7", EX,
    A $150.00

Duck on Wheels, late 1930s, open back, wooden wheels, 8" long, EX+, A, $200.00. (Photo courtesy Bertoia Auctions)

Easter Basket, lithoed nursery-rhyme characters, 1959, 7½" dia,
    NM...$125.00
Easter Egg, take-apart w/lithoed scenes, 5", NM $75.00
Globe, 10", NMIB..$125.00
Player Piano, electric, NM $275.00

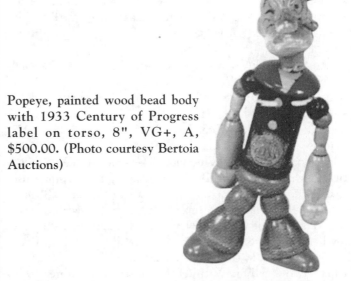

Popeye, painted wood bead body with 1933 Century of Progress label on torso, 8", VG+, A, $500.00. (Photo courtesy Bertoia Auctions)

Pull Toy, cat on 3-wheeled platform, 7½", EX $350.00
Sparkler, #95, 1930s, red, wht & bl, 4½", EXIB.............$100.00
Stop/Go Sign, 11", EX $400.00
Top, Gulliver's Travels, 1939, 5" dia, rare, NM $175.00
Top, various images of children's toys, 1930s, NM...........$75.00

Roly Poly, clown, 6¼", EX, A, $220.00; Roly Poly, rabbit, 6¼", EX, $190.00. (Photo courtesy Bertoia Auctions)

Traffic Cop, flat-sided figure on base next to traffic sign, 5", P..**$125.00**
Train Station, litho tin simulated brick building w/Grove Station sign, 6", EX **$75.00**

Coloring, Activity, and Paint Books

Coloring and activity books from the early years of the twentieth century are scarce indeed and when found can be expensive if they are tied into another collectibles field such as Black Americana or advertising; but the ones most in demand are those that represent familiar movie and TV stars of the 1950s and 1960s. Condition plays a very important part in assessing worth, and though hard to find, unused examples are the ones that bring top dollar — in fact, as much as 50% to 75% more than one even partially used.

A-Team Storybook/Coloring Book, Peter Pan, 1984, The Maltese Cow, unused, EX **$5.00**
Alvin & the Chipmunks in 'Pinocchio' Sticker Book, Landoll's, 1996, unused, M (NOS) **$5.00**
Anastasia Coloring & Water Paint Book, Golden Books, 1997, unused, M (NOS) **$5.00**
Andy Panda Paint Book, Whitman, 1944, some use, EX...**$35.00**
Ann Sheridan Coloring Book, Whitman, 1940s, some use, EX+...**$50.00**
Annette Coloring Box, Whitman, 1962, complete w/all 256 pgs, no crayons, some use, EX+IB.......................................**$50.00**
Baby Lamb Chop & Friends Paint With Water, Golden Book, 1993, unused, M (NOS) **$5.00**
Batman (Sticker Fun With...), Watkins-Strathmore, 1966, unused, EX+..**$25.00**
Batman Forever Coloring & Activity Book, Golden Books, 1995, unused, EX **$5.00**
Batman Forever Paint With Water, Golden Book, 1995, unused, M..**$5.00**
Batman Paint-By-Number Book, Whitman, 1966, EX+...**$25.00**

Bewitched Coloring Book, Treasure Books, 1965, unused, M, $125.00. (Photo courtesy Greg Davis and Bill Morgan)

Bing Crosby Coloring Book, Saalfield #2440, 1954, some use, NM...**$50.00**
Blondie Paint Book, Whitman, 1947, unused, NM+ **$175.00**
Bozo the Clown Paint Book, Whitman/Capitol Records, 1950, some use, NM **$50.00**
Buck Rogers Paint Book, Whitman #679, 1935, some use, VG+ **$250.00**
Captain Planet & the Planeteers Sticker Fun Book, Golden, 1991, unused, NM...**$6.00**
Charlie Chaplin Coloring Book, Saalfield #198, 1941, all pgs colored, EX **$100.00**
Crusader Rabbit Trace & Color Book, Whitman, 1959, some use, EX+ **$75.00**
Davy Crockett Frontier Cabin Punchout Book, Whitman/WDP #1943, 1955, unused, M **$100.00**
Donald Duck Color-By-Number Book, Whitman #1408, 1979, unused, NM+ **$15.00**
Donna Reed Coloring Book, Saalfield, 1964, unused, M..**$30.00**

Donny & Marie Coloring Book, Whitman, 1977, unused, M, $25.00. (Photo courtesy Greg Davis and Bill Morgan)

Dukes of Hazzard Stunt Show Coloring & Activity Book, Modern Promotions, 1981, unused, M (NOS) $7.00

Fame Coloring & Activity Book, Playmore Publishing, 1983, some use, VG $6.00

Flash Gordon Coloring Book, Whitman, 1952, some use, VG.$30.00

Flintstones Great Big Punchout Book, Whitman, 1961, some use, EX $30.00

Gene Autry Cowboy Paint Book, Merrill, 1940, some use, EX+ $40.00

Gene Autry Cowboy Punch-Out Book, Merrill #4802, 1940s, some use, EX $85.00

Gilligan's Island Coloring Book, Whitman, 1965, unused, M, $100.00. (Photo courtesy Greg Davis and Bill Morgan)

Gone With the Wind Paint Book, Merrill #3403, 1940, some use, G+ $50.00

Grace Kelly, Whitman, 1956, portrait photo on scroll w/floral detail, unused, EX $50.00

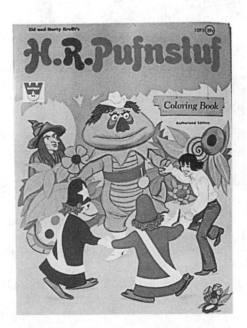

H.R. Pufnstuf Coloring Book, Whitman, 1970, unused, M, $75.00. (Photo courtesy Greg Davis and Bill Morgan)

Greer Garson Coloring Book, Merrill, 1940s, some use, EX+ ...$50.00

Haley Mills in Search of the Castaways Coloring Book, Whitman #1138, 1962, some use, EX+ $30.00

Hopalong Cassidy in Pirates on Horseback Coloring Book, Lowe, 1950s, some use, VG $25.00

Hopalong Cassidy Sticker Fun & Stencil, Whitman, 1951, some use, VG $25.00

Jack Webb's Safety Squad Dragnet Coloring Book, Abbott, 1957, some use, EX+ $35.00

Jackie Gleason Funny TV Coloring Book, Abbott #1314, 1956, some use, EX+ $50.00

Jackie Gleason's Dan Dan Dandy Coloring Book, Lowe #2370, 1950s, some use, EX+ $50.00

Jonny Quest Paint With Water Book, Landolls, 1994, unused, NM $50.00

Judy Garland Fashion Paint Book, Whitman/MGM #674, 1940, some use, scarce, VG $50.00

Jurrasic Park — The Lost World Paint With Water, Landoll's, 1997, unused, M (NOS) $5.00

Knight Rider Activity Book, Modern Publishing, 1983, unused, EX+ $8.00

Land of the Lost Coloring Book, Whitman #1045, 1975, unused, M, $30.00; Land of the Lost Coloring and Activity Book, Whitman #1271, 1975, unused, M, $30.00. (Photo courtesy Gred Davis and Bill Morgan)

Lassie Coloring Book, Whitman #1151-2, 1982, unused, EX ..$15.00

Love Bug Coloring Book, Walt Disney Studio, 1969, Hunt's Catsup promotion for Love Bug movie, unused, EX, P6 ..$24.00

Lucille Ball & Desi Arnez Coloring Book, Whitman #2079, 1953, some use, EX+ $75.00

Mickey Mouse Activity Book, Whitman, 1936, unused, EX+ ..$75.00

Mickey Mouse Club, Mouskartooner, Mattel, 1950s, EX (VG box featuring Roy Williams) $50.00

Mickey Mouse Club, Whitman, 1955, boxed set of 12 different books, 7x6", most have some coloring, EX $50.00

Mickey Mouse Club Old MacDonald Had a Farm Coloring Book, 1955, some use, EX, P6 ....$24.00

Mr Ed Coloring Book, Whitman #1135, 1963, some use, EX..$50.00

Munsters Sticker Fun Book, Whitman, 1965, some use, EX....$75.00

Our Gang Coloring Book, Saalfield, 1930s, color images used as guide for coloring, 15x11", some coloring, EX+.........$75.00

Peanuts Trace & Color Set, Saalfield, #6122, 1960s, 5-book set, unused, NM+...$75.00

Pink Panther Activity Book, Whitman, 1979, unused, NM+ ..$15.00

Pink Panther Coloring Book, Whitman, 1976, unused, NM+ $15.00

Pinocchio Paint Book, Disney, 1939, unused, NM+.......$100.00

Planet of the Apes, Saalfield, 1974, some use, EX $10.00

Playroom People Paint Book, Saalfield, 1941, unused, EX, P6...$28.00

Popeye Giant 24 Big Pictures Coloring Book, Merrigold Press, 1981, unused, NM+ $25.00

Popeye Paint With Water Book, Whitman, 1981, unused, NM+..$10.00

Porky Pig Coloring Book, Leon Schlesinger, 1930s, some use, EX, $125.00. (Photo courtesy Davis Longest)

Raggedy Ann & Andy (paper dolls), Whitman #1650, 1971..$20.00

Rambo Coloring & Activity Book, Modern Publishing, 1985, some use, EX+...$6.00

Reg'lar Fellers Story Paint Book, by Gene Byrnes, 1932, cb cover, unused, EX, P6 ....$35.00

Roy Rogers Paint Book, Whitman, 1948, some use, 15x11", VG..$30.00

Roy Rogers Rodeo Sticker Fun w/Dale Evans, Trigger & Bullet, Whitman, some use, EX+ $50.00

Sergeant Preston Coloring Book, Whitman, 1957, some use, NM...$25.00

Sesame Street Coloring Book, Whitman, 1975, unused, EX..$10.00

Shirley Temple's Blue Bird Coloring Book, Saalfield, 1939, some use, EX+..$40.00

Shirley Temples Busy Book, Saalfield #5326, 1958, some use, EX+...$45.00

Sid & Marty Krofft's Kaleidoscope Puppets Punch-out Book, As Presented by the Coca-Cola Co, 1968, unpunched, EX+......$50.00

Sleeping Beauty Sticker Fun Book, Whitman, 1959, unused, NM+ $50.00

Smokey Bear Coloring Book, Whitman, 1958, unused, NM+ ...$25.00

Spider-Man Coloring Book, Marvel, 1983, The Arms of Dr Octopus, some use, EX+ $15.00

Straight Arrow Indian Coloring Book, Stephens, 1949, some use, EX+...$50.00

Superman Coloring Book, Saalfield #4583, 1958, some use, EX $50.00

Superman Paint-By-Number Book, Whitman, 1966, unused, NM+ $35.00

Superman Sticker Book, Whitman, 1977, 4 pgs of stickers to be used on 16-pg Superman story, unused, M, P6...........$22.00

Superman to the Rescue, Whitman #1001, 1964, some use, EX+..$30.00

Thief of Bagdad, Saalfield, 1940, movie edition, Sabu on magic carpet on cover, some use, NM................................$50.00

Three Little Pigs Coloring Book, Playmore, 1984, unused, NM $8.00

Three Stooges Coloring Book, Lowe #2965, 1962, some use, EX $35.00

Three Stooges Coloring Book, Whitman #1135, 1964, some use, EX..$35.00

Three Stooges Funny Coloring Book, Lowe #2855, 1959, VG .$50.00

Tom Corbett Space Cadet Coloring Book, Saalfield, 1950s, Tom in foreground w/rocket center in back, some use, VG .$25.00

Tom Corbett Space Cadet Push Outs, Saalfield/Rockill, 1952, unused, NM+, A..$100.00

Tom Mix Paint Book, Whitman 1935, some use, VG $50.00

Toy Story Coloring Book, Golden Books, unused, M $6.00

Toy Story Paint w/Water Book, Golden Books, unused, M...$6.00

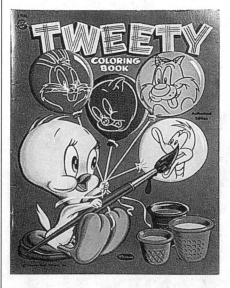

Tweety Coloring Book, Whitman, some use, EX, $25.00. (Photo courtesy Davis Longest)

Universal Monsters Paint 'N' Marker Book, Golden Book, 1991, some use, EX $5.00

Walt Disney Paint Book, Whitman/WDE #2080, 1937, some use, VG $50.00

Who Framed Roger Rabbit Paint & Water Book, Golden #1702, unused, NM+ $25.00

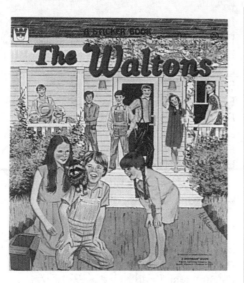

Waltons Sticker Book, Whitman, 1975, unused, NM+, $50.00. (Photo courtesy Greg Davis and Bill Morgan)

Winnie the Pooh & the Blustry Day Coloring Book, Whitman, 1965, unused, EX $15.00

Winnie the Pooh Coloring Book & Follow the Dots, Whitman, 1976, unused, EX $12.00

Winnie the Pooh Trace & Color Book, Whitman, 1973, unused, EX...$12.00

Wizard of Oz (Tales of) Coloring Book, Whitman, 1962, from cartoon TV show, unused, NM+ $25.00

Wizard of Oz Color-By-Number Book, Karas Publishing #A-116, 1962, unused, NM+ $50.00

Wizard of Oz Paint Book, Whitman, 1939, some use, EX+ ..$125.00

Wizard of Oz Sticker Fun Book, Whitman, 1976, unused, NM...$15.00

Woody Woodpecker's Fun-O-Rama Punch-Out Book, 1972, unused, NM+ $30.00

Young Indiana Jones Chronicles Color & Activity Book, Golden Book, 1992, unused, M $4.00

Comic Books

For more than a half a century, kids of America raced to the bookstand as soon as the new comics came in for the month and for 10¢ an issue kept up on the adventures of their favorite super heroes, cowboys, space explorers, and cartoon characters. By far most were eventually discarded — after they were traded one friend to another, stacked on closet shelves, and finally confiscated by Mom. Discount the survivors that were torn or otherwise damaged over the years and those about the mundane, and of those remaining, some could be quite valuable. In fact, first editions of high-grade comics books or those showcasing the first appearance of a major character often bring $500.00 and more. Rarity, age, and quality of the artwork are prime factors in determining value, and condition is critical. If you want to seriously collect comic books, you'll need to refer to a good comic book price guide such as *Overstreet's*.

Alvin & His Pals Merry Christmas, Dell, 1963, EX+ $55.00

Amazing Spider-Man, Marvel #43, 1966, VG..................$35.00

Andy Griffith, Dell Four-Color #1252, VG $75.00

Andy Panda, Dell Four-Color #280, 1950, EX..................$25.00

Aquaman, Dell #1, 1962, EX.......................................$200.00

Atom (The) in Master of the Plant World!, DC Comics #1, EX, $150.00.

Avengers, Marvel #1, 1963, EX......................................$500.00

Barbie & Ken, Dell #3, 1963, EX $50.00

Batman, Deathblow: After the Fire, DC Comics #1, NM...$15.00

Batman (Adventures of), DC Comics #1, NM $5.00

Beany & Cecil, Dell #2, 1962, rare, EX............................$35.00

Beatles Yellow Subamrine, Gold Key, 1968, w/poster, NM, from $150 to $200.00

Bewitched, Dell #2, 1965, NM, from $40 to $65.00

Bionic Woman, Charlton #1, 1977, NM..........................$15.00

Black Rider, Marvel #8, EX+ $20.00

Bonanza, Dell #20, 1962, EX $50.00

Brady Bunch, Dell #2, 1970, NM $75.00

Bugs Bunny, Dell Four-Color #164, VG $30.00

Bugs Bunny Christmas Funnies, Dell #7, NM...................$60.00

Captain Marvel (Adventures of), Fawcett #132, 1952, VG.$30.00

Captain Marvel, Marvel #1, 1968, NM............................$150.00

Cisco Kid, 1952, VG, $10.00.

Captain Midnight, Fawcett #37, NM..................$170.00
Christmas in Disneyland, Dell #1, EX+ $250.00
Cisco Kid, Dell #17, VG..$20.00
Dale Evans, National Periodical Publication #1, EX $100.00
Daredevil, Marvel Comics, #1, 1964, G.........................$175.00
Dark Shadows, Gold Key #5, 1970, NM $50.00

Dennis the Menace, Marvel #1, 1981, NM+ $15.00
Dick Tracy, Dell #4, NM..$120.00
Donald Duck Beach Party, Dell Giant #1, EX................$35.00
Donald Duck in Mathmagicland, Dell #1198, NM...........$45.00
Elmer Fudd, Dell #689, NM...$25.00
Family Affair, Gold Key #1, 1970, w/poster, NM $40.00
Felix the Cat, Dell #61, 1946, VG $40.00
Flash Gordon, Dell Four-Color #175, 1967, NM $130.00
Flintstones, Dell #2, NM $75.00
Flying Nun, Dell #4, 1968, NM.......................................$30.00
Gene Autry, Dell #51, VG..$20.00
Get Smart, Dell #1, 1966, NM $65.00
Green Hornet, Dell Four-Color #496, 1953, EX $70.00
Gunsmoke, Dell Four-Color #844, EX+ $45.00
Hawkman, National Periodical Publications #1, 1964, NM...$470.00
Hogan's Heroes, Dell #4, 1966, NM................................$25.00
HR Pufnstuf, Gold Key #2, 1971, EX $40.00
Human Torch Battling the Submariners, #8, 1942, NM..$2,200.00

David Cassidy, Charlton #1 – 3, 1972, EX, $12.00 each. (Photo courtesy Greg Davis and Bill Morgan)

Human Torch, Chipiden Publishing Vol 1 #38, August, 1954, EX, $250.00.

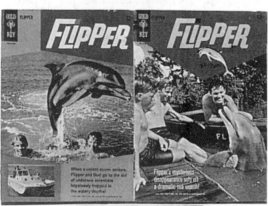

Flipper, Gold Key #1 – 3, 1966 – 1967, from $15.00 to $20.00 each. (Photo courtesy Greg Davis and Bill Morgan)

Hunchback of Norte Dame, Dell Four-Color #854, 1957, EX ..$40.00
I Dream of Jeannie, Dell #1, 1966, NM $100.00
I Love Lucy, Dell #5, 1955, EX+....................................$85.00
Incredible Hulk, Marvel #102, EX...................................$75.00
Jetsons, Gold Key #35, EX $15.00
John Carter of Mars, Gold Key #1, 1964, VG.................$20.00
Journey Into Mystery, Marvel #91, 1963, VG $40.00
Justice League of America, SC Comics #6, VG $50.00
Kid Montana, Charlton #10, EX+....................................$15.00
Kiss, Image Comics #1, 1997, NM..................................$10.00
Lady & the Tramp, Dell Four-Color #629, 1955, EX $30.00
Lassie, Dell #27, NM..$25.00
Lawman, Dell #8, 1961, VG+..$20.00
Lil' Abner, Harvey #61, 1947, NM $190.00
Lone Ranger, Dell #1, 1948, VG....................................$100.00
Lone Ranger, Dell #37, EX+...$45.00
Lone Rangers, March of Comics #310, photo cover, EX ..$45.00
Marge's Little Lulu, Dell #74, NM..................................$60.00
Marge's Little Lulu, Dell Four-Color #115, 1946, VG+ $90.00
Marvel Tales, Dell #121, 1954, VG.................................$50.00
Mary Poppins, Gold Key, 1964, EX $15.00

Maverick, Dell Four-Color #980, EX.................................$65.00
Mickey Mouse, Dell Four-Color #27, 1943, VG $160.00
Mod Squad, Dell #1, 1969, NM+ $50.00
Monkees, Dell #1, 1967-68, NM $65.00
Munsters, Gold Key #4, 1965, EX $20.00
Mysterious Adventures, Story #8, 1952, VG....................$75.00
Nancy & Sluggo, United Features Syndicate #100, 1953,
   VG..$15.00

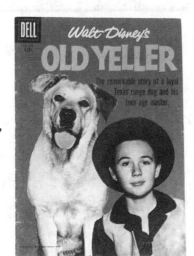

Old Yeller, Dell #869, 1957, EX, $30.00.

Outlaws of the West, Charlton #15, VG+ $15.00
Partridge Family, Charlton #19, 1973, EX.......................$15.00
Playful Little Audrey, Harvey #1, EX $80.00
Popeye, Dell #8, 1959, EX $40.00
Raggedy Ann & Andy, Dell #2, 1946, VG.......................$35.00
Rawhide, Dell #1160, 1960, VG+ $30.00
Rawhide Kid, Atlas/Marvel #12, EX $50.00
Red Ryder, Dell #69, 1949, NM $45.00
Restless Gun, Dell Four-Color #1146, VG+.....................$25.00
Rifleman, Dell #5, 1960, photo cover, EX $35.00
Robin Hood, Dell #1, 1963, EX+ $15.00
Roy Rogers & Trigger, Dell #1, 1948, EX $140.00
Savage Tales, Marvel #2, 1975, EX..................................$35.00

Scooby Doo, Marvel #1, 1977, NM+ $25.00
Silly Symphonies, Dell Giants #7, NM.............................$110.00
Six Million Dollar Man, Charlton #1, 1976, NM............$15.00
Space Busters, Ziff-Davis #2, 1952, EX $210.00
Star Trek, Gold Key #2, 1968, M $150.00
Strange Adventures, National Periodical Publications #39, EX.$100.00
Superman, DC Comics #1, 1939, G, minimum value ..$15,000.00
Superman, DC Comics #25, 1941, VG $225.00
Superman's Girlfriend Lois Lane, Dell #13, NM............$120.00
Tales to Astonish, Atlas #22, 1961, VG...........................$35.00

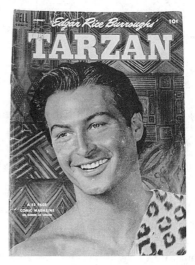

Tarzan, Dell Vol 1 #52, Lex Barker cover, EX, $55.00.

Tarzan's Jungle Annual, Dell #2, 1953, EX.....................$40.00
Tex Ritter Western, Fawcett #2, 1954, EX $60.00
Three Stooges, Dell Four-Color #1170, 1961, VG............$30.00
Tom & Jerry, Dell #115, EX..$20.00
Tom Mix Western, Fawcett #2, VG $100.00
Top Cat, Gold Key #5, 1963, NM $45.00
Tweety & Sylvester, Dell #11, NM..................................$25.00
Uncle Scrooge, Dell Four-Color #386, 1952, VG..........$140.00
Underworld Crime, Fawcett #3, 1952, EX+ $60.00
Voyage to the Bottom of the Sea, Gold Key #6, 1966, EX..$15.00

Star Trek: To Err Is Vulcan!, Gold Key #59, 1978, NM+, $30.00.

Wild Bill Hickok, #26, January – February 1956, EX, $35.00.

Voyage to the Deep, Dell #1, 1962, EX $15.00
Walt Disney's Picnic Party, Dell Giant #8, 1957, VG+ $50.00
Western Tales, Dell #32, 1956, EX+................................$80.00
Wild Wild West, Gold Key #2, 1966, G+ $12.00
Wonder Woman, National Periodical Publication #100, 1958, EX................................$45.00
Woody Woodpecker Back to School, Dell Giant #1, 1952, EX $25.00
Wyatt Earp, Dell Four-Color #860, NM.........................$75.00
X-Men, Marvel #13, 1965, VG.......................................$45.00
Zane Grey's Stories of the West, Dell Four-Color #511, 1954, EX.................................$25.00

Corgi

The Corgi legacy is a rich one, beginning in 1934 with parent company Mettoy of Swansea, South Wales. In 1956, Mettoy merged with Playcraft Ltd. to form Mettoy Playcraft Ltd. and changed the brand name from Mettoy to Corgi, in honor of Queen Elizabeth's beloved Welsh Corgis, which she could regularly be seen taking for walks around Buckingham palace.

In 1993, Mattel bought the Corgi brand and attempted, for a short time, to maintain the tradition of producing Corgi quality collectible toys. Shortly afterward, employees of the Welsh manufacturing center purchased back the Corgi Collectibles line from Mattel. In July 1999, the brand was purchased again, this time by Zindart, an American-owned company based in Hong Kong, where the Corgi Classics line is now produced.

Some of the most highly prized Corgi toys in today's collectors' market are the character-related vehicles. The assortment includes the cars of secret agent James Bond, including several variations of his Aston-Martin, his lotus Esprit complete with underwater maneuvering fins, and other 007 vehicles. Batman's Batmobile and Batboat, and the man from U.N.C.L.E.'s Thrushbuster are among the favorites as well.

Values represent models in new condition in their original package unless noted otherwise.

Advisor: Dana Johnson (J3)

#50, Massey-Ferguson 50B Tractor, from $60 to $75.00
#50, Massey-Ferguson 65 Tractor, from $100 to.............$125.00
#51, Massey-Ferguson Tipper Trailer, from $25 to............$40.00
#53, Massey-Ferguson Tractor Shovel, from $100 to $125.00
#54, Fordson Half-Track Tractor, from $150 to...............$175.00
#54, Massey-Ferguson Tractor Shovel, from $60 to $75.00
#55, David Brown Tractor, from $60 to...........................$75.00
#55, Fordson Power Major Tractor, from $100 to $125.00
#56, Plough, from $25 to $35.00
#57, Massey-Ferguson Tractor & Fork, from $100 to......$125.00
#58, Beast Carrier, from $50 to......................................$65.00
#60, Fordson Power Major Tractor, from $90 to $120.00
#61, Four-Furrow Plough, from $25 to............................$35.00
#62, Ford Tipper Trailer, from $25 to $35.00
#64, Conveyor on Jeep, from $90 to $120.00
#66, Massey-Ferguson 165 Tractor, from $75 to...............$95.00

#67, Ford 5000 Super Major Tractor, from $80 to...........$110.00
#69, Massey-Ferguson Tractor Shovel, from $90 to $120.00
#71, Fordson Disc Harrow, from $25 to............................$40.00
#72, Ford 5000 Tractor & Trencher, from $110 to..........$130.00
#73, Massey-Ferguson Tractor & Saw, from $100 to.......$125.00
#74, Ford 5000 Tractor & Scoop, from $100 to $125.00
#100, Dropside Trailer, from $25 to................................$40.00
#101, Platform Trailer, from $25 to $40.00
#102, Pony Trailer, from $25 to $40.00
#104, Dolphin Cabin Cruiser, from $30 to......................$45.00
#107, Batboat & Trailer, 1972-76, from $150 to............$175.00
#107, Batboat & Trailer, 1976-1980, from $90 to...........$110.00
#109, Pennyburn Trailer, from $50 to..............................$65.00
#112, Rice Horse Box, from $35 to $50.00
#150, Surtees TS9, from $45 to......................................$60.00
#150, Vanwall, regular, from $90 to $110.00
#151, Lotus XI, regular, from $90 to $110.00
#151, McLaren Yardley M19A, from $35 to.....................$50.00
#152, BRM Racer, from $85 to......................................$100.00
#152, Ferrari 312 B2, from $35 to..................................$50.00
#153, Bluebird Record Car, from $125 to $150.00
#153, Team Surtees, from $45 to....................................$60.00
#154, Ferrari Formula I, from $45 to $60.00
#154, Lotus John Player, from $40 to $55.00
#154, Lotus Texaco Special, from $40 to.........................$55.00

#155, Lotus-Climax F1 Racer, from $65.00 to $75.00; #156, Cooper Maserati F1 Racer, from $50.00 to $65.00.

#158, Tyrrell-Ford Elf, from $40 to $55.00
#159, STP Patrick Eagle Racer, from $45 to $60.00
#160, Hesketh Racer, from $45 to $60.00
#161, Elf-Tyrrell Project 34, from $45 to.........................$60.00
#161, Santa Pod Commuter Dragster, from $45 to $60.00
#162, Quartermaster Dragster, from $35 to $50.00
#162, Tyrell P34 Racer, from $40 to $55.00
#163, Santa Pod Dragster, from $40 to $55.00
#164, Wild Honey Dragster, from $40 to..........................$55.00
#165, Adams Bros Dragster, from $35 to $50.00
#166, Ford Mustang Organ Grinder Dragster, from $35 to...$50.00
#167, USA Racing Buggy, from $30 to..............................$45.00
#169, Starfighter Jet Dragster, from $45 to......................$60.00
#170, John Wolfe's Dragster, from $45 to $60.00
#190, Lotus John Player Special, from $60 to $75.00
#191, McLaren Texaco-Marlboro, from $60 to $75.00
#200, BMC Mini 1000, from $45 to $60.00
#200, Ford Consul, dual colors, from $175 to $200.00
#200, Ford Consul, solid colors, from $150 to.................$175.00

#200m, Ford Consul, w/motor, from $175 to $200.00
#201, Austin Cambridge, from $150 to..........................$175.00
#201, Austin Cambridge, from $175 to..........................$200.00
#201, Saint's Volvo, from $175 to $200.00
#201m, Austin Cambridge, w/motor, from $200 to $225.00
#202, Morris Cowley, from $125 to $150.00
#202, Renault 16TS, from $45 to $60.00
#202m, Morris Cowley, w/motor, from $150 to.............$175.00
#203, Detomaso Mangusta, from $40 to $55.00
#203, Vauxhall Velox, dual colors, from $175 to $200.00
#203, Vauxhall Velox, solid colors, from $150 to $175.00
#203, Vauxhall Velox, w/motor, dual colors, from $250 to...$275.00
#203, Vauxhall Velox, w/motor, red or yel, from $200 to...$225.00
#204, Morris Mini-Minor, bl, from $225 to $250.00
#204, Rover 90, other colors, from $175 to.....................$200.00
#204, Rover 90, wht & red, 2-tone, from $225 to $250.00
#204m, Rover 90, w/motor, from $200 to $225.00
#205, Riley Pathfinder, bl, from $150 to $175.00
#205, Riley Pathfinder, red, from $100 to $125.00
#205m, Riley Pathfinder, w/motor, bl, from $150 to......$175.00
#205m, Riley Pathfinder, w/motor, red, from $200 to.....$225.00

#211s, Studebaker Golden Hawk, gold-painted, suspension, from $100.00 to $125.00. (Photo courtesy June Moon)

#215, Ford Thunderbird Sport, no suspension, from $115 to...$140.00
#215s, Ford Thunderbird Sport, w/suspension, from $100 to...$125.00
#216, Austin A-40, red & blk, from $125 to $150.00
#216, Austin A-40, 2-tone bl, from $115 to $140.00
#216m, Austin A-40, w/motor, from $300 to.................$325.00
#217, Fiat 1800, from $70 to.......................................$85.00
#218, Aston Martin DB4 Saloon, from $100 to.............$125.00
#219, Plymouth Suburban, from $90 to $110.00

#206, Hillman Husky, metallic blue and silver, from $150.00 to $175.00. (Photo courtesy June Moon)

#206, Hillman Husky Estate, solid colors, from $125 to ...$150.00
#206m, Hillman Husky Estate, w/motor, from $150 to...$175.00
#207, Standard Vanguard, from $125 to $150.00
#207m, Standard Vanguard, w/motor, from $150 to.......$175.00
#208, Jaguar 2.4 Saloon, no suspension, from $120 to....$140.00
#208m, Jaguar 2.4 Saloon, w/motor, from $155 to..........$180.00
#208s, Jaguar 2.4 Saloon, w/suspension, from $140 to....$165.00
#209, Riley Police Car, from $100 to $125.00
#210, Citroen DS19, from $90 to................................$110.00
#210s, Citroen DS19, w/suspension, from $100 to $120.00
#211, Studebaker Golden Hawk, no suspension, from $125 to..$150.00
#211, Studebaker Golden Hawk, w/suspension, from $150 to....$175.00
#211m, Studebaker Golden Hawk, w/motor, from $150 to..$175.00
#213, Jaguar Fire Chief, from $150 to $175.00
#213s, Jaguar Fire Chief, w/suspension, from $200 to.....$225.00
#214, Ford Thunderbird, no suspension, from $115 to...$140.00
#214m, Ford Thunderbird, w/motor, from $300 to.........$325.00
#214s, Ford Thunderbird, w/suspension, from $95 to $120.00

#220, Chevy Impala, from $75.00 to $90.00. (Photo courtesy June Moon)

#221, Chevrolet Impala Taxi, from $100 to....................$125.00
#222, Renault Floride, from $90 to $110.00
#223, Chevrolet Police, from $120 to $140.00
#224, Bentley Continental, from $100 to $125.00

#229, Chevrolet Corvair, from $60.00 to $75.00. (Photo courtesy June Moon)

#225, Austin 7, red, from $100 to $125.00
#225, Austin 7, yel, from $300 to $325.00
#226, Morris Mini-Minor, from $100 to......................$125.00
#227, Mini-Cooper Rally, from $250 to $275.00
#228, Volvo P-1800, from $75 to..................................$90.00
#230, Mercedes Benz 220SE, blk, from $120 to.............$140.00
#230, Mercedes Benz 220SE, red, from $75 to $90.00
#231, Triumph Herald, from $100 to $125.00
#232, Fiat 2100, from $75 to...$90.00
#233, Heinkel Trojan, from $75 to...............................$90.00
#234, Ford Consul Classic, from $85 to $100.00
#235, Oldsmobile Super 88, from $70 to.....................$95.00
#236, Austin A60, right-hand drive, from $70 to...........$95.00
#237, Oldsmobile Sheriff's Car, from $95 to.................$120.00
#238, Jaguar MK10, metallic gr or silver, from $165 to ..$190.00
#238, Jaguar MK10, metallic red or bl, from $100 to......$125.00

#251, Hillman Imp, from $85 to....................................$100.00
#252, Rover 2000, metallic bl, from $80 to......................$95.00
#252, Rover 2000, metallic maroon, from $175 to $200.00
#253, Mercedes Benz 220SE, from $100 to....................$125.00
#255, Austin A60, left-hand drive, from $225 to $250.00
#256, VW 1200 East Africa Safari, from $225 to $250.00
#258, Saint's Volvo P1800, red hood, from $250 to........$275.00
#258, Saint's Volvo P1800, wht hood, from $175 to.......$200.00
#259, Citroen Le Dandy, bl, from $175 to $200.00
#259, Citroen Le Dandy, maroon, from $100 to $125.00
#259, Penguin Mobile, from $60 to $75.00
#260, Renault R16, from $60 to $75.00
#261, James Bond's Aston Martin DB5, from $250 to....$275.00
#261, Spiderbuggy, from $100 to $125.00
#262, Capt Marvel's Porsche, from $60 to......................$75.00
#262, Lincoln Continental Limo, bl, from $175 to $200.00
#262, Lincoln Continental Limo, gold, from $100 to.....$125.00

#239, VW Karman Ghia, from $75.00 to $90.00. (Photo courtesy June Moon)

#240, Fiat 600 Jolly, from $125 to $150.00
#241, Chrysler Ghia, from $65 to...................................$80.00
#242, Fiat 600 Jolly, from $150 to $175.00
#245, Buick Riviera, from $85 to $100.00

#263, Rambler Marlin Sports Fastback, from $75.00 to $100.00. (Photo courtesy June Moon)

#264, Incredible Hulk Mazda Pickup, from $65 to............$80.00
#264, Oldsmobile Toronado, from $100 to $125.00
#265, Supermobile, from $75 to.....................................$90.00
#266, Chitty-Chitty Bang-Bang, orig, from $375 to.......$425.00
#266, Chitty-Chitty Bang-Bang, replica, from $125 to ..$150.00
#266, Superbike, from $75 to..$90.00
#267, Batmobile, red 'Bat'-hubs, from $400 to................$450.00
#267, Batmobile, w/red whizzwheels, from $500 to $550.00
#267, Batmobile, w/whizzwheels, from $125 to..............$150.00
#268, Batman's Bat Bike, from $60 to $75.00
#268, Green Hornet's Black Beauty, from $350 to...........$400.00
#269, James Bond's Lotus Esprit, from $100 to $125.00
#270, James Bond's Aston Martin, w/tire slashers, 1/43 scale, from
    $275 to..$325.00
#270, James Bond's Aston Martin, w/whizzwheels, 1/43 scale, from
    $125 to..$150.00
#271, Ghia Mangusta De Tomaso, from $65 to................$80.00
#271, James Bond's Aston Martin, from $100 to $125.00
#272, James Bond's Citroen 2CV, from $50 to $65.00
#273, Honda Driving School, from $50 to $65.00
#273, Rolls Royce Silver Shadow, from $100 to $125.00
#274, Bentley Mulliner, from $80 to $100.00
#275, Mini Metro, colors other than gold, from $25 to $40.00
#275, Mini Metro, gold, from $65 to $80.00

#246, Chrysler Imperial, metallic turquoise, from $240.00 to $265.00. (Photo courtesy June Moon)

#246, Chrysler Imperial, red, from $100 to $125.00
#247, Mercedes Benz 600 Pullman, from $75 to $90.00
#248, Chevrolet Impala, from $80 to $95.00
#249, Morris Mini-Cooper, wicker, from $120 to $135.00

#275, Rover 2000 TC, gr, from $75 to..............................$90.00

#275, Rover 2000 TC, wht, from $150 to.......................$200.00

#275, Royal Wedding Mini Metro, from $25 to..............$40.00

#276, Oldsmobile Toronado, metallic gold, from $150 to...$200.00

#276, Oldsmobile Toronado, metallic red, from $75 to....$90.00

#276, Triumph Acclaim, from $25 to...............................$40.00

#277, Monkeemobile, from $300 to $350.00

#277, Triumph Driving School, from $30 to.....................$45.00

#279, Rolls Royce Corniche, from $35 to $50.00

#280, Rolls Royce Silver Shadow, colors other than silver, from $50 to..$65.00

#280, Rolls Royce Silver Shadow, silver, from $80 to.....$100.00

#281, Austin Mini, from $25 to..$40.00

#281, Rover 2000 TC, from $90 to $110.00

#282, Mini Cooper Rally Car, from $100 to $125.00

#283, DAF City Car, from $30 to......................................$55.00

#284, Citroen SM, from $50 to...$65.00

#285, Mercedes Benz 240D, from $30 to..........................$45.00

#286, Jaguar XJ12C, from $45 to......................................$60.00

#287, Citroen Dyane, from $30 to....................................$45.00

#288, Minissima, from $25 to $40.00

#290, Kojak Buick, with hat, from $60.00 to $90.00. (Photo courtesy June Moon)

#292, Starsky and Hutch Ford Torino, from $85.00 to $100.00. (Photo courtesy June Moon)

#289, VW Polo, from $25 to...$40.00

#290, Kojak Buick, no hat, from $125 to $150.00

#291, AMC Pacer, from $30 to...$45.00

#291, Mercedes Benz 240 Rally, from $35 to....................$50.00

#293, Renault 5TS, from $20 to.......................................$35.00

#294, Renault Alpine, from $20 to...................................$35.00

#298, Magnum PI's Ferrari, from $50 to $65.00

#299, Ford Sierra 2.3 Ghia, from $25 to...........................$40.00

#300, Austin Healey, red or cream, from $150 to...........$175.00

#300, Austin Healey Sports Car, bl, from $300 to..........$350.00

#300, Chevrolet Corvette Stingray, from $100 to..........$125.00

#300, Ferrari Daytona, from $25 to..................................$40.00

#301, Iso Grifo 7 Litre, from $65 to................................$80.00

#301, Lotus Elite, from $25 to $40.00

#301, Triumph TR2 Sports Car, from $150 to $175.00

#302, Hillman Hunter Rally, kangaroo, from $125 to $150.00

#302, MGA Sports Car, from $140 to...............................$155.00

#302, VW Polo, from $20 to...$35.00

#303, Mercedes Benz 300SL, from $100 to $125.00

#303, Porsche 924, from $25 to $40.00

#303, Roger Clark's Ford Capri, gold wheels w/red hubs, from $225 to...$275.00

#303, Roger Clark's Ford Capri, w/whizwheels, from $75 to..$100.00

#303s, Mercedes Benz 300SL, w/suspension, from $100 to....$125.00

#304, Chevrolet SS350 Camaro, from $75 to $90.00

#304, Mercedes Benz 300SL, yel, from $425 to $450.00

#304, Mercedese Benz 300SL, colors other than yel, from $100 to...$125.00

#304s, Mercedes Benz 300SL, w/suspension, from $100 to...$125.00

#305, Mini Marcos GT 850, from $75 to $90.00

#305, Triumph TR3, from $150 to...................................$175.00

#306, Fiat X1/9, from $35 to..$50.00

#306, Morris Marina, from $55 to $70.00

#307, Jaguar E Type, from $125 to..................................$150.00

#307, Renault, from $25 to..$40.00

#308, BMW M1 Racer, gold plated, from $100 to.........$125.00

#308, BMW M1 Racer, yel, from $25 to $40.00

#308, Monte Carlo BMC Mini Cooper S, from $100 to...$125.00

#309, Aston Martin DB4, from $100 to..........................$125.00

#309, Aston Martin DB4, w/spoked hubs, from $150 to...$200.00

#309, VW Polo Turbo, from $25 to..................................$40.00

#310, Chevrolet Corvette, bronze, from $150 to............$175.00

#310, Chevrolet Corvette, red or silver, from $70 to........$95.00

#310, Porsche 924, from $25 to $40.00

#311, Ford Capri, orange, from $110 to $135.00

#311, Ford Capri, red, from $70 to...................................$90.00

#311, Ford Capri, w/gold hubs, from $200 to..................$250.00

#312, Ford Capri S, from $35 to.......................................$50.00

#312, Jaguar E Type, from $100 to..................................$125.00

#312, Marcos Mantis, from $40 to....................................$60.00

#313, Ford Cortina, bronze or bl, from $90 to $120.00

#313, Ford Cortina, yel, from $275 to.............................$325.00

#314, Ferrari Berlinetta Le Mans, from $55 to................$70.00

#314, Supercat Jaguar, from $20 to.................................$35.00

#315, Lotus Elite, from $25 to $40.00

#315, Simca Sports Car, metallic bl, from $175 to.........$200.00

#315, Simca Sports Car, silver, from $55 to $70.00

#316, Ford GT 70, from $40 to..................................$55.00
#316, NSU Sports Prinz, from $75 to.......................$95.00
#317, Mini Cooper Monte Carlo, from $175 to.............$225.00
#318, Jaguar XJS, from $20 to.................................$35.00
#318, Lotus Elan, copper, from $275 to....................$325.00
#318, Lotus Elan, metallic bl, from $100 to.................$125.00
#318, Lotus Elan, wht, from $125 to........................$175.00
#319, Jaguar XJS, from $25 to.................................$40.00
#319, Lamborghini P400 GT Miura, from $30 to............$50.00
#319, Lotus Elan, gr or yel, from $125 to..................$150.00
#319, Lotus Elan, red or bl, from $75 to...................$100.00
#319 Lotus Elan, red, from $75 to...........................$100.00
#320, Saint's Jaguar XJS, from $80 to.......................$100.00
#321, Monte Carlo Mini Cooper, 1965, from $275 to....$325.00
#321, Monte Carlo Mini Cooper, 1966, w/autographs, from $575
     to..$625.00
#321, Porsche 924, metallic gr, from $60 to....................$75.00
#321, Porsche 924, red, from $40 to..........................$55.00
#322, Rover Monte Carlo, from $150 to.......................$190.00
#323, Citroen DS19 Monte Carlo, from $140 to...........$170.00
#323, Ferrari Daytona 365 GTB4, from $30 to..............$45.00
#324, Marcos Volvo 1800 GT, from $70 to...................$95.00
#325, Chevrolet Caprice, from $70 to........................$95.00
#325, Ford Mustang Competition, from $75 to.............$100.00
#326, Chevrolet Police Car, from $45 to.....................$65.00
#327, Chevrolet Caprice Cab, from $45 to..................$65.00
#327, MGB GT, from $125 to....................................$150.00
#328, Hillman Imp Monte Carlo, from $125 to.............$150.00
#329, Ford Mustang Rally, from $50 to........................$70.00
#329, Opel Senator, bl or bronze, from $45 to.............$60.00
#329, Opel Senator, silver, from $50 to......................$65.00
#330, Porsche Carrera 6, wht & bl, from $120 to..........$145.00
#330, Porsche Carrera 6, wht & red, from $65 to...........$80.00
#331, Ford Capri Rally, from $80 to...........................$100.00
#332, Lancia Fulvia Sport, red or bl, from $65 to...........$80.00
#332, Lancia Fulvia Sport, yel & blk, from $125 to........$150.00
#332, Opel, Doctor's Car, from $45 to........................$60.00
#334, Ford Escort, from $30 to.................................$45.00
#334, Mini Magnifique, from $70 to...........................$95.00
#335, Jaguar 4.2 Litre E Type, from $140 to................$160.00

#336, James Bond Toyota 2000GT, from $375.00 to $400.00. (Photo courtesy June Moon)

#337, Chevrolet Sting Ray, from $60 to........................$80.00
#338, Rover 3500, from $30 to..................................$45.00
#339, Rover 3500 Police Car, from $30 to....................$45.00
#339, 1967 Mini Cooper Monte Carlo, w/roof rack, from $275 to..$325.00

#338, Chevrolet SS350 Camaro, from $75.00 to $95.00. (Photo courtesy June Moon)

#340, Rover Triplex, from $25 to $40.00
#340, 1967 Sunbeam IMP Monte Carlo, from $125 to ..$150.00
#341, Chevrolet Caprice Racer, from $25 to.................$40.00
#341, Mini Marcos GT850, from $60 to $80.00
#342, Lamborghini P400 GT Miura, from $70 to $90.00
#342, Professionals Ford Capri, from $75 to.................$95.00
#342, Professionals Ford Capri, w/chrome bumpers, from $100
     to $125.00
#343, Pontiac Firebird, red hubs, from $100 to..............$125.00

#343, Pontiac Firebird, with whizwheels, from $60.00 to $75.00. (Photo courtesy June Moon)

#344, Ferrari 206 Dino Sport, from $75 to $90.00
#345, Honda Prelude, from $25 to $40.00
#345, MGC GT, orange, from $275 to.........................$325.00
#345, MGC GT, yel, from $125 to $150.00
#346, Citroen 2 CV, from $25 to $35.00
#347, Chevrolet Astro 1, red hubs, from $100 to $125.00
#347, Chevrolet Astro 1, w/whizwheels, from $40 to $60.00
#348, Flower Power Mustang Stock Car, from $125 to...$150.00
#348, Pop Art Mustang Stock Car, from $125 to $150.00
#348, Vegas Ford Thunderbird, from $85 to $105.00
#349, Pop Art Morris Mini, from $1,750 to................$2,250.00
#350, Thunderbird Guided Missile, from $100 to...........$125.00
#351, RAF Land Rover, from $95 to $120.00

#352, RAF Vanguard Staff Car, from $95.00 to $120.00. (Photo courtesy June Moon)

#391, James Bond 007 Ford Mustang, from $250.00 to $275.00. (Photo courtesy June Moon)

#353, Radar Scanner, from $65 to $80.00
#354, Commer Military Ambulance, from $100 to $125.00
#355, Commer Military Police, from $110 to $135.00
#356, VW Personnel Carrier, from $125 to $150.00
#357, Land Rover Weapons Carrier, from $145 to $195.00
#358, Oldsmobile Staff Car, from $125 to....................$150.00
#359, Commer Army Field Kitchen, from $150 to.........$175.00
#370, Ford Cobra Mustang, from $25 to $40.00
#371, Porsche Carrera, from $40 to $55.00
#373, Peugeot 505, from $25 to $40.00
#373, VW Police Car, Polizei, from $150 to $175.00
#374, Jaguar 4.2 Litre E Type, from $100 to..................$125.00
#374, Jaguar 5.3 Litre, from $80 to $95.00
#375, Toyota 2000 GT, from $100 to $125.00
#376, Chevrolet Stingray Stock Car, from $50 to..........$65.00
#377, Marcos 3 Litre, wht & gray, from $100 to $125.00
#377, Marcos 3 Litre, yel or bl, from $70 to $95.00
#378, Ferrari 308 GT, from $25 to $40.00
#378, MGC GT, from $150 to..$175.00
#380, Alfa Romeo P33, from $50 to $65.00
#380, Beach Buggy, from $45 to $60.00
#381, Renault Turbo, from $25 to $40.00
#382, Lotus Elite, from $30 to $45.00
#382, Porsche Targa 911S, from $60 to $75.00
#383, VW 1200, red or orange, from $65 to....................$80.00
#383, VW 1200, Swiss PTT, from $125 to......................$150.00
#383, VW 1200, yel ADAC, from $175 to $225.00
#384, Adams Bros Probe 15, from $60 to........................$75.00
#384, Renault 11 GTL, cream, from $25 to $40.00
#384, Renault 11 GTL, maroon, from $40 to $55.00
#384, VW 1200 Rally, from $70 to................................$85.00
#385, Porsche 917, from $35 to $50.00
#386, Bertone Runabout, from $60 to............................$75.00
#387, Chevrolet Corvette Sting Ray, from $90 to $115.00
#388, Mercedes Benz C111, from $50 to........................$65.00
#389, Reliant Bond Bug 700, gr, from $120 to................$140.00
#389, Reliant Bond Bug 700 ES, orange, from $65 to......$80.00
#392, Bertone Shake Buggy, from $45 to $60.00
#393, Mercedes Benz 350 SL, bl, from $50 to $65.00
#393, Mercedes Benz 350 SL, metallic gr, from $100 to ..$125.00
#393, Mercedes Benz 350 SL, wht, from $80 to $95.00

#394, Datsun 240Z, East African Safari, from $55 to........$70.00
#396, Datsun 240Z, US Rally, from $60 to......................$75.00
#397, Can Am Porsche Audi, from $30 to......................$45.00
#400, VW Driving School, bl, from $60 to......................$75.00
#400, VW Driving School, red, from $150 to..................$175.00
#401, VW 1200, from $60 to..$75.00
#402, Ford Cortina GXL, wht w/red stripe, from $70 to...$85.00
#402, Ford Cortina GXL Police, wht, from $60 to............$75.00
#402, Ford Cortina GXL Polizei, from $150 to................$175.00
#403, Bedford Daily Express, from $150 to $175.00
#403, Thwaites Dumper, from $50 to $65.00
#403m, Bedford KLG Plugs, w/motor, from $250 to $275.00
#404, Bedford Dormobile, cream, maroon & turq, from $100
    to $125.00
#404, Bedford Dormobile, yel & 2-tone bl, from $215 to ..$240.00
#404, Bedford Dormobile, yel w/bl roof, from $125 to....$150.00
#404m, Bedford Dormobile, w/motor, from $160 to $185.00
#405, Bedford Utilicon Fire Department, gr, from $160 to $185.00
#405, Bedford Utilicon Fire Department, red, from $200 to...$250.00
#405, Chevrolet Superior Ambulance, from $35 to..........$50.00
#405, Ford Milk Float, from $30 to $45.00
#405m, Bedford Utilicon Fire Tender, w/motor, from $235 to ..$265.00
#406, Land Rover Pickup, from $75 to............................$95.00
#406, Mercedes Ambulance, from $30 to........................$45.00
#406, Mercedes Benz Unimog, from $60 to $75.00
#407, Karrier Mobile Grocers, from $150 to $175.00
#408, Bedford AA Road Service, from $140 to $165.00
#409, Allis Chalmers Fork Lift, from $35 to $50.00
#409, Forward Control Jeep FC-150, from $45 to............$60.00
#409, Mercedes Dumper, from $55 to..............................$70.00
#411, Karrier Lucozade Van, from $150 to......................$175.00
#411, Mercedes 240D, orange, from $75 to......................$95.00
#411, Mercedes 240D Taxi, cream or blk, from $60 to $75.00
#411, Mercedes 240D Taxi, orange w/blk roof, from $45 to $60.00
#412, Bedford Ambulance, split windscreen, from $125 to...$150.00
#412, Bedford Ambulance, 1-pc windscreen, from $225 to..$275.00
#412, Mercedes Police Car, Police, from $50 to............$65.00
#412, Mercedes Police Car, Polizei, from $40 to $55.00
#413, Karrier Bantam Butcher Shop, from $130 to $165.00

#413, Mazda Maintenence Truck, from $50 to $65.00

#413s, Karrier Bantam Butcher Shop, w/suspension, from $210 to...$240.00

#414, Bedford Military Ambulance, from $100 to..........$125.00

#414, Coastguard Jaguar, from $45 to.......................$60.00

#415, Mazda Camper, from $45 to.............................$60.00

#416, Buick Police Car, from $45 to.........................$60.00

#416, Radio Rescue Rover, bl, from $110 to.................$140.00

#416, Radio Rescue Rover, yel, from $380 to $415.00

#416s, Radio Rescue Rover, w/suspension, bl, from $110 to $140.00

#416s, Radio Rescue Rover, w/suspension, yel, from $400 to...$450.00

#417 Land Rover Breakdown, from $110 to $140.00

#417s, Land Rover Breakdown, w/suspension, from $75 to..$100.00

#418, Austin Taxi, w/whizzwheels, from $45 to $60.00

#419, Ford Zephyr, Rijks Politei, from $350 to............$375.00

#419, Ford Zephyr Politei, from $300 to $325.00

#419, Jeep, from $40 to..$50.00

#420, Airbourne Caravan, from $80 to.......................$110.00

#421, Bedford Evening Standard, from $210 to.............$240.00

#422, Bedford Van, Corgi Toys, bl w/yel roof, from $525 to...$575.00

#422, Bedford Van, Corgi Toys, yel w/bl roof, from $200 to ..$250.00

#422, Riot Police Wagon, from $45 to $60.00

#423, Rough Rider Van, from $45 to..........................$60.00

#424, Ford Zephyr Estate Car, from $80 to.................$95.00

#424, Security Van, from $35 to...............................$50.00

#425, London Taxi, from $30 to...............................$45.00

#426, Chipperfield's Circus Booking Office, from $300 to..$350.00

#426, Pinder's Circus Booking Office, from $50 to $75.00

#428, Mister Softee's Ice Cream Van, from $225 to........$250.00

#428, Renault Police Car, from $25 to $40.00

#429, Jaguar Police Car, from $40 to........................$55.00

#430, Bermuda Taxi, metallic bl & red, from $375 to $425.00

#430, Bermuda Taxi, white, from $125.00 to $150.00. (Photo courtesy June Moon)

#430, Porsche 924 Polizei, from $30 to $45.00

#431, VW Pickup, metallic gold, from $300 to..............$350.00

#431, VW Pickup, yel, from $100 to...........................$125.00

#432, Vantastic Van, from $30 to..............................$45.00

#433, VW Delivery Van, from $100 to $125.00

#434, Charlie's Angels Van, from $60 to......................$75.00

#434, VW Kombi, from $100 to.................................$125.00

#435, Karrier Dairy Van, from $140 to.......................$165.00

#435, Superman Van, from $50 to...............................$75.00

#436, Citroen Safari, from $95 to.............................$120.00

#436, Spider Van, from $50 to..................................$70.00

#437, Cadillac Ambulance, from $95 to.......................$120.00

#437, Coca-Cola Van, from $55 to.............................$70.00

#438, Land Rover, gr, from $55 to $70.00

#438, Land Rover, Lepra, from $375 to.......................$425.00

#439, Chevrolet Fire Chief, from $100 to.....................$125.00

#440, Ford Consul Cortina Super Estate Car, w/golfer & caddy, from $150 to...$175.00

#440, Mazda Pickup, from $30 to..............................$45.00

#441, Jeep, from $25 to..$40.00

#441, VW Toblerone Van, from $125 to.......................$150.00

#443, Plymouth US Mail, from $125 to.......................$150.00

#445, Plymouth Sports Suburban, from $90 to..............$115.00

#447, Walls Ice Cream Van, from $300 to....................$350.00

#448, Police Mini Van, w/dog & handler, from $215 to ...$260.00

#448, Renegade Jeep, from $25 to.............................$40.00

#450, Austin Mini Van, from $85 to...........................$110.00

#450, Austin Mini Van, w/pnt grille, from $150 to $175.00

#450, Peugeot Taxi, from $25 to...............................$40.00

#452, Commer Lorry, from $125 to.............................$150.00

#453, Commer Walls Van, from $175 to.......................$225.00

#454, Commer Platform Lorry, from $125 to................$150.00

#455, Karrier Bantam 2-Ton, bl, from $115 to..............$140.00

#455, Karrier Bantam 2-Ton, red, from $300 to............$350.00

#456, ERF Dropside Lorry, from $115 to......................$140.00

#457, ERF Platform Lorry, from $100 to $125.00

#457, Talbot Matra Rancho, gr or red, from $30 to $45.00

#457, Talbot Matra Rancho, wht or orange, from $45 to...$60.00

#458, ERF Tipper Dumper, from $80 to $100.00

#459, ERF Moorhouse Van, from $350 to.....................$400.00

#459, Raygo Road Roller, from $40 to.........................$55.00

#460, ERF Cement Tipper, from $40 to $55.00

#461, Police Vigilant Range Rover, Police, from $40 to...$55.00

#461, Police Viligant Range Rover, Politei, from $75 to ..$90.00

#462, Commer Van, Co-op, from $150 to......................$175.00

#462, Commer Van, Hammonds, from $175 to $200.00

#463, Commer Ambulance, from $100 to $125.00

#464, Commer Police Van, City Police, minimum value, from $350 to...$400.00

#464, Commer Police Van, County Police, bl, from $115 to.$140.00

#464, Commer Police Van, Police, bl, from $115 to.......$140.00

#464, Commer Police Van, Police, gr, from $750 to.......$800.00

#464, Commer Police Van, Rijks Politei, bl, minimum value, from $350 to $400.00

#465, Commer Pickup Truck, from $65 to $80.00

#466, Commer Milk Float, Co-op, from $170 to............$200.00

#466, Commer Milk Float, wht, from $70 to...................$85.00

#467, London Routemaster Bus, from $80 to..................$95.00

#468, London Transport Routemaster, Church's Shoes, red, from $200 to...$225.00

#468, London Transport Routemaster, Design Centre, red, from $250 to...$275.00

#468, London Transport Routemaster, Gamages, red, from $200 to...$225.00

#468, London Transport Routemaster Bus, Corgi Toys, brn, gr or cream, from $1,000 to...................................$1,250.00

#468, London Transport Routemaster Bus, Corgi Toys, red, from $90 to..$120.00

#468, London Transport Routemaster Bus, Madame Tussand's, red, from $200 to..$250.00

#468, London Transport Routemaster Bus, Outspan, red, from $60 to..$75.00

#470, Disneyland Bus, from $45 to................................$65.00

#470, Forward Control Jeep FC-150 Covered Truck, from $60 to.$75.00

#470, Greenline Bus, from $25 to................................$40.00

#471, Silver Jubilee Bus, from $45 to..........................$60.00

#471, Smith's-Karrier Mobile Canteen, Joe's Diner, from $150.00 to $175.00. (Photo courtesy June Moon)

#471, Smith's-Karrier Mobile Canteen, Potato Frittes, from $300 to..$350.00

#471, Woolworth Silver Jubilee Bus, from $50 to.........$65.00

#472, Public Address Land Rover, from $150 to.........$175.00

#475, Citroen Ski Safari, from $150 to.......................$175.00

#477, Land Rover Breakdown, w/whizzwheels, from $60 to..$75.00

#478, Forward Control Jeep, Tower Wagon, from $100 to..$125.00

#479, Mobile Camera Van, from $150 to....................$175.00

#480, Chevrolet Impala Cab, from $85 to $100.00

#481, Chevrolet Police Patrol Car, from $110.00 to $140.00. (Photo courtesy June Moon)

#482, Chevrolet Fire Chief Car, from $95 to $120.00

#482, Range Rover Ambulance, from $55 to..................$70.00

#483, Dodge Tipper, from $60 to...................................$75.00

#483, Police Range Rover, Belgian, from $80 to...........$100.00

#484, AMC Pacer Rescue, from $40 to..........................$55.00

#484, AMC Pacer Secours, from $60 to..........................$75.00

#484, Livestock Transporter, from $70 to.....................$85.00

#484, Mini Countryman Surfer, w/silver grille, from $165 to....$190.00

#485, Mini Countryman Surfer, w/unpnt grille, from $250 to...$275.00

#486, Chevrolet Kennel Service, from $125 to $150.00

#487, Chipperfield's Circus Parade, from $200 to..........$250.00

#489, VW Police Car, from $45 to.................................$60.00

#490, Touring Caravan, from $30 to $45.00

#490, VW Breakdown Truck, from $100 to $125.00

#491, Ford Consul Cortina Estate, from $120 to $145.00

#492, VW Police Car, Politie, from $250 to $300.00

#492, VW Police Car, Polizei, from $85 to $100.00

#492, VW Police Car, w/gr mudguards, from $275 to.....$325.00

#493, Mazda Pickup, from $45 to $60.00

#494, Bedford Tipper, red & silver, from $175 to...........$200.00

#494, Bedford Tipper Truck, red and yellow, from $85.00 to $100.00. (Photo courtesy June Moon)

#495, Mazda Open Truck, from $30 to.............................$45.00

#497, Man From UNCLE, wht, minimum value, from $650 to..$700.00

#497, Man From UNCLE Gun Firing Thrush-Buster, from $275 to..$325.00

#499, Citroen, 1968 Olympics, from $200 to.................$250.00

#500, US Army Rover, from $450 to $500.00

#503, Chipperfield's Circus Giraffe Transporter, from $150 to..$175.00

#506, Sunbeam Imp Police, from $125 to.......................$150.00

#508, Holiday Minibus, from $115 to $140.00

#509, Porsche Police Car, Polizei, from $85 to $100.00

#509, Porsche Police Car, Ritjks Politie, from $150 to...$175.00

#510, Citroen Tour De France, from $125 to...................$150.00

#511, Chipperfield's Circus Poodle Pickup, from $600 to ..$675.00

#513, Alpine Rescue Car, from $350 to $400.00

#647, Buck Rogers' Starfighter, from $80 to...................$95.00

#648, Space Shuttle, from $45 to $60.00

#649, James Bond's Space Shuttle, from $85 to $100.00

#650, BOAC Concorde, all others (no gold logo on tail), from $60 to..$75.00

#650, BOAC Concorde, gold logo on tail, from $95 to..$110.00

#651, Air France Concorde, all others (no gold tail design), from $60 to..$75.00

#651, Air France Concorde, gold tail design, from $125 to..$150.00

#651, Japan Air Line Concorde, from $450 to................$500.00

#653, Air Canada Concorde, from $350 to.....................$400.00

#681, Stunt Bike, from $250 to.....................................$275.00

#700, Motorway Ambulance, from $35 to $45.00
#701, Intercity Minibus, from $35 to $45.00
#703, Breakdown Truck, from $35 to $45.00
#703, Hi Speed Fire Engine, from $35 to $45.00
#801, Ford Thunderbird, from $40 to.........................$55.00

#801, Noddy's Car, other than black-face Noddy, $350.00 to $400.00; black-face Noddy, from $650.00 to $700.00. (Photo courtesy June Moon)

#802, Mercedes Benz 300 Sl, from $35 to $45.00
#802, Popeye's Paddle Wagon, from $600 to.................$650.00
#803, Beatle's Yellow Submarine, from $700 to $750.00
#804, Jaguar XK120 Rally, from $35 to $45.00
#804, Jaguar XK120 Rally, w/spats, from $65 to..............$75.00
#804, Noddy's Car, Noddy only, from $250 to $300.00
#804, Noddy's Car, w/Mr Tubby, from $325 to $375.00
#805, Hardy Boy's Rolls Royce, from $300 to $350.00
#805, Mercedes Benz 300 SC, from $35 to....................$45.00
#806, Lunar Bug, from $150 to.................................$200.00
#806, Mercedes Benz 300 SC, from $35 to....................$45.00
#807, Dougal's Car, from $300 to $350.00
#808, Basil Brush's Car, from $250 to.........................$300.00
#809, Dick Dastardly's Racer, from $175 to $200.00
#810, Ford Thunderbird, from $35 to.........................$45.00
#811, James Bond's Moon Buggy, from $550 to $600.00
#831, Mercedes Benz 300 SL, from $35 to.....................$45.00
#851, Magic Roundabout Train, from $400 to...............$450.00
#852, Magic Roundabout Carousel, from $750 to $950.00
#853, Magic Roundabout Playground, from $1,500 to ..$1,750.00
#859, Mr McHenry's Trike, from $300 to....................$350.00
#900, German Tank Tiger Mk I, from $55 to $70.00
#901, British Centurion Mk III, from $55 to $70.00
#902, American Tank M60 A1, from $60 to....................$75.00
#903, British Chieftain Tank, from $60 to $75.00
#904, King Tiger Tank, from $60 to $75.00
#905, SU100 Tank Destroyer, from $60 to....................$75.00
#906, Saladin Armoured Car, from $60 to $75.00
#907, German Rocket Launcher, from $80 to..................$95.00

#908, French Recovery Tank, from $70 to $85.00
#909, Quad Gun Tank, Trailer & Field Gun, from $55 to ..$70.00
#920, Bell Helicopter, from $35 to.............................$45.00
#921, Hughes Helicopter, from $35 to $45.00
#922, Sikorsky Helicopter, from $35 to $45.00
#923, Sikorsky Helicopter Military, from $35 to..............$45.00
#925, Batcopter, from $80 to..................................$95.00
#926, Stromberg Helicopter, from $85 to....................$100.00
#927, Chopper Squad Helicopter, from $55 to $70.00
#928, Spidercopter, from $85 to..............................$100.00
#929, Daily Planet Helicopter, from $80 to...................$95.00
#930, DRAX Helicopter, from $80 to $95.00
#931, Jet Police Helicopter, from $55 to $65.00

CLASSICS

Mack Truck, from $30.00 to $40.00. (Photo courtesy June Moon)

Daimler 38HP, #9021, red w/4 figures, MIB, from $80 to...$95.00
St Mary's County Mack CF Pumper, #52004, MIB, from $30 to $40.00
1915 Ford Model T, #901, MIB, from $80 to $95.00

CORGITRONICS

#1001, Corgitronics Firestreak, from $85 to.................$100.00
#1002, Corgitronics Roadtrain, from $65 to $75.00
#1003, Ford Torino, from $50 to..............................$60.00
#1004, Corgitronics Beep Beep Bus, from $50 to.............$60.00
#1005, Police Land Rover, from $50 to........................$60.00
#1006, Roadshow, Radio, from $60 to.........................$70.00
#1007, Land Rover & Compressor, from $60 to...............$70.00
#1008, Chevrolet Fire Chief, from $50 to $60.00
#1009, Maestro MG1600, from $50 to $60.00
#1011, Firestreak, from $40 to $50.00

EXPLORATION MODELS

#2022, Scanotron, from $50 to................................$70.00
#2023, Rocketron, from $60 to................................$70.00
#2024, Lasertron, from $60 to $70.00
#2025, Magnetron, from $60 to...............................$70.00

GIFT SETS

#1, Car Transporter Set, from $800 to $1,000.00
#1, Ford Sierra & Caravan, from $40 to...........................$50.00
#1, Ford 500 Tractor & Beast Trailer, from $150 to $175.00

#2, Land Rover and Pony Trailer, from $175.00 to $200.00. (Photo courtesy June Moon)

#2, Unimog Dumper, from $150 to $175.00
#3, Batmobile & Batboat, w/'Bat'-hubs, from $425 to....$475.00
#3, Batmobile & Batboat, w/whizzwheels, from $225 to....$275.00
#3, RAF Land Rover & Missile, from $225 to $275.00
#4, Country Farm Set, from $75 to...............................$90.00
#4, RAF Land Rover & Missile, from $475 to $550.00
#5, Agricultural Set, from $275 to $325.00
#5, Country Farm Set, w/no hay, from $80 to................$100.00
#5, Racing Car Set, from $275 to $325.00
#6, Rocket Age Set, from $900 to..............................$1,250.00
#6, VW Transporter & Cooper Maserati, from $175 to....$200.00
#7, Daktari Set, from $150 to $175.00
#7, Tractor & Trailer Set, from $125 to $150.00
#8, Combine Harvester Set, from $375 to $425.00
#8, Lions of Longleat, from $175 to $225.00
#9, Corporal Missile & Launcher, from $575 to $625.00
#9, Tractor w/Shovel & Trailer, from $175 to................$225.00
#10, Centurion Tank & Transporter, from $125 to.........$150.00
#10, Jeep & Motorcycle Trailer, from $30 to...................$50.00
#10, Rambler Marlin, w/kayaks, from $200 to $225.00
#11, ERF Truck & Trailer, from $200 to.......................$225.00
#11, London Set, no Policeman, from $125 to $150.00
#11, London Set, w/Policeman, from $575 to.................$650.00
#12, Chipperfield's Circus Crane Truck & Cage, from $325 to.$350.00
#12, Glider Set, from $80 to $95.00
#12, Grand Prix Set, from $425 to $500.00
#13, Fordson Tractor & Plough, from $150 to $175.00
#13, Peugeot Tour De France, from $80 to....................$100.00
#13, Renault Tour De France, from $150 to..................$175.00
#14, Giant Daktari Set, from $475 to $525.00
#14, Tower Wagon, from $100 to $125.00
#15, Land Rover & Horsebox, from $95 to....................$120.00
#15, Silvertone Set, from $1,750 to $2,000.00
#16, Ecurie Ecosse Set, from $525 to............................$600.00

#17, Land Rover & Ferrari, from $175 to......................$225.00
#17, Military Set, from $80 to $95.00
#18, Emergency Set, from $80 to...................................$95.00
#18, Fordson Tractor & Plough, from $125 to $140.00
#19, Chipperfield's Circus Rover & Elephant Trailer, from $325
    to..$375.00
#19, Emergency Set, from $80 to...................................$95.00
#19, Flying Club Set, from $80 to $95.00
#20, Car Transporter Set, minimum value, from $1,000 to...$1,250.00
#20, Emergency Set, from $65 to...................................$80.00
#20, Golden Guinea Set, from $275 to $325.00
#21, Chipperfield's Circus Crane & Trailer, minimum value,
    from $1,700 to...$2,000.00
#21, ERF Milk Truck & Trailer, from $350 to.................$375.00
#21, Superman Set, from $250 to.................................$300.00
#22, James Bond Set, from $250 to $300.00
#23, Chipperfield's Circus Set, w/Booking Office, from $900 to..$1,250.00

#23, Spider-Man Set, from $225.00 to $250.00. (Photo courtesy June Moon)

#24, Constructor Set, from $150 to..............................$175.00
#24, Constructor Set, from $150 to..............................$175.00
#24, Mercedes & Caravan, from $60 to $75.00
#25, Mantra Rancho & Trailer, from $60 to $75.00
#25, Shell or BP Garage Set, minimum value, from $1,750
    to..$2,000.00
#25, VW Transporter & Cooper Masarati, from $150 to..$175.00
#26, Beach Bug Set, from $45 to $60.00
#26, Matra Rancho & Racer, from $70 to $85.00
#27, Priestman Shovel Set, from $200 to.......................$225.00
#28, Mazda Pickup & Dinghy, w/trailer, from $60 to........$75.00
#28, Transporter Set, from $750 to..............................$900.00
#29, Ferrari Racing Set, from $75 to $90.00
#29, Jeep & Horsebox, from $40 to $50.00
#29, Tractor & Trailer, from $125 to $150.00
#30, Grand Prix Set, from $250 to $300.00
#30, Pinder's Circus Rover & Trailer, from $125 to........$150.00
#3008, Crime Busters Gift Set, scarce, A, from $800 to..$850.00
#31, Buick Riviera & Boat, from $250 to.......................$300.00
#31, Safari Set, from $100 to $125.00
#32, Lotus Racing Set, from $100 to $125.00
#32, Tractor & Trailer, from $175 to...........................$200.00

#33, Fordson Tractor & Carrier, from $150 to $175.00
#35, Chopper Squad, from $60 to....................................$75.00
#35, London Set, from $175 to.......................................$200.00
#36, Tarzan Set, from $250 to..$275.00

#36, Toronado Set w/Swordfish Speedboat, from $250.00 to $275.00. (Photo courtesy June Moon)

#37, Fiat & Boat, from $60 to...$75.00
#37, Lotus Racing Team, from $500 to $550.00
#38, Jaguar & Powerboat, from $70 to $85.00
#38, Mini Camping Set, from $90 to $115.00
#38, Monte Carlo Set, from $575 to $650.00
#40, Avengers, red & wht vehicles, from $625 to..........$700.00
#40, Batman Set, from $250 to......................................$300.00
#41, Ford Transporter Set, from $825 to $900.00
#41, Silver Jubilee State Landau, from $45 to................$60.00
#42, Agricultural Set, from $75 to $90.00
#43, Silo & Conveyor, from $60 to $75.00
#44, Police Rover Set, from $60 to................................$75.00
#45, Royal Canadian Mounted Police, from $80 to..........$95.00
#46, All Winners Set, from $575 to $650.00
#46, Super Karts, from $25 to.......................................$40.00
#47, Ford 5000 Tractor & Conveyor, from $175 to $200.00
#47, Pony Club Set, from $45 to $60.00
#48, Ford Transporter Set, from $575 to $625.00
#48, Jean Richards' Circus Set, from $200 to.................$225.00
#48, Scammell Transport Set, from $925 to $1,000.00
#49, Flying Club Set, from $45 to $60.00

HUSKIES

Huskies were marketed exclusively through the Woolworth stores from 1965 to 1969. In 1970, Corgi Juniors were introduced. Both lines were sold in blister packs. Models produced up to 1975 (as dated on the package) are valued from $15.00 to $30.00 (MIP), except for the character-relat ed examples listed below.

#1001A, James Bond's Aston Martin, Husky on base, from $200 to..$250.00
#1001B, James Bond Aston Martin, Junior on base, from $150 to $200.00
#1002A, Batmobile, Husky on base, from $200 to $225.00
#1003A, Bat Boat, Husky on base, from $125 to $150.00
#1003B, Bat Boat, Junior on base, from $80 to $95.00
#1004A, Monkeemobile, Husky on base, from $200 to..$225.00
#1004B, Monkeemobile, Junior on base, from $175 to...$200.00
#1005A, UNCLE Car, Husky on base, from $175 to......$200.00
#1005B, UNCLE Car, Junior on base, from $1,500 to...$1,750.00

#1006A, Chitty-Chitty Bang-Bang, Husky on base, from $200 to $225.00
#1006B, Chitty-Chitty Bang-Bang, Junior on base, from $175 to $200.00
#1007, Ironside Police Van, from $125 to......................$150.00
#1008, Popeye Paddle Wagon, from $200 to..................$225.00
#1011, James Bond Bobsleigh, from $300 to..................$325.00
#1012, Spectre Bobsleigh, from $300 to........................$325.00
#1013, Tom's Go-Kart, from $70 to...............................$85.00
#1014, Jerry's Banger, from $70 to $85.00
#3008, Crime Busters Gift Set, scarce, from $825 to......$900.00

MAJOR PACKS

#1100, Carrimore Low Loader, red cab, from $150 to $175.00
#1100, Carrimore Low Loader, yel cab, from $250 to.....$275.00
#1100, Mack Truck, from $100 to $125.00
#1101, Carrimore Car Transporter, bl cab, from $250 to ..$300.00
#1101, Carrimore Car Transporter, red cab, from $150 to...$175.00
#1101, Hydrolic Crane, from $60 to...............................$75.00
#1102, Crane Fruehauf Dumper, from $70 to $85.00
#1102, Euclid Tractor, gr, from $150 to.........................$175.00
#1102, Euclid Tractor, yel, from $250 to........................$275.00
#1103, Airport Crash Truck, from $100 to $125.00
#1103, Euclid Crawler Tractor, from $150 to..................$175.00
#1104, Machinery Carrier, from $150 to.........................$175.00
#1104, Racehorse Transporter, from $125 to $150.00
#1105, Berliet Racehorse Transporter, from $70 to..........$85.00
#1106, Decca Mobile Radar Van, from $150 to..............$200.00
#1107, Berliet Container Truck, from $70 to $85.00
#1107, Euclid Tractor & Dozer, red, from $375 to.........$425.00
#1107, Euclid Trctor & Dozer, orange, from $300 to......$350.00
#1108, Bristol Bloodhound & Launching Ramp, from $125 to...$150.00
#1108, Michelin Container Truck, from $45 to................$60.00
#1109, Bristol Bloodhound & Loading Trolley, from $125 to..$150.00
#1109, Michelin Truck, from $60 to...............................$75.00
#1110, JCB Crawler Loader, from $60 to $75.00
#1110, Mobilgas Tanker, from $275 to...........................$325.00
#1111, Massey-Ferguson Harvester, from $200 to...........$250.00
#1112, Corporal Missile on Launching Ramp, from $150 to..$200.00
#1112, David Brown Combine, from $100 to $125.00
#1113, Corporal Erector & Missile, from $400 to...........$450.00
#1113, Hyster, from $60 to $75.00
#1113, Hyster Sealink, from $150 to..............................$175.00
#1115, Bloodhound Missile, from $100 to $125.00
#1116, Bloodhound Missile Platform, from $100 to $125.00
#1116, Refuse Lorry, from $35 to $50.00
#1117, Bloodhound Missile Trolley, from $70 to $85.00
#1117, Faun Street Sweeper, from $35 to........................$50.00
#1118, Airport Emergency Tender, from $80 to................$95.00
#1118, International Truck, Dutch Army, from $300 to...$350.00
#1118, International Truck, gr, from $150 to...................$175.00
#1118, International Truck, US Army, from $300 to.........$350.00
#1119, HDL Hovercraft, from $100 to...........................$125.00
#1120, Midland Coach, from $200 to $250.00
#1121, Corgimatic Ford Tipper, from $60 to...................$75.00

#1121, Chipperfield's Circus Crane, from $225.00 to $275.00.

#1123, Chipperfield's Circus Animal Cage, from $150 to...$175.00
#1124, Corporal Missile Launching Ramp, from $80 to ...$95.00
#1126, Ecurie Ecosse Transporter, from $200 to $250.00
#1126, Simon Snorkel Dennis Fire Engine, from $65 to ..$80.00
#1127, Simon Snorkel Bedford Fire Engine, from $125 to..$150.00

#1128, Priestman Cub Shovel, from $125.00 to $150.00. (Photo courtesy June Moon)

#1129, Mercedes Truck, from $35 to $50.00
#1129, Milk Tanker, from $300 to.................................$350.00
#1130, Chipperfield's Circus Horse Transporter, from $275 to...$325.00
#1130, Mercedes Tanker, Corgi, from $35 to $45.00
#1131, Carrimore Machinery Carrier, from $150 to $175.00
#1131, Mercedes Refrigerated Van, from $35 to $45.00
#1132, Carrimore Low Loader, from $250 to $300.00
#1132, Scania Truck, from $30 to.................................$40.00
#1133, Troop Transporter, from $250 to.........................$300.00

#1134, Army Fuel Tanker, from $450.00 to $500.00.

#1135, Heavy Equipment Transporter, from $450 to......$500.00
#1137, Ford Tilt Cab w/Trailer, from $150 to $200.00
#1138, Carrimore Car Transporter, Corgi, from $150 to...$200.00
#1140, Bedford Mobilgas Tanker, from $300 to $350.00
#1140, Ford Transit Wrecker, from $35 to........................$45.00
#1141, Milk Tanker, from $400 to....................................$450.00
#1142, Holmes Wrecker, from $135 to............................$180.00
#1143, American LaFrance Rescue Truck, from $130 to..$155.00
#1144, Berliet Wrecker, from $75 to $90.00
#1144, Chipperfield's Circus Crane Truck, from $750 to..$800.00
#1145, Mercedes Unimog Dumper, from $60 to $75.00
#1146, Tri-Deck Transporter, from $200 to....................$250.00
#1147, Ferrymaster Truck, from $125 to $150.00
#1148, Carrimore Car Transporter, from $150 to $200.00
#1150, Mercedes Unimog Snowplough, from $70 to........$85.00
#1151, Scammell Co-op Set, from $325 to $375.00
#1151, Scammell Co-op Truck, from $250 to $300.00
#1152, Mack Truck, Esso Tanker, from $90 to $110.00
#1152, Mack Truck, Exxon Tanker, from $150 to.........$175.00
#1153, Priestman Boom Crane, from $90 to $110.00
#1154, Priestman Crane, from $125 to $150.00
#1154, Tower Crane, from $85 to..................................$105.00
#1155, Skyscraper Tower Crane, from $75 to $90.00
#1156, Volvo Cement Mixer, from $60 to......................$75.00
#1157, Ford Esso Tanker, from $60 to $75.00
#1158, Ford Exxon Tanker, from $70 to $85.00
#1159, Ford Car Transporter, from $100 to...................$125.00
#1160, Ford Gulf Tanker, from $60 to $75.00
#1161, Ford Aral Tanker, from $90 to..........................$110.00
#1163, Circus Cannon Truck, from $75 to......................$90.00
#1164, Dolphinarium, from $150 to..............................$175.00
#1169, Ford Guiness Tanker, from $115 to $140.00
#1170, Ford Car Transporter, from $90 to $110.00

Diecast Vehicles

Diecast replicas of cars, trucks, planes, trains, etc., represent a huge corner of today's collector market, and their manufacturers see to it that there is no shortage. Back in the 1920s, Tootsietoy had the market virtually by themselves, but one by one other companies had a go at it, some with more success than others. Among them were the American companies of Barclay, Hubley, and Manoil, all of whom are much better known for other types of toys. After the war, Metal Masters, Smith-Miller, and Doepke Ohlsson-Rice (among others) tried the market with varying degrees of success. Some companies were phased out over the years, while many more entered the market with fervor. Today it's those fondly remembered models from the '50s and '60s that many collectors yearn to own. Solido produced well-modeled, detailed little cars; some had dome lights that actually came on when the doors were opened. Politoy's were cleanly molded with good detailing and finishes. Mebetoys, an Italian company that has been bought out by Mattel, produced several; and some of the finest come from Brooklyn.

In 1968 the Topper Toy Company introduced its line of low-friction, high-speed Johnny Lightning cars to be in direct competition with Mattel's Hot Wheels. To gain attention, Topper sponsored Al Unser's winning race car, the 'Johnny Lightning,' in the 1970 Indianapolis 500. Despite the popularity of their cars, the Topper Toy Company went out of business in 1971. Today the Johnny Lightnings are highly sought after, and a new company, Playing Mantis, is reproducing many of the original designs as well as several models that never made it into regular production.

If you're interested in Majorette Toys, we recommend *Collecting Majorette Toys* by Dana Johnson; ordering information is given with Dana's listing under Diecast, in the section called Categories of Special Interest in the back of the book. Dana is also the author of *Toy Car Collector's Guide* published by Collector Books.

Values are for examples in mint condition and in the original packaging unless noted otherwise.

Advisor: Dana Johnson (J4)

See also Corgi; Dinky; Farm Toys; Hot Wheels; Matchbox; Tootsietoy.

Anson, Porsche 911 Carrera 4 Cabriolet, black, mint, red, or yellow, from $25.00 to $40.00. (Photo courtesy Dana Johnson)

Ahi, Alfa Romeo Giuletta Sprint, from $20 to.................$25.00
Ahi, Buick, from $20 to...$25.00

Ahi, Dodge Military Crane Truck, from $12 to $16.00
Ahi, Dodge Military Radar Truck, from $12 to................$16.00
Ahi, Ford Model T (1915), from $15 to...........................$20.00
Ahi, Jaguar Mk IX, from $20 to......................................$25.00
Ahi, Maserati Racer, from $20 to $25.00
Ahi, Midget Racer, from $20 to.......................................$25.00
Ahi, Oldsmobile (1904), from $12 to...............................$16.00
Ahi, Rambler (1903), from $12 to $16.00
Ahi, Rolls Royce Silver Wraith, from $25 to....................$30.00
Ahi, 1903 Cadillac, from $12 to.......................................$16.00
Anker, Alfa Romeo 1300, from $20 to..............................$25.00
Asahi Model Pet, Datsun Bluebird, from $120 to...........$140.00
Asahi Model Pet, Mitsubishi Galant GTO, from $40 to ..$60.00
Asahi Model Pet, Yamaha Police Motorcycle, from $25 to..$35.00
Aurora Cigar Box, Ford J Car, yel, from $30 to................$40.00
Aurora Cigar Box, Thunderbird, yel, from $30 to............$40.00
Auto Pilen, Mercedes Taxi, from $40 to $50.00
Bandii, Nisson JAL Vacuum Car, from $6 to.....................$8.00
Bandii, Porsche 928, bl, from $16 to $20.00
Bang, Ferrari 250 GTO Thirty Years, chrome, from $30 to..$40.00
Bang, Ford AC Cobra Sebring, 1963, from $25 to............$35.00
Bang, Ford Mk II Le Mans, bl or blk, ea from $25 to........$35.00
Barclay, Ambulance, #50, from $45 to $55.00
Barclay, Mack Pickup Truck, 3½", from $30 to................$35.00
Barclay, Searchlight Truck, from $145 to........................$160.00
Barlay, Chrysler Airflow, 4", from $80 to $95.00
Barlux, Ferrari B2, from $9 to...$12.00
Barlux, Fiat Ambulance, from $25 to $35.00

BBR, Alfa Romeo 2900 Berlinetta (1939), from $140 to...**$170.00**
BBR, Ferrari 250 Europa Street (1954), red, from $140 to..**$170.00**
BBR, Ferrari 250 GTE (1959), from $150 to **$180.00**
BBR, Ferrari 288 GTO (1984), from $150 to **$180.00**
BBR, Ferrari 308 GTB Coupe, red, from $165 to **$185.00**
Bburago, Cement Mixer, 1500 series, from $30 to **$35.00**
Bburago, Dump Truck, 1500 series, M, from $30 to.........**$35.00**
Bburago, Lamborghini Countach, from $25 to **$30.00**
Bburago, Lumber Truck, 1500 series, M, from $30 to **$35.00**
Bburago, Range Rover Safari, from $25 to **$30.00**
Bburago, Renault RE20 Formula One, 1980, from $35 to...**$45.00**

Bburago, Rolls Royce Camargue, from $20.00 to $30.00. (Photo courtesy Dana Johnson)

Bburago Jaguar SS 100, 1937, from $30 to **$40.00**
Benbros, Bedford Articulated Petrol Tanker, from $40 to...**$65.00**
Benbros, Dodge Army Radar Truck, from $80 to **$95.00**
Benbros, Rolls Royce (1906), from $15 to **$20.00**
Bendros, Army Land Rover, from $20 to.........................**$30.00**
Bendros, Army Scout Car, from $15 to **$20.00**
Best Toys of Kansas, Racer #76, 4", from $30 to...............**$35.00**
Best Toys of Kansas, Racer #81, 4½", from $30 to **$35.00**
Best Toys of Kansas, Sedan #87, from $30 to **$35.00**
Best-Box of Holland, DAF Torpedo Dumo Truck, from $24 to..**$27.00**
Best-Box of Holland, Ford Model T Coupe, from $24 to..**$27.00**

Brooklins (British Issues), Buick Roadmaster Coupe (1949), from $75.00 to $200.00. (Photo courtesy Dana Johnson)

Brooklins (British Issues), Cadillac Eldorado Brougham (1957), from $185 to **$210.00**
Brooklins (British Issues), Chevrolet El Camino (1959), from $60 to **$75.00**

Brooklins (British Issues), Chrysler Airflow (1934), from $80 to **$125.00**
Brooklins (Canadian Issues), Chevrolet Coupe (1937), from $300 to..**$350.00**
Brooklins (Canadian Issues), Chrysler Newport 4-Door (1940), from $175 to **$225.00**
Brooklins (Canadian Issues), Packard (1932), from $300 to...**$350.00**
Brooklins (Lansdowne Models), Austin Healy Sprite Mk I (1958), from $60 to **$85.00**
Brooklins (Lansdowne Models), Sunbeam Alpine (1963), from $60 to **$85.00**
Brooklins (Robeddie Models), Saab 99 (1969), from $60 to ...**$85.00**
Brooklins (Robeddie Models), Volvo Amazon 120 (1957), from $60 to **$85.00**
Brumm, Fiat S 61 (1903), from $18 to **$24.00**
Brumm, Maserati 250F Muso Corto (1957), from $18 to....**$24.00**
Buby, VW Buggy, from $6 to..**$8.00**
CD, MG Record Car, from $100 to **$125.00**
Chad Valley, Ambulance, from $35 to **$40.00**
Chad Valley, Commer Breakdown Truck, from $150 to ...**$170.00**
Chad Valley, Commer Fire Engine, from $160 to **$180.00**
Chad Valley, Guy Ice Cream Truck................................**$250.00**
Charbens, Ambulance **$65.00**
Charbens, Tanker..**$65.00**
CIJ, Cattle Trailer, #3/28, 1962 ....**$55.00**
CIJ, Renault Floride, #3/58, 1960...................................**$55.00**

Classic Cast, Buick Delivery Van (1923), 8", M, A, $220.00. (Photo courtesy Bertoia Auctions)

Con-Cor, Ferrari Testarossa...**$8.00**
Con-Cor, Mustang (1969) **$10.00**
Conquest, Ford Country Squire Station Wagon (1963) ..**$200.00**
Conquest, Plymouth Fury (1960)...................................**$210.00**
Conrad, Volkswagen Polo C...**$10.00**
Conrad, Volkswagen Santana GL, from $ **$20.00**
Conrad, Volvo Titan L395 Flatbed Truck........................**$48.00**
Dali-Solido, Maderati 250F, red, yel, or gr, ea.................**$100.00**
Dalia, Lambretta Army Motor Tricycle, olive **$75.00**
Dalia, Vesper Scooter, gr..**$75.00**
Dalia-Solido, Jaguar D Le Mans, red, gr, or bl................**$100.00**

Dalia-Solido, Porsche F2, silver & red $125.00
Dalia-Tekno, Oldsmobile Toronado, from $60 to $75.00
Danbury Mint, Ferrari 250 Testa Rossa, red, from $110
    to..$135.00
Danbury Mint, Pontiac GTO (1965), lavender & wht, from
    $110 to..$135.00
Diapet, Airport Bus, #B32, from $15 to $20.00
Diapet, Corvette, #G76, from $65 to $80.00
Diapet, Datsun Tow Truck, #272, from $15 to $20.00
Diapet, Honda Acura NSX, #SV26, from $30 to.............$40.00
Diapet, Nissan Silvia Coupe, #G37, from $35 to.............$45.00
Doepke, MT Roadster, 1950s, 15", VG, A, from $185 to...$275.00
Doepke, Unit Mobile Crane, 11½", MIB, from $300 to..$400.00

Doepke, Victory 37 Bus (1972), $25.00. (Photo courtesy Dana Johnson)

Dugu, Benz Victoria (1893), 1964, from $35 to $45.00
Dugu, Fiat Open Tourer (1911), 1963, from $45 to $55.00
Dugu, Fiat 500A (1936), 1966, from $55 to.......................$65.00
Durham Classics, Chevy Suburban Niagara Falls (1941), from
    $100 to...$120.00
Durham Classics, Ford Coupe (1941), from $90 to $110.00
Durham Classics, Lincoln Zephyr Coupe (1938), blk, from $90
    to...$110.00
Efsi, Commer Ambulance, from $12 to..............................$16.00
Efsi, Porsche 911 S, from $16 to $18.00
Eligor, Ford Police Sedan (1932), from $30 to..................$35.00
Eligor, Ford Roadster Fire Chief (1932), from $30 to $35.00
Enchanted, Buick Riviera (1949), from $125 to.............$150.00
Enchanted, Chevy Nomad (1957), from $75 to $100.00
Enchanted, Kaiser Manhattan (1953), from $75 to........$100.00
Enchanted, Packard Victoria (1937), from $75 to $100.00
Enchantment Land Coach Builders, Pontiac Convertible
    (1968), from $90 to $120.00
Ertl, Buick (1912), red & blk, 1:43 scale, 1985, from $20 to ...$25.00
Ertl, Buick GSX (1971), blk & gold, 1:18 scale, from $30 to...$35.00
Ertl, Corvette Coupe (1963), dk bl, 1:18 scale, from $30 to...$35.00
Ertl, Dodge Ram Truck (1995), red or blk, 1:18 scale, ea from
    $30 to...$35.00
Ertl, Pontiac Trans Am Coupe (1996), metallic red, 1:18 scale,
    from $30 to..$35.00
Ertl, 1967 Corvette L-71 Roadster, Sunfire Yellow, 1:18 scale,
    from $35 to..$40.00

Ertl, Corvette Stingray, $20.00. (Photo courtesy Dana Johnson)

France Jouets, Army Jeep w/Searchlight, 1961, from $60
    to..$75.00
France Jouets, Police Jeep, 1965, from $60 to $75.00
France Jouets, Tow Truck, 1967, from $70 to....................$85.00
Franklin Mint, Benz Patent Motorwagon (1886), from $130
    to..$150.00
Franklin Mint (1:10 Scale), Indian 442 Motorcycle (1886), from
    $130 to...$150.00
Franklin Mint (1:16 Scale), Ford Model T (1913), from $120
    to..$140.00
Franklin Mint (1:24 Scale), Buick Riviera, lt bl-gray & gray,
    from $120 to...$150.00
Franklin Mint (1:24 Scale), Oldsmobile Petty NASCAR #43, bl
    & red, from $110 to..$125.00
Franklin Mint (1:32 Scale), Ahren Fox R-K-4 Fire Pumper
    Truck (1922), from $110 to..$125.00

Franklin Mint (1:43 Scale), Chrysler Town & Country (1950), from $55.00 to $70.00. (Photo courtesy Dana Johnson)

Franklin Mint (1:43 Scale), Ford Mustang (1964), from $65
    to..$75.00
Franklin Mint (1:43 Scale), Lincoln Sport Touring Car (1927),
    from $65 to...$75.00
Franklin Mint (1:43 Scale), Nash (1950), from $65 to $75.00
Franklin Mint (1:43 Scale), Studebaker Starliner (1953), from
    $65 to $75.00
Gama, Ford Taunus 17M, #901, 1959, from $45 to...........$55.00
Gama, Henschel Wrecker, #31, 1969, from $25 to $35.00

Gama, Mercedes-Benz 300CE, from $20 to $30.00
Goldvarg, Chevy Bel-Air Sedan (1954), from $85 to $100.00
Goldvarg, Ford Deluxe Sedan (1946), from $85 to $100.00
Goodee, Ford Fuel Truck (1955), 3", from $12 to.............$16.00
Goodee, Ford Fuel Truck (1955), 6", from $24 to.............$30.00
Goodee, Lincoln Capri Hardtop (1953), 3", from $16 to .$20.00

Goodee, Moving Van, $15.00. (Photo courtesy Dana Johnson)

Goodee, Studebaker Coupe (1953), 3", from $20 to.........$24.00
Guiloy, Indian Chief Motorcycle (1948), from $35 to......$45.00
Guisval, Chevy Camaro (1979), from $16 to....................$20.00
Guisval, Mercedes 406 Kombi, from $16 to $20.00
Guisval, Porsche 959, from $16 to...................................$20.00

Hubley, Convertible, nickel-plated fold-down top, 7", EX, A, $85.00. (Photo courtesy Bertois Auctions)

Hubley, Army Air Squadron Set, 5 planes w/box converting to
    hangar, lg plane is 10" L, EXIB, A, from $220 to.....$250.00
Hubley, Bell Telephone Truck w/Pole Trailer, 24", from $175
    to $200.00
Hubley, Chrysler Airflow, 5", from $80 to.........................$95.00
Hubley, LaSalle (1940), lt bl, WRT w/red hubs, 7", VG, A, from
    $215 to...$235.00

Hubley, Log Truck, 1950s, with logs, 11", EX+IB, $85.00.
(Photo courtesy Bertoia Auctions)

Hubley, Log Truck, 1960s, w/logs, 10", G, A, from $35 to ..$45.00
Hubley, Midget Racers Set, w/3 racers, 7" ea, NM+IB, A, from
    $875 to...$950.00
Hubley, Packard Sedan (1939-40), 5½", from $75 to $90.00
Hubley, Poultry Truck, w/accessories, 10", from $265 to...$300.00
Hubley, Sports Car, yel w/blk convertible top, 13", rare, from
    $850 to...$1,000.00
Hubley, TAT NC-31 Airplane, 5" W, from $90 to.........$110.00
Hubley, Tractor, orange w/blk rubber tires, 7", from $150 to...$175.00
Hubley, US Army Truck, 1960s, 12", missing canvas cover o/w
    VGIB, A, from $30 to...$40.00

Hubley Kiddie Toy, Convertible, blue, 7", EXIB, A, $165.00.
(Photo courtesy Bertoia Auctions)

Hubley Kiddie Toy, Dump Truck, #510, from $240 to **$265.00**
Hubley Kiddie Toy, MG Sports Car, 9", from $180 to **$200.00**
Hubley Kiddie Toy, Sedan, #452, 7", from $30 to **$45.00**
Hubley Kiddy Toy, DeLuxe Sports Car (T-Bird), red w/blk top, 9", NMIB, A, from $215 to **$240.00**
Hubley Mighty-Metal, Tow Truck, from $120 to **$135.00**
Jane Francis, Pickup Truck, 5", from $24 to **$28.00**
Joal, Adams Probe 16, from $35 to................................**$45.00**
Joal, Chevrolet Monza, from $35 to **$45.00**
Joal, Chrysler 150, from $35 to **$45.00**
Joal, Ferrari 250 Le Mans, from $30 to **$40.00**
Johnny Lightning, Custom El Camino, 1969, MIP **$1,250.00**
Johnny Lightning, Custom Eldorado, 1969....................**$125.00**
Johnny Lightning, Custom Eldorado, 1969, mirror finish, doors open, MIP...**$1,200.00**
Johnny Lightning, Custom Eldorado, 1969, standard finish, doors open, MIP **$400.00**
Johnny Lightning, Custom Eldorado, 1969, standard finish, doors cast shut, MIP **$1,750.00**
Johnny Lightning, Custom XKE, doors open, 1969........**$125.00**
Johnny Lightning, Custom XKE, mirror finish, MIP...**$1,250.00**
Johnny Lightning, Custom XKE, standard finish w/doors cast shut, 1969, MIP **$150.00**
Johnny Lightning, Custom XKE, standard finish w/opening doors, 1969, MIP **$750.00**
Johnny Lightning, Indy 500 Racing Set, w/original container, MIP...**$1,000.00**
Johnny Lightning, Jet Powered Screamer, 1970................**$35.00**
Johnny Lightning, Sand Stormer, 1970, blk roof............**$175.00**
Johnny Lightning, Sand Stormer, 1970, roof same color as body..**$150.00**
Jouef, Honda Acura NSX, gray, from $25 to **$35.00**
Jouef, Nissan 300ZX, red, from $25 to..............................**$35.00**
JRD, Citroen 2CV Fire Van, 1958, from $80 to **$100.00**
Kansas Toy & Novelty, Army Truck, #74, 2¼", from $50 to ..**$65.00**
Kansas Toy & Novelty, Bearcat Racer #3, 3", from $50 to..**$65.00**
Kansas Toy & Novelty, Chevrolet Sedan, 2", from $40 to..**$55.00**
Kansas Toy & Novelty, Truck, #20, 3⅛", from $30 to **$40.00**
Kiddie Car Classics, Ford Mustang (1964), 7" **$55.00**
Kiddie Car Classics, Murray Pontiac (1948), 6", from $50 to..**$60.00**
Kirk, Chevrolet Monza GT, from $65 to **$75.00**
Lansing Slik-Toys, Pickup Truck, #9601, 7", from $35 to ...**$45.00**
Lansing Slik-Toys, Roadster, #9701, 3½", from $35 to **$45.00**
Lansing Slik-Toys, Tanker Truck, #9705, 4", from $30 to ...**$40.00**
Lledo, Delivery Van, 1983, from $15 to **$20.00**

Lledo, Fire Engine, 1983, from $15 to **$20.00**
Lledo, Ford Model T Tanker, 1983, from $15 to **$20.00**
Lledo, Long Distance Coach, 1985, from $15 to.............**$20.00**
Lledo, Packard Town Van, 1986, from $15 to **$20.00**
Lledo, Rolls Royce Silver Ghost Tourer, 1987, from $15 to ..**$20.00**
Londontoy, City Bus, 4", from $30 to.............................**$35.00**
Londontoy, Dump Truck, lg, from $110 to....................**$125.00**
Londontoy, Ford Pickup (1941), 4", from $30 to **$35.00**
Londontoy, Ford Pickup (1941), 6", from $35 to **$45.00**
Lone Star, Cadillac Coupe de Ville, wht & bl, from $80 to..**$100.00**
Lone Star, Dodge Dart Phoenix, metallic bl, from $80 to **$100.00**
Maisto, Bugatti EB110 (1992), red or bl, 1:18 scale, ea from $30 to **$40.00**
Maisto, Ferrari F50 Barchetta (1995), yel, 1:18 scale, from $30 to **$40.00**
Maisto, Ferrari F50 Coupe, yel or red, ea from $25 to.......**$35.00**
Maisto, Mercedes-Benz 280SE (1966), wht, from $25 to...**$35.00**

Maisto, Volkswagen Export (Beetle) Sedan (1951), black, gray, or green, from $25.00 to $30.00. (Photo courtesy Dana Johnson)

Majorette, Chrysler 180, metallic gr, from $12 to **$15.00**
Majorette, Citreon Maserati SM, from $12 to **$15.00**
Majorette, Citreon DS 21, from $21 to **$24.00**
Majorette, Jeep 4x4 w/Motorcylce Trailer, from $16 to **$18.00**
Majorette, Mercedes-Benz 280SE, from $12 to **$16.00**
Majorette, Mercedes Utility Truck w/Compressor, from $15 to...**$18.00**
Majorette, Peugeot 404 & Horse Trailer, from $10 to.......**$13.00**
Majorette, Toyota Truck & Trailer, from $12 to...............**$15.00**
Majorette, VW Golf, red, from $5 to...............................**$6.00**
Majorette Club/Super Club, Jaguar E-Type, from $12 to ..**$15.00**
Majorette Magic Cars, Corvette Big Mouth Bruno, from $6 to **$8.00**
Majorette Sonic Flashers, Ambulance, from $8 to............**$12.00**
Majorette Special Forces Series, Missile Launcher, from $5 to..**$6.00**
Majorette Super Series, Mustang Hardtop, yel, from $5 to ...**$6.00**
Mandarin, Honda 9 Coupe, from $6 to **$8.00**
Manoil, Bus, 1945-55, from $35 to **$50.00**
Manoil, Roadster, 1935-41, from $85 to **$100.00**
Manoil, Wrecker, 1935-41, from $85 to..........................**$100.00**
Master Caster, Packard Convertible, w/orig windshield, 8", EX, A, from $425 to **$475.00**

Lledo, Greyhound Scenicruiser, from $18.00 to $20.00. (Photo courtesy Dana Johnson)

McGregor, Honda F1, brn & wht, from $15 to $18.00
Mebetoys, BMW 320 Rally, 1980, from $27 to $35.00
Mebetoys, Corvette Rondline, 1967, from $27 to...........$35.00
Mebetoys, 1966 Fiat 850, from $28 to............................$35.00
Mebetoys, 1974 Land Rover Fire Truck, from $40 to........$45.00
Mebetoys, 1974 Porsche 912 Rally, from $35 to $40.00
Mebetoys, 1974 Willys Fire Jeep, from $35 to..................$40.00
Mebetoys, 1981 Mercedes-Benz 280SE, from $28 to $35.00
Mebetoys, 1983 Ford Escort, from $30 to $40.00
Mebetoys, 1983 Pontiac Firebird, from $28 to $35.00
Mercury, Harley-Davidson Electra, from $35 to...............$45.00
Mercury, Stagecoach, from $80 to $95.00
Mercury, 1946 Caravan Trailer, from $45 to $65.00
Mercury, 1947 Lincoln Continental, from $165 to.........$200.00
Mercury, 1949 Cadillac 62 Sedan, from $140 to............$175.00
Mercury, 1969 Osi Silver Fox, from $50 to......................$60.00
Mercury, 1974 Fiat 131 Rally, from $24 to......................$36.00
Mercury, 1976 BMW 320 Police Car, from $25 to............$30.00
Mercury, 1977 Fiat 131 Wagon & Trailer, from $35 to.....$45.00
Micropet, 1960s Ford Falcon, from $150 to....................$175.00
Midgetoys, Army Ambulance, 1950s, 4", from $16 to......$20.00
Midgetoys, Jeep, 1960s, red, from $8 to..........................$12.00
Milton, Chevrolet Impala, from $32 to...........................$36.00
Milton, Ford Model T, from $27 to $30.00
Mira, Buick Century Convertible (1955), 2-tone, from $30
    to $40.00
Mira, Chevy Pickup (1953), from $30 to $40.00

Mira, Ford Panel Truck (1950), $25.00. (Photo courtesy Dana Johnson)

Mira, Ford Thunderbird (1956), from $30 to $40.00
Morestone, Austin-Healey 100, from $35 to.....................$50.00
Morestone, Packard Convertible, from $50 to $65.00
Nicky Toys, Bentley S Coupe, from $30 to $35.00
Nostalgic, Ford Mustang 2+2 (1965), blk, from $50 to $65.00
Nostalgic, Ford Roadster (1930), top down, from $50 to..$65.00
Nostalgic, Ford Van (1936), maroon, from $55 to $70.00
Nostalgic, Lincoln Continental (1941), from $55 to........$70.00
NZG, Kramer Tremo Utility Truck, from $25 to................$35.00
NZG, Porsche 911 Speedster, from $30 to $40.00
NZG, Scania City Bus CN112, from $45 to.......................$55.00

Playart, Chevrolet Blazer, Sears Roadmates #7242, from $6
    to..$8.00

Playart, Chevrolet Caprice Classic, metallic purple, $5.00. (Photo courtesy Dana Johnson)

Quiralu, Renault Etoile Filante (1958), w/decals, from $90
    to $115.00
Racing Champions, Chevy Impala (1964), wht, from $6 to......$8.00
Racing Champions, Dodge Ram (1969), #12, bl, from $6 to.....$8.00
Racing Champions, Ford Thunderbird (1956), pk, from $6 to..$8.00

Racing Champions, Plymouth Superbird (1970), red with black top, from $5.00 to $6.00. (Photo courtesy Dana Johnson)

Ralstoy, Safety-Kleen, M, from $40 to..............................$55.00
Renwal, Ford Crestline Sedan, friction, 8", NMIB, A, from $325
    to $350.00
Renwal, Ford Sunliner Convertible, from $40 to..............$55.00
Renwal, Pontiac Convertible, from $125 to $140.00
Replicars, Triumph TR6 (1974), from $55 to $70.00
Rextoys, Ford Coupe (1935), from $35 to.........................$45.00
Rio, Fiat 501 Tourer (1919), 1961, from $27 to................$32.00
Road Champs, Greyhound Eagle Coach, from $9 to $12.00
Sablon, BMW 1600 GT, from $30 to $36.00
Sakura, Toyota Land Cruiser, from $24 to.......................$27.00
Schabak, Audi 100 Avant, 5", from $20 to.......................$25.00
Schabak, Audi 80 Sedan (1992), from $20 to...................$25.00
Schabak, Ford Transit Van (1986), 1987, from $32 to......$36.00
Schuco, Audi 80 LS, 1972, from $30 to $35.00
Schuco, BMW 520 Police Car, 1976, from $30 to $35.00
Schuco, Ford Escort 1300 GT, 1971, 2", from $12 to........$16.00
Schuco, Krupp Cement Mixer, 3⅝", from $55 to $70.00
Schuco, Krupp Cement Mixer, 5½", from $65 to $80.00
Schuco, MGA Coupe, 1958, 2", from $55 to $75.00

Schuco, Volkswagen Polo, 1975, from $25 to $35.00
Scottoys, Fiat 600 Saloon, from $30 to $35.00
Siku, Ferrari Berlinetta, 1975-81, from $16 to $20.00
Siku, Ford Capri 1700GT, 1970-74, from $20 to $25.00
Siku, Ford 12M, 1963, from $36 to.............................$40.00
Siku, Ford 17M Station Wagon, 1968-70, from $40 to.....$50.00
Siku, Mercedes Water Service Van, 1972-74, from $30 to..$40.00
Siku, Police Bat Transporter, 1989, from $30 to $35.00
Siku, Porsche Carrea 906, 1975-82, from $15 to............$20.00
Siku, Porsche 901, 1964-69, from $45 to $60.00
Siku, Volkswagen Fire Rescue Bus, 1992, from $12 to......$16.00

**Siku, Volkswagen Vanagon Bus (1973 – 1974), $25.00.
(Photo courtesy Dana Johnson)**

Solido, Kaiser Jeep M 34, from $25 to $30.00
Solido, Mack R 600 Fire Engine, from $30 to $35.00
Solido, 1936 Ford Pickup, from $35 to $45.00
Solido, 1939 Rolls Royce Convertible, from $25 to.........$30.00
Solido, 1940 Dodge Fire Dept Recovery Truck, from $25 to ..$35.00
Solido, 1946 Chrysler Windsor, 1960s, from $30 to.........$40.00
Solido, 1963 Ford Thunderbird Grand Sport, from $30 to...$40.00
Solido, 1978 Jaguar XJ 12, from $12 to $16.00
Solido, 1989 Mercedes-Benz SL Convertible, from $20 to....$25.00
Spot-On, Aston Martin DB3, from $225 to $250.00
Spot-On, Austin A40, from $150 to $175.00
Spot-On, Jaguar Mk 10, from $180 to $210.00
Spot-On, Rolls Royce Silver Wraith, from $275 to $300.00
Sunnyside, BMW Z1 Roadster, from $6 to $8.00
Sunnyside, BMW 728 Sedan, from $6 to $8.00
Sunnyside, Porsche 959 Coupe, from $6 to $8.00
Tip Top Toy, Parcel Delivery Panel Truck, 2", from $32 to ..$36.00
Tip Top Toy, Stake Truck, 5", from $55 to....................$65.00
Tip Top Toy, 1923 Dodge Coupe, 3", from $32 to.............$36.00
Tomica, Cadillac Ambulance, #F-2, from $12 to $16.00
Tomica, Datsun 200SX, #235-6, from $6 to $8.00
Tomica, Honda Motorcycle, #42, from $7 to $9.00
Tomica, Lotus Elite, #F47, from $6 to..........................$8.00
Tomica, Porsche Turbo 935, #183-F31, from $5 to $6.00
Tomica, Toyota Land Cruiser, #83-02, from $9 to............$12.00
Tomica, Volkswagen Microbus, #166-F29, from $18 to $24.00
Tomica Dandy, Mini Cooper, #DJO15, from $25 to $30.00

Tomica Dandy, Nissan Skyline, from $20 to $25.00
Tomica Dandy, Toyota Landcruiser, from $22 to...........$27.00
Tri-Ang, 1935 Limousine, from $110 to........................$140.00
Tri-Ang, 1935 Town Coupe, from $120 to......................$150.00
Tri-Ang, 1937 Vauxhall Cabriolet, from $160 to...........$190.00
Tri-Ang, 1937 Vauxhall Town Coupe, from $120 to $150.00
Tri-Ang, 1938 Bentley Touring Car, from $120 to..........$150.00
Verem, Porsche Carerra, wht, from $18 to $21.00
Vitesse, 1947 Chrysler Windsor Sedan, from $30 to........$36.00
Vitesse, 1956 Ford Fairlane Victoria, from $30 to...........$36.00
Vitesse, 1959 Volkswagen 1200, w/sunroof, from $30 to...$36.00

**Yatming, Chevrolet Bel Air Nomad Station Wagon (1957),
$23.00. (Photo courtesy Dana Johnson)**

Ziss, Opal Stadt-Coupe (1908), 1963, from $24 to $32.00
Ziss, 1916 Chevrolet Phaeton, 1969, from $24 to............$32.00
Ziss, 1966 Volkswagen Van, 1970, from $48 to $56.00
Ziss, 1971 Opel Commodore Coupe, from $36 to............$48.00

Dinky

Dinky diecasts were made by Meccano (Britain) as early as
1933, but high on the list of many of today's collectors are those
from the decades of the '50s and '60s. They made commercial
vehicles, firefighting equipment, farm toys, and heavy equipment as well as classic cars that were the epitome of high style,
such as the #157 Jaguar XK120, produced from the mid-'50s
through the early '60s. Some Dinkys were made in France; since
1979 no toys have been produced in Great Britain. Values are
for examples mint and in the original packaging unless noted
otherwise.
    Advisor: Dana Johnson (J4)

#100, Lady Penelope's Fab 1, luminous pk, from $375 to..$425.00
#100, Lady Penelope's Fab 1, pk, from $225 to $275.00
#101, Sunbeam Alpine, from $275 to $325.00
#101, Thunderbird II & IV, gr, from $275 to $325.00
#101, Thunderbird II & IV, metallic gr, from $375 to $425.00
#102, Joe's Car, from $225 to....................................$260.00
#102, MG Midget, from $225 to $260.00
#105, Triumph TR2, from $225 to $260.00
#106, Austin Atlantic, bl or blk, from $195 to $240.00

#104, Spectrum Pursuit Vehicle, from $225.00 to $250.00.

#106, Austin Atlantic, pk, from $385 to........................$435.00
#106, Prisoner Mini Moke, from $375 to......................$425.00
#106, Thunderbird II & IV, from $200 to $250.00
#107, Sunbeam Alpine, from $200 to $250.00
#108, MG Midget, from $200 to $250.00
#108, Sam's Car, gold, red or bl, from $150 to $175.00
#108, Sam's Car, silver, from $150 to $175.00
#109, Austin Healey 100, from $225 to $250.00
#109, Gabriel Model T Ford, from $150 to $175.00
#110, Aston Martin DB5, from $180 to.........................$210.00
#111, Cinderella's Coach, from $150 to $175.00
#111, Triumph TR2, from $150 to $180.00
#112, Austin Healey Sprite, from $110 to $135.00
#112, Purdey's Triumph TR7, from $110 to $135.00
#113, MGB, from $135 to $160.00
#114, Triumph Spitfire, gray, gold or red, from $135 to..$160.00
#114, Triumph Spitfire, purple, from $155 to $180.00
#115, Plymouth Fury, from $225 to $250.00
#116, Volvo 1800S, from $160 to.................................$185.00
#117, Four Berth Caravan, from $150 to $175.00
#120, Happy Cab, from $120 to $145.00
#120, Jaguar E-Type, from $160 to $185.00
#121, Goodwood Racing Gift Set, from $2,000 to $2,500.00
#122, Touring Gift Set, from $2,000 to........................$2,500.00
#122, Volvo 265 Estate Car, from $120 to $145.00
#123, Mayfair Gift Set, from $2,850 to........................$3,250.00
#123, Princess 2200 HL, from $170 to $190.00
#124, Rolls Royce Phantom V, from $165 to $180.00
#125, Fun A'Hoy Set, from $315 to.............................$335.00
#128, Mercedes Benz 600, from $170 to $195.00
#129, MG Midget, from $950 to $1,250.00
#129, VW 1300 Sedan, from $160 to............................$175.00
#130, Ford Consul Corsair, from $145 to $160.00
#131, Cadillac El Dorado, from $195 to.......................$215.00
#131, Jaguar E-Type, 2+2, from $135 to.......................$160.00

#132, Ford 40-RV, from $130 to $155.00
#132, Packard Convertible, from $195 to......................$220.00
#133, Cunningham C-5R, from $180 to $210.00
#134, Triumph Vitesse, from $160 to $185.00
#135, Triumph 2000, from $140 to...............................$165.00
#136, Vauxhall Viva, from $140 to $165.00
#137, Plymouth Fury, from $180 to $210.00
#138, Hillman Imp, from $145 to.................................$170.00
#139, Ford Cortina, from $140 to.................................$165.00
#139a, Hudson Commodore Sedan, dual colors, from $325
    to $400.00
#139a, Hudson Commodore Sedan, solid colors, from $215
    to $250.00
#139a, US Army Staff Car, from $345 to.......................$375.00
#140, Morris 1100, from $130 to $155.00
#141, Vauxhall Victor, from $130 to $155.00
#142, Jaguar Mark 10, from $130 to $155.00
#143, Ford Capri, from $130 to $155.00
#144, VW 1500, from $140 to......................................$165.00
#145, Singer Vogue, from $130 to $155.00
#146, Daimler V8, from $160 to...................................$185.00
#147, Cadillac Series 62, from $150 to $195.00
#148, Ford Fairlane, gr, from $150 to $195.00
#148, Ford Fairlane, metallic gr, from $200 to $240.00
#149, Citroen Dyane, from $100 to $135.00
#149, Sports Car Gift Set, from $1,750 to...................$2,000.00
#150, Rolls Royce Silver Wraith, from $155 to $210.00
#151, Triumph 1800 Saloon, from $175 to $225.00
#151, Vauxhall Victor 101, from $150 to $185.00
#152, Rolls Royce Phantom V, from $150 to $185.00
#153, Aston Martin DB6, from $160 to $195.00
#153, Standard Vanguard-Spats, from $175 to $225.00
#154, Ford Taurus 17M, from $160 to $195.00
#155, Ford Anglia, from $160 to $195.00
#156, Mechanized Army Set, from $4,750 to $5,250.00
#156, Rover 75, dual colors, from $275 to $325.00
#156, Rover 75, solid colors, from $175 to....................$225.00
#156, Saab 96, from $150 to...$200.00
#157, BMW 2000 Tilux, from $150 to $185.00

#157-G, Jaguar XK120, 1954, M, from $145.00 to $160.00.
(Photo courtesy Dana Johnson)

#158, Riley, from $175 to $225.00
#158, Rolls Royce Silver Shadow, from $185 to $245.00
#159, Ford Cortina MKII, from $125 to........................$175.00

#159, Morris Oxford, dual colors, from $275 to..............$325.00
#159, Morris Oxford, solid colors, from $175 to $225.00
#160, Austin A30, from $175 to $225.00
#160, Mercedes Benz 250 SE, from $150 to $185.00
#161, Austin Somerset, dual colors, from $275 to $325.00
#161, Austin Somerset, solid colors, from $175 to $225.00
#161, Ford Mustang, from $165 to $200.00
#162, Ford Zephyr, from $185 to $210.00
#162, Triumph 1300, from $160 to................................$195.00
#163, Bristol 450 Coupe, from $145 to $160.00
#163, VW 1600 TL, metallic bl, from $200 to................$250.00
#163, VW 1600 TL, red, from $60 to.............................$80.00
#164, Ford Zodiac MKIV, bronze, from $175 to.............$225.00
#164, Ford Zodiac MKIV, silver, from $150 to $185.00
#164, Vauxhall Cresta, from $175 to.............................$225.00
#165, Ford Capri, from $160 to $195.00
#165, Humber Hawk, from $195 to................................$240.00
#166, Renault R16, from $135 to $170.00
#166, Sunbeam Rapier, from $175 to.............................$225.00
#167, AC Acceca, all cream, from $275 to $325.00
#167, AC Acceca, dual colors, from $200 to $240.00
#168, Ford Escort, from $135 to $165.00
#168, Singer Gazelle, from $175 to $225.00
#169, Ford Corsair, from $135 to $165.00
#169, Studebaker Golden Hawk, from $190 to...............$240.00
#170, Ford Fordor, dual colors, from $275 to $325.00
#170, Ford Fordor, solid colors, from $180 to.................$230.00
#170, Lincoln Continental, from $210 to.......................$250.00
#170m, Ford Fordor US Army Staff Car, from $340 to ..$365.00
#171, Austin 1800, from $135 to $160.00
#171, Hudson Commodore, dual colors, from $350 to ...$375.00
#172, Fiat 2300 Station Wagon, from $135 to...............$160.00
#172, Studebaker Land Cruiser, dual colors, from $300 to ...$350.00
#172, Studebaker Land Cruiser, solid colors, from $200 to...$250.00
#173, Nash Rambler, from $175 to.................................$225.00
#173, Pontiac Parisienne, from $140 to $195.00
#174, Mercury Cougar, from $140 to $195.00
#175, Cadillac El Dorado, from $140 to.........................$195.00
#175, Hillman Minx, from $180 to $210.00
#176, Austin A105, cream or gray, from $170 to............$220.00
#176, Austin A105, cream w/bl roof, or gray w/red roof, from $275 to..$325.00
#176, NSU Rho, metallic bl, from $160 to $195.00
#176, NSU Rho, metallic red, from $130 to...................$165.00

#177, Opel Kapitan, from $130 to.................................$165.00
#178, Mini Clubman, from $120 to $145.00

#178, Plymouth Plaza, blue with white roof, from $225.00 to $300.00.

#178, Plymouth Plaza, pk, gr or 2-tone bl, from $185 to..$220.00
#179, Opel Commodore, from $175 to $210.00
#179, Studebaker President, from $210 to $250.00
#180, Rover 3500 Sedan, from $120 to..........................$145.00
#181, Volkswagen, from $210 to $225.00
#182, Porsche 356A Coupe, cream, red or bl, from $230 to ..$260.00
#182, Porsche 356A Coupe, dual colors, from $315 to...$345.00
#183, Fiat 600, from $130 to $160.00
#183, Morris Mini Minor, from $130 to.........................$160.00
#184, Volvo 122S, red, from $160 to.............................$190.00
#184, Volvo 122S, wht, from $360 to $400.00
#185, Alpha Romeo 1900, from $180 to........................$230.00
#186, Mercedes Benz 220SE, from $185 to $235.00
#187, De Tomaso Mangusta 5000, from $130 to............$150.00
#187, Volkswagen Karmann-Ghia Coupe, from $195 to ..$240.00
#188, Ford Berth Caravan, from $135 to $175.00
#188, Jensen FF, from $145 to $185.00
#189, Lamborghini Marzal, from $145 to.......................$185.00
#189, Triumph Herald, from $145 to $185.00
#191, Dodge Royal Sedan, cream w/bl flash, from $280 to...$320.00
#191, Dodge Royal Sedan, cream w/brn flash, or gr w/blk flash, from $210 to $240.00
#192, DeSoto Fireflite, from $210 to.............................$240.00
#192, Range Rover, from $110 to..................................$130.00

#176, Austin A105, EX, from $40.00 to $50.00. (Photo courtesy Dana Johnson)

#193, Rambler Cross Country Station Wagon, 1961, M, from $85.00 to $100.00.

#194, Bentley S Coupe, from $150 to $180.00
#195, Range Rover Fire Chief, from $135 to $160.00
#196, Holden Special Sedan, from $135 to....................$160.00
#197, Austin Countryman, orange, from $300 to..........$350.00
#197, Morris Mini Traveller, dk gr & brn, from $400 to.$450.00
#197, Morris Mini Traveller, from $155 to.....................$200.00
#197, Morris Mini Traveller, lime gr, from $250 to........$325.00
#198, Rolls Royce Phantom V, from $160 to $200.00
#199, Austin Countryman, bl, from $130 to...................$170.00
#200, Matra 630, from $130 to.......................................$170.00
#201, Plymouth Stock Car, from $120 to.......................$135.00
#201, Racing Car Set, from $750 to............................$1,000.00
#202, Customized Land Rover, from $110 to.................$140.00
#202, Fiat Abarth 2000, from $45 to...............................$65.00
#203, Customized Range Rover, from $110 to...............$130.00
#204, Ferrari, from $115 to..$135.00
#205, Talbot Lago, in bubble pkg, from $310 to $350.00
#206, Customized Corvette Stingray, from $130 to........$160.00
#207, Triumph TR7, from $1130 to $160.00
#208, VW Porsche 914, from $110 to $135.00
#210, Alfa Romeo 33, from $190 to................................$220.00
#210, Vanwall, in bubble pkg, from $185 to $225.00
#211, Triumph TR7, from $110 to $140.00
#213, Ford Capri, from $110 to.....................................$140.00
#214, Hillman Imp Rally, from $110 to.........................$140.00
#215, Ford GT Racing Car, from $120 to $140.00
#216, Ferrari Dino, from $120 to...................................$140.00
#217, Alfa Romeo Scarabo, from $120 to $140.00
#218, Lotus Europa, from $120 to $140.00
#219, Jaguar XJS Coupe, from $120 to..........................$140.00
#220, Ferrari P5, from $125 to.......................................$145.00
#221, Corvette Stingray, from $140 to...........................$165.00
#222, Hesketh Racing Car, dk bl, from $120 to..............$140.00
#222, Hesketh Racing Car, Olympus Camera, from $135 to ..$160.00
#223, McLaren M8A Can-Am, from $110 to.................$135.00
#224, Mercedes Benz C111, from $120 to......................$145.00
#225, Lotus Formula 1 Racer, from $110 to $135.00
#226, Ferrari 312/B2, from $125 to $140.00
#227, Beach Bunny, from $115 to..................................$130.00
#228, Super Sprinter, from $115 to $130.00
#236, Connaught Racer, from $170 to $195.00
#237, Mercedes Benz Racer, from $160 to $185.00
#238, Jaguar Type-D Racer, from $160 to $185.00
#239, Vanwall Racer, from $175 to.................................$225.00
#240, Cooper Racer, from $135 to $170.00
#240, Dinky Way Gift Set, from $270 to $300.00
#241, Lotus Racer, from $120 to....................................$140.00
#241, Silver Jubilee Taxi, from $120 to..........................$140.00
#242, Ferrari Racer, from $145 to...................................$165.00
#243, BRM Racer, from $145 to.....................................$165.00
#243, Volvo Police Racer, from $120 to.........................$140.00
#244, Plymouth Police Racer, from $125 to...................$145.00
#245, Superfast Gift Set, from $275 to...........................$325.00
#246, International Car Gift Set, from $275 to $325.00
#249, Racing Car Gift Set, from $1,450 to $1,750.00
#249, Racing Car Gift Set, in bubble pkg, from $1,750 to...$2,000.00
#250, Mini Cooper Police Car, from $140 to.................$175.00

#251, USA Police Car, Pontiac, from $145 to...............$180.00
#252, RCMP Car, Pontiac, from $145 to.......................$180.00
#254, Austin Taxi, yel, from $170 to..............................$220.00
#254, Police Range Rover, from $120 to........................$140.00
#255, Ford Zodiac Police Car, from $100 to..................$130.00
#255, Mersey Tunnel Police Van, from $130 to.............$160.00
#255, Police Mini Clubman, from $110 to $135.00
#256, Humber Hawk Police Car, from $175 to..............$225.00
#257, Nash Rambler Canadian Fire Chief Car, from $160 to..$200.00
#258, USA Police Car, Cadillac, Desoto, Dodge, or Ford, from
    $175 to..$225.00
#259, Bedford Fire Engine, from $160 to $200.00
#260, Royal Mail Van, from $175 to $225.00
#260, VW Deutsch Bundepost, from $225 to $275.00
#261, Ford Taunus Polizei, from $300 to $350.00
#261, Telephone Service Van, from $150 to $200.00
#262, VW Swiss Post PTT Car, casting #129, from $300 to...$350.00
#262, VW Swiss Post PTT Car, casting #181, minimum value,
    from $900 to...$1,250.00
#263, Airport Fire Rescue Tender, from $120 to.............$145.00
#263, Superior Criterion Ambulance, from $180 to.......$210.00
#264, RCMP Patrol Car, Cadillac, from $195 to $225.00
#264, RCMP Patrol Car, Fairlane, from $195 to............$225.00
#265, Plymouth Taxi, from $195 to................................$225.00
#266, ERF Fire Tender, Falck, from $155 to..................$180.00
#266, ERF Fire Tender, from $140 to $165.00
#266, Plymouth Taxi, Metro Cab, from $175 to............$225.00
#267, Paramedic Truck, from $140 to $165.00
#267, Superior Cadillac Ambulance, from $150 to $180.00
#268, Range Rover Ambulance, from $105 to................$135.00
#268, Renault Dauphine Mini Cab, from $165 to..........$195.00
#269, Ford Transit Police Accident Unit, Faulk Zonen, from $50
    to $75.00
#269, Ford Transit Police Accident Unit, from $105 to ..$135.00
#269, Jaguar Motorway Police Car, from $165 to $195.00
#270, AA Motorcycle Patrol, from $115 to $140.00
#270, Ford Panda Police Car, from $120 to $145.00
#271, Ford Transit Fire, Appliance, from $115 to..........$140.00
#271, Ford Transit Fire, Falck, from $160 to..................$190.00

#278, Plymouth Yellow Cab, MIB, from $105.00 to $135.00.

#271, TS Motorcycle Patrol, from $275 to $350.00

#272, ANWB Motorcycle Patrol, from $325 to..............$375.00

#272, Police Accident Unit, from $120 to......................$140.00

#273, RAC Patrol Mini Van, from $175 to......................$225.00

#274, Ford Transit Ambulance, from $115 to..................$145.00

#275, Brink's Armoured Car, no bullion, from $110 to ..$140.00

#275, Brink's Armoured Car, w/gold bullion, from $175 to..$225.00

#275, Brink's Armoured Car, w/Mexican bullion, from $950 to $1,250.00

#276, Airport Fire Tender, from $150 to $175.00

#276, Ford Transit Ambulance, from $120 to $145.00

#277, Police Range Rover, from $120 to..........................$145.00

#277, Superior Criterion Ambulance, from $150 to.......$200.00

#278, Vauxhall Victor Ambulance, from $120 to...........$145.00

#279, Aveling Barford Diesel Roller, from $120 to.........$145.00

#280, Midland Mobile Bank, from $130 to......................$165.00

#281, Fiat 2300 Pathe News Camera Car, from $175 to..$225.00

#281, Military Hovercraft, from $115 to.........................$140.00

#282, Austin 1800 Taxi, from $110 to $135.00

#282, Land Rover Fire, Appliance, from $110 to $135.00

#282, Land Rover Fire, Falck, from $110 to....................$135.00

#283, BOAC Coach, from $160 to $185.00

#283, Single-Decker Bus, from $120 to..........................$145.00

#284, London Austin Taxi, from $120 to........................$145.00

#285, Merryweather Fire Engine, Falck, from $135 to....$160.00

#285, Merryweather Fire Engine, from $130 to $155.00

#286, Ford Transit Fire, Falck, from $145 to..................$170.00

#288, Superior Cadillac Ambulance, Falck, from $160 to ..$200.00

#288, Superior Cadillac Ambulance, from $150 to $175.00

#289, Routemaster Bus, Esso, purple, from $775 to $850.00

#289, Routemaster Bus, Esso, red, from $150 to $175.00

#289, Routemaster Bus, Festival of London Stores, from $225 to $250.00

#289, Routemaster Bus, Madame Tussaud's, from $175 to ..$200.00

#289, Routemaster Bus, Silver Jubilee, from $125 to......$150.00

#289, Routemaster Bus, Tern Shirts or Schwepps, from $150 to $175.00

#290, Double-Decker Bus, from $175 to $200.00

#290, SRN-6 Hovercraft, from $135 to...........................$160.00

#291, Atlantean City Bus, from $125 to $150.00

#292, Atlantean City Bus, Regent or Ribble, from $150 to...$175.00

#293, Swiss Postal Bus, from $120 to $140.00

#295, Atlantean City Bus, Yellow Pages, from $90 to $120.00

#296, Duple Luxury Coach, from $70 to.........................$90.00

#296, Police Accident Unit, from $175 to......................$200.00

#297, Silver Jubilee Bus, National or Woolworth, from $125 to..$150.00

#298, Emergency Services Gift Set, minimum value, from $1,000 to..$1,500.00

#299, Crash Squad Gift Set, from $150 to......................$175.00

#299, Motorway Services Gift Set, minimum value, from $1,250 to $1,750.00

#299, Post Office Services Gift Set, minimum value, from $750 to $1,250.00

#300, London Scene Gift Set, from $125 to $150.00

#302, Emergency Squad Gift Set, from $125 to..............$150.00

#303, Commando Gift Set, from $200 to $225.00

#304, Fire Rescue Gift Set, from $175 to........................$200.00

#305, David Brown Tractor, from $125 to......................$150.00

#308, Leyland 384 Tractor, from $125 to.......................$150.00

#309, Star Trek Gift Set, from $225 to...........................$275.00

#319, Week's Tipping Farm Trailer, from $125 to...........$150.00

#320, Halesowen Harvest Trailer, from $125 to..............$150.00

#321, Massey-Harris Manure Spreader, from $125 to.....$150.00

#322, Disc Harrow, from $115 to...................................$140.00

#323, Triple Gang Mower, from $115 to $140.00

#324, Hay Rake, from $115 to.......................................$140.00

#325, David Brown Tractor & Harrow, from $160 to.....$185.00

#340, Land Rover, from $140 to $165.00

#341, Land Rover Trailer, from $90 to...........................$115.00

#342, Austin Mini Moke, from $175 to.........................$200.00

#342, Moto-Cart, from $120 to.....................................$145.00

#344, Estate Car, from $145 to......................................$170.00

#344, Land Rover Pickup, from $130 to $155.00

#350, Tiny's Mini Moke, from $195 to...........................$235.00

#351, UFO Interceptor, from $180 to $210.00

#352, Ed Straker's Car, red, from $175 to.......................$205.00

#352, Ed Straker's Car, yel or gold-plated, from $225 to.$250.00

#353, Shado 2 Mobile, from $250 to $300.00

#354, Pink Panther, from $230 to $250.00

#355, Lunar Roving Vehicle, from $180 to $215.00

#357, Klingon Battle Cruiser, from $225 to $275.00

#358, USS Enterprise, from $225 to...............................$250.00

#359, Eagle Transporter, from $300 to $325.00

#360, Eagle Freighter, from $225 to $250.00

#361, Galactic War Chariot, from $210 to $235.00

#362, Trident Star Fighter, from $230 to........................$255.00

#363, Cosmic Zygon Patroller, for Marks & Spencer, from $230 to $255.00

#364, NASA Space Shuttle, w/booster, from $225 to $250.00

#366, NASA Space Shuttle, no booster, from $200 to...$220.00

#367, Space Battle Cruiser, from $210 to.......................$235.00

#368, Zygon Marauder, from $210 to $235.00

#370, Dragster Set, from $180 to...................................$205.00

#371, USS Enterprise, sm version, from $180 to $220.00

#372, Klingon Battle Cruiser, sm version, from $180 to.$220.00

#380, Convoy Skip Truck, from $120 to $145.00

#381, Convoy Farm Truck, from $120 to $145.00

#382, Wheelbarrow, from $105 to $130.00

#382 Convoy Dumper, from $120 to..............................$145.00

#383, Convoy NCL Truck, from $120 to $145.00

#384, Convoy Fire Rescue Truck, from $115 to................$140.00

#384, Grass Cutter, from $115 to $140.00

#384, Sack Truck, from $90 to $115.00

#385, Convoy Royal Mail Truck, from $115 to $140.00

#386, Lawn Mower, from $115 to...................................$140.00

#389, Med Artillery Tractor, from $90 to.......................$115.00

#390, Customized Transit Van, from $115 to.................$140.00

#398, Farm Equipment Gift Set, from $1,850 to $2,350.00

#399, Farm Tractor & Trailer Set, from $250 to.............$275.00

#400, BEV Electric Truck, from $115 to $140.00

#401, Coventry-Climax Fork Lift, orange, from $115 to ..$140.00

#401, Coventry-Climax Fork Lift, red, from $475 to......$550.00

#404, Conveyancer Fork Lift, from $115 to...................$140.00

#402, Bedford Coca-Cola Truck, from $265.00 to $310.00.

#430, Commer Breakdown Lorry, all colors other than tan and green, from $950.00 to $1,300.00.

#405, Universal Jeep, from $140 to $175.00
#406, Commer Articulated Truck, from $195 to $220.00
#407, Ford Transit, from $115 to.....................................$140.00
#408, Big Ben Lorry, bl & yel, or bl & orange, from $350 to ..$375.00
#408, Big Ben Lorry, maroon & fawn, from $300 to.......$325.00
#408, Big Ben Lorry, pk & cream, from $1,950 to.......$2,350.00
#409, Bedford Articulated Lorry, from $275 to...............$300.00
#410, Bedford Van, Danish Post or Simpsons, from $180 to...$210.00
#410, Bedford Van, MJ Hire, Marley or Collectors' Gazette, from
$160 to..$195.00
#410, Bedford Van, Royal Mail, from $115 to $140.00
#411, Bedford Truck, from $170 to..................................$195.00
#412, Bedford Van AA, from $115 to $140.00
#413, Austin Covered Wagon, lt & dk bl, or red & tan, from
$675 to..$750.00
#413, Austin Covered Wagon, maroon & cream, or med & lt bl,
from $220 to $250.00
#413, Austin Covered Wagon, red & gray, or bl or cream, from
$450 to..$500.00
#414, Dodge Tipper, all colors other than Royal bl, from $170
to $195.00
#414, Dodge Tipper, Royal bl, from $190 to $215.00
#416, Ford Transit Van, from $115 to $140.00
#416, Ford Transit Van, 1,000,000 Transits, from $210 to ..$240.00
#417, Ford Transit Van, from $115 to $140.00
#417, Leyland Comet Lorry, from $170 to $295.00
#419, Leyland Comet Cement Lorry, from $350 to........$375.00
#420, Leyland Forward Control Lorry, from $170 to $195.00
#421, Hindle-Smart Electric Lorry, from $170 to $195.00
#422, Thames Flat Truck, bright gr, from $225 to $250.00
#422, Thames Flat Truck, dk gr or red, from $170 to......$195.00
#425, Bedford TK Coal Lorry, from $225 to $250.00
#428, Trailer, lg, from $115 to $140.00
#429, Trailer, from $115 to $140.00
#430, Commer Breakdown Lorry, tan & gr, from $195 to...$225.00
#430, Johnson Dumper, from $115 to $140.00
#432, Foden Tipper, from $115 to $140.00

#432, Guy Warrior Flat Truck, from $450 to $525.00
#433, Guy Flat Truck w/Tailboard, from $550 to............$600.00
#434, Bedford Crash Truck, from $165 to $200.00
#435, Bedford TK Tipper, gray or yel cab, from $170 to .$210.00
#435, Bedford TK Tipper, wht, silver & bl, from $250 to...$275.00
#436, Atlas COPCO Compressor Lorry, from $145 to ...$170.00
#437, Muir Hill Loader, from $145 to $170.00
#438, Ford D 800 Tipper, opening doors, from $120 to ..$145.00
#439, Ford D 800 Snow Plough & Tipper, from $145 to...$170.00
#440, Mobilgas Tanker, from $170 to..............................$195.00
#441, Petrol Tanker, Castrol, from $195 to.....................$220.00
#442, Land Rover Breakdown Crane, Falck, from $145 to ..$270.00
#442, Land Rover Breakdown Crane, from $120 to $145.00
#442, Petrol Tanker, Esso, from $170 to..........................$195.00
#443, Petrol Tanker, National Benzole, from $170 to.....$195.00
#449, Chevrolet El Camino Pickup, from $145 to..........$170.00
#449, Johnson Road Sweeper, from $120 to $145.00
#450, Bedford TK Box Van, Castrol, from $270 to.........$295.00
#451, Johnston Road Sweeper, opening doors, from $120 to..$145.00
#451, Trojan Van, Dunlop, from $225 to $250.00
#452, Trojan Van, Chivers, from $250 to.......................$275.00
#454, Trojan Van Cydrax, from $225 to..........................$250.00
#455, Trojan Van, Brooke Bond Tea, from $600 to $750.00
#470, Austin Van, Shell-BP, from $225 to.......................$250.00
#475, Ford Model T, from $170 to...................................$195.00
#476, Morris Oxford, from $170 to $195.00
#477, Parsley's Car, from $170 to $195.00
#480, Bedford Van, Kodak, from $225 to $250.00
#481, Bedford Van, Ovaltine, from $225 to $250.00
#482, Bedford Van, Dinky Toys, from $225 to $250.00
#485, Ford Model T w/Santa Claus, from $225 to..........$250.00
#486, Morris Oxford, Dinky Beats, from $170 to...........$195.00
#490, Electric Dairy Van, Express Dairy, from $200 to ...$225.00
#491, Electric Dairy Van, NCB or Job Dairies, from $200 to..$225.00
#492, Election Mini Van, from $350 to $395.00
#492, Loudspeaker Van, from $180 to............................$200.00
#500, Citroen 2-CV, from $180 to $210.00

#501, Foden Diesel 8-Wheel, second cab, from $700.00 to $850.00.

#501, Citroen Police, DS-19, from $170 to $195.00
#502, Foden Flat Truck, 1st or 2nd cab, from $1,000 to..$1,250.00
#503, Foden Flat Truck, 1st cab, from $1,250 to $1,500.00
#503, Foden Flat Truck, 2nd cab, bl & orange, from $400 to ..$450.00
#503, Foden Flat Truck, 2nd cab, bl & yel, from $1,000 to ..$1,500.00
#503, Foden Flat Truck, 2nd cab, 2-tone gr, from $2,750 to ..$3,250.00
#504, Foden Tanker, red, from $750 to $950.00
#504, Foden Tanker, 1st cab, 2-tone bl, from $475 to $525.00
#504, Foden Tanker, 2nd cab, red, from $600 to.............$650.00
#504, Foden Tanker, 2nd cab, 2-tone bl, from $3,500 to $3,750.00
#505, Foden Flat Truck w/Chains, 1st cab, from $3,000 to...$3,250.00
#505, Foden Flat Truck w/Chains, 2nd cab, from $425 to........$475.00
#505, Maserati 2000, from $200 to.............................$225.00
#506, Aston Martin, from $200 to $225.00
#509, Fiat 850, from $175 to $200.00
#510, Peugeot 204, from $175 to..............................$200.00
#511, Guy 4-Ton Lorry, red, gr or brn, from $850 to ...$1,050.00
#511, Guy 4-Ton Lorry, 2-tone bl, from $350 to............$400.00
#512, Guy Flat Truck, all colors other than bl or red, from $750
        to $900.00
#512, Guy Flat Truck, bl or red, from $400 to................$450.00
#512, Lesko Kart, from $225 to $250.00
#513, Guy Flat Truck w/Tailboard, from $400 to $425.00
#514, Alfa Romeo Giulia, from $175 to.......................$200.00
#514, Guy Van, Lyons, from $2,000 to $2,500.00
#514, Guy Van, Slumberland, from $650 to $850.00
#514, Guy Van, Spratt's, from $650 to $850.00
#514, Guy Van, Weetabix, from $3,600 to $3,850.00
#515, Ferrari 250 GT, from $175 to...........................$200.00
#517, Renault R8, from $175 to...............................$200.00
#518, Renault 4L, from $150 to $175.00
#519, Simca 100, from $175 to................................$200.00
#520, Chrysler New Yorker, from $275 to.....................$325.00
#521, Bedford Articulated Lorry, from $175 to..............$200.00
#522, Big Bedford Lorry, bl & yel, from $350 to $375.00
#522, Big Bedford Lorry, maroon & fawn, from $200 to..$225.00
#522, Citroen DS-19, from $265 to $290.00
#523, Simca 1500, from $150 to...............................$175.00
#524, Panhard 24-CT, from $175 to..........................$200.00

#524, Renault Dauphine, from $175 to.........................$200.00
#525, Peugeot 403-U, from $225 to $250.00
#526, Mercedes-Benz 190-SL, from $200 to $225.00
#527, Alfa Romeo 1900, from $175 to..........................$200.00
#529, Vespa 2-CV, from $200 to...............................$225.00
#530, Citroen DS-23, from $125 to $150.00
#531, Leyland Comet Lorry, all colors other than bl or brn, from
        $275 to...$300.00
#531, Leyland Comet Lorry, bl or brn, from $650 to $700.00

#531, Leyland Comet Lorry, blue and orange, from $260.00 to $300.00.

#532, Bedford Comet Lorry w/Tailboard, from $275 to ..$300.00
#532, Lincoln Premiere, from $275 to $300.00
#533, Leyland Cement Wagon, from $225 to $300.00
#533, Peugeot, from $225 to...................................$250.00
#534, BMW 1500, from $200 to................................$225.00
#535, Citroen 2-CV, from $225 to $250.00
#538, Buick Roadmaster, from $350 to........................$375.00
#538, Renault 16-TX, from $175 to $200.00
#539, Citroen ID-19, from $225 to $250.00
#540, Opel Kadett, from $175 to..............................$200.00
#541, Simca Versailles, from $200 to $225.00
#542, Simca Taxi, from $200 to $225.00
#543, Renault Floride, from $185 to $210.00
#545, DeSoto Diplomat, from $210 to $235.00
#546, Austin-Healey, from $225 to $250.00
#548, Fiat 1800 Familiare, from $200 to $225.00
#550, Chrysler Saratoga, from $350 to $375.00
#551, Ford Taunus, Polizei, from $225 to $250.00
#551, Rolls Royce, from $300 to $325.00
#551, Trailer, from $75 to $90.00
#552, Chevrolet Corvair, from $230 to $255.00
#555, Fire Engine, w/extension ladder, from $150 to......$175.00
#555, Ford Thunderbird, from $265 to........................$280.00
#556, Citroen Ambulance, from $275 to $300.00
#558, Citroen, from $225 to...................................$250.00
#559, Ford Taunus, from $225 to..............................$250.00

#561, Blaw-Knox Bulldozer, from $125 to $150.00

#561, Blaw-Knox Bulldozer, plastic, from $600 to $625.00

#561, Citroen Van, Gervais, from $260 to.....................$285.00

#561, Renault Mail Car, from $175 to $200.00

#562, Muir-Hill Dumper, from $85 to............................$100.00

#563, Blaw-Knox Heavy Tractor, from $120 to $145.00

#563, Estafette Pickup, from $195 to $220.00

#564, Armagnac Caravan, from $150 to.........................$175.00

#564, Elevator Loader, from $150 to $175.00

#566, Citroen Police Van, from $205 to $230.00

#568, Ladder Truck, from $225 to $250.00

#569, Dump Truck, from $225 to $250.00

#570, Peugeot Van, from $200 to $225.00

#571, Coles Mobile Crane, from $150 to.......................$175.00

#572, Dump Truck, Berliet, from $225 to $250.00

#576, Panhard Tanker, Esso, from $350 to.....................$375.00

#577, Simca Van, Bailly, from $300 to $325.00

#578, Simca Dump Truck, from $250 to $275.00

#580, Dump Truck, from $250 to $275.00

#581, Container Truck, Bailly, from $250 to..................$275.00

#581, Horse Box, British Railway, from $260 to $285.00

#581, Horse Box, Express Horse Van, from $1,250 to ..$1,500.00

#582, Pullman Car Transporter, from $175 to.................$200.00

#584, Covered Truck, from $225 to $250.00

#585, Dumper, from $250 to..$275.00

#587, Citroen Van, Philips, from $250 to $275.00

#589, Berliet Wrecker, from $275 to $300.00

#590, City Road Signs Set, from $215 to $240.00

#591, AEC Tanker, Shell, from $225 to.........................$250.00

#591, Country Road Signs Set, from $215 to.................$240.00

#592, Gas Pumps, Esso, from $250 to............................$275.00

#593, Road Signs Set, from $250 to $275.00

#595, Crane, from $400 to...$425.00

#595, Traffic Signs Set, from $160 to $185.00

#597, Fork Lift, from $200 to $225.00

#601, Austin Para Moke, from $225 to..........................$250.00

#602, Armoured Command Car, from $150 to................$175.00

#603, Army Personnel, box of 12, from $115 to $140.00

#604, Land Rover Bomb Disposal Unit, from $135 to....$160.00

#609, 105mm Howitzer & Gun Crew, from $95 to.........$120.00

#612, Commando Jeep, from $95 to...............................$120.00

#615, US Jeep & 105mm Howitzer, from $120 to $145.00

#616, AEC Articulated Transporter & Tank, from $165 to...$190.00

#617, VW KDF w/Antitank Gun, from $195 to.............$220.00

#618, AEC Articulated Transporter & Helicopter, form $170 to $195.00

#619, Bren Gun Carrier & Antitank Gun, from $145 to...$170.00

#620, Berliet Missile Launcher, from $170 to $195.00

#621, 3-Ton Army Wagon, from $195 to.......................$220.00

#622, Bren Gun Carrier, from $125 to $150.00

#622, 10-Ton Army Truck, from $195 to $220.00

#623, Army Covered Wagon, from $195 to $220.00

#625, 6-Pounder Antitank Gun, from $120 to $145.00

#626, Military Ambulance, from $165 to........................$190.00

#640, Bedford Military Truck, from $325 to..................$350.00

#641, Army 1-Ton Cargo Truck, from $165 to $190.00

#642, RAF Pressure Refueller, from $195 to $220.00

#643, Army Water Carrier, from $200 to.......................$225.00

#650, Light Tank, from $225 to.....................................$250.00

#651, Centurion Tank, from $200 to $225.00

#654, Mobile Gun, from $125 to....................................$150.00

#656, 88mm Gun, from $125 to $150.00

#660, Tank Transporter, from $200 to............................$225.00

#661, Recovery Tractor, from $250 to............................$275.00

#662, Static 88mm Gun & Crew, from $125 to..............$150.00

#665, Honest John Missile Erector, from $275 to $300.00

#666, Missile Erector Vehicle w/Corporal Missile & Launching Platform, from $525 to $550.00

#667, Armoured Patrol Car, from $125 to $150.00

#667, Missile Servicing Platform Vehicle, from $350 to..$375.00

#668, Foden Army Truck, from $125 to.........................$150.00

#670, Armoured Car, from $200 to $225.00

#671, MKI Corvette (boat), from $125 to $150.00

#671, Reconnaissance Car, from $200 to $225.00

#672, OSA Missile Boat, from $150 to $175.00

#673, Scout Car, from $175 to.......................................$200.00

#674, Austin Champ, olive drab, from $170 to $195.00

#674, Austin Champ, wht, UN version, from $525 to ...$540.00

#674, Coast Guard Missile Launch, from $175 to $200.00

#675, Motor Patrol Boat, from $150 to..........................$175.00

#676, Armoured Personnel Carrier, from $175 to...........$200.00

#676, Daimler Armoured Car, w/speedwheels, from $150 to ...$175.00

#677, Armoured Command Vehicle, from $175 to $200.00

#677, Task Force Sct, from $180 to $210.00

#678, Air Sea Rescue, from $175 to...............................$200.00

#680, Ferret Armoured Car, from $120 to......................$145.00

#681, DUKW, from $170 to $195.00

#682, Stalwart Load Carrier, from $165 to.....................$190.00

#683, Chieftain Tank, from $175 to...............................$200.00

#686, 25-Pounder Field Gun, from $140 to $165.00

#687, Convoy Army Truck, from $125 to $150.00

#687, Trailer, from $45 to $60.00

#688, Field Artillery Tractor, from $145 to....................$170.00

#690, Mobile Antiaircraft Gun, from $170 to $195.00

#690, Scorpion Tank, from $175 to................................$200.00

#691, Striker Antitank Vehicle, from $175 to $200.00

#692, Leopard Tank, from $170 to $195.00

#692, 5.5 Med Gun, from $170 to..................................$195.00

#693, 7.2 Howitzer, from $170 to $195.00

#694, Hanomag Tank Destroyer, from $150 to $175.00

#695, Howitzer & Tractor, from $250 to $275.00

#696, Leopard Anti-aircraft Tank, from $175 to............$200.00

#697, 25-Pounder Field Gun Set, from $215 to.............$240.00

#698, Tank Transporter & Tank, from $335 to $360.00

#699, Leopard Recovery Tank, from $165 to.................$190.00

#699, Military Gift Set, from $1,000 to $1,250.00

#700, Spitfire MKII RAF Jubilee, from $165 to.............$190.00

#701, Shetland Flying Boat, from $875 to $925.00

#702, DH Comet Jet Airliner, from $240 to $265.00

#704, Avro York Airliner, from $190 to.........................$215.00

#705, Viking Airliner, from $165 to..............................$190.00

#706, Vickers Viscount Airliner, Air France, from $165 to..$190.00

#708, Vickers Viscount Airliner, BEA, from $165 to $190.00

#710, Beechcraft S35 Bonanza, from $165 to $190.00

#712, US Army T-42A, from $120 to $145.00

#715, Beechcraft C-55 Baron, from $170 to $195.00

#715, Bristol 173 Helicopter, from $170 to..................$195.00

#716, Westland Sikorsky Helicopter, from $85 to $110.00

#717, Boeing 737, from $80 to $95.00

#718, Hawker Hurricane, from $80 to...........................$95.00

#719, Spitfire MKII, from $80 to $95.00

#721, Junkers Stuka, from $75 to..................................$90.00

#722, Hawker Harrier, from $75 to................................$95.00

#723, Hawker Executive Jet, from $55 to $80.00

#724, Sea King Helicopter, from $70 to $95.00

#725, Phantom II, from $95 to $120.00

#726, Messerschmitt, desert camouflage, from $95 to $120.00

#726, Messerschmitt, gray & gr, from $190 to $215.00

#727, US Air Force F-4 Phantom II, from $295 to........$320.00

#728, RAF Dominie, from $75 to................................$100.00

#729, Multi-Role Combat Aircraft, from $70 to............$95.00

#730, US Navy Phantom, from $95 to.........................$120.00

#731, SEPECAT Jaguar, from $75 to...........................$100.00

#731, Twin-Engine Fighter, from $50 to.......................$75.00

#732, Bell Police Helicopter, M*A*S*H, from $100 to ..$125.00

#732, Bell Police Helicopter, wht & bl, from $60 to........$85.00

#733, German Phantom II, from $200 to.....................$225.00

#733, Lockhead Shooting Star Fighter, from $50 to $75.00

#734, Submarine Swift, from $60 to..............................$85.00

#735, Glouster Javelin, from $60 to $85.00

#736, Bundesmarine Sea King, from $90 to..................$115.00

#736, Hawker Hunter, from $60 to...............................$85.00

#737, P1B Lightning Fighter, from $90 to....................$115.00

#738, DH110 Sea Vixen Fighter, from $70 to...............$95.00

#739, Zero-Sen, from $100 to.....................................$125.00

#741, Spitfire MKII, from $100 to..............................$125.00

#749, RAF Avro Vulcan Bomber, from $3,450 to $3,750.00

#750, Call Telephone Box, from $50 to.........................$75.00

#751, Lawn Mower, from $100 to...............................$125.00

#752, Goods Yard Crane, from $75 to.........................$100.00

#752, Police Box, from $50 to $65.00

#755, Standard Lamp, single arm, from $25 to $40.00

#756, Standard Lamp, dbl arm, from $25 to..................$40.00

#760, Pillar Box, from $35 to.......................................$50.00

#766, British Road Signs, Country Set A, from $90 to...$115.00

#767, British Road Signs, Country Set B, from $90 to ...$115.00

#768, British Road Signs, Town Set A, from $90 to.......$115.00

#769, British Road Signs, Town B, from $90 to..............$115.00

#770, Road Signs, set of 12, from $140 to.....................$165.00

#771, International Road Signs, set of 12, from $150 to...$175.00

#772, British Road Signs, set of 24, from $185 to $210.00

#773, Traffic Signal, from $25 to $40.00

#777, Belisha Beacon, from $25 to $40.00

#781, Petrol Pumping Station, Esso, from $90 to $115.00

#782, Petrol Pumping Station, Shell, from $75 to...........$90.00

#784, Dinky Goods Train Set, from $150 to $175.00

#785, Service Station, from $385 to..............................$420.00

#786, Tire Rack, from $150 to.....................................$175.00

#787, Lighting Kit, from $70 to....................................$85.00

#796, Healy Sports Boat, from $170 to $195.00

#798, Express Passenger Train, from $250 to $275.00

#801, Mini USS Enterprise, from $120 to.....................$160.00

#802, Mini Klingon Cruiser, from $120 to....................$160.00

#815, Panhard Armoured Tank, from $245 to $270.00

#817, AMX 13-Ton Tank, from $220 to.......................$245.00

#822, M3 Half-Track, from $240 to $265.00

#893, UNIC Pipe-Line Transporter, from $450 to.........$475.00

#894, UNIC Boilot Car Transporter, from $400 to.........$425.00

#900, Building Site Gift Set, from $1,500 to...............$1,650.00

#901, Foden 8-Wheel Truck, from $450 to...................$475.00

#902, Foden Flat Truck, from $450 to..........................$475.00

#903, Foden Flat Truck w/Tailboard, from $750 to.........$800.00

#905, Foden Flat Truck With Chains, from $475.00 to $525.00.

#911, Guy 4-Ton Lorry, from $475 to...........................$500.00

#912, Guy Flat Truck, from $475 to $500.00

#913, Guy Flat Truck w/Tailboard, from $625 to...........$650.00

#914, AEC Articulated Lorry, from $200 to $225.00

#915, AEC Flat Trailer, from $175 to............................$200.00

#917, Guy Van, Spratts, from $650 to...........................$700.00

#917, Mercedes Benz Truck & Trailer, from $375 to $400.00

#917, Mercedes Benz Truck & Trailer, Munsterland, from $375 to..$400.00

#923, Big Bedford Van, Heinz 57 Varieties and Heinz Baked Beans Can, from $725.00 to $800.00.

#918, Guy Van, Ever Ready, from $800 to $950.00

#919, Guy Van, Golden Shred, from $2,000 to $2,250.00

#920, Guy Warrior Van, Heinz, from $3,000 to...........$3,250.00

#921, Bedford Articulated Lorry, from $325 to..............$350.00

#922, Big Bedford Lorry, from $325 to $350.00

#923, Big Bedford Van, Heinz Ketchup bottle, from $2,000 to $2,250.00

#924, Aveling-Barford Dumper, from $175 to................$200.00

#925, Leyland Dump Truck, from $250 to $275.00

#930, Bedford Pallet-Jekta Van, Dinky Toys, from $375 to ..$400.00

#931, Leyland Comet Lorry, all colors other than bl & brn, from $275 to...$300.00

#931, Leyland Comet Lorry, bl & brn, from $525 to $550.00

#932, Leyland Comet Wagon w/Tailboard, from $275 to ..$300.00

#933, Leyland Cement Truck, from $300 to $325.00

#934, Leyland Octopus Wagon, all colors other than bl & brn, from $650 to $700.00

#934, Leyland Octopus Wagon, bl & yel, from $2,000 to ..$2,250.00

#936, Leyland 8-Wheel Test Chassis, from $225 to........$250.00

#940, Mercedes Benz Truck, from $175 to $200.00

#943, Leyland Octopus Tanker, Esso, from $450 to $500.00

#944, Shell-BP Fuel Tanker, from $325 to $350.00

#944, Shell-BP Fuel Tanker, red wheels, from $675 to ...$725.00

#945, AEC Fuel Tanker, Esso, from $200 to $225.00

#945, AEC Fuel Tanker, Lucas, from $250 to $275.00

#948, Tractor-Trailer, McLean, from $400 to.................$425.00

#949, Wayne School Bus, from $400 to $425.00

#950, Foden S20 Fuel Tanker, Burmah, from $200 to $225.00

#950, Foden S20 Fuel Tanker, Shell, from $200 to........$225.00

#951, Trailer, from $125 to $140.00

#952, Vega Major Luxury Coach, from $200 to..............$240.00

#953, Continental Touring Coach, from $425.00 to $475.00.

#954, Fire Station, from $425 to $450.00

#954, Vega Major Luxury Coach, no lights, from $175 to ..$200.00

#955, Fire Engine, from $200 to $225.00

#956, Turntable Fire Escape, Bedford, from $200 to $225.00

#956, Turntable Fire Escape, Berliet, from $250 to........$275.00

#957, Fire Services Gift Set, from $650 to $725.00

#958, Snow Plough, from $325 to $350.00

#959, Foden Dump Truck, from $300 to $325.00

#960, Lorry-Mounted Concrete Mixer, from $200 to $225.00

#961, Blaw-Knox Bulldozer, from $175 to $200.00

#961, Vega Major Luxury Coach, from $350 to..............$375.00

#962, Muir-Hill Dumper, from $175 to $200.00

#963, Blaw-Knox Heavy Tractor, from $175 to $200.00

#963, Road Grader, from $150 to $175.00

#964, Elevator Loader, from $175 to $200.00

#965, Euclid Rear Dump Truck, from $200 to $225.00

#965, Terex Dump Truck, from $275 to $300.00

#966, Marrel Multi-Bucket Unit, from $175 to $200.00

#967, BBC TV Mobile Control Room, from $350 to $375.00

#967, Muir-Hill Loader & Trencher, from $150 to.........$175.00

#968, BBC TV Roving Eye Vehicle, from $350 to $375.00

#969, BBC TV Extending Mast Vehicle, from $350 to ..$375.00

#970, Jones Cantilever Crane, from $150 to...................$165.00

#971, Coles Mobile Crane, from $200 to $215.00

#972, Coles 20-Ton Lorry, mounted crane, yel & blk, from $225 to..$250.00

#972, Coles 20-Ton Lorry, mounted crane, yellow and orange, from $200.00 to $225.00.

#973, Eaton Yale Tractor Shovel, from $600 to $650.00

#973, Goods Yard Crane, from $200 to..........................$225.00

#974, AEC Hoyner Transporter, from $175 to................$200.00

#975, Ruston Bucyrus Excavator, from $375 to $400.00

#976, Michigan Tractor Dozer, from $275 to $300.00

#977, Commercial Servicing Platform Vehicle, from $325 to...$350.00

#977, Shovel Dozer, from $200 to $225.00

#978, Refuse Wagon, from $200 to $225.00

#979, Racehorse Transporter, from $625 to $675.00

#980, Coles Hydra Truck, from $225 to $250.00

#980, Horse Box, British Railways, from $375 to $400.00

#980, Horse Box Express, from $850 to $1,000.00

#984, Atlas Digger, from $200 to $225.00

#984, Car Carrier, from $475 to $525.00

#985, Trailer for Car Carrier, from $200 to $225.00

#986, Mighty Antar Low Loader w/Propeller, from $500 to..**$525.00**
#987, ABC TV Control Room, from $500 to **$550.00**
#988, ABC TV Transmitter Van. from $500 to **$550.00**
#989, Auto Transporters, from $2,000 to.....................**$2,250.00**
#990, Pullman Car Transporter w/4 Cars, from $2,500 to..**$2,750.00**
#991, AEC Tanker, Shell Chemicals, from $350 to........**$375.00**
#992, Avro Vulcan Delta Wing Bomber, from $3,500 to..**$3,750.00**
#994, Loading Ramp for #992, from $100 to **$125.00**
#997, Caravelle, Air France, from $375 to.....................**$400.00**
#998, Bristol Britannia Canadian Pacific, from $375 to ..**$400.00**
#999, DH Comet Jet, from $375 to **$400.00**

Disney

Through the magic of the silver screen, Walt Disney's characters have come to life, and it is virtually impossible to imagine a child growing up without the influence of his genius. As each classic film was introduced, toy manufacturers scurried to fill department store shelves with the dolls, games, battery-ops, and windups that carried the likeness of every member of its cast. Though today it is the toys of the 1930s and 1940s that are bringing top prices, later toys are certainly collectible as well, as you'll see in our listings. Even characters as recently introduced as Roger Rabbit already have their own cult following.

Since the advent of the Internet, condition and rarity are much more important than ever when it comes to evaluation. Disney limited editions purchased within the past ten years would probably get 75% of the their original purchase price. Vintage items, however, have remained steady in value over the past several years.

For more information we recommend *Disneyana* by Cecil Munsey (Hawthorne Books, 1974); *Disneyana* by Robert Heide and John Gilman; *Walt Disney's Mickey Mouse Memorabilia* by Hillier and Shine (Abrams Inc., 1986); *Tomart's Disneyana Update Magazine*; and *Elmer's Price Guide to Toys* by Elmer Duellman (L-W Books).

Advisor: Joel J. Cohen (C12)

See also Battery-Operated; Books; Bubble Bath Containers; Character and Promotional Drinking Glasses; Character Clocks and Watches; Chein; Coloring, Activity, and Paint Books; Fisher-Price; Games; Lunch Boxes; Marx; Pin-Back Buttons; Plastic Figures; Puzzles; Ramp Walkers; Records; Sand Toys; View Master; Western; Windups, Friction, and Other Mechanicals.

Art Paper w/Drawing Guide, Mickey & Donald cutting & pasting on front wrapper, complete, WDP, 1940s, 12x9" pkg, EXIP, P6 ....**$30.00**
Art Stamp Picture Set, Snow White & the Seven Dwarfs, Fulton/WDE, 1930s, VGIB...**$50.00**
Baby Rattle, Mickey Mouse, celluloid bead figure w/elastic string, bells for feet, vintage, 3½", VG, P6.................**$50.00**
Bank, Donald Duck seated & holding coin, ceramic, 7½", 1940s, NM...**$175.00**

Baby Rattle, Mickey seated atop ball, celluloid, Japan, 5", EX+, $200.00. (Photo courtesy Bertoia Auctions)

Bank, Donald Duck standing with arm around nautical object with rope and coin slot, painted composition, Walt Disney Productions, 1938, 6", VG, A, $185.00; Bank, Mickey Mouse standing and leaning forward on trunk, painted composition, Walt Disney Crown Toy, 6", VG, A, $165.00. (Photo courtesy Randy Inman Auctions)

Bank, Donald Duck, Second National Duck Bank, litho tin w/images of Donald, Micky & Minnie, Chein, NMIB..**$150.00**
Bank, Mickey, Minnie & Pluto featured in Post Office graphics on litho tin canister, Happynak/England, 6", NM, A **$75.00**
Bank, Mickey Mouse head, ceramic, 1950s, 6", EX+ **$50.00**
Bank, Pinocchio figure, plastic, Play Pal, 1960s, 12", EX+ .**$20.00**
Bank, Pinocchio head form, vinyl, Play Pal, 1970s, 10", NM+ .**$25.00**
Bank, Pinocchio leaning against tree stump, pnt compo, WDE, 1940s, 5½", NM...**$75.00**
Bank, Pooh's Honey Bank marked on pot between Pooh's legs, ceramic, Enesco/WDP, 1964, 6", EX, P6 ....**$85.00**
Bank, Uncle Scrooge head figure w/wire glasses, ceramic, Cuernavaca/WDP, 1960s, 11", rare, EX, P6 ....**$950.00**
Banner, Disneyland lettered above park scenes, linen w/wood dowl, WDP, 1960s, 28x16", NM+ **$75.00**

Barette, Snow White, Catalin plastic bow shape w/decaled bust image of Snow White flanked by 2 dwarfs, 2", EX+ ..**$30.00**

Birthday Party Kit, Donald Duck on box, Rendoll Paper Co, 1940s, some use, incomplete o/w VGIB, P6.............**$55.00**

Book, Disney on Parade ('73), Mary Poppins cover, 1973, M, P6...**$30.00**

Book, Forever Hold Your Banner High, by Jerry Bowles, 1976, 1st ed, hardback, 151 pgs, EX, P6...............................**$25.00**

Bracelet, Donald Duck, enameled image on wht heart on gold-&-silver tone flexible band, 1940s, EX, P6 ....**$55.00**

Bracelet, Snow White & the Seven Dwarfs, 8 enameled metal charm figures on chain, WD, 1938, 7", VG+.............**$50.00**

Bubble-Blowing Figure, Mickey Mouse, hard rubber, Tootsietoy, 1993, 5", MIP..**$5.00**

Camera, Donald Duck, blk plastic, Herbert George Co, 2½x4½", EX (w/partial box), A.............................**$135.00**

Candy Dispensers, Toy Story characters, sold at McDonald's, 1999, NM, ea **$5.00**

Card Game, Old Maid, box only, Mickey graphic on front, Whitman, 1930s, EX **$25.00**

Card Game, see also Playing Cards

Cereal Bowl, plastic w/image of Mickey in center, Warner-craft, 5½" dia, NM+IB (box reads MM Child's Cereal Bowl), A **$300.00**

Character Plaks, set of 6 w/Mickey, Donald, Bambi, Thumper, Flower & Pluto, die-cut cb, YPS, 1942, assembled, EX **$175.00**

Christmas Lights, 8 lamps w/decals of various characters, w/box, 1930s, EXIB **$225.00**

Color-By-Number Oil Set, Disneyland, Hasbro #2195, 1950s, unused, NMIB...**$65.00**

Colorforms Sew-Ons, 'Mickey and Minnie in lots of swell new clothes,' 6 unused cards, 1970s, EXIB, P6 ....**$30.00**

Dexterity Puzzle, Mickey Mouse, rectangular box w/image of Mickey on skis, complete w/18 balls, 1930s, 4x6", NM, A..........**$175.00**

Dexterity Puzzle, Mickey Mouse, rnd w/image of Mickey 'juggling' balls, BV Paris, 2" dia, EX+, A **$75.00**

Dolls, see Figures

Drum, Mickey, Minnie, Donald & Pluto parading w/instruments, litho tin, Ohio Art/WDE, 6½" dia, EX...................**$200.00**

Drum, Mickey Mouse, pnt wood w/paper top & bottom, w/drum stick, Nobel & Cooley/Borgfeldt, 1930s, 6½" dia, NM, A..**$225.00**

Egg Coloring Kit, 101 Dalmatians, Sunhill, complete & unused, MIP (sealed)..**$5.00**

Egg Cup, Donald Duck, ceramic, emb pnt image of Donald's head on side of footed cup, vintage, 4", VG, P6 ....**$65.00**

Egg Cup, Mickey Mouse, porcelain, figural w/pnt detail, 1930s, 3", EX, P6...**$125.00**

Figure, see also Figure Sets

Figure, Aladdin, beanbag type in purple & wht outfit, 11", EX..**$8.00**

Figure, Alice (Alice in Wonderland), hard plastic, standing on rnd base waving, WDP, 1960s, sold w/wristwatch, 5", EX...**$35.00**

Figure, Baloo (Jungle Book), beanbag type, 8", EX **$5.00**

Figure, Bambi, celluloid, attached to a metal holder stand, WD, 1940s, 4", EX, P6...**$75.00**

Figure, Beast (Beauty & the Beast), plush & felt, Mattel, 1992, 12", EX **$15.00**

Figure, Beast or Belle (Beauty & the Beast), PVC, Applause, 2½", NM, ea...**$4.00**

Figure, Belle (Beauty & the Beast), PVC, bendable, Just Toys, 4½", NM **$5.00**

Figure, Bianca (Rescuers Down Under), beanbag type, 8", NM+...**$5.00**

Figure, Brer Bear (Song of the South), ceramic, holding club, Walt Disney World, 1970s, 7", EX, P6 ....**$45.00**

Figure, Buzz Light Year (Toy Story), beanbag type, Kellogg's premium, 5", MIP..**$5.00**

Figure, Captain Hook, plastic, 8", NM+ **$20.00**

Figure, Chip (Chip 'N Dale Rescue Ranger), plush, brn coat w/fur trim, beige hat, w/orig tag, 10", EX....................**$8.00**

Figure, Chip (Chip 'N Dale), beanbag type, 8", NM **$8.00**

Figure, Christopher Robin (Winnie the Pooh), ceramic, beating drum while leaning on tree stump, Enesco, 1964, 6", EX, P6...**$55.00**

Figure, Cinderella, bl satin dress w/lace trim, 7", NM+ **$10.00**

Figure, Dale (Chip 'N Dale), PVC, cereal premium, sm, MIP..**$4.00**

Figure, Donald Duck, celluloid, roly poly figure w/push-down head causing squeaking noises, 1930s, 6⅓", EX, A..**$330.00**

Figure, Donald Duck, celluloid, string-jtd, 3", VG, A **$135.00**

Figure, Donald Duck, ceramic, pirate w/hands on hips, WDP, 1970s, 3½", EX, P6...**$30.00**

Figure, Donald Duck, ceramic, strutting w/head up, bl coat & hat, orange beak & feet, Japan, 3", G+, A **$50.00**

Figure, Donald Duck, compo, standing w/hands on hips, movable head, long bill, no base, Knickerbocker, 1930s, 5½", EX **$400.00**

Figure, Donald Duck, stuffed canvas with painted cloth eyes, stiched features, blue corduroy jacket and hat, Knickerbocker, 16", EX, A, $300.00; Figure, Donald Duck, stuffed, Drum Major, windup (nonworking), Knickerbocker, 14", G, A, $300.00. (Photo courtesy Bertoia Auctions)

Figure, Donald Duck, rubber, standing w/legs & arms spread, WDP/Hong Kong, 1970s, 5¼", EX, P6 ....$15.00

Figure, Donald Duck, squeeze rubber, Sun Rubber, 1950s, 10½", EX+ $65.00

Figure, Donald Duck, stuffed, Disney Baby, Playskool #70480, 1984, EX...$12.00

Figure, Donald Duck, stuffed, drum major, Knickerbocker, 1930s, 17", EX+ $350.00

Figure, Donald Duck, stuffed, talker, Mattel, 1970s, EX+ .$100.00

Figure, Donald Duck, vinyl, standing w/1 hand on chest & the other at side, feet apart, Holland Hall, 1950s, 7", EX, P6 ....$30.00

Figure, Donald's nephew, ceramic, standing w/hands on hips & billed hat turned to side, WDP, 1960s, 3½", EX, P6 ....$25.00

Figure, Donald's nephew (Louie), beanbag type, 8", EX $6.00

Figure, Dumbo, ceramic, seated w/trunk up & looking up, WDP, 1950s-60s, 5", EX, P6...$50.00

Figure, Dumbo, ceramic, sitting upright wearing bonnet, Shaw, 1940s, 6", VG...$75.00

Figure, Dumpo, squeeze rubber, Dell, 1950s, 5", EX+ $25.00

Figure, Elephant (Jungle Book), squeeze vinyl, WDP/Holland Hall Prod, 1960s, 6", EX, P6.......................................$28.00

Figure, Fates (Hercules), beanbag type, 5", EX...................$5.00

Figure, Ferdinand the Bull, bsk, 3½", NM+ $50.00

Figure, Ferdinand the Bull, compo w/cloth tail, jtd, Knickerbocker, 1930s, 9" L, EX+ $150.00

Figure, Ferdinand the Bull, seated with flower in mouth, chalkware, 1930s, $100.00. (Photo courtesy Michael Stern)

Figure, Flit the Bird (Pocahontas), cloth, Mattel, 1995, 9", EX .$5.00

Figure, Flounder (Little Mermaid), plush, 15" L, NM.......$10.00

Figure, Flower, soft rubber, 4½", VG+ $4.00

Figure, Genie (Aladdin), ceramic, Genie coming out of lamp, Disney/Japan, 7", EX, P6...$30.00

Figure, Geppetto (Pinocchio), wood fiber, sitting on box w/chin in hand, Multiproducts, 1940s, 5x3x3", EX $55.00

Figure, Geppetto (Pinocchio), wood fiber, standing on sq base w/name, Multiproducts/WDP, 1940s, 2¼", rare, EX, P6 ..$55.00

Figure, Goofy, cloth, holding Christmas cake (Merry Christmas-1999), 7", EX..$5.00

Figure, Goofy, stuffed, Jacob Marley (Mickey's Christmas Carol), issued by Hardee's, 1984, 6", EX $5.00

Figure, Goofy, stuffed, orange shirt & pk vest, gr hat, Mattel, 17", EX...$100.00

Figure, Goofy, stuffed plush with cloth overalls and shirt, Schuco, 1950s, 14", EX, $250.00.

Figure, Hercules, cloth, Mattel, 5", EX...............................$5.00

Figure, Hewy, Louie, or Dewy, see Donald's Nephew

Figure, Iago the Parrot (Aladdin), cloth, 6", EX $5.00

Figure, Jessica (Roger Rabbit), ceramic, leaning against fire hydrant, 5½", EX, P6...$30.00

Figure, Jiminy Cricket, ceramic, standing & looking up while tipping his hat, WDP, 1960s, 2¾", EX, P6 ....$30.00

Figure, Jiminy Cricket, injection molded wax made by novelty machines at Disneyland or 1964 World's Fair, 5", NM ..$30.00

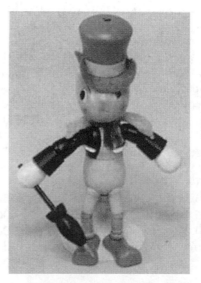

Figure, Jiminy Cricket, beaded wood with felt collar and hat brim, ribbon tie, Ideal, 1940, 9", EX, A, $410.00. (Photo courtesy Bertoia Auctions)

Figure, Joe Carioca, stuffed with cloth eyes, stitched mouth, cloth outfit, hat, and umbrella, 16", VG, A, $400.00. (Photo courtesy Bertoia Auctions)

Figure, Lady (Lady & the Tramp), ceramic, sitting upright w/head tilted up, collar, WDP, 1960s-70s, 4", EX, P6 ....$35.00

Figure, Lady (Lady & the Tramp), plush roly-poly style w/vinyl face, felt feet, Gund, 1950s, 8½", EX $35.00

Figure, Lampwick (Pinocchio), wood/compo, Multi-Wood Prod, 1940s, 5½", EX+ $75.00

Figure, Lucky (101 Dalmatians), squeeze vinyl, sitting upright w/head & ear cocked, Dell, from orig movie, 7", EX, P6 ....$25.00

Figure, Mary Poppins, bendable, Gund, 12", EX+ $60.00

Figure, Mickey Mouse, bsk, standing w/hand on hip, other arm articulated, red shorts, yel feet, 5", G+, A $200.00

Figure, Mickey Mouse, celluloid, movable head & arms, Borgfeldt, 1930s, 5½", VG, A $250.00

Figure, Mickey Mouse, ceramic, Santa Mickey hugging lg candy cane, Royal Orleans/WDP, older, 4¼", MIB, P6 ....$25.00

Figure, Mickey Mouse, ceramic, standing w/hands on hips, blk & wht w/red shorts & yel shoes, Enesco, 1960s, 5", EX, P6 ....$35.00

Figure, Mickey Mouse, rubber, Seiberling, 1930s, 6½", VG+ ..$75.00

Figure, Mickey Mouse, stuffed, cloth, blk & wht, red shorts w/wht buttons, yel felt shoes, England, 20", G, A......$90.00

Figure, Mickey Mouse, stuffed, pie eyes, stitched mouth, 4-fingered, cloth shoes, Knickerbocker, 10", VG, A $430.00

Figure, Mickey Mouse, stuffed, talker, Hasbro, 1970s, 8", NM+ $50.00

Figure, Mickey Mouse, stuffed, talker, Horsman, 1970s, 12", VG $25.00

Figure, Mickey Mouse, stuffed, toothy grin, button eyes, 5-fingered felt hands, felt shoes, Dean's/England, 6", VG $300.00

Figure, Mickey Mouse, stuffed velvet body and outfit with felt ears and silk-type hands, Charlotte Clark, 12", NM, A, $2,750.00. (Photo courtesy Bertoia Auctions)

Figure, Mickey Mouse, stuffed canvas with stenciled features, felt eyes and ears, large orange feet, Knickerbocker, 15", EX, A, $300.00; Figure, Mickey Mouse, stuffed canvas with felt ears, yarn-stitched mouth, wearing cowboy chaps, 20", G, A, $330.00. (Photo courtesy Bertoia Auctions)

Figure, Mickey Mouse, stuffed velvet with muslin face, velvet eyes, ears, and hands, brown overalls with wooden buttons, 14", G, A, $165.00; Figure, Mickey Mouse, stuffed velvet with stenciled features, felt ears and hands, rubber tail, velvet shorts, 12", VG, A, $400.00. (Photo courtesy Bertoia Auctions)

Figure, Mickey Mouse, stuffed, toothy grin, button eyes, 5-fingered felt hands, felt shoes, Dean's/England, 8", EX ..$375.00

Figure, Mickey Mouse, stuffed, toothy grin, cartoon eyes, 5-finger felt hands & shoes, Dean's/England, 1930s, 12", EX, A $1,050.00

Figure, Mickey Mouse, stuffed, velvet w/felt ears, decal eyes, 4-finger hands, Steiff, 7", EX, A $385.00

Figure, Mickey Mouse, stuffed, vinyl head, hands & feet, red pants, Applause #8528, 1981, 10½", EX+.................$15.00

Figure, Mickey Mouse, wood, jtd bead body, ball hands, blk & wht w/gr shorts, yel shoes, mk Walt Disney, 9½", EX, A ...$430.00

Figure, Mickey Mouse, wood, jtd bead body, lollipop hands, pie eyes, blk & red w/red shorts & shoes, 1930s, 7", EX+..$550.00

Figure, Mickey Mouse, wood, red body w/Mickey Mouse decal, blk arms & legs w/yel hands & feet, 5", VG, A $220.00

Figure, Mickey Mouse, wood & compo, blk & wht w/red shorts, pie eyes, wht bead hands, gold shoes, 1930s, 9½", VG+, A $500.00

Figure, Mickey Mouse Club Boy, cermaic, standing on rnd base wearing ears, Twinton, 1970s, 6¾", rare, EX, P6 .....$125.00

Figure, Minnie Mouse, bsk, looking at nest of Easter eggs & hen while holding basket, WDP, 3", EX, P6.....................$40.00

Figure, Minnie Mouse, bsk, sitting by typewriter & phone taking dictation, WDP, 1960s-70s, 4", EX, P6.......................$30.00

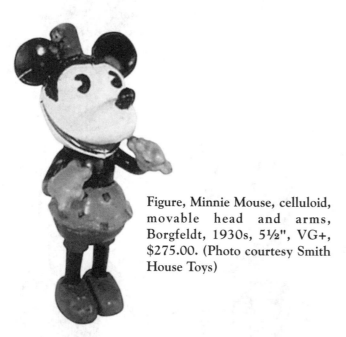

Figure, Minnie Mouse, celluloid, movable head and arms, Borgfeldt, 1930s, 5½", VG+, $275.00. (Photo courtesy Smith House Toys)

Figure, Minnie Mouse, ceramic, cheerleader w/red head bow & '50s skirt w/Pluto silhouette, Japan, 1987, 4½", EX, P6.........$28.00

Figure, Minnie Mouse, ceramic, hands clasped in front looking up, pk/wht polka-dot skirt, turq shoes, 1960s, 6", EX, P6 ....$40.00

Figure, Minnie Mouse, ceramic, playing parade drum while looking up, mc, Ucago, 3", EX, P6 ....$30.00

Figure, Mousketeer, Horsman, 1960s, 8", MIB................$150.00

Figure, Mulan, cloth, peach, bl & wht outfit, 12", NM $10.00

Figure, Mushu the Dragon (Mulan), cloth, red, 12", EX.....$8.00

Figure, Nala (Lion King), plush, Disney Store, 6x11", NM+...$15.00

Figure, Nala (Lion King), plush, lying down, Mattel, 1993, 7x12", EX...$12.00

Figure, Pegasus (Hercules), cloth, Applause, 5", EX $5.00

Figure, Peter Pan, Ideal, 1950s, 18", EX+ $95.00

Figure, Pinocchio, composition with felt outfit and hat, Ideal, 13", VG+, A, $285.00. (Photo courtesy James D. Julia Auctions, Inc.)

Figure, Pinocchio, compo, Ideal, 1940, 20", EX+ $450.00

Figure, Pinocchio, plaster, WDP, 1940, 4¼", EX, P6 ....$24.00

Figure, Pinocchio, plush, cloth mask face w/pnt features, wooden arms & legs, cloth outfit, 1940, 15", EX...................$165.00

Figure, Pinocchio, rubber, Pinocchio standing w/school books & an apple for the teacher, Dell, 1950s, 7", EX, P6 ....$30.00

Figure, Pinocchio, wood & compo, posable pnt bead body, w/compo head, decal on chest, Ideal, 8", VG+, A...$100.00

Figure, Pinocchio, wood & compo w/swivel neck & jtd body, brn silk tie, yel felt hat, Ideal, 1940, 12", EX, A.............$275.00

Figure, Pinocchio, wood fiber, standing w/hand in air on sq base, Multiproducts, 1940, 7", scarce, VG $75.00

Figure, Pluto, ceramic, curious crouching pose, Brayton Laguna, 1940s, 6½" L, NM $75.00

Figure, Pluto, composition, 8" long, G, A, $20.00. (Photo courtesy Randy Inman Auctions)

Figure, Pluto, ceramic, rump in air holding up left front paw, 1940s, 2¼" L, EX, P6.................................$100.00

Figure, Pluto, ceramic, sitting upright w/head turned & looking up, WDP/Japan, 1960s, 2½", EX, P6.........................$25.00

Figure, Pluto, plush, orange w/blk posable ears & tail, Gund, 1940s-50s, 9x13", NM.................................$150.00

Figure, Queen of Hearts (Alice in Wonderland), beanbag type, red & blk cape, Disney Store, 9", M.........................$10.00

Figure, Rafiki (Lion King), plush w/rubber head, Mattel, 1994, 8", EX.................................$8.50

Figure, Roger Rabbit, beanbag type, LJN, 1980s, 4", NM+..$15.00

Figure, Roger Rabbit, cloth, Amblin, 1987, 18", EX+......$20.00

Figure, Roger Rabbit, plush, Applause, 1987, 12", EX+....$15.00

Figure, Roger Rabbit, vinyl, bendable, Amblin, 1987, 6", EX+.................................$6.50

Figure, Scuttle (Little Mermaid), plush, 15", EX+.............$15.00

Figure, Sebastian (Little Mermaid), cloth, Mattel, 8x9", EX...$8.50

Figure, Sebastian (Little Mermaid), plush, 16", NM.........$15.00

Figure, Seven Dwarfs, beanbag type, any character, Applause, 7", EX+, ea.................................$6.50

Figure, Simba (Lion King), beanbag plush, Applause, 6x12", EX.................................$12.00

Figure, Simba (Lion King), cloth w/rubber head, young version, Applause, 6x7" L, VG+.................................$8.50

Figure, Simba (Lion King), plush, Mattel, 1993, EX.........$12.50

Figure, Sleeping Beauty w/rabbit, squeeze rubber, Dell, 1959, 5", EX+.................................$40.00

Figure, Snow White, chalkware, full figure w/glitter accents, 1940s-50s, 15", NM.................................$75.00

Figure, Snow White, compo, Knickerbocker, 1940, 12", VG+.................................$75.00

Figure, Snow White, stuffed cloth body, mask face with painted features, mohair wig, organdy dress, Ideal, 1930s, 16", EX, A, $400.00. (Photo courtesy McMasters Harris Doll Auctions)

Figure, Thomas O'Malley (Aristocats), plush, 7", NM+...$10.00

Figure, Thumper (Bambi), ceramic, yel, Goebel, 2", EX, P6..$30.00

Figure, Tigger, plush, issued by McDonald's, 12", EX........$15.00

Figure, Timon (Lion King II), cloth, Mattel, 1998, 6", EX+....$6.00

Figure, Timothy (Dumbo), beanbag type, orig tags, 8", NM..$10.00

Figure, Tinker Bell, open-close eyes, jtd arms & head, gr outfit w/wht wings, gold trim, Duchess Doll, 1950s, 8", EX+.............$150.00

Figure, Tinker Bell, rubber & plastic, Sutton, 1960s, 7", EX+...$35.00

Figure, Winnie the Pooh, cloth, Pooh lettered on red sweater, Mattel, 12", EX.................................$10.00

Figure, Woody (Toy Story), beanbag type w/rubber head & hat, Mattel/Star Bean, 12", EX.................................$10.00

Figure Set, Mickey, Goofy, Pluto, ceramic, 4" Goofy & 3" Pluto attached to 6" Mickey by chains, D Breckner, 1960s, EX..$125.00

Figure Set, Mickey, Minnie & Pluto, bsk, (The Three Pals), Borgfeldt/Japan, 1930s, 3"-3½", NM+IB, A.............$450.00

Figure Set, Mickey, Minnie & Pluto, lead, unpnt, Home Foundry Mfg, 1930s, 5", NM.................................$50.00

Figure Set, Mickey, Minnie & Pluto, wood, Fun-E-Flex/Borgfeldt, 1930s, 3¾", EX, A.................................$225.00

Figure Set, Mickey & Minnie, wood, Fun-E-Flex/Borgfeldt, 1930s, 7", EX+, A.................................$675.00

Figure Set, Mickey & Minnie, wood, Fun-E-Flex/Borgfeldt, 1930s, 4½", EX, A.................................$400.00

Figure Set, Mickey Mouse, bsk, 4 different poses, blk & wht w/purple shorts & yel shoes, 1½", EX, A.................$110.00

Figure Set, Minny Mouse, bsk, 3 minstrel figures, Japan, 3½" ea, NM+IB, A.................................$475.00

Figure Set, Seven Dwarfs, stuffed felt with white fur beards, painted features, original name tags, Chad Valley, 10", EX+, A, $2,475.00. (Photo courtesy McMasters Harris Doll Auctions)

Figure Set, Snow White & the Seven Dwarfs, bsk, Geo Borgfeldt/Japan, no sz given, VG+IB, A.................$440.00

Figure Set, Snow White & the Seven Dwarfs, plush, compo heads, cloth-dressed, SW w/blk mohair wig, 16" & 9", VG, A.................................$1,600.00

Figure Set, Snow White & the Seven Dwarfs, vinyl, 22" SW in cloth dress & rooted hair, pnt vinyl dwarfs, 1950s, NMIB, A.................................$350.00

Figure Set, Snow White and the Seven Dwarfs and the Prince, ceramic, Goebel small bee, 1970s, 3" to 5½", EX+, A, $465.00. (Goebel large bee, 1950s, would be valued at $975.00.) (Photo courtesy Bertoia Auctions)

Figure Set, Three Little Pigs, bsk, 3 minstrels, Japan/Borgfeldt, 3½" ea, NM+IB, A $365.00

Figure Set, Walt Disney's Miniature Figures, Mickey, Pluto, Donald, Dumbo & Goofy, pnt metal, 1¼", NMIB, A $200.00

Finger Puppet, Cri-Kee (Mulan), issued by Blockbuster Video, 1998, MIP...$3.00

Finger Puppet, Simba (Lion King), cloth, Mattel, 1994, EX ..$5.00

Fishing Kit, litho tin box w/hinged lid, shows Mickey & Minnie in boat catching a big fish, WDE, 1920s, 5x8", EX...$500.00

Flashlight, Mickey and Minnie Mouse, EX, A, $150.00. (Photo courtesy Randy Inman Auctions)

Flute, litho tin w/images of Mickey conducting barnyard animals, SFC/Italy, 1930s, 10", VG, A..........................$115.00

Game, Library of Games, 1946, EXIB, A $15.00

Game, Mickey Mouse Scatter Ball, Marks Bros, 1930s, complete, NM+, A $300.00

Game, Mickey Mouse Target Game, cb target w/image of Mickey on wooden props, Marx Bros, 24x24", VGIB, A........$330.00

Game, Mickey Mouse Tidley-Winks, Chad Valley, 1930s, unused, MIB, A $275.00

Game, Party Game for Young Folks, Donald Duck, Parker Bros/WDE, 1930s, EXIB...$75.00

Game, Pin the Tail on Mickey, Marks Bros, 1935, EXIB ..$80.00

Game, Put the Tail on Ferdinand the Bull, Whitman/WDE, 1938, EXIB...$100.00

Grow Chart, Ready Set Grow!, features Mickey, Donald & Pluto, Hallmark/Disney, 1970s, EX (w/orig envelope), P6...$18.00

Hand Puppet, Beast or Belle (Beauty & the Beast), flexible rubber, Pizza Hut issue, 1992, 7", EX, ea $6.00

Hand Puppet, Captain Hook, cloth w/vinyl head, Gund, 1950s, EX+ $50.00

Hand Puppet, Dopey (Snow White & the Seven Dwarfs), cloth w/vinyl head, Ivory Snow premium, 1960s, MIB.....$100.00

Hand Puppet, Esmerelda, Hugo, Phoebus, or Quasimodo (Hunchback of Notre Dame), issued by Burger King, 1996, EX, ea $5.00

Hand Puppet, Ferdinand the Bull, Crown Toy Co, 1930s, 9½", EX+ $75.00

Hand Puppet, Horace Horsecollar, cloth w/vinyl head, Gund, 1950s, EX+ $75.00

Hand Puppet, Jiminy Cricket, 1st version, Gund, 1950s, EX+...$50.00

Hand Puppet, Jiminy Cricket, 2nd version, Gund, 1960s, VG $25.00

Hand Puppet, Mad Hatter (Alice in Wonderland), cloth body w/vinyl head, 1960s, EX+ $30.00

Hand Puppet, Mickey Mouse, printed cloth body w/name on chest, vinyl head, Gund, EX......................................$25.00

Hand Puppet, Minnie Mouse, plush, red polka-dot dress, Mattel, 1993, 10", NM+ $10.00

Hand Puppet, Minnie Mouse, printed cloth body w/name on waist of dress, vinyl head, Gund, EX $25.00

Hand Puppet, Peter Pan, rubber, Oak, 1950s, EX+...........$40.00

Hand Puppet, Pinocchio, cloth body w/vinyl head, w/squeaker, Gund, 1950s, 10", EX+ $30.00

Hand Puppet, Pinocchio, Knickerbocker, 1962, EX+ $50.00

Hand Puppet, Tinker Belle, talker, cloth with vinyl head, Gund, EXIB, $75.00. (Photo courtesy Michael Stern)

Hand Puppet, Pluto, cloth body w/vinyl head, Gund, 1950s, EX+ $25.00

Hand Puppet, Pluto, WDP, 1970s, G..............................$10.00

Hand Puppet, Simba (Lion King), plush, Applause, 9", EX ..$10.00

Hand Puppet, Sword & the Stone, cloth body w/pnt vinyl head, WDP, 1963, 11", EX...$25.00

Hand Puppet, Three Little Pigs, printed cloth bodies w/compo heads (open-mouth smiles), 9", EXIB $250.00

Handkerchief, Donald Duck about to set sail w/3 nephews, 1950s, 8¼" sq, EX, P6...$28.00

Handkerchief Set, Snow White & the Seven Dwarfs, 4 different prints, WDE, 1930s, unused, MIB, A.......................$180.00

Hat Holder, Minnie Mouse, 2-sided die-cut wood figure of Minnie on rnd base, 1930s, 14", EX, A...........................$200.00

Jack-In-The-Box, Donald Duck pops up, Lakeside, 1960s, VG $50.00

Jack-In-The-Box, Winnie the Pooh, Carnival Toys, 1960s, EX+...$25.00

Jewelry Box, Ariel (Little Mermaid), musical, 5x6", NM+ ..$20.00

Lamp, Mickey Mouse figure w/1 hand on hip & waving w/other on base w/name, ceramic, w/shade, Dan Brechner, 1961, 15", EX...$165.00

Lamp, Pluto figure (ceramic) & shade w/Disney characters, 1950s, about 16" to 17", EX, P6 ....$175.00

Lamp Base, Pablo Penguin (Three Caballeros) figure waving, ceramic, 1940s, 7½" figure, EX, P6 ....$125.00

License Plate, Jessica (Who Framed Roger Rabbit), NM+ ..$15.00

Light Switch Plate, Three Little Pigs, plastic w/minstrel images, EX...$15.00

Lunar Flight Certificate, Disneyland souvenir given to Trip to the Moon riders, 1950s, 5x7", NM $25.00

Lunch Box, lithographed tin with Disney graphics, single handle, Walt Disney, 7½" long, G, A, $130.00. (Photo courtesy Randy Inman Auctions)

Magic Slate, Winnie the Pooh, Western Publishing, 1965, unused, NM+ $50.00

Make-Up Kit, Alice in Wonderland, cb box w/metal closure & hdl, Hasbro/WDP, 1950s, 11x6x4", NM $50.00

Marionette, Alice in Wonderland, Peter Puppet Playthings, MIB (2 different boxes), ea...$225.00

Marionette, Captain Hook, wood body w/pnt compo head & limbs, cloth clothes, metal hook, Peter Puppet, 1952, 16", VG $100.00

Marionette, Mickey Mouse and Donald Duck, Pelham, 1970s, Made in England, M (in blue box, numbered edition), $350.00 each. (Photo courtesy Joel Cohen)

Marionette, Donald Duck, Peter Puppet, 6½", EX+.........$75.00

Marionette, Dopey (Snow White), wood w/pnt compo head, cloth & felt outfit, Peter Puppet Playthings, 1950s, 12", VG...$100.00

Marionette, Jiminy Cricket, Pelham, 1950s, 10", EXIB..$250.00

Marionette, Mad Hatter (Alice in Wonderland), Peter Puppet Playthings, 1950s, MIB...$150.00

Marionette, Minnie Mouse, wood & compo w/cloth outfit, Peter Puppet Playthings, 1950s, 12", VG+ $75.00

Marionette, Peter Pan, wood & compo w/cloth outfit, Peter Puppet Playthings, 1950s, 15", NM $75.00

Marionette, Snow White, Tony Sarg/Alexander, 1930s, 12½", EX+ $100.00

Mask, Dopey (Snow White & the Seven Dwarfs), canvas, 1930s, EX, P6 ....$55.00

Mask, Figaro the Cat (Pinocchio), paper, Gillette Razor Blue Blades premium, 1939, 8x9", EX, P6 ....$25.00

Mask, Jiminy Cricket, pnt molded stiff gauze, Fishbach/WDP, 1940, 11x9", EX $50.00

Mask, Mickey Mouse, canvas, pie-eyed, 1930s, 8½x11", EX, P6...$55.00

Mask & Puppet, Pinocchio, litho paper, First National Stores premium, 1939-40, 16x10", uncut & unused, NM+ ..$65.00

Mechanical Toy, Ludwig Von Drake, push spring-action feet & head shoots off, plastic, Tigrett/WDP, 1961, 9", EX...$50.00

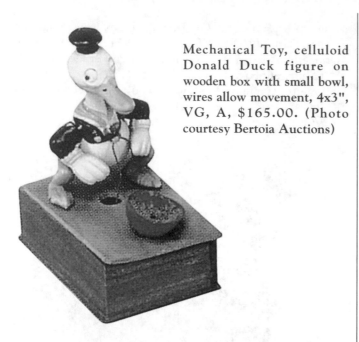

Mechanical Toy, celluloid Donald Duck figure on wooden box with small bowl, wires allow movement, 4x3", VG, A, $165.00. (Photo courtesy Bertoia Auctions)

Metal Craft Tapping Set, Pressman #1135, 1950s, EXIB ..$50.00

Mirror, Bambi & friends on molded & pnt plastic frame around irregularlly shaped mirror, 1970s, 24x21", EX, P6....$175.00

Movie Jector, Mickey Mouse, tin w/wooden base, decal on front, WDE, 1930s, 10", EX....................................$75.00

Mystery Art Set (Mickey Mouse), Dixon/WDE, complete & unused, MIB, A $400.00

Napkin Ring, Mickey Mouse, silver-plated w/engraved images of Mickey, Wm Rogers, 1930s, 1½" dia, NM+IB, A....$150.00

Necklace, Babes in Toyland, 3 mc toy soldiers & a pearl on gold-tone chain, WDP, 1961, MOC, P6............................$50.00

Newsreel, Mickey Mouse Club w/Micky graphics, complete w/film & records, 9", G (P box), A $55.00

Nodder Figure, Donald Duck, pnt compo, Brechner/WDP/Japan, 1960s, 6", NM+..$75.00

Nodder Figure, Mickey Mouse standing with hand on hip and banjo at side, celluloid, Japan, prewar, 7", EX, A, $800.00. (Photo courtesy James D. Julia Auctions)

Nodder Figure, Pluto, compo, seated on oval base, looking up, mouth partially open, Japan, 1950s, 5¾", EX, P6......$90.00

Ornament, Ariel (Little Mermaid), figural, 3¾", EX, P6..$18.00

Ornaments, Jacques the Mouse & Gus the Mouse (Cinderella), plush w/hooks, issued by McDonald's, 1987, 3", EX, ea...$6.00

Pail (Candy/Sand), Three Little Pigs, litho tin w/image of 3 pigs & advertising, w/scoop, Mayfair Candy Co, 3½", VG+...$175.00

Paint Box, Donald Duck, litho tin w/images of Donald, Mickey & Nephews, WDE, 1946, used contents, EX+...........$50.00

Paint Box, Snow White, litho tin, WD/MM Ltd, 1930s, 4x½x9½" L, unused, EX...$50.00

Paint Shop (Mickey Mouse), Fulton/WDE, complete, NMIB..$175.00

Paint-On Ceramic Plaque, Donald Duck, Leisuramics #8031, 1973 unused, NMIP..$25.00

Paint-On Ceramic Plaque, Pluto, Leisuramics #8030, 1973, partially pnt, EXIP $20.00

Party Decorations, Sword & the Stone, Disney, 1963, MIP (unopened), P6..$18.00

Pencil Box, Donald Duck holding tomahawk while flying plane on box, Dixon, 1¼x5x8½" L, EX+......................$75.00

Pencil Box, Mickey, Pluto & Goofy on rocket, Dixon, 1930s, 1x6x9" L, EX+ $75.00

Pencil Box, Snow White & the Seven Dwarfs, Venuz, 1x3x8" L, VG $50.00

Pencil Case, Mary Poppins, vinyl w/zipper, 1960s, EX+ ...$15.00

Pencil Holder, Mickey Mouse, compo figure w/pencil upright in shoe, blk & wht, pie eyes, WDE, 1930s, 5", EX+ $175.00

Pencil Sharpener, Mickey Mouse, pnt cowboy image on rnd Catalin plastic sharpener w/scalloped edge, 1¼", EX...$125.00

Pencil Sharpener, Mickey Mouse figure standing with hands on chest, round base, painted celluloid, 3", NM, $235.00. (Photo courtesy James D. Julia Auctions, Inc.)

Pencil Sharpener, Pooh, ceramic, Pooh's Pencil Pot & Sharpener, Enesco/WDP, 1964, 4¾", EX, P6.....................$60.00

Phonograph, Snow White & the Seven Dwarfs PortoFonic, litho tin, 14" dia, VG, A $185.00

Piano, Mickey Mouse, wood w/Mickey & Minnie decals, Marks Bros, 10", rare, VG, A $800.00

Pillow Cover, Mickey w/flower, blk, gray & yel on wht cloth, Vogue Needlecraft, 1930s, 17x15", EX.....................$50.00

Pin, Arial (Little Mermaid), enameled figure w/blk hair & aqua fish tail, mk Disney/Arthus Bertrand, 1½", EX, P6....$12.00

Pin, Dumbo & ringmaster, pnt enamel w/metal clasp, WDP, 1940s, 2½x1¾", NM $60.00

Pin, Dwarf (Snow White), pnt wood figure playing horn while resting against tree stump, 1938, 1½", VG, P6 ....$45.00

Pin, Goofy, enameled figure of Goofy as colonial (bicentennial) fife player, Kodak premium, 1989, 1½", EX, P6 ....$20.00

Pin, Mickey & Minnie heads w/crescent moon & star connected by chain, gold-tone w/rhinestones, Wendy Gell, EX ..$55.00

Pin, Mickey Mouse, enameled figure playing parade drum, gold-tone trim, WD Co, 1", EX, P6 ....$15.00

Pin, Mickey Mouse, enameled figure playing soccer, gold-tone trim, 1", EX, P6 ....$15.00

Pin, Mickey Mouse, enameled figure w/1 hand on hip & waving w/other, sterling silver backing, 1930s, 1½", VG, P6...$75.00

Pin, Mickey Mouse, stick pin w/Mickey figure standing in open heart form, gold-tone, WDP, 1970s, 2½", EX, P6 ......$25.00

Pin, Minnie Mouse, enameled figure of Minnie w/unbrella in front of cloud & rainbow, gold-tone base, 1980s, 1", EX, P6 ....$15.00

Pin, Snow White, wood compo figure sweeping w/broom, brn w/bl neck scarf & yel broom, 1930s, 1", EX $30.00

Place Mat, Disneyland, die-cut paper litho w/stand-up images of landmarks, 1950s-60s, NM $50.00

Plaque, see Paint-On Ceramic Plaque

Plate, Fantasia, ceramic, wht w/colorful floral border, Vernona Kilns/WD, 1940, 9½" dia, EX+ $100.00

Playing Cards, see also Card Game

Playing Cards, Snow White & the Seven Dwarfs, complete deck w/same illus on ea card, Western/WDE, 1930s, EX ...$30.00

Playsuit, Mickey Mouse, cloth top w/rnd decals, short pants w/buttons, cord tail, gauze mask, Ben Cooper, 1940s, EX+ $75.00

Playsuit, Mickey Mouse, sleeved vest, pants & guaze mask, Ben Cooper, 1940s, VG $50.00

Poster Paint Set (Donald Duck), Milton Bradley/WDE, 1930s, complete & unused, NMIB, A $200.00

Posters to Color, Toy Story, Golden Books, 1996, unused, MIP $5.00

Pull Toy, Mickey & Pluto cart, paper-litho-on-wood Pluto pulls rubber Mickey on 4-wheeled cart, Chad Valley, 12", EX, A $450.00

Purse, Little Mermaid, vinyl, 6" dia, NM+ $15.00

Push-Button Puppet, Bambi, Kohner, 1960s, EX $25.00

Push-Button Puppet, Donald Duck, Kohner, 1950s, EX+..$30.00

Push-Button Puppet, Mickey Mouse, Kohner, 1948, EX ..$70.00

Push-Button Puppet, Mickey Mouse with drum, Kohner, 1948, EX, $150.00.

Push-Button Puppet, Peter Pan, Kohner, 1960s, EX+.......$25.00

Push-Button Puppet, Pinocchio, Kohner, 1960s, EX+......$20.00

Push-Button Puppet, Pinocchio & Jiminy Cricket Duet Show Time, Marx/WDP, 1950s, MIB $175.00

Push-Button Puppet, Pluto, wood w/oilcloth ears & beaded tail, Fisher-Price Pop-Up Critter, 1930, 5", EX+ $95.00

Record Player, see Phonograh

Ring, Mickey Mouse, celluloid ¾" figure on gold-tone plastic open band, 1930s, EX, P6 ....$45.00

Ring, Mickey Mouse, enameled ¾" figure in wht jacket & red pants on gold-tone adjustable band, 1940s, EX, P6 ..$55.00

Ring, Mickey Mouse, plastic, flashes from Mickey Mouse Club to Mickey Mouse Member & WDP, premium, EX, P6.....$24.00

Rubber Toy, fire chief's car w/Mickey as driver, Sun Rubber, 6", VG, A $65.00

Scissors, Mickey Mouse Cut-Out Scissors, WDE, 1930s, NM+OC, A $250.00

Scrapbook, image of Mickey & Minnie on cover, Whitman/WDE, 1930s, 15x11", EX........................$100.00

Sewing Card Set, Snow White & the Seven Dwarfs, Whitman, 1950s, 3 different, EX $15.00

Sewing Set, see Yarn Sewing Set

Slippers, Bambi, fabric w/figural heads on top, Trimfoot/WDP, 1940s-50s, child-sz, VG, pr...$50.00

Slippers, Donald Duck, fabric w/figural heads on top, Trimfoot/WDP, 1940s-50s, child-sz, VG $50.00

Pull Toy, Pluto, wood, movable head, 12" long, EX, A, $150.00. (Photo courtesy Bertoia Auctions)

Scooter Jockey, plastic Mickey figure seated on scooter waving, head and legs move when skooter rolls, 6", EX+IB, A, $200.00. (Photo courtesy Bertoia Auctions)

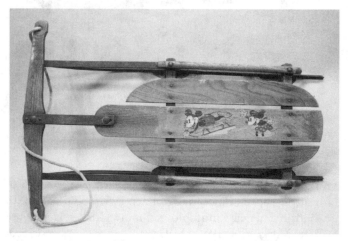

Sled, wood with painted images of Mickey and Minnie, metal runners, rope pull handle, 1930s, EX, $395.00.

Snap-Eeze Set, 12 different flat plastic figures, Marx, 1960s, EXIB..$75.00

Snow Dome, Little Mermaid, 4", M $25.00

Snow Dome, Mickey & Minnie, w/rainbow & pot of gold, 1970s, 3", EX+ $18.00

Snow Dome, The Wonderful World of Disney featuring Mickey & Minnie w/castle in background, plastic, 1970s, 3x4", EX, P6 ....$30.00

Soap Figure, Ferdinand the Bull, Lightfoot Schultz, 1938, EXIB $75.00

Soap Figure, Ugly Duckling, Lightfoot/WDE, 1939, 4", unused, VG+ (in illus box)..$75.00

Song Book, Peter Pan, Children's Album, 9 songs, 24 pgs, WD Music/British edition, 1953, EX $50.00

Souvenir Album, Pinocchio, features 10 songs, well illus cover, 40 pgs, Bourne, 1945, EX+ $50.00

Spoon, Donald Duck or Daisy Duck figural ceramic hdl on stainless steel spoon, 6", EX, P6, ea....................................$15.00

Stick Horse, Samson from Sleeping Beauty, gray-pnt plastic w/cloth reins & wood stick body, Bayshore/WDP, 1959, 36", EX+ $50.00

Talkie Jector, Mickey Mouse, complete w/4 orig rolls of film, G, A $225.00

Tambourine, Mickey & Minnie, tin & paper, Nobel & Cooley/Borgfeldt, 1930s, 9" dia, NM, A $250.00

Tambourine, Mickey Mouse Club, newer MMC logo w/head image of Mickey, litho tin w/paper top, 7" dia, EX, A $75.00

Tambourine, Mickey Mouse Club, vintage MMC logo w/head image of Mickey, litho tin w/paper top, 7" dia, VG+, A...........$150.00

Target Set, litho tin w/plastic figures & target gun, 9x14", EXIB, A $40.00

Tea Set, Alice in Wonderland, plastic, 2 place settings w/plates & saucers, teapot & flatware, Plasco, 1950s, EX........$50.00

Tea Set, Belle (Beauty & the Beast), 12-pc wht china set w/decal head images of Belle, Schmid, MIB, P6......$100.00

Tea Set, Mary Poppins, litho tin, Chein, 1960s, complete, NM+..$100.00

Tea Set, Mickey, Minnie & Pluto, litho tin, Mickey at piano on pitcher, trio on cups, Ohio Art, 1930s, complete, EXIB...$100.00

Tea Set, Mickey and Minnie on white china with tan lustre trim, 24 pieces, Walt Disney Enterprises/Japan, EXIB, A, $275.00. (Photo courtesy Bertoia Auctions)

Tea Set, Mickey Mouse, porcelain, wht 12-pc set w/Bavarian image of Mickey w/hands on hips, Reutter/Germany, NRFB.$100.00

Tea Set, Sleeping Beauty, plastic, service for 3 w/heart shaped images, Worchester Toy Co, 1959, EXIB, P6...........$250.00

Telephone, candlestick version w/flat-sided Mickey figure, steel & wood w/paper litho detail, 7", EX, A $150.00

Thermometer, Jiminy Cricket, Bakelite, decal image of Jiminy on base mk New York World's Fair, 1939, 3" T, NM, A...$225.00

Three-D Plastic Color-Plax 'Paint-Wash-Paint Again,' Peter Pan, Pancordion Inc, 1950s, unused, NMIB $75.00

Tie Rack, Mickey Mouse, die-cut wood image of Mickey, red, blk & wht, 1930s, 10½" T, NM, A..............................$200.00

Toothbrush Holder, Donald Duck, bsk, long-billed Donald on sq container w/2 holes, Japan, 1930s, rpt, VG, P6 ......$175.00

Tin Toy, Mickey Riding Pluto on rocker base, Linemar, 7", VG, A, $990.00. (Photo courtesy Bertoia Auctions)

Toothbrush Holder, Mickey, bsk, standing, jtd arm, 5", EX, A ...$180.00
Toothbrush Holder, Mickey, Minnie & Donald, bsk, standing on rectangular base, Japan, 1930s, 4", EX, A $150.00
Toothbrush Holder, Mickey & Minnie, bsk, standing on gr base, 4½", EX, A $150.00
Toothbrush Holder, Mickey & Pluto, bsk, Mickey drying Pluto w/towel on basc, 4¾", EX, A...................................$150.00
Toothbrush Holder, Three Little Pigs, bsk, mason w/flute & fife players on gr base, Japan/WD, 4", VG, A $100.00
Toothbrush Holder, Three Little Pigs, wood plaque w/pnt image showing 3 Pigs from back, Dibble Studio, 1938, EX, P6..$125.00
Top, Mickey Mouse Coral Top, litho tin, red w/Disney characters, Lakawanna Mfg/Borgfeldt, 1930s, 10" dia, rare, NM+IB, A $775.00

TV set, Mousketeers, lithographed tin with ten rolls and two records, T Cohn Inc., 10x9x13", VG, A, $355.00. (Photo courtesy Bertoia Auctions)

Top, Snow White & the Seven Dwarfs, litho tin, Chein, 9" dia, EX, A $250.00
Top, Three Little Pigs, litho tin, red, yel & gr w/images of the pigs, Chein, 4½" dia, EX, A $235.00
Toy, see Mechanical Toy, Rubber Toy, Tin Toy, etc
Transfer, Mickey Mouse, iron-on type w/arched name below standing image, red & blk, 1950s, unused, EX, P6.....$15.00
Tray, Lady & the Tramp, tin, 'spaghetti' scene in center w/characters around rim, Calif Metalware, 1950s, 13x17", EX+ ..$75.00
Tray, Mickey Mouse & Minnie musical scene on reverse-pnt glass, w/metal frame & hdls, 16x11", VG, A $150.00
TV Bulb, Mickey Mouse, WDE, 6", EXIB, A...................$55.00
Ventriloquist Doll, Mickey Mouse, Horsman, 1973, NM ..$75.00
Wall Plaque, Jose Carioca, litho on wood oval w/full figure image, 1940s, 7½", EX+ $25.00
Walt Disney's Television Playhouse, Marx, complete, NMIB, A...$375.00
Washing Machine, Seven Dwarfs, plastic w/up wringer type, Revell, 1940s-50s, 9x5" dia, VG................................$75.00

Washing Machine, Three Little Pigs, lithographed tin, Chein, 8", VG, $410.00. (Photo courtesy Randy Inman Auctions)

Watering Can, Donald Duck, litho tin, Ohio Art, 1930s, 6", EX+ $50.00
Wind-up Toys, see Mechanical Toys
Wood Burning Set, Disneyland, ATF/WDP, 1950s, VG+IB ..$50.00
Yarn Sewing Set (Mickey Mouse), Marks, 1930s, complete, EXIB, A $225.00
Yoyo, Buzz Lightyear, NM $5.00

Dollhouse Furniture

Back in the 1940s and 1950s, little girls often spent hour after hour with their dollhouses, keeping house for their imaginary families, cooking on tiny stoves (that sometimes came with scaled-to-fit pots and pans), serving meals in lovely dining rooms, making beds, and rearranging furniture, most of which was plastic, much of which was made by Renwal, Ideal, Marx, Irwin, and Plasco. Jaydon made plastic furniture as well but sadly never marked it. Tootsietoy produced metal items, many in boxed sets.

Of all of these manufacturers, Renwal and Ideal are considered the most collectible. Renwal's furniture was usually detailed; some pieces had moving parts. Many were made in more than one color, often brightened with decals. Besides the furniture, they made accessory items as well as 'dollhouse' dolls of the whole family. Ideal's Petite Princess line was packaged in sets with wonderful detail, accessorized down to the perfume bottles on the top of the vanity. Ideal furniture and parts are numbered, always with an 'I' prefix. Most Renwal pieces are also numbered.

Advisor: Judith Mosholder (M7)

Acme/Thomas, carriage, any color combo, M7, ea $6.00
Acme/Thomas, cat for dog sled, M7 ....$8.00
Acme/Thomas, dog for dog sled, cocker spaniel or dachshund, M7, ea...$8.00
Acme/Thomas, doll, baby in diaper, Thomas, 1¼", M7......$3.00
Acme/Thomas, doll, baby in diaper, Thomas, 1⅛", M7......$2.00
Acme/Thomas, doll, baby in diaper, Thomas, 2", M7 ....$4.00
Acme/Thomas, doll, baby sucking thumb, hard plastic, pk, Thomas, 1¼", M7 ....$3.00
Acme/Thomas, doll, Dutch girl, flesh-colored, Thomas, 2⅜", M7 ....$5.00
Acme/Thomas, doll, girl, hard plastic, yel dress, Thomas, 3½", M7 ....$20.00
Acme/Thomas, doll, little brother w/raised hand, Thomas, M7 .$3.00
Acme/Thomas, hammock, bl w/red supports, M7 ....$20.00
Acme/Thomas, rocker, yel w/gr or yel w/red, M7, ea $4.00
Acme/Thomas, seesaw, bl w/yel horseheads, M7 ....$6.00
Acme/Thomas, stroller, any color combo, M7, ea $6.00
Acme/Thomas, swing, single; red w/gr seat & yel 'ropes,' M7 ...$15.00
Acme/Thomas, tomy horse, gr w/wht seat, M7 ....$12.00
Allied/Pyro, bed, red w/wht spread, M7 ....$10.00
Allied/Pyro, chair, barrel; aqua, unmk, M7 ....$5.00
Allied/Pyro, chair, dining; pk, red or wht, M7, ea $3.00
Allied/Pyro, chair, kitchen; gray, pk or red, unmk, M7, ea..$3.00
Allied/Pyro, cupboard, corner; aqua, M7............................$8.00
Allied/Pyro, hutch, aqua or red, M7, ea.............................$4.00
Allied/Pyro, night stand, yel, M7......................................$4.00
Allied/Pyro, piano, blk (unmk) or lt bl (Allied), M7, ea ..$5.00
Allied/Pyro, radio, floor; yel, M7 ....$8.00
Allied/Pyro, radio, floor; yel, M7, ea.................................$8.00
Allied/Pyro, sofa, aqua or lt bl, unmk, M7, ea $5.00
Allied/Pyro, sofa, yel, unmk, M7 ....$8.00
Allied/Pyro, stove, wht, unmk, M7....................................$4.00
Allied/Pyro, table, kitchen; wht, M7.................................$4.00
Allied/Pyro, tub, lt bl, M7..$4.00
Allied/Pyro, vanity, aqua, bl or pk, M7, ea $4.00
Arcade, bath set (tub, sink, toilet), pnt CI, wht, VG pnt, A..$55.00
Arcade, bathtub, pnt CI, ivory, M7...............................$125.00

Arcade, Boone Kitchen Cabinet, cast iron, 8x5½", MIB, A, $1,650.00. (Photo courtesy Bertoia Auctions)

Arcade, breakfast nook set (Curtis), 3-pc (table & 2 benches), pnt CI, wht, G, A $100.00
Arcade, chair, bedroom; pnt CI, dk gr, VG pnt, M7.........$95.00
Arcade, cupboard (Boone), pnt CI, wht, 8", VG, A.........$90.00
Arcade, dresser, arched mirror, 4-drawer, 4-footed, gr, 6½", G, A $220.00

Arcade, Hotpoint Electric Range, cast iron, 6x5½", complete, MIB, A, $1,980.00. (Photo courtesy Bertoia Auctions)

Arcade, icebox (Leonard), pnt CI, wht, 6", VG, A $185.00
Best, bunk bed, bl or pk, M7, ea $5.00
Best, cradle, bl, M7...$2.00
Best, doll, baby, standing or sitting; hard plastic, M7, ea $2.00
Blue Box, bed, lt brn w/bl spread, M7................................$5.00
Blue Box, bookcase, w/clear sliding doors & 'books,' M7....$4.00
Blue Box, chair, dining; lt brn w/red seat, M7 ....$2.00
Blue Box, chest, 4-drawer, lt brn, M7.................................$4.00
Blue Box, hassock, lt brn w/bl seat, M7 ....$2.00
Blue Box, piano w/stool, M7..$8.00
Blue Box, stove, avocado w/silver top, M7 ....$3.00
Blue Box, vanity, resembles a miniature Petite Princess style, M7 ....$3.00

Blue Box, vanity, w/heart-shaped mirror, M7 ....$4.00
Blue Box, vanity stool, lt brn w/red seat, M7 ....$2.00
Casablanca, vanity w/mirror, brn, M7 ....$12.00
Cheerio, any hard plastic pc, M7, ea $4.00
Cheerio, any soft plastic pc, sm, M7, ea $2.00
Commonwealth, lamppost w/street sign & mailbox, blk or red, M7, ea...$15.00
Commonwealth, lawn mower, any color combo, M7, ea ..$30.00
Commonwealth, rake, any color, M7, ea $4.00
Commonwealth, spade, bright yel or wht, M7, ea..............$4.00
Commonwealth, watering can, red or wht, M7, ea $6.00
Commonwealth, wheelbarrow, bright yel w/red wheels, M7 ..$8.00
Donna Lee, chair, kitchen; wht, M7....................................$3.00
Donna Lee, sink, stove or kitchen table, wht, M7, ea.........$4.00

Fisher-Price, barbecue grill and patio lounge chair, #272, 1983 – 1984, MOC, $4.50. (Photo courtesy Brad Cassity)

Fisher-Price, chair, dining; brn w/tan seat, M7 ....$2.00
Fisher-Price, chair, kitchen; wht & yel, M7..........................$2.00
Fisher-Price, chair, kitchen; wht w/marbleized seat, M7 .....$1.00
Fisher-Price, cradle, wht, M7 ....$5.00

Fisher-Price, doll family, father (#275) or girl (#277), 1983-85, MOC, ea...$3.00

Fisher-Price, doll, Mother, #276, 1983 – 1985, MOC, $3.00. (Photo courtesy Brad Cassity)

Fisher-Price, dresser w/mirror, wht, M7 ....$5.00
Fisher-Price, refrigerator, wht w/yel, M7.............................$5.00
Fisher-Price, sink, kitchen; yel, wht & orange, M7 ....$5.00
Fisher-Price, stove w/hood, yel, M7 ....$5.00
Fisher-Price, table, kitchen; wht w/red marbleized top, M7 .$3.00
Fisher-Price, toilet/vanity, bright gr w/wht trim, M7 ....$10.00
Goldilocks, kitchen set, 6 pcs w/chair, cupboard, refrigerator, stool, stove & table, pnt ivory, M7.....................$175.00
Grand Rapids, dresser w/mirror, decals on drawers, M7 ....$12.00
Hasbro, kitchen sink or stove, M7, ea $2.00
Ideal, bench, lawn; bl, M7 ....$18.00
Ideal, bird bath, marbleized ivory, M7 ....$18.00
Ideal, buffet, dk brn or dk marbleized brn, M7, ea $10.00
Ideal, buffet, red, M7 ....$15.00
Ideal, chair, chaise lounge; wht, M7 ....$18.00
Ideal, chair, dining room; brn w/bl seat, dk marbleized maroon w/bl or yel seat, M7, ea $10.00
Ideal, chair, sq back, bl swirl, bright gr swirl or med gr swirl, all w/brn bases, M7, ea..$15.00
Ideal, china closet, dk brn swirl or dk marbleized maroon, M7, ea $15.00
Ideal, china closet, red, M7...$20.00
Ideal, clothes washer, front load, wht, M7..........................$22.00
Ideal, dishwasher, w/lettering, M7 ....$20.00
Ideal, doll, baby, pnt diaper, M7 ....$10.00
Ideal, electric ironer, wht w/blk, M7 ....$18.00
Ideal, hamper, bl, M7 ....$6.00
Ideal, hamper, ivory, M7 ....$4.00
Ideal, highboy, ivory w/bl, M7 ....$18.00
Ideal, highchair, collapsible, bl or pk, M7, ea.....................$25.00
Ideal, night stand, brn or dk marbleized maroon, M7, ea....$6.00
Ideal, piano w/bench, caramel swirl, M7 ....$35.00
Ideal, playpen, bl w/pk bottom or pk w/bl bottom, M7, ea..$25.00

Ideal, potty chair, pk, complete, M7...................................$15.00
Ideal, radiator, M7...$25.00
Ideal, radio, floor; brn or dk marbleized maroon, M7........$10.00
Ideal, refrigerator, Deluxe, wht w/blk, opening door, cb backing,
 M7..$30.00

Ideal, refrigerator, ivory with black, $15.00; kitchen sink, ivory with black, $15.00; stove, ivory with black, $15.00; kitchen table, ivory, $6.00; kitchen chairs, ivory with various colors of seats, $5.00 each.

Ideal, secretary, dk marbleized maroon, complete, M7......$40.00
Ideal, sewing machine, dk marbleized brn or dk marbleized
 maroon, M7, ea...$20.00
Ideal, shopping cart, bl w/wht baskets, wht w/red or bl baskets,
 M7, ea $40.00
Ideal, sink, bathroom; bl w/yel or ivory w/blk, M7, ea $8.00
Ideal, sofa, med, bl, med gr, med gr swirl or orange-red swirl, all
 w/brn bases, M7, ea..$22.00
Ideal, table, coffee; brn or dk marbleized maroon, M7, ea..$10.00
Ideal, table, picnic; gr, M7 ....$20.00
Ideal, table, umbrella; yel w/red umbrella & red pole, M7 ..$25.00
Ideal, television, dog picture, yel detail, M7 ....$45.00
Ideal, toilet, bl w/yel hdl, M7...$10.00
Ideal, toilet, ivory w/blk hdl, M7 ....$20.00
Ideal, tub, corner; bl w/yel, M7......................................$18.00
Ideal, tub, ivory w/blk, M7...$10.00
Ideal, vacuum cleaner, no bag, bl w/red or yel or gr w/red-yel,
 M7, ea $20.00
Ideal, vanity stool, ivory w/bl seat, M7 ....$6.00
Ideal, vanity w/mirror, dk marbleized maroon, mirror wear,
 M7 ....$12.00
Ideal, vanity w/mirror, ivory w/bl, mirror good, M7 ....$18.00
Ideal Petite Princess, bed, #4416-4, bl or pk, complete, w/otig
 box, M7, ea $30.00
Ideal Petite Princess, books & bookends, Heirloom #4428-9,
 M7, ea..$5.00
Ideal Petite Princess, Buddha, #4437-0, metal, M7...........$15.00
Ideal Petite Princess, buffet, Royal #4419-8, complete, in orig
 box, M7...$25.00
Ideal Petite Princess, buffet, Royal #4419-8, complete, M7 ..$4.00
Ideal Petite Princess, cabinet, Treasure Trove #4418-0, M7 ..$10.00

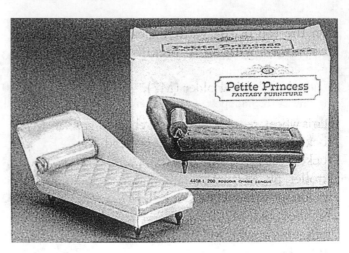

Ideal Petite Princess, boudoir chaise lounge, #4408-1, pink, MIB, $25.00.

Ideal Petite Princess, cabinet, Treasure Trove #4418-09, in orig
 box, M7...$12.00
Ideal Petite Princess, cabinet, Treasure Trove #4479-2, in orig
 box, M7...$12.00
Ideal Petite Princess, candelabra, Fantasia #4438-8, in orig box,
 M7...$22.00
Ideal Petite Princess, candelabra, Royal #4439-6, in orig box,
 M7...$15.00
Ideal Petite Princess, chair, dining; Host #4413-1, w/orig box,
 M7...$17.00
Ideal Petite Princess, chair, drum; Salon #4411-5, gold or gr,
 w/orig box, M7, ea $17.00
Ideal Petite Princess, chair, guest dining; #4414-9, in orig box,
 M7...$17.00
Ideal Petite Princess, chair, host dining; #4474-3, in orig box,
 M7...$17.00
Ideal Petite Princess, chair, hostess dining; #4415-6, M7....$8.00
Ideal Petite Princess, chair, wing; Salon #4410-7, w/orig box,
 M7...$15.00
Ideal Petite Princess, chair & ottoman, occasional; #4412-3, lt
 brn, w/orig box, M7 ....$22.00
Ideal Petite Princess, chest, Palace #4420-6, in orig box,
 M7...$17.00
Ideal Petite Princess, chest, Palace #4420-6, M7 ....$5.00
Ideal Petite Princess, clock, grandfather; #4423-0, M7.....$10.00
Ideal Petite Princess, clock, grandfather; #4423-0, w/folding
 screen, in orig box, M7..$20.00
Ideal Petite Princess, dressing table, #4417-2, bl, complete,
 M7...$20.00
Ideal Petite Princess, hearthplace, Regency, #4422-2, complete
 in orig box, M7 ....$18.00
Ideal Petite Princess, hearthplace, Regency #4422-2, complete,
 M7...$4.00
Ideal Petite Princess, lamp, table; Heirloom #4428-9, M7..$5.00
Ideal Petite Princess, piano & bench, grand; Royal #4425-5,
 M7...$25.00
Ideal Petite Princess, piano & bench, grand; Royal #4425-5, in
 orig box, M7..$30.00

Ideal Petite Princess, Doll Family, father, mother, girl, boy, #9170-5, MIB, $75.00 for the set. (Photo courtesy Judith Mosholder)

Ideal Petite Princess, planter, Salon #4440-4, M7 ....$15.00

Ideal Petite Princess, planter, Salon #9710-5, in orig box, M7 ....$18.00

Ideal Petite Princess, sofa, #4407-3, beige/gold, in orig box, M7 ....$25.00

Ideal Petite Princess, table, coffee; Salon #4433-9, w/assorted accessories, M7 ....$4.00

Ideal Petite Princess, table, dining room; #4421-4, M7 ....$15.00

Ideal Petite Princess, table, dressing; Royal #4417-2, pk, M7 ..$5.00

Ideal Petite Princess, table, dressing; Royal #4417-2, pk, no accessories, in orig box, M7 ....$8.00

Ideal Petite Princess, table, lyre; #4426-3, M7 ....$5.00

Ideal Petite Princess, table, occasional; #4437-0, M7 ....$5.00

Ideal Petite Princess, table, Palace #4431-3, M7 ....$5.00

Ideal Petite Princess, table set, Heirloom #4428-9, complete, in orig box, M7 ....$27.00

Ideal Petite Princess, table set, lyre; #4426-3, complete, M7 ..$15.00

Ideal Petite Princess, table set, occasional; #4437-0, complete, in orig box, M7 ....$27.00

Ideal Petite Princess, table set, Palace #4431-3, complete, M7 ..$20.00

Ideal Petite Princess, table set, pedestal; #4427-1, complete, in orig box, M7 ....$18.00

Ideal Petite Princess, table set, Salon #4433-9, complete, in orig box, M7 ....$27.00

Ideal Petite Princess, table set, tier; #4429-7, complete, in orig box, M7 ....$18.00

Ideal Petite Princess, tea cart, rolling, #4424-8, complete, in orig box, M7 ....$20.00

Ideal Petite Princess, telephone, Fantasy #4432-1, M7 ....$8.00

Ideal Petite Princess, telephone set, Fantasy #4432-1, complete, in orig box, M7 ....$20.00

Ideal Young Decorator, bathtub, corner; bl w/yel, M7 ......$35.00

Ideal Young Decorator, carpet sweeper, 2 rollers, red w/bl hadl, M7 ....$30.00

Ideal Young Decorator, chair, kitchen; wht, M7 ....$10.00

Ideal Young Decorator, china closet, dk marbleized maroon, M7 ....$25.00

Ideal Young Decorator, night stand, dk marbleized maroon, M7 .$15.00

Ideal Young Decorator, playpen, pk, M7 ....$45.00

Ideal Young Decorator, sofa, roght corner section, rose, M7 ...$12.00

Ideal Young Decorator, sofa, sm middle section, rose, M7...$12.00

Ideal Young Decorator, stove, wht, M7 ....$55.00

Ideal Young Decorator, table, coffee; dk marbleized maroon, M7 ....$18.00

Ideal Young Decorator, table, kitchen; wht, M7 ....$10.00

Ideal Young Decorator, television, complete, M7 ....$45.00

Ideal Young Decorator, television, no cb backing, M7......$25.00

Imagination, any pc except lawn set, M7, ea....................$3.00

Imagination, lawn set, 3-pc set w/barbecue, lawn sofa & table w/umbrella, rust, M7 ....$12.00

Irwin, broom, any color, M7, ea......................................$5.00

Irwin, clothes basket, bright yel, 3" across, M7 ....$4.00

Irwin, dustpan, any color, M7, ea....................................$4.00

Irwin, hoe, orange, M7..$3.00

Irwin, hoe, pitch fork, M7...$3.00

Irwin, pail, dk bl or gr, M7, ea...$4.00

Irwin, shovel, gr or orange, M7, ea $3.00

Irwin, spade, bright yel, M7 ....$3.00

Irwin, watering can, orange, M7......................................$10.00

Irwin Interior Decorator, bathtub, lt gr, M7 ....$5.00

Irwin Interior Decorator, plate, orange, M7 ....$3.00

Irwin Interior Decorator, refrigerator, under the counter; yel, M7 ....$3.00

Irwin Interior Decorator, refrigerator, yel, M7.................$5.00

Irwin Interior Decorator, toilet, lt gr, M7 ....$5.00

Irwin Interior Decorator, yel w/chrome, M7.....................$5.00

Jaydon, bed w/spread, bl spread, M7................................$15.00

Jaydon, chair, any color, M7, ea.......................................$1.00

Jaydon, chair, bedroom; bl or pk, M7, ea..........................$6.00

Jaydon, chair, living room; ivory w/brn base, M7 ....$8.00

Jaydon, chest, low w/2 opening drawers, reddish brn, M7...$5.00

Jaydon, cupboard, corner; red, M7...................................$5.00

Jaydon, hamper, red, M7 ....$5.00

Jaydon, lamp, table; ivory w/red shade or red w/red shade, M7, ea $15.00

Jaydon, nightstand, pk, M7 ....$4.00

Jaydon, piano, reddish brn swirl, M7 ....$12.00

Jaydon, piano bench, reddish brn swirl, M7 ....$3.00

Jaydon, refrigerator, ivory w/blk, M7 ....$15.00

Jaydon, sink, bathroom; ivory, M7...................................$10.00

Jaydon, sink, kitchen; ivory w/blk, M7.............................$15.00

Jaydon, table, dining; reddish brn swirl, M7 ....$5.00

Jaydon, toilet, ivory w/red lid, M7 ....$10.00

JP Co, chair, brn, M7 ....$1.00

JP Co, hutch, brn, M7..$4.00

Kage, cupboard, china; walnut, M7 ....$8.00

Kage, refrigerator, wht w/blk & red trim, M7 ....$8.00

Kage, sink, kitchen; ivory, M7 ....$5.00

Kage, table, coffee; walnut, M7..$3.00

Kage, table & chairs set, wire legs, red, larger scale, M7...$18.00

Kenton, stove (DOT), pnt CI, 4-footed, 4½", G+, A (Est: $25-$50) $35.00

Kilgore, baby carriage, CI, orange w/NP top, hdl & spoke wheels, 5½x5", EX, A..$355.00

Kilgor, Sally Ann nursery set, cast iron, complete, NMIB, $700.00.

Lundby, fireplace, 3¼x2¾" or 2¾x4¼", M7, ea $15.00

Lundby, table, living room; walnut, M7 ....$12.00

Marvi, boat ride, mc, M7 ....$20.00

Marvi, Ferris wheel, mc, M7 ....$15.00

Marx, hard plastic, ½" scale, any pc except barbecue, curved sofa, jukebox or milk bar, any color, M7, ea from $3 to $5.00

Marx, hard plastic, ½" scale, barbecue, patio; dk brn, M7 ..$8.00

Marx, hard plastic, ½" scale, curved sofa or milk bar, bright yel or red, M7, ea $15.00

Marx, hard plastic, ½" scale, juke box, bright yel or red, M7, ea..$20.00

Marx, hard plastic, ¾" scale, any pc except iron, swimming pool or upright sweeper, M7, ea, from, $3 to $6.00

Marx, hard plastic, ¾" scale, iron, wht, M7 ....$8.00

Marx, hard plastic, ¾" scale, swimming pool (red), upright sweeper (wht), M7, ea $10.00

Marx, soft plastic, ¾" scale, any pc except floor lamp, M7, ea from $3 to $4.00

Marx, soft plastic, ¾" scale, floor lamp, bright yel or lt yel, M7, ea $6.00

Marx Little Hostess, chair, bedroom occasional; ivory w/hot pk seat, M7 ....$8.00

Marx Little Hostess, chair, occasional; yel, M7 ....$12.00

Marx Little Hostess, chaise, ivory w/bright pk, M7...........$12.00

Marx Little Hostess, chest, block front, rust or ivory, M7, ea..$12.00

Marx Little Hostess, clock, grandfather; red, M7 ....$18.00

Marx Little Hostess, dresser, dbl; ivory, M7 ....$8.00

Marx Little Hostess, fireplace, ivory, M7...........................$20.00

Marx Little Hostess, lowboy, red, M7 ....$12.00

Marx Little Hostess, mirror, wall; M7 ....$5.00

Marx Little Hostess, refrigerator, avocado, M7 ....$25.00

Marx Little Hostess, rocker, reddish-brn, M7....................$12.00

Marx Little Hostess, sideboard, brn, M7 ....$12.00

Marx Little Hostess, table, coffee; rnd, brn, M7 ....$8.00

Marx Little Hostess, table, gate-leg; rust, M7....................$15.00

Marx Little Hostess, table, tilt-top; blk, M7.......................$12.00

Mattel Littles, armoire, M7..$8.00

Mattel Littles, doll, Belinda, w/4 chairs & pop-up room setting, M7...$25.00

Mattel Littles, doll, Hedy, w/sofa & pop-up room setting, M7 ....$22.00

Mattel Littles, sofa, M7 ....$5.00

Mattel Littles, sofa & Hedy doll, in orig box, M7 ....$15.00

Mattel Littles, table, drop-leaf; w/4 plates & cups, M7 .....$15.00

Mattle Littles, doll set, Littles Family (Mr & Mrs & baby), M7...$22.00

MPC, any pc, M7, ea..$3.00

Nancy Forbes, bathroom set, 5-pc w/medicine cabinet, scale, sink & vanity w/mirror, ivory, M7 ....$25.00

Nancy Forbes, buffet, walnut, M7......................................$3.00

Nancy Forbes, chair, kitchen; wht, M7...............................$2.00

Nancy Forbes, dresser w/mirror, walnut, M7 ....$4.00

Nancy Forbes, highboy, walnut, M7...................................$3.00

Nancy Forbes, lamp, table; gold, M7 ....$3.00

Nancy Forbes, night stand, walnut, M7..............................$2.00

Nancy Forbes, vanity, walnut, M7......................................$4.00

Nancy Forbes, vanity bench, walnut, M7............................$3.00

Plasco, bathroom set, complete, in orig box w/insert & floor plan, M7...$50.00

Plasco, bathtub, any color, M7, ea $4.00

Plasco, bed, yel spread & brn headboard, M7....................$3.00

Plasco, bedspread, any color, M7, ea $2.00

Plasco, buffet, any color, M7, ea $4.00

Plasco, chair, dining (w/ or w/o arms); brn or marbleized brn, M7, ea..$3.00

Plasco, chair, dining; tan w/paper seat cover, M7 ....$4.00

Plasco, chair, kitchen; any color, M7, ea $2.00

Plasco, chair, living room; no-base style, dk brn or yel, M7, ea ..$3.00

Plasco, chair, living room; w/base, bright gr, lt gr or mauve, M7, ea...$15.00

Plasco, chair, patio; bl w/ivory legs, M7 ....$3.00

Plasco, clock, grandfather; lt brn swirl or dk brn, cb face, M7, ea...$15.00

Plasco, highboy, tan, M7..$8.00

Plasco, kitchen counter, no-base style, pk, M7...................$3.00

Plasco, night stand, brn, med marbleized brn or tan, M7, ea.$3.00

Plasco, refrigerator, no-base style, pk or wht, M7, ea $3.00

Plasco, refrigerator, wht w/bl base, M7 ....$5.00

Plasco, sink, kitchen; no base style, lt gr w/rose trim, pk, or wht, M7, ea..$3.00

Plasco, sofa, no-base style, any color, M7, ea.....................$3.00

Plasco, stove, no-base style, pk, M7...................................$3.00

Plasco, stove, wht w/bl base, M7..$5.00

Plasco, table, coffee; brn, med marbleized brn or tan, M7, ea..$3.00

Plasco, table, coffee; tan w/leather top, M7.......................$5.00

Plasco, table, dining room side; tan w/yel, M7 ....$4.00

Plasco, table, kitchen; pk, M7...$5.00

Plasco, table, patio (sm); bl/ivory legs, M7........................$4.00

Plasco, table, umbrella; bl w/ivory, complete, M7.............$15.00

Plasco, toilet, turq w/wht, M7...$8.00

Plasco, vanity, w/ or w/o mirror style, any color, M7, ea $5.00

Plasco, vanity bench, any color, M7, ea..............................$3.00

Pyro, see Allied/Pryo

Reliable, bathtub, ivory w/bl trim, M7 ....$15.00

Reliable, chair, dining; rust, M7..$5.00

Reliable, chair, kitchen; ivory w/bl seat, M7.....................$5.00

Reliable, chair, living room; bl w/rust base or red w/rust base, M7, ea..$15.00

Reliable, doll, baby, jtd, hard plastic, pk, M7 ....$10.00
Reliable, doll, baby sucking thumb, hard plastic, 2¾", M7 ..$10.00
Reliable, highboy, rust, M7 ....$8.00
Reliable, piano bench, brn, M7 ....$4.00
Reliable, piano bench, rust, M7 ....$25.00
Reliable, radio, floor; rust, M7 ....$15.00
Reliable, refrigerator, ivory w/bl trim, M7 ....$5.00
Reliable, stove, ivory w/bl trim, M7.......................$5.00
Reliable, table, dining; rust, M7 ....$20.00
Reliable, table, kitchen; ivory, M7 ....$12.00
Reliable, toilet, ivory w/bl seat, M7 ....$5.00
Renwal, baby bath, bl or pk, duck decal, M7, ea...........$15.00
Renwal, baby crib, ivory, Alice, Irene or Mary, M7, ea.....$10.00
Renwal, baby crib, matt pk, M7.................................$10.00
Renwal, baby crib, pk, John, Mary or Peter, M7, ea..........$10.00
Renwal, bed, brn w/ivory spread, M7.........................$8.00
Renwal, blanket, M7...$5.00
Renwal, broom, witch's style, metallic bl hdl, M7 ....$10.00
Renwal, buffet, non-opening drawer, brn, M7................$6.00
Renwal, carriage, blanket insert, bl w/pk wheels, M7 ....$30.00
Renwal, carriage, doll insert, bl, stenciled, M7 ....$35.00
Renwal, carriage, doll insert, pk w/pk wheels or pk w/bl wheels,
    M7, ea $30.00
Renwal, chair, barrel; bl stenciled w/brn base, M7............$15.00
Renwal, chair, barrel; bl w/red base or ivory w/brn base, M7,
    ea...$8.00
Renwal, chair, barrel; med bl w/metallic red base, M7........$9.00
Renwal, chair, brn w/ivory, ivory w/red or red w/yel, M7, ea ..$3.00
Renwal, chair, club; bl w/brn base, lt bl w/brn base, pk w/ tallic
    red base or pk w/red base, M7, ea..............$8.00
Renwal, chair, club; dk bl base, M7 ....$15.00
Renwal, chair, folding; red w/gold seat, M7....................$15.00
Renwal, chair, ivory w/blk, M7 ....$5.00
Renwal, chair, teacher's; brn, M7 ....$15.00
Renwal, china closet, brn, reddish brn or med maroon swirl,
    M7 ....$5.00
Renwal, china closet, brn or reddish brn, stenciled, M7, ea ..$15.00
Renwal, clock, kitchen; ivory or red, M7, ea...................$20.00
Renwal, clock, mantel; ivory or red, M7, ea....................$10.00
Renwal, cocker spaniel (from animal hospital set), blk, M7 ...$22.00
Renwal, cradle, doll insert, bl, stenciled, M7 ....$25.00
Renwal, desk, student; bl, brn, red or yel, M7, ea $12.00
Renwal, desk, teacher's; bl, M7 ....$25.00
Renwal, doll, baby, flesh-colored w/pnt diaper, pk w/pnt diaper
    or plan, M7, ea...$8.00
Renwal, doll, baby, pnt suit, M7 ....$10.00
Renwal, doll, baby insert, M7 ....$5.00
Renwal, doll, chubby baby, pnt diaper, M7 ....$45.00
Renwal, doll, father, metal trivets, bl suit, M7 ....$25.00
Renwal, doll, father, plastic trivets, tan or brn suit, M7, ea ..$25.00
Renwal, doll, mother, metal trivets, rose dress, M7...........$25.00
Renwal, doll, nursery baby, rubber, M7........................$4.00
Renwal, doll, sister, metal trivets, yel dress, M7 ....$25.00
Renwal, dust pan, red or yel, M7, ea...........................$10.00
Renwal, garbage can, no decal, red w/yel or yel w/red, M7,
    ea $5.00
Renwal, garbage can, w/decal, yel w/red, M7 ....$8.00

Renwal, hamper, ivory, M7 ....$2.00
Renwal, hamper, opening lid, lt gr, M7 ....$10.00
Renwal, highboy, bl or pk, M7, ea.............................$12.00
Renwal, highboy, brn, M7......................................$6.00
Renwal, highboy, opening doors, brn, M7 ....$8.00
Renwal, highboy, opening drawers, blk, M7..................$22.00
Renwal, highchair, ivory, M7..................................$30.00
Renwal, ironing board, bl or pk, M7..........................$7.00
Renwal, ironing board w/iron, bl or pk, M7, ea..............$22.00

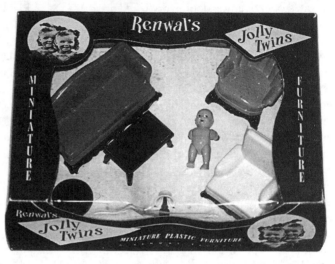

Renwal, Jolly Twins living room set, complete, MIB, from $100.00 to $125.00. (Photo courtesy Judith Mosholder)

Renwal, kiddie car, bl w/red & yel, M7 ....$55.00
Renwal, lamp, table; brn w/ivory shade, M7 ....$6.00
Renwal, lamp, table; carmel w/ivory shade, M7 ....$12.00
Renwal, lamp, table; metallic red w/ivory shade, M7........$12.00
Renwal, lamp, table; red w/ivory shade, M7.................$10.00
Renwal, lamp, table; yel w/ivory shade, M7 ....$10.00
Renwal, night stand/end table, caramel swirl or lt bl, M7, ea.$3.00
Renwal, night stand/end table, pk or matt pk, M7, ea $4.00
Renwal, piano, marbilized brn, M7............................$35.00
Renwal, piano bench, brn or lt gr, M7, ea $2.00
Renwal, playground slide, bl w/red steps or yel w/bl steps, M7,
    ea $22.00
Renwal, playpen, bl w/pk bottom or pk w/bl bottom, M7, ea ..$15.00
Renwal, radio, floor; brn, M7.................................$8.00
Renwal, radio, table; brn or red, M7, ea $15.00
Renwal, radio/phonograh, metallic red or red, M7, ea......$20.00
Renwal, refrigerator, ivory w/blk non-opening door, M7 ..$15.00
Renwal, rocker, blk, M7.......................................$18.00
Renwal, rocker, yel w/red, M7................................$8.00
Renwal, scale, ivory or red, M7, ea...........................$10.00
Renwal, server, brn, M7 ....$6.00
Renwal, server, opening door, brn, M7 ....$8.00
Renwal, server, opening drawer, brn or reddish brn, stenciled,
    M7 ....$12.00
Renwal, server, opening drawer, red, M7.....................$15.00
Renwal, sewing machine, bl w/yel & red, red w/bl & yel or yel
    w/red & bl, M7, ea..$30.00

Renwal, sewing machine, tabletop; red w/bl base, M7......$85.00
Renwal, sink, bathroom; dk turq w/blk, M7.......................$8.00
Renwal, sink, bathroom; ivory w/blk, pk w/bl or pk w/lt bl, M7, ea...$5.00
Renwal, sink, non-opening door, ivory w/blk door, M7....$15.00
Renwal, smoking stand, ivory w/red or red w/ivory, M7, ea...$12.00
Renwal, sofa, all red, bright pk w/metallic red base or dk burgundy w/brn base, M7, ea...$18.00
Renwal, stool, ivory w/red seat or red w/ivory seat, M7, ea..$10.00
Renwal, stove, non-opening door, ivory w/blk door or turq, M7, ea..$12.00
Renwal, stove, opening door, ivory w/red door, M7.........$18.00
Renwal, student desk, bl, brn, red or yel, M7, ea...............$12.00
Renwal, table, brn or yel, M7, ea..$8.00
Renwal, table, cocktail; brn, M7.......................................$10.00
Renwal, table, cocktail; reddish brn, M7............................$8.00
Renwal, table, dining; brn, M7..$18.00
Renwal, table, dining; orange or reddish orange, M7, ea..$15.00
Renwal, table, folding; gold, M7.......................................$20.00
Renwal, table, ivory or very deep ivory, M7, ea..................$5.00
Renwal, table (folding) & chair set, gold table, 4 red chairs w/gold seats, M7...$120.00
Renwal, telephone, yel w/red, M7.....................................$22.00
Renwal, toilet, ivory w/blk, M7..$10.00
Renwal, toilet, turq w/blk hdl, M7.......................................$8.00
Renwal, toydee, bl, matt bl or pk, M7, ea............................$4.00
Renwal, toydee, bl w/duck stencil, M7...............................$15.00
Renwal, tub, bathroom; ivory w/blk or pk w/bl, M7, ea......$7.00
Renwal, tub, bathroom; med bl & turq w/blk, M7.............$12.00
Renwal, vacuum cleaner, yel w/red hdl decal, M7.............$25.00
Renwal, vanity, simplified style w/mirror, brn w/stenciling, M7...$15.00
Renwal, vanity, simplified-style w/mirror, brn, M7............$12.00
Renwal, washing machine, bl w/pk or pk w/bl, both with bear decal, M7, ea...$30.00
Sounds Like Home, bed w/night clothes, M7.....................$12.00
Sounds Like Home, breakfront, brn, M7..............................$6.00
Sounds Like Home, chair, M7..$2.00
Sounds Like Home, dresser w/mirror, M7............................$6.00
Sounds Like Home, dresser w/music box, M7.....................$12.00
Sounds Like Home, hair dryer, bl, M7..................................$5.00
Sounds Like Home, night table w/electric alarm clock, M7..$8.00
Sounds Like Home, shower curtain rod, M7.........................$2.00
Sounds Like Home, sink, electronic; M7............................$12.00
Sounds Like Home, stove, electronic; M7...........................$12.00
Sounds Like Home, table, kitchen; M7.................................$5.00
Sounds Like Home, tissue box, M7......................................$5.00
Strombecker, bathtub, aqua, bl or ivory, ¾", M7, ea.........$10.00
Strombecker, bed, pk, 1940s, ¾" scale, M7.........................$8.00
Strombecker, chair, bedroom/dining; unfinished, 1930s, ¾", M7...$6.00
Strombecker, chair, living room; aqua, dk bl or red, 1940s-50s, ¾" scale, M7, ea...$10.00
Strombecker, clock, grandfather; bl w/blk trim or dk peach w/blk trim, ¾" scale, M7, ea...$15.00
Strombecker, lamp, floor; unfinished, ¾" scale, M7.........$10.00
Strombecker, lamp, table; gr w/ivory shade or yel w/ivory shade, M7, ea...$15.00

Strombecker, living room set, 8-pc w/sofa, chair, foot stool, end & library tables, radio, clock, bench, 1" scale, M7 ..$135.00
Strombecker, night stand, lt gr or pk, ¾" scale, M7, ea.......$6.00
Strombecker, scale, dk bl or gr, ¾" scale, M7, ea.............$15.00
Strombecker, sink, aqua or ivory, ¾" scale, M7..................$8.00
Strombecker, sink, bathroom; gr w/gold swirl, 1" scale, M7 ..$20.00
Strombecker, sofa, gr flocked, 1940s, ¾" scale, M7...........$18.00
Strombecker, sofa, gr flocked, 1950s, 1" scale, M7............$25.00
Strombecker, sofa, 1940s, gr flocked, M7 ....$18.00
Strombecker, sofa, 1940s-50s, aqua, peach or red, M7, ea...$10.00
Strombecker, stove, ivory w/blk trim, 1936, 1" scale, M7 ..$20.00
Strombecker, stove, lt gr, 1940s, ¾" scale, M7.................$15.00
Strombecker, stove, wht or wht w/blk, 1940-50s, ¾" scale, M7, ea $18.00
Strombecker, stove, wht w/ivory trim, 1961, ¾" scale, M7.$15.00
Strombecker, stove, 1940s, ivory, ¾" scale, M7..................$8.00
Strombecker, table, dining; walnut, 1930s, 1" scale, M7...$20.00
Strombecker, table & chair, trestle; red, 1940s, ¾" scale, M7.$10.00
Strombecker, table & chairs set, dining; wood finish, 1940s, ¾" scale, M7 ....$15.00
Strombecker, television, paper screen, ivory, 1961, ¾" scale, M7 ....$20.00
Superior, any soft plastic pc, sm, M7, ea from $1 to...........$2.00

Superior, chair, $5.00; vanity and bench, yellow, $9.00; chest of drawers, $5.00; bed, $5.00. (Photo courtesy Judith Mosholder)

Superior, dust pan, ¾" scale, red, M7 ....$8.00
Superior, most pcs except dust pan, ¾" scale, M7, ea $3.00
Thomas, see Acme/Thomas
Tomy-Smaller Home, cabinet w/dbl sink bowls, bathroom; M7..$20.00
Tomy-Smaller Homes, armoire, no hangers, M7..............$10.00
Tomy-Smaller Homes, armoire, w/hangers, M7 ....$15.00
Tomy-Smaller Homes, bathtub, M7 ....$15.00
Tomy-Smaller Homes, bed, canopy; M7..........................$15.00
Tomy-Smaller Homes, cabinet w/television, high, M7.....$55.00
Tomy-Smaller Homes, cat, M7 ....$10.00
Tomy-Smaller Homes, checkerboard, M7 ....$5.00
Tomy-Smaller Homes, diary, M7 ....$10.00
Tomy-Smaller Homes, dolls, father, sister or brother; M7, ea..$8.00

Tomy-Smaller Homes, lamp, table; M7.............$15.00
Tomy-Smaller Homes, mirror, standing; M7 ....$15.00
Tomy-Smaller Homes, night stand, M7 ....$8.00

Tomy-Smaller Homes, oven unit with microwave and cherry pie, $55.00; refrigerator, $15.00; sink/diswasher with two racks, $15.00; stove/hood unit, $15.00; kitchen table, $8.00; kitchen chairs, $3.00 each. (Photo courtesy Judith Mosholder)

Tomy-Smaller Homes, placemat, yel & orange, M7............$5.00
Tomy-Smaller Homes, plant, tall, M7 ....$8.00
Tomy-Smaller Homes, planter, bathroom; no towels, M7...$10.00
Tomy-Smaller Homes, range top w/hood, M7................$18.00
Tomy-Smaller Homes, refrigerator, w/drawers, M7 ....$12.00
Tomy-Smaller Homes, rocker, M7.............$10.00
Tomy-Smaller Homes, rug, throw; M7 ....$8.00
Tomy-Smaller Homes, scale, M7 ....$15.00
Tomy-Smaller Homes, sink w/dishwasher, no racks, M7.....$8.00
Tomy-Smaller Homes, sofa, 2-pc, M7.............$12.00
Tomy-Smaller Homes, sofa, 3-pc, M7.............$15.00
Tomy-Smaller Homes, speakers, M7.............$3.00
Tomy-Smaller Homes, stereo cabinet, M7 ....$15.00
Tomy-Smaller Homes, table, end; M7.............$8.00
Tomy-Smaller Homes, television, M7 ....$50.00
Tomy-Smaller Homes, toilet, M7 ....$10.00
Tomy-Schoenhut Homes, towel, M7 ....$5.00
Tomy-Smaller Homes, vanity, M7 ....$15.00
Tomy-Smaller Homes, vanity stool, M7 ....$6.00
Tootsietoy, bed, w/headboard, footboard & slats, bl or pk, M7, ea..$20.00
Tootsietoy, buffet, opening drawer, cocoa brn, M7.............$22.00
Tootsietoy, cabinet, medicine; ivory, M7.............$25.00
Tootsietoy, chair, bedroom; bl or pk, M7, ea.............$7.00
Tootsietoy, chair, club; bl, M7.............$8.00
Tootsietoy, chair, kitchen, ivory; M7 ....$7.00
Tootsietoy, chair, simple back, no arms, M7 ....$7.00
Tootsietoy, chair, simple back w/arms, dk brn, M7.............$8.00
Tootsietoy, chair, tufted look, dk red, M7 ....$20.00
Tootsietoy, chair, XX back, w/or w/o arms, M7, ea.............$7.00
Tootsietoy, cupboard, non-opening doors, ivory, M7 ....$20.00
Tootsietoy, icebox or stove, non-opening doors, ivory, M7, ea..$20.00
Tootsietoy, lamp, table; bl, M7 ....$45.00
Tootsietoy, night stand, pl, M7 ....$10.00

Tootsietoy, living room set, five-piece, $65.00.

Tootsietoy, piano bench, yel w/tan seat, M7 ....$15.00
Tootsietoy, rocker, bedroom; bl, M7 ....$12.00
Tootsietoy, rocker, wicker style w/cushion, gold or ivory, M7 ..$20.00
Tootsietoy, server, non-opening door, dk brn, M7.............$22.00
Tootsietoy, table, long, gr crackle, M7.............$22.00
Tootsietoy, table, rectangular, dk brn, M7 ....$22.00
Tootsietoy, tea cart, dk brn, M7 ....$22.00
Tootsietoy, vanity, blk, M7 ....$18.00
Tootsietoy (Midget), bed, pk, M7.............$18.00
Tootsietoy (Midget), dresser, pk, M7.............$10.00
Tootsietoy (Midget), piano, ivory, M7.............$25.00
Tootsietoy (Midget), sofa, 2-pc, right side, red, M7 ....$6.00
Tootsietoy (Midget), vanity, pk, M7.............$10.00
Toysville (Renwal mold), hutch, tan, M7 ....$5.00
Toysville (Renwal mold), radio, floor; tan, M7 ....$5.00
Wolverine, ½" scale, any pc, M7, ea.............$3.00

Dollhouses

Dollhouses were first made commercially in America in the late 1700s. A century later, Bliss and Schoenhut were making wonderful dollhouses that even yet occasionally turn up on the market, and many were being imported from Germany. During the 1940s and 1950s, American toy makers made a variety of cottages; today they're all collectible.

Key:
PLW — Paper lithograph on wood
PW — Painted wood

Bliss, Fire Station No 2, PLW, VG, A (Est: $1,000-$1,250) ..**$400.00**
Bliss, Victorian, 2-story, 2 rooms & attic, PLW, columned porch, electric lights, 30x15", VG, A (Est; $800-$1,000)...**$1,320.00**
Bliss, 2-story, PLW, lithoed detail in & out, roofed porch across front, gr, yel & red, 11x9", G, A (Est: $200-$400) ..**$190.00**
Bliss, 2-story, 2-room, PLW, railed porch, lithoed curtains in 2 upper windows, 17x12x8", VG, A (Est: 1,000-1,250)...........**$800.00**

Bliss, two-story, four rooms, paper lithograph on wood, front porch with railed veranda above, two chimneys, lace curtains, 20x11x23", VG, A (Est: $600.00 – $800.00), $1,200.00. (Photo courtesy Bertoia Auctions)

Christian Hacker, two-story mansion, four rooms and attic, painted wood with paper-lithographed mansard roof, 26x27x14", restored, A (Est: $2,500.00 – $3.500.00), $2,200.00. (Photo courtesy Bertoia Auctions)

English, 2 rooms, mansard roof, chimneys at ea end, gothic trim, 5 arched windows/door, 23", EX, A (Est: $1,500-$2,000) ..$2,750.00
McLoughlin Bros, Dolly's Playhouse, 2-story, heavy lithoed cb, 2 rooms, 20½" T, VGIB, A (Est: $200-$300) $550.00
Schoenhut, 2-story, 6 rooms, 3-room attic, 2 dormers, PW, cb shutters, window boxes, 23x25", VG+, A (Est: $600-$800)..$1,300.00

Unknown, suburban, 2-story, PW, clapboard siding, sm porch, basement windows, 16x23x11", VG, A (Est: $400-$500)..$1,100.00
Unknown, 3-story, pnt tin, chimneys at ea end, 2 bay windows, fenced courtyard, 24x20x22", G, A (Est: $1,000-$1,500) $935.00
Whitney Reed, 2-story, 2 rooms, PLW, guttered sides, 2 doors open, railed porch & balcony, 18", VG, A (Est: $600-$800)..$1,060.00

SHOPS AND SINGLE ROOMS

Butcher Shop, Germany, outdoor shop against storefront w/hanging meat, 2 figures, 19x31", EX, A (Est: $2,500-$3,500) $8,800.00
General Grocery, litho tin, sides fold out to open display, w/product boxes & separate counter, VG, A (Est: $300-$400)..$165.00
Grocery Shop, wood w/top rail & drawers w/porc knobs on back panel, counter, etc, 16x28", EX, A (Est: $800-$1,200) $1,650.00

General Store, Germany, wood with paper lithographed walls and floor, two dolls, many accessories, 30x15x14", EX, A (Est: $2,000.00 – $3,000.00), $3,035.00. (Photo courtesy Bertoia Auctions)

Hat Shoppe, mid-twentieth century shop with mid-nineteenth century doll, painted wood, many accessories, 10½" doll, 17x14" shop, EX, A (Est: $1,300.00 – $1,600.00), $1,540.00. (Photo courtesy Bertoia Auctions)

Journaux Amusants (News Stand), French, PLW, front opens to counter, w/accessories, 10x12x15", EX, A (Est: $800-$1,000) $1,320.00

Kitchen, German, wood, bl/wht wallpaper, wht furniture, bl trim, many accessories, 14x16x25", EX, A (Est: $1,000-$1,200) $2,200.00

Parlor, French, 3-sided foldup, no floor, wht & pk, ornate accessories, upholstery, 13x25", EX, A (Est: $1,200-$1,500) $1,760.00

Silversmith Shop, Kupjack, wood, detailed w/paned glass window & door, w/accessories, 15x12x7", EX, A (Est: $800-$1,000) $1,320.00

Sortie de L'Ecole, French, PLW & cb, mansard roof opens, back folds down, w/accessories, 13x18", VG+, A (Est: $800-$900)..$990.00

Stable, Bliss, PLW, 6 posts form open ground floor on base, opening loft door, 15" T, Fair+, A (Est: $150-$200)..........$220.00

Stable w/Dormer, Germany, lithoed paper on wood, opening door on upper level, 3 animals, 12x10", EX, A (Est: $200-$300)..$520.00

Dolls and Accessories

Obviously the field of dolls cannot be covered in a price guide such as this, but with the exception of Schoenhut and Shirley Temple, we wanted to touch upon some of the later dolls from the 1950s and 1960s, since a lot of collector interest is centered on those decades. For in-depth information on dolls of all types, we recommend those lovely doll books, all of which are available from Collector Books: *Doll Values, Antique to Modern*, by Barbara DeFeo and Carol Stover; *Madame Alexander Collector's Dolls Price Guide, Madame Alexander Store Exclusives and Limited Editions*, and *Collector's Encyclopedia of Madame Alexander Dolls, 1948 – 1965*, all by Linda Crowsey; *The World of Raggedy Ann Collectibles* by Kim Avery; *Collector's Encyclopedia of American Composition Dolls, 1900 – 1950*, by Ursula R. Mertz; *Encyclopedia of Bisque Nancy Ann Storybook Dolls* by Elaine M.

Pardee and Jackie Robertson; *Arranbee Dolls, "The Dolls That Sell on Sight,"* by Suzanne DeMillar and Dennis J. Brevik; *Modern Collectible Dolls* by Patsy Moyer; *Small Dolls of the 40s & 50s* by Carol J. Stover; *Collector's Guide to Horsman Dolls* by Don Jensen; *Collector's Guide to Ideal Dolls* and *American Character Dolls* by Judith Izen; *Collector's Encyclopedia of Vogue Dolls* by Judith Izen and Carol J. Stover; and *Dolls of the 1960s and 1970s, Vol. I* and *Vol. II*, by Cindy Sabulis. Other books are referenced in specific subcategories.

See also Action Figures; Barbie and Friends; Character, TV, and Movie Collectibles; GI Joe; and other specific categories.

BABY DOLLS AND OTHER FAVORITES

Remnants of dolls have been found in the artifacts of most primitive digs. Some are just sticks or stuffed leather or animal skins.

Dolls teach our young nurturing and caring. Mothering instincts stay with us — and aren't we lucky as doll collectors that we can keep 'mothering' even after the young have 'left the nest.'

Baby dolls come in all sizes and mediums: vinyl, plastic, rubber, porcelain, cloth, etc. Almost everyone remembers some doll they had as a child. The return to childhood is such a great trip. Keep looking and you will find yours.

Advisor: Marcia Fanta (M15)

Annabelle, Madame Alexander, complete with comb and curlers in pink box, EX, A, $350.00. (Photo courtesy McMasters Harris Doll Auctions)

Baby Beans, Mattel, 1970, several variations, NM, ea from $15 to $20.00

Baby Cheerful Tearful, Mattel, 1966, 6½", MIB $55.00

Baby Crawl-Along, Remco, 1967, all orig, 20", EX, from $25 to..$35.00

Baby First Step, Mattel, 1964, M.......................$95.00
Baby Fun, Mattel, 1968, all orig, complete, 7", EX, from $30
    to...$35.00
Baby Giggles, Ideal, 1967, 15", MIB..................$100.00
Baby Kissy, Ideal, 1962, 23", NRFB.....................$95.00
Baby Tender Love, Mattel, 1971, all orig, 16", VG..........$35.00
Baby Tippee Toes, Mattel, 1967, 16", MIB $100.00
Betsy Wetsy, Ideal, 1954-56, molded or rooted curly hair, 16",
    MIB, ea minimum value......................................$125.00
Cabbage Patch Preemie, Coleco, complete, VG+ $65.00
Chatterbox, Madame Alexander, 1961, MIB.................$125.00
Dancerella, Mattel, 1976, 15", MIN...............................$45.00

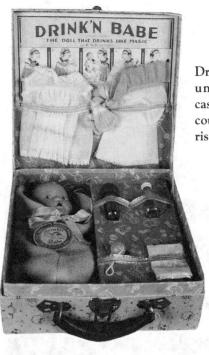

Drink 'N Babe, Arranbee, unplayed with, M (in case), A, $775.00. (Photo courtesy McMasters Harris Doll Auctions)

Dy-Dee Baby, Effanbee, 1935, w/wardrobe, 11", MIB.....$425.00
Gabbigale, Kenner, 1972, 18", MIB................................$85.00
Ginny, Vogue Dolls #101, 1950s, walker, hard plastic, wig,
    sleep eyes, several outfits, 7½", EXIB, A (Est: $300-
    $400)..$450.00
Johnny Playpal, Ideal, 1959, 24", NM...........................$425.00
Kissy, Ideal, 1960s, 22", MIB, from $100 to....................$125.00
Lil' Miss Fashion, Deluxe Reading, 1960, 20", MIB..........$75.00
Magic Baby Tender Love, Mattel, 1978, 14", MIB............$45.00
Marjorie (The Teenage Doll), Belle Doll & Toy Co, vinyl,
    MIB $125.00
Miss Ideal (The Photographer's Model), Ideal, complete w/Play-
    wave Kit, 25", MIB, from $250 to $300.00
Nancy Nonsense, Kenner, 1968, talker, 17", MIB $115.00
Patti Playful, Ideal, 1970, 16", EX, from $45 to.................$65.00
Patti Prays, Ideal, 1957, NM......................................$55.00
Patty Playpal (Nurse), Ideal, 1960s, 36", M $355.00
Pretty Curls, Ideal, 1981-82, all orig, EX...........................$25.00
Rub-A-Dub Dolly in Tugboat Shower, Ideal, 1974-78, 17",
    MIB..$95.00
Talking Baby Alive, Kenner, 1992, MIB........................$100.00

Revlon Doll, Ideal, EXIB, A, $300.00. (Photo courtesy McMasters Harris Doll Auctions)

Tearful Tender Love, Mattel, 1971, 16", VG+ $50.00
Thumbelina, Ideal, 18", NMIB, from $150 to.................$200.00
Thumbelina (Newborn), Ideal, 1967, pull string and she wiggles
    and squirms, 9½", M....................................$50.00
Thumbelina (Tiny), Ideal, 1962-68, 14", MIB................$185.00

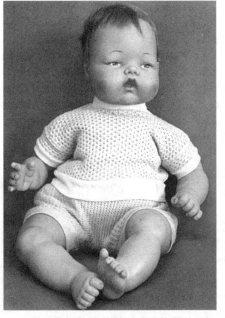

Thumbelina (Tiny), Ideal, 1962 – 1968, 21", NM, from $100.00 to $150.00. (Photo courtesy Cindy Sabulis)

Thumbelina (Toddler), Ideal, 1960s, complete w/walker, NMIB,
    from $75 to $100.00
Tickles, Deluxe Reading, 1963, talker, MIB.....................$75.00
Tiny Baby Tender Love, Mattel, all orig, 11½", VG $35.00
Tiny Tears, American Character, all orig, complete w/acces-
    sories, M (in case)..$350.00
Tiny Tears, American Character, 1950s, all orig, 12", VG ..$125.00

Tiny Tubber, Effanbee, 1976, all orig, 11", MIB $55.00
Toni Doll, Ideal, walker, 'The Doll With Magic Nylon Hair,'
   includes Simplicty dress patterns, unused, NMIB, A ..$425.00
Upsy Dazy, Ideal, 1973, 15", EX...$40.00
Winnie Walker, Advance, 1957, talker, 24", MIB..........$200.00

Betsy McCall

The tiny 8" Betsy McCall doll was manufactured by the American Character Doll Co. from 1957 through 1963. She was made from high-quality hard plastic with a bisque-like finish and hand-painted features. Betsy came in four hair colors — tosca, red, blond, and brunette. She had blue sleep eyes, molded lashes, a winsome smile, and a fully jointed body with bendable knees. On her back there is an identification circle which reads 'McCall Corp.' The basic doll wore a sheer chemise, white taffeta panties, nylon socks, and Maryjane-style shoes and could be purchased for $2.25.

There were two different materials used for tiny Betsy's hair. The first was a soft mohair sewn into fine mesh. Later the rubber skullcap was rooted with saran which was more suitable for washing and combing.

Betsy McCall had an extensive wardrobe with nearly one hundred outfits, each of which could be purchased separately. They were made from wonderful fabrics such as velvet, taffeta, felt, and even real mink. Each ensemble came with the appropriate footwear and was priced under $3.00. Since none of Betsy's clothing was tagged, it is often difficult to identify other than by its square snap closures (although these were used by other companies as well).

Betsy McCall is a highly collectible doll today but is still fairly easy to find at doll shows. Prices remain reasonable for this beautiful clothes horse and her many accessories.

Doll, Ideal, 14", hard plastic body, original gray and white checked dress, shoes, and socks, EX, A, $200.00. (Photo courtesy McMasters Harris Doll Auctions)

Doll, American Character, 8", hard plastic, rooted hair, 1957, EX (in basic chemise)...$350.00

Doll, American Character, 14", vinyl w/swivel waist or 1-pc torso, rooted hair, 1958, EX, ea $500.00
Doll, American Character, 19" to 20", vinyl, rooted hair, 1-pc torso, 1959, EX, ea...$500.00
Doll, American Character, 22", vinyl w/jtd limbs & waist, 5 different colors of rooted hair, 1961, EX, ea.................$225.00
Doll, American Character, 29", vinyl w/jtd limbs & waist, 5 different colors of rooted hair, 1961, EX, ea.................$300.00
Doll, American Character, 36", Linda McCall (Betsy's cousin), vinyl w/Betsy face, rooted hair, 1959, EX................$350.00
Doll, American Character, 36", vinyl w/Patti Playpal style body, rooted hair, 1959, EX..$325.00
Doll, American Character, 39", Sandy McCall (Betsy's brother), vinyl w/molded hair, red blazer & navy shorts, 1959, EX...........$350.00
Doll, Horsman, 12½", rigid plastic body w/vinyl head, w/extra hair pc & accessories, 1974, EX................................$50.00
Doll, Horsman, 29", rigid plastic teen body w/vinyl head, rooted hair w/side part, orig clothing mk BMc, 1974, MIB...$275.00
Doll, Uneeda, 11½", rigid vinyl body w/rooted hair, wore hip outfits, 1964, EX, minimum value............................$100.00

Blythe by Kenner

Blythe by Kenner is an 11" doll with a slender body and an extra large head. You can change her eye color by pulling a string in the back of her head. She came with different hair colors and had fashions, cases, and wigs that could be purchased separately. She was produced in the early 1970s which accounts for her 'groovy' wardrobe. In excellent condition, loose dolls are worth from $100.00 to $200.00.

Advisor: Dawn Diaz (P2)

Case, #33241, image of blond-haired doll wearing Pow-Wow Poncho, orange background, vinyl, EX, P2 ....$50.00
Doll, brunette hair, MIB $500.00
Doll, brunette hair, wearing Medieval Mood, EX, P2 .....$200.00
Doll, lt red hair, wearing Golden Goddess, EX, P2 ....$200.00
Doll, red hair, wearing Love 'N Lace, EX, P2 ....$200.00

Doll, MIB (sealed), $500.00. (Photo courtesy Cindy Sabulis)

Outfit, Aztec Arrival, complete, EX, P2 ....$100.00
Outfit, Golden Goddess, NRFB, P2 ....$150.00
Outfit, Kozy Kape, complete EX, P2 ....$100.00
Outfit, Lounging Lovely, NRFB, P2 ....$150.00
Outfit, Love 'N Lace, NRFB, P2 ....$150.00
Outfit, Pleasant Peasant, missing shoes, EX, P2 ....$75.00
Outfit, Pow-Wow Poncho, complete, EX, P2 ....$100.00
Wig, Lemon, complete w/instructions, M, P2 ....$250.00

CELEBRITY DOLLS

Celebrity dolls have been widely collected for many years. Except for the rarer examples, most of these dolls are still fairly easy to find, and the majority are priced under $100.00.

Condition is a very important worth-assessing factor, and if the doll is still in the original box, so much the better! Should the box be unopened (NRFB), the value is further enhanced. Using mint as a standard, add 50% for the same doll mint in the box and 75% if it has never been taken out. On the other hand, dolls in only good or poorer condition drop at a rapid pace. For more information, see *Collector's Guide to Celebrity Dolls* by David Spurgeon.

The dolls listed here are not character-related. For celebrity/character dolls see Action Figures; Character, TV, and Movie Collectibles; Rock 'N Roll.

Alan Jackson (Country Music Stars), Exclusive Premiere, 1998, 9", MIB, $30.00. (Photo courtesy David Spurgeon)

Abbott & Costello, vinyl in cloth baseball uniforms, w/cassette of the comedy routine 'Who's on First?,' MIB, set ...$250.00
Andy Gibb, Ideal, 1979, 7½", MIB $85.00
Ashley & Mary Kate Olsen, Mattel, 1st issue, Dance & Horeback Riding sets, 9½", MIB, ea....................................$30.00
Audrey Hepburn (Breakfast at Tiffany's), Mattel, 1998, 11½", MIB $50.00
Betty Grable, International Doll Co, 1940s, blond Dynel hair, w/tag, 19", NM, minimum value $400.00

Beverly Johnson (Real Model Collection), Matchbox, 1989, 11½", MIB $50.00
Boy George, LJN, 1984, 11½", rare, MIB $150.00
Brooke Shields, LJN, 1982, pk & gray casual outfit, 11½", MIB...$55.00
Brooke Shields, LJN, 1982, Prom Party, 11½", rare, MIB..$150.00

Brooke Shields, LJN, 1982, suntan doll, 11½", MIB, $65.00. (Photo courtesy Davis Spurgeon)

Captain & Tenille, Mego, 1977, 12½", MIB, ea $125.00
Charlie Chaplin (Little Tramp), Milton Bradley/Bubbles Inc, 1972, 19", MIB $100.00
Cher, Mego, 1976, Growing Hair, 12½", MIB.................$150.00
Cher, Mego, 1976, pk evening gown, 12½", MIB...........$125.00
Cher, Mego, 1981, swimsuit, 12", MIB.............................$50.00
Cheryl Ladd, Mattel, 1978, 11½", MIB............................$85.00
Cheryl Tiegs (Real Model Collection), Matchbox, 1989, 11½", MIB $50.00
Christy Brinkly (Real Model Collection), Matchbox, 1989, 11½", MIB $50.00
Christy Lane, long red velvet skirt w/wht blouse, 1965-70s, 14", M $25.00
Danny Kaye (White Christmas), Exclusive Premiere 1998, dressed as Santa, 9", MIB...$45.00
Debbie Boone, Mattel, 1978, 11½", MIB $100.00
Deidre Hall (Days of Our Lives), Mattel, 1999, 11½", MIB...$35.00
Dennis Rodman (Basketball Player), Street Players, 1990s, 12", MIB $30.00
Diana Ross, Mego, 1977, 12½", MIB, A $150.00
Diana Ross (of the Supremes), Ideal, 1969, 19", rare, MIB ..$600.00
Dick Clark, Juro, 1958, 26½", MIB..............................$450.00
Dionne Quintuplets Set, Madame Alexander, 7½", in pastel rompers & bonnets, EX $850.00
Dionne Quintuplets Set, M Alexander, pastel playsuits & bonnets, w/wood 3-wheeled cart, ea VG, A (Est: $1,000-$1,500)..$650.00

Dionne Quintuplets, Madame Alexander, 11", composition, VG to EX, all with original boxes, $1,300.00 for set. (Photo courtesy McMasters Harris Doll Auctions)

Dolly Parton, Goldberger, 1978, red & silver outfit, 11½", MIB..$100.00
Dolly Parton, Goldberger, 1990s, blk outfit w/silver boots, 12", MIB...$75.00
Donny & Marie Osmond, Mattel, 1976, 12", MIB, ea......$85.00
Dorothy Hamill (Olympic Ice Skater), Ideal, 1977, 11½", MIB...$100.00
Dorothy Lamour, Film Star Creations, 1940s-50s, stuffed print cloth w/mohair wig, cloth bathing suit, w/tag, 14", NM.........$135.00
Ekaterina 'Katia' Gordeeva (Olympic Ice Skater), Playmates, 1998, 11½", MIB $25.00
Eleanor Roosevelt, Effanbee, 1985, brn dress, 14½", MIB.....$125.00
Elizabeth Taylor (Butterfield 8), Tri-Star, 1982, 11½", MIB.$150.00
Elizabeth Taylor (National Velvet), Madame Alexander, 1990, 12", MIB $100.00
Elvis Presley, Eugene, 1984, issued in 6 different outfits, 12", MIB...$75.00
Elvis Presley, Hasbro, 1993, Jailhouse Rock, Teen Idol or '68 Special, numbered edition, 12", MIB, ea....................$50.00
Elvis Presley, World Doll, 1984, Burning Love, 21", MIB..$125.00
Farrah Fawcett-Majors, Mego, 1977, wht jumpsuit, 12½", MIB...$125.00
Farrah Fawcett-Majors, Mego, 1981, swimsuit, 12", MIB ..$50.00
Farrah Fawcett-Majors, see also Charlie's Angels in Character, TV & Movies category
Flip Wilson/Geraldine, Shindana, 1970, stuffed reversable talker, 15", MIB...$85.00
Florence Griffith Joyner, LJN, 1989, 11½", MIB $65.00
George Burns, Effanbee, 1996, blk tuxedo holding cigar, 17", MIB...$150.00
George Burns, Exclusive Premiere, 1997, w/accessories, 9", MIB...$25.00
Ginger Rogers, World Doll, 1976, limited edtion, MIB...$100.00
Grace Kelly (Swan or Mogambo), Tri-Star, 1982, 11½", MIB, ea...$100.00
Groucho Marx, Julius Henry/Effanbee, 1982, 18", MIB...$150.00
Harold Lloyd, 1920s, lithoed stuffed cloth of star standing w/hands in pockets, 12", EX+.................................$100.00
Humphery Bogart & Ingrid Bergman (Casablanca), Exclusive Premiere, 1998, 9", MIB, ea.......................................$30.00
Humphrey Bogart (Casablanca), Effanbee, 1989, 16", MIB..$150.00

Jaclyn Smith, Mego, 1977, 12½", MIB $200.00
Jaclyn Smith, see also Charlie's Angels in Character, TV & Movies category
James Cagney, Effanbee, 1987, pinstripe suit & hat, 16", MIB...$125.00
James Dean, DSI, 1994, sweater & pants, 12", MIB $55.00
Jerry Springer, Street Players, 1998, 12", MIB..................$50.00
Jimmy Osmond, Mattel, 1978, 10", MIB.........................$125.00
John Travolta (On Stage...Super Star), Chemtoy, 1977, 12", MIB...$100.00
John Wayne (Great Legends), Effanbee, 1981, Symbol of the West (cowboy outfit), 17", MIB..............................$150.00
John Wayne (Great Legends), Effanbee, 1982, Guardian of the West (cavalry uniform), 18", MIB..............................$150.00
Kate Jackson, Mattel, 1978, 11½", MIB...........................$85.00
Katerina Witt (Olympic Ice Skater), Playmates, 1998, 11½", MIB...$25.00
KISS, Mego, 1978, any from group, 12½", MIB, ea........$350.00

Kristi Yamaguchi, Playmates, 1998, 11½", MIB, $25.00. (Photo courtesy David Spurgeon)

Laurel & Hardy, Goldberger, 1986, bluejean overalls, 12", MIB, ea...$55.00
Laurel & Hardy, Hamilton Gifts, 1991, cloth suits, 16", MIB, ea...$65.00
Laurel & Hardy, 1981, cloth bodies w/porcelain heads, cloth suits, 18" & 21", MIB, ea.......................................$75.00
Leann Rimes (Country Music Stars), Exclusive Premiere, 1998, 9", MIB...$30.00
Leslie Uggams, Madame Alexander, 1966, lt pk dress, 17", MIB...$350.00
Liberace, Effanbee, 1986, glittery blk & silver outfit w/cape, 16½", MIB...$250.00
Linda Evans, see Character, TV & Movie category
Louis 'Satchmo' Armstrong, Effanbee, 1984, bl & blk tuxedo, 15½", MIB...$250.00
Lucille Ball, Effanbee, 1985, in blk tails & top hat, 15", MIB...$175.00

Lucille Ball (Hollywood Walk of Fame Collection), CAL-HASCO Inc, 1992, 20", MIB..............$350.00

Mae West, Hamilton Gifts, 1991, 17", M..........$50.00

Mae West (Great Legends), Effanbee, 1982, 18", MIB...$125.00

Mandy Moore, Play Along, 2000, 11½", MIB $20.00

Margaret O'Brien, Madame Alexander, 18", EX, $675.00. (Photo courtesy David Spurgeon)

Marie Osmond (Modeling Doll), Mattel, 1976, 30", MIB ..$150.00

Marilyn Monroe, DSI, 1993, blk gown & wht fur stole, 11½", MIB..............................$50.00

Marilyn Monroe, Tri-Star, 1982, pk gown & gloves, 16½", MIB $100.00

Marilyn Monroe, Tri-Star, 1982, 1st issue (same face mold as 16½" doll), 11½", MIB..............................$75.00

Marilyn Monroe, Tri-Star, 1982, 2nd issue (different face mold), 11½", MIB..............................$150.00

Marlo Thomas (That Girl), Madame Alexander, 1967, 17", rare, MIB..............................$800.00

Michael Jackson, LJN, 1984, bl & gold outfit holding microphone, 12", MIB $75.00

Muhammad Ali, Hasbro, 1997, 12", MIB $45.00

Muhammad Ali, Mego, 1976, 9", MOC $150.00

New Kids on the Block, dolls, Show Time Kids Rag Dolls, Hasbro, 1990, 5 different, 19", MIB, ea $65.00

New Kids on the Block, Hasbro, In Concert, 5 different, 12", MIB, ea..............................$50.00

Nicole Boebeck (Olympic Ice Skater), Playmates, 1998, 11½", MIB $25.00

Patty Duke, Horsman, 1965, 12", rare, MIB $450.00

Penny Marshall or Cindy Williams, see Character, TV & Movie category

Prince Charles, Goldberg, 1983, dress uniform, 12", MIB....$100.00

Prince William, Goldberg, 1982, christening gown, 18", MIB..$150.00

Prince William, House of Nisbet, 1982, as baby, 18", MIB..............................$200.00

Princess Diana, Danbury Mint, 1988, pk satin gown, 14", MIB..............................$125.00

Princess Diana, Effanbee (Fan Club), 1982, wedding dress, 16½", MIB..............................$225.00

Princess Diana, Goldberg, 1983, wht gown w/wht boa, 11½", MIB..............................$100.00

Princess Diana, Way Out Toys, 1990s, Royal Diana, pk dress, 11½", MIB $20.00

Princess Margaret, Dean's Rag Book Co, 1920s, papier-maché over cloth, mohair wig, cloth coat & hat, 14", unused, M..$350.00

Queen Elizabeth, Effanbee, 1980s, wht satin gown, 14", MIB...$75.00

Queen Elizabeth, Effanbee, 1989, red & wht satin gown, 14", MIB..............................$125.00

Randy Travis (Country Music Stars), Exclusive Premiere, 1998, 9", MIB..............................$30.00

Red Foxx, Shindana, 1976, 2-sided stuffed print cloth talker, 16", MIB $150.00

Robert Crippen (Astronaut), Kenner, 1997, 12", MIB $45.00

Rosemary Clooney (White Christmas), Exclusive Premiere, 1998, red gown, 8", MIB..............................$45.00

Rosie O'Donnell, Mattel, 1999, red outfit, 11½", MIB $30.00

Rosie O'Donnell, Tyco, 1997, The Rosie O'Doll, stuffed cloth w/outfit, 14", MIB..............................$40.00

Selena, Arm Enterprise, 1996, red jumpsuit, 11½", MIB..$85.00

Shari Lewis, Direct Connect International, 1994, rag doll holding Lambchop, 14", MIB $30.00

Shari Lewis, Madame Alexander, 1959, yel sweater w/gr skirt & hat, 21", MIB..............................$450.00

Shirley Temple, Armand Marseille, bsk, jtd, wht & red polka-dot dress, 22", VGIB..............................$135.00

Shirley Temple, Ideal, 1973, plastic, wht & red polka-dot dress, 17", MIB, A..............................$40.00

Sonny Bono, Mego, 1976, 12½", MIB $150.00

Soupy Sales, 1960s, yel sweater & red tie, 11½", MIB ...$250.00

Vanna White, HSC, 1990, gold dress & purple jumpsuit, 11½", MIB..............................$55.00

WC Fields, Effanbee, 1980, blk coat, checked pants & gray top hat, 15½", MIB..............................$125.00

WC Fields, Knickerbocker, 1972, stuffed print cloth talker, 16", MIB $75.00

Willie Nelson, Catena International Inc, 1989, stuffed cloth w/yarn hair & head bandana, 16", M $65.00

CHATTY CATHY

Chatty Cathy (made by Mattel) was introduced in the 1960s and came as either a blond or brunette. For five years, she sold very well. Much of her success can be attributed to the fact that Chatty Cathy talked. By pulling the string on her back, she could respond with many different phrases. During her five years of fame, Mattel added to the line with Chatty Baby, Tiny Chatty Baby and Tiny Chatty Brother (the twins), Charmin' Chatty, and finally Singin' Chatty, Charmin' Chatty had sixteen interchangable records. Her voice box was acitvated in the same manner as the above-mentioned dolls, by means of a pull string located at the base of her neck. The line was brought back in 1969, smaller and with a restyled face, but it was not well received.

Note: Prices given are for working dolls. Deduct half if doll is mute.

Carrying Case, Chatty Baby, bl or pk, NM, ea $50.00
Carrying Case, Tiny Chatty Baby, bl or pk, NM, ea $40.00
Doll, Charmin' Chatty, EX, from $75 to $150.00
Doll, Chatty Baby, EX, from $65 to $90.00
Doll, Chatty Cathy, any style except for unmarked 1st doll, EX $150.00
Doll, Chatty Cathy, 1970 reissue, MIB, from $75 to $100.00
Doll, Singin' Chatty, blond hair, M $250.00
Doll, Tiny Chatty Baby, EX from $35 to $50.00
Doll, Tiny Chatty Baby (Black), EX $75.00
Doll, Tiny Chatty Baby (Brother), EX, from $45 to $65.00
Outfit, Charmin' Chatty, Let's Go Shopping, MIP $75.00
Outfit, Charmin' Chatty, Let's Play Together, MIP $75.00
Outfit, Chatty Baby, Sleeper Set, MIP $50.00
Outfit, Chatty Cathy, Pink Peppermint Stick, MIP $125.00
Outfit, Chatty Cathy, Playtime, MIP $125.00
Outfit, Tiny Chatty Baby, Bye-Bye, MIP $75.00
Outfit, Tiny Chatty Baby, Pink Frill, MIP $100.00

CRISSY AND HER FAMILY

Ideal's 18" Crissy doll with growing hair was very popular with little girls of the early 1970s. She was introduced in 1969 and continued to be sold throughout the 1970s, enjoying a relatively long market life for a doll. During the 1970s, many different versions of Crissy were made. Numerous friends followed her success, all with the growing hair feature like Crissy's. The other Ideal 'grow hair' dolls in the line included Velvet, Cinnamon, Tressy, Dina, Mia, Kerry, Brandi, and Cricket. Crissy is the easiest member in the line to find, followed by her cousin Velvet. The other members are not as common, but like Crissy and Velvet loose examples of these dolls frequently make their appearance at doll shows, flea markets, and even garage sales. Only those examples that are in excellent or better condition and wearing their original outfits and shoes should command book value. Values for the rare Black versions of the dolls in the line are currently on the rise, as demand for them increases while the supply decreases.

Advisor: Cindy Sabulis (S14) author of *Dolls of the 1960s and 1970s, Vol. I* and *Vol. II*

Baby Crissy, 1973-76, pk dress, EX $65.00
Baby Crissy, 1973-76, pk dress, MIB $125.00
Baby Crissy (Black), 1973-76, pk dress, EX $80.00
Brandi (Black), 1972-73, orange swimsuit, EX $125.00
Cinnamon, Curly Ribbons, 1974, EX $45.00
Cinnamon, Curly Ribbons (Black), 1974, EX $75.00
Cinnamon, Hairdoodler, 1973, EX $40.00
Cinnamon, Hairdoodler (Black), 1973, EX $75.00
Crissy, Beautiful, 1969, orange lace dress, EX $40.00
Crissy, Country Fashion, 1982-83, EX $20.00
Crissy, Country Fashion, 1982-83, MIB $45.00
Crissy, Look Around, 1972, EX $40.00
Crissy, Magic Hair, 1977, EX $30.00
Crissy, Magic Hair, 1977, MIB, from $65 to $90.00

Baby Crissy, 1973 – 1977, re-dressed, from $35.00 to $45.00. (Photo courtesy Cindy Sabulis)

Crissy, Magic Hair, 1977, NRFB $90.00
Crissy, Magic Hair (Black), 1977, EX $125.00
Crissy, Movin' Groovin', 1971, EX $40.00
Crissy, Movin' Groovin' (Black), 1971, EX $100.00
Crissy, Swirla Curla, 1973, EX $35.00
Crissy, Swirla Curla (Black), 1973, EX $100.00
Crissy, Twirly Beads, 1974, MIB, M15 .... $65.00
Dina, 1972-73, purple playsuit, EX $50.00
Kerry, 1971, gr romper, EX $55.00
Mia, 1971, turq romper, EX $50.00
Tara (Black), 1976, yel gingham outfit, MIB $200.00
Velvet, Beauty Braider, 1973, EX $35.00
Velvet, Look Around, 1972, EX $35.00
Velvet, Look Around (Black), 1972, EX $100.00
Velvet, Movin' Groovin', 1971, EX $35.00
Velvet, reissue, 1982, EX $30.00
Velvet, Swirly Daisies, 1974, EX $35.00
Velvet, Swirly Daisies, 1974, MIB $65.00
Velvet, 1st issue, purple dress, 1970, EX $55.00

DAWN

Dawn and her friends were made by Deluxe Topper in the 1970s. They're becoming highly collectible, especially when mint in the box. Dawn was a 6" fashion doll, part of a series sold as the Dawn Model Agency. They were issued in boxes already dressed in clothes of the highest style, or you could buy additional outfits, many complete with matching shoes and accessories.

Advisor: Dawn Diaz (P2)

Accessory, Dawn's Apartment, complete $50.00
Doll, Dancing Angie, NRFB $50.00
Doll, Dancing Dale, NRFB $65.00
Doll, Dancing Dawn, NRFB $50.00
Doll, Dancing Gary, NRFB $50.00
Doll, Dancing Glori, NRFB $50.00
Doll, Dancing Jessica, NRFB $50.00
Doll, Dancing Ron, NRFB $50.00
Doll, Dancing Van, NRFB $80.00

Doll, Daphne, Dawn Model Agency, gr & silver dress, NRFB $100.00

Doll, Dawn Majorette, NRFB.....................................$100.00

Doll, Denise, NRFB...$100.00

Doll, Dinah, NRFB..$100.00

Doll, Gary, NRFB...$50.00

Doll, Jessica, NRFB..$50.00

Doll, Kip Majorette, NRFB...$65.00

Doll, Longlocks, NRFB...$50.00

Doll, Maureen, Dawn Model Agency, red & gold dress, NRFB $100.00

Doll, Ron, NRFB $50.00

Outfit, Bell Bottom Flounce, #0717, NRFB....................$25.00

Outfit, Green Slink, #0716, NRFB..............................$25.00

Outfit, Sheer Delight, #8110, NRFB...........................$25.00

DOLLY DARLINGS BY HASBRO

Dolly Darlings by Hasbro are approximately 4" tall and have molded or rooted hair. The molded-hair dolls were sold in themed hatboxes with small accessories to match. The rooted-hair dolls were sold separately and came with a small brush and comb. There were four plastic playrooms that featured the rooted-hair dolls. Hasbro also produced the Flower Darling series which were dolls in flower corsages. The Dolly Darlings and Flower Darlings were available in the mid to late 1960s.

Advisor: Dawn Diaz (P2)

Flower Darlings: Lily Darling and Daisy Darling, with flower pins, $20.00 to $25.00 each. (Photo courtesy Cindy Sabulis)

DD, Beth at the Supermarket, NRFB..............................$50.00

DD, Cathy Goes to a Party, M (EX case), from $35 to $45.00

DD, Daisy Darling, complete, EX $15.00

DD, Flying Nun, MIB, from $50 to $75.00

DD, Go-Team-Go, doll only, EX, from $25 to $35.00

DD, Hipster, doll only, EX, from $25 to $35.00

DD, Honey, NRFB..$50.00

DD, John & His Pets, M (in case), from $35 to $55.00

DD, Lemon Drop, doll only, EX, from $30 to..................$50.00

DD, Powder Puff, doll only, EX, from $15 to...................$25.00

DD, Rose Darling, NRFB...$50.00

DD, School Days, doll only, EX, from $15 to...................$25.00

DD, Shary Takes a Vacation, doll only, EX $10.00

DD, Slick Set, doll only, EX $25.00

DD, Slumber Party, doll only, EX $15.00

DD, Sunny Day, doll only, from $15 to $25.00

DD, Susie Goes to School, M (EX case), from $35 to $45.00

DD, Sweetheart, doll only, EX, from $15 to $25.00

DD, Tea Time, NRFB...$50.00

DD, Teeny Bikini, doll only, EX, from $15 to $25.00

DD, Violet Darling, doll only, EX.................................$10.00

FD, dolls, complete, MIP ea from $50 to.......................$75.00

FD, dolls w/o flower pins, ea from $7 to $12.00

FISHER-PRICE

Though this company is more famous for their ruggedly durable, lithographed wooden toys, they made dolls as well. Many of the earlier dolls (circa mid-'70s) had stuffed cloth bodies and vinyl heads, hands, and feet. Some had battery-operated voice boxes. In 1981 they introduced Kermit the Frog and Miss Piggy and a line of clothing for both. For company history, see the Fisher-Price category.

Advisor: Brad Cassity

See also Advertising; Character, TV, and Movie; Disney.

Doll, Audrey, #203, 1974-76, EX.................................$25.00

Doll, Baby Ann, #204, 1974-76, EX.............................$25.00

Doll, Billie, #242, 1979-80, EX...................................$10.00

Doll, Elizabeth (Black), #205, 1974-76, EX $25.00

Doll, Honey, #208, 1977-80, EX.................................$20.00

Doll, Jenny, #201, 1974-76, EX..................................$25.00

Doll, Joey, #206, 1975-76, EX....................................$25.00

Doll, Mandy, #4009, 1985, Happy Birthday, EX $50.00

Doll, Mary, #200, 1974-77, EX...................................$25.00

Doll, Mikey, #240, 1979-80, EX..................................$10.00

Doll, Miss Piggy, #890, Dress-Up Muppet, 1981-84, EX ...$12.00

Doll, Muffy, #241, 1979-80, EX...................................$10.00

Doll, My Baby Sleep, #207, 1979-80, EX......................$25.00

Doll, My Friend Becky, #218, 1982-84, EX $20.00

Doll, My Friend Christie, #8120, 1990, EX, from $40 to..$75.00

Doll, My Friend Mandy, #210 (1977-78), #211 (1979-81), #215 (1982-83), EX, ea...$25.00

Doll, My Friend Mandy, #216, 1984 only, EX $35.00

Doll, My Friend Nicky, #206, 1985, EX $30.00

Doll, Natalie, #202, 1974-76, EX $25.00

My Friend Mikey, #205, 1982-84, EX...........................$30.00

Outfit, Aerobics, #4110, 1985, EX...............................$10.00

Outfit, Let's Go Camping, #222, 1978-79, EX $10.00

Outfit, Miss Piggy's Sailor Outfit, #891, 1981-82, EX.......$12.00

Outfit, Party Dress Outfit & pattern, #221, 1978-79, EX....$10.00

Outfit, Rainy Day Slicker, #219, 1978-80, EX.................$10.00

Outfit, Springtime Tennis, #220, 1978-82, EX................$10.00

Outfit, Sunshine Party Dress, #237, 1984, EX.................$10.00

Outfit, Valentine Party Dress, #238, 1984-85, EX $10.00

FLATSYS

Flatsy dolls were a product of the Ideal Novelty and Toy Company. They were produced from 1968 until 1970 in 2", 5", and 8" sizes. There was only one boy in the 5" line; all were dressed in '70s fashions, and not only clothing but accessory items such as bicycles were made as well.

In 1994 Justoys reissued Mini Flatsys. They were sold alone or with accessories such as bikes, rollerblades, and jet skis.

Advisor: Dawn Diaz (P2)

Ali Fashion Flatsy, NRFP, from $45 to $65.00
Bonnie Flatsy, sailing, NRFP $55.00
Candy, Happy Birthday, complete, EX $25.00

Casey Flatsy, MIB, $55.00. (Photo courtesy Cindy Sabulis)

Cory Flatsy, print mini-dress, NRFP, from $45 to.............$65.00
Dale Fashion Flatsy, hot pk maxi, NRFP, froM $45 to $65.00
Dewie Flatsy, NRFP $60.00
Dewie Flatsy Locket, NRFP, from $35 to...........................$50.00
Filly Flatsy, complete, EX..$25.00
Grandma Baker, Flatsyville series, complete, M, from $35 to ..$50.00
Gwen Fashion Flatsy, NRFP, from $45 to..........................$65.00
Judy Flatsy, complete, NRFP, from $55 to $75.00
Kookie Flatsy, Flatsyville series, complete, M, from $35 to ..$50.00
Munch Time Flatsy, Mini Flatsy Collection, NRFP, from $50
    to...$85.00
Slumber Time Flatsy, Mini Flatsy Collection, NRFP, from $50
    to $85.00
Spinderella Flatsy, complete, M.......................................$50.00
Summer Mini Flatsy Collection, NFRP $65.00
Susie Flatsy, complete, EX $25.00

GERBER BABIES

The first Gerber Baby dolls were manufactured in 1936. These dolls were made of cloth and produced by an unknown manufacturer. Since that time, six different companies working with leading artists, craftsmen, and designers have attempted to capture the charm of the winsome baby in Dorothy Hope Smith's charcoal drawing of her friend's baby, Ann Turner (Cook). This drawing became known as the Gerber Baby and was adopted as the trademark of the Gerber Products Company, located in Fremont, Michigan. For further information see *Gerber Baby Dolls and Advertising Collectibles* by Joan S. Grubaugh.

Amsco, baby & feeding set, vinyl, 1972-73, complete, 14",
    NMIB $85.00
Amsco, baby & feeding set, vinyl, 1972-73, re-dressed, 14", M..$40.00

Amsco, pk & wht rosebud sleeper, vinyl, 1972-73, 10", NM,
    from $45 to..$55.00
Amsco, pk & wht rosebud sleeper (Black), vinyl, 1972-73, 10",
    NM, from $60 to...$100.00
Arrow Rubber & Plastic Corp, pk & wht bib & diaper, 1965-67,
    14", MIB, from $45 to..$60.00
Arrow Rubber & Plastic Corp, pk & wht bib & diaper, 1965-67,
    re-dressed, 14", EX $50.00
Atlanta Novelty, Baby Drink & Wet, 1979-81, 17", complete
    w/trunk & accessories, M, from $75 to.......................$85.00
Atlanta Novelty, Baby Drink & Wet (Black), 1979-81, 12",
    complete w/trunk & accessories, M..........................$100.00
Atlanta Novelty, Bathtub Baby, 1985, 12", MIB, from $70
    to..$85.00
Atlanta Novelty, bl or rose velour dress w/wht blouse (Black),
    1979-81, 17", M, ea from $75 to...............................$85.00
Atlanta Novelty, flowered bed jacket w/matching pillow & cov-
    erlet, 1979, 17", NRFB, from $75 to $100.00
Atlanta Novelty, mama voice, several different outfits, 1979-81,
    17", NRFB, ea from $75 to $85.00
Atlanta Novelty, mama voice (Black), 1979-81, 17", NRFB,
    from $75 to..$85.00
Atlanta Novelty, porcelain w/soft body, wht eyelet christening gown,
    limited edition, 1981, 14", NRFB, from $275 to $350.00
Atlanta Novelty, rag doll, pk or bl, 1984, 11½", EX.........$20.00
Atlanta Novelty, snowsuit w/matching hood, 1979, 17", NRFB,
    from $75 to..$95.00
Atlanta Novelty, snowsuit w/matching hood (Black), 1979-81,
    17", NRFB, from $75 to...$85.00
Atlanta Novelty, 50th Anniversary, eyelet skirt & bib, stuffed
    cloth & vinyl, 1978, 17", NRFB, from $75 to............$95.00
Lucky Ltd, Birthday Party Twins, 1989, 6", NRFB............$40.00
Lucky Ltd, christening gown, cloth & vinyl, 1989, 16", EX..$40.00
Sun Rubber, orig nightgown, 1955-58, M......................$175.00
Toy Biz, Baby Care Set, 1996, MIB $25.00
Toy Biz, Food & Playtime Baby, 1995, MIB, from $25 to...$35.00
Toy Biz, Potty Time Baby, vinyl, 1994-95, 15", NRFB......$25.00

HOLLY HOBBIE

Sometime around 1970 a young homemaker and mother, Holly Hobbie, approached the American Greeting Company with some charming country-styled drawings of children. Her concepts were well received by the company, and since that time over four hundred Holly Hobbie items have been produced, nearly all marked HH, H. Hobbie, or Holly Hobbie.

See also Clubs, Newsletters, and Other Publications.

Doll, Country Fun Holly Hobbie, 1989, 16", NRFB.........$20.00
Doll, Grandma Holly, Knickerbocker, 14", MIB...............$20.00
Doll, Grandma Holly, Knickerbocker, 24", MIB...............$25.00
Doll, Holly Hobbie, Heather, Amy, or Carrie, Knickerbocker, 6",
    MIB, ea...$5.00
Doll, Holly Hobbie, Heather, Amy, or Carrie, Knickerbocker, 9",
    MIB, ea...$10.00
Doll, Holly Hobbie, Heather, Amy, or Carrie, Knickerbocker,
    16", MIB, ea $20.00

Doll, Holly Hobbie, Heather, Amy, or Carrie, Knickerbocker, 27", MIB, ea $25.00

Doll, Holly Hobbie, Heather, Amy, or Carrie, Knickerbocker, 33", MIB, ea $35.00

Doll, Holly Hobbie, scented, clear ornament around neck, 1988, 18", NRFB..$30.00

Doll, Holly Hobbie, 25th Anniversary Collector's Edition, Meritus, 1994, 26", MIB...$55.00

Doll, Holly Hobbie Bicentennial, Knickerbocker, 12", MIB ..$25.00

Doll, Holly Hobbie Day 'N Night, Knickerbocker, 14", MIB ..$15.00

Doll, Holly Hobbie Dream Along, Holly, Carrie or Amy, Knickerbocker, 9", MIB, ea...$10.00

Doll, Holly Hobbie Dream Along, Holly, Carrie or Amy, Knickerbocker, cloth, 12", MIB, ea $15.00

Doll, Holly Hobbie Talker, 4 sayings, 16", MIB $25.00

Doll, Little Girl Holly, Knickerbocker, 1980, 15", MIB....$20.00

Doll, Robby, Knickerbocker, 9", MIB $15.00

Doll, Robby, Knickerbocker, 16", MIB $20.00

Dollhouse, M $200.00

Plate, 'Start each day in a happy way,' American Greetings Collectors Edition, 10½" $25.00

Sand Pail, Chein, 1974, 6", EX, N2................................$25.00

Sewing Machine, Durham, 1975, plastic & metal, battery-op, 5x9", EX $25.00

Sing-A-Long Electric Parlor Player, Vanity Fair, 1970s, complete w/booklet, scarce, NMIB $45.00

Valentine Activity Book, 1978, 5x8", unused, EX, N2 .....$10.00

JEM

The glamorous life of Jem mesmerized little girls who watched her Saturday morning cartoons, and she was a natural as a fashion doll. Hasbro saw the potential in 1985 when they introduced the Jem line of 12" dolls representing her, the rock stars from Jem's musical group, the Holograms, and other members of the cast, including the only boy, Rio, Jem's road manager and Jerrica's boyfriend. Each doll was posable, jointed at the waist, head, and wrists, so that they could be positioned at will with their musical instruments and other accessory items. Their clothing, their makeup, and their hairdos were wonderfully exotic, and their faces were beautifully modeled. The Jem line was discontinued in 1987 after being on the market for only two years.

Accessory, Backstager, M $25.00

Accessory, New Wave Waterbed, M....................................$35.00

Accessory, Star Stage, M $30.00

Doll, Aja, 1st issue, orig outfit, M....................................$45.00

Doll, Aja, 2nd issue, orig outfit, M $90.00

Doll, Ashley, orig outfit, M..$40.00

Doll, Clash, orig outfit, M...$25.00

Doll, Flash 'n Sizzle Jem, orig outfit, M $60.00

Doll, Glitter 'n Gold Jem, orig outfit, M $60.00

Doll, Jem/Jessica, star earrings, orig outfit, M....................$35.00

Doll, Jem/Jessica, 1st issue, orig outfit, M.........................$30.00

Doll, Jetta, orig outfit, M $40.00

Doll, Kimber, 1st issue, orig outfit, M..............................$40.00

Doll, Pizzazz, 1st issue, orig outfit, M $50.00

Doll, Pizzazz, 1st issue, NRFB, $65.00. (Photo courtesy Jennifer Dobb)

Doll, Raya, orig outfit, M..$150.00

Doll, Rock 'n Curl, NRFB $30.00

Doll, Stormer, orig outfit, M $45.00

Doll, Synergy, orig outfit, M $45.00

Doll, Video, orig outfit, M $45.00

Outfit, Award Night, MIP $30.00

Outfit, Designing Woman, MIP $35.00

Outfit, Electric Cords, MIP...$25.00

Outfit, Encore, MIP $35.00

Outfit, Friend or Stranger, MIP $50.00

Outfit, Let's Rock This Town, MIP $35.00

Outfit, Moraccan Magic, MIP $75.00

Outfit, Purple Haze, MIP..$30.00

Outfit, Rappin', MIP..$45.00

Outfit, She Makes an Impression, MIP $90.00

Outfit, Splashes of Sound, MIP $25.00

Outfit, We're Off & Running, MIP $35.00

LIDDLE KIDDLES

From 1966 to 1971, Mattel produced Liddle Kiddle dolls and accessories, typical of the 'little kid next door.' They were made in sizes ranging from a tiny ¾" up to 4". They were all posable and had rooted hair that could be restyled. Eventually there were Animiddles and Zoolery Jewelry Kiddles, which were of course animals, and two other series that represented storybook and nursery-rhyme characters. There was a set of extraterrestrials, and lastly in 1979, Sweet Treets dolls were added to the assortment.

In the mid-1970s Mattel reissued Lucky Locket Kiddles. The dolls had names identical to the earlier lockets but were not of the same high quality.

In 1994 – 1995 Tyco reissued Liddle Kiddles in strap-on, clip-on, Lovely Locket, Pretty Perfume, and baby bottle collections.

Loose dolls, if complete and with all their original accessories, are worth about 50% less than the same mint in the box. Dressed, loose dolls with no accessories are worth 75% less.

Advisor: Dawn Diaz (P2)

Alice in Wonderliddle, complete, NM $175.00

Animiddle Kiddles, MIP, ea...$75.00

Aqua Funny Bunny, #3532, complete, EX $20.00

Aqua Funny Bunny, #3532, MIP $75.00
Babe Biddle, #3505, complete, M....................................$75.00
Baby Din-Din, #3820, complete, M $50.00
Baby Rockaway, #3819, MIP $100.00
Beach Buggy, #5003, complete, NM..................................$35.00
Beat-A-Diddle, #3510, MIP $500.00
Blue Funny Bunny, #3532, MIP` $75.00
Calamity Jiddle, #3506, complete w/high saddle horse, M ..$75.00

Chitty Chitty Bang Bang Kiddles #3597, MOC, $150.00. (Photo courtesy McMasters Harris Doll Auctions)

Chocolottie's House, #2501, MIP $25.00
Cinderriddle's Palace, #5068, plastic window version, M ..$25.00
Cookin' Kiddle, #3846, complete, M $150.00
Dainty Deer, #3637, complete, M......................................$20.00
Florence Niddle, #3507, complete, M $75.00
Flower Charm Bracelet, #3747, MIP $50.00
Flower Pin Kiddle, #3741, MIP $50.00
Flower Ring Kiddle, #3744, MIP $50.00
Frosty Mint Kone, #3653, complete, M.............................$60.00
Greta Grape, #3728, complete, M $50.00
Greta Griddle, #3508, complete, M $85.00
Heart Charm Bracelet Kiddle, #3747, MIP $50.00
Heart Pin Kiddle, #3741, MIP $50.00
Heart Ring Kiddle, #3744, MIP $50.00
Henrietta Horseless Carriage, #3641, complete, M...........$60.00
Honeysuckle Kologne, #3704, MIP $75.00
Hot Dog Stand, #5002, complete, M $25.00
Howard Biff Biddle, #3502, complete, M $75.00
Howard Biff Biddle, #3502, NRFB....................................$300.00
Jewelry Kiddles, 3735 & #5166 Treasure Boxes, M, ea $25.00
Jewelry Kiddles Flower Charm Bracelet Kiddle, #3747, MIP...$50.00
Kampy Kiddle, #3753, complete, M $150.00
Kiddle & Kars Antique Fair Set, #3806, NRFB.............$300.00
Kiddle Komedy Theatre, #3592, EX...................................$35.00
Kiddles Kologne, #3710 Gardinia, MIP.............................$75.00
Kiddles Kologne Sweet Three Boutique, #3708, NRFB...$300.00
Kiddles Kolognes, #3705 Sweet Pea, NRFB......................$75.00
Kiddles Sweet Shop, #3807, NRFB.................................$300.00
King & Queen of Hearts, #3784, MIP................................$150.00
Kleo Kola, #3729, complete, M $50.00

Kola Kiddles Three-Pak, #3734, NRFB.............................$300.00
Kosmic Kiddles, M, ea $150.00
Lady Crimson, #A3840, NRFB..$75.00
Lady Lavendar, #A3840, NRFB...$75.00
Laffy Lemon, #3732, MIP $85.00
Larky Locket, #3539, complete, EX $25.00
Lenore Limousine, #3743, complete, M $60.00
Liddle Biddle Peep, #3544, complete, M $125.00
Liddle Diddle, #3503, complete, M $75.00
Liddle Kiddles Kabin, #3591, complete, EX $25.00
Liddle Kiddles Kastle, #3522, complete, M $55.00
Liddle Kiddles Klub, #3301, M $20.00
Liddle Kiddles Kolony, #3571, M $25.00
Liddle Kiddles Kottage, #3534, complete, EX $25.00
Liddle Kiddles Open House, #5167, MIB..........................$40.00
Liddle Kiddles Pop-Up Boutique, #5170, complete, M.....$30.00
Liddle Kiddles Pop-Up Playhouse, #3574, complete, M ...$30.00
Liddle Kiddles Talking Townhouse, #5154, MIB $50.00
Liddle Kiddles 3-Story House, complete, M $35.00
Liddle Lion Zoolery, #3661, complete, M $100.00
Liddle Red Riding Hiddle, #3546, complete, M $150.00
Lilac Locket, #3540, MIP $75.00
Limey Lou Spoonfuls, #2815, MIP $25.00
Lois Locket, #3541, complete, M $75.00
Lola Locket, #3536, MIP $75.00
Lolli-Grape, #3656, complete, M $60.00
Lolli-Lemon, #3657, MIP $75.00
Lolli-Mint, #3658, MIP $75.00
Lorelei Locket, #3717, MIP $75.00
Lorelei Locket, #3717, 1976 version, MIP $25.00
Lottie Locket, #3679, complete, M $35.00
Lou Locket, #3537, MIP $75.00
Luana Locket, #3680, complete, M $35.00
Luana Locket, #3680, Gold Rush version, MIP $85.00
Lucky Lion, #3635, complete, M $50.00
Lucky Locket Jewel Case, #3542, M $150.00
Lucky Locket Magic Paper Dolls, Whitman, 1968, EXIB..$30.00
Luscious Lime, #3733, glitter version, complete, M.........$75.00
Luscouis Lime, #3733, complete, M $55.00
Luvvy Duvvy Kiddle, #3596, MIP $50.00
Millie Middle, #3509, complete, M....................................$125.00
Miss Mouse, #3638, MIP..$75.00
Nappytime Baby, #3818, complete, M $60.00
Nurse 'N Totsy Outfit, #LK7, MIP $25.00
Olivia Orange Kola Kiddle, #3730, MIP $80.00
Peter Pandiddle, #3547, NRFB...$300.00
Pink Funny Bunny, #3532, MIP $75.00
Posies 'N Pink Skediddle Outfit, #3585, MIP $30.00
Rah Rah Skediddle, #3788, complete, M $150.00
Rapunzel & the Prince, #3783, MIP $150.00
Robin Hood & Maid Marion, #3785, MIP $150.00
Rolly Twiddle, #3519, complete, M....................................$175.00
Romeo & Juliet, #3782, MIP...$150.00
Rosebud Kologne, #3702, MIP $75.00
Rosemary Roadster, #3642, complete, M $60.00
Santa Kiddle, #3595, MIP...$40.00
Shirley Skediddle, #3766, MIP $75.00

Shirley Strawberry, #3727, complete, M $50.00
Sizzly Friddle, #3513, complete, M $75.00
Sizzly Friddle, MIP..$300.00
Sleep 'N Totsy Outfit, #LK5, MIP $25.00
Sleeping Biddle, #3527, complete, M..............................$100.00

Sleeping Biddle, #3527, MOC, $300.00. (Photo courtesy McMasters Harris Doll Auctions)

Slipsy Sliddle, #3754, complete, M $125.00
Snap-Happy Bedroom, #5172, complete, M $15.00
Snap-Happy Furniture, #5171, MIP $30.00
Snap-Happy Living Room, #5173, NMIP $20.00
Snoopy Skediddleer & His Sopwith Camel, M $150.00
Suki Skediddle, #3767, complete, M................................$25.00
Surfy Skediddle, #3517, complete, M...............................$75.00
Swingy Skediddle, #3789, MIP.......................................$200.00
Teeter Time Baby, #3817, complete, M $60.00
Teresa Touring Car, #3644, complete, M..........................$60.00
Tessie Tractor, #3671, complete, NM.............................$150.00
Tiny Tiger, #3636, MIP $75.00
Tracy Trikediddle, #3769, complete, M............................$50.00
Trikey Triddle, #3515, complete, M $75.00
Vanilla Lilly, #2819, MIP..$25.00
Violet Kologne, #3713, MIP...$60.00
Windy Fliddle, #3514, complete, M $85.00
World of the Kiddles Beauty Bazaar, #3586, NRFB $300.00

LITTLECHAP FAMILY

Carrying Case, EX...$40.00
Doll, Doctor John, MIB, from $65.00 to $70.00
Doll, Judy, MIB $75.00
Doll, Libby, MIB $45.00
Doll, Lisa, MIB...$65.00
Family Room, Bedroom or Doctor John's Office, EX, ea...$125.00
Outfit, Doctor John, complete, EX, from $15 to $30.00
Outfit, Doctor John, NRFB, from $30 to $50.00
Outfit, Judy, complete, EX, from $25 to $40.00
Outfit, Judy, NRFB, from $35 to.......................................$75.00
Outfit, Libby, complete, EX, from $20 to $35.00
Outfit, Libby, NRFB, from $35 to......................................$50.00
Outfit, Lisa, complete, EX, from $20 to.............................$35.00
Outfit, Lisa, NRFB, from $35 to $75.00

MATTEL TALKING DOLLS

For more information refer to *Talking Toys of the 20th Century* by Kathy and Don Lewis (Collector Books).
See also Character, TV, and Movie Collectibles; Disney.

Baby Beans, NM $25.00
Baby Cheryl, 1965, 16", MIB..$200.00
Baby Colleen, Sears Exclusive, 1965, 15½", MIB...........$100.00
Baby Drowsy (Black), 1969, plush hands, 15", MIB $175.00
Baby First Step, 1967, MIB...$225.00
Baby Flip-Flop, JC Penney Exclusive, 1970, MIB $85.00
Baby Secret, 1966, red hair, 18", EX $75.00
Baby See 'N Say, 1964, MIB...$150.00
Baby Sing-A-Song, 1969, 16½", MIB...............................$150.00
Baby Small Talk, 1968, MIB...$125.00
Baby Teenietalk, 1966, orig dress, 17", VG $75.00
Baby Whisper, 1968, 17½", MIB......................................$200.00
Chatty Patty, 1980s, MIB...$50.00
Cheerleader, 1970, several variations, MIB, ea $75.00
Cynthia, M..$45.00
Drowsy Sleeper-Keeper, 1966, MIB.................................$125.00
Gramma & Grampa, 1968, MIB, ea.................................$150.00
Hi Dottie, Black, 1972, complete w/telephone, NM $75.00
Little Sister Look 'N Say, Sears Exclusive, 18", M..........$150.00
Matty the Talking Boy, 1961, MIB...................................$300.00
Randi Reader, 1968, 19½", MIB $175.00
Sister Belle, 1961, MIB..$300.00
Sister Small Talk, 1968, blond hair, EX............................$55.00
Somersalty, 1970, MIB..$200.00
Tatters, M $85.00
Teachy Keen, Sears Exclusive, 1966, 16", MIB...............$125.00
Teachy Talk, 1970, MIB...$50.00
Teacy Keen, Sears Exclusive, 1966, 16", NM $50.00
Timey Tell, MIB..$110.00

ROCKFLOWERS BY MATTEL

Rockflowers were introduced in the early 1970s as Mattel's answer to Topper's Dawn Dolls. Rockflowers are 6½" tall and have wire articulated bodies that came with mod sunglasses attached to their heads. There were four girls and one boy in the series with eighteen groovy outfits that could be purchased separately. Each doll came with their own 45 rpm record, and the clothing packages were also in the shape of a 45 rpm record.
Advisor: Dawn Diaz (P2)

Case, Rockflowers on Stage, #4993 (3 dolls), vinyl, NM...$15.00
Case, Rockflowers, #4991 (single doll), vinyl, NM...........$10.00
Doll, Doug, #1177, NRFB, from $40 to............................$50.00
Doll, Heather, #NRFB, from $40 to $50.00
Doll, Iris, NRFB, from $40 to $50.00
Doll, Lilac, #1167, NRFB, from $35 to $50.00
Doll, Rosemary, #1168, NRFB..$50.00
Gift Set, Rockflowers in Concert, w/Heather, Lilac & Rosemary,
    NRFB $150.00

Rockflowers in Concert, Heather and Lilac, EX, $15.00 to $20.00 each. (Photo courtesy Cindy Sabulis)

Outfit, Flares 'N Lace, #4057, NRFP.......................................$15.00
Outfit, Frontier Gingham, #4069, NRFP..........................$20.00
Outfit, Jeans in Fringe, NRFP...$15.00
Outfit, Long in Fringe, #4050, NRFP...............................$15.00
Outfit, Overall Green, #4067, NRFP.................................$10.00
Outfit, Tie Dye Maxi, #4053, NRDP.................................$15.00
Outfit, Topped in Lace, #4058, NRFP...............................$15.00

SCHOENHUT

Schoenhut dolls are from the late nineteenth century to the early twentieth century. First came the all-wood dolls, then came the dolls with cloth bodies, and later the composition dolls. Their hair was carved or molded and painted or wigged. They had intaglio or sleep eyes, open or closed mouths.

The following listings are from auctions and include the auction estimates. Most of the dolls went over estimate, although some did sell in range.

Baby Girl, 13", pnt hair & eyes, bent arms & legs, lt pink dress & bonnet, EX, A (Est: $300-$400) $300.00
Boy, 14½", carved hair w/comb marks, intaglio eyes, mouth closed, redressed, EX, A (Est: $700-$900) $990.00
Boy, 14½", wig, intaglio eyes, mouth closed, lt gray & wht sailor suit w/hat, VG, A (Est: $300-$400) $330.00
Boy, 16", carved hair parted on side, intaglio eyes, 7 teeth, wht sailor suit, red boots, VG, A (Est: $800-$1,000) ..$1,870.00
Boy, 16", wig, intaglio eyes, open closed mouth, wht linen sailor suit, red tie, wht ankle boots, EX, A (Est: $600-$800) $1,200.00
Boy, 17", wig, intalio eyes, mouth closed, blk pea coat w/red knickers, plaid hat & satchel, VG, A (Est: $400-$600)........$715.00
Boy, 17", wig, sleep eyes, mouth open showing 2 teeth, in sweater & knit cap, EX, A (Est: $300-$400) $500.00
Boy, 20", wig, intaglio eyes, mouth closed, orig tan & wht striped suit & wht leather shoes, EX, A (Est: $700-$900)...$1,870.00
Character Boy, 16", carved hair combed forward w/curl, pnt eyes, mouth closed, button sweater, P, A (Est: $200-$300) ..$355.00
Character Girl, 14½", carved hair w/middle part, intaglio eyes, closed mouth, bl & wht strips, VG, A (Est: $500-$600)...........$825.00

Character Girl, 17", shoulder-length wig, 2 teeth, navy & wht houndstooth outfit, straw hat, EX, A (Est: $600-$800)..$1,320.00
Character Girl, 19", wig w/braids, mouth closed, orig dress & hat, EX, A (Est: $400-$600)....................................$825.00
Character Girl, 21", wig, intaglio eyes, mouth closed, orig dress & leather shoes, VG, A (Est: $300-$400) $465.00
Girl, 14", carved bobbed hair w/headband, intaglio eyes, mouth closed, orig union suit, EX, A (Est: $2,000-$3,000) $1,700.00
Girl, 14", carved hair parts in middle w/bow in back, mouth closed, orig dress, EX, A (Est: $600-$800)............$2,200.00
Girl, 15", carved bobbed hair, teeth showing, bl & wht gingham outfit, bl wool tam, VG, A (Est: $400-$600)...........$770.00
Girl, 15", wig w/bow in back, intaglio eyes, mouth closed, orig dress, EX, A (Est: $500-$700) $660.00
Girl, 16", carved hair parted in middle, intaglio eyes, re-dressed, rpt, A (Est: $200-$300) $385.00
Girl, 16", wig, intaglio eyes, mouth closed, orig dress, G, A (Est: $500-$700) $1,650.00
Girl, 16", wig, intaglio eyes, pouty mouth, red wool suit w/wht lace/embroidered trim, red hat, EX, A (Est: $300-$400) $440.00
Girl, 16", wig w/pigtails, intaglio eyes, mouth closed, rpl dress, orig shoes, P, A (Est: $100-$200) $350.00
Girl, 17", carved bobbed hair w/headband, intaglio eyes, mouth closed, striped dress w/collar, EX, A (Est: $800-$1000).............$1,540.00
Girl, 17", chin-length wig, mouth closed, orig dress, EX, A (Est: $400-$600) $550.00
Girl, 17", wig parted in middle, decal eyes, mouth slighty open w/teeth, redressed, VG, A (Est: $200-$300) $300.00
Girl, 19", wig parted on side w/curls, sleep eyes, slightly open mouth w/teeth, redressed, VG, A (Est: $300-$400) ..$330.00
Girl, 19½", wig parted on side, intaglio eyes, mouth closed, orig 'flapper' dress, G, A (Est: $300-$400) $880.00
Girl, 20", shoulder-length wig, intaglio eyes, mouth closed, orig dress, straw hat, EX, A (Est: $500-$700) $825.00
Graziana Boy, 16½", carved hair combed forward, intaglio eyes, mouth closed, orig outfit, VG, A (Est: $1,200-$1,500).............$1,980.00
Graziana Girl, 16", human-hair wig parted in middle, intaglio eyes, mouth closed, orig dress, Fair, A (Est: $400-$500) ...$3,575.00
Toddler Boy, 12", wig, pnt eyes, mouth closed, dressed in romper, EX, A (Est: $300-$400)....................................$330.00
Toddler Boy, 15", wig, pnt eyes, slightly open mouth, sailor suit & hat, brn side-button boots, EX, A (Est: $400-$500) ..$465.00
Toddler Boy, 16", wig, pnt eyes, mouth slightly open, knit cap, G, A (Est: $200-$300)...$275.00
Toddler Girl, 12", short wig, pnt eyes, closed mouth, orig dress, EX, A (Est: $300-$400) $465.00
Walking Boy, 16", wig, decal eyes, orig outfit, EX, A (Est: $400-$500)..$300.00
Walking Boy, 17", wig, pnt eyes, open closed mouth, sailor outfit w/hat, VG, A (Est: $300-$400).............................$410.00
Walking Girl, 17", chin-length wig, pnt eyes, slightly open mouth, orig dress, VG, A (Est: $300-$400) $410.00
Walking Toddler Girl, 16½", wig parted in middle, pnt eyes, slightly open mouth, dress, VG, A (Est: $200-$300) ..$220.00

SHIRLEY TEMPLE

The Shirley Temple doll made her first appearance in 1934. The Ideal Toy Company produced the composition doll in several sizes with Mollye Goldman designing outfits fashioned after Shirley's movies through 1936. In the 1950s, Ideal started making the vinyl doll in five different sizes. These dolls were outfitted with many accessories in keeping with other fashionable dolls of the time.

The following listings were taken from current auctions and the auction estimates have been included to give a better picture of price trends.

Note: The outfits described are original and complete with undergarments and shoes and socks unless noted otherwise.

Doll, 11", compo, cowgirl outfit, no hat, w/pin, VG, A (Est: $600) $1,380.00

Doll, 11", compo, wig, wht dress w/red dots, ruffled collar, red ribbons, button, EX, A (Est: $500-$800) $800.00

Doll, 12", vinyl, rooted hair, complete w/4 outfits & necklace, EXIB (TV box), A (Est: $400-$600) $350.00

Doll, 12", vinyl, rooted hair, sleep eyes, open mouth w/upper teeth, slip, shoes & socks, EX, A (no est) $200.00

Doll, 12", vinyl, rooted hair, sleep eyes, pinafore, purse, with original hang tag, unused, NM, A (Est: $100.00 – $300.00), $350.00. (Photo McMasters Harris Doll Auctions)

Doll, 13", compo, red curly wig, chubby face, 6 teeth, bl & wht pinafore, w/tag, VGIB, A (Est: $200-$300) $410.00

Doll, 13", compo, wig, sleep eyes, orig bl dress w/wht Scottie dogs, shoes & socks, unused, NM, A (Est: $400-$600).......$850.00

Doll, 15", vinyl, rooted hair, sleep eyes, bl dress w/flocked floral design, wht lace, unused, EX+, A (Est: $100-$300) $100.00

Doll, 15", Wards Yesterday's Darling, 1972, vinyl, rooted hair, sleep eyes, red & wht dress, MIB, A (Est: $100-$200) $125.00

Doll, 17", compo, cowgirl outfit, blk felt hat, w/pin, VG, A (Est: $500-$600) $1,265.00

Doll, 17", compo, wig, sleep eyes, pk pleated dress w/wht pleated collar, bl ribbons, button, EX, A (Est: $500-800) $450.00

Doll, 17", compo, wig, sleep eyes, wht dress w/bl dots, bl ribbon trim, ruffled collar, EX, A (Est: $400-$700)............$750.00

Doll, 18", compo, blond curly wig, lt pk dress, shoes & socks, unused, NMIB, A (Est: $600-$800).......................$1,150.00

Doll, 19", vinyl, rooted hair, blk & wht velvet dress, w/purse, name on dress, EX, A (Est: $200-$400) $375.00

Doll, 20", compo, wig, sleep eyes, yel taffeta dress w/blk velvet jacket, blk tam, EX, A (Est: $400-$600) $650.00

Doll, 21", compo, wig, turq & wht dress w/pin-back button, straw hat, shoes & socks, G, A (Est: $300-$500) $720.00

Doll, 21", compo w/cloth body, wig, pk lace-trimmed dress w/ruffled hem, bonnet, button, EX, A (Est: $1,000-$2,000) ...$1,300.00

Doll, 22", cloth body, compo head & limbs, wig, sleep eyes, pk dress, coat & bonnet, crier, EX, A, (Est: $1,000-$2,000) $1,600.00

Doll, 22", compo, wig, sleep eyes, blk & wht 'Curly Top' outfit w/blk tam, VG, A (Est: $500-$800)........................$650.00

Doll, 22", compo, wig, sleep eyes, plaid dress from 'Bright Eyes,' pinback button, EX, A (Est: $500-$800) $600.00

Doll, 22", compo, wig, sleeveless dress w/ruffled collar, shoes & socks, w/pin, all orig, VG+, A (Est: $900-$1,000) $1,380.00

Doll, 22", vinyl, rooted hair, sleep eyes, Scottish outfit from 'Wee Willie Winkie,' 1957, NM, A (Est: $200-$400) $250.00

Doll, 27", compo, wig, sleep eyes, wht dress w/red dots, red tie at waist, VGIB, A (Est: $700-$1,000) $900.00

Doll, 36", vinyl, sleep eyes, rooted hair, lt pk taffita dress w/floral applique, EX, A (Est: $800-$1,200) $900.00

Tea Set, pk & wht plastic, service for 3 w/teapot & silverware, Ideal, 1960s, unused, MIB, A (Est: $100-$200) $500.00

STRAWBERRY SHORTCAKE

It was around 1980 when Strawberry Shortcake came on the market with a bang. The line included everything to attract small girls — swimsuits, bed linens, blankets, anklets, underclothing, coats, shoes, sleeping bags, dolls and accessories, games, and many other delightful items. Strawberry Shortcake and her friends were short lived, lasting only until the middle of the decade.

Big Berry Trolley, 1982, EX...$40.00
Doll, Almond Tea, 6", MIB $30.00
Doll, Angel Cake & Souffle, 6", NRFB..............................$40.00
Doll, Apple Dumbling, 12", cloth w/yarn hair, EX+ $25.00
Doll, Apple Dumpling & Tea Time Turtle, 6", MIB $75.00
Doll, Apricot, 15", NM...$35.00
Doll, Baby Needs a Name, 15", NM...................................$35.00
Doll, Berry Baby Orange Blossom, 6", MIB.....................$35.00
Doll, Butter Cookie, 6", MIB...$25.00
Doll, Cafe Ole, 6", MIB $45.00
Doll, Cherry Cuddler, 6", NRFB.......................................$45.00
Doll, Huckleberry Pie, flat hands, 6", MIB.......................$45.00
Doll, Lemon Meringue, 6", MIB..$45.00

Doll, Lemon Meringue, 15", cloth w/yarn hair, EX...........$25.00
Doll, Lime Chiffon, 6", MIB...$45.00
Doll, Mint Tulip, 6", MIB..$50.00
Doll, Orange Blossom & Marmalade, MIB $45.00

Doll, Orange Blossom and Sleeping Marmalade, made in 1984 only, NM, $25.00 for the pair.

Doll, Peach Blush & Melonie Belle, 6", MIB..................$115.00
Doll, Purple Pieman w/Berry Bird, poseable, MIB $35.00
Doll, Strawberry Shortcake & Custard, 6", NRFB..........$150.00
Doll, Strawberry Shortcake & Strawberrykin, 6", NRFB...$295.00
Dollhouse, no accessories, M..$200.00
Figure, Almond Tea w/Marza Panda, PVC, 1", MOC.......$15.00
Figure, Cherry Cuddler w/Gooseberry, Strawberryland Minia-
    tures, MIP, from $15 to $20.00
Figure, Lemon Meringue w/Frappo, PVC, 1", MOC.........$15.00
Figure, Lime Chiffon w/balloons, PVC, 1", MOC $15.00
Figure, Merry Berry Worm, MIB......................................$35.00
Figure, Mint Tulip w/March Mallard, PVC, MOC $15.00
Figure, Raspberry Tart w/bowl of cherries, MOC..............$15.00
Figure, Sour Grapes w/Dregs, Strawberryland Miniatures, MIP,
    B5, from $15 to $20.00
Figurine, Strawberry Shortcake, ceramic, 5", EX...............$8.00
Ice Skates, EX $35.00
Motorized Bicycle, EX..$95.00
Pillow Doll, Huckleberry Pie, 9", EX...............................$10.00
Roller Skates, EX $35.00
Sleeping Bag, EX..$25.00
Storybook Play Case, M..$35.00
Stroller, Coleco, 1981, M...$85.00
Telephone, Strawberry Shortcake figure, battery-op, EX..$85.00

SUNSHINE FAMILY BY MATTEL

The Sunshine Family was produced and sold from 1974 to 1982. The first family consisted of the father, Steve, his wife, Steffie, and their daughter, Baby Sweets. In 1976 Mattel added The Happy Family (an African-American family consisting of mom, dad, and their two children). The line also included grandparents, playsets, vehicles, and lots of other accessories that made them so much fun to play with.

Camping Craft Kit, 1974, MIP, minimum value $35.00
Craft Store, 1976, MIB, minimum value.........................$70.00
Doll, Darlin', Honey Hill Bunch, 4", NM $10.00
Doll, Little Hon (Black), w/nursery set, 1977, MIB, minimum
    value...$35.00
Doll, Little Sweets, w/nursery set, 1975, MIB, minimum
    value...$35.00
Doll, New Baby, orig outfit, NM....................................$15.00
Doll, Sister, w/shoes, EX $20.00
Doll, Slugger, Honey Hill Bunch, 4", EX, from $5 to.......$10.00
Doll, Steffie, NM, from $15 to..$20.00
Doll, Steve, NM, from $15 to..$20.00
Doll & Craft Case, Sears Exclusive, 1977, EX, minimum
    value..$25.00
Doll Set, Grandparents, 1976, MIB, minimum value $60.00
Doll Set, Happy Family (Black), 1975, MIB, minimum
    value $60.00
Doll Set, Steve, Stephie & Baby Sweets, 1976, MIB, minimum
    value..$65.00
Doll Set, Watch 'Em Grow Greenhouse, w/3 dolls, craft
    kit & seeds, limited edition, 1977, MIB, minimum
    value...$100.00
Family Farm, 1977, rare, MIB, minimum value $140.00
Kitchen Craft Kit, 1974, MIB, minimum value $35.00
Nursery Craft Kit, 1976, MIP $25.00
Outfits, several variations, 1975-76, MIP, minimum value,
    ea..$15.00
Sunshine Family Home, 4 rooms w/furniture, 1974, EX, mini-
    mum value...$65.00
Surrey Cycle, 1975, MIB, minimum value $35.00
Van w/Piggyback Shack, 1975, MIB, minimum value $50.00

TAMMY

In 1962 the Ideal Novelty and Toy Company introduced their teenage Tammy doll. Slightly pudgy and not quite as sophisticated-looking as some of the teen fashion dolls on the market at the time, Tammy's innocent charm captivated consumers. Her extensive wardrobe and numerous accessories added to her popularity with children. Tammy had a car, a house, and her own catamaran. In addition, a large number of companies obtained licenses to issue products using the 'Tammy' name. Everything from paper dolls to nurse's kits were made with Tammy's image on them. Her success was not confined to the United States; she was also successful in Canada and several other European countries.

Interest in Tammy has risen quite a bit in the past few years according to our advisor Cindy Sabulis. Values have gone up and supply for quality mint-in-box items is going down. Loose, played-with dolls are still readily available and can be found for decent prices. Values are given for mint-in-box dolls.

Advisor: Cindy Sabulis (S14)

Accessory Pak, baseball bat, catcher's mask, mitt & ball,
    unknown #, NRFP $35.00
Accessory Pak, electric skillet & frying pan w/lids, unknown #,
    NRFP $50.00

Accessory Pak, luggage case, airline ticket & camera, #9183-0, NRFP $25.00

Accessory Pak, Misty Hair Color Kit, #9828-5, MIB........$75.00

Accessory Pak, pizza, princess phone, Tammy's Telephone Directory, wht scandals, #9184-80, NRFP $25.00

Accessory Pak, plate of crackers, juice, glasses, sandals & newspaper, #9179-3, NRFP $30.00

Accessory Pak, poodle on leash, red vinyl purse & wht sneakers, #9186-80, NRFP $25.00

Accessory Pak, tennis racket, score book & sneakers, #9188-8, NRFP, S14...$15.00

Case, Dodi, gr background, EX, S14 ....$30.00

Case, Misty, Dutch door-type, blk, EX $30.00

Case, Misty, pk & wht, EX $25.00

Case, Misty & Tammy, dbl telephone, gr or pk, ea $25.00

Case, Misty & Tammy, hatbox style, EX $30.00

Case, Papper & Patti, Montgomery Ward's Exclusive, red, EX $50.00

Case, Pepper, front snap closure, red or coral, EX $15.00

Case, Pepper, hatbox style, turq, EX $40.00

Case, Pepper, yel or gr, EX $20.00

Case, Pepper & Dodi, front opening, bl, EX $30.00

Case, Tammy, suitcase type w/doll compartment, closet & accessory compartment, red w/clear see-through front, EX..$50.00

Case, Tammy & Her Friends, pk or gr, EX $30.00

Case, Tammy Beau & Arrow, hatbox style, bl or red, EX...$40.00

Case, Tammy Evening in Paris, bl, blk or red, EX $20.00

Case, Tammy Model Miss, dbl trunk, red or blk, EX........$25.00

Case, Tammy Model Miss, hatbox style, bl or blk, EX $30.00

Case, Tammy Model Miss, red or blk, EX.........................$25.00

Case, Tammy Traveller, red or gr, EX $45.00

Doll, Bud, MIB, minimum value $600.00

Doll, Dodi, MIB $75.00

Doll, Glamour Misty the Miss Clairol Doll, MIB $150.00

Doll, Grown Up Tammy, MIB $85.00

Doll, Grown Up Tammy (Black), MIB $400.00

Doll, Misty, MIB $100.00

Doll, Misty (Black), MIB, minimum value $600.00

Doll, Patti, MIB $200.00

Doll, Pepper, MIB $65.00

Doll, Pepper ('carrot'-colored hair), MIB........................$75.00

Doll, Pepper (Canadian version), MIB $75.00

Doll, Pepper (trimmer body & smaller face), MIB............$75.00

Doll, Pos'n Dodi, M (decorated box) $150.00

Doll, Pos'n Dodi, M (plain box) $75.00

Doll, Pos'n Misty & Her Telephone Booth, MIB...........$125.00

Doll, Pos'n Pepper, MIB..$75.00

Doll, Pos'n Pete, MIB $125.00

Doll, Pos'n Salty, MIB $125.00

Doll, Pos'n Tammy & Her Telephone Booth, MIB........$100.00

Doll, Pos'n Ted, MIB $100.00

Doll, Tammy, MIB...$85.00

Doll, Tammy's Dad, MIB..$65.00

Doll, Tammy's Mom, MIB..$75.00

Doll, Ted, MIB...$50.00

Outfit, Dad & Ted, blazer & slacks, #9477-1, NRFP $20.00

Outfit, Dad & Ted, pajamas & slippers, #9456-5, MIB.....$20.00

Tammy's Mom, EX, from $45.00 to $50.00; Tammy's Dad, EX, from $25.00 to $30.00; Tammy's Brother, Ted, EX, from $20.00 to $25.00. (Photo courtesy Cindy Sabulis)

Outfit, Dad & Ted, sports car coat & cap, #9467-2, NRFP ..$20.00

Outfit, Dad & Ted, sweater, shorts & socks, #9476-3, MIP..$25.00

Outfit, Pepper, After School, #9318-7, complete, M $30.00

Outfit, Pepper, Anchors Away, #9316-1, complete, M $35.00

Outfit, Pepper, Flower Girl, #9332-8, complete, M $50.00

Outfit, Pepper, Happy Holiday, #9317-9, complete, M.....$40.00

Outfit, Pepper, Miss Gadabout, #9331-0, MIP $50.00

Outfit, Pepper & Dodi, Light & Lacy, #9305-4, MIP........$45.00

Outfit, Pepper & Dodi, Sun 'n Surf, #9321-1, MIP...........$75.00

Outfit, Tammy, Beach Party, #9056-3 or #9906-9, complete, M $45.00

Outfit, Tammy, Career Girl, #9945-7, complete, M..........$75.00

Outfit, Tammy, Cutie Coed, #9132-2 or 9932-5, complete, M $45.00

Outfit, Tammy, Jet Set, #9155-3 or #9943-2, MIP $75.00

Outfit, Tammy, Knit Knack, #9094-4 or #9917-6, complete, M..$25.00

Outfit, Tammy, Opening Night, #9954-9, MIP................$100.00

Outfit, Tammy, Private Secretary, #9939-0, MIP $100.00

Outfit, Tammy's Mom, Evening in Paris, #9421-9, complete, M $40.00

Outfit, Tammy's Mom, Lazy Days, #9418-5, MIP.............$50.00

Pak Clothing, afternoon dress & shoes, #9345-2, NRFP ..$45.00

Pak Clothing, nightgown, sandals & 3-pc fruit set, #9242-9, NRFP $30.00

Pak Clothing, pedal pushers, orange juice, newspaper & hanger, #9224-7, NRFP $30.00

Pak Clothing, sheath dress, blk belt, shoes & hanger, #9243-7, NRFP $45.00

Pak Clothing, short-sleeved blouse, red glasses & hanger, #9231-2, NRFP $20.00

Pak Clothing, skirt, belt, handkerchief, date book & hanger, #9220-5, MIP $30.00

Pak Clothing, skirt, shoes & hanger, #9221-3, NRFP.......$25.00

Pak Clothing, sleeveless blouse, necklace & hanger, #9222-1, NRFP $25.00

Pak Clothing, sweater, scarf & hanger, #9244-5, NRFP ...$25.00

Pepper's Jukebox, M $65.00

Pepper's Pony, MIB..$250.00

Pepper's Treehouse, MIB...$150.00

Tammy & Ted Catamaran, MIB...$200.00

Tammy Bubble Bath Set, NRFB...$75.00

Tammy Dress-Up Kit, Colorforms, 1964, complete, MIB ..$30.00

Tammy Hair Dryer, sq or rnd case, NM..............................$50.00

Tammy's Bed, Dress & Chair, MIB..$85.00

Tammy's Car, MIB...$75.00

Tammy's Ideal House, M, minimum value $100.00

Tammy's Jukebox, M $50.00

Tammy's Magic Mirror Fashion Show, Winthrop-Atkins, NRFB..$50.00

Tressy

American Character's Tressy doll was produced in this country from 1963 to 1967. The unique feature of this 11½" fashion doll was that her hair 'grew' by pushing a button on her stomach. Tressy also had a little (9") sister named Cricket. Numerous fashions and accessories were produced for these two dolls. Never-removed-from-box Tressy and Cricket items are rare, so unless indicated, values listed are for loose, mint items. A never-removed-from-box item's worth is at least double its loose value.

Advisor: Cindy Sabulis (S14)

Tressy in original outfit, MIB, $100.00. (Photo courtesy Cindy Sabulis)

Apartment $350.00

Beauty Salon $250.00

Case, Cricket, M $30.00

Case, Tressy $30.00

Doll, American Character Tressy, MIB.........................$100.00

Doll, Pre-Teen Tressy $50.00

Doll, Tressy & Her Hi-Fashion Cosmetics, MIB............$145.00

Doll, Tressy in Miss America Character outfit, NM $65.00

Doll, Tressy in orig dress $35.00

Doll, Tressy w/Magic Make-up Face, M............................$25.00

Doll Clothes Pattern..$10.00

Gift Pak w/Doll & Clothing, NRFB, minimum value $100.00

Hair Accessory Pak, NRFB $20.00

Hair Dryer $40.00

Hair or Cosmetic Accessory Kits, ea minimum value $50.00

Millinery $200.00

Outfits, MOC, ea $40.00

Outfits, NRFB, ea minimum value $65.00

Upsy Downsys by Mattel

The Upsy Downsy dolls were made by Mattel during the late 1960s. They were small, 2½" to 3½", made of vinyl and plastic. Some of the group were 'Upsies' that walked on their feet, while others were 'Downsies' that walked or rode fantasy animals while upside-down.

Advisor: Dawn Diaz (P2)

Baby So-High, #3828, complete, M $50.00

Downy Dilly, #3832, complete, M....................................$50.00

Downy Dilly, #3832, NRFB $75.00

Flossy Glossy, #3827, doll & playland, EX.....................$25.00

Funny Feeder, #3834, Gooey Chooey only, EX $25.00

Hairy Hurry Downsy Wizzer, #3838, complete, EX.........$100.00

Miss Information, #3831, NRFB..$75.00

Mother What Now, #3829, complete, EX.......................$50.00

Pocus Hocus, #3820, complete, M....................................$50.00

Pudgy Fudgy, #3826, NRFB $75.00

Tickle Pinkle & Her Bugabout Car, MIB, from $75 to ...$100.00

Farm Toys

It's entirely probable that more toy tractors have been sold than real ones. They've been made to represent all makes and models, of plastic, cast iron, diecast metal, and even wood. They've been made in at least 1/16th scale, 1/32nd, 1/43rd, and 1/64th. If you buy a 1/16th-scale replica, that small piece of equipment would have to be sixteen times larger to equal the size of the real item. Limited editions (meaning that a specific number will be made and no more) and commemorative editions (made for special events) are usually very popular with collectors. Many models on the market today are being made by the Ertl company.

Advisor: John Rammacher (S5)

See also Cast Iron, Farm; Diecast.

Ad-Chem Rogator Liquid Sprayer 1254, Ertl, #13173, 1/64 scale, MIB, S5 ....$7.00

Agco Allis Tractor 6690 w/Duals, Ertl, #1286, 1/64 scale, MIB, S5 ....$3.50

Agco Allis Tractor 6690 w/4-Post ROPS, Ertl, #1239, 1/64 scale, MIB, S5 ....$3.35

Agco Allis 6670 Row Crop, Ertl, #1214, 1/64 scale, MIB, S5...$3.50

Agco Tractor DT200, Ertl, #13377, 1/64 scale, MIB, S5 ....$5.20

Allis-Chalmers Tractor D-21 w/Duals, Ertl #13078, 1/16 scale, MIB, S5 ....$39.00

Allis-Chalmers Tractor G, 1/16 scale, MIB, $30.00.

Allis-Chalmers Tractor Hi-Crop D-19, Ertl, #13403, 1/64 scale, MIB, S5...$39.00

Allis-Chalmers Tractor WD-45, Ertl, #13080, 1/16 scale, MIB, S5 ....$23.50

Allis-Chalmers Tractor WD-45 Precision #7, Ertl, #13101, 1/16 scale, MIB, S5 ....$118.00

Allis-Chalmers Tractor 7060 w/Cab, Ertl, #13185, 1/16 scale, MIB, S5 ....$35.00

Case HI Round Baler, Ertl #14173, 1/64 scale, MIB, S5 .....$4.50

Case HI Tillage Plow, Ertl #14172, 1/64 scale, MIB, S5......$3.25

Case IH Combine Axial-Flow 2366, Ertl, #4614, 1/64 scale, MIB, S5 ....$10.50

Case IH Combine 2388, Ertl, #14176, 1/64 scale, MIB, S5...$11.00

Case IH Cotton Express Picker, Ertl, #4300, 1/64 scale, MIB, S5...$11.00

Case IH Hay Rake, Ertl, #210, 1/64 scale, MIB, S5 ....$3.00

Case IH Mower Conditioner 8312, Ertl, #4362, 1/64 scale, MIB, S5 ....$3.50

Case IH Planter 12-Row 900, Ertl, #656, 1/64, MIB, S5.....$4.50

Case IH Round Baler, Ertl, #274, 1/64 scale, MIB, S5 ....$3.25

Case IH Tractor Magnum MZ180, Ertl, #4550, 1/64 scale, S5...$4.00

Case IH Tractor Maxxum MX120, Ertl, #4487, 1997 Farm Show, 1/16 scale, MIB, S5 ....$45.00

Case IH Tractor MX120 w/Loader, Ertl, #14174, 1/64 scale, MIB, S5 ....$8.00

Case IH Tractor MX135, Ertl, #14158, 1/64 scale, MIB, S5..$5.00

Case IH Tractor MX220, Ertl, #4431, 1/64 scale, MIB, S5...$4.00

Case IH Tractor MX240 w/Triples, Ertl, #14103, 1/64 scale, MIB, S5 ....$5.00

Case IH Tractor MX270, Ertl, #14134, 1/64 scale, MIB, S5..$5.00

Case IH Tractor STX Tracked, Ertl, #14046, 1/64 scale, MIB, S5...$8.00

Case IH Tractor w/Enloader, Ertl, #212, 1/64 scale, MIB, S5 ..$5.00

Case IH Tractor 5130 Row Crop, Ertl, #229, 1991 Farm Show, 1/64 scale, MIB, S5..$10.00

Case IH Tractor 6670 Row Crop, Ertl, #229, 1/64 scale, MIB, S5...$3.00

Case IH Tractor 7130 Magnum, Ertl, #458, 1/64 scale, MIB, S5...$3.00

Case IH Tractor 7140 MFD, Ertl, #616, 1/64 scale, MIB, S5..$3.50

Case IH Tractor 7150 FWA, Ertl, #285, 1992 Farm Show, 1/64 scale, MIB, S5 ....$10.00

Case IH Tractor 7220 w/Loader, Ertl, #460, 1/64 scale, MIB, S5...$5.00

Case IH Tractor 9260 w/4-Wheel Drive, Ertl, #231, 1993 Farm Show, 1/64 scale, MIB, S5 ....$9.00

Case Skid Steer Loader 90XT, Ertl, #4216, 1/64 scale, MIB, S5...$25.00

Case Tractor L, Ertl, #2554, 1/43 scale, MIB, S5................$6.25

Case Tractor Maxxum MX100 w/Loader, Ertl #4270, 1/64 scale, MIB, S5 ....$5.00

Case Tractor STX3754 w/4-Wheel Drive, Ertl, #14003, 1/16 scale, MIB, S5 ....$70.00

Case Tractor 930 Precision #12, Ertl, #4284, 1/16 scale, MIB, S5...$107.00

Case Tractor 970 Agriking, Ertl, #4279, 1/16 scale, MIB, S5 .$32.50

Case Tractor 1470 Traction King, Ertl, #4332, 1/64 scale, MIB, S5...$6.00

Case Tractor 1930 Western SP Precision #15, Ertl, #14130, 1/16 scale, MIB, S5 ....$116.00

Caterpillar Flotation Liquid Fertilizer Spreader, Ertl, #2324, 1/64 scale, MIB, S5 ....$4.75

Caterpillar Flotation VFS50 w/Gravity Wagon, Ertl, #2326, 1/64 scale, MIB, S5 ....$4.85

Caterpillar Industrial Disk, Ertl, #2333, 1/64 scale, MIB, S5..$3.25

Chevy Cameo Pickup (1955) w/Crates, Ertl #2154, 1/43 scale, MIB $6.00

Deutz Allis Tractor 7085, Ertl, #1260, 1990 Farm Show Ed, 1/64 scale, MIB, S5 ....$11.00

Deutz Allis Tractor 9150 Orlando Show, Ertl, #1280, 1/16 scale, MIB, S5...$200.00

Farmall Crawler 340, Ertl, #4734, 1/16 scale, MIB, S5 .....$25.00

Farmall Tractor B, Ertl, #14113, 1/16 scale, MIB, S5........$23.50

Farmall Tractor H, Ertl, #4441, 1/16 scale, MIB, S5 ....$25.00

Farmall Tractor Super H, Ertl, #14269, 1/16 scale, MIB, S5..$17.00

Farmall Tractor Super M, Ertl, #14171, 1/64 scale, MIB, S5 ..$4.00

Farmall Tractor Super M, Ertl, #14270, 1/16 scale, MIB, S5 ..$22.00

Farmall Tractor 140, Ertl, #4741, 1995 Farm Show, 1/16 scale, MIB, S5 ....$35.00

Farmall Tractor 230, Ertl, #14040, 1/16 scale, MIB, S5 ....$25.50

Farmall Tractor 400 Precision, Ertl, #14007, 1/16 scale, MIB, S5...$110.00

Farmall Tractor 560 w/Mount Picker & Wagon, Ertl, #14073, 1/64 scale, MIB, S5 ....$10.50

Farmall Tractor 856, Ertl #14170, 1/64 scale, MIB, S5 ....$6.00

Ford Fordson Tractor, Ertl, #13573, 1/16 scale, MIB, S5 ..$27.00

Ford Tractor F, Ertl, #872, Collector's Ed, 1/16, MIB, S5..$45.00

Ford Tractor TW35, Ertl, #899, 1/64 scale, MIB, S5...........$3.00
Ford Tractor 8N, Ertl, #843, 1/16 scale, MIB, S5 ....$20.00
Ford Tractor 9N, Ertl, #926, 1/64 scale, MIB, S5 ....$3.50
Ford Tractor 621, Ertl, #13529, 1/16 scale, MIB, S5 ....$22.25
Ford Tractor 640, Ertl, #3054, 1/16 scale, MIB, S5 ....$22.00
Ford Tractor 640 Precision #8, Ertl, #13574, 1/16 scale, MIB,
    S5 ....$112.00
Ford Tractor 641 w/Precision Series Loader, Ertl, #383, 1/16
    scale, MIB, S5..$135.00
Ford Tractor 4000, Ertl, #3024, 1/64 scale, MIB, S5 ....$3.15
Ford Tractor 5000 Precision, Ertl, #13503, 1/64 scale, MIB,
    S5 ....$117.00
Ford Tractor 5000 Super Major, Ertl, #928, 1/64 scale, MIB,
    S5 ....$3.50
Ford Tractor 5640 w/Loader, Ertl, #334, 1/64 scale, MIB, S5 ..$5.00
Ford Tractor 6640 Row Crop, Ertl, #332, 1/64 scale, MIB, S5...$325.00
Ford Tractor 7740 Row Crop, Ertl, #873, Collector's Ed, 1/16
    scale, MIB, S5 ....$50.00
Ford Tractor 7740 w/Loader, Ertl, #387, 1/64 scale, MIB, S5 ..$5.00
Ford Tractor 7840, Ertl, #336, 1/64 scale, MIB, S5 ....$3.50
Ford Tractor 8240 w/4-Wheel Drive, Ertl, #389, 1/64 scale, MIB,
    S5 ....$4.00
Ford Tractor 8340 w/Duals, Ertl, #388, 1/64 scale, S5.........$3.50
Ford Tractor 8340 w/4-Wheel Drive, Ertl, #877, Collector's Ed,
    1/16 scale, MIB, S5 ....$50.00
Ford Tractor 901 Power Master, Ertl, #927, 1/64 scale, MIB,
    S5 ....$5.00
Genesis Tractor 8770, Ertl, #391, 1/64 scale, MIB, A $3.50
Genesis Tractor 8870 w/4-Wheel Drive, Ertl, #392, 1/64 scale,
    MIB, S5 ....$3.50

International Cub Tractor, Ertl, MIB, $18.00.

IH Tractor 756 w/Cab, Ertl, #14124, 1/16 scale, MIB, S5 ....$35.00
IH Tractor 756 WF, Ertl, #2308, 1/16 scale, MIB, S5........$31.00
IH Tractor 1456 Diesel w/Cab, Ertl #2311, 1/16 scale, MIB,
    S5 ....$31.00
IH Tractor 1466 Precision, Ertl, #14204, 1/16 scale, MIB, S5..$125.00
IH Tractor 9560 Gas, Ertl, #4830, 1/64 scale, MIB, S5 ....$3.50
IHC Famous Engine, Ertl, #615, 1/16 scale, MIB, S5 ....$19.00
John Deere Baler 338 (Rectangular), Ertl, #5646, 1/64 scale,
    MIB, S5 ....$3.50
John Deere C&J Liquid Fertilizer Spreader, Ertl #5089, 1/64
    scale, MIB, S5 ....$4.50
John Deere Combine 95, Ertl, #5819, 1/64 scale, MIB, S5 ..$10.00
John Deere Combine 9750 STS, Ertl #15038, 1/64 scale, MIB,
    S5 ....$11.00
John Deere Compact Utility Tractor, Ertl, #581, 1/16 scale, MIB,
    S5 ....$16.00
John Deere Cotton Picker 9986, Ertl, #15440, 1/64 scale, MIB,
    S5 ....$10.50
John Deere Crawler 40, Ertl, #5072, 1/16 scale, MIB, S5 ...$27.00
John Deere Crawler 430, Ertl, #5771, 1/16 scale, MIB, S5 ..$22.00
John Deere Field Cultivator 2200, Ertl, #15081, 1/64 scale, MIB,
    S5 ....$8.00
John Deere Flare Box Wagon, Ertl, #5637, 143 scale, MIB, S5...$5.25
John Deere Forage Blower Model 150, Ertl, #5728, 1/64 scale,
    MIB, S5 ....$3.35
John Deere Forage Harvester, Ertl, #566, 1/64 scale, MIB, S5..$3.00
John Deere Hydra-Push Spreader, Ertl, #574, 1/64 scale, MIB,
    S5...$3.20
John Deere Mower Conditioner, Ertl, #5657, 1/64 scale, MIB,
    S5...$3.00
John Deere Skid Steer Loader, Ertl, #569, 1/16 scale, MIB,
    S5...$18.50
John Deere Split Row Planter 1790, Ertl, #15380, 1/64 scale,
    MIB, S5 ....$7.75
John Deere Sprayer, Ertl, #5752, 1/64 scale, MIB, S5 ....$9.00
John Deere Sprayer, Ertl, #15180, 1/64 scale, MIB, S5 ....$8.00
John Deere Tractor D, Ertl, #5179, 1/16 scale, MIB, S5 ...$26.00
John Deere Tractor G, Ertl, #5104, 1/16 scale, MIB, S5 ...$20.00

Grain Truck, Ertl, 14½", EX, $100.00.

Hesston Skid Steer Loader SL-30, Ertl, #2267, 1/64 scale, MIB,
    S5 ....$4.25
IH Combine 815, Ertl, #4354, 1/64 scale, MIB, S5...........$10.50
IH Tractor I-D9, Ertl, #4611, 1993 Farm Show, 1/16 scale, MIB,
    S5 ....$36.50
IH Tractor 460 Precision #11, Ertl, #4355, 1/16 scale, MIB,
    S5...$110.00
IH Tractor 560, Ertl, #14035, 1/16 scale, MIB, S5 ....$29.00

John Deere Tractor A General Purpose (1934), Ertl, MIB, $75.00.

John Deere Tractor 70, Ertl, #5611, 1/16 scale, MIB, S5 ......**$21.00**

John Deere Tractor 430, Ertl, #5620, 1/64 scale, MIB, S5 .....**$3.75**

John Deere Tractor 630 w/Corn Picker & Wagon, Ertl, #15086, 1/64 scale, MIB, S5 ....**$10.50**

John Deere Tractor 2510, Ertl, #2510, 1/64 scale, MIB, S5 ....**$3.50**

John Deere Tractor 2510, Ertl, #5756, 1/64 scale, MIB, S5 ....**$3.50**

John Deere Tractor 4010, Ertl #5716, 1/16 scale, MIB, S5 ...**$25.00**

John Deere Tractor 4040, Ertl, #5133, 1/16 scale, MIB, S5 ...**$30.00**

John Deere Tractor 5020, Ertl, #5726, 1/64 scale, MIB, S5 ...**$3.75**

John Deere Tractor 6410 w/Loader, Ertl, #5069, 1/16 scale, MIB, S5 ....**$35.00**

John Deere Tractor 6410 w/Loader, Ertl, #5169, 1/64 scale, MIB.............................**$5.25**

John Deere Tractor 7800, Row Crop, Ertl, #5538, 1/64 scale, MIB, S5 ....**$3.75**

John Deere Tractor 8200, Ertl, #5064, 1/64 scale, MIB, S5 ...**$3.50**

John Deere Tractor 8300, Ertl, #5063, 1/64 scale, MIB, S5 ..**$375.00**

John Deere Tractor 8400T, Ertl, #5051, 1/64 scale, MIB, S5 ....**$6.75**

John Deere Utility Tractor w/Loader, Ertl, #517, 1/16 scale,MIB, S5 ....**$22.00**

John Deere Wing Disk, Ertl, #5615, 1/64 scale, MIB, S5 ....**$3.25**

Massey-Ferguson Tractor 1155, Ertl, #13170, 1/16 scale, MIB, S5.............................**$43.00**

Massey-Ferguson Tractor 3070 w/Front-Wheel Drive, Ertl, #1107, 1/64 scale, MIB, S5.............................**$3.50**

Massey-Ferguson Tractor 3070 w/Loader, Ertl, #1109, 1/64 scale, MIB, S5 ....**$5.00**

Massey-Ferguson Tractor 3120, Ertl, #1177, 1/64 scale, MIB, S5 ....**$3.00**

Massey-Ferguson Tractor 3120 w/Loader, Ertl #1109, 1/64 scale, MIB, S5 ....**$4.50**

Massey-Ferguson Tractor 3140 w/Front-Wheel Drive, Ertl, #1107, 1/64 scale, MIB, S5 ....**$3.50**

Massey-Ferguson Tractor 8280 w/Duals, Ertl, #13052, 1/64 scale, MIB, S5 ....**$5.85**

Massey-Harris Tractor 44 Precision #9, Ertl, #13082, 1/16 scale, MIB, S5 ....**$112.00**

New Hollad Baler, Ertl, #337, 1/64 scale, MIB, S5.............**$2.25**

New Holland Box Spreader, Ertl, #308, 1/64 scale, MIB, S5..**$3.00**

New Holland Combine CR960, Ertl, #13595, 1/64 scale, MIB, S5 ....**$11.00**

New Holland Combine TR 97, Ertl, #815, 1/64 scale, MIB, S5 ....**$10.00**

New Holland Hay Rake, Ertl, #369, 1/64 scale, S5 ....**$2.65**

New Holland Skid Loader, Ertl, #381, 1/64 scale, MIB.......**$4.25**

New Holland Skid Steer Loader LS170, Ertl, #13562, 1/64 scale, MIB, S5 ....**$4.00**

New Holland Tractor TG-255, Ertl, #13617, 1/64 scale, MIB, S5.............................**$5.00**

New Holland Tractor TM-150 w/4-Wheel Drive, Ertl, #13560, 1/16 scale, MIB, S5 ....**$40.00**

New Holland Tractor 7840 w/Loader, Ertl, #13588, 1/16 scale, MIB, S5 ....**$48.00**

New Holland Tractor 8260, Ertl, #3050, 1997 National Farm Show, 1/43 scale, MIB, S5 ....**$22.00**

New Holland Tractor 8560, Ertl, #3032, 1/43 scale, MIB, S5..**$11.00**

New Holland Wing Disk, Ertl, #3049, 1/64 scale, MIB, S5...**$4.00**

Oliver Crawler HG, Ertl, #13079, 1/16 scale, MIB, S5.....**$22.00**

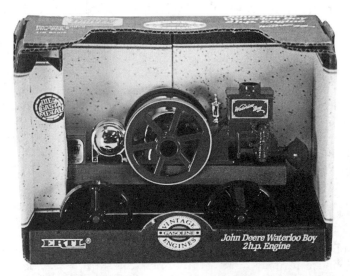

John Deere Waterloo Boy two-horsepower Engine, Ertl, 1992 special edition, 1/8 scale, MIB, $20.00.

Oliver Combine, SLIK, 1952, stamped S9830BAR, 5x12", EX, $25.00.

Oliver Crawler OC-3, Ertl, #13007, 1/16 scale, MIB, S5..**$22.25**
Oliver Tractor 88 w/Mounted Picker & Wagon, Ertl, #13051, 1/64 scale, MIB, S5......................................**$10.50**
Oliver Tractor 1655 w/Cab, Ertl, #13186, 1/16 scale, MIB, S5 ..**$35.00**
Steiger Super Wild Cat SP ED, Ertl, #2019, 1/32 scale, MIB, S5..**$31.00**

Fisher-Price

Fisher-Price toys are becoming one of the hottest new trends in the collectors' marketplace today. In 1930 Herman Fisher, backed by Irving Price, Elbert Hubbard, and Helen Schelle, formed one of the most successful toy companies ever to exist. Located in East Aurora, New York, the company has seen many changes since then, the most notable being the changes in ownership. From 1930 to 1968, it was owned by the individuals mentioned previously and a few stockholders. In 1969 it became an aquisition of Quaker Oats, and in June of 1991 it became independently owned. In November of 1993, one of the biggest sell-outs in the toy industry took place: Fisher-Price became a subdivision of Mattel.

There are a few things to keep in mind when collecting Fisher-Price toys. You should count on a little edge wear as well as some wear and fading to the paint. Pull toys found in mint condition are truly rare and command a much higher value, especially if you find one with its original box. This also applies to playsets, but to command higher prices, they must also be complete, with no chew/teeth marks or plastic fading. Another very important rule to remember is there are no standard colors for pieces that came with a playset. Fisher-Price often substituted a piece of a different color when they ran short. Please note that the dates on the toys indicate their copyright date and not the date they were manufactured.

The company put much time and thought into designing their toys. They took care to operate by their five-point creed: to make toys with (1) intrinsic play value, (2) ingenuity, (3) strong construction, (4) good value for the money, and (5) action. Some of the most sought-after pull toys are those bearing the Walt Disney logo.

The ToyFest limited editions are a series of toys produced in conjunction with ToyFest, an annual weekend of festivities for young and old alike held in East Aurora, New York. It is sponsored by the Toy Town USA Museum and is held every year in August. Fisher-Price produces a limited-edition toy for this event; these are listed at the end of this category. (For more information on ToyFest and the museum, write to Toy Town Museum, P.O. Box 238, East Aurora, NY 14052; see display ad this section.) For more information on Fisher-Price toys we recommend *Fisher-Price, A Historical Rarity Value Guide*, by John J. Murray and Bruce R. Fox; and *Fisher-Price Toys* by our advisor Brad Cassity.

Additional information may be obtained through the Fisher-Price Collectors' Club who publish a quarterly newsletter; their address may be found in their display ad (this section) and in the Directory under Clubs, Newsletters, and Other Publications.

Note: With the ever increasing influence of the Internet it is becoming harder and harder to establish book value. A toy can sell for 100% more than the book value or 75% less on the Internet. The prices we have listed here are derived from dealers, price lists, and toy shows and represent values for examples that show only a little edge and paint wear and minimal fading (VG).

Advisor: Brad Cassity (C13)

See also Building Blocks and Construction Toys; Catalogs; Character, TV, and Movie Collectibles; Dollhouse Furniture; Dollhouses; Dolls; Optical Toys; other specific categories.

#5 Bunny Cart, 1948-49, C13 ....$50.00
#6 Ducky Cart, 1948-49, C13...$50.00
#7 Doggy Racer, 1942-43, C13...$150.00
#7 Looky Fire Truck, 1950-53 & Easter 1954, C13...........$75.00
#8 Bouncy Racer, 1960-62, C13.......................................$30.00
#10 Bunny Cart, 1940-42, C13 ....$50.00
#11 Ducky Cart, 1940-42, C13...$50.00
#12 Bunny Truck, 1941-42, C13 ....$65.00
#14 Ducky Daddles, 1941, C13 ....$85.00
#15 Bunny Cart, 1946-48, C13...$50.00
#16 Ducky Cart, 1946-48, C13...$50.00
#20 Animal Cutouts, 1942-46, duck, elephant, pony or Scottie dog, C13, ea $50.00
#28 Bunny Egg Cart, 1950, C13.......................................$50.00
#50 Bunny Chick Tandem Cart, 1953-54, no number on toy, C13..$75.00
#51 Ducky Cart, 1950, C13 ....$50.00
#52 Rabbit Cart, 1950, C13...$50.00
#75 Baby Duck Tandem Cart, 1953-54, no number on toy, C13 ....$75.00
#100 Dr Doodle, 1931, C13..$700.00
#100 Dr Doodle, 1995, Fisher-Price limited edition of 5,000, 1st in series, C13..$50.00
#100 Musical Sweeper, 1950-52, plays Whistle While You Work, C13...$60.00
#101 Granny Doodle & Family, 1931-32, C13 ....$800.00

#102 Drummer Bear, 1931, C13......................................$700.00
#102 Drummer Bear, 1932-33, fatter & taller version, C13....$700.00
#103 Barky Puppy, 1931-33, C13....................................$700.00
#104 Looky Monk, 1931, C13..$700.00
#105 Bunny Scoot, 1931, C13..$700.00
#107 Music Box Clock Radio, 1971, plays Hickory Dickory Dock..$1.00
#109 Lucky Monk, 1932-33, C13.....................................$700.00
#110 Chubby Chief, 1932-33, C13 ....$700.00
#110 Puppy Playhouse, 1978-80, C13 ....$10.00
#112 Picture Disk Camera, 1968-71, w/5 picture disks, C13.....$20.00
#114 Music Box TV, 1967-83, plays London Bridge & Row Row Row Your Boat, C13 ....$1.00
#114 Sesame Street Music Box TV, 1984-87, plays People in Your Neighborhood, C13..$1.00
#117, Play Family Barnyard, 1972-74, complete, loose, C13....$5.00
#118 Tumble Tower Game, 1972-75, w/10 marbles, C13.....$5.00
#120 Cackling Hen, 1958-66, wht, C13............................$35.00
#120 Gabby Goose, 1936-37 & Easter 1938, C13 ....$350.00
#121 Happy Hopper, 1969-76, C13..................................$10.00
#122 Bouncing Buggy, 1974-79, 6 wheels, C13.................$1.00
#123 Cackling Hen, 1966-68, red litho, C13....................$35.00
#123 Roller Chime, 1953-60 & Easter 1961, C13 ....$30.00
#124 Roller Chime, 1961-62 & Easter 1963, C13 ....$25.00
#125 Music Box Iron, 1966, aqua w/yel hdl, C13 ....$40.00
#125 Music Box Iron, 1966-69, wht w/red hdl, C13.........$30.00
#125 Uncle Timmy Turtle, 1956-58, red shell, C13.........$75.00
#130 Wobbles, 1964-67, dog wobbles when pulled, C13....$35.00
#131 Milk Wagon, 1964-72, truck w/bottle carrier, C13....$45.00
#131 Toy Wagon, 1951-54, C13.......................................$200.00
#132 Dr Doodle, 1957-60, C13 ....$50.00
#132 Molly Moo Cow, 1972-78, C13 ....$10.00
#135 Play Family Animal Circus, 1974-76, complete, C13....$60.00
#136 Play Family Lacing Shoe, 1965-69, complete, C13....$60.00

#137 Pony Chime, 1965 – 1967, $40.00, (Photo courtesy Brad Cassity)

#111 Play Family Merry-Go-Round, 1972 – 1977, plays 'Skater's Waltz,' with four figures, $30.00. (Photo courtesy Brad Cassity)

#138 Jack-in-the-Box Puppet, 1970-73, C13 ....$20.00
#139 Tuggy Tooter, 1967-73, C13 ....$30.00
#139 Tuggy Turtle, 1959-60 & Easter 1961, C13 ....$75.00

#140 Coaster Boy, 1941, C13 ....$700.00
#140 Katy Kackler, 1954-56 & Easter 1957, C13.............$75.00
#141 Snap-Quack, 1947-49, C13 ....$200.00
#142 Three Men in a Tub, 1970-73, w/bell, C13 ....$10.00
#142 Three Men in a Tub, 1974-75, w/flag, C13 ....$5.00
#145 Humpty Dump Truck, 1963-64 & Easter 1965, C13 ....$30.00
#145 Husky Dump Truck, 1961-62 & Easter 1963, C13 ....$30.00
#145 Musical Elephant, 1948-50, C13 ....$200.00
#146 Pull-A-Long Lacing Shoe, 1970-73, w/6 figures, C13.....$50.00
#148 Ducky Daddles, 1942, C13 ....$225.00
#148 Jack & Jill TV Radio, 1959 & Easter 1960, wood & plastic, C13 ....$55.00
#149 Dog Cart Donald, 1936-37, C13 ....$700.00
#150 Barky Buddy, 1934-35, C13 ....$600.00
#150 Pop-Up-Pal Chime Phone, 1968-78, C13 ....$15.00
#150 Teddy Tooter, 1940-41, C13 ....$400.00
#150 Timmy Turtle, 1953-55 & Easter 1956, gr shell, C13.....$75.00
#151 Goldilocks & the Three Bears Playhouse, 1967-71, C13.........................$60.00
#151 Happy Hippo, 1962-63, C13...................................$85.00
#152 Road Roller, 1934-35, C13 ....$700.00

#154 Frisky Frog, 1971 – 1983, $10.00. (Photo courtesy Brad Cassity)

#154 Pop Goes the Weasel TV-Radio, 1964-67, wood & plastic, C13.........................$15.00
#155 Jack & Jill TV Radio, 1968-70, wood & plastic, C13 ....$25.00
#155 Moo-oo Cow, 1958-61 & Easter 1962, C13 ....$75.00
#155 Skipper Sam, 1934, C13 ....$850.00
#156 Baa-Baa Black Sheep TV-Radio, 1966-67, wood & plastic, C13.........................$50.00
#156 Circus Wagon, 1942-44, band leader in wagon, C13 ....$400.00
#156 Jiffy Dump Truck, 1971-73, squeeze bulb & dump moves, C13.........................$15.00
#158 Katie Kangaroo, 1976-77, squeeze bulb & she hops, C13..$15.00
#158 Little Boy Blue TV-Radio, 1967, wood & plastic, C13 ....$50.00

#159 Ten Little Indians TV-Radio, 1961-65 & Easter 1966, wood & plastic, C13 ....$20.00
#160 Donald & Donna Duck, 1937, C13 ....$700.00
#161 Creative Block Wagon, 1961-64, 18 building blocks & 6 wooden dowels fit into pull-along wagon, C13 ....$60.00
#161 Looky Chug-Chug, 1949-52, C13 ....$175.00
#161 Old Woman Who Lived in a Shoe TV-Radio, 1968-70, wood & plastic w/see-through window on back, C13..$30.00
#162 Roly Poly Boats Chime Ball, 1967-69, C13...............$1.00
#164 Chubby Cub, 1969-72, C13...................................$10.00
#164 Mother Goose, 1964-66, C13...................................$30.00
#165 Roly Poly Chime Ball, 1967-85, C13...................$1.00
#166 Bucky Burro, 1955-57, C13...................................$200.00
#166 Farmer in the Dell TV-Radio, 1963-66, C13...........$30.00
#166 Piggy Bank, 1981-82, pk plastic, C13 ....$10.00
#168 Magnetic Chug-Chug, 1964-69, C13...................$35.00
#168 Snorky Fire Engine, 1960 & Easter 1961, gr litho, C13.......$125.00
#169 Snorky Fire Engine, 1961 & Easter 1962, red litho, C13 ....$100.00
#170 American Airlines Flagship w/Tail Wing, 1941-42, C13 ....$900.00
#170 Change-A-Tune Carousel, 1981-83, music box w/crank hdl, 3 molded records & 3 figures, C13 ....$20.00
#171 Pull-Along Plane, 1981-88, C13...................................$5.00
#171 Toy Wagon, 1942-47, C13...................................$250.00
#172 Roly Raccoon, 1980-82, C13 ....$5.00
#175 Gold Star Stagecoach, 1954-55 & Easter 1956, C13....$250.00
#175 Kicking Donkey, 1937-38, C13 ....$450.00
#175 Winnie the Pooh TV-Radio, 1971-73, Sears only, C13.....$50.00
#177 Donald Duck Xylophone, 1946-52, 2nd version w/'Donald Duck' on hat, C13 ....$250.00

#177 Oscar the Grouch, 1977 – 1984, $10.00. (Photo courtesy Brad Cassity)

#178 What's in My Pocket Cloth Book, 1972-74, boy's version, C13.........................$20.00
#179 What's in My Pocket Cloth Book, 1972-74, girl's version, C13.........................$20.00
#180 Snoopy Sniffer, 1938-55, C13...................................$50.00

#183 Play Family Fun Jet, 1970, 1st version, C13 ....$15.00

#185 Donald Duck Xylophone, 1938, mk WDE, C13 ....$800.00

#189 Looky Chug-Chug, 1958-60, C13 ....$50.00

#189 Pull-A-Tune Blue Bird Music Box, 1969-79, plays Children's Prayer, C13 ....$8.00

#190 Gabby Duck, 1939-40 & Easter 1941, C13 ....$350.00

#190 Molly Moo-Moo, 1956 & Easter 1957, C13 ....$150.00

#190 Pull-A-Tune Pony Music Box, 1969-72, plays Shubert's Cradle Song, C13..$5.00

#191 Golden Gulch Express, 1961 & Easter 1962, C13.....$100.00

#192 Playland Express, 1962 & Easter 1963, C13 ....$100.00

#192 School Bus, 1965-69, new version of #990, C13....$125.00

#194 Push Pullet, 1971-72, C13 ....$15.00

#195 Peek-A-Boo Screen Music Box, 1965-68, plays Mary Had a Little Lamb, C13..$25.00

#195 Teddy Bear Parade, 1938, C13................................$600.00

#196 Peek-A-Boo Screen Music Box, 1964, plays Hey Diddle Diddle, C13..$45.00

#198 Band Wagon, 1940-41, C13 ....$300.00

#201 Woodsy-Wee Circus, 1931-32, complete, C13 ......$750.00

#205 Walt Disney's Parade, WDE, 1936-41, C13, ea......$250.00

#205 Woodsy-Wee Zoo, 1931-32, C13 ....$750.00

#207 Walt Disney's Carnival, 1936-38, Mickey, Donald, Pluto, or Elmer, complete, C13, ea $200.00

#207 Woodsy-Wee Pets, 1931, complete w/goat, donkey, cow, pig & cart, C13 ....$650.00

#208 Donald Duck, 1936-38, C13................................$175.00

#209 Woodsy-Wee Dog Show, 1932, complete w/5 dogs, C13..$650.00

#210 Pluto the Pup, 1936-38, C13 ....$150.00

#211 Elmer Elephant, 1936-38, C13 ....$175.00

#215 Fisher-Price Choo-Choo, 1955-57, engine w/3 cars, C13..$75.00

#225 Wheel Horse, 1935 & Easter 1936, C13 ....$500.00

#234 Nifty Station Wagon, 1960-62 & Easter 1963, removable roof, C13..$250.00

#237 Riding Horse, 1936, C13 ....$500.00

#250 Big Performing Circus, 1932-38, C13 ....$950.00

#300 Scoop Loader, 1975-77, C13................................$10.00

#301 Bunny Basket Cart, 1957-59, C13...........................$40.00

#301 Shovel Digger, 1975-77, C13................................$15.00

#302 Chick Basket Cart, 1957-59, C13 ....$40.00

#302 Husky Dump Truck, 1978-84, C13.........................$15.00

#303 Adventure People Emergency Rescue Truck, 1975-78, C13..$15.00

#303 Bunny Push Cart, 1957, C13 ....$75.00

#304 Adventure People Wild Safari Set, 1975-78, C13.....$50.00

#304 Chick Basket Cart, 1960-64, C13 ....$35.00

#304 Running Bunny Cart, 1957, C13.............................$60.00

#305 Adventure People Air-Sea Rescue Copter, 1975-80, C13 ....$10.00

#305 Walking Duck Cart, 1957-64, C13...........................$40.00

#306 Adventure People Daredevil Sport Plane, C13..........$5.00

#306 Bizzy Bunny Cart, 1957-59, C13 ....$40.00

#307 Adventure People Wilderness Patrol, 1975-79, C13....$30.00

#307 Bouncing Bunny Cart, 1961-63 & Easter 1964, C13 ...$35.00

#310 Adventure People Sea Explorer, 1975-80, C13........$20.00

#309 Adventure People TV Action Team, 1977 – 1978, $50.00. (Photo courtesy Brad Cassity)

#310 Mickey Mouse Puddle Jumper, 1953-55 & Easter 1956, C13 ....$100.00

#311 Bulldozer, 1976-77, C13................................$15.00

#311 Husky Bulldozer, 1978-79, C13 ....$15.00

#312 Adventure People Northwoods Trail Blazer, 1977-82, C13 ....$20.00

#312 Running Bunny Cart, 1960-64, C13 ....$40.00

#313 Husky Roller Grader, 1978-80, C13 ....$15.00

#313 Roller Grader, 1977, C13................................$15.00

#314 Husky Boom Crane, 1978-82, C13.........................$25.00

#314 Queen Buzzy Bee, 1956-58, C13...........................$20.00

#315 Husky Cement Mixer, 1978-82, C13.......................$15.00

#316 Husky Tow Truck, 1978-80, C13 ....$15.00

#317 Husky Construction Crew, 1978-80, C13 ....$20.00

#318 Adventure People Daredevil Sports Van, 1978-82, C13 ....$25.00

#319 Husky Hook & Ladder Truck, 1979-85, C13 ....$20.00

#320 Husky Race Car Rig, 1979-82, C13.........................$20.00

#322 Adventure People Dune Buster, 1979-82, C13 ....$10.00

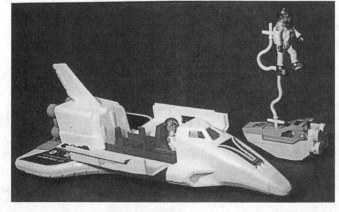

#325 Adventure People Alpha Probe, 1980 – 1984, $15.00. (Photo courtesy Brad Cassity)

#325 Buzzy Bee, 1950-56, 1st version, yel & blk litho, wooden wheels & antenna tips, C13 ....$25.00

#326 Adventure People Alpha Star, 1983-84, C13 ....$20.00

#327 Husky Load Master Dump, 1984, C13 ....$20.00

#328 Husky Highway Dump Truck, 1980-84, C13 ....$20.00

#329 Husky Dozer Loader, 1980-84, C13 ....$15.00

#331 Husky Farm Set, 1981-83, C13 ....$20.00

#332, Husky Police Patrol, 1981-84 ....$15.00

#333 Butch the Pup, 1951-53 & Easter 1954, C13 ....$55.00

#334 Adventure People Sea Shark, 1981-84, C13............$20.00

#336 Husky Fire Pumper, 1983-84, C13 ....$15.00

#337 Husky Rescue Rig, 1982-83, C13 ....$20.00

#338 Husky Power Tow Truck, 1982-84, C13 ....$20.00

#339 Husky Power & Light Service Rig, 1983-84, C13....$30.00

#344 Copter Rig, 1981-84, C13..$10.00

#345 Boat Rig, 1981-84, C13 ....$10.00

#345 Penelope the Performing Penguin, 1935, w/up, C13 ....$800.00

#347 Little People Indy Racer, 1983-90, C13 ....$5.00

#350 Adventure People Rescue Team, 1976-79, C13.......$15.00

#350 Go 'N Back Mule, 1931-33, w/up, C13..................$800.00

#351 Adventure People Mountain Climbers, 1976 – 1979, $20.00. (Photo courtsey Brad Cassity)

#352 Adventure People Construction Workers, 1976-79, C13 ....$15.00

#353 Adventure People Scuba Divers, 1976-81, C13.......$15.00

#354 Adventure People Daredevil Skydiver, 1977-81, C13 ....$10.00

#355 Adventure People White Water Kayak, 1977-80, C13 .....$10.00

#355 Go 'N Back Bruno, 1931, C13 ....$800.00

#356 Adventure People Cycle Racing Team, 1977-81, C13.....$10.00

#358 Adventure People Deep Sea Diver, 1980-84, C13 ....$10.00

#358 Donald Duck Back-Up, 1936, w/up, C13...............$800.00

#360 Adventure People Alpha Recon, 1982-84, C13 ......$10.00

#360 Go 'N Back Jumbo, 1931-34, w/up, C13 ....$900.00

#365 Puppy Back-up, 1932-36, w/up, C13 ....$800.00

#367 Adventure People Turbo Hawk, 1982-83, C13........$10.00

#368 Adventure People Alpha Interceptor, 1982-83, C13.....$10.00

#369 Adventure People Ground Shaker, 1982-83, C13 ....$10.00

#375 Adventure People Sky Surfer, 1978, C13 ....$25.00

#375 Bruno Back-Up, 1932, C13 ....$800.00

#377 Adventure People Astro Knight, 1979-80, C13.......$15.00

#400 Donald Duck Drum Major, 1946-48, C13............$250.00

#400 Donald Duck Drum Major Cart, 1946 only, C13...$250.00

#400 Tailspin Tabby, 1931-38, rnd guitar, C13 ....$75.00

#401 Push Bunny Cart, 1942, C13.................................$200.00

#402 Duck Cart, 1943, C13..$250.00

#404 Bunny Egg Cart, 1949, C13 ....$50.00

#405 Lofty Lizzy Pop-Up Kritter, 1931-33, C13..........$200.00

#406 Bunny Cart, 1950-53, C13 ....$50.00

#407 Chick Cart, 1950-53, C13 ....$50.00

#407 Dizzy Dino Pop-Up Kritter, 1931-32, C13 ....$200.00

#410 Stoopy Stork Pop-Up Kritter, 1931-32, C13.........$225.00

#415 Lop-Ear Looie Pop-Up Kritter, 1934, C13 ....$200.00

#415 Super Jet, 1952 & Easter 1953, C13......................$200.00

#420 Sunny Fish, 1955, C13 ....$150.00

#422 Jumbo Jitterbug Pop-Up Kritter, 1940, C13..........$200.00

#423 Jumping Jack Scarecrow, 1979, C13 ....$1.00

#425 Donald Duck Pop-Up, 1938 & Easter 1939, C13 ....$500.00

#433 Dizzy Donkey Pop-Up Kritter, 1939, C13 ....$125.00

#434 Ferdinand the Bull, 1939, C13 ....$600.00

#435 Happy Apple, 1979-84, short stem, C13 ....$1.00

#440 Goofy Gertie Pop-Up Kritter, 1935, C13...............$225.00

#440 Pluto Pop-Up, 1936, mk WDP, C13......................$75.00

#444 Fuzzy Fido, 1941-42, C13.....................................$225.00

#444 Puffy Engine, 1951-54, C13 ....$50.00

#444 Queen Buzzy Bee, 1959, red litho, C13 ....$30.00

#445 Hot Dog Wagon, 1940-41, C13............................$200.00

#445 Nosey Pup, 1956-58 & Easter 1959, C13 ....$50.00

#447 Woofy Wagger, 1947-48, C13.................................$75.00

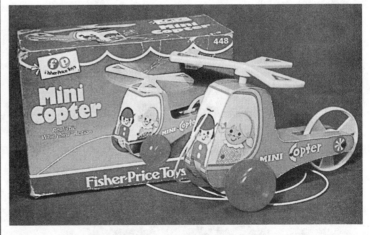

#448 Mini Copter, 1971 – 1984, blue lithograph, $5.00. (Photo courtesy Brad Cassity)

#450 Donald Duck Choo-Choo, 1941, 8½", C13...........$400.00

#450 Donald Duck Choo-Choo, 1942-45 & Easter 1949, C13.....$150.00

#450 Kiltie Dog, 1936, C13..$350.00

#450 Music Box Bear, 1981-83, Schubert's Cradle Song, C13 .....$1.00

#454 Donald Duck Drummer, 1949-50, C13 ....$250.00

#455 Tailspin Tabby Pop-Up Kritter, 1939-42, C13 ....$50.00

#456 Bunny & Container, 1939-40, C13.....................$225.00

#460 Dapper Donald Duck, 1936-37, no number on toy, C13..$600.00

#460 Movie Viewer, 1973-85, crank hdl, C13.............$1.00

#460 Suzie Seal, 1961-63 & Easter 1964, C13..............$20.00

#461 Duck Cart, 1938-39, C13.................................$225.00

#462 Busy Bunny, 1937, C13...................................$200.00

#465 Teddy Choo-Choo, 1937, C13.........................$350.00

#466 Busy Bunny Cart, 1941-44, C13........................$75.00

#469 Donald Cart, 1940, C13..................................$400.00

#469 Rooster Cart, 1938-40, C13.............................$350.00

#470 Tricky Tommy, 1936, C13...............................$350.00

#472 Jingle Giraffe, 1956, C13................................$200.00

#472 Peter Bunny Cart, 1939-40, C13......................$225.00

#473 Merry Mutt, 1949-54 & Easter 1955, C13............$50.00

#474 Bunny Racer, 1942, C13.................................$225.00

#476 Cookie Pig, 1966-70, C13.................................$40.00

#476 Mickey Mouse Drummer, 1941-45 & Easter 1946, C13..$300.00

#476 Rooster Pop-Up Kritter, 1936, C13...................$300.00

#477 Dr Doodle, 1940-41, C13................................$225.00

#478 Pudgy Pig, 1962-64 & Easter 1965, C13...............$40.00

#479 Donald Duck & Nephews, 1941-42, C13.............$400.00

#479 Peter Pig, 1959-61 & Easter 1962, C13................$40.00

#480 Leo the Drummer, 1952 & Easter 1953, C13........$225.00

#480 Teddy Station Wagon, 1942, C13......................$200.00

#485 Mickey Mouse Choo-Choo, 1949-54, new litho version of #432, C13.......................................$100.00

#488 Popeye Spinach Eater, 1939-40, C13.................$600.00

#495 Sleepy Sue Turtle, 1962-63 & Easter 1964, C13......$40.00

#499 Kitty Bell, 1950-51, C13.................................$100.00

#500 Donald Duck Cart, 1937, no number on toy, wheels not painted, C13..................................$700.00

#500 Donald Duck Cart, 1951-53, no baton, gr litho background, C13.......................................$350.00

#500 Donald Duck Cart, 1953, w/baton, yel litho background, C13..$350.00

#500 Pick-Up & Peek Puzzle, 1972-86, C13................$10.00

#500 Pushy Pig, 1932-35, C13.................................$500.00

#502 Action Bunny Cart, 1949, C13.........................$200.00

#503 Pick-Up & Peek Wood Puzzle, Occupations, 1972-76, C13...$10.00

#505 Bunny Drummer, 1946, bell on front, C13...........$225.00

#507 Pushy Doodle, 1933, C13................................$800.00

#508 Bunny Bell Drummer, 1949-53, C13....................$75.00

#510 Pick-Up & Peek Wood Puzzle, Nursery Rhymes, 1972-81, C13...$10.00

#510 Strutter Donald Duck, 1941, C13......................$250.00

#512 Bunny Drummer, 1942, C13.............................$225.00

#515 Pushy Pat, 1933-35, C13.................................$550.00

#517 Choo-Choo Local, 1936, C13...........................$550.00

#517 Pick-Up & Piece Wood Puzzle, Animal Friends, 1977-84, C13...$10.00

#520 Bunny Bell Cart, 1941, C13.............................$225.00

#520 Pick-Up & Peek Puzzle, Three Little Pigs, 1979-84, C13...$15.00

#525 Cotton Tail Cart, 1940, C13.............................$350.00

#525 Pushy Elephant, 1934-35, C13..........................$550.00

#530 Mickey Mouse Band, 1935-36, C13....................$800.00

#533 Thumper Bunny, 1942, C13.............................$500.00

#540 Granny Duck, 1939-40, C13.............................$225.00

#544 Donald Duck Cart, 1942-44, C13......................$300.00

#549 Toy Lunch Kit, 1962-79, red w/barn litho, w/thermos, C13...$25.00

#550 Toy Lunch Kit, 1957, red, wht & gr plastic barn shape, no litho, C13...$40.00

#552 Basic Hardboard Puzzle, Nature, 1974-75, C13........$15.00

#563 Basic Hardboard Puzzle, Weather, 1975, C13..........$10.00

#568 Basic Hardboard Puzzle, bear on log, C13............$10.00

#569 Basic Hardboard Puzzle, Airport, 1975, C13..........$10.00

#600 Tailspin Tabby Pop-Up, 1947, C13....................$250.00

#604 Bunny Bell Cart, 1954-55, C13.........................$100.00

#605 Donald Duck Cart, 1954-56, C13......................$200.00

#605 Woodsey Major Goodgrub Mole & Book, 1981-82, 32 pgs, C13...$15.00

#606 Woodsey Bramble Beaver & Book, 1981-82, 32 pgs, C13...$15.00

#607 Woodsey Very Blue Bird & Book, 1981-82, 32 pgs, C13...$15.00

#615 Tow Truck, 1960-61 & Easter 1962, C13..............$65.00

#616 Chuggy Pop-Up, 1955-56, C13..........................$75.00

#616 Patch Pony, 1963-64 & Easter 1965, C13.............$40.00

#617 Prancy Pony, 1965-70, C13.............................$25.00

#621 Suzie Seal, 1965-66, ball on nose, C13................$30.00

#625 Playful Puppy, 1961-62 & Easter 1963, w/shoe, C13....$45.00

#628 Tug-A-Bug, 1975-77, C13..................................$1.00

#491 Boom-Boom Popeye, $425.00. (Photo courtesy Brad Cassity)

#494 Pinocchio, 1939-40, C13.................................$600.00

#495 Running Bunny Cart, 1941, C13........................$200.00

#623 Suzie Seal, 1964 – 1965, umbrella on nose, $30.00. (Photo courtesy Brad Cassity)

#629 Fisher-Price Tractor, 1962-68, C13............................$30.00
#630 Fire Truck, 1959-62, C13....................................$45.00
#634 Drummer Boy, 1967-69, C13...................................$60.00
#634 Tiny Teddy, 1955-57, C13....................................$50.00
#637 Milk Carrier, 1966-85, C13 ....$15.00
#640 Wiggily Woofer, 1957-58 & Easter 1958, C13 ....$75.00
#641 Toot Toot Engine, 1962-63 & Easter 1964, bl litho, C13............................$60.00
#642 Bob-Along Bear, 1979-84, C13...................................$5.00
#642 Dinky Engine, 1959, blk litho, C13............................$60.00
#642 Smokie Engine, 1960-61 & Easter 1962, blk litho, C13 ....$60.00
#649 Stake Truck, 1960-61 & Easter 1962, C13...............$50.00
#653 Allie Gator, 1960-61 & Easter 1962, C13...............$75.00
#654 Tawny Tiger, 1962 & Easter 1963, C13 ....$75.00
#656 Bossy Bell, 1960 & Easter 1961, w/bonnet, C13......$50.00
#656 Bossy Bell, 1961-63, no bonnet, new litho design, C13 ....$40.00
#657 Crazy Clown Fire Brigade, 1983-84, C13 ....$45.00
#658 Lady Bug, 1961-62 & Easter 1963, C13 ....$50.00
#659 Puzzle Puppy, 1976-81, C13 ....$1.00
#662 Merry Mousewife, 1962-64 & Easter 1965, C13 ......$45.00
#663 Play Family, 1966-70, tan dog, MIP, C13 ....$170.00
#666 Creative Blocks, 1978-90, C13 ....$5.00
#674 Sports Car, 1958-60, C13 ....$75.00
#677 Picnic Basket, 1975-79, C13......................................$20.00
#678 Kriss Kricket, 1955-57, C13......................................$50.00
#679 Little People Garage Squad, 1984-90, MIP, C13......$15.00
#684 Little Lamb, 1964-65, C13 ....$45.00
#685 Car & Boat, 1968-69, wood & plastic, 5 pcs, C13 ....$65.00
#686 Car & Camper, 1968-70, C13 ....$65.00
#686 Perky Pot, 1958-59 & Easter 1960, C13..................$50.00
#694 Suzie Seal, 1979-80, C13 ....$10.00

#695 Lady Bug, 1982-84, C13...$1.00
#695 Pinky Pig, 1956-57, wooden eyes, C13.....................$75.00
#695 Pinky Pig, 1958, litho eyes, C13 ....$75.00
#698 Talky Parrot, 1963 & Easter 1964, C13....................$50.00
#700 Cowboy Chime, 1951-53, C13..................................$250.00
#700 Popeye, 1935, C13..$700.00
#700 Woofy Wowser, 1940 & Easter 1941, C13 ....$350.00
#703 Bunny Engine, 1954-56, C13.....................................$75.00
#703 Popeye the Sailor, 1936, C13....................................$700.00
#705 Mini Snowmobile, 1971-73, C13 ....$40.00
#705 Popeye Cowboy, 1937, C13 ....$700.00
#710 Scotty Dog, 1933, C13 ....$550.00
#711 Cry Baby Bear, 1967-69, C13 ....$15.00
#711 Huckleberry Hound, 1961, Sears only, C13 ....$300.00
#711 Raggedy Ann & Andy, 1941, C13 ....$850.00
#711 Teddy Trucker, 1949-51, C13 ....$225.00
#712 Fred Flintstone Xylophone, 1962, Sears only, C13.....$250.00
#712 Johnny Jumbo, 1933-35, C13 ....$550.00
#712 Teddy Tooter, 1957-58 & Easter 1959, C13 ....$200.00
#714 Mickey Mouse Xylophone, 1963, Sears only, C13 ....$275.00
#715 Ducky Flip Flap, 1964-65, C13.................................$50.00
#717 Ducky Flip Flap, 1937-39, C13 ....$400.00
#718 Tow Truck & Car, 1969-70, wood & plastic, C13....$45.00
#719 Busy Bunny Cart, 1936-37, C13................................$350.00
#719 Cuddly Cub, 1973-77, C13 ....$1.00
#720 Pinnochio Express, 1939-40, C13 ....$500.00
#721 Peter Bunny Engine, 1949-51, C13..........................$150.00
#722 Racing Bunny Cart, 1937, C13 ....$350.00
#722 Running Bunny, 1938-40, C13..................................$225.00
#723 Bouncing Bunny Cart, 1936, C13 ....$350.00
#724 Ding-Dong Ducky, 1949-50, C13.............................$200.00

#724 Jolly Jalopy, 1965, $5.00. (Photo courtesy Brad Cassity)

#725 Musical Mutt, 1935-36, C13 ....$350.00
#725 Play Family Bath/Utility Room Set, 1972, C13 ....$10.00

#726 Play Family Patio Set, 1970-73, C13 ....$10.00
#727 Bouncing Bunny Wheelbarrow, 1939, C13 ....$350.00
#728 Buddy Bullfrog, 1959-60, yel body w/red coat, C13 .....$50.00
#728 Pound & Saw Bench, 1966-67, C13 ....$30.00
#730 Racing Rowboat, 1952-53, C13 ....$150.00
#732 Happy Hauler, 1968-70, C13 ....$20.00
#732 Happy Whistlers, 1977-79, C13 ....$5.00
#733 Mickey Mouse Safety Patrol, 1956-57, C13 ....$250.00

**#734, Teddy Zilo, 1964 – 1966, $40.00.
(Photo courtesy Brad Cassity)**

#734 Teddy Zilo, 1965-66, w/coat, C13 ....$55.00
#735 Juggling Jumbo, 1958-59, C13 ....$150.00
#736 Humpty Dumpty, 1972-79, plastic, C13 ....$1.00
#737 Galloping Horse & Wagon, 1948-49, C13 ....$200.00
#737 Ziggy Zilo, 1958-59, C13 ....$50.00
#738 Dumbo Circus Racer, 1941 & Easter 1942, rubber arms, C13 ....$700.00
#738 Shaggy Zilo, 1960-61 & Easter 1962, C13 ....$50.00
#739 Poodle Zilo, 1962-63 & Easter 1964, C13 ....$50.00
#740 Pushcart Pete, 1936-67, C13 ....$600.00
#741 Teddy Zilo, 1967, C13 ....$35.00
#741 Trotting Donald Duck, 1937, C13 ....$800.00
#742 Dashing Dobbin, 1938-40, C13 ....$350.00
#744 Doughboy Donald, 1942, C13 ....$600.00
#745 Elsie's Dairy Truck, 1948-49, w/2 bottles, C13 ....$600.00
#746 Pocket Radio, 1977-78, It's a Small World, wood & plastic, C13 ....$10.00
#747 Chatter Telephone, 1962-67, wooden wheels, C13 .....$25.00
#747 Talk-Back Telephone, 1961 & Easter 1962, C13 .....$75.00
#749 Egg Truck, 1947, C13 ....$225.00
#750 Hot Dog Wagon, 1938, C13 ....$300.00
#750 Space Blazer, 1953-54, C13 ....$175.00
#755 Jumbo Rolo, 1951-52, C13 ....$200.00
#756 Pocket Radio, 1973, 12 Days of Christmas, wood & plastic, C13 ....$25.00

#757 Howdy Bunny, 1939-40, C13 ....$350.00
#757 Humpty Dumpty, 1957 & Easter 1958, C13 ....$150.00
#757 Snappy-Quacky, 1950, C13 ....$200.00
#758 Pocket Radio, 1970-72, Mulberry Bush, wood & plastic, C13 ....$10.00
#758 Pony Chime, 1948-50, C13 ....$175.00
#758 Push-Along Clown, 1980-81, C13 ....$5.00
#759 Pocket Radio, 1969-73, Do-Re-Me, wood & plastic, C13 ....$10.00
#760 Peek-A-Boo Block, 1970-79, C13 ....$1.00
#760 Racing Ponies, 1936, C13 ....$300.00
#761 Play Family Nursery Set, 1973, C13 ....$10.00
#762 Pocket Radio, 1972-77, Raindrops, wood & plastic, C13 ....$10.00
#763 Music Box, 1962, Farmer in the Dell, yel litho, C13 ....$40.00
#763 Pocket Radio, 1978, I Whistle a Happy Tune, wood & plastic, C13 ....$10.00
#764 Music Box, 1960-61 & Easter 1962, Farmer in the Dell, red litho, C13 ....$40.00
#764 Pocket Radio, 1975-76, My Name Is Michael, C13 ....$10.00
#765 Dandy Dobbin, 1941-44, C13 ....$175.00
#765 Talking Donald Duck, 1955-58, C13 ....$125.00
#766 Pocket Radio, 1968-70, Where Has My Little Dog Gone?, wood & plastic, C13 ....$10.00

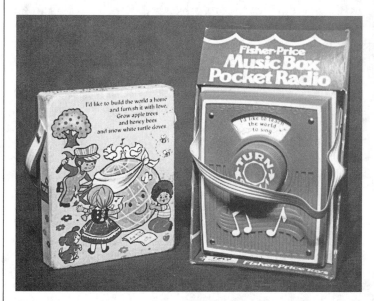

#766 Pocket Radio, 1977 – 1978, 'I'd Like To Teach the World To Sing,' $10.00. (Photo courtesy Brad Cassity)

#767 Pocket Radio, 1977, Twinkle Twinkle Little Star, C13 ....$25.00
#767 Tiny Ding-Dong, 1940, 6 wheels, C13 ....$400.00
#768 Pocket Radio, 1971-76, Happy Birthday, wood & plastic, C13 ....$10.00
#770 Doc & Dopey Dwarfs, 1938, C13 ....$1,000.00
#772 Pocket Radio, 1974-76, Jack & Jill, C13 ....$10.00
#773 Tip-Toe Turtle, 1962-77, vinyl tail, C13 ....$5.00
#775 Gabby Goofies, 1956-59 & Easter 1960, C13 ....$25.00
#775 Pocket Radio, 1967-68, Sing a Song of Six Pence, wood & plastic, C13 ....$10.00

#775 Pocket Radio, 1973-75, Pop Goes the Weasel, wood & plastic, C13 ....$10.00

#775 Teddy Drummer, 1936, C13 ....$675.00

#777 Pushy Bruno, 1933, C13.......................................$725.00

#777 Squeaky the Clown, 1958-59, C13 ....$175.00

#778 Ice Cream Wagon, 1940 & Easter 1941, C13 ....$300.00

#778 Pocket Radio, 1967-68, Frere Jacques, wood & plastic, C13..$10.00

#779 Pocket Radio, 1976, Yankee Doodle, wood & plastic, C13 ....$15.00

#780 Jumbo Xylophone, 1937-38, C13.....................$250.00

#780 Snoopy Sniffer, 1955-57 & Easter 1958, C13 ....$50.00

#784 Mother Goose Music Chart, 1955-56 & Easter 1957, C13 ....$50.00

#785 Blackie Drummer, 1939, C13 ....$625.00

#785 Corn Popper, 1957-58, red base, C13 ....$50.00

#786 Perky Penguin, 1973-75, C13..............................$10.00

#788 Rock-A-Bye Bunny Cart, 1940-41, C13 ....$300.00

#789 Lift & Load Road Builders, 1978 – 1982, $15.00. (Photo courtesy Brad Cassity)

#791 Tote-A-Tune Music Box Radio, 1979, Let's Go Fly A Kite, plastic, C13 ....$5.00

#792 Tote-A-Tune Music Box Radio, 1980-81, Teddy Bears' Picnic, plastic, C13 ....$5.00

#793 Jolly Jumper, 1963-64 & Easter 1965, C13...............$40.00

#793 Tote-A-Tune Music Box, 1981, When You Wish Upon a Star, plastic, C13 ....$5.00

#794 Big Bill Pelican, 1961-63, w/cb fish, C13 ....$75.00

#794 Tote-A-Tune Music Box, 1981-82, Over the Rainbow, plastic, C13 ....$5.00

#795 Micky Mouse Drummer, 1937, C13 ....$700.00

#795 Musical Duck, 1952-54 & Easter 1955, C13 ....$75.00

#795 Tote-A-Tune Music Box, 1984-91, Toyland, plastic, C13...$5.00

#798 Chatter Monk, 1957-58 & Easter 1959, C13 ....$50.00

#798 Mickey Mouse Xylophone, 1939, w/hat, C13 ....$350.00

#798 Mickey Mouse Xylophone, 1942, no hat, C13.......$350.00

#799 Duckie Transport, 1937, C13 ....$400.00

#799 Quacky Family, 1940-42, C13 ....$75.00

#800 Hot Diggety, 1934, w/up, C13 ....$800.00

#808 Pop'n Ring, 1956-58 & Easter 1959, C13 ....$75.00

#810 Hot Mammy, 1934, w/up, C13 ....$800.00

#810 Timber Toter, 1957 & Easter 1958, C13....................$75.00

#841, Kermit the Frog Stick Puppet $5.00

#841-849 are 1979-83..$.09

#842, Fozzie Bear Stick Puppet $5.00

#843, Rowlf Stick Puppet.......................................$5.00

#844, Miss Piggy Stick Puppet $5.00

#845 Farm Truck, 1954-55, w/booklet, C13.................$250.00

#846, The Muppet Show Players, 1979-83, MIB $30.00

#848, Scooter Stick Puppet......................................$5.00

#849, Gonzo Stick Puppet $5.00

#850, Kermit the Frog Puppet, 1977-83 ....$10.00

#851, Fozzie Bear, 1977-78, plush $10.00

#852, Rowlf, 1977-81, plush puppet $10.00

#853, Scooter, 1978-81, plush hand puppet $10.00

#854, Animal, 1978-82, plush hand puppet $20.00

#855, Miss Piggy Hand Puppet, 1979-80, mouth moves $10.00

#857, Kermit the Frog Dress-Up Muppet Doll, 1981-84 .....$10.00

#858, The Great Gonzo Dress-Up Muppet Doll, 1982-83 ....$15.00

#860, Kermit the Frog Hand Puppet, 1979-83, plush $10.00

#861, Fozzie Bear Hand Puppet, 1979-82, plush $10.00

#870 Pull-A-Tune Xylophone, 1957-69, w/song book, C13 ....$25.00

#875, Looky Push Car, 1962-65 & Easter 1966, C13........$45.00

#890, Miss Piggy Dress-Up Muppet Doll, 1981-84 ....$10.00

#900 Struttin' Donald Duck, 1939 & Easter 1940, C13 ....$650.00

#900 This Little Pig, 1956-58 & Easter 1959, C13...........$55.00

#902 Junior Circus, 1963-70, C13 ....$225.00

#904 Beginners Circus, 1965-68, C13 ....$60.00

#905 This Little Pig, 1959-62, C13 ....$30.00

#909 Play Family Rooms, 1972, Sears only, C13 ....$200.00

#910 Change-A-Tune Piano, 1969-72, Pop Goes the Weasel, This Old Man & The Muffin Man, C13....................$25.00

#931 Play Family Children's Hospital, 1976 – 1978, $115.00. (Photo courtesy Brad Cassity)

#915 Play Family Farm, 1968-79, 1st version w/masonite base, C13..$25.00

#919 Music Box Movie Camera, 1968-70, plays This Old Man, w/5 picture disks, C13................................$35.00

#923 Play Family School, 1971-78, 1st version, C13.......$20.00

#926 Concrete Mixer, 1959-60 & Easter 1961, C13......$175.00

#928 Play Family Fire Station, 1980-82, C13.................$50.00

#929 Play Family Nursery School, 1978-79, C13.............$30.00

#932 Amusement Park, 1963-65, C13..........................$300.00

#932 Ferry Boat, 1979-80, C13......................................$25.00

#934 Play Family Western Town, 1982-84, C13..............$60.00

#935 Tool Box Work Bench, 1969-71, C13....................$20.00

#937 Play Family Sesame Street Clubhouse, 1977-79, C13.....$70.00

#938 Play Family Sesame Street House, 1975-76, C13.....$75.00

#942 Play Family Lift & Load Depot, 1977-79, C13........$40.00

#943 Lift & Load Railroad, 1978-79, C13.......................$40.00

#944 Lift & Load Lumber Yard, 1979-81, C13................$40.00

#945 Offshore Cargo Base, 1979-80, C13........................$50.00

#960 Woodsey's Log House, 1979-81, complete, C13.......$20.00

#961 Woodsey's Store, 1980-81, complete, C13...............$25.00

#962 Woodsey's Airport, 1980-81, complete, C13............$10.00

#969 Musical Ferris Wheel, 1966-72, 1st version w/4 wooden straight-body figures, C13................................$50.00

#972 Fisher-Price Cash Register, 1960-72, C13.................$20.00

#979 Dump Truckers Playset, 1965-67, C13....................$75.00

#982 Hot Rod Roadster, 1983-84, riding toy w/4-pc take-apart engine, C13..$40.00

#983 Safety School Bus, 1959, w/6 figures, Fisher-Price Club logo, C13..$225.00

#992 Play Family Car & Camper, 1980-84, C13..............$35.00

#993 Play Family Castle, 1974-77, 1st version, C13.........$75.00

#994 Play Family Camper, 1973-76, C13........................$50.00

#996 Play Family Airport, 1972-76, 1st version w/bl airport & clear look-out tower, C13................................$45.00

#997 Musical Tick-Tock Clock, 1962 – 1963, $30.00. (Photo courtesy Brad Cassity)

#997 Play Family Village, 1973-77, C13..........................$50.00

#998 Music Box Teaching Clock, 1968-83, C13...............$10.00

#999 Huffy Puffy Train, 1958-62, C13...........................$50.00

#1005 Push Cone, 1937-38, C13.....................................$400.00

#1006 Floor Train, 1934-38, C13....................................$600.00

#2155 McDonald's Happy Meal, 1989-90, C13...............$15.00

#2352 Little People Construction Set, 1985, C13............$15.00

#2360 Little People Jetliner, 1986-88, C13.....................$10.00

#2361 Little People Fire Truck, 1989-90, C13................$10.00

#985 Play Family Houseboat, 1972 – 1976, complete, $35.00. (Photo courtesy Brad Cassity)

#987 Creative Coaster, 1964-82, C13..............................$40.00

#990 Play Family A-Frame, 1974-76, C13.......................$45.00

#991 Music Box Lacing Shoe, 1964-67, C13...................$50.00

#991 Play Family Circus Train, 1973-78, w/gondola car, C13..$15.00

#991 Play Family Circus Train, 1979-86, no gondola car, C13..$10.00

#2453 Little People Beauty Salon, 1990, $15.00. (Photo courtesy Brad Cassity)

#2454 Little People Drive-In Movie................................$15.00

#2455 Little People Gas Station, 1990............................$15.00

#2500 Little People Main Street, 1986-90, C13..............$30.00

#2501 Little People Farm, 1986-89, C13........................$15.00

#2504 Little People Garage, 1986, rare, C13 ....$55.00
#2524 Little People Cruise Boat, 1989-90, C13................$15.00
#2525 Little People Playground, 1986-90, C13 ....$10.00
#2526 Little People Pool, 1986-88, C13 ....$15.00
#2550 Little People School, 1988-89, C13 ....$20.00
#2551 Little People Neighborhood, 1988-90, C13 ....$40.00
#2552 McDonald's Restaurant, 1990, 1st version, C13 ....$65.00
#2552 McDonald's Restaurant, 1991-92, 2nd version, same pcs
    as 1st version but lg-sz figures, C13 ....$40.00
#2580 Little People Little Mart, 1987-89, C13................$15.00
#2581 Little People Express Train, 1987-90, C13 ....$10.00

**#2582 Little People Floating Marina, 1988 – 1990, $15.00.
(Photo courtesy Brad Cassity)**

#2712 Pick-Up & Peek Wood Puzzle, Haunted House, 1985-88,
    C13...$15.00
#2720 Pick-Up & Peek Wood Puzzle, Little Bo Peep, 1985-88,
    C13...$15.00
#4500 Husky Helpers Workmen, 1985-86, 6 different, MOC,
    C13, ea $15.00
#4520 Highway Dump Truck, 1985-86, C13....................$15.00
#4521 Dozer Loader, 1985-86, C13 ....$15.00

#4523 Gravel Hauler, 1985-86, C13 ....$15.00
#4550 Chevy S-10 4x4, 1985, C13................................$20.00
#4551 Pontiac Firebird, 1985, C13................................$20.00
#4552 Jeep CJ-7 Renegade, 1985, C13...........................$20.00
#4580 Power Tow, 1985-86, C13 ....$20.00
#6145 Jingle Elephant, 1993, ToyFest limited edition of 5,000,
    C13 ....$100.00
#6464 Gran'Pa Frog, 1994 ToyFest limited edition of 5,000,
    C13...$50.00
#6550 Buzzy Bee, 1987, ToyFest limited edition of 5,000,
    C13 ....$120.00
#6558 Snoopy Sniffer, 1988, ToyFest limited edition of 3,000,
    C13 ....$550.00
#6575 Toot-Toot, 1989, ToyFest limited edition of 4,800,
    C13...$65.00
#6588 Snoopy Sniffer, 1990, Fisher-Price Commemorative lim-
    ited edition of 3,500, Ponderosa pine, C13 ....$150.00
#6590 Prancing Horses, 1990, ToyFest limited edition of 5,000,
    C13...$75.00
#6592 Teddy Bear Parade, 1991, ToyFest limited edition of
    5,000, C13 ....$50.00
#6593 Squeaky the Clown, 1995, ToyFest limited edition of
    5,000, C13 ....$125.00
#6599 Molly Bell Cow, 1992, ToyFest limited edition of 5,000,
    C13 ....$150.00
#7001 Zummi Gummi Bear, 1986, plush $10.00
#7002 Zummi Gummi Bear, 1986, plush $10.00
#7003 Tummi Gummi Bear, 1986, plush $10.00
#7004 Sunni Gummi Bear, 1986, plush...........................$10.00
#7005 Guffie Gummie Bear, 1986, plush $10.00

**#4581 Power Dump Truck, 1985 – 1986,
$20.00. (Photo courtesy Brad Cassity)**

**#7006 Grammi Gummi Bear, 1986, $10.00.
(Photo courtesy Brad Cassity)**

#7016-#7021 Gummi Bear Bouncers, 1986, plush, ea.........**$5.00**
#7031-7036 Poseable Gummi Bears, 1986, jtd vinyl, ea **$5.00**
#76880 Raggedy Ann & Andy, 1997, ToyFest limited edition of 5,000, C13 ....**$150.00**

Games

Early games (those from 1850 to 1910) are very often appreciated more for their wonderful lithographed boxes than their 'playability,' and you'll find collectors displaying them as they would any fine artwork. Many boxes and boards were designed by commercial artists of the day.

Though they were in a decline a few years ago, baby-boomer game prices have leveled off. Some science fiction and rare TV games are still in high demand. Games produced in the Art Deco era between the World Wars have gained in popularity — especially those with great design. Victorian games have become harder to find; their prices have also grown steadily. Condition and rarity are the factors that most influence game prices.

When you buy a game, check to see that all pieces are there. The games listed below are complete unless noted otherwise. For further information we recommend *Board Games of the '50s, '60s and '70s* (L-W Book Sales). Note: In the listings that follow, assume that all are board games (unless specifically indicated card game, target game, bagatelle, etc.) and that each is complete as issued, unless missing components are mentioned.

See also Advertising; Black Americana; Barbie; California Raisins; Disney; Halloween; Political; Robots and Space Toys.

A-Team, Parker Brothers, 1984, EXIB, $25.00.

Abbott & Costello — Who's on First?, Selchow & Righter, 1978, NMIB...**$12.00**
Addams Family, Ideal, 1965, EXIB...................................**$50.00**
Addams Family (Cartoon Series), Milton Bradley, 1974, NMIB...**$35.00**
Addams Family Card Game, Milton Bradley, 1965, NMIB...**$25.00**
Advance to Boardwalk, Parker Bros, 1985, NMIB............**$15.00**
Air Defense Target Game, Wolverine, tin, 18" L, VG, A..**$275.00**

Alfred Hitchcock Presents Mystery Game Why?, Milton Bradley, 1958, EXIB...**$25.00**
Alien, Kenner, 1979, EXIB...**$25.00**
All in the Family, Milton Bradley, 1972, NMIB **$25.00**
Allen Sherman's Camp Granada, Milton Bradley, 1965, EXIB..**$45.00**
Ally Slooper, Milton Bradley, 1907, EXIB **$50.00**
Alvin & the Chipmunks Acorn Hunt, Hasbro, 1960, EXIB..**$35.00**
Amazing Chan & the Chan Clan, Whitman, 1973, NMIB..**$20.00**
Amazing Spider-Man, Milton Bradley, 1966, EXIB..........**$50.00**
American Heritage Battle-Cry Game, Milton Bradley, 1975, NMIB..**$45.00**
Angela Cartwright Buttons & Bows Game, Transogram, 1960, EXIB..**$75.00**
Annette's Secret Passage Game, Parker Bros, 1958, EXIB..**$20.00**
Annie Oakley Game, Milton Bradley, 1950s, lg sz, NMIB..**$45.00**
Annie Oakley Game, Milton Bradley, 1950s, sm sz, NMIB ..**$25.00**
Annie The Movie Game, Parker Bros, 1981, NMIB **$10.00**
Apple's Way, Milton Bradley, 1974, NMIB.......................**$35.00**
Aquanauts, Transogram, 1961, NMIB...............................**$75.00**
Archies, Whitman, 1969, NMIB..**$30.00**
Around the World in 80 Days, Transogram, NMIB..........**$25.00**
As the World Turns, Parker Bros, 1966, NMIB.................**$30.00**
Astro Launch, Ohio Art, 1960s, NMIB **$35.00**
Astro The Wizard From Mars Questions & Answers, Peerless Playthings, 1953, EXIB..**$35.00**
Atom Ant Saves the Day, Transogram, 1966, NMIB........**$50.00**
Auto Racing Game, Milton Bradley, VGIB, A................**$125.00**
B-17 Queen of the Skies, Avalon Hill, 1983, NMIB **$15.00**
Babe Ruth's Baseball Game, Milton Bradley, EXIB........**$500.00**
Babes in Toyland, Whitman, 1961, EXIB **$25.00**
Bamboozle, Milton Bradley, 1962, NMIB **$30.00**
Barbie Queen of the Prom, Mattel, 1960, NMIB............**$55.00**
Barbie's Keys to Fame, Mattel, 1963, EXIB **$35.00**
Barbie's Little Sister Skipper Game, Mattel, 1964, NMIB..**$45.00**
Baretta, Milton Bradley, 1976, NMIB **$30.00**
Bargain Hunter, Milton Bradley, 1981, NMIB.................**$20.00**
Barnabas Collins Dark Shadows Game, Milton Bradley, 1969, NMIB..**$50.00**
Barney Google & Spark Plug Game, Milton Bradley, 1923, EXIB..**$100.00**
Barney Miller, Parker Bros, 1977, NMIB.........................**$20.00**

Base Ball, Pan American Toy Company, 1920s, NMIB, $400.00.

Baseball Challenge, Tri-Valley Games, 1980, NMIB........$30.00

Baseball Game, Hustler, litho tin & wood w/spring-activated roller in top that gives outcome of play, 14x9", VG+, A.......$110.00

Baseball Pitching Game, Marx, 1940s, NMIB...............$225.00

Bash! Milton Bradley, 1965, NMIB....................$20.00

Bat Masterson, Lowell, 1958, NMIB...................$65.00

Batman, Milton Bradley, 1966, NMIB.................$50.00

Batman & Robin Game, Hasbro, 1965, EXIB.............$35.00

Batman & Robin Pinball Game, Marx, 1966, NM........$125.00

Batman Pinball Game, AHI, 1976, NMIB.................$100.00

Battle Cry, Milton Bradley, 1962, EXIB.............$30.00

Battle of the Planets, Milton Bradley, 1970s, NMIB........$30.00

Battlestar Galactica, Parker Bros, 1978, NMIB.............$20.00

Beany & Cecil Match It, Mattel, 1960s, EXIB.............$35.00

Beany & Cecil Ring Toss, Pressman, 1961, EXIB...........$50.00

Beat the Clock, Lowell, 1954, NMIB....................$35.00

Beat the Clock, Milton Bradley, 1960s, NMIB.............$15.00

Beatlemania, VGIB....................$40.00

Beatles Flip Your Wig Game, Milton Bradley, 1964, NMIB..$125.00

Beetle Bailey The Old Army Game, Milton Bradley, 1963, EXIB....................$35.00

Ben Casey, Transogram, 1961, MIB....................$20.00

Bermuda Triangle, 1976, EXIB.............$25.00

Betsy Ross Flag Game, 1960s, NMIB.............$30.00

Beverly Hillbillies, Standard Toykraft, 1963, NMIB........$50.00

Bewitched, T Cohn Inc, 1965, NMIB.............$85.00

Bewitched Card Game, Milton Bradley, 1965, EXIB........$30.00

Beyond the Stars, Game Partners, 1964, NMIB.............$50.00

Big Game, National, 1930s-40s, EXIB.............$20.00

Big Game (Pinball), Marx, 1950s, NM.............$60.00

Big Maze, Marx, 1955, MIB....................$50.00

Billionaire, Parker Bros, 1973, NMIB.............$12.00

Bionic Crisis, Parker Bros, 1975, NMIB.............$20.00

Bionic Woman, Parker Bros, 1976, NMIB.............$18.00

Black Ball Express, Schaper, 1957, NMIB.............$30.00

Black Beauty, Transogram, 1957, NMIB.............$25.00

Blast Off, Selchow & Righter, 1953, EXIB.............$75.00

Blondie, Parker Bros, 1970s, NMIB.............$12.00

Blow Your Cool, Whitman, 1969, NMIB.............$15.00

Bluff, Saalfield, 1964, EXIB.............$15.00

Bonanza Michigan Rummy Game, Parker Bros, 1964, EXIB....................$25.00

Bobbsey Twins, Milton Bradley, 1957, MIB, $25.00.

Boots & Saddles, Chad Valley, 1960, EXIB.............$40.00

Bop the Beetle, Ideal, 1963, EXIB.............$40.00

Boris Karloff's Monster Game, Gems, 1965, VGIB.............$75.00

Bozo Ed-U Cards, 1972, EXIB.............$15.00

Bozo the Clown in Circus Land, Transogram, 1960s, NMIB..$25.00

Brady Bunch, Whitman, 1973, MIB.............$100.00

Branded, Milton Bradley, 1966, EXIB.............$25.00

Buccaneers, Transogram, 1957, NMIB.............$45.00

Buck Rogers Adventures on the 25th Century Game, Transogram, 1965, NMIB.............$30.00

Buck Rogers Game, Milton Bradley, 1970, EXIB.............$15.00

Bug-A-Boo, Whitman, 1968, NMIB.............$25.00

Bugaloos, Milton Bradley, 1971, EXIB.............$30.00

Bullwinkle & Rocky Magic Dot Game, Transogram, 1962, NMIB....................$100.00

Bullwinkle Hide 'N Seek Game, Milton Bradley, 1961, NMIB.$50.00

Bullwinkle's Super Market Game, Whitman, 1970s, EXIB..$25.00

Burk's Law — Game of Who Killed?..., Transogram, 1963, EXIB....................$30.00

Buy & Sell, Whitman, 1953, EXIB.............$10.00

Cabbage Patch Kids, Parker Bros, 1984, EXIB.............$8.00

Calvin & the Colonel — Game of High Spirits, Milton Bradley, 1962, NMIB....................$20.00

Camp Granada, see Alan Sherman's Camp Granada

Can't Stop, Parker Bros, 1980, NMIB.............$15.00

Candid Camera, Lowell, 1963, NMIB.............$30.00

Candyland, Milton Bradley, 1955, NMIB.............$20.00

Captain & the Kids, Milton Bradley, 1947, NMIB.............$85.00

Captain America, Milton Bradley, 1977, NMIB.............$20.00

Captain Caveman Card Game, 1979, MIB.............$10.00

Captain Gallant of the Foreign Legion Adventure Game, Transogram, NMIB....................$40.00

Captain Kangaroo, Milton Bradley, 1956, NMIB.............$50.00

Captain Kangaroo TV Lotto, Ideal, 1961, EXIB.............$25.00

Captain Video, Milton Bradley, 1952, EXIB.............$50.00

Car 54 Where Are You?, Allison, 1963, NMIB.............$150.00

Careers, Park Bros, 1965, NMIB.............$20.00

Casey Jones, Saalfield, 1959, NMIB.............$50.00

Casper & His Pals Ed-U Cards, 1960s, NMIB.............$10.00

Casper the Friendly Ghost Game, Milton Bradley, 1959, NMIB....................$15.00

Cat & Mouse Game, Parker Bros, 1964, EXIB.............$10.00

Challenge the Chief, Ideal, 1973, NMIB.............$25.00

Charlette's Web Game, Hasbro, 1974, NMIB.............$30.00

Charlie's Angels (Farrah on Box), NMIB.............$25.00

Cheyenne, Milton Bradley, 1957, EXIB.............$30.00

Children's Hour, Parker Bros, 1946, EXIB.............$15.00

CHiPs, Ideal, 1981, MIB.............$15.00

CHiPs Game, Milton Bradley, 1977, NMIB.............$10.00

Chopper Strike, Milton Bradley, 1976, EXIB.............$10.00

Chutes & Ladders, Milton Bradley, 1956, NMIB.............$20.00

Cinderella, Parker Bros, 1964, EXIB.............$50.00

Clean Sweep, Schaper, 1960s, NMIB.............$25.00

Close Encounters of the Third Kind, Parker Bros, 1977, EXIB....................$10.00

Clue, Parker Bros, 1972, NMIB.............$10.00

Columbo, Milton Bradley, 1973, NMIB.............$12.00

Combat, Ideal, 1963, NMIB, $50.00. (Photo courtesy June Moon Collectibles)

Combat Card Game, Milton Bradley, EXIB......................$20.00
Comical Pete The New Ring Game, Spears/Germany, 1930s,
    EXIB..$65.00
Commercial Traveler, McLoughlin Bros, EXIB, A $330.00
Conflict, Parker Bros, 1960, EXIB...............................$50.00
Containment, Shamus Gamus, 1979, EXIB.....................$15.00
Count Down Space Game, Transogram, 1960, NMIB......$30.00
Countdown, Lowe, 1967, NMIB $45.00
Counter Point, Hallmark, 1976, NMIB $20.00
Crazy Clock, Ideal, 1964, NMIB $50.00
Creature From the Black Lagoon, Hasbro, 1963, EXIB ..$350.00
Crusader Rabbit TV Game, Tryne, 1960s, NMIB..........$125.00
Dallas, Marcura Industries, 1985, EXIB........................$25.00
Dangerous World of James Bond 007, Milton Bradley, 1965,
    NMIB...$60.00
Daniel Boone Ed-U Cards, 1965, NMIB.........................$40.00
Dark Crystal Game, Milton Bradley, 1982, NMIB............$25.00

Dark Shadows Game, Whitman, 1968, NMIB, $50.00.

Dark Tower, Milton Bradley, 1981, NMIB.....................$150.00
Dating Game, Hasbro, 1967, EXIB................................$15.00
Davy Crockett Adventures, Gardner, 1950s, EXIB..........$50.00
Davy Crockett Ed-U Cards, 1955, EXIB $30.00
Davy Crockett Radar Action, Ewing, 1955, EXIB............$50.00
Davy Crockett Rescue Race, Gabriel, 1950s, EXIB $25.00
Daytona 500 Race Game, Milton Bradley, 1989, NMIB ..$30.00

Dennis the Menace Baseball Game, MTP, 1960, NMIB ..$45.00
Deputy (The), Milton Bradley, Bell, 1960, NMIB............$50.00
Deputy Dawg, Milton Bradley, 1960, EXIB.....................$50.00
Derby Day, Parker Bros, 1959, NMIB...............................$50.00
Derby Steeple Chase, McLoughlin, EXIB, A $55.00
Detectives, Transogram, 1961, NMIB $35.00
Dick Tarcy Card Game, Whitman, 1934, EXIB................$75.00
Dick Tracy, The Master Detective, Selchow & Righter, 1961,
    MIB..$75.00
Dick Tracy 'Bagatelle' Pinball, Marx, 1967, EX $65.00
Dick Tracy Crime Stopper Game, Ideal, 1963, MIB.........$40.00

Dig, Parker Bros, 1930s, EXIB, $30.00.

Diner's Club Credit Card Game, Ideal, 1961, NMIB........$40.00
Disney's True Life Electric Quiz Game, 1952, VGIB $25.00
Disneyland Game, Transogram, 1954, EXIB $65.00
District Messenger Boy, McLoughlin, VGIB, A..............$575.00
Doc Holiday Wild West Game, Transogram, 1960, NMIB ..$35.00
Dogfight, Milton Bradley, 1962, EXIB...............................$85.00
Don't Have a Cow Dice Game (Simpsons), Milton Bradley,
    1990, NMIB $15.00
Don't Spill the Beans, 1967, EXIB $25.00
Donkey Kong Board Game, 1982, EXIB $30.00
Donnie & Marie Osmond Game Show, Mattel, 1977, NMIB....$30.00
Dr Kildare, Ideal, 1962, NMIB $40.00
Dragnet, Transogram, 1955, NMIB $50.00
Dream House, Milton Bradley, 1968, EXIB.....................$40.00
Dudley Do-Right's Find Snidley Game, Whitman, 1976,
    NMIB..$30.00
Dukes of Hazzard, Ideal, 1981, EXIB $20.00
Electric Sports Car Race, Tudor, 1959, NMIB $75.00
Electric Target Game, Marx, 1950s, unused, EXIB.........$300.00
Emergency, Milton Bradley, 1973, NMIB.......................$40.00
Ensign O'Toole USS Appleby Game, Hasbro, 1968, NMIB ..$30.00
Escape From New York, TSR, 1980, EXIB $20.00
Escort Game of Guys & Gals, Parker Bros, 1955, unused,
    MIB $30.00
Excuse Me! A Game of Manners, Parker Bros, EXIB $25.00
Eye Guess, 1966, EXIB..$25.00

Family Ties, Apple Street, 1986, EXIB............................$15.00

Fantastic Voyage, Milton Bradley, 1968, NMIB...............$30.00

Farmer Jones Pigs, McLoughlin Bros, VGIB..................$130.00

Felix the Cat, Milton Bradley, 1960, 1st version, EXIB....$35.00

Felix the Cat Target, Lido, 1960s, EXIB........................$25.00

Felix the Cat's Down on the Farm Game, Built-Rite, 1950s,
EXIB $25.00

Ferdinand's Chinese Checkers with the Bee!, Parker Bros.,
1939, EXIB, $150.00. (Photo courtesy Dunbar Auction
Gallery)

Flintstones, Milton Bradley, 1971, NMIB $20.00

Flintstones Brake Ball, Whitman, 1962, EXIB..................$85.00

Flintstones Stone Age Game, Transogram, 1961, NMIB..$55.00

Flipper Flips, Mattel, 1965, NMIB $70.00

Flying Nun Marble Maze Game, Milton Bradley, 1967,
NMIB $45.00

Fonz Hanging Out At Arnold's Card Game, Milton Bradley,
1976, MIB..$30.00

Football Game, Woolsey, folding cb & wood target w/7"
mechanical figure on steel base, EX, A $770.00

Formula 1 Car Racing Game, Parker Bros., 1968, NMIB,
$55.00.

Fox & the Hounds, Parker Bros, 1948, NM $25.00

Fugitive, Ideal, 1964, NMIB..$75.00

Fugitive Game, Ideal, 1966, VGIB..................................$80.00

Funny Finger, Ideal, 1968, NMIB....................................$15.00

G-Men Clue Games, Whitman #3930, 1930s, VGIB.......$75.00

Game of Baseball, McLoughlin Bros, c 1886, EXIB (paper litho
cover on wood box), A $2,300.00

Game of Coney Island, Selchow & Righter, 1956, EXIB..$55.00

Game of Famous Men, Parker Bros, VGIB........................$50.00

Game of Flags, McLoughlin Bros, VGIB..........................$75.00

Game of Golf, JH Singer, VGIB.....................................$550.00

Game of Innocence, Parker Bros, 1888, GIB.................$100.00

Game of Nosey, McLoughlin, VGIB, A..........................$175.00

Game of Red Riding-Hood, Parker Bros, 1895, VGIB ...$150.00

Game of Telegraph Boy, McLoughlin Bros, 1880s, EXIB (wood
box w/paper label), A $165.00

Game of Yuneek, McLoughlin Bros., VGIB, $100.00. (Photo
courtesy Randy Inman Auctions)

Games People Play, Alpsco, 1967, NMIB $25.00

Gee Whiz Horse Racing Game, Wolverine, tin, 15½", EXIB,
A...$100.00

Gee-Wiz Horse Race, Wolverine, EX.............................$100.00

Gene Autry Bandit Trail Game, Kenton, EXIB.............$200.00

Gene Autry Dude Ranch Game, Built-Rite #859, 1950s,
EXIB...$50.00

George of the Jungle, Parker Bros, 1968, NMIB...........$110.00

Get in That Tub, Hasbro, 1969, unused, NMIB...............$50.00

Get Smart, Ideal, 1966, NMIB $50.00

Get Smart Card Game, Ideal, 1966, EXIB $25.00

Gettysburg, Avalon Hill, 1960, EXIB...............................$20.00

Gidget, Standard Toykraft, 2965, MIB, from $75 to.......$100.00

Gilligan's Island, Game Gems/T Cohn, 1965, EXIB $375.00

Go Back, Milton Bradley, 1968, EXIB.............................$15.00

Godzilla, Mattel, 1978, EXIB..$60.00

Gomer Pyle, Transogram, 1964, EXIB.............................$35.00

Goodbye Mr Chips, Parker Bros, 1969, MIB....................$25.00

Gray Ghost, Transogram, 1958, NMIB $90.00

Great Obstacle Race Game, Spear's, VGIB $30.00

Groucho Marx TV Quiz, Pressman, 1950s, EXIB $70.00

Guliver's Travels, Milton Bradley, 1930s, VG+IB..........$135.00

Gulliver's Travels Card Game, Paramount/England, 1939,
w/instruction sheet, NMIB.......................................$75.00

Gumby & Poky Playful Trails, 1968, NMIB....................$25.00

Gunsmoke, Lowell, 1958, EX $45.00
Gunsmoke, Lowell, 1958, NMIB...$75.00
Hair Bear Bunch, Milton Bradley, 1971, NMIB................$30.00
Hang on Harvey, Ideal, 1969, EXIB $25.00
Hangman, Milton Bradley, 1976, NMIB...........................$12.00

Happy Days, Parker Bros., 1976, MIB, $28.00.

Hardy Boys Treasure, Parker Bros, 1960, VGIB $45.00
Hawaiian Eye, Lowell, 1960, EXIB..................................$130.00
Heckle & Jeckle 3-D Target Game, Aldon Industries, 1950s,
    EXIB...$40.00
Hector Heathcote the Minute-And-A-Half Man, Transogram,
    1963, NMIB..$85.00
Heidi Elevator, Remco, 1965, NMIB $30.00
Higgly Piggly, Cadaco, 1953, NMIB.................................$20.00
High Gear, Mattel, 1953, NMIB $40.00
Hippety-Hop, Corey, 1947, EXIB.....................................$40.00
Hoopla, Ideal, 1966, NMIB $60.00
Hopalong Canasta Card Game, Pacific, 1950, NM $200.00
Hopalong Cassidy Dominoes Western Style, Milton Bradley,
    1950, EXIB...$100.00
Hopalong Cassidy Game, Marx, 1950s, EXIB.................$115.00
Hopalong Cassidy Stage Coach Toss Game, Transogram, 1950s,
    EXIB...$65.00
Hoppity Hooper Pinball Game, Lidu, 1965, NMIB........$100.00
Hot Wheels Wipe Out Race Game, Mattel, 1968, NMIB..$50.00
Howdy Doody Bean Bag Game, Parker Bros, 1950s, EXIB ..$75.00
Howdy Doody Card Game, Russell, 1950s, EXIB $40.00

I Dream of Jeannie, Milton Bradley, 1965, MIB, $100.00.
(Photo courtesy Richard Barnes)

Howdy Doody's Own Game, Parker Bros, 1949, EXIB ...$100.00
Huckleberry Hound Spin-O-Game, 1959, EXIB..............$90.00
Huckleberry Hound Target, Knickerbocker, 1959, VGIB ..$50.00

I Spy, Ideal, 1965, NMIB, $85.00. (Photo courtesy American
Pie Collectibles)

Identipops, Playvalue, 1969, VGIB $200.00
Improved Game Fish Pond, McLoughlin Bros, 1890, VGIB ..$100.00
Indiana Jones in the Raiders of the Lost Ark, Kenner, 1981,
    NMIB...$25.00
Intrigue, Milton Bradley, 1954, NMIB $40.00
Ipcress File, Milton Bradley, 1966, MIB $40.00
Jack & Jill, Milton Bradley, VGIB....................................$100.00
Jackie Gleason & Away We Go! TV Fun Game, Transogram,
    1956, EX (G box) $75.00
Jackie Gleason's And Away We Go! TV Fun Game, Transogram,
    1956, EX $55.00
James Bond Live & Let Die Tarot Game, US Games, 1973,
    NMIB...$75.00
James Bond Secret Agent 007, Milton Bradley, 1964, NMIB..$45.00
James Bond 007 Thunderball, Milton Bradley, 1965, NMIB...$45.00
Jan Murray's Charge Account TV Word Game, Lowell, 1961,
    EXIB...$25.00
Jan Murray's Treasure Hunt, Gardner, 1950s, NMIB $30.00
Jeanne Dixon's Game of Destiny, Milton Bradley, 1968, NMIB..$15.00
Jeopardy, Milton Bradley, 1964, EXIB $25.00
Jeopardy, Milton Bradley, 1972, 10th edition, NMIB $15.00
Jerome Park Steeple Chase, McLoughlin Bros, EXIB $400.00
Jerome Park Steeple-Chase, McLoughlin Bros, VGIB....$200.00
Jetson's Fun Pad, Milton Bradley, 1963, NMIB.................$80.00
Jocko the Clown Pinball Game, 1960s, 13", VG+............$25.00
John Drake Secret Agent, Milton Bradley, 1966, EXIB....$35.00
Joker's Wild, Milton Bradley, 1973, NMIB $15.00
Jolly Jungleers, Milton Bradley, VGIB $100.00
Jonny Quest Card Game, Milton Bradley, 1964, EXIB.....$30.00
Jules Verne's Around the World With Nellie Bly, McLoughlin
    Bros, 1890, NMIB..$200.00
Jungle Book, Parker Bros, 1966, NMIB..........................$45.00
Junior Caster Mold Set, Rapaport, 1950s, EXIB $40.00
King Kong, Milton Bradley, 1966, NMIB........................$35.00
Knight Rider, Parker Bros, 1983, EXIB $18.00
Kojak Stake Out Detective Game, Milton Bradley, 1975,
    MIB...$40.00

Kukla and Ollie, Parker Bros., 1962, NMIB, $50.00.

Lame Duck, Parker Bros., 1928, VGIB...........................$125.00
Land of the Lost, Milton Bradley, 1975, NMIB $30.00
Lassie (Adventures of), Whiting, 1955, EXIB..................$50.00
Last Straw, Schaper, 1966, NMIB....................................$15.00
Leave It to Beaver Rocket to the Moon Space Game, Hasbro, 1959, NMIB $60.00
Legend of Jesse James, Milton Bradley, 1965, NMIB $85.00
Let's Drive, Milton Bradley, 1969, VGIB $20.00
Let's Face It, Hasbro, 1950s, NMIB $35.00
Letter Carrier, McLoughlin, VGIB................................$275.00
Li'l Stinker, Schaper, 1956, NMIB $20.00
Lie Detector, Mattel, 1961, NMIB $75.00
Lieutenant Combat Town, Transogram, 1963, NMIB $80.00
Literary Salad, Parker Bros, GIB.....................................$25.00
Little Orphan Annie Game, Parker Bros, 1981, NMIB....$18.00
Little Rascals Clubhouse Bingo, Gabriel, 1958, EXIB $50.00
Little Red Riding Hood, McLoughlin Bros, 1900s, EXIB..$200.00
Lone Ranger, Milton Bradley, 1966, NMIB $35.00
Lone Ranger Game, Milton Bradley, 1938, EXIB $50.00
Lone Ranger Silver Bullets, Whiting, 1956, MIB...........$150.00

Lone Ranger Target Game, Marx, 1946, EXIB, $250.00.

Looney Tunes, Milton Bradley, 1968, NMIB $60.00
Lost in Space, Milton Bradley, 1965, NMIB $75.00
Lucy Tea Party Game, Milton Bradley, 1971, EXIB..........$45.00
Mad's Spy vs Spy, Milton Bradley, 1986, NMIB................$25.00

Madame Planchette Horoscope Game, SelRight, 1967, NMIB $25.00
Magic Magic Magic Game Set, Remco, 1975, NMIB.......$30.00
Magic Robot, J&L Randall Ltd/England, 1950s, NMIB ...$75.00
Magnetic Fish Pond, McLoughlin Bros, 1890s, VGIB....$400.00
Magnetic Fish Pond Game, Milton Bradley, 1948, NM....$25.00
Man From UNCLE Secret Code Wheel Pin Ball Game, Sears/MGM, 1966, EXIB....................................$450.00
Man From UNCLE Target Game, Marx, 1965, NM.......$250.00
Man From UNCLE The Pinball Game, 1966, EX..........$110.00

Man From UNCLE Thrush Ray Gun Affair 3-D Game, Ideal, 1966, NMIB, $150.00. (Photo courtesy American Pie Collectibles)

Manson of Happiness, Parker Bros (version of the first board game published in America), c 1894, VG+IB, A $220.00
Margie The Game of Woopie, Milon Bradley, 1961, NMIB...$25.00
Masquerade Party, Bettye-B, 1955, EX $50.00
Masquerade Party, Bettye-B, 1955, MIB $110.00
Match Game, 3rd Edition, Milton Bradley, 1963, NM $50.00
Matchbox Traffic Game, Bronner, 1960s, MIB.................$60.00
McHale's Navy, Transogram, 1962, NMIB.......................$60.00
McKeever & the Colonel Bamboozle Game of Hide & Seek, Milton Bradley, 1962, NMIB....................................$30.00
Melvin Pervis' 'G'-Man Detective Game, Parker Bros, 1936, board only, EX..$50.00
Melvin the Moon Man, Remco, 1960s, NMIB.................$90.00
Merry Game of Fibber McGee & the Wistful Vista Mystery, VGIB...$55.00

Mighty Hercules Game, Hasbro, 1960s, NMIB, $325.00.

Merry Milkman, Hasbro, 1955, EXIB..............................$95.00
Miami Vice, Pepper Lane, 1984, EXIB............................$25.00
Mickey Mouse Circus, Marks Bros, EXIB........................$650.00
Mickey Mouse Club Game in Disneyland, Whitman, 1963,
    EXIB...$15.00
Mickey Mouse Kiddy Keno, Jaymar, 1950s-60s, NMIB $20.00
Mickey Mouse Pop Up Game, Whitman, 1970s, MIB $25.00
Mighty Comics Super Heroes Game, Transogram, 1966,
    NMIB..$85.00
Mighty Mouse, Milton Bradley, 1978, NMIB...................$30.00
Mighty Mouse Rescue Game, Harett-Gilmer, 1960s, EXIB ..$55.00
Mighty Mouse Skill Roll, Pressman/Terrytoons, 1950s, EXIB..$150.00
Military Tenpins, Ives, Pat 1885, EXIB........................$1,500.00
Milton the Monster, Milton Bradley, 1966, EXIB.............$35.00
Mind Maze, Parker Bros, 1970, NMIB $20.00
Mission Impossible, Ideal, 1967, EXIB...........................$120.00

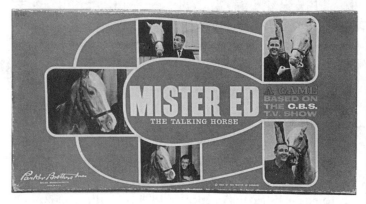

Mister Ed Game, Parker Bros., 1962, EXIB, $55.00. (Photo courtesy American Pie Collectibles)

Monkees Game, Transogram, 1968, EXIB $115.00
Monopoly, Parker Bros, 1964, M (lg maroon box)............$65.00
Monster Old Maid, Card Game, Milton Bradley, 1964, EXIB..$50.00
Mork & Mindy, Milton Bradley, 1978, NMIB $20.00
Morton Downy Jr Loudmouth Game, 1988, NMIB..........$10.00
Movie-Land Keeno, EXIB...$75.00

Munsters Card Game, Milton Bradley, EXIB, $50.00.

Moving Picture Game, Milton Bradley, EXIB.................$125.00
Mr Bug Goes to Town, Milton Bradley, 1955, NMIB $30.00
Mr Knovak, Transogram, 1963, NMIB............................$25.00
Mr Magoo's Maddening Misadventures, Transogram, 1970,
    NMIB..$70.00
Mr Ree! The Fireside Detective, SelRight, 1957, NMIB..$60.00
Ms Pac Man Board Game, 1982, EXIB............................$25.00
Muppet Show, Parker Bros, 1977, NMIB $20.00
Murder She Wrote, Warren, 1985, VGIB $10.00
My Favorite Martian, Transogram, 1963, VGIB $90.00
Mystery Date, Milton Bradley, 1965, NMIB $175.00
Mystic Skull The Game of Voodoo, Ideal, 1964, NMIB...$50.00
Nancy & Sluggo Game, 1944, rare, NMIB.....................$100.00
Nancy Drew Mystery Game, Parker Bros, 1957, NMIB...$160.00
National Velvet, Transogram, 1950s, NMIB.....................$45.00
Neck & Neck, Yaquinto, 1981, MIB $25.00
Newlywed Game, Hasbro, 1st Edition, 1967, NMIB $25.00
Newport Yacht Race, McLoughlin Bros, GIB..................$450.00
No Time for Sergeants, Ideal, 1964, EXIB.......................$25.00
Nurses, Ideal, 1963, NMIB $65.00
Office Boy The Good Old Days, Parker Bros, 1889, EXIB..$150.00
Oh Magoo, Warren, 1960s, NMIB $30.00

Orbit, Parker Bros., 1959, NMIB, $25.00.

Pac-Man, Milton Bradley, 1980s, NMIB, $20.00.

Our Country, 1880s, VGIB..............................$550.00
Our Game Tipple-Topple Game, All-Fair, c 1930, EXIB..$40.00
Outer Limits, Milton Bradley, 1964, EXIB.....................$240.00
Overland Trail, Transogram, 1960, NMIB $90.00
Park & Shop, Milton Bradley, 1960, NMIB....................$75.00
Parlor Croquet, Bliss, GIB $150.00
Partridge Family, Milton Bradley, 1974, NMIB................$45.00
Patty Duke Show, Milton Bradley, 1963, NMIB $40.00
Peanuts — The Game of Charlie Brown & His Pals, Selchow &
    Righter, 1959, EXIB..............................$35.00
Perils of Pauline, Marx, 1964, NMIB $120.00
Perry Mason, Case of the Missing Suspect, Transogram, 1959,
    NMIB $40.00
Peter Gunn Detective Game, Lowell, 1960, NMIB..........$55.00
Peter Pan, Transogram, 1953, EXIB $20.00

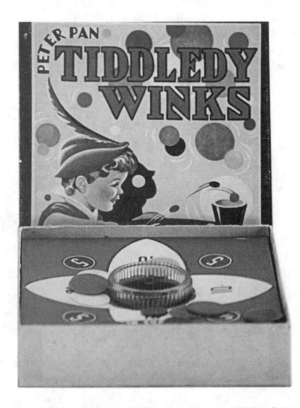

Peter Pan Tiddley Winks, Whitman #3035, EXIB, $25.00.

Petticoat Junction Game, Standard Toykraft, 1963, NMIB, $85.00.

Peter Potamus Game, Ideal, 1964, NMIB $70.00
Phantom's Complete 3 Game Set, Built-Rite #729, 1955,
    EXIB $85.00
Philip Marlow, Transogram, 1960, EXIB $60.00
Pied Piper of Hamelin — Walt Disney's Own Game, Parker
    Bros, 1930s, EXIB $100.00
Pin the Hat on Ko-Ko the Clown, All-Fair, 1940, EXIB ..$20.00
Pink Panther, Warren, 1977, NMIB.................................$25.00
Pinky Lee & the Runaway Frankfurters, Lisbeth Whiting Co
    #500, 1950s, NMIB...$75.00
Pirate & Traveler, Milton Bradley, 1953, NMIB..............$35.00
Pirate Ship, Lowe, 1940, EXIB $30.00
Pirates of the Caribbean, Parker Bros, 1967, EXIB $25.00
Planet of the Apes, Milton Bradley, 1974, EXIB..............$50.00
Play Ball! Game & TV Scorer, Colorforms, 1960s,
    NMIB $40.00
Play Sheriff, Milton Bradley, 1958, NMIB $30.00
Playing Department Store, Milton Bradley, VGIB $400.00
Poky the Clown Target Game, Wyandotte, 1950s, EXIB....$75.00
Pop the Chutes Target Game, NN Hill, NMIB $225.00
Pop Yer Top! Game of Suspense, Milton Bradley, 1968,
    EXIB $40.00
Pop-A-Puppet Pinball Game, Marx, 1960s, EX $25.00
Popeye Carnival (3 Games in 1), Toymaster, NMIB $200.00
Popeye Clobber Cans, Gardner, NMIB...........................$150.00
Popeye Jet Pilot Target Game, Japan, NMIB $150.00
Popeye Pipe Toss Game, Rosebud Art #17, 1935, VGIB..$40.00
Popeye Pipe Toss Game, Rosebud Art #17, 1935, MIB,
    A $100.00
Popeye Ring Toss, Transogram, EXIB.............................$165.00
Popeye's Game, Parker Bros, 1948, unused, NMIB.........$200.00
Popeye's Good Time/Blow Me Down, Built Rite, 1950, NMIB...$40.00

Popeye's Sliding Boards and Ladders Game, Built Rite, 1958, NMIB, $40.00.

Price Is Right, 1958, 1st edition, EXIB............................$25.00
Prince Valiant (Harold Foster), Transogram, 1950s, EXIB..$65.00
Prisoner of Zelda, Parker Bros, 1896, EXIB.....................$125.00
PT Boat 109, Ideal, 1963, VGIB $45.00

Quick Draw McGraw Ed-U Cards, 1961, NMIB $10.00
Quick Draw McGraw Private Eye Game, 1960, EXIB $25.00

Raggedy Ann Game, Milton Bradley, 1956, NMIB, $25.00. (Photo courtesy Kim Avery)

Raise the Titanic, Hoyle, 1987, EXIB................................$35.00
Rat Patrol, Transogram, 1966, NMIB...............................$90.00
Rebel, Ideal, 1961, NMIB...$75.00
Red Ryder Target Game, Daisy, VGIB $175.00
Red Ryders's Complete 3 Game Set, Built-Rite #729, 1950s,
    EXIB...$65.00
Restless Gun, Milton Bradley, 1950s, EXIB $50.00
Rich Uncle, The Stock Market Game, Parker Bros, 1955,
    EXIB...$50.00
Ricochet Rabbit Game, Ideal, 1965, EXIB.......................$80.00
Rifleman, Milton Bradley, 1959, NMIB $70.00
Rin-Tin-Tin (Adventures of), Transogram, 1955, EXIB ...$50.00
Rip Van Winkle, Parker Bros, VGIB...............................$125.00
Road Runner, Milton Bradley, 1968, NMIB.....................$35.00
Road Runner Card Game, 1976, NMIB.............................$10.00
Robin Hood, Parker Bros, 1970s, EX................................$10.00
Robin Hood (Adventures of), Betty-B, 1956, EXIB $65.00
Rocket Race to Saturn, Lido, 1950s, VGIB $25.00

Scottie, Pilot Plastics, 1950s, MIB, $25.00.

Rocky & His Friends, Milton Bradley, 1960, EXIB...........$75.00
Rondezvous, Create, 1965, NMIB....................................$25.00
Rootie Kazootie Ed-U Cards, 1953, unused, NMIB.........$25.00
Roulette Wheel, Marx, NMIB...$50.00
Rudolph the Red-Nosed Reindeer, Parker Bros, 1948, EXIB..$200.00
Ruff & Reddy Spelling Game, Exclusive Plaything, 1958,
    EXIB $30.00
Scarlett O'Hara — One of Her Problems Marble Game, Mari-
    etta Games/MGM, 1939, EXIB $75.00
Scooby Doo Where Are You?, Milton Bradley, 1973, NMIB ..$50.00
Scores 'N Stripes Bagatelle Game, Marx, 1949, NMIB ..$125.00
Screwball The Mad Mad Mad Game?, Trasnogram, 1960,
    NMIB $75.00
Sea Hunt, Lowell, 1961, EXIB...$75.00
Sealab 2020, Milton Bradley, 1973, NMIB $15.00
Secret Agent Man, Milton Bradley, 1966, EXIB...............$45.00
Shenanigans, Milton Bradley, 1964, EXIB $50.00
Shopping, John Ladell, 1973, NMIB.................................$20.00
Sigmund & the Sea Monsters, Milton Bradley, 1975,
    NMIB $40.00

Slap Stick, Milton Bradley, MIB, $25.00. (Photo courtesy Martin and Carolyn Berens)

Sleeping Beauty, see Walt Disney's Sleeping Beauty
Smack-A-Roo Game Set, Mattel, 1964, EXIB...................$40.00
Smokey Bear Forest Prevention Bear, Ideal, 1961, NMIB ..$95.00
Snake's Alive, Ideal, 1967, NMIB $35.00
Snoopy & the Red Baron, Milton Bradley, 1970, MIB.....$55.00
Snoopy Card Game, Idel, 1965, NMIB $25.00
Snoopy Snake Attack, Gabriel, 1980, MIB.......................$25.00
Snow White & the Seven Dwarfs, Cadaco, 1970s, EXIB ..$12.00
Soldiers on Guard, McLoughlin Bros, VGIB $125.00
Space Age Picture Checkers, Common, 1965, NMIB......$15.00
Space Mouse Card Game, Fairchild, 1964, NMIB...........$18.00
Space Pilot, Cadaco-Ellis, 1951, EXIB $75.00
Space: 1999, Milton Bradley, 1975, NMIB $25.00
Sparky Marble Maze, Built Rite, 1971, NMIB $30.00
Spear's 'Quick Change' Comic Pictures, VGIB................$65.00
Spider-Man, see also Amazing Spider Man

Spider-Man w/the Fantastic Four, Milton Bradley, 1977, NMIB..$35.00

Spot Shot Marble Game, Wolverine, 1930s, NM............$50.00

Spy Detector, Mattel, 1960, NMIB $75.00

Stagecoach, Milton Bradley, 1958, NMIB.....................$25.00

Stagecoach West Adventure Game, Transogram, 1961, NMIB..$90.00

Star Trek, Milton Bradley, 1979, EXIB...............................$45.00

Star Trek Adventure Game, West End Games, 1985, NMIB..$25.00

Star Trek Game, Milton Bradley, 1979, EXIB.....................$40.00

Star Wars Escape From Death Star, Kenner, 1977, NMIB..$25.00

Starsky & Hutch Detective, Milton Bradley, 1977, NMIB..$25.00

Steeple Chase, JH Singer, GIB..$125.00

Steeple Chase, McLoughlin Bros, VGIB.....................$200.00

Steve Canyon Exciting Air Force Game, Lowell, 1950s, NMIB..$50.00

Stop Thief, Parker Bros, 1979, NMIB $50.00

Submarine Search, Milton Bradley, 1977, EXIB.............$60.00

Super Heroes Card Game, Milton Bradley, 1978, EXIB ...$20.00

Superboy Game, Hasbro, 1960s, EX $50.00

Superboy Game, Hasbro, 1960s, NMIB $125.00

Superman (Adventures of), Milton Bradley, 1942, EXIB .$225.00

Superman Game, Hasbro, 1965, EXIB $90.00

Superman III, Parker Bros, 1983, MIB $25.00

Superstition, Milton Bradley, 1977, NMIB $35.00

Surfside 6, Lowell, 1961, unused, MIB $100.00

Tales of Wells Fargo, Milton Bradley, 1959, EXIB $85.00

Tennessee Tuxedo, Transogram, 1963, EXIB $150.00

That Girl, Remco, 1969, EXIB..$70.00

This Is Your Life, Lowell, 1954, EXIB $35.00

Tic-Tac Dough, Transogram, 1957, EXIB.........................$25.00

Tim Holt Rodeo Dart Games, American Toys, unused, NMIB..$100.00

Time Tunnel, Ideal, 1966, EXIB, $125.00. (Photo courtesy Apple Pie Collectibles)

Tiny Time Game of Beautiful Things, Parker Bros, 1970, MIB..$50.00

Tip It, 1965, VGIB...$20.00

To Tell the Truth, Lowell, 1957, EXIB $20.00

Tom & Jerry, Milton Bradley, 1977, EXIB.......................$30.00

Tom & Jerry Adventure in Blunderland, Transogram, 1965, EXIB..$55.00

Tom Sawyer and Huck Finn, (Adventures of), Stoll & Edwards, VGIB $125.00

Top Cat, Cadaco-Ellis, 1961, NMIB...............................$70.00

Touchdown Football, Wilder, GIB $75.00

Town & Country Traffic, Ranger Steel, 1940s, EXIB $50.00

Town Hall, Milton Bradley, 1939, NMIB.........................$20.00

Truth or Consequences, Ranger Steel, 1950, NMIB.......$135.00

Turn Over, Milton Bradley, EXIB.......................................$75.00

Twiggy, Milton Bradley, 1967, EXIB.................................$65.00

Uncle Sam's Mail, Milton Bradley, GIB, A $90.00

Uncle Wiggily, Parker Bros, 1979, NMIB $25.00

Untouchables, Marx, 1950s, NMIB $220.00

Untouchables Target Game, Marx, 1950s, NM $350.00

Virginian, Transogram, 1962, EXIB.................................$100.00

Voodoo Doll Game, Schaper, 1967, EXIB.......................$30.00

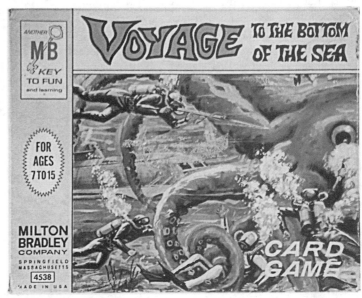

Voyage to the Bottom of the Sea Card Game, Milton Bradley, 1964, NMIB, $50.00.

Wagon Train, Milton Bradley, 1960, EXIB.......................$50.00

Walt Disney's Fantasyland, Parker Bros, 1950, MIB $50.00

Walt Disney's Sleeping Beauty, Whitman #4732:100, 1958, EXIB...$35.00

Walter Johnson Baseball Game, VGIB $200.00

Wanted Dead or Alive, Lowell, 1959, EXIB $110.00

Wally Gator Game, Transogram, 1963, NMIB, $100.00.

Which Witch?, Milton Bradley, 1970, NMIB.................$130.00

Who Framed Roger Rabbit?, Milton Bradley, 1987, NMIB...$50.00

Wide World Travel Game, Parker Bros, 1957, NMIB.......$25.00

Wild Bill Hickok's Cavalry & Indians Game, Built Rite, 1955, NMIB.................$40.00

Wilder's Football Game, GIB.................$125.00

Wink Tennis, Transogram, 1956, NMIB.................$15.00

Wonder Woman, Hasbro, 1967, NMIB.................$60.00

Woody Woodpecker Game, Milton Bradley, 1959, MIB..$50.00

Woody Woodpecker's Crazy Mix Up Color Factory, Whitman, 1972, EXIB.................$25.00

World's Fair Ed-U Cards, 1965, NMIB.................$15.00

Wow Pillow Fight Game, Milton Bradley, 1964, NMIB...$25.00

Wyatt Earp, Transogram, 1958, EXIB.................$70.00

Yogi Bear Cartoon Game, Milton Bradley, 1980, MIB.....$12.00

Yogi Bear Rummy Ed-U Cards, 1961, MIB (sealed).........$15.00

Yogi Bear Score-A-Matic Ball Toss, Transogram, EXIB....$65.00

You Don't Say, Milton Bradley, 1963, EXIB.................$20.00

Young America Target, Parker Bros, VGIB.................$275.00

Zamboola, Norstar, VGIB.................$85.00

Zorro, Parker Bros/Walt Disney, 1966, EXIB.................$55.00

4 Alarm Game, Milton Bradley, 1963, EXIB.................$20.00

10-4 Good Buddy, Parker Bros, 1976, EXIB.................$10.00

77 Sunset Strip, Lowell, 1960, EXIB.................$30.00

20,000 Leagues Under the Sea, Gardner, 1950s, EXIB......$30.00

$10,000 Pyramid, Milton Bradley, 1972, NMIB.................$25.00

$64,000 Question, Lowell, 1955, EXIB.................$25.00

Gasoline-Powered Toys

Two of the largest companies to manufacture gas-powered models are Cox and Wen-Mac. Since the late 1950s they have been making faithfully detailed models of airplanes as well as some automobiles and boats. Condition of used models will vary greatly because of the nature of the miniature gas engine and damage resulting from the fuel that has been used. Because of this, 'new in box' gas toys command a premium.

Richard Trautwein, our advisor for this category, tells us that the 'prices have softened some, but remain strong' on the most desirable of the gas-powered toys such as Dooling, McCoy, Reuhl, and Rexner. 'EBay,' he says, 'has some effect to drive down prices on the lower end gas-powered and has stopped sales on some of them.'

All-American Hot Rod, cast aluminum, 9", VG.............$250.00

Bremer Whirlwind #2, gr & wht, 1939, 18", NM........$2,900.00

Bremer Whirlwind #8, red w/yel detail, louvered belly pan & hood, ca 1940, 18", EX.................$2,300.00

Bremer Whirlwind #300, red, Brown Jr engine, 1939, VG...$1,250.00

Cameron Racer #4, red w/yel flame decals, 8", VG, from $200 to.................$275.00

Cessna UC 78 Bobcat (WWII-era Bamboo Bomber), w/pilot, co-pilot & 2 passengers, 42x57½" W, EX, from $300 to..$375.00

Cox AA Fuel Dragster, bl & red, 1968-70, M.................$125.00

Cox Acro-Cub, 1960s, MIB (sealed), from $60 to............$85.00

Cox Baja Bug, yel & orange, 1968-73, M.................$65.00

Cox Chopper, MIB, from $70 to.................$100.00

Cox Commanche, E-Z Flyer series, 1993-95, NMIB.......$35.00

Cox Delta F-15, Wing Series, gray, 1981-86, M.................$30.00

Cox E-Z Flyer Comanche, wht, NMIB.................$35.00

Cox Golden Bee, .49 engine, M.................$30.00

Cox ME-109 Airplane, 1994, MIB (sealed), from $40 to..$60.00

Cox Mercedes Benz W196 Racer, red, 1963-65, EX.........$85.00

Cox Navy Helldiver, 2-tone bl, 1963-66, EX, from $65 to...$80.00

Cox P-51 Bendix Racer, red & yel, molded landing gear, 1963-64, EX, from $65 to.................$80.00

Cox Pitts Special Biplane, wht, .20 engine, 1968, EX, from $35 to.................$50.00

Cox PT-19 Flight Trainer, yel & bl, EX.................$45.00

Cox QZ PT-19, Quiet Zone Muffler, red & wht, 1966-69, EX, from $50 to.................$70.00

Cox Ryan ST-3, w/pilot & co-pilot, wht & bl, .20 ignition power, M.................$65.00

Cox Sandblaster, brn & tan, 1968-72, M, from $45 to.....$65.00

Cox Shrike Bonneville Special, MIB, from $130 to.......$150.00

Cox Sky Jumper, helicopter w/pilot & parachute, olive, 1989-95, M.................$40.00

Cox Sky Raider, gray, EXIB.................$85.00

Cox Snowmobile, silver, 1968, M.................$100.00

Cox Stealth Bomber, blk, 1987-89, EX, from $30 to........$50.00

Cox Thimble Drome Comanche, metal w/plastic wings, .15 engine, 1960s, MIB, from $50 to.................$75.00

Cox Thimble Drome Prop Rod, plastic w/aluminum undercarriage, Friskies Flyer decal, 13", VG.................$150.00

Cox Thimble Drome Prop-Rod, yel & red, 12", EXIB....$200.00

Cox Thimble Drome Racer #54 O Forty-Five Special, 9", Fair (Poor box), A, from $150 to.................$190.00

Cox Thimble Drome TD-3 Airplane, all aluminum body, early 1950s, $85.00; Cox Thimble Drome TD-1 Airplane, plastic body with aluminum wings, from $95.00 to $125.00.

Cox Thunderbolt, E-Z Flyer Series, blk, w/muffler, 1993-95, M.................$30.00

Cox UFO Flying Saucer, Wings Series, wht, 1990-91, M ..$25.00

Cub-Kart, Harkimer Tool, 1961, go-cart w/plastic driver, 6½", unused, MIB, from $120 to......................................$150.00
Curtiss Jenny Airplane, WWI era, 65" W, EX, from $250 to...$300.00
Curtiss P-40D Tiger Shark, Comet Model Hobby Craft, Inc, plastic, 13½", MIB, from $95 to.............................$135.00
Dooling Bros F Racer #3, red, no engine, 1948, 16", EX, from $1,000 to...$1,350.00
Dooling Bros F Racer #3, red w/Knoxville Champ logo, 19", EX, from $1,000 to...$1,400.00

Dooling Bros F Style Sostilo Offy #54 Race, from $2,000.00 to $2,450.00.

Dooling Bros Mercury Racer #59, aluminum w/some pnt detail, Hornet engine, ca 1940, 18½", VG, from $1,800 to $2,300.00
Dooling Bros Racer #4, orange, articulated front end, McCoy engine, rstr, EX $1,500.00
Dooling Bros Racer #5, red, 16", EX $1,200.00
Dooling Bros Racer #6, bl, rear drive w/front drive conversion, Super Cyclone engine, 1941, 18", EX..................$2,300.00
Dooling Bros Racer #8, Atwood .60 Champion engine, 1939, 19", EX, from $1,500 to.......................................$1,800.00
Dooling Bros Tether Racing Boat, red w/stepped hull design, .61 engine, 1955, 35", EX, from $500 to $700.00
England Special Racer #8, gr-pnt aluminum w/leather seats, central clutch, ca 1948, 16", EX, from $825 to $1,000.00

Fairchild 22 Model Airplane, blue and cream, working shock absorber in landing gear, 47" wingspan, NM, from $250.00 to $350.00.

Hiller T Racer #19, yel w/Voit wheels & tires, Hiller .60 engine, 20", EX...$1,800.00

Hiller-Comet #5, red, 1942, 19", EX, $1,800.00.

Hot Rod Roadster, red, Hornet .60 engine, 15", EX $950.00
McCoy Invader #6, yel, McCot .49 engine, 17", EX ...$1,400.00
McCoy Streamliner, chrome-plated, 1950, 18", EX, from $525 to $900.00
McCoy Streamliner, gray, never drilled for engine, 17", NM..$800.00
Melcraft Racer, wht w/Champion tires, ignition engine, ca 1948, 16", EX, from $600 to $800.00
Miracle Power Special Racer #1, yel & blk w/red detail, Dooling Engine, 17", EX $1,600.00
Ohlsson & Rice Racer #54, red, modified w/direct O&R marine engine, w/cooling slots, 10", VG $600.00
Phantom Lady Speedboat, wood, Phantom P-30 engine, 21", EX $650.00

Railton Champion Racer #12, red and yellow, 17", NM, $2,700.00.

Reuhl Racer #39, Bakelite body, grille & seat, .49 McCoy engine, 1940, 17", EX..$2,200.00
Speed Demon #18, yel-pnt wood, Bunch .60 engine, 1937-38, 20", EXIB...$4,700.00
Testors Avion Mustang Fighter Airplane, NMIB...........$100.00
Testors Cosmic Wind, orange, MIB..................................$50.00
Testors Cosmic Wind, Spirit of '76, M $60.00
Testors Nitro Nightmare 0.49 Engine Funny Car, plastic, 19", EXIB, A $175.00

Testors OD P-51 Mustang, VG..............................$30.00
Testors Sopwith Camel, Fly 'Em Series, NM....................$35.00
Testors Sprite Indy Car, wht, 1966-68, M, from $75 to ..$100.00
Wen-Mac, P-63 King Cobra, chrome, 1962-64, EX..........$50.00
Wen-Mac, SBD-5 Navy Dive Bomber, 1962-64, EX $50.00
Wen-Mac '57 Chevy Racer, orange plastic w/decals, 12", VG,
    from $90 to $160.00
Wen-Mac A-24 Army Attack Bomberm 1962-64, EX $45.00
Wen-Mac Aeromite, blk, Baby Spitfire engine, EX..........$60.00
Wen-Mac Albatross, Flying Wing Series, red, wht & bl, EX..$40.00

Wen-Mac Automite Racer, plastic, with driver, 1960s, 9", complete, EXIB, A, $120.00. (Photo courtesy Randy Inman Auctions)

Wen-Mac Cutlass, bl, blk & yel, 1958-60, EX $50.00
Wen-Mac Falcon, red, wht & bl, 1963-64, EX.................$45.00
Wen-Mac Giant P-40 Flying Tiger, wht, 1959-60, EX......$45.00
Wen-Mac Marine Corsair, red, ca 1960s, EX $40.00
Wen-Mac P-63 King Cobra, chrome, 1962-64, EX..........$50.00
Wen-Mac RAF Day Fighter, wht, 1963-64, EX $50.00
Wen-Mac Yellow Jacket Corsair, yel, 1959-64, EX $40.00
Woodette Tornado Racer #3, red, Mot-Airette engine, 13",
    VG...$400.00

GI Joe

GI Joe, the most famous action figure of them all, has been made in hundreds of variations since Hasbro introduced him in 1964. The first of these jointed figures was 12" tall; they can be identified today by the mark each carried on his back: 'GI Joe T.M. (trademark), Copyright 1964.' They came with four different hair colors: blond, auburn, black, and brown, each with a scar on his right cheek. They were sold in four basic packages: Action Soldier, Action Sailor, Action Marine, and Action Pilot. A Black figure was also included in the line, and there were representa-

tives of many nations as well — France, Germany, Japan, Russia, etc. These figures did not have scars and are more valuable. Talking GI Joes were issued in 1967 when the only female (the nurse) was introduced. Besides the figures, uniforms, vehicles, guns, and accessories of many varieties were produced. The Adventure Team series, made from 1970 to 1976, included Black Adventurer, Air Adventurer, Talking Astronaut, Sea Adventurer, Talking Team Commander, Land Adventurer, and several variations. In 1974 Joe's hard plastic hands were replaced with kung fu grips, so that he could better grasp his weapons. Assorted playsets allowed young imaginations to run wild, and besides the doll-size items, there were wristwatches, foot lockers, toys, walkie-talkies, etc., made for the kids themselves. Due to increased production costs, the large GI Joe was discontinued in 1976.

In 1982, Hasbro brought out the smaller 3¾" GI Joe figures, each with its own descriptive name. Of the first series, some characters were produced with either a swivel or straight arm. Vehicles, weapons, and playsets were available, and some characters could only be had by redeeming flag points from the backs of packages. This small version proved to be the most successful action figure line ever made. Loose items are common; collectors value those still mint in the original packages at two to four times higher.

The 1990s through today has seen the exit and return of the 3¾" figures in various series along with the reintroduction of the 12" figure in a few different collections including the Classic

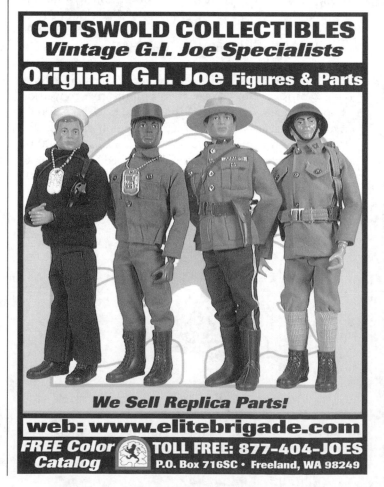

Collection and the 30th Anniversay, among others. Joe is still going strong today.

For more information we recommend *Encyclopedia to GI Joe* and *The 30th Anniversary Salute to GI Joe* both by Vincent San Telmo; *Official Collector's Guide to Collecting and Completing, Official Guide to Completing 3¾" Series and Hall of Fame: Vol II,* and *Official Guide to GI Joe: '64 – '78,* all by James DeSimone. Note: All items are American issue unless indicated otherwise. (Action Man was made in England by Hasbro circa 1960 into the 1970s.) All listings are complete unless noted.

Advisor: Cotswold Collectibles (C6)

See also Games; Lunch Boxes; Puzzles; Windups, Friction, and Other Mechanicals.

12" GI JOE FIGURES AND FIGURE SETS

Action Pilot, #7800, MIB, $550.00. (Photo courtesy Cotswold Collectibles, Inc.)

Action Marine, #7700, MIB, $400.00. (Photo courtesy Cotswold Collectibles, Inc.)

Action Pilot, 30th Anniversary, #81046, 1994, NRFB...$125.00
Action Sailor, #7600, NM..$250.00
Action Sailor, Breeches Bouy, #7625, EX $300.00
Action Sailor, Breeches Bouy, #7625, NM.....................$450.00
Action Sailor, Breeches Bouy, #7625, 1968 reissue, EX..$300.00
Action Sailor, Deep Freeze, #7623, EX $225.00
Action Sailor, Deep Sea Diver, #7620, NM.....................$400.00
Action Sailor, Landing Signal Officer, #7621, MIP........$540.00
Action Sailor, Landing Signal Officer, #7621, NM $360.00
Action Sailor, Navy Attack Set, #7607, NM...................$150.00

Action Sailor, Sea Rescue, #GIHLD-37, EX, $200.00. (Photo courtesy Cotswold Collectibles, Inc.)

Action Marine, #7700, EX $115.00
Action Marine, #8 (Talking), #7790, NM $200.00
Action Marine, Beachhead Assault Field Pack Set, #7713, EX...$100.00
Action Marine, Demolition Set, #7730, EX $60.00
Action Marine, Dress Blues Parade Set, #7710, EX..........$50.00
Action Marine, Jungle Fighter, #7732, NM....................$675.00
Action Marine, Medic, #7720, NM, C6............................$50.00
Action Marine, Medic Set, #7719, w/stretcher, MIP......$825.00
Action Marine, Paratrooper Helmet Set, #7707, NM $40.00
Action Marine, Tank Commander Set, #7731, EX $350.00
Action Marine, 30th Anniversary, #81`047, 1994, NRFB..$80.00
Action Nurse, #4200, EX $1,900.00
Action Nurse, #4200, MIB (sealed)............................$5,000.00
Action Pilot, Crash Crew Set, #7820, MIP $425.00
Action Pilot, Crash Crew Set, #7820, NM.....................$225.00
Action Pilot, Survival Life Raft, #7802, MIP $300.00
Action Pilot, Talking, #7890, NM $250.00
Action Pilot, USAF Dress Uniform, #7803, NM $625.00

Action Sailor, Shore Patrol Dress Jumper Set, #7613, NM ..$130.00
Action Sailor, Shore Patrol Dress Pant Set, #7614, MIP ..$160.00
Action Sailor, Talking, #7690, EX $225.00
Action Sailor, Talking, #7690, MIB.........................$1,175.00
Action Sailor, 30th Anniversary, #81048, 1994, NRFB ...$90.00
Action Soldier, #7500, MIB, from $275 to $375.00
Action Soldier, Bivouac Machine Gun, #7514, MIP......$400.00
Action Soldier, Bivouac Sleeping Bag, #7515, MIP $120.00
Action Soldier, Black, #7900, EX...............................$450.00
Action Soldier, Black, #7900, MIP $2,400.00
Action Soldier, Combat Field Jacket, #7505, MIP $325.00
Action Soldier, Command Post Poncho, 1964, #7519, NM ..$40.00
Action Soldier, Green Beret, #7536, EX.........................$250.00
Action Soldier, Heavy Weapons, #7538, EX $190.00
Action Soldier, Military Police Helmet & Small Arms, #7526,
    NM...$80.00
Action Soldier, Military Police Uniform Set, #7521, MIP ..$2,850.00
Action Soldier, Mountain Troops Set, #7530, MIP........$365.00
Action Soldier, Sabotage Set, #7516, NM.....................$260.00
Action Soldier, Ski Patrol Deluxe Set, #7531, NM........$340.00
Action Soldier, Snow Troops Set, #7529, NM.................$50.00
Action Soldier, Talking, #7590, MIP $800.00
Action Soldier, West Point Cadet Uniform Set, #7537, EX..$230.00
Action Soldier, West Point Cadet Uniform Set, #7537, MIP...$1,100.00
Action Soldier, 30th Anniversary, #81048, 1994, NRFB...$100.00
Adventure Team, Adventurer, Black, #7404, NMIB......$375.00
Adventure Team, Adventurer, Black, Kung Fu Grip, #7823,
    EX $80.00
Adventure Team, Adventurer, Hidden Treasure, #7308-1, EX ..$20.00

Adventure Team, Adventurer, Trouble at Vulture Pass, #59289,
    MIP $300.00
Adventure Team, Air Adventurer, #7403, EX...............$130.00
Adventure Team, Air Adventurer, #7403, MIP.............$400.00
Adventure Team, Air Adventurer, Fantastic Freefall, #7423,
    MIP $390.00
Adventure Team, Air Adventurer, Kung Fu Grip, #7823,
    MIB...$340.00
Adventure Team, Air Adventurer, Life-Like Hair & Beard,
    #7282, EX..$80.00
Adventure Team, Air Adventurer, White Tiger Hunt, #7436,
    NM..$190.00
Adventure Team, Air Adventurer Aerial Recon, #7345, EX ..$80.00
Adventure Team, Air Adventurer Dangerous Climb, #7309-2,
    MIP $85.00
Adventure Team, Bullet Man, #8026, NM $95.00
Adventure Team, Commander, Talking, #7290, MIP.....$475.00
Adventure Team, Commander, Talking, #7400, EX $75.00

Adventure Team, Commander, Talking, Life-Like Hair and Beard, #7400, MIP, $380.00. (Photo courtesy Cotswold Collectibles, Inc.)

Adventure Team, Demolition, #7370, EX.........................$25.00
Adventure Team, Demolition, #7370, MIP $135.00
Adventure Team, Desert Explorer, #7209-5, NM $45.00
Adventure Team, Eagle Eye Land Commander, #7276, MIP...$140.00
Adventure Team, Fight for Survival, #7431, EX.............$280.00
Adventure Team, Flying Space Adventure, #7425, NM ..$550.00
Adventure Team, Headquarters, #7490, MIP $275.00
Adventure Team, Jungle Survival, #7373, EX..................$20.00

Adventure Team, Adventurer, Life-Like Hair and Beard, #7401, MIB, $50.00. (Photo courtesy Cotswold Collectibles, Inc.)

Adventure Team, Jungle Survival, #7373, MIP $50.00
Adventure Team, Land Adventurer, Kung Fu Grip, #7280, NM..$75.00
Adventure Team, Land Adventurer, Life-Like Hair & Beard, #7401, EX..$50.00
Adventure Team, Land Adventurer, Life-Like Hair & Beard, #7401, MIP $210.00
Adventure Team, Man of Action, Life-Like Hair, #7500, EX...$60.00

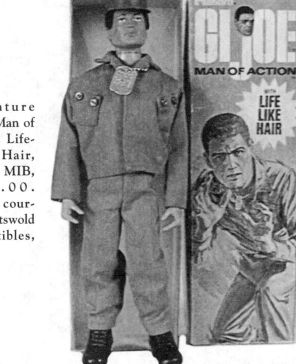

Adventure Team, Man of Action, Life-Like Hair, #7500, MIB, $200.00. (Photo courtesy Cotswold Collectibles, Inc.)

Adventure Team, Man of Action, Talking, #7590, NM ..$130.00
Adventure Team, Mike Power Atomic Man, #8025, MIP ..$140.00
Adventure Team, Photo Recon, #7609-4, EX...................$25.00
Adventure Team, Radiation Detection, #7341, MIP......$210.00
Adventure Team, Sea Adventurer, #7281, MIP, from $160 to $200.00
Adventure Team, Sea Adventurer, #7402, MIP $250.00
Adventure Team, Secret Rendezvous, #7308-4, EX..........$15.00
Adventure Team, Volcano Jumper, #7344, MIP $275.00
Adventure Team, White Tiger Hunt, #7436, MIB $350.00
Adventure Team, Winter Rescue, #7309-4, NM $80.00
Adventures of GI Joe, Astronaut, Hidden Missile Discovery, #7652, EX..$80.00
Adventures of GI Joe, Astronaut, Talking, #7615, EX ...$100.00
Adventures of GI Joe, Astronaut, Talking, #7615, MIP ..$950.00
Adventures of GI Joe, Mysterious Explosion Set, #7921, EX...$70.00
Australian Jungle Fighter, no equipment, #8205, MIP ..$1,100.00
Australian Jungle Fighter, no equipment, #8205, NM....$250.00
Australian Jungle Fighter, w/equipment, #8105, MIP ..$2,200.00
Australian Jungle Fighter, w/equipment, #8105, NM $375.00
British Commando, #8104, EX.......................................$325.00
British Commando, #8104, MIP $2,200.00
French Resistance Fighter, #8203, MIP $1,175.00

French Resistance Fighter, #8203, NM $230.00
German Storm Trooper, no equipment, #8200, NM $300.00
German Storm Trooper, w/equipment, #8100, MIP $2,300.00
Japanese Imperial Soldier, w/equipment, #8201, EX.......$275.00

Japanese Imperial Soldier, with equipment, #8201, NMIB (reproduction box), $700.00. (Photo courtesy Cotswold Collectibles, Inc.)

Japanese Imperial Soldier, w/equipment & medal, #8101, MIP...$2,550.00
Russian Infantryman, no equipment, #8202, MIP.......$1,100.00
Russian Infantryman, w/equipment, #8102, MIP $2,100.00

ACCESSORIES FOR 12" GI JOE

Boxed and packaged items are listed by name/title just as it appears on the box or card; loose pieces of clothing or equipment are listed by item first, followed by the name of of the series or the character it relates to (for instance 'Jacket & Trousers, Green Beret.')

Ammo Box, Tank Commander, gr w/orange US GI Joe stencil, issued for uniform set, NM, A $600.00
Armband, Army Airborne MP, snap connectors (rare), NM...$200.00
Armored Suit, Demolition, EX.......................................$15.00
Army Combat Engineer Set, #7571, 1967, MIP $650.00
Astronaut Boots, plastic, VG+, pr....................................$25.00
Astronaut Suit, multi-pocket, w/side tabs, EX $400.00
Belt, Action Man, brn web, EX $3.00
Binoculars, Hurricane Spotter, gray, EX, C6 ....$7.00

Binoculars, red w/string, 1960s, EX $14.00

Bivouac Set, sleeping bag, knife, spoon, fork, mess kit, canteen & cover, rifle, bayonet, belt & army field manual, MIB..$285.00

Boots, Flying Space Adventure, yel, EX, pr.......................$32.00

Camera, Secret Mission to Spy Island, blk w/elastic strap, EX, C6 ....$7.00

Canadian Mountie Set, outfit, rifle, ammunition belt, goggles, radio & mess kit, NM...$290.00

Canteen & Cover, British, EX......................................$35.00

Cap, Action Pilot, bl, EX..$14.00

Carrying Case/Play Set, Takara, VG+............................$100.00

Cobra, Search for the Golden Idol, EX $15.00

Coveralls, Landing Signal Officer, VG...........................$35.00

Crocodile, Adventure Team, EX $15.00

Diver Belt, 1st issue w/exposed weights & leg strap, EX ...$25.00

Entrenching Tool, Australian, EX $10.00

Fatigue Pants, Action Marine, #7715, camo, M (NM card)..$400.00

Fatigue Pants, Action Soldier, #7504, gr, NMOC $250.00

Fatigue Shirt, Action Marine, #7714, camo, MOC.......$400.00

Fatigue Shirt, Action Soldier, #7503, gr, MOC $435.00

First Aid Pouch, gr cloth, w/snap closure, EX $50.00

Flag, Army, EX...$35.00

Flag, USAF, EX $35.00

Flame Thrower, gr, EX $35.00

Flight Suit, Scramble, w/accessories, MIB $1,000.00

Flight Suit, Scramble, w/accessories, NM $250.00

Geiger Counter, Volcano Jumper, yel, EX $7.00

Goggles, Desert Patrol, amber, rpl elastic, EX $65.00

Green Beret Set, #7533, MOC.....................................$325.00

Green Beret Set, #7533, NM..$250.00

Grendade Launcher, Action Man, EX.............................$15.00

Handgun (.45), Action Man, EX.....................................$5.00

Head Gear, Landing Signal Officer, 1960s, EX $60.00

Helmet, A.S. (Air Security), bl w/wht lettering & trim, EX...$450.00

Helmet, British, EX..$18.00

Helmet Set, #7507, MOC...$110.00

Helmet Sticker, Soldier Helmet, #7507, EX $10.00

High Voltage Escape, 1972, MIP...................................$120.00

Jacket & Trousers, Airborne MP, gr, VG $85.00

Jacket & Trousers, Green Beret, VG $40.00

Jackhammer, EX+...$275.00

Jumpsuit, Adventure Team, mesh, EX.............................$12.00

Jumpsuit, Radiation Detection, gr, EX $15.00

Life Vest, orange, padded, 1960s...................................$29.00

Map Case & Map, Sandstorm Survival, silver, EX.............$7.00

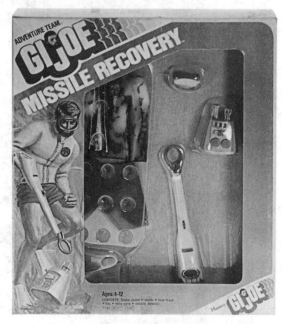

Missile Recovery, Adventure Team, #7348, MIP, $50.00. (Photo courtesy Cotswold Collectibles, Inc.)

Laser Rescue, Adventure Team, #7311, MOC, $75.00. (Photo courtesy Cotswold Collectibles, Inc.)

Panzer Captain Outfit, Action Man, MIB, $75.00.

Medal, Australian, Victoria Cross, Action Man, EX $10.00
Oar, Secret Mission to Spy Island, blk, for dinghy, EX........$6.00
Parachute Pack, Sky Dive to Danger, EX+ $125.00
Pup Tent, Marine, EX..$25.00
Pup Tent, White Tiger Hunt, orange/gr (1st version), no poles, EX..$15.00
Radio, Airborne MP, blk, mk Hong Kong, G+ $245.00
Rockblaster, Sonic Blaster, EX...$5.00
Scabbard, Annapolis Cadet, w/slings, no sword, EX.......$125.00
Scuba Gear, orange suit, tanks & fins, NM....................$150.00
Scuba Suit, MIP (sealed) $580.00
Scuba Top, Action Man, EX...$12.00
Shirt & Trousers, Japanese, EX.......................................$45.00
Shorts, Australian, EX $27.00
Space Capsule Collar, inflatable, Sears, EX $115.00
Stethoscope, Medic, EX...$19.00
Tripod, Combat Engineer, w/plumb bob, EX+ $250.00
Trousers, Capture of the Pygmy Gorilla, camo, EX $6.00
Tunic & Trouser Set, German, VG $30.00
Uniform, State Trooper, w/accessories, NM...................$500.00
Work Shirt, Action Sailor, #7608, MOC, from $200 to..$250.00

Volcano Jumper, Adventure Team, #7349, $50.00.

VEHICLES FOR 12" GI JOE

Action Pilot, Crash Crew Set, #7820, MIP $460.00
Action Pilot, Crash Crew Set, #7820, NM.....................$225.00
Action Sailor, Sea Sled & Frogman, #5957, Sears Exclusive, EX..$160.00
Action Sailor, Sea Sled & Frogman, #8050, no cave, MIP ..$525.00
Action Sildier, Amphibian Duck, #5693, NM $360.00
Adventure Soldier, Helicopter, #5395, NM...................$275.00

Adventure Team, ATV, #23528, MIP $130.00
Adventure Team, Avenger Pursuit Craft, Sears, NM $165.00
Adventure Team, Big Trapper, #7498, NM....................$100.00
Adventure Team, Capture Copter, #7480, NM...............$160.00
Adventure Team, Combat Jeep Set, #7000, w/trailer, EX..$75.00
Adventure Team, Combat Jeep Set, #7000, w/trailer, MIP ..$525.00
Adventure Team, Escape Car, #7360, MIP $80.00
Adventure Team, Sky Hawk, #7470, MIP $160.00
Adventure Team, Windboat Set, #7353, NM $25.00
Adventure Team Vehicle Set, #7005, MIP $225.00
Desert Patrol Jeep, #8030, NM......................................$375.00
Friendship VII Space Capsule, w/astronaut, complete, MIB...$165.00
German Staff Car, Action Man Task Force, MIB $275.00
Iron Knight Tank, M $135.00
Iron Knight Tank, VG $35.00

Jeep and Trailer Combat Set, #7000, EXIB, $350.00. (Photo courtesy Cotswold Collectibles, Inc.)

Jet Helicopter, Irwin, #5395, EXIB................................$175.00
Mobile Support Vehicle, EX..$250.00

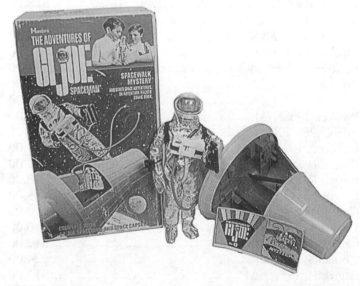

Spacewalk Mystery, Adventures of GI Joe, #7981, Made in Canada, EXIB, $350.00. (Photo courtesy Cotswold Collectibles, Inc.)

Mobile Support Vehicle, EX+IB..............$325.00
Motorcycle & Sidecar, Cherilea, gr, near complete, EX ...$50.00
Motorcycle & Sidecar, Irwin, rust colored, w/machine gun, EX $110.00
Night Raven, w/blueprints, EX..............$110.00
Panther Jet, EX..............$400.00
Sandstorm Jeep, gr, EXIB..............$275.00
Sea Wolf (submarine), EXIB..............$100.00
Space Capsule, VG+..............$55.00
Space Capsule & Suit, #8020, w/record, EXIB..............$345.00
Trouble Shooter ATV, orange, w/tracks, EX..............$210.00

3¾" GI Joe Figures

Aero-Viper, 1989, NM..............$1.10
Airborne, 1983, MOC..............$65.00
Airtight, 1985, MOC..............$15.00
Astro Viper, 1988, MOC..............$30.00
Backblast, 1989, MIP..............$15.00
Barbecue, 1985, EX..............$25.00
Barbecue, 1985, MOC..............$50.00
Baroness, 1984, EX..............$40.00
Baroness, 1984, MOC..............$160.00
Barricade, 1992, MOC..............$8.00
BAT, 1986, EX..............$12.00
BAT, 1990, MOC..............$30.00
Battle Force 2000 Dee-Jay, 1989, NM..............$7.00
Battle Force 2000 Dodger, 1987, NM..............$18.00
Battle Force 2000 Maverick, 1987, NM..............$16.00
Bazooka, 1985, EX..............$25.00
Bazooka, 1985, MOC..............$50.00
Beach Head, 1986, MOC..............$35.00
Beach Head, 1986, NM..............$20.00
Big Boa, 1987, EX..............$6.00
Blast-Off, 1993, MOC..............$10.00
Blast-Off, 1993, NM..............$7.00
Blaster, 1987, NM..............$18.00
Blizzard, 1988, MOC..............$22.00
Blocker, 1988, MOC..............$30.00
Blocker, 1988, NM..............$22.00
Blowtorch, 1984, MOC..............$55.00
Breaker, 1982, EX..............$22.00
Breaker, 1982, MOC..............$80.00
Breaker, 1982, NM..............$38.00
Budo, 1988, EX..............$6.00
Bullhorn, 1990, MOC..............$14.00
Buzzer, 1985, EX..............$12.00
Buzzer, 1985, MOC..............$70.00
Captain Grid Iron, 1990, NM..............$8.00
Carcass, 1994, MOC..............$10.00
Cesspool, Eco Warrior, 1991, MOC..............$10.00
Charbroil, 1988, NM..............$10.00
Chuckles, 1987, MOC..............$24.00
Chuckles, 1987, NM..............$15.00
Clutch, 1993, MIP..............$15.00
Cobra, 1983, MIP..............$100.00
Cobra Commander, 1984, hooded, NM..............$18.00

Cobra Commander, 1987, battle armor, MOC..............$28.00
Cobra Fire Fly, 1984, MOC..............$170.00
Cobra HISS w/driver, 1983, NM..............$60.00
Cobra Officer, 1982, MOC..............$130.00
Cobra Officer, 1983, EX..............$30.00
Cobra Stinger w/Officer, 1984, NM..............$35.00
Colonel Courage, 1993, MOC..............$12.00
Crazylegs, 1987, MOC..............$25.00
Crimson Guard, 1985, MOC..............$100.00
Crimson Guard Commander, 1993, NM..............$12.00
Crimson Guard Immortal, 1991, MOC..............$21.50
Croc Master, 1987, NM..............$12.00
Cross Country, 1993, NM..............$8.00
Cyber-Viper, 1993, NM..............$8.00
D.E.F. Cutter, 1992, NM..............$7.00
Deep-Six, 1984, NM..............$15.00
Deep Six, 1989, MOC..............$22.00
Destro, 1983, MOC..............$65.00

Crystal Ball, 1987, MOC, $18.00.

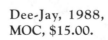

Dee-Jay, 1988, MOC, $15.00.

Dhalsim, Street Fighter, 1993, MOC $10.00
Dial-Tone, 1986, MOC..$45.00
Doc - Medic, 1983, NM..$30.00
Dr Mindbender, 1986, MOC..$35.00
Dr Mindbender, 1986, NM..$18.00
Drop-Zone, 1990, NM $17.00
Eco Warrior Ozone, 1991, EX $6.00
Eco Warrior Ozone, 1991, MOC................................$15.00

Low-Light,
1986, MOC,
$28.00.

Eels, 1985,
MOC, $55.00.

Mainframe, 1986, NM $18.00
Major Bludd, 1983, MIP $55.00
Mercer, 1991, MOC..$18.50
Monstro-Viper, 1993, NM $10.00
Mutt & Junkyard, 1984, MOC....................................$60.00
Ninja Force Banzai, 1993, MOC $15.00
Ninja Force Bushido, 1993, MOC................................$10.00
Ninja Force Dojo, 1992, MOC.....................................$28.00
Ninja Force Nunchuk, 1992, MOC $20.00
Outback, 1987, MOC..$24.00
Outback, 1988, NM..$18.00
Pedacon, Star Brigade, 1994, MOC $16.00
Psyche-Out, 1987, MOC...$25.00
Quick Kick, 1985, MOC..$100.00
Ranger-Viper, 1990, MOC..$19.00

Eels, 1985, NM...$28.00
Falcon, 1987, NM $17.00
Flint, 1985, MOC $85.00
Flint, 1985, NM $32.00
Footloose, 1985, MOC $50.00
Frag Viper, 1989, MOC $16.00
Free Fall, 1989, MOC $18.00
Fridge, 1986, mail-in, NM $18.00
Frostbite, 1985, MOC...$18.00
General Hawk, 1993, mail-in, MIP $12.00
Gnawgahyde, 1989, MOC...$15.00
Grunt, 1982, NM $30.00
Gung-Ho, 1983, NM $35.00
Gung-Ho, 1987, Version II, Marine Dress Blues, MOC ...$32.00
H.E.A.T-Viper, 1989, MOC $20.00
Hardball, 1988, NM..$12.00
Iceberg, 1986, NM $20.00
Incinerator, 1991, MOC...$18.00
Iron Granadier TARGAT, 1989, NM...........................$10.00
Iron Grenadier's Annihilator, 1989, NMOC $18.00
Jinx, 1987, MOC $28.00
Ken Masters, 1993, MOC..$10.00
Lady Jaye, 1985, MOC..$90.00
Lady Jaye, 1985, NM..$45.00
Law & Order, 1987, NM...$20.00
Leatherneck, 1986, MOC..$50.00
Low-Light, 1986, NM...$20.00

Red Star, 1991,
MOC, $20.00.

Raptor, 1987, MOC $24.00
Recoil, 1989, EX..$7.00
Recondo, 1984, MOC...................................$70.00
Repeater, 1988, MOC...................................$30.00
Ripcord, Halo Jumper, 1984, NM................$18.50
Ripper, 1985, EX $12.00
Road Pig, 1988, EX $8.00
Roadblock, 1984, MOC................................$60.00
Robo-Joe, Star Brigade, 1993, MOC $10.00
Rock 'n Roll, 1989, NM.................................$8.00
Ryu, Street Fighter, 1993, MOC....................$10.00
Scarlett, 1982, MOC $140.00
Sci-Fi, 1986, MOC $32.00
Sci-Fi, 1986, NM...$12.00
Scoop, 1989, MOC $20.00
Scrap Iron Cobra, 1984, NM $27.00
Shadow Ninja Lobotomaxx, 1994, MOC $15.00
Shipwreck, 1985, MOC...............................$100.00
Short-Fuze, 1982, NM $30.00
Sky Patrol Drop-Zone, 1990, MOC $25.00
Snake Eyes, w/Timber (wolf), 1985, MOC $160.00
Snake Eyes, w/Timber (wolf), 1985, NM $75.00
Sneak Peek, 1987, MOC $25.00
Snow Job, 1983, MOC..................................$65.00
Snow Serpent, 1985, MOC $60.00
Snow Serpent, 1985, NM $35.00
Snow Storm, 1994, MOC $15.00
Sonic Fighter Lampery, 1990, MOC $25.00
Spearhead & Max, 1988, NM $13.00
Spirit, 1984, MOC..$80.00
Stalker, 1982, MOC....................................$125.00
Stalker, 1982, NM..$35.00
Steel Brigadem 1987-94 mail-in, MOC $45.00
Storm Shadow, 1984, MOC.........................$170.00
Storm Shadow, 1984, NM $65.00
Sub-Zero, 1990, MOC $18.00
Techno-Viper, 1987, MOC............................$23.00

Tele-Viper, 1985, MOC................................$50.00
Tiger Force Road Block, 1988, NM...............$20.00
Tomax & Xamot, 1985, MOC $180.00
Topside, 1990, NM.......................................$14.00
Torch, 1985, EX...$15.00
Torpedo, 1983, NM......................................$30.00
Toxo Viper, 1988, MOC...............................$23.50
Toxo-Zombie, 1992, MOC $11.50
Tripwire, 1983, MOC $62.50
Tunnel Rat, 1987, MOC...............................$38.00
Wet Suit, 1986, NM $23.00
Wild Bill, 1992, MOC..................................$15.00
Wild Bill, 1993, NM $10.00
Zandar, 1986, NM.......................................$18.00
Zap, 1982, MOC..$90.00
Zarana, 1986, w/earring, MOC...................$115.00
Zartan, 1986, w/no earrings, MOC...............$30.00

VEHICLES AND ACCESSORIES FOR 3¾" GI JOE

Ammo Dump Unit, 1985, #6129-1, MIP $30.00
Arctic Blast, 1988, EX $12.00
Battlefield Robot Radar Rat, 1989, MIP $25.00
Bridge Layer (Toss 'N Cross), 1985, #6023, MIP $65.00
C.A.T Crimson Attack Tank, 1985, Sears, MIP............$110.00
Cobra Condor Z25, 1989, w/Aero-Viper Pilot, MIP.........$75.00

Cobra Night Raven S3P, 1986, MIB, $85.00.

Cobra Terror Dome, 1986, #6003, MIP..........................$325.00
Cobra Wolf w/Ice Viper, 1987, EX $15.00
Combat Jet Skystriker XP-14F, 1983, #6010, MIP..........$175.00
Crusader Space Shuttle, 1989, MIP $125.00
Dragon Fly XH-1, $4025, w/Wild Bill, MIP....................$135.00
Ghostrider X-16, Battle Corps, 1993, MOC $38.00
H.A.L Heavy Artillery Laser w/Grand Slam, 1982, #6052, MOC $110.00
Hovercraft, 1984 mail-in, MIP $40.00
Hovercraft Killer WHALE, 1984, #6005, MIP.................$150.00
Iron Granadiers AGP (Anti-Gravity Pods), 1988, w/Nulifier Pilot, MOC......................................$30.00
LCV Recon Sled, 1986, #6067, EX $14.00

Vipers, 1986, MOC, $32.00.

M.M.S. Mobile Missile System, 1982, #6054, MIP..........$65.00
Mauler MBT Tank, 1985, MIP $80.00
Mobile Command Center, 1987, #6006, MIP................$120.00
Mobile Command Center, 1987, #6006, NM $60.00
Motorized Battle Wagon, 1991, MIP...........................$30.00
Mountain Howitzer, 1984, #6125, EX $8.00
Polar Battle Bear, 1983, #6072, MIP.............................$30.00
Sky Patrol Sky Raven Set, 1990, MIB.............................$95.00
Skystriker XP-14F, w/Ace figure, MIP...........................$135.00
Swamp Skier w/Zartan, 1984, MOC.............................$130.00
Swamp Skier w/Zartan, 1984, NM $80.00

Thunderclap, 1989, MIB, $115.00.

Tiger Cat w/Frostbite, 1988, EX $20.00
Tiger Force Tiger Shark, 1988, MIP...............................$30.00
Transportable Tactical Battle Platform, 1985, NM $30.00
USS Flagg Aircraft Carrier, 1986, #6001, EX $160.00

Miscellaneous

Activity Box, 1965, complete, MIB, $125.00.

Adventure Locker, red footlocker, w/tray & inner lid illustration, NM+, A..$4,000.00
Air Manual, wide, EX, C6..$6.00
Backing Card, Takara, Gun Collection Series, EX, C6.....$15.00

Canteen, EX...$15.00
Catalog, Palitoy Retailer's, 1970, 34 pages, 10 showing Action Man, EX, A..$335.00
Coloring Book, Scramble, GI Joe Action Pilot, 1965, unused, EX, A..$55.00
Coloring Book, Whitman, 1965, Joes in various military garb, some coloring, EX+.....................................$18.00
Comic, Big Trapper Adventure, EX, C6............................$15.00
Comic, Secret Mission to Spy Island, EX, C6 ....$16.00
Comic Book, America's Movable Fighting Man, 1967, EX, C6..$5.00
Comic Book, Eight Ropes of Danger, EX, C6 ....$16.00
Comic Book, GI Joe, Vol 1 #18, 1952, Ziff-Davis, EX, A...$110.00
Comic Book, Mystery of the Boiling Lagoon, EX, C6 ......$17.00
Dog Tag w/Chain, NM...$20.00
Electric Drawing Set, Lakeside, 1965, NMIB...................$30.00
Flare Gun, EX..$8.00
Footlocker, wood, gr w/blank Name, Rank, Serial No fields, NM (EX rpr sleeve), A.....................................$250.00
Game, Capture of Hill 79, Hasbro, 1969, EXIB $60.00
Game, Let's Go Joe, Hasbro, 1966, EXIB $55.00
Instructions, Adventure Team Danger of the Depths, EX, C6..$12.00
Instructions, Revenge of Spy Shark Sonar Detector, EX, C6 ..$8.00
Knapsack, GI Joe US Army, Hassenfeld Bros/Hasbro, 1964, unused, NM+...$250.00
Manual, Counter-Intelligence, EX, C6 ....$25.00
Manual, Gear & Equipment, EX, C6.................................$3.00
Mess Kit, EX...$10.00
Official ID Bracelet, KMT Inc, 1982, rare, MOC.............$10.00
Package Ad Insert, Adventure Team, 1975, EX, C6 ....$8.00
Pinball Game, image of Frogman on litho cb w/plastic covering, Hasbro, 1965, 13x7", NM.............................$50.00
Puzzle, jigsaw, Whitman, 1965, beach landing, NMIB $25.00
Puzzle, jigsaw, Whitman, 1965, Joe in sea battle, NMIB...$25.00
Sticker Book, Action Man, Figurine Panini, 20 sticker sheets, unused, EX/NM, A $35.00
Sticker Book, Whitman, 1965, used, EX..........................$20.00
Trace & Color Book, Whitman, 1965, unused, NM.........$20.00
Walkie-Talkies, EX...$15.00

Guns

    Until WWII, most cap guns were made of cast iron. Some from the 1930s were nickel plated, had fancy plastic grips, and were designed with realistic details like revolving cylinders. After the war, a trend developed toward using cast metal, a less expensive material. These diecast guns were made for two decades, during which time the TV western was born. Kids were offered a dazzling array of toy guns endorsed by stars like the Lone Ranger, Gene Autry, Roy Rogers, and Hopalong Cassidy. Space guns made popular by Flash Gordon and Tom Corbett, kept pace with the robots coming from Japan. Some of these early tin lithographed guns were fantastic futuristic styles that spat out rays of sparks when you pulled the trigger. But gradually the space race lost its fervor and westerns ran their course, replaced with detective shows and sitcoms. Guns in disfavor is a recent phenomenon, not relevent before the mid-1980s. Since guns were meant to see a lot of action, most will show wear. Learn to be realistic when you assess condition; it's critical when evaluating the value of a gun.

Our advisor, Bill Hamburg says 'The Internet, and eBay in particular, continue to have a muting effect on the value of old toys, and cap guns are no exception. EBay has become a giant 'yard sale' of international scope. As a result, many once-hard-to-find items are presented in one grand marketplace.' He feels this is 'healthy for the hobby' as 'collectors can potentially snag that once-elusive cap gun for their collections, while at the same time, the values are lower than just a few years ago.' He goes on to say 'This doesn't mean prices are by any means overly depressed. They have just reached a new level of market value. Those truly 'rare' cap guns have actually increased in value as more collectors are competing to aquire them. All-in-all, it's a pretty happy and fun place out there for us cap gun collectors.'

American Cap Pistol, Kilgore, 1940s, 1st version, flying eagle on ivory-colored grips, 9", EX, A...................................$325.00
American Revolving Cap Pistol, Kilgore, 1940s, 2nd version w/PS cylinder, NP, eagle emb on ivory-colored grips, 9", VG..$200.00
Army .45 Cap Gun, Hubley, CI w/wht grips, EX $50.00

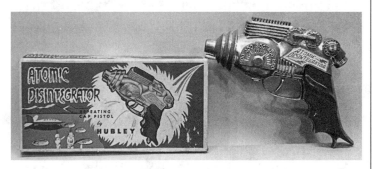

Atomic Disintegrater Repeating Cap Pistol, Hubley, 1950s, MIB, $350.00.

Atomic Ray Gun, MT, litho tin, b/o, 18½", EXIB..........$250.00
Automatic Repeater Paper Pop Pistol, Marx, 1930, PS, 7", unused, NM+IB $75.00
Baby Space Gun, Daiya, litho tin, 6", EXIB, A.................$45.00
Bang-O Cap Pistol, J&E Stevens, 1940s, NP w/horse heads & cowboys emb on blk grips, 7", unused, NM+IB, A ..$150.00
Big Game Rifle, Marx, unused, MIB $125.00
Big Horn Cap Gun, Kilgore, 1940s, 2nd version, CI w/PS revolving cylinder, brn grips, 9", VG, A $200.00
Bronco Six-Shooter Cap Pistol, Kilgore, 1950s, short barrel version w/mountian lion engraving, wht grip, 8", NMIB, A...$135.00
Buck'n Bronc Cap Guns w/Cowboy Double Holster Set, Russell, NMIB..$350.00
Champion Cap Pistol, Hubley, 1940s, lever opening, NP w/horse heads emb on wht grips, 9", EX, A $85.00

Colt .45 Cap Pistol, Hubley, NP w/wht grip, complete w/6 metal cartridges, 13½", NM+IB, A $250.00
Cork Shooting Submachine Gun, Marx, 1951, MIB......$175.00
Cowboy Cap Pistol, Hubley, 1950s, gold-tone finish, blk steer-head grips, 11½", rare, VG, A.................................$275.00
Cowboy Cap Pistol, Kenton, 1940s, 2nd version w/flat-sided plate, NP, dk reddish orange grips, 6½", rare, EX+, A $125.00
Cowboy Repeating Cap Pistol, Hubley, 1950s, NP, wht grips, 11½", unused, NMIB, A..$200.00

Cowboy 6-Shooter Water Pistol, Irwin, MIB, $75.00.

Coyote Cap Pistol, Hubley, 1960s, NP, checkered pattern on blk grips, unused, NM, A...$50.00
Crack Shot Dart Pistol, Wyandotte, 8", complete, VGIB, A...$65.00

Deputy Cap Pistol, Hubley, 1960s, allover nickel-plated finish, 10½", unused, MIB, $135.00. (Photo courtesy Smith House Toy and Auction Co.)

Derringer w/Dagger, Hubley, 1960s, NP w/red plastic push-out dagger, blk grips, 7", unused, NM, A $90.00
Dixie Cap Pistol, Kenton, 1930s, NP, checkered patterns on blk grips, red jewels, 6½", G+, A.................................$85.00
Duck Hunt Set, Japan, 1960s, litho tin, 18" L, missing darts o/w EXIB, A..$45.00

Flashy Ray Gun, TN, 1950s, b/o, 18", NMIB.................$200.00

Foxhole Tommy Gun Space Rifle, TN, 1950s, litho tin, b/o, 17", NMIB...$250.00

Hide-A-Mite Secret Holster and Nichols Cap Pistol, Carnell, MOC, $45.00.

Jupiter Signal Gun, Remco, 1950s, plastic, battery-operated, 9", EXIB, A, $165.00. (Photo courtesy Bertoia Auctions)

Little Burp Gurrilla Machine Gun, Mattel, NMIB........$125.00

Long Tom Cap Pistol, Kilgore, 1940s, 2nd version w/2-pc revolving cyclinder, ivory-colored grips, 10½", EXIB, A...$500.00

Mountie Repeating Cap Pistol, Hubley, 1960s, NP w/engraved grip, 7", NM+IB, A $45.00

Multi-Pistol 09, Topper Toys, NM+ (in case) $95.00

Padlock Cap Gun, Hubley, 1950s, barrel extends & fires when key is turned, silver finish, NM+ $75.00

Persuader Revolving Cap Pistol, Kenton, NP CI w/crisscross detail on grips, 6½", EX, A...$100.00

Pioneer Repeating Cap Pistol, Stevens, 1950s, NP, blk grips, 7½", rare, NMIB, A...$100.00

Ray Gun, Reliable Toys, 1950s-60s, air-pump, blk w/yel barrel, 8", NM+...$150.00

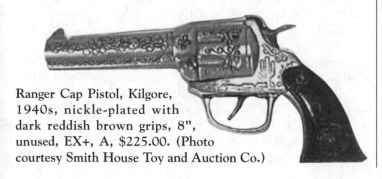

Ranger Cap Pistol, Kilgore, 1940s, nickle-plated with dark reddish brown grips, 8", unused, EX+, A, $225.00. (Photo courtesy Smith House Toy and Auction Co.)

Ric-O-Shay .45 Cap Pistol, Hubley, 1950s, revolving cyclinder, NP w/slick blk grips, 12", NM, A $125.00

Rodeo Cap Gun, Hubley, 1950s, nickel-plated with longhorn steer heads on white grips, 8", MIB, $100.00. (Photo courtesy Smith House Toy and Auction Co.)

Sharpshooter, Kilgore, 1940s, CI w/dk finish, rearing horses emb on wht grips, 6½", EX, A...$85.00

Sheriff Repeating Cap Pistol, J&E Stevens, 1940s, NP, blk horse head grips w/red jewels, 8", unused, NMIB, A.........$200.00

Shootin' Shell Cap Pistol, Mattel, EXIB.........................$300.00

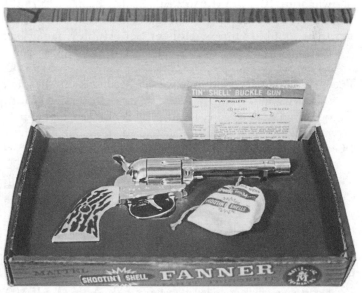

Shootin' Shell Fanner Cap Pistol, Mattel, MIB, $275.00.

Shootin' Shell Scout Rifle, Mattel, unused, MIB $350.00

Silver Eagle Tracer Machine Gun, w/automatic crank action, 21", EX+IB, A...$140.00

Space Cadet, Atomic Pistol (Flashlight), EXIB.............$200.00

Space Gun, Y, litho tin, 5", unused, MIB, A $75.00

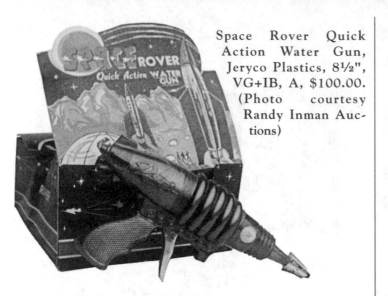

Space Rover Quick Action Water Gun, Jeryco Plastics, 8½", VG+IB, A, $100.00. (Photo courtesy Randy Inman Auctions)

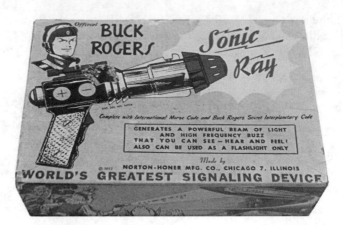

Buck Rogers Sonic Ray Gun, Norton-Horner, plastic, battery-operated, 7½", NMIB, $250.00.

Space Machine Gun, SY, 1950s, tin, friction, 12½", NMIB...$150.00

Space Super Jet Gun, KO, litho tin, 9", MIB.................$195.00

Spatz Cap Pistol, Lunde Arms Co, 1950s, walnut wood grips, 8", rare, VG, A..$100.00

Spinner Rifle, Marx, NMOC $125.00

Submachine Gun, see Cork Shooting Submachine Gun

Tetsujin Space Gun, TN, friction, mostly tin, 8¼", EX, A...$250.00

Tex Repeating Cap Pistol, Hubley, 1950s, lever opening, NP w/blk grips, 8", VG, A $50.00

Texan .38 Cap Pistol, Hubley, 1960s, NP, blk emb steer head on wht grips, 10½", MIB, A $300.00

Texan .38 Cap Pistol, Hubley, 1960s, NP, blk emb steer head on wht grips, 10½", VG+, A $75.00

Texan Double Gun & Holster Set, Halco, unused, MIB...$500.00

Texan Jr Double Gun & Holster Set, Hubley, fancy brn leather w/gold-pnt trim & silver studs, Hubley 8" guns, VG+, A..$195.00

Texan Pistol, Hubley, gold tone w/steer head emb on wht grips, star medallion, 9", EXIB, A $175.00

Warrior Cap Pistol, Kilgore, 1920s, NP, blk checked grips w/cross medallion, 9", G, A..$75.00

2 Guns in 1 Cap Pistol, Hubley, 1960s, w/2 interchangeable barrels, NP, wht grip w/red star, 8¼", NM+IB, A $150.00

CHARACTER

Agent Zero Radio-Rifle, Mattel, 1964, NMIB $80.00

Batman Freeze Ray Gun, Baravelli/Italy, plastic, b/o, unused, NMIB...$200.00

Bonanza Double Holster Set, engraved tan leather, 2 9" NP CI Leslie-Henry guns w/blk grips, lever openings, EX+, A $250.00

Buck Rogers Atomic Pistol, Daisy, bronze-colored PS, emits sparks, 9", EXIB, A $400.00

Buck Rogers Atomic Pistol, Daisy #U-235, 1936, metallic gold, 10", NMIB, A $500.00

Buck Rogers Pop Gun, Daisy, PS, name inscribed on hdl, 10", EX, A $200.00

Buck Rogers Rocket Pistol, Daisy, PS w/bl finish, emits popping sound, 9½", VG, A...$200.00

Buffalo Bill Repeating Cap Pistol, J&E Stevens, NP w/emb horse & heads & red jewels on wht grips, 8", NM+IB, A ..$175.00

Burk's Law Automatic Repeater Cap Pistol, Leslie-Henry, 1964, metal w/wht grip, 6½", NMOC....................................$50.00

Captain Gallant Foreign Legion Holster Outfit, Halco, complete with .45 cap gun, wallet, canteen, binoculars, etc., NMIB, $275.00. (Photo courtesy Smith House Toy and Auction Co.)

Cowboy King Revolving Cap Pistol, Stevens, 1940s, 2nd version, gold-tone, full-figure cowboy emb on wht grips, 9", VG, A $100.00

Dan Dare Planet Guns, Merit Toys, 1950s, complete, NMIB ..$150.00

Davy Crocket Double Gun & Holster Set, R&S Toys, tan & brn leather w/jeweled buckle, name & image on pockets, NMIB $200.00

Davy Crockett, Frontier Rifle, Marx/WDP, metal, 34", NMIB $175.00

Davy Crockett Cap Pistol, Marx, 1950s, pnt marbleized plastic w/working metal 'flintlock' hammer & trigger, 10½", NM+...........$75.00

Davy Crockett Pistol, Lacto, NP w/bronze-type floral grips, 10½", unused, NM+...$125.00

Day Crockett Cap Pistols, Schmidt, metal w/blk grips, 7½", EX, pr...$250.00

Detective Shoulder Holster (w/Gun), Rayline #36, 1950s, plastic & vinyl, complete w/wallet, bullets, etc, EXOC.....$125.00

Dick Tracy Jr Click Pistol #78, Marx, 1930s, aluminum, EX+ $65.00

Dick Tracy Power Jet Squad Gun, Mattel, 1962, 29", EX+ ..$75.00

Dragnet Cap Gun, Knickerbocker, 1955, diecast w/plastic hdls, 5½", unused, NMIB, A..$100.00

Flash Gordon Click Ray Gun, Marx, lithographed tin, 10", EXIB, $350.00.

G-Man Automatic Gun, Marx, pressed steel, w/up, 4", EX+, A $80.00

G-Man Gun, Marx, tin w/wood stock, w/up, 23" L, VG+, A ..$175.00

G-Man Gun (Siren Alarm Pistol), Marx, EXIB, $150.00. (Photo courtesy Smith House Toy and Auction Co.)

G-Man Machine Gun, Japan, 1950s, 18", unused, MIB ..$125.00

Gene Autry Cap Pistol, Kenton, 1940s, 3rd version, NP, red grips, 8", VG, A $150.00

Gene Autry Cap Pistol, Kenton, 1950s, short barrel, NP, dk orange grips, 6¼", EX+, A.......................................$125.00

Gene Autry Cap Pistol, Kenton, 1950s, short barrel, wht signature grips, 6½", VG, A $100.00

Gene Autry Cap Pistol, Leslie-Henry, 1950s, NP, transparent amber horse head grips, 11", unused, EX, A $175.00

Gene Autry Double Gun & Holster Set, blk leather w/silver studs & yel jewels, 2 Kenton 8½" CI guns w/wht grips, VG, A ..$325.00

Gene Autry Cap Pistol, Leslie-Henry, nickel-plated repeater with horse heads on white grips, 8", EXIB, $250.00.

Hi-Ranger Cap Pistol, J&E Stevens, 1940s, single shot, NP w/horse heads & cowboys emb on wht grips, 7½", NM+IB, A $125.00

Hopalong Cassidy Cap Pistol, Schmidt, blk grip w/emb wht silhouette bust image, unused, 9½", NM+ $275.00

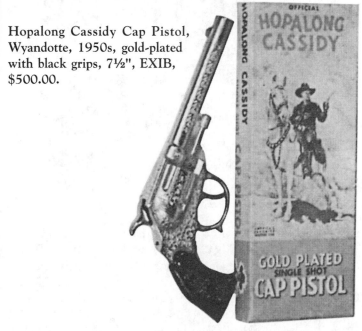

Hopalong Cassidy Cap Pistol, Wyandotte, 1950s, gold-plated with black grips, 7½", EXIB, $500.00.

James Bond 007 Multi-Buster Machine Gun, plastic, complete, 19", EXIB, $375.00.

Hopalong Cassidy Cap Pistol, Wyandotte, 1950s, NP, blk outlined bust image of Hoppy & signature on wht grips, 8", VG+, A...$195.00

Hopalong Cassidy Double Holster Set, Wyandotte, 1950s, blk leather w/silver studs & red jewels, 8" guns w/wht grips, G+.......$600.00

James Bond 007 Harpoon Gun, Lone Star, 1960s, EXIB ..$100.00

James Bond 007 Hideaway Pistol, Coibel, 1985, NMIB ...$75.00

Kit Carson Pistol, Kilgore, NP, lever opening, profile bust emb on blk grips, 9½", NM+IB, A................................$300.00

Lone Ranger Carbine Rifle, Leslie-Henry, plastic, shoots caps, 26", NMIB $350.00

Popeye Gun Set, Halco, 1961, complete double-gun and holster set, with diecut Popeye card, EX, $300.00. (Photo courtesy Randy Inman Auctions)

Lone Ranger Double Gun and Holster Set, Esquire, 1947, black leather with silver-look trim and red jewels, two Pony Boy cap guns, MIB (NOS), $300.00.

Roy Rogers Cap Pistol, Kilgore, 1950s, gold-tone finish with black horse-head grips, 8", VG, $175.00. (Photo courtesy Smith House Toy and Auction Co.)

Lone Ranger Official Outfit, Feinburg-Henry, 1938, leather holster w/compo gun, blk mask, red scarf, EXIB $200.00

Lone Ranger Pistol, Kilgore, dk metaql w/dk tan grips inscribed Hi-Yo Silver, 8½", EX..$275.00

Lone Ranger Single Gun & Holster Set, Esquire, blk leather w/silver-look trim & red jewels, Pony Boy cap gun, MIB...$250.00

Lone Ranger Sparkling Pop Pistol, Marx, 1938, metal, 7½", EXIB...$165.00

Lost in Space Helmet & Gun Set, Remco, 1966, EX+IB ..$500.00

Lost in Space Roto-Jet Gun, Mattel, 1966, 20", rare, EX+ ...$200.00

Man From UNCLE Napoleon Solo Gun Set, Ideal, converts into rifle, complete, NMIB...................................$500.00

Marshall Revolving Cap Pistol, Leslie-Henry, 1950s, NP, wht grips w/blk oval, 10½", EX+, A................................$150.00

Mirror Man Double Barrel Pop Gun, Takatoku, tin & plastic, 21", NMIB $100.00

Popeye Pirate Pistol, Marx/KFS, 1935, litho tin, 9", EXIB, A $500.00

Red Ranger, Wyandotte, 1950s, gold-tone finish, emb horseshoe & rope on red & gold swirl grips, 8½", VG, A $75.00

Red Ranger Jr Cap Pistol, Wyandotte, NP w/horse heads & star medallion on wht grips, 7½", NMIB, A.....................$75.00

Rin-Tin-Tin Cap Pistol, Actoy, copper-colored metal w/wht grips, 9", NM..$125.00

Roy Rogers Cap Pistol, Schmidt, emb Roy Rogers & RR, copper color metal grips w/red jewel, 9", EX.......................$250.00

Roy Rogers Double Gun & Holster Set, Classy, brn & wht leather w/silver pockets, jewels, 10" Schmidt guns, EXIB.......$600.00

Roy Rogers Revolving Cap Pistol, Leslie-Henry, 1950s, 2nd version, gold-tone finish w/blk grips, 9", VG+, A $190.00

Roy Rogers Shootin' Iron, Kilgore, simulated pearl hdl, 9", MIB $350.00

Stallion '38' Repeater Cap Pistol, Nichols, MIB, $150.00.

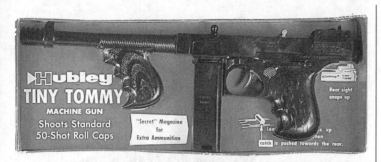

Tiny Tomy Machine Gun, Hubley, 10¼", MIB, $75.00.

Stallion .32 Six Shooter, Nichols, NP, 8", NM+IB, A....**$125.00**

Tom Corbett Cadet Space Gun, Marx, litho tin, 10", NMIB (box reads Official Space Patrol) **$300.00**

Tom Corbett Space Cadet Atomic Pistol Flashlite, Marx, plastic, 7½", NMIB..**$200.00**

Tom Corbett Space Cadet 1507-4 Official Space Gun, Marx, 1950s, tin& plastic, 21", NM+ **$275.00**

Wild Bill Hickok Cap Pistols, Leslie-Henry, Marshall Wild Bill Hickok on grips, 9½", EX, pr **$250.00**

Wild Bill Hickok Double Gun & Holster Set, 2-tone brn leather w/name in relief, 11" .44 cap pistols, EX.................**$450.00**

Wilma Deering's Gun & Holster (Buck Rogers), NM **$800.00**

Wyatt Earp Double Gun & Holster Set, Esquire, 1950s, blk leather w/silver-tone medallions & trim, wht grips, MIB.........**$400.00**

Wyatt Earp Double Gun & Holster Set, Esquire, 1950s, brn leather w/blk tooling & name, w/2 Actoy guns w/wht grips, EX, A...........**$225.00**

Zorro Cap Pistol, flintlock style, NM **$100.00**

2-Guns-In-1, Hubley, 1960s, with two interchangeable barrels, nickel-plated, white grips with red star, 8¼", NM+IB, $150.00. (Photo courtesy Smith House Toy and Auction Co.)

49-er Cap Pistol, J&E Stevens, 1940s, gold-tone finish, wht grips, 9", VG, A **$125.00**

EARLY CAST-IRON CAP SHOOTERS

The Early Cap Shooters listed are single shot and action unless noted otherwise.

Adams, unknown, 1890, ribbed hdl, no sz given, EX, A (Est: $1,000-$1,200) **$825.00**

Airplane, Arcade, monoplane w/pilot & revolving prop, NP, 4¼", VG, A (Est: $600-$800) **$725.00**

Alligator, unknown, Pat 1887, loop hdl, 3¼", VG, A (Est: $800-$1,000) **$1,760.00**

Bell Ringer, Pat May 22 1877, red pnt, multi-shot, dual action, 5", VG, A (Est: $800-$1,000) **$990.00**

Bomb, Lockwood, 1880, mk w/crescent moon, 4¼", G, A (Est: $200-$250) **$190.00**

Bulldog, Ives, ca 1887, bulldog's head on gun barrel, 4½", EX, A (Est: $250-$350) **$330.00**

Butting Match, Ives, 1995, 5", EX, A (Est: $700-$900)..**$1,045.00**

Cadet, Ideal (?), ca 1890, long barrel, 6½", VG, A (Est: $600-$800)..**$880.00**

Cat, unknown maker, 1882, marked Pat Mar 14 82 on looped tail handle, 4¾", EX, A (Est: $3,000.00 – $3,500.00), $5,775.00. (Photo courtesy Bertoia Auctions)

Chinese Must Go, Ives, 1880, 4¾", VG, A (Est: $700-$900)..**$880.00**

Clown & Mule Atop Barrel, Ives, 1882, 5¼", VG, A (Est: $800-$1,000) **$1,540.00**

Clown Seated on Keg Atop Barrel, Ives, 1892, 4", EX, A (Est: $800-$1,000) **$1,200.00**

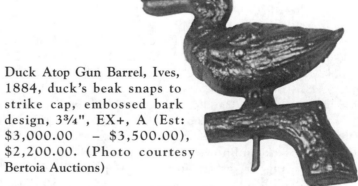

Duck Atop Gun Barrel, Ives, 1884, duck's beak snaps to strike cap, embossed bark design, 3¾", EX+, A (Est: $3,000.00 – $3,500.00), $2,200.00. (Photo courtesy Bertoia Auctions)

Filigree Cutout, unknown, 1872, blk pnt, firecracker, 4", EX, A (Est: $200-$300) **$165.00**

Five, see 5 at end of listings

Frontier, Ives, ca 1890, blk pnt, 5½", VG, A (Est: $250-$350)...**$250.00**

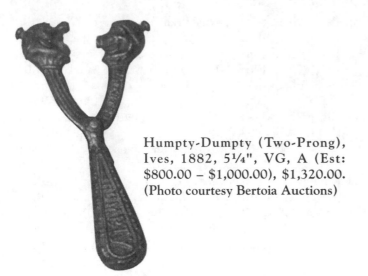

Humpty-Dumpty (Two-Prong), Ives, 1882, 5¼", VG, A (Est: $800.00 – $1,000.00), $1,320.00. (Photo courtesy Bertoia Auctions)

J&ES & Co, 1868, cut-out hdl, single rosette under emb name, no sz given, VG, A (Est: $400-$600) $410.00

Johnnie's Little Gun, Ives, 1888, 11", EX, A (Est: $600-$800) $440.00

Just Out, Ives, 1884, yel enameled chick comes out of egg, 5¾", VG, A (Est: $3,000-$3,500) $2,475.00

Lion, Ives, 1887, lion's head on gun barrel, 5¼", EX, A (Est: $250-$350) $220.00

Man on Alligator, Ives, 1883, painted mouth and hat, 5", EX, A (Est: $3,000.00 – $3,800.00), $3,850.00. (Photo courtesy Bertoia Auctions)

Monkey w/Coconut Atop Gun Barrel, J&E Stevens, 1890, pnt detail, 4¼", EX, A (Est: $600-$800).....................$1,100.00

Monkeys (2) Atop Gun Barrel, Lockwood, 1882, 4¼", VG, A (Est: $400-$500) $400.00

Moon Face Form w/Handle, unknown, 1890, pull string & nose snaps, red-pnt smile, 5½", VG, A (Est: $800-$1,000) $1,980.00

Pig on a Stick, unknown, mk Pat 1884, when string is pulled, pig strikes self in snout, 4" pig, VG, A (Est: $700-$900) $935.00

Seven, see 7 at end of lisitngs

Snap Shot Camera, Ives, 1893, 3¼", NM, A (Est: $1,200-$1,500)...$935.00

Surprise Box, Lockwood, 1882, when box is opened monkey strikes head on coconut, 3¼", EX+, A (Est: $2,000-$2,500) $3,025.00

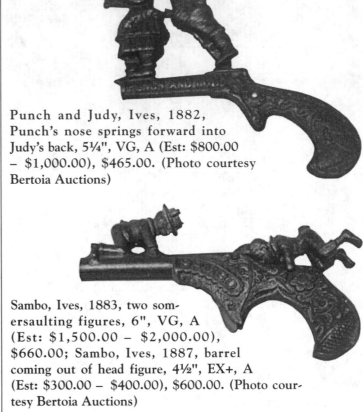

Punch and Judy, Ives, 1882, Punch's nose springs forward into Judy's back, 5¼", VG, A (Est: $800.00 – $1,000.00), $465.00. (Photo courtesy Bertoia Auctions)

Sambo, Ives, 1883, two somersaulting figures, 6", VG, A (Est: $1,500.00 – $2,000.00), $660.00; Sambo, Ives, 1887, barrel coming out of head figure, 4½", EX+, A (Est: $300.00 – $400.00), $600.00. (Photo courtesy Bertoia Auctions)

Tammany, Ives (?), 1890, animals' head w/open mouth on gun barrel, 4½", VG, A (Est: $300-$400).......................$520.00

Uncle Sam Says, Pat 1899 Franklin, Uncle Sam kicks man in rear atop gun barrel, crisscross handle, 4", EX, A (Est: $5,000.00 – $7,000.00), $8,800.00.

Washington, unknown, 1885, bust figure at end of axe, 3¾", EX+, A (Est: $300-$400) $825.00

Zip, J&E Stevens, 1890, 4⅞", EX+, A (Est: $250-$350) ..$135.00

5, J&E Stevens, 1875, 4", VG, A (Est: $150-$200) $65.00

7, J&E Stevens, 1879, 4", VG, A (Est: $100-$150) $100.00

1880, J&E Stevens, dbl-barrel, multi-shot, 4⅛", VG, A (Est: $200-$250) $165.00

BB Guns

Values are for BB Guns in excellant condition.

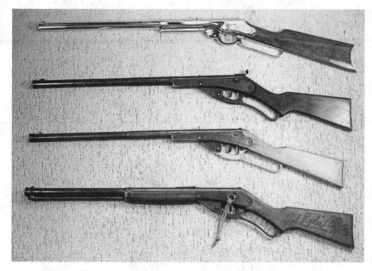

'1000' Shot Daisy, lever action, wood stock, $400.00; King No. 5536, lever action, wood stock, $35.00; Daisy No. 102, Model 36, lever action, wood stock, $50.00; Daisy No. 111 Model 40 'Red Ryder,' early model with iron cocking lever, $90.00. (Photo courtesy Jim Buskirk)

Daisy '0500 Shot Daisy,' lever action, wood stock $400.00
Daisy Action No 102, Model 36, lever action, wood stock, nickel finish $75.00
Daisy Model A, break action, wood stock......................$350.00
Daisy Model B, lever action, wood stock $100.00
Daisy Model B, lever action, wood stock, CI sight $200.00
Daisy Model C, break action, wood stock......................$300.00
Daisy Model H, lever action, wood stock.......................$125.00
Daisy Model 21, dbl barrel, plastic stock, 37", 1968 ....$400.00
Daisy Model 1938B, 'Christmas Story/Red Ryder,' $90.00
Daisy No 11, Model 29, lever action, wood stock.............$80.00
Daisy No 12, Model 29, lever action, wood stock.............$80.00
Daisy No 25, pump action, pistol grip, wood stock, many variations, ea..$65.00
Daisy No 25, pump action, straight stock, many variations, ea $75.00
Daisy No 30, lever action, wood stock $100.00
Daisy No 40, 'Military,' lever action, wood stock...........$200.00
Daisy No 40, 'Military,' lever action, wood stock, w/bayonet $500.00
Daisy No 50, 'Golden Eagle,' lever action, blk wood stock....$150.00
Daisy No 100, Model 38, break action, wood stock $80.00
Daisy No 101, Model 33, lever action, wood stock............$60.00
Daisy No 101, Model 36, lever action, wood stock............$50.00
Daisy No 103, Model 33, 'Buzz Burton,' nickel finish.....$250.00
Daisy No 103, Model 33, lever action, wood stock.........$300.00

Daisy No 104, Model 1938, dbl barrel, wood stock $650.00
Daisy No 105, 'Junio Pump Gun,' wood stock $250.00
Daisy No 106, break action, wood stock $40.00
Daisy No 107, 'Buck Jones Special,' pump action, wood stock..$150.00
Daisy No 107, pump action, plastic stock $30.00
Daisy No 108, Moel 39, 'Carbine,' lever action, wood stock ..$90.00
Daisy No 111, Model 40, 'Red Ryder,' aluminum lever $75.00
Daisy No 111, Model 40, 'Red Ryder,' plastic stock..........$50.00
Daisy No 140, 'Defender,' lever action, wood stock........$275.00
Daisy No 195, 'Buzz Burton,' lever action, wood stock ...$100.00
King No 1, break action, wood stock $200.00
King No 2, break action, wood stock...............................$65.00
King No 4, lever action, wood stock $250.00
King No 5, 'Pump Action, wood stock...........................$150.00
King No 5, lever action, wood stock $200.00
King No 10, break action, wood stock..............................$50.00
King No 17, break action, wood stock $175.00
King No 21, lever action, wood stock...............................$65.00
King No 22, lever action, wood stock...............................$70.00
King No 24, break action, wood stock $225.00
King No 24, lever action, wood stock...............................$75.00
King No 55, lever action, wood stock $85.00
King No 2136, lever action, wood stock $40.00
King No 2236, lever action, wood stock $40.00
King No 5533, lever action, wood stock $35.00
Markham/King 'Chicago,' break action, all wood...........$300.00
New King, repeater, break action, wood stock $250.00
New King, single shot, break action, wood stock...........$225.00

Related Items and Accessories

Holster on Belt, Dale Evans, unmk, 1950s, tan leather w/blk trim & silver-tone studs, VG, A................................$150.00
Holster Set, Wild Bill Hickok, unmk, blk & tan leather w/silver-tone studs, diamond detail, VG, A, pr $200.00
Spurs, Gene Autry, 1940s, NP, wht leather bootstraps w/red Autry signatures, EX, A, pr $115.00
Spurs, 1930s, NP, tan leather bootstraps w/silver studs & red jewels, EX, A, pr $85.00

'Posse' Shooting Galley, Wyandotte, complete, EXIB, A $135.00. (Photo Courtesy Bertoia Auctions).

Halloween

Halloween, the most colorful and fantasy filled of all the holidays is enjoying a popularity not known since the golden years of 1900 – 1920. Prices flucuated greatly because of the tremendous amount of reproductions and the fake pre-WWII items being made in Germany today and being sold as old. The folk art pieces made here in the U.S. have become some of the most desired items because production is so low and demand is great. Artists such as Jack Roads, Debee Thibault, Ram Pottery, the Millers, etc. cannot sufficiently supply the demand. Vintage pieces have leveled out in price because of so many investors cashing in on the high prices. Collectors will find this a welcome relief. As more collectors continue to discover the artistic as well as nostalgic joys of the holidays, more contemporary, mass-produced items have gone up in value, especially those that are character related. Artist-signed contemporary folk art seems to be the most coveted items that collectors are looking for.

For more information we recommend *Collectible Halloween; Halloween: Decorations and Games,* and *More Halloween Collectibles,* by our advisor, Pamela E. Apkarian-Russell, The Halloween Queen (H9).

See also Halloween Costumes.

Candy Container, composition, girl and cat playing 'peek-a-boo' around a pumpkin, 4", EX+, $800.00. (Photo courtesy James D. Julia, Inc.)

Candy Container, glass, policeman with pumpkin head, 1920s, 4", VG, A, $1,150.00. (Photo courtesy James D. Julia, Inc.)

Book, Dennison's Bogie Book, 1924, hardcover, 36 pages, VG, $125.00. (Photo courtesy Pamela Apkarian-Russell)

Book, Children's Party Book, 1940s, softcover, 23 pgs, EX...$35.00
Book, Hallowe'en Fun, Willis N Bugbee Co, hardcover, 104 pgs, EX..$45.00
Cake Decorations, 3 orange plastic figures w/blk accents, 1950s, 1½" to 1¾", EX+, set...$25.00
Candle Set, 5 orange jack-o'-lanterns w/wht candles, Gurley, 1950s, unused, NMIP (sealed)...................................$50.00
Candy Container, compo, blk cat coming out of pumpkin, toothy grin, bow tie, 6", VG, A.................................$375.00
Candy Container, compo, blk cat embedded in pumpkin w/back & tail protruding from top & back, toothy grin, 3" dia, G+, A....$290.00
Candy Container, compo, blk cat on spring on orange top hat hat, grinning face pnt on hat, 5", EX, A.................$465.00

Candy Container, compo, blk cat w/arched back, glass eyes, pnt open mouth & nose, leather ears, 8" L, VG+, A $718.00
Candy Container, compo, cat w/pumpkin face & stand-up tail, orange w/gr ears & legs, wht tail, holds candle, 4½", EX...........$2,350.00
Candy Container, compo, goblin & cat seated atop pumpkin, 5" T, G, A..$865.00
Candy Container, compo, pumpkin man seated atop tree stump, 4" T, VG, A $345.00
Candy Container, compo, watermelon, oblong w/rnd goggle eyes, teardrop nose & wide toothy grin, 4½", VG+, A $920.00
Candy Container, compo, witch holding broom, lt yel-orange head blk pnt-on glasses & gray hair, dk orange dress, 5", VG .$400.00
Candy Container, compo, witch in shoe, felt clothing, shoe w/pointy toe pointing upward, 4", EX, A $980.00
Candy Container, glass, bell-shaped goblin head, pnt features, lg loop on top, 1920s, VG, A $600.00
Candy Container, glass, witch w/pumpkin head, wearing glasses, rnd base, 1920s, 4¾", VG, A....................................$600.00
Change Purse, orange vinyl jack-o'-lantern form in blk top hat, zippered closure, w/chain, 1950s-60s, 5x3½", NM+ ..$50.00
Decoration, blk cat on jack-o'-lantern, die-cut cb, American, 1930s, 12", EX...$125.00

Decoration, cat face, die-cut cb, Germany, 1930s, 8", EX..$50.00

Decoration, cat face w/snarling look, die-cut cb, Dennison, 1920s, 16x18", EX+ $75.00

Decoration, figure set, 3-pc w/pumpkin man, cat & witch, molded plastic, orange w/blk detail, 1950s, 1½ to 1¾", EX......$25.00

Decoration, Halloween á Go Go Dancers, cardboard skeleton and girl in witch's hat, 14", unused, MIP, $55.00.

Decoration, jack-o'-lantern & crescent moon, die-cut cb, Germany, 1930s, 5" dia, NM $100.00

Decoration, scarecrow w/pumpkin head, die-cut cb w/shredded tissue paper arms & legs, Beistle, 1940s-50s, 28", NM $40.00

Doll, devil, silk-like stuffed cloth w/molded plastic face, 1950s, 29", NM+..$100.00

Figure, cat man, blk cloth-dressed figure w/orange pumpkin mask, squeeze body & mask moves to reveal cat's head, 7", G..$1,550.00

Figures, pumpkin man with nodding cat coming out of top of head, painted composition with cloth outfit, 13", VG, A, $1,680.00; veggie man astride nodding black flocked cat, 5x4", EX+, A, $1,500.00. (Photo courtesy James D. Julia, Inc.)

Figure, pumpkin girl, pnt compo w/cloth dress, w/up w/vibrating action, 6½", VG, A $230.00

Figure, pumpkin kids on seesaw, carved wood bodies w/cloth outfits, pumpkin heads, rocker base, 6x8", VG $2,040.00

Figure, pumpkin man, compo body & head w/glass eyes, pumpkin body w/leafy collar, gr arms & legs, 7", G+, A...$475.00

Figure, pumpkin man, felt-covered wood body, pull string & he rings hand-held bells, Germany, 10", VG, A $920.00

Figure, witch on broom, compo body w/orange & wht cloth outfit, blk hat, shoe & glasses, twig broom, 7", G+, A $230.00

Figure, witch on cat, cloth outfit & pnt hat, w/broom, blk felt cat w/glass eyes, Germany, 6", VG, A...................$1,035.00

Figure, witch on stick, cvd wood & compo w/cloth outfit, push body on hdl & arms move, 10", G, A $570.00

Game, Fortune Teller, Milton Bradley #4303, 1905, VGIB ..$75.00

Game, Fortune Telling Game, Whitman, 1930s, complete, EXIB..$75.00

Game, Halloween Party, Saalfield #702, unused, NM $125.00

Game, Witzi-Wits the Fortune Teller, Alderman Fairchild, 1928, EXIB..$100.00

Jack-in-the-Box, compositon pumpkin man pops up from wooden box with paper lithographed panels, 4", EX, $700.00. (Photo courtesy James D. Julia , Inc.)

Lantern, jack-o'-lantern, pulp, orange with black pilgrim-type hat, inserted paper features with round eyes and toothy grin, fiber hair, 6" tall, EX, $450.00. (Photo courtesy James D. Julia, Inc.)

Lantern, J-O-L, litho tin w/metal hdl, orange w/blk triangular eyes & nose, toothy grin, US Metal, 1940s, 5x5" dia, EX $50.00

Lantern, J-O-L, litho tin w/metal hdl, smiling face w/bats, owl & moon on back, US Metal Toy Mfg, 1940s, 5x6" dia, EX $60.00

Lantern, J-O-L, pnt glass J-O-L globe on blk metal base w/hdl, battery-op, Hong Kong, 1950s, 5", EX+ $50.00

Lantern, J-O-L, pulp, orange, inserted paper features, bl & wht eyes, toothy grin, wire hdl, 5", VG, A.......................$220.00

Lantern, J-O-L, pulp, orange, inserted paper features, cat eyes, open mouth w/tongue, wire hdl, Germany, 7", VG, A $220.00

Lantern, J-O-L, pulp, orange, pnt features, blk triangle eyes, toothy grin, blk top stem, Atco, 1950s, 4x5" dia, EX...$50.00

Lantern, J-O-L, pulp, orange, pnt features, rnd blk eyes & triangle nose, molded & pnt toothy grin, 1930s, 5" dia, VG+ ..$50.00

Lantern, skull, pulp, white with black airbrushed accents, inserted paper features, toothy grin, Germany, 5", VG+, A, $920.00. (Photo courtesy James D. Julia, Inc.)

Lantern, witch head on base w/hdl, tin & celluloid, blk & wht, b/o, 4½", NMIB, A...$175.00

Nodder, pumpkin man, cb body w/compo head & legs, blk top hat, cloth outfit, 10", VG, A $270.00

Nodder, pumpkin man, pnt compo, pumpkin head w/toothy grin wearing brn hat, brn suit & wht shirt, bl bow tie, 8½", G $150.00

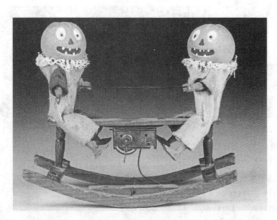

Mechanical Toy, pumpkin kids on seesaw, carved wood bodies with cloth outfits, pumpkin heads, rocker base, 6x8" long, VG, A, $2,040.00. (Photo courtesy James D. Julia, Inc.)

Noisemaker, pumpkin head, tongue moves as wooden noisemaker device is pressed, Germany, 1920s, 2½" dia, EX...........$50.00

Party Book, Weeny Witch, cb litho featuring franfurter promo of games, decorations, masks, Visking, 1950s, unused, EX+ ..$45.00

Party Favor, girl in pumpkin patch, celluloid & crepe paper, 1930s, 5", EX..$150.00

Plate, plastic with Halloween theme, McDonald's, 1995, M, $25.00. (Photo courtesy Pamela Apkarian-Russell)

Rattle, witch head, plastic w/wooden stick hdl, orange & blk, USA, 1950s, 12", EX+ $50.00

Roly Poly, black cat seated Buddha style atop orange base, celluloid, 4", G+, A, $375.00. (Photo courtesy James D. Julia, Inc.)

Roly Poly, pumpkin man w/felt & cotton clothing, red hat, 4½", VG, A $175.00

Sparkler, witch face, litho tin, Hale-Ness Corp, 1950s, 6½", NMOC...$50.00

Tambourine, litho tin w/textured paper top, festive border design, USA, 1940s, 6" dia, VG+..............................$50.00

Halloween Costumes

During the 1950s and 1960s, Ben Cooper and Collegeville made Halloween costumes representing the popular TV and movie characters of the day. If you can find one in excellent to mint condition and still in its original box, some of the better ones can go for over $100.00. MAD's Alfred E. Newman (Collegeville, 1959 – 1960) usually carries an asking price of $150.00 to $175.00, and The Green Hornet (Ben Cooper, 1966), upwards of $200.00. Earlier handmade costumes are especially valuable if they are 'Dennison-Made.'

Advisor: Pamela E. Apkarian-Russell, The Halloween Queen (H9)

Admiral Ackbar (Return of the Jedi), 1983, NMIB..........$25.00
Alf, Collegeville, MIB $35.00
Alfred E Newman, mask only, Ben Cooper, 1960s, NM ...$50.00
Aquaman, Ben Cooper, 1967, NMIB.........................$125.00
Archie, Collegeville, 1960, MIB $50.00
Barbarino (Welcome Back Kotter), Collegeville, 1976, MIB..$40.00
Barbie, TV Comic, Collegeville, 1975, MIB.................$55.00
Barbie Super Star Bride, Collegeville, 1975, MIP............$60.00
Batgirl, 1977, NMIB $35.00
Batman, Ben Cooper, 1969, NMIB $60.00

Batman (Super Heroes), Ben Cooper, 1973, EXIB, $35.00.

Beatles, any member, Ben Cooper, MIB, $450.00.

Beany & Cecil, Ben Cooper, 1950, NMIB.......................$50.00
Bewitched, Ben Cooper, 1965, MIB.............................$75.00
Boss Hogg (Dukes of Hazzard), Ben Cooper, 1982, MIB ..$40.00
Brady Bunch, any character, Collegeville, 1970s, MIB, ea from $25 to $35.00
C-3PO (Star Wars), Ben Cooper, 1977, MIB..................$45.00
Capser the Friendly Ghost, Collegeville, 1960s, EXIB $65.00
Charlie's Angels, Collegeville, 1976, any character, MIB, ea .$75.00
CHiPs, any character, Ben Cooper, 1978, MIB, ea $25.00
Cookie Monster, Ben Cooper, 1989, MIB.....................$30.00
Daffy Duck, Collegville, 1960s, EXIB..........................$25.00
Darth Vader, Ben Cooper, 1977, MIP.........................$25.00
Darth Vader, ESB, 1980, VGIB $35.00
Donny & Marie, Collegeville, 1977, MIB, ea $35.00
Droopy Dog, Collegeville, 1952, EXIB.........................$50.00
Electra Woman, Ben Cooper, 1976, MIB $60.00
Flipper, Collegeville, 1964, MIB.................................$80.00
GI Joe, Halco, 1960s, EXIB $65.00
Great Grape Ape, Ben Cooper, 1975, EXIB....................$50.00

Green Hornet, Ben Cooper, 1966, NMIB, $200.00.

Gumby, TV Comic, Collegeville, EXIB $65.00
Hardy Boys, Collegeville, 1978, MIB, ea..........................$45.00
He-Man, mask only, Mattel, M $10.00
Hong Kong Phooey, 1974, NMIB................................$20.00
HR Pufnstuf, Collegeville, 1970s, MIB $80.00
Hush Puppy, Shari Lewis Masquerade Costumes, Halco, 1961, EXIB..$60.00
Impossibles, Ben Cooper, 1967, NMIB..........................$50.00
Jeannie, TV Comic, Ben Cooper, 1974, MIB $65.00
Jimmy Osmond, Collegeville, 1977, MIB........................$20.00
Joker, vinyl, 1989, MIB...$35.00
King Kong, Ben Cooper, 1976, MIB..............................$95.00
Lambchop, mask only, Halco, 1961, NM $40.00
Land of the Giants, 1968, complete, EX+ $50.00
Laugh-In, Ben Cooper, MIP $40.00
Laverne & Shirley, Collegeville, 1977, MIB, ea................$30.00
Li'l Abner, Ben Cooper, 1957, NMIB $45.00

KISS, Gene Simmons, Collegeville, 1978, MIB, $100.00.

Li'l Tiger, 1960s, VGIB $25.00
Little Audrey, Collegeville, 1959, MIB $50.00
Lost in Space, silver flight suit, Ben Cooper, 1965, complete,
   EX $60.00
Luke Skywalker (Return of the Jedi), Ben Cooper, EXIB ..$125.00
Mandrake the Musician, Collegeville, 1950s, EXIB $85.00
Marie Osmond, 1977, NMIB..$35.00
Maverick, 1959, complete, EX...$50.00
Mickey Mouse, Ben Cooper, 1940s, w/vest, pants & gauze mask,
   VG (no box) $45.00
Miss Kitty (Gun Smoke), Halco, EXIB........................$125.00
Monkees, any member, Blan Charnas, 1967, NMIB, ea ..$200.00
Mork (Mork & Mindy), Ben Cooper, complete, NM $35.00
Morticia Addams, Ben Cooper, 1965, VG+IB.................$50.00
Morticia Addams, mask only, Ben Cooper, 1964, EX+.....$35.00

Mr. Spock (Star Trek), Ben Cooper, MIB, $50.00.

Raggedy Andy, Ben Cooper, 1965, MIB...........................$30.00
Reggedy Ann, Ben Cooper, 1965, MIB............................$30.00
Rin-Tin-Tin, 1950s, NMIB...$50.00

Sabrina the Teenage Witch, Ben Cooper, 1971, NMIB....$40.00
Samantha (Bewitched), Ben Cooper, 1965-67, VG $50.00
Six Million Dollar Man, Ben Cooper, 1965, MIB.............$40.00
Space: 1999, Commander Koenig, 1975, EXIB................$35.00
Spider-Man, Ben Cooper, 1972, NMIB.............................$35.00
Steve Canyon, Halco, 1959, NMIB $50.00
Superman, complete w/comic book, Ben Cooper, EXIB..$225.00
SWAT, Ben Cooper, 1975, NMIB $35.00
Tattoo (Fantasy Island), Ben Cooper, 1978, MIB $30.00
Top Cat, Ben Cooper, 1965, NMIB...................................$75.00
Underdog, Collegeville, 1974, NIB...................................$40.00
Winky Dink, Halco/Marvel Screen Ent, 1950s, EX..........$65.00

Witchiepoo, Collegeville, 1971, MIB, $75.00. (Photo courtesy Greg Davis and Bill Morgan)

Yoda (Empire Strikes Back), EXIB $35.00
Zorro, Ben Cooper #233/WDP, 1950s, scarce deluxe edition,
   EXIB..$100.00

Hartland Plastics, Inc.

Originally known as the Electro Forming Co., Hartland Plastics Ind. was founded in 1941 by Ed and Iola Walters. They first produced heels for military shoes, birdhouses, and ornamental wall decor. It wasn't until the late 1940s that Hartland produced their first horse and rider. Figures were hand painted with an eye for detail. The Western and Historic Horsemen, Miniature Western Series, Authentic Scale Model Horses, Famous Gunfighter Series, and the Hartland Sports Series of Famous Baseball Stars were a symbol of the fine workmanship of the '40s, '50s, and '60s. The plastic used was a virgin acetate. Paint was formulated by Bee Chemical Co., Chicago, Illinois, and Wolverine Finishes Corp., Grand Rapids, Michigan. Hartland figures are best known for their uncanny resemblance to the TV Western stars who portrayed characters like the Lone Ranger, Matt Dillon, and Roy Rogers.

Though in today's volatile marketplace, some categories of toys have taken a downward turn, Hartlands have remained strong. For more information we recommend *Hartland Horses and Riders* by Gail Fitch. See also Clubs, Newsletters, and Other Publications.

Alkine Ike, NM $150.00
Annie Oakley, NM $275.00
Bill Longley, NM $600.00
Brave Eagle, NM...$200.00
Brave Eagle, NMIB.......................................$300.00
Bret Maverick, miniature series.....................$75.00
Bret Maverick, NMIB....................................$600.00
Bret Maverick, w/coffeedunn horse, NM $500.00
Bret Maverick, w/gray horse, rare, NM $600.00
Buffalo Bill, NM $300.00
Bullet, NM $35.00
Bullet, w/tag, NM $150.00
Cactus Pete, NM...$150.00
Champ Cowgirl, very rare, NM $275.00
Cheyenne, miniature series, NM $75.00
Cheyenne, w/tag, NM $190.00
Chief Thunderbird, rare shield, NM $150.00

Cochise, NM,
$150.00.

Commanche Kid, NM $150.00
Dale Evans, bl, rare, NM $500.00
Dale Evans, gr, NM..$175.00
Dale Evans, purple, NM $250.00
Davy Crockett, NM $500.00
General Custer, NM $150.00
General Custer, NMIB $350.00
General George Washington, NMIB $175.00
General Lee, VG..$175.00
General Robert E Lee, NM............................$175.00
General Robert E Lee, NMIB........................$250.00
Gil Favor, prancing, very rare, NM $1,100.00
Gil Favor, semi-rearing, NM..........................$550.00
Hoby Gillman, NM $250.00

Jim Bowie, w/tag, NM....................................$250.00
Jim Hardy, EX+ $200.00
Jim Hardy, NMIB..$300.00
Jockey, NM $150.00
Josh Randle, NM...$650.00
Lone Ranger, Champ version, w/chaps, blk breast collar, NM $125.00
Lone Ranger, miniature series, NM $75.00
Lone Ranger, NM $150.00
Lone Ranger, rearing, NMIB $300.00
Lone Ranger, rearing, w/tag, NMIB $600.00
Matt Dillon, w/tag, NMIB.............................$300.00

Paladin, NMIB,
$350.00.

Rebel, miniature series, NM $125.00
Rebel, NM $250.00
Rebel, NMIB $1,200.00
Rifleman, miniature series, EX $75.00
Rifleman, NMIB $350.00
Ronald MacKenzie, NM...............................$1,200.00
Roy Rogers, semi-rearing, NMIB....................$600.00
Roy Rogers, walking, NMIB $300.00
Seth Adams, NM $275.00
Sgt Lance O'Rourke, NMIB...........................$300.00
Sgt Preston, NM $650.00
Tom Jeffords, NM $175.00
Tonto, miniature series, NM $75.00
Tonto, NM..$150.00
Tonto, semi-rearing, rare, NM.......................$650.00
Warpaint Thunderbird, w/shield, NMIB.........$350.00
Washington, EX+ $200.00
Wyatt Earp, NMIB..$250.00

STANDING GUNFIGHTERS

Bat Masterson, NMIB....................................$500.00
Bret Maverick, NM..$350.00
Chris Colt, NM..$150.00

Clay Holister, NM, $200.00.

Dan Troop, NM	$600.00
Jim Hardy, NM	$150.00
Johnny McKay, NM	$800.00
Paladin, NM	$400.00
Vint Bonner, NMIB	$850.00
Wyatt Earp, NM	$150.00

Hot Wheels

When introduced in 1968, Hot Wheels were an instant success. Sure, the racy style and flashy custom paint jobs were instant attention-getters, but what the kids loved most was the fact that the cars were fast! Fastest on the market! It's estimated that more than two billion Hot Wheels have been sold to date — every model with a little variation, keeping up with the big cars. The line has included futuristic vehicles, muscle cars, trucks, hot rods, racers, and some military vehicles. A lot of these can still be found for very little, but if you want to buy the older models (collectors call them 'Redlines' because of their red sidewall tires), it's going to cost you a little more, though many can still be found for under $25.00. By 1977, black-wall tires had become the standard and by 1978, 'Redlines' were no longer used.

A line of cars with Goodyear tires called Real Riders was made from 1983 until about 1987. (In 1983 the tires had gray hubs with white lettering; in 1984 the hubs were white.) California Customs were made in 1989 and 1990. These had the Real Rider tires, but they were not lettered 'Good Year' (and some had different wheels entirely).

Chopcycles are similar to Sizzlers in that they have rechargable batteries. The first series was issued in 1972 in these models: Mighty Zork, Blown Torch, Speed Steed, and Bruiser Cruiser. Generally speaking, these are valued at $35.00 (loose) to $75.00 (MIB). A second series issued in 1973 was made up of Ghost Rider, Rage Coach, Riptide, Sourkraut, and Triking Viking. This series is considerably harder to find and much more

expensive today; expect to pay as much as $600.00 to $1,000.00 for a mint-in-package example.

Though recent re-releases have dampened the collector market somewhat, cars mint and in the original packages are holding their values and are still moving well. Near mint examples (no package) are worth about 50% to 60% less than those mint and still in their original package, excellent condition about 65% to 75% less.

For more information we recommend *Hot Wheels, The Ultimate Redline Guide, Second Edition,* and *Hot Wheels, The Ultimate Redline Guide, Volume 2,* both by Jack Clark and Robert P. Wicker (Collector Books).

Advisor: Steve Stephenson (S25)

Aeroflash, 1990s, blk walls, purple, Gleam Team edition, MIP	$12.00
Air France Delivery Truck, 1990, blk walls, wht, M (International box)	$15.00
Alive '55 Chevrolet Station Wagon, 1973, redline, plum, EX+	$200.00

Alive '55 Chevrolet Station Wagon, 1974, redline, light blue with yellow tampo, NM, $175.00. (Photo courtesy Jack Clark and Robert P. Wicker)

American Hauler, 1976, redline, dk bl w/red & bl tampo, M.	$40.00
American Tipper, 1976, redline, red, M	$55.00
AW Shoot, 1976, redline, olive, NM+	$40.00
Backwoods Bomb, 1975, redline, lt bl, NM+	$58.00
Baja Bruiser, 1974, redline, orange, metal base, NM	$55.00
Beatnik Bandit, 1968, redline, creamy pk, VG	$75.00
Beatnik Bandit, 1968, redline, ice bl w/wht interior, NM	$95.00
Beatnik Bandit, 1968, redline, metallic aqua, M	$60.00
Blown Camaro, 1980s, blk walls, turq, MOC	$10.00
Bone Shaker, 1973, redline, wht, orig yel driver w/flesh face, goggles & yel helmet, training wheels, rare, M	$400.00
Boss Hoss, 1971, redline, chocolate brn, rare, MOC	$550.00
Boss Hoss, 1971, redline, metallic aqua, #2 tampo, M	$150.00
Boss Hoss, 1971, redline, olive w/blk roof, NM	$200.00
Breakaway Bucket, 1974, redline, bl, M	$100.00
Bugeye, 1971, redline, lt metallic gr w/cream interior, EX +	$24.00
Bye Focal, 1971, redline, lt gr, M	$275.00
Bywayman, 1979, blk walls, lt bl, NM+	$15.00
Cadillac Seville, 1983, blk walls, metal-flake gold, M	$5.00
Camaro Z-28, 1984, blk walls, metal-flake red, MIP	$10.00
Captain America, 1970, blk walls, red, wht & bl, NM	$20.00

Captain America Hot Bird, 1979, red, wht & bl, NM......$25.00
Carabo, 1970, redline, yel, NM+ $48.00
Cargoyle, 1986, blk walls, orange, M....................................$5.00
CAT Dump Truck, 1982, blk walls, yel, MIP $8.00
Cement Mixer, 1970, redline, metallic olive w/cream interior, complete, EX+ $35.00
Chaparral 2G, 1969, redline, metallic orange w/blk interior, NM $30.00
Chapparal 2G, 1969, redline, yel, NM+.............................$35.00
Chevy Stocker, metal-flake red, MIP $15.00
Chief's Special, 1976, redline, red w/red bar, NM............$45.00
Choppin' Chariot, 1972, orange, orig bl driver w/full-face mask, wht helmet, missing training wheels, NM $50.00
Classic '31 Ford Woody, 1969, redline, lt metallic magenta w/cream interior, smooth blk roof, NM.....................$65.00
Classic '31 Ford Woody, 1969, redline, orange, M............$45.00
Classic '31 Vicky, 1994, blk walls, metal-flake pk, M (NM card)..$8.00

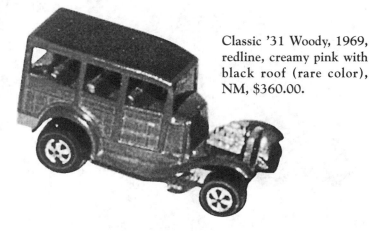

Classic '31 Woody, 1969, redline, creamy pink with black roof (rare color), NM, $360.00.

Classic '32 Ford Vicky, 1968, redline, rose w/wht interior, NM+ ..$48.00
Classic '35 Caddy, 1989, wht walls, silver w/beige interior, pk fenders, NM $25.00
Classic '57 T-Bird, 1969, redline, metallic red w/cream interior, EX+ $35.00

Classic Nomad, 1970, redline, red, MIP (unpunched), $225.00.

Classic Cobra, 1990s, blk walls, red, MOC $8.00
Classic Cord, 1971, redline, bl, NM+ $250.00
Classic Nomad, 1970, redline, bl, M $85.00
Classic Nomad, 1970, redline, magenta, NM+ $135.00
Cockney Cab, 1971, redline, bl, NM+ $120.00
Cool One, 1976, redline, plum w/yel & wht tampo, NM+ ...$55.00
Corvette Stingray, 1988, blk walls, yel w/mc tampo, MOC ..$12.00
Custom AMX, 1969, redline, bl, NM+ $85.00
Custom AMX, 1969, redline, yel, NM+.............................$90.00
Custom Baracuda, 1968, redline, metallic aqua, NM $100.00
Custom Camaro, 1968, redline, chocolate brn, rare, NM ...$180.00
Custom Charger, 1969, redline, gold, M $350.00
Custom Charger, 1969, redline, red, MIP $650.00
Custom Continental Mark III, 1969, redline, gold, NM+ ...$65.00

Custom Continental Mark III, 1969, redline, hot pink, NM, $225.00.

Custom Corvette, 1968, redline, gold w/wht interior, NM+...$160.00
Custom Corvette, 1968, redline, rose w/wht interior, NM+...$185.00
Custom Cougar, 1968, redline, metallic orange, MIP.....$400.00
Custom Eldorado, 1968, redline, olive w/wht interior, NM+...$100.00
Custom Eldorado, 1968, redline, yel w/wht interior, NM+ ...$75.00
Custom Firebird, 1968, redline, metallic gr w/blk roof, cream interior, NM...$75.00
Custom Firebird, 1968, redline, red w/brn interior, M....$100.00
Custom Fleetside, 1968, redline, lt purple, NM+ $125.00
Custom Mustang, 1968, redline, metallic bl, rare louvered rear window, EX...$350.00
Custom Mustang, 1968, redline, metallic red w/red interior, rare, open scoops, EX...$330.00
Custom Mustang, 1968, redline, red w/red interior, NM+ ...$135.00
Custom Mustang, 1968, redline, ice bl, NM $400.00
Custom Police Cruiser, 1969, redline, blk & wht w/cream interior, opaque light, rare prototype w/blk fenders, EX+ $300.00
Custom T-Bird, 1968, redline, gold, NM $600.00
Custom Volkswagen, 1968, orange, NM+.........................$75.00
Custom Volkswagen, 1968, redline, bl, M $60.00
Custom Volkswagen, 1968, redline, purple (rare color), EX ...$100.00
Demon, 1970, redline, olive w/wht interior, NM+ $45.00
Demon, 1994, blk walls, metal-flake bl, Toy Fair limited edition, scarce, M..$150.00
Double Vision, 1973, redline, lt gr, NM+ $180.00
Dump Truck, 1970, redline, metallic bl w/brn bed & yel dump, blk interior, EX $25.00
Dumpin' A, 1983, blk walls, gray w/chrome motor, M $50.00
Dumpin' A, 1983, blk walls, gray w/gray motor, M...........$15.00

Dune Daddy, 1973, redline, lt gr, NM+ $90.00
El Rey Special, 1974, redline, dk bl, NM+.....................$315.00
El Rey Special, 1974, redline, gr w/yel & orange #1 tampo, NM+..$55.00
Emergency Squad, 1982, blk walls, red, MIP..................$10.00
Evil Weevil, 1971, redline, red, #6 tampo, NM $110.00
Ferrari 312P, 1970, redline, red, M $45.00
Ferrarri, 312P, 1973, redline, pk, NM+ $400.00
Ferrari 312P, 1974, redline, red w/blk interior, bl & wht tampo, M (M Flying Colors card) $100.00
Ferrari 512S, 1972, redline gold, NM+ $125.00
Fiat Ritmo, France, 1983, blk walls, gray w/brn interior, blk tampo, M (EX card)...$30.00
Fire Eater, 1977, redline, red, M $20.00
Fire Eater, 1977, redline, red w/yel & blk tampo, EX+ $15.00
Ford Aerostar, 1991, blk walls, wht, M (NM International box)..$10.00
Ford J-Car, 1968, redline, metallic lavender w/blk interior, NM..$150.00
Ford J-Car, 1968, redline, wht, NM+ $65.00
Formula Fever, 1983, blk walls, yel, MIP $8.00
Formula PACK, 1976, blk walls, blk orange & yel tampo, M (EX+ Flying Colors card)..$50.00
Formula PACK, 1976, redline, blk w/orange & yel tampo, M (NM rare Japanese box) $60.00
Formula 5000, 1976, redline, wht w/bl & red #76 tampo, M (NM Flying Colors card) $50.00

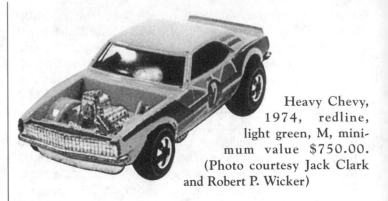

Heavy Chevy, 1974, redline, light green, M, minimum value $750.00. (Photo courtesy Jack Clark and Robert P. Wicker)

Heavy Chevy, 1970, redline, purple & wht, NM............$135.00
Heavy Chevy, 1974, redline, yel, NM+..........................$110.00
Heavyweight Cab, redline, metallic gr w/cream interior, no trailer, EX+ $5.00
Heavyweight Dump Truck, 1970, redline, bl, M $50.00

Funny Money, 1974, redline, plum, M, minimum value $80.00. (Photo courtesy Jack Clark and Robert P. Wicker)

Heavyweight S'Cool Bus, 1971, redline, yellow, NM+, minimum value $200.00. (Photo courtesy Jack Clark and Robert P. Wicker)

Heavyweight Scooper, 1971, redline, bl, NM+...............$135.00
Heavyweight Snorkle, 1971, redline, purple, NM+........$125.00
High Tailer, 1971, orange, orig bl driver w/wht full-face helmet, training wheels, M $75.00
Hiway Robber, 1973, redline, gr w/blk interior, NM $150.00
Hiway Robber, 1973, redline, red, NM+ $135.00

GMC Motor Home, Hong Kong, 1977, redline, orange w/bl, wht & yel tampo, rare, EX..$300.00
Grass Hopper, 1971, redline, metallic gr w/blk interior, scarce color, NM+ $60.00
Grass Hopper, 1975, redline, lt gr w/blk plastic base, orange & bl tampo, no engine exposed, scarce, NM.....................$90.00
Gremlin Grinder, 1975, redline, gr, NM+ $45.00
Gremlin Grinder, 1976, redline, Super Chrome, red, gr & blk tampo, M (EX rare Japanese box) $55.00
Gulch Stepper, 1985, blk walls, yel w/tan roof, mc tampo, MIP $6.00
Gulch Stepper, 1987, blk walls, red, MIP $18.00
Gun Slinger, 1975, redline, lt olive, M............................$55.00
Hairy Hauler, 1971, redline, lt gr, NM+ $40.00
Hairy Hauler, 1971, redline, magenta, NM+ $55.00

Indy Eagle, 1969, redline, orange, MIP (with button), minimum value $80.00.

Hot Heap, 1968, redline, orange, NM+ $45.00

Hummer, 1990s, blk walls, beige camouflage, MOC.........$10.00

Ice T, 1971, redline, lt yel, M...$50.00

Ice T, 1971, redline, yel w/blk interior, EX.......................$20.00

Incredible Hulk, blk walls, yel w/mc tampo, 2 rear windows, 1979, NM...$22.00

Indy Eagle, 1969, redline, aqua w/blk interior, NM+.......$30.00

Indy Eagle, 1969, redline, metallic gr w/blk interior, orig decal, NM $25.00

Inferno, 1976, redline, yel, M $60.00

Inside Story, 1980, blk walls, yel, MIP..............................$10.00

Jet Threat, 1971, redline, metallic yel, M $90.00

King Kuda, 1970, redline, Club Car, chrome, complete, NM $72.00

Lamborghini Diablo, red, MIP..$12.00

Light My Firebird, 1970, redline, metallic bl, complete, NM....$60.00

Lola GT-70, redline, metallic brown, back lifts to show engine, M, from $35.00 to $40.00.

Lola GT-70, 1969, metallic pk (rare color), NM $450.00

Lotus Turbine, 1969, redline, orange, NM+ $27.00

Mantis, 1970, redline, metallic gr, NM $35.00

Mantis, 1970, redline, metallic yel w/cream interior, NM+....$35.00

McClaren M6A, 1969, redline, antifreeze, M $60.00

Mercedes C-11, 1972, redline, metallic bl w/cream interior, NM $135.00

Mercedes SL, 1991, blk walls, M (NM International card)..$10.00

Mercedes 540K, blk, MIP $10.00

Mighty Maverick, 1970, redline, aqua, MOC................$200.00

Mighty Maverick, 1970, redline, metallic pk, rare, NM ...$150.00

Minitrek, 1983, blk walls, wht, NM+.................................$65.00

Mod Quad, 1970, redline, lt metallic gr w/blk interior, M ...$40.00

Mod Quad, 1970, redline, magenta, scarce, M.................$120.00

Mod Quad, 1970, redline, metallic yel w/blk interior, M...$40.00

Mongoose Funny Car, 1970, redline, red, NM+ $75.00

Mod Quad, 1970, redline, metallic magenta, M, $20.00.

Mongoose Rear Engine Dragster, 1972, redline, bl, clear front wheels, MOC..$550.00

Moving Van, 1970, redline, metallic gr w/blk interior & gray trailer, NM $55.00

Mutt Mobile, 1971, redline, magenta, NM+ $200.00

Mutt Mobile, 1971, redline, metallic aqua, complete, NM ...$50.00

Neet Streeter, 1977, blk walls, lt bl w/blk interior, mc tampo, M $30.00

Nitty Gritty Kitty, 1970, redline, metallic bl, complete, EX+ ...$28.00

Nitty Gritty Kitty, 1970, redline, metallic brn, NM $120.00

Noodlehead, 1971, redline, metallic magenta w/cream interior, scarce, EX..$55.00

Old Number 5, 1982, blk walls, red w/louvers, NM+..........$5.00

Old Number 5, 1982, blk walls, red w/out louvers, NM+ .$20.00

Olds 442, 1971, redline, metallic bl w/cream interior, rare, NM...$550.00

Omni 024, 1981, blk walls, gray, MIP................................$8.00

Open Fire, 1972, redline, magenta, NM+ $225.00

Packin' Pacer, 1980, blk walls, orange, MIP.....................$15.00

Paddy Wagon, 1970, redline, dk bl w/gold letters, M (NM card)..$75.00

Paramedic, 1975, redline, yel w/red tampo, MIP..............$65.00

Peeping Bomb, 1970, redline tires, metallic orange, M $50.00

Peterbilt Dump Truck, 1985, blk walls, metal-flake bl, M (NM Workhorses card) $7.00

Pit Crew, 1971, redline, wht w/cream interior, complete w/8 stickers, NM...$100.00

Pit Crew Car, 1971, redline, wht w/gray interior, NM+...$115.00

Poison Pinto, 1976, redline, lt gr w/yel, blk & wht tampo, NM..$30.00

Porsche Targa Christmas Car, 1996, blk walls, red, w/Santa & passenger, M (NM card) $20.00

Porsche 911, 1976, redline, Super Chromes, M $35.00

Porsche 917, 1970, redline, yel, NM+ $45.00

Porsche 959, 1991, blk walls, yel, Getty promotion, M (M bag) $5.00

Pro Circuit #2, 1993, blk walls, wht w/Texaco logo, gray Pro Circuit Indy wheels, NM+ $6.00

Purple Passion, 1990, ww walls, purple w/2-tone gr tampo, NM..$11.00

Python, 1968, redline, metallic blue with black top, M, $45.00.

Python, 1968, redline, yel w/wht interior, NM+..............$55.00

Rapid Transit School Bus, 1984, blk walls, yel, M (NM Team Bus card) $7.00

Ranger Rig, 1975, redline, dark green, M, $55.00. (Photo courtesy Jack Clark and Robert P. Wicker)

Red Baron, 1970, redline, metallic red w/blk interior, sharp point, EX $24.00

Rip Cord, 1973, bl, orig lime driver w/wht full-face helemt, training wheels, M (EX card) $375.00

Road King Truck, 1974, redline, yel, w/orig trailer, rear, EX+ ...$480.00

Rock Buster, 1976, redline, yel w/mc tampo, NM..............$35.00

Rocket Bye Baby, 1971, redline, aqua, NM+ $68.00

Rocket Bye Baby, 1973, redline, red, Shell promotion, MIB....$125.00

Sand Crab, 1970, redline, metallic pk w/blk interior, EX+....$75.00

Sand Crab, 1970, redline, yel, NM+ $30.00

Sand Drifter, 1975, redline, yel w/orange & magenta tampo, EX $45.00

Seasider, 1970, redline, metallic yel w/blk interior, NM+ ...$90.00

Shadow Jet, yel w/maroon accents, MIP $10.00

Sheriff Patrol, 1988, blk walls, blk, MIP...........................$10.00

Short Order, 1971, redline, bl (rare color), MIP, minimum value $250.00

Short Order, 1971, redline, gold w/blk interior, M............$80.00

Short Order, 1973, redline, dk bl, NM+ $110.00

Side Kick, 1971, redline, metallic gr w/chrome slide-out cockpit, Larry Wood concept design, NM $100.00

Side Kick, 1972, redline, magenta, NM+.........................$150.00

Silhouette, 1968, redline, lt gr, M $165.00

Six-Shooter, 1971, redline, magenta, EX $125.00

Snake, 1970, redline, yel, NM+......................................$75.00

Snake 2, 1971, redline, wht, NM $65.00

Snorkel, 1971, redline, wht w/blk interior, M.................$250.00

Special Delivery, 1971, redline, lt bl, M $70.00

Spider-Man, 1979, blk walls, blk, M................................$15.00

Spoiler Sport, 1977, redline, gr w/blk, yel & dk red tampo, scarce, M $50.00

Splittin' Image, 1969, redline, metallic green, M, $30.00.

Sting Rod, 1988, blk walls, olive, MIP $12.00

Street Beast, 1988, blk walls, red, MIP............................$8.00

Street Eater, 1975, redline, yel w/red & orange flame tampo, M (NM Flying Colors card) $300.00

Street Snorter, 1973, redline, fluorescent pk, EX............$195.00

Strip Teaser, 1973, redline, fluorescent pk, Shell promotion, complete, MIB $200.00

Sugar Caddy, 1971, redline, metallic gr, complete, NM....$70.00

SWAT Van Scene, 1979, blk walls, dk bl, VG $20.00

Sweet 16, 1973, redline, dk bl w/blk interior, EX+ $140.00

Sweet 16, 1973, redline, fluorescent lime gr, M $225.00

T-Bird Stocker, 1996, blk walls, red & wht, Bill Elliot, Kellogg's promotion, M (EX+ card) $18.00

T-4-2, 1971, redline, magenta, EX..................................$95.00

T-4-2, 1971, redline, metallic gr (scarce color), M...........$85.00

T-4-2, 1971, redline, metallic yel, NM $72.00

Team Trailer, 1971, redline, metallic red w/cream interior, NM $90.00

Thor Van, 1979, blk walls, yel, M....................................$12.00

Thrill Drivers Torino, 1977, blk walls, wht, NM $95.00

Thunderbird Stocker, 1984, blk walls, wht, MIP $35.00

TNT Bird, 1970, redline, metallic bl w/#3 tampo, NM $65.00

Top Eliminator, 1974, redline, bl w/orange, gr & yel tampo, MOC..$150.00

Torero, 1969, redline, metallic aqua w/cram interior, NM ...$24.00

Tough Customer, 1975, redline, olive w/wht Army tampo, MIP...$75.00

Tow Truck, 1970, redline, metallic gr w/blk interior, NM...$45.00

Turbo Mustang, 1982, blk walls, red, MIP.......................$10.00

Turbofire, 1970, redline, metallic red w/cream interior, NM ...$25.00

Turismo, 1983, blk walls, yel, MIP...................................$10.00

Twin Mill, 1973, redline, fluorescent pk, Shell promotion, MIB...$175.00

Vega Bomb, 1975, redline, orange w/red, yel & bl tampo, complete, NM...$60.00

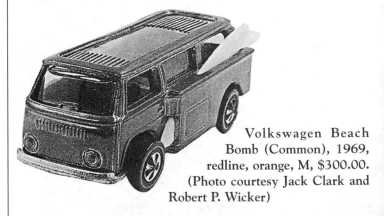

Volkswagen Beach Bomb (Common), 1969, redline, orange, M, $300.00. (Photo courtesy Jack Clark and Robert P. Wicker)

Volkswagen Bug, 1974, redline, orange w/blk, yel & gr tampo, M $80.00

Waste Wagon, 1971, redline, metallic aqua, NM $80.00

Whip Creamer, 1970, redline, metallic pk w/blk interior, NM....$80.00

Winnipeg, 1974, redline, yel w/bl & orange tampo, M...$130.00

'31 Doozie, 1986, wht walls, maroon w/red-brn fenders, MIP..$12.00

'32 Ford Delivery, 1989, blk walls, yel w/orange & magenta tampo, M..$10.00
'56 Flasher Pickup, 1990s, blk walls, turq, MIP..................$5.00
'57 Chevy, yel w/flame accents, 1984, MIP.....................$20.00
'65 Mustang Convertible, red w/tan interior, MIP...........$10.00
'65 Mustang Convertible, 1980s, blk walls, lt bl w/blk interior, MIP..$30.00

MISCELLANEOUS

Autorama, 1970, MIB, $250.00. (Photo courtesy Jack Clark and Robert P. Wicker)

Button, Beatnik Bandit, metal, NM, $8.00.

Action City, 1969, yel, EX+...$50.00
Button, Cement Mixer, metal, NM+............................$5.00
Button, Classic '31 Ford Woody, metal, NM................$5.00
Button, Custom Barracuda, metal, NM.........................$5.00
Button, Jet Threat, plastic, M.....................................$10.00
Button, Racer Rig, metal, NM+...................................$8.00
Button, S-Cool Bus, plastic, rare, NM.........................$10.00
Button, Short Order, plastic, M....................................$4.00
Button, Strip Tease, plastic, NM+................................$4.00
Case, 12-car, 1969, yel w/red car on front, NM...........$20.00
Case, 12-car pop-up, 1968, orange w/name on front, cars on back, EX...$35.00

Case, 24-car, 1969, yel w/wht & bl cars on front, adjustable, EX...$30.00
Case, 24-car, 1975, bl w/wht trays, Porsche 917, Super Van & Emergency Squad on front, NM...............................$40.00
Case, 48-car, 1969, yel, adjustable, NM.....................$40.00
Case, 72-car, 1970, blk w/Snake & Mongoose on front, EX..$40.00
Chopcycles, Mighty Zork, metallic gr, M (NM card).....$115.00
Chopcycles, Rip Rider Set, MOC.................................$75.00
City Machines, 1982, set of 6, MIB.............................$45.00
Collector's Button Book, Rumblers Are Coming, 1970, 3-fold cb, EX+..$70.00
Dual-Lane Rod Runner Hand-Shift Power-Booster, 1970, MIB.$35.00
Dual-Lane Speedometer, 1970, wht & orange, EX+.........$15.00
Farbs Human Race Set, 1972, MOC, from $15 to..........$30.00
Gran Toros, Chevy Astro II, 1970, gray, complete, NM..$125.00

Gran Toros, Match Race Set, 1970, complete, MIB, $450.00.

Gran Toros, Toyota 2000 GT, 1970, MOC, from $175 to...$225.00
Hot Line Great Freight Set, complete, MIB, from $150 to..$200.00
Hot Wheels Competition Pak, 1968, MIB (sealed)..........$25.00
Hot Wheels Dare Devil Loop, 1968, MIB (sealed)...........$20.00
Hot Wheels Dual-Lane Lap Counter, 1968, MIB.............$25.00
Iron-On Patch, 1969, Hot Wheels logo, NM...................$10.00
Mongoose & Snake Wild Wheelie Set, orig issue, complete, MIB...$600.00
Puzzle, 1970, jigsaw, shows race scene w/Jack Rabbit & 3 other cars, M (VG+ box)...$30.00
Revealers Sol-Aire CX-4, 1993-94, several color variations, MIP, ea..$5.00
Road King Highway Drive Ins, 1974, MIB...................$250.00
Sizzlers Fast Track Curve Pak, 1970, MIB....................$20.00
Sizzlers Laguna Oval Set, complete, MIB....................$250.00
Speedometer, 1970, EX..$15.00
Strip Action Set, 1969, MIB (sealed)..........................$125.00
Super-Charger Sprint Set, complete, EXIB..................$225.00
Talking Service Center, 1969, complete, scarce, NM.....$100.00
Treasure Hunt Series, 1995, several different, MOC, ea from $25 to...$35.00
Tune-Up Tower, 1970, MIB (sealed)...........................$400.00
Yoyo, 1990s, plastic tire shape w/imprint seal, MOC.......$12.00

Housewares

Back in the dark ages before women's lib and career-minded mothers, little girls emulated mommy's lifestyle, not realizing that by the time they grew up, total evolution would have taken place before their very eyes. They'd sew and bake, sweep, do laundry and iron (gasp!), and imagine what fun it would be when *they* were big like mommy. Those little gadgets they played with are precious collectibles today, and any child-size houseware item is treasured, especially those from the 1940s and 1950s.

See also Activity Sets, Character, TV, and Movie Collectibles, Disney.

CLEANING AND LAUNDRY

Clothes Presser, 1930s, yel & gr tin w/wooden roller, w/up & electric, EX..$85.00
Iron, Wolverine, 1950s, electric, MIB...............................$35.00
Ironing Board, Snow White, Wolverine, tin, EX+ $20.00
Ironing Board, Sunnie Miss, Ohio Art, 1960s, tin, 20", VG...$25.00

Super Cleaner Vacuum Cleaner, plastic, battery-operated, 13½", EXIB, $50.00. (Photo courtesy Randy Inman Auctions)

Sweeper, Little Queen, Bissel, tin w/wood hdl, functional, 25½", EX...$50.00
Sweeper, Mickey Mouse, litho tin w/Mickey at piano & Minnie singing, wood hdl, Ohio Art, 24", VG+..................$200.00
Sweeper, Mickey Mouse, WD, 1930s, litho tin over wood w/wood hdl, rolling action rotates sweeping brush, EX...........$400.00
Washboard & Tub, 4-legged wooden tub w/metal bands & hdls, corrugated tin & wooden scrub board, 8" dia, EX....$125.00
Washing Machine, Pretty Maid, Marx, EX $150.00
Washing Machine, Snow White & the Seven Dwarfs, Revell, 1940s-50s, plastic w/up wringer type, 9x5" dia, VG...$75.00
Washing Machine, Three Kittens, Ohio Art, litho tin, crank-op agitator, 7½", VG $175.00
Washing Machine, Three Little Pigs, Chein, litho tin wringer, VG $150.00
Washing Set, Sunny Monday, Parker Bros, complete, EXIB...$400.00

COOKING

Automatic Dollee Blender For the Little Mother, b/o, 7½", EXIB..$75.00
Baking Set, Mother's Helper, complete, MIB $150.00
Canister Set, Wolverine, tin, MIB $150.00
Children's Kitchen Set, Krest, complete, NMIB...............$50.00
Cooking Set, Farberware, Linemar, 1950s, NMIB $275.00
Cooking Set, Graniteware, bl, 8 pcs, EX........................$275.00
Easy-Bake Oven, Kenner, EXIB......................................$75.00
Freeze Queen Ice Cream Maker, Kenner, 1966, MIB........$75.00

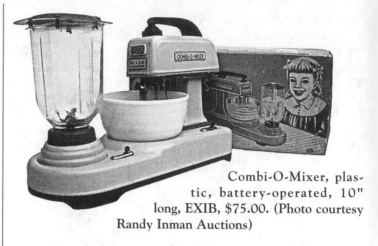

Combi-O-Mixer, plastic, battery-operated, 10" long, EXIB, $75.00. (Photo courtesy Randy Inman Auctions)

Refrigerator, Marx, metal, 14", EXIB, $125.00. (Photo courtesy Randy Inman Auctions)

Little Deb Toaster Set, Realistic Toys, chrome-look toaster w/2 glass trays, EXIB..$100.00
Refrigerator, Snow White, Wolverine, 1970s, wht w/yel border, 15", EX+...$35.00

Sink, Marx, metal, can have running water, 10" tall, EXIB, $125.00. (Photo courtesy Randy Inman Auctions)

Sink, Snow White, Wolverine, 1960s, tin, EX+ $20.00
Stove, Arcade Range, CI, emb Arcade & 1888, 11" L, VG...$1,045.00

Stove, Baby, Ideal, CI, w/many accessories, 16" W, VG+, A ..$230.00

Stove, Baby, Ideal, 1894, CI & steel, w/3-pc CI cookware set, 15½", rpt..$135.00

Stove, Beauty, CI w/name emb in oval on oven door, ornate casting w/back shelf, 4-footed, 16" L, VG+ $325.00

Stove, Beauty, Kenton, ca 1900, CI w/ornate design, 16" L, EX+ $400.00

Stove, Bess, CI, w/CI cookware, 10" L, EX $350.00

Stove, Blue Bird (2-in-1), Grey Iron, CI, w/cookware set, 10½" L, VG...$400.00

Stove, Blue Bird (3-in-1), Grey Iron, CI, 5½" L, VG.....$150.00

Stove, ca 1900, emb tin w/'brick' footed box exterior, oven door, back splash w/chimney, 9-pc pan set, VG.................$150.00

Stove, Charm, Grey Iron, NPCI, fluted trim, CI cookware set, 5" L, VG..$125.00

Stove, Charter Oak No 30, GF Filley (Excelsior Stove Works), CI w/blk finish, 24½" L, EX $200.00

Stove, Choice, Grey Iron, NPCI, w/CI cookware, 10½" L, VG...$300.00

Stove, Cory, Grey Iron, CI, w/CI cookware set, 9" L, EX...$400.00

Stove, Cotton Plant, Abendroth Bros, CI w/blk finish, w/CI cookware set, 11½" L, EX $2,000.00

Stove, Crescent, Grey Iron, CI w/copper or NP finish, w/CI cookware set, 13" L, EX...$450.00

Stove, Crown, Grey Iron, CI w/bl enamel & NP finish, w/CI cookware set, 13½" L, EX...$650.00

Stove, Daisy, Arcade, CI w/blk finish, w/cookware set, 6" L, EXIB...$375.00

Stove, Daisy, Kenton, CI w/blk finish, 17½" L, EX, A (Est: $700-$900) $600.00

Stove, Dictator Jr, Detroit Stove Works, dated 1870, CI w/blk finish, long stove pipe, 11", rpt, EX $1,100.00

Stove, Dolly's Favorite, Favorite Range & Stove Co, CI w/blk finish, w/CI cookware, 18½" L, G.............................$775.00

Stove, Eagle, Hubley, #887, NP w/ornate details, several accessories, 9½" L, VG $500.00

Stove, Globe, Kenton, NP CI, complete w/many accessories, 19x23", EX+ $2,000.00

Stove, Little Orphan Annie, tin, bl & wht w/2 graniteware pots, 8" W, EX $100.00

Stove, Muster-Schutz, CI w/3 NP front doors, 5 burners (3 rermovable), 5x11½", VG......................................$150.00

Stove, Raggedy Ann, plastic, 1978, 7x15x20" $25.00

Sugar Plum Quick Freeze, Hasbro, unused, MIB.............$50.00

Suzy Homemaker Grill, Topper, 1960s, unused, MIB $75.00

Toaster, chrome curved shape on dk metal base, electric, EX ..$50.00

Utensil Set, rolling pin, slotted spoon, spatula, masher, wht soap holder, etc, wht-pnt wood hdls, 9-pc, VG..................$75.00

FURNITURE

Breakfront, wood French style w/many glass-front doors, wht w/gold trim, footed, 27x17", VG.............................$350.00

Cupboard, wood, plain hutch top w/2 railed shelves, 2 bottom ornate panel doors, footed, 17", EX+ $200.00

Cupboard, wood, 2 doors w/vertical cutout fronts show shelving, 2 bottom drawers, ornate top, 27", EX $175.00

Desk (Roll-Top), oak w/orig finish, 6-drawer front, WJ Heath, 18" W, VG...$250.00

Dresser, wood, tall side swivel mirror beside 2 sm drawers atop 2 long drawers, metal pulls, 27", VG......................$300.00

Rocker, walnut w/woven cane seat & shield-shape back, geometric carved decor, low arms, 26", G............................$250.00

Secretary, wood, fold-down front, 19", EX, $325.00. (Photo courtesy Bertoia Auctions)

Victrola, tin body in wooden frame, side crank, windup turntable, 17x10x9", VG, $35.00. (Photo courtesy James D. Julia, Inc.)

Stove, Marx, metal, 10", EXIB, $125.00. (Photo courtesy Randy Inman Auctions)

Sideboard, oak w/orante trim, top mirror, 2 bottom side-by-side drawers & doors, wht porcelain pulls, 22", EX.........$750.00

Vanity, mahogany & tiger maple, fold-down mirror, tapered legs, swags on front drawer, 10x13", G.............................$800.00

Wardrobe, wood w/bamboo trim, mirrored front, turned finials, interior shelf, 11x6½x3", VG.................................$200.00

Nursery

Carriage, Joel Ellis, wood, 3-wheeled sleigh type w/blk leather fold-up hood, 29" L, VG.................................$250.00

Carriage, Marklin (?), pnt tin w/emb wicker design, folding top, 4 spoke wheels, 6" L, EX.................................$250.00

Carriage, wicker, chair-type w/scrolled arms, 2 lg wood spoke wheels & 2 sm, curved hdl, 27", G..........................$250.00

Carriage, wicker, curved & stepped box body, partially quilted interior, spoke wheels, 50" L, G $150.00

Carriage, wicker, sleigh type w/scroll design, 2 lg spoke wheels & 2 smaller, curved hdl, 36" L, EX......................$500.00

Carriage, wicker, wht sleigh type w/bl spoke wheels & hdl, parasol canopy, upholstered, 38" L, G.........................$100.00

Carriage, wood, box frame w/upholstered bench seat, flat fringed top on wire supports, 27" (to hdl), EX $300.00

Carriage, wood, sleigh body, blk oilcloth fold-down hood (horse buggy type), pnt/stenciled, 25" (to hdl), EX $200.00

Carriage, wood, sleigh body, flat fringed top on wire supports, pnt/stenciled, 30" (to hdl), EX $325.00

Carriage, wood, sleigh body, fringed top w/hang-down flap, cloth seat, pnt/stenciled, 25" (to hdl), EX....................$575.00

Carriage, wood, sleigh body w/blk oilcloth fold-down fringed top, upholstered seat, pnt/stenciled, 30" (to hdl), EX $575.00

Carriage, wood, surrey type w/rnd fringed top, upholstered seat bottom, wood spoke wheels, 24" L, VG $850.00

Carriage, wood, twin, curved box body w/2 pivoting fringed tops, pnt & stenciled, 55" L, VG, A (Est: $400-$600).....$475.00

Pram, England, 1890, wood w/leather top, spoke wheels (2 lg & 2 sm), 30" L, VG.......................................$200.00

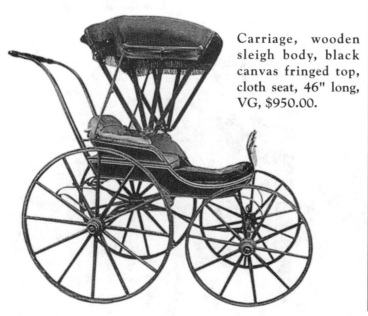

Carriage, wooden sleigh body, black canvas fringed top, cloth seat, 46" long, VG, $950.00.

Sewing

Cutting Machine, Singer, wht plastic w/suction cup foot, 5x6½", EX...$50.00

Sewing Basket, sq wicker w/lid & bottom shelf on 4 tall legs, 17x9", EX+...$75.00

Sewing Cabinet, Martha Wasington, ca 1930, dk wood w/3 drawers, flip-top side compartments, 18", EX $250.00

Sewing Kit, Victorian girls & Christmas pram illus on lid, w/mirror, needles, thread & button, MIB.....................$150.00

Sewing Machine, Jaymar, metal w/orange crinkle-pnt finish, b/o, EX, minimum value $50.00

Sewing Machine, Jr Miss, Sew-Rite/Hasbro, 1960s, NM (NM carrying case), minimum value.................................$50.00

Sewing Machine, Little Miss, Lindstrom, crank-operated, 8" long, EX, $100.00. (Photo courtesy Randy Inman Auctions)

Sewing Machine, Midget, decal-decorated CI, 7½", EX, A (Est: $100-$150) $300.00

Sewing Machine, Sew Master, LAYanEE, metal, crank-op, 8" L, EXIB...$100.00

Sewing Machine, Singer, Featherweight Bo 221-1, 1941, complete, EX $250.00

Table Service

Castor Set, 4 glass condiment bottles w/stoppers in metal stand, EX $100.00

Decanter Set, brass, service for 6, MIB..............$50.00

Dinner Set, Jeannette Jr, pk depression glass, 4 ea cups, saucers, lunch plates, creamer/sugar, EXIB.....................$250.00

House that Jack Built Dinner Set, Florence Cook Pottery, wht ceramic, character detail, gold trim, 22-pc, EX, A...$100.00

Percolator Set, Tootsietoy, 1920s, samovar, sugar bowl & creamer on tray, MIB.....................................$200.00

Silverware Set, Banner Metallone Tableware, 4 place settings w/butter knife & cake server, MIB $75.00

Tea Set, Little American Maid, Akro Agate, MIB.........$375.00

Tea Set, Little Hostess, Made in Japan, lustre ware, service for 4, EXIB..$200.00

Tea Set, Ohio Art, 1950s, litho tin w/circus animals & clowns on red background, 31 pcs, EX $250.00

Tea Set, Germany, deep pink floral pattern on white china with light blue airbrushing, gold trim, 12-piece, EXIB, $175.00. (Photo courtesy McMasters Harris Doll Auctions)

Tea Set, Sun Bonnet Babies, Japan, ceramic, wht w/mc detail, 24-pc, EX $125.00
Tea Set, Sunnie Miss, Ohio Art, 1976, litho tin, 6 pcs, MOC $35.00

MISCELLANEOUS

Crumb Set, Little Miss Muffett.../Little Jack Horner, aluminum, NM...$100.00
Doll Sled, wood sleigh type w/curved runners & hdl, red pnt w/gold trim, 32" L, G, A (Est: $100-$200) $175.00
Dresser Set, pitcher & bowl, soap dish, lotion, powder & pin containers, china w/purple & brn flowers, EX $250.00
Dresser Set, 1930s, mirror, brush & hair receiver, celluloid, doll sz, MIB $200.00
Scale, Arcade, mk Toledo, red-pnt CI, 5", EX $600.00
Tool Set, Ideal, 1960s, die-cast metal, 5-pc set, MIB $15.00
Typewriter, Unique Toy, 1940s-50s, tin w/lithoed keys, alphabet wheel, EXIB $50.00
Wagon, Paris/USA, natural wood w/Express stenciled on sides, red & gr trim, spoke wheels, 16x8", EX $450.00
Wagon, Wyandotte, 1940s, PS, lt gr w/pk wheel covers, 5½", EX $100.00

Wheelbarrow, SA Smith MFG, wood, iron-capped spoke wheels, 39", long, EX, $350.00. (Photo courtesy James D. Julia, Inc)

Japanese (and Other) Tin Vehicle Replicas

Listed here are the model vehicles (most of which were made in Japan during the 1950s and 1960s) that were designed to realistically represent the muscle cars, station wagons, convertibles, budget models, and luxury cars that were actually being made at the time. Most are tin and many are friction or battery operated, some have remote control. In our descriptions, all are tin unless noted otherwise.

Aston-Martin M101 Secret Ejector Car, r/c, 11", EX+IB .$350.00
Austin Healey 100 Six Coupe (1959), Bandai, friction, 8", EXIB...$250.00
BMW 600 Isetta (1950), Bandai, friction, 9", EX+ $375.00
Buick (1947), Gama/US Zone Germany, w/up, blk, 6½", NM+IB $150.00
Buick (1953), Marusan, friction, b/o headlights, WWT, 7", EX+ $185.00
Buick (1958), ATC, friction, 14½", NMIB $4,500.00
Buick (1958), Bandai, friction, 8", VG $75.00
Buick (1958), Ichiko, friction, 14½", NMIB $2,500.00
Buick (1960), Ichiko, friction, 17½", EXIB $850.00
Buick (1961), TN, friction, 11", NMIB $500.00
Buick (1966), A-1/Germany, b/o, 2 red lights on hood, bump-&-go action, 11½", NM+IB............................$225.00
Buick Century Wagon (1954), Irco, r/c, 8½", EX+IB.....$150.00
Buick Convertible (Model Auto Series), Bandai, friction, 6", NM+IB $150.00
Buick Invicta (1959), Daito, friction, roof slides into trunk, 9", NM+ $150.00
Buick LeSabre (1966), ATC, friction, 19", NM+IB....$1,000.00
Buick LeSabre Dream Car, Yonezawa, friction, 8", EX+ .$600.00
Buick Riveria Station Wagon (1960s), Asakusa, friction, 15", EX+ $230.00
Cadillac (1950), Marusan, friction, 11", NM.................$750.00
Cadillac (1954), Gama, friction, 12", EX+ $250.00

Cadillac Sedan (1955), Marusan, friction, 12", EX+IB, $1,400.00.

Cadillac (1960 Gold), Bandai, r/c, 17", EX+ $225.00
Cadillac (1965), ATC, friction, 17", NM+ $650.00
Cadillac Convertible (1954), Bandai, friction, 11", EX+IB .$385.00
Cadillac Convertible (1959), Bandai, friction, 11½" $425.00
Cadillac Convertible (1960), Bandai, friction, 11", unused,
    NM+IB $400.00
Cadillac Convertible (1963 Golden), Bandai, b/o, opening doors
    & trunk, working lights, etc, 17", NMIB $575.00
Cadillac Fleetwood Eldorado, ST, friction, 10½", MIB ..$375.00
Cadillac Sedan (1959), Bandai, friction, 11", EXIB $250.00
Cadillac Sedan (1961), Yonezawa, friction, bl-tinted windows,
    18", EX+ $2,100.00
Cadillac Sedan (1964), Y, friction, 22", NMIB $2,850.00
Chevy Corvair Bertone (1963, Bandai, b/o, 12", EX+....$175.00

Chevy Corvette (1963), Ichika, battery-operated, headlamps open, working horn, 12", NMIB, $300.00. (Photo courtesy Bertoia Auctions)

Chevy Corvette Sports Coupe (1958), Yonezawa, friction, 9½",
    NMIB $1,650.00
Chevy Corvette Sting Ray (1963), Ichida, b/o, headlamps open,
    working horn, 12½", NMIB $300.00
Chevy Impala (1961), ATC, friction, 12", NM+............$450.00
Chevy Impala (1963), Bandai, friction, working headlights, 18",
    NMIB...$300.00
Chevy Impala (1963), TN, friction, 17", NMIB............$725.00
Chevy Pickup (1958 El Camino), Yonezawa, friction, 8",
    EXIB...$150.00
Chevy Sedan (1959), ASC, friction, 10", NM $300.00
Chevy Sedan (1959), Japan, friction, no interior, 12", VG+.$200.00
Chevy Sedan (1960), IY, friction, 11", NMIB.............$1,400.00
Chevy Sedan (1963), Bandai, friction, 11", NM $150.00
Chevy Station Wagon (Model Auto Series #708), Bandai, fric-
    tion, 6", NM+IB $150.00
Chrysler Convertible, Gunthermann, friction, wht over red,
    WWT, w/orig compo driver, 11", EX $200.00
Chrysler Convertible (1950s), Gunthermann, w/up, b/o lights,
    compo driver, 11", NMIB $600.00

Chrysler Convertible (1958), Gunthermann, r/c, w/driver, 13½",
    NMIB...$350.00
Chrysler Imperial Sedan (1962), ATC, friction, 15½",
    NM $12,000.00
Chrysler Imperial Sedan (1962), ATC, friction, 15½",
    NMIB...$22,000.00

Chrysler New Yorker (1957), Alps, friction, 14", NM, $1,200.00. (Photo courtesy Randy Inman Auctions)

Chrysler New Yorker (1957), Alps, friction, 14", VG+ ...$600.00
Chrysler New Yorker (1958), Germany, friction, w/compo driver,
    14", scarce, EX $725.00
DeSoto Convertible (1961), Haji, friction, 8", VG+......$275.00
DeSoto Sedan (1958), Haji, friction, 8", NM.................$275.00
Dodge (1957), b/o, 9½", EXIB (box mk Streamline Electric
    Sedan)..$175.00
Dodge Charger Sonic Car, 1966, G/O, 16" EX+ $50.00

Dodge (Pickup) Truck (1959), Marusan #M-1050, friction, 19", NMIB, $4,500.00. (Photo courtesy Randy Inman Auctions)

Edsel City Cab (1958), friction, 7½", EX+ $225.00
Edsel Station Wagon (1958), TN, friction, 10½", NM+ .$275.00
Ferrari, Bandai, 1960s, battery-op, 11", EXIB $350.00
Ferrari, Bandai, 1960s, friction, 11½", EXIB..................$300.00
Ferrari (Gear Shift), Bandai, b/o, 11", NMIB $225.00

Ferrari Super America, Bandai, friction, 11", MIB $650.00
Ferrari Super America, Bandai, friction, 11", NM $200.00
Fiat 600 Sunroof Sedan, Bandai, friction, 7", NM+IB....$375.00
Ford (New), Ichiko, b/o, 8", NM+IB................................$80.00
Ford Capri Sedan, Aoshin, friction, BRT, 11", NM+IB..$200.00
Ford Convertible (1955), Haji, friction, 7½", VG..........$175.00
Ford Convertible (1956), Haji, friction, 12", EX.........$2,000.00
Ford Fairlane (1960), Haji, opening hood, 11", NM+IB .$350.00
Ford Fairlane (1961), friction, 11", EX+ $150.00
Ford Fairlane Victoria (1955), Marusan, friction, 13", EX .$2,500.00
Ford Flower Delivery Wagon (1955), Bandai, friction, 12",
   NMIB $1,100.00
Ford Flower Delivery Wagon (1955), Bandai, friction, 12", VG ..$275.00
Ford Mustang (1967), Bandai, b/o, 13", unused, NM+IB .$125.00
Ford Mustang Fastback (1965), Bandai, friction, 11", EX.$175.00
Ford Mustang Fastback (1966), TN, friction, 17", EX+ .$225.00
Ford Sedan, Gunthermann, w/up, 11", MIB $450.00

Ford Sedan (1956), Marusan, friction, 13", NMIB, $3,500.00. (Photo courtesy Randy Inman Auctions)

Ford Skyliner, Kosuge, b/o, 9", EX+IB.............................$350.00
Ford Skyliner, TN, friction, roof retracts into trunk, 7½",
   NMIB...$250.00
Ford Skyliner (1958), Normura, b/o, 9", NM..................$200.00
Ford Skyliner Sports Car, TN, b/o, top slides into trunk, 9",
   NMIB...$110.00
Ford Standard Coffee Station Wagon (1955), Bandai, friction,
   12", NM..$3,500.00
Ford Standard Coffee Station Wagon (1955), Bandai, friction,
   12", VG+ $2,100.00

Ford T-Bird Convertible (1964), Sears, friction, 15", NM+IB, $300.00.

Ford T-Bird (1956), friction, see-through roof, 8", EX+ ...$85.00
Ford T-Bird (1956), TN, b/o, working lights, 11", EX+ ..$200.00
Ford T-Bird (1959), Bandai, friction, 8", M $260.00
Ford T-Bird (1968), Ichiko, friction, BRT, 11", EX, A......$70.00
Ford Taunus 17M (1960s), Bandai, friction, 8½", NMIB...$125.00
Greyhound Senic Cruiser Bus, 1960s, friction, 14½",
   EXIB...$150.00
Henny-Packard Ambulance, plastic version, wht, 12½",
   EXIB..$450.00
Hudson Sedan (1950s), Tipp/US Zone Germany, w/up, Dunlop
   cord tires, 10", VG...$250.00
International Super Constructor Dump Truck (1960s), SSS, 6-
   wheeled, 23", EX+IB $2,500.00
Isetta, Bandai, friction, red & wht (scarce), front opens, 6½",
   NMIB...$350.00
Isuzu, ATC, friction, steering wheel on right side, 7", EX $200.00
Jaguar XKE, 1960s, Bandai, b/o, 10", EXIB....................$275.00
Jaguar 3.4 Convertible (1960s), Bandai, friction, 8", EX+ .$75.00

Lincoln Continental Mark II (1956), Linemar, friction, 11", EX, $1,375.00. (Photo courtesy Randy Inman Auctions)

Lincoln Continental Mark II (1956), Linemar, friction, 11",
   NMIB $5,250.00
Lincoln Continental Mark II (1956), Linemar, r/c, 11", MIB
   (rare yel box)..$6,500.00
Lincoln Sedan (1955), Yonezawa, friction, 13", NMIB.$3,500.00
Lincoln Sedan (1955), Yonezawa, friction, 13", VG+ $475.00

Mercedes-Benz 300SE (1970), Ichiko, friction, 25" MIB, $175.00.

Mercedes-Benz (Gullwing), Bandai, r/c, engine sound, opening doors, 8", VG+IB $200.00

Mercedes-Benz Sedan, Adenaur/West Germany, w/up, 9", EX $175.00

Mercedes-Benz SL, Bandai (for Sears), friction, 10", NMIB..$100.00

Mercedes-Benz 190 SL, KKS, r/c, 9", NM+IB $250.00

Mercedes-Benz 219 Convertible, Bandai, friction, 8", EX+ .$125.00

Mercedes-Benz 219 Sedan, Bandai, friction, 8", NM+IB.$225.00

Mercedes-Benz 230SL, Schuco, b/o, key ignition, intricate internal gearing beneath trunk, 10", NM $300.00

Mercedes-Benz 300 (1960s), Alps, b/o, working headlights, 9½", unused, NM+IB..$1,700.00

Mercury Cougar (1967), Asakusa, friction, 15", NMIB..$825.00

Mercury Station Wagon (1958), Bandai, friction, 8", EXIB.$150.00

MG (1953), Bandai, friction, 10½", EXIB $300.00

MG S-1018, friction, w/fold-down window, 6½", NMIB.$250.00

MG 1600 Roadster Convertible (1957), ATC, friction, 9½", EX+ $300.00

Oldsmobile (1958), ATC, friction, 12½", EX+ $450.00

Oldsmobile Rocket 88 2-Door (1960), friction, 13", VG+ .$350.00

Oldsmobile Sedan (1958), ACT, friction, 12½", NMIB .$550.00

Oldsmobile Toronado, ATC, friction, 15½", NM+IB $325.00

Oldsmobile Toronado (1968), Ichiko, friction, 17", unused, MIB $650.00

Packard Convertible (1952), Alps, friction, 16", NM+.$1,800.00

Packard Hawk Convertible (1957), Schuco, b/o, 11", EX .$575.00

Plymouth Fury (1964), Kusama, friction, 10", EX+ $75.00

Plymouth Fury Convertible (1959), Bandai, friction, 8½", NMIB...$400.00

Plymouth Station Wagon (1961), Ichiko, friction, 12", EXIB.$500.00

Plymouth Valiant (1960), Yonezawa, friction, working wipers, 9", NM $100.00

Pontiac Convertible, Yonezawa, friction, 8", NMIB.......$275.00

Pontiac Firebird (1967), Bandai, b/o, w/windshield wipers, 9½", EXIB..$125.00

Pontiac Star Chief (1954), Asahi, friction, 11", EXIB ...$600.00

Porsche (Fastback), Yanoman, friction, 15", EX $500.00

Porsche Electro Matic 7500 Convertible, Distler/W Germany, b/o, 10", NM+IB...$625.00

Porsche Speedster Electromatic 7500 Police-Polizei Model 356, Distler, 1950s, b/o, 10", EX+IB $2,000.00

Rambler Station Wagon w/Shasta Trailer & Viking Boat (Vacationer Set), Bandai/Fleet Line, 11" car, NM+IB......$725.00

Rolls-Royce Silver Cloud (1960s), Bandai, b/o, w/working headlights, 12", VG $125.00

Rolls-Royce Silver Cloud (1960s), Bandai, friction, 12", EX+ $175.00

Rolls-Royce Silver Cloud Convertible (1960s), Bandai, friction, 12", NM $200.00

Saab 93B (1960s), Bandai, friction, 7", EX+IB...............$125.00

Studebaker (1954), Yoshiva, friction, 9", EX+ $250.00

Subaru 360 (1960s), Bandai, friction, 7", VG+ $150.00

Toyota (1960s), Ichiko, friction, 16", NMIB..................$250.00

Triumph TR-3 Coupe (1960s), Bandai, friction, 8", EXIB.$200.00

Volkswagen Convertible (1950s), Taiyo, b/o, 10", MIB .$200.00

Volkswagen Karmann-Ghia (1960), Bandai, friction, 7½", EXIB, $275.00. (Photo courtesy Randy Inman Auctions)

Volkswagen Sedan, Bandai, b/o, w/driver, 10½", NM+IB..$225.00

Volkswagen Van w/Open Roof (1960s), Bandai, friction, 8", NM+ $175.00

Volkswagen 1600TL Fastback, Yanoman, r/c, opening hood & trunck, 13½", NM+IB..$675.00

Volvo PV444, KS, b/o, 7½", EX+IB................................$450.00

Volvo 1800 S, Ichiko, friction, opening doors, 9", NM+IB.$525.00

Keystone

Though this Massachusetts company produced a variety of toys during their years of operation (circa 1920 – late 1950s), their pressed-steel vehicles are the most collectible, and that's what we've listed here. As a rule they were very large, with some of the riders being around 30" in length.

Air Mail Plane NX-263, 24" W, VG, A (Est: $700-$900) .$925.00

Airplane (Rapid Fire Motor), 24" W, G, A (Est: $800-$1,000) $1,650.00

Airplane (Rapid Fire Motor), 24" W, VG, A $2,640.00

American Railway Express Truck, #43, 27", VG, A (Est: $800-$1,000) $1,045.00

Coast-To-Coast Bus, #84, rider, 32", G, A (Est: $2,500-$3,500) $6,900.00

Rolls-Royce Silver Cloud Convertible (1960s), Bandai, friction, 12", NMIB, $600.00.

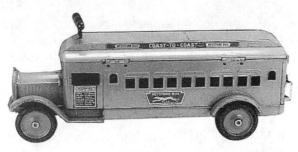

Coast-To-Coast Bus, #84, rider, 32", EX+ (G box), A (Est: $4,000.00 – $5,000.00), $24,200.00. (Photo courtesy Noel Barrett Antiques and Auctions, Inc.)

Dump Truck, open cab, side crank, BRT, 27", G, A (Est: $600-$700)..$420.00
Dump Truck, rider, cabover w/rear dual tires, 24", EX+, A (Est: $600-$900) $935.00

Dump Truck, rider, 24", VG, A (Est: $300.00 – $500.00), $650.00. (Photo courtesy Noel Barrett Antiques and Auctions)

Dump Truck, 1920s, doorless cab, front crank hydraulic lift, 26", VG, A (Est: $1,200-$1,500) $1,650.00
Fire Chemical Truck, #57, 29", P, A (Est: $400-$600)....$715.00
Fire Ladder Truck, #52, 28", amateur rstr/rpt, A (Est: $300-$500) $355.00
Fire Water Tower Truck, rider, cabover, fully equipt, wood hdls, high seat, 31", VG, A (Est: $700-$900) $1,870.00
Greyhound Bus, 18", G+, A (Est: $150-$250)................$385.00
Koaster Truck, #54, rider, 25", VG, A (Est: $800-$1,200) ..$715.00
Locomotive No 6400, rider, 25", VG, A $250.00
Moving Van, #58, early w/roof extending over open cab, MDW, 25", G, A (Est: $250-$450) $900.00
Moving Van, doorless cab, BRT, 26", rstr, ($1,000-$1,200)..$350.00
Police Patrol, #51, 27", P, A (Est: $200-$300) $200.00
Steam Roller, #60, 21", EX, A (Est: $500-$600).............$515.00
Steam Shovel, #46, 21", G, A (Est: $150-$250).............$100.00
Train, locomotive/tender, gondola & work crane on flatbed, 65" overall, EX, A (Est: $1,200-$1,400) $1,780.00
Truck Loader, #44, rare lt gr version, 18", Fair, A (Est: $150-$250)..$200.00
US Army Truck, 1920s, open seat, cloth cover, 26", rpt, A (Est: $250-$350) $300.00

US Mail Truck, #45, screened van, 26", rstr, A (Est: $600-$800)..$410.00
Water Tower Truck, 29", VG, A $2,750.00
Wrecker, #78, 27", older rpt, A (Est: $600-$800) $520.00

World's Greatest Circus Truck, 26", EX, A (Est: $7,000.00 – $9,000.00), $20,900.00. (Photo courtesy Bertoia Auctions)

Lehmann

Lehmann toys were made in Germany as early as 1881. Early on they were sometimes animated by means of an inertia-generated flywheel; later, clockwork mechanisms were used. Some of their best-known turn-of-the-century toys were actually very racist and unflattering to certain ethnic groups. But the wonderful antics they perform and the imagination that went into their conception have made them and all the other Lehmann toys favorites with collectors today. Though the company faltered with the onset of WWI, they were quick to recover and during the war years produced some of their best toys, several of which were copied by their competitors. Business declined after WWI. Lehmann died in 1934, but the company continued for awhile under the direction of Lehmann's partner and cousin, Johannes Richter.

Advisor: Scott Smiles (S10)

Acrobat, VG $750.00
Adam the Porter, EX $650.00
Adam the Porter, NM $1,200.00
Adam the Porter, NMIB...$1,350.00
Africa Ostrich Cart, EX $600.00
AHA Delivery Van, EX $650.00
Ajax, VG, A $850.00
Alabama Coon Jigger, G..$450.00
Alabama Coon Jigger, VGIB.....................................$650.00
ALSO Auto, NM...$500.00
ALSO Auto, VG $350.00
Anxious Bride, NMIB $2,000.00
Autin Pedal Car, 4", Fair, A $220.00
Autin Pedal Car, 4", NM (in box mk American Boy).$1,000.00
Auto Post Delivery Van, NMIB................................$1,400.00
Auto-Onkel, NMIB..$1,400.00

Ajax, EX, $1,400.00. (Photo courtesy Bertoia Auctions)

Autobus #590, EX, A $1,050.00
Autohutte w/2 Autos, VGIB, A.............................$1,200.00
Baker & Chimney Sweep, NMIB $3,000.00

Baker and Chimney Sweep, VG+, $1,000.00. (Photo courtesy Randy Inman Auctions)

Balky Mule, EX, A...$400.00
Balky Mule, EXIB, A $500.00
Berolina Convertible, NM $3,500.00

Bucking Bronco, EXIB, $1,000.00. (Photo courtesy Bertoia Auctions)

Bird, tin body w/pasteboard wings, EX+.........................$525.00
Boxer, 4 Chinese men mounted on base throw figure in cloth
     blanket, rare, NM, from $5,000 to $6,500.00
Bucking Bronco, G+...$600.00
Buster Brown in Auto, NM..................................$1,750.00
Buster Brown in Auto, VG.......................................$900.00
Captain of Kopenvil, NM $2,700.00
Climbing Monkey, NMIB..$300.00
Crawling Beetle, NM..$250.00
Crawling Beetle, VG, A..$125.00
Crocodile, Fair, A...$300.00
Crocodile, NMIB..$450.00
Dancing Sailor (Columbia), EX, A $600.00
Dancing Sailor (HMS Dreadnaught), EX+IB.............$1,300.00
Dancing Sailor (MARS), EXIB................................$900.00
Daredevil, EX..$550.00

Duo, EX, A, $935.00. (Photo courtesy Bertoia Auctions)

Duo, NM...$1,200.00
Echo Motorcycle w/Driver, EX.............................$1,500.00
Echo Motorcycle w/Driver, NMIB.......................$2,500.00
EHE & Co Truck, VG $500.00
EPL-I Dirigible, NMIB $800.00
EPL-I Dirigible, VG..$400.00
EPL-II Zeppelin, EX $800.00
Express Porter, NM $700.00
Express Porter, VG $450.00
Futurus Peace Chime, VG $650.00
Gala Sedan, bl & wht, rare, VG $750.00
Galop Racer #1 w/Garage, EX $650.00
Galop Zebra Cart, 1954 reissue, NMIB...................$525.00
Garage w/Gnome (Series) Racer & Sedan, VG.............$550.00
Garage w/Sedan, EX $600.00
Going to the Fair, G $1,000.00
Going to the Fair, NM..$3,000.00
Gustav the Miller, EX $275.00
Gustav the Miller, VGIB...$400.00
Halloh Motorcycle w/Rider, NM $2,400.00
Halloh Motorcycle w/Rider, VG $1,400.00

Heavy Swell (Dapper Fella), EX, $1,200.00. (Photo courtesy Bertoia Auctions)

Mandarin, EXIB, A, $3,300.00; Masyama, EXIB, $2,500.00. (Photo courtesy Bertoia Auctions)

Heavy Swell (Dapper Fella), NMIB.............................$2,000.00
Icarus (Plane), EXIB..$3,500.00
Icarus (Plane), G..$950.00
Icarus (Plane), VG+..$1,100.00
IHI Meat Van, EX $1,700.00
Jonny Lion, plastic, friction, MIB..................................$50.00
Jonny Sailor Boy, EXIB...$200.00
Kadi, EX...$1,700.00
Kadi, NMIB $2,000.00
Kadi, VG..$1,200.00

Marke Coach, G+...$350.00
Mensa Delivery Van, EX $2,200.00
Mice on Spiral Rod, EX...$250.00
Minstrel Man, 1906, flat tin, scarce, EX (in envelope) ..$800.00
Miss Blondin (Tightrope Walker), EX $3,000.00
Mixtum, EX...$1,500.00
Motor Car, EX..$750.00
Motor Car, EXIB $1,000.00
NA-OB, EX+..$775.00
Nani Cart, plastic, friction, MIB $50.00
Naughty Boy, EXIB...$1,000.00
Naughty Boy, VG...$650.00
New Century Cycle, EX $850.00
New Century Cycle, VG $475.00
Nu-Nu, NM (partial box) $1,300.00
Oh My, EX $650.00
OHO, EX+..$600.00
OHO, G..$400.00
Paak-Paak Quack-Quack Duck Cart, EX $500.00

Kamerun Ostrich Cart, EX, $850.00. (Photo courtesy Randy Inman Auctions)

Kimado Family, EX..$1,700.00
Lexus Sedan, VG..$2,300.00
Li La Hansom Cab, G $1,000.00
Li La Hansom Cab, NMIB..$2,000.00
Lo & Li, NM..$8,000.00
Lo & Li, VG $4,000.00
Lo Lo, G...$500.00
Lo Lo, VG..$750.00
Los Angeles Zeppelin, Fair $250.00
Los Angeles Zeppelin, VG+ $475.00

Paddy the Pig, NM, $2,500.00. (Photo courtesy Bertoia Auctions)

Paddy & the Pig, VG...$1,100.00
Performing Sea Lion, NMIB...$475.00

Performing Sea Lion, VG $275.00
Pilot Motorcycle w/Driver, VG $3,500.00
Primus Roller Skater, rare, NM, from $6,500 to $7,000.00
Rad Cycle, NM...$2,000.00
Rigi Cable Car, EX+IB $200.00
Roll Mops (Ball), VG $550.00
Royal Mail Van, NM $2,000.00
Sedan #765, VG $300.00
Ski Rolf, EX $2,800.00
Snik-Snak, EXIB $5,000.00
Stiller Berlin Truck, rare, EX $900.00
Stubborn Donkey, NMIB...................................$650.00
Susu (Realistic Turtle), NMIB............................$100.00
Tap-Tap, EX $650.00
Tap-Tap, G+ $450.00
Tap-Tap, NMIB...$900.00
Taxi, EX $850.00
Terra Sedan, NM..$1,250.00

Terra Sedan, VG, $800.00. (Photo courtesy Bertoia Auctions)

Titian Sedan, electric lights, G.........................$600.00
Titian Sedan, electric lights, NM.................$2,300.00
Tom the Climbing Monkey, plain vest, hand-pnt face, MIB.$375.00
Tom the Climbing Monkey, polka-dot vest, litho tin face, MIB..$400.00
Tut-Tut, EX, A..$1,350.00
Tut-Tut, EX+IB..$1,750.00
Tut-Tut, G...$850.00
Tut-Tut, VG, A...$1,150.00
Tyras the Walking Dog, NM.............................$850.00

Zig-Zag, VG, $1,000.00. (Photo courtesy Bertoia Auctions)

UHU Amphibious Car, EX $800.00
Velleda Touring Car, G $1,000.00
Vineta Monorail, EX...$850.00
Waltzing Doll, EXIB..$1,800.00
Wild West Bucking Bronco, see Bucking Bronco
Zig-Zag, EX $1,400.00
Zig-Zag, EXIB $1,800.00
Zirka Dare Devil, NM $1,200.00
Zirka Dare Devil, VG...$800.00
Zulu, VG..$650.00

Lunch Boxes

When the lunch box craze began in the mid-1980s, it was only the metal boxes that so quickly soared to sometimes astronomical prices. But today, even the plastic and vinyl ones are collectible. So pick a genre and have fun. There are literally hundreds to choose from, and just as is true in other areas of character-related collectibles, the more desirable lunch boxes are those with easily recognized, well-known subjects — western heroes, TV, Disney and other cartoon characters, and famous entertainers. Bottles are collectible as well.

The listings are ranged from excellent to mint values. Bottles for metal boxes are listed under each lunch box, plastic and vinyl listings are complete with bottles.

If you would like to learn more, we recommend *A Pictorial Price Guide to Metal Lunch Boxes and Thermoses* and a companion book *A Pictorial Guide to Vinyl and Plastic Lunch and Plastic Lunch Boxes* by Larry Aikins.

Advisor: Terry Ivers (I2)

METAL

A-Team, 1980s, from $25 to $40.00
A-Team, 1980s, plastic bottle, from $8 to $12.00
Adam-12, 1970s, from $50 to...........................$100.00
Adam-12, 1970s, plastic bottle, from $20 to $30.00
Addams Family, 1970s, from $75 to $125.00

Action Jackson, 1970s, from $550.00 to $750.00; metal bottle, from $100.00 to $175.00. (Photo courtesy Carole Bess White and L.M. White)

Addams Family, 1970s, plastic bottle, from $15 to...........$20.00
America on Parade, 1970s, from $25 to $50.00
America on Parade, 1970s, plastic bottle, from $15 to $25.00
Animal Friends, 1970s, from $25 to $40.00
Annie, 1980s, from $30 to...$40.00
Annie, 1980s, plastic bottle, from $5 to $10.00
Annie Oakley & Tag, 1950s, from $225 to $325.00
Annie Oakley & Tag, 1950s, metal bottle, from $50 to .$100.00
Apple's Way, 1970s, from $50 to $75.00
Apple's Way, 1970s, plastic bottle, from $15 to $25.00
Archies, 1969, from $75 to..$125.00
Archies, 1969, plastic bottle, from $20 to $40.00
Astronauts, 1960, dome, from $85 to............................$150.00
Astronauts, 1960, metal bottle, from $30 to $50.00
Astronauts, 1969, from $75 to......................................$125.00
Astronauts, 1969, plastic bottle, from $20 to $50.00
Atom Ant, 1960s, from $75 to.......................................$175.00
Atom Ant, 1960s, metal bottle, from $35 to.....................$65.00
Auto Race, 1960s, from $50 to $75.00
Auto Race, 1960s, metal bottle, from $15 to $25.00
Back in '76, 1970s, from $40 to $70.00
Back in '76, 1970s, plastic bottle, from $10 to $20.00
Batman & Robin, 1960s, from $150 to $200.00
Batman & Robin, 1960s, metal bottle, from $50 to.........$75.00
Battle of the Planets, 1970s, from $50 to $75.00
Battle of the Planets, 1970s, plastic bottle, from $15 to ...$20.00

Battlestar Galactica, 1970s, from $35.00 to $65.00; plastic bottle (not shown), from $15.00 to $25.00. (Photo courtesy Carole Bess White and L.M. White)

Beatles, 1960s, from $450 to..$600.00
Beatles, 1960s, metal bottle, from $125 to $225.00
Bee Gees, 1970s, from $50 to $75.00
Bee Gees, 1970s, plastic bottle, from $15 to $20.00
Berenstain Bears, 1980s, from $50 to $75.00
Berenstein Bears, 1980s, plastic bottle, from $10 to $20.00
Betsy Clark, 1970s, from $35 to......................................$55.00
Betsy Clark, 1970s, plastic bottle, from $10 to.................$20.00
Beverly Hillbillies, 1960s, from $100 to.........................$150.00

Beverly Hillbillies, 1960s, metal bottle, from $50 to........$75.00
Bionic Woman, 1970s, from $30 to.................................$60.00
Bionic Woman, 1970s, plastic bottle, from $10 to...........$20.00
Black Hole, 1970s, from $30 to $60.00
Black Hole, 1970s, plastic bottle, from $10 to $20.00
Bobby Sherman, 1970s, from $50 to...............................$75.00
Bobby Sherman, 1970s, metal bottle, from $25 to...........$35.00
Bonanza, 1960s, 3 versions, ea from $100 to..................$175.00
Bonanza, 1960s, 3 versions, metal bottle, ea from $50 to .$75.00
Bozo the Clown, 1960s, dome, from $175 to $225.00
Bozo the Clown, 1960s, metal bottle, from $25 to...........$50.00

Brady Bunch, 1970s, from $150.00 to $200.00; metal bottle, from $25.00 to $50.00. (Photo courtesy Greg Davis and Bill Morgan)

Brave Eagle, 1950s, from $150 to $200.00
Brave Eagle, 1950s, metal bottle, from $50 to................$100.00
Buccaneer, 1950s, dome, from $150 to...........................$225.00
Buccaneer, 1950s, metal bottle, from $75 to...................$120.00
Buck Rogers, 1970s, from $25 to $50.00
Buck Rogers, 1970s, plastic bottle, from $15 to $25.00
Bullwinkle & Rocky, 1960s, from $500 to $750.00
Bullwinkle & Rocky, 1960s, metal bottle, from $175 to.$275.00
Cabbage Patch Kids, 1980s, from $15 to.........................$30.00
Cabbage Patch Kids, 1980s, plastic bottle, from $5 to......$10.00
Campbell Kids, 1970s, from $125 to $175.00
Campbell Kids, 1970s, metal bottle, from $30 to.............$60.00
Campus Queen, 1960s, from $50 to $75.00
Campus Queen, 1960s, metal bottle, from $10 to...........$20.00
Captain Astro, 1960s, from $225 to...............................$275.00
Care Bear Cousins, 1980s, from $25 to $50.00
Care Bear Cousins, 1980s, plastic, from $5 to $10.00
Care Bears, 1980s, from $25 to $50.00
Care Bears, 1980s, plastic bottle, from $5 to..................$10.00
Carnival, 1950s, from $350 to $450.00
Carnival, 1950s, metal bottle, from $75 to $125.00
Cartoon Zoo Lunch Chest, 1960s, from $200 to $275.00
Cartoon Zoo Lunch Chest, 1960s, metal bottle, from $65 to .$115.00
Casey Jones, 1960s, dome, from $400 to........................$550.00
Casey Jones, 1960s, metal bottle, from $100 to $150.00
Chan Clan, 1970s, from $60 to $115.00

Charlie's Angels, 1970s, from $50.00 to $100.00; plastic bottle, from $10.00 to $20.00. (Photo courtesy Greg Davis and Bill Morgan)

Chan Clan, 1970s, plastic bottle, from $20 to $30.00
Chavo, 1970s, from $40 to...$90.00
Chavo, 1970s, plastic bottle, from $15 to...........................$25.00
Chitty Chitty Bang Bang, 1960s, from $75 to $125.00
Chitty Chitty Bang Bang, 1960s, metal bottle, from $20 to..$40.00
Chuck Conners, 1960s, Cowboy in Africa, from $150 to ..$200.00
Chuck Conners 1960s, Cowboy in Africa, metal bottle, from $75 to..$100.00
Clash of the Titans, 1980s, from $30 to............................$60.00
Clash of the Titans, 1980s, plastic bottle, from $10 to......$20.00
Close Encounters of the Third Kind, 1970s, from $50 to .$100.00
Close Encounters of the Third Kind, 1970s, plastic bottle, from $10 to..$20.00
Cracker Jack, 1970s, from $30 to.....................................$60.00
Cracker Jack, 1970s, plastic bottle, from $5 to..................$10.00
Cyclist, 1970s, from $25 to..$50.00
Cyclist, 1970s, plastic bottle, from $10 to........................$20.00
Daniel Boone, Aladdin, 1950s, from $300 to..................$350.00
Daniel Boone, Aladdin, 1950s, metal bottle, from $50 to .$75.00
Daniel Boone, Aladdin, 1960s, from $125 to..................$175.00
Daniel Boone, Aladdin, 1960s, metal bottle, from $55 to .$70.00
Daniel Boone, KST, 1960s, Fess Parker, from $125 to $175.00
Daniel Boone, KST, 1960s, Fess Parker, metal bottle, from $60 to...$80.00
Davy Crockett, 1955, At the Alamo, from $250 to........$350.00
Davy Crockett, 1955, At the Alamo, metal bottle, from $400 to...$600.00
Davy Crockett, 1955, gr rim, from $150 to.....................$200.00
Davy Crockett, 1955, gr rim, metal bottle, from $50 to .$100.00
Davy Crockett, 1955, Official (Fess Parker), no bottle, from $200 to..$300.00
Davy Crockett/Kit Carson, 1955, no bottle, from $150 to.$225.00
Dick Tracy, 1960s, from $125 to....................................$175.00
Dick Tracy, 1960s, metal bottle, from $25 to $50.00
Disney Express, 1970s, from $25 to $50.00
Disney Express, 1970s, plastic bottle, from $5 to $15.00
Disney on Parade, 1970s, from $30 to $60.00
Disney on Parade, 1970s, plastic bottle, from $15 to $25.00

Disney School Bus, 1960s-70s, dome, from $50 to $100.00
Disney School Bus, 1960s-70s, metal bottle, from $20 to.$30.00
Disney World, 1970s, 50th Anniversary, from $30 to.......$50.00
Disney World, 1970s, 50th Anniversary, plastic bottle, from $10 to $20.00
Disney's Magic Kingdom, 1970s, from $25 to $40.00
Disney's Magic Kingdom, 1970s, plastic bottle, from $10 to .$15.00
Disney's Wonderful World, 1980s, from $15 to.................$30.00
Disney's Wonderful World, 1980s, plastic bottle, from $5 to.$15.00
Disneyland, 1950s-60s, from $150 to $200.00
Disneyland, 1950s-60s, metal bottle, from $30 to.............$60.00

Doctor Dolittle, 1960s, from $75.00 to $125.00; metal bottle (not shown), from $20.00 to $40.00. (Photo courtesy Carole Bess White and L.M. White)

Double-Deckers, 1970s, from $50 to $75.00
Double-Deckers, 1970s, plastic bottle, from $15 to $30.00
Dr Seuss, 1970s, from $85 to...$135.00
Dr Seuss, 1970s, metal bottle, from $20 to.......................$40.00
Dudley Do-Right, 1960s, from $500 to $800.00
Dudley Do-Right, 1960s, metal bottle, from $225 to......$325.00
Dukes of Hazzard, 1980s, from $45 to..............................$65.00
Dukes of Hazzard, 1980s, plastic bottle, from $10 to.........$20.00
Dyno Mutt, 1970s, from $35 to $55.00
Dyno Mutt, 1970s, plastic bottle, from $10 to $20.00
Early West, 1982-84, ea from $65 to $100.00
Emergency!, 1973, from $50 to..$75.00
Emergency!, 1973, plastic bottle, from $20 to...................$40.00
Empire Strikes Back, 1980s, from $35 to..........................$65.00
Empire Strikes Back, 1980s, plastic bottle, from $10 to....$20.00
ET, 1980s, from $25 to $50.00
ET, 1980s, plastic bottle, from $5 to $10.00
Evel Knievel, 1970s, from $50 to $100.00
Evel Knievel, 1970s, plastic bottle, from $15 to...............$30.00
Fall Guy, 1980s, from $20 to...$40.00
Fall Guy, 1980s, plastic bottle, from $10 to.....................$20.00
Family Affair, 1960s, from $45 to $90.00
Family Affair, 1960s, metal bottle, from $20 to.................$40.00

Emergency! 1977, dome, from $150.00 to $200.00; plastic bottle (not shown), from $20.00 to $40.00.

Gunsmoke, 1959, from $100.00 to $200.00; metal bottle, from $50.00 to $100.00.

Flintstones, 1960s, from $125 to **$175.00**
Flintstones, 1960s, metal bottle, from $30 to **$60.00**
Flintstones, 1970s, from $100 to **$150.00**
Flintstones, 1970s, plastic bottle, from $20 to..................**$40.00**
Flintstones & Dino, 1960s, from $125 to **$175.00**
Flintstones & Dino, 1960s, metal bottle, from $30 to **$60.00**
Flipper, 1960s, from $100 to **$150.00**
Flipper, 1960s, metal bottle, from $20 to.........................**$40.00**
Flying Nun, 1960s, from $100 to.....................................**$150.00**
Flying Nun, 1960s, metal bottle, from $20 to **$40.00**
Fraggle Rock, 1980s, from $30 to **$60.00**
Fraggle Rock, 1980s, plastic bottle, from $5 to **$10.00**
Frontier Days, 1950s, from $125 to.................................**$175.00**
Gene Autry Melody Ranch, 1950s, from $175 to...........**$275.00**
Gene Autry Melody Ranch, 1950s, metal bottle, from $50 to.**$100.00**
Gentle Ben, 1960s, from $75 to **$115.00**
Gentle Ben, 1960s, metal bottle, from $20 to **$40.00**
Get Smart, 1960s, from $125 to **$175.00**
Get Smart, 1960s, metal bottle, from $25 to.....................**$50.00**
Ghostland, 1970s, from $25 to **$50.00**
GI Joe, 1960s, from $80 to..**$130.00**
GI Joe, 1960s, metal bottle, from $25 to **$50.00**
GI Joe, 1980s, from $25 to..**$40.00**
GI Joe, 1980s, plastic bottle, from $10 to.........................**$20.00**
Globe Trotters, 1950s, dome, from $175 to....................**$225.00**
Globe Trotters, 1950s, metal bottle, from $20 to **$40.00**
Gomer Pyle, 1960s, from $100 to **$150.00**
Gomer Pyle, 1960s, metal bottle, from $20 to..................**$40.00**
Goober & the Ghost Chasers, 1970s, from $30 to **$60.00**
Goober & the Ghost Chasers, 1970s, plastic bottle, from $15
   to **$25.00**
Great Wild West, 1950s, from $300 to...........................**$400.00**
Great Wild West, 1950s, metal bottle, from $65 to........**$115.00**
Green Hornet, 1960s, from $200 to **$300.00**
Green Hornet, 1960s, metal bottle, from $50 to.............**$100.00**
Gremlins, 1980s, from $20 to **$35.00**
Gremlins, 1980s, plastic bottle, from $5 to **$10.00**
Grizzly Adams, 1970s, dome, from $50 to **$75.00**
Grizzly Adams, 1970s, plastic bottle, from $15 to **$30.00**
Guns of Will Sonnet, 1960s, from $100 to **$150.00**

Guns of Will Sonnet, 1960s, metal bottle, from $25 to **$50.00**
Gunsmoke, 1959, Marshall (scarce version), from $200 to ..**$400.00**
Gunsmoke, 1959, Marshall (scarce version), metal bottle, from
   $50 to..**$100.00**
Gunsmoke, 1962, from $175 to.......................................**$225.00**
Gunsmoke, 1962, metal bottle, from $40 to......................**$80.00**
Gunsmoke, 1972, from $75 to..**$125.00**
Gunsmoke, 1972, plastic bottle, from $30 to **$60.00**
Gunsmoke, 1973, from $125 to..**$175.00**
Gunsmoke, 1973, plastic bottle, from $25 to **$50.00**
Hair Bear Bunch, 1970s, from $100 to............................**$150.00**
Hair Bear Bunch, 1970s, metal bottle, from $15 to **$30.00**
Hansel & Gretel, 1980s, from $40 to **$60.00**
Happy Days, 1970s, 2 versions, ea from $50 to **$75.00**
Happy Days, 1970s, 2 versions, plastic bottle, ea from $10 to..**$20.00**

Hardy Boys Mysteries, 1970s, from $25.00 to $50.00; plastic bottle, from $5.00 to $15.00. (Photo courtesy Greg Davis and Bill Morgan)

Harlem Globetrotters, 1970s, from $30 to **$60.00**
Harlem Globetrotters, 1970s, metal bottle, from $15 to...**$25.00**
Heathcliff, 1980s, from $20 to...**$30.00**
Heathcliff, 1980s, plastic bottle, from $5 to.....................**$10.00**

Hector Heathcote, 1960s, from $100 to..........................$200.00
Hector Heathcote, 1960s, metal bottle, from $25 to $50.00
Hee Haw, 1970s, from $50 to $100.00
Hee Haw, 1970s, metal bottle, from $15 to......................$30.00
Highway Signs, 1960s or 1970s, 2 versions, ea from $30 to..$75.00
Hogan's Heroes, 1960s, dome, from $200 to $300.00
Hogan's Heroes, 1960s, metal bottle, from $30 to.............$75.00
Holly Hobbie, 1970s, any version, from $30 to.................$40.00
Holly Hobbie, 1970s, plastic bottle, from $5 to $10.00
Hopalong Cassidy, 1950-53, bl or red w/cloud or sq decal, ea
     from $175 to $250.00
Hopalong Cassidy, 1950-53, metal bottle, ea from $50 to..$75.00
Hopalong Cassidy, 1954, from $275 to...........................$350.00
Hopalong Cassidy, 1954, metal bottle, from $85 to........$150.00
How the West Was Won, 1970s, from $30 to $50.00
How the West Was Won, 1970s, plastic bottle, from $10 to.$20.00
HR Pufnstuff, 1970s, from $100 to $150.00
HR Pufnstuff, 1970s, plastic bottle, from $20 to $40.00
Huckleberry Hound & Friends, 1960s, from $100 to......$175.00
Huckleberry Hound & Friends, 1960s, metal bottle, from $20
     to $40.00
Incredible Hulk, 1970s, from $20 to................................$80.00
Incredible Hulk, 1970s, plastic bottle, from $5 to............$15.00
Indiana Jones, 1980s, from $20 to...................................$40.00
Indiana Jones, 1980s, plastic bottle, from $5 to $15.00
James Bond 007, 1960s, from $150 to $225.00
James Bond 007, 1960s, metal bottle, from $25 to...........$50.00
Jet Patrol, 1950s, from $200 to $300.00
Jet Patrol, 1950s, metal bottle, from $50 to $100.00
Jetson's, 1960s, dome, from $900 to $1,400.00
Jetson's, 1960s, metal bottle, from $200 to $300.00
Johnny Lightning, 1970s, from $40 to.............................$75.00
Johnny Lightning, 1970s, plastic bottle, from $15 to........$30.00
Jr Miss, 1956, from $30 to..$65.00
Jr Miss, 1956, metal bottle, from $10 to $20.00
Jr Miss, 1960, from $25 to..$50.00
Jr Miss, 1960, metal bottle, from $15 to $20.00
Jr Miss, 1962, from $25 to..$75.00
Jr Miss, 1962, metal bottle, from $15 to $25.00
Jr Miss, 1966, from $25 to..$45.00
Jr Miss, 1966, metal bottle, from $15 to $20.00
Jr Miss, 1970, from $20 to..$40.00
Jr Miss, 1970, plastic bottle, from $5 to..........................$15.00
Jr Miss, 1973, from $15 to..$30.00
Jr Miss, 1973, plastic bottle, from $5 to..........................$15.00
Julia, 1960s, from $50 to...$100.00
Julia, 1960s, metal bottle, from $15 to $40.00
Jungle Book, 1960s, from $45 to.....................................$90.00
Jungle Book, 1960s, metal bottle, from $15 to $30.00
Knight Rider, 1980s, from $20 to $40.00
Knight Rider, 1980s, plastic bottle, from $5 to $15.00
Korg, 1970s, from $35 to...$65.00
Korg, 1970s, plastic, from $10 to $20.00
Krofft Supershow, 1970s, from $50 to $100.00
Krofft Supershow, 1970s, plastic bottle, from $15 to........$25.00
Kung Fu, 1970s, from $40 to...$80.00
Kung Fu, 1970s, plastic bottle, from $5 to......................$15.00

Lance Link Secret Chimp, 1970s, from $75 to $125.00
Lance Link Secret Chimp, 1970s, metal bottle, from $15 to..$30.00
Land of the Giants, 1960s, from $100 to.........................$160.00
Land of the Giants, 1960s, plastic bottle, from $20 to......$40.00
Land of the Lost, 1970s, from $75 to..............................$125.00
Land of the Lost, 1970s, plastic bottle, from $15 to.........$30.00
Lassie, 1970s, from $35 to...$55.00
Laugh-In, 1968, from $75 to...$125.00
Laugh-In, 1968, plastic bottle, ea from $15 to $30.00
Laugh-In, 1971, from $75 to...$150.00
Laugh-In, 1971, plastic bottle, from $15 to......................$30.00
Lawman, 1960s, from $75 to $150.00
Lawman, 1960s, metal bottle, from $20 to........................$40.00
Legend of the Lone Ranger, 1980s, from $45 to..............$75.00
Legend of the Lone Ranger, 1980s, plastic bottle, from $15
     to...$30.00
Little Dutch Miss, 1959, from $50 to.............................$100.00
Little Dutch Miss, 1959, metal bottle, from $20 to...........$40.00
Little Friends, 1980s, from $350 to................................$475.00
Little Friends, 1980s, plastic bottle, from $75 to.............$150.00

Little House on the Prairie, 1970s, from $50.00 to $100.00. (Photo courtesy Carole Bess White and L.M. White)

Little House on the Prairie, 1970s, plastic bottle, from $20
     to...$40.00
Little Orphan Annie, 1980s, from $25 to $50.00
Lone Ranger, 1950s, from $300 to..................................$450.00
Looney Tunes, 1959, from $175 to $250.00
Looney Tunes, 1959, metal bottle, from $30 to.................$60.00
Lost in Space, repro, dome, from $20 to...........................$40.00
Lost in Space, 1960s, dome, from $350 to.......................$450.00
Lost in Space, 1960s, metal bottle, from $30 to $60.00
Ludwig Von Drake in Disneyland, 1960s, $125 to.........$175.00
Ludwig Von Drake in Disneyland, 1960s, metal bottle, from $20
     to...$40.00
Magic of Lassie, 1970s, from $45 to................................$75.00
Magic of Lassie, 1970s, plastic bottle, from $15 to...........$30.00
Marvel Super Heroes, 1970s, from $25 to $50.00

Man From U.N.C.L.E., 1960s, from $100.00 to $150.00; metal bottle from $20.00 to $40.00. (Photo courtesy Carole Bess White and L.M. White)

Mary Poppins, 1960s, from $50 to $100.00
Mary Poppins, 1960s, metal bottle, from $15 to $30.00
Masters of the Universe, 1980s, from $30 to $60.00
Masters of the Universe, 1980s, plastic bottle, from $5 to .$10.00
Mickey Mouse & Donald Duck, 1950s, from $250 to.....$350.00
Mickey Mouse & Donald Duck, 1950s, metal bottle, from $75 to $150.00
Mickey Mouse Club, 1960s, from $65 to........................$100.00
Mickey Mouse Club, 1960s, metal bottle, from $15 to $30.00
Mickey Mouse Club, 1970s, from $30 to..........................$60.00
Mickey Mouse Club, 1970s, plastic bottle, from $5 to......$15.00
Miss America, 1970s, from $50 to $100.00
Miss America, 1970s, plastic bottle, from $15 to $30.00
Monkees, 1990s, from $25 to..$50.00
Monroes, 1960s, from $75 to...$150.00
Monroes, 1960s, metal bottle, from $25 to........................$50.00
Mr Merlin, 1980s, from $20 to $35.00
Mr Merlin, 1980s, plastic bottle, from $5 to $15.00

Munsters, 1960s, from $200 to $375.00
Munsters, 1960s, metal bottle, from $75 to.....................$125.00
Muppet Babies, 1980s, from $20 to $40.00
Muppet Babies, 1980s, plastic bottle, from $5 to $10.00
Muppets, 1970s, any, ea from $20 to $50.00
Muppets, 1970s, plastic bottle, from $5 to $10.00
Nancy Drew Mysteries, 1970s, from $30 to....................$60.00
Nancy Drew Mysteries, 1970s, plastic, from $10 to $20.00
Orbit, 1950s, from $50 to $125.00
Orbit, 1960s, metal bottle, from $25 to...........................$50.00

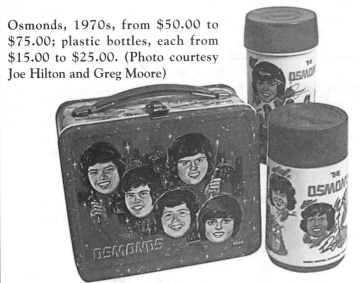

Osmonds, 1970s, from $50.00 to $75.00; plastic bottles, each from $15.00 to $25.00. (Photo courtesy Joe Hilton and Greg Moore)

Our Friends, 1980s, from $200 to $400.00
Our Friends, 1980s, metal bottle, from $50 to...................$75.00
Pac Man, 1980, from $20 to $35.00
Pac-Man, 1980s, plastic bottle, from $5 to.......................$10.00
Paladin, 1960s, from $150 to $225.00
Paladin, 1960s, metal bottle, from $40 to.........................$80.00
Pathfinder, 1959, from $300 to..$400.00
Pathfinder, 1959, metal bottle, from $75 to.....................$150.00

Mork and Mindy, 1970s, from $25.00 to $50.00; plastic bottle, from $5.00 to $15.00. (Photo courtesy Carole Bess White and L.M. White)

Partridge Family, 1970s, from $40.00 to $80.00; plastic bottle, from $15.00 to $30.00. (Photo courtesy Carole Bess White and L.M. White)

Peanuts, 1960, from $30 to $60.00
Peanuts, 1960, metal bottle, from $10 to $20.00
Peanuts, 1973, from $25 to $50.00
Peanuts, 1973, plastic bottle, from $5 to $15.00
Peanuts, 1976, from $20 to $35.00
Peanuts, 1976, plastic bottle, from $5 to $15.00
Peanuts, 1980, from $15 to $30.00
Peanuts, 1980, plastic bottle, from $6 to $12.00
Pebbles & Bamm Bamm, 1970s, from $40 to $80.00
Pebbles & Bamm Bamm, 1970s, plastic bottle, from $15 to..$30.00
Pele, 1970s, from $50 to $100.00
Pele, 1970s, plastic bottle, from $15 to...............$30.00
Pete's Dragon, 1970s, from $30 to $60.00
Pete's Dragon, 1970s, plastic bottle, from $10 to $20.00
Peter Pan, 1960s, from $50 to...........................$100.00
Peter Pan, 1960s, plastic bottle, from $20 to...........$40.00
Pigs in Space, 1970s, from $35 to $50.00
Pigs in Space, 1970s, plastic bottle, from $5 to $15.00
Pink Panther & Sons, 1980s, from $20 to.................$40.00
Pink Panther & Sons, 1980s, plastic bottle, from $5 to....$15.00
Pinocchio, 1970s, from $50 to...........................$100.00
Pinocchio, 1970s, plastic bottle, from $15 to...................$30.00
Pit Stop, 1960s, from $50 to $100.00
Planet of the Apes, 1970s, from $75 to $125.00
Planet of the Apes, 1970s, plastic bottle, from $15 to $25.00
Play Ball, 1960s, from $40 to $80.00
Play Ball, 1960s, metal bottle, from $15 to $30.00
Police Patrol, 1970s, from $125 to $175.00
Police Patrol, 1970s, plastic bottle, from $15 to..............$25.00
Polly Pal, 1970s, from $20 to $35.00
Polly Pal, 1970s, plastic bottle, from $5 to $10.00
Pony Express, 1950s, from $225 to $275.00

Popeye, 1962, from $350.00 to $550.00; metal bottle (not shown) from $175.00 to $250.00. (Photo courtesy Carole Bess White and L.M. White)

Popeye, 1964, from $100 to $150.00
Popeye, 1964, metal bottle, from $40 to.................$80.00
Popeye, 1980, from $40 to $80.00
Popeye, 1980, plastic bottle, from $10 to $20.00
Popples, 1980s, from $15 to $25.00

Popples, 1980s, plastic bottle, from $5 to $10.00
Porky's Lunch Wagon, 1959, from $200 to $300.00
Porky's Lunch Wagon, 1959, metal bottle, from $25 to....$50.00

Raggedy Ann and Andy, 1970s, from $20.00 to $40.00; plastic bottle, from $10.00 to $20.00. (Photo courtesy Carole Bess White and L.M. White)

Rambo, 1980s, from $20 to................................$30.00
Rambo, 1980s, plastic bottle, from $5 to................$10.00
Rat Patrol, 1960s, from $75 to...........................$125.00
Rat Patrol, 1960s, metal bottle, from $20 to $40.00
Rescuers, from $25 to....................................$50.00
Rescuers, 1970s, plastic bottle, from $15 to $25.00
Return of the Jedi, 1980s, from $30 to...................$60.00
Return of the Jedi, 1980s, plastic bottle, from $10 to $20.00
Rifleman, 1960s, from $275 to............................$350.00
Rifleman, 1960s, metal bottle, from $50 to......................$90.00
Road Runner, 1970, from $40 to $80.00
Road Runner, 1970s, metal bottle, from $15 to $30.00
Robin Hood, 1950s, from $125 to $200.00
Robin Hood, 1950s, metal bottle, from $20 to.................$40.00
Robin Hood, 1970s, from $30 to..........................$60.00
Robin Hood, 1970s, plastic bottle, from $8 to $18.00
Ronald McDonald, 1980s, from $15 to $30.00
Ronald McDonald, 1980s, plastic bottle, from $6 to $12.00
Rose Petal Place, 1980s, from $20 to.....................$40.00
Rose Petal Place, 1980s, plastic bottle, from $5 to...........$15.00
Rough Rider, 1970s, from $50 to $75.00
Rough Rider, 1970s, plastic bottle, from $18 to $28.00
Roy Rogers & Dale Evans, 1950s, many versions, ea from $150
    to..$250.00
Roy Rogers & Dale Evans, 1950s, metal bottle, ea from $45
    to $75.00
Satellite, 1950s, from $80 to............................$120.00
Satellite, 1950s, metal bottle, from $20 to $40.00
Satellite, 1960s, from $50 to............................$75.00
Satellite, 1960s, metal bottle, from $15 to $30.00
School Days, 1980s, from $350 to $450.00
School Days, 1980s, plastic bottle, from $65 to $125.00
Scooby Doo, 1970s, any, ea from $50 to.........................$100.00

Scooby Doo, 1970s, plastic bottle, from $22 to................$38.00
Secret Agent T, 1960s, from $50 to...................................$100.00
Secret Agent T, 1960s, metal bottle, from $25 to $50.00
Secret of NIMH, 1980s, from $15 to...............................$30.00
Secret of NIMH, 1980s, plastic bottle, form $5 to $10.00
Secret Wars, 1980s, from $50 to....................................$75.00
Secret Wars, 1980s, plastic bottle, from $18 to $28.00
Sesame Street, 1970s, from $25 to....................................$50.00
Sesame Street, 1970s, plastic bottle, from $5 to................$10.00
Sesame Street, 1980s, from $20 to....................................$40.00
Sesame Street, 1980s, plastic bottle, from $5 to...............$10.00
Sigmund & the Sea Monsters, 1970s, from $65 to $125.00
Sigmund & the Sea Monsters, 1970s, plastic bottle, from $25
    to...$45.00
Six Million Dollar Man, 1970s, any, ea from $35 to $55.00
Six Million Dollar Man, 1970s, plastic bottle, ea from $18 to.$28.00
Skateboarder, 1970s, from $35 to $65.00
Skateboarder, 1970s, plastic bottle, from $15 to $25.00
Smokey Bear, 1970s, from $225 to $300.00
Smokey Bear, 1970s, metal bottle, from $75 to.............$150.00
Smurfs, 1980s, from $100 to $150.00
Smurfs, 1980s, plastic bottle, from $5 to $15.00
Snoopy, 1969, dome, from $50 to......................................$100.00
Snoopy, 1969, metal bottle, from $15 to.............................$25.00
Snow White, 1975, from $35 to $70.00
Snow White, 1975, plastic bottle, from $10 to $20.00
Snow White, 1977 or 1980, ea from $25 to $50.00
Space Shuttle Orbiter Enterprise, 1970s, from $45 to $85.00
Space Shuttle Oribter Enterprise, 1970s, plastic bottle, from $15
    to $25.00
Space: 1999, 1970s, from $50 to.......................................$75.00
Space: 1999, 1970s, plastic bottle, from $15 to.................$25.00
Spider-Man & The Hulk, 1980, from $30 to $60.00
Spider-Man & The Hulk, 1980s, plastic bottle, from $10 to.$20.00
Sport Goofy, 1980s, from $20 to..$40.00
Sport Goofy, 1980s, plastic bottle, from $5 to..................$15.00
Star Trek, 1960s, dome, from $550 to $750.00
Star Trek, 1960s, metal bottle, from $250 to.................$350.00
Star Wars, 1970s, any, ea from $50 to $100.00

Star Wars, 1970s, plastic bottle, any, ea from $10 to.........$20.00
Steve Canyon, 1959, from $150 to...................................$250.00
Steve Canyon, 1959, metal bottle, from $55 to $85.00
Strawberry Shortcake, 1980s, from $20 to $40.00
Strawberry Shortcake, 1980s, plastic bottle, from $5 to ...$10.00
Street Hawk, 1980s, from $70 to.....................................$135.00
Street Hawk, 1980s, plastic bottle, from $20 to...............$40.00
Submarine, 1960, from $50 to $100.00
Submarine, 1960, metal bottle, from $15 to.....................$30.00

Super Friends, 1970s, from $40.00 to $80.00; plastic bottle, from $10.00 to $20.00. (Photo courtesy Carol Bess White and L.M. White)

Super Heroes, 1970s, from $35 to......................................$70.00
Super Heroes, 1970s, plastic bottle, from $10 to..............$20.00
Super Powers, 1980s, from $45 to......................................$85.00
Super Powers, 1980s, plastic bottle, 1980s, from $10 to ...$20.00
Superman, 1960s, from $100 to.......................................$175.00
Superman, 1960s, metal bottle, from $50 to $75.00
Superman, 1970s, from $40 to $80.00
Superman, 1970s, plastic bottle, from $15 to...................$25.00

Star Trek The Motion Picture, from $100.00 to $200.00; plastic bottle, from $20.00 to $30.00. (Photo courtesy Carol Bess White and L.M. White)

Tom Corbett Space Cadet, 1952, from $100.00 to $200.00; metal bottle, from $30.00 to $55.00. (Photo courtesy Carole Bess White and L.M. White)

Tarzan, 1960s, from $100 to..$150.00
Tarzan, 1960s, metal bottle, from $20 to.........................$40.00
Three Little Pigs, 1980s, from $40 to..............................$80.00
Thundercats, 1980s, from $25 to.....................................$50.00
Thundercats, 1980s, plastic bottle, from $5 to.................$10.00

Tom Corbett Space Cadet, 1954, from $125.00 to $275.00; metal bottle, from $35.00 to $65.00. (Photo courtesy Scott Bruce)

Transformers, 1980s, from $25 to.....................................$50.00
Transformers, 1980s, plastic bottle, from $5 to.................$15.00
Treasure Chest, 1960s, dome, from $175 to...................$275.00
Treasure Chest, 1960s, metal bottle, from $75 to...........$125.00
UFO, 1970s, from $50 to...$85.00
UFO, 1970s, plastic bottle, from $15 to...........................$30.00
Underdog, 1970s, from $350 to.......................................$750.00
Underdog, 1970s, metal bottle, from $150 to.................$250.00
US Mail/Zippy, 1969, dome, from $35 to..........................$65.00
US Mail/Zippy, 1969, plastic bottle, from $15 to.............$30.00
V, 1980s, from $75 to...$125.00
V, 1980s, plastic bottle, from $20 to................................$40.00
Voyage to the Bottom of the Sea, 1960s, from $175 to...$250.00
Voyage to the Bottom of the Sea, 1960s, metal bottle, from $50
    to..$75.00
Wagon Train, 1960s, from $100 to................................$200.00
Wagon Train, 1960s, metal bottle, from $25 to................$50.00
Waltons, 1970s, from $50 to...$75.00
Waltons, 1970s, plastic bottle, from $15 to.....................$30.00
Wild Bill Hickok & Jingles, 1950s, from $150 to............$200.00
Wild Bill Hickok & Jingles, 1950s, metal bottle, from $40 to .$80.00
Wild Wild West, 1960s, from $175 to.............................$250.00
Wild Wild West, 1969, plastic bottle, from $35 to............$65.00
Winnie the Pooh, 1970s, from $150 to...........................$200.00
Winnie the Pooh, 1970s, plastic bottle, from $25 to........$50.00
Woody Woodpecker, 1970s, from $100 to.......................$150.00
Woody Woodpecker, 1970s, plastic bottle, from $25 to....$50.00
Yankee Doodle, 1970s, from $25 to.................................$50.00
Yellow Submarine, 1960s, metal bottle, from $75 to......$150.00
Yellow Submarine, 1968, from $250 to...........................$500.00
Yogi Bear, 1970s, from $45 to..$85.00

Welcome Back Kotter, 1970s, from $50.00 to $75.00; plastic bottle, from $10.00 to $20.00. (Photo courtesy Greg Davis and Bill Morgan)

Yogi Bear, 1970s, plastic bottle, from $15 to...................$35.00
Yogi Bear & Friends, 1960s, from $85 to........................$135.00
Yogi Bear & Friends, 1960s, metal bottle, from, $20 to....$40.00

Zorro, 1950s or 1960s, each from $100.00 to $200.00; metal bottles, each from $40.00 to $75.00.

18 Wheeler, 1970s, from $50 to..$80.00
18 Wheeler, 1970s, plastic bottle, from $10 to.................$15.00
240 Robert, 1970s, from $2,500 to..............................$3,500.00
240 Robert, 1970s, plastic bottle, from $350 to.............$450.00

PLASTIC

A-Team, 1980s, from $15 to...$20.00
Astrokids, 1980s, from $15 to..$25.00
Barbie, 1990s, from $10 to...$15.00
Barney Baby Bop, 1990s, from $5 to.................................$10.00
Benji, 1970s, from $20 to...$30.00
Cabbage Patch Kids, from $15 to......................................$20.00
Casper the Friendly Ghost, 1990s, from $8 to..................$15.00
Chip 'n Dale, 1980s, from $5 to...$10.00
Chuck E Cheese, 1990s, from $25 to.................................$35.00
Crest Toothpast, 1980s, tubular, from $50 to....................$75.00
Dick Tracy, 1990s, red, from $10 to..................................$15.00

CHiPs, 1970s, dome, from $40.00 to $60.00. (Photo courtesy Greg Davis and Bill Morgan)

Disney School Bus, 1990s, from $20 to	$30.00
Dr Seuss, 1990s, from $20 to	$25.00
Fat Albert, 1970s, from $20 to	$30.00
Flintstones (A Day at the Zoo), Denny's logo, 1989, from $20 to	$30.00
Garfield, 1980s, from $15 to	$20.00

Happy Days, 1970s, Canada, dome, from $30.00 to $50.00. (Photo courtesy Greg Davis and Bill Morgan)

Holly Hobby, 1989, from $20 to	$25.00
Hot Wheels, 1990s, from $15 to	$20.00
Incredible Hulk, 1980s, dome, from $40 to	$50.00
Jabberjaw, 1970s, from $30 to	$40.00
Jem, 1980s, from $8 to	$15.00
Jurassic Park, 1990s, w/recalled bottle, from $25 to	$30.00
Keebler Cookies, 1980s, from $30 to	$50.00
Kermit the Frog, 1980s, dome top, from $30 to	$40.00
Little Orphan Annie, 1970s, dome, from $35 to	$45.00
Looney Tunes, 1970s, from $15 to	$25.00
Lucy Luncheonette, 1980s, dome, from $20 to	$30.00
Mickey Mouse, 1980s, head form, from $25 to	$35.00
Mickey Mouse & Donald Duck, 1980s, from $10 to	$15.00
Mighty Mouse, 1970s, from $25 to	$35.00
Minnie Mouse, 1980s, head form, from $30 to	$40.00

Muppet Babies, 1980s, from $15 to	$25.00
Muppets, 1990s, from $10 to	$18.00
Nestlé's Quik, 1980s, from $25 to	$30.00
New Kids on the Block, 1990s, from $15 to	$25.00
Nosey Bears, 1990s, from $10 to	$20.00
Pee Wee Herman, 1980s, from $20 to	$30.00
Pepsi, 1980s, from $30 to	$40.00
Popeye, 1979, dome, from $30 to	$40.00
Rap It Up, 1990s, from $20 to	$25.00
Robot Man, 1980s, from $20 to	$30.00

Rocky and Bullwinkle, 1990s, from $75.00 to $125.00. (Photo courtesy Carole Bess White and L.M. White)

Rocky Roughneck, 1970s, from $25 to	$35.00
Rover Dangerfield, 1990s, from $20 to	$30.00
Shadow, 1990s, from $10 to	$20.00
Smurfs, 1980s, dome, from $20 to	$30.00
Snoopy & Woodstock, 1970s, dome, from $20 to	$30.00
Snoopy as Joe Cool, 1970s, from $15 to	$25.00
Star Trek (TNG), 1970s, from $10 to	$20.00
Star Wars Ewoks, 1980s, from $20 to	$30.00
Sunnie Miss, 1970s, from $50 to	$75.00
Superman, 1980s, phone booth scene, from $30 to	$40.00
SWAT, 1970s, dome, from $30 to	$40.00
The Tick, 1990s, from $25 to	$50.00
Tom & Jerry, 1990s, from $10 to	$20.00
Train Engine #7, 1990s, from $15 to	$25.00
Winnie the Pooh, 1990s, from $15 to	$25.00
Yogi Bear, 1990s, EX, from $15 to	$25.00
Young Astronauts, 1980s, from $20 to	$30.00

VINYL

Annie, 1980s, from $50 to	$75.00
Barbie, 1970s, from $65 to	$85.00
Barbie Lunch Kit, 1960s, from $300 to	$400.00
Batman, 1990s, from $15 to	$25.00
Denim, 1970s, from $45 to	$65.00
Deputy Dawg, 1960s, from $325 to	$375.00
Donny & Marie, 1970s, from $80 to	$120.00
Fire Station Engine Co #1, 1970s, from $115 to	$135.00

Barbarino (Welcome Back Kotter), 1970s, from $125.00 to $150.00. (Photo courtesy Greg Davis and Bill Morgan)

Casper the Friendly Ghost, 1960s, from $400.00 to $500.00. (Photo courtesy Carole Bess White and L.M. White)

Holly Hobbie, 1970s, from $50 to $75.00
Jr Deb, 1960s, from $100 to...$150.00
Li'l Jodie, 1980s, from $50 to..$75.00
Lion in the Van, 1970s, from $50 to..................................$75.00
Little Old Schoolhouse, 1970s, from $50 to.....................$75.00
Mardi Gras, 1970s, from $50 to.......................................$110.00
Monkees, 1960s, from $300 to...$350.00

Mary Poppins, 1970s, from $75.00 to $100.00. (Photo courtesy Carole Bess White and L.M. White)

Pac Man, 1980s, from $40 to $60.00
Pepsi-Cola, 1980s, yel, from $50 to $75.00
Pink Panther, 1980s, from $75 to $100.00
Psychedelic Blue, 1970s, from $40 to $60.00
Ringling Bros & Barnum & Bailey Circus, 1970s, from $175 to $125.00
Ronald McDonald, 1980s, lunch bag, from $15 to $25.00
Snoopy, 1970s, brunch bag, from $75 to $125.00
Snoopy at Mailbox, 1969, red, from $65 to.....................$85.00
Soupy Sales, 1960s, from $300 to....................................$375.00
Speedy Turtle, 1970s, drawstring bag, from $15 to...........$25.00

Strawberry Shortcake, 1980, from $75.00 to $135.00. (Photo courtesy Carole Bess White and L.M. White)

The Sophisticate, 1970s, drawstring bag, from $50 to $75.00
Tic-Tac-Toe, 1970s, from $50 to.......................................$75.00
Wonder Woman, 1970s, from $100 to $150.00
World of Barbie, 1971, EX, from $50 to $75.00
Ziggy, 1979, from $50 to $75.00

Marbles

Antique marbles are divided into several classifications: 1) Transparent Swirl (Solid Core, Latticinio Core, Divided Core, Ribbon Core, Lobed Core, and Coreless); 2) Lutz or Lutz-type (with bands having copper flecks which alternate with colored or clear bands; 3) Peppermint Swirl (made of red, white, and blue opaque glass); 4) Indian Swirl (black with multicolored surface swirls); 5) Banded Swirl (wide swirling bands on opaque or transparent glass); 6) Onionskin (having an overall mottled appearance due to its spotted, swirling lines or lobes: 7) End-of-Day (single pontil, allover spots, either two-colored or multicolored); 8) Clambroth (evenly spaced, swirled lines on opaque glass); 9) Mica (transparent color with mica flakes added); 10) Sulfide (nearly always clear, colored examples are rare, containing figures). Besides glass marbles, some were made of clay, pottery, china, steel, and even semiprecious stones.

Most machine-made marbles are still very reasonable, but some of the better examples may sell for $50.00 and up, depending on the colors that were used and how they are defined. Guineas (Christensen agates with small multicolored specks instead of swirls) sometimes go for as much as $200.00. Mt. Peltier comic character marbles often bring prices of $100.00 and more with Betty Boop, Moon Mullins, and Kayo being the rarest and most valuable.

From the nature of their use, mint-condition marbles are extremely rare and may be worth as much as three to five times more than one that is near-mint, while chipped and cracked marbles may be worth half or less. The same is true of one that has been polished, regardless of how successful the polishing was. If you'd like to learn more, Everett Grist has written three books on the subject that you will find helpful: *Antique and Collectible Marbles, Machine Made and Contemporary Marbles,* and *Everett Grist's Big Book of Marbles.* Also refer to MCSA's *Marble Identification and Price Guide,* recently re-written by Robert Block (Schiffer Publishing). See Clubs, Newsletters, and Other Publications for club information.

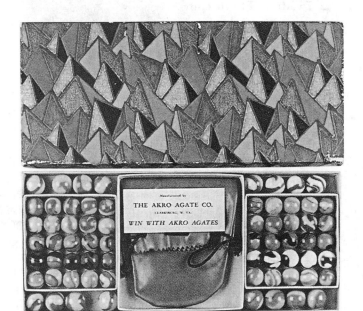

Akro Agate, Opaque Corkscrews with bag, complete set, NMIB, $2,000.00. (Photo courtesy Everett Grist)

Artist-Made, end-of-day w/lutz or mica, Mark Mathews, ⅝", to ¾", M $50.00
Artist-Made, swirls & ribbons, Harry Boyer, 1⅝", M........$50.00
Banded Opaque Swirl, wht w/red & bl swirls from top to bottom, ⅝", M $150.00
China, hand-painted, bull's-eye pattern in mc on wht, 1¾", M..$900.00
China, hand-painted circles w/lines surrounding them giving them 'eye-like' appearance on wht, 1¾", M $375.00
China, hand-painted flower on creamy wht, 2 hairline stripes running from pole to pole, ⅝", M $275.00
China, hand-painted, overlapping mc flowers on creamy wht, ⅝", M...$350.00

China, hand-painted plaid-like design on wht, ⅝", M $45.00
Clambroth Swirl, bl w/wht swirls, rare, ⅝", M...............$400.00
Clambroth Swirl, opaque wht swirls in 1 to 4 colors, ⅝", ea, M..$225.00
Clay, commonly found, some are dyed, others natural, 1¾", ea, M..$5.00
Cloud, wht, red, yel & bl bits floating in clear, 1¾", M.$2,000.00
Cloud, wht, red, yel & bl bits floating in clear, ⅝" (rare sz), M..$150.00

Comic, top row: Skeezix, $100.00; Herbie, $100.00; Smitty, $110.00; Emma, $85.00; middle row: Ko Ko, $100.00; Moon Mullins, $275.00; Betty Boop, $275.00; Kayo, $375.00; bottom row: Andy Gump, $85.00; Bimbo, $90.00; Sandy, $90.00; Annie, $100.00. (Photo courtesy Everett Grist)

Comic, Tom Mix, Peltier Glass, M, minimum value $500.00
Crockery, wht w/random mc zigzag lines throughout, ⅝", M..$15.00
Divided Core Swirl, peewee, any variation, ⅜" to ½", M, ea...$25.00
Divided Core Swirl, 4 yel puter bands w/3 mc inner bands, 1 1/16", NM..$100.00
End-of-Day, clear w/surface color of 2 feathery wing-like sections, 1 red & 1 wht, 1 9/16", M............................$2,500.00
End-of-Day, cobalt w/silver mica, all cased in clear, 1⅝", M.$2,000.00
End-of-Day, predominately bl w/sm mc specks & lots of mica, 2⅜", M..$3,800.00
End-of-Day, red & wht w/yel & bl flowing down center, single pontil, 2", M...$1,800.00
End-of-Day, red & yel w/blue specks w/mottling at top cascades down to blur at bottom, 1¾", M $1,950.00
End-of-Day, wht w/bl & red specks, dashes of yel w/deep bl at base, 1¾", M...$2,500.00
End-of-Day w/mica, red, wht, bl globules suspended in clear, 1⅞", M..$4,000.00
Gooseberry, transparent gr base w/wht swirls, ⅝", M......$275.00
Indian Swirl, blk w/outer bands in earth tones of red, orange, yel & burnt umber, ⅝", M..$150.00
Indian Swirl, blk w/turq bl & earth-tone bands, 1¾" ..$2,000.00
Joseph's Coat, clear base w/mc swirl, shrunken core w/aventurine, M..$165.00

Joseph's Coat, transparent bl base w/mc swirl, ¹⁵⁄₁₆", VG ..$65.00

Lucky Boy Marble Set, 28 tiger-eyes, MIB $300.00

Lutz Ribbon Core, amber & brn w/golden border surrounding gold swirl, 1⅜", M $3,500.00

Lutz Ribbon Core, blood red w/single wht-bordered gold swirl, ⅝", M $300.00

Lutz Ribbon Core, emerald gr w/mint-bordered gold swirl, ⅝", M $300.00

Lutz-Type 1, clear swirl, bright bl & wht-bordered gold surface swirls, ⅝", M $125.00

Lutz-Type 2, transparent, wht & wht-bordered gold surface swirls on aqua, 1¾", M $2,500.00

Lutz-Type 2, wht & gold surface swirls on amber, ⅝", M .$225.00

Lutz-Type 3, wht & wht-edged gold surface swirls on blk, ⅝", M ..$300.00

Lutz-Type 3, wht & wht-edged gold surface swirls on aqua, ⅝", M $350.00

Lutz-Type 3, ⅝", $225.00 each; 1¾", $2,700.00. (Photo courtesy Everett Grist)

Lutz-Type 5 (Onionskin), sapphire bl w/wht & gold spirals, slight lustre look (possibly from use), ⅝", M $275.00

Lutz-Type 6 (single color), gr w/gold slightly S-shaped swirls, ⅝", M $300.00

Lutz-Type 7, Indian Swirl w/gold-colored flakes added, ⅝", M $450.00

Machine-Made, Carnelian Agate containing oxblood, ⁹⁄₁₆" to ¹¹⁄₁₆", M $100.00

Machine-Made, Christensen Agate known as Flame, red 'flames' on gr, M $175.00

Machine-Made, Christensen Agate known as Hurricane, tangled mc swirls, M, from $100 to $225.00

Machine-Made, clear or transparent w/ribbon corkscrew, ⁹⁄₁₆" to ¹¹⁄₁₆", M, ea from $15 to $25.00

Machine-Made, corkscrew, clear, wht, yel & bl, Akro Agate, M, from $30 to $40.00

Machine-Made, corkscrew, wht w/red swirl, Akro Agate, M .$7.00

Machine-Made, corkscrew, 3-color, ⁹⁄₁₆" to ¹¹⁄₁₆", M, ea....$40.00

Machine-Made, Ketchup & Mustard, yel & red swirls on wht, Peltier Glass, M, from $60 to $275.00

Machine-Made, lemonade oxblood, Akro Agate, ⁹⁄₁₆" to ¹¹⁄₁₆", M, ea $130.00

Machine-Made, limeade corkscrew or swirl, Akro Agate, ⁹⁄₁₆" to ¹¹⁄₁₆", M $30.00

Machine-Made, Moss Agate, Akro Agate & other companies, M, ea ....$.50

Machine-Made, Orange Peel, opaque blk base w/orange & yel triangular patch, M, rare $250.00

Machine-Made, Popeye corkscrew, clear & wht w/gr & yel, ⁹⁄₁₆" to ¹¹⁄₁₆", M $30.00

Machine-Made, Rocket, blk & orange translucent swirls, ¹¹⁄₁₆", M $250.00

Mica, transparent bl (or gr) w/mica added, old, ⅝", VG ..$25.00

Onionskin, gr w/slender swirls of red, yel & gr, 1⅞", M..$1,200.00

Onionskin, mica (very heavy) over red, yel & bl ribbons, 1¾", M $3,500.00

Onionskin, mica flecks overlaid on red, gr & wht, slightly swirled, 1¾", M $2,500.00

Onionskin, mica over red & wht, ribbons laid end-to-end in slight swirl, 1¾", M $2,000.00

Onionskin, red, yel & gr, 1¾", M $1,200.00

Onionskin, red & bl w/yel streaks, lots of mica, 2⅜", M..$2,600.00

Onionskin, red and white with a touch of blue and a hint of pink, 1¾", $2,750.00. (Photo courtesy Everett Grist)

Onionskin, 4-lobed, 1 yel swirl w/red flecks, 1 wht swirl w/wht & gr flecks, over spatter w/blk flecks & mica, 1¾", M.$750.00

Onionskin, 4-lobed swirl, Christmas like w/bright red, yel & dk gr, 1¾", M $900.00

Peppermint Swirl, opaque glass w/red, wht, bl swirls, ⅝", M.$100.00

Peppermint Swirl, opaque glass w/red, wht & bl swirls, 1¾", M $3,500.00

Peppermint swirl, opaque glass w/red, wht & bl swirls & mica, ⅝", M $500.00

Solid Opaque, various colors, 2 pontil points, ⅝", ea, M..$35.00

Sulfide, angel holding wreath, figure stops at knees, 1¾", M $750.00

Sulfide, bear standing, 1¾", M $200.00

Sulfide, buffalo (American Bison), EX detail & design, 1¾", M $300.00

Sulfide, child in crawling position, knickers & sailor-collar shirt, bobbed haircut, 1¾", M $600.00

Sulfide, child in long dress, 1¾", M $650.00

Sulfide, child seated in chair, 1¾", M $650.00

Sulfide, clown in Harlequin outfit, peaked hat, few details, 1¾", M $1,000.00

Sulfide, Crucifix, figure on cross, crudely made, 1¾", M .$650.00

Sulfide, dog w/blk spots sitting on grassy mound, rare, M .$3,500.00

Sulfide, fish, 1¾", M $200.00

Sulfide, girl seated w/hammer, pleated skirt, fine details, 1¾", M $600.00

Sulfide, horse standing, 1¾", M $175.00

Sulfide, Little Boy Blue seated w/horn, 1¾", M $750.00

Sulfide, numeral 2, 1¾", M $400.00

Sulfide, owl, 1¾", M $200.00

Sulfide, peacock in gr grass, rare, 1¾", M $8,000.00

Sulfide, elephant with head erect, 1¾", $300.00. (Photo courtesy Everett Grist)

Sulfide, pony running in field of grass, 1¾", M..............$200.00

Sulfide, rabbit in crouching position, EX details & form, 1¾", M...$250.00

Sulfide, Santa standing in short coat & snug breeches, EX detail, 1¾", M..$1,300.00

Transparent Swirl, bl & orange outer bands, wht latticinio core, 1¾", M...$275.00

Transparent Swirl, deep bl w/even-spaced swirls, ¾", M.$3,500.00

Transparent Swirl, latticinio core (yel), 6 red & wht outer bands, 1⅝", NM..$150.00

Transparent Swirl, latticinio core (gr), lt bl base w/4 mc outer bands, 9/16", EX $125.00

Transparent Swirl, latticinio core (wht), red, wht & bl outer bands w/inner yel lines, 1¾" $425.00

Transparent Swirl, latticinio core (yel), red, wht & bl outer bands, 1¾", M..$250.00

Transparent Swirl, latticinio core (yellow), outer bands of red and white, ⅝", $325.00. (Photo courtesy Everett Grist)

Transparent Swirl, ribbon core, mc tight swirls, ⅝", M ..$200.00

Transparent Swirl, ribbon core (oversize) w/coating of transparent glass, 1 9/16" $2,500.00

Transparent Swirl, ribbon core (wht, red, bl & wht), lg red throat, ⅝", M..$150.00

Transparent Swirl, solid core (red & wht) surrounded by yel threads, wht & bl outer lines, ⅝" $60.00

Transparent Swirl, solid core (wht, gr, yel & red), wht outer lines, 1¾", M.......................................$450.00

Transparent Swirl, split core, clustered interior bands, wide mc outer bands, lg...$600.00

Marx

Louis Marx founded his company in New York in the 1920s. He was a genius not only at designing toys but also marketing them. His business grew until it became one of the largest toy companies ever to exist, eventually expanding to include several factories in the United States as well as other countries. Marx sold his company in the early 1970s; he died in 1982. Though toys of every description were produced, collectors today admire his mechanical toys above all others.

Advisors: Scott Smiles (S10), windups; Tom Lastrapes (L4), battery-ops

See also Advertising; Banks; Character, TV, and Movie Collectibles; Dollhouse Furniture; Games; Guns; Plastic Figures; Playsets; and other categories. For toys made by Linemar (Marx's subsidiary in Japan), see Battery-Operated Toys; Windups, Friction, and Other Mechanicals.

BATTERY-OPERATED

Alley the Roaring Stalking Alligator, 18", NMIB $275.00

Barking Terror Dog, plush, w/collar, 8", EXIB, A $100.00

Baseball Pitching Game, EXIB $75.00

Bengali Tiger, r/c, 13", EXIB, A...............................$100.00

Brewster the Rooster, plush, 10", EXIB, A $75.00

Buttons (The Puppy w/a Brain), plush & tin, 1960s, 12", EX..$250.00

Colonel Hap Hazard, litho tin, 12", NMIB, A...............$975.00

Fred Flintstone on Dino, plush Dino, 12x14", MIB, A.$1,225.00

Fred Flintstone on Dino, plush Dino, 12x14", VGIB, A, $465.00. (Photo courtesy Randy Inman Auctions)

Jetspeed Racer, tin w/vinyl driver, 17", NMIB, A, $500.00. (Photo courtesy Smith House Toys)

Great Garloo, r/c, 24", EXIB $425.00
Hootin' Hollow Haunted House, 11", EXIB $875.00
Hootin' Hollow Haunted House, 11", VG, A................$485.00
Locomotive, r/c, 6", EXIB, A..................................$88.00
Mighty King Kong Big Mouth Ball Blowing Target Game, EXIB,
    A $545.00
Mighty Kong, plush, r/c, 11", EXIB.........................$500.00
Mr Mercury, r/c, 13", EX+IB, A $400.00
Nutty Mad Car, 9½", EX, A $150.00
Nutty Mad Indian, EX $100.00
Nutty Mad Indian, VG+IB......................................$175.00
Peppy Puppy, Y, plush, r/c, 7", EXIB, A....................$40.00
Scootin'-Tootin' Hot Rod, 13", P+IB, A....................$150.00

Cities Service Tow Truck, litho tin with black rubber tires, 20½", VG, $250.00.

Walking Tiger, plush, remote control, 12", EXIB, $325.00. (Photo courtesy Randy Inman Auctions)

Coupe, pressed steel with black rubber tires, electric lights, wind-up action, 15", M, A, $1,980.00. (Photo courtesy Bertoia Auctions)

Whistling Spooky Kooky Tree, rare 'winter' version, 14", NMIB
    (rare correct box), A $1,500.00
Whistling Spooky Kooky Tree, 14", EXIB, A $1,320.00
Whistling Spooky Kooky Tree, 14", VG, A $600.00
Yeti the Abominable Snowman, r/c, 11", EXIB, A.........$750.00

PRESSED-STEEL AND TIN VEHICLES

A&P Super Markets Semi, 1950s, red cab w/silver trailer, 8-
    wheeled, 27", G, A $90.00
Aero Oil Co Tanker, tin, 5½", VG+, A......................$215.00
Ambulance, 1930s, wht, w/bell, covered wheel wells, 10", G..$150.00
Ambulance (Military), gr w/gray fenders, cross on sides & top,
    medical symbol on doors, 14", G, A.....................$330.00
Auto, 1940s, red w/gr top, wht-pnt tin metal wheels w/lettering
    & numbers, 11", P+, A......................................$200.00
Auto Transport, 1950s, w/2 plastic autos & loading ramp, 22",
    NMIB, A...$350.00
Contractor's Truck, front loader, spring-loaded dumping action,
    20", EX, A...$200.00
Delivery Pickup Truck, 1950s, 14", EX, A $330.00
Deluxe Delivery Super Service Truck, 1950s, covered wheel
    wells, red & bl, 4-wheeled, 13", G, A $100.00
Dump Truck, DUMP lettered on sides of bed, 12", EX, A .$90.00
Dump Truck, 1940s, flat top cab, covered wheel wells, swinging
    side-dump bed, red, 10½", VG, A $130.00

Dump Truck, 1950s, red & bl w/yel frame, 4-wheeled, 18",
    EX+IB, A...$355.00
Dump Truck w/Front Scoop, 1940s, red, yel & bl, covered wheel
    wells, 4-wheeled, 20", G+, A...............................$85.00
Emergency Searchlight Unit Truck, 1950s, wht, 18", VG+,
    A $150.00
Fire Chief Car, w/up, w/siren, red, 14", G+, A...............$190.00
Heavy Duty Express Truck, 1950s, plastic cab, red & bl, 10-
    wheeled, 19", MIB, A (Est: $100-$200)..................$250.00

Fire Engine, pressed steel with black rubber tires, electric headlights and hood lamp, 15", EX+, $770.00. (Photo Bertoia Auctions)

Hi Way Express Truck, 1940s, red & yel, covered wheel wells, 16", VG, A (Est: $150-$250) $230.00

Inter City Delivery Service Stake Truck, 1940s, red, bl & yel lithoed detail, 4-wheeled, 18", VG, A $120.00

Lazy Day Farms Stake Truck, 1950s, red, yel & bl lithoed detail, 4-wheeled, 17", EX, A $130.00

Lumar Construction Dump Truck, 1950s, 17½", VG $75.00

Lumar Construction End Loader, 1950s, 16", EX.............$35.00

Lumar Utility Service Truck, 1950s, olive gr w/yel trim, #18 on sides of bed, 4-wheeled, 19½", EX $150.00

Mammoth Zeppelin, tin, 27", VG, $625.00. (Photo courtesy Bertoia Auctions)

Meadow Farm Dairy Truck, 13", VG, A..........................$150.00

Mystery Car, 1930s, spring-op drive mechanism, red, 10", G, A $200.00

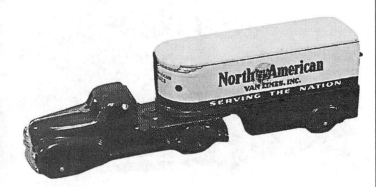

North American Van Lines Semi, windup action, 14", EX, $300.00. (Photo courtesy Bertoia Auctions)

Polar Ice Co Stake Truck, 4-wheeled, wheels covered, 13", EX, A $275.00

Public Utility Service Truck, complete w/accessories, 17" L, NMIB, A..$575.00

Railway Express Agency, w/'Hi-Lift' tailgate, complete w/accessories, 20", NM+IB, A..$1,225.00

Reversible Coupe, heavy tin, w/up, 15½", EX, A $500.00

Roy Rogers Semi, litho tin w/graphics of Roy on rearing Trigger, opening doors, 1950s, 15", EX+ $275.00

Sand Dump Truck, PS cab w/litho tin dump bed, wheels covered, 4-wheeled, 13", G, A $50.00

Sand Dump Truck, PS cab w/litho tin dump body, 4-wheeled, wheeles covered, 1950s, 13", G+, A $100.00

Sears Roebuck & Co Semi, opening rear doors, 2-tone gr, 25", VG, A $225.00

Shop-Rite Super Markets Semi, 25", NM+IB, A............$275.00

Sinclair Tanker, litho tin, gr w/red & wht detail, 10-wheeled, 18", Fair+, A...$175.00

Sturdy Construction Co Steam Shovel & Transport Truck, 1950s, 20", EX, A $110.00

Toy Town Express Van Lines, box van, 4-wheeled, wheels covered, 1950s, 12", G, A $130.00

Tri-City Express Service Stake Truck, lithoed detail, 13½", NM, A $170.00

US Army Stake Truck, dk bl w/lt bl detail, mk USA 41573147, 4-wheeled, 14", EX, A...$85.00

US Army Stake Truck, gr w/wht detail, open tailgate, 4-wheeled, 18", G, A $65.00

US Army Stake Truck & Flatbed Trailer, gr w/wht detail, ea 4-wheeled, 36" overall, VG, A $65.00

US Army Stake Truck & Howitzer Cannon, gr w/wht detail, cloth canopy, complete w/8 shells, 25", MIB (NOS), A $450.00

US Army Stake Truck & Searchlight Trailer, gr w/wht detail, cloth canopy, b/o searchlight, 30" overall, VG, A ...$110.00

US Army Stake Truck & US Army Convoy Trailer, gr w/wht detail, cloth canopies, ea 4-wheeled, 30" overall, VG, A.........$165.00

US Army Transport Truck With Searchlight Trailer, 1950s, pressed steel with black rubber tires, cloth canopy, 30" overall, NM+, $200.00.

US Navy Jeep & Searchlight Trailer, 23" overall, VG+IB, A..$400.00

Willy's Jeep, 13", VG+IB, A...$200.00

WINDUPS, FRICTION, AND OTHER MECHANICALS

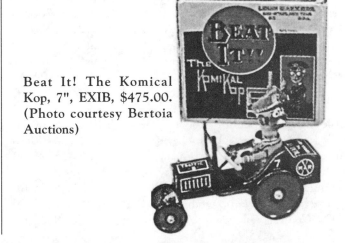

Beat It! The Komical Kop, 7", EXIB, $475.00. (Photo courtesy Bertoia Auctions)

Acrobat Marvel, monkey on wire attached to based lithoed
    w/circus theme, 12", EX, A $150.00
Amos 'N Andy Fresh Air Taxi, 8", EXIB, A...............$1,200.00
Amos 'N Andy Fresh Air Taxi, 8", G..........................$475.00
Amos Walker, 11½", EX..$550.00
Animal Express, 15", MIB.......................................$650.00
Army Tank #12, 1930s, 10", EX, A $115.00
Balky Mule (Pulling Cart w/Driver), 8", EXIB................$225.00
Ballerina, see Twinkle Toes Ballet Dancer
Be-Bop Jigger, 10", EX+, A....................................$250.00
Bear Cyclist, EXIB...$275.00
Big Parade, 24" L, EX, A $700.00
Big Show Circus Wagon, 9", EX...............................$500.00
Big-3 Aerial Acrobats, 12", VGIB.............................$200.00
Blondie's Jalopy, 16", G...$950.00
BO Plenty, 9", EX $250.00

City Cab, friction, 7", EX+, $175.00.

Coo-Coo Car, 8", VG $250.00
Coupe, flat top, side spare, w/driver, 11", EX $450.00
Cowboy Whoopee Car, see Whoopee Car (Cowboy)
Dagwood the Driver, 8", unused, NM+IB, A...............$1,700.00
Dagwood's Solo Flight (Aeroplane), 9", EXIB............$1,050.00
Dan Dipsy Car, celluloid nodder figure, 6" L, EX..........$225.00
Dapper Dan Coon Jigger, 10½", G $425.00
Dare Devil Flyer, 13", G..$350.00
Dare Devil Flyer, 13, EX+IB..................................$1,750.00
Delivery Cyle, 3-wheeled cycle w/driver, 10", G+ $225.00
Dept of Police Car, friction, 8½", VG.......................$175.00

Buck Rogers 25th Century Rocket Police Patrol, 12", EX+IB, $2,000.00. (Photo courtesy Skinner, Inc.)

Buck Rogers 25th Century Rocket Ship, 12", EX...........$850.00
Buck Rogers 25th Century Rocket Ship, 12", G+ $450.00
Busy Bridge, 24", VG, A..$400.00
Busy Miners, 1930s, 16", NMIB $350.00
Butter & Egg Man, 1930s, 8", EX............................$700.00
Captain Marvel Tricycle, 4", NM, A..........................$250.00
Charleston Trio, dtd 1921, 10", EX, A $700.00
Charlie McCarthy & Mortimer Snerd Private Car, 15",
    NMIB $3,500.00
Charlie McCarthy & Mortimer Snerd Private Car, 15",
    VG $1,500.00
Charlie McCarthy Benzine Mobile, 1930, 7", EXIB.......$700.00
Charlie McCarthy Benzine Mobile, 1930, 7", VG.........$400.00
Charlie McCarthy Walker, 9", EX.............................$325.00
Chicken Snatcher, see Hey! Hey! the Chicken Snatcher
Climbing Fireman, 22" (extended), EX $225.00
Climbing Fireman, 22" (extended), EXIB....................$325.00
Coast-to-Coast Double-Decker Bus, litho tin, 10", VG .$525.00

Dick Tracy Police Station, with car, 9" long, EXIB, $500.00.

Dick Tracy Police Station, w/car, 9" L, G+ $250.00
Dick Tracy Siren Squad Car #1, 11", EXIB..................$375.00
Dick Tracy Sparkling Riot Car, 6½", NMIB, A $300.00
Disney Kart (Donald Duck), friction, 6" L, VG, A.........$300.00
Disney Parade Roadster, 11", NMIB, A.....................$750.00
Disney Train, engine mk 376, 15", G+........................$225.00
Donald Duck Duet, 10", EXIB.................................$700.00
Donald Duck on Tractor, friction, plastic, 4" L, EX $75.00
Donald Duck the Drummer, plastic w/litho tin drum, 10",
    EX..$200.00
Donald Duck the Skier, plastic figure w/tin skis & poles, 10",
    EX..$300.00
Donald Duck w/Whirling Tail, plastic, 7", EX $100.00
Dopey Walker, WDE, 1938, 8", EXIB $600.00
Dopey Walker, 8", EX..$400.00
Dottie Driver, celluloid nodder figure, 8" L, EXIB..........$100.00
Doughboy Tank, 1940s, 10", EX................................$225.00

Drive-Ur-Self Car, 14", EX $300.00
Drive-Ur-Self Car, 14", NMIB $375.00
Electric Lighted Car, plastic, w/up, b/o headlights, Canada, 10",
     EXIB, A $350.00
Falcon Sports Car, friction, tin w/plastic windshield & side win-
     dows, yel w/blk plastic 'canvas' top, 21", EX+, A $350.00
Ferdinand the Bull, 1938, 6" L, NMIB, A $400.00
Fire Chief Car, lithoed windows, BRT, 11", EX+IB, A ...$300.00
Flash Gordon Rocket Fighter #5, 12" L, VGIB...............$750.00
Flintstone Car (Fred), 4", EX+IB $450.00
Flintstone Car (Wilma), friction, 4", NMIB...................$525.00

Gorilla (in Shackles and Chains), plush, 8", EXIB, $325.00. (Photo courtesy Randy Inman Auctions)

Flintstone Pals on Dino, Fred, 8", VGIB, $300.00; Barney, 8", EXIB, $350.00.

Flintstone Tricycle (Dino), 4", NM+IB $400.00
Flintstone Tricycle (Fred), 4", NM+IB............................$500.00
Flintstone Tricycle (Wilma), 4", NM+IB.........................$300.00
Fred Flintstone Flivver, 7", NMIB, A..............................$450.00

Funny Flivver, 7", EXIB, A, $600.00.

Funny Russian Drummer, 7", EXIB $125.00
George the Drummer Boy, moving eyes, 9", EX..............$225.00
George the Drummer Boy, stationary eyes, 9", NM $225.00
Goofy the Gardener, 8½" L, VG $400.00
Harold Lloyd Funny Face Walker, 10", EX......................$475.00
Hey! Hey! the Chicken Snatcher, 9", EX $1,100.00
Hi-Yo Silver the Lone Ranger, no base, 7", G.................$150.00

Hi-Yo Silver the Lone Ranger, rocker base, 9", EXIB $675.00
Honey-Moon Express, 1940s, 9" dia, VG........................$125.00
Honey-Moon Express, 1940s, 9" dia, VGIB.....................$200.00
Hopalong Cassidy, rocker base, 10", EXIB $475.00
Hopalong Cassidy, rocker base, 10", VG $350.00
HQ Staff Car, 15", EX, A $745.00

Huckleberry Car, Yogi or Quick Draw McGraw, tin with vinyl heads, friction, 4" long, NMIB, A, $250.00 each. (Photo courtesy Smith House Toy and Auction Company)

International Agent Car, friction, 1960s, 4", NM+IB $125.00
Jetson Express, litho tin, 12", EXIB................................$325.00
Jetson Rollover Tank, litho tin, 4", VG, A $275.00
Jetsons Hopping Rosey, litho tin, 4", VGIB, A $500.00
Joe Penner & His Duck, 8", NM+IB...........................$1,200.00
Joe Penner & His Duck, 8", VG......................................$350.00
Joy Rider (Jalopy), 7", VG+, A $125.00
Jumbo Climbing Monkey, 10", VGIB, A $100.00
Jumpin' Jeep, 5½", EXIB $250.00
King Racer, w/driver, 9", EXIB $675.00
Komical Kop, see Beat It! the Komical Cop
Lone Ranger w/Lasso On Rearing Silver, 8" T, G $175.00
Lonesome Pine Trailer, 8", G...$100.00
Looping Plane, 8", EXIB..$175.00
Main Street, 24", EXIB..$475.00

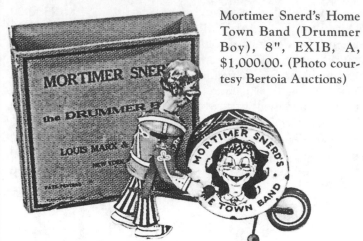

Mortimer Snerd's Home Town Band (Drummer Boy), 8", EXIB, A, $1,000.00. (Photo courtesy Bertoia Auctions)

Little Orphan Annie and Sandy, 5", EX, pair, $650.00. (Photo courtesy Bertoia Auctions)

Main Street, 24", VG..$275.00
Marvel Car, see Reversible Coupe
Marvel Car, 16", G+ $400.00
Merry Makers, conductor on piano, no marquee, VG $900.00
Merry Makers, conductor on piano, w/marquee, VG ..$1,200.00
Mickey Mouse Dipsy Car, 6", EXIB, A..........................$750.00
Mickey Mouse Express, 10" dia, EXIB...........................$775.00
Mickey Mouse Express, 10" dia, VG.............................$400.00
Mickey Mouse Express Train, 5-pc, 16" L overall, EX, A$275.00

Parade Roadster (Disney Characters), litho tin w/3 plastic
    figures, 11", NMIB, A.......................................$850.00
Pinched!, 10" sq, EX, A..$650.00
Pinched!, 10" sq, EXIB $900.00
Pinocchio & His Famous Pet Figaro, NMIB...............$1,000.00
Pinocchio the Acrobat, 17", VG+ $350.00
Pinocchio Walker, 8½", VG.......................................$275.00
Pinocchio Walker, 9", EXIB $425.00
Planet Patrol Tank, 10½", EX $325.00
Pluto the Drum Major, 7", EX....................................$250.00
Pluto w/Spinning Tail, plastic, 1950s, 6", VG................$125.00
Police Squad Motorcycle #3, 9", VG............................$225.00
Police Squad Motorcycle #3 w/Sidecar, 9", EX $275.00
Poor Fish, 8", EXIB $525.00

Mickey Mouse Meteor Train, five-piece, 43" overall, EX+, A, $700.00. (Photo courtesy Bertoia Auctions)

Mickey Mouse Meteor Train, 5-pc, 43" L overall, VG ...$450.00
Mickey the Driver, 1950s, 6½", EXIB............................$450.00
Midget Climbing Fighting Tank, 5½", NMIB, A $175.00
Midget Racer, plastic, 6½", EXIB, A............................$175.00
Milton Berle Crazy Car, 6", EX+IB $400.00
Milton Berle Crazy Car, 6", G+..................................$150.00
Monkey Acrobat, see Acrobat Marvel
Monkey Cyclist, 6", EXIB, A......................................$375.00
Moon Mullins & Kayo Handcar, 6", EX.........................$450.00
Moon Mullins & Kayo Handcar, 6", EX+IB, A $650.00
Mortimer Snerd Tricky Auto, 7", EX+, A......................$450.00
Mortimer Snerd Tricky Auto, 7", EXIB, A $650.00
Mortimer Snerd Walker, 1939, 9", EX $250.00
Mortimer Snerd Walker, 1939, 9", NMIB......................$375.00
Nutty Mad Indian, 7", EXIB......................................$150.00
Old Jalopy, 8", EX $175.00

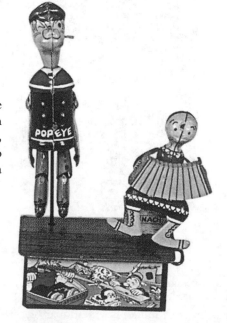

Popeye and Olive Oyl Jiggers on Roof, 10", EX, A, $875.00. (Photo courtesy Bertoia Auctions)

Popeye & Olive Oyl Jiggers on Roof, 10", VG...............$675.00
Popeye Dippy Dumper, 9", EXIB.................................$1,300.00
Popeye Express, 1935, 9½" dia, EXIB, A $4,000.00

Popeye the Champ, 8" square, NMIB, A, $3,000.00. (Photo courtesy Bertoia Auctions)

Sandy's Doghouse, 8", EXIB, A, $385.00. (Photo courtesy Bertoia Auctions)

Short Snort the Mystery Drinking Monkey, 12", VGIB, A, $110.00. (Photo courtesy Bertoia Auctions)

Popeye Express, 9" dia, EXIB....................................$1,200.00
Popeye Express (Baggage), 9", EXIB, A.....................$1,125.00
Popeye Express (Baggage), 9", G.................................$475.00
Popeye the Pilot, 8" W, EX+...$775.00
Popeye the Pilot, 8" W, EXIB, A....................................$825.00
Porky Pig w/Lasso, 1939, 8", EX+IB.............................$550.00
Porky Pig w/Umbrella, 8½", EX.....................................$325.00
Porky Pig w/Umbrella, 8½", VG.....................................$225.00
Porter, see Red Cap Porter
Racer #2, yel & red w/checked pattern on grille, w/driver, 13½",
   EX..$400.00
Racer #27, mk 1948 Indy 500 Winner, 12", EXIB..........$375.00
Racing Coupe, top up, rear spare & radiator mascot, w/driver, 9",
   VG+...$375.00
Ranger Rider (Cowboy), 11" L, VGIB............................$225.00
Ranger Rider (Lone Ranger), 9", NMIB, A....................$525.00
Red Cap Porter (Carrying Luggage), 8", EX...................$550.00
Red Cap Porter (Carrying Luggage), 8", VG, A.............$300.00
Red Cap Porter (Pushing Trunk on Cart), 6", VG..........$550.00
Reversible Coupe (The Marvel Car), 16", EX, A............$350.00
Ring-A-Ling Circus, 8" dia, EX....................................$1,200.00
Ring-A-Ling Circus, 8" dia, EXIB................................$1,600.00
Roadster, see Mechanical Roadster
Rocket Racer, 16½", G, A..$125.00
Roll Over Airplane, 6" W, EX...$100.00
Roll Over Cat, 6", EXIB..$125.00
Roll Over Pluto, 8" L, VG...$200.00
Roll Over Tank, 8", EX..$150.00
Royal Bus Lines Bus, 10", G..$325.00
Sam the City Gardener, 8" T, G..$75.00
Sandy (Little Orphan Annie's Dog), 5", EXIB, A...........$250.00
Scottie the Guid-A-Dog, 12" L, EX................................$125.00
Scottie the Guid-A-Dog, 12" L, NM+IB.........................$225.00
Sheriff Sam & His Woopie Car, 6", NM+IB....................$250.00
Siren Police Patrol Car, b/o lights, 21", EX....................$350.00
Skyhawk Tower, 8x18" W, EX...$225.00
Snoopy & Gus Hook & Ladder Truck, 9", NM+........$2,000.00
Snoopy & Gus Hook & Ladder Truck, 9", VG...............$800.00

Sparkling Climbing Fighting Tank, 10", NMIB..............$250.00
Sparkling Soldier, soldier on camp motorcycle, 8", EXIB...$500.00
Speed Boy Delivery Cycle, 10", EX................................$375.00
Speed Boy Delivery Cycle, 10", G, A.............................$250.00
Speedway Racer #2, 4", EXIB...$100.00
Spic & Span, 10", VG, A..$1,100.00
Sportster Car, 1940s, friction, 20", VG, A.....................$175.00
Streamline Auto, extra-long nose, bl w/wht trim, 13", G,
   A...$200.00
Streamline Speedway, figure-8 track w/2 cars, 17x13" track, GIB,
   A...$100.00
Superman Turnover Plane, bl/yel, 6", VG+....................$700.00
Superman Turnover Plane, gold/silver, 6", EX+..........$1,100.00
Superman Turnover Plane, red/yel, 6", EX.....................$800.00
Superman Turnover Tank, 4", EXIB................................$500.00
Tidy Tim Street Sweeper, 8", EX....................................$550.00
Tidy Tim Street Sweeper, 8", G......................................$350.00
Tiger, see also Walking Tiger
Tiger on Handcart, friction, dressed tiger on 4-wheeled cart mk
   Marx, 6" L, EX...$125.00
Tom Corbett Space Cadet #2 Spaceship, NMIB............$925.00
Tom Tom Jungle Boy, 6", EXIB......................................$125.00
Toyland's Farm Products Horse-Drawn Milk Wagon, 10",
   VG+...$200.00
Tricky Taxi, 5", EXIB..$225.00

Twinkle Toes Ballet Dancer, 5", VGIB, A, $100.00. (Photo courtesy Bertoia Auctions)

Tricky Tom Dog, 6" L, EXIB	$75.00
Tumbling Monkey, 5", VG+	$175.00
Uncle Wiggly Car, 1935, 8", EX	$725.00
Uncle Wiggly Car, 1935, 8", VG	$450.00
US Army Tank No 3, G	$150.00
US Army Turnover Tank, wood wheels, 8", EXIB, A	$220.00
Walking Tiger (All Fours), plush, 9", EXIB	$125.00
Walking Tiger (Upright), plush, 8", EXIB, A	$175.00
Watch Me Roll Over Pluto, see Roll Over Pluto	
Whoopee Car (College Student), 8" L, VG, A	$275.00
Whoopee Car (Cowboy), 8½", VG, A	$300.00
Wise Pluto, WDE, 1939, 8" L, EXIB	$425.00
Wonder Cyclist, boy on tricycle, 9" T, NMIB	$575.00
Wonder Cyclist, boy on tricycle, 9" T, VG	$275.00
Yellow Cab #15, 6½", EX	$100.00

MISCELLANEOUS

Brightlite Filling Station, 1940s, litho tin, 2 pumps, in/out signs & oil & grease display case on curved base, 9" L, EX.....$550.00

Fire Department Headquarters, litho tin, complete w/accessories fire chief's car, EXIB...$550.00

Gas Station Island, litho tin, w/gas pump, oil case & air pump, b/o, 9" L, P+, A...$100.00

General Alarm Firehouse w/Firechief Car & Patrol Truck, litho tin, postwar, 11"x17" base, VG+IB.........................$575.00

Glendale Depot, litho tin, complete with accessories, VG, A, $250.00. (Photo courtesy Bertoia Auctions)

Glendale Depot, litho tin, complete w/accessories, VGIB, A...$400.00

Midtown Service Station, complete, 15x28", unused, MIB (NOS)...$450.00

Oil Tank, litho tin, 100% Penna Oil, 3½", G, A............$100.00

Sunny Side Service Station, litho tin, b/o gas globes, w/lift rack, 10x13", G, A...$225.00

Tractor Sales & Service Farm Machinery Set, litho tin tractor w/driver & 2 implements, 13" L tractor, EXIB.........$375.00

TV and Radio Station, tin an plastic, NMIB, $300.00.

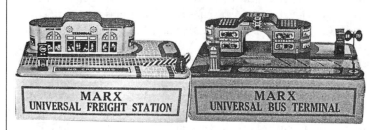

Universal Freight Station, tin, NMIB, A, $650.00; Universal Bus Terminal, tin, EXIB, A, $400.00.

Universal Airport, litho tin, complete w/accessories, EXIB..$400.00

Van Truck, plastic, red cab w/clear see-thru box van, 10", NMIB, A...$50.00

Matchbox

The Matchbox series of English and American-made autos, trucks, taxis, Pepsi-Cola trucks, steamrollers, Greyhound buses, etc., was very extensive. By the late 1970s, the company was cranking out more than five million cars every week, and while those days may be over, Matchbox still produces about seventy-five million vehicles on a yearly basis.

Introduced in 1953, the Matchbox Miniatures series has always been the mainstay of the company. There were seventy-five models in all but with enough variations to make collecting them a real challenge. Larger, more detailed models were introduced in 1957; this series, called Major Pack, was replaced a few years later by a similar line called King Size. To compete with Hot Wheels, Matchbox converted most models over to a line called SuperFast that sported thinner, low-friction axles and wheels. (These are much more readily available than the original 'regular wheels,' the last of which were made in 1969). At about the same time, the King Size series became known as Speed Kings; in 1977 the line was reintroduced under the name Super Kings.

In the early '70s, Lesney started to put dates on the baseplates of their toy cars. The name 'Lesney' was coined from the first names of the company's founders, Leslie and Rodney Smith. The last Matchbox toys that carried the Lesney mark were made in 1982. Today many models can be bought for less than $10.00, though a few are priced much much higher.

In 1988, to celebrate the company's fortieth anniversary, Matchbox issued a limited set of five models that except for minor variations were exact replicas of the originals. These five were repackaged in 1991 and sold under the name Matchbox Originals. In 1993 a second series expanded the line of reproductions.

Another line that's become very popular is their Models of Yesteryear. These are slightly larger replicas of antique and vintage vehicles. Values of $20.00 to $60.00 for mint-in-box examples are average, though a few sell for even more.

Sky Busters are small-scale aircraft measuring an average of 3½" in length. They were introduced in 1973. Models currently being produced sell for about $4.00 each.

The Matchbox brand has changed hands several times, first to David Yeh and Universal Toy Company in 1982, then to Tyco Toys in 1992, and finally to Mattel, who purchased Tyco, and along with it, Matchbox, Dinky, and several other Tyco subsidiaries, such as Fisher-Price, Milton-Bradley, and View Master.

To learn more, we recommend *Matchbox Toys, 1947 to 2003, Fourth Edition,* and *The Other Matchbox Toys, 1947 – 2004,* by Dana Johnson, our advisor for this category.

To determine values of examples in conditions other than given in our listings, based on MIB or MOC prices, deduct a minimum of 10% if the original container is missing, 30% if the condition is excellent, and as much as 70% for a toy graded only very good.

The 1 – 75 Series listings are for regular wheels unless otherwise indicated with the abbreviations LS (Laser Wheels) or SF (SuperFast Wheels).

1 – 75 Series

AEC Ergomatic Horse Box, see Ergomatic Horse Box
AMC Javelin AMX, #9, 1971, red w/blk hood scoop, doors don't open, MIP, from $40 to $50.00
AMC Javelin AMX Pro Stocker, #17, 1983, metallic gray w/red & blk stripes, MIP, from $3 to.......................................$5.00
Aston Martin DB2 Saloon, #53, 1958, metallic lt gr w/gray plastic wheels, MIP, from $65 to $85.00

Akfa Carabo, #75, 1971, metallic pk with no tampo, MIP, from $12.00 to $18.00. (Photo courtesy Dana Johnson)

Aston Martin Racer, #19, decal #5, #41 or #52, 1961, gray or wht driver, MIP, from $145 to $160.00
Aston Martin Racer, #19, 1961, gray or wht driver, MIP, from $60 to $80.00
Atlantic Trailer, #16, 1957, tan w/tan towbar, gray plastic wheels, MIP, from $65 to $85.00
Atlas Skip Truck, #37, 1976, orange w/red skip, MIP, from $90 ....$120.00
Austin Mk 2 Radio Truck, #68, 1959, olive w/blk plastic wheels, MIP, from $70 to $90.00
Aveling Barford Road Roller, #1, 1962, gr w/red plastic rollers, MIP, from $30 to $40.00
Aveling Bradford Diesel Road Roller, #1, 1953, dk gr, MIP, from $100 to $150.00
Aveling Bradford Diesel Road Roller, #1, 1953, lt gr, MIP, from $175 to $225.00
Badger Exploration Truck, #16, 1974, Rolomatic radar, metallic orange-red, MIP, from $6 to.......................................$10.00
Baja Dune Buggy, #13, 1971, lt metallic gr w/police shields decal, MIP, from $35 to..$50.00
Beach Buggy, #30, 1971, pk & wht, MIP, from $20 to $35.00
Bedford 'Matchbox Removal' Van, #17, 1956, maroon body, MIP, from $425 to..$475.00
Bedford Duplé Long Distance Coach, #21, 1956, MIP, from $80 to..$100.00
Bedford Lomas Ambulance, #14, 1962, silver plastic wheels, MIP, from $325 to..$375.00
Bedford Wreck Truck, #13 (cast into base), 1958, tan w/gray plastic wheels, MIP, from $80 to $110.00
Bedford Wreck Truck, #13 (not cast into base), 1955, tan metal wheels, MIP, from $75 to $90.00
Berkley Cavalier Travel Trailer, #23, 1956, lime gr, MIP, from $100 to..$125.00
Berkley Cavalier Travel Trailer, #23, 1956, pale bl, MIP, from $60 to..$80.00
Big Bull Bulldozer, #12, 1975, orange rollers, MIP, from $5 to..$7.00
Case Bulldozer, #16, 1969, dk red w/blk treads, MIP, from $40 to $55.00
Caterpillar Bulldozer, #18, 1961, silver plastic rollers, MIP, from $175 to..$225.00
Caterpillar DB Bulldozer, #18, 1956, yel w/red blade, MIP, from $80 to..$110.00
Caterpillar Tractor, #8, 1955, orange w/orange driver, no blade, MIP, from $175 to..$225.00

Case Bulldozer, #16, 1969, green treads, MIP, from $9.00 to $12.00. (Photo courtesy Dana Johnson)

Caterpillar Tractor, #8, 1959, yel w/metal rollers, MIP, from, $85 to..$110.00

Caterpillar Tractor, #8, 1961, silver plastics rollers, MIP, from $90 to..$115.00

Cement Mixer, #3, 1953, bl w/gray plastic wheels, MIP, from $85 to..$100.00

Cement Mixer, #3, 1953, bl w/orange metal wheels, MIP, from $60 to...$85.00

Chevrolet Impala Taxi Cab, #20, 1965, orange w/gray wheels, MIP, from $1,250 to $1,500.00

Chevy Bel Air ('57), #4, 1979, metallic maganta, MIP, from $6 to...$8.00

Commer Pickup, #50, 1958, lt or dk tan w/metal or plastic wheels, MIP, ea from $75 to..$90.00

Corvette ('97), #4, 1997, metallic bl, MIP, from $5 to........$7.00

Corvette Convertible, #14, 1987, metallic purple w/lt orange interior, wht accents, 3", MIP, from $2 to.....................$4.00

Corvette T-Roof, #62, 1980, blk w/opaque windows, gr & orange stripes, MIP, from $9 to..$12.00

Crane Truck, #49, 1976, red, MIP, from $80 to..............$100.00

Crane Truck, #49, 1976, yel, MIP, from $6 to $8.00

DAF Girder Truck, #58, 1968, MIP, from $12 to $16.00

DAF Girder Truck, #58, 1970, cream, SF, MIP, from $75 to .$90.00

DAF Girder Truck, #58, 1970, pale metallic gr, SF, MIP, from $25 to $35.00

DAF Tipper Truck, #47, 1970, SF, siver & yel, M, from $30 to $45.00

Daimler Ambulance, #14, 1956, gray plastic wheels, MIP, from $80 to...$100.00

Datsun 280ZX, #24, 1983, wht w/red & bl Turbo 33 tampo, MIP, from $6 to...$8.00

Dennis Fire Escape, #9, 1955, no front bumper, no number cast, MIP, from $45 to...$60.00

Dennis Refuse Truck, #15, 1963, dk bl w/gray container, port-hole in rear hatch, MIP, from $45 to $60.00

DeTomaso Pantera, #8, 1975, wht w/bl base, MIP, from $10 to ..$15.00

Diesel Road Roller, see Aveling Bradford Diesel Road Roller

Dodge BP Wreck Truck, #13, 1970, SF, MIP, from $65 to..$85.00

Dodge Challenger, #1, 1976, hood grilles, no scoop, red w/silver interior, MIP, from $6 to $8.00

Dodge Crane Truck, #63, 1968, yel, M, from $12 to........$16.00

Dodge Dump Truck, #48, 1966, MIP, from $10 to $15.00

Dodge Stake Truck, #4, 1970, SF, MIP, from $20 to.........$30.00

Dumper, #2, 1953, gr metal wheels, MIP, from $185 to..$235.00

Dumper, #2, 1953, unpnt metal wheels, MIP, from $65 to.$90.00

Dune Man Volkswagen Beetle, #49, 1984, from $4 to $5.00

Eight-Wheel Tipper Truck, #51, 1969, Pointer decal, MIP, from $30 to..$50.00

Ergomatic Cab Horse Box, #17, 1969, w/2 horses, MIP, from $9 to..$12.00

Ergomatic Horse Box (AEC), #17, 1970, SF, MIP, from $25 to..$40.00

Euclid Quarry Truck, #6, 1964, yel, MIP, from $15 to.......$25.00

Ferrari F1 Racer, #73, 1962, w/driver, MIP, from $20 to ...$30.00

Ferret Scout Car, #61, 1959, olive green with black plastic wheels, MIP, from $15.00. to $25.00. (Photo courtesy Dana Johnson)

Fiat 1500 w/Luggage on Roof, #56, 1965, red, MIP, from $85 to..$100.00

Field Car, #18, 1969, gr plastic hubs, MIP, from $900 to..$1,200.00

Field Car, #18, 1970, SF, olive drab, MIP, from $75 to......$90.00

Flying Bug, #11, 1972, MIP, from $15 to $20.00

Foden Concrete Truck, #21, 1970, SF, MIP, from $25 to ..$40.00

Ford Capri, #54, 1971, MIP, from $12 to $18.00

Ford Esso Wreck Truck, #71, 1968, amber windows, MIP, from $200 to..$300.00

Ford Fairlane Station Wagon, #31, 1960, gr w/pk roof, silver or gray plastic wheels, MIP, ea from $45 to.....................$60.00

Ford Fairlane Station Wagon, #31, 1960, yel w/silver plastic wheels, MIP, from $275 to.....................................$325.00

Ford Galaxie Police Car, #55, 1966, bl dome light, MIP, from $50 to..$65.00

Ford Galaxie Police Car, #55, 1966, red dome light, MIP, from $16 to..$24.00

Ford Group 6, #45, 1970, SF, dk gr, MIP, from $1,250 to .$1,750.00

Ford Group 6, #45, 1970, SF, metallic gr, MIP, from $12 to .$16.00

Ford Group 6, #45, 1970, SF, purple, MIP, from $12 to.....$16.00

Ford Mustang Fastback, #8, 1966, SF, orange, MIP, from $320 to..$360.00

Ford Mustang Wildcat Dragster, #8, 1970, MIP, from $25 to..$40.00

Ford Pickup, #6, 1968, wht grille, MIP, from $10 to $15.00

Ford Refuse Truck, #7, 1966, blk plastic wheels, MIP, from $12 to..$16.00

Ford Refuse Truck, #7, 1970, SF, MIP, from $30 to $40.00

Ford T-Bird, #75, 1960, cream & pk w/blk plastic wheels, MIP, from $225 to $300.00

Ford Thames Estate Car, #70, 1959, yel & turq w/gr windows, blk plastic wheels, MIP, from $65 to.........................$80.00

Ford Thames Trader Wreck Truck, #13, 1961, gray wheels, from $115 to...$140.00

Ford Tractor, #39, 1967, yellow and blue, MIP, from $15.00 to $20.00. (Photo courtesy Dana Johnson)

Ford Transit, #66, 1977, orange, no towing tab on base, MIP, from $7 to...$10.00

Ford Transit, #66, 1977, orange, towing tab on base, MIP, from $45 to..$60.00

Ford Zodiac Mk II Sedan, #33, 1957, lt bl, lt bl-gr or dk gr, no windows, metal wheels, MIP, ea from $100 to........$125.00

Ford Zodiac Mk II Sedan, #33, 1957, silver-gray & orange, no windows, gray plastic wheels, MIP, from $160 to.....$185.00

Fork Lift Truck, #15, 1972, Landing Bagnall decals, no steering wheel, MIP, from $9 to...$12.00

Formula 1 Racing Car, #34, 1971, bl, MIP, from $12 to....$16.00

Formula 5000, #36, 1975, wht w/Texaco on hood, MIP, from $375 to...$475.00

GMC Refrigerator Truck, #44, 1967, MIP, from $12 to....$16.00

Horse-Drawn Milk Float, #7, 1955, orange with gray plastic wheels, MIP, from $145.00 to $170.00. (Photo courtesy Dana Johnson)

GMC Tipper Truck, #26, 1968, MIP from $7 to $10.00

Gruesome Twosome, #4, 1971, gold w/amber windows, MIP, from $12 to..$16.00

Harley-Davidson Motorcycle, #50, 1980, MIP, from $5 to .$7.00

Hay Trailer, #40, 1967, beige (rare color), from $175 to..$225.00

Hay Trailer, #40, 1967, common color, MIP, from $6 to...$10.00

Honda ATC, #23, 1985, red, MIP, from $10 to................$12.00

Hoveringham Tipper, #17, 1963, red cab, orange tipper, MIP, from $30 to..$45.00

Iron Fairy Crane, #42, 1969, MIP, from $45 to $75.00

Jaguar XKE, #32, 1961, metallic red w/gray plastic wheels, clear windows, MIP, from $100 to....................................$120.00

Jaguar XKE, #32, 1961, red w/gray plastic wheels, gr windows, MIP, from $80 to..$110.00

Jeep Hot Rod, #2, 1971, pk or red, MIP, from $16 to........$20.00

John Deere Tractor, #50, 1964, gray plastic wheels, MIP, from $25 to $35.00

Jumbo Jet Motorcycle, #71, 1973, MIP, from $15 to.........$20.00

Land Rover, 12, 1955, olive gr, metal wheels, w/driver, MIP, from $60 to..$85.00

Land Rover Fire Truck, #57, 1970, SF, MIP, from $50 to..$65.00

Leyland Site Office Truck, #60, 1966, MIP, from $15 to...$20.00

Lincoln Continental, #31, 1970, Super-Fast wheels, green-gold, MIP, from $50.00 to $65.00. (Photo courtesy Dana Johnson)

London Bus, #5, 1954, red, MIP, from $80 to $100.00

London Bus, #5, 1954, red w/Buy Matchbox Series decal, metal wheels, MIP, from $80 to.......................................$100.00

Lotus Europa, #5, 1969, SF, blk, MIP, from $16 to $20.00

Lotus Europa, #5, 1969, SF, pk, unpnt base, MIP, from $12 to $16.00

Lotus Racing Car, #19, 1970, Super-Fast wheels, MIP, from $45.00 to $60.00. (Photo courtesy Dana Johnson)

Mack Dump Truck, #28, 1968, red wheel hubs, MIP, from $25 to **$35.00**

Maserati 4CL T/1948 Racer, #52, 1958, red w/blk plastic wheels, MIP, from $80 to..................................**$100.00**

Maserati 4CL T/1948 Racer, #52, 1958, yel w/blk tires, MIP, from $110 to **$130.00**

Massey-Harris Tractor, #4, 1954, w/fenders, MIP, from $80 to.**$100.00**

Massey-Harris Tractor, #4, 1957, metal wheels, no fenders, MIP, from $60 to..**$80.00**

Mechanical Horse & Trailer, #10, 1955, red cab w/gray trailer, metal wheels, MIP, from $80 to................................**$100.00**

Mercedes Benz Ambulance, #3, 1968, opening rear hatch, MIP, from $18 to...**$24.00**

Mercedes Trailer, #2, 1969, SF, metallic gold w/orange canopy, MIP, from $25 to..**$30.00**

Mercedes Trailer, #2, 1969, SF, metallic gold w/yel canopy, MIP, from $18 to..**$24.00**

Mercury Cougar, #62, 1970, SF, doors open, MIP, from $30 to..**$45.00**

Merryweather Fire Engine, #35, 1969, SF, metallic red, from $16 to..**$20.00**

Merryweather Marquis Fire Engine, #9, 1959, red w/gold ladder, gray plastic wheels, MIP, from $65 to **$85.00**

MG Midget Sports Car, #19, 1956, cream, w/driver, MIP, from $85 to..**$105.00**

MG Midget Sports Car, #19, 1956, wht w/driver, MIP, from $175 to..**$225.00**

MG 1100 w/Driver & Dog, #64, 1970, SF, gr, MIP, from $225 to..**$275.00**

MGA Sports Car, #19, 1958, wht w/gold grille, metal wheels, MIP, from $450 to...**$525.00**

Mobile Canteen Refreshment Bar, #74, 1959, pk w/lt bl base & interior, gray wheels, MIP, from $475 to **$525.00**

Mobile Canteen Refreshment Bar, #74, 1959, silver w/blk plastic wheels, MIP, from $35 to **$50.00**

Pickford Removal Van, #46, 1960, dk bl w/gray plastic wheels, MIP, from $65 to...**$80.00**

Plymouth Grand Fury Police, #10, 1979, wht w/Metro tampos, MIP, from $5 to...**$7.00**

Pontiac Fiero, #2, 1985, blk over red w/2 Dog Racing Team decal, MIP, from $12 to...**$16.00**

Pontiac Grand Prix, #22, 1964, blk plastic wheels, MIP, from $24 to...**$28.00**

Pony Trailer w/Two Horses, #43, 1968, MIP, from $9 to...**$12.00**

Porsche 910, #68, 1970, wht, MIP, from $24 to **$28.00**

Porsche 911 Turbo, #3, 1978, metallic brn w/unpnt base, MIP, from $45 to..**$60.00**

Porsche 911 Turbo, #3, 1978, red w/opaque windows, MIP, from $8 to...**$12.00**

Prime Mover Truck Tractor, #15, 1956, yel w/metal wheels, MIP, from $1,000 to...**$1,500.00**

Quarry Truck, #6, 1964, 6-wheeled, yel, MIP, from $24 to..**$28.00**

Racing Mini, #26, 1970, orange, MIP, from $12 to..........**$16.00**

Rallye Royale, #14, 1973, MIP, from $8 to......................**$12.00**

Road Dragster, #19, 1970, red, MIP, from $16 to **$20.00**

Road Tanker, #11, 1955, red with gold trim, metal wheels, Esso decal on rear, MIP, from $60.00 to $75.00. (Photo courtesy Dana Johnson)

Road Tanker, #11, 1955, yel w/metal wheels, MIP, from $125 to...**$150.00**

Mod Rod, #1, 1971, yellow with black wheels, wildcat label, MIP, from $20.00 to $25.00. (Photo courtesy Dana Johnson)

Monteverdi Hai #6, #3, 1973, orange w/blk base, MIP, from $18 to..**$24.00**

Mustang GT350, #23, 1979, MIP, from $12 to **$16.00**

Nissan Fairlady Z, #5, 1981, red, MIP, from $18 to..........**$24.00**

Pannier Tank Locomotive, #47, MIP, from $8 to.............**$12.00**

Peterbilt Wrecker, #61, 1982, bl w/amber windows, blk boom, no markings, MIP, from $50 to **$75.00**

Safari Land Rover, #12, 1965, green with brown luggage rack on roof, MIP, from $20.00 to $25.00. (Photo courtesy Dana Johnson)

Saab Sonnet, #65, 1973, wht, MIP, from $225 to $275.00

Saab 9000, #15, 1988, LW, metallic bl, MIP, from $9 to...$12.00

Safari Land Rover, #12, 1965, gold w/tan luggage, MIP, from $85 to...$100.00

Safari Land Rover, #12, 1970, SF, bright bl, luggage on roof, MIP, from $1,000 to $1,250.00

Scaffolding Truck, #11, 1970, SF, silver, complete, M, from $28 to..$34.00

Scammell Mountaineer Dump Truck, #16, 1964, gray plastic wheels, MIP, from $85 to...$100.00

Seasprite Helicopter, #74, reg, 1977, dk gr or dr cream, MIP, ea from $285 to $340.00

Setra Coach, #12, 1970, metallic gold w/tan roof, MIP, from $25 to..$30.00

Sports Boat & Trailer w/Outboard Motor, #48, 1961, gray wheels, MIP, from $70 to...$85.00

Stake Truck, #20, 1956, maroon w/silver grille & fuel tanks, gray plastic wheels, MIP, from $110 to $130.00

Standard Jeep CJ5, #72, 1966, red interior, MIP, from $16 to..$20.00

Standard Jeep CJ5, #72, 1966, wht interior, MIP, from $1,000 to..$1,250.00

Standard Jeep CJ5, #72, 1970, SF, MIP, from $32 to.........$44.00

Stingeroo Cycle, #38, 1973, purple w/chrome handlebars, MIP, from $325 to $375.00

T-Bird Turbo Coupe, #59, 1988, LW, metallic gold w/Motorcraft decal, MIP, from $7 to..$10.00

Taylor Jumbo Crane, #11, 1965, yel weight box, MIP, from $20 to..$40.00

Toyman Dodge Challenger, #1, 1983, MIP, from $5 to.......$8.00

Toyota Mini Pickup Camper, #22, 1983, MIP, from $6 to...$8.00

Tyre Fryer Jaffa Mobile, #42, 1972, bl, MIP, from $100 to..$125.00

US Mail Jeep, #5, 1978, US Mail tampo, MIB, from $6 to.$8.00

Volkswagen Camper, #23, 1970, turq, opening roof, M, from $20 to..$30.00

Volkswagen Rabbit, #7, 1976, yel w/red interior, rack & surf-boards, MIP, from $8 to..$10.00

Volkswagen 1500 Saloon, #15, 1970, SF, metalllic red, MIP, from $30 to $45.00

Volkswagen 1600TL, #67, 1970, SF, MIP, from $35 to $50.00

Wells Fargo Armored Truck, #69, 1978, red w/bl windows, MIP, from $6 to...$8.00

Wells Fargo Armored Truck, #69, 1978, red w/clear windows, MIP, from $35 to $50.00

1957 T-Bird, #42, 1982, red, MIP, from $6 to.....................$8.00

8-Wheel Crane Truck, #30, 1965, mint gr, MIP, from $1,000 to $1,250.00

CONVOY, HIGHWAY EXPRESS, SUPER RIGS

Blue Grass Farms Kenworth Horse Box Transporter, #CY-6, 1982, gr cab, MIP, from $12 to $16.00

DAF Aircraft Transporter, #CY-21, 1987, wht w/Airtrainer decal, MIP, from $12 to...$16.00

DAF Box Truck, #CY-24, 1988, orange & red w/Parcel Post decal, MIP, from $16 to...$20.00

DARTS Kenworth Aircraft Transporter, #CY-12, 1984, wht & bl w/dk gr or brn tampos, bl plane, England cast, MIP, ea.$20.00

Ford Aeromax Superstar Transporter, #CY-109, 1991, red w/Melling Performance or Motorcraft decal, MIP, ea from $20 to..$24.00

Kenworth Car Transporter, #CY-1, 1982, red w/beige ramp, wht stripes, MIP, from $12 to...$16.00

Kenworth COE Power Launch Transporter, #CY-14, wht w/wht boat, MIP, from $10 to...$15.00

Kenworth Rocket Transporter, #CY-2, 1982, silver-gray w/wht plastic rocket, MIP, from $10 to $15.00

Kenworth Superstar Transporter, #CY-104, 1989, any Indy 500 version except K-Mart/Havoline, MIP, ea from $10 to $15.00

Kenworth Superstar Transporter, #CY-104, 1989, Indy 500 version, wht w/K-Mart/Havoline decal, MIP, from $15 to.........$20.00

Kenworth Superstar Transporter #51, #CY-104, 1989, black with red and white trim, 'Days of Thunder' version, MIP, from $30.00 to $40.00. (Photo courtesy Dana Johnson)

Mack Shovel Transporter, #CY-32, 1992, orange & yel w/29-F Shovel Nose tractor, MIP, from $8 to........................$12.00

Midnight X-Press Kenworth Box Truck, #CY-9, 1982, blk, England cast, MIP, from $45 to...$60.00

Peterbilt Conventional Double Container Truck, #CY-3, wht w/Federal Express decals, MIP, from $12 to...............$16.00

Peterbilt Fire Engine, #CY-13, 1984, fluorescent orange w/ City Fire Dept 15 decals, Thailand cast, MIP, from $9 to..$12.00

Peterbilt Fire Engine, #CY-13, 1984, red w/8/Fire Dept decals, Macau cast, MIP, from $12 to.....................................$16.00

Peterbilt Fire Engine, #CY-13, 1984, red w/8/Fire Dept decals, Thailand cast, MIP, from $8 to...................................$10.00

Peterbilt MBTV News Remote Truck, #CY-15, 1989, olive w/Strike Team/LS2009 decal, MIP, from $20 to.........$35.00

Peterbilt MBTV News Remote Truck, #CY-15, 1989, bl, MIP, from $12 to..$16.00

Scania Container Truck, #CY-18, 1986, bl w/blk interior, Varta Batteries decal, MIP, from $35 to $50.00

Scania Container Truck, #CY-18, 1986, bl w/gray interior, Varta Batteries decal, MIP, from $16 to $20.00

Scania Covered Truck, #CY-23, 1988, yel w/Michelin decal, MIP, from $10 to..$15.00

Scanoa Petrol Transporter, #CU-17, 1985, wht w/FEOSO decal, MIP, from $45 to..$60.00

KING SIZE, SPEED KINGS, AND SUPER KINGS

Airport Rescue Fire Tender, #K-075, 1980, MIP, from $12 to..$16.00

Allis-Chalmers Earth Scraper, #K-006, 1961, MIP, from $45 to..$60.00

Articulated Horse Box, #K-018, 1967, complete, NM+, from
$45 to $60.00
Articulated Tipper Truck, #K-018, 1974, metallic red cab, MIP,
from $16 to...$20.00
Auto Transport, #K-010, 1976, from $20 to......................$30.00
Barracuda Custom Racer, #K-051, 1973, MIP, from $20 to..$25.00
Breakdown Tow Truck, #K-011, 1976, red, MIP, from $50 to.$65.00
Camping Cruiser, #K-027, 1971, MIP, from $16 to...........$20.00
Cargo Hauler, #K-033, 1978, MIP, from $25 to.................$35.00
Caterpillar Bulldozer, #K-003, 1960, MIP, from $45 to.....$60.00
Citreon SM, #K-033, 1972, MIP, from $12 to...................$16.00
Curtiss-Wright Rear Dumper, #K-007, 1961, from $40 to .$55.00
Dodge Charger, #K-022, 1969, MIP, from $24 to..............$32.00
Dodge Custom Van, #K-080, 1980, from $18 to $24.00
ERF Simon Snorkel Fire Engine, #K-039, 1980, from $26 to.$32.00
Farm Unimog Livestock Trailer, #K-032, 1978, MIP, from $18
to $24.00
Fire Tender, #K-009, 1973, MIP, from $12 to....................$16.00
Ford Mustang, #K-060, 1976, MIP, from $18 to................$24.00
Fuzzy Buggy, #K-041, 1973, MIP, from $18 to $24.00
Gus's Gulper, #K-038, 1973, MIP, from $12 to.................$16.00
Heavy Breakdown Truck, #K-014, 1977, MIP, from $12 to..$16.00
Hercules Mobile Crane, #K-012, 1975, yel, MIP, from $18
to $24.00
Javelin Drag Racing Set, #K-057, 1975, MIP, from $30 to.$40.00
KW Dart Dump Truck, #K-002, 1964, MIP, from $40 to..$55.00

KW Dart Dump Truck, #K-2-B, 1964, MIP, from $75.00 to $90.00. (Photo courtesy Dana Johnson)

KW Dump Cart, #K-002, 1964, MIP, from $35 to $50.00
Lamborghini Miura, #K-024, 1969, bronze, mag wheels, NM+,
from $20 to...$30.00
Log Transport, #K-043, 1981, MIP, from $18 to...............$24.00
Londoner Bus, #K-15, The Royal Wedding, 1981, M, from $30
to $45.00
Marauder Racer, #K-045, 1973, MIP, from $18 to.............$24.00
Matra Rancho, #K-090, 1982, MIP, from $18 to...............$24.00
Mercury Cougar, #K-021, 1968, red interior, MIP, from $40
to $55.00
Merryweather Fire Engine, #K-015, 1964, MIP, from $65 to.$80.00
Michelin Scammell Container Truck, #K-024, 1977, MIP, from
$25 to $40.00
Milligan's Mill, #K-039, 1973, MIP, from $12 to..............$18.00
Miura Seaburst Set, #K-029, 1971, MIP, from $40 to $60.00

Mercury Commuter Fire Station Wagon, #K-23-A, 1969, black plastic tires, $45.00 to $70.00; SuperFast, from $20.00 to $35.00. (Photo courtesy Dana Johnson)

Motorcycle Racing Set, #K-091, 1982, MIP, from $45 to .$65.00
Motorcycle Transporter, #K-006, 1975, MIP, from $18 to..$24.00
Muir Hill Tractor-Trailer, #K-005, 1972, yel, MIP, from $25
to $35.00
O&K Excavator, #K-001, 1970, MIP, from $20 to $30.00
Pepsi Delivery Truck, #K-040, 1980, wht, MIP, from $25 to .$35.00
Petrol Tanker, #K-016, 1974, Total decal, MIP, from $30 to.$40.00
Pipe Truck, #K-010, 1967, MIP, from $20 to.....................$30.00
Pipe Truck, #K-010, 1967, w/4 orig pipes, EX, from $25 to.$35.00
Power Boat & Transport, #K-027, 1978, MIP, from $25 to.$35.00
Quaker State Patrol Tanker, #K-016, 1966, gr cab, MIP, from
$85 to $110.00
Racing Car Transporter, #K-005, 1967, MIP, from $35 to..$50.00
Racing Porsche, #K-101, 1983, metallic beige, MIP, from $20
to $30.00
Refuse truck, #K-007, 1967, blk wheels, MIP, from $35 to .$50.00
Road Construction Set, #K-137, 1986, MIP, from $35 to.$50.00
Sandcart, #K-037, 1973, orange or red, MIP, ea from $12 to.$18.00
Scammel Tipper Truck, #K-019, 1967, MIP, from $40 to .$55.00
Seaspeed SRN6 Hovercraft, #K-022, 1974, bl & wht, NM, from
$6 to $10.00
Security Truck, #K-019, 1979, MIP, from $18 to..............$24.00
Shovel Nose Custom Car, #K-032, 1972, MIP, from $20 to.$30.00
Taylor Jumbo Crane, #K-014, 1964, yel weight box (scarce),
MIP, from $40 to $55.00
Thunderclap Racer, #K-034, 1972, MIP, from $18 to $24.00
Weatherhill Hydraulic Shovel, #K-001, 1960, MIP, from $70
to $90.00

MODELS OF YESTERYEAR

Albion 6-Wheeler (1938), #Y-42, 1991, MIP, from $18 to .$24.00
Allchin Traction Machine (1926), #Y-1, 1956, diagonal unpnt
treads, silver boiler door, MIP, from $175 to $225.00
Atkinson Blue Circle Portland Cement Steam Wagon (1920),
#Y-1, yel, MIP, from $18 to.......................................$24.00
Auburn 851 Boattail Speedster (1933), #Y-19, 1980, beige &
cream w/chrome spoke wheels, MIP, from $25 to $30.00
Benz Limousine (1910), #Y-3, 1966, lt gr w/pale lime gr roof,
MIP, from $40 to..$55.00
Bugatti Type 35 (1932), #Y-11, 1987, MIP, from $20 to ...$30.00
Bugatti T44 (1927), #Y-24, 1983, gray w/tan interior & plum
accents, MIP, from $25 to $35.00

B-Type London Bus (1911), #Y-2-A, 1956, MIP, from $250.00 to $300.00. (Photo courtesy Dana Johnson)

Busch Steam Fire Engine (1905), #Y-43, 1991, MIP, from $65 to **$80.00**

Cadillac (1913), #Y-6, 1967, gold-plated, MIP, from $225 to .**$275.00**

Cadillac Fire Engine (1933), #Y-61, 1992, MIP, from $25 to..**$35.00**

Crossley (1918), #Y-13, 1973, bl-gray w/tan roof & canopy, RAF decal, MIP, from $65 to...**$80.00**

Crossley Beer Lorry (1918), #Y-26, 1984, any color & decal, MIP, ea, from $20 to **$30.00**

Deusenberg Model J Town Car (1930), #Y-4, 1976, brn & beige, lt bl or silver & bl (Macau cast), MIP, ea from $20 to.**$30.00**

Ferrari Dino 246/V12 (1957), #K-16, 1986, MIP, from $20 to **$30.00**

Foden Steam Lorry (1922), #Y-27, 1985, bl w/tow hook, Pick- fords decal, MIP, from $35 to.....................................**$50.00**

Ford Model A Van (1930), #Y-22, 1982, beige w/red roof, Toblerone decal, MIP, from $18 to **$24.00**

Ford Model A Woody Wagon (1929), #Y-21, 1981, yel & brn, MIP, from $24 to...**$32.00**

Ford Model T (1911), #Y-1, 1965, cream, MIP, from $20 to .**$28.00**

Ford Model T Tanker (1912), #Y-3, 1982, gr & wht roof & tank, gold spoke wheels, Zerolene decal, MIP, from $100 to.**$135.00**

Ford Model T Truck (1912), #Y-12, 1979, cream w/blk roof, sil- ver wheels, Coca-Cola decal, MIP, from $75 to **$90.00**

Garrett Steam Truck (1931), #Y-37, 1990, MIP, from $18 to .**$24.00**

Garrett Steam Wagon (1931), #Y-48, 1996, MIP, from $55 to **$70.00**

Grand Prix Mercedes (1908), #Y-10, 1958, cream, MIP, from $125 to...**$175.00**

Hispano Suiza (1938), #Y-17, 1973, gr, MIP, from $24 to.**$28.00**

Horse-Drawn London Bus (1899), #Y-12, 1959, beige driver & seats, MIP, from $115 to **$140.00**

Horse-Drawn Royal Mail Coach (1820), #Y-39, 1990, MIP, from $65 to...**$80.00**

Jaguar SS 100 (1936), #Y-1, lt yel w/wht-wall tires, England-cast, MIP, from $110 to...**$140.00**

Jaguar SS 100 (1936), #Y-1-C, silver & bl, MIP, from $16 to.**$20.00**

Lagonda Drophead Coupe (1938), #Y-11, 1973, plum w/blk inte- rior, from $28 to..**$34.00**

Lemans Bentley (1929), #Y-5, 1958, gr tonneau, MIP, from $85 to **$100.00**

Leyland Van (4-Ton), #Y-7, 1957, 2 lines of text, cream roof, metal wheels, MIP, from $1,250 to **$1,650.00**

Lincoln Zephyr (1938), #Y-64, 1992, MIP, from $30 to....**$45.00**

Mack Tanker (1930), #Y-23, 1989, MIP, from $20 to **$30.00**

Mercedes Benz SS Coupe (1911), #Y-16, 1972, metallic gray w/red chassis, blk roof, MIP, from $75 to....................**$90.00**

Mercedes Benz 540K (1937), #Y-20, 1981, metallic gray w/red disk or spoke wheels, MIP, from $40 to **$55.00**

MG TC (1945), #Y-8, 1978, cream w/tan top, MIP, from $15 to..**$20.00**

Morris Pantechicon Van (1933), #Y-31, 1990, MIP, from $18 to..**$24.00**

Packard Landaulet (1912), #Y-11, 1964, beige & brn, MIP, from $25 to..**$35.00**

Peugeot (1907), #Y-5, 1969, yel w/clear windows, blk rook, MIP, from $80 to **$100.00**

Prince Henery Vauxhall (1914), #Y-2, 1970, bl w/wht seats, from $25 to..**$35.00**

Renault Type AG (1910), #Y-25, 1983, gr w/gold spoke wheels, Perrier decal, MIP, from $18 to................................**$24.00**

Riley MPH (1934), #Y-3, 1974, lt metallic red w/red 12-spoke wheels, from $40 to..**$55.00**

Rolls Royce Silver Ghost (1907), #Y-15, 1960, silver-gr w/gray tires, MIP, from $60 to **$80.00**

Scania Vabis Postbus (1922), #Y-16, MIP, from $40 to.....**$60.00**

Sentinel Steam Wagon, #Y-4, 1956, unpnt metal wheels, MIP, from $45 to...**$60.00**

Shand-Mason Horse-Drawn Fire Engine, #Y-004, 1960, Kent, gray horses, MIP, from $375 to **$450.00**

Simplex (1912), #Y-9, 1968, pale gold w/blk roof, MIP, from $50 to..**$70.00**

Stutz Bearcat (1931), #Y-14, 1974, cream & red w/red wheels, MIP, from $35 to...**$50.00**

Sunbeam Motorcycle & Milford, #Y-008, 1962, dk gr sidecar seat, MIP, from $50 to..**$70.00**

Talbot Van (1927), #Y-5, 1978, bl w/blk roof, Frasers decal, MIP, from $400 to **$450.00**

Type 35 Bugatti (1923), #Y-6, 1961, red & wht dash & floor, MIP, from $60 to...**$75.00**

Unic Taxi (1907), #Y-28, 1984, maroon, bl or wht, MIP, ea from $16 to...**$20.00**

1911 Renault 2-Seater, #Y-002, 1963, silver-plated, MIP, from $70 to...**$85.00**

SKYBUSTERS

Air Malta A300 Airbus, #SB-027, 1981, wht, MIP, from $15 to .**$20.00**

Alpha Jet, #SB-011, 1973, bl & red, MIP, from $10 to **$15.00**

Army Helicopter, #SB-020, 1977, olive, MIP, from $10 to .**$15.00**

Bell Jet Ranger Helicopter, #SB-33, 1990, wht & bl, MIP, from $6 to **$8.00**

Boeing 747-400, #SB-031, 1990, any, MIP, from $7 to **$9.00**

Cessna 210, #SB-014, 1973, orange-yel & wht, MIP, from $9 to...**$12.00**

Cessna 402, #SB-009, 1973, lt gr & wht, MIP, from $9 to .**$12.00**

Circus-Circus Boeing Stearman Biplane, #SB-039, 1992, wht, MIP, from $6 to **$8.00**

Corsair A7D, #SB-002, 1973, khaki & wht w/brn & gr camou-
flage, MIP, from $8 to $10.00
Corsair F4U, #SB-016, 1975, metallic bl or orange, MIP, ea from
$8 to $10.00
F-16, #SB-024, 1979, any, MIP, from $9 to $12.00
Harrier Jet, #SB-027, 1981, wht & red, MIP, from $8 to ..$10.00
Heinz 57 SST Super Sonic Transport, #SB-023, 1979, wht, MIP,
from $24 to..$32.00
James Bond Cessna 210 Float Plane, #SB-026, 1981, wht, MIP,
from $12 to..$16.00
Junkers 87B, #SB-007, 1973, blk w/swastikas, MIP, from $80
to...$100.00
Learjet, #SB-001, 1973, red w/Datapost decal, MIP, from $8
to...$12.00
Lightning, #SB-0212, 1977, olive or silver-gray, MIP, ea from $8
to...$12.00

Lockheed A130/C-130 Hercules, #SB-34-A, 1990, MIP, from $4.00 to $6.00. (Photo courtesy Dana Johnson)

Lockheed F-117A Stealth, #SB-036, 1991, wht, no markings,
MIP, from $7 to...$10.00
Marine Phantom F4E, #SB-015, 1975, pk, MIP, from $7 to.$10.00
Mig 21, #SB-006, 1973, bl & wht, MIP, from $8 to $12.00
MiL M24 Hind-D Chopper, #SB-035, 1990, any, MIP, ea from
$6 to $8.00
Mirage F1, #SB-004, 1973, red w/bull's-eye on wings, MIP, from
$12 to $16.00
NASA Space Shuttle, #SB-003, 1980, wht & gray, MIP, from $9
to...$12.00
Piper Comanche, #SB-019, 1977, beige & dk bl, Macau cast,
MIP, from $7 to...$10.00
Pitts Special Biplane, #SB-012, 1980, any, MIP, from $16 to .$20.00
Ram Rod, #SB-016, 1976, red, MIP, from $7 to...............$10.00
Royal Air Force Hawk, #SB-037, 1992, red, MIP, from $7 to.$10.00
Spitfire, #SB-008, 1973, dk brn & gold, MIP, from $18 to.$24.00
Starfighter F104, #SB-005, 1973, red & wht w/maple leaf labels,
MIP, ea from $9 to $12.00
Tornado, #SB-022, 1978, lt gray & wht, dk gray & wht or red &
wht, MIP, ea , from $9 to $12.00
Tornado, #SB-022, 1978, lt purple & wht, MIP, from $7 to.$10.00
USAF Lockheed SR-71 Blackbird, #SB-029, 1989, blk, MIP,
from $4 to..$6.00
UTA Douglas DC-10, #SB-013, 1973, wht, MIP, from $70 to..$85.00
Wild Wind, #SB-018, 1976, lime gr & wht, MIP, from $8 to.$12.00
007 Rescue Helicopter, #SB-025, 1979, red & wht, MIP, from
$10 to $15.00

Model Kits

Though model kits were popular with kids of the '50s who enjoyed the challenge of assembling a classic car or two or a Musketeer figure now and then, when the monster series hit in the early 1960s, sales shot through the ceiling. Made popular by all the monster movies of that decade, ghouls like Vampirella, Frankenstein, and the Wolfman were eagerly assembled by kids everywhere. They could (if their parents didn't object too strongly) even construct an actual working guillotine. Aurora had other successful series of figure kits, too, based on characters from comic strips and TV shows as well as a line of sports stars.

But the vast majority of model kits were vehicles. They varied in complexity, some requiring much more dexterity on the part of the model builder than others, and they came in several scales, from 1/8 (which might be as large as 20" to 24") down to 1/43 (generally about 3" to 4"), but the most popular scale was 1/25 (usually between 6" to 8"). Some of the largest producers of vehicle kits were AMT, MPC, and IMC. Though production obviously waned during the late 1970s and early 1980s, with the intensity of today's collector market, companies like Ertl (who now is producing 1/25 scale vehicles using some of the old AMT dies) are proving that model kits still sell very well.

As a rule of thumb, assembled kits (built-ups) are priced at about 25% to 50% of the price range for a boxed kit, but this is not always true on the higher-priced kits. One mint in the box with the factory seal intact will often sell for up to 15% more than if the seal were broken, though depending on the kit, a sealed perfect box may add as much $100.00. Condition of the box is crucial. Last but not least, one must factor in Internet sales, which could cause some values to go down considerably.

For more information, we recommend *Collectible Figure Kits of the '50s, '60s, and '70s* by Gordy Dutt.

See also Plasticville.

Addar, Planet of the Apes, Cornelius, MIB, $50.00.

Adams, Around the World in 80 Days Balloon, 1960, MIB..$325.00
Adams, Hawk Missile Battery, 1958, MIB........................$70.00

Addar, Evel Knievel, 1974, MIB......................................$50.00

Addar, Planet of the Apes, Gen Ursus, 1973-74, MIB......$40.00

Addar, Planet of the Apes, Stallion & Soldier, 1974, MIB .$100.00

Addar, Planet of the Apes, 1974, Caesar or Gen Alod, MIB, ea..$50.00

Addar, Planet of the Apes, 1974, Dr Zaius, MIB...............$40.00

Addar, Planet of the Apes, 1975, Tree House, NMIB.......$45.00

Addar, Super Scenes, 1975, Jaws in a Bottle, MIB............$60.00

Addar, Super Scenes, 1975, Spirit in a Bottle, MIB..........$50.00

Airfix, Bigfoot, 1978, MIB...$75.00

Airfix, Bristol Bloodhound, 1992, MIB............................$15.00

Airfix, Corythosaus, 1970, MIB (sealed)...........................$30.00

Airfix, James Bond & Odd Job, 1966, MIB.....................$200.00

Airfix, Sam-2 Missile, 1973, MIB...................................$40.00

Airfix, Yeoman of the Guard, 1978, MIB.........................$10.00

Airfix, 2001: A Space Odyssey, 1970, Orion, MIB $75.00

Airfix, 2001: A Space Odyssey, 1980, Orion, NMIB $25.00

AMT, Farrah's Foxy Vet, 1977, MIB................................$65.00

AMT, Flintstones, 1974, MIB...$75.00

AMT, Flintstones Rock Crusher, 1974, MIB.....................$75.00

AMT, Get Smart Sunbeam Car, 1967, MIB......................$75.00

AMT, Girl From UNCLE Car, 1974, MIB.......................$300.00

AMT, KISS Custom Chevy Van, 1977, MIB.....................$75.00

AMT, Laurel & Hardy, '27 Touring Car, 1976, MIB........$65.00

AMT, Man From UNCLE Car, MIB...............................$225.00

AMT, My Mother the Car, 1965, MIB..............................$45.00

AMT, Sonny & Cher Mustang, 1960s, MIB.....................$325.00

AMT, Star Trek, Klingon Cruiser, #S952-802, 1968, MIB..$225.00

AMT, Star Trek, Romulan Bird of Prey, 1975, MIB........$125.00

AMT, Star Trek, Spock, 1973, NMIB (sm box)...............$150.00

AMT, Star Trek, USS Enterprise Command Bridge, 1975, MIB..$80.00

AMT, Wackie Woodie Krazy Kar, 1960s, MIB.................$85.00

AMT/Ertl, A-Team Van, 1983, MIB................................$30.00

AMT/Ertl, Back to the Future, Delorian, 1991, MIB (sealed).$35.00

AMT/Ertl, Batman (movie), Batman Cocoon, 1989, MIB..$20.00

AMT/Ertl, Batman (movie), Batwing, 1990, MIB (sealed) .$30.00

AMT/Ertl, Monkeemobile, 1990, MIB (sealed) $100.00

AMT/Ertl, Peterbilt 359 Truck, MIB...............................$35.00

AMT/Ertl, Robocop 2, Robo 1 Police Car, 1990, MIB.....$25.00

AMT/Ertl, Star Trek (TV), Kirk, 1994, MIB (sealed) $25.00

AMT/Ertl, Star Trek (TV), McCoy, 1994, MIB (sealed)..$25.00

AMT/Ertl, Star Trek, U.S.S. Enterprise, Chrome Set, Special Edition #6005, MIB, $35.00.

AMT/Ertl, Star Trek: Deep Space Nine, Defiant, 1996, MIB $20.00

AMT/Ertl, Star Trek: TNG, USS Enterprise, 1988, MIB.$30.00

AMT/Ertl, Star Wars, Cut-Away Millenium Falcon, 1996, MIB $25.00

Anubis, Jonny Quest, Robot Spy, 1992, MIB....................$60.00

Anubis, Jonny Quest, Turu the Terrible, 1992, MIB.........$60.00

Arii, Orguss Flier, MIB...$15.00

Arii, Regult Missile Carrier, MIB $25.00

Arii, Southern Cross, NAD-Jun Yamashita, MIB $25.00

Arii-Macross, Valkyrie VF-1J, MIB $20.00

Aurora, Addams Family Haunted House, 1964, assembled but not pnt, EX $275.00

Aurora, Addams Family Haunted House, 1964, MIB.....$850.00

Aurora, Alfred E Newman, 1965, EXIB (unused) $165.00

Aurora, Archie's Car, 1969, MIB $100.00

Aurora, Banana Splits 1969, Banana Buggy, MIB...........$525.00

Aurora, Batman, 1964, MIB (sealed) $250.00

Aurora, Big Frankie (Frankenstein), #470, 1964, 1:5 scale, assembled, 19", EX...$275.00

Aurora, Big Frankie (Frankenstein), #470, 1964, 1:5 scale, 19", MIB...$1,200.00

Aurora, Bloodthirsty Pirates, 1965, Blackbeard, MIB.....$225.00

Aurora, Bride of Frankenstein, 1965, MIB....................$750.00

Aurora, Captain Action, 1966, MIB..............................$300.00

Aurora, Captain America, 1966, MIB $330.00

Aurora, Castle Creatures, 1966, Vampire, MIB $225.00

Aurora, Chitty Chitty Bang Bang, 1965, assembled, EX ..$40.00

Aurora, Creature From the Black Lagoon, 1963, MIB ...$450.00

Aurora, Creature From the Black Lagoon, 1969, glow-in-the-dark, MIB...$200.00

Aurora, Dick Tracy in Action, 1968, MIB.....................$350.00

Aurora, Dr Jekyll as Mr Hyde, 1964, MIB....................$375.00

Aurora, Dr Jekyll as Mr Hyde, 1969, glow-in-the-dark, MIB..$200.00

Aurora, Dracula, 1962, MIB...$300.00

Aurora, Dracula, 1975, Monsters of the Movies, MIB....$250.00

Aurora, Flying Sub, 1968, NMIB $200.00

Aurora, Flying Sub, 1975, MIB $100.00

Aurora, Forgotten Prisoner, 1966, MIB.........................$425.00

Aurora, Forgotten Prisoner, 1969, Frightning Lightning, glow-in-the-dark, MIB $200.00

Aurora, Forgotten Prisonser, 1969, Frightning Lightning, MIB $450.00

Aurora, Frankenstein, see also Big Frankie

Aurora, Frankenstein, 1971, glow-in-the-dark, MIB $150.00

Aurora, Frankenstein, 1971, Monster Scenes, MIB........$125.00

Aurora, Frankenstein, 1975, Monsters of the Movies, MIB .$325.00

Aurora, George Washington, 1965, MIB (sealed) $100.00

Aurora, Ghidrah, 1975, Monsters of the Movies, MIB...$325.00

Aurora, Gladiator, see Roman Gladiator w/Trident

Aurora, Godzilla, 1964, MIB..$550.00

Aurora, Godzilla's Go-Cart, 1966, assembled, NM.........$750.00

Aurora, Godzilla's Go-Cart, 1966, MIB......................$3,000.00

Aurora, Gold Knight of Nice, 1957, MIB $325.00

Aurora, Gold Knight of Nice, 1965, MIB $275.00

Aurora, Green Beret, 1966, NMIB................................$175.00

Aurora, Green Hornet's Black Beauty, 1966, MIB..........$500.00

Aurora, Godzilla, 1964, glow-in-the-dark, assembled, EX, $100.00; MIB, $350.00.

Aurora, Gruesome Goodies, 1971, Monster Scenes, MIB..$100.00
Aurora, Guys & Gals, 1957, Indian Chief, MIB.............$125.00
Aurora, Guys & Gals, 1959, Caballero, MIB.................$100.00
Aurora, Hunchback of Notre Dame, 1964, Anthony Quinn, MIB...$300.00
Aurora, Hunchback of Notre Dame, 1969, glow-in-the-dark, MIB...$150.00
Aurora, Incredible Hulk, 1966, MIB.............................$325.00
Aurora, Incredible Hulk, 1974, Comic Scenes, MIB......$100.00
Aurora, Invaders, 1968, UFO, MIB...............................$100.00
Aurora, Invaders, 1975, UFO, MIB.................................$75.00
Aurora, James Bond 007, 1966, MIB..............................$350.00
Aurora, Jesse James, 1966, MIB......................................$200.00
Aurora, John F Kennedy, 1965, MIB................................$150.00
Aurora, King Kong, 1964, MIB $475.00
Aurora, King Kong, 1969, glow-in-the-dark, MIB..........$300.00
Aurora, Land of the Giants, Space Ship, 1968, MIB......$425.00
Aurora, Land of the Giants, 1968, Diorama, MIB..........$450.00
Aurora, Lone Ranger, 1967, MIB.....................................$175.00
Aurora, Lone Ranger, 1974, Comic Scenes, MIB (sealed).$65.00
Aurora, Lost in Space, 1968, Robot, MIB.......................$850.00
Aurora, Man From UNCLE, 1966, Illya Kuryakin, MIB .$225.00
Aurora, Man From UNCLE, 1966, Napoleon Solo, MIB..$275.00
Aurora, Mummy, 1963, MIB $325.00
Aurora, Mummy, 1969, glow-in-the-dark, MIB..............$200.00
Aurora, Mummy's Chariot, 1965, MIB $525.00
Aurora, Munsters, 1964, Living Room, MIB...............$1,200.00
Aurora, Odd Job, 1966, MIB $450.00
Aurora, Pendulum, 1971, Monster Scenes, MIB..............$90.00
Aurora, Phantom of the Opera, 1969, Frightning Lightning, MIB...$375.00
Aurora, Phantom of the Opera, 1969, glow-in-the-dark, MIB...$175.00
Aurora, Phantom of the Opera, 1972, glow-in-the-dark, MIB..$75.00
Aurora, Prehistoric Scenes, 1971, Cro-Magnon Man, MIB.$75.00
Aurora, Prehistoric Scenes, 1971, Neanderthal Man, MIB..$50.00
Aurora, Prehistoric Scenes, 1972, Tar Pit, MIB.............$160.00
Aurora, Rat Patrol, 1967, MIB..$115.00
Aurora, Robin, 1966, MIB..$125.00

Aurora, Robin, 1974, Comic Scenes, MIB.....................$100.00
Aurora, Rodan, 1975, Monsters of the Movies, rare, MIB .$375.00

Aurora, Roman Galdiator With Trident, 1959, Famous Fighters, MIB, $175.00.

Aurora, Spider-Man, 1966, MIB $300.00
Aurora, Spider-Man, 1974, Comic Scenes, MIB (sealed) ..$120.00
Aurora, Steve Canyon, 1958, Famous Fighters, MIB $200.00
Aurora, Superboy, 1964, MIB..$250.00
Aurora, Superboy, 1974, Comic Scenes, MIB................$100.00
Aurora, Superman, 1963, assembled, EX..........................$45.00
Aurora, Superman, 1963, MIB...$350.00

Aurora, Tarzan, 1967, MIB, $200.00.

Aurora, Tonto, 1967, MIB...$250.00
Aurora, Tonto, 1974, Comic Scenes, MIB.......................$75.00
Aurora, Viking, 1959, Famous Fighters, MIB.................$250.00
Aurora, Voyage to the Bottom of the Sea, 1966, Seaview, MIB $325.00
Aurora, Voyager (Fantastic Voyage), 1969, MIB $500.00

Aurora, Whoozis?, 1966, Alfalfa, MIB $85.00
Aurora, Whoozis?, 1966, Denty, MIB $85.00
Aurora, Whoozis?, 1966, Suzie, MIB $75.00
Aurora, Witch, 1965, MIB $325.00
Aurora, Witch, 1969, glow-in-the-dark, MIB $200.00
Aurora, Wolfman, 1969, glow-in-the-dark, MIB $175.00
Aurora, Wonder Woman, 1965, MIB $500.00
Bachmann, Animals of the World, Lion, 1959, MIB $50.00
Bachmann, Birds of the World, Scarlet Tanager, 1990, MIB.$20.00
Bachmann, Dogs of the World, Basset Hound, 1960s, MIB.$30.00
Bachmann, Fisher Boy, 1962, MIB $80.00
Bandai, Godzilla, 1984, MIB $50.00
Bandai, Kinggidrah, 1984, MIB $50.00
Bandai, Pegila, 1990, MIB $15.00
Bandai, Thunderbird, 1984, MIB $40.00
Billiken, Frankenstein, 1988, MIB $150.00
Billiken, Laser Blast Alien, 1988, vinyl, MIB $100.00
Billiken, Mummy, 1990, MIB $175.00
Billiken, She-Creature, 1989, MIB $175.00
Chitty Chitty Bang Bang, 1965, MIB $150.00
Dark Horse, King Kong, 1992, vinyl, MIB $75.00
Dark Horse, Mummy, 1995, MIB $150.00
Dark Horse, Predator II, 1994, MIB $175.00
Eldon, Pink Panther, 1970s, MIB $75.00
Entex, Message From Space, 1978, Comet Fire, MIB $25.00
Geometric Design, Boris Karloff as The Mummy, MIB.....$50.00
Geometric Design, Lon Chaney Jr as the Wolfman, MIB.$50.00
Hawk, Bobcat Roadster, 1962, MIB $30.00
Hawk, Cherokee Sports Roadster, 1962, MIB $35.00
Hawk, Cobra II, 1950s, MIB....................................$75.00
Hawk, Francis the Foul, 1963, MIB..........................$60.00

Hawk, Freddy Flameout the Way Out Jet Jockey, 1963, Weird-Ohs, MIB, $85.00.

Hawk, Indian Totem Poles, 1966, Thunderbird, MIB.......$50.00
Hawk, Monte Carlo Sports Roadster, 1962, MIB.............$75.00
Hawk, Woodie on a Surfari, 1964, MIB.........................$100.00
Horizon, Bride of Frankenstein, 1990s, MIB.................$65.00
Horizon, Dracula (Bela Lugosi), MIB...........................$65.00
Horizon, Frankenstein, MIB......................................$100.00
Horizon, Invisible Man, NMIB...................................$50.00
Horizon, Marvel Universe, 1933, Cyclops, MIB $50.00
Horizon, Marvel Universe, 1988, Punisher, MIB............$50.00
Horizon, Marvel Universe, 1988, Spider-Man, MIB.........$40.00
Horizon, Marvel Universe, 1990, Incredible Hulk, MIB ..$40.00

Horizon, Marvel Universe, 1991, Dr Doom, MIB.............$45.00
Horizon, Marvel Universe, 1991, Thing, MIB $50.00
Horizon, Mole People, 1988, Mole Man #2, MIB.............$75.00
Horizon, Robocop, 1989, ED-209, MIB $70.00
Horizon, Robocop, 1992, Robocop #30, MIB $70.00
Imai, Batman Boat, 1960s, MIB (box in Japanese), A....$300.00
Imai, Captain Blue, 1982, MIB...................................$15.00
Imai, Orguss, 1990, Incredible Hulk, MIB $45.00
Imai, Orguss, 1994, Cable, MIB.................................$40.00
Imai, Orguss, 1994, Spider-Man, new pose, MIB $30.00
ITC, Dog Champions, 1959, German Shepard, MIB $35.00
ITC, Neanderthal Man, 1959, MIB..............................$50.00
Life-Like, Ankylosaurus, 1968, MIB............................$35.00
Life-Like, Corythosaurus, 1970s, MIB $20.00
Life-Like, Roman Chariot, 1970s, MIB.........................$20.00
Lindberg, Coo Coo Clock, 1965, MIB $40.00
Lindberg, Douglas X-3 Supersonic Stiletto, 1950s, MIB...$60.00
Lindberg, Flying Saucer, 1952, MIB $200.00
Lindberg, Scuttle Bucket, 1964, Lindy Loonys, MIB......$100.00
Lindberg, SST Continental, 1958, MIB........................$175.00
Lindberg, Tyrannosaurus, 1987, MIB..........................$15.00
Lindberg, US Space Station, 1958, MIB........................$200.00
Lunar Models, Angry Red Planet, Giant Amoeba, MIB .$100.00
Lunar Models, Lost in Space, Space Pod, MIB $125.00
Monogram, Bad Machine, 1970s, MIB..........................$60.00
Monogram, Bathtub Buggy, 1960s, MIB (sealed)...........$100.00
Monogram, Blue Thunder Helicopter, 1984, MIB...........$30.00
Monogram, Buck Rogers, 1970, Marauder, MIB $70.00
Monogram, Dracula, 1983, MIB (sealed) $40.00
Monogram, Elvira Macabre Mobile, 1988, MIB $25.00
Monogram, Giraffes, 1961, MIB..................................$50.00
Monogram, Godzilla, 1978, MIB.................................$100.00
Monogram, NASA Space Shuttle, 1986, MIB $25.00
Monogram, Sand Crab, 1969, MIB $50.00
Monogram, Snoopy & Motorcycle, 1971, snap-tite, MIB..$100.00
Monogram, Snoopy as Joe Cool, 1971, MIB...................$100.00
Monogram, Space Buggy, 1969, MIB $100.00
Monogram, TV Orbiter, 1959, MIB...............................$150.00
Monogram, Tyannosaurus Rex, 1987, MIB.....................$25.00
Monogram, Voyage to the Bottom of the Sea, 1979, Flying Sub, MIB...$175.00
Monogram, Wolfman, 1983, MIB (sealed).....................$50.00
Monogram, Young Astronauts, 1987, Mercury/Gemini Capsules, MIB (sealed) $50.00
Monogram, Young Astronauts, 1987, X-15 Experimental Aircraft, MIB...$35.00
MPC, Alien, 1979, MIB (sealed) $100.00
MPC, Barnabas, 1968, Dark Shadows, MIB..................$400.00
MPC, Barnabas Vampire Van, 1969, Dark Shadows, MIB..$250.00
MPC, Batman, 1984, MIB (sealed) $40.00
MPC, Beverly Hillbillies Truck, 1968, MIB..................$200.00
MPC, Bionic Woman, 1976, Bionic Repair, NMIB.........$40.00
MPC, Dukes of Hazzard, 1980, Daisy's Jeep CJ, NMIB.....$30.00
MPC, Dukes of Hazzard, 1982, Sheriff Rosco's Police Car, NMIB $40.00
MPC, Fonzie & Dream Rod, 1976, NMIB $40.00
MPC, Hogan's Heroes Jeep, 1968, MIB $125.00

MPC, Incredible Hulk, 1978, MIB (sealed) $50.00
MPC, Incredible Hulk Van, 1977, MIB $25.00
MPC, Mannix Roadster, 1968, MIB...............................$50.00
MPC, Pirates of the Caribbean, 1972, Freed in the Nick of Time,
   NMIB..$75.00
MPC, Road Runner & the Beep-Beep T, 1972, MIB........$75.00
MPC, Space: 1999, 1976, Alien Creature & Vehicle, MIB .$55.00
MPC, Space: 1999, 1976, Eagle 1 Transporter, NMIB....$100.00
MPC, Space: 1999, 1977, Hawk Spaceship, MIB $55.00
MPC, Spider-Man, 1978, NMIB $35.00
MPC, Star Wars, 1978, Darth Vader TIE Fighter, MIB $35.00
MPC, Star Wars, 1979, R2-D2, NMIB............................$35.00
MPC, Star Wars, 1981, AT-AT, MIB (sealed)...................$35.00
MPC, Star Wars, 1982, Boba Fett's Slave I, MIB (sealed) .$35.00
MPC, Star Wars, 1983, Shuttle Tydirium, MIB (sealed) ..$25.00
MPC, Strange Changing Time Machine, 1974, MIB $65.00
MPC, Strange Changing Vampire, 1974, MIB.................$55.00

Pyro, Classic Auburn Speedster, MIB, $75.00.

Pyro, Gladiator Show Cycle, 1970, MIB..........................$50.00
Pyro, Indian Warrior, 1960s, MIB...................................$60.00
Pyro, Peacemaker 45, 1960, MIB (sealed).......................$100.00
Pyro, Prehistoric Monsters Gift Set, 1950s, MIB $125.00
Pyro, Restless Gun, 1959, Deputy Sheriff, MIB $70.00
Pyro, Surf's Up!, 1970, MIB..$40.00
Remco, Flintstones, any kit, 1961, MIB, ea $200.00
Revell, Alien Invader, 1979, w/lights, MIB (sealed).........$50.00
Revell, Amazing Moon Mixer, 1970, MIB $35.00
Revell, Apollo Astronaut on Moon, 1970, MIB.............$125.00
Revell, Apollo Columbia/Eagle, 1969, MIB (sealed)......$100.00
Revell, Ariane 4 Rocket, 1985, MIB $35.00
Revell, Baja Humbug, 1971, MIB....................................$85.00
Revell, Beatles, 1965, George Harrison, MIB $250.00
Revell, Beatles, 1965, John Lennon, MIB.......................$250.00
Revell, Beatles, 1965, Paul McCartney, MIB..................$200.00
Revell, Beatles, 1965, Ringo Starr, MIB..........................$200.00
Revell, CHiPs, 1980, Helicopter, MIB $35.00

MPC, Sweathogs 'Dream Machine,' 1976, MIB, $45.00.

Precision, Cap'n Kidd the Pirate, 1959, MIB, $115.00.

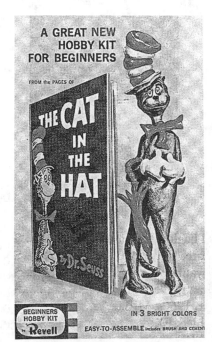

Revell, Cat in the Hat, 1960, MIB, $150.00.

Revell, CHiPs, 1980, Jon's Chevy 4x4, MIB....................$35.00
Revell, CHiPs, 1980, Kawaski Motorcycle, MIB.............$35.00
Revell, CHiPs, 1981, Ponch's Firebird, MIB (sealed).......$30.00
Revell, Code Red, 1981, Fire Chief's Car, MIB................$20.00
Revell, Disney's Love Bug Rides Again, 1974, MIB.......$100.00
Revell, Disney's Robin Hood Set #1, 1974, MIB...........$100.00
Revell, Dr Seuss Zoo, 1959, Kit #1 w/Gowdy, Norbal & Tingo, MIB..$400.00
Revell, Dr Seuss Zoo, 1960, Kit #2 w/Busby, Grickily & Rosco, MIB..$500.00
Revell, Dune, 1985, Ornithopter, MIB (sealed)..............$60.00
Revell, Dune, 1985, Sand Worm, MIB (sealed)...............$75.00
Revell, Ed 'Big Daddy' Roth, 1960, Road Agent, MIB.....$80.00
Revell, Ed 'Big Daddy' Roth, 1963, MIB..........................$80.00
Revell, Ed 'Big Daddy' Roth, 1963, Mr Grasser, NMIB....$75.00
Revell, Ed 'Big Daddy' Roth, 1965, Angel Fink, MIB....$180.00
Revell, Ed 'Big Daddy' Roth, 1965, Fink-Eliminator, MIB..$125.00
Revell, Endangered Animals, 1991, Gorilla, MIB.............$30.00
Revell, Flash Gordon & the Martian, 1965, MIB...........$150.00
Revell, Flipper, 1965, MIB..$150.00
Revell, History Makers, 1983, Jupiter C, MIB (sealed)....$50.00
Revell, Love Bug, 1970s, MIB..$50.00
Revell, Magnum PI, 1981, TC's Helicopter, MIB (sealed).$60.00
Revell, Magnum PI, 1982, 308 GTS Farrari, MIB............$60.00
Revell, Moon Ship, 1957, MIB..$225.00
Revell, Moonraker Space Shuttle, 1979, MIB..................$25.00
Revell, Penny Pincher VW Bug, 1980, MIB....................$35.00
Revell, Peter Pan Pirate Ship, 1960, #377, MIB...........$100.00
Revell, Rif Raf & Hid Spitfire, 1971, MIB.......................$50.00
Revell, Robotech, 1984, Commando, 1984, MIB (sealed).$50.00
Revell, Robotech, 1985, VF-1J Fighter, MIB (sealed)......$60.00
Revell, Space Explorer Solaris, 1969, MIB....................$125.00
Revell, Terrier Missile, 1958, MIB.................................$200.00
Revell, US Army Nike Hercules, 1958, MIB....................$60.00
Revell, USN Bendix Talos Missile, 1957, MIB.................$85.00
Screamin', Contemplating Conquest, 1995, MIB (sealed).$50.00
Screamin', Friday the 13th's Jason, MIB.......................$125.00
Screamin', Mars Attacks, Target Earth, assembled, NM...$30.00
Screamin', Mary Shelly's Frankenstein, 1994, assembled, EX.$30.00
Screamin', Star Wars, Stormtrooper, 1993, MIB..............$45.00
Screamin', Werewolf, MIB..$100.00
Strombecker, Disneyland Stagecoach, 1950s, MIB.........$200.00
Strombecker, Walt Disney's Spaceship, 1958, MIB........$300.00
Superior, Beating Heart, 1959, MIB.................................$35.00
Superior, Seeing Eye, 1959, MIB.....................................$35.00
Testors, Weird-Ohs, Endsville Eddie, 1993, MIB (sealed).$35.00
Toy Biz, Ghost Rider, 1996, MIB.....................................$30.00
Toy Biz, Storm, 1996, MIB...$20.00
Toy Biz, Thing, 1996, MIB...$20.00
Toy Biz, Wolverine, 1996, NMIB.....................................$20.00
Tsukada, Ghostbusters, Stay Puft Man (sm), 1984, MIB..$40.00
Tsukuda, Creature From the Black Lagoon, MIB...........$150.00
Tsukuda, Frankenstein, 1985, MIB................................$100.00
Tsukuda, Ghostbusters Terror Dog, MIB.......................$125.00
Tsukuda, Metaluna Mutant, MIB...................................$100.00
Tsukuda, Mummy, MIB...$100.00
Tsukuda, Wolfman, MIB...$100.00

Musical Toys

Whether meant to soothe, entertain or inspire, musical toys were part of our growing-up years. Some were as simple as a wind-up music box, others as elaborate as a lacquered French baby grand piano.

See also Character, TV, and Movie Collectibles; Disney; Rock 'n Roll; Western.

Accordion, Horner, 2-octave, leatherette case, 10", NM..$250.00
Church Organ, Chein, litho tin, hand crank, 10", EXIB.$150.00
Drum, Chein, circus graphics, litho tin w/paper heads, spring-tension body, wooden sticks, 11" dia, EX+..............$100.00
Drum, Chein, 1970s, Revolutionary graphics, litho tin w/cb insert, designed by Gene Bosch, NM+....................$425.00
Drum, Ohio Art, Noah's Art, Litho tin, NM..................$150.00

Farmer in the Dell Music Maker, Mattel, 1950s, lithographed tin with crank handle, EX, $125.00.

Golden Banjo, Emenee, 1960s, NMIB.............................$125.00
Golden Piano Accordion, Emenee, EX+IB.......................$75.00
Harmonica, Strauss, 1925, detachable horn, EXIB.........$150.00
Junior Jazz Band, A&A American Metal Toys, 1930s, litho tin, 10", EXIB..$200.00
Kiddyphone Record Player, litho tin, w/up, 7½" dia, VG..$300.00
Melody Player Roller Organ, litho tin w/hand-op paper roller player, w/2 rolls, 6", EX...$100.00
Piano, Bliss, grand style w/internal xylophone, 16", EX.$115.00
Piano, Bliss, litho front, 9½", VG.................................$100.00
Piano, Chein, Electric Player Piano, NM.....................$300.00
Piano, Schoenhut, upright, EX+...................................$400.00
PlaRola Organ, litho tin & wood, 4", EXIB..................$200.00
Play-A-Way Piano, Marx, songbook w/16 tunes to play, 10x9", EXIB, A..$100.00
Rol Monica, harmonica mounted on Bakelite player housing, 5", VGIB...$200.00
Showboat Band Set #50, Spec-Toy-Culars Inc, 1952, plastic, EXIB...$35.00
Tambourine, T Cohn, litho tin w/clown face, 8" dia, NM...$100.00

Toyland Band Deluxe Drum Sey, Ohio Art, litho tin, complete, 7½", MIB..$100.00

Tuneyville Player Piano, Tomy, 1978, plastic, b/o, complete w/4 records, 8½", EX $30.00

Optical Toys

Compared to the bulky viewers of years ago, contrary to the usual course of advancement, optical toys of more recent years have tended to become more simplified in concept.

See also Character, TV, and Movie Collectibles; Disney; View-Master and Tru-View; Western.

Automatic Space Viewer, Stephens, 1950s, EX $175.00

Charlie Chaplin Ombro-Cinema, France, early 1900s, turn hdl for flickering blk & wht celluloid silhouettes, EX....$600.00

Columbus Lantern, Germany, pnt tin egg shape w/eagle & lettered decals, kerosene lamp base, 10", EX $3,400.00

Comicscope Viewer, Remington Moris, 1900s, comic strip viewer w/3 comic strips, EX...$50.00

Easy Show Motorized Movie Projector, Kenner, 1960s, battery-op, MIB..$110.00

Famous Komics Movie Viewer & Films, Cheerio/Canadian version of Acme Films, 1946, complete, rare, VGIB.$1,500.00

Flashy Flickers Magic Picture Gun, Marx, EXIB.............$125.00

Give a Show Projector, Kenner, 1971-73, features Josie & the Pussycats, MIB $75.00

Irwin Projector, Irwin, 1930s, steel w/baked-on blk enamel, celluloid filmstrip features several characters, 5", NMIB...$175.00

Irwin Projector, Irwin, 1940s, w/projector & 1 film, NMIB..$35.00

Kaleidoscope, Bush, cb tube w/brass element housing, impressed logo, 4-ftd wood base, 14", EX..................................$500.00

Kaleidoscope, Du-All Product, 1940s, camera shape, leatherette, glass interior stems, VG+ $250.00

Kiddie Kamera, Allied Mgf, 1930s, plain blk metal film viewer, sm version, features Dick Tracy, Annie, Kayo, etc, NMIB .$125.00

Komic Kamera, Allied, 1934, features various comic characters, EX...$75.00

Magic Lantern, Bing, tin, w/orig glass sliders & instructions, 6½x6½", EX (in cb box) $80.00

Magic Lantern, Ernst Plank, box shape w/all orig components, 9 lg slides, G (in fitted box) $110.00

Magic Lantern, Ernst Plank, tin & brass, w/orig glass slides, 7½x10½", VG (in cb box w/hinged lid)..................$100.00

Magic Lantern, JS, tin w/CI ft, kerosene lamp w/glass chimney, lens & slides, 9", EXIB...$150.00

Magic Lantern, Plank, w/star drive shutter mechanism & sprocket drive, took film, 12", VG+, A $80.00

Magic Mirror, McLoughlin Bros, paper litho image appears on mercury glass tube, EX (in wooden box) $1,500.00

Movie Viewer Theater, Fisher-Price, 1977 – 86, #463, MIB, $25.00. (Photo courtesy Brad Cassity)

Movieland Drive-In Theatre, Remco, complete, EXIB ..$225.00

Optical Illusions Science Kit, Remco, 1961, NM (orig can).$25.00

Play 'N Show Phono Projector, Kenner, 1969, complete, MIB.$35.00

Real Sound Movie Projector, Kenner, 1968, comes w/3 movie reels, EXIB $200.00

See-Action Football, Kenner, 1973, NMIB $25.00

Starmaster Astronomy Set, complete w/projector & early space film, Reed, 1950s, EX+IB $45.00

Tantalizer the Optical Puzzler, Northern Signal Co, 1960s, game, EXIB...$25.00

Zoetrope, tin drum on brass & wood base, w/6 animated strips mounted to heavy paper, 17", EX...........................$850.00

Paper Dolls

Turn-of-the-century paper dolls are seldom found today and when they are, they're very expensive. Advertising companies used them to promote their products, and some were printed on the pages of leading ladies' magazines. By the late 1920s most paper dolls were being made in book form — the doll on the cover, the clothes on the inside pages. Because they were so inexpensive, paper dolls survived the Depression and went on to peak in the 1940s. Though the advent of television caused sales to decline, paper doll companies were able to hang on by making paper dolls representing Hollywood celebrities and TV stars. These are some of the most collectible today. Even celebrity

Magic Lantern, Ernst Plank, complete, VG+IB, $250.00.

dolls from more recent years like the Brady Bunch or the Waltons are popular. Remember, condition is very important; if they've been cut out, even when they're still in fine condition and have all their original accessories, they're worth only about half as much as an uncut book or box set. Our values are for mint and uncut dolls unless noted otherwise.

For more information, refer to *Price Guide to Lowe and Whitman Paper Dolls*, *Price Guide to Saalfield and Merrill Paper Dolls* and *20th Century Paper Dolls* by Mary Young, our advisor for this category, and *Paper Dolls of the 1960s, 1970s, and 1980s* by Carol Nichols.

A Walt Disney Silly Symphony Cut-Out, Whitman #989, 1933, from $300 to **$500.00**
Airline Stewardess, Lowe #4913, 1957........................**$45.00**
Annette, Whitman #1971, 1960 ....**$75.00**
Annette in Hawaii, Whitman #1969, 1961, used, VG+...**$30.00**
Annie (& Sandy), Happy House #84979-5, 1982, from $4 to..**$10.00**
Annie Oakley, Whitman #2056, 1955 ....**$75.00**
Archies, Whitman #1987, 1969 ....**$50.00**
Army Nurse & Doctor, Merrill #3425, 1942, from $100 to.**$125.00**
Baby Beans & Pets, Whitman #1950, 1978 ....**$12.00**
Baby First Step, Whitman #1997, 1965 ....**$35.00**
Baby Nancy, Whitman #966, 1935................................**$75.00**
Baby Sparkle Plenty, Saalfield #2500, 1948 ....**$50.00**
Baby Sue, Lowe #2786, 1969 ....**$15.00**
Betty, Jane & Dick, Lowe #130, 1943 ....**$22.00**
Betty Bo-Peep/Billy Boy Blue, Lowe #1043, 1942............**$75.00**
Betty Buttercup, Lowe #2754, 1964 ....**$15.00**
Betty Grable, Whitman #962, 1946................................**$200.00**

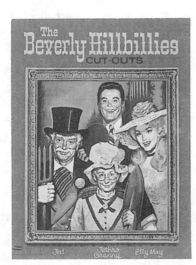

Beverly Hillbillies, Whitman #1955, 1964, $85.00. (Photo courtesy Greg Davis and Bill Morgan)

Big & Little Sister, Whitman #4411, 1962 ....**$25.00**
Blondie, Whitman #975, 1943 ....**$150.00**
Brady Bunch, Whitman #1997, 1973, EX **$55.00**
Brenda Lee, Lowe #2785, 1961, from $50 to.................**$75.00**
Bride & Groom, Lowe #2493, 1959 ....**$50.00**
Buffy, Whitman #1985, 1969..**$35.00**
Career Girls, Lowe #958, 1950 ....**$35.00**
Carol Lynley, Whitman #2089, 1960 ....**$70.00**

Charlie Chaplin & Paulette Goddard, Saalfield #2356, 1941..**$300.00**
Cheerleaders, Lowe #2741, 1962 ....**$25.00**
Cinderella, Saalfield #2590, 1950.................................**$75.00**
Cinderella Steps Out, Lowe #1242, 1948......................**$60.00**

Circus Paper Dolls, Saalfield #2610, 1952, from $35.00 to $50.00. (Photo courtesy Mary Young)

Clothes Crazy, Lowe #1046, 1945.................................**$35.00**
Coke Crowd, Merrill #3445, 1946.................................**$100.00**
Connie Francis, Whitman #1956, 1963 ....**$70.00**
Cowboys & Indians, Lowe #2104, 1961, stand-ups..........**$15.00**
Cuddles & Rags, Lowe #1283, 1950..............................**$50.00**
Cyd Charisse, Whitman #2084, 1956 ....**$150.00**
Debbie Reynolds, Whitman #1178, 1953 ....**$125.00**
Dionne Quints Cut-Out Dolls, Whitman #2190, 1937..**$125.00**
Dolls of Many Lands, Whitman #3046, 1931, MIB **$85.00**
Doris Day Doll, Whitman #1977, 1957 ....**$100.00**
Dotty Dimple, Lowe #2711, 1957.................................**$15.00**
Dy-Dee Baby Doll, Whitman #969, 1938 ....**$125.00**
Elizabeth Taylor, Whitman #2057, 1957.......................**$150.00**
Elly May, Watkins-Strathmore #1819A, 1963 ....**$50.00**
Family Dolls, Whitman #4574, 1960..............................**$40.00**
Farmyard, Lowe #1254, 1943, stand-ups.......................**$10.00**
Fashion Previews, Lowe #1246, 1949 ....**$40.00**
Flintstones, Whitman #4796, 1962 ....**$50.00**
Flying Nun, Saalfield #5121, 1968 ....**$65.00**

Fonzie, Toy Factory, #105, 1976, $25.00.

Gene Tiereny, Whitman #992, 1947 ....$175.00
Glamour Girl, Whitman #973, 1942 ....$50.00
Gloria's Make-Up, Lowe #2585, 1952 ....$50.00
Golden Girl, Merrill #1543, 1953 ....$75.00
Good Neighbor, Saalfield #2487, 1944 ....$40.00
Grace Kelly, Whitman #2049, 1955 ....$125.00
Green Acres, Whitman #1979, 1967 ....$65.00
Gretchen, Whitman #4613, 1966 ....$15.00
Gulliver's Travels, Saalfield #1261, 1939 ....$125.00
Hello Patti, Lowe #1877, 1964 ....$18.00
Henry & Henrietta, Saalfield #2189, 1938 ....$25.00
High School Dolls, Merrill #1551, 1948, from $75 to $100.00
Honey Hill Bunch, Whitman #1976-1, 1977, from $10 to ..$18.00
It's a Date, Whitman #1976, 1956 ....$40.00

Julia, Saalfield #6055, 1970 ....$50.00
June Allyson, Whitman #970, 1950 ....$125.00
Laugh-Inn Party, Saalfield #6045, 1969, from $40 to......$65.00
Lennon Sisters, Whitman #1979, 1958 ....$75.00
Linda Darnell, Saalfield #1584, 1953 ....$100.00
Little Brothers & Sisters, Whitman #971, 1953 ....$25.00
Little Friends From History, Rand McNally #186, 1936 ...$40.00
Little Lulu & Tubby, Whitman #1987, 1974, from $15 to .$25.00
Little Orphan Annie, Saalfield #299, 1943 ....$100.00
Little Women, Artcraft #5127, from $30 to $40.00

Lucy, Whitman #1963, 1964, from $65.00 to $85.00. (Photo courtesy Carol Nichols)

Jane Russell, Saalfield #4328, 1955, $95.00. (Photo courtesy Mary Young)

Janet Leigh, Lowe #2405, 1957 ....$75.00
Janet Lennon, Whitman #4613, 1962 ....$50.00
Joan's Wedding, Whitman #990, 1942 ....$75.00
Josie & the Pussycats, Whitman #1982, 1971, EX $30.00
Judy Garland, Whitman #999, 1940 ....$100.00

Magic Mary Ann, Milton Bradley #4010-2, 1950, NMIB..$25.00
Magic Mindy, Whitman #1991, 1970 ....$15.00
Magic Stay-On Doll, Whitman #4618, 1963 ....$20.00
Mary Hartline, Whitman #2104, 1952 ....$125.00

Mary Poppins, Whitman #1977, 1973, from $25.00 to $45.00. (Photo courtesy Carol Nichols)

Little Miss America, Saalfield #2358, 1941, $75.00. (Photo courtesy Mary Young)

Me & Mimi, Lowe #L144, 1942 ....$40.00
Mickey & Minnie Steppin' Out, Whitman #1979, 1977..$25.00
Miss America, Whitman #7410D, 1980, from $12 to.......$15.00

Mother & Daughter, Lowe #1860, 1963..........................$18.00
Mother & Daughter, Saalfield #1330, 1962 ....$25.00
Mousketeers, Whitman #1974, 1963...............................$75.00
Movie Starlets, Whitman #960, 1946 ....$150.00
My Baby Book, Whitman #1011, 1942 ....$50.00

Nanny and the Professor, Saalfield #1213, 1970, $50.00. (Photo courtesy Greg Davis and Bill Morgan)

National Velvet, Whitman #1958, 1961 ....$65.00
One Hundred & One Dalmatians, Whitman #1993, 1960.$60.00
Patti Page, Lowe #2488, 1958.......................................$75.00
Patty Duke, Whitman #4775, 1965................................$50.00
Penny's Party, Lowe #4207, 1952...................................$40.00
Peter Rabbit, Saalfield #963, 1934, stand-ups $40.00
Pink Prom Twins, Merrill #2583, from $55 to..................$65.00
Pippi Longstockings, Whitman #4390/7409, 1976 ....$25.00
Pixie Doll & Pup, Lowe #2764 ....$25.00
Playmates, Lowe #1829, 1961......................................$10.00
Punky Brewster, Golden #1532, 1986, from $5 to............$10.00
Riders of the West, Saalfield #2716, 1950.......................$35.00
Rita Hayworth Dancing Star, Merrill #3478, 1942.........$350.00
Roy Rogers & Dale Evans, Whitman #998, 1950...........$140.00
Sally, Sue & Sherry, Lowe #2785, 1969...........................$10.00
Shari Lewis & Her Puppets, Saalfield #6060, 1960, from $50
    to..$65.00
Sheree North, Saalfield #4420, 1957...............................$90.00
Shirley Temple Dolls & Dresses, Saalfield #2112, 1934 .$250.00
Sleeping Beauty, Whitman #4723, 1958, from $75 to....$100.00
Slumber Party, Merrill #4854, 1943, from $65 to.............$90.00
Soldiers & Sailors, Lowe #2573, 1943, stand-ups..............$40.00
Sonny & Sue, Lowe #522, 1940 ....$35.00
Square Dance, Lowe #2707, 1957 ....$20.00
Stardancer, Rand McNally #09052-6, 1984, from $8 to ...$15.00
Strawberry Sue, Whitman #1976-2, 1979 ....$10.00
Sunshine Family, Whitman #1980, 1977 ....$12.00
Sweet-Treat Kiddles, Whitman #1993, 1969 ....$55.00
Sweetie Pie, Lowe #2482, 1958 ....$25.00
Tammy & Pepper, Whitman #1997, 1965, from $60 to....$75.00
Teen Queens, Lowe #2710, 1957....................................$20.00

Tender Love 'N Kisses, Whitman #1944-1, 1978..............$15.00

That Girl, Saalfield #1351, 1967, from $45.00 to $75.00. (Photo courtesy Carol Nichols)

Three Little Sisters, Whitman #996, 1943.......................$75.00
Tom the Aviator, Lowe #1074, 1941 ....$75.00
Tony Hair-Do Dress-Up Dolls, Lowe #1251, 1951...........$75.00
Trixie, Lowe #3920, 1961 ....$45.00
Tropical Barbie, Golden #1523-1, 1986, from $12 to $15.00
Tuesday Weld, Saalfield #4432, 1960 ....$70.00
Turnabout Dolls, Lowe #1025, 1943................................$50.00
TV Tap Stars, Lowe #990, 1952 ....$35.00
Twins Bob & Jean, Lowe #128, 1944..............................$30.00
Umbrella Girls, Merrill #2562, 1956...............................$75.00
Vera Miles, Whitman #2086, 1957 ....$125.00
Virginia Weidler, Whitman #1016, 1942, from $60 to $80.00
Walt Disney's Mary Poppins, Whitman #1982, 1964 ....$40.00

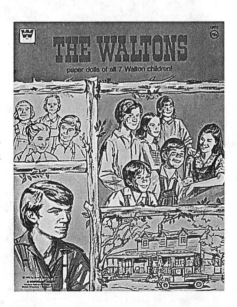

Waltons, Whitman #1995, 1975, from $35.00 to $50.00.

Waltons, Whitman #4334, 1974, boxed set $30.00
Wedding Dolls, Whitman #1953, 1958, from $60 to........$85.00

Winnie the Pooh, Whitman #1977-24, 1980, from $25 to ..$30.00
Wonderful World of Brothers Grimm, Saalfield #1336, 1963,
    from $35 to..$50.00
Woody Woodpecker & Andy Panda, Saalfield #1391, 1960s,
    from $25 to..$40.00
Ziegfield Girl, Merrill #3466, 1941 ....$400.00

Paper-Lithographed Toys

Following the development of color lithography, early toy makers soon recognized the possibility of using this technology in their own field. By the 1800s, both here and abroad, toys ranging from soldiers to involved dioramas of entire villages were being produced of wood with colorful and well detailed paper lithographed surfaces. Some of the best known manufactures were Crandell, Bliss, Reed, and McLoughlin. This style of toy remained popular until well after the turn of the century.

Advisors: Mark and Lynda Suozzi (S24)

See also Black Americana; Dollhouses; Games; Puzzles; Schoenhut.

ABC Blocks, McLoughlin Bros, ABC's and various images of
    exotic birds, 10x12", VGIB, A $715.00
ABC Little Word Blocks, McLoughlin Bros, 6-pc, EXIB, A .$500.00

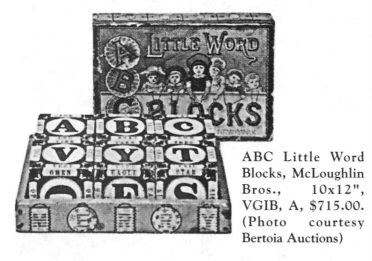

ABC Little Word Blocks, McLoughlin Bros., 10x12", VGIB, A, $715.00. (Photo courtesy Bertoia Auctions)

Adirondack Railroad Train, locomotive & 2 cars, 25", Fair,
    A $60.00
Architectural Building Blocks, Bliss, plain wood blocks, paper litho
    label on sliding wood box top, complete, VG+IB, A...$120.00
Battleship Conqueror, Bliss, 21", G+, A $600.00
Battleship Iowa, Bliss, on wheels, 30", G+, A.................$600.00
Bowling Game, 1900s, 3 figures (Chinaman, Black man &
    clown) & 3 pins, hit the pin & figure falls down, 9", EX+,
    A $630.00
Chicago Limited Vestibule Train, Bliss, w/locomotive, tender &
    3 passenger cars, 54" overall, VG+, A....................$770.00
Four Footed Friends Cubes, McLoughlin Bros, various images of
    cats, dogs, etc, 11x8½", EXIB, A $330.00

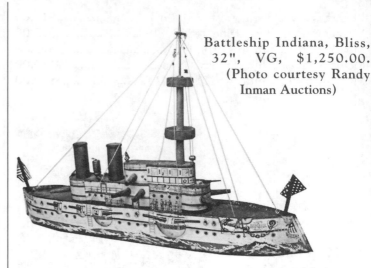

Battleship Indiana, Bliss, 32", VG, $1,250.00. (Photo courtesy Randy Inman Auctions)

Church Building, Bliss, 1890s, pieces come apart for rebuilding, 12x9", VG, $875.00. (Photo courtesy Bertoia Auctions)

Horse-Drawn Coach, Bliss, 4 horses pulling well-detailed coach,
    29" overall, VG, A...$550.00
Noah's Ark Play Box, Spears, GIB $225.00
Palmer Cox Brownies Picture Puzzle Cubes, McLoughlin Bros, 1890s,
    20 blocks form various scenes, 10x13", VGIB, A..............$165.00
Picture (Puzzle) Cubes, 9 cubes w/4 different images of farm ani-
    mals, 8x8", EXIB, A...$165.00
Picture Blocks, Gilmour & Co, 1910s, various scenes of children &
    letters on 2 sides stacked vertically, 4-pc, EXIB, A $330.00

Pickwick Ten Pins, Horsman, EX+IB, A, $2,420.00. (Photo courtesy Bertoia Auctions)

Picture Puzzle Cubes, scenes with children, 24-piece, 8x11", VGIB, A, $465.00. (Photo courtesy Bertoia Auctions)

Picture Puzzle Cubes, peasant scenes, 48-pc, 15x11", VGIB, A..$465.00
Pretty Village Set, McLoughlin Bros, 1897, EXIB $300.00
Red Robin Farm, Converse, lg barn w/2 sm sheds, 10 flat-sided animals on bases, 10½x8½x14" barn, EX, A $200.00
Reed's Cathedral/Sunday Blocks, blocks form cathedral, VGIB $350.00
Roller Chimes, Pat 1884, rolling barrel w/wire pull hdl, 26½", VG $250.00
Roosevelt Stock Farm, barn w/removable roof, sliding doors, 6 stalls, 6 prs of farm animals, 19½", VG $700.00
Soldiers on Parade Set #3, McLoughlin, complete, NMIB .$300.00

Stacking Blocks, graduated five-piece set with images of children at playground, 10", G, A, $155.00. (Photo courtesy Bertoia Auctions)

Target Game, Schoenhut, 6-pc jungle animal set & cannon, VG to EX $225.00
The Flyer Train, Milton Bradley, 1880s, w/Hercules locomotive, tender & passenger car, 47", EX.............................$3,250.00
Trinity Chimes, Schoenhut, musical toy w/8 chimes, 17", G+, A..$150.00
World's Columbian Exposition Trolley, Bliss, 18", EX.$1,200.00

Pedal Cars and Other Wheeled Vehicles

Just like Daddy, all little boys (and girls as well) are thrilled and happy to drive a brand new shiny car. Today both generations search through flea markets and auto swap meets for cars, boats, fire engines, tractors, and trains that run not on gas but pedal power. Some of the largest manufacturers of wheeled goods were AMF (American Machine and Foundry Company), Murray, and Garton. Values depend to a very large extent on condition, and those that have been restored may sell for $1,000.00 or more, depending on the year and mode. The following listings are in original condition unless noted otherwise.

Advisor: Nate Stoller (S7)

Army Scout Airplane, Gendron, 1920s, 41", $2,000.00. (Photo courtesy Randy Inman Auctions)

Astrojet, Evans, seat on open chassis w/4 disk wheels, steer stick w/hand grips, red w/wht detail, wht hubs, 38", G, A .$65.00

Austin A40 Sports Car, England, 1950s, opening hood and trunk, electric lights, 56", restored, $995.00. (Photo courtesy Bertoia Auctions)

Boat, mk Moncano, ca 1910, wood w/metal seat, long oar-type push hdls, 2 lg spoke wheels & 2 sm, 39", EX, A..$2,090.00
Bugatti, Eureka/France, 1930s, NP steering wheels & trim, thin rubber tread on metal disk wheels, 32", rpt, A $1,430.00
Bugatti, France, 1930s, NP steering wheel & trim, thin rubber tread on metal disk wheels, w/fenders, 43", overpt, A...........$520.00
Buick, Steelcraft, V-shaped windshield, chrome-like bumper, lights, hood trim & hubs, disk wheels, 45", EX+ rstr, A...$1,320.00
Buick, Steelcraft, 1920s, full-fendered, disk wheels, 35", EX rstr, A $715.00
Cadillac, Sidway Topliff, early, glass windshield & headlights, rear gas tank, wooden running boards, 36", G+, A........$3,500.00
Car, Am National, arched hood w/winged ornament, flat grille w/emb detail, headlights, disk wheels, 42", P, A $600.00

Car, Eureka, 1930s, oval-shaped w/cut-out disk wheels, dk red, 44", older rstr, A $385.00

Car, Steelcraft, arched hood w/flat grille, metal seat, disk wheels, license plate reads B5-29..., 32", P, A $275.00

Car, Tri-Ang, 1930s, door opens, running boards/fenders, pnt disk wheels, 36", no bumper or steering, old rpt, A .$245.00

Centurian, Tri-Ang, 1950s, opening trunk, windshield frame, rubber tires, NP hubs & trim, 47", rpt......................$700.00

Chevrolet, 1930, NP mascot windshield, curved seat, fenders & running boards, rubber tires on disk wheels, 36", rstr, A .$1,540.00

Chrysler, Steelcraft, 1941, maroon & cream, 37", rstr, A.$1,430.00

Chrysler Airflow, Steelcraft, w/hood ornament, windshield & horn, 46", rstr, A $1,265.00

Coupe, Argyle/England, 1930, opening driver's door, fenders & running boards, windshield, rubber tires, 33", G, A..$650.00

Deusenberg, chrome detail with side pipes, gear shift, and horn, white pneumatic tires with spoke wheels, 69", restored, A, $2,200.00. (Photo courtesy Randy Inman Auctions)

Early Wooden Car, England, ca 1905, wood steering wheel, tin lantern on hood, rubber tires w/spoke wheels, 33", Fair, A $825.00

Earth Mover With Playland Dump, yel w/blk & wht detail, 47", VG, A $200.00

Erskine (1927 – 1930), Toledo, 37", VG, $3,500.00. (Photo courtesy Bertoia Auctions)

Essex #31-644, Steelcraft, 1930s, electric headlights, 34", VG, A $2,420.00

Fire Dept Kidillac Car, Garton, red w/wht detail, 45", P+, A..$245.00

Fire Ladder Truck, Murray, 1960s, bell on hood, rear railed platform w/2 wooden ladders, 39", G, A $990.00

Fire Truck, Murray, red w./wht wooden ladders, 43", EX, A .$255.00

Ford, early wood & steel construction w/barrel-nosed hood, adjustible seat, spoke wheels, 42", G+, A $2,530.00

Ford, Steelcraft, 1930s, no fenders (flat bottom), solid disk wheels, 30", older rpt, A...$385.00

Ford, Steelcraft, 1930s, w/fenders, disk wheels w/cut-out circle detail, 33", need rstr, A...$770.00

Good Humor Cycle, 3-wheeled, chain-drive, w/bell, wht w/lt bl, orig decals, 36", VG+, A $1,430.00

Graham (Shark-Nose), Am National, disk wheels, rear spare, 53", EX rstr, A $1,375.00

GTO, AMF-510, 389 license plate, 36", restored, $350.00. (Photo courtesy Jackson's International Auctioneers and Appraisers)

Hook & Ladder Pumper 519, red w/wht plastic ladders, 46", rstr, A $230.00

Hot Rod, Garton, 37", G, A..$330.00

Hot Rod Style Car, 1940s-50s, open seat w/cone-shaped frontend, open wheels, 2 bars attached to seat/frame, 43", overpt..$85.00

Jeep, aluminum, gray w/bl star stenciled on hood, pnt headlights, rubber tires w/disk wheels, 38", P, A......................$120.00

John Deere Tractor, diecast aluminum, gr, 38", P, A.......$130.00

Murrey Weston Coupe, Steelcraft, 1930s, vinyl seat & top cover, rear spare, NP trim, fenders & running boards, 48", rstr $1,980.00

Police Sergeant Car, Murray, 36", restored, $350.00. (Photo courtesy Jackson's International Auctioneers and Appraisers)

Navy Patrol Plane, Murray, 3-wheeled, red, wht & bl, 47" L, EX, A $880.00

Packard, Am National, 1920s, 45", G+, A $4,025.00

Racer, BMC, 1940s, 40", P+ orig orange pnt, A $275.00

Racer #60, Garton, orig red w/wht 60 on sides & back, wht perforated disk wheels, 46", Fair+, A $500.00

Roadster, Am National, open bench seat, all-in-one fenders & running boards, rubber tires, spoke wheels, 46", overpnt, A...$1,375.00

Runabout, Keystone, 1910, metal & wood, 2 lg rubber tires w/spoke wheels in back & 2 smaller in front, 33", Fair, A...$1,540.00

Sand & Gravel Dump Truck, Murray, working dump bed, yel, mk Jet Flow Drive, wht-line tires w/chrome hubs, 45", G+, A...$255.00

Speedway 500 Pace Car, Murray, wht w/orange & blk detail, 35", rstr, A $285.00

Sports Coupe, Tri-Ang, 1960s, rubber wht-wall tires w/NP hubs, hood opens to expose engine, 39", rpt, A $110.00

Station Wagon, Murray, w/rear rails, front bumper, windshield, metal disk wheels, 42", P, A....................................$600.00

Tin Lizzie, Garton, 40", restored, A, $515.00. (Photo courtesy Jackson's International Auctioneers and Appraisers)

Torpedo, Murray, 1940s, 39", Fair+, A $630.00

Tractor, Garton, 1950s, red w/wht 'vent' stripes, rubber tires w/wht hubs, 38", P, A..$35.00

Wagons

Skippy Airflow, 1930s, pressed steel, electric lights, 48", restored, $795.00. (Photo courtesy Randy Inman Auctions)

Auto-Wheel Coaster, wood w/stenciled name on sides, metal spoke wheels, 42", G, A..$385.00

Buckboard Wagon, pnt wood w/iron hardware, spoke wheels, red, gr & blk, 17x48", some rstr, A $1,320.00

Flyer, Fisher, wood, disk wheels, 45", G, A $100.00

Miscellaneous

Scooter, w/fenders, red w/wht hdl grips, wht hubs, 39", G, A.$65.00

St Bernard on Wheels Ride-On, straw-stuffed w/brn & wht fur, steel chassis frame w/WRT, glass eyes, 24x25" L, G+, A $175.00

Penny Toys

Penny toys were around as early as the late 1800s and as late as the 1920s. Many were made in Germany, but some were made in France as well. With few exceptions, they ranged in size from 5" on down; some had moving parts, and a few had clockwork mechanisms. Though many were unmarked, you'll sometimes find them signed 'Kellermann,' 'Meier,' 'Fischer,' or 'Distler,' or carrying an embossed company logo such as the 'dog and cart' emblem. They were made of lithographed tin with exquisite detailing — imagine an entire carousel less than 2½" tall. Because of a recent surge in collector interest, many have been crossing the auction block of some of the country's large galleries. Our values are prices realized at several of these auctions. We have also included the auction estimate at the end of each listing.

Airplane Roundabout Whistle, w/3 planes, red, bl & gold, 4¼" L, VG, A (Est: $200-$250)......................................$300.00

Airplane Spiral Toy, Einfalt, 6½", EX, A (Est: $300-$400).$350.00

Airplane Whistle Toy, 4¼x3" W, VG, A (Est: $250-$300)..$200.00

Bear w/Penny Whistle Toy, Germany, bear standing holding pole in hand, gold-pnt, 4", VG, A (Est: $300-$350) $325.00

Bird Cage, Meier, bottom lever activates pecking motion, 3x2", G, A (Est: $150-$250)...$100.00

Boat, Meier, pnt tin, w/pilot house, flag & standing figure, 4½", VG, A (Est: $300-$400)..$350.00

Dentist Clicker, Germany, 3", VG, A (Est: $75.00 – $125.00), $275.00. (Photo courtesy James D. Julia, Inc.)

Boat (Passenger), Fischer, bl w/2 yel stacks, spoke wheels & trim, 4¼", G, A (Est: $300-$400) $200.00

Boxers, Germany, hand-held squeezing action causes figures to fight, 5¾", VG, A (Est: $300-$400) $110.00

Boy Seated on Sled, Levy, VG, A (Est: $200-$250) $200.00

Clown w/Stick Chasing Donkey, Meier, 3¾", G, A (Est: $150-$250) $200.00

Delivery Stake Truck, Germany, open cab w/driver, 3½", VG+ (Est: $125-$250) $150.00

Dog (Spinning) Whistle, France, 4", G, A (Est: $150-$250) .$150.00

Donkey on Four-Wheeled Platform, Meier, 3" L, EX, A (Est: $125-$200) $200.00

Double-Decker Bus, long nose w/railed top, spoke wheels, sun visor, w/driver, yel & orange, 4½", EX, A (Est: $175) $175.00

Fire Ladder Truck, w/up, open w/overhead ladder, red w/NP bumpers & fenders, 5 firemen, 4¼", VG, A (Est: $200-$300) $325.00

Girls (2) Spiral Down Pole, lever action, open seats, 8½", EX, A (Est: $300-$350) $300.00

Globe on Stand, Germany, swivels, mc, 2¾", EX+, A (Est: $150-$200) $110.00

Gnomes (2) Sawing Wood, Meier, beveled oblong base, 4" L, VG, A (Est: $250-$300) $250.00

Goat on Four-Wheeled Platform, Meier, 3" L, EX, A (Est: $125-$200) $220.00

Goose on 4-Wheeled Platform, Distler, articulated neck, spoke wheels, 3" T, EX, A $325.00

Horse-Drawn (2) Open Carriage w/Driver, Meier, 4", EX, A (Est: $250-$350) $225.00

Horse-Drawn Cart with Driver, 3½", VG, A (Est: $75.00 – $150.00), $125.00. (Photo courtesy James D. Julia, Inc.)

Horse-Drawn Dray Wagon w/Driver, Fischer, spoke wheels, 4¾", G, A (Est: $150-$250) $135.00

Horse-Drawn Wagon, Meier, open-slat wagon w/emb side lanterns, spoke wheels, 4½", EX, A (Est: $100-$200) $110.00

Locomotive (Self Moving), wind rubber band to axle, stamped tin, 3", VG, A (Est: $200-$250) $225.00

Man Smoking Pipe & Pushing Wheelborrow, Germany, 2¾" L, EX, A (Est: $200-$300) $135.00

Merry-Go-Round (Souvenir From Universal Theatres... Chicago), 2½", EX+, A (Est: $250-$350) $450.00

Monkey Climbing Pole, Distler, pull-string action, U-shaped pole on fluted base, 6¾", VG, A (Est: $300-$350) ..$110.00

Motorcycle w/Rider, Velocette/Spain, 1925, 4", EX, A (Est: $100) $225.00

Noah's Ark, hinged roof, lithoed detail, 4¾", EX, A (Est: $400-$600) $650.00

Ox-Drawn Wagon, Meier, red rail-sided wagon w/open front & back, gray canopy, spoke wheels, 6", EX, A (Est: $250-$300) ..$225.00

Pool Player, Kellerman, player ready to strike ball into slots, 4", EX, A (Est: $200-$300) $225.00

Race Car, CKO/Germany, open boattail w/driver, 3", VG, A (Est: $125-$250) $150.00

Saloon Auto, Meier, open front seat w/enclosed back, die-cut figures, 4¼", VG, A (Est: $500-$700) $355.00

Squirrel in Cage Whistle, France, 4½", EX, A (Est: $150-$250) $165.00

Stake Truck, Fischer, open seat w/driver, curved roof, 5-sided nose, lithoed bed, gray & red, VG, A (Est: $100-$150) $85.00

Stake Truck, open seat, flat roof, tapered nose, red & blk, 4½", VG, A (Est: $50-$100) $125.00

Swing (Gondola w/Couple), Meier, A-frame on platform, 3⅛", EX, A (Est: $330-$350) $325.00

Tank on Wheels, Germany, camo detail, 4-wheeled, 2½", EX, A (Est: $100-$200) $200.00

Taxi Touring Car, J.D./Germany, circa 1910, with driver, 3", VG, A (Est: $125.00 – $250.00), $450.00. (Photo courtesy James D. Julia, Inc.)

Touring Car, Meier, open, w/passenger, yel w/red interior, red spoke wheels, 4½", VG, A (Est: $200-$250) $225.00

Train, Hess, locomotive & tender w/stake car & 3 coach cars, 14½" overall, VG, A (Est: $250-$350) $225.00

Train on Oval Track, Schuhlmann, w/signals, tunnel & bridge, 8½" L, NMIB, A (Est: $225) $275.00

Velocette Motorcycle w/Rider, 4⅛", EX, A (Est: $300-$400).$350.00

Vis-A-Vis, Meier, emb, w/driver, red & yel, spoke wheels, 3", VG, A (Est: $200-$300) $275.00

Pez Dispensers

Pez was originally designed as a breath mint for smokers, but by the '50s, kids were the target market, and the candies were packaged in the dispensers that we all know and love today. There is already more than three hundred variations to collect, and more arrive on the supermarket shelves every day. Though early on collectors seemed to prefer the dispensers without feet, that attitude has changed, and now it's the character head they concentrate on. Feet were added in 1987, so if you were to limit yourself to only 'feetless' dispensers, your collection would be far from complete. Some dispensers have variations in color and design that can influence their values. Don't buy any that are damaged, incomplete, or that have been tampered with in any way; those are nearly worthless. For more information refer to *A Pictorial Guide to Plastic Candy Dispensers Featuring Pez* by David Welch.

Advisor: Richard Belyski (B1)

Aardvark, w/ft $5.00
Angel, no ft..$75.00
Arlene, w/ft, pk, from $3 to $5.00
Asterix Line, Asterix, Obelix, Roman or Getafix, ea from $4
    to $6.00
Baloo, w/ft $20.00
Bambi, no ft...$50.00
Barney Bear, no ft...$40.00

Barney Bear, w/ft...
Baseball Glove, no ft $150.00
Batgirl, no ft, soft head $150.00
Batman, no ft $10.00
Batman, no ft, w/cape $100.00
Batman, w/ft, bl or blk, ea from $3 to $5.00
Betsy Ross, no ft..$125.00
Bouncer Beagle, w/ft $6.00
Boy, w/ft, brn hair...$3.00
Bozo, no ft, diecut $175.00
Bubble Man, w/ft..$3.00
Bubble Man, w/ft, neon hat $3.00
Bugs Bunny, no ft $15.00
Bugs Bunny, w/ft, from $1 to $3.00
Bullwinkle, no ft $200.00
Candy Shooter, red & wht, w/candy & gun license, unused .$125.00
Captain America, no ft.....................................$90.00
Captain Hook, no ft...$75.00
Casper, no ft...$175.00

Charlie Brown, Snoopy, and Lucy, with feet, each from $1.00 to $3.00. (Photo courtesy Mary Jane Lamphier)

Charlie Brown, w/ft & tongue $20.00
Chicago Cubs 2000, Charlie Brown in pkg w/commerative
    card $30.00
Chick, w/ft, from $1 to.......................................$3.00
Chick in Egg, no ft..$15.00
Chick in Egg, no ft, w/hair $125.00
Chip, w/ft...$45.00
Clown, w/ft, whistle head $6.00
Clown w/Collar, no ft $60.00
Cockatoo, no ft, bl face, red beak $60.00
Cool Cat, w/ft $75.00
Cow (A or B), no ft, bl, ea, from $80 to $90.00
Creature From the Black Lagoon, no ft..............$300.00
Crocodile, no ft...$95.00
Crystal Hearts, eBay, limited edition, set of 4, ea.............$10.00
Daffy Duck, no ft..$15.00
Daffy Duck, w/ft, from $1 to $3.00
Dalmatian Pup, w/ft..$50.00
Daniel Boone, no ft $175.00
Dino, w/ft, purple, from $1 to $3.00
Dinosaur, w/ft, 4 different, ea from $1 to $3.00

Doctor, no ft...$200.00
Donald Duck, no ft, die-cut..........................$150.00
Donald Duck, no ft, from $10 to $15.00
Donald Duck's Nephew, no ft $30.00
Donald Duck's Nephew, w/ft, gr, bl or red hat, ea $10.00
Donkey, w/ft, whistle head...............................$6.00
Droopy Dog (A), no ft, plastic swivel ears $25.00
Droopy Dog (B), w/ft, pnt ears, MIP..................$6.00
Duck Tales, any character, w/ft, ea....................$6.00
Dumbo, w/ft, bl head......................................$25.00
Eerie Spectres, Air Spirit, Diabolic or Zombie (no ft), ea.$185.00
Fat-Ears Rabbit, no ft, pk head $20.00
Fat-Ears Rabbit, no ft, yel head........................$15.00

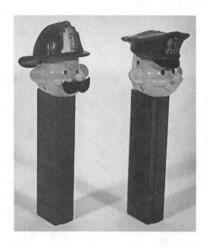

Fireman, no feet, $80.00; Policeman, no feet, $60.00.

Fishman, no ft, gr..$185.00
Foghorn Leghorn, w/ft $65.00
Football Player...$175.00
Fozzie Bear, w/ft, from $1 to $3.00
Frankenstein, no ft.......................................$225.00
Fred Flintstone, w/ft, from $1 to $3.00
Frog, w/ft, whistle head $40.00
Garfield, w/ft, orange w/gr hat, from $1 to $3.00
Garfield, w/ft, teeth, from $1 to $3.00
Garfield, w/ft, visor, from $1 to $3.00
Gargamel, w/ft...$5.00
Ghosts (Glowing), Happy Henry, Naughty Neil, or Slimy Sid, ea $1.00
Ghosts (Non-Glowing), Happy Henry, Naughty Neil, or Slimy Sid, ea..............$2.00
Girl, w/ft, yel hair..$3.00
Gonzo, w/ft, from $1 to $3.00
Goofy, no ft, ea..$15.00
Gorilla, no ft, blk head...................................$80.00
Green Hornet, 1960s, from $200 to $250.00
Gyro Gearloose, w/ft $6.00
Henry Hawk, no ft $75.00
Hulk, no ft, dk gr..$40.00
Hulk, no ft, lt gr, remake $3.00
Indian, w/ft, whistle head $20.00
Indian Brave, no ft, reddish $125.00
Indian Chief, no ft, yel headdress.......................$90.00

Indian Maiden, no ft...................................$125.00
Inspector Clouseau, w/ft..................................$5.00
Jerry Mouse, w/ft, plastic face $15.00
Jerry Mouse, w/ft, pnt face $6.00
Jiminy Cricket, no ft.....................................$175.00
Joker (Batman), no ft, soft head $175.00
Jungle Mission, interactive dispenser.................$3.00
Kermit the Frog, w/ft, red, from $1 to $3.00
Koala, w/ft, whistle head................................$40.00

King Louie, orange, no feet, $30.00.

Krazy Animals, Blinky Bill, Lion, Hippo, Elephant, or Gator, ea, from $4 to...........................$6.00
Lamb, no ft...$15.00
Lamb, w/ft, from $1 to......................................$3.00
Lamb, w/ft, whistle head.................................$20.00
Lazy Garfield, w/ft...$5.00
Li'l Bad Wolf, w/ft..$25.00
Lion w/Crown, no ft $100.00
Lion's Club Lion, minimum value...................$2,000.00
Make-A-Face, works like Mr Potato Head $2,500.00
Mary Poppins, no ft $500.00
Merlin Mouse, w/ft...$15.00
Merry Melody Makers, rhino, donkey, panda, parrot, clown, tiger or penguin, w/ft, MOC, ea.........$6.00
Mexican, no ft..$225.00
Mickey Mouse, no ft, removable nose or cast nose, ea from $10 to..$15.00
Mickey Mouse, w/ft, from $1 to.........................$3.00
Mimic Monkey (monkey w/ball cap), no ft, several colors, ea..$50.00
Miss Piggy, w/ft, ea from $1 to...........................$3.00
Miss Piggy, w/ft, eyelashes................................$15.00
Monkey Sailor, no ft, w/wht cap $50.00
Mowgli, w/ft..$15.00
Muscle Mouse (gray Jerry), w/ft, plastic nose $15.00
Nermal, w/ft, gray...$3.00
Nintendo, Diddy Dong, Koopa Trooper, Mario, Yoshi, ea from $4 to...................................$6.00
Nurse, no ft, brn hair.....................................$175.00
Octopus, no ft, blk $85.00
Odie, w/ft...$5.00

Olive Oyl, no ft..$200.00
Panda, no ft, diecut eyes $20.00
Panda, w/ft, remake, from $1 to......................$3.00
Panda, w/ft, whistle head $6.00
Papa Smurf, w/ft, red $6.00
Parrot, w/ft, whistle head $6.00
Pebbles Flintstone, w/ft, from $1 to $3.00
Penguin, w/ft, whistle head $6.00
Penguin (Batman), no ft, soft head $175.00
Peter Pez (A), no ft...$50.00
Peter Pez (B & C), w/ft, from $1 to $3.00
Pilgrim, no ft...$125.00
Pink Panther, w/ft $5.00
Pinocchio, no ft $125.00

Pirate, no feet, $65.00; Elephant, no feet, orange and
blue, flat hat, $85.00; Mr. Ugly, no feet, $45.00.

Pluto, no ft $15.00
Pluto, no ft, red $15.00
Pluto, w/ft, from $1 to $3.00
Pokemon (non-US), Kottins, Meowith, Mew, Pikachu, or Psy-
    duck, ea from $5 to $10.00
Policeman, no ft...$60.00
Popeye (B), no ft..$90.00
Popeye (C), no ft, w/removable pipe...............$110.00
Practical Pig (B), no ft.......................................$30.00
Psychedelic Eye, no ft......................................$350.00
Psychedelic Eye, remake, blk or pk, MOC, ea............$20.00
Psychedelic Flower, no ft $300.00
Pumpkin (A), no ft, from $10 to $15.00
Pumpkin (B), w/ft, from $1 to............................$3.00
Raven, no ft, yel beak $70.00
Rhino, w/ft, whistle head $6.00
Ringmaster, no ft..$350.00
Road Runner, no ft...$25.00
Road Runner, w/ft..$15.00
Rooster, w/ft, whistle head $35.00
Rooster, w/ft, wht or yel head, ea......................$30.00

Rudolph, no ft..$50.00
Santa Claus, w/ft, from $1 to $3.00
Santa Claus (A), no ft, steel pin $125.00
Santa Claus (B), no ft $125.00
Santa Claus (C), no ft, from $5 to....................$15.00
Santa Claus (C), w/ft, B1, from $1 to $3.00
Scrooge McDuck (A), no ft $35.00
Scrooge McDuck (B), w/ft $6.00
Sheik, no ft...$55.00
Skull (A), no ft, from $10 to $15.00
Skull (B), w/ft, from $1 to $3.00
Smurf, w/ft...$5.00
Smurfette, w/ft...$5.00
Snow White, no ft $225.00
Snowman (A), no ft...$15.00
Snowman (B), w/ft, from $1 to $5.00
Space Trooper Robot, no ft, full body $300.00
Spaceman, no ft $150.00
Speedy Gonzales (A), w/ft.................................$15.00
Speedy Gonzales (B), no ft, from $1 to...............$3.00
Spider-Man, no ft, from $10 to $15.00
Spider-Man, w/ft, from $1 to $3.00
Spike, w/ft, B1 ....$6.00
Star Wars, Boba Fet, Ewok, Luke Skywalker, or Princess Leia, ea
    from $1 to $3.00
Star Wars, C3PO, Chewbacca, Darth Vader, or Storm Trooper,
    ea from $1 to $3.00
Sylvester (A), w/ft, cream or wht whiskers, ea $5.00
Sylvester (B), w/ft, from $1 to............................$3.00
Teenage Mutant Ninja Turtles, 8 different, w/ft, ea from $1 to.$3.00
Thor, no ft...$300.00
Thumper, w/ft, no copyright $45.00
Tiger, w/ft, whistle head $6.00
Tinkerbell, no ft...$225.00
Tom, no ft...$35.00
Tom, w/ft, plastic face $15.00
Tom, w/ft, pnt face $6.00
Truck, many variations, ea, minimum value.....................$1.00
Tweety Bird, no ft $15.00
Tweety Bird, w/ft, from $1 to $3.00
Tyke, w/ft..$15.00
Uncle Sam, no ft...$175.00
Valentine Heart, B1, from $1 to $3.00
Wal-Mart Smiley Pez, ea from $1 to $2.00
Whistle, w/ft, from $1 to $3.00
Wile E Coyote, w/ft...$60.00
Winnie the Pooh (A), w/ft...................................$75.00
Winnie the Pooh (B), Eeore, Piglet, Pooh, or Tigger, ea from $1
    to $2.00
Witch, 3-pc, no ft...$15.00
Wolfman, no ft...$275.00
Wonder Woman, no ft, soft head $175.00
Wonder Woman, w/ft, from $1 to........................$3.00
Woodstock, w/ft, from $1 to $3.00
Woodstock, w/ft, pnt feathers $15.00
Yappy Dog, no ft, orange or gr, ea $80.00
Yosemite Sam, w/ft, from $1 to $3.00

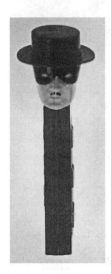

Zorro, no feet, $65.00.

MISCELLANEOUS

Bank, truck #1, metal	$200.00
Bank, truck #2, metal	$40.00
Body Parts, fit over stem of dispenser & make it look like a person, many variations, ea	$1.00
Bracelet, pk	$5.00
Bubble Wand	$3.00
Clicker, US Zone Germany, 1950, litho tin, 3½", NM	$300.00
Clicker, 1960s, metal, 2", EX, N2	$45.00
Coin Plate	$15.00
Coloring Book, Safety #2, non-English	$15.00
Power Pez, rnd mechanical dispenser	$5.00
Puzzle, Ceaco, 550 pcs, MIB	$30.00
Puzzle, Springbok/Hallmark, 500 pcs	$15.00
Refrigerator Magnet Set	$10.00
Snow Dome, Bride & Groom, 4½", M	$20.00
Snow Dome, ringmaster & elephant, M	$20.00
Tin, Pez Specials, stars & lines on checked background, gold colors, 2½x4½", rare, EX	$225.00
Toy Car, Johnny Lightning Psychedelic Eye racer	$20.00
Toy Car, Johnny Lightning Racing Dreams PEZ racer	$10.00
Watch, pk face w/yel band or yel face w/bl band, ea	$10.00
Watch, Psychedelic Hand	$10.00
Yo-yo, 1950s, litho metal w/peppermint pkg, rare, NM	$300.00

Pin-Back Buttons

Pin-back buttons produced up to the early 1920s were made with a celluloid covering. After that time, a large number of buttons were lithographed on tin; these are referred to as tin 'lithos.'

Character and toy-related buttons represent a popular collecting field. There are countless categories to base a collection on. Buttons were given out at stores and theatres, offered as premiums, attached to dolls or received with a club membership.

In the late '40s and into the '50s, some cereal companies packed one in each box of their product. Quaker Puffed Oats offered a series of movie star pin-backs, but probably the best known are Kellogg's Pep Pins. There were eighty-six in all, so theoretically if you wanted the whole series as Kellogg hoped you would, you'd have to buy at least that many boxes of their cereal. Pep pins came in five sets, the first in 1945, three more in 1946, and the last in 1947. They were printed with full-color lithographs of comic characters licensed by King Features and Famous Artists — Maggie and Jiggs, the Winkles, and Dagwood and Blondie, for instance. Superman, the only D.C. Comics character, was included in each set. Most Pep pins range in value from $10.00 to $15.00 in NM/M condition, but some sell for much more.

Nearly all pin-backs are collectible. Be sure that you buy only buttons with well-centered designs, well-alligned colors, no fading or yellowing, no spots or stains, and no cracks, splits, or dents. In the listings that follow, sizes are approximate.

Advisors: Michael and Polly McQuillen (M11)

Alfred E Newman for President/What — Me Worry?/I'm Voting MAD, face image on red/bl colors, 1950s, 2½" dia, EX	$35.00
Bugs Bunny/What's Up Doc, head image of Bugs on blk w/red rim band, 1950s, 1½" dia, EX	$25.00
Charlie Brown/Chex Mix, shows Charlie Brown holding bowl of Chex Mix, 1996, 3" dia, NM	$4.00
Charlie McCarthy/Licenses by Edgar Bergen, head image on wht center w/red tim, blk trim, 1¼" dia, VG+	$50.00
Creepy Magazine Fan Club, lettering around monster's head on orange, 1960s, 2½" dia, EX+	$12.00
Equal Rights for Smurfettes, w/Smurfette graphics, Peyo, 1980, 2½" dia, EX	$4.00
ET, image of ET in center, 1980s, 2" dia, EX	$5.00
Flash Gordon/Ming the Merciless, mc image of the 2 sword fighting on orange background, 1970s, 3" dia, EX	$10.00
GAFC/PCP (Gene Autry Fan Club), bl lettering on wht, 1950s, 1¼" dia, VG	$50.00
Help Archie & Inspector Sammy Terry Make the Right Connections, head images on wht center, bl rim, 1970s, 1¾" dia, NM	$15.00

Huckleberry Hound for President, head image on yellow background, 1960s, 3" dia, $20.00.

I'm Smokey's Helper (Smokey Bear), 3" dia, EX	$5.00
Junior Forest Ranger (Smokey Bear), bl & wht plastic, 2" T, EX	$5.00
Junior Salesmens' Club/Fleers Dubble Bubble Gum, red, wht & bl graphics on wht, 1¼" dia, EX+	$50.00

Justice League of America/Member, Superman, Batman & Wonder Woman head images in center, yel, 1980s, 2" dia, EX $12.00

Looney Tunes Little Wilbur, image encircled by phrase, 1930s, EX+ $30.00

New Kids on the Block, image of Joseph, 6" dia, NM $5.50

Only 25 Years Old and They're Doing My Life Story!, full image of Charlie Brown on pitcher's mound, 1975, 4" dia, $30.00.

Peter Pan A Paramount Picture encircles image of Betty Broson as Peter Pan seated on stump, 1924, ¾" dia, EX+ $35.00

Pride/Courage, image of Simba (Lion King), 2¼" dia, MOC.$4.00

Rocky Jones Space Ranger/Silvercup Bread, premium button, 1950s, bust image on blue background, $35.00. (Photo courtesy June Moon)

Safety First/Stop/Drive Carefully, phrase encircles half-length image of Spanky McFarland waving, 1930s, 1¼" dia, EX $50.00

Snow White Jingle Club/Member, red & bl image of Snow White & dwarfs on wht, WDE/Kay Kamen, 1930s, 1¼" dia, EX+ $30.00

Superman Muscle Building Club, w/image, Peter Puppet Playthings, 1954, EX+ $75.00

Superman of America, phrase encircles half-length image, 1¼" dia, 1938-42, VG $50.00

Virginia Slade for Congress (Doonsbury character), head imge in center w/red, wht, bl detail, blk rim, 1970s, 4" dia, EX .$25.00

Walt Disney's Dumbo D-X, red, blk & gray image on wht, 1¼" dia, EX...$25.00

KELLOGG'S PEP PINS

BO Plenty, NM $30.00

Corky, NM $16.00

Dagwood, NM...$30.00

Dick Tracy, NM...$30.00

Fat Stuff, NM $15.00

Felix the Cat, NM...$60.00

Flash Gordon, NM...$25.00

Flat Top, NM...$23.00

Goofy, NM $10.00

Gravel Gertie, NM...$15.00

Harold Teen, NM...$15.00

Inspector, NM...$12.50

Jiggs, NM...$25.00

Judy, NM...$10.00

Kayo, NM...$12.00

Little King, NM...$15.00

Little Moose, NM...$15.00

Maggie, NM $25.00

Mama De Stross, NM...$30.00

Mama Katzenzammer, NM $25.00

Mamie, NM...$15.00

Moon Mullins, $10.00. (Photo courtesy Doug Dezso)

Olive Oyle, NM $18.00

Orphan Annie, NM...$25.00

Pat Patton, NM...$10.00

Perry Winkle, NM $15.00

Phantom, NM...$60.00

Pop Jenks, NM...$15.00

Popeye, NM...$30.00

Popeye, NM...$30.00

Rip Winkle, NM...$20.00

Skeezix, NM...$15.00

Superman, NM...$25.00

Toots, NM...$15.00

Uncle Walt, NM...$20.00

Uncle Willie, NM...$12.50

Winkle Twins, NM $25.00

Winnie Winkle, NM...$15.00

Plastic Figures

Plastic figures were made by many toy companies. They were first boxed with playsets, but in the early '50s, some became available individually. Marx was the first company to offer single figures (at 10¢ each), and even some cereal companies included one in boxes of their product. (Kellogg offered a series of 16 54mm Historic Warriors, and Nabisco had a line of ten dinosaurs in marbleized, primary colors.) Virtually every type of man and beast has been modeled in plastic; today some have become very collectible and expensive. There are lots of factors you'll need to be aware of to be a wise buyer. For instance, Marx made cowboys during the mid-'60s in a flat finish, and these are much harder to find and more valuable than the later figures with a waxy finish. Marvel Super Heroes in the fluorescent hues are worth about half as much as the earlier, light gray issue. Beware that Internet sales may cause values to change greatly.

Because of limited space, it isn't possible to evaluate more than a representative few of these plastic figures in a general price guide, so if you would like to learn more about ehem, we recommend *Geppert's Guide* by Tim Geppert.

See also Clubs, Newsletters, and Other Publications for information concerning *Prehistoric Times* magazine for dinosaur figure collectors, published by our advisor, Mike Fredericks.

Advisor: Mike Fredericks (F4)
Note: All listings are figures by Marx unless noted otherwise.
See also Playsets.

Size Conversion:
20mm — ¾"   54mm — 2⅛"
45mm — 1¾"   60mm — 2½"
50mm — 2"   70mm — 2¾"

ACTION AND ADVENTURE

Captain Video, Lido, 1950s, various poses and colors, 2", $25.00. each. (Photo courtesy June Moon)

Apollo Astronaut Explorers, set of 8 in 7 poses, 54mm, orange, NM...$33.00
Apollo Astronaut Moon Walking, 6", lt bl, EX..................$6.50
Apollo Astronaut w/American Flag, 6", wht, NM............$14.50
Ben Hur, set of 16, 54mm, NM..$70.00
Deep Sea Diver, Ideal, 3" $35.00
Fox Hunt, fox running, 60mm, NM $10.00
Fox Hunt, hound sniffing, 60mm, NM............................$10.00
Man From UNCLE, Alexander Waverly, Illya Kuryakin, or Napoleon Solo, 6", steel bl, NM, ea from $12 to.......$20.00
Man From UNCLE, Illya Kuryakin or Napoleon Solo, 6", lt gray, NM (Watch for Mexican copies in near exact gray), ea .$25.00
Royal Canadian Police, Dulcop, NM $5.00
Space Patrol, driver seated, 45mm, tan & orange, NM, ea .$15.00
Spaceman, 3", various poses & colors, Premier, ea..............$5.00
Spaceman, 45mm, metallic bl or yel, NM, ea....................$5.00
Sports, bowler, boxer, figure skater, golfer or runner, 60mm, wht, NM, ea from $2.50 to.....................................$3.00

Sports, hockey player, 60mm, matt lt bl, NM $12.00
Untouchables, 54mm, NM, ea...$15.00

ANIMALS

Champion Dogs, any, 84mm, NM, ea...............................$6.50
Circus Animals, elephant w/howdah, NM.......................$10.00
Circus Animals, giraffe, tan, NM $10.00
Circus Animals, gorilla, NM..$3.00
Farm Stock, any, 60mm, NM, ea from $2 to.......................$5.00
Farm Stock, any from 2nd issue, NM, ea $2.00
Ice-Age Mammals, any, NM, from $10 to $20.00
Prehistoric Dinosaurs, Dimetrodon, marbled gray, NM, from $5 to..$10.00
Prehistoric Dinosaurs, Parasaurolphus, brn, NM, from $5 to.$10.00
Prehistoric Dinosaurs, Plateosaurus, lt gr, NM, ea...............$5.00
Prehistoric Dinosaurs, Styacosaurus, tan, NM, from $10 to .$14.00
Prehistoric Dinosaurs, Trachodon, marbled gray, NM, from $5 to .$10.00
Prehistoric Dinosaurs, Tyrannosaurus Rex, brn, NM $12.50
Ranch & Rodeo, bronco bucking, 60mm, reddish brn, NM, from $4 to $6.00
Ranch & Rodeo, Indian pony running, 54mm, various colors, EX..$3.50
Ranch & Rodeo, longhorn steer haulting, 60mm, reddish brn, NM, from $5 to $10.00

CAMPUS CUTIES AND AMERICAN BEAUTIES

American Beauties, ballerina, 1955, NM.........................$20.00
American Beauties, hula dancer, NM $20.00
American Beauties, reclining nude, M..............................$40.00

Campus Cuties, Lazy Afternoon, Lodge Party, and Stormy Weather, M, $8.00 each.

COMIC, DISNEY, AND NURSERY CHARACTERS

Disneykids, Wendy, M $35.00
Disneykings, Donald Duck, MIB $20.00
Disneykings, Goofy, MIB $20.00
Disneykins, Alice in Wonderland, M $10.00
Disneykins, Brer Rabbit, gold label, NM........................$15.00
Disneykins, Daisy Duck, M...$10.00
Disneykins, Dumbo, NM $10.00

Disneykins, Bambi, MIB, $15.00.

Disneykins, King Louie, rare, MIB $45.00
Disneykins, Peter Pan, NM..$15.00
Disneykins, Snow White & the Seven Dwarfs, 8-pc set, ea
     NMIB, A, set $55.00
Fairykins, set of 21, w/book, EXIB..................................$125.00
Fun on Wheels, set of 5 Disney characters, 1950s, VG+ to NM .$75.00
Nursery Rhymes, Humpty Dumpty, 60mm, gr or pk, NM, ea.$5.00
Nursery Rhymes, Humpty Dumpty, 60mm, matt gr, NM..$12.50
Nursery Rhymes, Humpty Dumpty, 70mm, NM $12.50
Nursery Rhymes, Little Jack Horner, 70mm, NM.............$10.00
Nursery Rhymes, Little Miss Muffet, 70mm, NM $12.50
Nursery Rhymes, Simple Simon, 60mm, NM $4.00
Oz-Kins, set of 10 different characters, Aurora/MGM, 1967,
     unused, NMOC $100.00
Rolykins, Donald Duck or Pluto, NM, ea from $10 to......$15.00
Tinykins, Benny, NM...$20.00
Tinykins, Flintstones, Barney, NMIB $30.00
Tinykins, Hoky Wolk, NM $18.00
Tinykins, Jinx, NM $18.00
Tinykins, Officer Dibble, NM...$20.00
Tinykins, Peter Pan, any character, NM, ea $15.00
Tinykins, Spook, NM...$20.00
Tinykins, Yogi Bear, NM..$18.00

FAMOUS PEOPLE AND CIVILIANS

**Cameraman, 2½",
$15.00.**

Civilians & Workman, racetrack pit crewman, 54mm, cream,
     NM...$10.00

Civilians & Workman, railroad station people, 45mm, cream, set
     of 5, NM..$20.00
International VIPs, Prince Charles, 60mm, wht, NM $20.00
International VIPs, Princess Anne, 60mm, wht, NM.......$20.00
International VIPs, Princess Margaret, 60mm, wht, NM .$20.00
International VIPs, Queen Elizabeth II, 60mm, wht, NM.$30.00
Politicians, Adlai Stevens, NM $50.00
Religious Leaders, Cardinal Spellman, NM $20.00
US Presidents, Eisenhower, 60mm, NM...........................$20.00
US Presidents, Lincoln, 60mm, NM...................................$6.50
US Presidents, Nixon, 60mm, NM..................................$12.50
US Presidents, Washington, 60mm, NM $8.00

MILITARY AND WARRIORS

**Tim-Mee Toys,
WWII Soldier,
grenade launcher,
green, 4¼", $3.00;
Marx, German Sol-
dier, green with
orange face and
hands, 1960s,
$3.00.**

American Heroes, Gen Arnold, 60mm, wht.....................$20.00
American Heroes, Gen Bradley, 60mm, wht....................$20.00
American Heroes, Gen Eisenhower, 60mm, wht, NM $20.00
American Heroes, Gen Grant, 60mm, pnt, NM...............$15.00
American Heroes, Gen Grant, 60mm, wht, NM $30.00
American Heroes, Gen Gruenther, 60mm, wht, NM $15.00
American Heroes, Gen Jackson, 60mm, wht, NM $40.00
American Heroes, Gen Lee, 60mm, wht, rpt $15.00
American Heroes, Gen Lemay, 60mm, wht, flat face $10.00
American Heroes, Gen MacArthur, 60mm, wht, NM......$20.00
American Heroes, Gen Pershing, 60mm, wht, NM $40.00
American Heroes, Gen Pickett, 60mm, wht $50.00
American Heroes, Gen Ridgeway, 60mm, wht, NM.........$25.00
American Heroes, Gen Sheridan, 60mm, wht, NM $40.00
American Heroes, Gen Spaatz, 60mm, wht, NM $20.00
American Heroes, Gen Taylor, 60mm, wht, NM $40.00
American Heroes, Gen Washington, 60mm, wht, NM $25.00
Civil War, Confederate officer mounted, Andy Guard, NM..$4.00
Civil War, Confederate soldier bayonetting, Andy Guard,
     NM..$3.00
Civil War, Confederate soldier being shot, Andy Guard, NM..$3.00
Civil War, Confederate soldier clubbing, Andy Guard, NM.$3.00
Civil War, Confederate soldier kneeling & firing, Andy Guard,
     NM..$4.00
Civil War, Confederate soldier lying dead, Andy Guard, NM..$3.00
Civil War, Confederate soldier prone & firing, Andy Guard,
     NM..$4.00

Civil War, Confederate soldier standing & firing, Andy Guard, NM $4.00
Civil War, Confederate soldier w/ramrod & pistol, Andy Guard, NM $3.00
Civil War, Union officer mounted, Andy Guard, NM........$8.00
Civil War, Union soldier advancing, Andy Guard, NM $6.00
Civil War, Union soldier bayonetting, Andy Guard, NM ..$6.00
Civil War, Union soldier being shot, Andy Guard, NM.....$6.00
Civil War, Union soldier clubbing, Andy Guard, NM........$6.00
Civil War, Union soldier kneeling & firing, Andy Guard, NM $8.00
Civil War, Union soldier lying dead, Andy Guard, NM $6.00
Civil War, Union soldier prone & firing, Andy Guard, NM.$8.00
Civil War, Union soldier w/ramrod & pistol, Andy Guard, NM................................$6.00
Plastic Toys, bugler, EX $6.00
Plastic Toys, hand gernade thrower, M $8.00
Plastic Toys, machine gunner kneeling, some pnt, EX........$6.00
Plastic Toys, soldier in gas mask w/rifle, some pnt, EX........$6.00
Plastic Toys, soldier standing firing rifle, some pnt, EX.......$6.00
Plastic Toys, soldier standing firing rifle, some pnt, M $8.00
Warriors of the World, Cadets, set of 6, NMIB...............$120.00
Warriors of the World, US Combat Soldiers, set of 6, NMIB.$120.00
Warriors of the World, Viking, EXIB $45.00

NUTTY MADS

The Thinker, dark green, NM, $35.00; Suburban Sidney, maroon, first issue, NM, $35.00; Bullpen Boo Boo, dark green, NM, $30.00.

All Heart Hogan, pk w/cream swirl, NM $20.00
Dippy the Sea Diver, cobalt, 1st issue, EX................................$10.00
End Zone Football Player, dk gr, 1st issue, NM, from $15 to.$20.00
Lost Teepee, flourescent red, NM, from $15 to $20.00
Manny of the Wrechless Mariner, lt gr, 1st issue, NM $35.00
Manny of the Wreckless Mariner, lime gr, NM................$20.00
Rocko the Champ, lime gr, 1st issue, NM, from $15 to $20.00
Rocko the Champ, pk, NM $16.50
Roddy the Hotrod, chartreuse gr, 1st issue, NM................$35.00
Waldo the Weight Lifter, pk, 1st issue, NM $25.00

WESTERN AND FRONTIER HEROES

Buffalo Bill, Atlantic #1202, MIP (sealed) $50.00

Buffalo Bill, 60mm, beige, EX................................$5.00
Cavalry (7th), mounted, 60mm, ea $18.00
Cowboy, mounted w/rifle, 45mm, NM $27.00
Cowboy, mounted w/rope, 45mm, NM $36.00
Cowboys, 6", Crescent, NM, ea $10.00
Dale Evans, 60mm, cream, NM $22.00
Davy Crockett, 50mm, cream, NM $25.00
Gunsmoke, Chester, NM................................$375.00
Gunsmoke, cowboys, bl, NM, ea from $75 to $100.00
Gunsmoke, cowboys, tan, NM, ea $3.00
Gunsmoke, Doc, NM................................$375.00
Gunsmoke, driver seated, bl, NM................................$100.00
Gunsmoke, Marshal Dillon, NM, minimum value $700.00
Gunsmoke, Miss Kitty, NM................................$375.00
High Chaparral, 42-pc set, ½", Airfix, unused, MIB $25.00
Indian Cheif, w/club, 54mm, NM $10.00
Lone Ranger & Tonto, 54mm, NM $65.00
Pioneer, clubbing, 60mm, NM................................$5.00
Ranch Hand, walking, 60mm, NM $60.00
Rough Rider, mounted, 60mm, NM $18.00
Roy Rogers, hands on hips, NM $27.00
Roy Rogers on Trigger, 5", Ideal, M................................$150.00
Sky King or Sheriff, NM, ea $18.00
Tonto, cream, 60mm, NM $110.00
Town Cowboys, 19-pc matched set, 60mm, NM $110.00
Wagon Driver, cream, 6", NM $5.00
Zorro w/Horse Tornado, NM $60.00

Plastic Toys

During the 1940s and into the 1960s, plastic was often the material of choice for consumer goods ranging from dinnerware and kitchenware items to jewelry and even high-heel shoes. Toy companies used brightly colored plastic to produce cars, dolls, pull toys, banks, games, and thousands of other types of products. Of the more imaginative toys, those that have survived in good collectible condition are beginning to attract a considerable amount of interest, especially items made by major companies.

Authentic Mighty Construction Series, Japan, three-piece set with dump truck, cement truck, and bulldozer, friction, 7" each, EXIB, A, $75.00. (Photo courtesy Randy Inman Auctions)

Bunny Rabbit on Scooter w/Sidecar, Canada, 1940s-50s, 5" L, NM..$40.00

Buzzy Airplane, w/pilot in open cockpit, pull cord, red & yel, VGIB..$150.00

Drawbridge Set #155, Renwal, crank-op bridge, 2 cars & 2 boats, unused, NM+IB, A.......................................$175.00

Fix-It Stagecoach, Ideal, 1950s, complete, NMIB...........$75.00

Hardy Farm, complete, EXIB...$75.00

Hot Rod, Nosco, mc plastic w/pistons exposed in clear plastic, w/driver, 9½", EX, A (Est: $75-$100)....................$130.00

Ice Cream Trike, red, wht & bl w/yel trim, spoke wheels, w/bell, 4½", EX, A...$35.00

International Stake Truck, PMC, 1950s, 11½", EX+IB, $200.00.

International Truck Cab, PMC, 1950s, 9", EXIB............$175.00

Jetgo Freedom Plane, Nosco, EXIB (box mk United Nations Peace Toy)...$150.00

Lady Penelope's Fab 1 Car, Hong Kong, friction, futuristic car w/4 front wheels, w/driver & passenger, 10", NMIB.......$235.00

Li'l Beep Bus, beeps when squeezed, w/pull string, Arrow, 1960s, 11", EX...$20.00

Mayflower Moving Van, Con-Cor, 1.87 scale, MIB..........$15.00

Modern Toys Autos & Planes Set, Kilgore, ca 1937, w/sedan, coupe, truck & 2 planes, 5" to 12", EXIB................$350.00

Revell Plumbing Service Truck, Revell, complete, 9½", unused, MIB..$90.00

Rocket Tank, red, gr & yel, 6", EXIB...............................$30.00

Satellite Launcher, Ideal, w/radar & 4 satellites, 17" L, NMIB, A.$250.00

Service & Hi-Way Fleet, Gilmark, 10-pc vehicle set in various colors, EXIB, A...$75.00

Steam Shovel Construction Kit, Lido #475, complete, EXIB.$250.00

Steer-O Car, Product Miniature Co Inc., convertible w/wht-wall tires, chrome-look hubs, 12", EXIB........................$250.00

Terrier, eyes open & close, w/squeaker, 9", EX.............$15.00

Witch on Rocket, 1950s-60s, 4", NM+............................$175.00

XP-600 Fix-It Car of Tomorrow, Ideal, complete w/repair kit, 16" L, EXIB..$250.00

Plasticville

From the 1940s through the 1960s, Bachmann Brothers produced plastic accessories for train layouts such as buildings, fences, trees, and animals. Buildings often included several smaller pieces — for instance, ladders, railings, windsocks, etc. — everything you could ever need to play out just about any scenario. Beware of reissues.

Advisor: Gary Mosholder, Gary's Trains (G1)

Airport Administration Building, #AD-4, EXIB, G1 ....$55.00

Bank, #BK-1, EXIB, G1..$18.00

Bank, #1801, EXIB, G1...$28.00

Barn, #BN-1, wht w/red roof, chrome silo top, EXIB, G1.$18.00

Barn, #BN-1, wht w/red roof, EXIB, G1.........................$15.00

Barnyard Animals #1606, VGIB, G1...............................$18.00

Bridge (Trestle), #BR-2, EXIB, G1.................................$18.00

Bridge & Pond, #BL-2, EXIB, G1.....................................$6.00

Cape Cod, #HP-9, VGIB, G1...$8.00

Cathedral, #C-18, EXIB, G1..$35.00

Cathedral, #C-18, GIB, G1..$20.00

Church, #CC-9, EXIB, G1...$12.00

Church, #1600, EXIB, G1..$16.00

Church, #1818, MIB, G1..$14.00

Church (Littletown), #113, EXIB, G1.............................$25.00

Colonial (2-Story), #LH-4, red w/wht trim, gray roof, MIB, G1...$29.00

Colonial (2-Story), #LH-4, tan w/brn trim, red roof, MIB, G1..$19.00

Colonial Mansion, #1703, bl roof, GIB, G1...................$24.00

Corner Store, #1626, gray w/wht roof, EXIB, G1.............$65.00

Diner, #DE-7, red, EXIB, G1...$18.00

Farm Implements, #1302, MIB, G1.................................$45.00

Fence (Picket), #FG-12, 12-pc set, EXIB, G1.................$10.00

Fire House, #FH-4, w/hollow siren, EXIB, G1................$25.00

Fire House, #FH-4, w/lg base siren, EXIB, G1...............$16.00

Fire House, #FH-4, w/sm base siren, EXIB, G1.............$16.00

Five & Ten Cent Store, #CS-5, EXIB, G1.......................$15.00

Freight Station, #LM-3, brn platform, EXIB, G1...........$8.00

Frosty Bar, #FB-1, yel w/chrome bar, EXIB, G1..............$18.00

Gas Station, #1800, w/yel auto, EXIB, G1......................$18.00

Gas Station, sn, EX, G1...$10.00

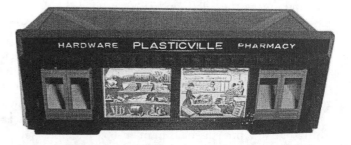

Hardware-Pharmacy, #DH-2, EXIB, $18.00. (Photo courtesy Gary Mosholder)

Hospital, #HS-6, w/furniture, EXIB, G1..........................$35.00

Hospital, #HS-6, w/o furniture, EXIB, G1.......................$22.00

Lionel Figure Set, #953, VGIB, G1.................................$65.00

Log Cabin, #LC-2, w/chimney & rustic fence, EXIB, G1.$18.00

Motel, #1621, any color variation, EXIB, G1..................$15.00

New England Ranch House, #MH-2, wht w/yel trim, brn roof, MIB, G1...$22.00

New England Ranch House, #MH-2, wht w/yel trim, brn roof, VGIB..$17.00
Plasticville Hall, #PH-1, tan w/red roof, EXIB, G1...........$35.00
Playground, #1406, EXIB, G1...$30.00
Police Dept, #PD-3, dk gray, EXIB, G1 ....$25.00
Police Dept, #PD-3, lt gray, EXIB, G1.............................$20.00
Railroad Accessories, #5605, complete, EXIB, G1............$65.00
Railroad Accessories Kit, #RA-6, EXIB, G1 ....$18.00
Railroad Signal Bridge, #SG-3, MIB, G1 ....$15.00

Ranch House, #1603, turquoise with white roof, GIB, $18.00. (Photo courtesy Gary Mosholder)

School, #SC-4, EXIB, G1 ....$18.00
Split-Level, #1908, turq, EXIB, G1 ....$22.00
Suburban Station, #RS-8, brn platform, GIB, G1............$10.00
Union Station, #1901, EXIB, G1.....................................$25.00
Watchman's Shanty, #1407, EXIB, G1............................$12.00

Playsets

Louis Marx is given credit for developing the modern-age playset and during the 1950s and 1960s produced hundreds of boxed sets, each with the buildings, figures, and accessories that when combined with a child's imagination could bring any scenario alive, from the days of Ben Hur to medieval battles, through the cowboy and Indian era, and on up to Cape Canaveral. Marx's prices were kept low by mass marketing (through retail giants such as Sears and Montgomery Wards) and overseas production. But on today's market, playsets are anything but low priced; some mint-in-box examples sell for upwards of $1,000.00. Just remember that a set that shows wear or has even a few minor pieces missing quickly drops in value. The listings below are for complete examples unless noted otherwise.

See the Clubs, Newsletters, and Other Publications section for information on how to order *Prehistoric Times*, by Mike and Kurt Fredericks, and *Playset Magazine*, published six times a year.

African Warrior's Canoe, Multiple Toys, 1950s, MIP $75.00
AGY Arctic Satellite Base, Marx #4800, Series 1000, 1959, NMIB..$800.00

Alamo, Marx, 1957, #3546, EXIB..................................$150.00
Alaska, Marx, 1960, #2755-6, EX+IB $350.00

American Airlines International Jetport, Marx, Series 1000, EXIB, $175.00.

Anzio Beach, Aurora, HO scale, VGIB.............................$50.00
Arctic Explorer, Marx #3702, Series 2000, 1957, NM+IB.$500.00
Army Combat Training Center, Marx #4153, 1958, NM+IB..$75.00
Battle of Iwo Jima, Marx #4147, 1964, NM+IB..............$300.00
Battleground, Marx #4754, 1962, EXIB $50.00
Ben Hur, Marx #4696, 1959, EX+IB $250.00

Ben-Hur, Marx #4702, Series 2000, EX+IB, $450.00.

Beyond Tomorrow Lunar Space Station, Multiple Toys, 1975, EXIB, $125.00.

Big Top Circus, Marx #4310, 1952, NM+IB....................$375.00
Blue & Gray, Marx #4744, 1963, NMIB......................$750.00

Cape Canaveral, Marx, #4521, NMIB, $225.00.

Captain Space Solar Port, Marx #7018, 1954, NMIB $275.00
Castle, Elastolin #9756, EXIB $300.00
Construction Camp, Marx #4439, 1954, NMIB.............$300.00
Cragstan International Airport, cb terminal w/13 tin planes & vehicles & 8 airport signs, complete, NM, A..........$200.00
Custer's Last Stand, Marx #4779, Series 500, 1956, NMIB.$375.00
Daktari, Marx #3720, 1967, EX+IB $200.00
Daniel Boone Wilderness Scout, Marx #0670, 1964, NMIB.$250.00
Davy Crockett at the Alamo, Marx #3544, 1955, NMIB.$600.00
Davy Crockett at the Alamo #3530, 1955, EX+IB.........$150.00
Desert Fox, Marx #4177, 1966, EX+IB $150.00
Desert Patrol, Marx #4174, 1967, NMIB $200.00
Evel Knievel Stunt World, Ideal, 1975, NMIB..............$125.00
Farm Set, Marx #3953, 1969, EXIB................................$125.00
Fire House, Marx #4820, EX+IB $800.00
Fort Apache, Marx #3685, NMIB $500.00
Fort Apache, Marx/Sears #59093C, 1972, EXIB..............$50.00
Fort Apache Stocade, Marx #3660, Series 2000, 1960, EXIB.$100.00
Fort Dearborn, Marx #3688, NMIB $275.00
Fort Pitt, Marx #3741, Series 750, 1959, EX+IB $125.00

Gallant Men, Marx #4634, NMIB $300.00
Gunsmoke, MPC #1117, EXIB...$250.00
Gunsmoke Dodge City, Marx #4268, Series 2000, EX+IB.$800.00
Happi-Time Farm Set, Marx #3480, EXIB $50.00
Happi-Time Roy Rogers Rodeo Ranch, Marx #3990, 1953, NMIB..$200.00
Johnny Apollo Moon Launcher Center, Marx #4630, 1970, EXIB...$75.00
Jungle, Marx/Sears #3716, 1960, NMIB.........................$100.00
Jungle Jim, Marx #3705-6, Series 1000, 1957, EXIB $350.00
Knights & Vikings, Marx #4733, 1973, NMIB $175.00
Legend of the Lone Ranger, MPC, later issue, MIB (sealed).$75.00
Little Big Horn, Marx #4679MO, 1972, EXIB................$150.00
Lone Ranger Ranch, Marx #3969, Series 500, NMIB $300.00
McDonaldland, Remco, 1976, unused, MIB $135.00
Medieval Castle, Marx/Sears #4734, EXIB $125.00
Midtown Service Station, Marx #3420, 1960, EX+IB......$75.00
Mobile Army Battlefront, MPC #3501, EXIB $150.00
Modern Farm Set, Marx #3932, 1967, EXIB....................$74.00
Modern Service Station, Marx #6044, 1966, EXIB $50.00
Mountain Assault, Atlantic #202, unused, MIB.............$175.00
Navarone Mountain Battleground Set, Marx #3412, 1976, NMIB..$150.00
Operation Moon Base, Marx #465304, 1962, EXIB $150.00
Pet Shop, Marx #4209-10, 1953, EXIB $125.00
Pirate's Canoe, Multiple Toys, 1950s, MIP $100.00
Planet of the Apes, MPC, unused, MIB $125.00
Prehistoric Times, Marx #3389, Series 500, EXIB.............$50.00
Prince Valiant Castle, Marx #4705, 1955, EXIB.............$100.00
Project Mercury Cape Canaveral, Marx #4524, 1959, EXIB.$150.00
Revolutionary War Set, Marx #3404, Series 1000, 1950s, EXIB $250.00

Rifleman Ranch, Marx #3997-8, 1959, EX+IB, $300.00.

Roy Rogers Rodeo Ranch, Marx #3992, NMIB, $300.00.

Fort Liberty, Hong Kong, 1970s, MIB, $100.00.
(Photo courtesy June Moon)

Rin Tin Tin Fort Apache, Marx #3686R, Series 5000, 1956, NMIB..$800.00
Robin Hood Castle, Marx #4717, 1956, NMIB.............$400.00
Robin Hood Castle, Marx #4718, 1958, EXIB................$200.00
Roy Rogers Double R Bar Ranch, Marx #3982, 1962, EXIB.$150.00
Roy Rogers Rodeo Ranch, Marx #3996, Series 2000, NMIB .$425.00
Roy Rogers Western Town, Marx #4216, NMIB.............$275.00
Sands of Iwo Jima, Marx, Miniature Play, VGIB............$325.00
Service Station, Marx #3485, EXIB.................................$200.00
Silver Ciy Western Town, Marx #4220, 1956, NMIB $175.00
Super Circus, Marx #4320, 1952, EXIB.........................$115.00
Tactical Air Command, Marx #4106, 1970s, NMIB.........$45.00
Tales of Wells Fargo Train Set, Marx #54752, 1959, NMIB.$700.00
Tank Battle, Marx/Sears #6056, 1964, NMIB.................$125.00
Tom Corbett Space Academy Set, Marx #7012, 1952, NMIB..$825.00
Undersea Attack, Atlantic #206, EXIB $100.00
Untouchables, Marx #4676, 1961, EXIB $350.00
US Armed Forces, Marx #4151, NMIB..........................$225.00
US Armed Forces Training Center, Marx #4158, 1956, NMIB $375.00
US Army Mobile Set, Marx #3655, 1956, EXIB..............$30.00
Viking Ship, Eldon, 1960s, 18" L, unused, MIP (sealed) .$125.00
Wagon Train, Marx #4805, 1960s, Series 1000, NMIB ..$500.00
Wagon Train, Marx #4888, Series 5000, NMIB..........$1,000.00

Walt Disney's Television Playhouse, Marx #4349, NMIB, $500.00.

Walt Disney's Television Playhouse, Marx #4352, 1953, NMIB..$450.00
Ward's Service Station, Marx #3488, 1959, NMIB $275.00
Western Frontier Town, Ideal #3298, EXIB....................$475.00
Western Ranch Set, Marx #3980, NMIB........................$100.00
Wyatt Earp Dodge City Western Town, Marx #4228, Series 1000, NMIB..$475.00
Yogi Bear at Jellystone National Park, Marx #4363-4, 1962, EXIB...$175.00
Zorro, Marx #3754, Series 1000, 1958, EXIB $1,000.00

Political Toys

As far back as the nineteenth century, children's toys with a political message were on the market. One of the most familiar was the 'Tammany Bank' patented by J. & E. Stevens in 1873. The message was obvious — a coin placed in the man's hand was deposited in his pocket, representing the kickbacks William Tweed was suspected of pocketing when he was the head of Tammany Hall in New York during the 1860s.

Advisors: Michael and Polly McQuillen (M11)

Ronald Reagan, doll, Horsman, 1987, 17", MIB, $100.00.

Agnew, Spiro; Presidential semi-trailer, Winross, 1972, MIB $35.00
Agnew, Spiro; The Spiro Agnew Jigsaw Puzzle, as Superman, 1970s, NMIB...$25.00
Agnew, Spiro; wristwatch, All American Time Co, caricature face, non-working $25.00
Bush, George; doll, stuffed cloth w/vinyl caricature head, blk jacket, striped shirt & pants, red tie, 1990s, 9½", M .$20.00
Carter, Amy; coloring book, 1977, unused, EX................$15.00
Carter, Jimmy; radio, peanut shape, transistor, MIB.........$60.00
Carter, Jimmy; ring, peanut, EX.....................................$15.00
Clinton, Hillary; doll, Draft Evader, MIB.......................$15.00
Clinton/Gore, yo-yo, Humphery, 1990s, NM....................$10.00
Clout, American Political Game, Scofield, 1985, EXIB...$18.00
Eisenhower, Dwight D; figure, Excel, 1974, fully jtd, complete w/pistol & uniform, 9½", NMIB $15.00
Eisenhower, Dwight D; nodder, 1950s, pnt compo elephant w/I'm for Ike, 6½", NM $100.00
Goldwater, Barry; board game, 1964 Presidential Election, MOC $30.00
Gorbachev, doll, Dreamworks, 1990, 11", MIB................$45.00
Jackson, Andrew; doll, in military uniform, Effanbee, 1990, 16", MIB $125.00
Johnson, Lyndon B; doll, Remco, 1964, plastic, 6", MIB..$40.00
Kennedy, Jackie; doll, 1960s, 14", M.............................$450.00
Kennedy, John F; jigsaw puzzle, Tuco, 1960s, 350 pcs, EXIB..$12.50
Kennedy, John F; model kit, Aurora #851-149, 1965, unassembled, NMIB...$105.00

MacArthur, Gen Douglas; bank, Save for Victory & portrait flanked by flags, glass & cb, 7", EX..............................$55.00

MacArthur, Gen Douglas; puzzle, Forward America, Tuco, 320 pcs, EXIB..$85.00

Mao/Nixon, ping-pong paddle set, 1970s, EXIP $55.00

Miss Liberty, doll, stuffed cloth body w/pnt compo head & limbs, cloth outfit, 1940s, 23", EX $100.00

Mr President, board game, 3M, 1970s, EXIB....................$22.50

Nixon, Richard; hand puppet, cloth body w/plastic head, 1968, NM..$35.00

Powell, Colin; doll, 1980s, 8", NMIB.............................$30.00

Reagan, Ronald; doll, stuffed print cloth (Reaganomics), Dots Okay, 1982, 10", MIB $25.00

Reagan, Ronald; yo-yo, plastic, NM..............................$10.00

Roosevelt, Eleanor; doll, 1980s, 14", MIB.......................$85.00

Roosevelt, Franklin D; puzzle, Forward America, Tuco, 320 pcs, EXIB...$85.00

Truman, Harry S; doll, in suit & hat w/red bow tie, Effanbee, 1988, 16", MIB $125.00

Uncle Sam, doll, stuffed cloth body w/pnt compo head & limbs, cloth outfit, 1940s, 20", EX $100.00

Washington, George & Martha; figures, Japan, prewar, celluloid, 7", NM $85.00

Washington, George; action figure, Fun-World, Collectors Series of Great Americans #1776-1, fully jtd, 7½", NRFB...$23.50

Washington, George; puzzle, Washington Pleading for Democracy, Perfect Picture Puzzle, 400 pcs, NMIB...............$35.00

Washington, George; toy soldier, Elastolin #7080, plastic, MIB $27.50

Premiums

Those from the pre-boomer era must remember waiting in anticipation for a silver bullet ring, secret membership kit, decoder pin, coloring book, or whatever other wonderful item seen advertised in a favorite comic book or heard about on the Tom Mix show. Tom wasn't the only one to have these exciting premiums, though, just about any top character-oriented show from the 1930s through the 1940s made similar offers, and even through the 1950s some were still being distributed. Often they could be had free for a cereal boxtop or an Ovaltine inner seal, and if any money was involved, it was usually only a dime. Not especially durable and often made in somewhat limited amounts, few have survived to the present. Today some of these are bringing fantastic prices, but the market at present is very volatile. Note: Those trademark/logo characters created to specifically represent a cereal product or company (for example Cap'n Crunch) are listed in the Advertising category.

Condition is very important in assessing value; items in pristine condition bring premium prices.

Advisor: Bill Campbell (C10)

See also Advertising; Pin-back Buttons.

Alvin & the Chipmunks, Alvin's Christmas Cards, Nestlé's Quik, 1965, unused set of 4, complete, VG+ (w/envelope)...$35.00

Amos 'N Andy, Weber City Map, Pepsodent, 1930s, 15x20", EX+ (w/orig mailing envelope), NM+ $75.00

Annie, decoder, 1935, EX...$35.00

Annie, decoder, 1936, EX, $40.00.

Annie, decoder, 1937, EX...$50.00

Annie, decoder, 1938, EX...$50.00

Annie, decoder, 1939, EX...$55.00

Annie, decoder, 1940, EX...$125.00

Annie, manual, Secret Society, 1935, with original mailer, EX, $125.00.

Annie, mask, die-cut litho paper, Ovaltine/Einson-Freemon, 1933, 8½x7½", EX (w/envelope)...........................$65.00

Annie, ring, face, NM+ $100.00

Annie, ring, initial, EX..$125.00

Annie, ring, Mystic Eye, w/instructions, EX $200.00

Annie, ring, secret message, EX $250.00

Annie, ring, silver star, EX $350.00

Annie, Shake-Up mug, 1931, ivory & orange, EX............$50.00

Annie, Shake-Up mug, 1935, beige & orange, EX $75.00

Annie, Shake-Up mug, 1938, aqua & orange, EX $175.00

Annie, Shake-Up mug, 1939, brn & orange, EX............$150.00

Annie, Shake-Up mug, 1940, gr & red, EX $150.00

Batman, ring, Nestlé, M...$90.00

Batman, rubber stamp set, set of 6 plastic stamps of various characters, w/2x5" plastic case, Kellogg's, 1960s, EX+......$75.00

Buck Jones, badge, Buck Jones Club, horseshoe spape, litho on brass, Grape-Nuts/Hoofbeats radio show, 1930s, 1½", EX $35.00

Buck Jones, Club Badge, litho brass horseshoe shape w/head image & name, Post Grape-Nuts, 1937, 1½x1¼", EX+ $50.00

Buck Rogers, badge, Chief Explorer, Cream of Wheat, 1936, NM, from $150 to...$175.00

Buck Rogers, badge, Solar Scout, Cream of Wheat, 1936, 1½", VG+, A..$50.00

Buck Rogers, badge, Solar Scouts, Cream of Wheat, 1936, EX+, from $150.00 to $175.00.

Buck Rogers, Cut-Out Adventure Book, Cocomalt, 1933, unused, VG...$375.00

Buck Rogers, Official Punch-O-Bag, Morton's Salt/Lou Fox, 1930s, unused, EX+ (sealed envelope).......................$65.00

Buck Rogers, ring, birthstone, EX $565.00

Buck Rogers, ring, Saturn, NM+ $600.00

Buck Rogers Space Ranger Kit, Sylvania, 1950s, unused, with original envelope, $135.00.

Buffalo Bill, jigsaw puzzle, Cocomalt, 1930s, NM+ (w/envelope) $50.00

Buster Brown, bandana, Buster & Tige & pals images around Smilin' Ed McConnel in center, mc, 1940s, 23x20", VG $50.00

Captain Kangaroo, Grandfather Clock Puppet, cb, Keeshan Miller Ent/Buster Brown Shoes, 1950s, 17x11", unpunched, M .$50.00

Captain Marvel, key ring, Captain Marvel Club, EX $75.00

Captain Marvel Magic Whistle, EX $50.00

Captain Midnight, badge, Mysto-Magic Weather Forecasting Wings, w/litmus paper, Skelly Oil, 1939, EX.............$50.00

Captain Midnight, badge, pilot's wings, 24k gold-finished brass, 1943, EX $225.00

Captain Midnight, badge, Secret Squadron Decoder, brass-plated tin, 2¼", EX..$125.00

Captain Midnight, decoder, 1945, EX.............................$125.00

Captain Midnight, decoder, 1947, whistle, EX $75.00

Captain Midnight, decoder, 1955, EX.............................$175.00

Captain Midnight, manual, 1945, EX $75.00

Captain Midnight, manual, 1948, NM, $100.00.

Captain Midnight, manual, 1957, G $75.00

Captain Midnight, membership kit, 1957, complete, EX .$575.00

Captain Midnight, ring, Flight Commander, EX $495.00

Captain Midnight, ring, Marine Corps, EX $400.00

Captain Midnight, ring, Mystic Sun God, EX $800.00

Captain Midnight, ring, secret compartment, EX...........$140.00

Captain Midnight, ring, Whirlwind Siren, EX $400.00

Captain Midnight, Shake-Up mug, 1955, orange & bl, EX .$225.00

Captain Midnight, Shake-Up mug, 1957, red & bl, EX .$100.00

Captain Video, ring, photo, EX $325.00

Cisco Kid, ring, saddle, EX $500.00

Davy Crockett, ring, compass, w/expansion band, EX....$175.00

Davy Crockett, ring, TV flicker, M $150.00

Dick Tracy, book, Dick Tracy & the Invisible Man, Big Little Book, softcover, Whitman/Quaker, 1939, EX+..........$75.00

Dick Tracy, manual, Jr Detective, style B version, EX $50.00

Dick Tracy, ring, secret compartment, EX......................$200.00

Dragnet, badge, Sergeant 714, brass-plated tin, NM.........$25.00

Flash Gordon, ring, Post Toasties, MIP $75.00

Flintstones, comic book, March of Comics #243, 1963, NM .$15.00

Frank Buck, ring, black leopard, bronze, NM, $3,200.00.

Gabby Hayes, movie viewer & filmstrip, Quaker Cereals, rare, VG $100.00

Gabby Hayes, ring, cannon, EX $250.00

Gene Autry, Adventure Story Trail Map, poster for displaying bread labels, Schafer's Bread, 1950s, EX....................$75.00

Gene Autry, Pop Pistol, die-cut cb w/Gene Autry Show insert, 1950s, 9", NM..$40.00

Gene Autry, ring, flag, NM+ $100.00

Green Hornet, ring, rubber stamp seal, EX $100.00

Green Hornet, ring, seal/secret compartment, EX..........$850.00

Green Lantern, ring, FX, solid gr metal w/gr stone, EX $85.00

Green Lantern, ring, glow-in-dark, gr plastic, DC, EX $15.00

Hopalong Cassidy, badges, 12 different in a series, metal, Post Raisin Bran, 2x1½", EX, ea $20.00

Hopalong Cassidy, ring, hat/compass, EX $275.00

Hopalong Cassidy, Western Badges, metal, 12 different, Post Raisin Bran, 1950-51, 1", ea from $15 to $20.00

Howdy Doody, bread label album, American History, Wonder Bread, 1950s, 8 pgs, unused, NM+ $65.00

Howdy Doody, Coloring Comics #1 (The Bee Breaks Clarabelles Balloon), Blue Bonnet Margarine box insert, 1950s, VG...$15.00

Howdy Doody, mug, Ovaltine, NM, $75.00.

Howdy Doody, ring, Clarabelle horn, EX........................$385.00

Huckleberry Hound, ring, plastic, NM+ $65.00

Jack Armstrong, pedometer, EX $25.00

Jack Armstrong, ring, Egyptian siren, NM+ $125.00

Lassie, ring, friendship, EX $150.00

Lassie, wallet/membership card, brn vinyl w/color image of Lassie, w/Get-Up-And-Go Club card, Campbell's Soup, 1950s, EX...$50.00

Little Orphan Annie, Orphan Annie Circus, die-cut litho cb, w/accessory pcs, Ovaltine, 1930s, EX+ $100.00

Little Orphan Annie, see Annie

Lone Ranger, badge, copper star, EX, $35.00.

Lone Ranger, belt, glow-in-dark, EX $25.00

Lone Ranger, coloring book, Lone Range Health & Safety Club, Merita Bread, 1955, 5x7", unused, NM...................$50.00

Lone Ranger, flashlight gun, plastic, w/horseshoe logo & secret compartment, Morton's Salt, 6", M $75.00

Lone Ranger, hat, wht cloth soda-jerk type w/Hi-Yo Silver in bl & Ranger graphics, TLR, 1942, 11" L, VG $50.00

Lone Ranger, pedometer, w/ankle strap, EX $25.00

Lone Ranger, ring, atomic bomb, EX $215.00

Lone Ranger, ring, flashlight, w/instructions, EX...........$150.00

Lone Ranger, ring, gold ore/meteorite, EX...................$2,000.00

Lone Ranger, ring, Six Shooter, 1947, EX......................$150.00

Melvin Pervis, manual, Secret Operator's, Post Toasties, 1937, EX..$50.00

Melvin Pervis, ring, Jr G-Men Corps, EX........................$85.00

Melvin Pervis, Secret Operator's Manual, Post Toasties, 1937, 28 pgs, 5x7", EX...$50.00

Mighty Mouse, Merry Pack punchouts, Post Cereal/CBS-TV Ent, 1956, unused, EX $75.00

Orphan Annie, see Annie

Our Gang, Fun Kit, 12 die-cut pgs featuring the gang and different activities, Morton Salt, 1930s, 10x7", NM........$175.00

Phantom, ring, skull, brass w/red eyes, 1950s, EX $800.00

Pinocchio, puppet, paper litho, 1st National Stores, 1939-40, promoting the Pinocchio movie, uncut & unused, NM $50.00

Popeye, membership card, Theatre Club, blk & wht, WSOC TV, 1958, EX..$30.00

Radio Orphan Annie, see Annie

Red Skelton, masks, Kaddiddlehopper, Sheriff & Freddy the Freeloader, Pet Milk, 1960, VG (w/mailer box) $125.00

Rin-Tin-Tin, ballpoint pen, rifle shape, Nabisco Shredded Wheat, 5½", MIP $50.00

Rin-Tin-Tin, ring, magic, w/pencil, EX...........................$550.00

Roger Wilco, ring, Flying Tiger, w/whistle & glow top, EX.$325.00

Roger Wilco, ring, MagniRay, glow-in-dark, 1940s, EX....$80.00

Roy Rogers, badge & membership card, star compartments, EX $85.00

Roy Rogers, calendar, Nestlé's Quik, 1960, complete, 8x7", EX...$110.00

Roy Rogers, calendar, Roy Rogers Ranch, 1960, Nestlé's Quik, Canadian version, 14", VG $75.00

Roy Rogers, Double R Bar Ranch, cb punch-out set, Post Cereals, 1953-55, EX (w/mailer) $75.00

Roy Rogers, Paint-by-Number Kit, Roy & Bullet plaque in relief, sq w/rope-like border, Nestlé's Quik, 1960, unused, EXIB.$100.00

Roy Rogers, Paint-by-Number Paint Set, Post's Sugar Crisp, 1954, complete, some use, EX $75.00

Roy Rogers, Ranch Calendar, 1959, Nestlé's Quik, 1958, 14", EX..$75.00

Roy Rogers, ring, microscope, EX...................................$125.00

Roy Rogers, ring, saddle, silver, EX $350.00

Roy Rogers, Wild West Action Toy, punch-out cb, free in boxes of RR Cookies, 1950s, unused, 5x7", NM+...............$75.00

Scrappy, Scrappy's Animated Cartoon Puppets, 4-pg punch-out book, Pillsbury's Farina, 1936, unused, EX..............$100.00

Sgt Preston, pedometer, 1952, EX $25.00

Shadow, ring, Blue Coal, EX $650.00
Shadow, ring, bust, EX...$150.00
Shadow, ring, Diamond Co, EX.....................................$200.00
Sky King, Deteco-Microscope, 1950s, complete, NM (EX mailer) $225.00
Sky King, Deteco-Writer, aluminum or brass, EX, ea $125.00
Sky King, ring, Aztec, EX...$800.00
Sky King, ring, MagniGlo Writing, EX.........................$115.00
Sky King, ring, radar, EX..$125.00
Sky King, ring, Telebinger, EX.......................................$255.00
Sky King, Stamping Kit, Your Personal Name & Address..., litho tin, 1953, complete, EX $50.00
Smokey the Bear, badge, Jr Forest Ranger, 1960s, 2", NM.$25.00
Smokey the Bear, Jr Forest Ranger Kit, US Dept of Agriculture, 1956-57, complete, EX+ (w/mailer)...........................$65.00
Snow White & the Seven Dwarfs, game board, Tek Toothbrush/WDE, 1930s, EX $60.00

Space Patrol, badge, red, white, and bue under plastic, EX, $350.00.

Space Patrol, binoculars, Ralston, 1953, 5", NM............$150.00
Space Patrol, decoder belt buckle, brass & aluminum, Ralston, 1950s, EX...$185.00
Space Patrol, ring, Hydrogen Ray Gun, Wheat Chex, 1950s, EX..$250.00
Straight Arrow, ring, face, EX...$70.00
Straight Arrow, ring, Nugget Cave w/photo, EX $275.00
Superman, airplane, Kellogg's Pep, EX...........................$200.00
Superman, ring, Crusader, EX $235.00
Superman, ring, S logo, gold finish, Nestlé's, 1978, EX+..$25.00
Superman, Stereo Pix, Kellogg's, 1954, 8", NM, ea from $10 to..$15.00
Terry & the Pirates, ring, gold detector, EX $125.00
Tom Corbett, patch (from Tom Corbett membership kit), bl, gold & red stitched fabric, Kellogg's, 1951, NM+......$50.00
Tom Corbett, ring, face, EX..$125.00
Tom Corbett, ring, rocket, w/expansion band, unused, M.$475.00
Tom Mix, badge, Deputy Sheriff of Dobie County whistler, w/papers, EX..$75.00
Tom Mix, badge, Straight Shooter, EX............................$60.00
Tom Mix, badge, Straight Shooter, MOC (w/catalog & mailer) $150.00
Tom Mix, postcard promoting premiums to Ralston dealers, reads 'Check your stock...build Ralston displays!,' 1940s, NM..$50.00
Tom Mix, puzzle, 125-pc jigsaw, Rexall, 1920s, complete, NM (w/envelope)...$150.00

Tom Mix, ring, Look Around, EX $125.00
Tom Mix, ring, Marlin, EX..$300.00
Tom Mix, ring, Straight Shooter, EX...............................$100.00
Tom Mix, Straight Shooters Periscope, cb w/tin cap ends, Ralston, 1939, 9", EX...$50.00
Wild Bill Hickok, Colt 6-Shooter Pistol, Sugar Pops, 1958, 10", MIB...$300.00
Wild Bill Hickok, Secret Treasure Guide & Map, Kellogg's, NM+ (w/envelope)..$50.00
Wonder Woman, ring, Nestlé, 1977, EX........................$110.00
Woody Woodpecker, ring, Club Stamp, EX....................$150.00
Zorro, ring, silver plastic w/logo on blk top, EX...............$60.00

Pressed Steel

Many companies were involved in the manufacture of pressed-steel automotive toys which were often faithfully modeled after actual vehicles in production at the time they were made. Because they were so sturdy, some from as early as the 1920s have survived to the present, and those that are still in good condition are bringing very respectable prices at toy auctions around the country. Some of the better-known manufacturers are listed in other sections or their own categories.

The following listings are from current auctions and the estimates have been given at the end of the line as a comparison to the actual price.

See also Aeronautical; Buddy L; Keystone; Marx; Pedal Cars and Other Wheeled Goods; Structo; Tonka; Wyandotte.

CARS

Auto Pulling Leisure Trailer, Kingsbury, 1930s, w/up, BRT, 23", rstr, A (Est: $200-$400)...$150.00

Brougham, Kingsbury, #345, windup, 13", restored, A (Est: $400.00 – $600.00), $500.00. (Photo courtesy Noel Barrett Antiques and Auctions, Ltd.)

Cadillac Sedan, Kingsbury, 1940s, w/up, sliding sunroof, lt gr w/NP grille/bumpers, WRT, 14½", VG, A (Est: $250-$500) $345.00
Chrysler Airflow, Cor-Cor, 1930s, w/up, b/o headlights, red, BRT, chrome hubs, 17", G, A (Est: $1,000-$1,200) $1,150.00
Chrysler Airflow, Kingsbury, b/o headlights, WRT, 14", G, A (Est: $300-$400)...$330.00

Chrysler Airflow Coupe, Cor-Cor, 1930s, w/up, b/o headlights, blk, BRT, 17", P rpt, A (Est: $300-$500) $300.00

Chrysler Airflow Sedan, Cor-Cor, w/up, b/o lights, NP grille, bumpers & hood ornament, BRT, 17", G, A (Est: $800-$900) $715.00

Chrysler Airflow Sedan (1934), Kingsbury, w/up, dummy headlights, maroon, WRT, 15", VG+, A (Est: $400-$600) $550.00

Chrysler Airflow Sedan (1935), Kingsbury, w/up, b/o headlights, tan, BRT, 15", G+, A (Est: $300-$400) $520.00

Chrysler Airflow Sedan (1936-37), Kingsbury, w/up, b/o headlights, maroon, WRT, 15", VG, A (Est: $400-$600) .$770.00

Citroen Racer, France, w/up, NP grille, BRT w/silver hubs, compo driver's head, 16½", VGIB, A (Est: $1,000-$1,200) $880.00

Coupe, Girard, w/up, b/o headlights, wht top w/gr body, orange fenders & running boards, BRT, 14", G, A (Est: $100-$200) $175.00

DeSoto Sedan, Cor-Cor, w/up, b/o headlights, 17½", G, A (Est: $300) $545.00

DeSoto Sky Roof Sedan, Kingsbury, 1939, sliding sky roof, WRT, gr, 14", EX, A (Est: $900-$1,000) $1,100.00

Golden Arrow Racer, Kingsbury, w/up, red w/lithoed wheels, orig CI driver, 19", no windshield, G+, A (Est: $300-$400)...$465.00

Graham Sedan, Cor-Cor, battery-operated headlights, 19½", EX, A (Est: $2,500.00 – $3,000.00), $2,750.00. (Photo courtesy Bertoia Auctions)

Limousine, Dayton, 1920s, flywheel motor, spoke wheels, CI driver, 12", VG, A (Est: $175-$250) $465.00

Lincoln Touring Sedan, Turner, dummy lights, bl w/blk roof, BRT, red hubs, 26", VG, A (Est: $2,500-$3,000) .$3,300.00

Pierce Arrow (1934), Girard, w/up, b/o headlights, blk disk wheels, 13½", G, A (Est: $300-$500) $220.00

P2 Alfa Romeo Racer #2, CIJ/France, 1920s, leather hood straps, side pipes, BRT, spokes, 21", EX, A (Est: $2,000-$2,500) $3,850.00

Roadster, Dayton, 1920s, friction, blk w/red hubs, 18", old rpt, A (Est: $150-$250) $245.00

Roadster, Dayton, 1920s, friction, open high seat w/CI driver, luggage on back, MSW, 8", P, A (Est: $25-$50).......$110.00

Roadster, Dayton, 1920s, friction, open seat, no windshield, red & gold, disk wheels, 11", G+, A (Est: $75-$125) $100.00

Roadster, Kingsbury, w/up, b/o headlights, tan & red, WRT w/gr hubs, 13", VG, A (Est: $300-$400)....................$350.00

Roadster, Republic, open rumble seat, 2 windshields, MDW, yel & red, gr hubs, driver, 18", VG, A (Est: $1,500-$2,000) $1,430.00

Sedan w/Boat, Kingsbury, orange car & trailer w/gr boat, orig oars, blk disk wheels, 21½", EX, A (Est: $1,000-$1,200)..$2,750.00

Sunbeam Racer, Kingsbury, w/up, red w/American flag decals, BRT, NP driver, 18", G, A ($400-$500) $715.00

Touring Car, Dayton, oblong w/sq back, open w/2 front 'bucket' seats, MSW, bl, gold trim, 10½", G, A (Est: $150-$200).........$110.00

Touring Hillclimber, Clark, friction, open bench seats, CI spoke wheels, w/passenger, 8", G, A (Est: $300-$400) $165.00

Transitional (Hansom) Taxi, Converse, w/up, blk w/yel trim & MSW, open bench seat, 10", EX, A (Est: $500-$700) .$220.00

Yellow Taxicab, Turner, friction, 9", EX, A (Est: $350.00 – $450.00), $330.00. (Photo courtesy Bertoia Auctions)

Zephyr Towing Camper Trailer, Kingsbury, gr, BRT, 23", VG, A (Est: $250-$300)..$275.00

CONSTRUCTION

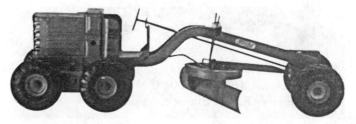

Adams Road Grader, 26", VG, A (Est: $150.00 – $200.00), $165.00. (Photo courtesy Noel Barrett Antiques and Auctions, Ltd.)

Barber-Greene Bucket Loader, Doepke, 1950s, 17½", MIB, A (Est: $300-$400)..$715.00

Barber-Greene Loader & Conveyor, Doepke, 1950s, 23", EX, A (Est: $150-$200)..$385.00

Barber-Greene Loader & Conveyor, Doepke, 1950s, 23", G, A (Est: $75-$125)..$100.00

Cement Mixer, Doepke, Jaeger style, 14", VG, A (Est: $200-$300).....................$265.00

Derrick, Kiddie Toy, 20", G, A (Est: $100-$200)...........$190.00

Derrick, Tri-Ang, 1930s, derrick atop 4-footed stand, 36", VG, A (Est: $100-$200)......................$520.00

Emmets No 50 Concrete Truck, 20", VG+, A (Est: $800.00 – $1,200.00), $1,150.00. (Photo courtesy Randy Inman Auctions)

Euclid, Doepke, 27", Fair, A (Est: $50-$75).....................$25.00

Heiliner Earth Mover, Doepke, BRT, 30", VG, A (Est: $200-$300)......................$185.00

Kingsbury Motor-Driven Tractor, w/up, on/off lever, gr w/red wheels, metal treads, 8", EX (Est: $200-$300).........$400.00

Lorain Steam Shovel, Reuhl, very detailed, 14", G, A (Est: $200-$400).......................$385.00

Marion Steam Shovel Truck (Little Jim), Steelcraft/J.C. Penney, 28", G+, A (Est: $1,500.00 – $2,000.00), $1,200.00. (Photo courtesy Randy Inman Auctions)

Payloader, Ny-Lint, 1950s, rubber treads, 17", G+, A (Est: $50-$75).......................$120.00

Payloader, Ny-Lint, 1960s, 4-wheeled, 17", EX (w/orig tag), A (Est: $75-$125).......................$165.00

Payloader, Ny-Lint, 1960s, 4-wheeled, 17", VG, A (Est: $50-$100).......................$75.00

Steam Shovel, Turner, 1930s, 4-wheeled platform, 15" (shovel not extended), G, A (Est: $50-$75).......................$55.00

Telescoping Crane, Ny-Lint, 1950s, boom mk Austin Western, red & yel, 4-wheeled, 22", G, A (Est: $75 to $125)...$45.00

Travel Loader, Ny-Lint, 1960s, orange, 28", EX+IB, A (Est: $150-$250).......................$300.00

Woolridge Bottom Dump, Doepke, 1950s, 26", G, A (Est: $150-$200).......................$130.00

FIREFIGHTING

Aerial Ladder Truck, Doepke, 1950s, open cab, red w/aluminum ladders, BRT, 4-wheeled, 34", EX, A (Est: $150-$200).......................$200.00

Aerial Ladder Truck, Kingsbury, motor-driven version, open bench seat, 35", Fair+, A (Est: $600-$800)..........$1,265.00

Aerial Ladder Truck, Kingsbury, 1920s, open seat & frame, running boards, red, WRT, 35", G, A (Est: $1,200-$1,500).......................$1,650.00

Aerial Ladder Truck, Kingsbury, 1930s, Airflow, open, w/driver, automatic ladders, 4-wheeled, 24", G, A (Est: $100-$200).......................$150.00

City Fire Dept. Hose and Ladder Truck, Steelcraft, 27", VG, A (Est: $1,750.00 – $2,250.00), $1,800.00. (Photo courtesy James D. Julia, Inc.)

Fire Chief Car, Girard, w/up, b/o headlights, BRT, red w/side decals, 14", EXIB, A (Est: $350-$500).....................$715.00

Fire Chief Car, Hoge, w/up, b/o headlights, rear spare, red & blk, 14", EX, A (Est: $500-$700).......................$600.00

Fire Chief Car, Hoge, w/up, b/o lights, red & blk, 14½", EX, A (Est: $400).......................$500.00

Fire Chief Coupe #243, Kingsbury, w/up, b/o lights, red, WRT (rpl), 12", G, A (Est: $200-$300)...........................$465.00

Little Jim Pumper Truck, 20", VG, A (Est: $400.00 – $500.00), $300.00. (Photo courtesy Bertoia Auctions)

Ladder Truck, Dayton, friction, open bench seat w/driver, MDW, w/ladders, 18", VG, A ($150-$250) $485.00

Ladder Truck, Dayton, friction, open seat w/flat grille front, cut-out sides, MSW, 3 ladders, 20", G, A (Est: $150-$250) $165.00

Ladder Truck, w/up, open frame & seat w/CI driver, MDW, wht w/red wooden ladders & hubs, 19", VG, A (Est: $400-$500) $275.00

Ladder Truck, Wilkens, open frame w/4 spoke wheels, tin driver, bump action causes ladders to rise, 18½", G, A.......$200.00

Pumper Truck, Dayton, 1920s, friction, open cab w/driver, red, gold pumper, MDW, 4-wheeled, 8½", G, A (Est: $75-$125) ..$230.00

Pumper Truck, Kingsbury, w/up, open-framed w/driver at center steering wheel, MSW, 4-wheeled, VG, A (Est: $175-$225)..$385.00

Pumper Truck (Aherns-Fox), Turner, open bench seat, yel & red, yel hubs, 16", G, A (Est: $300-$500) $990.00

Rossmoyne Fire Truck, Doepke, 1940s, open cab w/windshield, 4-wheeled, 19", incomplete o/w VG, A (Est: $75-$125)...$140.00

Water Tower Truck, Sturditoy, 33", EX, A (Est: $2,200.00 – $2,500.00), $5,290.00. (Photo courtesy James D. Julia, Inc.)

TROLLEYS AND BUSSES

Bus, Cor-Cor, 1930s, long nose, cut-out windows, front fenders, gr, red hubs, MDW, 4-wheeled, 24", G, A (Est: $200-$300) $300.00

Bus #788, Kingsbury, w/up, bl & blk w/orange stripe, WRT, red hubs, 16", Fair+, A (Est: $300-$500) $440.00

Double-Decker Bus, Tri-Ang, 1940s, 93...Epsom Stn, red, BRT, 4-wheeled, 23", G+, A (Est: $150-$150) $275.00

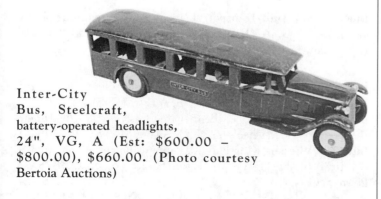

Inter-City Bus, Steelcraft, battery-operated headlights, 24", VG, A (Est: $600.00 – $800.00), $660.00. (Photo courtesy Bertoia Auctions)

Inter-City Bus, Steelcraft, luggage rack on top, spare tires on ea side, bl w/red hubs, BRT, 24", G, A (Est: $600-$800).$500.00

New York-San Francisco Bus, streamline style, NP grille, BRT, 21", VG, A (Est: $200-$300) $430.00

TRUCKS AND VANS

Acme Markets Semi, bl & wht cab w/logos on silver van body, 14-wheeled, 25", EXIB, A (Est: $250-$350) $520.00

American Railway Express, Sturditoy, van roof extends over open seat, blk, gr & red, 26", rstr, A (Est: $1,000-$1,200)..$825.00

Armored Truck, Sturditoy, 1920s, roof extends over open cab, red w/red hubs, 24", old rpt, A (Est: $800-$1,200) $1,650.00

Auto Transport, Dunwell, 1950s, red cab, gr trailer w/cutouts on sides, open back, 26", no cars, VG, A (Est: $150-$250)............$185.00

Auto Transport, Lincoln, 1940s, red cab w/gray trailer, 6-wheeled, 24", no ramp or accessories o/w VG, A (Est: $75-$125)..$245.00

Bloomingdale's Delivery Van, Steelcraft, roof extends over open cab, b/o lights, gr, BRT, G+, A (Est: $800-$1,200).$2,970.00

Bronco w/Safari Animal Trailer, Ny-Lint, 1960s, gr w/wht top, WWT, chrome hubs, w/3 animals, 23", EX, A (Est: $125-$150)..$65.00

Buckeye Livestock Transport Truck, 1950s, red, 23", VG+, A (Est: $200-$300) $150.00

Buckeye Pickup Truck, bl w/NP grille w/emb name, opening tailgate, BRT, 13", EX, A (Est: $200-$250)...................$275.00

Bull Dog Mack Dump Truck, Toledo, front crank, 27", VG, A (Est: $2,500.00 – $3,500.00), $2,300.00. (Photo courtesy James D. Julia, Inc.)

Cannon Truck, Kingsbury, 1940s, w/up, olive w/chrome headlights & grille, 4-wheeled, 16", G, A (Est: $50-$100).$60.00

City Tank Lines Truck, Steelcraft, 26", restored, A (Est: $800.00 – $1,200.00), $880.00. (Photo courtesy Randy Inman Auctions)

Cannon Truck, Ny-Lint, 1960s, olive w/yel trim & wht stars on doors, 4-wheeled, 23", incomplete, G, A (Est: $25-$50).**$55.00**

Cement Mixer Truck, SSS, opening doors, red & yel w/steel bl drum, yel hubs, 6-wheeled, 19", VG, A (Est: $300-$400)........**$275.00**

City Trucking Co Dump Truck, Steelcraft, 1940s, red & wht w/Deco styling, 4-wheeled, 21", Fair, A (Est: $75-$125)...........**$330.00**

Coal Truck, Sturditoy, high dump bed w/dividers, doorless cab, orange, red hubs, rstr, 24", G, A (Est: $700-$900) .**$1,100.00**

Coal Truck, Sturditoy, side-dump, no-headlights version, 25", VG, A (Est: $1,800.00 – $2,200.00), $3,190.00. (Photo courtesy Noel Barrett Antiques and Auctions, Ltd.)

Coast To Coast Delivery, Truck, Holland, 1950s, flat-top cabover w/flat-top van, 4-wheeled, 20", G, A (Est: $75-$100)......................................**$110.00**

Delivery Truck, Dayton, 1920s, friction, doorless cab, MSW, Carlysle Drygoods emb on sides, 12", VG, A (Est: $300-$500)......................................**$575.00**

Delivery Truck, Turner, 1940s, tan & blk cab, red bed w/railed sides, open back, 4-wheeled, 20", rst, A (Est: $75-$125) **$150.00**

Drink Smile Stake Truck, Metalcraft, red, BRT, 12", G, A (Est: $150-$200) **$355.00**

Dump Truck, Cor-Cor, 1930s, beveled bed, gr & blk w/chrome bumper/grille, red hubs, 4-wheeled, 24", P, A (Est: $50-$75)...**$140.00**

Dump Truck, Cor-Cor, 1930s, straight-sided bed, gr & blk w/red lights & hubs, 4-wheeled, 24", old rpt, A (Est: $75-$125)......................................**$300.00**

Dump Truck, Dayton, 1920s, friction, MDW, side crank, blk w/yel hubs, 19", nonworking, older rpt, A (Est: $75-$125)...**$165.00**

Dump Truck, Holland, 1950s, flat-top cabover w/dump bed even w/cab top, gr & yel, 4-wheeled, 20", G, A (Est: $75-$100) **$80.00**

Dump Truck, Kingsbury, w/up, blk & orange, BRT w/orange hubs, 11", VG, A (Est: $150-$200)......................**$385.00**

Dump Truck, Roberts, 1960s, yel w/red front scoop, 18", EXIB, A (Est: $100-$200)......................................**$200.00**

Dump Truck, SSS, red long-nosed cab w/yel dump bed, yel hubs, 6-wheeled, 23", EX, A (Est: $350-$450)..................**$385.00**

Dump Truck, Sturditoy, 1920s, doorless cab, blk & gr w/red hubs, MDW, 4-wheeled, 27", VG, A (Est: $1,200-$1,500).**$1,375.00**

Dump Truck, Turner, 1920s, enclosed Mack cab, red & gr, red hubs, 6-wheeled, 27", P, A (Est: $100-$200) **$175.00**

Dump Truck, Turner, 1930s, enclosed cab, yel & gr cab w/red dump bed, 6-wheeled, 27", rstr, A (Est: $150-$200).**$100.00**

Dump Truck, Turner, 1930s, Mack cab, dump bed w/side crank, gr & red, 4-wheeled, 23", Fair, A (Est: $75-$125) ...**$220.00**

Dump Truck, Turner, 1940s, red w/gr bed, NP dome hubs, 6-wheeled, 27", no tailgate, older rpt, A (Est: $75-$125).**$75.00**

Dunwell Dump Truck, Metal Prod, side lever dumping action, red cab w/gr bed, rear duals, 13", EX, A (Est: $200-$300)......................................**$245.00**

Flatbed Tractor-Trailer, Tri-Ang, 1950s, red & wht die-cast cab w/turq trailer, 6-wheeled, 24", G+, A (Est: $50-$100).**$190.00**

Ford Truck & Trailer w/Race Car, Ny-Lint, 1960s, red & wht truck w/red plastic racer, WWT, 21", G (Est: $75-$125).......**$165.00**

Grain Hauler, SSS, hydraulic dump action, 6-wheeled, side mirrors, opening doors, red & orange, 23", EX, A (Est: $600)......................................**$600.00**

Heavy Machinery Service Truck, 1950s, gr & wht, BRT, 6-wheeled, 20", VG+, A (Est: $150-$200).................**$120.00**

Heinz Delivery Truck, Metalcraft, b/o headlights, wht w/advertising on sides, BRT, 12", G, A (Est: $200-$300) **$300.00**

Heinz Delivery Truck, Metalcraft, b/o headlights, wht w/advertising on sides, BRT, 12", VG+, A (Est: $400-$700) **$850.00**

Hi-Way Emergency Unit, 1960s, red & wht Ford truck w/red boom, WWT, 4-wheeled, 16", G, A (Est: $50-$100)..**$65.00**

International Dump Truck, SSS, friction, enclosed cab, spring-activated bed, BRT, 23", EX+, A (Est: $600-$800) .**$935.00**

Kroger Food Express Delivery Truck, Metalcraft, orange box van, MDW, emb grille, 12", Fair, A (Est: $150-$250) **$190.00**

Lincoln Auto Transport, Canada, 1-tiered w/2 PS autos, 6-wheeled, 24", VG, A (Est: $150-$250)..................**$1,100.00**

Lincoln Toys Auto Transport, Canada, two-tiered, four plastic cars, 25", VG, A (Est: $300.00 – $400.00), $1,100.00. (Photo courtesy Bertoia Auctions)

Lincoln Van Lines Semi, 1940s, bl cab, lt bl trailer w/yel & red advertising, 14-wheeled, 23", G, A (Est: $75-$125).**$165.00**

Little Jim Mack Truck, JC Penney, red C-style cab w/blk frame body, BRT, red wheels, 22", VG, A (Est: $150-$200).**$245.00**

Little Jim/Wrecker, Kingsbury/JC Penney, lime gr, orange rubber tires & hubs, 11", G+, A (Est: $150-200) **$875.00**

Lowney's Chocolate Bars Semi, Lincoln, red 1940s or 1950s cab w/gr trailer, yel lettering, 24", VG+, A (Est: $200-$300).....**$1,650.00**

Metalcraft Delivery Truck, early blk cab w/name stenciled on lt gr box van, MDW, 12", VG, A (Est: $200-$300) **$300.00**

Milk Truck, Tri-Ang, 1950s, wht w/bl flat bed, Tri-Ang decal on door, BRT, 14", no accessories o/w VG+, A (Est: $50-$75) **$30.00**

Mobile Home, see Truck Pulling Mobile Home

Motor Driven (Stake) Truck, Kingsbury, early blk cab w/red stake bed, wht wheels, 25", Fair+, A ($800-$1,200)........**$1,650.00**

Parcel Delivery (Divco) Truck, Kingsbury, w/up, open side doors, orange, orig decal, BRT, 9", G+, A (Est: $150-$200)..**$330.00**

Pickup Truck #359, Kingsbury, w/up, blk, WRT w/orange hubs, scarce, 14", G, A (Est: $800-$1,200) **$1,100.00**

Pure Oil Co Tank Truck, Metalcraft, b/o headlights, bl w/wht stenciling, BRT, 15", G, A (Est: $500-$700) **$355.00**

Railway Express Truck, Steelcraft, 1920s, roof extends over open cab, screened sides, 25", Fair, A (Est: $600-$800) ...**$935.00**

Rossmoyne Searchlight Truck, Doepke, 1950s, open cab, rear platform, wht, BRT, 4-wheeled, 19", VG, A (Est: $600-$800)..**$520.00**

Sand & Gravel Truck, Slik-Toy, red aluminum cab w/gr PS beveled dump bed, BRT, 10-wheeled, 13", EX, A (Est: $50-$100)..**$135.00**

Sealtest Milk Rider Truck, Roberts Co, gray w/red decals, frame & top steering wheel, 22", EX+IB, A (Est: $400-$600) ..**$880.00**

Sedan, friction, vehicle w/straight back & flat roof, running boards, MDW, red & wht, driver, 11", G, A (Est: $150-$175)..**$165.00**

Shell Motor Oil Stake Truck, Metalcraft, red & yel, BRT, 5 barrels, 12½", G, A (Est: $300-$400) **$410.00**

Shell Motor Oil Stake Truck, Metalcraft, red & yel, BRT, 8 barrels, 12½", VG, A (Est: $500-$750) **$770.00**

Son-ny USA 1120 Cannon Truck, Dayton, 1920s, open bench seat, MDW, 23", G, A (Est: $200-$300) **$440.00**

Speed Boy Delivery Cycle, 1930s, no lights, 10", EX, A..**$440.00**

Stake Truck, Ny-Lint, 1960s, red & wht, oval farm decal on door, WWT, 4-wheeled, 14", EX, A (Est: $50-$100)..........**$150.00**

Steel Carrier Co Hauler, Dunwell, 1950s, red cab w/gr open bed, 14-wheeled, 23", EX, A (Est: $125-$150)................**$220.00**

Stix Baer & Fuller Toy Dept Delivery Truck, van roof extends over open seat, MSW, red & wht, 14", F, A (Est: $200-$300)..**$245.00**

Sunshine Biscuits Delivery Truck, Metalcraft, yel w/red lettering on box van, BRT, 12", G, A (Est: $250-$300).........**$330.00**

Tanker Truck, Am National, 1920s version, doorless cab w/oval cutouts, red & blk, BRT, 28", rstr, A (Est: $1,000-$1,200)..**$1,375.00**

Tank Department Tanker Truck, Kelmet, 1920s, 27", restored, A (Est: $1,200.00 – $1,500.00), $1,650.00. (Photo courtesy Randy Inaman Auctions)

Tanker Truck, Sturditoy, 1920s, doorless cab, tank on trailer, red w/BRT, 10-wheeled, 33", VG, A ($4,000-$6,000) .**$8,250.00**

Telephone Service Truck, Lincoln, snub-nosed cab, gr w/yel ladder, BRT, 12", EXIB, A (Est: $200-$300).................**$520.00**

Tow Truck, Lincoln, 1950s, covered wheel wells, Dunlop Tires decal on bed, red, 4-wheeled, 14", VG, A (Est: $75-$125) **$300.00**

Traveling Store Truck, Sturditoy, 1920s, roof extends over open seat, 4-wheeled, 26", old rpt, A (Est: $300-$500)....**$575.00**

Tru-Scale Dump Truck, 1950s, BRT, 10-wheeled, 12", Fair, A (Est: $75-$125) **$130.00**

Tru-Scale Pickup Truck, 1960s, bl & cream cab, cream bed w/bl fenders, WWT, 12", some rpt, A (Est: $25-$50)........**$55.00**

Truck Pulling Mobile Home, Ny-Lint, 1960s, no accessories, 29", G, A (Est: $50-$75)..**$65.00**

Truck Pulling Mobile Home, Ny-Lint, 1960s, complete with plastic furniture, 29" overall, EXIB, A (Est: $200.00 – $300.00), $360.00. (Photo courtesy Randy Inman Auctions)

Truck w/Horse Van, Ny-Lint, 1960s, metallic gold & wht, 23", EXIB, A (Est: $125-$175) **$220.00**

U-Haul Pickup Truck & Trailer, Ny-Lint, 1960s, 21", VG, A (Est: $75-$125) **$75.00**

Uranium Hauler, Ny-Lint, olive gr w/yel trim, lg tread tires, 23", VG, A (Est: $200-$250) **$75.00**

US Mail Truck, Kingsbury, w/up, van roof extends over open seat, MSW, driver at center wheel, 7", G, A (Est: $400-$500)..**$355.00**

US Mail Truck, Oh-Boy, 1920s, screened van roof extends over open cab, doors open, NPDW, 22", VG, A (Est: $500-$800)..**$650.00**

US Mail Truck, Scheible, van roof extends over open seat, 6 MSW, emb oval on sides, 11½", G, A (Est: $150-$250)........**$135.00**

US Mail Truck, Sturditoy, 1920s, roof extends over open cab, screened sides, gr w/red hubs, 26", G, A (Est: $400-$600) **$740.00**

Weston's English-Quality Biscuits Delivery Truck, Metalcraft, BRT, red & yel, 12", G, A (Est: $150-$200) **$255.00**

Wrecker, see Tow Truck and other specific names

Pull and Push Toys

Pull and push toys from the 1800s often were hide- and cloth-covered animals with glass or shoe-button eyes on wheels or wheeled platforms. Many were also made of tin or wood. The cast-iron bell toys of that era can be found in the Cast Iron category under Bell Toys.

See also Character, TV, and Movie Collectibles; Disney; Fisher-Price.

American Milk Co Milk Wagon, horse on 4-wheeled platform, wooden wagon, 24", VG, A (Est: $350-$450) **$770.00**

Bear on All Fours, brn stuffed plush w/wht snout & neck, metal rod base w/4 wheels, 23" L, VG, A (Est: $150-$200)..**$55.00**

Bear on Wheels, brown mohair covered papier-maché with glass eyes, muzzle, and growler, 10½", EX, A (Est: $200.00 – $300.00), $400.00. (Photo courtesy Noel Barrett Antiques and Auctions, Ltd.)

Borden's Milk Wagon, Rich Toys, pnt wood w/stenciled detail, disk wheels, horse-drawn, 10" L, EX, A (Est: $100-$150).................**$935.00**

Borden's Milk Wagon, Rich Toys, pnt wood w/stenciled detail, disk wheels, horse-drawn, 29", VG, A (Est: $500-$650)....**$385.00**

Boy in Boat on Wheeled Platform, boy w/bsk head & cloth outfit in wood boat w/oars, 12" L, EX, A (Est: $1,500-$2,000)..**$3,025.00**

Boy Riding Clown's Back on Platform, articulated, wood platform & wheels, cloth outfits, 9", VG, A (Est: $500-$700)..**$275.00**

Boy Traveler on Four-Wheeled Cart, stuffed body w/papier-maché head, w/suitcases, wood cart, 12", G, A (Est: $150-$250).................**$110.00**

Circus Band Wagon, Converse, tin w/circus band scene lithoed on sides, 2 horses, 18", VG, A (Est: $125-$175)......**$500.00**

Circus Cage Wagon, Arcade, red-pnt wood cage body w/gold tin bars, CI driver/2 horses, MSW, 14", EX, A (Est: $600-$800).................**$465.00**

Clown Seated w/Bells on Box Platform, Germany, pnt compo w/cloth outfit, wood platform, 7½", EX, A (Est: $600-$800).................**$500.00**

Covered Cart, Francis Field, 1850s, tin, wheeled horse pulls 2-wheeled cart, 7", Fair, A (Est: $250-$350)..............**$515.00**

Covered Wagon, tin & wood wagon w/canvas top, paper litho-on-wood horses, 19", EX, A (Est: $200-$300) **$250.00**

Cow on Platform, leather hide, glass eyes, wooden hooves, wood platform w/4 sm spoke wheels, 11", G, A (Est: $150-$250).................**$190.00**

Dog Carrying Pail w/Bell on Back on 4-Wheeled Platform, pnt tin, brn, gold & gr, 5½" L, G, A (Est: $150-$250) ..**$135.00**

Dolls on Wheeled Musical Box Platform, 6 fully clothed bsk-head dolls, string pull, 9x13", EX, A (Est: $1,000-$1,200)..**$1,430.00**

Elephant on Wheels, compo, nodding head, dk gray, 8" L, Fair, A (Est: $50-75) **$75.00**

Elephant Performing Tricks on Barrel on Wheeled Platform w/Bell, 8", G, A (Est: $200-$400) **$300.00**

Elephant Pulling Circus Wagon, Courtland, litho tin, 12" L, EX, A (Est: $50-$100)..**$120.00**

Elephant-Drawn Carriage, Fallows, pnt tin, ornate high-back carriage w/4 sm spoke wheels, 11", VG, A (Est: $800-$1,000)..**$715.00**

Elephants (Mother & Baby) on Wheeled Platform Bell Toy, Fallows, pnt tin w/wood platform, 6" L, VG, A (Est: $800-$1,000)..**$660.00**

Express Wagon, American, Express emb on sides, 4 sm spoke wheels, horse-drawn, 12½", VG, A (Est: $300-$400)..**$220.00**

Girl & Butterfly in Two-Wheeled Platform, compo figure w/cloth dress, tin butterfly, 8", EX, A (Est: $400-$600)..........**$770.00**

Hillside Farm Wagon, 24", VG, A (Est: $150-$200) **$330.00**

Horse (2) on Two Spoke Wheels (Le Petit Postillon), France, 1880s, compo horses gallop on rod when pulled, 13", EXIB, A..**$1,650.00**

Horse & Jockey on Platform, pnt tin, 4 sm spoke wheels, 10" L, G, A (Est: $300-$500)...............................**$770.00**

Horse & Rider on 4-Wheeled Platform, Stevens & Brown, 1870s, pnt tin, spoke wheels, 7" L, G, A (Est: $350-$450)...**$220.00**

Horse on Wheeled Platform, cloth-covered, wood legs, horse hair mane/tale, wood platform, 4 sm MSW, 12", VG, A (Est: $250-$300) **$220.00**

Horse on Wheeled Platform, Geo Brown, tin, wht w/red-pnt blanket & yel-pnt saddle, gr platform, 9", G, A ($250-$350) **$245.00**

Horse on Wheeled Platform, pnt tin, brn w/red saddle, gr platform, spoke wheels, 4", VG, A (Est: $150-$200).....**$110.00**

Horse on Wheels, wht plush w/brn spots, wht rubber wheels w/red hubs, hdl on back of neck, 23" L, VG, A (Est: $100-$150)..**$190.00**

Horse w/Black Jockey on 4-Wheeled Platform, pnt tin, horse & jockey rock back & forth, 5" T, G, A (Est: $150-$300) **$450.00**

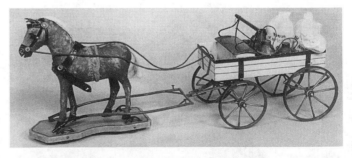

Horse-Drawn Supply Wagon, Marklin, hide-covered horse on wooden platform pulling painted tin wagon with supplies, 22", EX+, A (Est: $2,000.00 – $2,500.00), $2,640.00. (Photo courtesy Bertoia Auctions)

Horse-Drawn Cart, Geo Brown (?), pnt tin, trotting horse pulls 2-wheeled arched covered cart, 8", G, A (Est: $150-$300)..$100.00

Horse-Drawn Cart, Hull & Stafford, pnt tin, 2-wheeled cart w/3 straight sides & open seat, 11", G, A (Est: $150-$250).$77.00

Horse-Drawn Cart, USA, pnt tin, trotting horse pulls cart w/roof & open sides, 2 sm wheels, 13", G, A (Est: $150-$300) $90.00

Horse-Drawn Stake Cart, Hull & Stafford, pnt tin, 2-wheeled cart w/open ends, 10¾", VG, A (Est: $250-$350)...$245.00

Horse-Drawn Trolley, Hull & Stafford, pnt tin, 2 horses & 4-wheeled trolley w/driver, 12", EX, A (Est: $2,500-$3,500) $6,325.00

Horse-Drawn Wagon, Hull & Stafford, 4-wheeled wagon w/ornate cut-out sides, 8", VG, A (Est: $150-$250).$165.00

Jester on 2-Part Duck w/Bells on Each Side, 2 plain wire wheels, 4", G, A (Est: $50-$100) $200.00

Man on Trike, France, cloth w/pnt compo head & wood legs on wire-framed cycle, spoke wheels, 7", EX+, A (Est: $500-$700)..$715.00

Milk Wagon, open w/tin barrels, spoke wheels, felt-covered horse on wheels, 7", G+, A (Est: $200-$400) $175.00

Monkey as Parade Leader on Frog's Back on 4-Wheeled Platform, papier-maché & wood, 5½" L, G, A (Est: $125-$250)..$1,035.00

Nanny w/Baby on Wheeled Platform, fully dressed bsk head dolls on wood platform w/MSW, 14" T, EX, A (Est: $500-$700)..$880.00

Noah's Ark Deluxe, Milton Bradley-Bumpa Toys, pressed wood ark w/removable roof, 32 wood animals, 12", NMIB (Est: $100)..$150.00

Plantation Cart, Wilkens, PS V-shaped cart w/2 CI spoke wheels, w/driver & horse, 13", VG, A (Est: $250-$350) $385.00

Rich's Milk Wagon, Rich Toys, tin wagon w/wood roof & wheels, rear door opens, 19", EX, A (Est: $150-$200)...........$165.00

Ringling Bros Circus Wagon, pnt & stamped wood, w/team of horse, wagon & animals, 37" overall, G+, A (Est: $100-$200)..$60.00

Sheep on Platform, Germany, wool body w/papier-maché face, wood platform, 4 MSW, 13" L, EX, A (Est: $1,500-$2,000)..$1,950.00

Sheep on Platform, pnt tin, wht sheep on gr platform w/4 spoke wheels, 11½" L, VG, A (Est: $400-$500) $385.00

Sheffield Farms Delivery Wagon, wood w/stenciled detail, 5 bottles in case, 21", EX, A (Est: $250-$350) $330.00

Tractor, Hubley, composition tractor w/BRT, driver w/CI head, 5½", NMIB (Tractor Pull-Toy on box), A (Est: $300-$400) ..$190.00

Train Lococmotive (Puck) w/Tender, Flatbed & Blue Line Box Car, Ives, tin, 7", VG, A (Est: $800-$1,000) $2,090.00

Train Locomotive (America), Fallows, tin, mk A-1 on boiler, 11", VG, A (Est: $200-$250) $330.00

Train Locomotive (Dexter), Fallows, pnt & stenciled tin w/CI heart-shaped spoke wheels, 8", EX, A (Est: $700-$800) $330.00

Train Locomotive (Union), A Bergman, 1870s, pnt/stenciled tin w/CI heart spoke wheels, 12", EX, A (Est: $2,000-$2,500)...$2,475.00

Train Locomotive & 2 Passenger Cars, Fallows, tin, integral tender, sm spoke wheels, 20", VG, A (Est: $200-$300).$275.00

US Express Wagon, litho tin, horse w/articulated legs, 14", VG, A (Est: $200-$300)..$465.00

US Mail Train, Fallows, 1880s, tin, 22" overall, EX+, $3,000.00.

Yankee Notions Wagon, Geo Brown, 1880s, pnt tin, 2 horses pull stenciled wagon, 11" L, G, A (Est: $500-$750) $920.00

Puzzles

Jigsaw puzzles have been around almost as long as games. The first examples were handcrafted from wood, and they are extremely difficult to find. Most of the early examples featured moral subjects and offered insight into the social atmosphere of their time. By the 1900s jigsaw puzzles had become a major form of home entertainment. Cube puzzles or blocks were often made by the same companies as board games. Early examples display lithography of the finest quality. While all subjects are collectible, some (such as Santa blocks) often command prices higher than games of the same period.

Because TV and personality-related puzzles have become so popular, they're now regarded as a field all their own apart from character collectibles in general, and these are listed here as well, under the subtitle 'Character.'

Note: All puzzles are complete unless indicated otherwise.

Advisor: Bob Armstrong (A4), non-character related

See also Advertising; Barbie; Black Americana; California Raisins; Paper-Lithographed Toys; Political; and other specific catagories.

Afternoon Tea, Parker Bros/Pastime/P Phillippi (artist), 1920s, plywood, 516 pcs, 16x19", rpl box..........................$220.00

Arriving at Grandfather's for Christmas (colonial scene), JLG Ferris (artist), 1930s, plywood, 208 pcs, 9x14", orig box.....$60.00

Autumn Along the Seine, Joseph Straus, 1930s, plywood, 300 pcs, orig box $40.00

Auvers-Sur Oise (cathedral), Jumbo International/Van Vogh (artist), 1980-90, plastic, 210 pcs, 7x7", orig box.......$15.00

Bamboo Walk (Asian farm scene), Parker Bros/Pastime, 1930s, 108 pcs, 7x10", orig box...$40.00

Beautiful Garden of Dreams (idyllic/women), Madmar Quality Co/Interlox, 1930s, plywood, 250 pcs, 10x13", orig box .$65.00

Blooms & Blossoms (house & garden), 1930s, pressed board, 1930s, 505 pcs, 18x26", rpl box...............................$150.00

Buffeting the Billows (clipper ships), Milton Bradley/Premier, 1930s, plywood, 158 pcs, 9x12", orig box...................$50.00

Camping (night stream), Austin McKay (maker)/Maple Leaf, 1930s, plywood, 76 pcs, 5x7", orig box......................$15.00

Cattle in Pasture (farming), Julien Dupre (artist), 1930s, plywood, 188 pcs, 10x14", rpl box...............................$45.00

Celestial Glories (thatched cottage), Milton Bradley/Mayfair Jig, 1930s, cb, 200 pcs, 11x15", orig box.........................$14.00

Cenotaph (early 20th century London street scene), Chad Valley, 1930s, 200 pcs, 10x14", orig box $40.00

Church/Stark Village, NH (winter), Roland Chesley, 1950s, plywood, 269 pcs, 10x14", orig box $50.00

Colonial Picture (Washington & colonists), Percy Morgan (?), 1910-20, wood, 380 pcs, 11x15", rpl box $120.00

Cromwell at the Blue Boar (historical), 1930s, J Salmon/Acadamy (maker), 1930s, plywood, 300 pcs, orig box $50.00

Dairy Pride (cow in pasture), Pulver Novelty Co/Idle-Hour, 1930s, plywood, 301 pcs, 12x18", orig box.................$60.00

David Copperfield Bids Farewell, Parker Bros/Pastime/Ludovici (artist), plywood, 362 pcs, 12x20", rpl box $175.00

Deer in Mountain Valley, Edward Leggett Clark (maker), 1930s, plywood, 850 pcs, 16x22", orig box.........................$250.00

Departure (medieval/scenery), Spear/Hayter/Victory Artist, plywood, 1500 pcs, 23½x36½", orig box $260.00

Derby Day (19th century scene w/many figures), Tuck/Zag-Zaw/BP Smith (artist), 1930s, plywood, 211 pcs, 7x15", orig box $70.00

Dessert of Fruit, Louise Scribner/Currier & Ives, plywood, 246 pcs, 8½x12", orig box $60.00

Fire Engine Picture Puzzle, McLoughlin Bros, 1887, EXIB, A, $400.00. (Photo courtesy David Longest)

George Washington's Ancestral Home (garden), Lloyd Clift/Miloy, 1930s, plywood, 607 pcs, 16x20", orig box $175.00

Girl From Arizona, Louise Scribnerm 1950-60, plywood, 193 pcs, 7x12", orig box...$50.00

Gleaners (farming scene), Jean Francois Millet (artist), cb, 325 pcs, 12x16", orig box...$10.00

Grosvenor Hunt-1763 (fox hunt), Mrs Enid Leisure Stockton, 1930s, plywood, 495 pcs, 10½x15½", orig box........$200.00

Happy Family (home scene w/peasants), E Zampighi (artist), 1930s, 12x16", rpl box $105.00

High Society (stylized carriage), Par Co, 1950s, plywood, 825 pcs, 17x25", orig box $1,200.00

Household Cavalry (horses/humor), Thomson (artist), 1909, wood, 200 pcs, 12x18", orig box...............................$220.00

Hunting (fall scene w/dog & hunter), 1930s, plywood, 162 pcs, 8x10", rpl box...$35.00

In Golden Hunting Grounds (sunset/moose), Joseph Straus/Hintermeister (artist), 1930s, plywood, 300 pcs, 12x16", rpl box $35.00

In Northern Climes (fjord scene), Gruittefiem (artist ?), 1930s, plywood, 204 pcs, 10x12", orig box $40.00

In the Gloaming (countryside at sunset), Qualitee Jig-Saw Puzzles, 1930s, plywood, 334 pcs, 12x16", orig box $80.00

In the Park (WWI/horse & rider), Vallentine Sandberg (artis t), 1909, wood, 63 pcs, 5x7", orig box.....................$15.00

Indian Paradise (Indians/women), R Atkinson Fox (artist), 1930s, cb, 250 pcs, 10x13½", orig box $15.00

Invocation (Eastern women), Phyllis McLellan (maker), 1930s, plywood, 280 pcs, 10x12", orig box $75.00

Jewel Case (women), Parker Bros/Pastime, 1926, plywood, 257 pcs, 10x13", orig box $110.00

Juawles Pius (Picasso abstract), James Browning, 1960s, plywood, 1000 pcs, 24x30", orig box $375.00

King's Cavalier, Joseph Straus/Regal/Doheny (artist), 1940-50, plywood, 1000 pcs, 22x28", orig box................$200.00

Lagoon at Night (Venice), Saybold (artist), 1930s, 500 pcs, orig box $110.00

Lanterns (female pirate), Pressler (artist), 1930s, plywood, 321 pcs, 11x14", rpl box $75.00

Mallards (ducks in marsh), Joseph Straus/C Blinks (artist), 1930s, plywood, 300 pcs, 12x16", orig box.................$35.00

Mill House (cabin on lake at sunset), Will Thompson (artist), 1930-40, plywood, 550 pcs, 20x16", orig box...........$110.00

Modern Travel Series Picture Puzzles, Milton Bradley, EXIB, A $165.00

Moonlight Beams (harbor scene), JM Hayes (maker), 1940s, plywood, 540 pcs, 14x18", orig box $110.00

Moses in the Bullrushes, Parker Bros/Pastime/Relyea (artist), 1920s, plywood, 354 pcs, 12x16½", rpl box $150.00

Mountain Lake, Spear/Hayter/Victory Artistic, 1970s, plywood, 800 pcs, orig box $130.00

Mountain Lodge (winter), Jig-Jig/Will Thompson (artist), 1930s, cb, 165 pcs, 8½x12", orig box.................................$10.00

Mountain Train, Parker Bros/Kohler's Puzzles, 1930s, plywood, 412 pcs, 16x19", orig box $150.00

My Garden Is a Glory, Joseph Straus, plywood, 325 pcs, 15½" dia, orig box $50.00

Mystic Lures of the Orient (Arabian women), S Sedlacik (artist), 1930s, plywood, 666 pcs, 16x20", orig box .$120.00

News of Peace (Civil War/town), Clyde O Deland (artist), 1910s, wood, 321 pcs, 12x16", orig box $140.00

Ocean (children), Parker Bros/M Kirk (artist), 1910s, plywood, 28 pcs, 5½x7½", rpl box.......................................$20.00

Old Mill (stream), Macy's, 1930s, plywood, 200 pcs, 9x12", orig box $70.00

On the High Seas (clipper ship), James C Tyler (artist), 1940s, plywood, 358 pcs, 11x14", rpl box...........................$85.00

Oriental Traders in Venice (harbor), Milton Bradley, 1930s, plywood, 1009 pcs, orig box $330.00

Out for a Sail, Parker Bros/Pastime, 1932, plywood, 100 pcs, 7x10", orig box..$50.00

Over Field & Fence (fox hunt scene), Jewel Puzzle Co, 1930s, plywood, 134 pcs, 8x10", orig box $30.00

Over the Fence & Away (humor/boy & goose), Leisure Hour, 1909, wood, 111 pcs, 6x8", orig box $45.00

Peaceful Hours (romantic colonial courtship), Parker Bros/Pastime, 1933, plywood, 255 pcs, 10x15½", orig box ...$110.00

Peaceful Valley (family w/Christmas tree), Josep Straus/Lee (artist), 1940s, plywood, 500 pcs, 16x20", orig box ...$65.00

People's Advocate (Lincoln addressing court), Griswald Fang (artist ?), 1920s, wood, 540 pcs, 16x21", rpl box......$150.00

Pride of the Litter (18th century drawing room w/dogs), Joseph Straus, 1930s, plywood, 500 pcs, orig box $60.00

Proposal (courtship scene), Parker Bros/Pastime, 1930s, 317 pcs, 1930s, 9x17", orig box $125.00

Rounding the Capes (clipper ship), Joseph Straus, 1930s, plywood, 300 pcs, 12x16", orig box.................................$40.00

Scene in Brussels (Flemish town & river), 1930s, plywood, 240 pcs, 9x12", rpl box $85.00

Sheep Sheering & Reaping, Hayter (maker)/Victory Super-Cut, 1930s, plywood, 500 pcs, 15x19", orig box...............$125.00

Silvery Afternoon (Dutch harbor scene), Mairaux (artist?)/Ed Smith Mfg, 1930s, plywood, 150 pcs, 10x13", orig box ..$30.00

Simple Simon (humor/children), Isabel Ayer/Picture Puzzle Ex/GG Wiederseim (artist), 1909, 185 pcs, 11x13", orig box......$85.00

Sir Galahad (knight beside horse), Parker Bros/Pastime, 1910s, plywood, 162 pcs, 7x14½", orig box...........................$65.00

Squire & His Daughter (country/horse), Fred Hedger (maker)/Leigham Puzzle Club, 1930s, plywood, 203 pcs, 8x11", orig box..$65.00

Steady (setters at point), Olive Novelty, 1909, plywood, 121 pcs, 6x8", orig box...$50.00

Summer Harvest, Hayter/Victory/Artistic/Shepherd (artist), 1950s, plywood, 500 pcs, 14x20", orig box.................$80.00

Summer on the Riviera (sailing scene), Parker Bros/Pastime, G Roger (artist), 1930s, plywood, 1000 pcs, 24x35", rpl box...........$450.00

Sunday in Plymouth (Puritan courtship), JLG Ferris, 1909, wood, 161 pcs, 8x10", orig box $60.00

Sunlight in Paris, Parker Bros/Pastime, 1930s, plywood, 257 pcs, 12x15½", orig box $110.00

Sunset in Japan, Parker Bros/Pastime/Armitoka (artist), 1930s, plywood, 205 pcs, 9x12", orig box.............................$100.00

Sunshine & Shadows (countryside w/stream), Weber (artist), 1930s, plywood, 467 pcs, rpl box................................$120.00

Surprised (bears raiding tent), Saalfield, 1940s, cb, 500 pcs, orig box $12.00

Three Graces (closeup of girl by water w/swans), att to Chad Valley, 1930s, plywood, 727 pcs, 20x16", rpl box $170.00

Tranquility (scenery w/12 figures), 1930s, plywood, 210 pcs, 9x12", orig box...$40.00

Treasure Ships (galleons), Deltagram Puzzle Co/Hadlan (artist), 1930s, plywood, 100 pcs, 10x12", orig box.................$35.00

Trouble on the Trail, Tuco/Deluxe, 1940s, cb, 357 pcs, 15x19½", orig box $16.00

Union w/Scotland (historical), Hayter/Victory/Artistic, plywood, 1000 pcs, 21x22", orig box.............................$170.00

Untitled (bears raiding canoe camp), 1930s, plywood, 75 pcs, 6x9", rpl box...$12.00

Untitled (Chartres), Parker Bros/Pastime/C Eishling (artist), 1930s, plywood, 763 pcs, 21x29", rpl box $350.00

Untitled (colonial patriots), ca 1909, wood, 36 pcs, 6x8", orig box $12.00

Untitled (cowboy surprising bear family), McCallist (artist), cb, 54 pcs, 10x13", rpl box...$8.00

Untitled (dog eyeing stuffed pheasant over fireplace), 1930s, plywood, 260 pieces, 18x14", replaced box, $50.00. (Photo courtesy Bob Armstrong)

Untitled (ride 'em cowboy action scene w/5 figures), 1930s, plywood, 140 pcs, 7x9", rpl box......................................$45.00

Untitled (ships at sea), Joseph Straus, 1930s, plywood, 750 pcs, 18x23½", rpl box $85.00

Untitled (singing in church), 1909, wood, 134 pcs, 10x12", rpl box $55.00

Untitled (spanking scene), Frondeker (artist ?), 1930s, masonite, 269 pcs, 9x12", rpl box $70.00

Untitled (Starting the Walk), 1909, wood, 200 pcs, 11x20½", rpl box $75.00

Untitled (tinkering w/early auto), Jaymar/Norman Rockwell (artist), 1940s, cb, 500 pcs, 17½x17½", orig box.......$14.00

Untitled (town by stream), Norton & Curtis (maker)/Moran (artist), 1930s, plywood, 209 pcs, orig box.................$30.00

Untitled (Winter Fashions), English, 1910s, 393 pcs, 11x17", rpl box $100.00

Untitled (16th century couple), Parker Bros/Pastime, 1910s, plywood, 156 pcs, 11½x9", rpl box $60.00

Unwelcome Visitor, AVN Jones (maker)/Delta, 1930s, plywood, 375 pcs, 14x18", rpl box $60.00

Unwelcome Visitors (bears observe fishermen), Consolidated Paper Box/Perfect, cb, 250 pcs, 10x14", orig box.......$12.00

Venetian Sunset, Webers Novelty Shop/Ribowsky (artist ?), 510 pcs, 16x20", orig box $100.00

Vorarlberg Austria (winter town scene), Wester/Whitman/ Deluxe, 1940-50, cb, 500 pcs, 15½x18", orig box......$12.00

Washington & His Birthplace (1732-1932), Adelaide Hiebal (artist), 1930s, plywood, 716 pcs, 17x21", rpl box ...$200.00

Washington at Valley Forge, Joseph Straus, 1930s, plywood, 200 pcs, 9x12", orig box...$25.00

Water Gates Haarlem, (European town scene), 1928, plywood, 500 pcs, 14x2½", orig box $210.00

Welcome Guest (camp scene w/bear), Zig-Zag Puzzle Co, 1930s, plywood, 500 pcs, 16x20", orig box............................$135.00

Where 'Seconds' Mean 'Minutes' (river action), Philip R Goodwin (artist), 1910s, plywood, 11½x16", rpl box.........$35.00

White Horse Tavern, Madmar Quality Co, 1930s, plywood w/paper back, 200 pcs, rpl box.....................................$40.00

Winter Morning in the Country (sleigh scene), Louise Scribner/ Currier & Ives, 1950s, 127 pcs, 8½x12", orig box.........$25.00

York Coach (coaching scene), Victor Venner (English artist), 1909, wood, 14x24", orig box...................................$250.00

CHARACTER

Angela Cartwright — America's Little Darling on TV — The Danny Thomas Show, fr-tray, Saalfield #7030, 1962, EX...............$40.00

Aquaman, jigsaw, Whitman, 1968, Aquaman & Mera, 100 pcs, EXIB...$30.00

Archie, jigsaw, Jaymar, 1960s, malt shop scene, 60 pcs, NMIB..$75.00

Babes in Toyland, jigsaw, WDP, 1961, 70 pcs, EXIB, P6...$28.00

Batman, fr-tray, Whitman, 1966, Batman & Robin fighting the Joker, 14x11", EX+ $25.00

Captain Kangaroo, jigsaw, Fairchild #1560, 1960s, EXIB.$20.00

Captain Kangaroo, jigsaw, Fairchild #4430, 1970s, EXIB.$18.00

Charlie's Angels, jigsaw, Pro Arts, 1977, Farrah holding flower, 11x17", EXIB $18.00

Cheyenne Puzzle Set, jigsaw, Milton Bradley #4705-2, set of 3, NMIB...$50.00

Chip 'N Dale Rescue Rangers, fr-tray, Golden #4664C-14, 11x14", NM...$6.00

Dukes of Hazzard, fr-tray, 1980s, plastic, 4x4", EX $6.00

Dukes of Hazzard, jigsaw, American Publishing #1600, 1981, 200 pcs, NMIB...$15.00

Flip the Frog, jigsaw, Saalfield/Celebrity Prod, 1932, boxed set of 4, EXIB...$75.00

Gulliver's Travels, jigsaw, Saalfield, 1930s, set of 2, EXIB..$100.00

Gulliver's Travels, jigsaw, Saalfield, 1930s, set of 3, EXIB.$125.00

Hopalong Cassidy, jigsaw, Milton Bradley, 1950, 12x9", set of 3, NMIB...$75.00

Huckleberry Hound Puzzles (4), jigsaw, Milton Bradley/Hanna-Barbera, 1960, boxed set of 4, 14x10½" ea, EXIB, P6.$40.00

Jungle Book, fr-tray, Golden, 8x11", EX $5.00

Katzenjammer Kids, jigsaw, Featured Funnies, 1930s, 14x10", EXIB...$80.00

Lady & the Tramp, fr-tray, Whitman, 1954, EX+ $25.00

Lamb Chop, fr-tray, Golden #8206, 1993, 8x11", EX.........$6.00

Lindy Loonys Picture Puzzle, Lindberg, 1965, features Big Wheeler, EXIB..$50.00

Marvel Superheroes, jigsaw, Milton Bradley, 1967, 100 pcs, EXIB...$50.00

Mary Poppins, fr-tray, Jaymar, 1964, NM+ $25.00

Masters of the Universe, jigsaw, Monstrous Meeting, 1984, 100 pcs, EXIB...$8.00

Monkees Greatest Hits, jigsaw, Sunsout Inc, 500 pcs, 19x19", MIB (sealed) $15.00

My Little Pony, jigsaw, Milton Bradley #4576-10, 1989, EXIB..$8.00

Our Gang, jigsaw, Saalfield #912, set of 3, EX (G+ window box) $100.00

Peanuts, fr-tray, Milton Bradley, c 1965, Snoopy on top of doghouse w/Woodstock on toes, EXIB......................$6.00

Pink Panther, jigsaw, Whitman, 100 pcs, EXIB $25.00

Pinocchio Picture Puzzles, Whitman, 1939, set of 2, 10x8½", NMIB...$50.00

Popeye in 4 Picture Puzzles, jigsaw, Saalfield/KFS #908, few pcs missing, VGIB..$65.00

Raggedy Ann and Andy Picture Puzzles, Milton Bradley, 1944, set of three, 11x14", NMIB, $75.00.

Flipper, frame-tray, Whitman, 1965 – 1966, $20.00 each. (Photo courtesy Greg Davis and Bill Morgan)

Glo Bugs (Glo Worms), fr-tray, Playskool, 1985, images of Glo Bug & Glow Snugbug, EX+ $8.00

Goldfinger/James Bond 007, jigsaw, Milton Bradley, 1965, confrontation w/Odd Job by car, 600 pcs, NMIB.............$50.00

Rescuers, jig saw, Golden, 200 pcs, NMIB............................$6.00

Robert Louis Stevenson Puzzle Box, Saalfield #575, 1930s, 7 complete puzzles, EXIB...$65.00

Rootie (Kazootie) Wins the Soap Box Race..., fr-tray, Fairchild Corp, 1940s, 10x14", EX, P6 ....$30.00

Smokey Bear, jigsaw, Whitman #4610, 1971, 100 pcs, EXIB..$15.00

Smurfs, jigsaw, Milton Bradley, 1983, toboggan scene, EX+IB $8.50

Smurfs, jigsaw, Milton Bradley #4278-2, 1982, beach scene, NMIB..$10.00
Smurfs, jigsaw, Peyo, 1988, camping scene, EXIB..............$8.00
Smurfs, Milton Bradley #4190-5, 1987, Papa Smurf & Smurfs at table, NMIB..$10.00
Superman, fr-tray, Whitman, 1966, various scenes, EX+, ea.$30.00
Superman Saves a Life, jigsaw, Saalfield, 1940s, 500 pcs, EX+IB...$300.00
Superman the Man of Tomorrow, jigsaw, Saalfield, 1940, 300 pcs, EX+IB..$200.00
Thunderball/James Bond 007, jigsaw, Milton Bradley, 1965, over 600 pcs, NMIB...$50.00
Wizard of Oz, fr-tray, Jaymar, 1960s, NM+.......................$25.00
Wizard of Oz, fr-tray, Whitman, 1976, NM+....................$10.00
Wizard of Oz, jigsaw, Jaymar, 1970s, Departure From Oz, 19x19", EXIB..$55.00
Wizard of Oz, jigsaw, Milton Bradley, 1990, 1000 pcs, image of 1989 Norman James Co Poster, EX+IB.....................$10.00
Zorro, fr-tray, Whitman, 1957, Zorro standing by tree, 15x11½", NM..$40.00

Radios, Novelty

Many novelty radios are made to resemble a commercial product box or can, and with the crossover interest into the advertising field, some of the more collectible, even though of recent vintage, are often seen carrying very respectible price tags. Likenesses of famous personalities such as Elvis or characters like Charlie Tuna house transistors in cases made of plastic that scarcely hint at their actual function. Others represent items ranging from baseball caps to Cadillacs.

Alf, rectangular w/image on front, NMIP $75.00
Annie & Sandie, 1980s, red & wht plastic, NM, MIB $75.00
Archie, Vanity Fair/Archie Co, 1977, shaped like a jukebox, 6", M..$50.00
Batman, 1973, bust figure, NMIB....................................$35.00
Bozo the Clown, 1970s, head & shoulders form, NM, EX .$50.00
Bubo the Owl, Japan, 1981, cast metal & plastic owl form, 6½", EX..$75.00
Bugs Bunny, w/sing-along microphone, finger points to dial, AM, VG..$50.00
Bugs Bunny & Elmer Fudd, plastic, EX............................$50.00
Bullwinkle, 1969, 12", NM...$150.00
Cabbage Patch Kids, Original Appalachian Artworks, 1983, purse style, 4½", NM+..$45.00
Cap 'n Crunch, Isis, model #39, NM+ $45.00
Charlie McCarthy, Majestic, 1930s, brown Bakelite with Charlie seated in front, EX..$500.00
Charlie Tuna, 1970s, w/clamp for handlebar, AM, EX $65.00
Dick Tracy, Creative Creations, 1970s, wristband type, AM, EX...$225.00
Fonz Jukebox, AM, G..$20.00
Hopalong Cassidy, Arvin, 1950s, model #441T, electric, red steel case w/silver decals front & back, EX, A $350.00

Casper the Friendly Ghost, Harvey Cartoons/ Sutton, 1972, M, $50.00.

Hugga Bunch, Nasta/Hallmark, 1984, wristwatch shape, NM+..$20.00
Incredible Hulk, Marvel Comics, 1978, 7", M $75.00
King Kong, Amico, 1986, 13", M......................................$35.00
Lone Ranger, Airliner, 1950, white plastic with colorful molded image of Lone Ranger on Silver, red dial, NM+...$1,100.00
Masters of the Universe, mouth moves w/music, 5½", EX+..$50.00
McDonald's, metal & plastic cylinder w/speaker on top, Burger Man mascot holding sign, red & bl on wht, 1980s, 5", NM $50.00
McDonald's Big Mac, GE, sm, EX $60.00

Mighty Mouse on Cheese Wedge, Vanity Fair/Viacom International, 1978, 5", M, $150.00. (Photo courtesy Marty Bunis and Robert F. Breed)

Mork From Ork Eggship, Concept 2000, 1979, MIB........$35.00
Pac Man, w/headphones, NM..$50.00
Popeye, Hong Kong, 1960, plastic head figure, b/o, 6½", EXIB .$75.00
Poppin' Fresh, Pillsbury, w/headphones, MIB, from $60 to.$75.00
Power Rangers, Micro Games of America, 6", NM...........$25.00
Raggedy Ann and Andy, Bobbs-Merrill/Hong Kong, 1975, 8x7", NM+ $50.00
Raid Bug, 1980s, figural clock radio, NM.......................$200.00
Rambo, Talbot Toys, w/headphones, EX $40.00
R2-D2 Robot, Kenner, figural, AM, MIB.........................$150.00
Scooby Do, 1972, brn head w/gr collar & red tongue hanging out of his mouth, NM+...$30.00
Smurfs, bl & wht plastic w/image of Smurf singing, wht tuner w/blk musical note, w/belt clip, Nasta, 1982, 3x5", EX+...........$15.00
Snoopy Doghouse, Determined, 1970s, plastic, 6x4", NMIB .$55.00
Snoopy Wearing Headphones, Determined, 1970s, 3-D, MIB $150.00

Snoopy's Spaceship, Concept 2000, 1970s, EX $75.00
Snow White & the Seven Dwarfs, Emerson, 1938, 8x8", VG .$500.00
Superman Exiting Phone Booth, Vanity Fair, 1970s, b/o, AM, EX+ $50.00
Superman From Waist-Up, 1970s, transistor, EX+ $50.00
Yogi Bear, Hanna-Barbera/Markson, NM+ $125.00

Ramp Walkers

Ramp walkers date back to at least 1873 when Ives produced two versions of a cast-iron elephant walker. Wood and composition ramp walkers were made in Czechoslovakia and the U.S.A. from the 1930s through the 1950s. The most common were made by John Wilson of Pennsylvania and were sold worldwide. These became known as 'Wilson Walkies.' Most are two-legged and stand approximately 4½" tall. While some of the Wilson Walkies were made of a composite material with wood legs (for instance, Donald, Wimpy, Popeye, and Olive Oyl), most are made with cardboard thread-cone bodies with wood legs and head. The walkers made in Czechoslovakia are similar but they are generally made of wood.

Plastic ramp walkers were primarily manufactured by the Louis Marx Co. and were made from the early 1950s through the mid-1960s. The majority were produced in Hong Kong, but some were made in the United States and sold under the Marx logo or by the Charmore Co., which was a subsidiary of the Marx Co. Some walkers are still being produced today as fast-food premiums.

The three common sizes are small, about 1½" x 2"; medium, about 2¾" x 3"; and large, about 4"x 5". Most of the small walkers are unpainted while the medium or large sizes were either spray painted or painted by hand. Several of the walking toys were sold with wooden, plastic, or colorful lithographed tin ramps.

Unless another manufacturer is noted within the descriptions, all of the following Disney ramp walkers were made by the Marx company.

Advisor: Randy Welch (W4)

ADVERTISING

Captain Flint, Long John Silvers, 1989, w/plastic coin weight $15.00
Choo-Choo Cherry, Funny Face drink mix, w/plastic coin weight $60.00
Flash Turtle, Long John Silvers, 1989, w/plastic coin weight..$15.00
Goofy Grape, Funny Face drink mix, w/plastic coin weight..$60.00
Jolly Ollie Orange, Funny Face drink mix, w/plastic coin weight $60.00
Quinn Penguin, Long John Silvers, 1989, w/plastic coin weight $15.00
Root'n Toot'n Raspberry, Funny Face drink mix, w/plastic coin weight..$60.00
Sydney Dinosaur, Long John Silvers, 1989, yel & purple, w/plastic coin weight $15.00
Sylvia Dinosaur, Long John Silvers, 1989, lavender & pk, w/plastic coin weight $15.00

CZECHOSLOVAKIAN

Bird $35.00
Bird (lg, store display)..$200.00
Chicago World's Fair (1933), wood, G, T1 ....$100.00
Cow $35.00
Dog $30.00
Dutch Girl..$60.00
Man w/Carved Wood Hat..$45.00
Monkey $45.00
Pig $30.00
Policeman..$60.00

DISNEY CHARACTERS

Big Bad Wolf & Mason Pig..$50.00
Big Bad Wolf & Three Little Pigs $150.00
Donald Duck & Goofy Riding Go-Cart $40.00
Donald Duck Pulling Nephews in Wagon........................$35.00
Donald Duck Pushing Wheelbarrow, all plastic $25.00
Donald Duck Pushing Wheelbarrow, plastic w/metal legs, sm.$25.00
Donald's Trio, France, Huey, Louie & Dewey dressed as Indian Chief, cowboy & 1 carrying flowers, NMOC, A $150.00
Fiddler & Fifer Pigs $50.00
Figaro the Cat w/Ball $30.00
Goofy Riding Hippo..$45.00

Jiminy Cricket With Cello, $30.00. (Photo courtesy Randy Welch)

Mad Hatter w/March Hare $50.00
Mickey Mouse & Donald Duck Riding Alligator $40.00
Mickey Mouse & Minnie, plastic w/metal legs, sm $40.00
Mickey Mouse & Pluto Hunting $40.00
Mickey Mouse Pushing Lawn Roller $35.00
Minnie Mouse Pushing Baby Stroller $35.00
Pluto, plastic w/metal legs, sm $35.00

HANNA-BARBERA, KING FEATURES & OTHER CHARACTERS BY MARX

Astro $150.00
Astro & George Jetson $75.00
Astro & Rosey..$75.00
Bonnie Braids' Nursemaid $50.00
Chilly Willy, penguin on sled pulled by parent................$25.00

Fred & Wilma Flintstone on Dino $60.00
Fred Flinstone & Barney Rubble $40.00
Fred Flintstone on Dino...$75.00
Hap & Hop Soldiers $25.00
Little King & Guard $60.00
Pebbles on Dino $75.00
Popeye, Irwin, celluloid, lg $60.00
Popeye & Wimpy, heads on springs, MIB $85.00
Popeye Pushing Spinach Can Wheelbarrow $30.00
Santa, w/gold sack...$45.00
Santa, w/wht sack $40.00
Santa, w/yel sack $40.00
Santa & Mrs Claus, faces on both sides...........................$50.00
Santa & Snowman, faces on both sides............................$50.00
Spark Plug..$200.00
Top Cat & Benny..$65.00

Yogi Bear and Huckleberry Hound, $50.00. (Photo courtesy Randy Welch)

Marx Animals With Riders Series

Ankylosaurus w/Clown $40.00
Bison w/Native $40.00
Brontosaurus w/Monkey $40.00
Hippo w/Native..$40.00
Lion w/Clown $40.00
Stegosaurus w/Black Caveman $40.00
Triceratops w/Native..$40.00
Zebra w/Native...$40.00

Plastic (Boxes Complete With Bottles)

Baby Walk-A-Way, lg $40.00
Bear $20.00
Boy & Girl Dancing..$45.00
Bull $20.00
Bunnies Carrying Carrot..$35.00
Bunny on Back of Dog $50.00
Bunny Pushing Cart $60.00
Camel w/2 Humps, head bobs..$20.00
Chicks Carrying Easter Egg..$35.00
Chinese Men w/Duck in Basket $30.00
Chipmunks Carrying Acorns..$35.00
Chipmunks Marching Band w/Drum & Horn $35.00

Cow, w/metal legs, sm $20.00
Cowboy on Horse, w/metal legs, sm $30.00
Dachshund $20.00
Dairy Cow $20.00
Dog, Pluto look-alike w/metal legs, sm...........................$20.00
Double Walking Doll, boy behind girl, lg........................$60.00
Duck $20.00
Dutch Boy & Girl $40.00
Elephant $20.00
Elephant, w/metal legs, sm $30.00
Farmer Pushing Wheelbarrow $30.00
Firemen $35.00
Frontiersman w/Dog...$95.00
Goat $20.00
Horse, circus style $20.00
Horse, lg $30.00
Horse, yel w/rubber ears & string tail, lg $30.00
Horse w/English Rider, lg...$50.00
Kangaroo w/Baby in Pouch $30.00
Mama Duck w/3 Ducklings $35.00
Marty's Market Lady Pushing Shopping Cart...................$65.00
Mexican Cowboy on Horse, w/metal legs, sm $30.00
Milking Cow, lg $40.00
Monkeys Carrying Bananas $60.00
Mother Goose $45.00
Nursemaid Pushing Baby Stroller $20.00
Pig $20.00
Pigs, 2 carrying 1 in basket..$40.00
Reindeer $45.00

Pumpkin Head Man and Woman, faces on both sides of head, $100.00. (Photo courtesy Randy Welch)

Sailors SS Shoreleave $25.00
Sheriff Facing Outlaw $65.00
Slugger the Walking Bat Boy, w/ramp & box....................$250.00
Teeny Toddler, walking baby girl, Dolls Inc, lg $40.00
Tin Man Robot Pushing Cart $150.00
Walking Baby, in Canadian Mountie uniform, lg $50.00
Walking Baby, w/moving eyes & cloth dress, lg................$40.00
Wiz Walker Milking Cow, Charmore, lg $40.00

Wilson

Clown..$30.00
Donald Duck...$175.00

Eskimo..$100.00
Indian Chief..$70.00
Little Red Riding Hood..............................$40.00
Mammy..$40.00
Nurse...$30.00
Olive Oyl..$175.00

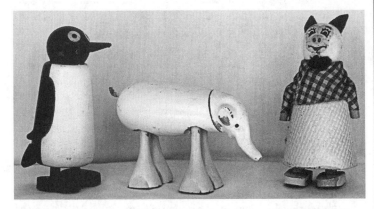

Penguin, $25.00; Elephant, $30.00; Pig, $40.00. (Photo courtesy Randy Welch)

Pinocchio..$200.00
Popeye..$200.00
Rabbit..$75.00
Sailor..$30.00
Santa Claus...$90.00
Soldier..$30.00
Wimpy...$175.00

Records

Most of the records listed here are related to TV shows and movies, and all are specifically geared toward children. The more successful the show, the more collectible the record. But condition is critical as well, and unless the record is excellent or better, its value is lowered very dramatically. The presence of the original sleeve or cover is crucial to establishing collectibility.

Advisor: Peter Muldavin (M21) 45 rpm, 78 rpm, and Kiddie Picture Disks

33⅓ RPM RECORDS

Addams Family (Original Music), RCA Victor #LPM-3421, EX (w/sleeve)......................................$75.00
Adventures of Batman & Robin, Leo/MGM, 1966, EX (w/sleeve)......................................$30.00
Adventures of the Lone Ranger, Decca, 1957, EX (w/sleeve) .$25.00
Aristocats, Stereo, 1970, orig soundtrack, complete w/booklet, EX (w/sleeve)...................................$12.00
At Home w/the Munsters, Golden #LP139, 1960s, EX (w/sleeve)......................................$50.00

At Home w/the Munsters, Golden #LP139, 1960s, VG (w/sleeve)......................................$30.00
Car 54 Where Are You?, Golden Records, 1963, EX (w/sleeve)......................................$35.00
Charlie Brown's All Star, 1978, EX (w/sleeve) $15.00
Chimpmunks Sing w/Children, Liberty, 1965, EX (w/sleeve)......................................$12.00
Christmas is for the Family (Jack Benny & Dennis Day), Design Records #DLPX-1, 1950s, EX (w/sleeve) $25.00
Clarabelle Clowns w/Jazz, Golden Crest CR-3030-LP, EX (w/sleeve)......................................$75.00
Dr Seuss Presents Yertle the Turtle, RCA/Stereo, 1960s, EX (w/sleeve)......................................$15.00
Famous Monsters Speak, AA Records, 1974, EX (w/sleeve) ..$40.00
Flash Gordon, 1980, soundtrack, EX........................$25.00
Get Along Gang & the Big Bully, Am Greetings, 1984, complete w/booklet, EX (w/sleeve)......................$12.00
He's Your Dog Charlie Brown, 1978, EX (w/sleeve) $15.00
Hefti in Gotham City (Batman), RCA, 1966, VG (w/sleeve)......................................$30.00
Huckleberry Hound & the Great Kellogg's TV Show, Colpix, 1960, EX (w/sleeve)......................................$35.00
I Love You (Wolfman-Dracula), Buzza/Cardoza/Universal Pictures, 1960s, vinyl coated picture disk, EX................$50.00
Indiana Jones & the Temple of Doom, 1984, NM (w/sleeve) .$15.00
It's a Small World, #ST-3925, 1970s, MIP $20.00
Jetsons New Songs of the TV Family of the Future, Golden, 1960s, EX (w/sleeve)......................................$85.00
Jiminy Cricket Multiply & Divide, 1963, G (w/sleeve) $5.00
Lady & the Tramp, Decca, 1955, EX (w/sleeve) $40.00
Merry Merry Merry Christmas From Captain Kangaroo, Golden #GLP 26, 1950s, EX......................................$25.00
Mickey Mouse Club, 1975, VG+ (w/sleeve) $10.00
Mister Ed, 1962, soundtrack, EX (w/sleeve).....................$40.00
Nikki the Wild Dog of the North, 1961, VG+ (w/sleeve) .$15.00
Original Music From the Addams Family, RCA, LPN-3421, 1965, VG (w/sleeve)......................................$30.00
Paddington Bear & Friends, 1982, M $20.00
Pink Panther, RCA, 1963, orig soundtrack, EX (w/sleeve)..$10.00
Pirates of the Caribbean, #3937, 1970s, no book, MIP.....$40.00
Popeye & Friends, Merry Records, 1980s, NM+ (w/jacket)..$20.00
Popeye the Sailor Man, Peter Pan, 1976, EX+ (w/jacket) .$10.00
Popeye's Favorite Stories, RCA Camden, 1960, EX+ (w/jacket)......................................$15.00
Roger Ramjet & the American Eagles, RCA, 1966, EX (w/sleeve), from $40 to......................................$50.00
Ruff & Reddy Adventures in Space, Colpix, 1958, EX (w/sleeve)......................................$35.00
Scooby Doo Christmas Stories, 1978, EX........................$25.00
Six Million Dollar Man, Peter Pan #8166, 1976, includes 4 stories, EX (w/sleeve)......................................$8.00
Space: 1999, 1975, 3 stories, EX........................$25.00
Spidey Super Stories, Peter Pan, 1977, EX (w/sleeve) $25.00
Star Trek The Motion Picture, 1979, NM (w/sleeve) $20.00
Strawberry Shortcake Let's Dance, 1982, NM (w/sleeve).$20.00
Superman, Power Records, 1975, EX (w/sleeve)..............$25.00
Thor, Golden, 1966, EX (w/sleeve)................................$25.00

Uncle Wiggily, 1970, EX (w/sleeve) $25.00

Voices of Marvel, Marvel Comics, 1964-65, EX (w/sleeve) .$50.00

Walt Disney Song Fest (Mouseketeers), 1960s, NM (w/sleeve) $20.00

Wonder Woman, Batman & Superman Christmas, 1977, EX (w/sleeve) $45.00

Wonder Woman, Peter Pan, 1977, EX (EX sleeve), $25.00.

Woody Woodpecker & His Friends, Cricket, 1962, EX (w/sleeve) $20.00

45 RPM RECORDS

Addition Made Easy, Disney, 1964, EX (w/sleeve) $5.00

Banana Splits, Doin' the Banana Splits & I Enjoy Being a Boy, Kellogg's premium, 1969, EX (w/sleeve) $45.00

Barbie (Busy Buzz/My First Date), 1961, NM (w/sleeve) ..$10.00

Batman, SPC, 1966, EX (w/sleeve), from $20 to $25.00

Bing Crosby Sings Mother Goose, Golden, 1957, EX (w/sleeve) $6.00

Casper the Friendly Ghost & Little Audrey Says, Little Golden, 1960s, EX (w/sleeve), from $25 to.............................$35.00

Dracula, Peter Pan, 1970s, EX (w/sleeve) $5.00

Felix the Cat, Cricket Records, 1958, EX (w/sleeve)........$20.00

Flintstones Lullaby of Pebbles, Golden, 1960s, VG (w/sleeve) $15.00

Fred Flintstone and Good, Old, Unreliable Dino, Peter Pan #1978, dated 1976, book and record set, EX (EX sleeve), $10.00.

Flipper the King of the Sea, MGM, 1960s, EX (w/sleeve) .$20.00

Hopalong Cassidy & the Two-Legged Wolf, Capitol, 1950s, EX (w/sleeve)..$50.00

HR Pufnstuf, Capitol, Kellogg's mail-in premiums, 1969, EX (w/sleeve)..$65.00

Jumbo's Lullaby, 1950s, red, EX (w/sleeve).....................$10.00

King Leonardo & His Short Subjects, Golden, 1961, EX (w/sleeve)..$20.00

Laurel & Hardy Chiller Diller Thriller, Peter Pan, 1962, EX (w/sleeve)..$15.00

Mary Poppins (Super Cali), 1964, EX (w/sleeve) $20.00

Miss Peach, RCA, 1960, EX (w/sleeve) $12.00

Olive Oyl on Troubled Waters, Peter Pan, 1976, NM+ (w/jacket)..$30.00

Popeye on Parade/Strike Me Pink, Cricket, 1950s, NM+ (w/jacket)..$35.00

Popeye the Sailor Man, Golden, 1959, EX (w/jacket)......$10.00

Raggedy Ann & Andy at the Circus, Kid Stuff, 1980, complete w/booklet, NM (w/sleeve) $15.00

Raggedy Ann & Andy on a Trip to the Stars, Hallmark, complete w/booklet, EX (w/sleeve) $35.00

Robin Hood, Disneyland, 1973, complete w/booklet, EX (w/sleeve)..$12.00

Roy Rogers Had a Ranch, Golden, 1950s, EX (w/sleeve) .$45.00

Roy Rogers Souvenir Record Album, RCA Victor WP-215, 1940s, 3 transparent gr vinyl records, EX (w/photo box) $50.00

Smokey Bear, Peter Pan, NM (w/sleeve)..........................$20.00

Swamp Fox, Golden, 1959, EX (w/sleeve) $12.00

Tom Terrific!, 1959, 3 on 1, rare, NM (w/sleeve) $95.00

Wagon Train, Golden, 1950s, EX (w/sleeve) $25.00

War of the Worlds, 1978, EX (w/sleeve) $10.00

Winnie the Pooh & Heffalumps, 1968, complete w/booklet, EX (w/sleeve)..$15.00

Wonder Woman Christmas Island, 1978, EX (w/sleeve) ..$25.00

78 RPM PICTURE AND NON-PICTURE RECORDS

Adventures of Mighty Mouse, Rocking Horse, 1957, EX (w/sleeve)..$15.00

Alice in Wonderland, Decca, 1944, 3-record set, EX (w/sleeve), from $25 to...$35.00

Annie Oakley Sings Ten Gallon Hat & I Gotta Crow, Golden, 1950s, EX+ (w/sleeve) $10.00

Art Carney, Columbia #40400, 1950s, performs Santa & the Doodle Li-Boop/Twas the Night Before Christmas, NM (w/sleeve)..$30.00

Blue-Tail Fly, 1953, EX (w/sleeve showing black banjo player on front), P6 ....$30.00

Bongo 'Fun & Fancy Free,' Columbia Records #MJ-41, 1940s, 3 record set, G (w/jacket), P6.....................................$45.00

Bozo Under the Sea, Capitol, 1950, w/20-pg booklet, EX (w/sleeve), from $40 to...$60.00

Brave Little Sambo, Peter Pan Records, 1950, EX (w/colorful sleeve) $55.00

Bugs Bunny & the Tortoise, Capitol, 1949, EX (w/sleeve), from $25 to $35.00

Casper the Friendly Ghost & Little Audrey Says, Golden, 1959, EX (w/sleeve)..**$15.00**

Cinderella, Golden, 1950s, EX (w/sleeve) **$10.00**

Davy Crockett at the Alamo, Columbia #C-518, 1950s, 2-record set, EX (w/photo sleeve)..**$50.00**

Dennis the Menace, Playtime, 1954, NM (w/sleeve) **$15.00**

Elmer Elephant, Capitol, 1940s, EX (w/sleeve), from $15 to..**$20.00**

Flipper the Fabulous Dolphin, Golden, EX (w/sleeve)........**$6.00**

Foodini Goes a Huntin', Caravan, 1949, VG+ (w/sleeve).**$35.00**

Froggy the Gremlin, Capitol, 1947, VG (w/sleeve) **$40.00**

Gabby Hayes 1001 Western Nights, RCA #Y-420, EX (w/sleeve) **$35.00**

Gene Autrey's Western Classics, Columbia, 1947, 4 records w/8 songs, NM+ (w/sleeve folio in photo box).................**$40.00**

Genie The Magic Record, Decca #CV102, 1946, 12", EX (EX sleeve), $15.00. (Photo courtesy Peter Muldavin)

Great Locomotive Chase, Golden, 1950s, EX (w/sleeve).**$10.00**

Hey Diddle Diddle, Peter Pan, 1948, EX (w/sleeve), from $20 to **$30.00**

Howdy Doody & Mother Goose, RCA-Little Nipper, 1950s, 2-record set, EX (w/sleeve) **$85.00**

Howdy Doody's Laughing Circus, RCA Victor, 1950, EX (w/sleeve)..**$25.00**

I Taut I Taw a Puddy Tat, Capitol, 1950s, EX (w/sleeve), from $35 to **$50.00**

It's Howdy Doody Time, RCA Victor, 1951, EX (w/sleeve), from $75 to..**$100.00**

Little Lulu & Her Magic Tricks, Golden, 1954, EX (w/sleeve) **$25.00**

Lone Ranger — He Saves the Booneville Gold, Decca, 1952, No 6 in series, EX (w/sleeve), from $60 to.................**$80.00**

Marge's Little Lulu & Lavender's Blue, Golden, 1951, EX (w/sleeve), from $15 to..**$20.00**

Mickey & the Beanstalk, Capitol, 1948, complete w/booklet, EX (w/sleeve)..**$30.00**

Mickey Mouse Picture House Song, Golden, 1950s, EX (w/sleeve)..**$15.00**

Mighty Mouse First Adventure, RCA, 1950s, EX (w/sleeve).**$45.00**

Mouseketunes, Disneyland Records, 1955, EX (w/sleeve), from $25 to **$35.00**

Mr Jinks & Boo Boo Bear, Golden, 1959, NM (w/sleeve).**$20.00**

Pinocchio, RCA Victor #349, 1940, VG (w/sleeve).........**$65.00**

Poky Little Puppy, Little Golden, 1947, EX (w/sleeve), from $7 to **$12.00**

Raggedy Ann's Sunny Songs, RCA, 1933, 3-record set, EX (w/sleeve)..**$150.00**

Roy Rogers in the Television Ambush, RCA Victor, 1951, EX (w/sleeve), from $35 to..**$50.00**

Ruff & Reddy, Golden, 1959, EX+ (w/sleeve) **$15.00**

Scuffy the Tugboat, Golden, 1948, EX (w/sleeve), from $8 to.**$12.00**

Simpsons Deep Deep Trouble, Geffen, M (w/sleeve)........**$45.00**

Sleeping Beauty, Golden, 1959, VG (w/sleeve) **$15.00**

Songs of the Flintstones, Golden, 1961, EX (w/sleeve) **$25.00**

Songs of the Jetsons, Little Golden, 1963, EX (w/sleeve), from $20 to **$30.00**

Tales of Uncle Remus, Capitol, 1947, 3 records, EX (w/sleeve)..**$30.00**

Trick or Treat, Disneyland, 1974, NM (w/sleeve)............**$12.00**

Tweetie Pie, Capitol, EX (w/sleeve), from $25 to **$30.00**

Uncle Remus, Disneyland, 1963, orig soundtrack to Song of the South, EX (w/sleeve) **$15.00**

Willie the Whale, Columbia, 1946, 3 records, EX (w/sleeve) .**$30.00**

Wizard of Oz, Decca, 1939, set of 4, EX (w/sleeve)...........**$65.00**

Woody Woodpecker Song/Woodpecker Dance, Golden, 1951, NM (w/sleeve) **$10.00**

Yankee Doodle Mickey, Disneyland, 1980, EX (w/sleeve).**$12.00**

KIDDIE PICTURE DISKS

Listed here is a representative sampling of kiddie picture disks that were produced through the 1940s. Most are 6" to 7" in diameter and are made of cardboard with plastic-laminated grooves. They are very colorful and seldom seen with original sleeves. Value ranges are for items in very good to near-mint condition. Ultimately, the value of any collectible is what a buyer is willing to pay, and prices tend to fluctuate. Our values are for records only (no sleeves except where noted). Unlike other records, the value of a picture disk is not diminished if there is no original sleeve.

A Birthday Song to You, Voco #35215, 5" square, NM (no mailing envelope), $20.00. (Photo courtesy Peter Muldavin)

A Birthday Song to You, Voco #35215, 1948, 5" sq, NM (w/mailer envelope), from $30 to.............................**$40.00**

Alice in Wonderland, Toy Toon Records, 1952, NM, from $10 to **$15.00**

Bible Storytime, Standard Publishing, 78rpm, ca 1948, 7", EX/NM, ea from $5 to **$10.00**

Bunny Easter Party, Vovo #EB-1, 1948, EX.......................**$15.00**

Cinderella, Toy Toon Records, 1952, NM, from $10 to **$15.00**

Disneyland Main Street Electrical Parade, 1973, 7", VG+...**$60.00**

Flash Gordon 'City of Caves,' Record Guild of America, 1948, scarce, NM..**$75.00**

Flash Gordon 'City of Sea Caves' Part I, Record Guild of American/King Features, 1948, EX......................................**$50.00**

Gilbert & Sullivan Series, Picture Tone Record Co, 1948, 78 rpm, rare, 6½", EX/NM, ea from $30 to......................**$40.00**

Greetings & Here's Good Wishes for a 14 Carrot Christmas, features Bugs Bunnys dressed as Santa, Capitol, 1948, 8", NM...**$125.00**

Jack in the Beanstalk, Toy Toon Records, 1952, NM, from $10 to **$15.00**

Kitty Cat, Voco, ca 1948, 7", EX/NM, from $4 to.............**$8.00**

Kitty Cat, Voco 'Dic Disc,' ca 1948, 6" (rare sz), EX/NM, from $15 to **$25.00**

Lionel Train Sound Effects, 1951, NM, M21, from $40 to.**$60.00**

Red River Valley, Record Guild of America #2002P, 1949, EX (EX rare sleeve), from $15 to.....................................**$25.00**

Round & 'Round the Village, Voco 'Pic Disc,' 1948, 78rpm, 6" (rare sz), EX/NM, from $15 to.................................**$25.00**

Round & 'Round the Village, Vovo 'Pic Disc,' 1948, 78rpm, 7", EX/NM, from $4 to...**$8.00**

Rover the Strongman, Voco, 1948, from $25.00 to $30.00. (Photo courtesy Peter Muldavin)

Shepherd Boy, Bible Storytime, 1948, NM, from $8 to **$10.00**

Songs From Mother Goose, Toy Toon Records, 1952, NM, from $10 to **$15.00**

Swing Your Partner, Picture Play Records #PR11A/Record Guild of America, 1948, NM, from $75 to.........................**$100.00**

Terry & the Pirates, Record Guild of America, F501, 1949, 6½", EX/NM, from $35 to...**$45.00**

The Fox, Talking Book Corp, 1917, 78rpm, very rare, EX/NM, from $90 to **$150.00**

Three Bears With Uncle Henry, Kidisks, KD-77A, 1948, rare, NM, from $50 to...**$75.00**

Trial of 'Bumble' the Bee Part I, Vogue #R-745, 1947, 10", EX, from $50 to **$60.00**

Winnie the Pooh & Christopher Robin Songs, RCA Victor, 1933, very rare, NM, from $300 to.............................**$500.00**

Reynolds Banks

Reynolds Toys began production in 1964, at first making large copies of early tin toys for window displays, though some were sold to collectors as well. These toys included trains, horse-drawn vehicles, boats, a steam toy, and several sizes of Toonerville trolleys. In the early 1970s, they designed and produced six animated cap guns. Finding the market limited, by 1971 they had switched to a line of banks they call 'New Original Limited Numbered Editions (10 – 50) of Mechanical Penny Banks.' Still banks were added to their line in 1980 and figural bottle openers in 1988. Each bank design is original; no reproductions are produced. Reynolds' banks are in the White House and the Smithsonian as well as many of the country's major private collections. *The Penny Bank Book* by Andy and Susan Moore (Schiffer Publishing, 1984) shows and describes the first twelve still banks Reynolds produced. Values are given for mint-condition banks.

Advisor: Charlie Reynolds (R5)

MECHANICAL BANKS

Uncataloged, elephant (conversion), 1970, edition of 4 .**$100.00**

1M, Train Man, 1971, edition of 30 ....**$350.00**

2M, Trolley, 1971, edition of 30 ....**$450.00**

3M, Drive-In, 1971, edition of 10 ....**$1,000.00**

4M, Pirate, 1972, edition of 10....................................**$725.00**

5M, Blackbeard, 1972, edition of 10 ....**$650.00**

6M, Frog & Fly, 1972, edition of 10...........................**$1,200.00**

7M, Toy Collector, 1972, unlimited edition **$650.00**

8M, Balancing Bank, 1972, edition of 10.....................**$725.00**

9M, Save the Girl, 1972, edition of 10 ....**$2,000.00**

10M, Father Christmas, 1972, 1 made ea year at Christmas..**$850.00**

11M, Gump on a Stump, 1973, edition of 10...............**$1,100.00**

12M, Trick Bank, 1973, edition of 10.........................**$1,000.00**

13M, Kid Savings, 1973, edition of 10.......................**$1,200.00**

14M, Christmas Tree, 1973, edition of 10......................**$725.00**

15M, Foxy Grandpa, 1974, edition of 10 ....**$975.00**

16M, Happy Hooligan, 1974, edition of 10.................**$1,075.00**

17M, Chester's Fishing, 1974, edition of 10...................**$900.00**

18M, Gloomy Gus, 1974, edition of 10 ....**$2,800.00**

19M, Kids' Prank, 1974, edition of 10 ....**$1,100.00**

20M, Mary & Her Little Lamb, 1974, edition of 20 ....**$850.00**

21M, Spook, 1974, edition of 10....................................**$800.00**

22M, Decoy, 1974, edition of 10 ....**$600.00**

23M, Decoy Hen, 1974, edition of 10 ....**$600.00**

24M, Comedy Bank, 1974, edition of 10 ....**$975.00**

25M, Bozo, 1974, edition of 10 ....**$950.00**

26M, Reynolds Foundry, 1974, edition of 15 ....**$3,400.00**

27M, Toonerville, 1974, edition of 10 ....**$1,200.00**

28M, Bank of Reynolds Toys, 1974, edition of 10 ....**$425.00**

29M, Simple Simon, 1975, edition of 10 ....**$925.00**

30M, Humpty Dumpty, 1975, edition of 20.................**$1,250.00**

31M, Three Blind Mice, 1975, edition of 15 ....$1,100.00
32M, Clubhouse, 1975, edition of 10........................$1,100.00
33M, Boat, 1975, edition of 10 ....$1,500.00
34M, St Nicholas, 1975, edition of 50 ....$775.00
35M, Forging America, 1976, edition of 13................$1,200.00
36M, Suitcase, 1979, edition of 22......................$825.00
37M, North Wind, 1980, edition of 23........................$1,100.00
39M, Quarter Century, 1982, edition of 25 ....$4,000.00
40M, Columbia, 1984, edition of 25...........................$1,350.00
41M, Whirligig, 1985, edition of 30.........................$1,300.00
42M, Miss Liberty, 1986, edition of 36 ....$1,300.00
42M, Miss Liberty on a Pedestal, 1986, edition of 4....$1,600.00
43M, Auto Giant, 1987, edition of 30.......................$2,250.00
45M, Campaign '88, 1988, edition of 50 ....$3,000.00
46M, Hollywood, 1989, edition of 35 ....$825.00

47M, Buffalos Revenge, 1990, edition of 35, $900.00. (Photo courtesy Charlie Reynolds)

48M, Williamsburg, 1991, edition of 35........................$850.00
49M, Duel at the Dome, 1992, edition of 50...............$1,000.00
50M, '92 Vote, 1992, edition of 50 ....$3,000.00
51M, Oregon Trail, 1993, edition of 50 ....$800.00
52M, Norway (Lillehammer), 1994, edition of 50..........$825.00
53M, Shoe House, 1994, edition of 50...........................$950.00
54M, J&E Stevens Co, 1995, edition of 50 ....$1,850.00
55M, Hyakutake (The Comet), 1996, edition of 50.......$625.00
56M, '96 Political Wish, 1996, edition of 50 ....$900.00
58M, Uncle Louie, 1997, edition of 50 ....$350.00
60M, Wall Street, 1998, edition of 98............................$750.00
61M, De Bug (Y2K Bug), 1999, edition of 50.................$495.00
64M, Decision 2000, Bush-Gore, edition of 50 ....$595.00
65M, The Lawyer, 2001, edition of 50 ....$600.00
66M, Bank of Uncle Sam, 2002, edition of 60...............$600.00
67M, Ben Franklin & the Liberty Bell, 2003, edition of 50 ....$495.00
69M, Tug-Over-War in 2004, 2004, edition of 50 ....$595.00

STILL BANKS

1S, Amish Man, 1980, edition of 50 ....$135.00
2S, Santa, 1980, edition of 50 ....$95.00

3S, Deco Dog, 1981, edition of 50................................$85.00
4S, Jelly Bean King, 1981, edition of 100 ....$265.00
5S, Hag, 1981, edition of 50...$160.00
6S, Snowman, 1981, edition of 50..................................$110.00
7S, Mark Twain, 1982, edition of 50...............................$200.00
8S, Santa, 1982, edition of 50 ....$125.00
9S, Anniversary, 1982, special edition $200.00
10S, Redskins Hog, 1983, edition of 50 ....$125.00
11S, Lock-Up Savings, 1983, edition of 50......................$55.00
12S, Miniature Bank Building, 1983, edition of 50 ....$195.00
13S, Santa in Chimney, 1983, edition of 50 ....$90.00
14S, Santa w/Tree (bank & doorstop), 1983, edition of 25..$325.00
15S, Redskins NFC Champs, 1983, edition of 35...........$185.00
16S, Chick, 1984, edition of 50.......................................$80.00
17S, Ty-Up, 1984, edition of 35 ....$225.00
18S, Tiniest Elephant, 1984, edition of 50.....................$110.00
19S, Baltimore Town Crier, 1984, edition of 50 ....$75.00
20S, Father Christmas Comes to America, July 4th, 1984, edition of 25 ....$325.00
21S, Campaign '84, edition of 100 ....$250.00
22S, Santa, 1984, edition of 50 ....$100.00
23S, Reagan '85, 1985, edition of 100............................$310.00
24S, Columbus Ohio, 1985, edition of 50.........................$60.00
25S, Austrian Santa (bank & doorstop), 1985, edition of 25 .$350.00
26S, Halloween, 1985, edition of 50...............................$210.00
27S, 1893 Kriss Kringle, 1985, edition of 20 ....$2,000.00
27S, 1893 Kriss Kringle (w/tree & candle decorations), 1985, edition of 20 ....$2,400.00
28S, Santa Coming to a Child, 1985, edition of 50........$165.00
29S, Halley's Comet, 1986, edition of 50......................$190.00
30S, 20th Anniversary, 1986, edition of 86 ....$165.00
31S, Father Christmas (bank & doorstop), gr, edition of 25.$280.00
32S, Santa & the Reindeer, 1986, edition of 50 ....$185.00
33S, Charlie O'Conner, 1987, edition of 50 ....$90.00
34S, Chocolate Rabbit, 1987, edition of 50....................$110.00
35S, St Louis River Boat, 1987, edition of 60 ....$75.00
36S, German Santa (bank & doorstop), 1987, edition of 25.$275.00
37S, Graduation, 1987, special edition $200.00
38S, Old Stump Halloween, 1987, edition of 50 ....$95.00
39S, Santa in Race Car, 1987, edition of 100 ....$130.00
40S, Technology Education, edition of 88 ....$65.00
41S, Super Bowl XXII Redskins, 1988, edition of 50........$90.00
42S, Easter Rabbit, 1988, edition of 50 ....$55.00
43S, Florida Souvenir, 1988, edition of 75 ....$90.00
44S, Father Christmas w/Lantern (bank & doorstop), 1988, edition of 35 ....$260.00
45S, Halloween Spook, 1988, edition of 50 ....$90.00
46S, NCRPBC (National Capitol Region Club), 1988, edition of 20 ....$300.00
48S, Bush-Quayle, 1989, edition of 100..........................$260.00
49S, Shuffle Off to Buffalo, 1989, edition of 75 ....$70.00
50S, Pocket Pigs, 1989, edition of 75 ....$125.00
51S, Regal Santa (bank & doorstop), 1989, edition of 35...$275.00
52S, Tiniest Snowman, 1989, edition of 75 ....$85.00
53S, Santa on Motorcycle, 1989, edition of 75..............$150.00
54S, Rabbit w/Mammy, 1990, edition of 75....................$225.00
55S, Antique Row Sign Post, 1990, edition of 75............$70.00

56S, Duck w/Puppy & Bee, 1990, edition of 75 ....**$110.00**
57S, 1895 Santa w/Wreath, 1990, edition of 35 ....**$250.00**
58S, Santa on a Pig, 1990, edition of 75 ....**$140.00**
60S, Santa w/Wassail Bowl, 1991, edition of 35 ....**$250.00**
61S, Santa Express, 1991, edition of 55 ....**$125.00**
62S, Pig on Sled, 1992, edition of 55 ....**$85.00**
63S, Santa About to Leave, 1992, edition of 25 ....**$290.00**
64S, Jack-O'-Lantern, 1992, edition of 60 ....**$80.00**
65S, Santa in Zeppelin, 1992, edition of 100..................**$145.00**
66S, Clinton, 1993, edition of 100..................................**$310.00**
67S, Windy City (Chicago Convention), 1993, edition of
     60 ....**$85.00**
68S, Santa & the Bad Boy (Summer Santa), 1993, edition of
     50..**$225.00**
69S, Arkansas President, 1994, edition of 100................**$325.00**
70S, Santa & the Good Kids, 1994, edition of 35 ....**$260.00**
71S, Penny Santa, 1994, edition of 60 ....**$125.00**
72S, School Days, 1995, edition of 100 ....**$110.00**
73S, 1880 Snow Santa, 1995, edition of 50 ....**$220.00**
75S, Santa on Donkey, 1995, edition of 50......................**$110.00**
76S, Clinton/Dole '96 (SBCCA '96), 1996, edition of
     100 ....**$280.00**
77S, Foxy Grandpa & Egelhoff Safe, 1997, edition of
     60 ....**$200.00**
78S, Halloween Witch, 1997, edition of 50 ....**$95.00**
79S, Christmas Time, 1997, edition of 50........................**$110.00**
80S, Portland Chicks, 1998, edition of 20, pr................**$155.00**
81S, Old St Nicholas, 1998, edition of 20 ....**$450.00**
82S, Little League Home Bank, 1999, edition of 50.......**$145.00**
83S, Santa's Last Check, 1999, edition of 30................**$200.00**
84S, Presidential 2000 Campaign Bank, edition of 60 ...**$150.00**

85S, See Your Savings, 2001, edition of 50, $150.00. (Photo courtesy Charlie Reynolds)

86S, The Conventioneer, 2002, edition of 50 ....**$135.00**
87S, We're Making Chicago Famous, 2003, edition of 50 .**$95.00**
89S, Holidays Bank (Christmas & Hanukkah), 2003, edition of
     50 ....**$200.00**
90S & 91S, George Washington on Horse & Martha Washington, 2004, edition of 30, ea pr **$195.00**

Robots and Space Toys

Space is a genre that anyone who grew up in the '60s can relate to, but whether you're from that generation or not, chances are the fantastic robots, space vehicles, and rocket launchers from that era are fascinating to you as well. Some emitted beams of colored light and eerie sounds and suggested technology the secrets of which were still locked away in the future. To a collector, the stranger, the better. Some were made of lithographed tin, but even plastic toys (Atom Robot, for example) are high on the want list of many serious buyers. Condition is extremely important, both in general appearance and internal workings. Mint-in-box examples may be worth twice as much as one mint-no-box, since the package art was often just as awesome as the toy itself.

Because of the high prices these toys now command, many have been reproduced. Beware!

Note: The following listings are from recent auctions and the auction estimates have been added at the end of the listings for comparison. Estimates with single prices are minimum estimates.

See also Marx; Guns.

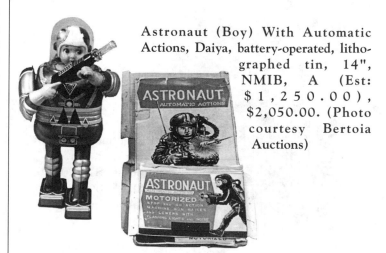

Astronaut (Boy) With Automatic Actions, Daiya, battery-operated, lithographed tin, 14", NMIB, A (Est: $1,250.00), $2,050.00. (Photo courtesy Bertoia Auctions)

Airport Saucer, Japan, b/o, litho tin, rnd w/scenes of famous places, plastic dome, 8" dia, EXIB, A (Est: $75-$125) .**$50.00**
Answer Game Robot, see Battery-Operated category
Apollo II Eagle Lunar Module, DSK, 1960s, b/o, litho tin, door opens to reveal astronaut, 10", EX, A (Est: $400-$500).**$75.00**
Apollo Space Craft, Masudaya, b/o, astronaut circles above craft, 11" L, EXIB, A (Est: $150)......................................**$225.00**
Apollo-Z Moon Traveler Capsule, Alps, 1960s, b/o, litho tin, 12" L, EXIB, A (Est: $300-$400) **$165.00**
Astroman, TN, w/up, tin, 11", NM, A (Est: $4,750) ..**$4,750.00**
Astronaut, Ahi, crank action, tin, 6½", NMIB, A (Est: $200)..**$625.00**
Astronaut (Boy) w/Automatic Actions, Daiya, b/o, litho tin & plastic, 14", EX, A (Est: $400) **$400.00**
Astronaut w/Gun, Japan, w/up, litho tin, gray w/red arms & feet, 9", incomplete, G+, A (Est: $100-$200)..................**$275.00**

Astronaut w/Gun, TN, b/o, litho tin, yel, silver helmet, red detail, 9", nonworking, G+, A (Est: $300-$400) $375.00

Atom Robot, friction, litho tin, gray w/red, wht, bl & yel detail, 7", EXIB, A (Est: $200-$400)................................$485.00

Atomic Reactor, Linemar, b/o & steam-powered, metal, 10x12", EXIB, A (Est: $300-$500) $410.00

Atomic Robot, Y, w/up, litho tin, 6½", NM, A (Est: $200) .$350.00

Atomic Robot, Y, w/up, litho tin, 6½", NM+IB, A (Est: $400)..$500.00

Attacking Martian Robot, SS, b/o, tin, 11½", EX+IB, A ($200-$300)..$250.00

Aurora Expedition Car, Y, b/o, litho tin, 14", NMIB, A (Est: $600)..$950.00

Battery-Operated Tractor w/Robot Driver, tin, rubber treads, pistons light & fan spins, 10", NMIB, A (Est: $275) ...$450.00

Blazer Shogun Robot, Japan, w/up, red litho tin w/silver plastic chest & red plastic head, 9", EX+IB, A (Est: $200-$400)........$300.00

Blink-A-Gear Robot, Taiyo, b/o, blk tin w/red arms, mc gears in clear plastic chest cover, 14½", NMIB, A................$900.00

Brazer Robot, Bullmark, w/up, litho tin, rubber head w/lg bug eyes, wrench hands, 8½", EX+IB, (Est: $500-$700) .$275.00

Capsule 6, Masudaya, b/o, litho tin, 10", NMIB, A (Est: $375) $825.00

Cragstan Astronaut, Daiya, battery-operated, lithographed tin, 13", VG, A (Est: $400.00 – $600.00), $385.00. (Photo courtesy Don Hultzman)

Cragstan Astronaut, Y, crank action, litho tin, 10", EXIB, A (Est: $1,500)................................$2,800.00

Cragstan Astronaut, Y, crank action, litho tin, 10", VG, A (Est: $600-$800) $525.00

Chief Robotman, KO, battery-operated, tin, 12", EX, A (Est: $1,000.00), $990.00. (Photo courtesy Bertoia Auctions)

Cragstan Moon Explorer M-27, Y, remote control, lithographed tin, 8" long, scarce, EX+IB, A (Est: $500.00), $725.00. (Photo courtesy Bertoia Auctions)

Chief Robotman, KO, b/o, tin, 12", NM+IB, A (Est: $1,000)..$1,600.00

Chief Smoky Advanced Robotman, KO, b/o, tin, 12", EXIB, A (Est: $1,800)..$5,700.00

Circus Car #8, ATC, friction, litho tin, robot driving sports car, 8" L, VG, A (Est: $300-$500) $500.00

Columbia Space Shuttle, Spain, b/o, litho tin, Columbia/NASA/United States, 14" L, NMIB, A (Est: $125) ..$200.00

Cragstan Astronaut, b/o, litho tin, 13", missing dome & nonworking o/w VG, A (Est: $200-$00) $485.00

Cragstan Astronaut, Daiya, b/o, litho tin, 11", EX+IB, (Est: $850) $1,300.00

Cragstan Mr Robot, b/o, tin, wht (scarce), 11", NMIB, A (Est: $850) $1,300.00

Cragstan Talking Robot, Y, b/o talking action, friction, tin, 11", nonworking o/w NMIB, A (Est: $500) $875.00

D Fighter Robot, ST, w/up, mc litho tin body, plastic head w/'horns,' 9½", EX, A (Est: $150-$250) $190.00

Deep Sea Robot (Scarce Variation of Space Captian), AN, w/up, litho tin, 8", EX, A (Est: $1,300) $1,900.00

Diaparon Robot, Bullmark, w/up, litho tin w/plastic helmet & torso shield, 8", EX+IB, A (Est: $350-$450)............$245.00

Directional Robot, see Robot (Directional)

Door Robot, Alps, r/c, litho tin w/clear plastic head, 9½", NM+IB, A (Est: $1,750)................................$3,800.00

Dino-Robot, SH, battery-operated, lithographed tin, 11", EX+IB, A (Est: $600.00 – $800.00), $1,320.00. (Photo courtesy Bertoia Auctions)

Door Robot, Alps, r/c, litho tin w/clear plastic head, 9½", VG, A (Est: $650-$750) $800.00

Driving Robot/Flying Man, SY, w/up, litho tin, 5½" T, NMIB, A (Est: $275) $350.00

Dynamic Fighter Robot, Junior Toy Co, 1960s, battery-operated, plastic, 10", EX, $225.00. (Photo courtesy Don Hultzman)

Dux Astroman, West Germany, b/o, plastic, nonworking o/w NMIB, A (Est: $400)..$400.00

Easel Back Robot, see Robot (Easel Back)

Electric Remote Control Robot, Linemar, litho tin, 8", EXIB, A (Est: $275) $475.00

Fire Bird #308 Space Rocket, Masudaya, friction, litho tin, 12½", VG+IB, A (Est: $100) $150.00

Flying Jeep N-365, ATC, friction, litho tin, 8" L, EX+IB, A (Est: minimum $150)..$365.00

Flying Saucer #8, Haji, friction, litho tin w/2 pilots under clear plastic dome, 7" dia, EXIB, A (Est: $175)...............$225.00

Flying Saucer w/Space Pilot, KO, b/o, litho tin, 7½" dia, NM+IB, A (Est: $150) $225.00

Flying Saucer w/Space Pilot, KO, bump-&-go action, 8" dia, EX, A $135.00

Friendship 7 Rocket Ship, Japan, friction, litho tin, pointed nose, red & wht checked band, 13" L, VG, A (Est: $25-$50) $220.00

Friendship 7 Space Capsule, SH, friction, tin w/plastic nose cone, w/astronaut, 6½", VG+, A (Est: $65) $80.00

Gear Robot, SH, b/o, litho tin, 11", NM+IB, A (Est: $275) .$450.00

Gear Robot, SH, w/up, tin & plastic, 9", MIB, A (Est: $150)..$425.00

Getta (Japanese Super Hero), w/up, tin w/vinyl head, walks & arms swing, 9", EX+IB (Japanese box), A (Est: $125) $175.00

Gettsuko Kamen Robot, Bullmark, windup, lithographed tin, 9", EX+IB, A (Est: $700.00 – $900.00), $550.00. (Photo courtesy Bertoia Auctions)

Giant Sonic Robot (Train Robot), Masudaya, 1959, battery-operated, lithographed tin, 16", EXIB, A (Est: $7,000.00 – $9,000.00), $6,050.00. (Photo courtesy Randy Inman Auctions)

Ground Zero Robot, ST, w/up, litho tin w/vinyl head, 9½", NMIB, A (Est: minimum $150) $175.00

Gurendaiza (UFO), Popy, w/up, tin w/vinyl head, 9", NMIB, A (Est: $150) $175.00

High-Wheel Robot, Yoshiya, w/up, blk litho tin w/mc gear box in chest, red hands & feet, 10", EX+IB, A (Est: $400-$500)..$412.00

ICBM Launching Station, Horikawa, crank action, litho tin, 19" L, EXIB, A (Est: $250) $250.00

Inter-Planet Space Captain, Naito Shoten, 1950s, w/up, litho tin, wht w/bl, blk & red, 8", EX, A (Est: $1,200-$1,500) $1,430.00

Interceptor #230, S&E, b/o, litho tin & plastic, 14½", EXIB, A (Est: $150-$250) $355.00

Interplanet Space Captain, AN/Japan, w/up, litho tin, deep-sea type helmet, w/space gun, 8", VG+, A (Est: $475)..$1,000.00

Interplanetary Explorer Robot, Naito Shoten, w/up, litho tin, deep-sea looking helmet, 8", EX+, A (Est: minimum $550) $725.00

Jet Racer, TKK, friction, litho tin, driver under clear bubble canopy, 12" L, EXIB, A (Est: $875) $1,950.00

Journey to the Moon From Space Station to the Moon, Mego, b/o, 36" L, EX+IB, A $275.00

Jumping Robot, SY, w/up, tin, 6", NM+IB, A (Est: $200) .$350.00

Jupiter Robot, Japan, w/up, plastic w/tin chest graphics, 7", EX+IB, A (Est: $250-$350)..........................$165.00

Jupiter Rocket, Japan, friction, litho tin, mc, 9", EXIB, A (Est: $25-$50) $100.00

Kamen Rider, Bullmark, 1960s, friction, tin, vinyl & plastic, advances on feet or stomach, 7", NMIB, A (Est: $250) .$400.00

King Jet #8, TKK, friction, litho tin w/driver under clear plastic dome, 12", G, A (Est: $150-$250) $300.00

King Jet #8, TKK, friction, litho tin w/driver under clear plastic dome, 12", EXIB, A (Est: $775) $850.00

Krome Dome, Y, b/o, plastic, 9½", NM+IB, A (Est: $200)...$350.00

Lantern Robot (Powder Robot), Linemar, r/c, 8", VG, A (Est: $850) $1,475.00

Laser Robot, Daiya, crank action, tin w/plastic arms, w/block head, 7", NM, A (Est: $350) $675.00

Lavender Robot, see Non Stop Robot

Lilliput Robot, see Robot Lilliput

Lunar Captain, TN, 1960s, battery-operated, lithographed tin, 13½", EXIB, $275.00. (Photo courtesy Don Hultzman)

Man From Mars (Shooting), Irwin, w/up, plastic figure in red suit, clear bubble helmet, 11", EXIB, A (Est: $50-$100)...$300.00

Man in Space, Alps, b/o, tin & celluloid, 36" L, NMIB, A (Est: $675)....................................$760.00

Martin the Martian, Y, b/o, plastic, 15", NM+IB, A (Est: $200)....................................$450.00

Marvelous Mike Electromatic Tractor #1000, Saunders, b/o, tin w/plastic robot driver, 13", NMIB, A (Est: $350) $650.00

Mechanized Robot (The Original Robbie), TN, 1950s, battery-operated, tin and plastic, 13", EX, $2,250.00.

Lost in Space Robot, Remco, 1960s, battery-operated, 13", EXIB, $300.00. (Photo courtesy Don Hultzman)

Lunar Loop, Japan, b/o, plastic, Space Craft vehicle travels loop, 14", GIB, A (Est: $50-$100) $75.00

Machine Man, Masudaya, b/o, tin, 15", NM, A (Est: $35,000) $38,000.00

Man From Mars, USA, w/up, plastic, red spacesuit w/human head under bl-tinted bubble helmet, 11", VG, A (Est: $300-$500)....................................$100.00

Mechanized Robot (The Original Robbie), TN, b/o, tin & plastic, 13", NMIB, A (Est: $2750)....................$5,700.00

Mego Man, SY, w/up, tin, 7", NM+IB, A (Est: $350) $575.00

Mekanda, Bullmark, w/up, tin w/vinyl head, walks & arms move, 8½", NM+IB (Japanese box), A (Est: $175) $250.00

Mekanda, Bullmark, w/up, tin w/vinyl head, walks & moves arms, 8½", NM+IB (Japanese box), A (Est: $175)..$250.00

Mercury X-1 Space Saucer (M-164), Y, b/o, 8" dia, NMIB, (Est: $125)....................................$200.00

Mighty Robot, Diato, w/up, litho tin, 5", NMIB, A (Est: $125) $500.00

Mighty Robot, Yoshiya, b/o, litho tin, 12", EX, A (Est: $200-$400) $1,100.00

Mirror Man, Bullmark, b/o, tin w/vinyl head, complete w/mask, 14", MIB (Japanese box), A (Est: $1,000) $2,000.00

Mirror Man, Bullmark, w/up, tin w/vinyl head, complete w/mask, 10", NM+IB, A (Est: $250) $350.00

Monster Robot, Taiwan, b/o, plastic, 2-tone gr w/yel arms, chest controls, 9", EXIB, A (Est: $25-$50) $20.00

Moon Detector M27, Y, b/o, litho tin, 6x10" L, EX+, A (Est: $250) $445.00

Moon Explorer, Cragstan, r/c, litho tin & plastic, 8" L, EX, A (Est: $1,200-$1,500)........................$1,045.00

Moon Explorer, KO, crank action, tin, rare bl version w/lt bl helmet, 7", NM+IB, A (Est: $1,300) $2,600.00

Moon Globe Orbiter, Y/Mego, b/o, plastic space ship circles see-through globe, 10x6" dia, NM+IB, A (Est: $175) $1,750.00

Moon Patrol 11 (Flying Saucer), Y, 1960s, battery-operated, lithographed tin, 9" diameter, EX, $225.00. (Photo courtesy Don Hultzman)

Moon Rocket ZX18, Marusan/Japan, string activated, litho tin, w/sparking action, 9", EXIB, A (Est: $400-$600) $770.00

Moon Space Ship (Moon Car), b/o, tin, 13", EXIB, A (Est: $1,200) $1,400.00

Moon Traveler Apollo Z, TN, b/o, tin & plastic, w/3 astronauts, 12" L, NM+, A $200.00

Moonlight Man Scooter, Masudaya, b/o, litho tin w/vinyl head, bump-&-go w/flashing lights, rare, 9", NMIB (Est: $1,000) $1,400.00

Mr Atomic, Y, b/o, litho tin, 9", EX, A (Est: $1,200)..$2,325.00

Mr Mercury, Y, r/c, litho tin, 13", EX+IB, A..................$935.00

Mr Mercury Robot, Marx, r/c, tin, 13", NMIB, A (Est: $275) .$600.00

Mr Robot, ATC, w/up, 7", NM+IB, A (Est: $500) $575.00

Mr Zerox, SH, 1960s, b/o, litho tin, 9½", NMIB, A (Est: $200)..$200.00

Mystery Moon Man, see Chief Robotman

Non Stop Robot (Lavender Robot), Masaduya, b/o, litho tin, 15", NMIB, A (Est: $4,500.00) $6,600.00

Non Stop Robot (Lavender Robot), Masudaya, b/o, litho tin, 15", EX, A (Est: $2,500) $3,700.00

NP5357 Robot, see Robot Lilliput

Orbit Explorer (w/Airborne Satellite), KO, w/up, litho tin, 8½" L, NMIB, A (Est: $275) $400.00

Pete the Space Man (Mini-Mate Series), Bandai, b/o, tin & vinyl, NMIB, A (Est: $75)..................................$75.00

Piston Action Robot, TN, r/c, tin, Robbie look-alike, NMIB, A (Est: $900) $1,550.00

Planet Robot, KO, r/c, tin, 9", NMIB, A (Est: $700) $925.00

Planet Robot, KO, r/c, tin, 9", nonworking o/w EX, A (Est: $200)..$300.00

Planet Robot, KO, w/up, similar to Robbie, blk body w/red arms & feet, 9", MIB, A (Est: $150) $175.00

Powder Robot, see Lantern Robot $1,475.00

R-1 Robotank Z Robot, TN, b/o, 1960s, tin, rare plastic arm version, 11", NM+IB, A (Est: $250) $575.00

R-1 Robotank Z Robot, TN, 1960s, lithographed tin, 10", A (Est: $200.00 – $400.00), $250.00. (Photo courtesy Bertoia Auctions)

Rachet Robot, TN, w/up, tin, 8", NMIB, A (Est: $500).$900.00

Radar Robot, TN, r/c, tin, coil on head w/antenna, 10", NM+IB, A (Est: $1,200)....................................$1,600.00

Radar Robot (Pinocchio/Topolino Robot), b/o, litho tin w/plastic Pinocchio-type nose, mc, 11", NM+IB, A (Est: $14,000)..$15,000.00

Radar Scope Space Scout, SH, 1960s, b/o, litho tin, w/chest screen, 9", EX+, A (Est: $250-$350) $220.00

Radicon Robot, Masudaya, r/c, tin, 15", EXIB, A (Est: $9,000) $9,000.00

Robbie the Robot (The Original Robbie), see Mechanized Robot

Robert the Robot, Ideal, r/c, tin, skirted bottom, 16", EXIB, A $220.00

Robot Spaceship and Saucers, Cragstan, windup, lithographed tin, 8" overall, EX+, A (Est: $250.00 – $350.00), $330.00. (Photo courtesy Bertoia Auctions)

Robo Tank (Mini), TN, b/o, tin & plastic, 4¾", NMIB, A (Est: $125)..$150.00

Robot (Directional), Y, 1960s, b/o, litho tin, skirted bottom, red light atop head, 11", VG, A (Est: $400-$600).........$440.00

Robot (Directional), Y, 1960s, b/o, litho tin, skirted bottom, red light atop head, 11", EX+IB, A (Est: $1,200-$1,500)..........$1,430.00

Robot (Easel Back), Linemar, 1950s, r/c, litho tin w/clear plastic bubble helmet, 6", EX+IB, A (Est: $3,000-$3,500).$3,300.00

Robot Lilliput, KT, w/up, litho tin, 6", NMIB, A (Est: $5,000)...$8,200.00

Robot Lilliput, KT, w/up, litho tin, 6", VG, A (Est: $375).$1,325.00

Robot Torpedo, Marusan, crank action, tin, 11½", NM, A (Est: $375)..$475.00

Robot Torpedo, Marusan, crank action, tin, 11½", NMIB, A (Est: $750) $825.00

Robot w/Spark (Walking), SY, w/up, 7", EXIB, A (Est: $175) ...$200.00

Robot/Shoot Him, see Shoot Him Robot

Robotank Z Robot, see R-1 Robotank Z Robot

Robotrac, Japan, b/o, litho tin, robot at controls of bulldozer, 9½" L, VG+, A (Est: $200-$300) $160.00

Rocket Man (in Space Armor), Alps, 1960s, r/c, litho tin, 14", VGIB, A (Est: $750) $975.00

Rocket Racer, Masudaya, friction, litho tin, pilot on open cockpit, EXIB, A (Est: $125) $325.00

Rocket Ship, Holdeakete, friction, litho tin, upright w/pointed nose, fold-down ladder, 16", VG, A (Est: $25-$50) ...$55.00

Rockety Man in Space Armor, Alps, b/o, tin & plastic, complete w/4 rockets, 13½", NMIB, A (Est: $750) $1,535.00

Rotate-O-Matic Super Astronaut, Horikawa, b/o, litho tin, chest opens to reveal guns, 11½", EX, A (Est: $300-$500)..$165.00

Satellite, Japan, b/o, 3 red plastic rockets encircling litho tin globe on wire supports, 10", EXIB, A (Est: $75-$150)..........$430.00

Satellite Fleet, TPS, w/up, litho tin, mother ship pulling w/3 smaller ships, 12" L overall, NM, A (Est: $175) $415.00

Satellite Launcher (USA Army Truck), TN, friction, tin w/2 plastic satellites, 8", NM, A......................................$200.00

Satellite Launching Truck, Japan, friction, litho tin, plastic dome, complete w/accessories, 12", EX, A (Est: $100-$200)..$200.00

Secret Weapon Space Scout, Horikawa, b/o, litho tin w/face behind oval mask, guns in chest, 9", VG, A (Est: $400-$600)...$245.00

See-Thru Robot, Hong Kong, b/o, plastic, 12", VGIB, A (Est: $85)..$475.00

Shoot Him Robot, Masudaya, b/o, litho tin, shoot w/gun & he changes direction, 15", NMIB, A (Est: $7,000) ...$8,500.00

Shoot Him Robot, Masudaya, b/o, litho tin, shoot w/gun & he changes direction, 15", EX+, A (Est: $3,000) $3,500.00

Sky Patrol, TN, b/o, litho tin, 13", EX+IB, A (Est: $225) .$450.00

Smoking Robot w/Lantern, Linemar, r/c, tin, silver w/red detail, 8", EX, A (Est: $200) $2,000.00

Smoking Space Man, Linemar, b/o, tin, silver, 12", NMIB, A (Est: $1,500) $2,000.00

Sonicon Rocket, MT, litho tin, 13" L, NMIB, A............$675.00

Space Capsule (New), Japan, b/o, litho tin & plastic, doors open to reveal astronaut, 9", EXIB, A (Est: $150-$250) ..$110.00

Space Captain, AN, w/up, litho tin, holding space rifle, 8", A (Est: $750)...$1,300.00

Space Controlled Tractor, Hong Kong, b/o, plastic, bulldozer w/robot driver, 12", EXIB, A $425.00

Space Dog, Y, 1950s, friction, robotic look w/flat head, 'bulging' eyes, 7" L, EX, A (Est: $150-$250).....................$175.00

Space Elephant, KO, w/up, lith tin, 5", NMIB, A (Est: $1,000) $1,200.00

Space Elephant, KO, w/up, litho tin, 5", EX+, A (Est: $375).$425.00

Space Explorer (Robot), Y, battery-operated, lithographed tin, head and limbs retract into square body, 7½", EX+IB, A (Est: $800.00 – $1,000.00), $1,760.00. (Photo courtesy Bertoia Auctions)

Space Explorer (Robot), Y, b/o, tin, astronaut is at controls on screen in robot's chest, 12", NMIB, A (Est: $700) .$1,000.00

Space Explorer (Robot/Astronaut), SH, b/o, tin & plastic, flight of Apollo on screen, 12", NM+IB, A (Est: $100) $250.00

Space Explorer Vehicle, Japan, friction, litho tin, resembles train engine, lithoed detail, 13", EX, A (Est: $50-$100) $90.00

Space Man, Linemar, w/up, tin & plastic, 6", EX, A (Est: $100) $225.00

Space Man, Yonezawa, friction, litho tin, 9½", G+, A (Est: $275)..$775.00

Space Man, Yoshia, w/up, litho tin, full lithoed face shown in helmet, 6", EX+IB, A (Est: $250-$350) $330.00

Space Man (w/Spark), Noguchi, w/up, litho tin, 5½", EXIB, A (Est: $85) $150.00

Space Man (Walking), Tomiyama, w/up, tin & plastic, 5½", NMIB, A (Est: $375)..$525.00

Space Man Car, Usagiya, friction, tin, subamrine body w/sq robot head, bl w/red & yel, 6½", NM+IB, A (Est: $600)..$1,025.00

Space Man Robot, Japan, w/up, litho tin, gray w/red eyes, ears & feet, controls on chest, 7", EXIB, A (Est: $75-$125) ..$745.00

Space Patrol (Space Robot Patrol), Cragstan, friction, litho tin, robot in car, 8", EX+IB, A (Est: $1,500-$2,500) ..$2,300.00

Space Patrol (Walking), TT, w/up, tin, 4½" dia, NM, A.$250.00

Space Patrol R-10 Car, TN, b/o, litho tin, driver in Volkswagen-type convertible, 13", EX+IB, A $3,750.00

Space Patrol Super Cycle, Bandai, friction, tin, 12", NM, A $1,850.00

Space Patrol X-11, Y, b/o, litho tin, 8", NMIB, A (Est: $150).$350.00

Space Patrol/King Flying Saucer, Japan, b/o, rnd litho tin ship w/plastic dome, 7½" dia, EXIB, A (Est: $75-$125)....$90.00

Space Pioneer (Super Sonic), Modern Toys, b/o, litho tin, 12", EXIB, A (Est: $200-$300) $200.00

Space Racer, TN, b/o, tin & plastic, 6½" L, NM+IB, A..$150.00

Space Ranger-7, Taiwan, b/o, rnd litho tin vehicle w/plastic dome, 8" dia, EXIB, A (Est: $50-$100) $90.00

Space Refuel Station, Japan, 1950s, battery-operated, lithographed tin, 13", nonworking otherwise EXIB, A (Est: $1,200.00 – $1,500.00), $1,430.00. (Photo courtesy Randy Inman Auctions)

Space Robot X-70 (Tulip Head), see X-70 (Space Robot/Tulip Head)

Space Rocket, Masuya, r/c, litho tin, Blue Eagle jet w/moving wings & flashing engine light, 15", NMIB, A (Est: $425) $450.00

Space Rocket, SY, friction, tin, robot driver in rocket car, friction, tin, 6", EXIB, A (Est: $175).............................$225.00

Space Rocket Car X, Masudaya, 1950s, friction, litho tin, 6" L, NMIB, A (Est: $150)...$575.00

Space Scout (Radar-Scope), Horikawa, b/o, tin & plastic, space scenes on screen in chest, 10", NMIB, A (Est: $75) ..$140.00

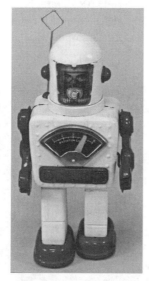

Space Scout, Y, 1960s, battery-operated, tin, white and red (rare version), 9½", EX+, A (Est: $2,500.00 – $3,000.00), $2,860.00. (Photo courtesy Bertoia Auctions)

Space Scout Robot, Y, tin, wht & red (rare version), Radiation Count dial in chest, 10", VG, A (Est: $1,500-$2,000) $1,870.00

Space Ship Discoverer XX3, Alps, friction, tin & plastic, 13", EXIB, A $400.00

Space Ship SS-18, S&E, friction, litho tin w/clear plastic dome, 10", EX+IB, A...$250.00

Space Ship X-5, MT, b/o, rnd litho tin vehicle w/plastic dome, 8" dia, EXIB, A (Est: $75-$125) $75.00

Space Ship X-8, Tada, b/o, litho tin w/plastic bubble cockpit, 8" L, VGIB, A (Est: $200-$300)................................$275.00

Space Station, Japan, b/o, litho tin, rnd w/figure in clear plastic dome, 9" dia, VG+, A (Est: $200-$300) $230.00

Space Station/NASA, Horikawa, early version, b/o, litho tin, 5 rooms, 11" dia, EXIB, A (Est: $700).....................$1,340.00

Space Tank (Robot Driver), Japan, friction, litho tin w/clear plastic dome, 6" L, nonworking o/w VG, A (Est: $75-$125) $90.00

Space Tank M-18, Masudaya, b/o, litho tin, bump-&-go action, 8½", NMIB, A (Est: $225) $400.00

Space Traveling Monkey, see Battery-Operated category

Space Trip Station, Y, b/o, litho tin, 14" L, NMIB, A (Est: $875)..$1,325.00

Space Trooper, Haji, 1950s, w/up, litho tin, holds gun, 7", VG, A (Est: $300-$500) $465.00

Space Vehicle #28905, Japan, b/o, litho tin, tank form, 4-wheeled, driver in dome, 8½", VG+, A (Est: $150-$250) $190.00

Spacecraft Jupiter, K/Japan, w/up, litho tin saucer w/clear plastic dome, 5" dia, EXIB, A $85.00

Spaceship, Ashi, friction, lithographed tin with astronaut under clear plastic dome, tail fin, 8½", VG, A (Est: $200.00 – $500.00), $135.00. (Photo courtesy Bertoia Auctions)

Spaceship, Japan, b/o, litho tin, rnd w/figure in dome, spiral coil & 2 antenna, red, 7½" dia, G, A (Est: $75-$125) $55.00

Spaceship Pulling Three Smaller Saucers, Cragstan, w/up, litho tin, no sz given, EX+, A (Est: $250-$350) $330.00

Spacetrooper Robot (Robby-Type), Yoshiya, 1950s, r/c, tin, 6½", EX, A (Est: $700-$1,000) $660.00

Sparking Robot, N, w/up, tin, 6½", NMIB, A (Est: $200).$225.00

Sparkling Space Dog, KO, friction, litho tin, 4¼", NMIB, A (Est: $475) $600.00

Sparky Robot, Japan, w/up, tin, silver w/red feet & head phones, 7½", EXIB, A (Est: $500-$800) $675.00

Special Man X-15 Saucer, Masudaya, friction, litho tin, man in saucer w/Japanese lettering, 8" dia, NMIB, A..........$575.00

SS Space Rocket, J KO, friction, litho tin, 13½" L, NMIB, A $1,300.00

Star Robot, Hong Kong, b/o, plastic, blk w/mc chest detail, 12", EXIB, A (Est: $25-$50) $35.00

Super Hero Robot, Bullmark, w/up, red & silver litho tin, 9", EX+IB, A (Est: $200-$300).............................$770.00

Super Jet V-7, TN, b/o, tin, 12" L, VG+, A (Est: $250) .$500.00

Super Moon Explorer (Robot), Hong Kong, b/o, plastic, blk, red feet, lithoed face in helmet, 12", EXIB, A (Est: $25-$50)..$90.00

Super Robot, M, w/up, litho tin, 5½", NMIB, A (Est: $125)..$200.00

Super Robot, SH, b/o, tin & plastic, 12", NMIB, A (Est: $125)...$125.00

Ultra Man Leo Robot, Bullmark, windup, red tin body, green rubber head with yellow eyes, 9", EX+, A (Est: $800.00 – $1,000.00), $825.00. (Photo courtesy Bertoia Auctions)

Super Space Capsule Apollo, SH, 1960s, battery-operated, lithographed tin, 9", NMIB, $300.00. (Photo courtesy Don Hultzman)

Super Space Giant (Robot), Japan, contemporary version, b/o, litho tin & plastic, 18", EX+IB, A (Est: $100-$200) .$230.00

Swinging Baby Robot, Japan, w/up, litho tin robot on swing, 12", EXIB, A (Est: $400-$500)..............................$550.00

Target Robot, see Shoot Him Robot

Television Space Man, Alps, w/up, litho tin, 6", EXIB, A (Est: $200-$300) $330.00

Tetsujin Robot, Japan, b/o, tin, gray w/red & gr detail, Japanese characters on belt, 13", NM, A (Est: $750)..........$1,550.00

Tetsujin 28 #3, TN, w/up, tin w/rubber nose, walks w/engine noise, 10", EX+, A (Est: $500)..............................$890.00

Thunder Robot, Asakusa, b/o, tin, w/spinning antenna on top, blk w/gr eyes & red detail, 12", NM+IB, A (Est: $7,500) $7,500.00

Tin Man Robot, see Battery-Operated category

Train Robot, see Giant Sonic Robot

Tulip Head Robot, see X-70 (Space Robot/Tulip Head)

Two-Stage Earth Satelite, Linemar, crank-op, litho tin, 9" L, EX+IB, A (Est: $225) $350.00

Two-Stage Rocket Launching Pad, TN, b/o, 8x7x4", NMIB, A (Est: $375) $650.00

UFO X05, MT, Japan, b/o, rnd litho tin vehicle w/plastic dome, 8" dia, EXIB, A (Est: $75-$125) $55.00

Ultra Man Leo Robot, Bullmark, b/o, litho tin w/vinyl head, 12½", NMIB, A (Est: $750)................................$2,000.00

Universe Car (Mystery Action), China, b/o, litho tin w/opaque wht plastic dome, 10" L, EXIB, A (Est: $50-$75) $65.00

Universe Teleboat #7, China, b/o, litho tin & plastic, astronaut w/camera seated in rocket, 15" L, EX, A (Est: $75-$125) $50.00

Urutora Man, Bullmark, w/up, red & silver tin body, gray vinyl head w/yel bug eyes, 9½", EX+IB, A (Est: $300-$400) $600.00

USA NASA Gemini, Masudaya, b/o, astronaut circle spacecraft, 9½" L, EX+IB, A $150.00

V-3 Rocket, Cragstan, 1950s, friction, litho tin, 3", NM ..$75.00

Video Robot, Japan, b/o, litho tin, blk w/red feet, lg screen in chest, mc lithoed controls, 9", EXIB, A (Est: $75-$125) $260.00

Vureiza (Blazer), Bullmark, w/up, tin w/vinyl head, walks as arms move, 8½", NM+IB (Japanese box), A (Est: $200)...$450.00

Walking Astroman w/Sparks, TN, w/up, litho tin, human form in spacesuit, 10½", rare, NM+IB, A (Est: $10,000) .$16,000.00

Walking Space Man, Linemar, b/o, litho tin, 7½", VG+, A (Est: $475) $1,000.00

X-70 (Space Robot/Tulip Head), TN, 1960s, battery-operated, tin and plastic, 12", EX, A (Est: $800.00 – $1,000.00), $715.00.

Walking Space Man, SY, w/up, tin, 9", NMIB, A (Est: $400) .$725.00

Winky Robot, Y, w/up, tin w/rubber ears, gray w/red detail, meter in chest, winky eyes, 10", NM+IB, A (Est: $2,000) $2,800.00

Winner #23 Rocket Vehicle, KDP, 1960s, b/o, litho tin, 5½", EX, A (Est: $75-$125)......................................$115.00

X-15 Spaceship, KO, 1960s, w/up, litho tin w/pilot under clear plastic dome, 6" dia, NM+ $150.00

X-70 (Space Robot/Tulip Head), TN, 1960s, b/o, tin & plastic, NMIB, A (Est: $650) $1,825.00

XX-2 Rocket, Cragstan, 1960s, friction, litho tin & plastic, 13", NM..$125.00

Z-01 Space Ship, Japan, friction, litho tin w/plastic dome, rnd w/2 wheels, red figure, 6" dia, VG, A (Est: $75-$125)........$90.00

Zabitan, TT, w/up, tin w/vinyl head, 9", NMIB (Japanese box), A (Est: $175) $225.00

Zero of Space Robot, Hong Kong, 1970s, b/o, plastic, NM+IB $375.00

MISCELLANEOUS

Bank, 'Plan-It,' depicts solar system, die-cast, 8½" dia, EX, A (Est: $300-$450)...$220.00

Blast-Off Space Game, Replogle Globe-Chicago, 1953, unused, NM+IB, A $675.00

Figure, ceramic w/clear celluloid space helmet, wide stance with head slightly turned, Kreiss, 1957, 6", VG $50.00

Kite, paper w/wood supports, various space graphics, Alox Mfg, 1950s, 28x22", unused, EX+ $20.00

Lamp, rnd-headed robot w/short body & feet, lg rnd bug eyes, litho tin w/chrome & gold trim, electric, 10", NM..$175.00

Missile Saving Bank, Japan, missile shoots coin into moon, litho tin, 7" L, NMIB, A (Est: $425) $525.00

Rocket Patrol Target Game, American Toy Prod, 1950s, EX+..$75.00

Space Money Bank, SI, lithogrpahed tin, 6½" dia, NMIB, A $725.00.

Space Scope, TN, paper kalidescope w/3 snap-on heads, MIB, A (Est: $85) $85.00

Spaceport USA Punch-Out Book, Whitman, 1953, unused, VG...$35.00

Spaceship Cap Toy, plastic rocket form w/raised spaceman on sides, Hong Kong, 1950s, NMIP (Plastic Toy on header card) $30.00

Spinaround Planet Bank, Vacumet, die-cast & plastic, planets on disc around sun bank, 8" dia, NMIB, A (Est: $65)......$65.00

Top, litho tin w/wooden hdl, allover space images, 1950s-60s, 5x5" dia, EX+...$50.00

Rock 'n Roll

From the 1950s on, rock 'n roll music has been an enjoyable part of many of our lives, and the performers themselves have often been venerated as icons. Today some of the biggest artists such as Elvis, the Beatles, KISS, and the Monkees, for instance, have fans that not only continue to appreciate their music but actively search for the ticket stubs, concert posters, photographs, and autographs of their favorites. More easily found, through, are the items that sold through retail stores at the height of their careers — dolls, games, toys, books, magazines, etc. In recent years, some of the larger auction galleries have sold personal items such as guitars, jewelry, costumes, automobiles, contracts, and other one-of-a-kind items that realized astronomical prices. If you're an Elvis fan, we recommend *Elvis Collectibles* and *Best of Elvis Collectibles* by Rosalind Cranor (Overmountain Press).

See also Action Figures; Bubble Bath Containers; Character and Promotional Drinking Glasses; Coloring, Activity, and Paint Books; Lunch Boxes; Model Kits; Paper Dolls; Pin-Back Buttons.

Andy Gibb, doll, wht suit & red vest, Ideal, 1979, 7½", MIB..$85.00

Andy Gibb, Wireless FM Microphone, LJN, 1978, MIB, from $55 to $75.00

Beatles, ball, blk w/faces & faux signatures on wht oval, 9" dia, EX $850.00

Beatles, banjo, Mastro, 22", EXIB..............................$3,000.00

Beatles, Beatlephones, Koss Electronics, EXIB............$2,000.00

Beatles, Beatles Colouring Set, Kitfix, 1964, complete, rare, MIB, $2,000.00. (Photo courtesy Joe Hilton and Greg Moore)

Beatles, bongos, red plastic w/blk & wht photo decals, Mastro, VG, from $2,500 to $3,500.00

Beatles, brooch, group photo set in plastic, EXOC...........$60.00

Beatles, bulletin board, Yellow Submarine, Unicorn Creations, 24x24", MIP, from $800 to $1,000.00

Beatles, chair, Yellow Submarine, inflatable vinyl, NM....$50.00

Beatles, Colorforms Cartoon Kit, 1966, complete, MIB, from $800 to..$1,000.00

Beatles, decals, blk & orange on yel, unused, set of 11 .....$90.00

Beatles, dolls, Beatles Forever, Applause, Raggedy Ann style, set of 4 w/stands & cb stage, 22", M..................................$400.00

Beatles, dolls, Remco, soft bodies, set of 4, NM............$375.00

Beatles, drum, blk outline of Ringo's head, hand & signature, w/stand, New Beat, 14" dia, EX............................$675.00

Beatles, figures, cartoon series, pnt resin, 1985, set of 4, 6", NM $150.00

Beatles, figures, Swingers Music Set, set of 4, 4", MOC (sealed), from $125 to..$150.00

Beatles, figures from gumball machine, rubber, red, bl or blk, 3", set of 4..$60.00

Beatles, game board, Flip Your Wig, Milton Bradley, 1960s, EX+..$75.00

Beatles, guitar, Four Pop, head images of group & name, NM...$650.00

Beatles, guitar, Junior by Selcol, red plastic w/group photo, paper label, 14", rare, EX..$1,500.00

Beatles, guitar strings, Hofner, NMIP..............................$80.00

Beatles, key chain, Love Songs promo, record shape w/logo, EX $15.00

Beatles, nesting dolls, hand-pnt wood w/Sgt Pepper costumes, EX..$50.00

Beatles, nodders, plastic, set of 4, 4" $40.00

Beatles, pencil case, oversized, beige leather w/cloth fringe across top, name & group w/instruments, 5x12", EX $280.00

Beatles, pennant, I Love the Beatles, felt, 29", EX $200.00

Beatles, pop-out art book, Yellow Submarine, 10 pgs w/20 popouts for multiple uses, KF/Subafilms, 1968, unused, M $65.00

Beatles, Poster Put-Ons, Yellow Submarine, unused, MIP .$225.00

Beatles, purse, blk vinyl clutch-type w/wht printed photo & names, orig leather strap, rare, EX............................$400.00

Beatles, record player, inside lid displays group w/insruments, 1964, VG $4,700.00

Beatles, scrapbook, The Beatles Scrap Book, 4 head images, Whitman/Nems, 1964, 13½x11", EX........................$75.00

Beatles, spatter toy, 16", rare, MIP $300.00

Beatles, squirt gun, 1960s, yel plastic submarine, 6", EX...$40.00

Beatles, switch plate cover, Yellow Submarine, cb litho of Turtle Turk, EXOC..$65.00

Beatles, wallet, red vinyl w/portrait & signatures, w/coin slots, comb & nail file, zipper closure, VG $50.00

Beatles, watercolor set, Yellow Submarine, Craftmaster, complete, MIB..$150.00

Beatles, wig, Lowell, MIP (sealed) $125.00

Bee Gees, fan club kit, 1979, complete, NM, from $75 to .$100.00

Bee Gees, record case, Vanity Fair, 1979, photo image on wht, for 45 rpm, EX, from $40 to..................................$50.00

Bobby Sherman, Love Beads, 1971, M, from $40 to.........$50.00

Bobby Sherman, ring, Love & Peace, 1971, M $25.00

Boy George, doll, LJN, 1984, 11½", rare, MIB $150.00

Boy George, puffy stickers, set of 6, 1984, M....................$15.00

Captain & Tennille, dolls, Mego, 1977, 12½", MIB, ea .$125.00

Chubby Checker, party game, Limbo Under the Bar, Wham-O, 1961, complete, NM..$100.00

David Cassidy, Dress-Up Set, 1972, MIP, $30.00. (Photo courtesy Greg Davis and Bil Morgan)

David Cassidy, guitar, Carnival Toys, 1973, plastic, 31", MIB.$250.00

David Cassidy, slide-tile puzzle, 1970s, M........................$35.00

Dick Clark, diary, vinyl, 1958, 4x4", EX $125.00

Dick Clark, doll, Juro, 1958, 24", MIB........................$250.00

Donny & Marie, AM pocket radio, LJN, 1977, 5", NM, from $35 to $45.00

Donny & Marie, iron-ons, 1970s, several different, ea from $10 to $15.00

Donny & Marie, marionettes, in bl show outfits, Osbro Prod, 1978, 12", MIB, ea..$100.00

Donny & Marie, Poster Pen Set, Craft House, 1977, unused, MIP $20.00

Donny & Marie, Show Biz Wireless Microphone, LJN, 1977, MIP, from $50 to..$75.00

Donny & Marie, tambourine, Lapin, 1977, 6" dia, M, from $30 to..$40.00

Elvis, autograph book, EP Enterprises, 1956, EX, minimum value $500.00

Elvis, beach hat, 1956, orig photo hang tag, EX $150.00

Elvis, bracelet, dog tag, EP Enterprises, 1950s, MOC (beware of repros) $150.00

Elvis, Coloring Contest page, line drawing of Elvis & girls from Girls! Girls! Girls!, Paramount, 1962, unused, M......$35.00

Elvis, doll, Elvis in Concert, Starr, 1987, plays micro-cassettes (4), 17", MIB..$90.00

Elvis, earrings, Loving You..., gold-framed portraits w/pierced backs, MIP $225.00

Elvis, flasher ring, 1957, EX, minimum value $100.00

Elvis, guitar, Lapin, 1984, MOC (sealed)........................$75.00

Elvis, Hound Dog, plush w/Elvis lettered on wht neck ribbon, Smile Toy Co, NM $250.00

Elvis, necklace, Love Me Tender, EP Enterprises, 1956, NMOC, from $175 to $225.00

Elvis, overnight case, simulated leather w/images of Elvis & signatures, EP Enterprises, 1956, EX $750.00

Elvis, pillow, Love Me Tender, print of Elvis singing & playing guitar & faux signature, EP Enterprises, 1956, NM .$400.00

Elvis, purse, bl foldover carryall w/Elvis playing guitar, EP Enterprises, 1956, 5x10", M, from $600 to $1,000.00

Herman's Hermits, doll, Peter Noone, Show Biz Babies, NMIB..$250.00

Jackson Five, banner, 1960s-70s, I Love Jackson 5, blk felt w/wht lettering & red trim, 29", NM $25.00

John Travolta, scrapbook, Sunridge, 1978, EX.................$10.00

KISS, backpack, photo on red canvas, Thermos, 1979, EX, $100.00. (Photo courtesy June Moon)

KISS, belt buckle, 1977, blk w/silver letters & border, M.$30.00

KISS, Colorforms, 1979, complete, MIB..........................$85.00

KISS, costume, Gene Simmons, 1978, sm, EXIB............$160.00

KISS, Your Face Makeup, Remco, 1978, MIB (sealed)...$200.00

KISS, 3-Function Van, radio controlled, 1979, unused, MIB..$600.00

Led Zeppelin, blimp, inflatable vinyl, distributed to music stores for record promo, M....................$100.00

Mamas & Papas, Show Biz Babies, Remco, MOC, ea.....$200.00

Marie Osmond, Hair Care Set, Gordy, 1976, MOC $25.00

Marie Osmond, Marie's Vanity Set, Standard Pyroxoloid Corp, 1977, MOC..................$25.00

MC Hammer, Rap Mike, Impact Toy, 1991, MIB.............$25.00

Michael Jackson, AM radio w/headphones, Ertl, 1984, MIB .$35.00

Michael Jackson, belt, red cloth w/wht stitched name & gloved hand, blk trim, disc buckle w/photo image, US, 1984, M.................$30.00

Monkees, tambourine, NM, $125.00. (Photo courtesy Bob Guttuso)

Monkees, charm bracelet, rnd disk charms w/photo head images, gold-tone chain-link band, Raybert, 1967, MOC......$90.00

Monkees, clothes hanger, heavy cb w/diecut blk & wht head photo of Mike Nesmith, Reybert Prod, 1960s, EX.....$35.00

Monkees, finger puppets, 1970, EX, ea..............................$35.00

Monkees, guitar, Mattel, 1966, 14", NM......................$150.00

Monkees, Monkeemania Oil Paint Set, Art Award, 1967, unused, MIB..................$250.00

Monkees, rings, flicker, several different, Kellogg's, 1967, EX, ea..................$30.00

New Kids on the Block, cassette player, Big Step Prod, 1990, MIB $35.00

New Kids on the Block, Colorforms Deluxe Playset, 1991, MIB..................$15.00

New Kids on the Block, dolls, In Concert, 5 different, Hasbro, 12", MIB, ea..................$45.00

New Kids on the Block, Fashion Plates, Hasbro, 1990, unused, MIB..................$35.00

Osmonds, frisbee, The Osmonds Zoom-O, group image in center, 1970s, EX..................$35.00

Rick Nelson, Picture Patch, 1950s, MOC.......................$20.00

Rolling Stones, dolls, Play Pals, 1963, rare, M, ea $125.00

Rolling Stones, Rad-A-Tattoos, Brockman, 1991, MOC .$15.00

Rolling Stones, sticker album, Stanley, 1983, NM+ $20.00

Shaun Cassidy, guitar, Carnival Toys, 1978, MIP $100.00

Shaun Cassidy, record case, Vanity Fair, 1978, cb, EX......$35.00

Van Halen, binoculars, plastic w/VH logo, EX $20.00

Village People, guitar, Carnival Toys, 1978, 36", MIP....$150.00

ZZ Top, mirror, 1980s, 6x6", M...$10.00

Roly Polys

Popular toys with children around the turn of the century, roly polys were designed with a weighted base that caused the toy to automatically right itself after being kicked or knocked over. Their popularity faded to some extent, but they continued to be produced until WWI and beyond. Most were made of papier-mache, though some Japanese toy makers used celluloid later on. Schoenhut made some that are especially collectible today in a variety of sizes — up to almost a foot in height. They represented clowns, animals, and children, as well as some well known story book characters.

Austrian Boy & Girl, 8", compo, musical, molded heads & arms, colorful ethnic costumes w/real feathers in caps, EX, pr $225.00

Baby Boy, 11½", compo, movable head, hands on belly, orange outfit w/wht shirt, yel & red trim, Schoenhut, VG .$300.00

Buster Brown, 2¼", compo, Schoenhut, EX $165.00

Clown, 6", litho tin, hands on belly, cone hat, lithoed ruffled collar, Chein, NM $400.00

Clown, 8", compo, hands on belly, sm rnd derby hat cocked to side, bl-pnt pointed collar, red, wht & bl body, VG..$200.00

Clown, 14", compo, hands on belly, cone hat, wht jacket w/gr vest, brn bottom, heavily rouged cheeks, VG..........$350.00

Clown, 11½", composition, hands on belly, cone hat, half green and half red, EX, $375.00. (Photo courtesy James D. Julia, Inc.)

Clown, 15", compo, hands on belly, cone hat, cloth collar, red, wht & bl, Schoenhut, VG.......................................$925.00
Clown, 15", compo, hands on belly, cone hat w/2 pompons, checkerboard suit, pnt collar, Germany, rpt.............$300.00

Donald Duck, 6", celluloid, mouth open, push down on head for squeaking sound (nonworking), EX, $325.00. (Photo courtesy Bertoia Auctions)

Drummer Boy, 4½", compo, holding drum sticks, long hair, bl uniform, wht hat, VG..$100.00
Foxy Grandpa, 10", compo, hands on belly, EX.............$500.00
Golliwog, 4", compo, gray suit, Schoenhut, EX $85.00
Happy Hooligan, 4", compo, hands in pockets, exaggerated face w/arched eyebrows & lg eyes, gr & red, EX.............$200.00
Indian Baby, 4", compo, pnt markings on face, yel outfit w/red trim, wht hood, Schoenhut, G $85.00
Keystone Cop, 5", compo, hands on belly, bl single-breasted jacket & hat, detailed face w/mustache, EX............$125.00
Keystone Cop, 10", compo, musical, hands on belly, bl single-breasted jacket, lg buttons, mustache, VG..............$165.00
Monkey, 6¼", litho tin, red cone hat, red & yel outfit, Chein, EX $250.00
Mother Goose, 8½", holding goose, bl & wht w/red trim, Schonhut, EX...$165.00
Popeye, 5", celluloid, hands on hips & pipe in mouth standing on filled base, mk CSA, rare, NM...........................$300.00
Rabbit, 6¼", litho tin, red jacket w/yel neck bow, Chein, EX...$200.00

Revolutionary Soldier, 15", compo, hands on belly, cloth collar, red & yel, Schoenhut, VG $650.00
Sailor Boy, 9¼", compo, hands on belly, bl suit & hat w/wht trim, Schoenhut, EX...$525.00
Santa, 5", compo, hands on belly, red suit w/pointed hood, wht beard w/long dk gray pnt mustache, EX $125.00

Santa, 10½", composition, hands on belly, molded detailed features, Schoenhut, EX, $1,975.00. (Photo courtesy Bertoia Auctions)

Santa, 11", compo, hands in front holding toy bag on back, red/gr/wht w/blk trim, Schoenhut, VG................$1,375.00

Sand Toys and Pails

By 1900, companies were developing all sorts of sand toys, free-standing models. The Sand Toy Company of Pittsburgh patented and made 'Sandy Andy' from 1909 onward. The company was later bought by the Wolverine Supply & Manufacturing Co. and continued to produce variations of the toy until the 1970s.

Today if you mention sand toys, people think of pails, spades, sifters, and molds.

We have a rich heritage of lithographed tin pails with such wonderful manufacturers as J. Chein & Co., T. Cohn Inc., Morton Converse, Kirchoff Patent Co., Marx Toy Co., and Ohio Art Co. plus the small jobbing companies who neglected to sign their wares. Sand pails have really come into their own and are now recognized for their beautiful graphics and designs. The following listings are lithographed or painted tin. For more information we recommend *Pails by Comparison, Sand Pails and Other Sand Toys, A Study and Price Guide*, by Carole and Richard Smyth.

Bowler Andy Mill, Wolverine #57A, 20", NMIB...........$400.00
Captain Sandy Andy, Wolverine #63C, 13½", MIB $375.00
Coal Loader, Wolverine, elevator & crane, 11", MIB.....$400.00
Crane, Wolverine #020, 17½", MIB $375.00
Dandy Sandy Andy, Wolverine, 11", G $75.00
Dutch Mill, Mac #26 (McDowell), 1930s, 12", EX.........$100.00
Dutch Mill, Mac #26 (McDowell), 1930s, 12", NMIB...$200.00
Pail, Donald Duck, Mickey, etc on yel, Happynak, 1930s, 4½", EX+, A..$225.00

Pail, Donald Duck at the beach, Ohio Art, 4", VG........$200.00

Pail, Donald Duck in angry pose while nephews play instruments, 5" (to top of hdl), VG...................................$200.00

Pail, Donald Duck in staw hat on the beach, Ohio Art/WDP, 1939, 4½" (to top of hdl), EX $225.00

Pail, elephant family on boardwalk, 3", VG.....................$50.00

Pail, Mickey, Minnie, Donald & Pluto in rowboat, Ohio Art/WDE, 1930s, 5", EX...$350.00

Pail, Mickey, Minnie, Horace Horsecollar & Clarabelle Cow at Atlantic City, Ohio Art/WDE, 1930s, 4", EX+ $825.00

Pail, Mickey, Minnie, Pluto & Clarabelle Cow at drink stand w/sign reading Ice Cold Drinks, Ohio Art, 1930s, 3", NM+ $400.00

Pail, Mickey, Minnie & Donald at the beach, Happynak, 10½" (to top of hdl), EX $150.00

Pail, Mickey (as pirate), Minnie & 2 of Donald's nephews burying treasure on desert island, Happynak, 1950s, 4½, EX .$200.00

Pail, Mickey & Donald on yel background w/red & bl stars, Happynak, 1950s, 3½", NM...............................$150.00

Pail, Pail Face/Right Side Up/Up Side Down, 4", EX.....$100.00

Pail, Popeye at the beach, Chein, 1936, 3¾", VG..........$150.00

Pail, Sea Side, red, wht & bl patriotic detail, 3", EX $250.00

Pail, Snow White & the Seven Dwarfs (lettered at bottom of pail), Ohio Art/WDE, 1938, 6", NM $350.00

Pail, Snow White and the Seven Dwarfs, Ohio Art, 1930s, 10" (largest of the Snow White pails), NM, $275.00. (Photo courtesy David Longest and Michael Stern)

Pail, squirrels (dressed) in landscape, Ohio Art, 3", EX....$75.00

Pail, Three Little Pigs, litho tin, Ohio Art, 1930s, 4½", EX+...$100.00

Sand Lift, Ohio Art, 11", VG...$50.00

Sand Lift, Ohio Art, 11", VGIB.....................................$100.00

Sand Loader, Wolverine, elevator w/crane, 11", MIB.....$400.00

Sandy Andy Merry Miller Mill, 12", VG $100.00

Sandy Andy Sand Loader (Large Can), Wolverine #50, w/seated figure, 13½", EX...$30.00

Sandy Andy Sand Loader (Small Can), Wolverine, VGIB...$30.00

Shovel, Mickey & Minnie Mouse at the beach, Mickey Mouse lettered at bottom, Ohio Art, 1930s, 8", EX............$175.00

Shovel, Micky Mouse, litho tin, Mickey dives into wave as Minnie watches, Ohio Art/WDE, 1930s, 8", NM $275.00

Sunny Andy Fun Fair No 65, Wolverine, 14" L, NMIB.$500.00

Sunny Andy Kiddy Kampers No 66, 13½" L, EXIB........$300.00

Teeter-Totter, center tower w/boy & girl on teeter-totter, 14" T, EX $150.00

Water Pump, lithoed w/children & elephant, Ohio Art, 10", EX, A $100.00

Schoenhut

Albert Schoenhut & Co. was located in Philadelphia, Pennsylvania. From as early as 1872, they produced toys of many types including dolls, pianos and other musical instruments, games, and a good assortment of roly polys (which they called Rolly Dollys). In 1902 and 1903 they were granted patents that were the basis for toy animals and performers that Schoenhut designated the 'Humpty Dumpty Circus.' It was made up of circus animals, ringmasters, acrobats, lion tamers, and the like, and the concept proved to be so successful that it continued in production until the company closed in 1935. During the nearly thirty-five years they were made, the figures were continually altered either in size or by construction methods, and these variations can greatly affect their values today. Besides the figures themselves, many accessories were produced to go along with the circus theme — tents, cages, tubs, ladders, and wagons, just to mention a few. Teddy Roosevelt's 1909 African safari adventures inspired the company to design a line that included not only Teddy and the animals he was apt to encounter in Africa but native tribesmen as well. A third line in the 1920s featured comic characters of the day, all with the same type of jointed wood construction, many dressed in cotton and felt clothing. There were several, among them were Felix the Cat, Maggie and Jiggs, Barney Google and Spark Plug, and Happy Hooligan. (See Character, TV, and Movie Collectibles.)

Several factors come into play when evaluating Schoenhut figures. Foremost is condition. Since most found on the market today show signs of heavy wear, anything above a very good rating commands a premium price. Missing parts and retouched paint sharply reduce a figure's value, though a well done restoration is usually acceptable. The earlier examples had glass eyes; by 1920 eyes were painted. In the early 1920s the company began to make their animals in a reduced size. While some of the earlier figures had bisque heads or carved wooden heads, by the '20s, pressed wood heads were the norm. Full-size examples with glass eyes and bisque or carved heads are generally more desirable and more valuable, though rarity must be considered as well.

During the 1950s, some of the figures and animals were produced by the Delvan Company, who had purchased the manufacturing rights.

For more information we recommend *Schoenhut Toy Price Guide* in full color by Keith Kaonis and Andrew Yaffee. Mr. Kaonis is listed in the Directory under Schoenhut.

Advisors: Keith and Donna Kaonis (K6)

See also Character, TV, and Movie Collectibles; Roly Polys.

HUMPTY DUMPTY CIRCUS ANIMALS

Humpty Dumpty Circus animals with glass eyes, circa 1903 – 1914, are more desirable and can demand much higher prices than the later painted-eye versions. As a general rule, a glass-eye version is 30% to 40% more than a painted-eye version. (There are exceptions.) The following list suggests values for both glass eye and painted eye versions and reflects a low painted eye price to a high glass eye price.

There are other variations and nuances of certain figures: bulldog — white with black spots or brindle (brown); open-and closed-mouth zebras and giraffes; ball necks and hemispherical necks on some animals such as the pig, leopard, and tiger, to name a few. These points can affect the price and should be judged individually.

Alligator, PE/GE, from $200 to $650.00
Arabian Camel, 1 hump, PE/GE, from $250 to $750.00
Bactrian Camel, 2 humps, PE/GE, from $200 to $1,200.00
Brown Bear, PE/GE, from $200 to....................................$800.00
Buffalo, cloth mane, PE/GE, from $300 to.....................$900.00
Buffalo, carved mane, PE/GE, from $200 to $1,200.00
Bulldog, PE/GE, from $400 to..$1,500.00
Burro (made for farm set, no harness), PE/GE, from $250 to.$700.00
Burro (made to go w/chariot & clown), PE/GE, from $200 to..$700.00
Cat, PE/GE, rare, from $600 to.....................................$3,000.00
Cow, PE/GE, from $300 to..$1,200.00
Deer, PE/GE, from $300 to..$1,400.00
Donkey, PE/GE, from $75 to...$300.00
Donkey w/Blanket, PE/GE, from $100 to........................$500.00
Elephant, PE/GE, from $75 to..$300.00
Elephant w/Blanket & Head Tapestry, PE/GE, from $200 to..$600.00
Gazelle, PE/GE, rare, from $500 to...............................$2,750.00

Giraffe, painted or glass eyes, from $200.00 to $900.00. (Photo courtesy Keith and Donna Kaonis)

Goat, PE/GE, from $150 to $400.00
Goose, PE only, from $200 to...$600.00

Gorilla, PE only, from $1,500 to $4,000.00
Hippo, PE/GE, from $250 to $800.00
Horse, brn, saddle & stirrups, PE/GE, from $200 to $500.00
Horse, wht, platform, PE/GE, from $190 to $550.00
Hyena, PE/GE, rare, from $1,000 to $6,000.00
Kangaroo, PE/GE, from $300 to.................................$1,800.00
Leopard, PE/GE, from $300 to....................................$1,400.00
Lion, cloth mane, GE only, from $400 to $1,000.00
Lion, carved mane, PE/GE, from $250 to $1,200.00
Monkey, 1-part head, PE only, from $250 to..................$600.00
Monkey, 2-part head, wht face, from $300 to $900.00
Ostrich, PE/GE, from $250 to $900.00
Pig, 5 versions, PE/GE, from $200 to $900.00
Polar Bear, PE/GE, from $400 to................................$2,000.00
Poodle, cloth mane, GE only, from $150 to...................$450.00
Poodle, carved mane, GE, from $400 to.....................$1,200.00
Poodle, PE, from $100 to..$200.00
Rabbit, PE/GE, rare, from $700 to..............................$3,500.00
Rhino, PE/GE, from $250 to $900.00
Sea Lion, PE/GE, from $400 to....................................$1,500.00
Sheep (lamb) w/bell, PE/GE, from $200 to....................$800.00
Tiger, PE/GE, from $250 to..$1,400.00
Wolf, PE/GE, rare, from $500 to $6,000.00
Zebra, PE/GE, from $250 to $1,200.00
Zebu, PE/GE, rare, from $600 to $3,000.00

HUMPTY DUMPTY CIRCUS CLOWNS AND OTHER PERSONNEL

Clowns with two-part heads (a cast face applied to a wooden head) were made from 1903 to 1916 and are most desirable — condition is always important. There have been nine distinct styles in fourteen different costumes recorded. Only eight costume styles apply to the two-part headed clowns. The later clowns, ca. 1920, had one-part heads whose features were pressed, and the costumes were no longer tied at the wrists and ankles.

Note: Use the low end of the value range for items in only fair condition. Those in good to very good condition (having very minor scratches and wear, good original finish, no splits or chips, no excessive paint wear or cracked eyes and, of course, complete) may be evaluated by the high end.

Black Dude, reduced size, from $100 to...........................$400.00
Black Dude, 1-part head, purple coat, from $250 to $700.00
Black Dude, 2-part head, blk coat, from $400 to.........$1,000.00
Chinese Acrobat, 1-part head, from $400 to $800.00
Chinese Acrobat, 2-part head, rare, from $400 to.......$1,600.00
Clown, early, 2-part head, G, from $150 to....................$600.00
Clown, reduced size, from $75 to $125.00
Gent Acrobat, bsk head, rare, from $300 to $750.00
Gent Acrobat, 2-part head, very rare, from $600 to....$2,000.00
Hobo, reduced size, from $200 to $400.00
Hobo, 1-part head, from $200 to....................................$400.00
Hobo, 2-part head, curved-up toes, blk coat, from $500 to..$1,200.00
Hobo, 2-part head, facet toe ft, from $400 to.................$900.00
Lady Acrobat, bsk head, from $400 to............................$800.00
Lady Acrobat, 1-part head, from $200 to.......................$400.00
Lady Rider, 1-part head, from $200 to............................$400.00

Lady Rider, bisque head, from $250.00 to $550.00.

Lady Rider, 2-part head, very rare, from $700 to **$1,800.00**
Lion Tamer, bsk head, rare, from $500 to **$1,000.00**
Lion Tamer, 1-part head, from $400 to **$750.00**
Lion Tamer, 2-part head, early, very rare, from $700 to ..**$1,500.00**
Ringmaster, bsk, from $400 to **$700.00**
Ringmaster, 1-part head, from $200 to.........................**$450.00**
Ringmaster, 2-part head, early, very rare, from $800 to...**$1,800.00**

HUMPTY DUMPTY CIRCUS ACCESSORIES

There are many accessories: wagons, tents, ladders, chairs, pedestals, tight ropes, weights, and various other items.

Circus Cage Wagon, 1920, red w/Schoenhut's...Greatest Show on
    Earth stenciled in yel, 10" & 12", EX, from $300 to .**$1,200.00**
Menagerie Tent, early, ca 1904, from $1,500 to...........**$2,500.00**
Menagerie Tent, later, 1914-20, from $1,200 to **$2,000.00**
Oval Litho Tent, 1926, from $3,000 to........................**$6,000.00**
Sideshow Panels, 1926, pr, from $2,000 to **$5,000.00**

Schuco

A German company noted for both mechanical toys as well as the teddy bears and stuffed animals we've listed here, Schuco operated from the 1930s well into the 1950s. Items were either marked Germany or US Zone, Germany.

See also Aeronautical; Battery-Operated; Character, TV, and Movie Collectibles; Diecast; Disney; Windups, Friction, and Other Mechanicals.

Bear, 2½", blk, shoe-button eyes, felt pads, G+, A (Est: $125-$250).**$200.00**
Bear, 2½", cream, metal eyes, tan nose & mouth, 1920s, VG.**$150.00**
Bear, 2½", pale gold, metal eyes, paper label, 1950s, NM.**$225.00**
Bear, 3½", cinnamon, orig ribbon, 1950s, M **$250.00**
Bear, 4", lt gold, 1940s-50s, EX....................................**$125.00**
Bear, 12", yel, metal eyes, 1920s, VG **$350.00**
Bingo-Bello Dog, 14", orig clothes, NM..........................**$150.00**

Black Scottie, 3", Noah'a Ark, 1950s, MIB **$225.00**
Blackbird, 3", Noah's Ark, 1950s, MIB **$200.00**
Dalmatian, 2½", Noah's Ark, rare, M **$375.00**
Elephant, 2½", Noah's Ark, 1950s, NM **$125.00**
Monkey, 8", brn & wht shaggy mohair, glass eyes, posable fingers
    & toes, EX...**$650.00**
Monkey (Talisman ?), 3½", lavender, 1920s-30s, VG **$200.00**
Monkey Acrobat, 5", brn, flocked tin face, felt ears, hands &
    feet, jtd, w/up action, VG, A....................................**$110.00**
Mouse, 6", mc dress w/gr shoes, EX+ **$200.00**
Orangutan, 3", Noah's Ark, 1950s, rare, MIB..................**$300.00**
Owl, 3", Noah's Ark, 1950s, M...**$75.00**
Penguin, 3", Noah's Ark, 1950s, EX..............................**$150.00**
Perfume Bear, 3½", gold, 1920s, no bottle o/w VG **$150.00**
Perfume Bear, 5", bright gold, orig bottle, 1920s-30s, NM.**$650.00**
Perfume Bear, 5", imprinted Niagara Falls/Germany, orig bottle,
    mid-20th C, EX, A...**$350.00**
Perfume Bellboy Monkey, 5", all orig, EX **$650.00**
Raccoon, 3½", Noah's Ark, 1950s, M **$200.00**
Squirrel, 2½", Noah's Ark, 1950s, M **$150.00**
Tiger, 3½", Noah's Ark, EX **$125.00**
Turtle, 3", Noah's Ark, NM **$110.00**
Two-Faced Bear, 3½", brn, blk shoe-button eyes, 1950s, EX..**$250.00**
Yes/No Bear, 5", caramel, glass eyes, 1950s, NM.............**$450.00**
Yes/No Bear, 5", caramel, glass eyes, 1950s, VG **$200.00**
Yes/No Bear, 17", carmel, amber glass eyes, VG **$1,000.00**

Yes/No Bellboy Bear with Cello, 15", VG, A, $1,150.00. (Photo courtesy James D. Julia, Inc.)

Yes/No Bellboy Monkey, 9", 1920s-30s, EX **$350.00**
Yes/No Bellboy Monkey, 14", 1920s-30s, G **$125.00**
Yes/No Bulldog, 7", cream & brn, glass eyes, 1930s, NM.**$1,200.00**
Yes/No Cat, 5", M...**$650.00**
Yes/No Donkey, 5", 1950s, NM **$475.00**
Yes/No Elephant, 5", 1948, EX **$400.00**
Yes/No Fox, 13", 1920s, NM **$1,200.00**
Yes/No Monkey, 5", cinnamon, blk glasses, G+, A.........**$200.00**
Yes/No Monkey, 5", pk, flock-covered tin face, metal-framed
    sunglasses, head turns w/lever on back, jtd, VG, A ...**$65.00**

Yes/No Panda, 3½", 1950s, NM.................................$1,000.00
Yes/No Panda, 8", 1940-50, rare, EX.........................$850.00
Yes/No Parrot, 11", 1926, rare, NM...........................$650.00
Yes/No Rabbit, 5", NM...$650.00
Yes/No Rooster, 12", 1950s, NM $350.00
Yes/No Tricky Bear, 8", 1950, NM $950.00
Yes/No Tricky Bear, 13", 1948, M $1,200.00
Yes/No Tricky Monkey, 10", orig tag, 1940s-50s, EX $350.00
Yes/No Tricky Monkey, 14", NM.................................$450.00
Yes/No Tricky Orangutan, 8", EX...............................$375.00
Yes/No Tricky Orangutan, 14", NM $950.00

Slot Cars

Slot cars first became popular in the early 1960s. Electric raceways set up in retail storefront windows were commonplace. Huge commercial tracks with eight and ten lanes were located in hobby store and raceways throughout the United States. Large corporations such as Aurora, Revell, Monogram, and Cox, many of which were already manufacturing toys and hobby items, jumped on the bandwagon to produce slot cars and race sets. By the end of the early 1970s, people were loosing interest in slot racing, and its popularity diminished. Today the same baby boomers that raced slot cars in earlier days are revitalizing the sport. The popularity of the Internet has stabilized the pricing of collectible slots. It can confirm prices of common items, while escalating the price of the 'rare' item to new levels. As the Internet grows in popularity, the accessibility of information on slots also grows. This should make the once hard-to-find slot cars more readily available for all to enjoy. Slot cars were generally well used, so finding vintage cars and race sets in like-new or mint condition is difficult. Slot cars replicating the 'muscle' cars from the '60s and '70s are extremely sought after, and clubs and organizations devoted to these collectibles are becoming more and more commonplace. Large toy companies such as Tomy and Tyco still produce some slots today, but not in the quality, quantity, or variety of years past.

Aurora produced several types of slots: Screachers (5700 and 5800 number series, valued at $5.00 to $20.00); the AC-powered Vibrators (1500 number series, valued at $20.00 to $150.00); DC-powered Thunderjets (1300 and 1400 number series, valued at $20.00 to $150.00); and the last-made AFX SP1000 (1900 number series, valued at $15.00 to $75.00).

Advisor: Gary Pollastro (P5)

COMPLETE SETS

AMT, Cobra Racing Set, NMIB $185.00
Atlas, Racing Set #1000, HO scale, GIB $100.00
Aurora, Home Raceway by Sears, #79N9513C, VG........$225.00
Aurora, Mario Andretti GP International Challenge, GIB .$55.00
Aurora, Stirling Moss #1313 Table Top Racing Set, 1968, NMIB $125.00
Aurora AFX, Devil's Ditch Set, EX................................$40.00
Aurora AFX, Jackie Stewart Challenger Raceway, NMIB.$75.00

Aurora AFX, Jackie Stewart Day & Night Enduro, complete, EXIB..$75.00
Aurora AFX, Ultra 5, complete, EXIB $75.00
Cox, Ontario 8, #3070, w/Eagle & McLaren, GIB...........$75.00
Eldon, Challenge Cup Sport 'N Stock, 1/32 scale, complete, NMIB..$85.00

Eldon Dodge Charger Road Race Set, complete, NMIB, $75.00.

Eldon, Raceway Set #24, 1/24th scale, VG $75.00
Eldon, Sky High Triple Road Race, w/Ferrari, Lotus, Stingray & Porsche, GIB..$75.00
Ideal, Alcan Highway Torture Track, 1968, complete, MIB..$50.00
Ideal, Mini-Motorific Set, #4939-5, EX $85.00
Marx, Race & Road Cross-Over Trestles, complete, w/Corvette & Thunderbird, NMIB...$150.00
Motorific, GTO Torture Track, lg, EXIB........................$100.00
Remco, Mighty Mike Action Track, NMIB.....................$50.00
Revell, HiBank Raceway Set #49-9503, w/Cougar GTE & Pontiac Firebird, EXIB...$150.00
Scaletrex, Electric Motor Racing Set, Officially Approved by Jim Clark, made in England, NMIB.........................$400.00
Strombecker, Plymouth Barracuda, 1/32 scale set...........$150.00
Strombecker, Thunderbolt Monza, Montgomery Ward, VGIB..$150.00
Strombecker, 4 Lane Mark IV Race Set, VGIB.............$250.00
Tyco, Collector Edition #6994, Petty '92 STP Special #43 & Petty '70 Superbird #43, bl, twin pk..........................$48.00
Tyco, Racing Bandits, EX $30.00

SLOT CARS ONLY

Aurora, Ford Baja Bronco, #1909, red, EX......................$15.00
Aurora, Ford Street Van, #1943, lt bl & brn, NM $15.00
Aurora, Snowmobile, #1485-400, yel w/bl figure, MIB........$55.00
Aurora AFX, '55 Chevy Bel Air, #1913, yel, VG $16.00
Aurora AFX, Autoworld McLaren XIR, #1752, bl & wht, EX $14.00
Aurora AFX, Autoworld Porsche #5, wht w/bl stripes, EX .$12.00
Aurora AFX, Blazer, #1917, bl & wht, VG $12.00
Aurora AFX, BMW 3201 Turbo, #1980, yel & orange, EX .$20.00
Aurora AFX, Camaro Z-28, #1901, red, wht & bl, EX $20.00
Aurora AFX, Chevelle Stock Car, #1704, yel, red & blk, EX..$16.00

Aurora AFX, Chevy Nomad, #1760, orange, EX..............$20.00
Aurora AFX, Corvette Funny Car, orange & purple, G ...$10.00
Aurora AFX, Datsun Baja Pickup, #1745, bl & blk, EX ...$20.00
Aurora AFX, Dodge Challenger, #1773, lime & bl, NM..$35.00
Aurora AFX, Dodge Charger Stock Car, #1910, wht w/blk hood,
    EXIB..$25.00
Aurora AFX, Dodge Fever Dragster, wht & yel, EX..........$15.00
Aurora AFX, Dodge Police Van, wht w/blk stripe, VG $15.00
Aurora AFX, Dodge Rescue Van, #1937, red, gr & wht, EX.$15.00
Aurora AFX, Ferrari #2, #1763, red & wht or wht & bl, EX,
    ea..$10.00
Aurora AFX, Ferrari 512M #1763, wht & bl, MIB $25.00
Aurora AFX, Ferrari 612, #1751, yel & blk, EX...............$10.00
Aurora AFX, Ford Baja Bronco, #1901, red, EX $14.00
Aurora AFX, Ford Thunderbird Stock Car, NMIB...........$25.00
Aurora AFX, Furious Fueler Dragster, #1774, wht & yel, EX.$15.00
Aurora AFX, Jeep CJ-7 Flamethrower, #1987, orange & red,
    NM..$18.00
Aurora AFX, Mario Andretti NGK Indy Car, blk, M.......$35.00
Aurora AFX, Mazda Taxi, wht, EX...............................$20.00
Aurora AFX, Monza GT, #1948, wht & gr, EX.................$15.00
Aurora AFX, Peterbilt Shell Rig, #1155, yel, red & wht, EX.$25.00
Aurora AFX, Plymouth Roadrunner #43, #1762, bl & wht,
    EX $20.00
Aurora AFX, Pontiac Firebird #9, wht, bl & blk, EX........$25.00
Aurora AFX, Pontiac Grand Am, #10-191, red, wht & bl,
    EX $15.00
Aurora AFX, Porsche Carrera #3, #1933, wht, red & blk, NM.$12.00
Aurora AFX, Porsche 917-10, #1747, wht, red & bl, EX..$12.00
Aurora AFX, Rallye Ford Escort, #1737, gr & bl, EX $15.00
Aurora AFX, Shadow Cam Racer, blk, EX.........................$20.00
Aurora AFX, Speed Banner #11, red, wht & bl, NM $15.00
Aurora AFX, Speed Beamer, red, wht & bl stripe, VG.....$10.00
Aurora AFX, Twi-Night Beamer, wht, red & bl stripe, VG .$10.00
Aurora AFX, Vega Van Gasser, #1754, yel & red, EX $15.00
Aurora AMX, Chevy Nomad, #1760, chrome, EX............$25.00
Aurora Cigarbox, Dino Ferrari, red, EX $20.00
Aurora Cigarbox, Ford GT, wht w/blk stripe, NM+ $20.00
Aurora Cigarbox, Ford Lola GT, red w/wht stripe, G+ $10.00
Aurora G-Plus, Amrac Can Am, yel & blk w/wht stripe, EX.$15.00
Aurora G-Plus, Corvette, #1011, red, orange & wht, EX .$15.00
Aurora G-Plus, Ferrari F1, #1734, red & wht, EX.............$25.00
Aurora G-Plus, Indy Valvoline, blk, VG..........................$12.00
Aurora G-Plus, Lotus F1, #1783, blk & gold, EX.............$20.00
Aurora G-Plus, Rallye Ford Escort, #1737, gr & bl, EX....$15.00
Aurora G-Plus, Shadow Can Am, #1744, wht, red, orange & yel,
    EX $15.00
Aurora Thunderjet, Chaparral 2F #7, #1410, lime & bl, EX.$25.00
Aurora Thunderjet, Cobra #1375, yel w/blk stripe, VG+.$30.00
Aurora Thunderjet, Cougar, #1389, wht, EX $40.00
Aurora Thunderjet, Dune Buggy, wht w/red striped roof, EX.$30.00
Aurora Thunderjet, Ferrari GTO 250, #1368, red w/wht stripes,
    EX $25.00
Aurora Thunderjet, Ford Car, #1382, wht & bl, VG........$25.00
Aurora Thunderjet, Ford GT 40, #1374, red w/blk stripe, EX.$25.00
Aurora Thunderjet, Ford GT 40, #1395, candy-colored bl,
    VG..$40.00

Aurora Thunderjet, Ho Dune Buggy, wht w/red & wht stripe
    top, EX $30.00
Aurora Thunderjet, International Tow Truck, wht & blk w/red
    stripe, EX+ $100.00
Aurora Thunderjet, Lola GT, #1378, turq & wht w/bl stripe,
    VG..$25.00
Aurora Thunderjet, Lola GT (Tuff Tones) #3, #1471, blk,
    orange & wht, EX $45.00
Aurora Thunderjet, Mangusta Mongoose, #1400, yel, EX.$45.00
Aurora Thunderjet, McLaren Elva, #1397, wht, red & blk,
    EX $28.00
Aurora Thunderjet, Sand Van Dune Buggy, #1483, pk & wht,
    EX $25.00
Aurora Thunderjet, Thunderbird Sports Roadster, #1355,
    EX $45.00
Aurora Tomy AFX, Speed Beamer #11, #8763, red, wht & bl,
    EX $15.00
Aurora Vibrator, Mercedes, #1542, yel, EX....................$50.00
Bauer, BMW 501 Police, #4303, gr, MIB.......................$65.00
Strombecker, Pontiac Bonneville, EX $40.00
TCR, Mack Truck, wht & red, EX $15.00
TCR, Maintenance Van, red & wht, EX...........................$15.00

Tomy, Camaro GT #88 Auto Tech, M, from $10.00 to $20.00.

Tyco, '40 Ford Coupe, #8534, blk w/flames, EX $20.00
Tyco, '57 Chevy, red & orange w/yel stripes, EX...............$20.00
Tyco, '83 Corvette Challenger #33, silver & yel, EX $25.00
Tyco, Autoworld Carrera, wht & red w/bl stripe, G..........$10.00
Tyco, Bandit Pickup, blk & red, EX $12.00
Tyco, Blazer, red & blk, VG..$10.00
Tyco, Caterpillar #96, blk & yel, EX $20.00
Tyco, Chaparral 2G #66, #8504, VG................................$14.00
Tyco, Corvette #12, wht & red w/bl stripes, EX................$12.00
Tyco, Corvette Cliffhanger #2, yel & blk, EX $10.00
Tyco, Firebird, #6914, cream & red, VG $12.00
Tyco, Firebird Turbo #12, blk & gold, EX $10.00
Tyco, Funny Mustang, orange w/yel flame, EX.................$25.00
Tyco, Highway Patrol #56, blk & wht, w/sound, EX.........$16.00
Tyco, Jam Car, yel & blk, EX...$10.00
Tyco, Lamborghini, red, VG..$12.00
Tyco, Lighted Porsche #2, silver w/red nose, EX $20.00
Tyco, Lighted Super America, #8525, red, wht & bl, EX .$20.00
Tyco, Military Police #45m wht & bl, EX.........................$30.00
Tyco, Pinto Funny Car Goodyear, red & yel, EX $20.00
Tyco, Pinto Funny Cargotcha, dk red w/gold stripe, VG ..$20.00

Tyco, Rokar 240-Z #7, blk, EX..............................$10.00
Tyco, Silverstreak Pickup, silver w/pk & orange stripes,
 EX $15.00
Tyco, Superbird, #8533, red, wht & bl, VG+ $15.00
Tyco, Turbo Firebird, blk & gold, NM.....................$12.00
Tyco, Turbo Hopper #27, red, EX $12.00
Tyco, Volvo 850 #3, wht & bl, EX............................$20.00
Tyco US1, Peterbilt Cab, red & wht, EX $20.00

MISCELLANEOUS

AMT Service Parts Kit, #2000, VG $65.00
Aurora AFX Billboard Retaining Walls, set of 8, EXIB $15.00
Aurora AFX Pit Kit, G $15.00
Aurora AFX Terminal Track, plug-in or wire-type, EX, ea .$5.00
Aurora AFX 45 OHM Hand Controller w/Brakes, EXIB .$15.00
Aurora Model Motoring Hill Track, 9", EX.................$8.00
Aurora Model Motoring Loop the Loop Track Set, #1504,
 EXIB $20.00
Aurora Model Motoring Thumb-Style Controller, EX $6.00
Aurora Model Motoring Y Turn-Off Track w/Switch, EX .$20.00
Aurora Model Motoring 4-Way Stop Track, 9", EX..........$15.00
Aurora Thunderjet Country Bridge Roadway, EXIB.........$20.00
Books, 'Here Is Your Hobby Slot Car Racing' & 'Complete Book
 of Model Raceways & Roadways,' VG, ea.................$50.00
Eldon Power Track, MOC $10.00
Gilbert Automatic Lap Counter, #19339, MIB.............$35.00
Gilbert Autorama Fly Over Chicane Kit, #19342, MIB ...$40.00
Gilbert Autorama Grand Stand #19340, MIB $25.00
Monogram Lane Change Track, MIB..........................$20.00
Monogram Tapered Chicane Track, MIB......................$20.00
Strombecker Scale Lap Counter, 1/32 scale, MIB..........$25.00
Tyco HO Scale 1973-74 Handbook, EX......................$10.00
Tyco Trigger Controller, orange, EX $8.00

Smith-Miller

Smith-Miller (Los Angeles, California) made toy trucks
from 1944 until 1955. During that time they used four basic cab
designs, and most of their trucks sold for about $15.00 each.
Over the past several years, these toys have become very popular, especially the Mack trucks which today sell at premium
prices. The company made a few other types of toys as well, such
as the train toy box and the 'Long, Long Trailer.'
 See also Advertising.

Army Materials Truck, L Mack, 1950s, 20", EX+ $400.00
Bank of America Truck, 1940s, 14", G.....................$175.00
Bekins Van Lines Co Semi, L Mack, 1950s, 25", NM .$1,700.00
Blue Diamond Dump Truck, 1940s, L Mack, wht, 19", G..$450.00
Drive-O Dump Truck, GMC, 1940s, EX.....................$250.00
Dump Truck, GMC, r/c, 12", EX+..........................$525.00
Dump Truck, GMC, 1950s, crank action, 7½", rstr........$175.00
Dump Truck, GMC, 1950s, crank action, 12", NM........$275.00
Dump Truck w/Front Scoop, GMC, 14", G+.................$650.00

**Fire Aerial Ladder Truck (LAFD), Mack, open cab, opening
doors, 24", NMIB, $1,100.00 (Photo courtesy Randy Inman)**

Fire Aerial Ladder Truck (MIC/LAFD), Mack, open cab, 28",
 VG+, A (Est: $600-$800) $600.00
Fire Aerial Ladder Truck No 3 (SMFD), L Mack, 36",
 G $385.00
Fire Aerial Ladder Truck No 5 (SMFD), L Mack, 36",
 EX $550.00
Fruehauf Lowboy, GMC, 26", rstr $275.00
Hollywood Film-Ad Truck & Searchlight Trailer, GMC, 27",
 EX+ $875.00
Kraft Foods Delivery Truck, GMC, box van, yel w/blk & wht ad
 detail, 4-wheeled, 14", EX $250.00
Lincoln Two-Door Hard Top Pulling House Trailer, bl & wht,
 w/accessories, 40" L, EX..................................$875.00
Log Truck w/Pup Trailer, L Mack, wooden flat beds, w/logs &
 chains, 32" overall, G+...................................$600.00
Lumber Truck & Trailer, B Mack, 1950s, 6-wheeled w/single rear
 axle, w/lumber, 30" overall, NM $825.00
Materials Truck, GMC, aluminum body w/chains across cut-out
 sides, 6-wheeled, 14", NM+ $225.00
Materials Truck, L Mack, metal cab, wood body, canvas tarp, 10-
 wheeled w/dbl rear duals, 20", rstr.......................$550.00
Mobiloil Tanker, GMC, all red, 14-wheeled w/3 sets of duals on
 tank, 22", EX...$375.00
Official Tow Car, Mack, MIC on doors, 17", EX $300.00
PIE Semi, GMC, 1940s, aluminum trailer, 14-wheeled, 25",
 EX+ $350.00
Silver Streak Express Truck, GMC, 1950s, open U-shaped silver
 trailer, 14-wheeled, 24", EX..............................$325.00
Silver Streak Semi, 1940s, GMC, 24", EX...................$200.00
Tanker Truck w/Pup Tank, L Mack, aluminum tanks, 10-
 wheeled w/dbl rear duals, 8-wheeled pup, 34", EX...$450.00
Teamster's Dump Truck, MIC, hydraulic dumping, doors open,
 10-wheeled w/dbl rear duals, 17", rstr $250.00
Texaco Tanker, GMC, aluminum tank w/wht lettering, 10-
 wheeled w/dbl rear duals, 15", EX $300.00
Train Box Car Toy Box, sliding doors, removable roof, 33" L,
 NM $1,150.00
Trans-Continental Freighter, GMC, 1940s, 24", EX+ $500.00
Triton Oil Truck, GMC, aluminum body w/chains across cut-out
 side, 6-wheeled, 14", EX $350.00
US Army Personnel Carrier, L-Mack, 19", VG $350.00
West Coast Fast Freight Truck, L Mack, 1940s, aluminum box
 van, 6-wheeled w/rear duals, EX $500.00

Soldiers and Accessories

'Dimestore' soldiers were made from the 1920s until sometime in the 1960s. Some of the better-known companies who made these small-scale figures and vehicles were Barclay, Manoil, and American Metal Toys, formerly known as Jones (hollow cast lead); Grey Iron (cast iron); and Auburn Rubber. They are 3" to 3½" high and were sold in Woolworth's, Kresge's, and other 5 & 10 stores for a nickel or a dime, hence the name 'Dimestore.' Marx made tin soldiers for use in target gun games; these sell for about $8.00 to $20.00. Condition is most important as these soldiers saw a lot of action. They are most often found with much of the paint worn off and with some serious 'battle wounds' such as missing arms or rifle tips. Nearly two thousand different figures were made by the major manufacturers, plus a number of others by minor makers such as Tommy Toy and All-Nu.

Another very popular line of toy soldiers has been made by Britains of England since 1893. They are smaller and usually more detailed than 'Dimestores,' and variants number in the thousands. Serious collectors should refer to *Collecting American Made Toy Soldiers* for 'Dimestore' soldiers, and *Collecting Foreign-Made Toy Soldiers* for Britains and others not made in America. Both books are by Richard O'Brien (1997).

You'll notice that in addition to the soldiers, many of our descriptions and values are for the vehicles, cannons, animals, and cowboys and Indians made and sold by the same manufacturers. Note: Percentages in the 'Dimestore' description lines refer to the amount of original paint remaining, a most important evaluation factor.

      Advisors: Sally and Stan Alekna (A1) 'Dimestore'
      See also Dinky; Plastic Figures.

Key:
AFB — American Family on the Beach
AFF — American Family on the Farm
AFH — American Family at Home
AFT — American Family Travels
AMR — American Family on the Ranch
CH — cast helmet
GK — Greyklip
HF — Happy Farm Set
LS — long stride
MCR — My Ranch Corral
PF — pod foot
PH — pot helmet
SS — short stride
TH — tin helmet
unpt — unpainted
USD — Uncle Sam's

DIMESTORE

American Metal Toys, calf, 97%, A1 ....$14.00
American Metal Toys, cow resting, 99%, A1 ....$19.00
American Metal Toys, farmer, 99%, A1 ....$20.00
American Metal Toys, farmer's wife, 96%, A1 ....$17.00
American Metal Toys, German soldier firing long rifle on bended knee, very scarce, 99%, A1..........................$225.00
American Metal Toys, horse, blk, sm, 99%, A1 ....$18.00
American Metal Toys, horse, blk & wht, sm, 99%, A1 ....$19.00
American Metal Toys, soldier AA gunner, khaki, scarce, 98%, A1 ....$115.00
American Metal Toys, soldier AA gunner, silver, scarce, NM, A1 ....$65.00
American Metal Toys, soldier ammo carrier, khaki, very scarce, 98%, A1 ....$98.00
American Metal Toys, soldier flagbearer, khaki, 97%, A1 ....$275.00
American Metal Toys, soldier grenade thrower, 97%, A1..$170.00
American Metal Toys, soldier kneeling at searchlight, khaki, scarce, 99%, A1 ....$133.00
American Metal Toys, soldier machine gunner firing from tree stump, 97%, A1 ....$90.00
American Metal Toys, soldier machine gunner prone, scarce, A1..$89.00
American Metal Toys, soldier w/rifle leaning forward in wide stance firing, khaki, scarce, 97%, A1 ....$126.00
Auburn Rubber, bugler, 95%, A1 ....$20.00
Auburn Rubber, calf, early, lg, 98%, A1 ....$12.00
Auburn Rubber, calf, later, sm, 98%, A1....................... $12.00
Auburn Rubber, collie, lg, 95%, A1 ....$18.00
Auburn Rubber, collie, sm, 98%, A1................................$14.00

Auburn Rubber, doctor, wht, red cross on cap, scarce, 95%, A1 ....$45.00

Auburn Rubber, farmer's wife (milk maid), 99%, A1 ....$29.00

Auburn Rubber, football center, scarce, 97%, A1 ....$60.00

Auburn Rubber, football lineman, scarce, 97%, A1 ....$55.00

Auburn Rubber, hen, NM, A1 ....$13.00

Auburn Rubber, infantry private, scarce, 98%, A1 ....$22.00

Auburn Rubber, officer, 98%, A1 ....$20.00

Auburn Rubber, signalman, very scarce, 95%, A1 ....$45.00

Auburn Rubber, soldier bomb thrower, khaki, scarce, 97%, A1.$57.00

Auburn Rubber, soldier lying wounded, 97%, A1 ....$47.00

Auburn Rubber, soldier machine gunner, 98%, A1 ....$21.00

Auburn Rubber, soldier marching at port arms, khaki, early, NM, A1 ....$21.00

Auburn Rubber, soldier w/binoculars observing, 97%, A1.$25.00

Auburn Rubber, soldier w/tommy gun charging, 2nd version, 97%, A1 ....$26.00

Auburn Rubber, sound detector, 90-92%, A1 ....$36.00

Auburn Rubber, US infantry officer, M, A1 ....$35.00

Auburn Rubber, White Guard officer, 92-94%, A1 ....$18.00

Auburn Rubber soldier tanker running w/amo boxes, very scarce, 97%, A1 ....$35.00

Barclay, armored truck, khaki, WRT, 98%, A1 ....$27.00

Barclay, aviator, PF, khaki, 98%, A1 ....$24.00

Barclay, aviator, 95%, A1 ....$28.00

Barclay, boy, orange/tan (rare color), 99%, A1 ....$18.00

Barclay, boy, 98%, A1 ....$16.00

Barclay, Boy Scout saluting, 98%, A1 ....$61.00

Barclay, Boy Scout signaling and Boy Scout hiking, NM, $65.00 each. (Photo courtesy Bertoia Auctions)

Barclay, boy skater, M, A1 ....$20.00

Barclay, bride & groom, 97%, A1, ea $26.00

Barclay, cannon, coastal defense; 5-man crew, working firing mechanism, very scarce, 98%, A1 ....$175.00

Barclay, cannon, field; variant w/diagonal pattern on gun carriage, very scarce, 98%, A1 ....$78.00

Barclay, cannon, long range; rubber tires, 96%, A1 ....$41.00

Barclay, cannon, mobile; 2-man crew, PF, 99%, A1 ....$42.00

Barclay, cavalryman, 1930s, 2¼", 98%, A1 ....$36.00

Barclay, couple in horse-drawn sleigh, 98%, A1 ....$102.00

Barclay, couple seated on bench (summer), 99%, A1 ....$43.00

Barclay, couple seated on bench (winter), 99%, A1 ....$43.00

Barclay, cow grazing, 98%, A1 ....$17.00

Barclay, cow standing w/head straight, tan & wht, 98%, A1..$17.00

Barclay, cowboy, TH brim, 97%, A1 ....$27.00

Barclay, cowboy rider (masked) w/gun drawn, 98%, A1 ...$51.00

Barclay, cowboy rider (masked) w/lasso, 97%, A1 ....$66.00

Barclay, cowboy rider w/gun drawn, 97%, A1 ....$60.00

Barclay, cowboy w/gun, right arm high, early version, 90-92%, A1 ....$19.00

Barclay, cowboy w/lasso (no lasso), gray, 95%, A1 ....$21.00

Barclay, cowboy w/lasso (no lasso), PF, 98%, A1 ....$21.00

Barclay, cowboy w/lasso (orig), 97%, A1 ....$23.00

Barclay, cowboy w/rifle, midi PF, scarce, NM, A1 ....$83.00

Barclay, cowboy w/rifle, PF, NM, A1 ....$22.00

Barclay, cowboy w/2 guns, 1 pointed outward, 97%, A1...$27.00

Barclay, cowboy w/2 guns, 1 raised in air, PF, blk, M, A1..$25.00

Barclay, cowboy w/2 guns, 1 raised in air, scarce, 97%, A1 .$72.00

Barclay, doctor, flat base, brn, 95%, A1.............................$26.00

Barclay, elderly lady, pk, 97%, A1 ....$19.00

Barclay, elderly man w/cane, 98%, A1 ....$20.00

Barclay, fireman w/axe, 98%, A1 ....$42.00

Barclay, girl, 99%, A1 ....$20.00

Barclay, girl figure skater, M, A1 ....$23.00

Barclay, girl in rocker, bl, M, A1 ....$25.00

Barclay, girl in rocker, lt bl (rare color), 97%, A1 ....$23.00

Barclay, girl in rocker, red, NM, A1 ....$24.00

Barclay, girl on skis, 99%, A1 ....$28.00

Barclay, girl on sled, NM, A1 ....$28.00

Barclay, girl skater, 99%, A1...$19.00

Barclay, highlander marching, very scarce, 96%, A1 ....$75.00

Barclay, HO brakeman, 99%, A1 ....$11.00

Barclay, HO conductor, 99%, A1 ....$11.00

Barclay, HO dining steward, 98%, A1 ....$10.00

Barclay, HO engineer, 99%, A1 ....$11.00

Barclay, HO fireman, NM, A1 ....$19.00

Barclay, HO hobo, 99%, A1 ....$11.00

Barclay, HO mailman, 99%, A1 ....$11.00

Barclay, HO man, 99%, A1 ....$11.00

Barclay, HO newsboy, 99%, A1 ....$11.00

Barclay, HO oiler, NM, A1 ....$11.00

Barclay, HO policeman, NM, A1 ....$12.00

Barclay, HO porter, 99%, A1..$11.00

Barclay, HO redcap, 99%, A1 ....$11.00

Barclay, HO woman, red, no dog, 99%, A1 ....$11.00

Barclay, HO woman carring baby, 99%, A1 ....$19.00

Barclay, horse, grazing, NM, A1 ....$20.00

Barclay, Indian chief w/arm across chest, 95%, A1 ....$20.00

Barclay, Indian chief w/rifle, PF, scarce, 98%, A1 ....$40.00

Barclay, Indian chief w/tomahawk & shield, 94%, A1 ....$19.00

Barclay, Indian rider, 98%, A1 ....$39.00

Barclay, Indian w/bow & arrow, PF, 98%, A1 ....$19.00

Barclay, Indian w/bow & arrow, scarce, 93-95%, A1 ....$29.00

Barclay, Indian w/bow & arrow on bended knee, 99%, A1..$24.00

Barclay, Indian w/rifle across waist, 95%, A1 ....$23.00

Barclay, Indian w/rifle aiming, midi PF, scarce, 95%, A1..$78.00

Barclay, Indian w/tomahawk, midi PF, scarce, 99%, A1 ...$82.00

Barclay, Indian w/tomahawk & shield, PF, NM, A1 ....$19.00

Barclay, Indian w/tomahawk & shield, scarce, 90-92%, A1 .$26.00

Barclay, Japanese soldier advancing w/rifle, scarce, 95%, A1 .$45.00

Barclay, Japanese soldier marching w/rifle, scarce, 95%, A1 .$45.00

Barclay, knight (blk) w/shield, 99%, A1 ....$42.00

Barclay, knight w/shield, 99%, A1....................................$25.00

Barclay, knight w/shield & sword over shoulder, PF, 99%, A1 .$41.00

Barclay, lady w/dog & bag, bl, 98%, A1 ....$21.00

Barclay, lady w/dog & bag, yel (rare color), 97%, A1 ....$20.00

Barclay, mailman, NM, A1 ....$22.00

Barclay, man on skis, NM, A1 ....$29.00

Barclay, man on sled, 98%, A1 ....$26.00

Barclay, man pulling kids on sled, scarce, 99%, A1 ....$63.00

Barclay, man putting skates on girl seated on bench, scarce, NM, A1 ....$190.00

Barclay, man speed skater, 99%, A1 ....$21.00

Barclay, man w/overcoat slung over arm, gray, 98%, A1...$21.00

Barclay, marine marching w/rifle, 95%, A1.........................$24.00

Barclay, marine officer, CH, bl, 85-88%, A1......................$86.00

Barclay, marine officer, LS, wht cap, scarce, 99%, A1 ......$55.00

Barclay, minister walking, scarce, 99%, A1........................$82.00

Barclay, Mountie, very scarce, 90-92%, A1.......................$70.00

Barclay, navel officer, LS, 95%, A1 ....$28.00

Barclay, newsboy, 99%, A1 ....$21.00

Barclay, nurse w/water bowl & towel, PF, red hair, scarce, 96%, A1 ....$41.00

Barclay, officer, khaki, 93-95%, A1 ....$21.00

Barclay, officer, PF, khaki, 97%, A1....................................$18.00

Barclay, officer w/binoculars, midi PF, gr, scarce, M, A1.$135.00

Barclay, officer w/sword marching, gr PH, 99%, A1 ....$32.00

Barclay, officer w/sword marching, LS, TH, 97%, A1.......$30.00

Barclay, officer w/sword marching, SS, TH, 94%, A1.......$34.00

Barclay, pirate, bl, scarce, 93-95%, A1 ....$32.00

Barclay, pirate, red, scarce, 93-95%, A1 ....$32.00

Barclay, plane, single engine, red, wht & bl (rare), 99%, A1..$45.00

Barclay, policeman, figure-8 base, M, A1 ....$27.00

Barclay, policeman, 93-95%, A1 ....$19.00

Barclay, ram, M, A1 ....$20.00

Barclay, sailor w/rifle marching, broad shoulders, bl, scarce, 99%, A1 ....$57.00

Barclay, sailor w/rifle marching, early, 97%, A1 ....$24.00

Barclay, sailor w/rifle marching, PF, wht, 98%, A1 ....$26.00

Barclay, Santa on tin skis, 96%, A1....................................$67.00

Barclay, Santa seated on sled, 99%, A1 ....$54.00

Barclay, Santa seated w/toy bag, scarce, 99%, A1............$325.00

Barclay, sentry in overcoat, 95%, A1 ....$95.00

Barclay, sheep resting, M, A1 ....$21.00

Barclay, sheep standing, head straight, M, A1 ....$20.00

Barclay, shoeshine boy, scarce, 94%, A1 ....$38.00

Barclay, sleigh, 98%, A1 ....$38.00

Barclay, soldier AA gun crew (2), PF, 98%, A1 ....$42.00

Barclay, soldier AA gunner, CH, 98%, A1........................$30.00

Barclay, soldier AA gunner, gr PH, 97%, A1 ....$27.00

Barclay, soldier AA gunner, PF, red, scarce, 96%, A1.....$120.00

Barclay, soldier AA gunner, plow base, CH, 97%, A1......$32.00

Barclay, soldier at order arms, gr WWII PH, 98%, A1......$29.00

Barclay, soldier at searchlight standing, smooth lens, no elevation wheel, very scarce, M rpt, A1 ....$85.00

Barclay, soldier bomb thrower, PF, gr, 95%, A1 ....$25.00

Barclay, soldier bomb thrower, PF, khaki, 97%, A1..........$24.00

Barclay, soldier bomb thrower, TH, 98%..........................$30.00

Barclay, soldier bugler, LS, TH, 93%, A1 ....$25.00

Barclay, soldier bullet (shell) loader, 94%, A1 ....$21.00

Barclay, soldier clarinetist, wht helmet, scarce, 97%, A1 .$74.00

Barclay, soldier dispatcher w/dog, 97%, A1......................$90.00

Barclay, soldier drummer, SS, TH, 97%, A1 ....$36.00

Barclay, soldier drummer, wht helmet, scarce, 97%, A1 ...$74.00

Barclay, soldier eating & sitting, scarce, 93-95%, A1 ....$40.00

Barclay, soldier field phone operator leaning out, gr CH (rare color, scarce, 98%, A1 ....$96.00

Barclay, soldier field phone operator leaning out, silver CH, scarce, 99%, A1 ....$92.00

Barclay, soldier field phone operator on bended knee, 96%, A1 .$30.00

Barclay, soldier flagbearer, earlier version, 96%, A1 ....$27.00

Barclay, soldier flagbearer, SS, TH, 97%, A1 ....$39.00

Barclay, soldier French horn player, 94%, A1 ....$24.00

Barclay, soldier grenade thrower, 96%, A1 ....$23.00

Barclay, soldier machine gunner charging, CH, 99%, A1.$47.00

Barclay, soldier machine gunner prone, gr PH, 99%, A1..$28.00

Barclay, soldier machine gunner prone, khaki, PF, 97%, A1.$20.00

Barclay, soldier machine gunner prone, TH, 95%, A1 .....$27.00

Barclay, soldier range finder crew (3), PF, 95%, A1 ....$38.00

Barclay, soldier sentry in overcoat, 95%, A1....................$29.00

Barclay, soldier sharpshooter standing firing, LS, TH, 98%, A1 ....$28.00

Barclay, soldier signalman w/flags, 97%, A1......................$38.00

Barclay, soldier tubist, wht helmet, scarce, 99%, A1 ....$76.00

Barclay, soldier w/bazooka on bended knee, midi PF, gr, scarce, M, A1..$135.00

Barclay, soldier w/binoculars (short) prone, TH, very scarce, 90-92%, A1..$105.00

Barclay, soldier w/pack marching, CH, scarce, 98%, A1 ..$43.00

Barclay, soldier w/pack marching, TH, 95%, A1 ....$29.00

Barclay, soldier w/pistol crawling, PF, gr, 99%, A1............$40.00

Barclay, soldier w/rifle & gas mask charging, CH, 96%, A1.$39.00

Barclay, soldier w/rifle & gas mask charging, 97%, A1 .....$31.00

Barclay, soldier w/rifle across waist charging, 96%, A1.....$23.00

Barclay, soldier w/rifle at order arms, CH, 85-88%, A1 ....$15.00

Barclay, soldier w/rifle at side pointed down walking, midi PF, gr, scarce, 99%, A1 ....$132.00

Barclay, soldier w/rifle bayonetting (no bayonet), CH, 97%, A1..$325.00

Barclay, soldier w/rifle charging, PF, gr, M, A1 ....$24.00

Barclay, soldier w/rifle charging, PF, red, scarce, 95%, A1..$129.00

Barclay, soldier w/rifle marching, PF, khaki, 99%, A1.......$21.00

Barclay, soldier w/rifle marching, PF, LS, TH, 97%, A1 ...$66.00

Barclay, soldier w/rifle on bended knee firing, PF, gr, 99%, A1 .$28.00

Barclay, soldier w/rifle running, 1 foot up, TH, 95%, A1..$32.00

Barclay, soldier w/rifle running looking back & up, PF, khaki, 99%, A1..$20.00

Barclay, soldier w/rifle slung marching, CH, 99%, A1......$43.00

Barclay, soldier w/rifle slung marching, gr PH, 97%, A1 ..$27.00

Barclay, soldier w/rifle slung marching, midi PF, gr, scare, 98%, A1 ....$130.00

Barclay, soldier w/rifle standing firing, PF, gr, 98%, A1.....$22.00

Barclay, soldier w/rifle standing firing, PF, khaki, 94%, A1.**$14.00**

Barclay, soldier wireless operator, w/separate antenna, 98%, A1 ....**$53.00**

Barclay, train conductor, 98%, A1.....................................**$18.00**

Barclay, train redcap w/bags, 98%, A1 ....**$30.00**

Barclay, US Army truck, scarce, 98%, A1.........................**$42.00**

Barclay, wagon, field; closed hitch, unmk, sm, 95%, A1...**$18.00**

Barclay, West Point cadet, SS, 97%, A1 ....**$28.00**

Barclay, West Point Officer, SS, 97%, A1.........................**$28.00**

Barclay, workhorse, NM, A1...**$19.00**

Gery Iron, Colonial soldier, postwar, 96%, A1 ....**$31.00**

Gery Iron, soldier w/rifle marching, GK, EX, A1 ....**$4.00**

Grey Iron, Aviation Corps pilot, GK, scarce, EX+, A1 ....**$28.00**

Grey Iron, aviator, orange harness, very scarce, 96%, A1.**$92.00**

Grey Iron, Battery F gunner, GK, EX+, A1 ....**$11.00**

Grey Iron, Battery F loader bending, GK, EX, A1 ....**$11.00**

Grey Iron, Battery F set, cannon, gunner, loader bending, loader standing, shell stack, GK, complete, EX+, A1..........**$79.00**

Grey Iron, bench, AFH, 96%, A1 ....**$16.00**

Grey Iron, bench, AFT, A1 ....**$95.00**

Grey Iron, black cook, AFH, scarce, 97%, A1 ....**$36.00**

Grey Iron, boy flying kite (no kite), AFH, 98%, A1 ....**$25.00**

Grey Iron, boy in summer suit, AFB, very scarce, 95%, A1.**$67.00**

Grey Iron, boy in traveling suit, AFT, NM, A1 ....**$18.00**

Grey Iron, Boy Scout saluting, 99%, A1 ....**$40.00**

Grey Iron, Boy Scout walking, 99%, A1 ....**$40.00**

Grey Iron, boy w/beach ball, AFB, very scarce, 95%, A1.**$67.00**

Grey Iron, boy w/life preserver, AFB, very scarce, 99%, A1.**$71.00**

Grey Iron, cadet, bl, 98%, A1..**$35.00**

Grey Iron, cadet, early, bl, 96%, A1 ....**$33.00**

Grey Iron, cadet, early, gray, 93-95%, A1.........................**$31.00**

Grey Iron, cadet officer, bl, early, 98%, A1 ....**$24.00**

Grey Iron, cadet officer, bl, 97%, A1................................**$37.00**

Grey Iron, cadet officer, early, bl, 98%, A1 ....**$24.00**

Grey Iron, cadet officer, wht, 96%, A1 ....**$36.00**

Grey Iron, calf, AFF, 99%, A1...**$18.00**

Grey Iron, calf (head turned), AFR, very scarce, A1 ....**$97.00**

Grey Iron, cannon, field; NP barrel, red spoke wheels, 98%, A1 ....**$34.00**

Grey Iron, collie, AFF, 98%, A1..**$17.00**

Grey Iron, Colonial foot officer, 97%, A1........................**$29.00**

Grey Iron, colt (for ranch scene), AFR, very scarce, 99%, A1.**$72.00**

Grey Iron, Company A officer charging, GK, EX, A1 ....**$7.00**

Grey Iron, Company A set, bugler, drummer, flagbearer, officer, 5 rifleman (1 missing) at attention, GK, EX, A1.......**$55.00**

Grey Iron, Company B set, bugler, drummer, flagbearer, officer, 6 riflemen (complete), GK, EX, A1 ....**$59.00**

Grey Iron, Company C drummer charging, GK, EX, A1....**$7.00**

Grey Iron, cow, AFF, NM, A1 ....**$19.00**

Grey Iron, cowboy, later, 96%, A1 ....**$24.00**

Grey Iron, cowboy on bucking bronc, early, scarce, 97%, A1 ....**$74.00**

Grey Iron, cowboy rider coming to a halt, scarce, 97%, A1.**$57.00**

Grey Iron, cowboy w/lasso (no lasso), AFR, very scarce, 97%, A1 ....**$70.00**

Grey Iron, cowboy w/lasso (no lasso), prewar, scarce, M, A1 .**$49.00**

Grey Iron, delivery boy, AFH, 96%, A1............................**$24.00**

Grey Iron, doctor carrying bag, wht suit, scarce, 96%, A1.**$43.00**

Grey Iron, elderly man sitting, AFH, 99%, A1 ....**$16.00**

Grey Iron, elderly woman sitting, AFH, 99%, A1 ....**$16.00**

Grey Iron, Ethiopian chief, 97%, A1 ....**$76.00**

Grey Iron, Ethiopian Tribesman, scarce, 99%, A1...........**$78.00**

Grey Iron, farmer, AFF, 98%, A1......................................**$19.00**

Grey Iron, flagbearer, 1950s version, no flag, 98%, A1.....**$75.00**

Grey Iron, Foreign Legion bomber crawling w/pistol, 97%, A1.**$64.00**

Grey Iron, Foreign Legion machine gunner on bended knee, 96%, A1 ....**$51.00**

Grey Iron, Foreign Legion officer, 97%, A1 ....**$62.00**

Grey Iron, girl catching ball, AFB, very scarce, 98%, A1.**$70.00**

Grey Iron, girl in riding suit, very scarce, 98%, A1..........**$70.00**

Grey Iron, girl in slacks, AFB, very scarce, 97%, A1 ....**$69.00**

Grey Iron, girl in traveling suit, AFT, 97%, A1 ....**$15.00**

Grey Iron, girl skipping rope (orig rope), AFH, NM, A1 .**$35.00**

Grey Iron, girl w/sand pail, AFB, very scarce, 97%, A1....**$69.00**

Grey Iron, hired man digging, AFF, 98%, A1 ....**$23.00**

Grey Iron, hold-up man, postwar, 97%, A1 ....**$36.00**

Grey Iron, hold-up man (Hoppy), M, A1 ....**$51.00**

Grey Iron, horse, AFF, 98%, A1 ....**$17.00**

Grey Iron, horse (stallion), AFR, very scarce, NM, A1....**$73.00**

Grey Iron, Indian chief w/hand on knife, 95%, A1 ....**$31.00**

Grey Iron, Indian chief w/tomahawk, gr pants, early, 95%, A1...**$19.00**

Grey Iron, knight in armor, NM, A1.................................**$45.00**

Grey Iron, Legion bulger, early, 99%, A1.........................**$35.00**

Grey Iron, Legion color bearer, 95%, A1 ....**$39.00**

Grey Iron, Legion drum major, early, scarce, 98%, A1 .....**$52.00**

Grey Iron, Legion drum major, 98%, A1...........................**$30.00**

Grey Iron, Legion drummer, early, 99%, A1 ....**$34.00**

Grey Iron, life guard, AFB, very scarce, 94%, A1 ....**$66.00**

Grey Iron, life guard chair, AFB, very scarce, 99%, A1 ....**$75.00**

Grey Iron, machine gunner seated, USD, brn, unpt face, 96%, A1...**$18.00**

Grey Iron, man in traveling suit, AFT, M, A1 ....**$18.00**

Grey Iron, man lying w/paper over face, AFB, 98%, A1 ..**$70.00**

Grey Iron, man w/watering can, AFH, 96%, A1 ....**$17.00**

Grey Iron, milkman, AFH, 98%, A1..................................**$26.00**

Grey Iron, newsboy, AFT, 99%, A1...................................**$17.00**

Grey Iron, nurse (Red Cross), 97%, A1 ....**$31.00**

Grey Iron, officer saluting, USD, brn, unpt face, 99%, A1 .**$21.00**

Grey Iron, pig, AFF, 98%, A1 ....**$17.00**

Grey Iron, pirate w/dagger, 97%, A1 ....**$39.00**

Grey Iron, pirate w/sword, 97%, A1 ....**$37.00**

Grey Iron, policeman, AFT, 99%, A1 ....**$17.00**

Grey Iron, postman, AFT, 98%, A1...................................**$16.00**

Grey Iron, preacher, AFT, NM, A1....................................**$19.00**

Grey Iron, Royal Canadian Mounted Police mounted, horse's head turned, early, 96%, A1 ....**$50.00**

Grey Iron, Royal Canadian Mounted Police standing at port arms, early, 97%, A1 ....**$37.00**

Grey Iron, ski trooper, 99%, A1 ....**$60.00**

Grey Iron, soldier flagbearer, USD, brn, pnt face, very scarce, 94%, A1...**$75.00**

Grey Iron, soldier w/rifle at attention, USD, brn, unpt face, 99%, A1...**$20.00**

Grey Iron, soldier w/rifle charging, USD, brn, unpt face, 99%, A1 ....$20.00

Grey Iron, soldier wounded (on crutches), 96%, A1 ....$75.00

Grey Iron, stretcher bearer, scarce, 94%, A1....................$45.00

Grey Iron, train conductor, AFT, 99%, A1 ....$17.00

Grey Iron, train engineer, AFT, 99%, A1 ....$17.00

Grey Iron, train porter, AFT, 98%, A1...............................$19.00

Grey Iron, Troop D officer mounted, GK, EX+, A1 ....$79.00

Grey Iron, US cavalry officer, early, 95%, A1 ....$49.00

Grey Iron, US cavalry officer, 85-88%, A1 ....$35.00

Grey Iron, US doughboy ammo carrier, very scarce, 98%, A1 ....$135.00

Grey Iron, US doughboy bomber crawling, 98%, A1 ....$34.00

Grey Iron, US doughboy charging, early, 98%, A1...........$26.00

Grey Iron, US doughboy combat trooper, 98%, A1..........$38.00

Grey Iron, US doughboy combat tropper, postwar, 98%, A1 .$38.00

Grey Iron, US doughboy grenade thrower, postwar, 98%, A1.$57.00

Grey Iron, US doughboy officer, early, 98%, A1...............$24.00

Grey Iron, US doughboy officer, 99%, A1 ....$28.00

Grey Iron, US doughboy officer w/field glasses, 97%, A1.$42.00

Grey Iron, US doughboy plunging rifle w/bayonet downward, scarce, 97%, A1 ....$40.00

Grey Iron, US doughboy port arms, early, 97%, A1.........$23.00

Grey Iron, US doughboy sentry, 97%, A1 ....$36.00

Grey Iron, US doughboy sharpshooter, scarce, 80-85%, A1 .$17.00

Grey Iron, US doughboy shoulder arms, 98%, A1 ....$24.00

Grey Iron, US doughboy signaling, postwar, 98%, A1......$43.00

Grey Iron, US doughboy signaling, 97%, A1 ....$43.00

Grey Iron, US doughboy w/field glasses, postwar, 95%, A1 .$39.00

Grey Iron, US infantry charging, early, 98%, A1..............$24.00

Grey Iron, US infantry officer, early, 98%, A1..................$26.00

Grey Iron, US infantry port arms, early, 97%, A1 ....$22.00

Grey Iron, US infantry shoulder arms, early, 99%, A1 .....$22.00

Grey Iron, US machine gunner on bended knee, early, 97%, A1...$32.00

Grey Iron, US machine gunner on bended knee, postwar, 96%, A1 ....$19.00

Grey Iron, US marine, early, NM, A1 ....$33.00

Grey Iron, US Naval officer, dk bl, early, 98%, A1...........$28.00

Grey Iron, US naval officer, wht, early, 93-95%, A1 ....$22.00

Grey Iron, US naval officer, wht, 90-92%, A1...................$19.00

Grey Iron, US sailor, bl, early, 98%, A1 ....$26.00

Grey Iron, US sailor, wht, early, 97%, A1 ....$25.00

Jones, cowboy on galloping horse firing pistol, NM, A, $50.00. (Photo courtesy Bertoia Auctions)

Grey Iron, woman in bathing suit seated w/legs out to side, AFB, very scarce, 94%, A1 ....$66.00

Grey Iron, woman w/basket, AFH, 99%, A1 ....$20.00

Grey Iron, wounded patient, 95%, A1 ....$45.00

Jones, British marine of 1775 firing musket at an angle, 54mm, scarce, 94%, A1 ....$25.00

Jones, Midshipmen of 1928 Set #544, 8-pc, MIB, A1 ....$250.00

Jones, Scot Highlander of 1814, 54mm, scarce, 98%, A1.$29.00

Jones, US Infantry Set #5413, 8-pc, MIB, A1 ....$250.00

Jones, US infantry soldier w/sling arms & pack, scarce, A1 .$35.00

Jones, US Marines of 1809 Set #5436, 7-pc, MIB, A1 ...$250.00

Jones, Waynes Legion soldier on guard w/bayonet, 54mm, M, A1..$34.00

Lincoln Log, caveman (Big Tooth) w/bow, scarce, 96%, A1.$68.00

Lincoln Log, caveman (Og), scarce, 99%, A1 ....$99.00

Lincoln Log, cavewoman (Nada), scarce, 96%, A1 ....$70.00

Lincoln Log, cowboy standing w/lasso, 98%, A1 ....$18.00

Lincoln Log, cowboy w/raised gun, 97%, A1 ....$17.00

Lincoln Log, dinosaur (Three Horn), very scarce, 85-88%, A1..$68.00

Lincoln Log, farmer, 99%, A1 ....$22.00

Lincoln Log, foot soldier of 1812 w/rifle, NM, A1 ....$19.00

Lincoln Log, Indian brave standing w/bow & arrow, 88-90%, A1..$29.00

Lincoln Log, Indian brave w/rifle (1 feather), 97%, A1 ...$19.00

Lincoln Log, Indian Chief w/bow & arrow facing straight ahead, 97%, A1..$17.00

Lincoln Log, Indian chief w/rifle, 98%, A1......................$18.00

Lincoln Log, officer (1918 uniform) mounted, 97%, A1 ..$39.00

Lincoln Log, pioneer standing w/gun, thin, 95%, A1 ....$18.00

Lincoln Log, pioneer standing w/gun, 98%, A1 ....$19.00

Lincoln Log, Royal Canadian Mounted Police standing, very scarce, 95%, A1...$33.00

Lincoln Log, sailor w/rifle at attention, scarce, 97%, A1..$30.00

Lincoln Log, soldier machine gunner, concave base, scarce, 99%, A1 ....$22.00

Lincoln Log, telegraph messenger, dk bl, scarce color, 98%, A1.$19.00

Lincoln Log, telegraph messenger, tan, NM, A1..............$19.00

Lincoln Log, train conductor, thin base, 94%, A1 ....$14.00

Lincoln Log, train engineer, NM, A1................................$19.00

Lincoln Log, train redcap, 98%, A1 ....$18.00

Lincoln Log, traveling man, 98%, A1 ....$17.00

Manoil, aviator, scarce, 97%, A1......................................$69.00

Manoil, aviator w/bomb, standing, 98%, A1 ....$52.00

Manoil, bench, HF, 98%, A1...$15.00

Manoil, Black man eating watermelon, HF, scarce, 95%, A1 .$100.00

Manoil, blacksmith making horseshoes, HF, 98%, A1......$29.00

Manoil, blacksmith w/wheel, HF, 97%, A1 ....$28.00

Manoil, boy carrying wood, HF, 98%, A1 ....$29.00

Manoil, bull w/head turned, MRC, 97%, A1 ....$24.00

Manoil, caisson, V-support stand, metal wheels, 98%, A1.$34.00

Manoil, calf bawling, MRC, 99%, A1 ....$19.00

Manoil, cannon, action; camouflaged, later, NM, A1 ......$27.00

Manoil, cannon, action; silver, early, scarce, 97%, A1 .....$35.00

Manoil, cannon, action; silver, later, 99%, A1 ....$25.00

Manoil, cannon, gray w/wood wheels, hitch flange on bottom, 97%, A1 ....$27.00

Manoil, carpenter carrying door, HF, scarce, 98%, A1......$72.00

Manoil, carpenter sawing lumber, HF, 98%, A1...............$29.00

Manoil, castus, MRC, lg, 97%, A1 ....$38.00

Manoil, cobbler making shoes, HF, scarce, 98%, A1 ....$42.00

Manoil, colt, MRC, M, A1...$32.00

Manoil, cow feeding, MRC, 99%, A1 ....$26.00

Manoil, cowboy rider, MRC, 95%, A1................................$26.00

Manoil, cowboy w/gun raised in air, hollow base, 93-95%, A3.$49.00

Manoil, doctor, wht, 99%, A1 ....$34.00

Manoil, fence section w/blanket, MRC, scarce, 96%, A1..$70.00

Manoil, General Patton saluting on podium, gr helmet, scarce, 94%, A1...$175.00

Manoil, girl picking berries, HF, early, scarce, 92%, A1....$63.00

Manoil, girl picking berries, HF, later, scarce, 95%, A1 ....$66.00

Manoil, girl watering flowers, HF, 98%, A1 ....$29.00

Manoil, gun, 5-barreled on wheels, 97%, A1 ....$36.00

Manoil, hod carrier w/bricks, HF, 98%, A1......................$43.00

Manoil, hostess, gr, scarce, 97%, A1 ....$76.00

Manoil, hostess, wht, very scarce, 96%, A1 ....$300.00

Manoil, Hot Papa (firefighter), gray, scarce, 92-94%, A1.$193.00

Manoil, hound dog, HF, 98%, A1......................................$29.00

Manoil, Indian chief w/knives, 90-92%, A1 ....$26.00

Manoil, lady holding baby, HF, 97%, A1 ....$44.00

Manoil, man at water pump, HF, 99%, A1.........................$30.00

Manoil, man blowing out lantern, HF, 95%, A1...............$28.00

Manoil, man carrying pumpkin, HF, 99%, A1 ....$30.00

Manoil, man carrying sack on back, HF, 98%, A1 ....$29.00

Manoil, man carrying sheaves, HF, 97%, A1 ....$28.00

Manoil, man chopping wood, HF, 95%, A1 ....$26.00

Manoil, man cutting corn, HF, 97%, A1............................$28.00

Manoil, man cutting w/scythe, HF, 97%, A1 ....$28.00

Manoil, man dumping wheelbarrow, HF, early, 98%, A1..$42.00

Manoil, man dumping wheelbarrow, HF, later, 97%, A1 ..$41.00

Manoil, man laying bricks, HF, cream, early, 98%, A1 .....$43.00

Manoil, man planting tree, HF, scarce, M, A1 ....$68.00

Manoil, man seated (for bench), HF, 98%, A1 ....$15.00

Manoil, man sharpening scythe, HF, 97%, A1...................$28.00

Manoil, man sowing grain, HF, 97%, A1 ....$28.00

Manoil, man w/barrel of apples, HF, dk gray, scarce, 96%, A1.$73.00

Manoil, man w/barrel of apples, HF, khaki, 98%, A1 ....$89.00

Manoil, navy deck gunner w/bare feet, 90-92%, A1.........$35.00

Manoil, navy ensign, 92-94%, A1.....................................$27.00

Manoil, nurse, 98%, A1...$31.00

Manoil, officer w/sword marching, 2nd version, 98%, A1.$31.00

Manoil, scarecrow in straw hat, HF, 97%, A1 ....$28.00

Manoil, scarecrow in top hat, HF, 99%, A1 ....$30.00

Manoil, school teacher, HF, scarce, 98%, A1....................$56.00

Manoil, shepard w/flute, HF, scarce, 97%, A1...................$71.00

Manoil, soldier AA gunner, post-WWII, 97%, A1...........$52.00

Manoil, soldier AA gunner, 98%, A1 ....$34.00

Manoil, soldier AA gunner camouflaged, compo, scarce, 95%, A1..$79.00

Manoil, soldier bomb thrower, 2 grenades, 99%, A1 ....$37.00

Manoil, soldier bullet feeder, 97%, A1 ....$30.00

Manoil, soldier butting w/rifle, scarce, NM, A1...............$73.00

Manoil, soldier cook's helper, WW2 helmet, very scarce, 89%, A1..$165.00

Manoil, soldier cook's helper w/ladle, scarce, 89%, A1 ..$165.00

Manoil, soldier digging trench, scarce, 97%, A1...............$69.00

Manoil, soldier eating, seated, scarce, 98%, A1 ....$61.00

Manoil, soldier flagbearer, post-WWII, LS, thin, unpt, A1..$18.00

Manoil, soldier flagbearer, post-WWII, LS, thin, 94%, A1..$36.00

Manoil, soldier flagbearer standing forward w/both hands on pole, post-WWII, 99%, A1 ....$54.00

Manoil, soldier grenade thrower in wide stance aiming upward, post-WWII, 98%, A1 ....$56.00

Manoil, soldier guard in poncho, post-WWII, 99%, A1...$56.00

Manoil, soldier loading bazooka rocket, prone, post-WWII, thin, 98%, A1...$42.00

Manoil, soldier machine gunner prone, post-WWII, thin, 98%, A1 ....$115.00

Manoil, soldier machine gunner prone, post-WWII, 98%, A1.$48.00

Manoil, soldier machine gunner prone w/backpack, 97%, A1..$33.00

Manoil, soldier machine gunner seated, compo, scarce, 96%, A1...$80.00

Manoil, soldier machine gunner seated leaning forward, post-WWII, 98%, A1 ....$48.00

Manoil, soldier machine gunner seated w/legs bent, 94%, A1..$28.00

Manoil, soldier machine gunner seated w/legs straight, post-WWII, thin, unpt, A1 ....$25.00

Manoil, soldier machine gunner seated w/legs straight, post-WWII, thin, scarce, 93-95%, A1 ....$113.00

Manoil, soldier paymaster, NM, $375.00. (Photo courtesy Bertoia Auctions)

Manoil, soldier sentry w/head turned, 97%, A1..............$115.00

Manoil, soldier sniper firing carbine, post-WWII, thin, scarce, 90%, A1...$62.00

Manoil, soldier sniper on bended knee, longer thicker rifle, 98%, A1 ....$36.00

Manoil, soldier sniper on bended knee w/legs apart, post-WWII, 99%, A1 ....$55.00

Manoil, soldier sniper prone w/camo cover, pnt flowers, 98%, A1 ....$41.00

Manoil, soldier sniper standing & leaning forward in wide stance, 98%, A1...$33.00

Manoil, soldier sniper standing & leaning forward in wide stance, post-WWII, 98%, A1 ....$48.00

Manoil, soldier sniper w/carbine on bended knee & legs spread shooting upward, post-WWII, 88-90%, A1 ....$29.00

Manoil, soldier stretcher bearer w/wounded soldier, very scarce, 97% overall, set $475.00

Manoil, soldier tommy gunner crouching, post-WWII, 94%, A1 ....$49.00

Manoil, soldier tommy gunner standing & firing, post-WWII, thin, unpt, A1 ....$18.00

Manoil, soldier tommy gunner standing & firing, post-WWII, 98%, A1 ....$42.00

Manoil, soldier w/barbed wire, wide face, 98%, A1 ....$65.00

Manoil, soldier w/bayonet charging, scarce, 98%, A1 ......$64.00

Manoil, soldier w/bazooka on bended knee, legs apart, post-WWII, 98%, A1 ....$42.00

Manoil, soldier w/bazooka on bended knee, legs together , post-WWII, 96%, A1 ....$46.00

Manoil, soldier w/bincoulars on bended knee, post-WWII, 99%, A1 ....$55.00

Manoil, soldier w/binoculars in wide stance looking upward, post-WWII, 88-90%, A1 ....$29.00

Manoil, soldier w/cannon (mk Manoil USA 2) running, 98%, A1 ....$56.00

Manoil, soldier w/gas mask & flare gun pointing upward standing, 95%, A1 ....$35.00

Manoil, soldier w/gas mask & rifle advancing, 93%, A1 ..$30.00

Manoil, soldier w/gas mask firing flare gun, post-WWII, NM, A1 ....$56.00

Manoil, soldier w/mine detector, 99%, A1 ....$46.00

Manoil, soldier w/periscope prone, 98%, A1 ....$56.00

Manoil, soldier w/rifle (M-1) standing in wide stance glancing sideways, post-WWII, 94%, A1 ....$48.00

Manoil, soldier w/rifle (M-1) standing w/legs closer together glancing sideways, post-WWII, 94%, A1 ....$49.00

Manoil, soldier w/rifle & backpack marching, 98%, A1...$38.00

Manoil, soldier w/rifle at attention presenting arms, post-WWII, 97%, A1 ....$42.00

Manoil, soldier w/rifle charging, scarce, 98%, A1 ....$67.00

Manoil, soldier w/rifle on bended knee firing straight up, post-WWII, 92-94%, A1 ....$52.00

Manoil, soldier w/rifle parade marching, post WWII, thin, 99%, A1 ....$48.00

Manoil, soldier w/rifle parade marching, stocky, M, A1 ...$30.00

Manoil, soldier w/rifle parade marching, thin, hollow base, very scarce, 92-94%, A1 ....$70.00

Manoil, soldier w/rifle parade marching w/curved rifle barrel, open between arm and body, post-WWII, 99%, A1 ..$55.00

Manoil, soldier w/rifle parade marching w/straight rifle barrel, closed between arm & body, post-WWII, 98%, A1...$29.00

Manoil, soldier w/trench mortar, 98%, A1 ....$36.00

Manoil, soldier writing letter, seated w/cigarette in mouth, scarce, 97%, A1 ....$98.00

Manoil, soup kitchen, lg or sm, NM, A1, ea $36.00

Manoil, woman at butter churn, HF, M, A1 ....$32.00

Manoil, woman laying out wash, HF, 98%, A1 ....$29.00

Manoil, woman lifting hen from nest, HF, 99%, A1 ....$30.00

Manoil, woman sweeping w/broom, HF, 99%, A1 ....$28.00

Marx, cavalry officer mounted, tin, M, A1 ....$13.00

Marx, cowboy drawing pistol, tin, postwar, scarce, NM, A1 .$26.00

Marx, cowboy rider, tin, oval base, postwar, scarce, EX+, A .$23.00

Marx, cowboy w/rifle, tin, oval base, postwar, NM, A1 ....$26.00

Marx, French infantry, tin, M, A1....................................$13.00

Marx, Gordon Highlander, tin, NM, A1 ....$8.00

Marx, Indian brave w/hatchet, tin, postwar, EX, A1 ....$20.00

Marx, Indian chief w/spear, tin, postwar, scarce, EX, A1 ..$20.00

Marx, Indian standing, tin, EX, A1 ....$12.00

Marx, infantry private at attention, tin, M, A1 ....$10.00

Marx, infantry private marching, tin, EX, A1 ....$9.00

Miller Plaster, General McArthur, 99%, A1 ....$58.00

Miller Plaster, rifle required by several figures, M, A1 ......$12.00

Miller Plaster, soldier flagbearer, 99%, A1 ....$55.00

Miller Plaster, soldier flagbearer planting flag, M, A1.......$44.00

Miller Plaster, soldier stretcher bearer, 99%, A1 ....$31.00

Miller Plaster, soldier w/rifle prone, 99%, A1 ....$33.00

Miller Plaster, soldier wounded, w/stretcher, 99%, A1 .....$46.00

FOREIGN-MADE

Britains, Argyll & Sutherland Highlanders Set #2063, 6-pc, EXIB, A (Est: $150-$200) $200.00

Britains, Army Lorry Set #1334, 2-pc, VGIB, A (Est: $150-$175)..$110.00

Britains, Artillery Set #2026, 7-pc, EXIB, A (Est: $225-$275) .$70.00

Britains, Belgian Cavalry Mounted Set #190, 5-pc, Fair (Fair+ box), A (Est: $200-$250) $200.00

Britains, Bikanier Camel Corps Set #123, 3-pc, VGIB, A (Est: $350-$450) $440.00

Britains, Black Watch Charging Set #11, 8-pc, EXIB, A (Est: $150-$200)..$150.00

Britains, British Army Staff Car Set #1448, 2-pc, VG, A (Est: $300-$350) $440.00

Britains, British Infantry in Steel Helmets & Gas Masks Set #258, 8-pc, VGIB, A (Est: $175-$225) $280.00

Britains, British Infantry Set #195, 8-pc, VGIB, A (Est: $150-$200)..$90.00

Britains, British Infantry w/Gas Masks Charging Set #1613, 10-pc, EXIB, A (Est: $150-$200) $190.00

Britains, Carden-Lloyd Tank w/Squad of Royal Tank Corps Set #1322, 9-pc, VGIB, A (Est: $200-$250)..................$260.00

Britains, Clockwork Van Set #2045, 1948-59, GIB, A (Est: $250-$350) $110.00

Britains, Cold Stream Guards Band Set #0037, 21-pc, VG+IB, A (Est: $300-$400)..$300.00

Britains, Coldstream Guards Firing Set #120, 8-pc, MIB, A (Est: $150-$200)..$90.00

Britains, Coldstream Guards Marching Set #1515, 8-pc, EXIB, A (Est: $150-$200)..$170.00

Britains, Coldstream Guards Set #8880, 6-pc, MIB, A (Est: $150-$175) $175.00

Britains, Colour Party of the Scots Guards Set #2084, 6-pc, EXIB, A $160.00

Britains, Devonshire Regiment Marching Set #110, 8-pc, GIB, A (Est: $250-$350)..$220.00

Britains, Drum & Pipe Band of the Scots Guards Marching Set #1722, 20-pc, VG, A (Est: $400-$600)....................$500.00

Britains, Drums & Bugles of the Line Set #0030, 6-pc, EXIB, A (Est: $150-$200) $88.00

Britains, Footmen From Attentants to the State Coach Set #9104, 6-pc, 1965, EX+IB, A (Est: $80-$120)........$130.00

Britains, French Foreign Legion in Action Set #2095, 16-pc, EXIB, A (Est: $250-$350) $220.00

Britains, French Infantry of the Line Set #141, 8-pc, EXIB, A (Est: $200-$300) $300.00

Britains, General Service Limbered Wagon Set #1330, 1955, 4 pieces, NMIB, A (Est: $600.00 – $800.00), $650.00. (Photo courtesy Bertoia Auctions)

Britains, German Infantry Set #432, 11-pc, VGIB, A (Est: $140-$160) $70.00

Britains, Gordon Highlanders Set #0157, 8-pc, EXIB, A (Est: $150-$200) $330.00

Britains, Grenadier Guards Set #41, 13-pc, EXIB, A (Est: $200-$250) $220.00

Britains, Honourable Artillery Co Set #5291 Set (Limited Ed), 8-pc, 1991, MIB, A (Est: $100-$150) $190.00

Britains, Horse-Drawn General Service Wagon w/Detachment Set #8920 (Primier Series), 7-pc, MIB, A (Est: $200-$250)..$200.00

Britains, Hussars (11th) Mounted, 5-pc, EXIB, A (Est: $250-$300)...$330.00

Britains, Hussars (4th) Mounted Set #9, 5-pc, EX+IB, A (Est: $150-$200) $120.00

Britains, Irish Guards Set #2096, 12-pc, VG+ (worn box), A (Est: $150-$250) $410.00

Britains, Medical Corps Figures Set #137, 27-pc, GIB, A (Est: $250-$350) $220.00

Britains, Miniature Barrage Balloon Unit w/Winch Lorry Set #1855, 2-pc, HO scale, VGIB, A (Est: $200-$300) .$280.00

Britains, Mountain Gun of the Royal Artillery Set #28, 12-pc, VG, A (Est: $175-$225) $140.00

Britains, Open State Landau Set #2094, 10-pc, MIB, A (Est: $350-$450) $320.00

Britains, Queen's Bays (2nd Dragoon Guards) Set #44, 5-pc, GIB, A $110.00

Britains, Queen's Own Cameron Highlanders Marching Set #114, 8-pc, VGIB, A (Est: $150-$175) $180.00

Britains, Queen's Own Royal West Surry Regiment Firing Set #121, 10-pc, GIB, A (Est: $300-$350) $360.00

Britains, Royal Air Force Marching Set #240, 8-pc, 1926-40 version, VGIB, A (Est: $300-$400) $400.00

Britains, Royal Air Force Marching Set #240, 8-pc, 1940-41, EXIB, A (Est: $300-$400) $280.00

Britains, Royal Air Force Marching Set #2073, 8-pc, EX+IB, A (Est: $150-$200) $180.00

Britains, Royal Army Medical Corps Ambulance Set #1450, 7-pc, 1932, 2nd version, NM (VG box), A $650.00

Britains, Royal Army Ambulance Set #1512, 4-pc, Fair (Fair box), A (Est: $125-$175) $190.00

Britains, Royal Army Medical Corps Horse-Drawn Ambulance Set #145, 7-pc, NMIB, A (Est: $300-$400) $560.00

Britains, Royal Army Medical Corps Unit Set #1723, 13-pc, Fair (Fair+ box), A (Est: $100-$150) $120.00

Britains, Royal Artillery Mountain Battery Set #8857 (Limited Ed), 11-pc, MIB, A (Est: $175-$225).....................$140.00

Britains, Royal Artillery Set #1730, 8-pc, EXIB, A (Est: $150-$225)...$165.00

Britains, Royal Engineers Limbered Wagon Set #1330, VG, A (Est: $150-$200) $110.00

Britains, Royal Fusiliers, Hussers & Scots Guards Set #1818, 26-pc, EXIB, A (Est: $500-$700) $1,200.00

Britains, Royal Lancers Mounted (12th) Set #128, 5-pc, EXIB, A (Est: $200-$250)...$280.00

Britains, Royal Lancers Mounted (12th) Set #1796, 6-pc, EXIB, A (Est: $200-$300) $600.00

Britains, Royal Regiment of Artillery (Gunners) Set #0313, 8-pc, EXIB, A (Est: $150-$200) $300.00

Britains, Royal Scots Dragoon Guards Set #5290, 8-pc, 1990, MIB, A (Est: $125-$150)......................................$90.00

Britains, Royal Scots Greys Mounted Set #32, 5-pc, GIB, A (Est: $150-$200)..$90.00

Britains, Royal Welsh Fusiliers Marching Set #74, 7-pc, GIB, A (Est: $90-$120) $80.00

Britains, Royal Welsh Fusiliers Set #5191 (Ltd Ed), 10-pc, 1991, MIB, A (Est: $125-$150) $130.00

Britains, Royal West Surrey Set #0121, 10-pc, 1908, EX (G box), A..$550.00

Britains, Seaforth Highlanders Set #5188 (Ltd Ed), 11-pc, 1988, MIB, A (Est: $125-150) $120.00

Britains, Sentrys & Sentry Boxes Set #0329, 8-pc w/4 Welsh Guards & 4 boxes, EX, A (Est: $100-$150) $65.00

Britains, Ski Troopers in White Snow Uniforms #2017, 4-pc, G, A (Est: $300-$350)..$160.00

Britains, Spanish Infantry (Infanteria Española) Set #92, 8-pc, NMIB, A $525.00

Britains, State Coach of England Set #1470, 10-pc, NMIB, A (Est: $250-$350)...$200.00

Britains, State Open Road Landau Set #2094, 10-pc, EXIB, A (Est: $300-$400)..$150.00

Britains, Underslung Heavy Duty Lorry w/Driver Set #1641, 2-pc, GIB, A (Est: $300-$400) $340.00

Britains, US Army Air Corps Marching Set #2041, 8-pc, Fair (G box), A (Est: $100-$125) $60.00

Britains, US Marines Marching Set #399, 8-pc, GIB, A (Est: $350-$450) $625.00

Britains, USA Army/West Point Cadets Set #0713A, 8-pc, EXIB, A (Est: $175-$225) $330.00

Britains, USA Infantry Set #0718A, 8-pc set, EXIB, A (Est: $150-$250) $275.00

Britains, Volunteer Corps Ambulance Set #1513, 3-pc, 1948-56, VG, A (Est: $500-$700)......................................$700.00

Britains, WWI British Thornycroft Anti-Aircraft Truck w/Gun Detachment Set #8926, 5-pc, MIB, A (Est: $200-$300)..$110.00

Britains, York & Lancer Regiment Running From Set #96, 10-pc, VGIB, A (Est: $200-$250) $240.00

Britains, Zoo Set #112, 11-pc w/animals, M (M box), A..$300.00

Brtiains, Zouaves Charging Set #142, 7-pc, G, A...........$100.00

Comet, Brigadiers Set #E824, 8-pc, EX (Est: $100-$150) $75.00

Elastolin, searchlight truck w/8 seated German soldiers, w/up, b/o lights, camo detail, 13", VG+, A (Est: $1,500-$2,000)..$1,045.00

French Cuirassiers Mounted Set #138, 5-pc, EXIB, A (Est: $175-$225)...$130.00

Lineol, Transport Truck w/Field Stove, 4 German soldiers, camo detail, 12", VG, A (Est: $300-$400) $385.00

Mignot, Band of the Dutch Grenadiers of the Guard Marching (1810), postwar, 12-pc, EXIB, A (Est: $225-$225)...$280.00

Mignot, Dutch Grenadiers of the Imperial Guard, 31-pc, postwar, G, A (Est: $350-$450) $425.00

Mignot, English Line Infantry Advancing (1812), 4-pc, MIB, A (Est: $60-$80) $40.00

Mignot, Farewell at Fountain Blue, 15-pc, ca 1980, EX-M, A $350.00

Mignot, French Colonial Infantry Marching (1890-1914), 8-pc, postwar, MIB, A (Est: $130-$160) $70.00

Mignot, French Napoleonic Field Artillery Caisson (1810), 5-pc, prewar, G, A (Est: $200-$250) $180.00

Mignot, French Napoleonic Infantry Marching, 8-pc, postwar, VG, A (Est: $100-$125)......................................$100.00

Mignot, French North African Goumiers, 5-pc, postwar, NMIB, A (Est: $200-$250)..$140.00

Mignot, Medieval Men-At-Arms Marching, 12-pc, postwar, E, A (Est: $175-$225) $80.00

Mignot, Napoleonic French Voltigeurs, 35-pc, postwar, G, A (Est: $350-$400) $380.00

Mignot, Napoleonic French 5th Hussars, 9-pc, postwar, EX, A (Est: $250-$300) $240.00

Mignot, Napoleonic-Era Italian Infantry Marching, 17-pc, postwar, G, A (Est: $175-$225) $130.00

Mignot, Prussian Infantry Marching (1810), 4-pc, postwar, MIB, A ($70-$90)...$60.00

Mignot, Russian Grenadiers Marching (1812), 8-pc, glossy pnt, ca 1970, EXIB, A (Est: $150-$175)..........................$190.00

Mignot, Standard Bearer, wooden bases, 4-pc, 1 base missing, G, A..$300.00

Mignot, Sappers & Drummer of the Imperial Guard Marching (1812), 8-pc, ca 1970, MIB, A (Est: $125-$175).......$60.00

Tipp & Co, Military Motorcycle w/Sidecar, litho tin w/compo German soldier driver, w/up, 5½", VG, A (Est: $250-$350) $465.00

Star Trek

The Star Trek concept was introduced to the public in the mid-1960s via a TV series which continued for many years in syndication. The impact it had on American culture has spanned two generations of loyal fans through its animated TV cartoon series (1977), six major motion pictures, Fox network's 1987 TV show, 'Star Trek, The Next Generation,' and two other television series, 'Deep Space 9,' and 'Voyager.' As a result of its success, vast amounts of merchandise (both licensed and unlicensed) have been marketed in a wide variety of items including jewelry, clothing, calendars, collector plates, comics, costumes, games, greeting and gum cards, party goods, magazines, model kits, posters, puzzles, records and tapes, school supplies, and toys. Packaging is very important; an item mint and in its original box is generally worth 75% to 100% more than one rated excellent.

See also Character and Promotional Drinking Glasses; Comic Books; Halloween Costumes; Lunch Boxes; Model Kits.

FIGURES

Galoob, ST V, any character, 1989, M, ea.........................$12.00

Galoob, ST V, any character, 1989, MIB, ea $28.00

Galoob, STNG, Antican, Ferengi, Q, or Selay, M, ea $30.00

Galoob, STNG, Antican, Ferengi, Q, or Selay, MOC, ea .$65.00

Galoob, STNG, Data, bl face, M.......................................$50.00

Galoob, STNG, Data, bl face, MOC...................................$75.00

Galoob, STNG, Data, brn face, M $25.00

Galoob, STNG, Data, brn face, MOC.................................$50.00

Galoob, STNG, Data, flesh face, M....................................$15.00

Galoob, STNG, Data, flesh face, MOC $25.00

Galoob, STNG, Data, spotted face, M $18.00

Galoob, STNG, Data, spotted face, MOC...........................$32.00

Galoob, STNG, LaForge, Lt Worf, Picard, or Riker, M, ea.$6.00

Galoob, STNG, LaForge, Lt Worf, Picard, or Riker, MOC, ea.$18.00

Galoob, STNG, Tasha Yar, M...$12.00

Galoob, STNG, Tasha Yar, MOC..$24.00

Mego, 3¾", Acturian, Betelgeusian, Klingon, Megarite, Rigelluian, or Zatanite, Series 2, M, ea................................$50.00

Mego, 3¾", Acturian, Betelgeusian, Klingon, Megarite, Rigelluian, or Zatanite, Series 2, MOC, ea $125.00

Mego, 3¾", Capt Kirk, Decker, Dr McCoy, Illia, Mr Spock, or Mr Scott, Series 1, M, ea..$10.00

Mego, 3¾", Capt Kirk, Decker, Dr McCoy, Illia, Mr Spock, or Mr Scott, Series 1, MOC, ea $30.00

Mego, 8", Andorian, 1970s, M..$300.00

Mego, 8", Andorian, 1970s, MOC $600.00

Mego, 8", Capt Kirk, 1970s, M $30.00

Mego, 8", Capt Kirk, 1970s, MOC $60.00

Mego, 8", Cheron, 1970s, M..$75.00

Mego, 8", Cheron, 1970s, MOC $150.00

Mego, 8", Dr McCoy, 1970s, M $75.00

Mego, 8", Dr McCoy, 1970s, MOC $150.00

Mego, 8", Gorn, 1970s, M..$95.00

Mego, 8", Gorn, 1970s, MOC $175.00

Mego, 8", Klingon, 1970s, M $25.00
Mego, 8", Klingon, 1970s, MOC $50.00
Mego, 8", Lt Uhura, 1970s, M $65.00
Mego, 8", Lt Uhura, 1970s, MOC $130.00
Mego, 8", Mr Scott, 1970s, M $40.00
Mego, 8", Mr Scott, 1970s, MOC $90.00
Mego, 8", Mr Spock, 1970s, M $30.00
Mego, 8", Mr Spock, 1970s, MOC $60.00
Mego, 8", Mugato, 1970s, M $300.00
Mego, 8", Mugato, 1970s, MOC $550.00
Mego, 8", Neptunian, 1970s, M $125.00
Mego, 8", Neptunian, 1970s, MOC $200.00
Mego, 8", Romulan, 1970s, M $800.00
Mego, 8", Romulan, 1970s, MOC...................................$1,200.00
Mego, 8", Talos, 1970s, M $300.00
Mego, 8", Talos, 1970s, MOC $525.00
Mego, 8", The Keeper, 1970s, M $80.00
Mego, 8", The Keeper, 1970s, MOC $160.00
Mego, 12½", Arcturian, 1979, M $65.00
Mego, 12½", Arcturian, 1979, MIP $130.00
Mego, 12½", Capt Kirk, 1979, M $40.00
Mego, 12½", Capt Kirk, 1979, MIP.....................................$80.00
Mego, 12½", Decker, 1979, M $60.00
Mego, 12½", Decker, 1979, MIP $120.00
Mego, 12½", Ilia, 1979, M...$40.00
Mego, 12½", Ilia, 1979, MIP $80.00
Mego, 12½", Klingon, 1979, M $60.00
Mego, 12½", Klingon, 1979, MIP $120.00
Mego, 12½", Mr Spock, 1979, M $40.00

Mego, 12½", Mr. Spock, 1979, MIP, $80.00.

Playmates, DS9, Chief Miles O'Brien, Commander Sisko, Major
    Kira Nerys, Morn, Odo, or Quark, 1994, M, ea............$5.00
Playmates, DS9, Chief Miles O'Brien, Commander Sisko, Major
    Kira Nerys, Morn, Odo, or Quark, 1994, MIP, ea $10.00
Playmates, DS9, Dr Julian Bashir, 1994, M......................$10.00

Playmates, DS9, Dr Julian Bashir, 1994, MIP $20.00
Playmates, DS9, Lt Jadzia Dax, 1994, M $6.00
Playmates, DS9, Lt Jadzia Dax, 1994, MIP........................$15.00
Playmates, First Contact, 5", Borg, Dr Beverly Crusher, Capt
    Picard, or Lily, 1996, M, ea.....................................$10.00
Playmates, First Contact, 5", Borg, Dr Beverly Crusher, Capt
    Picard, or Lily, 1996, MOC, ea................................$16.00
Playmates, First Contact, 5", Data, Deanna Troi, La Farge, Cpat
    Piccard, Riker, Worf, or Cochrane, 1996, M, ea $8.00
Playmates, First Contact, 5", Data, Deanna Troi, La Forge, Capt
    Piccard, Riker, Worf, or Cochrane, 1996, MOC, ea ..$14.00
Playmates, First Contact, 9", Capt Picard in 21st C outfit or
    Cochrane, 1996, M, ea $20.00
Playmates, First Contact, 9", Capt Picard in 21st C outfit or
    Cochrane, 1996, MIP $26.00
Playmates, First Contact, 9", Data, Capt Picard, or Riker, 1996,
    M $15.00
Playmates, First Contact, 9", Data, Capt Picard, or Riker, 1996,
    MIP, ea $20.00
Playmates, Insurrection, any character, 1998, 9", M, ea from $6
    to $8.00
Playmates, Insurrection, any character, 1998, 9", MIP, ea from
    $10 to $15.00
Playmates, Insurrection, any character, 1998, 12", M, ea....$8.00
Playmates, Insurrection, any character, 1998, 12", MIP, ea from
    $12 to $16.00
Playmates, STNG, 1st Series, Borg, Capt Picard, Commander Riker,
    Lt Commander Data, or Lt Worf, 1992, MOC, ea $22.00
Playmates, STNG, 1st Series, Deanna Troi or Romulan, 1992,
    M, ea $20.00
Playmates, STNG, 1st Series, Deanna Troi or Romulan, 1992,
    MOC, ea $35.00
Playmates, STNG, 1st Series, Ferengi, Gowron, or Lt Comman-
    der La Forge, M, ea $15.00
Playmates, STNG, 1st Series, Ferengi, Gowron, or Lt Comman-
    der La Forge, 1992, MOC, ea $30.00
Playmates, STNG, 2nd Series, any character, 1993, M, ea from
    $5 to $10.00
Playmates, STNG, 2nd Series, any character, 1993, MOC, ea
    from $12 to...$18.00

Playmates, Star Trek Next Generation, Second Series, Lt. Commander Geordi La Forge, 1993, MOC, $16.00.

Playmates, STNG, 3rd Series, any character except Esoqq or Data in red Redemption outfit, 1994, M, ea from $6 to **$12.00**

Playmates, STNG, 3rd Series, any character except Esoqq or Data in red Redemption outfit, 1994, MOC, ea from $16 to **$22.00**

Playmates, STNG, 3rd Series, Data in red Redemption outfit, 1994, M...**$125.00**

Playmates, STNG, 3rd Series, Data in red Redemption outfit, 1994, MOC..**$325.00**

Playmates, STNG, 3rd Series, Esoqq, 1994, M **$40.00**

Playmates, STNG, 3rd Series, Esoqq, 1994, MOC **$80.00**

Playmates, STNG, 4th Series or 5th Series, any character, 1995, M, from $8 to **$12.00**

Playmates, STNG, 4th Series or 5th Series, any character, 1995, MOC, ea from $12 to **$22.00**

Playmates, Voyager, Capt Janeway or Lt B'Elanna Torres, 5", M, ea..**$18.00**

Playmates, Voyager, Capt Janeway or Lt B'Elanna Torres, 5", MOC, ea...**$30.00**

Playmates, Voyager, Chakotay, Kazon, Lt Carey, Meelix, Seska, Tom Paris, Torres as Klingon, Tuvok, or Vidian, 5", M, ea **$10.00**

Playmates, Voyager, Chakotay, Kazon, Lt Carey, Neelix, Seska, Tom Paris, Torres as Klingon, Tuvok, or Vidian, 5", MIP, ea ...**$12.00**

Playmates, Voyager, Chakotay the Maquis, Doctor, or Harry Kim, 1995-96, 5", M, ea...**$10.00**

Playmates, Voyager, Chakotay the Maquis, Doctor, or Harry Kim, 5", MIP, ea...**$18.00**

PLAYSETS AND ACCESSORIES

Command Communications Console, Mego, 1976, MIB, from $125 to...**$150.00**

Communications Set, Mego, 1974, MIB........................**$150.00**

Engineering, Generations Movie, Playmates, MIB **$35.00**

Mission to Gamma VI, Mego, 1975, rare, MIB...............**$400.00**

Telescreen Console, Mego, 1975, MIB............................**$125.00**

Transporter Room, Mego, 1975, MIB.............................**$125.00**

USS Enterprise Bridge, Mego, 1975, complete w/3 figures, EX.**$80.00**

USS Enterprise Bridge, STNG, Playmates, 1991, MIB.....**$50.00**

VEHICLES

Borg Ship (sphere), Playmates, MIB **$60.00**

Ferengi Fighter, STNG, Galoob, 1989, NRFB.................**$75.00**

Klingon Bird of Prey, TNG, Playmates, 1995, MIB **$80.00**

Klingon Cruiser, Mego, 1980, 8" L, MIB........................**$70.00**

Klingon Warship, Star Trek II, Corgi #149, MOC...........**$30.00**

Romulan Warbird, Playmates, MIB.................................**$50.00**

USS Enterprise, Star Trek II, Corgi, 1982, MOC, from $25 to .**$30.00**

USS Enterprise B, Motion Picture, Playmates, M.............**$65.00**

USS Enterprise E, Motion Picture, Playmates, NMIB....**$135.00**

MISCELLANEOUS

Action Toy Book, Motion Picture, 1976, unpunched, EX.**$30.00**

Bank, Spock, plastic, Play Pal, 1975, 12", MIB................**$60.00**

Belt Buckle, marked 200th Anniversary USS Enterprise on back, 3½", M..**$15.00**

Book, Star Trek Pop-Up, Motion Picture, 1977, EX.........**$25.00**

Book, Where No One Has Gone Before, a History in Pictures, Dillard, M (sealed)..**$25.00**

Bop Bag, Spock, 1975, MIB..**$80.00**

Classic Science Tricorder, Playmates, MIB **$65.00**

Colorforms Adventure Set, MIB (sealed) **$35.00**

Coloring Book, Adventure, Wanderer Books, 1986, unused, NM+...**$8.00**

Comic Book, Gold Key #1, 1967, EX **$75.00**

Comic Book, Gold Key #1, 1967, M...............................**$215.00**

Communicators, bl plastic, Mego, 1976, MIB **$175.00**

Decanter, Mr Spock bust, ceramic, M **$40.00**

Flashlight Gun, plastic, 1968, NM **$50.00**

Kite, Spock, Hi-Flyer, 1975, unused, MIP **$35.00**

Metal Detector, Jetco, 1976, EX.....................................**$150.00**

Mix 'n Mold Casting Set, Kirk, Spock, or McCoy, MIB, ea.**$65.00**

Model Kit, Romulan Scoutship, resin, Amaquest, MIB....**$50.00**

Patch, America 1977 Convention, M **$40.00**

Patch, command insignia, w/instructions for uniform, M.**$25.00**

USS Enterprise Bridge, Mego, 1975, MIB, $130.00.

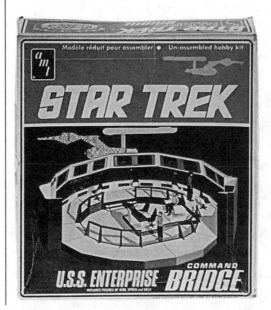

Model Kit, USS Enterprise Command Bridge, AMT, 1975, unused, MIB, $75.00.

Patch, Motion Picture, Kirk or Spock, M.........................$35.00
Pennant, Spock Lives, blk, red & yel on wht, Image Products, 1982, 30", M $15.00
Phaser Battle, Mego, 1976, NMIB $200.00
Phaser Ray Gun, clicking flashlight effect, 1976, MOC ...$75.00
Phaser Water Gun, Motion Picture, 1976, MOC $55.00
Puzzle Book, Wanderer Books, 1986, unused, NM+ $8.00
Starfleet Phaser, Motion Picture, Playmates, MIB..........$150.00
Trading Cards, 25th Anniversary, Series I, Impel, 1991, complete set of 160 different cards, NM+ $15.00
Tricorder, Mego, 1976, tape recorder, EXIB..................$125.00
Utility Belt, Remco, 1975, M $55.00
Wastebasket, Motion Picture, M $35.00
Water Gun, Motion Picture, Azrak Hamway Int'l, 1976, MOC..$50.00

Star Wars

The original 'Star Wars' movie was a phenomenal box office hit of the late 1970s, no doubt due to its ever-popular space travel theme and fantastic special effects. A sequel called 'Empire Strikes Back' (1980) and a third hit called 'Return of the Jedi' (1983) did just as well. Interest has been sustained through the release of three more films, 'Episode I, The Phantom Menace'; 'Episode II, Attack of the Clones'; and 'Episode III, The Revenge of the Sith.' As a result, an enormous amount of related merchandise was released — most of which was made by the Kenner Company. Palitoy of London supplied England and other overseas countries with Kenner's products and also made some toys that were never distributed in America. Until 1980 the logo of the 20th Century Fox studios (under whom the toys were licensed) appeared on each item; just before the second movie, 'Star Wars' creator, George Lucas, regained control of the merchandise rights, and items inspired by the last two films can be identified by his own Lucasfilm logo. Since 1987 Lucasfilm, Ltd., has operated shops in conjunction with the Star Tours at Disneyland theme parks.

The first action figures to be introduced were Luke Skywalker, Princess Leia, R2-D2, and Chewbacca. Because of delays in production that prevented Kenner from getting them on the market in time for Christmas, the company issued 'early bird' certificates so that they could be ordered by mail when they became available. In all, more than ninety action figures were designed. The 'Power of the Force' figures came with a collector coin on each card.

Original packaging is very important in assessing a toy's worth. As each movie was released, packaging was updated, making approximate dating relatively simple. A figure on an original 'Star Wars' card is worth more than the same character on an 'Empire Strikes Back' card, etc.; and the same 'Star Wars' figure valued at $50.00 in mint-on-card condition might be worth as little as $5.00 'loose.'

Especially prized are the original 12-back Star Wars cards (meaning twelve figures were shown on the back). Second issue cards showed eight more, and so on. Unpunched cards tend to be valued at about 15% to 20% more than punched cards, and naturally if the proof of purchase has been removed, the value of the card is less. (These could be mailed in to receive newly introduced figures before they appeared on the market. Remember, pricing is not a science — it hinges on many factors.

The following 'MOC' and 'MIB' listings are for mint items in mint packaging. Loose items are complete unless noted otherwise.

Because of the vast amount of Star Wars collectibles, listings are of vintage Kenner items only, including 'Power of the Force.'

For more information we recommend *Star Wars Super Collector's Wish Book Identification & Values, Third Edition*, by Geoffrey T. Carlton (Collector Books).

See also Character and Promotional Drinking Glasses; Halloween Costumes; Lunch Boxes; Model Kits.

Key:
ESB — Empire Strikes Back   POTF — Power of the Force
ROTJ — Return of the Jedi   SW — Star Wars

FIGURES

Ben (Obi-Wan) Kenobi, SW, 12", complete, M, $175.00. (Photo courtesy Linda Baker)

A-Wing Pilot, Droids, M $50.00
A-Wing Pilot, Droids, MOC..$150.00
A-Wing Pilot, POTF, M $50.00
A-Wing Pilot, POTF, MOC..$175.00
Admiral Ackbar, ROTJ, M..$10.00
Admiral Ackbar, ROTJ, MOC...$60.00
Amanaman, POTF, M...$100.00
Amanaman, POTF, MOC $325.00
Anakin Skywalker, M (in sealed mailer bag) $40.00
Anakin Skywalker, POTF, M..$35.00
Anakin Skywalker, POTF, MOC............................$2,250.00
AT-AT Commander, ESB, MOC.....................................$90.00
AT-AT Commander, ROTJ, M..$10.00
AT-AT Commander, ROTJ, MOC....................................$60.00
AT-AT Driver, ESB, MOC $125.00
AT-AT Driver, ROTJ, M..$10.00
AT-AT Driver, ROTJ, MOC $75.00
AT-ST Driver, POTF, M $15.00
AT-ST Driver, POTF, MOC..$95.00
AT-ST Driver, ROTJ, M...$10.00
AT-ST Driver, ROTJ, MOC $45.00
B-Wing Pilot, POTF, M..$10.00

B-Wing Pilot, POTF, MOC $55.00
B-Wing Pilot, ROTJ, M...$10.00
B-Wing Pilot, ROTJ, MOC...$65.00
Barada, POTF, M..$45.00
Barada, POTF, MOC $175.00
Ben (Obi-Wan) Kenobi, ESB, gray hair, M........................$15.00
Ben (Obi-Wan) Kenobi, ESB, gray hair, MOC $225.00
Ben (Obi-Wan) Kenobi, ESB, wht hair, MOC................$175.00
Ben (Obi-Wan) Kenobi, POTF, M...$30.00
Ben (Obi-Wan) Kenobi, POTF, MOC..................................$295.00
Ben (Obi-Wan) Kenobi, ROTJ, gray or wht hair, MOC, ea .$75.00
Ben (Obi-Wan) Kenobi, ROTJ, gray or wht hair, MOC (tri-
    logo), ea $200.00
Ben (Obi-Wan) Kenobi, ROTJ, wht hair, M $10.00
Ben (Obi-Wan) Kenobi, SW, gray hair, MOC (12-back).$710.00
Ben (Obi-Wan) Kenobi, SW, MOC (12-back) $750.00
Ben (Obi-Wan) Kenobi, SW, MOC (21-back) $190.00
Ben (Obi-Wan) Kenobi, SW, 12", MIB $450.00
Bespin Security Guard, ESB, Black, M.............................$10.00
Bespin Security Guard, ESB, Black, MOC.......................$70.00
Bespin Security Guard, ESB, White, M $10.00
Bespin Security Guard, ESB, White, MOC $125.00
Bespin Security Guard, ROTJ, Black, MOC.....................$75.00
Bespin Security Guard, ROTJ, White, MOC $50.00
Bib Fortuna, ROTJ, M $10.00
Bib Fortuna, ROTJ, MOC $40.00
Biker Scout, POTF, M...$15.00
Biker Scout, POTF, MOC $275.00
Biker Scout, ROTJ, M...$18.00
Biker Scout, ROTJ, MOC $125.00
Boba Fett, Droids, MOC $1,085.00
Boba Fett, ESB, MOC $425.00
Boba Fett, ESB, 12", MIB $625.00
Boba Fett, ROTJ, MOC (desert scene)............................$365.00
Boba Fett, ROTJ, MOC (fireball) $335.00
Boba Fett, ROTJ, MOC (tri-logo) $635.00
Boba Fett, SW, M..$45.00
Boba Fett, SW, MOC $775.00
Boba Fett, SW, 12", MIB..$1,225.00
Bobba Fett, Droids, M..$25.00
Bossk, ESB, M...$15.00
Bossk, ESB, MOC...$175.00
Bossk, ROTJ, MOC...$90.00
C-3PO, Droids, MOC..$95.00
C-3PO, ESB, removable limbs, M $10.00
C-3PO, ESB, removable limbs, MOC................................$110.00
C-3PO, POTF, removable limbs, M....................................$15.00
C-3PO, POTF, removable limbs, MOC $125.00
C-3PO, ROTJ, removable limbs, M $8.00
C-3PO, ROTJ, removable limbs, MOC $50.00
C-3PO, SW, MOC (12-back)..$425.00
C-3PO, SW, MOC (21-back)..$125.00
C-3PO, SW, 12", MIB $425.00
Chewbacca, ESB, MOC $275.00
Chewbacca, POTF, M..$20.00
Chewbacca, POTF, MOC $225.00
Chewbacca, ROTJ, MOC $225.00

Chewbacca, ROTJ, MOC (Endor photo) $95.00
Chewbacca, SW, M...$15.00
Chewbacca, SW, MOC (12-back) $360.00
Chewbacca, SW, MOC (21-back) $290.00
Chewbacca, SW, 12", MIB $235.00
Chief Chirpa, ROTJ, M $10.00
Chief Chirpa, ROTJ, MOC $50.00
Cloud Car Pilot, ESB, M $22.00
Cloud Car Pilot, ESB, MOC $130.00
Cloud Car Pilot, ROTJ, M $15.00
Cloud Car Pilot, ROTJ, MOC $75.00
Darth Vader, ESB, MOC...$145.00
Darth Vader, POTF, MOC...$295.00
Darth Vader, ROTJ, MOC (light saber drawn).................$65.00
Darth Vader, ROTJ, MOC (pointing) $115.00
Darth Vader, ROTJ, MOC (tri-logo)...............................$1,250.00
Darth Vader, SW, MOC (12-back) $625.00
Darth Vader, SW, MOC (21-back) $335.00
Darth Vader, SW, 12", MIB $270.00
Death Squad Commander, ESB, MOC..............................$140.00
Death Squad Commander, SW, M $15.00
Death Squad Commander, SW, MOC (12-back) $425.00
Death Squad Commander, SW, MOC (21-back) $225.00
Death Star Droid, ESB, MOC...$325.00
Death Star Droid, ROTJ, MOC..$125.00
Death Star Droid, SW, MOC $325.00
Dengar, ESB, M...$10.00
Dengar, ESB, MOC $195.00
Dengar, ROTJ, MOC $45.00
Dulok Scout, Ewoks, M...$10.00
Dulok Scout, Ewoks, MOC $35.00
Dulok Shaman, Ewoks, M..$16.00
Dulok Shaman, Ewoks, MOC $35.00
Emperor, POTF, MOC..$105.00
Emperor, ROTJ, M..$14.00
Emperor, ROTJ, MOC...$50.00
Emperor's Royal Guard, ROTJ, M.....................................$11.00

**Emperor's Royal Guard,
ROTJ, MOC, $55.00.**

EV-9D9, POTF, M...$90.00
EV-9D9, POTF, MOC $225.00

FX-7, ESB, M $10.00
FX-7, ESB, MOC $95.00
FX-7, ROTJ, MOC $75.00
Gammorrean Guard, ROTJ, M......................................$8.00
Gammorrean Guard, ROTJ, MOC $45.00
General Madine, ROTJ, M $8.00
General Madine, ROTJ, MOC......................................$50.00
Greedo, ESB, MOC..$125.00
Greedo, ROTJ, MOC..$100.00
Greedo, SW, M $15.00
Greedo, SW, MOC...$275.00
Hammerhead, ESB, MOC..$150.00
Hammerhead, ROTJ, MOC $100.00
Hammerhead, SW, M $12.00
Hammerhead, SW, MOC...$250.00
Han Solo, ESB, Bespin outfit, M $15.00
Han Solo, ESB, Bespin outfit, MOC...........................$225.00
Han Solo, ESB, MOC...$250.00
Han Solo, POTF, Carbonite Chamber, M....................$115.00
Han Solo, POTF, Carbonite Chamber, MOC...............$280.00
Han Solo, POTF, trench coat, M.................................$25.00
Han Solo, POTF, trench coat, MOC $565.00
Han Solo, ROTJ, Bespin outfit, MOC.........................$125.00
Han Solo, ROTJ, Hoth gear, M..................................$26.00
Han Solo, ROTJ, Hoth gear, MOC..............................$90.00
Han Solo, ROTJ, MOC (Death Star)..........................$210.00
Han Solo, ROTJ, MOC (Mos Eisley) $190.00
Han Solo, ROTJ, MOC (tri-logo) $125.00

Han Solo, ROTJ, trench coat, MOC (tri-logo), $60.00.

Han Solo, SW, lg head, MOC (12-back)....................$1,000.00
Han Solo, SW, MOC (21-back)................................$590.00
Han Solo, SW, sm head, M.......................................$35.00
Han Solo, SW, sm head, MOC (12-back) $860.00
Han Solo, SW, sm head, MOC (12-back) $860.00
Han Solo, SW, 12", MIB...$595.00
IG-88, ESB, MOC..$175.00
IG-88, ESB, 12", MIB..$1,200.00
IG-88, ROTJ, MOC $80.00
Imperial Commander, ESB, MOC................................$85.00
Imperial Commander, ROTJ, M..................................$10.00

Imperial Commander, ROTJ, MOC.............................$65.00
Imperial Dignitary, POTF, M $35.00
Imperial Dignitary, POTF, MOC...............................$110.00
Imperial Gunner, POTF, M..$95.00
Imperial Gunner, POTF, MOC..................................$195.00
Imperial Storm Trooper, ESB, Hoth weather gear, MOC ..$125.00
Imperial Storm Trooper, ROTJ, Hoth weather gear, MOC..$95.00
Jann Tosh, Droids, M...$25.00
Jann Tosh, Droids, MOC...$65.00
Jawa, ESB, MOC..$125.00
Jawa, POTF, MOC..$160.00
Jawa, ROTJ, MOC..$50.00
Jawa, SW, cloth cape, MOC (12-back)......................$425.00
Jawa, SW, MOC (21-back)......................................$200.00
Jawa, SW, plastic cape, M.......................................$280.00
Jawa, SW, plastic cape, MOC (12-back) $3,500.00
Jawa, SW, 12", M...$95.00
Jawa, SW, 12", MIB..$315.00
Jord Dusat, Droids, M $22.00
Jord Dusat, Droids, MOC $65.00
Kea Moll, Droids, M $26.00
Kea Moll, Droids, MOC $65.00
Kez-Iban, Droids, M $16.00
Kez-Iban, Droids, MOC..$75.00
King Gorneesh, Ewoks, MOC.....................................$35.00
Klaatu, ROTJ, Palace outfit, M $10.00
Klaatu, ROTJ, Palace outfit, MOC $45.00
Klaatu, ROTJ, Skiff outfit, M $12.00
Klaatu, ROTJ, Skiff outfit, MOC $45.00
Lady Ugrah Gorneesh, Ewoks, M $12.00
Lady Ugrah Gorneesh, Ewoks, MOC...........................$35.00
Lando Cairissian, ESB, MOC....................................$195.00
Lando Cairissian, ESB, no teeth, M............................$15.00
Lando Cairissian, ESB, no teeth, MOC $175.00
Lando Cairissian, POTF, General Pilot, M....................$65.00
Lando Cairissian, POTF, General Pilot, MOC $145.00
Lando Cairissian, ROTJ, MOC...................................$45.00
Lando Cairissian, ROTJ, Skiff outfit, M.......................$19.00
Lando Cairissian, ROTJ, Skiff outfit, MOC...................$65.00
Lobot, ESB, M..$9.00
Lobot, ESB, MOC..$85.00
Lobot, ROTJ, M...$10.00
Lobot, ROTJ, MOC...$95.00
Logray, Ewoks, M..$10.00
Logray, Ewoks, MOC..$35.00
Logray, ROTJ, M...$25.00
Logray, ROTJ, MOC...$50.00
Luke Skywalker, ESB, Bespin fatigues, blond hair, M $24.00
Luke Skywalker, ESB, Bespin fatigues, blond hair, MOC (looking)..$150.00
Luke Skywalker, ESB, Bespin fatigues, blond hair, MOC (walking)..$255.00
Luke Skywalker, ESB, Bespin fatigues, brn hair, M...........$26.00
Luke Skywalker, ESB, Bespin fatigues, brn hair, MOC (looking) $210.00
Luke Skywalker, ESB, Bespin fatigues, brn hair, MOC (walking) $260.00

Luke Skywalker, ESB, blond hair, MOC $425.00
Luke Skywalker, ESB, brn hair, MOC.............................$325.00
Luke Skywalker, ESB, Hoth battle gear, MOC $200.00
Luke Skywalker, ESB, X-Wing Pilot, MOC....................$175.00
Luke Skywalker, POTF, battle poncho, M.......................$10.00
Luke Skywalker, POTF, battle poncho, MOC $130.00
Luke Skywalker, POTF, Stormtrooper outfit, M $235.00
Luke Skywalker, POTF, Stormtrooper outfit, MOC $480.00
Luke Skywalker, POTF, X-Wing Pilot, MOC $145.00
Luke Skywalker, ROTJ, Bespin fatigues, blond hair, MOC (look-
    ing)..$150.00
Luke Skywalker, ROTJ, blond hair, MOC (Falcon Gunwell)..$275.00
Luke Skywalker, ROTJ, blond hair, MOC (Tatoonie) $295.00
Luke Skywalker, ROTJ, brn hair, M $26.00
Luke Skywalker, ROTJ, brn hair, MOC..........................$300.00
Luke Skywalker, ROTJ, Hoth battle gear, M $14.00
Luke Skywalker, ROTJ, Hoth battle gear, MOC $50.00
Luke Skywalker, ROTJ, X-Wing Pilot, M $15.00
Luke Skywalker, ROTJ, X-Wing Pilot, MOC $85.00
Luke Skywalker, ROTJ, X-Wing Pilot outfit, MOC (tri-logo)..$200.00
Luke Skywalker, SW, blond hair, MOC (12-back) $750.00
Luke Skywalker, SW, blond hair, MOC (21-back) $265.00
Luke Skywalker, SW, telescoping saber, M....................$275.00
Luke Skywalker, SW, telescoping saber, MOC (12-back) .$4,800.00
Luke Skywalker, SW, X-Wing Pilot, MOC.....................$340.00
Luke Skywalker, SW, 12", MIB $435.00
Luke Skywalker Jedi, POTF, gr light saber, MOC $95.00
Luke Skywalker Jedi, ROTJ, bl light saber, M..................$65.00
Luke Skywalker Jedi, ROTJ, bl light saber, MOC...........$225.00
Luke Skywalker Jedi, ROTJ, gr light saber, M $50.00
Luke Skywalker Jedi, ROTJ, gr light saber, MOC.............$95.00
Lumat, POTF, M $22.00
Lumat, POTF, MOC..$125.00
Lumat, ROTJ, M $21.00
Lumat, ROTJ, MOC...$85.00
Nien Nunb, M (in sealed mailer bag)..............................$20.00
Nien Nunb, ROTJ, M $10.00
Nien Nunb, ROTJ, MOC..$75.00
Nikto, ROTJ, M...$15.00
Nikto, ROTJ, MOC..$60.00
Paploo, POTF, M...$20.00
Paploo, POTF, MOC $125.00
Paploo, ROTJ, M...$20.00
Paploo, ROTJ, MOC...$95.00
Power Droid, ESB, MOC...$200.00
Power Droid, ROTJ, MOC $95.00
Power Droid, SW, M..$12.00
Power Droid, SW, MOC..$200.00
Princess Leia, ESB, Bespin crew neck, M $22.00
Princess Leia, ESB, Bespin crew neck, MOC (front view).$185.00
Princess Leia, ESB, Bespin turtleneck, M......................$20.00
Princess Leia, ESB, Hoth outfit, M................................$28.00
Princess Leia, ESB, Hoth outfit, MOC.........................$225.00
Princess Leia, ESB, MOC..$375.00
Princess Leia, POTF, combat poncho, M $18.00
Princess Leia, POTF, combat poncho, MOC $115.00
Princess Leia, ROTJ, Boushh outfit, M $26.00

Princess Leia, ROTJ, Boushh outfit, MOC $85.00
Princess Leia, ROTJ, combat poncho, MOC $70.00
Princess Leia, ROTJ, Hoth outfit, MOC $100.00
Princess Leia, ROTJ, MOC $465.00
Princess Leia, ROTJ, MOC (tri-logo) $200.00
Princess Leia, SW, MOC (12-back) $625.00
Princess Leia, SW, 12", MIB..$285.00
Princess Leis, SW, MOC (21-back)................................$295.00
Pruneface, ROTJ, M $12.00
Pruneface, ROTJ, MOC $75.00
Rancor Keeper, ROTJ, M $10.00
Rancor Keeper, ROTJ, MOC $55.00
Rebel Commander, ESB, M...$10.00
Rebel Commander, ESB, MOC.......................................$115.00
Rebel Commander, ROTJ, MOC......................................$75.00
Rebel Commando, ROTJ, M...$10.00
Rebel Commando, ROTJ, MOC.......................................$65.00
Rebel Soldier, ESB, MOC $90.00
Rebel Soldier, ROTJ, M $10.00
Rebel Soldier, ROTJ, MOC..$50.00
Ree-Yees, ROTJ, M..$10.00
Ree-Yees, ROTJ, MOC...$45.00
Romba, POTF, M...$25.00
Romba, POTF, MOC...$100.00
R2-D2, Droids, M $55.00
R2-D2, Droids, MOC $150.00
R2-D2, ESB, MOC $175.00
R2-D2, ESB, w/sensorscope, M.......................................$12.00
R2-D2, ESB, w/sensorscope, MOC $135.00
R2-D2, MOC (12-back) $425.00
R2-D2, POTF, w/pop-up light saber, M $100.00
R2-D2, POTF, w/pop-up light saber, MOC....................$225.00
R2-D2, ROTJ, w/pop-up light saber, MOC (tri-logo) $200.00
R2-D2, ROTJ, w/sensorscope, MOC................................$50.00
R2-D2, SW, 12", MIB...$285.00
R5-D4, ESB, MOC $150.00
R5-D4, ROTJ, MOC $95.00
R5-D4, SW, MOC $350.00
Sandpeople, ESB, MOC $145.00
Sandpeople, SW, MOC (12-back) $375.00
Sandpeople, SW, MOC (21-back) $165.00
Sise Fromm, Droids, MOC...$175.00
Snaggletooth, ESB, MOC $195.00
Snaggletooth, ESB or ROTJ, M, ea................................$10.00
Snaggletooth, ROTJ, MOC..$65.00
Snaggletooth, SW, bl body, M $350.00
Snaggletooth, SW, MOC..$110.00
Squidhead, ROTJ, M $10.00
Squidhead, ROTJ, MOC $45.00
Star Destroyer Commander, ESB, MOC........................$125.00
Star Destroyer Commander, ROTJ, MOC $80.00
Stormtrooper, ESB, MOC $185.00
Stormtrooper, POTF, MOC...$275.00
Stormtrooper, ROTJ, MOC...$65.00
Stormtrooper, SW, MOC (12-back)................................$450.00
Stormtrooper, SW, MOC (21-back)................................$178.00
Stormtrooper, SW, 12", MIB $345.00

Stormtrooper, SW, 12", M, $145.00.

Bespin Control Room, Micro Collection, MIB, $60.00.

Sy Snootles & the Max Rebo Band, ROTJ, 3-pc, M $65.00
Sy Snootles & the Max Rebo Band, ROTJ, 3-pc, MIB ..$150.00
Teebo, POTF, MOC..$240.00
Teebo, POTH or ROTJ, M, ea..$15.00
Teebo, ROTJ, MOC..$55.00
Thall Joben, Droids, MOC..$65.00
TIE Fighter Pilot, ROTJ, M..$18.00
TIE Fighter Pilot, ROTJ, MOC..$65.00
Tig Fromm, Droids, M..$60.00
Tig Fromm, Droids, MOC $165.00
Tusken Raider, ROTJ, MOC $75.00
Ugnaught, ESB, MOC..$100.00
Ugnaught, ESB or ROTJ, M, ea $10.00
Ugnaught, ROTJ, MOC..$40.00
Uncle Gundy, Droids, M..$18.00
Uncle Gundy, Droids, MOC...$55.00
Walrus Man, ESB, MOC..$195.00
Walrus Man, ROTJ, MOC...$75.00
Walrus Man, SW, MOC..$300.00
Warok, POTF, M...$26.00
Warok, POTF, MOC $125.00
Weequay, ROTJ, M...$20.00
Weequay, ROTJ, MOC $32.00
Wicket, Ewoks, M...$28.00
Wicket, Ewoks, MOC..$50.00
Wicket Warrick, POTF, MOC $260.00
Wicket Warrick, ROTJ, MOC $75.00
Yak Face, POTF, w/weapon, MOC.............................$2,180.00
Yoda, ESB, brn snake, MOC $365.00
Yoda, ESB, orange snake, MOC...$250.00
Yoda, POTF, MOC $585.00
Yoda, ROTJ, MOC...$150.00
Zuckuss, ESB, MOC...$150.00
Zuckuss, ROTJ, MOC...$65.00

PLAYSETS AND ACCESSORIES

Cantina Adventure Set, SW, complete, EX....................$175.00
Cantina Adventure Set, SW, MIB $700.00

Cloud City, ESB, complete, EX $135.00
Cloud City, ESB, MIB...$475.00
Creature Cantina, SW, complete, EX..............................$75.00
Creature Cantina, SW, MIB...$360.00
Dagobah, Darth Vadar & Luke Battle, ESB, complete, EX ..$25.00
Dagobah, Darth Vadar & Luke Battle, ESB, MIB...........$150.00
Darth Vader's Star Destroyer, ESB, MIB $245.00
Death Star Space Station, SW, complete, EX...............$115.00
Death Star Space Station, SW, MIB $295.00
Droid Factory, ESB, complete, EX $60.00
Droid Factory, ESB, MIB $170.00
Droid Factory, SW, MIB $145.00
Ewok Village, ROTJ, complete, EX $35.00
Ewok Village, ROTJ, MIB $225.00
Hoth Ice Planet, ESB, complete, EX $60.00
Hoth Ice Planet, ESB, MIB $335.00
Imperial Attack Base, ESB, complete, EX $40.00
Imperial Attack Base, ESB, MIB $145.00
Jabba the Hut, ROTJ, complete, EX $20.00
Jabba the Hut, ROTJ, MIB (Sears) $75.00
Jabba the Hut Dungeon w/Amanaman, ROTJ, complete, EX.$135.00
Jabba the Hut Dungeon w/Amanaman, ROTJ, MIB......$335.00
Jabba the Hutt Dungeon w/8D8, ROTJ, complete, EX.....$55.00
Jabba the Hutt Dungeon w/8D8, RTOJ, MIB.................$145.00
Land of the Jawas, SW, complete, EX...............................$55.00
Land of the Jawas, SW, MIB...$185.00
Rebel Command Center, ESB, complete, EX $80.00
Rebel Command Center, ESB, MIB.................................$350.00
Turret & Probot, ESB, complete, EX................................$35.00
Turret & Probot, ESB, MIB $160.00

VEHICLES

A-Wing Fighter, Droids, complete, EX $175.00
A-Wing Fighter, Droids, MIB..$550.00
All Terrain Attack Transport, complete, EX $90.00
All Terrain Attack Transport (AT-AT), ESB, MIB.........$350.00
All Terrain Attack Transport (AT-AT), ROTJ, MIB......$285.00
Armored Sentinel Transport (AST-5), ROTJ, complete, EX..$6.00
Armored Sentinel Transport (AST-5), ROTJ, mini-rig, MIB .$45.00

ATL Interceptor, Droids, complete, EX.............................$25.00
ATL Interceptor, Droids, MIB...$125.00
B-Wing Fighter, ROTJ, complete, EX $65.00
B-Wing Fighter, ROTJ, MIB $250.00
Captivator (CAP-2), ESB, mini-rig, MIB $35.00
Captivator (CAP-2), mini-rig, complete, EX......................$10.00
Captivator (CAP-2), ROTJ, mini-rig, MIB $20.00
Darth Vader's TIE Fighter, SW, complete, EX...................$55.00
Darth Vader's TIE Fighter, SW, MIB...............................$140.00
Darth Vader's TIE Fighter, SW, MIB (w/collector series
    sticker) $225.00
Desert Sail Skiff, ROTJ, complete, M $12.00
Desert Sail Skiff, ROTJ, mini-rig, MIB $45.00
Endor Forest Ranger, ROTJ, complete, EX $12.00
Endor Forest Ranger, ROTJ, mini-rig, MIB.......................$75.00
Ewok Battle Wagon, POTF, complete, EX $60.00
Ewok Battle Wagon, POTF, MIB $325.00
Imperial Cruiser, ESB, complete, EX.................................$50.00
Imperial Cruiser, ESB, MIB $150.00
Imperial Shuttle, ROTJ, complete, EX $100.00
Imperial Shuttle, ROTJ, MIB...$650.00
Imperial Shuttle Pod (ISP-6), ROTJ, complete, EX $10.00
Imperial Shuttle Pod (ISP-6), ROTJ, mini-rig, MIB $25.00
Imperial Sniper, POTF, complete, EX $30.00
Imperial Sniper, POTF, MIB...$110.00
Imperial Troop Transport, complete, EX $48.00
Imperial Troop Transport, ESB, MIB...............................$128.00
Imperial Troop Transport, SW, MIB................................$135.00
Interceptor (INT-4), complete, EX....................................$10.00
Interceptor (INT-4), ESB, mini-rig, MIB..........................$30.00
Interceptor (INT-4), ROTJ, mini-rig, MIB $45.00
Landspeeder, Sonic, SW, complete, EX............................$185.00
Landspeeder, Sonic, SW, MIB...$620.00
Landspeeder, SW, complette, EX.......................................$20.00
Landspeeder, SW, MIB...$85.00
Millennium Falcon, complete, EX $100.00
Millennium Falcon, ESB, MIB..$255.00

Millennium Falcon, Micro Collection, MIB, $540.00.

Millennium Falcon, ROTJ, MIB $285.00
Millennium Falcon, SW, MIB $375.00

Mobile Laser Cannon (MLC-3), ESB, mini-rig, MIB.......$40.00
Mobile Laser Cannon (MLC-3), ROTJ, mini-rig, complete,
    EX $10.00
Mobile Laser Cannon (MLC-3), ROTJ, mini-rig, MIB....$30.00
Multi-Terrain Vehicle (MTV-7), complete, EX $10.00
Multi-Terrain Vehicle (MTV-7), ESB, mini-rig, MIB.......$35.00
Multi-Terrain Vehicle (MTV-7), ROTJ, mini-rig, MIB....$25.00
One-Man Sand Skimmer, POTF, complete, EX...............$38.00
One-Man Sand Skimmer, POTF, MIB.............................$100.00
Personnel Deployment Transport (PDT-8), complete, EX.$10.00
Personnel Deployment Transport (PDT-8), ESB, mini-rig, MIB .$30.00
Personnel Deployment Transport (PDT-8), ROTJ, mini-rig,
    MIB..$20.00
Rebel Armored Snowspeeder, ESB, bl background, MIB.$185.00
Rebel Armored Snowspeeder, ESB, pk background, MIB.$195.00
Rebel Transport, ESB, bl background, MIB $190.00
Rebel Transport, ESB, yel background, MIB....................$175.00
Sandcrawler, radio-controlled, complete, EX..................$175.00
Sandcrawler, radio-controlled, ESB, MIB $500.00
Sandcrawler, radio-controlled, SW, MIB $665.00
Scout Walker (AT-ST), complete, EX...............................$35.00
Scout Walker (AT-ST), ESB, MIB...................................$175.00
Scout Walker (AT-ST), ROTJ, MIB.................................$150.00
Security Scout, POTF, complete, EX.................................$25.00
Security Scout, POTF, MIB...$115.00
Side Gunner, Droids, complete, EX..................................$25.00
Side Gunner, Droids, MIB $85.00
Slave I, ESB, complete, EX...$60.00
Slave I, ESB, MIB..$185.00
Speeder Bike, ROTJ, complete, EX...................................$15.00
Speeder Bike, ROTJ, MIB..$50.00
Tatooine Skiff, POTF, complette, EX..............................$250.00
Tatooine Skiff, POTF, MIB..$670.00
TIE Fighter, complete, EX $75.00
TIE Fighter, ESB, MIB...$265.00
TIE Fighter, SW, MIB..$150.00
TIE Fighter, SW, MIB (Free Figures Inside).....................$950.00
TIE Fighter (Battle Damage), ESB, MIB.........................$195.00
TIE Fighter (Battle Damage), ROTJ, complete, EX $45.00
TIE Fighter (Battle Damage), ROTJ, MIB......................$135.00
TIE Interceptor, ROTJ, complete, EX...............................$55.00
TIE Interceptor, ROTJ, MIB $250.00
Twin-Pod Cloud Car, ESB, complete, EX $45.00
Twin-Pod Cloud Car, ESB, MIB.....................................$130.00
X-Wing Fighter, complete, EX..$65.00
X-Wing Fighter, ESB, MIB...$495.00
X-Wing Fighter, SW, MIB..$425.00
X-Wing Fighter (Battle Damage), complete, EX $40.00
X-Wing Fighter (Battle Damage), ESB, MIB...................$295.00
X-Wing Fighter (Battle Damage), ROTJ, MIB.............$165.00
Y-Wing Fighter, ROTJ, complete, EX $60.00
Y-Wing Fighter, ROTJ, MIB..$225.00

MISCELLANEOUS

Bank, Chewbacca (kneeling), Sigma, M...........................$45.00
Bank, C3-PO, Roman Ceramics, M $75.00

Bank, R2-D2, Roman Ceramics, M..................................$50.00

Bank, Yoda, SW, Sigma, M...$90.00

Book, Empire Strikes Back, pop-up, Random House, M...$16.00

Book, Return of the Jedi — Things To Do & Make, Random House, 1983, paperback, EX+..$5.00

Book, Return of the Jedi Pop-Up Book, Random House, 1983, hardback, MIB..$18.00

Book, Splinter of the Mind's Eye, by A Foster, Del Ray Books, 1978, hardback, NM+...$12.00

Bop Bag, Darth Vader, Kenner, MIB............................$125.00

Bop Bag, Jawa, Kenner, MIB..$225.00

Card Game, Return of the Jedi-Play for Power, Parker Bros, 1983, MIB...$15.00

Case, Darth Vader, EX $15.00

Chewbacca Bandolier Strap, ROTJ, EXIB.....................$25.00

Chewbacca Bandolier Strap, ROTJ, MIB $40.00

Color 'N Clean Machine, Craftmaster, M.......................$50.00

Coloring Book, Ewoks, Kenner #18240, 1985, unused, NM+.$12.00

Doll, Chewbacca, Kenner, 1978-79, synthetic fur w/plastic eyes & nose, 20", EX $25.00

Doll, Latara the Ewok, plush, 1984, 16", MIB.................$50.00

Doll, Paploo the Ewok, ROTJ, plush, MIB $135.00

Doll, R2-D2, Kenner, 1978-79, stuffed cloth, w/speaker, 10", EX...$25.00

Doll, Wicket the Ewok, plush, w/cape, Kenner, 1983, 15", EX+..$30.00

Eraser & Sharpener, Ewok, 1983, MOC..........................$15.00

Erasers, ROTJ, 3-pc, 1983, MOC...................................$10.00

Game, Destroy Death Star, Kenner, MIB.........................$55.00

Game, ESB Yoda Jedi Master, Kenner, 1981, NMIB.........$75.00

Game, Escape From Death Star, Kenner, 1977, NMIB.....$40.00

Game, Laser Battle, SW, Kenner, MIB............................$85.00

Give-A-Show Projector, ESB, Kenner, complete, MIB $95.00

Gum Wrapper, 1977, 5x6", VG+....................................$10.00

Laser Pistol, SW, Kenner, 1978-83, plastic, b/o, 18½", EX .$40.00

Laser Rifle, ESB, Kenner, 1980, plastic, b/o, 18½", EX.....$75.00

Magnets, ROTJ, set of 4, MOC......................................$25.00

Movie Viewer, SW, Kenner, 1978-79, plastic w/snap-in cartridge, 7", EX $35.00

Night Light, Yoda (Return of the Jedi), 1980s, MOC $12.00

Paint Kit, Craftmaster, Luke Skywalker or Han Solo, MOC, ea...$16.00

Pencil, ROTJ, Butterfly Originals, 4-pack, 1983, 7½", MOC...$5.00

Poster Set, Craftmaster, 1979, w/2 posters, MIB (sealed) .$30.00

Puppet, Yoda, Kenner, 1981, hollow vinyl, 10", EX..........$25.00

Puzzle, Return of the Jedi Match Blocks, fr-tray, Craft Master, 1983, MIP (sealed) $12.00

Radio Watch, Lucasfilm/Bradley, 1982, R2-D2 & C-3PO on face, MIB..$50.00

Ruler, ROTJ, shows 8 characters, 1983, 12", EX.............$10.00

Scissors, ROTJ, MOC...$10.00

Sew 'N Show Cards, Wicket & Friends, MIB $18.00

Sit 'N Spin, Ewoks, MIB...$80.00

Speaker Phone, Darth Vader, MIB $95.00

Stick Pin, Darth Vader's mask, die-cast metal, 1977, MOC.$25.00

Stickers, ROTJ, 12-pc, 1983, MOC $10.00

Talking Telephone, Ewoks, MIB....................................$50.00

Yo-yo, Darth Vader, Dairy Queen promo, Humphrey, 1970s, rare, NM $25.00

Yo-yo, Stormtrooper, Spectra Star, sculpted plastic, MIP....$6.00

Steam Powered

During the early part of the century until about 1930, though not employed to any great extent, live steam power was used to activate toys such as large boats, novelty toys, and model engines. See also Boats; Trains.

Airplane Runabout, WK, planes suspended from canopy w/2 flags, round base, 10½", EX......................................$325.00

Artist, Germany, man w/pnt palette on stool at easel, gr base, 4", EX..$1,000.00

Blacksmiths, Ives, die-cut paper litho figures of 2 blacksmiths working, 9x10", EXIB..$500.00

Boiler, Weeden #3, ca 1910, stamped metal, 8½x10" dia, VG .$250.00

Butcher at Chopping Block, Bing, pnt tin, beveled base, 5" L, VG $85.00

Butter Churn, Marklin, model #4206, 1902, red & silver pin-striping, 7", VG..$925.00

Clown Acrobat, pnt tin, 5½", G+..................................$165.00

Clown in Barrel w/Hoop, pnt tin, hand-crank causes clown to spin, sq base, 6", EX..$475.00

Cyclone Pump, tin windmill w/electric motor on base, 16½", VG+...$375.00

Drill Press, Bing, 9", EX..$500.00

Eureka Steam Engine, Weeden, horizontal w/brass boiler in tin covering w/diecut stars, NP valves & lenses, 14", EX .$500.00

Ferris Wheel, Falk/Germany, tin with compo figures, steam or hand crank, 12½" T, overpt $900.00

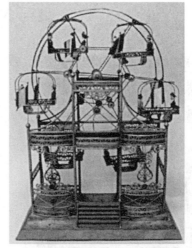

Ferris Wheel, Germany, six gondolas with composition figures on metal framework, 29x21", VG, A, $8,800.00. (Photo courtesy Bertoia Auctions)

Ferris Wheel, pnt tin, 6 gondolas w/2 figures in ea, 19", EX $2,100.00

Ferris Wheel, pnt tin, 8 gondolas w/lithoed children, steam or hand crank, 16" T, G $175.00

Fire Pumper, Weeden, Pat 1885, pnt CI w/brass boiler, engine w/dbl cylinders on wrist pins, 17", EX..................$2,000.00

Fodder Cutter, Marklin, 1902, mk Futterschneidmaschine, gr & red, 9" L, rare, EX $900.00

Fountain, Germany, sq ftd base w/railing at 4 corners, side fly-wheels, 8" sq, GIB..$110.00

Grindstone, CI, 6", VG $325.00

Hercules Engine & Machine Tool Set, Ernst Plank, 1902, vertical pillar-type engine w/fly-ball governor, EXIB $850.00

Kaleidoscope, Germany, glass face w/brass frame mounted on wood base, 7½", NMIB $850.00

Locomotive, Weeden, brass boiler w/NP valves & smoke stack, red-pnt spoke wheels & flywheel, 11½", EX............$475.00

Mill Engine, Doll, 1925-30, bl & blk w/red & bl pinstriping, fly-ball governor, 12x11" base, EX.................................$575.00

Pickup Truck, Doll, blk & yel tin, rubber tires w/spoke wheels, chain-driven live steam mechanism, 19", EX.......$3,300.00

Pillar Engine, Ernst Plank, 1895-1900, blk boiler w/brass high-lights, 6" sq wood base, EX $600.00

Roundabout, Doll, 4 compo figures in open chairs suspended from canopy, pulley on side of base, 9", EX..............$415.00

Seed Sorter, Marklin, model #4207, 1902, mk Trieur, gr & yel, repro tin base, 8" L, VG......................................$350.00

Shoeshine Boy, Germany, Black boy working on shoe in front of brick wall, 4½", G $385.00

Sled Ride, Doll, tiny figure on sled rides down slope, chain driven, 5", G+ $110.00

Steam Car, pressed steel & CI, early type w/open bench seat, spoke wheels, 15½", VG+ $180.00

Steam Engine, Bing #130/272, overtype, VG+..............$875.00

Steam Engine, CG&C, horizontal boiler w/CI bracket supporting NP flywheel & levers, CI base, 9", NM $575.00

Steam Engine, Doll, horizontal boiler w/dual flywheel, NP detail to levers & rods, CI base, 11½", NM $650.00

Steam Engine, Doll Co, horizontal boiler w/dual flywheel, much nickel detail, level glass tube, CI base, 11½", M $650.00

Steam Engine, Ernst Plank #420, Rapid Boch, VG $250.00

Steam Engine, Marklin #4106/7, mk ABC, vertical, 16", VG $600.00

Steam Engine, Schoenner, vertical, 19½", EX $1,265.00

Steam Engine, Weeden, single cylinder, NP base, 8" L, EX $850.00

Steam Engine, Weeden, tin horizontal boiler, 1-cylinder, nickled valves/whistle, CI support, no-veiw valve, EX.........$250.00

Steam Engine, Weeden #38 Walking Beam, w/wooden base & engine platform, GIB..$135.00

Steam Plant, Bing #10/110/3, w/6" flywheel, VG........$2,100.00

Steam Plant, Marklin, horizontal brass boiler on pnt tin 'brick' burner, engine on cast base, 14" sq, VGIB...............$450.00

Steam Plant, Weeden, w/5 workshop accessories mounted on 16x12" board, EX...$300.00

Steam Plant w/Dynamo, Doll, 1925-30, bl & blk w/red pin-striping, DC trademarks on cylinder, 13x8" base, EX $500.00

Steam Roller, Bing #130/740, w/reversing gear & whistle, 6¾", VG $350.00

Steam Roller, Fleischmann #155/1, incomplete o/w VG ..$200.00

Steam Roller, Weeden #646, VG $150.00

Thresher, Bing, pnt tin, yel w/red highlights & gr cranks, red funnel, 9" L, G...$150.00

Thresher, Marklin, gr & red w/wooden rollers under rear cap, wire mesh bottom, 8" L, EX....................................$475.00

Tractor, brass & steel, early model w/roof over driver's seat, spoke wheels, 12½", Fair+ $125.00

Tricycle, yel-pnt tin w/copper boiler, spoke wheels, tailgate opens for dbl wick burner, 11", VG......................$2,900.00

Turnip Cutter, Marklin, model #4204, 1902, gr & red w/yel pin-striping, 5", rare, VG $350.00

Well, Germany, pnt tin w/corrugated roof over rnd well w/crank & pulley system, beveled base, 12", G+ $130.00

Wheat Sifter, Bing, pnt tin, red & yel w/bl base, 5½" L, VG..$685.00

Windmill, Doll, pnt tin, simulated brick base, 19", EX ..$600.00

Windmill, PS & tin w/CI water pump & flywheel, 24", G, A $125.00

Winnowing Machine, Marklin, model #4202, 1902, red, internal fan & mechanical sifter, 6" L, rare, EX....................$500.00

Woman at Trough, Germany, tin, woman & 2 chickens at trough, 8½", EX..$200.00

Workshop, Marklin, model #4281, 1906-07, CI tools on gr litho base, 23x10", rare, VG $4,400.00

Workshop, Weeden #65, complete, VG..........................$100.00

Steiff

Margaret Steiff made the first of her felt toys in 1880, stuffing them with lamb's wool. Toys of velvet, plush, and wool followed later, and in addition to the lamb's wool stuffing, she used felt scraps, excelsior, and kapok as well. In 1897 and 1898 her trademark was a paper label printed with an elephant; from 1900 to 1905 her toys carried a circular tag with an elephant logo that was different than the one she had previously used. The most famous 'button in ear' trademark was registered on December 20, 1904. Both 1904 and 1905 saw the use of the button with an elephant (extremely rare) and the blank button (which is also rare). The button with Steiff and the underscored or trailing 'F' was used until 1948, and the raised script button is from the 1950s.

Steiff Teddy bears, perhaps the favorite of collectors everywhere, are characterized by their long thin arms with curved wrists and paws that extend below their hips. Buyer beware: The Steiff company is now making many replicas of their old bears. For more information about Steiff's buttons, chest tags, and stock tags as well as the inspirational life of Margaret Steiff and the fascinating history of Steiff toys, we recommend *Button in Ear Book* and *The Steiff Book of Teddy Bears*, both by Jurgen and Marianne Cieslik; *Teddy Bears and Steiff Animals 2nd* and *3rd Series* by Margaret Fox Mandel; *4th Teddy Bear and Friends Price Guide* by Linda Mullins; *Collectible German Animals Value Guide* by Dee Hockenberry; and *Steiff Sortiment 1947 – 1995* by Gunther Pefiffer. (This book is in German; however, the reader can discern the size of the item, year of production, and price estimation).

See also Character, TV, and Movie Collectibles; Disney.

Bear, 6", 1960s, beige, stitched nose & mouth, button eyes, jtd, no ID, VG..$350.00

Bear, 6½", 1950s, gold, glass eyes, stitched nose & mouth, no-pad style, jtd, EX..$250.00

Bear, 7", 1905, beige, button eyes, stitched nose, mouth & claws, felt pads, jtd, EX $825.00

Bear, 7½", light beige, glass eyes, stitched reddish nose, mouth, and claws, ear button, NM, $1,775.00. (Photo courtesy James D. Julia, Inc.)

Bear, 8", 1960s, blond w/red neck bow, button eyes, stitched nose, mouth & claws, felt pads, jtd, EX $450.00

Bear, 10", apricot, early, blk shoe-button eyes, blk stitched mouth, felt pads, jtd, G..$550.00

Bear, 10", blond, glass eyes, stitched claws w/felt pads, ear button, G...$600.00

Bear, 10", 1920s (?), beige, button eyes, pads on feet, No ID, VG+ $1,200.00

Bear, 12", lt beige, shoe-button eyes, felt pads, stitched claws, G $475.00

Bear, 13½", 1960s, dk brn, brn glass eyes, blk stitched nose, mouth & claws, tan felt pads, jtd, VG $200.00

Bear, 14", 1950s (?), beige, blk button eyes, stitched mouth, nose & claws, gold ear button & tag, VG $150.00

Bear, 15", early, tan, pointy nose, stitched eyes, Fair.......$200.00

Bear, 17", beige, button eyes, stitched nose & mouth, felt pads (redone), jtd, no ID, G $225.00

Bear, 20", gold, 1915, shoe-button eyes, stitched nose, mouth & claws, felt pads (rpl), jtd, G $500.00

Bear, 26", 1940s-50s, honey gold mohair, glass eyes, partial cloth tag, EX+..$2,250.00

Bear, 28", 1910(?), cinnamon, shoe-button eyes, stitched nose & mouth, w/pads, no ID, VG+ $12,000.00

Bear, 9½", 1905, blond, shoe-button eyes, stitched nose, mouth & claws, blank ear button, jtd, G...........................$450.00

Bear on Wheels, 44" L, ca 1903, glass eyes, stitched nose & paws, felt pads, jtd neck, EX................................$9,200.00

Bear Set (Collector's Editon 1983), 7" to 16", dk brn w/leather-padded feet, sold at Stron Museum, EX+IB............$250.00

Boy Doll, 16", stuffed felt body w/felt-covered face, pnt features, cloth knickers, sweater & stocking cap, Fair............$250.00

Bull Yale Bull Dog, 10½", 1950s, 3 shades of brn, glass eyes, felt 'Y' blanket & red leather collar, EX $525.00

Cat Seated Upright, 7", tan w/wht chest & brn stripes, stitched nose & mouth, gr button eyes, collar, ear button, tag, G.......$150.00

Elephant, 7½", gray plush, red blanket w/bells, orig ear & neck tags, EX $75.00

Elephant Train, 40" overall, elephant on wheeled platform, 1 cage wagon & 1 windowed wagon, VG+ $475.00

Fox Terrier, 10", 1920s-30s, standing, wht w/brn ears, glass eyes, blk stitched nose & mouth, brn leather collar, VG .$175.00

Giraffe, 24", old, off wht w/orange spots, ear tag, VG.....$300.00

Goat, 11", 1920s, gr glass eyes, blk stitched nose, mouth & hooves, felt ears & foot pads, neck ribbon & bell, EX $700.00

Kitten, 11", 1920s, gray striped, gr glass eyes, stitched nose, mouth & claws, jtd, EX $350.00

Koala Bear, 14½", 1960s, cream, brn eyes, gray felt nose, shaved hands & feet, EX $225.00

Lamb, 11½", 1950s, wht w/pk felt inner ears, gr eyes, stitched nose & mouth, neck ribbon & bell, not jtd, EX $175.00

Lion, 20", 1930s, long mane & end of tail, amber glass eyes, stitched nose & mouth, not jtd, VG $150.00

Llama, 16½", 1960s, cream w/blk & brn striping, brn glass eyes, shaved muzzle & lower legs, EX $125.00

Monkey on Handcart, 10½x9", dk brn mohair w/lt tan felt face, ears, hands & feet, articulated movement, VG........$150.00

Rabbit Skittles Game, 9 stuffed rabbits on wood bases w/ball, 9½" T, EX $8,000.00

Stick Horse, 40", 1940s, felt head w/mane, harness & rein, wooden stick hdl, EX+..$75.00

Teddy Roosevelt (Rough Rider) on Rearing Horse, 27x38" long, G, $6,900.00. (Photo courtesy James D. Julia, Inc.)

Tiger, 10", 1950s, lying down, airbrushed details, gr eyes, pk nose, paper label, ear tag & button, VG $125.00

Zebra, 14", 1950s, blk airbrushed stripes, glass eyes, ear button, VG $150.00

Zotty Bear, 16", 1950s (?), beige, curly, glass eyes, brn stitched nose, open felt mouth, peach felt pads, VG $175.00

Strauss

Imaginative, high-quality, tin windup toys were made by Ferdinand Strauss (New York, later New Jersey) from the onset of World War I until the 1940s. For about fifteen years prior to his becoming a toymaker, he was a distributor of toys he imported from Germany. Though hard to find in good working order, his toys are highly prized by today's collectors, and when found in even very good to excellent condition, many are in the $500.00 and up range.

Advisor: Scott Smiles (S10)

Air Devil, w/pilot, from $500 to $550.00
Alabama Coon Jigger, EX, A...$425.00
Auto Dump Cart EX...$300.00
Big Show Circus Truck, VG $900.00
Boob McNutt, flat-hat version, EX $500.00

Boob McNutt, flat-hat version, EXIB, A, $900.00.

Boob McNutt, VG...$400.00
Bus De Luxe #105, G...$400.00
Circus Wagon, VG $800.00
Dandy Jim Clown Dancer, EX...$700.00
Dizzy Lizzy, NMIB $500.00
Emergency Tow Car #54, VG $1,200.00
Flying Air Ship, NMIB..$800.00
Graf Zeppelin Jr #2, EXIB, from $600 to.............................$750.00
Ham & Sam, EX, A $800.00
Ham & Sam, NMIB $1,200.00
Ham & Sam, VG, A $550.00
Inter-State (Double-Decker) Bus, EX, A $525.00
Jackee the Hornpipe Dancer, EXIB, A.................................$900.00
Jackee the Hornpipe Dancer, G, A $400.00
Jazzbo Jim (Banjo Player), G+, A..$425.00
Jazzbo Jim (Jigger), EX, A...$500.00
Jazzbo Jim (Jigger), EXIB $700.00

Jenny the Balking Mule, 9" L, EXIB, A $375.00
Jitney Bus, EX $425.00
Jolly Pals, EX...$475.00
Knock Out Prize Fighters, G...$275.00
Knock-Out Prize Fighters, EX, A $400.00
Leaping Lena Car, EX, from $450 to $550.00
Leaping Lena Car, VG, A...$300.00
Locomotive & Tender, VG, A...$150.00
Long Haulage Truck #71, G+ $350.00
Lumber Tractor-Trailer, no mumber, G $375.00
Parcel Post Truck, NM $1,250.00
Play Golf, nonworking o/w EX, A......................................$900.00
Play Golf, 12", no golf balls o/w EX (P box), A $375.00
Play Golf (Just Like Daddy), VGIB....................................$300.00
Porter Pushing Pup in Truck, VG......................................$600.00
Red Flash Racer #31, EX, from $700 to $750.00
Rollo-Chair, litho tin, NMIB...$1,200.00
Santee Claus Sleigh, EXIB...$1,750.00
Santee Claus Sleigh, VG+, A...$900.00
Sparko, EXIB $300.00
Spirit of St Louis, 7" W, VG $350.00
Standard Oil Truck #73, VG, A...$400.00
Thrifty Tom's Jigger Bank, EX.......................................$2,100.00
Thrifty Tom's Jigger Bank, VGIB, A...............................$3,900.00
Timber Truck, VG $500.00
Tip Top Dump Truck, NM $1,000.00
Tip Top Dump Truck, 10", G...$250.00
Tip Top Porter, EXIB $350.00
Tip Top Porter, G, A $250.00
Tombo Alabama Coon Jigger, see Alabama Coon Jigger
Trackless Trolly/Twin Trolleys, VG $250.00
Travelchiks Boxcar, EX..$500.00
Travelchiks Boxcar, EXIB $700.00
Trik Auto, EX, A $550.00
Trik Auto, no driver, VG..$300.00
Water Sprinkler Truck #72, VG+, A $425.00
What's It?, NMIB...$850.00
Wildfire, EXIB $350.00
Yell-O Taxi #59, EX, A...$575.00
Yell-O Taxi #59, VG, A...$350.00

Structo

Pressed steel vehicles were made by Structo (Illinois) as early as 1920. They continued in business well into the 1960s, producing several army toys, trucks of all types, and firefighting and construction equipment.

Airport Mail Truck, 1920s, 24", G $1,100.00
American Airlines Sky Chief Truck, bl cab & base, wht box van
 w/scissor lift action, BRT, 12", VGIB.....................$250.00
Army Truck, open bench seat, gr w/brn canvas cover, b/o lights,
 WWT, 17", EX...$275.00
Auto Builder Roadster, w/up, open seat, MDW, 16",
 VG $350.00
Auto Transport, 1950s, w/2 Cadillacs, 22", EXIB.......$125.00

Bearcat Roadster, 15", EX, $750.00.

Car Carrier, 1950s, flat bed w/chain winch & loading ramp, opening hood, red, 21", EXIB....................................$250.00

Communications Center Truck, 1960s, 21", EX+...........$250.00

Concrete Mixer, 1950s, red w/yel drum, 10-wheeled, 21", VG $125.00

Dump Truck, lt gr, WWT, 22", VG $350.00

Fire Aerial Ladder Truck, 1960s, mk Structo on lg wht lettering, wht-wall tires, 30", VG+IB $150.00

Furniture Truck, 1960s, cabover w/10-wheeled van, 23", EX+IB $300.00

Guided Missile Launcher Truck, 1960s, 14", EXIB.........$200.00

Hydraulic Hook & Ladder, 1950s, 32", G $100.00

Motor Dispatch Truck, airplane decals on sides of van, bl, BRT, red hubs, 23", G $325.00

Racer, w/up, 2-seater, PMSW, Structo decal on radiator, 12½", EX+ $550.00

Roadster (DeLuxe), top down, spring motor w/rear wheel drive, Structo decal on radiator, 15½", VG+ $450.00

Sanitation Dept Truck, 1960s, 16", VG+.........................$125.00

Semi, 1960s, red cab w/wht trailer mk Structo Toys Live Action in red, wht-walls, 24", VG+IB..................................$175.00

Speedwagon, 1930s, 16", roof extends over open cab, yel w/turq disk wheels, EX $600.00

St Louis Dairy Truck, blk & wht, Phillips 66 decal on top, 18", EX $500.00

Steam Shovel, 1950s, rubber treads, 18", VG+IB...........$125.00

Structo Rid-er Dumper, 1960s, 20", complete, VG+ $75.00

Tank, w/up, gr w/red turret & wheels, w/treads, 11½", VG+ .$450.00

Tow Truck, 1950s, open curved back, BRT, red w/yel ad detail, 6-wheeled, 12", EXIB...$150.00

Structo 66 Tank Truck, windup motor, 13½", VG, $175.00.
(Photo courtesy Randy Inman Auctions)

Tractor, spring motor, open seat, yel & bl w/red wheels, rubber treads, 12", G $350.00

Tractor, w/up, open seat, yel & bl w/red wheels, rubber treads, NP driver, 8", VG+..$450.00

Tractor, 1920s, open seat w/vertical steer wheel, blk treads, clockwork motor, 12", EX+ $750.00

Tractor Pulling Trailer, w/up, gr w/red wheels, metal treads, red 2-wheeled trailer, 15", VG+ $250.00

Teddy Bears

The history of old teddy bears goes way back to about 1902 – 1903. Today's collectors often find it difficult to determine exactly what company produced many of these early bears, but fortunately for them, there are many excellent books now available that contain a wealth of information on those early makers.

Because most teddies were cherished childhood toys and were usually very well loved, many that survived are well worn, so an early bear in mint condition can be very valuable.

The following listings are from recent auctions with the auction estimates added at the end of each line just before the price to give a better idea of price trends.

We would like to direct your attention to the books on the market that are the most helpful on the detailed history and identification of teddies. *A Collectors History of the Teddy Bear* by Patricia Schoonmaker; *Teddy Bears Past and Present (Volumes I and II)* and *American Teddy Bear Encyclopedia* by Linda Mullins; *Teddy Bears — A Complete Guide to History, Collecting, and Care*, by Sue Pearson and Dottie Ayers; *Teddy Bear Encyclopedia* and *Ultimate Teddy Bear Book* by Pauline Cockrill; *Teddy Bear Treasury, Vol. II*, by Ken Yenke; and *Big Bear Book* by Dee Hockenberry. The reader can easily see that a wealth of information exists and that it is impossible in a short column such as this to give any kind of a definitive background. If you intend to be a knowledgeable teddy bear collector, it is essential that you spend time in study. Many of these books will be available at your local library or through dealers who specialize in bears.

See also Schuco; Steiff.

12", carmel, swivel head w/amber glass eyes, blk stitched nose & paws, felt pads, VG, A (Est: $200-$300)..................$250.00

14", beige w/red neck bow, button eyes, stitched nose & mouth, felt pads, jtd, Gund (?), Fair, A (Est: $50-$75) $100.00

14", lt beige, shoe-button eyes, stitched nose & mouth, w/pads, jtd, nonworking squeak box o/w VG, A (Est: $200-$300) $200.00

15", beige mohair w/glass eyes, stitched nose & mouth, dk velvet pads, mild hump back, Germany, G, A (Est: $250-$500).........$200.00

15", golden short mohair, boot button eyes, long snout, cloth pads, jtd w/swivel head, Am, early, G, (Est: $200-$300)......$200.00

16", carmel, brn glass eyes, velvet pads, stitched detail, jtd, hump back, swivel head, VG, A (Est: $200-$400) $225.00

16", cinnamon mohair w/center seam, sm glass eyes, brn pads, jtd, swivel head, Germany, G, A (Est: $200-$300)..$470.00

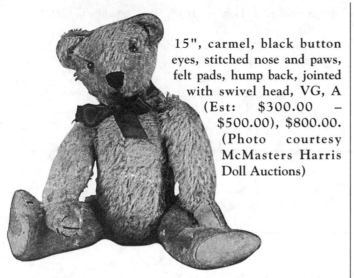

15", carmel, black button eyes, stitched nose and paws, felt pads, hump back, jointed with swivel head, VG, A (Est: $300.00 – $500.00), $800.00. (Photo courtesy McMasters Harris Doll Auctions)

16", wht mohair w/blk button eyes, blk stitched nose & mouth, stiched paws w/felt pads, jtd, VG+, A (Est: $100-$200) .$300.00
18", wht mohair, glass eyes, brn stitched nose, open mouth, orange felt pads, jtd, 1950s (?), VG...........................$150.00

18", Winnie the Pooh, honey beige mohair with rose-colored shirt, one of 2,500 made by R John Harris, MIB, A (Est: $800.00 – $1,000.00), $550.00. (Photo courtesy Bertoia Auctions)

21", beige mohair, blk button eyes, pointed snout w/oilcloth nose, suede pads, jtd, G, A (Est: $200-$300)...........$390.00
21", lt brn, glass eyes, felt snout & feet, stitched hands, jtd, 1920s, VG, A (Est: $600-$800) $990.00
22", brn short mohair, glass eyes, stitched nose, felt pads, jtd w/swivel head, growler, G, A (Est: $300-$400) $250.00
22", lt brn mohair w/brn button eyes, stitched nose & mouth, stubby ears, jtd, G, A (Est: $100-$200)....................$140.00
23", golden short mohair, blk button eyes, stitched nose, mouth & pads, G, A (Est: $200-$300) $220.00
25", brn mohair w/glass eyes, stitched nose & mouth, jtd, Fair, A (Est: $150-$250) $100.00
27½", lt beige mohair w/glass eyes, stitched nose & mouth, felt paws, jtd limbs, head turns, VG, A (Est: $400-$600) .$115.00

Telephones, Novelty

Novelty phones representing a well-known advertising or cartoon character are proving to be the focus of a lot of collector activity — the more recognizable the character the better. Telephones modeled after a product container are collectible too, and with the intense interest currently being shown in anything advertising related, competition is sometimes stiff and values are rising.

Alvin (Alvin & the Chipmunks), 1984, MIB..................$50.00
Bart Simpson, Columbia Tel-Com, 1990s, MIB...............$35.00
Batmobile, Columbia, 1990, MIB, from $25 to.................$35.00
Beetle Bailey, plastic figure in dk gr fatigues, wht rectangular base, Com VUI, 1982, 10", MIB $65.00
Cabbage Patch Girl, 1980s, EX, from $65 to....................$75.00
Crest Sparkle, MIB, from $50 to....................................$75.00
Dale Earnhardt, #3 Goodwrench car, headlights flash when phone rings, 9x3½", MIB $60.00
Ghostbusters, wht ghost inside red circle, receiver across center, Remco, 1987, EX $20.00
Keebler Elf, NM, from $60 to $70.00
Kermit the Frog, AT&T/Henson, 1980s, EXIB.............$100.00
Little Orphan Annie & Sandy, Columbia Pictures, 1982, 11", EX $100.00
M&M Candy, talking w/red & gr figures sitting by M&M dial, bl figure holds up yel receiver, MIB $50.00
Mickey Mouse, American Telecommunications Corp, 1976, VG+ $75.00
Mickey Mouse, Western Electric, 1976, EX $175.00
Oscar Mayer Weiner, EX $65.00
Pillsbury's Poppin' Fresh, figure on bl base, 1980s, VG...$100.00
Power Rangers, NM...$25.00
Roy Rogers, 1950s, plastic wall-type, 9x9", EX $50.00
R2-D2 (Star Wars), top spins when phone rings, 12" $35.00
Snoopy & Woodstock, Am Telephone Corp, 1976, touch-tone, EX $100.00
Star Trek Enterprise, 1993, NM.....................................$25.00
Strawberry Shortcake, M $55.00

Spider-Man, MIB (box not shown), $35.00.

Superman, ATE, 1979, MIB, ...$950.00
Ziggy, 1989, MIB..$75.00

Tonka

Since the mid-'40s, the Tonka Company (Minnesota) has produced an extensive variety of high-quality painted metal trucks, heavy equipment, tractors, and vans.

The following listings are from recent auctions and are in original condition unless noted otherwise.

Allied Van Lines, 1950s, red cabover w/aluminum trailer, 24", VG, A $140.00
Auto Transport, 1960s, yel dbl-decker w/side lever that lowers ramp, WWT, w/1 car, 28", VG, A...........................$100.00
Big Mike Hydraulic Dump Truck w/Snow Plow, 1950s, V-shaped plow, 20", VG, A.......................................$575.00
Cement Truck, 1960s, 10-wheeled, 16", EX, A................$85.00
Construction Utility Tractor w/Tandem Trailers, 1940s, 3-pc, orange, BRT, 6-wheeled, 24", G+, A..........................$75.00
Dump Truck & Sand Loader, 1950s, 13" red & gr, w/25" metal-framed sand loader, G................................$165.00
Grain Hauler, 1940s, 22", VG, A $120.00
Grain Hauler, 1950s, 23", VG+, A.................................$100.00
Log Truck, 1940s, w/chains & logs, 16-wheeled, 21", EX, A...$140.00
Log Truck, 1950s, gr cab w/silver bar trailer, 14-wheeled, 24", rstr, A $55.00
Motor Transport, 1950s, 28", VG....................................$100.00
Pickup Truck, 1950s, dk bl w/oval Tonka decal on door, 13", G $110.00
Pickup Truck w/Tonka Farms Horse Trailer, 1960s, WWT, chrome hubs, 21" overall, G $55.00
Rescue Squad, 1960s, 13", VG+, A.................................$120.00
Sportsman Truck, 1960s, w/plastic boats, 13", VG $100.00
State Hi-Way Dept Dump Truck w/Snow Plow, 1950s, V-shaped plow, 4 wheels, 18", older rpt & rstr.........................$155.00
State Hi-Way Dept Lowboy Truck & Dragline, 1960s, 26", incomplete, G...$110.00

Steam Shovel on Lowboy Truck, 1950s, red & bl, 25½", missing rear ramp, G, A..$130.00
Steel Carrier, 1950s, 16-wheeled, 24", rpt, A....................$55.00
Thunderbird Express Semi, wht w/red & blk decals, BRT, 14-wheeled, 24", EX+, A..................................$275.00
Tonka Farms Livestock Truck, 1960s, wht cab w/red high-sided stake bed, BRT, rear duals, 17", EX, A $220.00
Tonka Farms Stake Truck, 1960s, 14", G, A $75.00
Tonka Marine Service, 1960s, w/boat, 25", VG, A...........$75.00
Tonka Sanitary System Truck, wht garbage truck w/blk dump bucket, rear dual wheels, 17", EX, A.......................$525.00
Tonka Tanker, 1950s, PS cab w/plastic trailer, 27", G, A..$65.00
Truck w/Interchangable Bed, 1960s, changes from flatbed to stake body, dual rear wheels, 16", rpt, A $185.00

Tootsietoy

The first diecast Tootsietoys were made by the Samuel Dowst Company in 1906 when they reproduced the Model T Ford in miniature. Dowst merged with Cosmo Manufacturing in 1926 to form the Dowst Manufacturing Company and continued to turn out replicas of the full-scale vehicles in actual use at the time. After another merger in 1961, the company became known as the Stombecker Corporation. Over the years, many types of wheels and hubs were utilized, varying in both style and material. The last all-metal car was made in 1969; recent Tootsietoys mix plastic components with the metal and have soft plastic wheels. Early prewar mint-in-box toys are scarce and now command high prices on today's market.

Airport Hangar & 3 Planes, tin hangar w/diecast trimotor, biplane & UX24, 6" W hangar, VG+, A (Est: $200-$300) $550.00
Auto Carrier, Mack C-style cab & trailer w/MDW, 1 sedan & 2 coupes, 8½" overall, VG+, A (Est: $150-$200)......$200.00
Bild-A-Truck Set, NMIB, A (Est: $150-$250) $440.00
Boat Fleet Set, includes 12 war ships, EX (EX 15x10" box), A (Est: $200-$300)..$250.00
Camping Set, diecast & plastic, 7-pc, EXIB, A (Est: $150-$225) $275.00

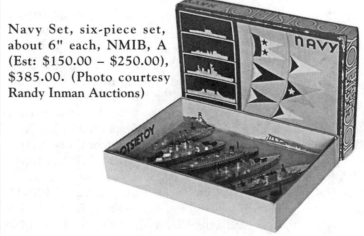

Navy Set, six-piece set, about 6" each, NMIB, A (Est: $150.00 – $250.00), $385.00. (Photo courtesy Randy Inman Auctions)

Tonka Cargo Line Truck, 1950s, U-shaped open trailer, 14-wheeled, 23", VG, A (Est: $75.00 – $125.00), $400.00. (Photo courtesy Randy Inman Auctions)

Fleet Set, 12 navy ships, approx: 6" ea, EX+IB, A (Est: $200-$300)..$440.00

Kayo Ice Truck, 3", VG+, A (Est: $200-$250)................$260.00

Mack Auto Transport, 1930s, w/4 cars, 11", G, A (Est: $50-$100)..$220.00

Moon Mullins in Police Wagon, Moon Mullins being hauled off to jail, 3", VG+, A (Est: $200-$250) $275.00

Motors Set, includes 8 smaller vehicles, NMIB, A (Est: $200-$300)..$385.00

Motors Set, 4 larger vehicles including a convertible, sedan, bus & tanker truck, NM (EX 11x8" box), A (Est: $200-$250)..$385.00

Navy Fleet Set, 12-pc, approx: 6" ea, EX+IB, A (Est: $200-$300)..$440.00

Pan American Airport Set, 1950s, complete, NMIB, A (Est: minimum $200)..$300.00

Railway Express Truck w/Wrigley's Gum Advertising, WRT, 4", EX, A (Est: $200-$250)..$400.00

Service Station Set, w/car elevator ramp, pump island & 8 vehicles, missing 4 traffic signs, EX+IB, A (Est: $200-$300)......$275.00

Sky Fleet Set, 1920s, 5-pc, EXOC, A (minimum $75).....$75.00

Smitty & Herby Motorcycle, Smitty driving and Herby in sidecar, 3", EX, A (Est: $200-$250)..............................$440.00

Smitty Delivery Cycle, side car has opening lid, 3", VG+, A (Est: $200-$250)..$275.00

Tootsie Toy Dairy, truck w/3 tank trailers, WRT, 12" L overall, VG+, A (Est: $200-$250) $385.00

Trailer Truck Set, cab w/2 box trailers, 8", NMIB, A (Est: $150-$250)..$600.00

Uncle Walt Roadster (Gasoline Alley), 3", VG+, A (Est: $200-$300)..$330.00

Trains

Some of the earliest trains (from ca 1860) were made of tin or cast iron, smaller versions of the full-scale steam-powered trains that transversed America from the east to the west. Most were made to simply be pushed or pulled along, though some had clockwork motors. Electric trains were produced as early as the late nineteenth century. Three of the largest manufacturers were Lionel, Ives, and American Flyer.

Lionel trains have been made since 1900. Until 1915 they produced only standard gauge models (measuring 2½" between the rails). The smaller O gauge (1¼") they introduced at that time proved to be highly successful, and the company grew until by 1955 it had become the largest producer of toys in the world. Until discontinued in 1940, standard gauge trains were produced on a limited scale, but O and 027 gauge models dominated the market. Production dwindled and nearly stopped in the mid-1960s, but the company was purchased by General Mills in 1969, and they continue to produce a very limited number of trains today.

The Ives company had been a major producer of toys since 1896. They were the first to initiate manufacture of the O gauge train and at first used only clockwork motors to pro-

pel them. Their first electric trains (in both O and #1 gauge) were made in 1910, but because electricity was not yet a common commodity in many areas, clockwork production continued for several years. By 1920, #1 gauge was phased out in favor of standard gauge. The company continued to prosper until the late 1920s when it floundered and was bought jointly by American Flyer and Lionel. American Flyer soon turned their interest over to Lionel, who continued to make Ives trains until 1933.

The American Flyer company had produced trains for several years, but it wasn't until it was bought by AC Gilbert in 1937 that it became successful enough to be considered a competitor of Lionel. They're best noted for their conversion from the standard (wide gauge) three-rail system to the two-rail S gauge (⅞") and the high-quality locomotives, passenger, and freight cars they produced in the 1950s. Interest in toy trains waned during the space-age decade of the 1960s. As a result, sales declined, and in 1966 the company was purchased by Lionel. Today both American Flyer and Lionel trains are being made from the original dies by Lionel Trains Inc., privately owned.

For more information we recommend *Collecting Toy Trains, An Identification and Value Guide*, by Richard O'Brien.

Advisor: Gary Mosholder

See also Buddy L (for that company's Outdoor Railroad); Cast Iron, Trains; Paper-Lithographed Toys; Pull and Push Toys.

AMERICAN FLYER

Accessory, aircraft beacon, #769A, NMIB....................$200.00

Accessory, church, #166, MIB, from $800 to.................$900.00

Accessory, controller for animated station, #789C, NM...$70.00

Accessory, controller for operating dump car, #919C, NM.$35.00

Accessory, freight & passenger station w/crane, #612, EX.$195.00

Accessory, freight station, #91, EX.............................$200.00

Accessory, freight station, #95, EX.............................$200.00

Accessory, Gabe the Lamplighter, #23780, NMIB......$1,500.00

Accessory, highway flasher, #760, EX...........................$125.00

Accessory, Mystic Talking Station, red & wht w/gr roof, gray base, orig record & stylus, EX................................$125.00

Accessory, switchtower #108, prewar, VG, A, $450.00.
(Photo courtesy Stout Auctions)

Accessory, passenger station, #102, EXIB $350.00

Accessory, station & baggage smasher, #23789, G..........$200.00

Accessory, station platform, #160, Chicklets advertising, MIB $950.00

Accessory, street light, #279, EX $75.00

Accessory, talking station, #709, EXIB $450.00

Accessory, transformer, #12B, 250 watts, EXIB................$75.00

Accessory, whistling billboard, #566, EX $150.00

Car, auto unloader/Manoil, #815, EX.............................$100.00

Car, boxcar (MKT), #24106, VG......................................$550.00

Car, boxcar (Northern Pacific), #24409, EX+IB.........$1,250.00

Car, caboose, #4011, yel & brn, VGIB............................$275.00

Car, caboose (10th Anniversary), #484, NM..................$100.00

Car, flatcar (Monon) w/2 American Flyer trailers, #24536, EX $1,300.00

Car, hopper, #4006, red, EXIB...$450.00

Car, hopper (Lehigh), #632, gray, EX................................$40.00

Car, lumber loader, #751, VGIB......................................$175.00

Car, rocket sled car, #25515, NMIB $500.00

Car, steel girder, #909, EX...$65.00

Car, tank car (Gilbert Chemicals), #910, EXIB.............$325.00

Car, tank car (Gulf), #24309, EX $75.00

Loco, New Haven EP-5, #499, EX....................................$375.00

Loco & Tender, #302A, EX $175.00

Loco & Tender, #343, VG $350.00

Loco & Tender, DC Northern, #332, G..........................$250.00

Loco & Tender, loco w/Golden State tender, #4694, VG.$500.00

Loco & Tender, NYC, #151, MIB (sealed) $400.00

Loco & Tender, Pennsylvania 0-6-0 & tender, #21004, NMIB $475.00

Loco & Tender, stream engine 4-8-4 & tender, #336, VG+ $450.00

Loco & Tender, 4-4-0 Burlington, #21166, M $100.00

Locomotive and tender, #4696, prewar, restored, $1,100.00. (Photo courtesy Stout Auctions)

Set, Burlington Zephyr, loco (#9900) & 4 cars, litho tin, silver & blk, VG..$225.00

Set, Comet, loco & 3 cars, VG...$450.00

Set, engine, tender, baggage car & 2 passenger cars, #12, G.$130.00

Set, Golden State, loco (#3115) & 3 cars, VGIB...........$575.00

Set, loco (#805) & 2 coaches, w/track, EXIB $230.00

Set, loco (#3115), 2 passenger cars (#3281), 1 passenger car (#3282), EX $825.00

Set, loco (#4000), 2 Bunker Hill Pullmans (#4151), Yorktown observation car (#4152), VGIB.............................$900.00

Set, locomotive #4670, tender #4671, passenger car #4331, and passenger car #4332, G to VG, $1,800.00. (Photo courtesy Stout Auctions)

Set, Macy's Electric Speed Special, red, NMIB $1,300.00

Set, Minnie Ha-Ha, loco & 3 cars, VG...........................$300.00

Set, Reliable Freight w/loco & 3 cars, #30705, EXIB $150.00

Set, Tru-Model Freight w/loco, tender & 7 cars, #101, VGIB..$250.00

Set, Warrior, loco w/tender (#4693), Hancock combine (#4380), coach (#4381), observation car (#4382), VG $4,600.00

Set #1492RC, with locomotive #49692X, tender #4963, passenger cars #4340, #4341, #4342, and #4343, each EX+, with original boxes, $14,500.00. (Photo courtesy Stout Auctions)

LIONEL PREWAR

Accessory, circuit breaker, #91, EX.................$75.00
Accessory, country estate (#911) w/villa (#191), EX+ .$1,150.00
Accessory, crane (magnetic), #165, gray & gr, EX.........$150.00
Accessory, crossing gate, #46, EX $100.00
Accessory, figure set, #550, 6 pnt figures, 1932-36, EXIB .$675.00
Accessory, Lionelville station, #136, 10", NM...............$550.00
Accessory, phone pole, #60, G...............................$60.00
Accessory, power station, #436, NM+IB $6,000.00

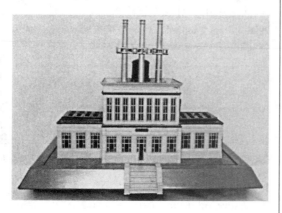

Accessory, power station #840, G, A, $825.00. (Photo courtesy Stout Auctions)

Accessory, Scenic Park layout, #921, VG+.................$7,000.00
Accessory, signal bridge, #440, silver & red w/NP trim, G.$275.00
Accessory, standard crossing track, #20, G.................$60.00
Accessory, station, #116, EX+IB...........................$3,100.00
Accessory, telegraph set, #86, NMIB $1,300.00
Accessory, tunnel, #120L, EXIB...........................$300.00
Accessory, tunnel, #140L, EX $1,950.00
Accessory, watchman's shanty w/bell, #76, G $100.00
Car, boxcar, #214, yel w/orange roof, EXIB....................$525.00
Car, boxcar, #2814, VGIB..................................$1,300.00
Car, caboose, #2672, brn, EX $25.00
Car, cattle car, #13, early vision, EX $450.00
Car, Pullman, #2640, bl & silver, NMIB....................$195.00
Car, tender, #217, orange & maroon, EX+IB.................$900.00
Car, tender, #2817, red, NMIB.............................$400.00
Loco, Commodore Vanderbilt, #265, rstr....................$600.00
Loco & Tender, #253, bl-gr, rare, VG $300.00
Loco & Tender, #256, orange, VG $950.00
Loco & Tender, #400, 2-tone bl w/wht stripe, G.........$1,400.00
Loco & Tender, #402E, VG...............................$500.00
Loco & Tender, engine (#226E) & tender (#2226W), NMIB...$5,500.00
Loco & Tender, 0-6-0 switcher (#228) & tender (2228B), NMIB...$2,100.00
Loco & Tender, 0-6-0 switcher (#8976) & tender (#2228B), VGIB..$1,100.00
Set, loco (#1700), tender (#1702) & caboose (#1702), yel & brn, VG...$1,750.00
Set, loco (#252), 2 Pullman cars (#529) & observation car (#530), terra cotta, rare, EX...................$1,700.00
Set, loco (#262) w/tender, observation car (#608), 2 Pullman cars (#607), gr w/blk roofs, EX $650.00

Set, loco (#402E) & 3 cars, rstr, EX $600.00
Set, Silver Streak (#265E) w/loco, tender & 2 cars, 1935 only, EX $2,250.00

Set #9E, standard gauge, four-piece, complete with individual boxes, EX, A, $5,600.00. (Photo courtesy Stout Auctions)

LIONEL POSTWAR

Accessory, control button, #90, EX $5.00
Accessory, crane (gantry), #282, EXIB.................$300.00
Accessory, crane (magnetic), #182, EX................$250.00
Accessory, dispatch board, #334, operating, EXIB..........$400.00

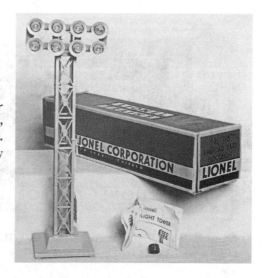

Accessory, floodlight tower #195, NMIB, $100.00. (Photo courtesy Stout Auctions)

Accessory, gateman (automatic), #45N, EX................$50.00
Accessory, ice cream station, #352, w/controller, NMIB.$200.00
Accessory, milk set, #3662, complete, EX $65.00
Accessory, missile firing range, #448, NMIB..............$300.00
Accessory, oil derrick, #455, w/accessories, EXIB $450.00
Accessory, sawmill, #464, EX $145.00
Accessory, snowplow (Great Northern), #58, rotary, EX.$600.00
Accessory, transfer table, #350, MIB......................$625.00
Accessory, transformer, #1025, 45 watts, EX................$15.00
Accessory, transformer, #1033, 90 watts, NM $50.00
Accessory, transformer (LW), 125 watts, w/whistle, EX....$85.00

Accessory, tree assortment, #972, NMIB $1,050.00
Accessory, turnpike set, #962, complete, NM $60.00
Accessory, water tower, #30, EX.................................$125.00
Accessory, water tower, #193, MIB $375.00
Car, baggage car (Western & Atlantic), NM $50.00
Car, barrel car, #3562-50, yel, NMIB $75.00
Car, barrel ramp car, #6343, VG.................................$40.00
Car, boxcar (Frisco), #6014, wht, EX $12.00
Car, boxcar (MP), #6464-150, type IIb body, solid yel door
    w/eagle to the left, EXIB..............................$325.00
Car, boxcar (Pennsylvania), #X2454, EX.....................$175.00
Car, boxcar (PRR Baby Ruth), #X2454, NMIB............$200.00
Car, boxcar (Rutland), #6464-300, EXIB.....................$325.00
Car, boxcar (State of Maine), #6464-275, type III variation,
    NMIB..$400.00
Car, boxcar (Timken), #6464-500, type IIb body, NMIB.$225.00
Car, boxcar (Western Pacific), #6464-275, type IV body,
    NMIB..$300.00
Car, caboose, #6517, bay window, EXIB $700.00
Car, caboose (AT&SF), #6357 (father & son set), EX ...$925.00
Car, caboose (PRR), #6427-500 (girl's set), NMIB.........$550.00
Car, caboose (wrecker), #6119, gray, EX $75.00
Car, capsule launch car, #3413, NM+ $425.00
Car, crane, #6560, red, VG...$45.00
Car, crane (burro), #3360, NMIB...............................$600.00
Car, gondola (Erie), #3444, unrun, MIB $150.00
Car, Lackawanna FM, #2321, maroon top, GIB $500.00

**Car, Lehigh Valley caboose #6417, VGIB, A, $2,200.00.
(Photo courtesy Stout Auctions)**

Car, lumber car, 6264, EXIB $70.00
Car, observation car (Santa Fe), #2410, NM $75.00
Car, refrigerator car, #6472, EX $30.00
Car, searchlight car, #6822, gray, EXIB $55.00
Car, snowplow (Rio Grande), #53, VGIB.....................$225.00
Car, target launcher, #3469, G $45.00
Car, tender (NY Central), #773W, NMIB $300.00
Car, trolley car, #60, VGIB.......................................$250.00
Loco, AEC switcher, #57, NM...................................$1,700.00
Loco, Baltimore & Ohio F3 AB units, #2368, EX.......$3,100.00
Loco, Burlington GP, #2328, silver, EX+ $475.00
Loco, Milwaukee Road GP, #2338, EX.........................$375.00

Loco, Rock Island A unit, #231P, MIB (sealed).............$400.00
Loco, Santa Fe AA Alco units, #218, silver & red, NMIB.$650.00
Loco & Tender, #682 & #2046W, EXIB $525.00
Loco & Tender, Alaska NW2 switcher, #682, w/dynamic brake
    unit, EXIB..$350.00
Loco & Tender, Hudson (#773) & tender (#2426W), VG.$900.00
Loco & Tender, Norfolk & Western, #746, VGIB $1,300.00
Loco & Tender, Norfolk & Western steam engine & tender,
    #746, short stripe version, EX $725.00
Loco & Tender, Wabash GP7, #2339, MIB.................$1,000.00
Set, Berkshire Freight, #2573, NMIB........................$4,200.00
Set, Hiawatha, #1000, MIB......................................$825.00
Set, loco & 3 cars, #254, olive gr w/red trim, NM $525.00
Set, Santa Fe Alco, #1649, MIB $1,950.00

LIONEL MODERN ERA 1970 – 1996

Accessory, antenna (rotating rotary), #12749, EXIB $35.00
Accessory, billboard, #12809, animated, NM.................$25.00
Accessory, crane (burro), #3360, MIB..........................$100.00
Accessory, crane (gantry), #2316, remote control, EXIB..$125.00
Accessory, horn shack, #2127, diesel, EX.....................$25.00
Accessory, microwave tower, #12723, EXIB.................$20.00
Accessory, oil drum loader, #12862, EXIB $100.00
Accessory, signal (block target), #2117, NM $25.00
Car, boxcar, (Jersey Central), #7404, NMIB.................$45.00
Car, boxcar (Conrail), EXIB......................................$25.00
Car, boxcar (Mail Express), #9229, MIB......................$30.00
Car, boxcar (Rio Grande), #9739, yel, no stripe, EX+....$275.00
Car, caboose (Reading), #17605, MIB $30.00
Car, Christmas car, #9400, 1985, MIB $850.00
Car, club car (Lionel Railroader), #784, MIB $55.00
Car, fire car, #52, MIB..$75.00
Car, flat car (Delaware & Hudson), #9226, w/trailer, EXIB.$45.00
Car, flat car (MKT liquid oxygen), #16368, EXIB $25.00
Car, flat car w/construction crane kit, #9157, NMIB........$35.00
Car, flat car w/steam shovel, #9158, NMIB...................$35.00
Car, freight car, Minneapolis & St Louis, MIB $50.00
Car, handcar, #18401, diesel, orange, MIB....................$40.00
Car, quad hopper (L&N), #16411, w/coal load, #EXIB....$30.00
Car, reefer (Hershey billboard), #9867, NMIB $35.00
Car, reefer (Pacific Fruit Express), #17306, EXIB $30.00
Car, tank car, (Pennsylvania), #6307, MIB....................$50.00
Car, tank car (LRRC 1995), #782, M...........................$45.00
Car, tank car (Santa Fe), #9321, MIB $50.00
Car, vat car (Lionel Railroader), #19940, MIB $25.00
Loco, Amtrack GG1 diesel, #18303, MIB.....................$400.00
Loco, Burger King GP-20 diesel engine, #8160, EX $125.00
Loco, GP-9 Railscope diesel, #33000, MIB...................$225.00
Loco, Rock Island 0-4-0 steam engine, #18610, MIB.....$150.00
Loco & Tender, Chessie, #18011, MIB.........................$575.00
Loco & Tender, New York Central 4-6-4 Hudson, #18002,
    MIB...$400.00
Loco & Tender, Reading 2-4-2, #8402, EX $50.00
Loco & Tender, Southern 2-8-2 Mikado '4501' (#8309) & ten-
    der (#18018), w/RailSounds, MIB $550.00
Set, Burlington Northern Limited, #8585, NMIB..........$300.00

Set, Conrail Limited, #18200, MIB.............................$250.00
Set, CSX Freight Train, #11779, MIB............................$275.00
Set, Maple Leaf Limited, #8152, MIB............................$200.00

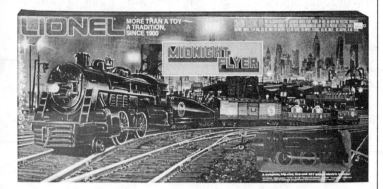

Set, Midnight Flyer #1960, MIB (sealed), $100.00.

Set, New Englander, #1050, NM.............................$200.00
Set, Southern Pacific FM Trainmaster, #8951, NMIB....$500.00
Set, SSS Santa Fe Work Train, #1632, MIB..................$275.00
Set, Western Maryland, MIB...................................$500.00

MISCELLANEOUS

Bing, accessory, Freight Station, litho tin, O gauge, VG+ $250.00
Bing, baggage car, 8-wheeled, hinged roof, O gauge, G $75.00
Bing, boxcar, gr & orange, #2 gauge, G+ $140.00
Bing, set, Miniature Table Railway, litho tin, 3 passenger cars & 16 pcs of track, NMIB $600.00
Bing, train station, emb litho tin, 8x15", EX $800.00
Boucher, loco & tender, #1200, G $2,000.00
Carette, loco & tender, steam-powered, gr w/brass boiler, emb coal compartment on tender, 11", VG.....................$450.00
Carette, loco & tender, 4-2-0 engine w/6-wheeled tender, live steam, #3 gauge, scarce, VG.............................$2,500.00
Carette, set, loco & tender w/coaches, steam-powered, blk w/red trim & cow cather, O guage, G $900.00
Carlisle & Finch, car, Electric Railway Inter Urban, G.$4,500.00
Carlisle & Finch, loco (#171) & tender, VG $1,100.00
Cor-Cor, set w/loco, tender & passenger car, blk & red, 54", EX...$1,100.00
Dayton, loco, tender & Pullman car, friction, red w/gold trim, blk cow catcher, 1930s, 28" L, old rpt, A $160.00
Ernst Plank, set, Vulkan dribbler loco, tender & baggage car, #32 gauge, rpt $925.00
Fallows, loco, mk Nero, pnt & stenciled tin w/CI wheels, clockwork, 10", VG...$725.00
Fleischmann, New Haven #1215, electric, red, wht & blk, VG $250.00
Gilbert, set #30320, Pennsylvania steam freight w/0-6-9 tender (#433), 3 cars, track & instruction book, NMIB $300.00
Gunthermann, loco & tender, mk 999, litho tin, clockwork, 11", F..$200.00
Hafner, set, complete w/loco, 4 cars & tracks, EXIB, A .$130.00

Hafner, set, Overland Flyer w/loco, tender & 3 passenger cars, CI & litho tin, w/up, EX.............................$200.00
Hafner, set, Sunshine Special w/loco, tender & 3 passenger cars, CI & litho tin, w/up, EX.............................$300.00

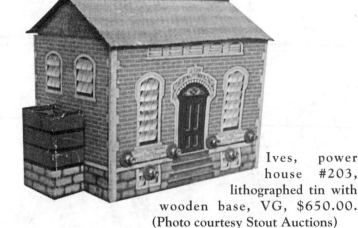

Ives, power house #203, lithographed tin with wooden base, VG, $650.00.
(Photo courtesy Stout Auctions)

Ives, set, Blue Vagabond, w/loco, tender & 3 cars, CI, G .$225.00
Ives, set, loco (#3), coal car (#11), Brooklyn passenger car (#51), Iroquois passenger car (#51), 3 mail cars (#50), VG..$3,000.00
Ives, station, single story, litho tin, no accessories, 21" L, VG+ $300.00
Ives, ticket office, litho tin, lithoed window, opening doors, w/base, 11½" L, EX..................................$55.00
Ives, Union Station, w/glass-domed canopy platform, VG..$1,430.00
Marklin, baggage handcart, no drawer, hdls, driver's platform, NM (partial box) $225.00
Marklin, freight car, #1929, w/guardhouse, brn, VG $150.00
Marklin, freight car, #1991, mk Seefishe, w/guardhouse, wht w/red, VG $325.00
Marklin, freight car (Jamaica Bababeb Bremen), #1992, w/guardhouse, #1 gauge, VG+, A $185.00
Marklin, gondola, open, gr & orange, #2 gauge, G+ $175.00
Marklin, goods station #2047, pnt tin w/corrugated roof, twin cranes, platforms & sliding doors, 1906, 15", EX...$4,500.00
Marklin, loco, #1802, clockwork, #1 gauge, VG+ $625.00
Marklin, loco TNM 65, #1302, #1 gauge, VG $465.00
Marklin, loco 0-40 & tender, blk & gr w/red striping, clockwork, #1 gauge, G+ $775.00
Marklin, loco 2-4-0 LMS, electric, rstr, A (Est: $300-$600) $385.00
Marklin, log carrier car w/logs, #1 gauge, VG $150.00
Marklin, mail van, gr-pnt tin w/orange trim, blk roof, brn interior, 6½", NM..$1,200.00
Marklin, mail van, gr-pnt w/orange trim, blk roof, brn interior, 6½", NM $1,200.00
Marklin, passenger car #1888, hinged roof, VG+ $275.00
Marklin, set #E3020 w/4-4-0 loco, LMS tender (#2879), Midland baggage car (#2879) & 3 LMS coaches (#2875), O gauge, VG..$1,100.00
Marklin, set w/loco, tender, 3 cars & rack, pnt & litho tin, EXIB..$850.00

Marklin, signal & signal bell, Ankunft/Abfahrt, enameled tin sign on gate-type base, crank-op bell, 7", VG+ $650.00

Marklin, ticket rack, pnt & stenciled w/city destinations, slots contain cb tickets, 7½", NM....................................$500.00

Marx, accessory, water tower, plastic, gray tank w/red & blk support, 8", EX (Poor box), A..$30.00

Marx, Rock Island Freight, #40845, 7-pc, VGIB............$125.00

Marx, set, Happi-Time Santa Fe Freight/Passenger #05944, VGIB $200.00

Marx, set, NY Central Passenger, #35250, 5-pc, VGIB ..$200.00

Marx set, passenger train, with streamline locomotive, tender, two coaches, and observation car, blue, VG, $375.00. (Photo courtesy Stout Auctions)

Marx, set, Santa Fe Passenger, #44544, 6-pc, VGIB.......$225.00

Marx, set, Western Pacific Passenger, #44464, 6-pc, MIB $600.00

Weeden, set, loco, tender & coach, live steam, G+........$825.00

Williams, loco (#5601 Norfolk & Western 4-8-4) & tender, MIB $400.00

Transformers

Made by the Hasbro Company, Transformers were introduced in the United States in 1984. Originally there were twenty-eight figures — eighteen cars known as Autobots and ten Decepticons, evil robots capable of becoming such things as a jet or a handgun. Eventually the line was expanded to more than two hundred different models. Some were remakes of earlier Japanese robots that had been produced by Takara in the 1970s. (These can be identified through color differences and in the case of the Diaclone series, the absence of the small driver or pilot figures.)

The story of the Transformers and their epic adventures were told through several different comic books and animated series as well as a highly successful movie. Their popularity was reflected internationally and eventually made its way back to Japan. There the American Transformer animated series was translated into Japanese and soon inspired several parallel series of the toys which were again produced by Takara. These new Transformers were sold in the U.S. until the line was discontinued in 1990.

In 1993, Hasbro reintroduced the line with Transformers: Generation 2. Transformers once again had their own comic book, and the old animated series was brought back in revamped format. In 1996, Hasbro reinvented the series by introducing Beast Wars that went from robot to animal. Now, Transformers have returned to their roots with the Armada series that transforms from robot to vehicle. Sustained interest in them has spawned a number of fan clubs with chapters worldwide.

Because Transformers came in a number of sizes, you'll find a wide range of pricing. Our values are for Transformers that are mint in mint or nearly mint original boxes. One that has been used is worth much less — about 25% to 75%, depending on whether it has all its parts (weapons, instruction book, tech specks, etc.), and what its condition is — whether decals are well applied or if it is worn. A loose Transformer complete and in near-mint condition is worth only about half as much as one mint in the box.

Advisor: David Kolodny-Nagy (K2)

SERIES 1, 1984

Autobot Car, Bluestreak (Datsun), bl $350.00

Autobot Car, Bluestreak (Datsun), silver........................$300.00

Autobot Car, Camshaft (car), silver, mail-in $40.00

Autobot Car, Downshaft (car), wht, mail-in....................$40.00

Autobot Car, Hound (jeep), MIB $235.00

Autobot Car, Jazz (Porsche) $300.00

Autobot Car, Mirage (Indy car) $235.00

Autobot Car, Overdrive (car), red, mail-in.....................$40.00

Autobot Car, Powerdasher #1 (jet), mail-in...................$20.00

Autobot Car, Powerdasher #2 (car), mail-in..................$20.00

Autobot Car, Powerdasher #3 (drill), mail-in.................$40.00

Autobot Car, Prowl (police car)....................................$400.00

Autobot Car, Rachet (ambulance)..................................$200.00

Autobot Car, Sunstreak (Countach), yel $300.00

Autobot Car, Trailbreaker (camper) $235.00

Autobot Car, Wheeljack (Mazzerati).............................$335.00

Autobot Commander, Optimus Primus w/Roller (semi)..$350.00

Cassette, Frenzy & Lazerbreak $50.00

Cassette, Ravage & Rumble $50.00

Collector's Case..$15.00

Collector's Case, red 3-D version $25.00

Collector's Showcase...$15.00

Decepticon Communicator, Soundwave & Buzzsaw, w/tape player & gold condor......................................$250.00

Decepticon Communicator, Soundwave w/Buzzsaw & Rumble, Japanese edtion w/headphones................................$350.00

Decepticon Jet, Skywrap, blk $225.00

Decepticon Jet, Starcream, gray, MIB $150.00

Decepticon Jet, Thundercracker, bl $230.00

Decepticon Leader, Megatron, Walther P-38 ....$350.00

Minicar, Brawn (jeep), gr..$35.00

Minicar, Bumblebee (VW Bug), red...............................$25.00

Minicar, Bumblebee (VW Bug), w/minispy, yel $40.00

Minicar, Bumblejumper (Bumblebee card) $40.00

Minicar, Bumblejumper (Cliffjumper card).....................$50.00

Minicar, Cliffjumper (race car), gr or yel, ea	$35.00
Minicar, Gears (truck), bl	$35.00
Minicar, Huffer (semi), orange cab	$35.00
Minicar, Windcharger (Firebird), red	$35.00
Watch, Time Warrior, w/Autobot insignia, mail-in	$80.00

Motorvator Lightspeed, $85.00. (Photo courtesy David Kolodny-Nagy)

Series 2, 1985

Autobot, Red Alert (fire chief)	$250.00
Autobot Air Guardian, Jetfire (F-14 jet)	$400.00
Autobot Car, Grapple (crane)	$250.00
Autobot Car, Hoist (tow truck)	$200.00
Autobot Car, Inferno (fire engine)	$250.00
Autobot Car, Skids (Le Car)	$250.00
Autobot Car, Smokescreen (Datsun), red, wht & bl	$250.00
Autobot Car, Tracks (Corvette)	$250.00
Autobot Car, Tracks (Corvette), red	$400.00
Autobot Commander, Blaster (radio/tapeplayer)	$145.00
Autobot Scientist, Perceptor (microscope)	$60.00
Constructicon, Bonecrusher (1)	$60.00
Constructicon, Devastator, gift set	$300.00
Constructicon, Hook (4)	$50.00
Constructicon, Long Haul (5)	$50.00
Constructicon, Mixmaster (6)	$50.00
Constructicon, Scavenger (2)	$50.00
Constructicon, Scrapper (3)	$50.00
Decepticon Jet, Dirge	$110.00
Decepticon Jet, Ramjet	$110.00
Decepticon Jet, Thrust, maroon	$120.00
Decepticon Military Operations Commander, Shockwave (lazer gun)	$200.00
Deluxe Insecticon, Beno (bee)	$90.00
Deluxe Insecticon, Chop Chop (beetle)	$90.00
Deluxe Insecticon, Ransack (grasshopper)	$125.00
Deluxe Vehicle, Roadster (off-road vehicle)	$60.00
Deluxe Vehicle, Whirl (helicopter), lt bl	$70.00
Dinobot, Grimlock (Tynnosaurus)	$250.00
Dinobot, Slag (Triceratops)	$125.00
Dinobot, Sludge (Brontosaurus)	$175.00
Dinobot, Snarl (Stegosaurus)	$175.00

Insecticon, Bombshell	$50.00
Insecticon, Sharpnel	$50.00
Insecticon, Venom	$50.00
Jumpstarter, Topspin	$45.00
Jumpstarter, Twin Twist (drill tank)	$50.00
Minicar, Beachcomber (dune buggy)	$30.00
Minicar, Brawn (jeep), gr	$40.00
Minicar, Bumblebee (VW Bug), red	$45.00
Minicar, Bumblebee (VW Bug), w/minispy, red	$30.00
Minicar, Bumblebee (VW Bug), yel	$50.00
Minicar, Cliffjumper (race car), red or yel, ea	$45.00
Minicar, Cliffjumper (race car), w/minispy, red or yel, ea	$50.00
Minicar, Cosmos (spaceship)	$30.00
Minicar, Gears (truck), bl	$35.00
Minicar, Gears (truck), w/minispy	$35.00
Minicar, Huffer (semi), orange cab	$45.00
Minicar, Huffer (semi), w/minispy	$50.00
Minicar, Powerglide (plane)	$25.00
Minicar, Seaspray (hovercraft)	$25.00
Minicar, Warpath (tank)	$30.00
Minicar, Windcharger (Firebird), red	$45.00
Minicar, Windcharger (Firebird), w/minispy	$50.00
Motorized Autobit Defense Base, Omega Supreme	$300.00
Triple Charger, Astrotrain (shuttle/train)	$80.00
Triple Charger, Blitzwing (tank/plane)	$80.00
Watch, Autoceptor, Kronoform (watch car)	$25.00
Watch, Deceptor, Kronofrom (watch jet)	$25.00
Watch, Listen 'N Fun, w/tape & yel Cliffjumper	$35.00

Series 3, 1986

Aerialbot, Air Raid (1)	$25.00
Aerialbot, Fireflight (3)	$25.00
Aerialbot, Silverbot (5)	$50.00
Aerialbot, Skydive (2)	$25.00
Aerialbot, Superion, gift set	$275.00
Autobot Car, Blurr (futuristic car)	$90.00
Autobot Car, Hot Rod (race car), red	$375.00
Autobot Car, Kup (pickup truck)	$100.00
Autobot City Commander, Refelctor, Spectro, Viewfinder & Spyglass into camera, mail-in	$225.00
Autobot City Commander, STARS Control Center, mail-in	$225.00
Autobot City Commander, Ultra Magnus (car carrier)	$135.00
Battlecharger, Runabout (Trans Am)	$30.00
Battlecharger, Runamuck (Corvette)	$35.00
Cassette, Ramhorn & Eject (robot & rhino), gold weapons	$65.00
Cassette, Ratbat & Frenzy (robot & bat), bl	$60.00
Cassette, Rewind & Steeljaw (robot & lion), gold weapons	$60.00
Cassette, Rewind & Steeljaw (robot & lion), silver weapons	$65.00
Combaticon, Blast Off (3)	$30.00
Combaticon, Brawl (1)	$35.00
Combaticon, Bruticus, gift set	$450.00
Combaticon, Onslaught (5)	$40.00
Combaticon, Swindle (3)	$40.00
Combaticon, Vortex (4)	$35.00
Heroes, Rodimus Prime (futuristic RV)	$150.00
Heroes, Wreck-Car (futuristic motorcycle)	$125.00

Decepticon City Commander, Galvatron, $225.00.

Jet, Cyclous Space Jet	$175.00
Jet, Scrouge (hovercraft)	$125.00
Minicar, Hubcap (race car), yel	$35.00
Minicar, Outback (jeep), brn	$35.00
Minicar, Pipes (semi), bl cab	$35.00
Minicar, Swerve (truck), red	$35.00
Minicar, Tailgate (Firebird), wht	$35.00
Minicar, Wheelie (futuristic car)	$35.00
Motorized Autobot Space Shuttle, Sky Lynz	$135.00
Motorized Decepticon City/Battle Station, Trypticon	$225.00
Predacon, Gnaw (futuristic shark)	$70.00
Predacon, Headstrong (5)	$70.00
Predacon, Rampage (2)	$70.00
Predacon, Razorclaw (1)	$70.00
Predacon, Tantrum (4)	$70.00
Predocon, Divebomb (3)	$70.00
Stunticon, Breakdown (2)	$30.00
Stunticon, Dead End (1)	$30.00
Stunticon, Drag Strip (4)	$30.00
Stunticon, Menasor, gift set	$450.00
Stunticon, Motormaster (semi)	$75.00
Stunticon, Wildrider (Ferrari)	$30.00
Triple Charger, Broadside (aircraft carrier/plane)	$100.00
Triple Charger, Octane (tanker truck/jumbo jet)	$85.00
Triple Charger, Sandstorm (dune buggy/helicopter)	$100.00
Triple Charger, Springer (armored car/copter)	$150.00

SERIES 4, 1987

Cassette, Slugfest & Overkill (Stegasaurus & Tyranosaurus)	$25.00
Clone, Fastlane & Cloudraker (dragster & spaceship)	$65.00
Clone, Pounce & Wingspan (puma & eagle)	$45.00
Double Spy, Punch-Counterpunch (Fiero)	$75.00
Duocon, Battlestap (jeep/copter)	$50.00
Duocon, Flywheels (jet/tank)	$25.00
Headmaster Autobot, Brainstorm w/Arcana (jet)	$75.00
Headmaster Autobot, Chromedome w/Stylor (futuristic car)	$200.00
Headmaster Autobot, Hardhead w/Duros (tank)	$120.00
Headmaster Autobot, Highbrow w/Gort (copter)	$120.00
Headmaster Base, Fortress Maxiumus w/Cerebros & Spike, Gasket, Grommet (battle station/city)	$800.00

Headmaster Base, Scorponok w/Lord Zarak & Fastrack	$225.00
Headmaster Decepticon, Mindwipe w/Vorath (bat)	$70.00
Headmaster Decepticon, Skullrunner w/Grax (alligator)	$70.00
Headmaster Decepticon, Weirdwolf w/Monzo (wolf)	$80.00
Headmaster Horrorcon, Apeface w/Spasma (jet/ape)	$100.00
Headmaster Horrorcon, Snapdragon w/Krunk (jet/dinosaur)	$100.00
Monsterbot, Doublecross (2-headed dragon)	$40.00
Monsterbot, Grotusque (tiger)	$50.00
Monsterbot, Repugnus (insect)	$90.00
Sixchanger, Sixshot (starfighter jet, winged wolf, laser pistol, armored carrier, tank)	$75.00
Targetmaster Autobot, Blurr w/Haywire (futuristic car & gun)	$90.00
Targetmaster Autobot, Crosshairs w/Pinpointer (truck & gun)	$30.00
Targetmaster Autobot, Hot Rod & Firebolt (race car & gun)	$150.00
Targetmaster Autobot, Kup & Recoil (pickup truck & gun)	$60.00
Targetmaster Autobot, Pointblank w/Peacemaker (race car w/gun)	$30.00
Targetmaster Autobot, Sureshot w/Spoilsport (off-road buggy & gun)	$30.00
Targetmaster Decepticon, Misfire w/Aimless (spaceship & gun)	$60.00
Targetmaster Decepticon, Scrouge w/Fracas (hovercraft & gun)	$125.00
Targetmaster Decepticon, Slugslinger w/Caliburts (twin jet & gun)	$50.00
Technobot, Afterburner, w/decoy	$30.00
Technobot, Afterburner (1)	$25.00
Technobot, Lightspeed, w/decoy	$25.00
Technobot, Lightspeed (4)	$20.00
Technobot, Nosecone, w/decoy	$30.00
Technobot, Nosecone (2)	$25.00
Technobot, Scattershot (5)	$40.00
Technobot, State, w/decoy	$30.00
Technobot, State (3)	$20.00
Terrocon, Blot (monster), w/decoy	$30.00
Terrocon, Blot (4)	$25.00
Terrocon, Cutthroat (Vulture), w/decoy	$30.00
Terrocon, Cutthroat (3)	$25.00
Terrocon, Hun-gr (5)	$40.00
Terrocon, Rippersapper, w/decoy	$30.00
Terrocon, Rippersapper (1)	$25.00
Terrocon, Sinnertwin, w/decoy	$20.00
Terrocon, Sinnertwin (2)	$25.00
Throttlebot, Chase (Ferrari)	$12.00
Throttlebot, Chase (Ferrari), w/decoy	$18.00
Throttlebot, Freeway (Corvette)	$15.00
Throttlebot, Freeway (Corvette), w/decoy	$20.00
Throttlebot, Goldbug (VW bug)	$15.00
Throttlebot, Rollbar (jeep)	$15.00
Throttlebot, Rollbar (jeep), w/decoy	$20.00
Throttlebot, Searchlight (race car)	$15.00
Throttlebot, Shearchlight (race car), w/decoy	$20.00
Throttlebot, Wideload (dump truck)	$15.00
Throttlebot, Wideload (dump truck), w/decoy	$20.00

SERIES 5, 1988

Cassette, Grand Slam & Raindance (tank & jet)............$40.00
Cassette, Squawkalk & Beastbox (hawk & gorilla) $40.00
Firecon, Cindersaur (dinosaur)..................................$15.00
Firecon, Flamefeather (monster bird)........................$15.00
Firecon, Sparkstalker (monster) $10.00
Headmaster Autobot, Hosehead w/Lug (fire engine) $40.00
Headmaster Autobot, Nightbeat w/Muzzle (race car).......$40.00
Headmaster Autobot, Siren w/Quig (fire chief car).........$50.00
Headmaster Decepticon, Fangry w/Brisko (winged wolf) .$40.00
Headmaster Decepticon, Horri-Bull w/Kreb (bull)..........$40.00
Headmaster Decepticon, Squeezeplay w/Lokos (crab)......$40.00
Powermaster Autobot, Getaway w/Rev (Mr2)..................$60.00
Powermaster Autobot, Joyride w/Hotwire (off-road buggy) .$70.00
Powermaster Autobot, Slapdash w/Lube (Indy car)..........$70.00
Powermaster Autobot Leader, Optimus Prime w/HiQ (semi)..$200.00
Powermaster Decepticon, Darkwing w/Throttle (jet), dk
    gray $60.00
Powermaster Decepticon, Dreadwing w/Hi-Test (jet, lt gray ..$60.00
Powermaster Mercenary, Doubledealer w/Knok & Skar (missile
    launcher)..$75.00
Pretender, Bomb-burst (spaceship), w/shell $60.00
Pretender, Cloudburst (jet), w/shell $60.00
Pretender, Finback (sea skimmer), w/shell $25.00
Pretender, Groundbreaker (race car), w/shell $40.00
Pretender, Iguanus (motorcycle), w/shell $40.00
Pretender, Landmine (race car), w/shell........................$60.00
Pretender, Skullgrin (tank), w/shell $40.00
Pretender, Sky High (jet), w/shell $40.00
Pretender, Splashdown (sea skimmer), w/shell $40.00
Pretender, Submarauder (submarine), w/shell..................$60.00
Pretender, Waverider (submarine), w/shell $40.00
Pretender Beast, Carnivac (wolf), w/shell.....................$30.00
Pretender Beast, Catilla (sabertooth tiger), w/shell $30.00
Pretender Beast, Chainclaw (bear, w/shell $30.00
Pretender Beast, Snarler (boar), w/shell........................$30.00
Pretender Vehicle, Gunrunner (jet) w/vehicle shell, red..$40.00
Pretender Vehicle, Roadgrabber (jet) w/vehicle shell, purple.$40.00
Seacon, Nautilator (3)...$15.00
Seacon, Overbite (1)..$15.00
Seacon, Piracon, gift set, minimum value $200.00
Seacon, Seawing (2)..$15.00
Seacon, Skalor (4)...$15.00
Seacon, Snaptrap (6)..$35.00
Seacon, Tenakil (5)...$15.00
Sparkbot, Fizzle (off-road buggy) $10.00
Sparkbot, Guzzle (tank)..$10.00
Sparkbot, Sizzle (funny car).......................................$10.00
Target master Autobot, Landfill w/Flintlock & Sliencer (dump
    truck & 2 guns)..$35.00
Targetmaster Autobot, Quickmix w/Boomer & Ricochet (cemet
    mixer & 2 guns)...$30.00
Targetmaster Autobot, Scoop w/Tracer & Holepunch (front-end
    loader & 2 guns)...$35.00
Targetmaster Decepitcon, Needlenose w/Sunbeam & Zigzag (jet
    & 2 guns) $50.00

Targetmaster Decepticon, Quaker w/Tiptop & Heater (tank & 2
    guns)..$30.00
Targetmaster Decepticon, Spinster & Singe & Hairsplitter (heli-
    copter & 2 guns) $40.00
Tiggerbot, Backstreet (race car)..................................$15.00
Tiggerbot, Override (motorcycle).................................$15.00
Triggercon, Crankcase (jeep)......................................$15.00
Triggercon, Rucus (dune buggy)..................................$15.00
Triggercon, Windsweeper (B-1 bomber) $15.00

SERIES 6, 1989

Legends (K-Mart Exclusive), Bumblebee (VW bug) $35.00
Legends (K-Mart Exclusive), Grimlock (dinosaur)...........$35.00
Legends (K-Mart Exclusive), Jazz (Porsche)...................$35.00
Legends (K-Mart Exclusive), Starscream (jet) $40.00
Mega Pretender, Crossblades (copter w/shell).................$35.00
Mega Pretender, Thunderwing (jet w/shell)....................$35.00
Mega Pretender, Vroom (dragster w/shell) $35.00
Micromaster Base, Countdown (Rocket Base & Micromaster
    Lunar Box)..$50.00
Micromaster Base, Groundbreaker & Micromaster (self-pro-
    pelled cannon & stealth fighter) $35.00
Micromaster Base, Skyhopper w/Micromaster (copter & F-15).$50.00
Micromaster Base, Skystalker (Space Shuttle Base & Micromas-
    ter Porsche)...$55.00
Micromaster Patrol, Battle Patrol Series, 4 different, ea ...$30.00
Micromaster Patrol, Off-Road Series, 4 different, ea $25.00
Micromaster Patrol, Sports Car Patrol Series, 4 different, ea.$25.00
Micromaster Station, Greasepit, pickup w/gas station $20.00
Micromaster Station, Ironworks (semi w/construction site)..$20.00
Micromaster Transport, Flattop (aircraft carrier) $20.00
Micromaster Transport, Overload (car carrier) $20.00
Micromaster Transport, Roughstuff (military transport)...$20.00
Pretender, Bludgeon (tank), w/shell............................$125.00
Pretender, Doubleheader (twin jet), w/shell $45.00
Pretender, Longtooth (hovercraft), w/shell....................$35.00
Pretender, Pincher (scorpion), w/shell $35.00
Pretender, Stanglehold (rhino), w/shell $35.00
Pretender Classic, Bumblebee (VW bug), w/shell $50.00
Pretender Classic, Grimlock (dinosaur), w/shell..............$50.00
Pretender Classic, Jazz (Porsche), w/shell......................$40.00
Pretender Classic, Starcream (jet), w/shell $50.00
Pretender Monster, Icepick (1).....................................$12.00
Pretender Monster, Wildfly (3).....................................$12.00
Ultra Pretender, Roadblock (tank w/figure & vehicle).....$40.00
Ultra Pretender, Skyhammer (race car w/figure & vehicle) .$40.00

SERIES 7, 1990

Action Masters, Blaster: Blaster, Flight-Pack (jet pack) ...$30.00
Action Masters, Devastator: Devastator, Scorpulator (scorpion)..$30.00
Action Masters, Grimlock: Grimlock, Anti-Tank Cannon (tank
    gun)...$30.00
Action Masters, Gutcruncher: Stratotronic Jet................$50.00
Action Masters, Inferno: Inferno, Hydro-Pack (laser back-
    pack) $30.00

Action Masters, Kroc, MOC, $30.00. (Photo courtesy David Kolodny-Nagy)

Action Masters, Optimus Prime: Optimus Prime, Armored Convoy $100.00
Action Masters, Over-Run: Over-Run, Attack Copter $40.00
Action Masters, Prowl: Prowl, Turbo Cycle $60.00
Action Masters, Rad: Rad, Lionizer (lion) $15.00
Action Masters, Shockwave: Shockwave, Fistfight (mini-robot) $30.00
Action Masters, Skyfall: Skyfall, Top-Heavy Rhino $30.00
Action Masters, Soundwave: Soundwave Wingthing $15.00
Action Masters, Wheeljack: Wheeljack, Turbo Racer......$70.00
Micromaster Combiner, Anti-Aircraft Base: Anti-Aircraft Base, Blackout & Spaceshot $25.00
Micromaster Combiner, Battle Squad: Meltdown, Half-Track, Direct Hit, Power Punch, Fireshot & Vanguish.........$25.00
Micromaster Combiner, Metro Squad: Wheel Blaze, Road Runner, Oiler, Slide, Power Run & Strike Down $25.00
Micromaster Combiner, Missile Launcher: Missile Launcher, Retro Surge $25.00
Micromaster Combiner, Tanker Truck: Tanker Truck, Pipeline & Gusher $30.00
Micromaster Patrol, Air Patrol: Thread Bolt, Eagle Eye, Sky High & Blaze Master $10.00
Micromaster Patrol, Hot Rod Patrol: Big Daddy Trip-Up, Greaser & Hubs $10.00
Micromaster Patrol, Military Patrol: Bombshock, Tracer, Dropshot 7 Growl $10.00
Micromaster Patrol, Race Track Patrol: Barricade, Roller Force, Ground Hog Motorhead...$10.00

BEAST WARS

Maximal, Airrazor, M..$25.00
Maximal, Blackarachina, 1996, MOC $85.00
Maximal, Cheeter, MOC..$18.00
Maximal, Depth Charge, MIB...$20.00
Maximal, Optimus Primal (Gorilla), MIB $110.00
Maximal, Polar Claw, 1995, MIB $15.00
Maximal, Rattrap, MOC...$100.00
Predacon, Dinobot, 1995, MOC $110.00

Predacon, Inferno, 1996, MIB $35.00
Predacon, Megatron (Dragon), Transmetal II, MIB..........$20.00
Predacon, Megatron (T-Rex), MIB $110.00
Predacon, Scorponok, dk purple/bl, MIB (Japanese) $85.00
Predacon, Shokaract, BotCon 2000 exclusive, MIB.........$70.00
Predacon, Terroraur, MOC..$90.00
Predacon, Tripedacus, w/instructions, loose, M................$60.00
Predacon, Waspinator, rare, MOC...................................$110.00

GENERATION 2, SERIES 1, 1992 – 1993

Autobot Car, Inferno (fire truck) $30.00
Autobot Car, Jazz (Porsche)..$35.00
Autobot Leader, Optimus Prime w/Roller (semi w/electronic sound effect box) $150.00
Autobot Minicar, Bumble (VW bug), metallic................$30.00
Autobot Minicar, Hubcap, metallic $20.00
Autobot Minicar, Seaspray (hovercraft), metallic $15.00
Autobot Obliterator (Europe only), Spark.......................$45.00
Color Change Transformer, Deluge $20.00
Color Change Transformer, Gobots.................................$20.00
Constructicon, Bonecrusher (1), orange $12.00
Constructicon, Bonecrusher (1), yel $10.00
Constructicon, Long Haul (5), orange $12.00
Constructicon, Long Haul (5), yel $10.00
Constructicon, Scrapper (3), orange $12.00
Constructicon, Scrapper (3), yel $10.00
Decepticon Jet, Starscream (jet w/electronic light & sound effect box), gray $30.00
Decepticon Leader, Megatron (tank w/electonic sound-effect treads) $45.00
Decepticon Obliterator (Europe only), Colossus $75.00
Dinobot, Grimlock (Tyrannosaurus), bl $25.00
Dinobot, Grimlock (Tyrannosaurus), turq $90.00
Dinobot, Snarl (Stegosaurus), gray or bl, ea....................$50.00
Small Autobot Car, Skram $15.00
Small Autobot Car, Turbofire...$15.00
Small Decepticon Jet, Afterburner $15.00
Small Decepticon Jet, Terredive......................................$15.00
Small Decepticon Jet, Windrazor $15.00
Small Decpeticon Jet, Eagle Eye.....................................$15.00

GENERATION 2, SERIES 2, 1994

Aerialbot, Fireflight (3) $10.00
Aerialbot, Silverbot (5) $25.00
Aerialbot, Skydive (1) $15.00
Aerialbot, Superion $225.00
Combaticon, Blast Off (3) $10.00
Combaticon, Brawl (1) $10.00
Combaticon, Onslaught (5) $25.00
Heroes, Autobot Hero Optimus Prime.............................$20.00
Heroes, Autobot Hero Optimus Prime, Japanese box.......$35.00
Heroes, Decepticon Hero Megatron.................................$20.00
Laser Rod Transformer, Electro.......................................$15.00
Laser Rod Transformer, Electro, Japanese box.................$20.00
Laser Rod Transformer, Jolt $15.00

Laser Rod Transformer, Jolt, Japanese box $20.00
Lead Force, Leadfoot, Manta Ray, or Ransack, ea $7.00
Rotor Force, Leadfoot $7.00
Stunticon, Breakdown (2), BotCon '94 Exclusive $100.00
Watch, Superion, Ultra Magnus, or Scorpia, ea...............$12.00

JAPANESE REMAKES

Blot, MIB $70.00
GodGinrai, MIB (sealed), K2 ....$70.00
Hot Rod, MIB, K2..$60.00
Jazz, MIB (sealed)..$35.00
Megatron, MIB...$90.00
Optimus Prime, New Year's edition.........................$150.00
Prowl, MIB (sealed), K2 ....$35.00
Ratchet, MIB (sealed)..$50.00
Red Alert, MIB (sealed) $90.00
Rodimus Prime, MIB (sealed), K2 ....$60.00
Sixshot, MIB (sealed) $60.00
Skids, MIB (sealed), K2 ....$35.00
Skywrap, MIB (sealed), K2....................................$120.00
Tracks, MIB (sealed) $35.00
Ultra Magnus, NRFB, K2 ....$80.00

Trolls

The first trolls to come to the United States were modeled after a 1952 design by Marti and Helena Kuuskoski of Tampere, Finland. The first trolls to be mass produced in America were molded from wood carvings made by Thomas Dam of Denmark. They were made of vinyl, and the original issue was marked 'Dam Things Originals copyright 1964 – 1965 Dam Things Est.; m.f.g. by Royalty Designs of Fla. Inc.' (Other marks were used as well; look on the troll's back or on the bottom of his feet for the Dam trademark. As the demand for these trolls increased, several US manufacturers were licensed to produce them. The most noteworthy of these were Uneeda Doll Company's Wishnik line and Inga Scandia House True Trolls. Thomas Dam continued to import his Dam Things line.

The troll craze from the '60s spawned many items other than dolls such as wall plaques, salt and pepper shakers, pins, squirt guns, rings, clay trolls, lamps, Halloween costumes, animals, lawn ornaments, coat racks, notebooks, folders, and even a car.

In the '70s, '80s, and '90s, new trolls were produced. While these trolls are collectible, the avid troll collector still prefers those produced in the '60s.

Condition is a very important worth-assessing factor.

Astronaut Pencil Sharpener, Scandia House, 1967, MIP .$65.00
Beatle, JN Reisler, bl jumpsuit, w/guitar, 3", VG..............$70.00
Belle of the Ball, Dam, 1960s, long blond mohair, gr lace, 2½",
    EX...$35.00
Bo Peep, Storybook Collection, Norfin, 1977, 9", M.......$35.00
Born to Ski, Russ, 3½", EX $12.00
Boy, Dam, 1960s, gr vest, orange pants, 2½", EX.............$30.00

Boy, Dam, 1960s, long yel hair, felt outfit, 2½", EX..........$30.00
Boy, Dam, 1964, nude, 2¾", EX $18.00
Boy, Dam #604, 1977, striped sweater, patched burlap pants, 8",
    EX...$50.00
Bride & Groom, Uneeda Wishnik, 1970s, EX, pr $35.00
Caveman, Dam, 1960s, nude, 3", EX $135.00
Cow, Dam, wht hair & brn eyes, 3½", EX.....................$55.00
Cow, Dam (unmk), Dam tag around neck, 7", EX............$80.00
Donkey, Dam Things, 1964, head swivels, 8½", VG......$110.00
Elvis, Norfin, 1977, wht satin outfit w/gold trim, guitar, 9", M .$25.00
Eskimo Boy, Scandia House (unmk), 6", VG....................$90.00
Eskimo Girl, Dam Things, 1960s, wht hair & skirt, red attire, 6",
    EX...$80.00
Fire Chief, Treasure Trolls, bl hair & eyes, 4", NM..........$12.00
Fox, Lephrechaun Ltd, 1970s, 6½", EX.........................$30.00
Giraffe, Dam (European), seated, 11", EX......................$95.00
Girl, Dam, 1960s, red dress w/apron & lace cap, 7", EX ...$50.00
Girl, Dam, 1979, seated, 18", NM $65.00
Girl, Uneeda, long-sleeved pk shirt, checked bibbed pants, 17",
    EX...$50.00
Girl Bank, Dam, 1960s, pk hair, 7", VG........................$50.00
Girl Scout, Dam Things, 1960s, 12", VG......................$55.00
Goo-Goo Baby, Russ Trolls, 1990s, 9", NM $13.00
Green Monster, L Khem, 1964, pk hair, wht robe, 3½", EX..$60.00
Henry, TH Dam/Made in Denmark, 1979, shaggy hair, bib over-
    alls, 18", EX...$60.00
Hobo Clown, Russ #18716, 6", EX..............................$70.00
Hula Dancer, Scandia House (unmk), 8", VG $75.00
Hunt-Nik, Totsy Wishnik, w/rifle, NM, from $20 to $25.00

Ice Skater, Dam Things, 1960s, white jacket and skates, red scarf and skirt, 3", EX, $145.00. (Photo courtesy Miss Kitty at The Cat's Pajamas Vintage)

Iggy Normous, Dam Things, 1960s, in 'leopard skin,' 13",
    NM $65.00
Lady, Dam/Made in Denmark, very long yel hair, 2½", EX..$25.00
Lion, Dam, 1968-72, 6¾x8¼" $60.00
Lion, keychain, rare, sm $15.00
Little Red Riding Hood, Russ Storybook, 4½", NM.........$14.00
Mermaid, Russ, iridescent hair & outfit, 5", EX...............$25.00
Mouse, 1968, allover orange hair, w/bl hang cord, 3½", EX .$35.00
Old Man, Nyrform, toothy smile, gr longjohns, 26", EX...$90.00

Gonk #953577/England, allover red animal fur, w/hang cord, sm, EX $20.00

Petal People, Wishnik, 1964, 7", EX $10.00

Piggy Bank, Dam, 1984, bl felt necktie, 6½" L, NM........$30.00

Redhead, Dam Things, 1960s, gr jumper w/lime gr shirt, 12", EX...$95.00

Santa, Wishnik, 7", NM $35.00

Seal, Norfin Pets/Dam, 1984, 6½", NM......................$50.00

Seal Bank, Dam/Made in Denmark, 1984, 6", EX...........$18.00

Snorkler, Russ, w/goggles & swim fins, 4", EX................$15.00

Sock-It-To-Me, Uneeda Wishnik, 6", NM....................$50.00

Squeek Mouse, Norfin/Dam, 1985, troll in mouse costume, 3½", EX...$15.00

St Louis Cardinals Troll Nodder, Russ, 1992, EX.............$14.00

Teenage Mutant Ninja Turtle, 1992, 7", MIB $8.00

Troll Lying on Log, Nyform, 5x5", EX.........................$75.00

Turtle, Norfin/Dam, 1984, amber eyes, 4", NM $50.00

Two-Headed Troll, Uneeda, 1965, nude, 3", EX $35.00

Viking Dam Things, 1960s, 5½", EX............................$90.00

View-Master and Tru-Vue

View-Master, the invention of William Gruber, was introduced to the public at the 1939 – 1940 New York World's Fair and the Golden Gate Exposition in California. Since then, View-Master reels, packets, and viewers have been produced by five different companies — the original Sawyers Company, G.A.F (1966), View-Master International (1981), Ideal Toys, and Tyco Toys (the present owners). Because none of the non-cartoon single reels and three-reel packets have been made since 1980, these have become collectors' items. Also highly sought after are the three-reel sets featuring popular TV and cartoon characters. The market is divided between those who simply collect View-Master as a field all its own and collectors of character-related memorabilia who will often pay much higher prices for reels about Barbie, Batman, The Addams Family, etc. Our values tend to follow the more conservative approach.

The first single reels were dark blue with a gold sticker and came in attractive gold-colored envelopes. They appeared to have handwritten letters. These were followed by tan reels with a blue circular stamp. Because these were produced for the most part after 1945 and paper supplies were short during WWII, they came in a variety of front and back color combinations, tan with blue, tan with white, and some were marbleized. Since print runs were low during the war, these early singles are much more desirable than the printed white ones that were produced by the millions from 1946 until 1957. Three-reel packets, many containing story books, were introduced in 1955, and single reels were phased out. Nearly all viewers are very common and have little value except for the very early ones, such as the Model A and Model B. Blue and brown versions of the Model B are especially rare. Another desirable viewer, unique in that it is the only focusing model ever made, is the Model D. For more information we recommend *View-Master Single Reels, Volume I*, by Roger Nazeley. Unless noted otherwise, values are for reels complete with cover and book.

Adam-12, #B-593, MIP $10.00

Apple's Way, #B558, MIP $15.00

Astrix & Cleopatra, #B-457, MIP $26.00

Bad News Bears (Breaking Training), #H-77, MIP...........$10.00

Barbar the Elephant, #B-419, MIP...............................$16.00

Barbie's Around the World Trip, #B-500, MIP $28.00

Batman, #1086, MIP...$10.00

Battle of the Planets, #BD-185, MIP...........................$16.00

Benji's Very Own Christmas, #J-51, MIP.......................$10.00

Beverly Hillbillies, #B-570, MIP.................................$22.00

Bonanza, #BB0487, MIP...$22.00

Brave Eagle, #B-466, MIP...$26.00

Bugs Bunny (Road Runner Show), #M-10, MIP.............$5.00

Bullwinkle, #B-515, MIP...$22.00

Captain Kangaroo, #B-560, MIP $10.00

Care Bears, #BD-264, MIP...$8.00

Charlie Brown (It's a Bird), #B-556, MIP......................$6.00

Cinderella, #B-318, MIP...$10.00

Close Encounters of the Third Kind, #J-47, MIP.............$15.00

Danger Mouse, #BD-214, MIP $20.00

Dark Crystal, #4036, MIP $12.00

Davy Crockett, #935abc, MIP $70.00

Deputy Dawg, #B-519, MIP.......................................$45.00

Disneyland (Fantasyland), #A-178, MIP.......................$22.00

Dr Shrinker & Wonderbug, #H-2, MIP $15.00

Dr Who, #BD-216, MIP...$70.00

Dukes of Hazzard, #L-17, MIP....................................$10.00

Dumbo, #J-60, MIP...$10.00

Eight Is Enough, #K76, MIP, $18.00. (Photo courtesy Greg Davis and Bill Morgan)

Electra Woman & Dyna Girl, #H-3, MIP $8.00

Emergency, #B-597, MIP $10.00

Family Affair, #B-571, MIP...$26.00

Ferdy, #BD-269, MIP...$8.00

Flintstone Kids, #1066, MIP $5.00

Fonz, #BJ-103, MIP...$10.00

Fox & the Hound, #L-29, MIP......................................$8.00

Full House, #4119, MIP $5.00

Goonies, #4064, MIP $10.00

Grimm's Fairy Tales, MIP..$10.00

Gunsmoke, #B-589, MIP..$26.00

Hair Bear Bunch, #B-552, MIP $10.00

Hawaii Five-O, #B-590, MIP..$18.00

Here's Lucy, #B-588, MIP $45.00

Happy Days, #B586, MIP, $12.00; Happy Days, #J13, MIP, $10.00. (Photo courtesy Greg Davis and Bill Morgan)

Sigmond and the Sea Monsters, #B595, MIP, $20.00. (Photo courtesy Greg Davis and Bill Morgan)

Huckleberry Finn, B-343, MIP	$10.00
Inspector Gadget, #BD-232, MIP	$8.00
Isis, #T-100, MIP	$10.00
James Bond (Live & Let Die), #B-393, MIP	$18.00
Jimbo & the Jet Set, #BD-261, MIP	$10.00
Julia, #B-572, MIP	$22.00
King Kong, #B-392, MIP	$10.00
Land of the Lost, #B-579, MIP	$12.00
Lassie Rides the Log Flume, #B-489, MIP	$14.00
Laugh-In, #B-497, MIP	$18.00
Lone Ranger, #962abc, MIP	$26.00
Lost in Space, #B-482, MIP	$55.00
M*A*S*H, #B-J11, MIP	$12.00
Man From UNCLE, #B-484, MIP	$22.00
Meteor, #K-46, MIP	$10.00
Mickey Mouse Jubilee, #J-29, MIP	$12.00
Mork & Mindy, #K-67, MIP	$10.00
Mr Magoo, #H-56, MIP	$8.00
Muppets Go Hawaiian, #L-25, MIP	$6.00
New Mickey Mouse Club, #H-9, MIP	$5.00
New Zoo Revue, #B-566, MIP	$14.00
One of Our Dinosaurs Is Missing, #B-377, MIP	$10.00
Partridge Family, #BB-5924, MIP	$18.00
Pinocchio, #B-311, MIP	$10.00
Pippi Longstocking, #B-322, MIP	$14.00
Pluto, #B-529, MIP	$12.00
Pluto, #BB-529, MIP	$9.00
Popeye's Fun, #B-527, MIP	$10.00
Poseidon Adventure, #N-391, MIP	$22.00
Power Rangers, #36870, MIP	$5.00
Raggedy Ann & Andy, #B-406, MIP	$12.00
Red Riding Hood, #FT-1, MIP	$4.00
Robin Hood Meets Friar Tuck, #B-373, MIP	$18.00
Roy Rogers, #N-462, MIP	$26.00
Rugrats, #36343, MIP	$5.00
Search, #B-591, MIP	$18.00
Secret Valley, #BD-208, MIP	$10.00
Sesame Street Circus Fun, #4097, MIP	$6.00
Shazam, #B-550, MIP	$8.00
Siegfried & Roy, MIP	$10.00
Silverhawks, #1058, MIP	$6.00
Smith Family, #B-490, MIP	$25.00
Smurfs, #BD-172, MIP	$5.00
Snow White, #B-300, MIP	$8.00
Space Mouse, #B-509, MIP	$18.00
Space: 1999, #BB-451, MIP	$20.00
Spider-Man, #BH-011, MIP	$10.00
Star Trek the Motion Picture, #K-57, MIP	$10.00
Steve Canyon, #B-582, MIP	$70.00
Superman the Movie, #J-78, MIP	$20.00
SWAT, #BB-453, MIP	$10.00
Tarzan, #B-580, MIP	$8.00
Tarzan of the Apes, #976-abc, MIP	$20.00
Teenage Mutant Ninja Turtles, #4109, MIP	$6.00
Thunderbirds, #B-453, MIP	$45.00
Tom & Jerry (Two Musketeers), #B-511, MIP	$12.00
Tom Sawyer, #B-340, MIP	$10.00
Tripods, #BD-242, MIP	$10.00
UFO, #B-417, MIP	$40.00
Voyage to the Bottom of the Sea, #B-483, MIP	$10.00
Waltons, #BB-596, MIP	$10.00
Wild Bill Hickock & Jingles, #B-473, MIP	$32.00
Winnetou, #BB-731, MIP	$22.00
Wizard of Oz, #FT-45-abc, MIP	$16.00
X-Men (Captive Hearts), #1085, MIP	$15.00

Western Heroes and Frontiersmen

No friend was ever more true, no brother more faithful, no acquaintance more real to us than our favorite cowboys of radio, TV, and the silver screen. They were upright, strictly moral, extremely polite, and tireless in their pursuit of law and order in the American West. How unfortunate that such role models are practically extinct nowadays.

For more information and some wonderful pictures, we recommend *Guide to Cowboy Character Collectibles* by Ted Hake and *The W.F. Cody Buffalo Bill Collector's Guide* by James W. Wojtowicz (Collector Books).

Advisors: Donna and Ron Donnelly (D7)

See also Advertising Signs, Ads, and Displays; Books; Character and Promotional Drinking Glasses; Character Clocks and

Watches; Coloring, Activity, and Paint Books; Guns; Lunch Boxes; Premiums; Puzzles, Windups, Friction, and Other Mechanicals.

Bat Masterson, cane, chrome-covered plastic hdl w/name emb across top, 1958, EX+ $35.00
Bat Masterson, outfit w/shirt, pants & tie, Gene Barry labels, Kaynee, MIB..$160.00
Cisco Kid, belt, blk leather w/brn embellishments & name tags, 1950s, NM $55.00
Dale Evans, washcloth mitt, terry cloth w/color image of Dale & inscribed name & Queen of the West, EX $25.00
Dale Evans, Western Dress-Up Kit, Colorforms/Roy Rogers Ent, 1959, EXIB...$50.00
Daniel Boone, coonskin cap, vinyl top w/fur sides, American Tradition Co, 1960s, mk A Fess parker Hat..., EX $75.00
Daniel Boone, figure, pnt plastic w/soft vinyl head, fur cap & powder horn, American Tradition Co, 1964, 5½", NM $50.00

Davy Crockett, Auto Magic Picture Gun, 1950s, complete, EX+IB, $175.00.

Davy Crockett, binoculars, plastic, Harrison, MIB.........$175.00
Davy Crockett, Dart Gun Target, Knickerbocker, unused, MIB..$80.00
Davy Crockett, doll, pnt hard plastic w/realistic outfit & hat, plastic rifle, Fortune Toy/WDP, 1950s, 7", EX+IB...$100.00
Davy Crockett, Frontierland Pencil Case, brn vinyl holster w/gun-shaped pencil case, 1950s, 8", VG...................$50.00
Davy Crockett, guitar, plastic w/yarn strap, mc paper litho label on front, w/up mechanisim plays music, Mattel, 14", EX $50.00
Davy Crockett, lamp, chalkware figural base with mountain scened painted on shade, 18", VG $100.00
Davy Crockett, marionette, compo w/cloth outfit, 'coonskin' cap, guitar & gun, Peter Puppet Playthings, 14", EX........$150.00
Davy Crockett, marionette, talker, Hazelle's, 15", MIB..$350.00
Davy Crockett, napkins, Beach Prod, 1950s, 30-ct in unopened pkg, 5" sq, MIP...$40.00

Davy Crockett, lamp, rotating cylinder, Econolite, 11", $275.00. (Photo courtesy Smith House Toys)

Davy Crockett, outfit, shirt, pants & skirt, brn cloth w/plastic fringe, Davy & Alamo scene on shirt, WDP, 1950s, EX $65.00
Davy Crockett, pencil case, marked Walt Disney's Official...Frontierland..., slide-out box, Hassenfeld, 1950s, 5x8", EX...$50.00
Davy Crockett, pin, diecast metal rectangle w/scalloped border, crossed swords emb on front, NMOC, A $65.00
Davy Crockett, play horse, Pied Piper Toys, MIB...........$125.00
Davy Crockett, tent, brn & wht Davy graphics on tan canvas, Empire Mfg/WDP, 1950s, complete, NM.................$135.00
Davy Crockett, tie clip, sq copper-tone metal w/emb image of musket & powder horn w/name, 1950s, M, P6 ....$18.00
Davy Crockett, towel, wht terry w/litho bust image of Davy/Fess Parker, Cannon/WDP, 1950s, 37x20", NM+ $40.00
Davy Crockett, tray, litho tin w/image of Davy fighting Indian, WDP, 1955, 13x17", VG.......................................$75.00
Davy Crockett, wallet, brn vinyl w/profile of Davy in 'fur' coonskin cap, WDP, 1955, 5x4", EX+IB..........................$75.00
Davy Crockett, Woodburning Set, Frontier..., ATF/USA, MIB..$175.00

Gene Autry, doll, composition, cloth outfit and felt hat, Terry Lee, 16", NM+, $500.00. (Photo courtesy Smith House Toys)

Gabby Hayes, Champion Shooting Target, Haccker/Ind, 1950s, NMIB...$225.00

Gabby Hayes, doll, stuffed cloth w/fur beard & felt hat, name on belt, 1960s, 13", M...$40.00

Gabby Hayes, Fishing Outfit, steel 2-part rod & reel, litho tin cylindrical container, VG...$175.00

Gene Autry, figure, ceramic, charicature-like standing figure on horseshoe base w/faux signature, 1950s, 8½", EX $400.00

Gene Autry, figure, pnt compo w/name emb on sides of chaps, w/lasso, wood base, 12", EX, A.................................$275.00

Gene Autry, flashlight, Cowboy Lariat, EXIB.................$100.00

Gene Autry, guitar, plastic, Emenee, 32", NMIB...........$225.00

Gene Autry, rug, tan chenille w/signature name & Champ above & below image of horse's head, 37x25", EX+.............$75.00

Gene Autry, wallet, leather w/zipper closure, image of Gene & Champion, Aristocrat, 1950s, VGIB..........................$75.00

Gunsmoke, cowboy hat, brn felt w/Gunsmoke & Marshall Matt Dillon emblem on front, vinyl trim, tie string, 1950s, EX $65.00

Gunsmoke, slippers, blk vinyl w/yel & red image of Matt, Chester & Doc, Columbia, 1959, unused, NM+IB .$200.00

Hopalong Cassidy, bank, plastic bust figure w/removable hat, copper plastic, Savings Club, Ohio S&L, 1950s, 4", EX.....$50.00

Hopalong Cassidy, boots, three-color leather, Acme, EXIB, $800.00. (Photo courtesy Smith House Toys)

Hopalong Cassidy, coin, front w/emb image of Hoppy, back marked Good Luck From Hoppy, 1¼" dia, VG.........$15.00

Hopalong Cassidy, Crayon & Stencil Set, Transogram, 1950s, complete, some use, EXIB.....................................$50.00

Hopalong Cassidy, doll, rubber head, cloth outfit, w/gun & holster, 1950s, 21", NM...$300.00

Hopalong Cassidy, drinking straws, cut-out photo of Hoppy on back of box, 1950s, unused, NM $75.00

Hopalong Cassidy, Figure & Paint Set, Laurel Ann, complete, used, EXIB $250.00

Hopalong Cassidy, hand puppet, cloth body w/vinyl head, 1950s, scarce, NM..$200.00

Hopalong Cassidy, lamp, rotating cylinder picturing Hoppy & Topper chasing stagecoach, plastic, Econolite, 10", NM+...$500.00

Hopalong Cassidy, night light, figural glass gun in holster w/image of Hoppy, Aladdin, 1950s, NM.................$350.00

Hopalong Cassidy, pants, blk cloth chaps-like w/2 images of Hoppy & Topper, covered wagons & steer heads, 1950s, VG..$50.00

Hopalong Cassidy, playhouse, 4 lithoed panels, William Boyd/Charcook, 1950, EX+...............................$650.00

Hopalong Cassidy, scrapbook, tan vinyl hardcover w/emb image of Hoppy on Topper, string-bound pgs, 1950s, unused, NM...$125.00

Hopalong Cassidy, spurs, silver-tone and brass with black leather straps, NM, $200.00.

Hopalong Cassidy, Stagecoach Toss beanbag target, litho tin & Masonite, Transogram, 1950s, 24x18", incomplete o/w EX $75.00

Hopalong Cassidy, stationary folio, w/paper & envelopes, complete, VG+ $50.00

Hopalong Cassidy, sweater, tan w/color graphics, shows Hoppy and name, 1950s, child-sz, EX.................................$100.00

Hopalong Cassidy, TV set, plastic w/pull-out knob, film strips revolve inside TV, Automatic Toy, 5x5", EXIB $250.00

Hopalong Cassidy, wallet, brn leather w/color litho head images of Hoppy & Topper, zippered closure, 1950s, 4x5", VG+..$50.00

Hopalong Cassidy, wallet, vinyl w/colorful images of stagecoach & Hoppy on Topper, 3x7½", 1950s, EX.....................$60.00

Hopalong Cassidy, Western Frontier Set, Milton Bradley, 1950s, complete, NMIB..$300.00

Hopalong Cassidy, Woodburning Set, American Toy, 1950s, unused, EXIB..$100.00

Johnny Ringo, hand puppet, Laura (girlfriend), cloth body w/vinyl head, felt hands, Tops in Toys, 1959-60, 10", EX+ $40.00

Lone Ranger, binoculars, plastic, Harrison, EX_IB.........$135.00

Lone Ranger, guitar, heavy cb w/wooden neck, Jefferson, 1950s, 28½" L, EX $100.00

Lone Ranger, Hi-Yo Silver the Lone Ranger Target Game, Marx, EXIB, A...$65.00

Lone Ranger, horseshoe set, rubber, Gardner, NMIB........$85.00

Lone Ranger, doll, stuffed body with composition head and hands, cloth outfit, cast-iron gun and holster, Dollcraft Novelty Company, 15", hat missing otherwise EX+, $600.00.

Lone Ranger, neck scarf & concho slide, purple silk-type material w/images of Lone Ranger & Silver, 1940s-50s, EX......$50.00

Lone Ranger, outfit (Official), w/chaps, vest, hat, wrist cuffs, mask, shirt, neckerchief & lasso, Henry, 1940s, NMIB, A...$480.00

Lone Ranger, push-button puppet, Lone Ranger on Silver, Press Action Toys, 1939, NMIB, from $125 to $175.00

Lone Ranger, record player, wood case, Decca Lone Ranger Inc., 10x12", EX, $350.00. (Photo courtesy Smith House Toys)

Lone Ranger, ring-toss, die-cut cb, complete, Rosebud Art, MIB...$250.00

Lone Ranger, school bag, canvas w/plastic hdl, image of Lone Ranger on side pocket, 1950s, EX $100.00

Lone Ranger, snow dome, Lone Ranger Round Up, glass globe on plastic base, Driss/TLR, 1950s, 4", VG+ $50.00

Lone Ranger, soap figure, Kerk Guild, 1939, 4½", unused, EXIB $65.00

Lone Ranger, soap figure set, Lone Ranger, Tonto & Silver, Kerk, 1939, 4", VG $50.00

Lone Ranger, Target, litho tin w/metal support, Marx, TLR Inc, 1930s, 9½" sq, EX $50.00

Maverick, Eras-O-Picture Book, Hasbro, 1958, complete, EX.$40.00

Maverick, Oil Painting by Numbers, Hasbro, 1958, complete, partially used, EXIB $75.00

Red Rider, gloves, Playmates, brn, red & bl cloth, tag w/premium offers, Wells Lamont Corp & SS, 1950s, NM..$30.00

Rin-Tin-Tin, Corporal Rusty 101st Cavalry Outfit, with gun and holster, Iskin/Screen Gems, EXIB, $225.00.

Rin-Tin-Tin, figure, Rinny, pnt plaster w/blk & bronze-tone finish, rhinestone eyes, 1939, 11x8x4", EX $75.00

Rin-Tin-Tin, outfit, Fighting Blue Devil 101st Cavalry, shirt, leather belt, pouch w/bullets & holster, NMIB........$185.00

Roy Rogers, archery set, Ben Pearson, 37", scarce, unused, NMOC..$185.00

Roy Rogers, bank, metal boot form w/copper finish, Almar Metal Arts Co, 1950s, 5½", EX................................$75.00

Roy Rogers, Branding Set/Ink Pad, 1950s, tin container, 1950s,½x2" dia, unused, EX $65.00

Roy Rogers, Crayon Set, Standard Toykraft #940, 1950s, VGIB...$75.00

Roy Rogers, flashlight, Signal Siren, tin, Usalite, 7", unused, MIB..$150.00

Roy Rogers, fountain pen, name on blk plastic barrel, gold trim, 1950s, 5", VG...$50.00

Roy Rogers, guitar, wood & pressed wood, red w/wht silhouette images, Range Rhythm/Rich Toys, 31", NMIB........$200.00

Roy Rogers, hand puppet, cloth w/vinyl head & hat, 1950s, 7", EX+ $75.00

Roy Rogers, lamp base, pnt plaster figure of Roy on rearing Trigger on rnd base, Plasto, 1950s, 10½", EX+ $100.00

Roy Rogers, Lucky Horseshoe Game, Ohio Art, 1950s, EX.$75.00

Roy Rogers, modeling clay set, complete, unused, NM (in box w/image of Roy on rearing Trigger) $150.00

Roy Rogers, paint-by-number paint set, RRE Set C/Post Sugar Crisp, 1954, used, EXIB...$40.00

Roy Rogers, paint-by-number paint set, RRE Set C/Post Sugar Crisp, 1954, unused, MIB...$75.00

Roy Rogers, lantern, lithographed tin, 8" with handle up, EX, $50.00.

Tonto, doll, stuffed body with composition head, cloth outfit, guns and holster set, 20", missing headband and feather otherwise EX, $500.00.

Roy Rogers, pencil case, vinyl w/wht stitching, name & image of Roy & Trigger on front, flap top w/snap closure, 8", EX..$50.00

Roy Rogers, Pony Contest entry form, Hudson's Bay Co, 1950s, 12x9", unused, NM $50.00

Roy Rogers, postcard, image of Roy on rearing Trigger, acknowledges contest entry, Quaker Oats, 1948, NM.............$50.00

Roy Rogers, pull toy, horse-drawn covered wagon, paper litho on wood, removable cloth cover, NN Hill, 20", EX......$250.00

Roy Rogers, rodeo program, Chicago Stadium, 1946, 20 pg w/back showing Tom Mix, Buck Jones, etc, EX $75.00

Roy Rogers, scarf, red & gold silk-like material w/vignette graphics, King of the Cowboys, 1950s, 25x25", EX.............$75.00

Roy Rogers, school bag, brn textured vinyl w/brn leather strap, badge above graphics on front pocket flap, 1950s, G+..$100.00

Roy Rogers, telescope, plastic, H George, 9", MIB.........$200.00

Roy Rogers, Trick Lasso, Classy Products, 1950s, complete, EXIP $75.00

Roy Rogers, wagon train, plastic stagecoach w/driver & horses leading 3 litho tin wagons, w/up, 14" L, VG, A.......$135.00

Roy Rogers, Woodburning Set, Burn-Rite, complete, EXIB..$175.00

Roy Rogers & Dale Evans, school tablets, Frontiers Inc, 1950s, 10x8", unused, EX, ea $25.00

Tonto, soap figure, Kerk Guild, 1939, 4", EXIB (unopened) ..$50.00

Wild Bill Hickok, wallet, fastens w/western buckle, NM+..$75.00

Zorro, accessory set w/mask, whip, lariat & ring, Shimmel/WDP, M (w/24" L card picturing Guy Williams) $150.00

Zorro, bolo tie, metal medallion w/plastic inset featuring Zorro portrait on red logo, NM $50.00

Zorro, bowl & plate, Sun-Valley Melmac, 1950s-60s, 5" dia & 7¼" dia, EX, set $40.00

Zorro, hand puppet, vinyl head w/cloth body, felt hat, Gund/WDP, 1950s, EX+..$75.00

Zorro, magic slate, Watkins/Strathmore/WDP, 1950s-60s, complete, EX..$75.00

Zorro, Oil-Painting-By-Number Set, Hassenfeld Bros, 1960s, complete, VGIB..$65.00

Zorro, Target Shoot, Lido/WDP, MIB $225.00

Zorro, tote bag, red vinyl, EX $275.00

Windups, Friction, and Other Mechanicals

Windup toys represent a fun and exciting field of collecting — our fascination with them stems from their simplistic but exciting actions and brightly colored lithography, and especially the comic character or personality-related examples are greatly in demand by collectors today. Though most were made through the years of the 1930s to the 1950s, they carry their own weight against much earlier toys and are considered very worthwhile investments. Various types of mechanisms were used — some are key wound while others depend on lever action to tighten the mainspring and release the action of the toy. Tin and celluloid were used in their production, and although it is sometimes possible to repair a tin windup, experts advise against investing in a celluloid toy whose mechanism is not working, since the material is usually too fragile to withstand the repair.

 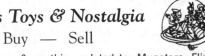

Many of the boxes that these toys came in are almost as attractive as the toys themselves and can add considerably to their value.

Advisor: Scott Smiles (S10)

See also Aeronautical; Boats; Chein; Japanese and Other Replica Vehicles; Lehmann; Marx; Robots and Space Toys; Strauss.

AMERICAN

Airplane, Unique Art, w/up, litho tin, flat-sided pilot's head, single lg prop, orange & yel, 7" L, A..............................$100.00
Airport, Ohio Art, w/up, litho tin, 2 airplanes spiral down center rod atop rnd 2-tiered building, 9" T, EXIB, A..........$275.00

Artie the Clown in Crazy Car, Unique Art, windup, lithographed tin, 7" long, EX, A, $500.00. (Photo courtesy Bertoia Auctions)

Artie the Clown in Crazy Car, Unique Art, w/up, litho tin, 7" L, G, A $250.00
Auto, Hess, w/up, tin, open body w/tiller steering, spoke wheels, goggled driver & lady passenger, 5", G, A................$300.00
Auto Lift, Wolverine, w/up, litho tin, 10½", EX, A $250.00

Barnacle Bill Rowboat, Emmert-Hammes & Co., rubber-band activated, lithographed tin, 10" long, EX+IB, A, $500.00. (Photo courtesy Bertoia Auctions)

Bear, Ives, w/up, blk fur w/wooden face & hands, colored paper teeth, VGIB, A...$600.00
Billard Table, Ranger Steel Prod, w/up, litho tin, 2 men at either end of table w/cues, 13½" L, EX+IB $350.00
Black Diamond Coal Co Truck, w/up, litho tin & plastic, 10½", EX, A..$125.00
Bombo the Monk, Unique Art, w/up, litho tin, VGIB...$125.00
Boy on Sled, Clark, friction, pnt pressed steel, 9" L, VG, A.$300.00
Boy on Tricycle (Wonder Cyclist), Unique Art, w/up, litho tin, 7½" L, VG, A $250.00
Bulldozer w/Plow & Rock Cart, Ranger Steel, w/up, litho tin, w/rubber treads, w/driver, 9½", EX+IB, A $100.00
Capitol Hill Racer, Unique Art, w/up, litho tin, 11" L, EXIB, A $135.00

Carnival, Wyandotte, crank-operated, lithographed tin, merry-go-round and other objects on flat base, 11x16", EX, $800.00. (Photo courtesy Bertoia Auctions)

Carnival, Wyandotte, crank-op, litho tin, merry-go-round & other objects on flat base, 11x16", VG, A $500.00
Carousel, Wolverine, w/up, litho tin, red, wht & bl w/circus theme, 12" dia, VG, A..$300.00
Convertible, Wyandotte, 1950s, w/up, litho tin, w/retractable roof, 13", VG, A $175.00
Coupe (Mystery Car), Wolverine, press-down action, tin, 3 windows, disk wheels, 13", G, A $150.00
Crawling Baby, Irwin, w/up, plastic w/cloth outfit, 5½", VGIB, A $75.00
Dancing Senorita, Irwin, w/up, plastic, 10", EXIB, A $75.00
Dandy Jim the Jolly Clown Dancer, Unique Art, w/up, litho tin, clown performs on roof, 10", EX $800.00
Dandy Jim the Jolly Clown Dancer, Unique Art, w/up, litho tin, clown performs on roof, 10", NMIB, A $1,100.00
Donald Duck Hand Car, Lionel, w/up, compo Donald standing behind doghouse w/Pluto figure, 11" L, EXIB, A.....$825.00
Donald Duck Hand Car, Lionel, w/up, compo Donald standing behind doghouse w/Pluto figure, 11" L, VG.............$425.00

Doin' the Howdy Doody, Unique Art, windup, lithographed tin, 8" long, EXIB, A, $825.00. (Photo courtesy Bertoia Auctions)

Horse-Drawn Fire Pumper, George Brown, windup, painted tin, 15" long, A, $14,300.00. (Photo courtesy Bertoia Auctions)

Dream Car, Mattel, 1950s, friction, plastic w/clear removable top, 10½", EX+IB, A $200.00
Dream Car, see also XP-1960 Dream Car
Drum Major, Wolverine, w/up, litho tin, 14", EX, A $275.00
Express Wagon, Wilkens, w/up, tin buckboard type w/embossed stake sides, CI spoke wheels, driver on bench seat, 7", G, A $165.00
Flying Circus, Unique Art, w/up, litho tin, elephant balancing clown & plane on rod, 24" (extended), VG, A $675.00
Futurmatic Airport, Automatic Toy Co, 1950s, w/up, litho tin, 15x15", NMIB $150.00

General Butler, Ives, Pat 1875, windup, painted-lead head and hands, cloth uniform, cast-iron shoes, 10", EXIB, $6,500.00. (Photo courtesy Bertoia Auctions)

George Washington Bridge, Fritz Bueschel, w/up, litho tin, w/Greyhound bus, 25" L, EX, A $600.00
GI Joe & His Jouncing Jeep, Unique Art, w/up, litho tin, 7", EXIB, A $275.00
GI Joe & His Jouncing Jeep, Unique Art, w/up, litho tin, 7", VG..$150.00
GI Joe & His K-9 Pups, Unique Art, w/up, litho tin, 9", EXIB, A $275.00
GI Joe & His K-9 Pups, Unique Art, w/up, litho tin, 9", VG, A $150.00
Hoky & Poky Handcar, Wyandotte, w/up, litho tin, 6½" L, EXIB, A $300.00
Howdy Doody, see Doin' the Howdy Doody
Howdy Doody Cart, Ny-Lint, w/up, litho tin, 9", VG, A...$300.00

Humphery Mobile, Wyandotte, w/up, litho tin, 9", G, A ..$200.00
Humphery Mobile, Wyandotte, w/up, litho tin, 9" L, EXIB, A.$475.00
Injun Chief, Ohio Art, w/up, EX+IB, A $175.00
Jackie Gleason Bus, Wolverine, 1955, press-down action, litho tin, 14", NMIB...$900.00
Jazzbo Jim (Banjo Player), Unique Art, w/up, litho tin, 10", EXIB..$500.00
Jazzbo Jim (Jigger & Fiddler), Unique Art, w/up, litho tin, 10", VG+ $350.00
Jet Roller Coaster, Wolverine, w/up, PS & litho tin, 12" L, EXIB, A $175.00
Johnny (Clown) Walker, Lindstrom, w/up, litho tin, red/yel suit w/pointed hat, 8", EX $200.00
Jungle Pete the Mechanical Alligator, Automatic Toy, w/up, litho tin, 15" L, VGIB, A $150.00
Kiddie Kampers, Wolverine, 1930s, w/up, litho tin, 14" L, VG+IB...$425.00
Kiddy Cyclist, Unique Art, w/up, litho tin, boy on tricycle, 8½" T, VG+IB $300.00
Li'l Abner & His Dogpatch Band, Unique Art, w/up, litho tin, 6x9", EX $400.00
Li'l Abner & His Dogpatch Band, Unique Art, 1940s, w/up, litho tin, 6x9", NMIB, A...$700.00
Li'l Abner & Lonesome Polecat in Canoe, Ideal, w/up, plastic, 12" L, NM+IB..$300.00
Lincoln Tunnel, Unique Art, w/up, litho tin, 24" L, complete, EX $250.00
Lincoln Tunnel, Unique Art, w/up, litho tin, 24" L, EXIB..$350.00
Lincoln Tunnel, Unique Art, w/up, litho tin, 24" L, G+ .$150.00
Locomotive (New York), George Brown, w/up, pnt tin w/wooden stack & base, 2 lg spoke front wheels, 10½", G $550.00
Locomotive (Union), Althof Bergman, w/up, pnt tin, very ornate w/heart-shaped spoke wheels, 9½", VG, A.............$1,870.00
Locomotive (Vulcan), Fallows, w/up, pn tin w/4 CI spoke wheels, V-shaped cow catcher, 10", EX, A $1,320.00

Loop the Loop, McDowell, w/up, litho tin, w/auto, 13" L, VGIB..$250.00

Mammy Walker, Lindstrom, w/up, litho tin, 8", VG $300.00

Man on the Flying Trapeze, Wyandotte, w/up, litho tin, 9", NM+IB..$250.00

Man on the Flying Trapeze, Wyandotte, w/up, litho tin, 9", VG+IB..$100.00

Man Pushing 2-Wheeled Cart, Girard, 1930s, w/up, 6", EX, A.$175.00

Mattel Music Maker Toy (Musical Man on the Flying Trapeze), 'Whirling Twirling Action,' 12", EXIB, A..................$75.00

Merry-Go-Round, #31A, Wolverine, spring motor, litho tin, w/horses & planes, 12x11" dia, VG..........................$200.00

Merry-Go-Round, see also Sunny Andy Merry-Go-Round

Merry-Go-Round, Wolverine #31A, spring motor, litho tin, w/horses & planes, 12x11" dia, EXIB, A..................$300.00

Mickey Mouse Circus Train, Lionel, compo Mickey figure on litho tin train w/loco, tender & 3 cars, 28", EX, A..........$1,320.00

Mickey Mouse Hand Car, Lionel, w/up, compo Mickey & Minnie figures on PS base, EXIB, A $825.00

Mickey Mouse Race, Lindstrom, w/up, litho tin w/WRT, Mickey driver, 4", VG, A $330.00

Mr Machine, Ideal, w/up, mc plastic, VGIB, A $200.00

Overland Trail Bus Line, Girard, ca 1921, w/up, litho tin, w/luggage rack, disk wheels, driver, 13¾", EX+, A $2,200.00

Skeeter-Bug Bumper Car, Lindstrom, 1940s, w/up, litho tin couple in PS car, 9½", EXIB, A $425.00

Ski Slope, Wolverine, litho tin & paperboard, skier on 4 wheels goes down slope, G, A..$125.00

Sky Rangers, Unique Art, w/up, litho tin, 24", EX+IB, A .$400.00

Sky Rangers, Unique Art, w/up, litho tin, 24", VG, A...$175.00

Spiral Speedway, Automatic Toy, w/up, 2 3¾" buses travel speedway, NMIB, A..$200.00

Steam Roller, Lindstrom, w/up, tin, 11½" L, VG+IB, A .$200.00

Street Sweeper, Ny-Lint, w/up, litho tin w/rubber wheels, plastic driver, 8" L, EXIB, A..$300.00

Sunny Andy Kiddie Campers, Wolverine, 1920s, litho tin, Scout camping scene w/marbles rolling down shoot, 14" L, EXIB, A $350.00

Sunny Andy Merry-Go-Round, Wolverine, spring-loaded action, litho tin, chrome center tower, 12x11" dia, EX+IB, A..$300.00

Target Shooter (Buffalo Bill Cody), rear lever action controls lifting of gun, pnt tin figure holding gun, 9", VG, A $550.00

TC 600 Custom Cruiser, Sears, 1950s, friction, plastic stylized body w/functioning rear luggage deck, 11½", NMIB.$125.00

Trailer Truck Assortment #376, Courtland, friction, tin & plastic, 2 12" (approx) vehicles, VGIB (box becomes building) $300.00

Train Set, Unique Art, w/up, litho tin, 4-pc w/10" L locomotive w/tender, boxcar & caboose, w/tracks, NMIB, A.....$300.00

Peter Rabbit Chick-Mobile, Lionel, windup, O gauge, 9" long, EXIB, A, $1,430.00. (Photo courtesy Bertoia Auctions)

Walking Zobave, Martin & Runyon of NYC, windup, painted composition head, cloth uniform, brass shoes, 11", NMIB, A, $3,025.00. (Photo courtesy Bertoia Auctions)

Phaeton Auto (1911), Wilkins, w/up, CI & PS, open vehicle w/MSW, CI lady driver at right steering wheel, 9", G, A $770.00

Police Chief Car, Hoge, friction, b/o headlights, litho tin, 2-tone gr, BRT, 14", G+, A $650.00

Popeye Walker Carrying 2 Parrot Cages, w/up, litho tin, 8½", VG, A $275.00

Rap & Tap in a Friendly Scrap, Unique Art, w/up, litho tin, 2 boxers in ring, 5½" T, EX, A $400.00

Rodeo Joe, Unique Art, w/up, litho tin, 8" L, EX $225.00

Royal Couple Waltzing, Irwin, w/up, plastic, 5½", NM+IB, A $75.00

Sandy (Orphan Annie), Harold Gray, w/up, litho tin dog w/valise in mouth, 5" L, EXIB (box shaped like doghouse w/name) $350.00

Whistling Boy, Irwin, w/up, plastic figure w/hands in pockets, 9½", EXIB, A..$120.00

Woman Chasing Duck w/Whip, Clark, friction, pnt steel, figures on 4-wheeled platform, 11", G+, A $400.00

Woman Churning on Box, Ives, w/up, figure in cloth dress at wood churn on wood box, 11", rstr, A (Est: $2,500-$3,000) $2,750.00

Wonder Cyclist, see Boy on Tricycle

XP-1960 Dream Car, Mattel, friction, plastic futuristic convertible, 8½", EXIB, A...$220.00

Zilotone, Wolverine, w/up, litho tin, figure plays along with records and hits keys, 8", VG+, A............................$600.00

ENGLISH

Austin Saloon Auto, Ranlite, w/up, Bakelite body w/PS running boards, NP trim, BRT, adjustable steering, 10", VG, A.$935.00

Bubble Blower, crank-operated, painted tin, 6½" tall, EX, $1,870.00. (Photo courtesy Randy Inman Auctions)

Charlie Chaplin, Fairylite, w/up, litho tin, stands w/cane & whiskey bottle under arm, neck rises, 6", EX, A......$275.00
Clown on Motorcycle (First Prize), Mettoy, w/up, litho tin w/diecast head, 7½", VG, A....................................$525.00

Clowns on Motorcycle (OU2), Mettoy, windup, lithographed tin, 8½", EX+, A, $1,870.00. (Photo courtesy Bertoia Auctions)

Coupe, Mettoy, w/up, litho tin, tan w/bl roof & top of hood, side vents, NP grille, MDW, 8", nonworking o/w EX, A .$250.00
Fire Engine, Chad Valley, w/up, litho tin, 8", EX, A $150.00
Ford Van, Minic, prewar, w/up, tin, BRT, spare gas tank on running board, orig decal, 3", VG+IB, A $150.00

Coupe, Wells, windup, lithographed tin, red and silver with black running boards, nickel-plated grille and bumpers, 12", EX, A, $1,430.00. (Photo courtesy Bertoia Auctions)

Joytown Fire Station, Mettoy, 8x8x5" firehouse w/2 5" vehicles, VG+IB, A $300.00
Limousine, Wells, w/up, litho tin, flat roof, tapered nose, side spares, rear luggage box, 3 side windows, 8", EX+, A.$600.00
Lincoln Zephyr, Brim Toy, w/up, plastic w/tin chassis, 6", EXIB $200.00
Mickey Mouse Circus Train Set, A Wells & Co, 1930s, w/up, litho tin, 3-pc train w/collapsible circus tent, EX $450.00
Motor Garage w/Open Touring Car, 1920s, w/up, litho tin, 12" L garage, G+, A..$400.00
Moving Van, Minic, w/up, tin, Carter-Patterson advertising, BRT, 5½", EXIB, A..$250.00
Nautilus Submarine, w/up, gr tin, from Disney's 20,000 Leagues Under the Sea, 9½", NMIB, A $200.00
Police Patrol Motor Cycle, Coral Plastics, friction, lt baby bl & wht plastic, 9" L, NMIB, A $200.00
Racer #3, w/up, litho tin boattail w/working steering, lithoed thick spoke wheels, no driver, 15½", G+, A............$460.00
Roadster, Chad Valley, w/up, litho tin, metal tires, rear spare, 12½", VG+, A..$650.00
Saloon Car, Chad Valley, w/up, litho tin, MDW, 9", EX+IB, A $500.00
Sedan, Chad Valley, w/up, litho tin, MDW, 9", G..........$175.00
Shell Oil Tank Truck, Minic, w/up, tin, BRT, w/spare gas can, 6", VGIB, A $250.00
Taxi, Minic, w/up, tin, BRT, 4", EXIB, A........................$250.00
Vauxhall Tourer, Minic, prewar, w/up, tin, WRT, top down, w/driver & 2 passengers, 5", GIB, A $400.00
Wells Brimtoy Distributors LTD Transport Double-Decker Bus, litho tin, red, 4½", EX (Poor box), A $125.00

FRENCH

Acrobats (2) on Bars, hand-op, pnt wood, figures flip head-over-heels on trapeze bar, 8½", VG, A............................$375.00
Advocate (Figure at Podium), Martin, early, figure in cloth robe standing at litho tin podium, 9", nonworking o/w EX, A..$1,760.00
Auto Garage, Muller & Kaderer, litho tin hangar-type garage, arched tressle entry w/flag above, 7½x12" L, VG, A $1,200.00

Auto Garage & Peugot Auto, Carl Rossignol, w/up auto, litho tin, electric light in copula, 14" auto, 15" L garage, EX, A...$1,980.00

Bambino Moto-Scooter, JML, w/up, pnt heavy tin, 11", EX, A..$355.00

Barber, Martin, ca 1903, w/up, 2 cloth-dressed figures on tin base, 8", VG, A $1,650.00

Bear Drinker, De Champs, 1880s, windup, brown fur, bear pouring from bottle into cup, 12", EX, A, $935.00. (Photo courtesy Bertoia Auctions)

Bear Walker, De Champs, w/up, blk & wht rabbit fur w/papier-maché hands, glass eyes, celluloid nose, 12", VG+, A ..$450.00

Bugatti Racer #2, JEP, w/up, litho tin, boattail rear, MDW, w/driver, 8½", EX, A $1,000.00

Bugatti Racer #3, JEP, w/up, litho tin, MSW, w/driver, 13", EX, A..$1,320.00

Cat Ironing, De Champs, windup, white rabbit fur covering, wooden base, 12", EX, $750.00. (Photo courtesy Bertoia Auctions)

Cat Walker, De Champs, w/up, wht rabbit fur covering, 12½" L, VG, A $350.00

City Bus, Carl Rossignol, w/up, litho tin, motor-driven trolley type w/4 MDW, open rear platform, w/driver, 12", VG, A ..$550.00

Coupe, Carl Rossignol, w/up, litho tin, red over bl, 2 side spares, 13½", VG $650.00

Delage, JEP, w/up, enameled tin, start & stop switch, opening door, electric lights, 13", EX+IB, A.......................$935.00

Drunkard, Martin, early, w/up, tin & lead w/cloth outfit, 7½", VGIV, A...$550.00

Fire Aerial Ladder Truck, w/up, red tin w/NP ladders, open cab, electric headlights, swivel base, BRT, 15", EX, A $300.00

Fish Toy, lever activated, colorful fish w/movable tail fin, 15½", EXIB, A $880.00

Fruit Seller, Martin, w/up, pnt tin, fully jtd blk figure pushing fruit wagon, 6½" L, G, A....................................$400.00

Greyhound Observation Car (Bus), Joustra, w/up, litho tin, 5½", EX+IB, A $550.00

JML Delivery Cart, w/up, litho tin 3-wheeled cart w/integral driver, 14", VG, A (Est: $800-$1,000) $935.00

Le Petit Livreur (Delivery Boy), Martin, w/up, cloth-dressed boy pushing 2-wheeled delivery card w/box, 7", EXIB, A.$1,650.00

Les Jouets Citroen Set, w/up, metal, truck cab interchanges w/flatbed, dump bed, pickup & oil tank, NMIB, A.$2,970.00

Limousine, Carl Rossignol, w/up, litho tin, curved back, 2 side spares, back wheel covers, 13½", EX, A...................$990.00

Limousine w/Right-Side Driver, JDP, w/up, tin, roof extends over open seat, flat roof w/3-sided rail, MSW, 11", VG, A..$1,760.00

Motorcycle w/Sidecar (SFA), w/up, litho tin, w/civilian driver, 6½", VG+, A...$250.00

Orange Vendor, Martin, w/up, pnt tin lady w/cloth dress pushing 2-wheeled cart w/spoke wheels, 6½" L, EX, A $1,540.00

Patisserie (Street Vendor w/Wagon), flywheel activated, pnt & lithoed tin, lady w/2-wheeled enclosed cart, 7" L, VG, A $1,045.00

Peugeot 601 Roadster w/Rumble Seat, Rossignol, w/up, litho tin, metal tires mk Michelin, 14½", VG+, A..............$1,100.00

Pianist, Martin, early, windup, cloth-dressed figure seated at tin upright piano on lithographed tin base, 5" wide, VG, $2,000.00. (Photo courtesy Bertoia Auctions)

Rabbit in Cabbage Head, De Champs, w/up, rabbit w/wht rabbit fur, compo cabbage head w/gr pnt fabric leaves, 9", EX, A...$1,430.00

Rabbit w/Maracas, De Champs, w/up, plush, 11", VG....$335.00

Racer #05, w/up, tin, back curves downward, NP side pipes, lithoed side vents, lithoed MSW, w/driver, 13½", EX+IB, A $1,200.00

Racer #25, Carl Rossignol, w/up, litho tin, front wheels on frame extended past hood, tapered back, driver, 17", EX, A...$1,100.00

Racer #63, w/up, litho tin boattail w/lithoed side vent pipes, flat front w/grille, MDW, w/driver, 10", G, A $275.00

Renault Viva Sport, CIJ, w/up, enameled tin w/cloth top, opening door, working steering, bsk driver, 12½", EX, A $875.00

Renault Work Truck, CIJ, w/up, tin, early model w/flat roof & tapered nose, opening doors, BRT, w/wood tools, 17", EX, A $1,430.00

Super Racer #42, 1950s, friction, litho tin w/BRT, w/driver, red flame version, 19", nonworking o/w VG+, A.......$1,760.00

Super Racer #42, 1950s, friction, litho tin w/BRT, w/driver, red flame version, 19", EX, A................$3,080.00

Tiger, De Champs, w/up, fur-covered, glass eyes, crouches, nods head & lunges forward, 16½" L, G, A $230.00

Tow Truck, Charles Rossignol, w/up, litho tin, spare tires on bothe sides, w/driver, 16", rare, EX, A.....................$950.00

Town Car, Carl Rossignol, windup with battery-operated lights, open front seat with enclosed back, metal disk wheels, rear spare, with driver, 15", VG, $2,200.00. (Photo courtesy Bertoia Auctions)

Vegetable Vendor, Martin, w/up, pnt tin lady w/cloth dress pushing 2-wheeled cart, 6", L, VG, A $1,200.00

Viva Sport Coupe, CIJ, w/up, tin, gr w/lt tan roof, NP grille & lights, BRT, 11½", EX...$650.00

GERMAN

Airplane Circling Tower, Bing, spring-activated tower allows plane to circle on rod w/counter weight, 12" T, EX, A $550.00

Airplane w/Pilot in Open Cockpit, Gunthermann, w/up, litho tin, runs forward then flips, 6½" L, EX, A $175.00

Akustico 2002 Roadster Convertible, Schuco, w/up, tin, 5½", EXIB, A $245.00

Alpine Express, Techno Fix, 24" L, VG (Poor box), A ..$125.00

Ambulance, Bing, w/up, litho tin, flat roof w/4-sided rail extends over doorless front seat w/driver, MSW, 8", EX+, A ..$1,430.00

Atlantic City Rollo Chair, w/up, litho tin, black porter pushing 3-wheeled chair, yel w/red trim, no sz given, VG, A.....$725.00

Auto #5300 w/Road Signs, Schuco, w/up, w/additional steering mechanism, 9" L, EX (w/box bottom only), A $250.00

Autos (2) & Garage, Orobr, w/up, litho tin, open touring car & sedan w/2-bay garage, 6" cars & 7x4x6" garage, EX+, A $1,870.00

Balloon & Toy Vendor, w/up, litho tin, man on platform holds bunch of balloons, toys & satchel, 7", EX, A...........$355.00

Barney Google on Spark Plug, Nifty, windup, lithographed tin, 7" long, G, $725.00. (Photo courtesy Bertoia Auctions)

Barnum & Bailey's Circus Cage Truck w/Animals, Lindstrom, w/up, litho tin, EX, A..$650.00

Bear Performing, Ives, w/up, cloth-covered tin figure w/muzzle & collar holding stick, 8", incomplete, Fair+, A..........$245.00

Betty Walker, Lindstrom, w/up, litho tin, 7½", VG, A ..$355.00

Bico Bus to Joyville, Distler, windup, lithographed tin, 7", EX, A, $2,475.00. (Photo courtesy Bertoia Auctions)

Bicyclist, w/up, litho tin, 2-D figure on bicycle w/headlight, lead spoke wheels, 6" L, VG, A $1,430.00

Billiards Player, w/up, litho tin, man w/pool cue at end of table, 6" L, EX, A...$375.00

Blue Bird Land Speed Racer, Gunthermann, litho tin, bl w/yel trim, w/driver, 20", VG, A $1,265.00

Boy & Little Girl (Dancing?) Schuco, w/up, boy w/tin face & felt outfit, celluloid girl in dress, 5", EX, A $175.00

Boy on Scooter, Fisher, w/up, litho tin, boy working 2 pedals on 3-wheeled platform, 8", EX, A $770.00

Boy Pushing Hoop, w/up, pnt tin, boy on 2-wheeled base pusing solid wheel, 7" L, G, A $440.00

Boy w/Stick in Hand on Rocking Dog, w/up, pnt tin, dog is on curved runners, 7" L, VG, A $1,050.00

Bus, Tipp & Co, w/up, litho tin, long-nosed w/curved top & back, NP grille, wide front fenders & bumper, 11½", EX, A..$1,100.00

Bus ('Bonnet'), Distler, w/up, litho tin, long nose, flat roof, MDW, 14½", VG, A $715.00

Buster Brown & Tige, w/up, pnt tin figures under lamppost on beveled sq base, 8", Fair, A........................$1,100.00

Busy Lizzie, w/up, litho tin, full-figured lady bent at waist pushing mop, red & gr, 6½", EX, A $575.00

Buttercup Crawler, w/up, litho tin baby on all fours, 7", some rpt, A $385.00

Cabrio (VW Bug Convertible), CKO, w/up, litho tin w/compo driver, 6", VGIB, A.......................................$300.00

Carousel, Bing, w/up, pnt tin, children on horses, flag atop, 12" T, EX, A $520.00

Carousel, Bing, w/up, pnt tin, children on horses, flag atop, 12" T, EX+IB, A $1,430.00

Castle With Swan, Fleischmann, windup, painted tin, 10" wide, restored, A, $825.00. (Photo courtesy Bertoia Auctions)

Castle w/Swan, Fleischmann, w/up, pnt tin, castle w/center tower, swan circles on rod in rnd pan, 8½" dia, EX, A $300.00

Cavalryman w/Sword Drawn on Horse, Gunthermann, w/up, pnt tin, 6", nonworking o/w VG, A $520.00

Charlie Chaplin Dancer, hand lever or steam-powered, litho tin, stands on platform, 6¼", EX, A $465.00

Charlie Chaplin Walker, w/up, litho tin w/CI shoes, 9", VG, A $725.00

Charlie Chaplin Walker, w/up, tin w/cloth outfit, 6½", EXIB, A $800.00

Child Pushing Baby Swing, early, w/up, pnt tin, figures on beveled base, 7", VG, A $385.00

Chinese Man Balancing Flag on Globe on Forehead, w/up, bsk head, cloth outfit, stands on rnd base, 16", EX, A.$4,950.00

Chinese Man Pulling Two-Wheeled Box Cart, w/up, litho tin, figure pops up like a jack-in-the-box, 6", VG, A $500.00

City Bus, Tipp, w/up, litho tin, electric hedalamp, retractable roof, MDW w/Dunlop litho, 2 figures, 12", Fair, A..$220.00

Clown Acrobat, arms revolve to perform tricks, pnt tin, 7", Fair, A $165.00

Clown Crawling, early, w/up, pnt tin, clown w/outstretched arms & legs, 5½", G, A $410.00

Clown Doing Handstand, Issmayer, w/up, litho tin, 7", VG, A $700.00

Clown Drummer, Schuco, w/up, litho tin w/cloth outfit, 4½", EX (P box), A..$185.00

Clown Guitar Player, Distler, w/up, litho tin, standing on rnd base, 8", NM, A...$500.00

Clown Head Talker on Block Base, w/up, litho tin head, 7" T, EX, A $770.00

Clown Holding Pig by the Ears, Gunthermann, w/up, pnt tin, pig on 2 spoke wheels, 8", nonworking, G, A.......$1,200.00

Clown Juggler, Schuco, w/up, cloth outfit, 4¾", EX+IB, A..$385.00

Clown Musicians, Gunthermann, early, windup, painted tin, 8½" long, VG, A, $2,585.00. (Photo courtesy Bertoia Auctions)

Clown Operating Ferris Wheel, Becker, pnt tin, clown cranks wheel that allows 3-seat Ferris wheel revolve, 10x12" L, VG $2,200.00

Clown Operating Gondola Ride, Becker, w/up, pnt tin, clown & 3 gondolas w/figures on beveled base, 12" W, Fair, A ...$825.00

Clown Performing Handstand on Drum, Erco #600, w/up, litho tin, 8", EX, A $920.00

Clown Saxophone Player, Distler, w/up, litho tin, stands on rnd base, 8", EX+, A $410.00

Clown w/Umbrella, w/up, litho tin, spins in circles, 6", G, A.$300.00

Cominato 4003 Car, Schuco, w/up, tin, 7½", VG+, A ..$225.00

Coupe, Karl Bub, w/up, electric lights, litho tin, flat roof, lithoed spoke wheels, w/driver, 20", some rpt, A $1,980.00

Coupe, Karl Bub, w/up, electric lights, tires lithoed Dunlop Balloon Tires w/spoke wheels, 12", VG, A $1,430.00

Coupe, Tipp & Co, w/up, litho tin, yel & gr, 'Dunlop Cord' tires w/simulated spoke wheels, w/driver, 13", VG, A $550.00

Crane, w/up, litho tin, crane boom atop 4-legged housing w/lithoed windows showing interior, 18" T, G, A....$200.00

Delahaye, JF, w/up, diecast metal, working steering, 10", NMIB, A..$650.00

Disneyland Alweg-Monorail, Schuco, electrically powered, 14", unused, MIB, A...$400.00

Donald Duck, w/up, wht plush w/felt jacket & hat, 8", EX, A..$65.00

DPR Six Roadster, prewar (?), w/up, diecast metal, 4", VG+IB, A..$120.00

Elephant Performing, w/up, litho tin, catches celluloid balls in tub as they sprial up & out of tower, 10", EXIB, A ..$300.00

Essomobile Racer #3, w/up, litho tin w/lithoed spoke wheels, w/diver, 12", Fair+, A $850.00

Examico II 400 Convertible, Schuco, w/up, tin, w/operable steering, 7", NMIB, A.................................$330.00

Felix the Cat on Scooter, 1922, w/up, litho tin, 3-wheeled scooter, 7", EX, A.....................................$525.00

Felix the Cat Walker, w/up, litho tin, 6½", Fair, A $325.00

Fire Aerial Ladder Truck & Trailer, friction, tin, w/figure, 14½" L overall, NM+IB.................................$350.00

Fire Brigade Ladder Truck, Distler, w/up, litho tin, red w/yel extension ladder, open, w/figures, 11", Fair, A.........$245.00

Fire Pumper Truck, Orobr, w/up, litho tin, open seat, MSW, 6", Fair+, A $220.00

Fire Pumper Truck, R&B Co, w/up, litho tin, driver in open seat at center wheel, spoke wheels, red & gr, 6½", EX, A......$825.00

Fire Pumper Truck, w/up, litho tin, open driver's seat, gold boiler, driver & 2 firemen, 8", EX+, A.....................$355.00

Fire Truck, Distler, w/up, litho tin, open w/4 figures seated on back & ladder, bell on wire support, 4½", EX, A.....$130.00

Ford Model T Coupe, Bing, w/up, litho tin, blk w/wht-pnt metal spoke wheels, w/lady driver, 6½", EX, A.................$465.00

Ford Model T Roadster, Bing, w/up, litho tin, blk w/wht-pnt metal spoke wheels, w/lady driver, 6½", EX, A........$465.00

Ford Model T Touring Car, Orobr, w/up, litho tin, blk, MSW, 8", EX, A $355.00

Ford Model T w/Center Door, Bing, blk w/spoke wheels, w/driver, 6½", VG, A $300.00

Ford Model Touring Car, Bing, w/up, litho tin, blk w/wht-pnt spoke wheels, w/lady driver, 6½", EX, A.................$500.00

Fox, w/up, pnt tin, crawls in crouched position, pnt tin, 7½", rpt, A..$165.00

Gama Motorcycle Cop, US Zone, friction, litho tin w/compo driver, 7", EX+IB, A.................................$600.00

Giant Packard Convertible, JNF, w/up, litho tin, lt bl, WWT, working gearshift, 11½", EX, A.....................$275.00

Go Kart, Schuco #1055, w/up, tin car w/plastic driver, 6", NMIB, A..$245.00

Grinding Wheel Worker, w/up, pnt tin, flat-sided figure sharpening scissors at wheel, 5½" T, G.....................$100.00

Guitar Player, see Clown Guitar Player

Happy the Clown, Distler, w/up, litho tin, stands w/hands in pockets of bl plaid jacket, red & wht striped pants, 6", EX..$300.00

Harold Lloyd Bell Toy, lever activated, litho tin head, 6", G, A..$220.00

Harp Player, Gunthermann, early, w/up, pnt tin, figure seated at harp on rnd musical base, 7", G $400.00

Hessmobile Open Roadster w/Driver, Hess, w/up, litho tin, MSW, 7", EX, A $600.00

Hobo Walker, Gama, w/up, litho tin, toes exposed through shoe, hands in pockets, scarf around neck, 7", EX+.........$225.00

Horn Player & Dancer, Gunthermann, early, w/up, pnt tin, figures on beveled musical base, 8½" L, G, A $1,100.00

Howdy Doody Acrobat, Arnold, lever action, papier-maché & tin, Howdy performs on acrobat bar, 13" T, G+.......$100.00

Hupmobile (1934 model), w/up, litho tin, BRT, 6¼", VG, A.$330.00

Jackie Coogan 'The Kid' Walker, windup, lithographed tin, 7", VG, $400.00. (Photo courtesy Bertoia Auctions)

Foxy Grandpa, Gunthermann, early, windup, painted tin, grandpa on wheels does the splits, 8", VG, A, $1,320.00. (Photo courtesy Bertoia Auctions)

Jiggs Jazz Car, Nifty, 1920s, w/up, litho tin, Jiggs driving car, 6¾" L, P+, A $200.00

Jockey on Horse, w/up, litho tin, toy is mounted on 3 wheels, 5" L, VG, A $300.00

Lady (Old) Walking w/Broom & Basket on Back, Gunthermann, w/up, pnt tin, figure leans forward, 7", G, A.$400.00

Lighthouse w/Boat, w/up, pnt tin, lighthouse suspended over rnd pan w/boat on rod, 11½x10" dia, VG+, A...............$700.00

Limousine, Bing, w/up, litho tin, flat roof, long hood, MDW, w/driver, 11", EX+, A $220.00

Limousine, Bing, w/up, litho tin, flat roof over doorless cab, MSW, right-side driver, 7", EX, A $550.00

Limousine, Carette, w/up, tin, doorless front w/enclosed back, railed top, glass windows, NP trim, MSW, driver, 16", EX $5,500.00

Limousine, Distler, w/up, litho tin, b/o lights, flat roof, long hood, lithoed spoke wheels, driver, 10", EX+, A ..$1,650.00

Limousine, Distler, w/up, litho tin, b/o lights, flat roof, rear opening luggage box, MDW, driver, 14", EX, A ...$3,300.00

Limousine, Gunthermann, w/up, litho tin w/roll-down cloth top, electric lights, w/driver, 17½", VG+, A $2,200.00

Limousine, Karl Bub, w/up, litho tin, b/o lights, early model w/visor, lithoed spoke wheels, rear spare, drive, 10", VG $465.00

Limousine, Karl Bub, w/up, litho tin, b/o lights, later model w/visor, lithoed spoke wheels, rear spare, driver, 16", VG $990.00

Limousine, Karl Bub, w/up, litho tin, flat roof extends over open front seat w/driver, MSW, 14", EX, A $1,045.00

Limousine, Orbor, w/up, litho tin, rear opening doors, MSW, w/driver, 6", EX, A $650.00

Mac 700 Motorcycle w/Civilian Driver, Arnold, w/up, litho tin, red & silver version, 8", VG, A $900.00

Mac 700 Motorcycle w/Civilian Driver, Arnold, w/up, litho tin, blk & silver version, VG $700.00

Maggie & Jiggs, Nifty, w/up, litho tin, figures facing on wheeled platforms connected by wire, 7" L, EX, A $1,000.00

Maggie & Jiggs, Nifty, w/up, litho tin, figures facing on wheeled platforms connected by wire, 7" L, G, A $450.00

Magico Alfa Romeo, Schuco, w/up w/remote steering, 'magic' start & stop action, 9½", NMIB, A $650.00

Mercedes 1088, Schuco, w/up, tin, 9", nonworking o/w NM, A $150.00

Merry-Go-Round, Gunthermann, w/up, litho tin, 2 horse w/riders on red base w/red, wht & bl canopy, 7" T, EX, A $715.00

Mice Dancers, Schuco, w/up, plush papa bear in pants swings baby bear in grass skirt, 4", EX, A $385.00

Mickey Mouse Jazz Drummer, Nifty, plunger action, lithographed tin, 7", VG, A, $1,320.00. (Photo courtesy James D. Julia, Inc.)

Mickey Mouse Hurdy Gurdy w/Dancing Minnie Mouse, 1930s, w/up, litho tin, 8", VG, A $4,950.00

Military Searchlight Truck, Tipp & Co, w/up, litho tin w/camo pattern on open bed truck w/2 German soldiers, 10", EX, A $465.00

Mirako-Pat (Girl on Motorcycle), Schuco, w/up, litho tin, realistic hair, 5" L, EXIB, A $825.00

Mirakomot 1012 Cyclist, Schuco, w/up, litho tin, 4", EX, A.$275.00

Model T Sedan, Orber, w/up, litho tin, blk, MSW, 6", G+, A.$140.00

Monkeys on Seesaw, w/up, litho tin, monkeys tip their hats while on seesaw that sits on 2 lg wheels, 11" L, VG, A $325.00

Monocoupe (Rollover), Gunthermann, w/up, litho tin, 7" L, G, A $135.00

Mother Cradling Baby in Her Arms, w/up, compo w/cloth dress, 8½", GIB (plain brn cb box), A $100.00

Motodrill 1006 (Motorcycle), Schuco, w/up, litho tin, 5", VGIB, A $325.00

Motorcycle #2 w/Rider Leaning Forward, Schuco, w/up, litho tin, 5", EX, A $825.00

Motorcycle A 560 w/Rider, Arnold, w/up, litho tin, gr cycle w/extensive engine graphics, 7½" L, EX, A $1,430.00

Motorcycle A-754 w/German Soldier, w/up, litho tin, camo detail, lg red sparkling headlight, 7½" L, EX, A $825.00

Motorcycle Curvo 1000 w/Civilian Rider, Schuco, w/up, litho tin, 5", EX+, A $425.00

Motorcycle w/Couple & Child in Sidecar, Tipp & Co, w/up, Dunlop Cord lithoed on tin tires, 9½" L, VG, A .$1,980.00

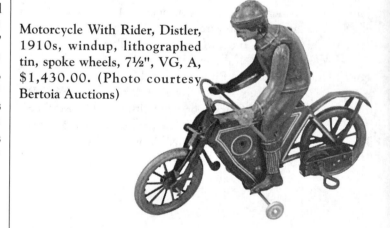

Motorcycle With Rider, Distler, 1910s, windup, lithographed tin, spoke wheels, 7½", VG, A, $1,430.00. (Photo courtesy Bertoia Auctions)

Motorcycle w/Sidecar, CKO, w/up, litho tin, mk K-342 on sidecar, w/driver & rider, 4", EX, A $350.00

Motorcyclist Doing Tricks (Trick Motorcycle), Technofix, w/up, litho tin, no sz given, EX+IB, A $575.00

Mountain Express Train, Technofix, litho tin, 16" L, EXIB, A $90.00

Mouse Acrobat, Schuco, articulated mouse on tin platform, 4", VG, A $275.00

Nifty Bus, Nifty, w/up, litho tin, 9½", VG, A $550.00

Opel 'Kaptain' Sedan, Gama, friction, tin w/lithoed interior, NP trim, 10", EXIB, A $400.00

Packard Convertible, see Gigant Packard Convertible

Peacock Walking, Hans Eberle, w/up, litho tin, 10" L, VG, A $350.00

Pheasant, w/up, litho tin, bird on 3 wheels, mostly red & bl, 10½", EX, A $220.00

Porter Carrying Bananas, Distler, w/up, litho tin, Black man in striped jacket w/bananas in ea hand, 7½", EX, A $990.00

Powerful Katrinka Holding Jimmy, Nifty, w/up, litho tin, 7", VG, A $1,200.00

Puss 'N Boots, 1950s, w/up, litho tin, 5", NM+ $225.00

Racer #2, Tipp, w/up, litho tin boattail w/lithoed Dunlop Cord tires, side spare, w/electric spot light, 15", G+, A....$900.00

Racer #7, Marklin, w/up, tin w/BRT, highly detailed, no driver, 14½", VG+, A $800.00

Radio 4012 Car, Schuco/US Zone, w/up, tin, turn on switch on switch on dash and car plays music, 6", NM+IB, A.$300.00

Roadster (Open), Tipp & Co, w/up, litho tin, celluloid windshield, lithoed MSW, lrear spare, lady driver, 12", EX, A $2,000.00

Rocket Express, Technofix, w/up, litho tin, w/1 car, 15" L, VG, A $100.00

Roundabout w/Parachutist, Muller & Kadeder, w/up, pnt tin, circles tower w/counter weight, 12", A $1,430.00

Ruck-Ruck Auto, Tellus, w/up, litho tin, 6½", EX, A $550.00

Rudy the Ostrich, Nifty, windup, lithographed tin, 8", EX, $550.00. (Photo courtesy Bertoia Auctions)

Sailor Walker, Gama, w/up, litho tin, wht hair, hands in pockets, 7", EX, A $250.00

Saloon Auto, Bing, w/up, litho tin, glass windshild, dummy headlights, MDW, right-side driver, 13", VG, A $900.00

Saloon Auto, Bing, w/up, litho tin, open windshield, MSW, right-side driver, 11", rpt, A $550.00

Saloon Auto, Tipp & Co, w/up, litho tin, flat roof, lithoed spoke wheels, w/driver, 15½", VG, A $2,200.00

Saxophone Player, see Clown Saxophone Player

Scull w/Man Holding Oars, w/up, litho tin, yel & red, 11", VG+, A $550.00

Sedan, Bing, w/up, litho tin, lt bl w/blk roof & running boards, MDW, opening side doors, 6", VG, A.....................$400.00

Shuttling Train, Arnold, w/up, litho tin, steam engine moves car back & forth, 15" L, EXIB, A $150.00

Skidoodle, Nifty, w/up, litho tin, 8", VG, A $1,100.00

Steam Tractor, Orbor, w/up, litho tin, front roller w/spokes, 2 lg rear spoke wheels, red & gr, 6", EX, A $125.00

Stork w/Baby, w/up, litho tin 'brick' housing w/plastic stork on rod, 13", L, NM+IB, A $200.00

Studio Racer, Schuco, modern edition, w/up, tin, complete w/ramp & tools, 5½", MIB, A $200.00

Swanberg, see Castle w/Swan

Tandem Cyclists, Niedemeier, w/up, litho tin, 2 uniform cyclists in shared platform, 6", EX, A $475.00

Taxi, Bing, w/up, litho tin, flat roof extends over doorless front seat, MSW, right-side driver, 7", EX, A....................$550.00

Taxi, Carette, windup, lithographed tin, 13", EX+, $3,575.00. (Photo courtesy Bertoia Auctions)

Taxi, Fisher, w/up, litho tin w/roof over driver's seat, open back, spoke wheels, driver & 2 lady passengers, 12", EX, A............$2,640.00

Taxi, Karl Bub, w/up, litho tin, blk & orange, w/disk wheels, 7½", VG, A $425.00

Taxi, RB Co, w/up, litho tin, luggage rack atop simulated wood roof over doorless cab w/driver, spoke wheels, 8", VG $825.00

Teddy, w/up, plush dog w/shoe in mouth, 5" L, EXIB, A .$300.00

Telesteering Car 3000, Schuco, w/up, tin, 4", complete, VG+IB, A $125.00

Tellus Horse Cart, Gunoka & Kelch, w/up, litho tin, seated driver, 2 spoke wheels, 6½", VG, A $300.00

Three Little Pigs as Musicians, Schuco, w/up, felt over tin bodies, 4½", VG, A, set...$600.00

Thunderbird Convertible Coupe, 1950s, friction, litho tin w/compo driver, working wipers, 13", EX.................$125.00

Tippco Bus, Tippco, w/up, litho tin, steerable wheels, 9¼", VG+, A $200.00

Toboggan, Technofix, w/up, litho tin figure-8 track w/cars, 22", EXIB, A $150.00

Toonerville Trolley, Distler, 1922, litho tin, 5" L, G, A..$500.00

Toonerville Trolley, Nifty, w/up, litho tin, 7", VG, A.....$750.00

Touring Car (Open), w/up, litho tin, long nose, full running boards, w/driver, 11", VG, A $200.00

Touring Car, Carette #50, windup, tin, with four figures, 8", VG, A, $2,475.00. (Photo courtesy Bertoia Auctions)

Touring Car (Open) w/Right-Side Driver, Bing, w/up, tin w/lithoed arched radiator & hood, MSW, 11", EX, A $1,000.00

Touring Cycle w/Rider, Fisher, w/up, litho tin, MSW, 7½", VG, A...$1,200.00

Tractor w/Wagon & Roller, Gunthermann, w/up, litho tin, farmer driving tractor w/wagon & roller 14" overall, EX, A..$190.00

Trick Motorcyclist, see Motorcyclist Doing Tricks

Yellow Taxi, Bing, w/up, litho tin, blk & orange, 8½" L, A..$450.00

Yellow Taxi #11249, Gunthermann, w/up, litho tin, orange & blk w/orange hubs, w/driver, 9", EX, A.................$1,320.00

JAPANESE

Acrocycle, Alps, w/up, litho tin, clown performs tricks on motorcycle, 6", EXIB, A $400.00

Agajanian #98 Race, see Midget Racers

Air Carousel (Kiddie City Amusement Park), AHI, w/up, litho tin, 7", NM+IB, A $175.00

Airplane, w/up, bl litho tin top-wing w/celluloid pilot's head, single sm prop, orange star decal, 4" W, VG, A $50.00

Airplane w/Boy Pilot, w/up, lg celluloid figure w/goggles atop pilot's hat in 3-wheeled litho tin plane w/bell, 5", EX+ $450.00

Airport Limousine, Ichiko, friction, litho tin Chevy Impala w/luggage rack on top, 7½", NM+IB, A $125.00

All Star (Baseball) Victory Car, TK, friction, litho tin, 9", NM+IP, A $150.00

All State Express Bus (See America First), Masudaya, friction, litho tin, open windows, 8½", EXIB, A $150.00

American Bus Lines (Bonnet) Bus, AN (Naito), friction, litho tin, 12", EX, A $825.00

Androcles Lion, Linemar, w/up, plush lion appearing to lick his paw, 6", VG+IB, A $115.00

Animal Carousel, Y, w/up, litho tin, dogs & cats go around in 4 carousel cars as bell rings on tower, 6", EXIB, A......$135.00

Animal Train, see Express Animal Train

Anti-Aircraft, SSS, friction, litho tin, w/driver & soldiers, 11½", MIB, A...$150.00

Armored Car, Kawahara (K), friction, tin, gunner standing behind 2 ack-ack cannons, silver tone, 7½", NM+IB, A $150.00

Armored Car, prewar, w/up, litho tin, turret on top & side guns, gray & orange, 9", VG+, A $425.00

Armored Car, Tomiyama, prewar, w/up, litho tin, bl, yel & red detail, gun turret on top, 6-wheeled, 13", G, A $685.00

Army Combat Carrier, 1960s, friction, tin, 19" L, EXIB, A ..$60.00

Atom Jet Racer #58, Y, friction, lithographed tin, 28", EX+, A, $3,850.00. (Photo courtesy Bertoia Auctions)

Atom Racer #153, Y, friction, litho tin, WWT, driver in open seat w/windshield, 16", NM+IB, A $4,950.00

Austin A50 Cambridge Deluxe (1955), K, friction, 8", NMIB, A (Est: $450) $825.00

Auto Pulling House Trailer, 1930s, w/up, litho tin w/NP trim, kidney-shaped trailer w/2 wheels, 8" overall, EX+, A $550.00

Automatic Racing Game, Haji, lever mechanisim, litho tin, no sz given, EXIB, A $300.00

Avenue Bus, see Sight Seeing Bus

Babes in Toyland Marching Soldier, Linemar, windup, lithographed tin, 6", EX+IB, A, $425.00. (Photo courtesy Bertoia Auctions)

Baby Scooter, Y, friction, litho tin, 6½", EX+IB, A........$990.00

Baby Super Express (Train), friction, litho tin, 20", NMIB, A $115.00

Baby Swinging, prewar, w/up, celluloid figure on wire swing apparatus, 6½", EX+, A...$100.00

Banjo Player, late 1800s-early 1900s, pendulum & spring-driven w/up, litho tin flat figure on base, 6x5x3", EX, A.$1,900.00

Banjo Player (Monkey), w/up, plush in cloth outfit, 6", EXIB, A..$50.00

Barky (Dog), Kanto, friction, litho tin, 6½" L, EXIB.......$30.00

Bear Golfer, TPS, w/up, litho tin, 4¼", VGIB, A...........$125.00

Best Made Marionette Theatre, 2 celluloid marionette dancers, 6x14", EXIB, A..$465.00

Big Joe Chef, w/up, litho tin figure w/bell at waistline, 6½", EXIB, A..$125.00

Black Smith Teddy, w/up, plush, 6", EXIB, A.................$180.00

Blue Ribbon (5th Ave) Bus, TN, friction, b/o lights, tin w/passengers lithoed in windows, 10½", NMIB, A..........$250.00

Bobo the Magician (Happy-Go-Lucky Magician), TN, litho tin, 8", VGIB, A..$325.00

Boxing (Figures), w/up, 2 celluloid figures on 2-wheeled litho tin bases connected by wire, 6" L, EX+IB, A.................$175.00

Boxing Bear, TN, w/up, plush & tin, bear punches bag on sq platform, 6½", MIB, A..$100.00

Boxing Monkey, #697, w/up, plush monkey in shorts & boxing gloves standing on platform w/punching bag, 8", EXIB, A $100.00

Boy Feeding Chicken on Platform, w/up, litho tin, 7" T, EX .$400.00

Boy Lying on Sled, w/up, litho tin w/felt outfit, 6" L, VG, A..$75.00

Boy on Rabbit Scooter, friction, litho tin, no sz given, EX, A.$770.00

Boy on Scooter, Kuramochi (CK), prewar, w/up, celluloid boy figure on tin scooter, bell rings, 7½", EX, A $625.00

Bruno, Alps, w/up, bear w/plush head, cloth jacket & litho tin pants cleaning eye glasses, 6", EXIB, A.....................$160.00

Bubble Blowing Bear, Alps, w/up, tin, plush & plastic, 8", EX+, A $150.00

Bubble Boy, w/up, litho tin, boy standing on tree stump, 8", EXIB, A $125.00

Cadillac Convertible w/Driver & Lady Passenger, friction, tin w/lithoed interior, NP trim, 13", EX+, A.................$550.00

Cameraman Bear, w/up, tin & plush w/cloth pants & hat, standing holding camera, 7", NMIB, A $170.00

Campus Express (Auto), Linemar, w/up, litho tin, 9½", G, A .$88.00

Car (Convertible) Pulling Boat & Trailer, Haji, friction, tin, boat is friction & crank-op, 16½" overall, EX+IB, A $225.00

Car (Convertible) Pulling House Trailer, Haji, friction, tin, 16" overall, VG+IB, A..$250.00

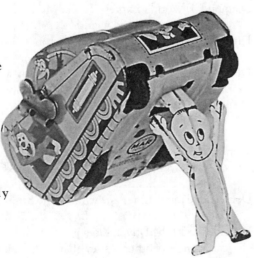

Casper the Friendly Ghost Rollover Tank, Linemar, windup, lithographed tin, VG, A, $325.00. (Photo courtesy Randy Inman Auctions)

Caterpillar, see Green Caterpillar

Champion Racers, see Midget Racer

Champion! (Stunt Car), SY, friction, w/pop-up driver, 8½", EXIB, A $200.00

Chef on Roller Skates, TPS, w/up, Black litho tin figure w/articulated arms, 6", G, A..$300.00

Chicken Feeding From Farmer's Pan on Base, Toyodo Seizo, 1920s, w/up, litho tin, chicken rocks while feeding, 5", VG, A $350.00

Choo Choo Train, Linemar, w/up, litho tin, 12", EXIB, A .$115.00

Chrysler Airflow Sedan, w/up, pnt tin w/NP grille, bumpers & rear spare, 5", VG, A..$165.00

Chrysler Convertible (1950s), Hadson, friction, litho tin, w/driver, 10", NM+IB, A..$800.00

Chrysler Sedan, Kuramochi, ca 1931, w/up, litho tin w/NP grille, bumper & headlights, side-mount spare, 8¾", VG, A .$600.00

Circus (Car w/Elephant Driver Balancing Globe w/Trunk), friction, litho tin, 8", EX, A..$100.00

Circus Boy, w/up, litho tin, 6", EXIB, A.........................$150.00

Circus Car, friction, litho tin, clown driver, 6" L, EXIB, A .$125.00

Circus Car w/Clown, TET, friction, litho tin, clown rocks back & forth as car does wheelies, 5½", EXIB, A $200.00

Circus Car w/Performing Seal, friction, litho tin, 8", EX, A.$100.00

Circus Clown, Cragstan, clown moves along string, cloth suit w/litho tin head & limbs, celluloid feet, 9", EXIB, A .$135.00

Circus Clown, w/up, litho tin w/cloth suit, rubber hands, hangs from bar & flips over, 6", EXIB, A $100.00

Circus Coaster, w/up, litho tin, 12" L, EXIB, A..............$225.00

Circus Hoop, MT, windup, lithographed tin, 6" dia, EXIB, A, $300.00. (Photo courtesy Bertoia Auctions)

Circus Jeep, Excelo, friction, litho tin, w/clown driver & elephant passenger balancing a globe, 5¾", NMIB, A.$200.00

Circus Parade, TPS, w/up, litho tin, elephant leads 3 performing clowns, 11" L, EXIB, A..$175.00

Circus Plane, w/up, litho tin, clown pilot, 4" W, EXIB, A .$100.00

Circus Trailer, AHI, friction, tin, truck pulls cage trailer w/crank-op platform, 11½", NM+, A $250.00

Circus Tricycle, Y, w/up, tin trike w/celluloid rider, front tire rises off the ground, 4", NM+IB, A.........................$125.00

Circus Trio Clown, Alps, w/up, plastic w/cloth outfit, 6½", VGIB, A..$30.00

Circus Truck, friction, litho tin cage truck w/animals, red & yel, 10" L, EXIB, A $125.00

Clever Puppy, TN, w/up, blk litho tin Scottie dog, 6" T, EXIB..$35.00

Clown Circus Cyclist, TPS, w/up, litho tin figure in cloth costume on lg-wheeled cycle w/sm back wheel, 6½", EX, A $300.00

Clown Hobo (Musical Band), w/up, plush & vinyl, 6½, EXIB, A..$65.00

Clown Magician, TN, w/up, tin w/cloth outfit, clown lifts hat & rabbit disappears, 7", EXIB, A $325.00

Clown on Motorcycle, w/up, litho tin, 6" L, EX, A $275.00

Clown on Roller Skates, w/up, litho tin, 7", VG+IB, A.$300.00

Convertible, Chiko, friction, tin, with driver, 14", EX+, A, $600.00. (Photo courtesy Bertoia Auctions)

Clown on Tricycle, TPS, windup, lithographed tin with cloth outfit, EX, A, $220.00. (Photo courtesy Bertoia Auctions)

Clown Performing on Donkey (Donkey Clown), w/up, celluloid clown on litho tin donkey, EXIB..............................$200.00

Clown Performing w/Balls & Balancing Plate, w/up, compo & litho tin w/cloth outfit, 11", G, A $125.00

Clown Standing on Hands (w/shoes on hands) & Balancing Ball on Feet, w/up, cloth costume, 10", EX $125.00

Clown Standing w/Tambourine, w/up, litho tin w/cloth costume, clown bends as he shakes instruments, 7", EX, A $75.00

Clown Trainer & His Acrobatic Dog, TPS, w/up, litho tin, 4½", EXIB, A $275.00

Clown w/Tambourine, see Tambourine Clown

Clown w/Umbrella on Unicycle, w/up, litho tin, clown performs atop 6" dia circus tub, EX, A $175.00

Condor Motorcycle, IY, friction, litho tin w/BRT, integral driver, 12", NM, A...$1,150.00

Coney Test Driver, KO, crank-op, tin, driver in bump-&-go car, 5½", EX+IB, A $125.00

Convertible w/Giant Boat, SSS, 1950s, friction, 17" overall, EX (partial box), A...$175.00

Cowboy on Horse, prewar, w/up, celluloid, horse has jtd legs, 6" T, unused, NM+IB, A...$200.00

Cowboy on Rocking Horse, Cragstan, w/up, litho tin, wht horse w/red rocker, 7" L, EXIB, A.......................................$245.00

Cowboy w/Lasso on Horse, w/up, celluloid figure w/tin lasso on tin horse, 7" T, VG, A $125.00

Cragstan Camper Truck, friction, litho tin, 8", EXIB, A .$140.00

Cragstan Galaxie Stock Racing Car #5, NGS, 1960s, friction, tin, 405 HP & flames on hood, 9½", NMIB, A.......$365.00

Cragstan Highway Patrol (PD) Car, Ichiko, friction, litho tin Oldsmobile w/speedometer on trunk, 13", NMIB, A.$175.00

Cragstan Police Car Chase, w/up, litho tin, 9" L, VG+IB, A.$75.00

Cubby the Reading Bear, Alps, w/up, plush w/cloth overalls, 7", EXIB, A $195.00

Dancing Girl, w/up, celluloid, sm rnd 4-wheeled platform, 8½", NM+, A...$425.00

Dancing Sam, S&E, w/up, litho tin figure w/cane on drum base, 8½", EX, A $125.00

Dandy, Mikuni, w/up, litho tin figure w/rubber walking stick, 5½", EX+IB, A $150.00

DC Transit Bus, ATC, friction, litho tin w/celluloid wheels, 15", VG, A $275.00

DC Transit Bus (GM), ATC, 1960s, friction, tin, 17", EX+IB, A $400.00

DC Transit/Arcticooler Bus, ATC, friction, 17", EX, A .$250.00

DeSoto Sedan, Asahito, 1950, friction, tin, maroon w/NP trim, 7½", EX+, A $110.00

Diamond Racer, Y, friction, litho tin, flashing lights, BRT, w/driver, 15½", NM+IB, A $1,260.00

Diamond T Gasoline Tanker, 1930s, w/up, litho tin w/NP trim, yel & red w/gr, 8", EX, A $770.00

Diamond T World's Express Truck, Modern Toys, w/up, litho tin w/NP trim, yel & red w/gr, 8½", NMIB, A...........$2,090.00

Dino-the-Dinosaur From the Flintstones, Linemar, w/up, litho tin, 9", VGIB, A $440.00

Disney Bus, Masudaya/WDP, friction, tin w/Disney characters lithoed in windows, 16", EX+IB (Japanese box), A.$500.00

Disney Electric Line Street Car, Masudaya, 1950s, friction, tin w/Disney characters lithoed in windows, 11", NMIB, A..$675.00

Disneyland Volunteers Fire Aerial Ladder Truck, Linemar, friction, Pluto driver w/Mickey, Donald & Nephew, 18", EX, A $875.00

Dockyard Crane, Linemar, w/up, litho tin, complete w/logs & pallet, 9" L, EXIB, A...$100.00

Donald (Duck) the Driver, Linemar, w/up, litho tin, Donald driving car w/imges of other Disney charcters, 7", EXIB, A $650.00

Donald Duck, Linemar, squeeze hdl & Donald opens bill & quacks, litho tin & plush, 6", EX, A $135.00

Donald Duck Car, Linemar, push down head to operate, tin w/lithoed Disney characters, 5½", G+, A $170.00

Donald Duck Climbing Fireman, Linemar, litho tin, 12" (including ladder), EX, A..$300.00

Donald Duck Delivery Wagon, Linemar, friction, litho tin w/plastic head, 5½", EX, A $355.00

Donald Duck Drummer, Linemar/WDP, w/up, litho tin, 6½", EXIB, A $425.00

Donald Duck in Convertible, Linemar, w/up, litho tin, bobbin' head, Minnie & Mickey lithoed on hood, 7", VG, A.$250.00

Donald Duck on Dipsey Car (Disney Dipsey Car), Linemar, w/up, litho tin, 5½" L, EXIB, A $525.00

Donald Duck on Motorcycle, Linemar/WDP, friction, litho tin, Donald figure intagral w/motorcycle, 3¾", EX, A ...$200.00

Donald Duck on Tricycle, Linemar, w/up, celluloid figure on litho tin tricycle w/bell, 4" L, EXIB, A.....................$300.00

Donald Duck the Drummer, Linemar, w/up, litho tin, 6", EX, A...$425.00

Donald Duck Walker, Borgfeldt, w/up, celluloid long-billed Donald w/slit eyes, 5½", NMIB, A $2,100.00

Donald Duck Walker, Borgfeldt, w/up, celluloid long-billed Donald w/slit eyes, 5½", VGIB, A $1,700.00

Donald Duck Walker, Borgfeldt/Lewis & Scott, 1930s, w/up, 11", EXIB, A $500.00

Donald Duck Whirligig, windup, celluloid, 10½", NM, A, $3,300.00. (Photo courtesy Bertoia Auctions)

Donald Duck's Go Power Gasoline Co Tanker Truck, Linemar, friction, litho tin, Mouseketeer emblem on back, 13", EX, A $450.00

Donkey, Marusan, w/up, standing upright, plush w/cloth outfit, smoking pipe, 10", EXIB, A..................................$125.00

Donkey Clown, see Clown Performing on Donkey

Donkey Truck, friction, litho tin, donkey playing drum on back on flatbed truck, 8" L, G, A.................................$75.00

Dream Car, 1950s, friction, lithographed tin, with driver, 16", NMIB, $4,950.00. (Photo courtesy Bertoia Auctions)

Dragon Fly, Cragstan, w/up, litho tin & plastic, 8½" L, VG+IB, A $75.00

Dream Car, 1950s, friction, litho tin, w/driver, 16", G ...$550.00

Drummer Boy, w/up, compo body w/celluloid head & hands, cloth outfit & hat, wood base, 11", EX, A $200.00

Drummer Jolly (Clown), w/up, clown in cloth costume standing & beating on drum, 6½", EXIB, A...........................$130.00

Duck, see Strutting Duck

Duck on Skis, Linemar, 1950s, w/up, litho tin, 4½", NM+ $125.00

Duck Postman, TBS, w/up, litho tin, 4½", EX, A $245.00

Dugan's Bakery Truck, HTC, friction, tin, wht w/blk hood, blk advertising on sides, EX, A.......................................$200.00

Dum-Dum & His Drum, w/up, plush elephant in red vest seated w/drum, 6", EXIB, A..$40.00

Dump Truck (Bonnet), Y, friction, litho tin, lever-op bed, NMIB, A..$425.00

Easter on Parade, friction, tin & celluloid, bunny pulling chicks on sleigh, 5½", NMIB, A $100.00

Eat At Joes Sign Man, see Ko-Ko Mechanical Sandwich Man

Electric Train, Daiya, friction, lime gr tin w/recessed windows & rubber tires, 17½", NM, A $130.00

Excursion Motor Cab, Modern Toys, prewar, w/up, tin, long nose, w/driver & 4 diecut passengers, 9", EX, A $825.00

Express Animal Train, friction, litho tin, 15", EXIB, A....$45.00

Farm Truck, friction, tin, high-sided stake bed w/2 horses, opening rear gate, 5" L, NMIB, A $65.00

Fast Freight Continental Express Truck, MT, friction, litho tin, NMIB (box reads Transport), A (Est: $25-$50) $155.00

Ferdinand the Bull, Linemar, w/up, litho tin, 6", VG, A .$125.00

Ferris Wheel Truck, TN, friction, litho tin, 8", EXIB, A .$300.00

Figaro (Pinocchio), Linemar, 1950, friction, litho tin figure, 3", EX+ $75.00

Fighting Bull, Alps, w/up, plush, EXIB, A.........................$40.00

Fire Aerial Ladder Truck, friction, litho tin, open cab, w/driver, side figure & 2 back figures, red w/yel boom, 10", EX...$100.00

Fire Engine w/Aerial Extension Ladders, friction, litho tin, right-sided driver's cab w/light, 7½", EXIB, A $55.00

Fire Wings, see Pontiac Fire Wings

Fishing Boy, Linemar, w/up, 5", NMIB, A......................$450.00

Fishing Monkey on Whale, TPS, w/up, litho tin, 9" L, EXIB, A...$250.00

Flintstones Semi-Truck, friction, litho tin, 12", VG, A..$330.00

Flower (Skunk), Linemar, friction, litho tin, 3" L, EX......$50.00

Flying Birds, TPS, w/up, litho tin, 2 birds suspended on wire above rnd base, 4" birds, 7½" T, EXIB, A $325.00

Ford Convertible (1958) w/Dog Driver, Alps, friction, tin, 8", EX, A $135.00

Ford Delivery Van (FK1000/15), friction, tin, BRT, 8¼", NMIB, A $275.00

Ford Sedan (A Souvenir of the Century of Progress Chicago 1934 Ford V8), w/up, litho tin, 7", nonworking, G, A $600.00

Ford Sedan (1935), Kuramochi, w/up, litho tin w/NP grille, 7¾", VG, A $385.00

Ford Stake Truck, Marusan, friction, tin, w/rubber mud flaps, Ford hubcaps, 8", NM+IB, A $150.00

Fox the Magician, TN, w/up, plush & tin, 6", EXIB, A..$225.00

Fred Flintstone on Dino, Linemar/Hanna-Barbera, 1960s, w/up, litho tin, NMIB, A $400.00

G-Men Motorcycle w/Rider, friction, litho tin, rubber front tire, 9½" L, EX, A $750.00

Galaxie Stock Racing Car, see Cragstan Galaxie Stock Racing Car

Gasoline Tanker, see Diamond T

General (Stake) Truck, Y, 1950s, friction, GMC cab, NMIB, A $300.00

Giant Bus, Yonezawa, friction, litho tin w/bl-tinted windows, 23", VG, A $400.00

Go-Round Tram Car, Yonezawa, w/up, litho tin, 5½" sq, NMIB, A $150.00

Golden Apples Delivery Truck, 1960s, friction, litho tin, rear door opens, gr & wht, 6½", NM+ $100.00

Golden Bear, GW Products, windup, plush, tin feet, 6½", EX, A, $135.00. (Photo courtesy Bertoia Auctions)

Golden Jet Racer #10, 1960s, litho tin w/tin driver's head, BRT, 10", EXIB $50.00

Good Time Charlie (Clown Blows Party Favor), Alps, w/up, cloth outfit, 12½", NM+IB, A $125.00

Goofy on Tricycle, Linemar/WDP, 1950s, 7", EX $1,000.00

Gordon's Farm Products Truck, MSK, friction, wht tin w/advertising on sides, 7" L, EX, A $225.00

Graham Paige Police Car, Kuramochi, ca 1936-37, w/up, litho tin w/NP grille & headlights, 11", EX, A $1,045.00

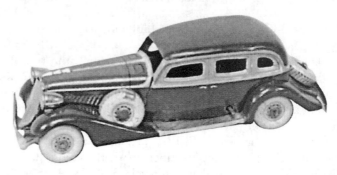

Graham Paige Sedan (1932), Kuramochi, windup, lithographed tin with nickel-plated detail, 11", EX, A, $3,025.00. (Photo courtesy Bertoia Auctions)

Graham Paige Sedan (1933), Kosuge, w/up, litho tin, NP detail & luggage rack, 8½", EX, A $825.00

Graham Paige Sedan (1933), Kosuge, w/up, litho tin, NP detail & luggage rack, 8½", G, A $400.00

Grasshopper, Marusan, w/up, mostly tin, realistic walking motion, 7", MIB, A $250.00

Great Swanee Paddle Boat, friction, litho tin, 11", EXIB, A $55.00

Greyhound Bus, friction, litho tin, wht, bl & silver w/driver lithoed in windshield, 10", VG, A $55.00

Ham 'N Sam (Black Jigger & Piano Player), Linemar, litho tin, 4x5", EXIB, A $1,250.00

Hand Standing Pierrot (Clown Standing on Hands), Occupied, Japan, w/up, cloth costume, celluloid head/hands, 7", NMIB, A $150.00

Happy Bunny, Nomura, w/up, litho tin rabbit in lithoed outfit beats on drums while standing, 8", EX+IB, A..........$520.00

Happy Bunny at Piano, w/up, plush & litho tin, 8" T, EXIB, A $220.00

Happy Car (Convertible Sedan), Alps, friction, BRT, 9", EXIB, A $100.00

Happy Doggy, Rosko, w/up, plush dog chewing on bone, 6" L, EX $50.00

Happy-Go-Lucky Magician, see Bobo the Magician

Harley-Davidson Auto Cycle, TN, friction, litho tin, BRT, 9", NM+IB $600.00

Harley-Davidson Auto Cycle, TN, friction, litho tin, BRT, 9", VG+, A $155.00

Harley-Davidson Motorcycle, friction, litho tin, BRT, integral driver, 15", EX, A $1,540.00

Henry & Porter on Elephant, Borgfeldt, prewar, w/up, celluloid, Henry on elephant's trunk w/porter on back, 8" L, EX, A..........$600.00

Highway Patrol Car (w/Broderick Crawford), MS, friction, litho tin, blk & wht, 5½", EXIB, A $225.00

Honk-A-Long Children Bus, Kanto, friction, litho tin scenicruiser, 9", EXIB, A $90.00

House Trailer, see Car (Convertible) Pulling House Trailer

Hudson Sedan, 1950s, friction, tin w/NP trim, BRT, 9½", EX, A..$175.00

Hulla Girl, w/up, celluloid & pnt tin figure w/spun yarn skirt, twists at waist, 8¼", EX, A..................................$110.00

Hungry Cub, Alps, w/up, plush bear seated w/milk bottle & cup, 6", EXIB, A..$50.00

Hurricane Racer #58, MT, 1950s, friction, litho tin, 13", EX+..$775.00

Ice Cream Truck (Ford FK 1000 Van), KTS, friction, tin, wht w/lithoed bl & wht awning & serving window, 8", VG+, A..$300.00

Ice Cream Vendor, Ohta, friction, litho tin, figure seated on 3-wheeled ice-cream cart, 5½", NMIB, A....................$425.00

Indian on Horse, prewar, celluloid, horse has jtd legs, 6" T, NM+IB, A..$250.00

Indian Train, Mitsuhashi, friction, litho tin, 10", NMIB, A..$100.00

Indy 500 Racer #8, friction, litho tin, realistic w/removable hub spinners & tires, orange & wht, 15", EX, A.............$450.00

Inflatable Bear-Cat Driver, S&E, friction, bear driver in inflatable '57 Corvette, 8" L, NMIB, A.............................$65.00

Iszuzu Dump Truck, ATC, friction, litho tin, 9½" L, EXIB, A..$100.00

Japan Sight-Seeing Bus, 1960s, friction, litho tin, 10½", NMIB, A..$200.00

Joe's Kitchen Wagon, H, friction, litho tin, side of van opens to reveal Joe in his kitchen, 10", EX, A......................$225.00

JTY Dump Truck (GMC Cab), Y, 1950s, friction, tin, red & wht w/yel hubs, 14", NM+IB, A..$175.00

J.T.Y. Y53 Racer, Y, friction, lithgraphed tin, with driver, 13", EX, A, $450.00. (Photo courtesy Randy Inman Auctions)

Judo Man, w/up, tin w/cloth judo outfit, 9½", NMIB, A..$575.00

Juggling Clown, Alps, w/up, clown in cloth suit twirling balls & plates on sticks, 6", EXIB, A..............................$300.00

Juggling Clown, TN, w/up, clown in cloth suit twirling rings on sticks, 6", EXIB, A..$115.00

Jumping Rabbit w/Baby, Y, w/up, litho tin, baby on mother's back, 5" L, EXIB, A..$135.00

Jumping Racer, Marusan, friction, 2 litho tin racers mk Jauar & Tiger, complete w/cb ramp, 4¾" ea, NMIB, A.........$250.00

Jupiter Jeep w/Cart, SSS, 1950s, friction, 12" L, NMIB, A..$135.00

King Scooter, Yonezawa, friction, litho tin, BRT, 9", EX, A..$1,540.00

Knitting Cat, TN, w/up, wht plush, 6", EX, A................$125.00

Ko-Ko Mechanical Sandwich Man, TN, w/up, litho tin & vinyl w/cloth outfit, 7", EXIB, A....................................$125.00

Land Rover, Cragstan, friction, gr tin, realistic detail, NMIB, A..$350.00

Lester the Jester, Alps, w/up, celluloid & tin clown figure in cloth costume twirls cane, 9½", NMIB, A...............$250.00

Limousine, w/up, litho tin, roof extends over open front seat, long nose w/flat front, MSW, w/driver, 7", VG+, A..$550.00

Lion, see Roaring Lion

Little Monkey Artist, TN, plush w/cloth jacket & hat, seated w/artist's palette, 7", EXIB, A................................$200.00

Little Monkey Shiner, TN, w/up, plush figure w/vinyl face, 6", EXIB, A..$100.00

Little Shoemaker, w/up, litho tin figure w/realistic wht hair, cloth jacket, EXIB, A..$170.00

Lucky (Flying Man), SY, w/up, litho tin, sq-headed figure in space car w/Playland flag, 6" L, NMIB, A..............$450.00

Lucky Baby (Sewing) Machine, windup, celluloid baby seated at lithographed tin sewing machine, 5x5", EX+IB, A, $400.00. (Photo courtesy Bertoia Auctions)

Lucky Monkey Playing Billiards, TPS, w/up, litho tin, 4½", NMIB, A..$300.00

Lullaby Mother, Alps/Rock Valley, w/up, tin & vinyl, mother in cloth dress holding baby, 10", unused, NM+IB, A...$150.00

Mary & Her Little Lamb, w/up, celluloid figure holding umbrella w/twirling balls, 6½", EX, A..................................$275.00

Merry Tourist Land, K, w/up, litho tin, 6" sq, NMIB, A..$100.00

Merry-Go-Round, Kuramochi (CK), w/up, tin w/celluloid riders & balls spinning as ride goes around, 6" sq base, VG+, A..$825.00

Merry-Go-Round, w/up, celluloid & wood, chicks-&-balls, lithoed base, 7", EXIB, A..$100.00

Merry-Go-Round Truck, friction, litho tin, 8" L, EX, A..$150.00

Mickey Mouse (Walking), Borgfeldt, w/up, celluloid, 6", EXIB, A..$11,000.00

Mickey Mouse & Minnie Acrobats, WD, w/up, celluloid figures on wire apparatus, 12", VGIB....................................$650.00

Mickey Mouse & Minnie on Seesaw, wind rubber band & celluloid figures seesaw back & forth, EX........................$900.00

Mickey Mouse Carousel, Borgfeldt, w/up, celluloid, Mickey on wheeled platform w/beaded 'whirling' umbrella, 8", VG+IB, A..$2,200.00

Mickey Mouse Dipsey Car, Linemar, w/up, litho tin, 5", VG+IB, A..$400.00

Mickey Mouse on Four-Wheeled Horse, w/up, celluloid, 7½", EX, A..$2,185.00

Mickey Mouse on Scooter, Linemar/WDP, w/up, tin, 4½", EX, A $450.00

Mickey Mouse Rambling, Whirling Tail, and Walking, w/up, celluloid, plump blk & wht Mickey w/red shorts & shoes, articulated arms & head, 7", NM+ $1,600.00

Mickey Mouse Riding Pluto, Occupied Japan, w/up, celluloid, Pluto w/lg front wheels & 2 sm back wheels, 6½", NM+, A..$1,900.00

Mickey Mouse Roller Skater, Linemar, w/up, litho tin w/cloth pants, 6", EX $650.00

Mickey Mouse Roller Skater, Linemar, windup, lithographed tin with cloth pants, 6", NMIB, A, $3,575.00. (Photo courtesy Bertoia Auctions)

Mickey Mouse Unicyclist, Linemar, w/up, litho tin w/cloth pants, 5½", VG, A..$450.00

Mickey Mouse Walking, Borgfeldt/WDE, 1930s, w/up, celluloid figure w/string-jtd arms & wire tail, 7", EXIB, A..$6,600.00

Mickey Mouse Whirling Tale, Linemar, w/up, litho tin, 6½", EXIB, A $600.00

Mickey Mouse Xylophone Player, Linemar, 1950s, w/up, litho tin, 6", EX, A $350.00

Mickey Mouse Xylophone Player, Linemar, 1950s, w/up, litho tin, 6", NMIB..$550.00

Mickey's Delivery, Linemar, friction, litho tin, 5½" L, EX, A..$300.00

Mid West Hauling Co (Van Trailer), Linemar, friction, litho tin, 12", NM+IB, A..$150.00

Midget Racer (Agajanian #98), Champion, 1950s, friction, lithographed tin, 19", MIB (box label reads Agajanian on car), A, $13,750.00. (Photo courtesy Bertoia Auctions)

Midget Racer (Agajanian #98), friction, litho tin, BRT, w/driver, 19", EX+IB (box reads Champions on car), A $7,370.00

Midget Racer (Champion #3), friction, litho tin, BRT, w/driver, 6", nonworking, P, A..$75.00

Midget Racer (Champion #63), friction, litho tin, BRT, w/driver, 7", VG, A..$350.00

Midget Racer (Champion #63), friction, litho tin, BRT, w/driver, 7", NM, A..$935.00

Midget Racer (Champion's Racer #98), Y, friction, litho tin, BRT, w/driver, 19", NM, A $3,850.00

Midget Racer (Champion's Racer #98), Y, friction, litho tin, BRT, w/driver, 19", VG, A $1,760.00

Midget Racer (Special #3), friction, litho tin, BRT, w/driver, 7", G+, A..$350.00

Midget Racer (Special #4), friction, litho tin, BRT, w/driver, 7", EX+, A..$630.00

Midget Racer (Special #7), friction, litho tin, BRT, w/driver, 7", Fair, A..$275.00

Midget Racer (Special #8), friction, litho tin, BRT, w/driver, 7", nonworking o/w EX+, A....................................$460.00

Mighty Robot (With Spark), w/up, litho tin, 6", EXIB, A.$135.00

Military Motorcycle, friction, litho tin, rider in uniform & helmet w/gun sticking through windshield, 5½", EX, A........$100.00

Minnie Mouse Seated in Rocking Chair Knitting, Linemar, w/up, litho tin, EXIB, A $550.00

Monkee Mobile, ASC, friction, tin car w/vinyl figures, 12", NMIB, A..$575.00

Monkey, see Wandering Chimpanzee

Monkey Carousel, Yone, w/up, litho tin, 4 monkeys spin & flip, 6", EX+IB, A..$110.00

Monkey on Seal Fishing, Cragstan, w/up, litho tin, 5", EXIB, A..$250.00

Monkey Rider, see Motorcyclist w/Monkey Rider

Monkey Scooter, MT, w/up, plush monkey in cloth outfit on litho tin scooter, 5", EX, A $55.00

Monkey w/Banjo, Occupied Japan, w/up, plush w/cloth outfit, 4½", VG, A..$50.00

Motorcycle (3-Wheeled) w/Boy Rider, Wakimura, prewar, w/up, litho tin, celluloid head, no sz given, EX, A.........$3,520.00

Motorcycle w/Boy Rider, w/up, litho tin cycle w/celluloid boy in helmet, 7¾", EX+, A $1,750.00

Motorcycle w/Rider Crouching Forward, Yachio, friction, litho tin, 5", EX+, A..$500.00

Motorcycle w/Sidecar, Masudaya, 1930s, w/up, litho tin, no driver, 9½", G, A $990.00

Motorcyclist w/Monkey Rider (Monkey Rider), Kanto, w/up, litho tin, no sz given, EXIB, A $880.00

Mr Caterpillar, w/up, litho tin, 12" L, EXIB, A.................$80.00

Mr Cragstan (Cragstan's The Man), Daiya, w/up, tin & plastic, 6½", NMIB, A..$225.00

Mr Dan the Hot Dog Eating Man, TN, 1960s, w/up, litho tin w/vinyl head, 7", NM+IB $150.00

Mr Lucky, Marusan, w/up, figure in cloth outfit & vinyl head standing at gambling table & sipping martini, 10", NMIB, A..$200.00

Musical Bear, w/up, plush bear seated on barrel playing 8½", EX, A..$100.00

Musical Chimp, Alps, w/up, plush, 6", EXIB, A $50.00
Musical Merry Go-Round, w/up, litho tin, 5x5", EX+IB, A.$400.00
Mystery Police Cycle, KO, crank-op, 6", EX, A..............$425.00
Nash Automobile, see New Nash
NBC Television Truck, friction, litho tin, brn & wht, 6", EX,
   A..$175.00
New Nash (1932), ET Co, w/up, litho tin w/NP grille & head-
   lights, 7½", EX, A..$935.00
News Pup, Normura, w/up, litho tin, upright pup in lithoed
   overalls & hat holds newspaper & bell, 6", EX, A..$165.00
NY World's Fair Escorter, 1964-65, friction, litho tin w/Grey-
   hound logo, 6" L, EXIB, A $100.00
O-Sen Fighter Pilot, ATD, 1960s, w/up, litho tin figure w/vinyl
   head w/goggles, 10", NMIB, A $675.00
Oldsmobile Convertible (Friction Car With Siren), Y, friction,
   tin w/chrome detail, 11", VGIB $500.00
Olive Oyl Ballet Dancer, Linemar, friction w/pull-rod, 5½",
   EXIB, A $600.00
Ostrich Pulling 2-Wheeled Cart, see Sunday Stroller
Packard (1936), Kosuge, w/up, litho tin w/NP trim, w/rear lug-
   gage rack & dummy lights, 8", G, A $330.00

Packard Sedan, Kosuge, prewar, windup, lithographed tin luxury model, 11½", EX, A, $6,600.00. (Photo courtesy Bertoia Auctions)

Peace Car (Bonnet Bus), friction, 7½", VG, A $500.00
Peace Corps Man, Sy Toys, w/up, litho tin robotic featured man
   w/bell on chest, 7", EXIB, A....................................$275.00
Peacock, see Proud Peacock
Phantom Dream Car, Tippco, friction, tin, 1950s replica of
   Buick dream car, metallic bl w/silver top, WWT, 14", NM,
   A..$1,475.00
Pigeon Scooter, Marusan, friction, litho tin w/celluloid wind-
   shield, 6", EX+IB, A $990.00
Pinocchio Walker, Linemar, w/up, litho tin, 6", EX, A ..$350.00
Pluto, Linemar, friction, litho tin, articulated legs, 4½", VG,
   A $90.00
Pluto Drum Major, Linemar, w/up, litho tin, sitting upright in hat
   w/horn in mouth, bell & wand in paws, 6", EXIB, A..$400.00
Pluto Drum Major, Linemar, w/up, litho tin, sitting upright in
   hat w/horn in mouth, bell & wand in paws, 6", EX.$200.00
Pluto on Tricycle w/Bell, Linemar, w/up, celluloid Goofy figure
   on litho tin trike w/bell on rear, 4", NM+IB, A.......$600.00
Pluto the Band Leader, Linemar, w/up, litho tin, 6", G ..$175.00

Pluto and Goofy, Linemar, windup, lithographed tin, separate figures about 5", EXIB, A, $1,200.00. (Photo courtesy Bertoia Auctions)

Polar Bear, w/up, plush, standing on all fours, 6", EXIB....$30.00
Polar Bear Balancing Ball on Nose, w/up, litho tin, standing
   upright w/red lithoed jacket, 6", EXIB, A $50.00
Police Car, friction, litho tin, 2-tone gr w/figures lithoed in win-
   dows, Police on sides & top, guns on hood, 7", G......$75.00
Police Car, friction, tin w/police figures lithoed on windows,
   POLICE lettered on top & sides, 10", NMIB, A $175.00
Police Car, Hadson, friction, tin w/police figures lithoed on windows,
   POLICE on sides, red light on top, 6", NM+IB, A...........$85.00
Police Car, see also Graham Paige Police Car
Police Man, w/up, litho tin policeman directing traffic w/whistle
   in mouth, 6½", EX..$225.00
Police Patrol Jeep, Y, friction, wht w/BRT, rear spare and water
   can, 17" L, EX, A..$200.00
Ponitac Firebird III, Alps, 1950s, friction, litho tin w/drivers
   under 2 clear domes, 11", EX..................................$300.00
Pontiac Fire Wings, Marusan, 1950s, friction, litho tin jet-like
   vehicle w/driver under clear dome, 4 BRT, 8", VG+ ..$175.00
Pontiac Sedan, Kosuge, prewar, w/up, litho tin luxury model
   w/NP detail, lithoed spoke wheels, 11½", EX, A...$3,575.00

Popeye Roller Skating Waiter, Linemar, windup, lithographed tin with cloth pants, 7", VG, A, $600.00. (Photo courtesy Bertoia Auctions)

Popeye & Olive Oyl Playing Catch w/Ball, Linemar, w/up, litho tin figures on long platform, 19" L, VG, A (Est: $650).......$925.00

Popeye Basketball Player, Linemar, w/up, litho tin, 9", EX+, A...$825.00

Popeye Roller Skating Waiter, Linemar, w/up, litho tin w/cloth pants, 7", EX+IB, A...$2,475.00

Popeye Turnover Tank, Linemar, w/up, litho tin, 4", NM+IB, from $550 to $600.00

Power Shovel, Linemar, friction, litho tin truck w/steam shovel on back, 12", EXIB, A $175.00

Prehistoric Animal (Dinosaur), Linemar, w/up, litho tin, walks & opens mouth, 6x8", EX+IB, A $330.00

Proud Peacock, Alps, w/up, litho tin, 7", EX+IB, A $225.00

Rabbit and Bear Playing Ball, windup, lithographed tin, 18½", EXIB, 225.00. (Photo courtesy Bertoia Auctions)

Rabbit w/Baby Rabbit on Back, see Jumping Bunny w/Baby Racer, see also Midget Racer

Racer #2, w/up, litho tin boattail type w/side vents, flat front w/grille, lithoed spoke wheels, w/driver, 7½", EX, A .$575.00

Racer #32, friction, litho tin w/BRT, wht w/red & bl detail, NP grille, side pipes extend to rear, w/driver, 8½", G+ $85.00

Rail Road Hand Car, see Tom & Dick Rail Road Hand Car

RCA TV Service Truck, SN, friction, litho tin, 9", EX, A..$375.00

Roadster (Open), prewar, w/up, litho tin, celluloid windshield, NP trim, lithoed MSW, driver & passenger, 12", EX, A .$9,350.00

Roaring Lion, Alps, w/up, plush, 6" L, VG+IB, A $50.00

Rocky (Fred Flintstone Look-A-Like), w/up, litho tin, 4", EXIB, A $165.00

Rollicking Sailor, Fairylite, w/up, celluloid figure w/compo legs, head bobs & rocks back & forth, 8", NMIB, A $200.00

San Francisco Cable Car #504 (Bay & Taylor Street), friction, litho tin w/tin passengers, bell noise, 7", NMIB, A ...$50.00

Santa Claus on Sled, w/up, celluloid, 8" T, EXIB, A $110.00

Santa Claus Standing Ringing Bell, Alps, w/up, cloth suit w/fur trim, fuzzy beard, blk belt, red gloves, 7", EXIB, A $80.00

Santa in Sleigh, w/up, litho tin sleigh & Santa w/wht celluloid reindeer, 8" L, EX+, A...$75.00

School Line (Bonnet) Bus, Marusan, friction, litho tin, 7½", NMIB, A..$775.00

Sedan, Kosuge, w/up, litho tin w/NP trim, flat turn signal opens when operated, 6", VG, A...$600.00

Sedan, w/up, tin w/NP grille & headlights, w/turn signals & front wheels controlled by lever action, 6½", EX, A $300.00

See America First Bus, see All State Express...

Sharp Shooter, Alps, w/up, celluloid figure in army gr uniform & helmet on belly w/rifle, 7", EXIB, A.........................$50.00

Shy-Anne (Indian Chief), Linemar/WDP, windup, lithographed tin with cloth outfit, rubber hands, nose, and arrowhead, 6", EX, $300.00. (Photo courtesy Bertoia Auctions)

Sight Seeing (Avenue) Bus, Yonezawa, friction, litho tin, 9", VG+IB, A...$125.00

Sight Seeing Bus, Masudaya, friction, tin w/passengers lithoed in windows, 14", NMIB, A $300.00

Silver Pigeon Motorcycle, friction, litho tin w/celluloid windshield, w/driver & passenger, no sz given, EX, A $935.00

Singing Warbler, w/up, litho tin bird w/realistic detail, 5", EXIB, A $175.00

Skip Rope Animals, TPS, w/up, litho tin, dog & squirrel twirl rope as baby bear jumps, 4¾" T, NMIB, A $175.00

Skipper (Squirrel) in the Forest, w/up, plush, 8", EXIB, A $50.00

Skippy the Tricky Cyclist, w/up, litho tin clown in cloth cuit, 5½", EXIB, A...$150.00

Smiling Sam the Carnival Man, Alps, w/up, litho tin w/cloth outfit, 9", EX, A..$125.00

Smiling Sam the Carnival Man, Alps, w/up, tin w/cloth outfit, 9", NM+IB, A...$300.00

Snapping Alligator (w/Leaping Fish in His Mouth), Cragstan, w/up, litho tin, 12" L, VG+IB $100.00

Special #8 Midget Racer, see Midget Racer

Speed King Racer #61, friction, litho tin, w/driver, 11", G+ .$50.00

Squirrel, see Skipper (Squirrel) in the Forest

Strutting Duck, Alps, w/up, plush w/cloth outfit, 7" T, EXIB .$30.00

Strutting Parade, Alps, rabbit taking pictures, w/up, plush w/cloth outfit, plastic camera, 8", EXIB, A $120.00

Sumo Wrestlers in Ring, air-bulb activated, celluloid & cb, 4½" T, NM+, A...$275.00

Sunday Stroller, ostrich pulling figure w/umbrella in 2-wheeled cart, w/up, litho tin, 9", EXIB, A...........................$250.00

Super Constructor Cement Mixer Truck, SSS, friction, mc tin, w/accessories, 20", NMIB, A..............................$4,620.00

Super Sonic Race Car #36, MT, w/up, litho tin, 9", EX+IB, A $275.00

Super Truck, IY, friction, litho tin, 'Studebaker' w/emb stake bed, 16", NMIB, A $3,960.00

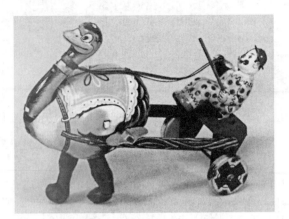

Susie the Ostrich, TPS, windup, lithographed tin with rubber legs, 6" long, EX, $650.00. (Photo courtesy Bertoia Auctions)

Tambourine Clown, TN, w/up, clown in cloth costume w/tambourine, 6", EXIB, A $50.00

Tap Dancer, Alps, Occupied Japan, w/up, celluloid figure in cloth outfit dances under street sign, 8½", NMIB, A..........$250.00

Taxi Cab, friction, tin, yel w/blk top, w/siren, 6", EXIB, A.$55.00

Teacup Merry-Go-Round, w/up, litho tin & plastic, 3 plush bears on cups on rnd lithoed base, 8", EXIB, A...................$85.00

Telephone Service Car (Truck), KO, friction, litho tin, w/telescoping platform, 7½", EXIB, A..............................$175.00

The Typist, Kanto, w/up, litho tin, 5½", EX, A $110.00

Thirsty Monkey, TN, w/up, plush w/vinyl face, 6", EXIB, A.$70.00

Thirsty Rabbit, Alps, plush w/cloth outfit, 8", VGIB, A ..$55.00

Tiger Target Game, 1950s, w/up w/growling sound, emb die-cut tin tiger's head w/mouth open revealing target, 14x12", NM $75.00

Tiger Trike (w/Revolving Bell), w/up, litho tin trike w/plastic tiger, 4" T, EXIB...$55.00

Tom & Dick Rail Road Hand Car, litho tin, car mk Rail Road, 6", EXIB, A $65.00

Toto the Acrobat, w/up, celluloid clown figure on wire frame, 12", VGIB, A $55.00

Tourist Motorcycle, Marusan, friction, tin w/clear plastic windhield, Tourist lettered on front, w/driver, 7", EX+ ...$500.00

Traveller, Alps, w/up, plush monkey in cloth outfit w/camera, 6", EXIB, A $185.00

Trolley Bus, Marusan, friction, tin w/passengers lithoed in windows, cable line attached to top, 11", NMIB, A......$665.00

Trucks on Parade Assortment, TN, friction, tin, 6-pc set w/moving van, dump, farm & delivery trucks & wrecker, 5", NMIB...$150.00

Tugboat (Betty Jane), Linemar, friction, litho tin, 10", NMIB, A (Est: $125) $235.00

Twirly Clown, w/up, clown in cloth costume looking up as he twirls balls on 2 rods, 7", EXIB, A $65.00

United Airlines Jeep, KO, friction, litho tin, BRT, w/driver, 7", VGIB, A $85.00

Venus Motorcycle, friction, litho tin, blk w/wht & silver trim, 9½", P, A (Est: $25-$50)...$65.00

Volvo Sedan, Rosko, friction, litho tin, 8", EXIB $400.00

Walking Drummer Clown, windup, lithographed tin with cloth suit, plastic hands, horn, and drumstick, 10½", EX, A, $220.00. (Photo courtesy Bertoia Auctions)

Walking Duck, Mama w/2 ducklings trailing behind, w/up, litho tin, 8", EXIB, A $140.00

Walt Disney's Mechanical Tricycle, see Donald Duck

Wandering Chimpanzee, w/up, plush w/vinyl face, hands & feet, 5", EXIB, A $125.00

Whirling Tale Mickey Mouse, see Mickey Mouse (Whirling Tale)

Wiggling Dachshund, S&E, w/up, litho tin, 8", EXIB, A .$45.00

Wonder Acrobat, CK, w/up, celluloid boy figure on wire aparatus, 10", EXIB, A $110.00

Wonder MG, Marusan, w/up, litho tin, driver w/umbrella, 12½", NMIB, A...$300.00

World's Express Truck, see Diamond T...

Xylophone Player, Linemar, w/up, hefty clown w/articulated arms, 5", G, A $325.00

Yellow Cab, TN, friction, b/o light on top, yel litho tin, 8½" L, NMIB, A...$275.00

Yogi Bear Go-Kart, Linemar, 1961, friction, tin w/vinyl head, 6", EX+...$150.00

Yogi Bear in Cadillac, Linemar, 1961, friction, litho tin car w/vinyl headed Yogi, 9", NM, A $350.00

SPANISH

Boy in Four-Wheeled Cart, Paya, windup, lithographed tin, 6½" long, EX, $650.00. (Photo courtesy Bertoia Auctions)

Campsa Oil Truck, RSA, w/up, litho tin, 7", nonworking o/w
   EX, A $85.00
Chrysler Airflow Sedan, Paya, w/up, tin w/NP grille & bumpers,
   lithoed tin spoke wheels, 13", VG, A $300.00

**Limousine, Paya, windup, painted tin, electric lights,
20", G, $900.00. (Photo courtesy Bertoia Auctions)**

Motorcycle & Rider, Paya, w/up, litho tin, does circus stunts, 5",
   EX $100.00
Sedan, Paya, w/up, litho tin, 'VW Bug' style w/longer nose
   &back curves outward, MSW, red & bl, 11", EX, A.$330.00
Vagabundo (Vagabond), w/up, plastic figure w/bedroll, umbrella
   & suitcase, 7", VG, A $65.00

Wyandotte

Wyandotte produced toys mostly of heavy gauge steel with a
few being tin or plastic. The following listings are of vehicles
and related toys from the 1920s to the 1960s. All are steel unless
noted otherwise.

See also Aeronautical; Boats; Character, TV, and Movie Collectibles; Guns; Windups, Friction, and Other Mechanicals.

Airflow Coupe, 1930s, friction, 5½", G, A (Est: $50-$75) .$100.00
Allied Van Lines, 1950s, Chieftan Lines on door, aluminum
   trailer w/advertising, 14-wheeled, 24", VG, A (Est: $50-
   $100) $75.00
Ambulance, 1930s, streamlined styling w/Ambulance imprinted
   on top, 4-wheeled, 6", EX, A (Est: $100-$150) $385.00
Ambulance, 1940s, wht w/red decals, NP grille, blk-pnt
   wooden wheels, rear opening door, 11", VG, A (Est: $150-
   $200) $190.00
Ambulance, 1950s, plastic w/friction motor, wht w/red lettering
   & cross symbol, 9", VG, A (Est: $25-$50) $25.00
Army Supply Corps No 42 Truck, 1940s, w/cloth cover, 4-
   wheeled, 18", EX, A (Est: $50-$75) $130.00
Auto Transport, 1950s, rnd-nosed cab, 8-wheeled, 23", EX, A
   (Est: $50-$75)..$110.00
Auto Transport #455, 1950s, 6-wheeled, 9", VG, A (Est: $25-
   $50) $65.00

**Auto Pulling
Leisure Trailer, 1930s,
26" overall, G, A (Est:
$400.00 – $600.00), $500.00. (Photo
courtesy Randy Inman Auctions)**

Auto-Transport, 1950s, rnd-nosed cab, 8-wheeled, 23", VG, A
   (Est: $50-$100) $75.00
Auto-Transport, 1950s, sq-nosed cab, 8-wheeled, 23", EX (P
   box), A (Est: $125-$175) $100.00
Automatic Loading Dump Truck, 1950s, front loader, 4-wheeled,
   15", EX, A (Est: $75-$125) $240.00
Automobile Society Tow Truck, 1950s, blk & yel checked band,
   4-wheeled, 10", EX, A (Est: $100-$125)..................$275.00

**Car-A-Van Automobile Transport, 1950s, eight-wheeled, 22",
EX, A (Est: $75.00 – $125.00), $120.00. (Photo courtesy
Randy Inman Auctions)**

Cargo Lines Motor Transport Fleet Semi, 1950s, 6-wheeled, 26",
   VG, A (Est: $75-$125)..$155.00
Circus Cage Truck Pulling Cage Trailer, Greatest Show on
   Earth, 2 paper animals, 20" overall, EX, A (Est: $350-
   $450) $880.00
Coal Truck, 1950s, whole truck slants forward, 4-wheeled, 11",
   VG, A (Est: $50-$75) $65.00
Construction Endloader & Dump Trailer, 1950s, orange w/blk
   seat & engine, 4-wheeled, 21", EX, A (Est: $25-$50).$40.00
Construction Set, 1940s, dump truck, sand hopper & steam
   shovel, about 10" ea, all EX, A (Est: $75-$125) $110.00
Construction Supply Co Stake Truck, 1950s, 14-wheeled, 23",
   EX, A (Est: $75-$125) $185.00
Cord Auto Pulling Leisure Trailer, 1940s, streamline styling, 23"
   overall, rstr, A (Est: $200-$350)...........................$330.00
Cord Coupe, w/up, yel w/gr roof, BRT, red wooden hubs, 13",
   VG, A (Est: $400-$475)..$275.00
Delivery Truck, 1930s, bed sides slanted, 4-wheeled, 6", EX, A
   (Est: $50-$100) $185.00
Delivery Truck, 1930s, slanted nose w/chrome grille & bumper,
   4-wheeled, 6", EX, A (Est: $50-$75) $85.00

Ducky Waddles, 1950s, 3-wheeled duck, litho tin, 9" L, VG, A (Est: $25-$50) $75.00

Dump Truck, 1930s, short-nosed w/grille and bumper, straight sides w/tailgate, four-wheeled, 17", EX, A (Est: $75.00 – $125.00), $85.00. (Photo courtesy Randy Inman Auctions)

Dump Truck, 1930s, slanted bed sides, orange, MDW, 4-wheeled, 12", EX, A (Est: $75-$125) $200.00

Dump Truck, 1930s, slanted bed sides, orange, WRT, 4-wheeled, 15", G, A (Est: $100-$150) $165.00

Dump Truck, 1930s, slanted bed sides, orange, WRT, 4-wheeled, 15", EX, A (Est: $150-$200) $300.00

Dump Truck, 1930s, slanted bed sides, orange & red w/blk, MDW, 6-wheeled, 15", EX, A (Est: $125-$150)......$275.00

Dump Truck, 1930s, slanted bed sides, red, WRT (rpl), 4-wheeled, 7", G, A, (Est: $10-$20) $60.00

Dump Truck, 1940s, cab slants forward, slanted bed sides, cab wheels covered, 4-wheeled, 12", EX+, A (Est: $75-$125) $140.00

Dump Truck, 1940s, side dump, cream cab w/tan V-shaped dump bed, 6-wheeled, 11", EX, A (Est: $50-$75) $130.00

Dump Truck, 1950s, blk & yel check, high dump bed w/tailgate, front wheels covered, 4-wheeled, 11", EX, A (Est: $25-$50) $130.00

Dump Truck, 1950s, blk & yel check, open back, front wheels covered, 4-wheeled, 10", EX, A (Est: $25-$50) $140.00

Dump Truck, 1950s, cab slants forward, slanted bed sides, cab wheels covered, 4-wheeled, 12", VG+, A (Est: $50-$75)............$65.00

Dump Truck, 1950s, front loader, straight sides w/slanted open back, 4-wheeled, 12", G, A (Est: $25-$50) $30.00

Dump Truck, 1950s, front loader, straight sides w/tailgate, all wheels covered, 4-wheeled, 13", G, A (Est: $50-$75) .$60.00

Dump Truck, 1950s, front loader, straight sides w/tailgate, front wheels covered, 4-wheeled, 13", EX, A (Est: $75-$100)..............$150.00

Dump Truck, 1950s, short-nosed w/grille & bumper, straight sides w/tailgate, 4-wheeled, 17", EX, A (Est: $75-$125) $85.00

Dump Truck, 1950s, side-dump, rnd-nosed cab, oblong bed, cab wheels covered, 6-wheeled, 17", EX, A (Est: $75-$125) $175.00

Dump Truck, 1950s, side-dump, short-nosed cab w/grille & bumper, V-shaped bed, 6-wheeled, 20", EX, A (Est: $75-$125)..$190.00

Dump Truck, 1950s, snub-nosed plastic cab, DUMP on side of bed, 4-wheeled, 11", EX, A (Est: $50-$75) $110.00

Dump Truck, 1950s, sq-nosed, straight-sided w/tailgate, all wheels covered, 4-wheeled, 13", G, A (Est: $25-$50) $65.00

Dump Truck, 1960s, hydraulic, long-nosed sq cab, straight sided w/tailgate, 6-wheeled, 22", EX, A (Est: $75-$125) $65.00

Dump Truck, 1960s, side crank, long-nosed sq cab, straight sides w/tailgate, 4-wheeled, 22", EX, A ($50-$100) $88.00

Easter Bunny Delivery, bunny on cycle w/2-wheeled side cart, litho tin, 10", VG, A (Est: $100-$200) $165.00

Emergency Auto Service Tow Truck, 1950s, plastic cab, boom w/2 wheels, 4-wheeled, 15", EX, A (Est: $75-$125) .$200.00

Express Co Stake Truck, 1940s, yel & orange cab w/lt gray U-shaped stake trailer, 6-wheeled, 22", EX, A (Est: $75-$125)..$88.00

Express Service Delivery Truck, 1950s, snub-nosed cab w/wheels covered, 4-wheeled, 10", G, A (Est: $25-$50) $100.00

Express Service Delivery Truck, 1950s, snub-nosed cab w/wheels covered, 4-wheeled, 10", EXIB, A (Est: $100-$150) .$300.00

Fire Dept #5 Truck, 1950s, 4-wheeled, 10", VG, A (Est: $25-$50)..$100.00

Fire Engine Co No 01, 1950s, 6-wheeled, 24", VG, A (Est: $75-$125)..$275.00

Fire Engine Co No 04, 1940s, long-nosed, red w/yel & gr trim, 4-wheeled, 12", VG, A (Est: $50-$75) $140.00

Fire Engine Co No 04, 1950s, cab slants forward, red w/yel trim, 4-wheeled, 11½", VG, A (Est: $25-$50) $110.00

Fire Engine Co No 10, 1940s, 4-wheeled, 18", VG, A (Est: $50-$75)..$120.00

Fire Hook & Ladder No 1, plastic cab, 6-wheeled, 20", VG, A, (Est: $50-$75)..$100.00

Flash Strat-O-Wagon, litho tin, 6", EXIB, A (Est: $85).$175.00

Flatbed Truck, 1950s, all wheels covered, 4-wheeled, 13", EX, A (Est: $50-$75) $80.00

Gas pumps, 1930s, steel with glass cylinders, crank action, 9", VG to EX, A (Est: $150.00 – $250.00), $450.00 each. (Photo courtesy Randy Inman Auctions)

Giant Construction Co Dump Truck, 1950s, 6-wheeled, 19", G, A (Est: $50-$100) $88.00

Giant Construction Co Dump Truck, 1950s, 6-wheeled, 19", VG+, A (Est: $75-$125) $130.00

Grader, 1950s, open seat, orange, 20", EX, A (Est: $25-$50) .$30.00

Grader (Power Charger), 1950s, enclosed cab, orange, 18", EX, A (Est: $25-$50) $20.00

Great Plains Cattle Ranch Stake Truck, 1950s, 6-wheeled, 23", EX, A (Est: $50-$75) $150.00

Green Valley Stock Ranch Stake Truck, 1950s, 6-wheeled, 17", EX, A (Est: $50-$75) $165.00

Grey Van Lines Semi, 1950s, 14-wheeled, 24½", P old rpt, A (Est: $50-$75) $90.00

High-Lift Loader, 1950s, orange, 15", EX, A (Est: $25-$50) .$25.00

Igloo Ice Co Truck, 1950s, lithoed detail, cab wheels covered, 4-wheeled, 10", EX, A (Est: $75-$125) $150.00

Jiffy Painting/Decorating Truck, 1950s, w/ladders, 4-wheeled, 10", EX, A (Est: $75-$125) $120.00

LaSalle Sedan Pulling Trailer, 1930s, gr w/NP grille & bumpers, WRT, 26", VG, A (Est: $300-$500) $715.00

Log Truck, 1950s, open-framed trailer w/logs, 14-wheeled, 26", VG, A (Est: $50-$75) $75.00

Log Truck, 1950s, yel & blk checks, front wheels covered, 4-wheeled, w/logs, 10", EX, A (Est: $50-$75) $120.00

Lowboy Machinery Re-Hauler, 1940s, 4 cab wheels covered, open trailer wheels, 6-wheeled, 22", G, A (Est: $50-$75).....$75.00

Mobile Artillery Flatbed Truck, 1950s, mk USA 5 on door, all wheels covered, 4-wheeled, 13", EX, A (Est: $25-$50)..$75.00

Moto-Fix Towcar, 1950s, 15", EX, A (Est: $125.00 – $175.00), $230.00. (Photo courtesy Randy Inman Auctions)

Motor Bus, 1930s, chrome grille & bumper, all wheels covered, 4-wheeled, 6", EX, A (Est: $75-$125)......................$440.00

Motor Freight Lines Semi, 1950s, 23", EX, A (Est: $75.00 – $125.00), $240.00.

Motor Fleet Hauling Service Dump Truck, 1950s, side-dump, front wheels covered, 6-wheeled, 17", VG, A (Est: $75-$125)...$100.00

Nation-Wide Air Rail Service Delivery Van, 1950s, plastic cab, 4-wheeled, 11", Fair, A (Est: $25-$50)......................$100.00

North American Van Line Semi, long-nosed cab, wheels covered, red, yel & blk, 6-wheeled, 14", EX, A (Est: $75-$125)..$185.00

Official Service Car Tow Truck, 1940s, cab slants forward, front wheels covered, 4-wheeled, 13", G+, A (Est: $50-$100) .$55.00

Parcel Service (Anywhere Anytime), 1950s, cab wheels covered, 4-wheeled, 9½", missing grille, G+, A (Est: $25-$50).$33.00

Pickway Pastures Livestock Dairy Cows Stake Truck, 1950s, 4-wheeled, EX, A (Est: $75-$125)...............................$120.00

Pickway Projects Building Co Dump Truck, 1950s, side-dump, 6-wheeled, 17", VG, A (Est: $150-$200) $55.00

Racer, b/o lights, pontoon wheel covers, World's Fair decal on hood, WRT, 8½", EX, A (Est: $200-$300) $440.00

Racer, 1940s, b/o lights, pontoon wheel covers, red, 8½", VG, A (Est: $125-$175)..$275.00

Railway Express Agency Delivery Truck, 1940s, Wyandotte Toys Good & Safe, 4-wheeled, 12", VG+, A (Est: $75-$125) .$120.00

Railway Express Agency Delivery Truck, 1950s, Wyandotte Toys For Boys & Girls, 4-wheeled, 6½", EX, A (Est: $25-$50) $100.00

Roadster, Deco style w/fin-like covered wheels, b/o lights, red, WRT, 9", VG, A (Est: $150-$200)...........................$140.00

Roadster, wht top w/lt bl body, NP trim, BRT, red hubs, 13", Fair+, A (Est: $200-$300) $300.00

Roadster Pulling Trailer, 1940s, streamline styling w/driver in open seat, gr, 11", EX (Est: $150-$250) $1,200.00

Sand Truck #443, 1950s, whole truck slants forward, front loader, 4-wheeled, 13", VG, A (Est: $75-$125).......$110.00

Sedan, PS, long pointed opening hood, electric lights, WRT, 15" L, VG, A (Est: $600-$800)......................................$600.00

Semi, 1950s, rnd-nosed cab, front wheels covered, streamlined trailer, 6-wheeled, 17", EX, A (Est: $75-$125) $130.00

Shady Glenn Stock Ranch Cattle Truck, 1950s, six-wheeled, 17", EX, A (Est: $75.00 – $125.00), $150.00.

Sit & Ride Truck, flatbed truck w/high seat & steer stick, 4-wheeled, 16", G, A (Est: $75-$125)......................$385.00

Soap Box Derby #226 Racer, wood wheels, 6", G, A (Est: $75-$125)...$110.00

Stake Truck, 1930s, slanted nose w/chrome grille & bumper, front wheels covered, 4-wheeled, 6", rstr, A (Est: $25-$50)...$60.00

Stake Truck, 1930s, straight-nosed w/chrome grille & bumper, front wheels covered, 4-wheeled, 6", EX, A (Est: $50-$100) $90.00

Stake Truck, 1950s, cab wheels covered, 4-wheeled, 16", VG, A (Est: $75-$125) $90.00

Stake Truck (All Purpose), 1950s, U-shaped trailer w/tailgate, cab wheels covered, 8-wheeled, 9", EX (Est: $25-$50).......$35.00

Sunshine Dairy Wagon (Early Bird Milk Wagon & Horse), 1950s, plastic, 8" L, NMIB, A (Est: $25-$50) $30.00

Super Service Garage, litho-graphed tin, 8½x8½", VG, A (Est: $50.00 – $100.00), $250.00. (Photo courtesy Randy Inman Auctions)

Tank Truck, 1930s, chrome grille & bumper, covered wheels, 4-wheeled, 6", EX, A (Est: $75-$125) $385.00

Tow Truck, 1950s, rnd-nosed cab, cab wheels covered, 4-wheeled, 14", EX, A (Est: $75-$125) $250.00

Tow Truck, 1950s, rnd-nosed cab, cab wheels covered, 4-wheeled, 14", G, A (Est: $25-$50) $50.00

Tow Truck, 1950s, short-nosed cab w/grille & bumper, 2-wheeled boom, open wheels, 4-wheeled, 15", rstr, A (Est: $50-$75)..$65.00

Tow Truck, 1950s, snub-nosed cab w/lithoed grille & bumper, front wheels covered, 4-wheeled, 10", VG, A (Est: $25-$50) $55.00

Towing Service Nite Day Tow Truck, 1950s, cab wheels covered, 4-wheeled, 9½", EX, A (Est: $75-$125) $260.00

Towing Service Tow Truck, 1950s, 2-wheeled boom, 4-wheeled, 15", EX, A (Est: $125-$175) $440.00

Toy Town Delivery Wagon, tin w/driver lithoed in window, red w/yel detail, BRT, doors open, 21", EX, A (Est: $275-$350)....$300.00

Toy Town Ice Co Truck, 1940s, cab slants forward, cab wheels covered, 4-wheeled, 12", G+, A (Est: $75-$125).......$75.00

Transmobile Jr, 1950s, 6-wheeled, 13", no accessory autos o/w VG, A (Est: $50-$75) $65.00

Truck w/Three Trailers, 1930s, w/box van, tanker & side dumper, 24" L overall, G, A (Est: $75-$125)...........$175.00

Turn Pike Semi, 1950s, rnd-nosed cab, streamlined trailer, 6-wheeled, 17", EX, A (Est: $75-$125) $165.00

Valley Farms Livestock Produce Stake Truck, 1950s, plastic cab, 6-wheeled, 8½", EX, A (Est: $25-$50).......................$75.00

Wagon, 1940s, gr w/pk wheel covers, 5½", EX (Est: $25-$50)..$90.00

Wagon, 1940s, U-shaped back, streamlined wheel covers, wooden pull hdl, 12", EX, A (Est: $75-$125) $65.00

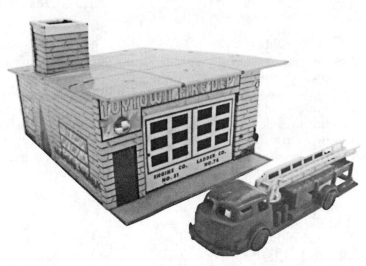

Toy Town Fire Dept, lithographed tin building with plastic firetruck, building is 6½x8", VG+, A (Est: $50.00 – $75.00), $50.00. (Photo courtesy Randy Inman Auctions)

Woody Convertible, lithoed detail, top goes up and down, 12½", VG+, A (Est: $150-$200) $250.00

Wrecker & Service, 1950s, all wheels covered, 4-wheeled, 6", VG, A $110.00

Wrecker Car, 1950s, cab slants forward, wooden wheels, 4-wheeled, 13", Poor, A (Est: $25-$50) $50.00

Wyandotte #7 Racer, lithoed detail, 8", Fair, A (Est: $10-$20)...$20.00

Wyandotte City Airport, litho tin, b/o search lights, w/2 PS planes, 16" L, VG+, A (Est: $400-$500) $440.00

Wyandotte Construction Co Dump Truck, 1940s, 4-wheeled, 21", G, A (Est: $50-$100) $100.00

Wyandotte Construction Co Dump Truck, 1950s, side-dump, 6-wheeled, 17", NM, A (Est: $100-$150) $330.00

Wyandotte Construction Co Dump Truck, 1950s, side-dump, 6-wheeled, 17", EX, A (Est: $75-$125) $275.00

Wyandotte Construction Co Hopper, 1950s, 10" T, EX, A (Est: $25-$50)..$50.00

Wyandotte Construction Co Semi & Steam Shovel, 1950s, 12-wheeled, 25", rstr, A (Est: $150-$200)....................$100.00

Wyandotte Construction Co Semi & Steam Shovel, 1950s, 6-wheeled, 23", VG+, A (Est: $150-$250)................$150.00

Wyandotte Construction Co Stake Truck, 1950s, 14-wheeled, 23", EX, A (Est: $125-$175) $385.00

Wyandotte Express Co Stake Truck, 1950s, curved trailer, 6-wheeled, 17", EX, A (Est: $75-$125) $175.00

Wyandotte Truck Lines/Construction Semi, 1950s, 6-wheeled, 23", VG, A ($75-$125) $75.00

Wyandotte Van Lines, 1940s, whole truck slants forward, 6-wheeled, 15", VG, A (Est: $75-$125) $120.00

Wyandotte Van Lines, 1950s, plastic cab, 6-wheeled, 15", EX, A (Est: $50-$100)...$200.00

Wyandotte Van Lines Coast To Coast Truck, 1940s, cab wheels covered, 6-wheeled, 8", EX, A (Est: $50-$100) $220.00

Wyndot (sic) Package Delivery Truck, 1950s, all wheels covered, 4-wheeled, 12", Fair+, A (Est: $25-$50) $55.00

Categories of Special Interest

If you would like to be included in this section, send us a list of your 'for sale' merchandise. These listings are complimentary to those who participate in the preparation of this guide by doing so. Please understand that the people who are listed here want to buy and sell. They are not appraisers.

Some of our description lines contain a letter/number code just before the suggested price. They identify the dealer or collector who sent his current inventory list to be included in this edition. If you correspond with any of them, please send a self-addressed, stamped envelope for their reply. Because our data was entered several months before this book hit the shelves, many of the coded items will have already sold, but our dealers tell us that they are often able to restock some of the same merchandise. If they don't have it themselves, they may be able to locate a dealer who does. Please bear in mind that because they may have had to pay more to restock, they may also have to charge a little more than the price quoted in their original sales list. The letter in the dealer's code will indicate the first letter of his last name or business name. The narratives to each category with an advisor will also contain their name as well as their code.

A1, see Soldiers
A4, see Puzzles
A7, see Bubble Bath Containers
B1, see Pez Candy Dispensers
B3, see Beatles Memorabilia;
 Character Collectibles
B6, see Guns
C2, see Character and Promo-
 tional Drinking Glasses
C3, see Advertising
C6, see GI Joe
C10, see Character Clocks and
 Watches
C12, see Character Collectibles
C13, see Fisher-Price
D7, see Character Collectibles
G1, see Trains

H1, see Guns
H3, see Building Blocks and Con-
 struction Toys
H9, see Halloween Collectibles
I2, see Character Collectibles;
 Halloween Collectibles
I3, see Banks
J3, see Diecast
K2, see Transformers
K6, see Schoenhut
L4, see Battery-Operated
M2, see Cast Iron
M7, see Dollhouse Furniture
M8, see Character Collectibles
M11, see Political Toys
M15, see Dolls
M21, see Records

P2, see Dolls
P5, see Schoenhut
P6, see Character Collectibles
R5, see Banks
S5, see Diecast
S7, see Pedal Cars
S10, see Windups
S14, see Dolls
S24, see Banks; Cast Iron; Paper
 Lithograph
S25, see Diecast
T3, see Character Collectibles
V2, see Dolls
W4, see Ramp Walkers
W7, see Cracker Jack
Y2, see Paper Dolls

Advertising

California Raisins, M&M Toppers, and all fast-food
Ken Clee (C3)
8 Agnus Drive
Stevens, PA 17578
waxntoys@aol.com
http://hometown.aol.com/waxn
toys/main/kidsmeal.htm

Banks

Ertl; sales lists available
Homestead Collectibles
Art and Judy Turner
P.O. Box 173
Mill Hall, PA 17751
570-726-3597
jturner@cub.kcnet.org

Modern mechanical banks: Reynolds, Sandman Designs, James Capron, Book of Knowledge, Richards, Wilton; sales lists available
Dan Iannotti (I3)
212 W. Hickory Grove Rd.
Bloomfield Hills, MI 48302-1127S
248-335-5042
modernbanks@prodigy.net

Penny banks (limited editions: new, original, mechanical, still, or fig-ural; also bottle openers
Reynolds Toys
Charlie Reynolds (R5)
2836 Monroe St.
Falls Church, VA 22042-2007
703-533-1322
reynoldstoys@erols.com

Antique tin and iron mechanical penny banks; no reproductions or limited editions; cast-iron architec-tural bank buildings in Victorian form. Buy and sell, list available upon request
Mark and Lynda Suozzi (S24)
P.O. Box 102
Ashfield, MA 01330
phone/fax: 413-628-3241 (9 am – 5 pm)
marklyn@valinet.com
www.marklynantiques.com

Barbie and Friends

Wanted: Mackie dolls as well as vin-tage Barbie dolls; buying and selling circa 1959 dolls to present issues
Marl & B Inc.
Marl Davidson

10301 Braden Run
Bradenton, FL 34202
941-751-6275
fax: 941-751-5463
www.marlbe.com

Battery-Operated
Tom Lastrapes (L4)
P.O. Box 2444
Pinellas Park, FL 33782
727-545-2586
tomlas1@fastmail.fm

Beatles Memorabilia
Buying and selling old and new mem-
orabilia; 1 piece or collection
Bojo (B3)
P.O. Box 1403
Cranberry Township, PA 16066-0403
phone/fax: 724-776-0621
bojo@zbzoom.net

Books
Specializing in Little Golden Books
and look-alikes
Steve Santi
19626 Ricardo Ave.
Hayward, CA 94541
510-481-2586
Author of *Collecting Little Golden*
Books, Volumes I and II. Also publishes
newsletter, *Poky Gazette*, primarily for
Little Golden Book collectors

Breyer
Author of book, order direct
Felicia Browell
123 Hooks Lane
Cannonsburg, PA 15317
fbrowell@nauticom.net

Bubble Bath Containers
Including foreign issues; also charac-
ter collectibles, character bobbin'
head nodders, and Dr. Dolittle,
*write for information or send **SASE***
for Bubble Bath Bulletin
Tatonka Toys
Matt and Lisa Adams (A7)

8155 Brooks Dr.
Jacksonville, FL 32244
904-772-6911
matadams@bellsouth.net

Building Blocks and Construction Toys
Anchor Stone Building Blocks by Richter
George Hardy (H3)
6 Deer Path Rd.
Palmyra, VA 22963
434-589-8752
georgeh@ankerstein.org
www.ankerstein.org

Cast Iron
Pre-war, large-scale cast-iron toys
and early American tinplate toys
John McKenna (M2)
701 W Cucharres
Colorado Springs, CO 80905
719-520-9125

Victorian bell toys, horse-drawn wag-
ons, fire toys, carriages, penny
banks, pull toys, animated coin-
operated machines. Buy and sell,
list available upon request, mail
order and shows only
Mark and Lynda Suozzi (S24)
P.O. Box 102
Ashfield, MA 01330
phone/fax: 413-628-3241 (9 am to 5 pm)
marklyn@valinet.com
www.marklynantiques.com

Character and Promotional Glasses
Especially fast-food and sports glasses
Mark Chase (C2)
P.O. Box 308
Slippery Rock, PA 16057
mark@glassnews.com
www.glassnews.com

Character Clocks and Watches
Also radio premiums and decoders,
P-38 airplane-related items from
World War II, Captain Marvel and

Hoppy items, Lone Ranger books
with jackets, selected old comic
books, toys and cap guns; buys and
sells Hoppy and Roy items
Bill Campbell (C10)
3501 Foxbriar Lane
Cibalo, TX 78108
830-626-1077
fax: 830-626-8092
captainmarvel1940@satx.rr.com

Character Collectibles
Dolls, rock 'n roll personalities (espe-
cially the Beatles), related character
items, and miscellaneous toys
Bojo (B3)
Bob Gottuso
P.O. Box 1403
Cranberry Twp., PA 16066-0403
phone/fax: 724-776-0621
bojo@zbzoom.net

Disney, books, animation art
Cohen Books and Collectibles
Joel J. Cohen (C12)
P.O. Box 810310
Boca Raton, FL 33481-0403
561-487-7888
disney@disneycohen.com
www.disneycohen.com

Early Disney, Gone with the Wind,
Western heroes, premiums and
other related collectibles
Saturday Heroes
Ron and Donna Donnelly (D7)
6302 Championship Dr.
Tuscaloosa, AL 35405

Any and all, also Hartland figures
Terri's Toys & Nostalgia
Terri Ivers (I2)
114 Whitworth Ave.
Ponca City, OK 74601
580-762-8697
toylady@cableone.net

Action figures, diecast, Strawberry
Shortcake, Nightmare Before

*Christmas, Star Wars, TV &
    Movie Character Toys*
June Moon
143 Vine Ave.
Park Ridge, IL 60068
junmoonstr@aol.com
www.junemooncollectibles.com

*Especially bendy figures and the
    Simpsons*
Simpson Mania
485 S. 12th St.
St. Helens, OR 97051

Especially Disney
The Mouse Man Ink (M8)
P.O. Box 3195
Wakefield, MA 01880
781-246-3876
mouse_man@msn.com
www.mouseman.com

*Especially pottery, china, ceramics,
    salt and pepper shakers, cookie jars,
    tea sets and children's china; with
    special interest in Black Americana
    and Disneyana; illustrated sales
    lists available*
Judy Posner (P6)
P.O. Box 2194
Englewood, FL 34295
judyandjef@yahoo.com
www.judyposner.com

*Especially tinplate toys and cars, bat-
    tery-op toys and toy trains*
Toys N Such
Richard Trautwein (T3)
437 Dawson St.
Sault Ste. Marie, MI 49783
906-635-0356
rtraut@up.com

Cracker Jack
Author of *Cracker Jack Toys* and
    *Cracker Jack, The Unauthorized
    Guide to Advertising Collectibles*
Larry White (W7)
108 Central St.

Rowley, MA 01969-1317
978-948-8187
larrydw@erols.com

Diecast
*Diecast and other automotive toys;
    editor of magazine*
Dana Johnson, publisher (J3)
Toy Car Collector magazine
c/o Dana Johnson Enterprises
P.O. Box 1824
Bend, OR 97709-1824
541-318-7176
toynutz@earthlink.net
www.toynutz.com

Ertl, banks, farm, trucks, and construction
Son's a Poppin' Ranch
John Rammacher (S5)
1610 Park Ave.
Orange City, FL 32763-8869
386-775-2891
sonsapoppin@earthlink.net
www.sonsapoppin.com

Hot Wheels
Steve Stephenson (S25)
11117 NE 164th Pl.
Bothell, WA 98011-4003
425-488-2603
fax: 425-488-2841

Dolls
*Ad dolls, Barbie and other Mattel
    dolls, premiums, character memo-
    rabilia, modern dolls, related items*
Marcia's Fantasy
Marcia Fanta (M15)
4275 33rd St. SE
Tappen, ND 58487-9411
701-327-4441
tofantas@bektel.com

Betsy McCall
Marci Van Ausdall (V2)
4532 Fertile Valley Road
Newport, WA 99156
509-292-1311
betsymcallfanclub@hotmail.com

*Liddle Kiddles and other small dolls
    from the late '60s and early '70s*
Dawn Diaz (P2)
20460 Samual Dr.
Saugus, CA 91350-3812
661-263-TOYS (8697)
jamdiaz99@earthlink.net

*Dolls from the 1960s – 70s, including
    Liddle Kiddles, Barbie, Tammy,
    Tressy, etc.*
Cindy Sabulis (S14)
P.O. Box 642
Shelton, CT 06484
203-926-0176
toys4two@snet.net
www.dollsntoys.com
Author of *Collector's Guide to Dolls
of the 1960s and 1970s* and co-
author of *The Collector's Guide to
Tammy, the Ideal Teen* (both from
Collector Books)

Dollhouse Furniture
Renwal, Ideal, Marx, etc.
Judith A. Mosholder (M7)
186 Pine Springs Camp Road
Boswell, PA 15531
814-629-9277
jlytwins@floodcity.net
www.renwaltoys.com

Fisher-Price
Brad Cassity (C13)
2391 Hunters Trail
Myrtle Beach, SC 29579

GI Joe
Also Diecast and Star Wars
Cotswold Collectibles (C6)
P.O. Box 716
Freeland, WA 98249
877-404-5637 (toll free)
fax: 360-331-5344
www.elitebrigade.com

Guns
*Pre-WWII American spring-air BB
    guns, all Red Ryder BB guns, cap*

guns with emphasis on Western six-shooters; especially wanted are pre-WWII cast iron six-guns
Jim Buskirk (B6)
3009 Oleander Ave.
San Marcos, CA 92069
760-599-1054

Specializing in cap guns
Happy Memories Collectibles
Bill Hamburg (H1)
P.O. Box 536
Woodland Hills, CA 91367
818-346-1269
fax: 818-346-0215
WHamburg@aol.com

Halloween Collectibles

Also postcards, author of books
C.J. Russell and The Halloween
Queen Antiques
Pamela E. Apkarian-Russell (H9)
P.O. Box 499
Winchester, NH 03470
603-239-8875
halloweenqueen@cheshire.net
The Tastes & Smells of Halloween, a
Trick or Treat Trader Publication
cookbook — Bogie book for collectors, regularly $25.00, order
from the author at $20.00 plus
shipping.

Terri's Toys
Terri Ivers (I2)
114 Whitworth Ave.
Ponca City, OK 74601
580-762-8697
toylady@cableone.net

Marx

Figures, playsets, and character toys
G.F. Ridenour
Fun House Toy Co.
P.O. Box 444
Warrendale, PA 15086
phone/fax: 724-935-1392
info@funhousetoy.com
www.funhousetoy.com

*Plastic figures and parts from play-sets; Also figures from about 100
other old manufacturers*
Phoenix Toy Soldier Co.
Bob Wilson
8912 E. Pinnacle Peak Rd.
PMB 552
Scottsdale, AZ 85255
480-699-5005
877-269-6074 (toll free)
fax: 480-699-7628
bob@phoenixtoysoldier.com
www.phoenixtoysoldier.com

Paper Dolls

Author of books
Mary Young (Y2)
Box 9244
Dayton, OH 45409
937-298-4838

Paper Lithograph

*Antique McLoughlin games, Bliss
and Reed boats, toy wagons, Ten
Pin sets, cube blocks, puzzles and
Victorian doll houses. Buy and sell;
lists available upon request. Mail
order and shows only*
Mark and Linda Suozzi (S24)
P.O. Box 102
Ashfield, MA 01330
phone/fax: 413-628-3241 (9am – 5pm)
marklyn@valinet.com
www.marklynantiques.com

Pedal Cars

*Also specializing in Maytag col-
lectibles*
Nate Stoller (S7)
960 Reynolds Ave.
Ripon, CA 95366
209-599-5933
multimotor@aol.com
www.maytagclub.com

Pez Candy Dispensers

Richard Belyski (B1)
P.O. Box 14956
Surfside Beach, SC 29587

peznews@juno.com
www.pezcollectorsnews.com

Plastic Figures and Playsets

*Plastic figures and parts from play-sets; Also figures from about 100
old manufacturers other than Marx*
Phoenix Toy Soldier Co.
Bob Wilson
8912 E. Pinnacle Peak Rd.
PMB 552
Scottsdale, AZ 85255
480-699-5005
877-269-6074 (toll free)
fax: 480-699-7628
bob@phoenixtoysoldier.com
www.phoenixtoysoldier.com

Also GI Joe, Star Trek and dinosaurs
Mike and Kurt Fredericks
145 Bayline Circle
Folsom, CA 95630-8077
916-985-7986

Political Toys

McQuillen's Collectibles
Michael and Polly McQuillen (M11)
P.O. Box 50022
Indianapolis, IN 46250-0022
317-845-1721
michael@politicalparade.com
www.politicalparade.com

Puzzles

Wood jigsaw type, from before 1950
Bob Armstrong (A4)
15 Monadnock Rd.
Worcester, MA 01609
508-799-0644
raahna@oldpuzzles.com
www.oldpuzzles.com

Ramp Walkers

*Specializing in ramp-walking figures,
also mechanical sparklers and other
plunger-type toys*
Raven'tiques
Randy Welch (W4)
27965 Peach Orchard Rd.

Easton, MD 21601-8203
410-822-5441

Records

78 rpm children's records and picture disks; buys, sells, and trades records as well as makes cassette recordings for a small fee
Peter Muldavin (M21)
173 W 78th St., Apt. 5-F
New York, NY 10024
212-362-9606
kiddie78s@aol.com
http://members.aol.com/kiddie78s/

Schoenhut

Keith and Donna Kaonis (K6)
P.O. Box 344
Centerport, NY 11721-0344
613-261-4100 (daytime)
631-351-0982 (evening)
fax: 631-261-9864

Specializing in slots and model racing from the '60s – '70s; especially complete race sets in original boxes
Gary Pollastro (P5)
5047 84th Ave. SE
Mercer Island, WA, 98040
206-232-3199

Soldiers

Barclay, Manoil, Grey Iron, other Dimestores and accessories; also Syroco figures
Stan and Sally Alekna (A1)
732 Aspen Lane

Lebanon, PA 17042-9073
717-228-2361
fax: 717-228-2362

Also vehicles, model kits, GI Joes, games, ad figures, View-Master, non-sports cards, Star Trek, advertising, antiques, fine art, and much more
June Moon
Jim and Nancy Frugoli
143 Vine Ave.
Park Ridge, IL 60068
junmoonstr@aol.com
www.junemooncollectibles.com

Trains

Lionel, American Flyer and Plasticville
Gary's Trains (G1)
186 Pine Springs Camp Road
Boswell, PA 15531-2421
814-629-9277
gtrains@floodcity.net
www.garystrains.com

Trains of all types; holds cataloged auctions, seeking quality collections for consignment
Stout Auctions
Greg Stout
11 West Third Street
Williamsport, IN 47993-1119
765-764-6901
fax: 765-764-1516
stoutauctions@hotmail.com
www.stoutauctions.com

Transformers

Specializing in Transformers, Robotech, Shogun Warriors, Gadaikins, and any other robot; want to buy these MIP — also selling
Toy Hell
David Kolodny-Nagy (K2)
6525 La Mirada Ave. #110
Hollywood, CA 90038
toyhell@yahoo.com
www.toyhell.com

Windups

Also friction and battery-operated; fast-food toys, displays
Scott Smiles (S10)
157 Yacht Club Way, Apt. #112
Hypoluxo, FL 33462-6048
561-582-6016
ssmiles@msn.com

Yo-yos

Lucky J. Meisenheimer, M.D.
7300 Sand Lake Commons Blvd.
Suite 105
Orlando, FL 32819
407-352-2444
fax: 407-363-2869
LuckyJ@MSN.com
www.yo-yos.net
Author of book, *Lucky's Collectors Guide to 20th Century Yo-Yos*. To order call 1-877-969-6728. Cost is $29.95 + $3.20 postage.

Clubs, Newsletters, and Other Publications

There are hundreds of clubs, newsletters, and magazines available to toy collectors today. Listed here are some devoted to specific areas of interest. You can obtain a copy of many newsletters simply by requesting a sample.

We will list other organizations and publications upon request. Please send your information to us by June 1.

Antique Advertising Association
of America
Pastimes newsletter
P.O. Box 1121
Morton Grove, IL 60053
aaa@aol.com
subscription: $35

Antique Doll Collector
Keith and Donna Kaonis
6 Woodside Ave., Suite 300
Northport, NY 11768
631-261-4100 (daytime)
888-800-2588 (toll free)
fax: 631-251-9684
antiquedollcoll@aol.com
www.antiquedollcollector.com

Antique Trader Weekly
Nancy Crowley, editor
P.O. Box 1050
Dubuque, IA 52004
collect@krause.com
www.collect.com
subscription: $38 (52 issues)
800-334-7165 (subscriptions only)

Association of Game and Puzzle
   Collectors
197M Boston Post Road W.
Marlborough, MA 01752
membership@agpc.org
membership: $30 per year (US);
$40 (Canada and overseas)
www.agca.com

Barbie Bazaar
5711 Eighth Ave.
Kenosha, WI 53140
262-658-1004
fax: 262-658-0433
www.barbiebazaar.com

subscription: $24.95 (US); $38.95
(Canada); $58.95 (foreign) for 6
issues per year

Betsy's Fan Club (Betsy McCall)
P.O. Box 946
Quincy, CA 95971-0946
916-283-2770
dreams@psln.com
subscription: $16 per year (quarterly)

*Beyond the Rainbow Collector's
   Exchange*
P.O. Box 31672
St. Louis, MO 63131
314-217-2727
www.jgdb.com/mfaq4.htm

Beatlefan
PO Box 33515
Decatur, GA 30033
subscription: $7 (US) 6 issues; $21
(Canada/Mexico)
www.beatlefan.com

Big Little Times
Big Little Book Collectors Club of
   America
Larry Lowery
P.O. Box 1242
Danville, CA 94526
925-837-2086
www.biglittlebooks.com

Bojo
P.O. Box 1403
Cranberry Township, PA 16066-0403
724-776-0621 (9 am to 9 pm EST)
bojo@zbzoom.net
Issues fixed price catalog containing Beatles and Rock 'n Roll memorabilia; catalog: $3
Buckeye Marble Collectors Club

Brenda Longbrake, secretary
brenda@wcoil.com
www.buckeymarble.com

Candy Container Collectors of
   America
The Candy Gram newsletter
Betty MacDuff
2711 De La Rosa St.
epmac27@aol.com or
Jeff Bradfield
90 Main St.
Dayton, VA 22821
www.candycontainer.org
membership: $25

Collector's Life
The world's foremost publication
   for Steiff enthusiasts
Beth Savino
P.O. Box 798
Holland, OH 43528
419-473-9801
800-862-TOYS (toll free)
fax: 419-473-3947
www.toystorenet.com

Cracker Jack Collectors Association and *Prize Insider Newsletter*
Theresa Richter
5469 S. Dorchester Ave.
Chicago, IL 61615
waddytmr@aol.com
www.tias.com/mags/cjca
subscription/membership: $20 per
year (single); $24 (family)

Doll Castle News
P.O. Box 247
Washington, NJ 07882
908-689-7042
fax: 908-689-6320
www.dollcastlemagazine.com

Doll News
United Federation of Doll Clubs
10900 N. Pomona Ave.
Kansas City, MO 65153
816-891-7040
ledward@ufdc.org

Dollhouse Toys 'N Us
Dollhouse and Miniatures newsletter
Bob and Geraldine Scott
Geraldine@Collector.org

The Fisher-Price Collector's Club
The Gabby Goose newsletter
Jeanne Kennedy
1840 N. Segnal Butte Rd.
Mesa, AZ 85204
FPClub1@cs.com or
FPClub@aol.com
www.fpclub.org
membership: $20 ($30 for first
class mailing); $25 (international)

Friends of Hoppy club and *Hoppy
  Talk* newsletter
Laura Bates
6310 Friendship Dr.
New Concord, OH 43762-9708
614-826-4850
LBates1205@cs.com
www.hopalong.com/home.asp
membership: $20 (4 newsletters
and free ads)

Game Times
Gene Autry Star Telegram
Gene Autry Museum
P.O. Box 67
Gene Autry, OK 73436
www.cow-boy.com/museum.htm

Hopalong Cassidy Fan Club International
Laura Bates
6310 Friendship Dr.
New Concord, OH 43762
614-826-4850; e-mail
LBates1250Acs.com
www.hopalong.com/home.asp

subscription: $20 (US) or $25
(overseas); includes quarterly
newsletter and information on
annual Cambridge, Ohio, festival

John's Collectible Toys and Gifts
  catalog
John DeCicco
1323 Main St.
Lancaster, MA 01524
800-505-TOYS
www.johns-toys-store.com/store
$1 for catalog

Liddle Kiddle Konvention
Paris Langford
415 Dodge Ave.
Jefferson, LA 70121
bbean415@aol.com
liddlekiddlesnewsletter@yahoo.com
www.vintagelane.com/kiddles_
news.htm

Marl & B catalog (Barbie dolls)
Marl Davidson
10301 Braden Run
Bradenton, FL 34202
941-751-6275
fax: 941-751-5463
Marlbe@aol.com
www.marlbe.com
subscription: $25 (US — sample
copy $7.95); $30 (Canada); $40
(foreign — sample copy $12.95)

McDonald's Collector Club
Joyce and Terry Losonsky
7506 Summer Leave Ln.
Columbia, MD 21046-2455
401-381-3358. Authors of *Illustrated
Collector's Guide to McDonald's®
Happy Meal® Boxes, Premiums &
Promotions* © ($9 plus $2 postage),
and *Illustrated Collector's Guide to
McDonald's McCaps* ($3 plus $2),
both available from the authors

McDonald's Collector's Club
(Florida Sunshine Chapter)

Bill and Pat Poe
220 Dominica Circle E.
Niceville, FL 32578-4085
850-897-4163
fax: 580-897-2606
McPoes@aol.com
Patpoetoys@aol.com
membership: $15 (individual); $20
(family/couple); $7 (junior); $20
(international)

Model and Toy Collector Magazine
Toy Scouts, Inc.
137 Casterton Ave.
Akron, OH 44303
330-836-0668
fax: 330-869-8668
toyscouts@toyscouts.com
www.toyscouts.com

National Fantasy Fan Club (Disney)
Dept. AC, Box 19212
Irvine, CA 92623-9212
714-731-4705
www.nffc.org
membership: $24 (US); $30
(Canada); $40 (foreign)
Includes newsletters, free ads,
chapters, conventions, etc.

Paper Dolls
Golden Opportunities
Nan Moorehead
P.O. Box 252
Golden, CO 80402
subscription: 4 issues for $24 US
(sample copy $7); $26 Canada;
$32 foreign

Pez Collector's News
Richard and Marianne Belyski
P.O. Box 14956
Surfside Beach, SC 29587
peznews@juno.com
www.pezcollectorsnews.com

Playset Magazine
1240 Marlstone Place
Colorado Springs, CO 80904

playsetmagazine@aol.com
www.playsetmagazine.com

The Prehistoric Times
Mike and Kurt Fredericks
145 Bayline Circle
Folsom, CA 95630
916-985-7986
www.prehistorictimes.com
subscription: $28 (6 issues), $7
(lates edition); $5 (back issue)

The Puppet Collector's Newsletter
Steven Meltzer
1255 2nd St.
Santa Monica, CA 90401
310-656-0483
steve@puppetmagic.com
www.puppetmagic.com

The Replica
Craig Purcell, Editor
Hwys 136 & 20
Dyersville, IA 52040
319-875-2000
www.toytractorshow.com/the_
replica.htm
Now a free online newsletter
Marketing tool that previews
upcoming diecast releases and articles of interest to collectors;
included are Wm Britain pewter figures, Ertl diecast automotive replicas
and John Deere kits (Pre-School)

Schoenhut Collectors Club
Patricia J. Girbach
1003 W Huron St.
Ann Arbor, MI 48103-4217
aawestie@provide.net

Shirley Temple Collectors Convention, Inc.
Marge Meisinger
11 S. 767 Book Rd.
Naperville, IL 60564

The Silver Bullet
Terry and Kay Klepey
P.O. Box 553
Forks, WA 98331
360-327-3726
slvrbllt@olypen.com
subscription: $20 per year; $5
(sample issue)
Back issues are available.

Snow Biz newsletter
Nancy McMichael
P.O. Box 53262
Washington, DC 20009
subscription; $10 (3 times a year)
Club has annual meeting and swap
meet.

Star Wars online newsletter
Host: Brian's Toys
www.brianstoys.com (sign up for
newsletter)

Still Bank Collectors Club of America
Larry Egelhoff
4175 Millersville Rd.
Indianapolis, IN 46205
317-846-7228
egelhoff1@juno.com
www.stillbankclub.com
membership: $35

Toy Car Collector Magazine
Dana Johnson Enterprises

P.O. Box 1824
Bend, OR 97709-1824
541-318-7176
toynutz@earthlink.net
www.toynutz.com
subscription: $29.95 (US); $39.95
(Canada and Mexico); $49.95
(foreign)

Toy Collector Club of America
(SpecCast toys)
P.O. Box 368
Dyersville, IA 52040
563-875-8706
fax: 563-875-8056
www.speccast.com

Toy Shop
Mark Williams, publisher
700 E State St.
Iola, WI 54990-0001
715-445-2214
fax: 715-445-4087
www.toyshopmag.com
subscription: $33.98 (26 issues)

Toy Soldier Collectors of America
Charles L. DuVal
P.O. Box 179
New Ellenton, SC 29809-0179
toysoldiercollectorsamerica@
yahoo.com
www.toysoldiercollectors.home
stead.com
membership: $10 (US and
Canada); $15 (overseas)

Train Collectors Association/
National Toy Museum
John V. Luppino

P.O.Box 248
300 Paradise Lane
Strasburg, PA 17579-0248
717-687-8623 (business office)
717-687-8976 (Toy Museum)
fax: 717-687-0742
toytrain@traincollectors.org
www.traincollectors.org

The Trick or Treat Trader
CJ Russell and the Halloween
Queen Antiques
P.O. Box 499
4 Lawrence St. and Rt. 10
Winchester, NH 03470
603-239-8875
halloweenqueen@cheshire.net
subscription: $15 (4 issues); $4
(sample issue)

The Working Class Hero (Beatles
  newsletter)
3311 Niagara St.
Pittsburgh, PA 15213-4223
Alternate address: 59 Crescent St.
Winsted, CT 06098
Published 3 times a year, send
SASE for information.

Auction Sources

We would like to thank the following auction houses for letting us use their catalogs, online sources, and photographs for this guide. They have been an invaluable source for all ten editions.

Noel Barrett Antiques & Auctions
Box 300
6183 Carversville Rd.
Carversville, PA 18913
215-297-5109
fax: 215-297-0457
www.noelbarrett.com

Bertoia Auction Gallery
2141 DeMarco Dr.
Vineland, NJ 08360
856-692-1881
fax: 856-692-8697
www.bertoiaauctions.com

James D. Julia Inc.
PO Box 830
Fairfield, ME 04937
207-453-7125
fax: 207-453-2502
www.juliaauctions.com

McMasters Harris Auction Co.
PO Box 1755
Cambridge, OH 43725
740-432-7400
800-842-3526
www.mcmastersharris.com

Randy Inman Auctions
PO Box 726
Waterville, ME
207-453-6444
fax: 207-453-6663
www.inmanauctions.com

Smith House Toy & Auction Company
PO Box 280
Somerdale, NJ 08083
856-428-8010
fax: 856-428-9832
www.smithhousetoys.com

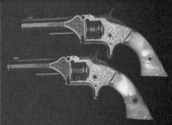

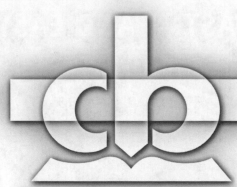

5615	Florences' **Glassware Pattern Identification** Guide, Vol. II	$19.95
6142	Florences' **Glassware Pattern Identification** Guide, Vol. III	$19.95
6643	Florences' **Glassware Pattern Identification** Guide, Vol. IV	$19.95
6641	Florences' **Ovenware** from the 1920s to the Present	$24.95
6226	**Fostoria** Value Guide, Long/Seate	$19.95
5899	**Glass & Ceramic Baskets**, White	$19.95
6460	**Glass Animals**, 2nd Edition, Spencer	$24.95
6127	The **Glass Candlestick** Book, Volume 1, Akro Agate to Fenton, Felt/Stoer	$24.95
6228	The **Glass Candlestick** Book, Volume 2, Fostoria to Jefferson, Felt/Stoer	$24.95
6461	The **Glass Candlestick** Book, Volume 3, Kanawha to Wright, Felt/Stoer	$29.95
6648	**Glass Toothpick Holders**, 2nd Edition, Bredehoft/Sanford	$29.95
6329	**Glass Tumblers**, 1860s to 1920s, Bredehoft	$29.95
5827	**Kitchen Glassware** of the Depression Years, 6th Edition, Florence	$24.95
6133	**Mt. Washington Art Glass**, Sisk	$49.95
6556	Pocket Guide to **Depression Glass** & More, 14th Edition, Florence	$12.95
6448	Standard Encyclopedia of **Carnival Glass**, 9th Ed., Edwards/Carwile	$29.95
6449	Standard **Carnival Glass** Price Guide, 14th Ed., Edwards/Carwile	$9.95
6035	Standard Encyclopedia of **Opalescent Glass**, 4th Ed., Edwards/Carwile	$24.95
6644	Standard Encyclopedia of **Pressed Glass**, 4th Ed., Edwards/Carwile	$29.95
6241	Treasures of **Very Rare Depression Glass**, Florence	$39.95
6476	**Westmoreland Glass**, The Popular Years, 1940 – 1985, Kovar	$29.95

POTTERY

4929	**American Art Pottery**, Sigafoose	$24.95
4851	Collectible **Cups & Saucers**, Harran	$18.95
6326	Collectible **Cups & Saucers**, Book III, Harran	$24.95
6344	Collectible **Vernon Kilns**, 2nd Edition, Nelson	$29.95
6331	Collecting **Head Vases**, Barron	$24.95
6621	Collector's Encyclopedia of **American Dinnerware**, 2nd Ed., Cunningham	$29.95
4931	Collector's Encyclopedia of **Bauer Pottery**, Chipman	$24.95
5034	Collector's Encyclopedia of **California Pottery**, 2nd Ed., Chipman	$24.95
6629	Collector's Encyclopedia of **Fiesta**, 10th Ed., Huxford	$24.95
3431	Collector's Encyclopedia of **Homer Laughlin China**, Jasper	$24.95
1276	Collector's Encyclopedia of **Hull Pottery**, Roberts	$19.95
5609	Collector's Encyclopedia of **Limoges Porcelain**, 3rd Ed., Gaston	$29.95
6637	Collector's Encyclopedia of **Made in Japan** Ceramics, First Ed., White	$24.95
2334	Collector's Encyclopedia of **Majolica Pottery**, Katz-Marks	$19.95
5677	Collector's Encyclopedia of **Niloak**, 2nd Edition, Gifford	$29.95
5679	Collector's Encyclopedia of **Red Wing Art Pottery**, Dollen	$24.95
5618	Collector's Encyclopedia of **Rosemeade Pottery**, Dommel	$24.95
5841	Collector's Encyclopedia of **Roseville Pottery**, Vol. 1, Huxford/Nickel	$24.95
5842	Collector's Encyclopedia of **Roseville Pottery**, Vol. 2, Huxford/Nickel.	$24.95
5917	Collector's Encyclopedia of **Russel Wright**, 3rd Edition, Kerr	$29.95
6646	Collector's Ency. of **Stangl Artware**, Lamps, and Birds, 2nd Ed., Runge	$29.95
3314	Collector's Encyclopedia of **Van Briggle Art Pottery**, Sasicki	$24.95
5680	Collector's Guide to **Feather Edge Ware**, McAllister	$19.95
6124	Collector's Guide to **Made in Japan Ceramics**, Book IV, White	$24.95
6634	Collector's Ultimate Ency. of **Hull Pottery**, Volume 1, Roberts	$29.95
6829	The Complete Guide to **Corning Ware & Visions Cookware**, Coroneos	$19.95
1425	**Cookie Jars**, Westfall	$9.95
6316	Decorative **American Pottery & Whiteware**, Wilby	$29.95
5909	**Dresden Porcelain** Studios, Harran	$29.95
5918	Florences' Big Book of **Salt & Pepper Shakers**	$24.95
6320	Gaston's **Blue Willow**, 3rd Edition	$19.95

6630	Gaston's **Flow Blue China**, The Comprehensive Guide	$29.95
2379	Lehner's Ency. of **U.S. Marks** on Pottery, Porcelain & China	$24.95
4722	**McCoy Pottery**, Collector's Reference & Value Guide, Hanson/Nissen	$19.95
5913	**McCoy Pottery**, Volume III, Hanson & Nissen	$24.95
6333	**McCoy Pottery Wall Pockets** & Decorations, Nissen	$24.95
6135	**North Carolina Art Pottery**, 1900 – 1960, James/Leftwich	$24.95
6335	Pictorial Guide to **Pottery & Porcelain Marks**, Lage	$29.95
5691	**Post86 Fiesta**, Identification & Value Guide, Racheter	$19.95
1440	**Red Wing Stoneware**, DePasquale/Peck/Peterson	$9.95
6037	**Rookwood Pottery**, Nicholson/Thomas	$24.95
3443	**Salt & Pepper Shakers** IV, Guarnaccia	$18.95
3738	**Shawnee Pottery**, Mangus	$24.95
6828	The Ultimate Collector's Encyclopedia of **Cookie Jars**, Roerig	$29.95
6640	Van Patten's ABC's of Collecting **Nippon Porcelain**	$29.95
5924	**Zanesville Stoneware** Company, Rans/Ralston/Russell	$24.95

OTHER COLLECTIBLES

5838	Advertising **Thermometers**, Merritt	$16.95
5898	Antique & Contemporary **Advertising Memorabilia**, Summers	$24.95
5814	Antique **Brass & Copper** Collectibles, Gaston	$24.95
1880	Antique **Iron**, McNerney	$9.95
6622	The Art of American **Game Calls**, Lewis	$24.95
1128	**Bottle** Pricing Guide, 3rd Ed., Cleveland	$7.95
6345	**Business & Tax Guide** for Antiques & Collectibles, Kelly	$14.95
3718	Collectible **Aluminum**, Grist	$16.95
6342	Collectible **Soda Pop** Memorabilia, Summers	$24.95
5060	Collectible **Souvenir Spoons**, Bednersh	$19.95
5676	Collectible **Souvenir Spoons**, Book II, Bednersh	$29.95
5666	Collector's Encyclopedia of **Granite Ware**, Book 2, Greguire	$29.95
5836	Collector's Guide to **Antique Radios**, 5th Edition, Bunis	$19.95
3966	Collector's Guide to **Inkwells**, Identification & Values, Badders	$18.95
4947	Collector's Guide to **Inkwells**, Book II, Badders	$19.95
5681	Collector's Guide to **Lunchboxes**, White	$19.95
6558	The Encyclopedia of Early American **Sewing Machines**, 2nd Ed., Bays	$29.95
6561	Field Guide to **Fishing Lures**, Lewis	$16.95
5683	**Fishing Lure** Collectibles, Volume 1, Murphy/Edmisten	$29.95
6328	**Flea Market Trader**, 14th Edition, Huxford	$12.95
6458	**Fountain Pens**, Past & Present, 2nd Edition, Erano	$24.95
6631	**Garage Sale** & Flea Market Annual, 13th Edition, Huxford	$19.95
4945	**G-Men and FBI Toys** and Collectibles, Whitworth	$18.95
2216	**Kitchen Antiques**, 1790–1940, McNerney	$14.95
6639	**McDonald's Drinkware**, Kelly	$24.95
6028	Modern **Fishing Lure** Collectibles, Volume 1, Lewis	$24.95
6131	Modern **Fishing Lure** Collectibles, Volume 2, Lewis	$24.95
6322	Pictorial Guide to **Christmas Ornaments** & Collectibles, Johnson	$29.95
6839	**Schroeder's Antiques** Price Guide, 24th Edition	$14.95
5007	**Silverplated Flatware**, Revised 4th Edition, Hagan	$18.95
6647	**Star Wars** Super Collector's Wish Book, 3rd Edition, Carlton	$29.95
6139	Summers' Guide to **Coca-Cola**, 4th Edition	$24.95
6827	Summers' Pocket Guide to **Coca-Cola**, 5th Edition	$12.95
4935	The W.F. Cody **Buffalo Bill** Collector's Guide, Wojtowicz	$24.95
6632	Value Guide to **Gas Station Memorabilia**, 2nd Ed., Summers & Priddy	$29.95
6841	Vintage **Fabrics**, Gridley/Kiplinger/McClure	$19.95
6036	Vintage **Quilts**, Aug/Newman/Roy	$24.95

1-800-626-5420 Fax: 1-270-898-8890

www.collectorbooks.com

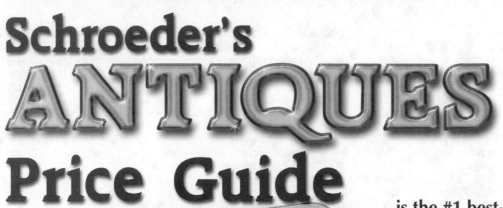
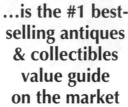